# PROFESSOR McDONALD'S
# CONVEYANCING MANUAL

# PROFESSOR McDONALD'S CONVEYANCING MANUAL

**A. J. McDONALD** ws
*Solicitor, Emeritus Professor of Conveyancing,
University of Dundee*

With

**STEWART BRYMER** ws
*Solicitor, Partner, Thorntons* ws
*Dundee*

**DOUGLAS J. CUSINE**
*Solicitor, Professor of Conveyancing
and Professional Practice of Law,
University of Aberdeen*

**ROBERT RENNIE**
*Solicitor, Professor of Conveyancing,
University of Glasgow*

T&T CLARK
EDINBURGH
1997

T&T CLARK LTD
59 GEORGE STREET
EDINBURGH EH2 2LQ
SCOTLAND

www.tandtclark.co.uk

First Edition 1982
Second Edition 1983
Reprinted with minor corrections 1984
Third Edition 1986
Fourth Edition 1989
Reprinted 1991
Fifth Edition 1993
Sixth Edition 1997
Reprinted 1999


British Library Cataloguing-in-Publication Data
A catalogue record for this book is available from the British Library


ISBN  0 567 00523 2  paperback
ISBN  0 567 00522 4  cased


Typeset by Fakenham Photosetting Ltd, Fakenham, Norfolk
Printed and bound in Great Britain by MPG Books Ltd, Bodmin, Cornwall

This edition of the Manual is dedicated to the memory of
David Marriott McDonald

# CONTENTS

# PREFACE TO SIXTH EDITION

Since it was first published in 1982, the Manual has become a familiar source of reference for students and for practitioners. Of particular value to both are the Reading List and the Digest of Cases which contain a comprehensive set of references and cases of interest.

The decision to prepare a sixth edition of the Manual was accelerated by the changes which came about as a result of the Requirements of Writing legislation. At the same time, it was felt that it would be helpful if a set of companion volumes were published. In due course Professor McDonald's Conveyancing Opinions and his Conveyancing Case Notes will appear.

This edition has been prepared under the supervision of an Editorial Board consisting of Professor Douglas Cusine of the Department of Conveyancing and Professional Practice of Law in the University of Aberdeen, Professor Robert Rennie of the University of Glasgow, and myself, a partner of Thorntons WS and a part-time lecturer in the Conveyancing Diploma Course at the University of Dundee. There has, however, been an (unofficial) fourth member of the Editorial Board – Professor McDonald himself.

The amount of work involved in updating the Manual – reflecting the volume of new law in the last four years – has been substantial. Several volunteers assisted us. Michael Blair, a partner of Thorntons WS, revised Chapter 26. Mrs Janette Langley, a senior solicitor with the City of Dundee Council, revised Chapter 19 and the 'Right to Buy' material in Chapter 28. Alec M Falconer, formerly senior legal adviser in the Registers of Scotland Executive Agency, checked the accuracy of the text with reference to Register House practice. Alan Barr and Charlotte Waelde of the Legal Practice Unit at the University of Edinburgh, revised Chapter 5 and Chapters 30 and 35 respectively. Particular thanks are due to Colin Graham, also a partner of Thorntons WS, who had responsibility for a number of chapters in Part 5 and assisted in the painstaking task of checking and rechecking the draft material. I am extremely grateful to Thorntons WS for allowing Professor McDonald and me use of the services of Pat Hay and Lynne Ness who have worked tirelessly and prodigiously, mostly in their own time, in assembling this edition. Thanks are also due to Kirstie Rae, a student at the University of Glasgow, Claire Langlands, a trainee at Thorntons WS, and Iain Pritty, a recent graduate of the University of Dundee for their proofreading. The Board are greatly indebted to each of these people for their valued and valuable contributions. Without them, the book would not have come to fruition.

I must also thank T&T Clark for agreeing to publish the sixth edition and the companion volumes referred to above. Their thoroughly professional approach and patience have been much appreciated.

Finally, a few words of personal thanks are due to Professor McDonald with whom I have had the pleasure of working for the past 17 years. He is a constant source of energy and inspiration – a professor of the old school who has strived for perfection in everything he has done. The publication of six editions of this Manual is testimony to the work of the man.

The sixth edition has been revised and updated to 1 January 1997. Some significant matters after that date have been briefly noted.

Stewart Brymer
*Chairman, Editorial Review Board*
September 1997

# READING LIST


## Part 1 – PRELIMINARY MATTERS


### Chapter 1. General Introduction

*References*

| | |
|---|---|
| Agnew of Lochnaw | – Agricultural Law in Scotland (1996) |
| Bell | – Lectures on Conveyancing (1882) ('Bell's Lectures') |
| Burns J. | – Handbook of Conveyancing (5th edn. 1938) ('Burns' Handbook') |
| Burns J. | – Conveyancing Practice (4th edn. 1957) ('Burns' Practice') |
| Butterworths | – Local Government Handbook (1990) |
| Butterworths | – Guide to Council Tax in Scotland |
| Connell | – The Agricultural Holdings (Scotland) Acts (7th edn. by Rennie and Agnew of Lochnaw, 1996) |
| Coull D. | – The Law of Bankruptcy in Scotland (1989) |
| Craigie J. | – Elements of Conveyancing – Heritable Rights (1908) ('Craigie's Elements') |
| Craigie J. | – Scottish Law of Conveyancing – Heritable Rights (1899) ('Craigie's Heritable Rights') |
| Craigie J. | – Conveyancing Statutes 1214–1894 ('Craigie's Statutes') |
| Currie | – Confirmation of Executors (8th edn. 1996) |
| Cusine D. J. | – Standard Securities (1991) |
| Cusine D. J. (ed.) | – A Scots Conveyancing Miscellany (1987) ('Conveyancing Miscellany') |
| Cusine and Rennie | – Missives |
| Duncan A. G. M. | – The Agricultural Holdings (Scotland) Act 1991 |
| Erskine | – An Institute of the Law of Scotland ('Erskine') |
| Farran C. D. | – The Principles of Scots and English Land Law (1958) |
| Flint | – Liquidation in Scotland (1990) |
| Gamble | – Obligations in Context (1990) |
| Garbutt | – Waste Management Law (1992) |
| Gill B. | – Law of Agricultural Holdings in Scotland (2nd edn. 1990) |
| Gloag & Henderson | – Introduction to the Law of Scotland (9th edn. 1987) ('Gloag & Henderson') |
| Gloag | – Contract (2nd edn. 1929) |
| Gordon W. M. | – Scottish Land Law (1989) ('Gordon') |
| Green | – Conveyancing Statutes (current edn.) |
| Green | – Scots Statutes – Children; Husband and Wife; Succession and Trusts. (current edn.) |
| Green | – Encyclopaedia of the Laws of Scotland 16 vols. (1926–35 with Supplements 1952) ('Green's Encyclopaedia') |
| Green | – Property Law Bulletin ('Greens PLB') |

Greene & Fletcher – The Law and Practice of Receivership in Scotland (2nd edn. 1992)
Gregory – Stamp Duties for Conveyancers (1990 – an English text)
Gretton G. L. – Guide to Searches (1991)
Gretton & Reid – Conveyancing (1993)
Gretton G. L. – The Law of Inhibition and Adjudication (2nd edn. 1996) ('Gretton on Inhibitions')
Halliday J. M. – The Land Tenure Reform (Scotland) Act 1974 ('Halliday's 1974 Act')
Halliday J. M. – The Conveyancing and Feudal Reform (Scotland) Act 1970 (2nd edn. 1977) ('Halliday's 1970 Act')
Halliday J. M. – The Land Registration (Scotland) Act 1979 ('Halliday's 1979 Act')
Halliday J. M. – Conveyancing Law and Practice (4 vols. (1985–1989)) ('Halliday's Practice' (Note: 2nd edn. 1996 incorporates first edition and Vols. I and IV updated. All references to 'Halliday's Practice' are to the first edition unless otherwise specified.))
Halliday J. M. – The Conveyancing Opinions of J. M. Halliday (edited by D. J. Cusine – 1992) ('Halliday's Opinions')
Himsworth C. – Housing Law in Scotland (4th edn. 1994)
HMSO – Registration of Title Practice Book (looseleaf 1981, regularly updated) – ('the RTPB')
Jauncey, The Hon. Lord – Fishing in Scotland – Law for the Angler (2nd edn. 1984)
Kolbert & Mackay – History of Scots and English Land Law
McAllister A. – Scottish Law of Leases – an Introduction (2nd edn. 1995)
McAllister & Guthrie – Scottish Property Law (1992)
McBryde W. W. – The Law of Contract in Scotland (1987) ('McBryde on Contract')
McBryde W. W. – The Bankruptcy (Scotland) Act 1985
McBryde W. W. – Bankruptcy (1989)
MacCuish & Flyn – Crofting Law (1990)
McDonald A. J. – Conveyancing Case Notes Vols. 1 and 2 ('Case Notes')
McDonald A. J. – Registration of Title Manual (1986)
Maher & Cusine – The Law and Practice of Diligence (1990)
Menzies A. – Lectures on Conveyancing (Sturrock's Edition 1900) ('Menzies Lectures')
Meston M. C. – The Succession (Scotland) Act 1964 (4th edn. 1993)
Mitchell – Eviction & Rent Arrears (1995)
Mullan – Scottish Housing Law Handbook (1992)
Nichols & Meston – The Matrimonial Homes (Family Protection) (Scotland) Act 1981 (2nd edn. 1986)
Ockrent – Scottish Land Registration (1942)
Palmer – Company Law (Current edition)
Palmer – Insolvency Law (1993)
Paton & Cameron – The Law of Landlord and Tenant in Scotland (1967)
Rankine – The Law of Landownership in Scotland (4th edn. 1909) ('Rankine – Landownership')
Rankine – The Law of Leases in Scotland (3rd edn. 1916) ('Rankine – Leases')
Reid K. G. C. – The Law of Property in Scotland (1996)
Reid K. G. C. – The Requirements of Writing (Scotland) Act 1995
Reid L. T. – Green's Guide to Environmental Law (1992)
Rennie & Cusine – The Requirements of Writing (1995)
Robson P. – Residential Tenancies (1994)
Robson P. – The Housing (Scotland) Act 1988
Robson & Miller – Property Law (1991)

| | |
|---|---|
| Ross | – Lectures on the Law of Scotland (1822) ('Ross' Lectures') |
| Ross (R.L.C.) | – Leading cases (3 vols. 1849) |
| Ross & McKichan | – Drafting and Negotiating Commercial Leases in Scotland (2nd end. 1993) |
| Rowan-Robinson J. | – Compulsory Purchase and Compensation (1990) |
| Rowan-Robinson & Young | – Planning by Agreement (1989) |
| Scott Robinson | – The Law of Game Salmon and Freshwater Fishing in Scotland (1990) |
| Scott Robinson | – The Law of Interdict (1987) |
| Scottish Rights of Way Society Limited | – Rights of Way – A Guide to the Law in Scotland (1986) |
| Sinclair J. H. | – Handbook of Conveyancing Practice in Scotland (2nd edn. 1990) ('Sinclair's Handbook') |
| Smith T. B. | – A Short Commentary on the Law of Scotland (1962) ('Smith's Commentary') |
| St. Clair & Drummond Young | – The Law of Corporate Insolvency in Scotland (2nd edn. 1992) |
| Stair | – Institutions ('Stair') |
| Stair Society | – Volume 1 Sources and Literature of Scots Law (1936) |
| | Volume 20 Introduction to the History of Scots Law (1959) |
| Stair Memorial Encyclopaedia | – The Laws of Scotland – Various Volumes ('Stair Encyclopaedia') (1987–; in particular: Vol. 6 paras. 401–800 Conveyancing, including Registration of Title, Vol. 13 Landlord and Tenant, Vol. 18 Property, Vol. 20 Rights in Security) |
| Thomson J. M. | – The Law Reform (Miscellaneous Provisions) (Scotland) Act 1985 |
| Thomson J. M. & Ors | – The Law Reform (Miscellaneous Provisions) (Scotland) Act 1990 (1991) |
| Tolley | Stamp Duties and Stamp Duty Reserve Tax (1990) |
| Walker D. M. | – The Law of Contracts & Related Obligations in Scotland (3rd edn. 1995) ('Walker's Contract') |
| Walker D. M | – Principles of Scottish Private Law (4th edn. 1988) ('Walker's Principles' or 'Walker') |
| Walker D. M. | – The Law of Prescription and Limitation of Actions in Scotland (5th edn. 1996) ('Walker's Prescription') |
| Walker D. M. | – Civil Remedies |
| Watchman P. Q. | – The Housing (Scotland) Act 1987 |
| Wilson W. A. | – The Scottish Law of Debt (2nd edn. 1991) |
| Wilson & Duncan | – Trusts, Trustees and Executors |
| Wood | – Lectures on Conveyancing (1903) ('Wood's Lectures') |
| Young E. | – Scottish Planning Appeals (1990) |
| Young & Rowan-Robinson | – Scottish Planning Law and Procedure |

*Styles*
Encyclopaedia of Scottish Legal Styles 10 Vols. (1935) ('Styles')
Diploma in Legal Practice – Conveyancing Styles ('Diploma Styles')
McDonald – Conveyancing Manual – Appendix A

*Conveyancing statutes*
Royal Mines Act 1424
Leases Act 1449
Registration Act 1617
Real Rights Act 1693

Registration of Sasines Act 1693
Infeftment Act 1845
Transference of Lands Act 1847
Transference of Burgage Lands Act 1847
Crown Charters Act 1847
Registration of Leases (Scotland) Act 1857 ('1857 Act')
Titles to Lands (Scotland) Act 1858 ('1858 Act')
Titles to Land (Scotland) Act 1860
Registration of Writs (Scotland) Act 1868
Land Registers (Scotland) Act 1868
Titles to Land Consolidation (Scotland) Act 1868 ('1868 Act')
Titles to Land Consolidation (Scotland) Amendment Act 1869
Conveyancing (Scotland) Act 1874 ('1874 Act')
Writs Execution (Scotland) Act 1887
Conveyancing Amendment (Scotland) Act 1887 ('1887 Act')
Feudal Casualties (Scotland) Act 1914
Conveyancing (Scotland) Act 1924 ('1924 Act')
Burgh Registers (Scotland) Act 1926 ('1926 Act')
Conveyancing Amendment (Scotland Act) 1938 ('1938 Act')
Public Registers and Records (Scotland) Acts 1948 and 1950
Tenancy of Shops (Scotland) Acts 1949 and 1964
Succession (Scotland) Act 1964 ('1964 Act')
Conveyancing & Feudal Reform (Scotland) Act 1970 ('1970 Act')
Redemption of Standard Securities (Scotland) Act 1971
Prescription & Limitation (Scotland) Acts 1973 and 1984
Land Tenure Reform (Scotland) Act 1974 ('1974 Act')
Land Registration (Scotland) Act 1979 ('1979 Act')
Law Reform (Miscellaneous Provisions) (Scotland) Act 1980
Matrimonial Homes (Family Protection) (Scotland) Act 1981
Law Reform (Miscellaneous Provisions) (Scotland) Act 1985
Prescription (Scotland) Act 1987
Register of Sasines (Scotland) Act 1987
Term and Quarter Days (Scotland) Act 1990
Property Misdescriptions Act 1991
Coal Industry Act 1994
Requirements of Writing (Scotland) Act 1995
Contract (Scotland) Act 1997


*Reports*
Reid Committee Report      – Registration of Title to Land 1963 Cmnd. 2032
Henry Committee Report     – Registration of Title to Land 1969 Cmnd. 4137
Halliday Committee Report  – Conveyancing Legislation and Practice 1968 Cmnd. 3118
White Paper                – Land Tenure in Scotland 1969 Cmnd. 4009
Green Paper                – Land Tenure Reform in Scotland (1972)


Scottish Law Commission Memoranda
No. 69  – Intestate Succession and Legal Rights
No. 70  – The Making and Revocation of Wills
No. 71  – Some Miscellaneous Topics in the Law of Succession
No. 72  – Floating Charges and Receivers
No. 91  – Law of the Tenement
No. 93  – Abolition of the Feudal System
Scottish Law Commission Consultation Paper
Mutual Boundary Walls (1992)
Scottish Law Commission Reports

No. 92 – Obligations – Report on Negligent Misrepresentation
No. 110 – The Legal Capacity and Responsibility of Minors and Pupils
No. 112 – The Requirements of Writing
No. 118 – Recovery of Possession of Heritable Property
No. 127 – Passing of the Risk in Contracts of Sale
No. 135 – Family Law (for Matrimonial Homes Act)
Scottish Law Commission Paper – The Reform of the Law of the Tenement:
 'The Management of Tenement Property' August 1995

## Chapter 2. Authentication

*References*

| | |
|---|---|
| Burns | Practice Chap. 1 |
| Burns | Handbook Chaps. 2 and 3 |
| Gloag | Contract Chaps. 10 and 11 |
| Green | Encyclopaedia Vol. 2 paras. 651–662 – Blanks in Documents |
| | Vol. 5 paras. 1071–1101 – Execution of Deeds |
| Halliday | Practice 2nd edn. Ch. 3. |
| Menzies | Lectures Part 1 Chaps. 1–6 |
| Reid K.G.C. | The Requirements of Writing (Scotland) Act 1995 |
| Rennie & Cusine | The Requirements of Writing (1995) |
| Stair Encyclopaedia | Vol. 6 paras. 401–433 |
| Walker | Law of Evidence in Scotland Chaps. 9–12, 16–19, 21, 22 |
| Styles | Vol. 4 Execution of Deeds |

Scottish Law Commission – Memo No. 66 (1985) – Constitution of Obligations and
 Authentication and Report thereon (No. 112)

*Statutes*

Subscription of Deeds Acts 1540, 1579 and 1584
Execution of Deeds Act 1593
Lyon King of Arms Act 1672
Subscription of Deeds Act 1681
Deeds Act 1696
Blank Bonds & Trusts Act 1696
Forms of Deeds (Scotland) Act 1856
1868 Act ss. 20, 139, 140, 144
1874 Act ss. 38, 39, 54
1924 Act s. 18 and Sch. 1
1970 Act s. 44
Wills Act 1861
Wills Act 1963
Partnership Act 1890 s. 6
Local Government (Scotland) Act 1973 s. 194
Companies Act 1985 s. 36B
Law Reform (Miscellaneous Provisions) (Scotland) Act 1985, ss. 8, 9
Requirements of Writing (Scotland) Act 1995

*Articles*

| | |
|---|---|
| 1 Conveyancing Review 216 | – Adopted as holograph |
| 1963 SLT (News) 161 | – The Wills Act 1963 |
| 1963 JLS 99 | – The Wills Act 1963 |
| 1979 SLT (News) 173 | – Notarially executed Wills |
| 1980 JLS 448 | – Testamentary Writings deemed to be Probative |

| | |
|---|---|
| 1985 JLS 308 | – What is a probative writ? |
| 1986 SLT (News) 129 | – Execution or revocation? |
| 1987 JLS 148 | – Execution of deeds |
| 1988 JLS 228 | – Comments on Scottish Law Commission Report No. 112 |
| 1989 JLS 135 | – Execution of Deeds by Companies |
| 1990 JLS 358 | – Execution of Documents by Companies |
| 1990 JLS 498 | – Execution of Documents by Companies |
| 1990 SLT 241 | – Execution of Deeds by Companies: the New Law |
| 1990 SLT 369 | – Execution of Deeds by Companies: the Replacement Provisions |
| 1991 SLT 283 | – Bad Company: Companies' Executions |
| 1991 SLT 457 | – Good Company: Companies' Executions Once Again |
| 1991 JLS 73 | – Who signs for the Firm? |
| 1993 JLS 270 | – Execution of Deeds by a Mark |
| 1994 JLS 191 | – A note on the Foreign Companies (Execution of Deeds) Regulations 1994 |
| 1994 JLS 450 | – Conveyancing – What's coming? An article on the proposed new statute on requirements of writing |
| 1995 JLS 221 | – A Commentary on the 1995 Act |
| Greens PLB Issue 15 p. 4 | – The Requirements of Writing Act |
| Greens PLB Issue 17 p. 7 | – The Requirements of Writing Act – Comment by the Keeper |
| 1995 JLS 405 | – The Requirements of Writing Act – Note by the Keeper |
| 1996 SLT (News) 49 | – Constructing Ambiguities? – Some problems of the 1995 Act |

## Chapter 3.  Capacity

*References*

| | |
|---|---|
| Burns | Practice pp. 308–323 |
| Gloag & Henderson | 9th edn. Chap. 6 |
| Halliday | Practice Chap. 2 |
| Walker | Judicial Factors |
| Wilson | Trusts |
| McBryde | Bankruptcy |
| Stair Encyclopaedia | Vol. 24 paras. 1–300 |

*Statutes*

Judicial Factors (Scotland) Acts 1849, 1880, 1889
Guardianship of Children Acts 1886, 1925 and 1973
Married Woman's Property (Scotland) Act 1920
1938 Act s. 1
Succession (Scotland) Act 1964
Trusts (Scotland) Acts 1921 and 1961
Family Law (Scotland) Act 1985 s. 24
Companies Act 1985 s. 35
Law Reform (Parent and Child) (Scotland) Act 1986
Age of Legal Capacity (Scotland) Act 1991
Requirements of Writing (Scotland) Act 1995

*Articles*

| | |
|---|---|
| 1984 JLS 357 | – The Title of a Liquidator |
| 1984 JLS 400 | – Delivery of Deeds and the Race to the Register |
| 1985 JLS 20 | – Bankruptcy etc. and the Race to the Register |
| 1985 JLS 109 | – Insolvency and Title – a Reply |
| 1987 JLS 62 | – Pupil Child Infeft |

1987 JR 163    – Who Owns Partnership Property
1989 JLS 414    – Why Can't Partnerships Own Heritage?
1991 JLS 232    – Problems in Partnership Conveyancing
1992 JLS 346    – Aspects of Insolvency Conveyancing
1994 JLS 205    – A cautionary note – sequestrations

## Chapter 4. Delivery

*References*
Burns                 Handbook p. 39
Green's Encyclopaedia Vol. 5 paras. 1200–1215 – Delivery of Deeds
Gloag                Contract Chap. 4
Halliday            Practice Chap. 9
McBryde           Contract Chap. 7

*Articles*
1981 JLS 132 and 181      – Delivery of Deeds
1982 SLT (News) 149      – Ownership on Delivery
1984 JLS 400              – Delivery of Deeds etc.
1985 SLT (News) 165      – Ownership on Delivery
1985 SLT (News) 280      – Ownership on Registration
1986 SLT (News) 177      – Constitution of Trust
1994 SLT (News) 183      – Dead on Delivery – Comment on *Sharp* v. *Thomson* by
                            Professor Rennic
1994 JLS 356, 371, 384, 444    – Various Comments on *Sharp* v. *Thomson*
1994 SLT (News) 313      – An article by Professor Gretton on *Sharp* v. *Thomson*
1995 SLT (News) 91 and 101    – Further Comments on *Sharp* v. *Thomson*
1995 SLT (News) 75       *Sharp* v. *Thomson* – A Civilian Perspective by Professor
                            Reid
1995 JLS 256              – *Sharp* v. *Thomson*: What now?
1995 JLS 323 Caveat      – Delivery of Documents
1995 JLS 311              – A commentary on *Sharp* v. *Thomson*
1996 SLT (News) 373      – Intimation – The Equivalent Delivery of What?
1996 SLT (News) 365      – The Perils of a Trusting Disposition
1997 SLT (News) 79       – Jam Today: *Sharp* in the House of Lords
Greens PLB Issue 26 p. 5    – *Sharp* v. *Thomson* – The House of Lords strikes back
1997 JLS 130              – *Sharp* v. *Thomson*: The Final Act
(and see Articles under Chapter 3 above)

## Chapter 5. Stamp Duties and VAT

*References*
Tolley                  Stamp Duties and Stamp Duty Reserve Tax (5th edn. 1996)
Tolley                  VAT on Construction, Land and Property (2nd edn. (looseleaf))
Goy & Walters        VAT and Property Law (2nd edn. 1993)
De Souza & Gillington   The Property Investor and VAT (1990)
Gammie & De Souza    Land Taxation (looseleaf)
Monroe & Nock       Stamp Duties (looseleaf)
Scott & McLellan      VAT and Property (looseleaf)
Sergeant & Sims       Stamp Duties (11th edn. 1996)
Soares                  VAT Planning for Property Transactions (6th edn. 1995)
Stair Encyclopaedia    Vol. 7 paras. 1281–1461 – Value Added Tax

Walker                              Evidence, Chap. 20


*Articles*

| | |
|---|---|
| Taxation – 29 August 1991 – p. 569 | – Transaction Interaction |
| 1992 JLS 35 | – VAT – Buildings and Land |
| 1992 PQLE | – VAT on Property |
| Inland Revenue Statement of Practice | – 12 September 1991 – Stamp Duty and VAT – Interaction (SP 11/91) |
| Inland Revenue Statement of Practice | – 12 July 1993 – Stamp Duty; New Buildings (SP 8/93) |
| HM Customs and Excise | – Notice 742 December 1995, as amended; Property Development |
| HM Customs and Excise | – Notice 742/3/95 April 1995: Scottish Law Terms |
| Taxation – 27 May 1993 – p. 199 | – The Option to Tax |
| Greens PLB Issue 4 p. 4 | – (Missives – VAT) |
| Greens PLB Issue 5 p. 2 | – (Missives – VAT Part 2) |
| 1994 JLS 64 | – VAT on Surrenders of Leases |
| 1994 JLS 101 | – Stamp Duty on VAT |
| 1994 JLS 217 | – Stamp Duty – Property Transactions |
| 1994 JLS 381 | – VAT News |
| Taxation – 23 March 1995 – p. 579 | – The Latest VAT Changes – I |
| Taxation – 30 March 1995 – p. 614 | – The Latest VAT Changes – II |
| 1996 JLS 75 | – Stamp Duty – Finance Act 1994 |
| 1996 JLS 232 | – Stamp Duty – Finance Act 1994: The Scottish Position |
| 1996 JLS 398 | – VAT: Statement of Practice on Transfer of a Property-letting Business as a Going Concern |
| Update – November 1995 | – VAT on Property |


*Statutes*

Stamp Act 1891 as amended
Finance Acts, various
Value Added Tax Act 1994 as amended


Part 2 – FEUS


## Chapter 6.  Creation of the New Feudal Estate


Gordon's Scottish Land Law Chaps. 2 and 3

| | |
|---|---|
| Stair Encyclopaedia | Vol. 6 paras. 401–411 – History of reform |
| | Vol. 18 paras. 41–113 – Feudalism |
| | Vol. 24 paras. 301–329 – Udal Law |


*References*

| | |
|---|---|
| Burns | Handbook Chaps. 10, 11 and 12 |
| Burns | Practice Chaps. 11, 12 and 16 |
| Green's Encyclopaedia | Vol. 2 paras. 1066–1101 – Burgage |
| | Vol. 3 paras. 236–296 – Casualties |
| | Vol. 3 paras. 518–554 – Charter – Feudal |
| | Vol. 12 paras. 758–863 – Registration and Records |
| Halliday | Practice Chap. 16 – Feudal Tenure |
| Stair Society | Vol. 20 Chap. 14 |

1976 SLT (News) 257  – Infeftment
1992 JLS 306  – Barony Title

*Statutes*
Land Registers (Scotland) Act 1868
1868 Act ss. 3, 5–10, 12–15, 17, 20, 21, 100, 138, 141–145, 147, 163
1874 Act ss. 4, 15, 16, 18, 20, 21, 22, 23, 25, 26, 27, 28, 32
Feudal Casualties (Scotland) Act 1914
1924 Act ss. 8–10, 12, 14, 48
Burgh Registers Act 1926
1938 Act ss. 8, 9
1970 Act Part 1
1974 Act ss. 1, 2, 3
1979 Act

*Miscellaneous*
Reid Committee Report  – Registration of Title to Land 1963 Cmnd. 2032
Henry Committee Report  – Registration of Title to Land 1969 Cmnd. 4137
Halliday Committee Report  – Conveyancing Legislation and Practice 1968 Cmnd. 3118
White Paper  – Land Tenure in Scotland 1969 Cmnd. 4009
Green Paper  – Land Tenure Reform in Scotland – 1972
Scottish Law Commission  – Discussion Paper No. 93: Abolition of the Feudal System
Greens PLB Issue 11 p. 8  – Comments by Professor Reid on the Law Commission proposals to abolish the feudal system
1995 JR 321  – The Feudal System – Going, Going, Gone? A commentary by Professor Robert Rennie on the proposals of the Scottish Law Commission for the abolition of the feudal system

**Chapters 7 to 12. The Feu Charter and content thereof**

*References*
Erskine         Bk. II
Craigie         Heritable Rights I, Chap. 3
Burns           Practice Chaps. 11, 24
Rankine         Landownership Chaps. 5–11, 18, 19, 25–27
Gloag           Contract – Chaps. 13, 14, 34
Green's Encyclopaedia Vols. as follows:
    1 paras. 104–112       – Accretion
    2 paras. 864–897       – Boundaries and Fences
    2 paras. 876–987       – Building Restrictions
    3 paras. 555–647       – Charter, Feudal
    7 paras. 361–385       – Fixtures
    10 paras. 1–54         – Mines and Minerals
    10 paras. 1252–1307    – Parts and Pertinents
    13 paras. 619–629      – Sea, Seashore (Part)
    13 paras. 1215–1267    – Servitudes
    14 paras. 246–255      – Singular Successor
    14 paras. 616–671      – Superior and Vassal
    14 paras. 677–720      – Support
    15 paras. 1107–1125    – Warrandice
    1949 Supplement Appendix – Coal Mines

Halliday      Practice
          Ch. 17– Feus
          Ch. 18 – Description of land conveyed
          Ch. 19 – Reservations, etc.
          Ch. 20 – Servitudes
          Ch. 24 – Infeftment and registration

Gordon      Scottish Land Law
          Ch. 4 – Descriptions
          Ch. 6 – Minerals
          Ch. 7 – Water
          Ch. 8 – Fishings
          Ch. 9 – Game
          Ch. 10 – Separate tenements
          Ch. 15 – Co-ownership and law of the tenement
          Ch. 22 – Inherent conditions
          Ch. 23 – Real burdens
          Ch. 24 – Servitudes and public rights of way

Stair Encyclopaedia    Vol. 6 paras. 401–641 – Conveyancing in general
          Vol. 11 paras. 1–64 – Salmon and freshwater fisheries
              paras. 801–961 – Game
          Vol. 12 paras. 1213–1262 – Interpretation of Deeds
          Vol. 18 paras. 17–40 – Co-ownership
              paras. 199–213 – Parts and pertinents
              paras. 214–226 – Boundary walls and fences
              paras. 227–251 – Law of the tenement
              paras. 252–272 – Minerals and support
              paras. 273–343 – Water
              paras. 344–353 – Real conditions
              paras. 354–374 – Common interest
              paras. 375–438 – Real burdens
              paras. 439–493 – Servitudes
              paras. 494–513 – Public rights of way
              paras. 514–529 – Public rights of navigation etc.
              paras. 701–714 – Warrandice etc.
          Vol. 19 paras. 801–882 – Public registers and records
          Vol. 25 paras. 301–447 – Water

Conveyancing Miscellany p. 152. Warrandice etc.
S. Scott Robinson    The Law of Game, Salmon and Freshwater Fishing in Scotland
(and see also References for Chapters 18 and 19 below.)

*Styles*
  Vol. 5 Feus
  Vol. 5 Fishings
  Vol. 7 Mines and Minerals
  Vol. 8 Servitudes

*Articles and Miscellaneous*
Scottish Law Commission Discussion Paper No. 91: Law of the Tenement
Scottish Law Commission Consultation Paper: Mutual Boundary Walls
Scottish Law Commission Discussion Paper No. 93: Abolition of the Feudal System

**Chapter 7. The Feu Charter**

*Destinations*
1984 JLS 103          – Heirs, Executors and Assignees

1985 SLT (News) 57      – Common Property
1989 JLS 299      – Destinations


*Joint and common property and common interest*
1 Conveyancing Review 17    – Property Commonly Called Joint
1 Conveyancing Review 105 – The Law of the Tenement
1 Conveyancing Review 143 – Maintenance of Tenement Roofs
1 Conveyancing Review 239 – The Law of the Tenement
1 Conveyancing Review 260 – The Limitations of Common Interest
2 Conveyancing Review 102 – The Law of the Tenement
1958 JLS 217      – Plans
1973 SLT (News) 68      – Support of Buildings
1980 JLS 141      – Mutual Gable Walls
1983 JLS 472      – The Law of the Tenement
1985 SLT (News) 57      – Common Property
1990 JLS 368      – Law of the Tenement
1993 SLT (News) 61      – Joint or Common Property
1993 JLS 465      – Joint Property – Is this the best advice?
1993 JLS 402      – Maintenance of tenement roofs
1994 JLS 423      – A note from the Professional Practice Committee as to accounting on the sale of joint property
1994 JLS 398      – Spousal Defences to division and sale
Greens PLB Issue 11 p. 6 – Law Reform : A comment by Professor Reid on Law Commission Paper 91 on the Law of the Tenement.
The Tenement Handbook – A Practical Guide (Royal Institute of Architects in Scotland)


**Chapter 8. Descriptions**

*General*
1971 JLS 62      – Descriptions in Feu Dispositions
1979 Act s. 19      – Agreement as to common boundary


*Tenements*
See Articles under Chapter 7 – Joint and common property and common interest


*Water rights, fishings and game*

*Statutes and Statutory Instruments*
Land Drainage (Scotland) Acts 1930 and 1958
Flood Prevention (Scotland) Act 1961
Rivers (Prevention of Pollution) (Scotland) Acts 1951 and 1965
Control of Pollution Act 1974
Water Act 1989
Environmental Protection Act 1990
Trout (Scotland) Acts 1902 and 1933
Salmon and Fresh Water Fisheries (Protection) (Scotland) Act 1951
Freshwater and Salmon Fisheries (Scotland) Act 1976
Game (Scotland) Act 1772
Night Poaching Acts 1828 and 1844
Day Trespass Act 1832
Ground Game Act 1880
Agricultural Holdings (Scotland) Act 1991
Units of Measurement Regulations 1995

## Chapter 9. Reservations

## Chapter 10. Burdens

| 1989 JR 69 | – Defining Real Conditions |
| 1992 JLS 397 | – Planning by Agreement and the Conveyancer. A commentary on the use of the 1972 Act s. 50 Agreement |

## Chapter 11. Servitudes

*Articles*

| 2 Conveyancing Review 97 | – Servitudes |
| 1993 JLS 490 Caveat | – A problem of access |
| 1993 SLG 127 | – Servitudes of access |
| Greens PLB Issue 4 p. 6 | – New buildings and old servitudes |
| 1994 SLT (News) 349 | Liability of an occupier to a person using a right of way |
| 1995 SLT (News) 228 | – The extinction of servitudes through confusion |

## Chapter 12. Subordinate Clauses

*Statute*
1979 Act s. 16

*Warrandice*

| 3 Conveyancing Review 144 | – Latent Defects in Heritable Property |
| 1972 SLT (News) 41 | – An Aspect of Warrandice |
| 1983 JR 1 | – The Scope of Warrandice in Conveyance of Land |
| 1983 JLS 228 | – Warrandice and Latent Defects in Heritage |
| Greens PLB Issue 5 p. 6 | – Warrandice |

## Chapter 13. Registration

*References*

| Halliday | The 1979 Act |
| McDonald | Registration of Title Manual (1986) |
| Burns | Handbook Chaps. 13 and 18 |
| Green's Encyclopaedia | Vol. 4 paras. 387–390, 418–431, 449, 457 – Completion of Title |
| | Vol. 12 paras. 804–847 – Registration and Records (part) |
| Burns | Practice Chaps. 12 and 18 |
| Stair Encyclopaedia | Vol. 6 paras. 448–53 (Sasines registration) |
| | paras. 701–86 (Registration of title) |

Registration of Title (PQLE Papers: February 1991)

| Wood | 'Lectures in Conveyancing' (1903) pp. 44–60 |
| Simpson | Land Law and Registration 1976 |

Minutes of Evidence. Royal Commission on Registration of Title (1907) (Dunedin Committee)
Memorandum of Evidence to be Submitted by the Council of the Law Society of Scotland to the Reid Committee pp. 6–26
Reid Committee Report 1963 Cmnd. 2632
Registration of Title to Land in Scotland (Henry Report) 1969 Cmnd. 4137
Registration of Title Practice Book, HMSO 1981

*Statutes*
Registration Act 1617
1681 c. 11 (Registration in Burghs)
Real Rights Act 1693

Register of Sasines Act 1693
Land Registers Act 1868
Burgh Registers Act 1926
1868 Act ss. 12, 15, 141–145
1874 Act s. 54
1924 Act ss. 10, 48
1979 Act
Register of Sasines (Scotland) Act 1987
Land Registration (Scotland) Rules 1980
Land Registration (Scotland) Amendment Rules 1988


*Articles*
| | |
|---|---|
| 2 JLS 29 | – The Register of Sasines |
| 3 JLS 217 | – The Register of Sasines |
| 1967 JLS | – The Sasine Register |
| 3 Conveyancing Review 108 | – Accretion |
| 1976 SLT (News) 257 | – Infeftment |
| 1964 JLS 285 and 320 | – The Torrens System in its Place of Origin. Registration of Title to Land in South Australia |
| 1 Conveyancing Review 13 | – Registration of Title in England |
| 2 Conveyancing Review 83 | – Registration of Title in England |
| 1963 SLT (News) 193 | – Registration of Title to Land in Scotland – J. M. Halliday |
| 14 JLS 352 | – Registration of Title Pilot Scheme |
| 15 JLS 8 | – Registration of Title |
| 1979 JLS 225 | – Registration of Title |
| 1981 JLS 219 | – Introduction of Registration of Title to Scotland |
| 1982 JLS 109 | – Titles to Land – The New System Considered |
| 1984 JLS 171, 212 and 260 | – Registration of Title – Comments on the 1979 Act |
| 1988 JLS 331 | – Note on the Land Registration Rules 1988 |
| 1988 JLS 98 | – What is a Real Right? |
| 1990 JLS 200 | – *Brookfield Developments Limited* v. *The Keeper* – A commentary |
| 1991 JR 70 | – *A Non Domino* Conveyances and the Land Register |
| 1992 JLS 120 | – Registration of Title – A comment on P16 reports |
| 1993 SLT (News) 97 | – Registration or Rectification? (discussing *Short's Tr*) |
| 1993 Greens Property Law Bulletin | – Issue 2 (Note on *Short's Tr*) |
| 1994 SLT (News) 183 | – Dead on Delivery – Comment on *Sharp* v. *Thomson* by Professor Rennie |

(Note: Further Articles on *Sharp* v. *Thomson* are listed under Chapter 4 – Delivery.)

| | |
|---|---|
| Greens PLB Issue 12 p. 3 | – Comments by the Keeper on Recording of Deeds in Sasines |
| 1995 JLS 15 | – Comments by the Keeper on the new questions in Land Register Form 1 |
| 1995 JLS 283 | – A Comment by the Keeper on proposed changes in fees in the Registers of Scotland Executive Agency |
| Greens PLB Issue 17 p. 12 | – ROT – A note on the extension of operational areas; and a comment on digital mapping |
| 1995 JLS 482 | – A note by the Keeper on the introduction of pre-payment of fees in the Land Register and Sasines Register |
| Greens PLB Issue 16 p. 8 | – A note on VAT in relation to registration fees referring to *Glenrothes Development Corporation* v. *IRC* – Chapter 5 above |
| 1995 JLS 481 | – A note on the Keeper's proposed practice in accepting standard securities for recording or registration following on the decision in *Bennett* v. *The Beneficial Bank plc* |

| 1996 JLS 272 | – A note by the Keeper on Requisition Policy in the Land Register, and his discretion in accepting applications without all the necessary documentation |
| Greens PLB Issue 19 p. 12 | – A note on the House of Lords decision in *Short's Trustees* |

## Chapter 14. The Effects of Possession: Prescription

*References*

| Burns | Practice Chap. 10 (part) |
| Millar | Prescription |
| Napier | Prescription |
| Rankine | Landownership Chaps. 1–4 |
| Green's Encyclopaedia | Vol. 12 paras. 41–88 – Prescription |
| Walker | Prescription (4th edn. 1990) |
| Gordon | Scottish Land Law paras. 12–15 – 12–53 (prescription) paras. 14–01–14–61 (possession) |
| Stair Encyclopaedia | Vol. 18, paras. 114–192 (possession) |

*Statutes*
Prescription Act 1469
Prescription Act 1474
Prescription Act 1617
1874 Act s. 34
1924 Act ss. 16, 17
1938 Act s. 4
1970 Act s. 8
Prescription and Limitation (Scotland) Act 1973
1979 Act s. 10

*Articles*

| 1994 SLT 261 | – Possession: nine-tenths of the law. A commentary on the decision in *Hamilton* v. *MacIntosh Donald Ltd.* |

## Part 3 – RESULTING RIGHTS OF SUPERIOR AND VASSAL

## Chapter 15. The Estate of Superiority

*References* (for Chapter 15–17)

| Gordon | Scottish Land Law, Chaps. 21–23 and 25. |
| Burns | Handbook Chap. 11 |
| Green's Encyclopaedia | Vols. as follows: |
| | 3 paras. 555–647 – Charter Feudal |
| | 9 paras. 968–9991 – Irritancies |
| | 8 paras. 1361–1374 – *Jus Quaesitum Tertio* |
| | 14 paras. 616–671 – Superior and Vassal |
| Burns | Practice Chap. 13 |
| Gloag | Contract Chaps. 13, 14, 37 |
| Halliday | 1970 Act Chaps. 2 and 3 |
| Halliday | 1974 Act |

Halliday                             Practice Chap. 16
Conveyancing Miscellany   p. 9 – Enforcement of Title Conditions
                                       p. 67 – Variation and Discharge of Land Obligations
Stair Encyclopaedia           Vol. 18. Property Chaps. 1–10, 12, 13

*Statutes*
Feuduty Act 1597
1874 Act s. 8
1887 Act s. 4
1924 Act s. 13
1938 Act s. 6
1970 Act ss. 1–7
1974 Act ss. 4–7, 15, 19, 21

*Articles*
1957 34 SLG                      – Interest to Enforce Building Restrictions
1 Conveyancing Review 239   – Redemption or Discharger of Feuduties
2 Conveyancing Review 121   – Irritancy by Over-superior
2 Conveyancing Review 225   – Some Aspects of Allocation of Feuduty
1969 JLS 45                      – Superior's Interest to Enforce
1971 SLT (News) 57           – The Lands Tribunal
1971 JLS 281                     – Allocation of Feuduty
1973 JLS 109                     – The Lands Tribunal for Scotland
1976 JLS 364                     – Redemption of Feuduty
1977 JR 89                        – Acquiescence, Singular Successors etc.
1977 JLS 127                     – The Lands Tribunal
1979 JLS 282                     – Function and Working of the Lands Tribunal in Scotland
1983 JLS 137                     – *Jus Quaesitum Tertio*
1984 JLS 232                     – Rights of Pre-emption
1988 JLS 434                     – Land Obligations, Planning Permission, etc.
Greens PLB Issue 3 p. 3     – Procedure in the Lands Tribunal
Green's PLB Issue 12 p. 4   – Greedy Superiors
The Scottish Office Central – Feuing Conditions in Scotland
   Research Unit 1995


## Chapter 18. The Estate of the Vassal


*References*
Gordon          Scottish Land Law, Chaps. 7, 15, 17 and 18
Burns            Practice Chap. 16 – Dispositions
Rankine         Landownership Chaps. 9, 11, 18, 24 and 28–33
Garbutt         Waste Management Law (1992)
Green's Guide to Environmental Law in Scotland (1992)
Green's Encyclopaedia Vols. as follows:
      2 paras. 310–326      – Barony Title
      3 paras. 1350–1376    – Common Gable
      3 paras. 1377–1395    – Common Property and Common Interest
      6 paras. 1–7           – Division and Sale
      7 paras. 1041–1111    – Game Laws
      10 paras. 687–766     – Nuisance and Non-natural Use of Property (Part)
      15 paras. 1126–1205   – Water and Water Rights
Henderson/Hogarth            Scottish Planning Sourcebook (1984)

| | |
|---|---|
| Jauncey | Fishing in Scotland (1984) |
| Scott Robinson | Law of Game, Salmon and Freshwater Fishing in Scotland (1990) |
| Walker | Principles Vol. III Chap. 4.39 – Injuries in respect of Heritable Property |
| Walker | Civil Remedies |
| Young & Rowan-Robinson | Scottish Planning Law and Procedure (1985) |
| Himsworth | Housing Law in Scotland (4th edn. 1994) |
| Lyall | Air, Noise, Water and Waste: a Summary of the Law in Scotland (1982) |
| Scottish Rights of Way Society | Rights of Way (1996) |
| Stair Encyclopaedia | Vol. 18.97 Property |
| | Vol. 18. Chap. 5 – Landownership (paras. 193–272) |
| | Vol. 25.127 Water and water rights |
| Rowan-Robinson & Lloyd | Land Development and the Infrastructure Lottery (1988) |

*Articles*

| | |
|---|---|
| 1992 JLS 306 | – Barony Title |
| 1993 JLS 187 | – Wheel Clamping on Private Property |
| 1993 JLS 156 | – Barony Title: a Response |
| Greens PLB Issue 9 p. 10 | – The New Law of Trespass |
| 1994 JR 283 | – The Theory and Ethics of Irritancy |
| 1995 JR 321 | – The Feudal System – Going, Going, Gone |
| 1995 JLS 63 | – Collective Trespass and Related Issues |

## Chapter 19. Restrictions on the Use of Land

*References*

| | |
|---|---|
| Young and Rowan-Robinson | Scottish Planning Law and Procedure (1985) |
| Himsworth | Housing Law in Scotland (4th edn. 1994) |
| Stair Encyclopaedia | Vol. 13.14 – Building controls |
| | Vol. 18 – Chap. 7 Real conditions etc. (paras. 344 438) |
| | Vol. 23.11 – Town and country planning |
| Scottish Rights of Way Society | Rights of Way (1996) |
| Rowan-Robinson | Compulsory Purchase and Compensation (1990) |
| Brodies | Scots Law and the Environment (1992) |
| Young, Eric | Greens Planning Acts (1993) |
| Collar, Neil | Planning (1994) |
| Young & Rowan-Robinson | Permitted Development (1997) |

*Statutes*

Ancient Monuments and Archaeological Areas Act 1979
Pests Act 1954
Weeds Act 1959
Factories Act 1961
Offices, Shops and Railway Premises Act 1963
Rivers (Prevention of Pollution) (Scotland) Acts 1951 and 1965
Countryside (Scotland) Act 1967
Building (Scotland) Acts 1959 and 1970
Fire Precautions Act 1971
Field Monuments Act 1972
Town and Country Planning (Scotland) Act 1972
Local Government (Scotland) Act 1973

Town and Country Amenities Act 1974
Health and Safety at Work etc. Act 1974
Mines (Working Facilities and Support) Act 1974
Control of Pollution Act 1974
Water (Scotland) Act 1980
Local Government Planning and Land Act 1980
Countryside (Scotland) Act 1981
Local Government (Miscellaneous Provisions) (Scotland) Act 1981
Local Government and Planning (Scotland) Act 1982
Civic Government (Scotland) Act 1982
Roads (Scotland) Act 1984
Housing (Scotland) Act 1986
Housing and Planning Act 1986
Abolition of Domestic Rates etc. (Scotland) Act 1987
Housing (Scotland) Act 1987
Housing (Scotland) Act 1988
Housing Act 1988
Farm Land and Rural Development Act 1988
Environmental Assessment (Scotland) Regulations 1988
Local Government and Housing Act 1989
Water Act 1989
Environmental Protection Act 1990
Planning and Compensation Act 1991
Natural Heritage Act 1991
Clean Air Act 1993
Radio Active Substances Acts 1993
Local Government etc. (Scotland) Act 1994
Environment Act 1995

*Articles*

| | |
|---|---|
| (1985) 15 SPLP 41 | – Section 50 Agreements: Procedural Provisions |
| (1987) 32 SPLP 56 | – The Award of Expenses at Planning Enquiries |
| (1988) 25 SPLP 65, 67 and 75; | (1989) 26 SPLP 11 – The Use Classes Order |
| 1989 JLS 206 | – Planning and Building Control Warranties |
| 1987 PQLE | – Role of Planning Law |
| 1987 PQLE | – Sources of Planning Law |
| 1987 PQLE | – Applying for Planning Permission |
| 1987 PQLE | – Conditions and Agreements |
| 1987 PQLE | – Role of the Solicitor in Planning Appeals |
| 1987 PQLE | – Role of the Reporter in Planning Appeals |
| 1987 PQLE | – Enforcement of Planning Provisions |
| 1987 PQLE | – Judicial Review |
| 1987 PQLE | – Planning and Building Control Clauses in Missives |
| 1988 PQLE | – Conveyancing – Planning and Building Control |
| 1989 PQLE | – Listed Building |
| 1989 PQLE | – Planning by Agreement |
| 1989 PQLE | – Planning Gain |
| 1989 PQLE | – Conveyancing and Planning |
| 1989 PQLE | – Compensation |
| 1989 PQLE | – Conveyancing: Planning and Building Control |
| (1990) 31 SPLP 68 | – The loss of rights to use or develop land |
| 1990 PQLE | – The view from the Scottish Office on Planning |
| 1990 PQLE | – Enforcement Notices and Appeals |
| 1990 PQLE | – Building Control Problems |
| 1990 PQLE | – Countryside Controls |
| 1990 PQLE | – Planning Gain |

| | |
|---|---|
| 1990 PQLE | – Changes in Planning Law |
| 1990 PQLE | – Recent Developments in Judicial Review |
| (1991) 32 SPLP 4 and 33 SPLP 39 | – Judicial Review in Planning |
| 1991 PQLE | – Environment Law |
| (1992) 35 SPLP 5 | – Contaminated Land |
| (1992) 35 SPLP 7 | – Environmental Assessment and Private Legislation |
| (1992) 35 SPLP 8 | – Pollution Control in Scotland |
| (1992) 35 SPLP 10 | – SSSI's and Part II of the Wildlife and Countryside Act 1981 |
| 1992 JLS 397 | – Planning by Agreement and the Conveyancer |
| (1992) 37 SPLP 68 | – Why use Section 50 Agreements? |
| (1993) 39 SPEL 37 | – Basics of Pollution Control |
| (1993) 39 SPEL 39 | – Conveyancing & Planning Matters |
| (1993) 38 JLS 312 | – Planning Appeals – Written Submissions |
| (1993) 38 SPLP 8 | – Use of Planning Agreements in Scotland |
| (1994) 42 SPEL 20 | – Enforcement – two years on |
| 1994 Conv. 31 | – Planning Decisions and Planning Agreements |
| Greens PLB Issue 7 p. 7 | – Validity of Planning Permission |
| 1995 SCOLAG 22 | – Planning, Pollution Control |
| (1995) 50 SPEL 60 | – The Limits of Planning Agreements |
| Greens PLB Issue 23 p. 7 | – Compulsory Purchase and Compensation |
| Greens PLB Issue 24 p. 3 | – Contaminated Land: Environmental Protection Act 1990 |

## Part 4 – SUBORDINATE RIGHTS IN THE FEU-SECURITIES AND LEASES

### Chapter 20. Securities

*References*

| | |
|---|---|
| Gordon | Scottish Land Law – Chap. 20 |
| Gloag & Irvine | Rights in Security (1897) |
| Green's Encyclopaedia | Vols. as follows: |
| | 1 paras. 1–50 — Absolute Disposition |
| | 2 paras. 790–814 — Bond |
| | 2 paras. 1049–1065 — Burdens |
| | 5 paras. 1024–1035 *Debita Fundi* |
| | 7 paras. 1292–1319 — Ground Annual |
| | 7 paras. 1420–1453 — Heritable Securities |
| | 13 paras. 777–845 — Securities |
| Burns | Handbook Chaps. 4, 20 |
| Burns | Practice Chaps. 14, 25, 27, 29–34 |
| Halliday | 1970 Act Chaps. 5–10 |
| Halliday | Practice Vol. 3 Part II – Heritable Securities (1987) |
| Conveyancing Miscellany | p. 33 – The Coming of the Floating Charge |
| | p. 126 – The Concept of Security |
| Cusine | Standard Securities (1991) |
| Stair Encyclopaedia | Vol. 6. paras. 617–700 |
| | Vol. 20. paras. 108–272 |

*Articles*

| | |
|---|---|
| 1993 JLS 185 | – Mandates, Assignations and Arrestments |

*Statutes*
Bankruptcy Act 1696
Blank Bonds and Trusts Act 1696

Heritable Securities (Scotland) Acts 1845 and 1847
Debt Securities (Scotland) Act 1856
1868 Act ss. 117–135
1874 Act ss. 47–49
Heritable Securities (Scotland) Act 1894
1924 Act ss. 23, 25, 43
Succession (Scotland) Act 1964
1970 Act Parts II and III
Redemption of Standard Securities (Scotland) Act 1971

*Articles*

| | |
|---|---|
| 1962 SLT (News) 149 | – Campbell's J.F. v. National Bank of Scotland |
| 1 Conveyancing Review 5 | – The *Ex Facie* Absolute Disposition |
| 2 Conveyancing Review 129 | – The Bondholder's Final Remedy |
| 2 Conveyancing Review 177 | – Securities over Reversions of Heritable Property |
| 3 Conveyancing Review 51 | – *Ex Facie* Absolute Disposition in Security of Loans |
| 3 Conveyancing Review 132 | – Completion of Title to Heritable Securities |
| 1967 JLS 32 | – *Ex Facie* Absolute Dispositions – The Fall of the House of Usher |
| 1972 JLS 370 | – Secured Loans and Restraint of Trade |
| 1979 JLS 462 | – *Ex* Facie Absolute Dispositions and their Discharge |
| 1980 JLS 54 | – *Ex Facie* Absolute Dispositions and their Discharge |

## Chapter 22. Standard Securities

*Articles*

| | |
|---|---|
| 1980 JLS 275 | – Ranking of Heritable Creditors |
| 1981 JLS 26 and 280 | – Ranking of Heritable Creditors |
| 1983 50 SLG 81 | – Securities over leases |
| 1983 JR 177 | – Prescription and the foreclosure of adjudications |
| 1983 SLT (News) 169 & 189 | – Real Conditions in Standard Securities |
| 1985 JLS 130 and 181 | – The Consumer Credit Act 1974 |
| 1985 JLS 159 | – Bridging Loans and the Consumer Credit Regulations |
| 1985 JLS 222 | – The Consumer Credit Act 1974 – Loan Agreements and Standard Securities |
| 1985 SLT (News) 125 | – Inhibitions and Standard Securities |
| 1986 PQLE | – The Consumer Credit Act and its implications for conveyancers |
| 1988 PQLE | – Lending and Financial Packages |
| 1989 PQLE | – Exercise of Power of Sale by Creditors Under Standard Securities |
| 1989 SLT (News) 201 | – Creditor's Remedies under a Standard Security |
| 1990 PQLE | – Security Transactions and Related Matters |
| 1990 JLS 97 and 127 | – Descriptions in Standard Securities |
| 1991 SLT (News) 195 | – Discharge of a Debtor and Securities |
| 1991 JR 169 | – Power of Sale Under a Standard Security |
| 1993 JLS 158 | – A Note on Ranking Agreements |
| 1993 JLS 199 Caveat | – Discharging Loans and Ranking Agreements |
| 1994 JR 18 | – Expenses under a Standard Security |
| 1994 JLS 52 | – Inhibitions, Standard Securities and Further Advances |
| 1994 SLT (News) 93 | – Controlling Creditors' Rights under Standard Securities |
| 1994 JLS 135 | – The Lender and the Solicitor's Duty of Care |
| Greens PLB Issue 7 p. 5 | – Advertising Requirements in a Sale by a Heritable Creditor |
| 1994 JLS 257 | – The Duties of a Standard Security Holder |

| | |
|---|---|
| 1994 SLT (News) 207 | – Assignation of All Sums Standard Securities |
| 1994 JLS 263 | – Note on *AIB Finance* (see 22.17) |
| 1995 JLS 58 | – Negligence, Securities and the Expanding Duty of Care |
| 1995 JLS 245 | – Lending Institutions, Loan Instructions and Reports on Title |
| 1995 JLS 363 Caveat | – Undisclosed Securities |
| 1995 JLS 357 | – Descriptions in Standard Securities |
| 1995 JLS 400 | – Enforcing Standard Securities |
| 1995 JLS 481 | – Descriptions in Standard Securities – (Note by the Keeper) |
| 1995 221 Scolag 41 | – Mortgages Explained |
| 1996 JLS 209 | – Descriptions in Standard Securities – Where Now? |
| 1996 JLS 232 Caveat | – Inadequate instructions from lenders |
| 1996 JLS 404 | – Certificates of Title |

## Chapter 23. Floating Charges

*References*

| | |
|---|---|
| Greene & Fletcher | The Law and Practice of Receivership in Scotland (2nd edn. 1992) |
| St. Clair & Drummond Young | The Law of Corporate Insolvency in Scotland (2nd edn. 1992) |
| Stair Encyclopaedia | Vol. 4, paras. 647–715 |

*Statutes*

Companies Act 1985 ss. 410–424, 462 and 466
Insolvency Act 1986 ss. 50–72
Companies Act 1989 ss. 92–107 and 140

*Articles*

| | |
|---|---|
| 1981 JLS 57 and 102 | – Diligence, Trusts and Floating Charges |
| 1982 SLT (News) 177 | – The Registration of Charges |
| 1983 SLT (News) 253 | – Floating Charges and Fraudulent Preferences |
| 1984 SLT (News) 25 | – The Receiver and effectually executed diligence |
| 1984 SLT (News) 105, 172, 117 | – The Nature of Receivership; Floating Charges; Receivers and Arresters |
| 1985 JLS 242 | – Future Assets and Double Attachments |
| 1986 SLT (News) 325 | – Should Floating Charges and Receivership be Abolished? |
| 1987 SLT (News) 113 | – Trusts and Floating Charges |
| 1988 SLT (News) 194 | – Trusts and Liquidators – Further Thoughts |
| 1988 JLS 53 | – Using Trusts as Commercial Securities |
| 1988 SLT (News) 81 | – Restitution and Property Law |
| 1988 JLS 357 | – Set–off and Receivership |
| 1989 JLS 50 | – Searches: (1) Companies |
| 1989 SLT (News) 143 | – Trusts and Liquidators |
| 1992 Update (April) | – Heritable and Moveable Securities: Floating Charges, some problems of constitution and enforcement |
| 1993 JLS 199 Caveat | – Discharging Loans and Ranking Agreements |
| Greens PLB Issue 2 p. 5 | – Guidance on completion of forms for Register of Charges |
| 1994 SLT (News) 183 | – Dead on Delivery |
| 1994 JLS 356 | – *Sharp v. Thomson* – difficulties at settlement |
| 1994 JLS 372 | – Comments on *Sharp* v. *Thomson* |
| 1994 JLS 384 | – *Sharp* v. *Thomson*, declaration of trust and stamp duty |
| 1994 JLS 444 | – *Sharp* v. *Thomson*, comments on ranking |
| 1994 SLT (News) 313 | – Sharp cases make good law |

1994 SLT (News) 75      – *Sharp* v. *Thomson* – A civilian perspective
1995 JLS 7      – *Sharp* v. *Thomson*: Feudal Purism, but is it Justice?
1995 JLS 92      – *Sharp* v. *Thomson*
1995 SLT (News) 79      – *Sharp* v. *Thomson* – Identifying the mischief
1995 JLS 256      – *Sharp* v. *Thomson* – What Now?
1996 SLT (News) 365      – The Perils of a Trusting Disposition
1997 SLT (News) 79      – Jam Today: *Sharp* in the House of Lords
                                (On *Sharp* v. *Thomson*, see also Ch. 4)
(and see Articles listed under Chapters 3 and 4)

## Chapter 24. Leases

*References*

| | |
|---|---|
| Gordon | Scottish Land Law, Chap. 19 |
| Burns | Practice Chap. 35 |
| Burns | Handbook Chap. 21 |
| Gloag & Henderson | Chap. 33 |
| Himsworth | Housing Law in Scotland (4th edn. 1994) |
| McAllister | The Scottish Law of Leases: An Introduction (2nd edn. 1995) |
| Megarry, R. E. | The Rent Acts (11th edn. 1988) |
| Menzies | Lectures Chap. 29 |
| Paton and Cameron | The Law of Landlord and Tenant in Scotland (1967) |
| Rankine | Leases |
| Watchman | The Housing (Scotland) Act 1987 (1991) |
| Green's Encyclopaedia | Vol. 9 paras. 140–248 Leases |
| Stair Encyclopaedia | Vol. 13. paras. 101–548 |

*Statutes*
Leases Act 1449
Registration of Leases (Scotland) Act 1857
Hypothec Abolition (Scotland) Act 1880
Removal Terms (Scotland) Act 1886
Heritable Securities (Scotland) Act 1894
Sheriff Courts (Scotland) Act 1907
Conveyancing (Scotland) Act 1924
Tenancy of Shops (Scotland) Act 1949 and 1964
Long Leases (Scotland) Act 1954
Succession (Scotland) Act 1964
Conveyancing and Feudal Reform (Scotland) Act 1970
Land Tenure Reform (Scotland) Act 1974
Crofting Reform (Scotland) Act 1976
Land Registration (Scotland) Act 1979
Tenants' Rights etc. (Scotland) Act 1980
Law Reform (Miscellaneous Provisions) (Scotland) Act 1985
Term and Quarter Days (Scotland) Act 1990
Requirements of Writing (Scotland) Act 1995

*Articles*
2 Conveyancing Review 47      – The Tenancy of Shops Act 1949
1962 Conveyancing Review 39      – *Rei interitus* in Leases
1972 JLS 121      – Crofting Law
1980 JLS 319      – The Tenants' Rights, etc. (Scotland) Bill
1980 SLT (News) 125      – The Tenants' Rights, etc. (Scotland) Bill

| | |
|---|---|
| 1981 JLS W 215,<br> W 223, W 231 | Calculating Fair Rents |
| 1981 SLT (News) 101 | – The Tenants' Rights etc. (Scotland) Act 1980 – Part IV |
| 1981 JLS 376 and 1982 JLS 21 | – How irritating are Landlords actually? |
| 1981 JLS 383 | – The Tenants' Rights etc. (Scotland) Act 1980 – Part II |
| 1982 JLS 161 | – The Tenants' Rights etc. (Scotland) Act 1980 – Part I |
| 1983 86 Scolag 169 | – Methods of Calculating Fair Rents |
| 1983 2 CSW 534 | – Scots Law – Irritancies in Leases |
| 1989 SLT (News) 431 | – Termination date in Notice to Quit |
| 1990 160 Scolag | – Security of Tenure |
| 1990 SLT (News) 257 | – Term and Quarter Days defined |
| 1991 173 Scolag 30, 174<br> Scolag 42 | – Resident Landlords and their Tenants |
| 1992 Update (April) | – Securities and Leases: Heritable and Moveable Securities |
| Greens PLB Issue 9 p. 6 | – A Landlord's Common Law Obligations |
| Greens PLB Issue 15 p. 8 | – Extraordinary Repairs |
| Greens PLB Issue 16 p. 3 | – Tenancy of Shops (Scotland) Act 1949 |
| Greens PLB Issue 18 p. 3 | – Landlord's Hypothec |
| Greens PLB Issue 21 p. 4 | – Tenant's Repairing Obligation |
| Greens PLB Issue 22 p. 7 | – Notices to Quit |
| Greens PLB Issue 24 p. 6 | – Tacit Relocation |
| 1996 SLPQ 1(3) | – Requirements of Writing: Problems of Practice |

## Chapter 25. Commercial Leases

*References*

| | |
|---|---|
| Ross and McKichan | Drafting and Negotiating Commercial Leases in Scotland (2nd edn. 1993) |
| Halliday's Practice Vol. III | Leases, esp. Chap. 29 |
| McAllister | The Scottish Law of Leases (2nd edn. 1995) |
| Lewison, K. | Drafting Business Leases (1980) |
| Clarke, D. N. and Adams, J. E. | Rent Reviews and Variable Rents (1981) |
| Aldridge, T. M. | Letting of Business Premises 4th edn. |
| Stair Encyclopaedia | Vol. 13. paras. 555–589 |

*Articles*

| | |
|---|---|
| 1976 JLS (Jan) 4 | – Irritancies in Leases |
| 1976 JLS (Oct) 368 | – Irritability of the Rash Tenant |
| 1977 JLS 20 | – Rent Review – A Search for the True Purpose |
| 1977 JLS 309 | – Disaster in Leases – *Rei Interitus* |
| 1979 JLS (Workshop) 38 | – Policy Decisions – Analysis of Insurance Provisions in Leases |
| 1979 JLS (Workshop) (xxi) | – Ground Leases – A consideration of pitfalls |
| 1979 JLS (Workshop) (xlv) | – Ground Leases – Further consideration |
| 1979 JLS (Workshop) (v) | – Assigning and subletting |
| 1979 JLS (Workshop) (lv) | – Findings by Arbiters |
| 1979 NLJ 839 | – The Lessons of Ravenseft |
| 1980 JLS (Workshop) 117 | – Styles Committee Lease |
| 1980 JLS (Workshop) 171 | – Comment on Style Lease |
| 1981 JLS 295 | – Less Irritating – Scottish Law Commission Memorandum No. 52 – Irritancies in Leases (1981) |
| 1982 NLJ 993 | – Drafting Rent Review Clauses – A Cautionary Tale |
| 1982 NLJ 677 | – Major Structural Repairs |
| 1982 NLJ 786 | – Tenant's Right to Remove Fixtures |

| | |
|---|---|
| 1983 JLS (Workshop) April April *et seq* | – Rent Review Clauses in Commercial Lease |
| 1983 JLS 519 | – The Scottish Commercial Lease: The Way Ahead |
| 1985 JLS 99 | – The Scottish Commercial Lease Grows Up |
| 1985 JLS 432 | – Enter the Fair and Reasonable Landlord |
| 1988 PQLE | – Commercial Conveyancing and Licensing Course |
| 1989 PQLE | – Commercial Leasing Course |
| 1989 PQLE | – Commercial Conveyancing Course |
| 1989 PQLE | – Landlord and Tenant Legislation Course |
| 1990 PQLE | – Commercial Leasing Course |
| 1990 PQLE | – Commercial Conveyancing Course |
| 1991 PQLE | – Commercial Leasing Course |
| 1991 PQLE | – Landlord and Tenant Course |
| 1991 PQLE | – General Conveyancing Course |
| 1992 PQLE | – Commercial Missives Seminar |
| 1992 PQLE | – Commercial Leasing |
| Greens PLB Issue 1 p. 3 | – Essential Aspects of Rent Review |
| Greens PLB Issue 2 p. 6 | – Essential Aspects of Rent Review |
| Greens PLB Issue 9 p. 6 | – A Landlord's Common Law Obligations |
| 1994 SLT (News) 1 | – Limited Interests in Property, Covenants to Insure and Subrogation |
| Greens PLB Issue 13 p. 10 | – Rent-Free Periods and Rent Review – The case so far |
| Greens PLB Issue 15 p. 2 | – Keep-Open Clauses |
| Greens PLB Issue 15 p. 8 | – Extraordinary Repairs |
| Greens PLB Issue 16 p. 3 | – Tenancy of Shops (Scotland) Act 1949 |
| Greens PLB Issue 17 p. 5 | – Assignation/Sub-Letting: Consent |
| Greens PLB Issue 18 p. 3 | – Landlord's Hypothec |
| 1995 JLS 349 | – Rent Review – Headline Rents v. Open Market Rents |
| Greens PLB Issue 19 p. 10 | – Rent Review and Waiver |
| Greens PLB Issue 20 p. 11 | – Schedules of Condition of Repair |
| Greens PLB Issue 21 p. 4 | – Tenant's Improvements |
| Greens PLB Issue 22 p. 7 | – Notices to Quit |
| Greens PLB Issue 23 p. 5 | – Tenant's Default: What are the Landlord's Options? |
| Greens PLB Issue 24 p. 6 | – Tacit Relocation |
| 1996 SLPQ 166 | – Assignation: Approaches to the Reasonable Landlord |
| 1996 JLS 228 | – Enforcing Keep-Open Clauses |
| Greens PLB Issue 25 p. 2 | – *Taylor Woodrow Property Co. Ltd.* |
| Scottish Law Commission Report No. 75 | – Irritancies in Leases (1983) |

**Chapter 26. Agricultural Leases**

*References*

| | |
|---|---|
| Agnew of Lochnaw | Agricultural Law in Scotland (1996) |
| Connell | The Agricultural Holdings (Scotland) Acts (7th edn. by Rennie & Agnew of Lochnaw, 1996) |
| Gill, B. | The Law of Agricultural Holdings in Scotland (2nd edn. 1990) |
| The Law Society of Scotland | Aspects of Agricultural Law |
| Duncan | The Agricultural Holdings (Scotland) Act 1991 |

*Statutes*
Hill Farming Act 1946
Agriculture (Scotland) Act 1948
Agriculture Act 1958

Succession (Scotland) Act 1964
Agriculture (Miscellaneous Provisions) Act 1968
Agriculture (Miscellaneous Provisions) Act 1976
Agricultural Holdings (Amendment) (Scotland) Act 1983
Agricultural Holdings (Scotland) Act 1991
Scottish Land Court Act 1993

*Articles*

| | |
|---|---|
| 1980 JLS (Workshop) 135 | – Style Agricultural Lease |
| PQLE 1992 and 1989 | – Advanced Agricultural Law |
| 1991 PQLE | – Agricultural Law (basic) |
| 1988 SLT (News) 65 | The Crofter and his Right to Buy |
| 1989 SLT (News) 256 | – Special Destinations and Agricultural Leases |
| 1990 JLS 463 | – Land Tenure 40 years on |
| 1990 JLS 434 | – The value of an agricultural tenancy |
| 1991 JLS 465 | – The value of an agricultural tenancy – update |
| 1992 SLT (News) 1 | – The Agricultural Holdings (Scotland) Act 1991 |
| 1993 SLT (News) 351 | – Unforeseen consequences of the Agricultural Holdings (Scotland) Act 1991 |
| Greens PLB Issue 2 p. 4 | – Procedure in the Scottish Land Court |
| 1996 JLS 249 | – The Agricultural Holdings (Scotland) Act 1991 – Is there a case for change? |

## Chapter 27. Residential Leases

*References*

| | |
|---|---|
| Himsworth | Housing Law in Scotland (4th edn. 1994) |
| McAllister | The Scottish Law of Leases: An Introduction (2nd edn. 1995) |
| McKerrell | The Rent Acts (1985) |
| Mitchell | Eviction and Rent Arrears (1995) |
| Robson | The Housing (Scotland) Act 1988 (1989) |
| Robson | Residential Tenancies (1994) |

*Statutes*

Rent (Scotland) Act 1984
Housing (Scotland) Act 1988
Leasehold Reform, Housing and Urban Development Act 1994

*Articles*

| | |
|---|---|
| 1989 SLT (News) 245 | – The Housing (Scotland) Act 1988 and Private Sector Rented Accommodation |
| 1990 SLT (News) 93 | – Assured and Short Assured Tenancies |
| 1990 JLS 425 | – The Rights of Secure Tenants |
| 1992 SLT (News) 21 | – Assured Tenancies: Notices to Quit and Form AT6 |
| Greens PLB Pilot p. 5 | – Residential Leases – Notices to Quit |
| Greens PLB Issue 3 p. 8 | – Assured Tenancy Statutory Forms |
| Greens PLB Issue 14 p. 2 | – Holiday Lettings |
| 1994 JLS 333 | – More Tenants' Rights |
| 1995 JLS 435 | – Ejection *brevi manu* and Hostel Dwellings |

Part 5 – TRANSMISSION OF THE FEU

**Chapters 28 and 29. Contracts of Sale and Purchase of Heritage and the Special Disposition**

*References*

| | |
|---|---|
| Halliday | Practice – Chap. 15 – Contracts for Sale and Purchase of Heritable Property |
| Halliday | Practice – Chap. 22 – Dispositions |
| Burns | Handbook Chaps. 14, 17 |
| Cusine and Rennie | Missives |

Green's Encyclopaedia Vols. as follows:
   4 paras. 500–526 Completion of Title (part)
   4 paras. 922–939 Consolidation
   5 paras. 1320–1369 Disposition (part)
   6 paras. 952–971 Excambion
   13 paras. 317–451 Sale of Heritable Property (part)

| | |
|---|---|
| Stair Society | Vol. 20 |
| Burns | Practice Chaps. 9, 16, 19, 23 |
| Gloag | Contract Chaps. 10, 20, 23 |
| Conveyancing Miscellany | p. 91 – Delays in Settlement of Conveyancing Transactions |
| McBryde on Contract | Chaps. 14 and 20 |
| Walker | Damages Chap. 12 |
| Walker | Principles Vol. III – Chap. 5 |
| Stair Encyclopaedia | Vol. 18 Property – Transfer of Ownership |
| Sinclair's Handbook | Chaps. 3 to 6 |
| Obligations in context | Essays in Honour of Prof. D. M. Walker: Suspensive and Resolutive Conditions in the Scots Law of Contract |
| Scottish Law Commission | Report No. 127 (1990) – Passing of Risk in Contracts for the Sale of Land |
| Scottish Law Commission | Discussion Paper 97 – Contract Law, Extrinsic Evidence, Supersession and the *actio quanti minoris* |
| Scottish Law Commission | Report No. 152 – Three bad rules in contract law. This is a follow-up to the preceding discussion paper No. 97 and deals with the same topics. |
| Walker | The Law of Contracts and related obligations in Scotland (3rd edn. 1995) |
| Woolman | Contract (2nd edn. 1994) |

The Law Society of Scotland Guidance Notes 1994
   Coal Mining Searches

*Statutes*
1868 Act ss. 5, 8, 141–143
1874 Act ss. 4, 6, 32
1924 Act ss. 8–11, 48

*Articles*
1956 SLT (News) 137
2 Conveyancing Review 165 – Mineral Reservations and the Unwilling Purchaser
2 Conveyancing Review 193 – Personal Rights
2 Conveyancing Review 189 – Delays in Settlement
3 Conveyancing Review 13 – Situation of Seller under Missives
3 Conveyancing Review 129 – Remedies for Breach of Missives
1966 JLS 124 – The *Actio Quanti Minoris*

1966 JLS 264 — *Rei Interventus* Reconsidered
1967 SLT (News) 231 — The Reserved Right to Bid
1968 JLS 46 — Sale by Instalments
1969 JLS 138 — Division of Large Industrial Units
1969 JLS 70 — Delayed Settlement
1970 JLS 10 — Sale of Heritage
1971 JLS 179 — The Purchase and Sale of Houses
1972 JLS 315 — Missives
1972 JLS 316 — Sale and Purchase of Heritage
1973 JLS 29 — Sale of Heritage: Fair Dealing
1976 JLS 317 — Notices of Change of Ownership
1976 JLS 282 — Conditions in Missives
1978 JLS 277 — Sale of Heritage – Interest
1979 JLS 485 — Housebuilders' Missives
1979 JLS Workshop vii — Liability to Pay Interest
1980 JLS 17 — Housebuilders' Missives
1980 JLS W.103 — A Question of Interest
1980 SLG 68 — Delay in Settlement
1980 NLJ 171, 195, 219 — NHBC Scheme Revision
1980 SLG 86 — NHBC (Scotland)
1981 JLS 414 — Winston v Patrick
1982 JLS 37 — Winston v Patrick Again
1982 JLS Workshop 313 — Recent Authority on Missives
1983 JLS 45 — The New Missives
1983 JLS 49 — The Lord Chancellor's Fixtures
1983 JLS 116 & 273 — Delays in Settlement
1983 JLS Workshop 339 — Avoiding Winston v Patrick
1984 JLS 103 — Heirs, Executors and Assignees
1984 JLS 448 — The Use of Referential Bids in Offers
1986 SLT (News) 137 — *Rei Interventus* Revisited
1986 SLT (News) 293 — Disclaiming Liability for Negligent Property Surveys
1986 SLT (News) 317 — Error Revisited
1986 JLS 316 — Five Years On – Living with Winston v Patrick
1988 SLT (News) 221 — Commercial Practice and the Formation of Contracts
1988 JLS 7 — Winston v Patrick etc.
1988 JLS 57 — Missives and the Disposition
1988 JLS 89 — House Valuations and Surveys
1988 JLS 102 — Winston v Patrick etc.
1988 JLS 162 — Good and Marketable Title
1988 JLS 285 — The *Actio Quanti Minoris* and Conveyancing Practice
1988 JLS 431 — Date of Entry or Date of Settlement
1988 JLS 484 — Surveyors' Negligence – The Assessment of Damages
1989 JLS 175 — Date of Entry or Date of Settlement
1989 JLS 206 — Planning and Building Control Warranties
1990 JLS 349 — Discharges in Land Registration
1990 JLS 482 — Fees for Forms 10 to 13
1990 JLS 146 — The right to buy
1990 SLT (News) 337 — The future liability for defective buildings
1990 JLS 412 — Matrimonial Homes Act conveyancing
1991 JLS 73 — Who signs for the Firm?
1991 SLT 77 — Gratuitous Alienations and Unfair Preferences under the 1985 Act
1991 JLS 405 — The Property Misdescriptions Act
1991 JLS 334 — VAT on the Purchase and Sale of Heritage
1991 SLT (News) 185 and 253 — Protestative Conditions in Contracts of Sale and Purchase of Heritage

| | |
|---|---|
| 1995 JLS 175 | – Matrimonial Homes Affidavits and Blind Persons. Responding to a letter in 1995 JLS 135 |
| 1995 JLS 142 | – Standard Missives – A Success Story |
| 1995 JLS 267 | – Commercial Law Update (Comments on *Sharp* v. *Thomson* and *Fortune* v. *Fraser*) |
| 1995 JLS 282 Caveat | – 'Disposal' under The Housing (Scotland) Act 1987 of a Local Authority house previously purchased and then donated which may be treated as a disposal resulting in a clawback |
| 1995 JLS 273 | – Unfair Contracts – A comment on the terms of builders' missives with particular reference to the Unfair Terms in Consumer Contracts Regulations 1994 (S.I. 1994 No 3159). These regulations may apply to missives, particularly builders' missives, and as a result may cause problems |
| Greens PLB Issue 19 p. 2 | – Setting missives up and apart. A discussion on the problem of identifying what is intended to be part of a contract and what is not, following the relaxations under the 1995 Act |
| 1996 JLS 9 | – A comment on the same topic |
| Greens PLB Issue 19 p. 11 | – Waiver of suspensive conditions. A note on *Manheath Ltd.* |
| 1995 JLS 326 | – A note on Coal Mining Searches |
| 1996 JLS 150 | – A note on the Construction (Design and Management) Regulations 1994 |
| 1996 JLS 8 | – A comment in two letters on the foregoing regulations |
| 1995 JLS 316 | – Property Enquiry Certificates. A suggestion that, with the new councils coming into operation, this whole area should be standardised |
| 1996 JLS 191 Caveat | – The problem of a purchaser's future plans for development etc. not disclosed to the solicitors at the time of purchase, resulting in a claim for negligence for failing to provide for access etc. |
| Greens PLB Issue 17 p. 2 | – Rescission of missives and in particular materiality |
| 1995 JLS 428 | – Liquidate damages – provision in missives. A follow-up to *Lloyds Bank plc* v. *Bamberger* |
| 1996 JLS 32 Caveat | – A warning against allowing phrases like 'as shown to the purchaser' in missives, which applies both to seller and purchaser |
| Greens PLB Issue 16 p. 2 | – Purchasing residential property for unmarried couples |
| Greens PLB Issue 20 p. 2 and 21 p. 2 | – The Construction (Design and Management) Regulations 1994 |
| 1996 SLT (News) 365 | – The perils of a Trusting Disposition |
| Greens PLB Issue 24 p. 11 | – Preparing deeds for conveyancing |
| Greens PLB Issue 23 p. 2 | – *Winston* v. *Patrick* Revisited: The Two Year Enforceability Clause |
| Greens PLB Issue 26 p. 1 | – The Seller's Remedies |

**Chapter 30. Statutory Titles**

*References*

| | |
|---|---|
| Burns | Handbook Chap. 19 |
| Burns | Practice Chap. 15 |
| Law Society of Scotland | Compulsory Purchase in Scotland |
| Coull | Bankruptcy (2nd edn. 1995) |
| Graham Stewart | Diligence |

Green's Encyclopaedia Vols. as follows:
  1 paras. 298–372 Adjudication
  4 paras. 564–567 Completion of Title
  4 paras. 607–626 and 684–686 Compulsory Purchase;
    1949 Supplement – Part 1 Acquisition of Land (Authorisation Procedure) (Scotland) Act 1947
  12 paras. 736–752 Reduction

| | |
|---|---|
| Gretton | The Law of Inhibitions and Adjudications (2nd edn. 1996) |
| Halliday | Conveyancing Law and Practice 2nd edn. Chap. 25 |
| Maher and Cusine | The Law and Practice of Diligence (1990) |
| McBryde | Bankruptcy (2nd edn. 1995) |
| Scott-Robinson | The Law of Interdict (1987) |
| Stair Encyclopaedia | Vol. 5.24 – Compulsory acquisition |
| | Vol. 2.11 – Bankruptcy |
| | Vol. 8.34 – Diligence, etc. |

(i) *Judicial titles*
*Statutes*
1868 Act ss 59, 62, 129
1924 Act s. 46

*Articles*

| | |
|---|---|
| 1979 JLS 101 | – Ranking of Inhibitors |
| 1982 JLS 13 and 68 | – Inhibitions, Securities, Reductions and Multiplepoindings |
| 1983 SLT (News) 145 & 177 | – Inhibitions and Company Insolvencies |
| 1983 JR 177 | – Prescription and Foreclosure of Adjudications |
| 1983 JLS 495 | – Inhibitions and Securities for Future Advances |
| 1984 JLS 357 | – The Title of a Liquidator |
| 1984 JLS 400 | – Delivery of Deeds and the Race to the Register |
| 1985 JLS 20 | – Bankruptcy etc. and the Race to the Register |
| 1985 JLS 109 | – Insolvency and Title: a Reply |
| 1986 SLT (News) 125 | – Reduction of Heritable Titles |
| 1990 JLS 52 | – Property Transfer Orders under the Family Law (Scotland) Act 1985 |
| 1990 JLS 236 | – Statutory Conveyances and Examination of Title |
| 1990 JLS 453 and 510 | – Positive and Negative Interdicts |
| 1990 SLT 77 | – Gratuitous Alienations and Unfair Preferences under the 1985 Act |
| 1991 SLT (News) 258 | – Bankruptcy (Scotland) Act 1985 |
| 1991 SLT (News) 219 | – Development in Personal Insolvency Law |
| 1992 JLS 346 | – Aspects of Insolvency Conveyancing |
| 1992 JLS 326 | – A note on the Bankruptcy (Scotland) Bill |
| 1992 SLT (News) 215 | – Error Revised |
| 1993 JLS 141 | – Gratuitous Alienations and Unfair Preferences in Insolvency |
| 1993 JLS 205 | – A cautionary note for conveyancers – the warrant to cite in the personal registers |
| 1993 JLS 261 | – Trust Deeds for Creditors |

1994 JLS 205                    – A cautionary note for conveyancers – sequestration
1994 SLT (News) 185            – Dead on Delivery – a comment on *Sharp* v. *Thomson*


(ii) *Compulsory purchase*
Stair Encyclopaedia Vol. 5     – Compulsory Acquisition


*Statutes*
Lands Clauses (Consolidation) (Scotland) Act 1845
Railways Clauses (Consolidation) (Scotland) Act 1845
Acquisition of Land (Authorisation Procedure) (Scotland) Act 1947
Town and Country Planning (Scotland) Act 1972 as amended
Land Compensation (Scotland) Acts 1963 and 1973
Housing (Scotland) Act 1987
Planning and Compensation Act 1991


*Articles*
1956 SLT (News) 103            – Schedule Conveyances
1964 SLT (News) 205            – Schedule Conveyances
1969 JLS 321                   – Statutory Conveyances
1973 SLT (News) 47            – Schedule Conveyances and the 1845 Act
1980 JLS Workshop 142         – Statutory Conveyances
1985 SLT (News) 205           – Compulsory Purchase and the Valuation Date
1990 JLS 236 and 1992         – The effect of Schedule Conveyances under the Land Clauses
    JLS 5, 68 and 182             Act 1845 with particular reference to examination of title
Greens PLB Issue 23 p. 7      – Planning


## Chapter 31. Transmission on Death


*References*
Halliday                      Practice Vol. IV
Burns                         Handbook Chaps. 24–27
Meston                        Chap. 8
Currie                        Confirmation of Executors (7th edn. 1972)
Burns                         Practice Chaps. 22, 38, 39, 45
Green's Encyclopaedia Vols. as follows:
    3 paras. 1236–1241 – Commissary Court
    4 paras. 463–499, 549–556 – Completion of Title (part)
    4 paras. 812–880 – Confirmation of Executors
    6 paras. 1116–1148 – Executor
    15 paras. 1083–1097 – Vitious Intromission
Walker                        Principles Vol. III – Chap. 7.6
Scottish Law Commission   Report on Succession (No. 124–1990)


*Statutes*
Confirmation of Executors (Scotland) Act 1823
1868 Act ss. 19, 20, 27–50, 101–103, 125–128
1874 Act ss. 9, 10, 29, 31, 46
Executors (Scotland) Act 1900
Trusts (Scotland) Act 1961 s. 2
1924 Act s. 5
1964 Act ss. 14–22, 30, 36
Law Reform (Miscellaneous Provisions) (Scotland) Act 1968 s. 19
Administration of Estates Act 1971

Acts of Sederunt – Confirmation of Executors Amendment 1966
Confirmation of Executors 1967

*Articles*

| | |
|---|---|
| 1977 SLT (News) 197 | – Survivorship Destinations |
| 1977 JLS 16 | – What makes a Destination Special? |
| 1979 SLT (News) 257 | – Deduction of Title – A Recurring Problem |
| 1984 JLS 103 | – Heirs, Executors and Assignees |
| 1984 SLT (News) 133, 180 and 299 | – Special Destinations and Liability for Debt |
| 1984 JLS 154 | – Debts and Destinations |
| 1984 SLT (News) 245 | – Notes on Petitions for Service of Heirs |
| 1985 SLT (News) 57, 92 and 98 | – Common Property |
| 1987 JLS 111 | – Trust and Executry Conveyancing |
| 1989 SLT (News) 256 | – Special Destinations and Agricultural Leases |
| 1989 JLS 299 | – Destinations |
| 1990 JLS 189 | – Special Destinations in Scotland |
| 1991 SLT (News) 395 | – Age of Capacity under the 1991 Act. Can they or can't they? |
| 1992 SLT (News) 77 and 91 | – Age of Capacity - Pitfalls |

## Chapter 32. Completion of Title

| | |
|---|---|
| Halliday | Practice Chaps. 45 and 48 |
| Burns | Practice Chaps. 21, 33, 45 and 46 |

*References*

Conveyancing Miscellany p. 57 – Completion of Title
Currie – Confirmation of Executors (8th edn. 1996 *passim*)
Green's Encyclopaedia
    Vol. 4 paras. 432–448 and 527–548 Completion of Title (parts)
    Vol. 5 paras. 1370–1378, 1433–1440 Disposition (parts)
Styles Vol. 7. Notice of Title
      Vol. 9. Trusts
Scottish Law Commission Report on Succession (No. 124–1990)

*Statutes*

1868 Act ss. 17, 19, 20, 22, 23, 25, 26, 125–128
1874 Act ss. 31, 45
1924 Act ss. 3–7
1938 Act s. 1
1970 Act ss. 12, 48

*Articles*

| | |
|---|---|
| 1978 JLS 438 | – Completion of Title |
| 1980 SLT (News) 257 | – Deduction of Title – A Recurring Problem |
| 1987 JLS 111 | – Trust and Executry Conveyancing |
| 1989 SLT 256 | – Special Destinations in Agricultural Leases |
| 1989 JLS 299 | – Destinations |
| 1990 JLS 62 | – Appointing and Removing Executors |
| 1990 JLS 189 | – Special Destinations in Scotland |
| 1993 JLS 482 | – Continuity of infeftment. |
| 1995 JLS 30 | – Who is the heir of provision in trust? |

## Chapter 33. Examination of Title

| | |
|---|---|
| Halliday | Practice Chap. 21 |
| Burns | Practice Chaps. 10, 13, 15, 19, 24 |

Green's Encyclopaedia Vols. as follows:
  13 paras. 452–478 Sale of Heritable Property (part)
  13 paras. 682–776 Searches
  8 paras. 413–445 Inhibitions
  9 paras. 719–722 Litigiosity

| | |
|---|---|
| Sinclair | Handbook Chaps. 7 and 8 |

*Articles*

| | |
|---|---|
| 1971 JLS 104 | – Enquiries of Local Authorities |
| 1972 SLT 213 | – Period of Search |
| 1975 JLS 260 | – Letters of Obligation |
| 1977 JLS 212 | – Heritable Transactions by Companies |
| 1978 JLS 209 and 306 | – A Conveyancing Trap |
| 1979 JLS Workshop i | – Heritable Transactions by Companies |
| 1979 JLS Workshop xxiv | – Inhibition and Search |
| 1982 JLS 13 and 68 | – Inhibitions, Securities, Reductions and Multiplepoindings |
| 1984 JLS 369, 455 and 1984 JLS 75 | – The Matrimonial Homes (Family Protection) (Scotland) Act 1981 |
| 1985 SLT (News) 125 | – Inhibitions and Standard Securities |
| 1985 SLT (News) 177 | – The Law Reform (Miscellaneous Provisions) (Scotland) Act 1985 |
| 1985 JLS 392 | – Inhibitions and Conveyancing Practice |
| 1986 JLS 486 | – Occupancy Rights in the Land Register |
| 1987 JLS 66 | – Further Thoughts on Inhibitions |
| 1988 JLS 162 | – Good and marketable Title |
| 1989 JLS 50 and 85 | – Searches I and II |
| 1989 JLS 206 | – Planning and Building Control Warranties |
| 1990 SLT 104 | – Letters of Obligation |
| 1991 JLS 179, 349 and 450 | – Letters of Obligation |
| 1991 JLS 471 | – Inhibitions and Partnerships |
| 1991 JLS 444 | – Matrimonial Homes Deeds Furth of Scotland |
| 1991 JLS 23, 1992 JLS 107 and 120 | – Recording and Registration |
| 1991 JLS 450 Caveat | – The cover provided by the Master Policy for letters of obligation |
| 1992 JLS 439 | – Conveyancing – The Profit Motive |
| 1992 JLS 448 Caveat | – Unsigned deed presented for recording along with a standard security |
| 1992 JLS 323 | – A note by the Law Society on the appropriate practice at settlement, particularly in relation to telegraphic transfers. This has since been amended by a Law Society circular. See also 1996 JLS 485. |
| 1992 JLS 232 Caveat | – A discussion on the basis of quantum following on defective survey |
| Greens PLB Issue 1 p. 6 | – Comment on the Property Misdescriptions Act 1991 |
| Greens PLB Issue 11 p. 9 | – Comment on the Property Misdescriptions Act one year on |
| Greens PLB Issue 12 p. 7 | – Conflict of Interest in Conveyancing |
| 1992 JLS 107 | – Computerisation of the Presentment Book |
| 1992 JLS 120 | – Registration of Title – A comment on P16 reports |
| 1992 JLS 51 | – Comments from correspondents on the liability of surveyors and solicitors for procuring confirmation on building warrants etc., following on an earlier letter in 1991 JLS 467 |

| | |
|---|---|
| 1992 JLS 500 | – When to get Forms 10–14 Reports |
| 1993 JLS 158 | – A Note on Letters of Obligation |
| 1993 SLT (News) 354 | – Inhibitions: The Problem of Designation |
| 1993 JLS 240 | – Searches in the Registers – Computerised Presentment Book |
| 1993 JLS 406 Caveat | – Matrimonial Homes Affidavits |
| 1993 JLS 409 | – Inhibitions – a Comment on Atlas Appointments Limited |
| 1993 JLS 431 | – Letters of Obligation |
| 1993 JLS 465 | – Joint Property – Is this the best advice? |
| 1994 JLS 99 | – Time limits in letters of obligation, commenting on the article in 1993 JLS 431 |
| 1994 JLS 52 | – Inhibitions, Standard Securities and Further Advances |
| Greens PLB Issue 8 p.10 | – Negative prescription |
| 1994 JLS 260 Caveat | – A note on letters of obligation and the wording thereof following *Warners* v. *Beveridge and Kellas* |
| 1994 JLS 356 | – Heritable property conveyed by a company |
| 1994 JLS 371 | – Commercial Law update – securities and insolvency |
| 1994 JLS 384 | – Conveyancing Practice – *Sharp* v. *Thomson* |
| 1994 JLS 444 | – Heritable property conveyed by a Company |
| 1994 SLT (News) 313 | – Sharp cases make good law |
| Greens PLB Issue 13 p. 2 | – Transactions with limited companies – caveat emptor? |
| 1994 SLT (News) 183 | – Dead on Delivery. A comment on *Sharp* v. *Thomson*. The Article also defines the 'classic' letter of obligation |
| The Law Society of Scotland Guidance Notes 1994 – Coal Mining Searches | |
| Greens PLB Issue 10 p. 6 | – 'To be held as undelivered' |
| 1994 JLS 135 | – Negligence, Instructions and the Lender's need to know |
| 1994 JLS 470 Caveat | – Domestic Conveyancing – Settlement Cheques |
| 1994 JLS 331 | – Pre-emption clauses and the right to buy |
| 1994 JLS 341 Caveat | – Mortgages, securities and searches |
| 1994 JLS 205 | – A cautionary note for solicitors |
| 1995 JLS 155 Caveat | – Grant of Security over Matrimonial Home by Joint Proprietors. |
| 1995 JLS 234 | – Local Authority sales and pre-emption rights |
| Green's PLB Issue 14 p. 11 | – The Register of Inhibitions and Adjudications: A Guide to Indexing Practice by the Manager of the Register at Meadowbank House |
| 1995 JLS 316 | – Property Enquiry Certificates |
| 1995 JLS 323 Caveat | – Delivery of Documents |
| 1995 JLS 323 Caveat | – Letters of Obligation |
| 1995 JLS 58 | – Negligence, securities and the duty of care |
| 1995 JLS 363 Caveat | – Undisclosed securities |
| 1995 JLS 377 | – Certificate of Title: Legal Context |
| 1995 JLS 482 | – Pre-payment of fees in the Land Register and Sasines Register – the new provisions |
| 1996 JLS 150 | – The Construction (Design and Management) Regulations 1994 – implications for solicitors |
| 1996 JLS 232 Caveat | – If in doubt ask |
| 1996 JLS 255 | – A Further Cautionary Note for Conveyancers (hazards of transactions with companies) |
| Greens PLB Issue 20 p. 2 and 21 p. 2 | – Construction (Design and Management) Regulations 1994 |
| Greens PLB Issue 24 p. 2 | – Surveyors' Conditions of Engagement |
| Greens PLB Issue 24 p. 3 | – Contaminated Land |
| 1996 SLT (News) 365 | – The perils of a Trusting Disposition |
| 1996 JLS 298 | – A short history of Conveyancing fees |
| 1996 JLS 341 | – Conveyancing Fees – Are we selling ourselves short? |

| | |
|---|---|
| 1996 JLS 379 | – Conveyancing Fees – The Real Answer |
| 1996 JLS 436 | – Conveyancing quality standards |
| Greens PLB Issue 25 p. 2 | – Landfill Tax |
| 1997 SLT (News) 79 | – Jam Today: *Sharp* in the House of Lords |
| Greens PLB Issue 26 p. 5 | – *Sharp* v. *Thomson*: The House of Lords strikes back |

## Chapter 34. A Typical Sasines Conveyancing Transaction

*Reference*

| | |
|---|---|
| Butterworths | Guide to Council Tax in Scotland |

*Articles*

| | |
|---|---|
| 1985 JLS 25 | – Repair and Improvement Grants – Breach of Conditions |
| 1985 JLS 155 | – Property Enquiry Certificates – The Responsibility of Local Authorities |
| 1985 JLS 159 | – Bridging Loans and Consumer Credit Relations |
| 1992 JLS 323 | – Domestic Conveyancing: Settlement Cheques |
| 1992 JLS 486 | – The Property Misdescriptions Act 1991 |

(See also Articles listed under Chapters 28 and 33)

## Chapter 35. Transactions with Companies

*References*

| | |
|---|---|
| Palmer | Company Law (25th edn. loose leaf and updated to 1992) Chaps. 8, 14 and 15 |
| Greene and Fletcher | Law and Practice of Receivership in Scotland (2nd edn. 1992) Chaps. 1 to 4, 7, 8 and 9 |
| St. Clair and Drummond Young | The Law of Corporate Insolvency in Scotland (2nd edn. 1992) Chaps. 3 to 5 and 8 |
| Gretton | The Law of Inhibitions and Adjudications (2nd edn. 1996) Chaps. 11 and 12 |
| Gretton | A Guide to Searches (1991) |
| Halliday Practice | Vol. 1. Chapters 2–100 to 120 (1985) |
| Palmer | Insolvency Law (1993) |
| Thomson J. M. & Others | The Law Reform (Miscellaneous Provisions) (Scotland) Act 1990 (1991) S. 72 |
| Stair Encyclopaedia | Vol. 4. paras. 221–744 |

*Statutes*

Bankruptcy (Scotland) Act 1985
Companies Act 1985
Insolvency Act 1986
Companies Act 1989
Law Reform (Miscellaneous Provisions) (Scotland) Act 1990
Requirements of Writing (Scotland) Act 1995

*Articles*

| | |
|---|---|
| 1977 JLS 212, 334 and 1978 JLS 45 | – Heritable Transactions by Companies |
| 1988 JLS 357 and 392 | – Set-off and Receivership |
| 1989 JLS 50 and 85 | – Searches |

1990 JLS 358 and 498 — Execution of Deeds by Companies
1991 SLT 283 and 257 — The Company Execution Provisions
1992 JLS 346 — Aspects of Insolvency Conveyancing
1992 JLS 262 — Set-off in receivership
1993 JLS 199 Caveat — Discharging loans and Ranking Agreements
1994 JLS 191 — A note on the Foreign Companies (Execution of Documents) Regulations 1994
1994 JLS 356 — *Sharp* v. *Thomson*
1994 JLS 371 — Notes on recent company cases
1994 JLS 372 — *Sharp* v. *Thomson*
1994 JLS 384 — *Sharp* v. *Thomson*
1994 JLS 400 — *Sharp* v. *Thomson*
1994 JLS 444 — *Sharp* v. *Thomson*
1994 JLS (News) 183 — *Sharp* v. *Thomson*
1994 JLS (News) 313 — *Sharp* v. *Thomson*
1994 JLS 256 — *Sharp* v. *Thomson* – What Now?
Greens PLB Issue 13 p. 2 — Transactions with limited companies – caveat emptor?
1995 JLS 438 — Voluntary dissolution or liquidation? An ethical dilemma for practitioners
1995 SLT (News) 79 — *Sharp* v. *Thomson*: Identifying the Mischief
1995 SLT (News) 11 — Proceedings involving dissolved companies
1995 SLT (News) 75 — *Sharp* v. *Thomson* – A Civilian Perspective
1995 SLT (News) 91 and 101 — *Sharp* v. *Thomson*
1996 JLS 141 — Cross Border Liquidations
1996 JLS 255 — A cautionary note for conveyancers when dealing with an administrator, receiver or liquidator
1996 SLT (News) 203 — The assignation of Floating Charges
1996 SLT (News) 365 — The Perils of a Trusting Disposition
1997 SLT (News) 79 — Jam Today: *Sharp* in the House of Lords
Greens PLB Issue 26 p. 5 — *Sharp* v. *Thomson*: The House of Lords strikes back
1997 JLS 103 — *Sharp* v. *Thomson* : The Final Act

# DIGEST OF CASES

## NOTES

1. The cases in this digest are intended to illuminate the text. The list of cases included is by no means exhaustive.
2. The headings in the digest do not correspond exactly with the headings in the text. Where a case is referred to in the text under a different heading, this may be indicated at the end of the case note thus: '(Text 2.25)' etc.
3. An alphabetical table of cases follows this digest.

### Chapter 1. General Introduction

#### 1.3 The role of solicitors in heritable property transactions
Negligence

*Watson* v. *Swift & Co's JF* 1986 SC 55. Marketability of seller's title. Defect therein. Seller already committed to both sale and purchase. Both contracts were then rescinded. *Held* that the resulting loss was reasonably foreseeable and a claim against the solicitors was therefore relevant.

*Ferguson* v. *McIntyre* 1993 SLT 1269. A solicitor failed to ensure that the title carried a share of common grazings. The purchaser claimed damages. Proof before answer allowed. (Text 28.56)

*Paterson* v. *Sturrock & Armstrong* 1993 GWD 27–1706. The purchasers' solicitor knew that they intended to use property as a guest house but failed to advise them as to planning permission *etc*. Negligence was conceded. Quantum of damages discussed.

*Moffat* v. *Milne* 1993 GWD 8–572. A solicitor failed to reserve a servitude of access to retained ground on a part sale. Proof before answer allowed. (Text 11.7)

*Higginbotham* v. *Paul Gebal & Co.* 1993 GWD 3–221. A solicitor who failed to advise the seller of a council house within the three-year period that there would be a clawback was held liable for negligence to the extent of the clawback amount.

*MacQueen* v. *J. M. Hodge & Son* 1989 GWD 29–1365. Advice given by solicitors to a client affected a third party. *Held* that the solicitor was not liable to make reparation to a third party who might be injured by his negligent acts or omissions when acting for his own client.

*Bolton* v. *Jameson & Mackay* 1987 SLT 291. Heritable property stood in name of a husband alone. With his wife's consent, he instructed solicitors to prepare an agreement to the effect that it was jointly owned. The husband later sold the house and disappeared with the whole proceeds. *Held* that the wife had failed to establish that the solicitors had acted on her behalf as well as on behalf of her husband but that in disposing of all the free proceeds to the husband the solicitors may have acted improperly and proof before answer allowed.

*Central Govan Housing Association Ltd.* v. *Maguire Cook & Co.* 1988 SC 137. Purchasers sued their solicitors for negligence at settlement of a transaction. *Held* that the only outstanding obligation at settlement was conditional and the solicitors were not at fault and could not have insisted either on retention or a letter of obligation.

*Mason* v. *A. & R. Robertson & Black* 1993 SLT 773. The pursuers claimed damages against their solicitors for failing to advise on the merits and effect of a counterclaim. (Text 28.96, 28.102)

*Glasper* v. *Rodger* 1996 SLT 44. A claim against solicitors was restricted on the footing that it had prescribed. *Held* that the claimants had shown sufficient evidence to demonstrate that their ignorance of a potential claim might have been reasonable.

Measure of damages

*Haberstitch* v. *McCormick & Nicholson* 1975 SLT 181. Solicitors acting for a purchaser accepted a title which was not marketable. The sheriff assessed damages on the basis of the difference between the value of the house with a good title and its value with a defective title, and was upheld on appeal.

*Pollard* v. *Speedie* 1971 SLT (Sh Ct) 54. Solicitors bungled missives of sale and purchase but a settlement was subsequently agreed. There was no agreement as to expenses. *Held* that the parties' solicitors should each be personally liable for half of the whole expenses of the action.

*Paterson* v. *Sturrock & Armstrong* 1993 GWD 27–1706. See under Negligence above.

*Moffat* v. *Milne* 1993 GWD 8–572. See under Negligence above.

*Higginbotham* v. *Paul Gebal & Co.* 1993 GWD 3–221. See under Negligence above.

*Stewart* v. *Wright Johnston & MacKenzie* 1994 GWD 22–1331. In an action for damages for negligence against a solicitor on the footing that he had failed to bid for property at an auction as instructed, proof before answer allowed with particular reference to *quantum*.

*Di Ciacca* v. *Archibald Sharp & Sons* 1994 SLT 421, and, on appeal, 1995 SLT 380. Whether damages could include increased value of a comparable property to which the title was defective.

Prescription of claim – *terminus a quo*

*Dunlop* v. *McGowans* 1980 SC (HL) 73. An action was raised in November 1976 against solicitors for failing to serve a timeous notice at Whitsunday 1971. *Held* that even if negligence were established, the claim had prescribed, and claim dismissed.

*Duncan* v. *Aitken, Malone & Mackay* 1989 SCLR 1. Solicitors argued that a claim for damages had prescribed. The client argued that she had suffered no loss, and therefore had no actionable claim, until her husband's sequestration which caused her loss, and that the claim had not prescribed. Her argument was upheld.

**Agency**

*Hopkinson* v. *Williams* 1993 SLT 907. Solicitors took instructions from the sister of the owner of heritable property and the seller later repudiated the bargain. Proof before answer allowed. (Text 28.4)

*McCabe* v. *Skipton BS* 1994 SC 467. A solicitor fraudulently obtained a joint loan for himself and his wife and forged the wife's signature. *Held* that he was not acting as agent within the scope of his authority.

*Bolton* v. *Jameson & Mackay* 1987 SLT 291. See under Negligence above.

*Stewart* v. *Wright Johnston & MacKenzie* 1994 GWD 22–1331. See under Measure of damages above.

**Chapter 2.   Authentication**

**2.8   Probativity**

*Stewart's Exrs.* v. *Stewart* 1993 SLT 440. Informal deed, proof by writ or oath. (Text 33.79)

*Sereshky* v. *Sereshky* 1988 SLT 426. Forged signature. (Text 30.10)

*McLeod* v. *Cedar Holdings Ltd.* 1989 SLT 620. Forged signature. (Text 30.11)

*Royal Bank of Scotland* v. *Purvis* 1990 SLT 262. Grantor bound by her signature of deed she had not read; uninduced unilateral error of grantor as to content irrelevant.

**2.10   Form of deed**

*Simsons* v. *Simsons* (1893) 10 R 1247. Writing in pencil curable under 1874 Act s. 39.

*Munro* v. *Butler Johnstone* (1868) 7 M 250. Essential word interlined but not authenticated; whole deed invalidated.

*Gollan* v. *Gollan* (1863) 1 M (HL) 65. Inessential words on erasure not authenticated; whole deed not invalidated.

*Cattanach's Trs.* v. *Jamieson* (1884) 11 R 972. Inessential words on erasure not authenticated; deed not invalidated. (Text 8.19)

*Pattison's Trs.* v. *University of Edinburgh* (1888) 16 R 73. Will altered in testator's own hand. (Text 2.15)

*Syme's Exrs.* v. *Cherrie* 1986 SLT 161. Unauthenticated deletion and interlineation made to a will at the time of execution held unauthenticated. (Text 2.15)

*Manson* v. *Edinburgh Royal Institution* 1948 SLT 196. Alterations by testator to copy will.

*Thomson's Trs.* v. *Bowhill Baptist Church* 1956 SC 217. Alterations by testator to copy will duly authenticated; effective to revoke the will.

## 2.19 Execution by parties

*Stuart* v. *Crawford's Trs.* (1885) 12 R 610. Signature illegible; touched up; stamp.

*Donald* v. *McGregor* 1926 SLT 103. Partial signature and mark invalid.

*Morton* v. *French* 1908 SC 171. Signature by mark on a testamentary nomination invalid.

*American Express Europe Ltd.* v. *Royal Bank of Scotland plc* 1989 SLT 266. Question whether an abbreviated signature complied with the 1672 Act.

*American Express Europe Ltd.* v. *Royal Bank of Scotland plc (No.2)* 1989 SLT 650. Signature by surname only valid execution.

*Rhodes* v. *Peterson* 1971 SC 56. Signature 'Mum' on a testamentary letter held valid. (Text 2.46)

*Draper* v. *Thomason* 1954 SC 136. Abbreviated signature competent in special circumstances; but see *American Express Europe Ltd. (No. 2)* above.

*Brown* v. *Duncan* (1888) 15 R 511. Signature on erasure valid.

*Gardner* v. *Lucas* (1878) 5 R (HL) 105. Signatures on last page, initials on preceding pages, invalid.

*Lowrie's JF* v. *McMillan's Exx.* 1972 SC 105. Signature by initials.

*Elwick Bay Shipping Co. Ltd.* v. *Royal Bank of Scotland plc* 1982 SLT 62. Signature 'pro general manager' not equivalent to signature of general manager.

*Moncrieff* v. *Moneypenny* (1710) M 15936. Signature must be spontaneous.

*Crosbie* v. *Picken* (1749) M 16814. Signature must be spontaneous.

*Noble* v. *Noble* (1875) 3 R 74. The hand must not be guided below the wrist

*Ker* v. *Hotchkis* (1837) 15 S 983. A blind person can validly subscribe.

*Drummond* v. *James Farquhar* 6 July 1809, FC 392. Status of bishops; but see *American Express Europe Ltd. (No. 2)* above.

*Dunlop* v. *Greenlee's Trs.* (1863) 2 M 1. Married women may subscribe their maiden surname; but see *American Express Europe Ltd. (No. 2)*.

*Bank of Scotland* v. *Graham's Tr.* 1992 SC 79. Application for rectification of standard security held relevant where grantor signed once as debtor, but failed to sign again as proprietor. (Text 30.14)

Subscription

*McLay* v. *Farrell* 1950 SC 149. Holograph will subscribed; clause added below signature held unauthenticated.

*Robbie* v. *Carr & Ors.* 1959 SLT (Notes) 16. Holograph will; signature in margin; invalid.

*Baird's Trs.* v. *Baird* 1955 SC 286. Signatures on reverse page; invalid.

*McNeill* v. *McNeill* 1973 SLT (Sh Ct) 16. Signatures on reverse page; valid.

*Ferguson, Petitioner* 1959 SC 56. Writing on first page, signatures on third; valid. *Baird's Trs.*, above, distinguished. (Text 2.22, 2.29)

## 2.20 Attestation

*Allan & Crichton, Petitioners* 1933 SLT (Sh Ct) 2. Witness signing 'Mrs. Bernard' invalid.

*Young* v. *Paton* 1910 SC 63. Allegation that witness did not see deed signed, nor hear acknowledgement; onus of proof.

*Walker* v. *Whitwell* 1916 SC (HL) 75. Witness signing after death of grantor; invalid. (Text 2.19, 2.27, 2.30, 2.42)

*Murray, Petitioner* (1904) 6 F 840. Witness signing *ex intervallo*; valid.

*MacDougall* v. *MacDougall's Exrs.* 1993 SCLR 832. Whether will validly attested. (Text 28.46, 31.26)

*Grant* v. *Keir* (1694) M 16 913. Sufficiency of designation of witness. (Text 2.25)

*Williamson* v. *Williamson* 1996 SLT 92. A will was attested by two witnesses. One signed 'D.C.R. Williamson'. In the testing clause he was named D.C.R. Wilson. *Held* that the document failed to meet the requirements of probativity. (Text 2.19, 2.23, 2.34)

*Lindsay* v. *Milne* 1995 SLT 487. A will was reduced as improperly attested, the second witness having not been present nor heard an acknowledgement of subscription.

## 2.28 The testing clause

*Blair* v. *Assets Co. Ltd.* (1896) 23 R (HL) 36. Operative words inserted in testing clause invalid. (Text 2.25)

*Gibson's Trs.* v. *Lamb & Ors.* 1931 SLT 22. Holograph provision in testing clause held valid in special circumstances.

*McDougall* v. *McDougall* (1875) 2 R 814. Names in testing clause written on erasure did not invalidate.

*Blair* v. *Earl of Galloway* (1827) 6 S 51. Thirty-two-year interval in completing testing clause did not invalidate. (Text 2.30)

## 2.31 Notarial execution

*Hynd's Tr.* v. *Hynd's Exr.* 1955 SC (HL) 1. Statutory procedure not strictly observed; will invalidated.

*Finlay* v. *Finlay's Trs.* 1948 SC 16. Interest of notary in will; power to charge; will invalidated. (Text 2.33)

*Irving* v. *Snow* 1956 SC 257. Interest of notary in will; deed executed in England; will not invalidated.

*McIldowie* v. *Muller* 1979 SC 271. Interest of notary in will; no power to charge; will not invalidated.

## 2.34 Informality of execution

*Addison, Petitioner* (1875) 2 R 457. Omitted testing clause may be added later; 1874 Act s. 39 petition probably unnecessary.

*Elliot's Exrs., Petitioners* 1939 SLT 69. Witnesses' designations omitted; alterations not authenticated; deed curable under s. 39.

*Grieve's Trs.* v. *Japp's Trs.* (1917) 1 SLT 70. Parties inaccurately designed; not sufficient to invalidate; s. 39 petition not necessary.

*Simsons* v. *Simsons* (1893) 10 R 1247. Writing in pencil curable under s. 39.

*McLaren* v. *Menzies* (1876) 3 R 1151. Deed on several sheets signed on last page only; curable under s. 39.

*McNeill* v. *McNeill* 1973 SLT (Sh Ct) 16. Signatures on reverse page; will held validly subscribed.

*Baird's Trs.* v. *Baird* 1955 SC 286. Signatures on reverse page; document held not subscribed; compare *McNeill* above.

*Walker* v. *Whitwell* 1916 SC (HL) 75. Defect in solemnities not curable under s. 39. (Text 2.19, 2.27, 2.30, 2.42)

*Hynd's Tr.* v. *Hynd's Exr.* 1955 SC (HL) 1. Defect in solemnities in notarial execution not curable under s. 39. (Text 2.31)

*Thomson's Trs.* v. *Easson* (1878) 6 R 141. Failure to complete testing clause before registration or founding on not necessarily fatal. (Text 2.30)

**2.35   The effect of *ex facie* probativity**

*Boyd* v. *Shaw* 1927 SC 414. Latent defect in probativity of onerous deed; personal bar.


**2.37   Holograph writings**

*Harper* v. *Green* 1938 SC 198. Onus of proof lies on proponer, not challenger.

*Harley* v. *Harley's Exr.* 1957 SLT (Sh Ct) 17. Holograph will invalidly attested; valid notwith-standing.

*Tucker* v. *Canch's Tr.* 1953 SC 270. Will partly printed, partly holograph; invalid.

*Gillies* v. *Glasgow Royal Infirmary* 1960 SC 438. Will partly printed, partly holograph; valid.

*Campbell, Petitioner* 1963 SLT (Sh Ct) 10. Will partly printed, partly holograph; cases reviewed.

*Merrick Homes Ltd.* v. *Duff* 1996 SLT 932. Missives subscribed and adopted as holograph; validly executed. (Text 28.7)

*Barker's Exrs.* v. *Scottish Rights of Way Society* 1996 SLT 1319. Whether documents partly printed and partly handwritten duly executed.

Adoption

*Shiell* v. *Shiell* (1913) 1 SLT 62. Holograph docquet subscribed on backing ; invalid.

*Campbell's Exrs.* v. *Maudsley* 1934 SLT 420. Holograph docquet subscribed on backing; valid.

*Craik's Exx.* v. *Samson* 1929 SLT 592. Improbative will adopted by separate holograph codicil.

*Stenhouse* v. *Stenhouse* 1922 SC 370. Improbative will in envelope bearing holograph signed docquet; invalid.

*Chisholm* v. *Chisholm* 1949 SC 434. Typewritten document subscribed; 'Adopted as holo-graph' typed at foot but no statement *in gremio*; invalid.


**2.38   Writings *in re mercatoria***

*Caledonian Bank plc* v. *St. Aubyn* 1994 GWD 30–1818. Question whether document solemnly executed or *in re mercatoria*.


**Chapter 3.   Capacity**


**3.5   Trustees**

*Darwin's Trs., Petitioners* 1924 SLT 778. Whether sale at variance with terms or purposes.

*Campbell, Petitioner* 1958 SC 275. Petition to court under nobile officium for power of sale. (Text 3.10)

*Horne's Trs., Petitioners* 1952 SC 70. Petition by English trustees to court under *nobile offi-cium* for power of sale; retrospective sanction of earlier sale not granted.

*Fletcher's Trs., Petitioners* 1949 SC 330. Petition to court under Trusts Acts for power to purchase heritage.


**3.11   Pupils and minors**

*Cunningham's Tutrix, Petitioner* 1949 SC 275. Tutor's power of sale. (Text 3.12)


**3.14   Curators and judicial factors**

*Inland Revenue* v. *McMillan's. CB* 1956 SC 142. Nature of office of curator.

*Bristow, Petitioner* 1965 SLT 225, 1965 SLT (Notes) 42. Curator's power to purchase. (Text 3.9, 3.12)

*Barclay, Petitioner* 1962 SC 594. Curator may still require power from court to sell heritage, not for the purpose of giving title, but to exclude claims by beneficiaries.

*Lothian's CB, Petitioner* 1927 SC 579. Whether sale at variance with terms or purposes.

*Leslie's JF, Petitioner* 1925 SC 464. Power of JF to sell heritage; but see now 1938 Act s. 1.

*Cooper & Sons' JF, Petitioner* 1931 SLT 26. Power of JF to sell heritage.

*Dunlop & Sons' JF* v. *Armstrong* 1995 SLT 645. Court declined to interfere in dispute between judicial factor and heritable creditor.

### 3.15 Corporations

*James Finlay Corporation Ltd.* v. *R. & R. S. Mearns* 1988 SLT 302. Whether standard security to guarantee debts of another company *ultra vires*.

*General Auction Co.* v. *Smith* [1891] 3 Ch 432. A trading company has implied power to borrow.

*In re Introductions* v. *National Provincial Bank Ltd.* [1969] 1 All ER 887. A creditor cannot rely on a power to borrow if the loan is patently for an *ultra vires* purpose.

*Cockenzie Community Council* v. *East Lothian DC* 1996 SCLR 209. Community council failed to prevent the sale by district council of part of common good under Local Government (Scotland) Act 1973 s. 75 (2).

*West Dunbartonshire Council* v. *Harvie* 1996 GWD 33–1986. Petition by council for authority to dispose of area of common ground, under 1973 Act s. 75, rejected on amenity grounds.

### 3.18 Sequestration

*Simpson's Tr.* v. *Simpson* 1993 SCLR 867. Division and sale of a matrimonial home; 1985 Act s. 40.

*Clark's Tr., Noter* 1993 SLT 667. In exceptional circumstances, interim trustee in sequestration may be given power of sale under Bankruptcy (Scotland) Act 1985 s. 18 (3) (c).

### 3.22 Partnerships

*Cameron* v. *Lightheart* 1995 SCLR 443. Title taken in name of A and B as trustees for their firm, but a special clause was added authorising either to sell and dispone without the consent of the other. B, acting alone, sold the subjects. A challenged the sale by an action of reduction but failed.

### 3.23 Unincorporated associations

*Lauder College, Petitioners* 1996 GWD 12–719. Petition for judicial review of decision of a Commissioner regarding transfer of property and responsibility dismissed.

*Piggins & Rix Ltd.* v. *Montrose Port Authority* 1995 SLT 418. *Held* that in the particular circumstances it would be *ultra vires* for a port authority to sell surplus land. (Text 3.2, 3.15, 35.4)

### Chapter 4.  Delivery

### 4.1  The need for delivery

*Gibson* v. *Hunter Home Designs Ltd.* 1976 SC 23. Undelivered feu disposition held invalid although price paid and possession given. (Text 33.51)

*Sharp* v. *Thomson* 1995 SC 45. A company executed and delivered a disposition of property to a bona fide purchaser for value. The company had already granted a floating charge which included that property. A receiver under the floating charge was appointed to the granter of the disposition before the purchaser had recorded it. *Held* in the Inner House that the property was attached by the floating charge. This was reversed on appeal to the House of Lords – see 1997 SLT (HL) 636. The House of Lords decision in no way affects the *ratio* of the opinion of the Lord President in the Inner House. (Text 12.4, 23.4, 29.33, 33.51, 35.7, 35.12, 35.15, 35.18)

*Russo's Tr.* v. *Russo's Tr.* 1996 GWD 21–1245. Alleged that shop premises in name of B were truly held in trust for A. Credibility of witnesses was suspect. Purported letters of trust rejected as evidence was dubious and insufficient to prove alleged trust. Accordingly, A's trustee in sequestration held entitled thereto.

*Life Association of Scotland* v. *Black's Leisure Group plc.* 1989 SC 166. Discussion on effect of delivery of disposition as divesting disponer.

*Life Association of Scotland* v. *Douglas* (1886) 13 R 910. Deed not delivered at granter's death held undelivered.

*Walker's Exr.* v. *Walker* (1878) 5 R 965. Deed in favour of donor's wife undelivered; held donor not divested.

*Connell's Trs.* v. *Connell's Trs.* 1955 SLT 125. Bond to trustees of wife of donor not exempt from need for delivery.

*Clark's Exr.* v. *Clark* 1943 SC 216. Delivery of testamentary writing does not prevent subsequent revocation. (Text 4.10)

*McManus's Tr.* v. *McManus* 1981 SC 233. Deed to wife of donor in hands of his agent, but intimated to her, not sufficient to infer delivery.

*Clark's Exr.* v. *Cameron* 1982 SLT 68. Disposition improperly executed but delivered to grantor's agent did not, *per se*, constitute homologation.

*Grant's Tr.* v. *Grant* 1986 SC 51. In bankruptcy, under 1696 Act (now repealed), date of recording disposition, not the date of delivery, determining date for fraudulent preferences. (Text 30.9)

#### 4.2 Presumptions arising from custody of the deed

*McAslan* v. *Glen* (1859) 21 D 511. Deed held by donee not sufficient to infer delivery.

*Mair* v. *Thom's Trs* (1850) 12 D 748. Deed held by common agent not sufficient to infer delivery.

*Lombardi's Tr.* v. *Lombardi* 1982 SLT 81. Delivery of disposition to common agent who intimated delivery to grantee. Deed held to be delivered.

#### 4.6 Equivalents to delivery
#### Registration
(a) In Sasines

*Linton* v. *Inland Revenue* 1928 SC 209. Registration in Sasines in names of donees held sufficient to imply delivery.

*Cameron's Trs.* v. *Cameron* 1907 SC 407. Registration in Sasines in name of donor as trustee for donee did not create valid trust. (Text 4.7)

(b) In Books of Council and Session

*Tennent* v. *Tennent's Trs.* (1869) 7 M 936. Registration in Books of Council and Session is ordinarily equivalent to delivery. (Text 4.7)

(c) In books of company

*Inland Revenue* v. *Wilson* 1928 SC (HL) 42. Registration in name of donee in books of company is a factor implying delivery.

#### 4.8 Intimation to the debtor in an obligation

*Smith* v. *Place D'Or* 1988 SLT (Sh Ct) 5. Assignation of lease *held* effective following intimation, despite the fact that the deed of assignation was not physically delivered.

#### 4.9 Intimation to donee

*Carmichael* v. *Carmichael's Exrs.* 1920 SC (HL) 195. Undelivered deed intimated to donee and held to create a *jus quaesitum tertio*. (Text 4.7)

*Allan's Tr.* v. *Lord Advocate* 1971 SC (HL) 45. Intimation to donee equivalent to delivery. (Text 4.11)

*Kerr's Trs.* v. *Lord Advocate* 1974 SC 115. Intimation to agent for donee equivalent to delivery.

*Clark Taylor & Co. Ltd.* v. *Quality Site Dev. (Edinburgh) Ltd.* 1981 SC 111. Contractual obligation, as 'continuing intimation' to obligee, is not equivalent to delivery.

#### 4.11 Acceptance of delivery

*Dowie & Co.* v. *Tennant* (1891) 18 R 986. Need for acceptance of delivery.

*Allans Trs.* v. *Lord Advocate* 1971 SC (HL) 45. Intimation to one donee, accepted, implies acceptance by all.

#### Chapter 5. Stamp Duties and VAT

#### 5.11 Rate of duty

*Cohen* v. *Attorney-General* [1937] 1 KB 478. Definition of a series of transactions.

**5.17 Voluntary dispositions**

*Kildrummy (Jersey) Ltd.* v. *IRC* 1991 SC 1. A complex arrangement involving an allegedly voluntary disposition, a declaration of trust, a disposition and lease *in gremio* intended to avoid stamp duty failed in its purposes and duty *held* to be payable. (Text 12.19, 14.7, 26.3)

*Jaymarke Development Ltd.* v. *Elinacre Ltd.* 1992 SLT 1193. Construction of missives. Missives of sale and purchase were entered into between two companies. The purchase price was stipulated as a single sum stated to be deemed to be inclusive of VAT. The purchase price was duly paid at the date of entry as required by the missives. The sellers, however, did not elect to waive exemption from VAT. The purchaser then sought to recover from the sellers the VAT component in the purchase price. The court construed the missives as requiring payment by the purchasers of the full amount of the purchase price, whether the sellers paid VAT or not. The case also contains an excellent review of the operation of VAT on transfers of heritable property. (Text 5.32)

**5.32 The election to waive exemption**

*Jaymarke Development Ltd.* v. *Elinacre Ltd.*, above. Construction of clause dealing with purchase price in missives to ascertain whether VAT element was refundable when sellers did not elect to waive exemption from VAT.

**5.35 The interaction between VAT and stamp duty**

*Glenrothes Development Corporation* v. *IRC* 1994 SLT 1310. Obligation on purchasers of heritage to pay VAT is part of price for stamp duty purposes.

**Chapter 7. The Feu Charter**

**7.3 Grantor**

*Swans* v. *Western Bank* (1866) 4 M 663. Accretion can operate even where grantor had no title to subjects at the time of grant.

**7.12 Joint property**

*Magistrates of Banff* v. *Ruthin Castle* 1944 SC 36. Joint property or common property. (Text 31.14)

*Munro* v. *Munro* 1972 SLT (Sh Ct) 6. Joint property or common property. (Text 31.14)

**7.13 Common property**

General rules

*Cargill* v. *Muir* (1837) 15 S 408. Nature of common property; multiplication of superiors. (Text 7.12)

*Deans* v. *Woolfson* 1922 SC 221. Common property; demolition and reconstruction.

*Sutherland* v. *Barbour* (1887) 15 R 62. Common property or common interest; alterations to buildings.

*Schaw* v. *Black* (1889) 16 R 336. Rights of individual *pro indiviso* proprietors; collecting rents.

*Lade* v. *Largs Banking Co.* (1863) 2 M 17. Right of *pro indiviso* proprietors to sue and defend.

*Fearnan Partnership* v. *Grindlay* 1992 SC (HL) 38. Where property is owned in common, all proprietors must concur in granting servitude rights over the common property. (Text 11.3)

*Grozier* v. *Downie* (1871) 9 M 826. Two out of three *pro indiviso* proprietors cannot remove a tenant without the participation of the third.

*Price* v. *Watson* 1951 SC 359. Sale of *pro indiviso* share. Effect on other *pro indiviso* proprietors. Whether ejection of purchaser competent.

*Bailey's Exrs.* v. *Upper Crathes Fishing Ltd.* 1991 SC 30. Interdict is an appropriate remedy in dispute between co-proprietors of common property.

*Wells* v. *New House Purchasers Ltd.* 1964 SLT (Sh Ct) 2. Whether obligation to repair personal or real as between owners in common. (Text 10.5, 10.6, 10.7, 29.12, 29.18, 29.19)

*Carlton Place Properties* v. *Richmond* 1991 SCLR 151. Question whether single ownership of tenement property previously separately owned, with rights in common *inter se,* extinguishes those rights absolutely or whether they revive *sub silentio* on subsequent subdivision.

*Midlothian DC* v. *McCulloch* 1993 SCLR 152. Two properties were separated by a road serving both. One proprietor was held entitled to a right of access over the half of the road belonging to his neighbour.

*Church of Scotland General Tr.* v. *Phin* 1987 SCLR 240. Liability for the cost of repairs to mutual fence and standard of repair required.

Division and sale

*Grant* v. *Heriot's Trust* (1906) 8 F 647. Common property and common interest. Exclusion of right of division and sale. (Text 7.12)

*D. & S. Miller* v. *Crichton* (1893) 1 SLT 262. On the division and sale of common property, one of the several proprietors who has been in possession may recover expenditure on maintenance but may be liable to pay rent.

*Upper Crathes Fishings Ltd.* v. *Bailey's Exrs.* 1991 SC 30. Absolute right to division or division and sale.

*Morrison* v. *Kirk* 1912 SC 44. Division.

*Scrimgeour* v. *Scrimgeour* 1988 SLT 590. Division and sale; purchase by co-proprietor.

*Berry* v. *Berry (No. 2)* 1989 SLT 292. Purchase by co-proprietor not allowed; sale to be on the open market; *Scrimgeour,* above, not followed.

*Miller Group* v. *Tasker* 1993 SLT 207. No fixed rule that judicial sale should be either by roup or by private bargain. Choice depends on which will achieve the highest price.

*Williams* v. *Cleveland & Highland Holdings Ltd.* 1993 SLT 398. Discussion of circumstances in which a *pro indiviso* owner can object to a report to the Court on the respective merits of physical division and division and sale.

*Hall* v. *Hall* 1987 SLT (Sh Ct) 15. Division and sale; matrimonial home.

*Berry* v. *Berry* 1988 SLT 650. Division and sale; matrimonial home; divorce.

*Milne* v. *Milne* 1994 SLT (Sh Ct) 57. *Held* that the Court had discretion under the 1981 Act. Application for division and sale refused on basis of balance of convenience.

*Simpson's Tr.* v. *Simpson* 1993 SCLR 867. Action of division and sale of a matrimonial home, and the Bankruptcy (Scotland) Act 1985 s. 40.

*Burrows* v. *Burrows* 1996 GWD 25–1439. *Held* that, on divorce, one party had an absolute right to division and sale.

*Grieve* v. *Morrison* 1993 SLT 852. Two parties purchased heritage jointly in contemplation of marriage which did not take place. The question was whether division and sale was appropriate or whether one party could purchase from the other.

*Langstane Housing Association Ltd* v. *Alan Davie* 1994 SCLR 158. A housing association, as *pro indiviso* proprietor, sought repossession of the other *pro indiviso* share from a defaulting owner/tenant and ran into procedural difficulties. *Held* that the action was incompetent in the circumstances.

*Riddell* v. *Morrisetti* 1994 GWD 38–2238. A dispute involving two adjoining plots of land purchased for building, and question of access.

*Gray* v. *Kerner* 1996 SCLR 331. Unmarried, cohabiting couple purchased a house in joint names. *Held* that the woman, who wished to remain in occupation, was entitled to purchase the *pro indiviso* share of the other cohabitee.

### 7.14 Common interest

*Grant* v. *Heriot's Trust* (1906) 8 F 647. Common interest.

*George Watson's Hospital* v. *Cormack* (1883) 11 R 320. Common interest in garden in square. Management.

*Donald & Sons* v. *Esslemont & Macintosh* 1923 SC 122. Common interest in public street.

*Calder* v. *Merchant Co. of Edinburgh* (1886) 13 R 623. Common interest in tenement.

*Taylor's Trs.* v. *McGavigan* (1896) 23 R 945. Prohibition against buildings.

*Gray* v. *MacLeod* 1979 SLT (Sh Ct) 17. Common property or common interest, boundary wall.

*Gill* v. *Mitchell* 1980 SLT 48. Common property or common interest, mutual wall.

*Thom* v. *Hetherington* 1988 SLT 724. Whether boundary wall mutual; consequences attaching to mutuality of wall.

*Church of Scotland General Tr.* v. *Phin* 1987 SCLR 240. Liability for the cost of repairs to a mutual fence and standard of repair required.

### 7.17   The special destination
(See also Ch. 31.10)

*Hay's Tr.* v. *Hay's Trs.* 1951 SC 329. Criticism of use of special destinations. (Text 7.17, 31.13)

*Redfern's Exrs.* v. *Redfern* 1996 SLT 900. Under a separation agreement, both parties relinquished any rights of succession in the estate of the other. *Held* that the agreement in its terms impliedly waived the normal prohibition against evacuation of a survivorship destination. (Text 31.17)

## Chapter 8.   Descriptions

(See also Ch. 14 – The Effects of Possession: Prescription – and Ch. 18 – The Estate of the Vassal)

### 8.2   The extent of the grant
*Hay* v. *Aberdeen Corporation* 1909 SC 554. 'Right and interest'. (Text 6.10)

*Gordon* v. *Grant* (1851) 13 D 1. Parts and pertinents.

### 8.3   Separate tenements
*McKendrick* v. *Wilson* 1970 SLT (Sh Ct) 39. Salmon fishings; need for conveyance. (Text 8.3, 28.33)

*Munro Ferguson* v. *Grant* (1900) 8 SLT 326. Salmon fishings; illustration of express grant.

### 8.6   The law of the tenement
Solum, front and rear ground

*Johnston* v. *White* (1877) 4 R 721. An express conveyance of the right in common to the solum, on which a tenement is built, gives no right of ownership in the front area.

*Barclay* v. *McEwan* (1880) 7 R 792. Same circumstances as in *Johnston*, above.

*Boswell* v. *Edinburgh Magistrates* (1881) 8 R 986. Express conveyance of back ground; right to build.

*Turner* v. *Hamilton* (1890) 17 R 494. Express conveyance of right to solum; proposed alterations thereon. (Text 17.6)

*Arrol* v. *Inches* (1886) 14 R 394. Whether proprietor can build out over front area.

*Bredero Aberdeen Centre Ltd* v. *Aberdeen DC* 1993 GWD 3–191. A small part of a building was constructed on the ground at ground-floor level. The remainder of that part of the building was supported by buildings on the ground floor in other ownerships. Held that the 'solum' thereof extended to the whole area over which the upper floors were constructed.

Main walls

*Todd* v. *Wilson* (1894) 22 R 172. Alteration to main wall; no special provision in titles.

Floor and ceiling

*Alexander* v. *Butchart* (1875) 3 R 156. Division line between upper and lower floors.

Roofs

*Taylor* v. *Dunlop* (1872) 11 M 25. Where the roof of a tenement is not owned in common, the whole roof space and the roof itself belong exclusively to the top-floor proprietor.

*Sanderson's Trs.* v. *Yule* (1897) 25 R 211. Ownership of roof; conversion of attics.

*Watt* v. *Burgess's Trs.* (1891) 18 R 766. Ownership of roof; extension of attic upwards.

*Duncan, Smith & MacLaren* v. *Heatly* 1952 JC 61. Maintenance; no provision in titles.

*Duncan* v. *Church of Scotland General Trs.* 1941 SC 145. Maintenance; partial provision in titles.

*Dunedin Property Management Services Ltd* v. *Glamis Property Co. Ltd.* 1993 GWD 31–2006.

In a dispute as to the meaning of the term 'roof', the Sheriff dismissed evidence based on leases as not forming part of the shop owner's title and was upheld on appeal. (Text 10.12)

Common passages and stairs
*WVS Office Premises Ltd.* v. *Currie* 1969 SC 170. Ownership of passage; no express provision in title.
*Deans* v. *Woolfson* 1922 SC 221. Destruction of common stair; right to rebuild.

Common gables
*Robertson* v. *Scott* (1886) 13 R 1127. Common gable; right to recompense; singular successor.
*Houston* v. *McLaren* (1894) 21 R 923. Whether wall a common gable.
*Lamont* v. *Cumming* (1875) 2 R 784. Adjoining proprietor is entitled to make vents in a mutual gable.
*Baird* v. *Alexander* (1898) 25 R (HL) 35. Rights attaching to common gable at common law may be modified or excluded by contract.
*Jack* v. *Begg* (1875) 3 R 35. One proprietor may not, without consent, remove a mutual boundary wall and erect a mutual gable in its place encroaching on a neighbouring property.
*Wilson* v. *Pottinger* 1908 SC 580. Whether common gable encroaching on adjoining property.
*Troup* v. *Aberdeen Heritable Securities Co. Ltd.* 1916 SC 918. Common gable resting on garden wall.
*Trades House of Glasgow* v. *Ferguson* 1979 SLT 187. Liability for cost of demolition and reconstruction of exposed gable.

Demolition and reconstruction
*Smith* v. *Giuliani* 1925 SC (HL) 45. Dangerous building; liability for cost of demolition.
*Barr* v. *Bass Ltd.* 1972 SLT (Lands Tr.) 5. Partial demolition; resulting rights of several proprietors. (Text 16.13)
*Deans* v. *Woolfson* 1922 SC 221. Common stair.

Liability for damage caused by alterations and reconstructions
*Thomson* v. *St. Cuthbert's Co-op Assn. Ltd.* 1958 SC 380. Nature and extent of obligation of support -(Text 8.7)
*Kerr* v. *McGreevy* 1970 SLT (Sh Ct) 7. Nature and extent of obligation of support.
*Doran* v. *Smith* 1971 SLT (Sh Ct) 46. Nature and extent of obligation of support.
*Macnab* v. *McDevitt* 1971 SLT (Sh Ct) 41. Nature and extent of obligation of support. (Text 8.8)
*Kennedy* v. *Glenbelle Ltd.* 1996 SLT 1186. Contrary to professional advice, tenants in basement of tenement removed load-bearing wall with resulting damage to the upper floors. Pursuer claimed damages from occupiers and their consulting engineers, founding on nuisance and *culpa*. Proof allowed. (Text 8.8)

Management and repairs
*Wells* v. *New House Purchasers Ltd.* 1964 SLT (Sh Ct) 2. Liability for repairs, personal or real. (Text 10.5, 10.6, 10.7, 29.12, 29.18, 29.19)
*Deans* v. *Woolfson* 1922 SC 221. Whether repairs necessary.
*McNally & Miller* v. *Mallinson* 1977 SLT (Sh Ct) 33. Whether repairs necessary. 'Majority of proprietors'.
*Schaw* v. *Black* (1889) 16 R 336. Discussion on right of one of several proprietors to collect rents.
*Taylor* v. *Irvine* 1996 SCLR 937. Servitude right of access must be constituted by express provision or by implication. (Text 8.7)
*Geary* v. *Tellwright* 1994 GWD 17–1077. Discussion on 'common repairs' between upper and lower proprietors.

### 8.9 Water rights
Surface water

*Campbell* v. *Bryson* (1864) 3 M 254. Lower property not entitled to surface water from upper tenement as of right.

*Anderson* v. *Robertson* 1958 SC 367. Lower property must accept natural flow of water from upper property.

*Logan* v. *Wang (UK) Ltd.* 1991 SLT 580. Upper proprietor entitled to collect water together and send it down in one body to lower property, provided the right is not 'over-stretched'.

*Crichton* v. *Turnbull* 1946 SC 52. Servitude of water; interference by drainage.

*Noble's Trs.* v. *Economic Forestry (Scotland) Ltd.* 1988 SLT 662. No liability, *ex dominio* and without *culpa*, for actings of a contractor causing damage by water; but interdict may be appropriate. (Text 19.2, 19.3)

*Scottish Highland Distillery* v. *Reid* (1887) 4 R 1118. Servitude of dam and aqueduct; interference therewith.

*McLaren* v. *British Railways Board* 1971 SC 182. Circumstances where proprietor may have a duty to maintain his banks to prevent flooding his neighbour's land.

Rights in rivers and streams

*Tidal and navigable waters*
*Bowie* v. *Marquis of Ailsa* (1887) 14 R 649. Fishings; express Crown grant.

*Buchanan & Geils* v. *Lord Advocate* (1882) 9 R 1218. Right to foreshore of tidal river.

*Lindsay* v. *Robertson* (1868) 7 M 239. Mussel fishing in tidal river; barony title and possession.

*Mull Shellfish Ltd.* v. *Golden Sea Produce Ltd.* 1992 SLT 703. Mussel farming in the sea; reparation for damage to mussel larvae.

*Walford* v. *David* 1989 SLT 876. Fish farm cages not a material interference with public right of navigation in the sea.

*Shetland Salmon Farmers Association* v. *Crown Estate Commissioners* 1990 SCLR 484. The seabed within territorial waters belongs to the Crown by virtue of the prerogative, and may be alienated or leased by the Crown. This includes the sea around Shetland.

*Lennox* v. *Keith* 1993 GWD 30–1913. The general public have no right to fish for trout in non-tidal waters, but may in tidal waters.

*Non-tidal, navigable rivers*
*Wills' Trs.* v. *Cairngorm Canoeing & Sailing School Ltd.* 1976 SC (HL) 30. Right of public navigation in rivers.

*Scammell* v. *Scottish Sports Council* 1983 SLT 462. Right of public navigation in rivers.

*Campbell's Trs.* v. *Sweeney* 1911 SC 1319. Right of public to anchor and moor in rivers.

*Orr Ewing* v. *Colquhoun's Trs.* (1877) 4 R (HL) 116. Private rights in alveus.

*Grant* v. *Henry* (1894) 21 R 358. Fishings in navigable river.

Non-navigable rivers
*Gibson* v. *Bonnington Sugar Refining Co. Ltd.* (1869) 7 M 394. 'Bounded by' a river implies ownership up to the medium filum. (Text 8.13)

*Bicket* v. *Morris* (1866) 4 M (HL) 44. Opposite heritors; operations in alveus.

*Menzies* v. *Breadalbane* (1901) 4 F 55. Opposite heritors; medium filum; main and subsidiary channel.

*Cowan* v. *Lord Kinnaird* (1865) 4 M 236. Upper and lower heritor; operations in alveus.

*Hood* v. *Williamsons* (1861) 23 D 496. Common interest in flow of water.

*Young* v. *Bankier Distillery Co.* (1893) 20 R (HL) 76. Pollution.

*Macintyre Bros.* v. *McGavin* (1893) 20 R (HL) 49. Pollution; prescriptive right.

*Hardie* v. *Walker* 1948 SC 674. Operations in alveus interfering with passage of salmon.

Lochs
*Macdonell* v. *Caledonian Canal Commissioners* (1830) 8 S 881. Loch surrounded by property of one proprietor.

*Scott* v. *Lord Napier* (1869) 7 M (HL) 35. Competing titles of adjoining proprietors; joint or exclusive right.

*Menzies* v. *MacDonald* (1856) 19 D (HL) 1. Joint right in loch; disposition 'with lakes and pertinents'.
*Meacher* v. *Blair-Oliphant* 1913 SC 417. Competing titles; joint or exclusive right.
*Mackenzie* v. *Bankes* (1878) 5 R 278. One loch or two.
*Magistrates of Ardrossan* v. *Dickie* (1907) 14 SLT 349. Loch or stagnum.
*Leith Buchanan* v. *Hogg* 1931 SC 204. Navigation on loch.
*Menzies* v. *Wentworth* (1901) 3 F 941. Regulation of joint rights of fishing in lochs.

**8.10 Fishings and game**
Salmon fishings
*Munro Ferguson* v. *Grant* (1900) 8 SLT 326. Express title.
*McKendrick* v. *Wilson* 1970 SLT (Sh Ct) 39. Separate tenement; need for conveyance. (Text 8.3, 28.34)
*Stuart* v. *McBarnett* (1868) 6 M (HL) 123. Crown grant with 'fishings'; construction.
*Bowie* v. *Marquis of Ailsa* (1887) 14 R 649. Crown grant; tidal and navigable river; competing public rights.
*Lord Advocate* v. *Cathcart* (1871) 9 M 744. Possession on barony title.
*Farquharson* v. *Lord Advocate* 1932 SN 28. Competing titles. (Text 18.2)
*Warrand's Trs.* v. *Makintosh* (1890) 17 R (HL) 13. Competing title.
*Magistrates of Tain* v. *Murray* (1887) 15 R 83. Boundaries between fishings.
*Lord Advocate* v. *Balfour* 1907 15 SLT 7. Udal law; salmon fishings not *inter regalia* in Orkney.
*Gay* v. *Malloch* 1959 SC 110. River; regulation of rights of opposite heritors.
*Fothringham* v. *Passmore* 1984 SC (HL) 96. River; *medium filum*; regulation of rights of opposite heritors.
*Roxburghe* v. *Waldie's Trs.* (1879) 6 R 663. Method of exercising right.
*Lord Advocate* v. *Lovat* (1880) 7 R (HL) 122. Express grant; possession; mode of exercise of right.
*Lord Advocate* v. *Sharp* (1878) 6 R 108. Sea fishings exercisable from foreshore; right of access over adjoining land.
*Middletweed Ltd.* v. *Murray* 1989 SLT 11. Rights of access are those necessary for beneficial enjoyment of the fishings. Circumstances in which held that there was no right of vehicular access.

Trout fishings
*Galloway* v. *Duke of Bedford* (1902) 4 F 851. Nature of right; lease of fishings.
*Don District Board* v. *Burnett* 1918 SC 37. Nature of right.
*Johnstone* v. *Gilchrist* 1934 SLT 271. Whether right of fishing and fowling real right or personal privilege.
*Harper* v. *Flaws* 1940 SLT 150. Whether right of trout fishings a servitude or real burden.
*Patrick* v. *Napier* (1867) 5 M 683. Whether right of angling right of property, burden or servitude.
*Wemyss Water Trs.* v. *Lawson* 1924 SLT 162. Reservation of fishings; whether enforceable against a statutory successor.
*Menzies* v. *Wentworth* (1901) 3 F 941. Regulation of joint rights of trout fishings in loch.
*Meacher* v. *Blair Oliphant* 1913 SC 417. Whether trout fishings in loch owned in common or exclusively.

Game
*Welwood* v. *Husband* (1874) 1 R 507. Nature of right.
*Johnstone* v. *Gilchrist* 1934 SLT 271. Nature of right.
*Beckett* v. *Bissett* (1921) 2 SLT 33. Shooting rights as real burden.
*Palmer's Trs.* v. *Brown* 1988 SCLR 499. Lease of shootings, if registered, transmits against singular successors of landlord. (Text 24.8)

**8.12 Methods of description: general description**
*Macdonald* v. *Keeper of the General Register of Sasines* 1914 SC 854. Description in general terms. (Text 8.11, 13.6)

*Houldsworth* v. *Gordon Cumming* 1910 SC (HL) 49. General description.
*Johnston's Trs.* v. *Kinloch* 1925 SLT 124. General description.

### 8.13 Particular description: boundaries

*Brown* v. *N.B. Ry. Co.* (1906) 8 F 534. Extrinsic evidence to identify boundary.
*Oliver* v. *Cameron* 1994 GWD 8–505. Access road described as shown within red boundary
  lines on plan; ownership and servitude of access discussed.(Text 11.3)
*Bennett* v. *Beneficial Bank plc.* 1995 SLT 1105. Discussion on what constitutes a particular
  description for purposes of standard security. (Text 8.11, 22.6, 31.21, 33.88)
*Beneficial Bank plc.* v. *McConnachie* 1996 SC 119. *Held* that description by postal address was
  not a particular description in standard security over a mid-terrace villa. (Text 8.11, 8.13,
  8.18, 8.21, 22.6, 33.88)
*Beneficial Bank plc.* v. *Wardle* 1996 GWD 30–1825. Rectification of defective description in
  standard security ordered. (Text 8.11)
*Reid* v. *McColl* (1879) 7 R 84. 'Bounded by the lands of A.'
*Strang* v. *Steuart* (1864) 2 M 1015. March fences.
*Thom* v. *Hetherington* 1988 SLT 724. Mutual boundary wall; comments on nature of owner-
  ship of respective proprietors.
*Gray* v. *MacLeod* 1979 SLT (Sh Ct) 17. Mutual wall.
*Lord Advocate* v. *Wemyss* (1899) 2 F (HL) 1. 'Bounded by the sea.'
*Gibson* v. *Bonnington Sugar Co.* (1869) 7 M 394. 'Bounded … along the Water of Leith';
  boundary was medium filum.
*Menzies* v. *Breadalbane* (1901) 4 F 55. River.
*Magistrates of Hamilton* v. *Bent Colliery* 1929 SC 686. River.
*Stirling* v. *Bartlett* 1992 SCLR 994. Effect on boundary of river changing course.
*Magistrates of Ayr* v. *Dobbie* (1898) 25 R 1184. Public road.
*Houstoun* v. *Barr* 1911 SC 134. Public road.
*Louttit's Trs.* v. *Highland Ry. Co.* (1892) 19 R 791. Private road. (Text 28.43, 28.98)
*Harris* v. *Wishart* 1996 SLT 12. Bounded by private road *prima facie* excludes whole road.
  (Text 11.9)
*Butt* v. *Galloway Motor Co. Ltd* 1996 SLT 1343. *Held* on appeal that word 'driveway' was
  bounding and excluded hedge and intervening verge. Boundary line lay along edge of
  tarmac of drive.
*Suttie* v. *Baird* 1992 SLT 133. Written description ambiguous; shape of area possessed did not
  match plan; title not bounding. (Text 8.15, 14.7)
*Mackenzie* v. *Emms* 1994 GWD 22–1363. Proof allowed in boundary dispute with strong
  recommendation to seek another form of resolution.
*Boyd* v. *Hamilton* 1907 SC 912. Lane; conflicting titles; actings of parties.
*Campbell* v. *Paterson* (1896) 4 SLT 79. Bounded by gable wall excludes the wall.
*Hetherington* v. *Galt* (1905) 7 F 706. Line of trees.

### 8.15 Repugnancies and ambiguities

*Currie* v. *Campbell's Trs.* (1888) 16 R 237. Boundaries and measurement inconsistent.
*North British Railway* v. *Moon's Trs.* (1879) 6 R 640. Written description and plan inconsistent.

### 8.16 Description by reference

*Murray's Trs.* v. *Wood* (1887) 14 R 856. Inept description by reference. (Text 8.19)
*Maclachlan* v. *Bowie* (1887) 25 SLR 734. Lost plan. (Text 8.13)
*Matheson* v. *Gemmell* (1903) 5 F 448. Description by reference at common law. (Text 8.19)
*Cattanach's Trs.* v. *Jamieson* (1884) 11 R 972. Error in date of recording deed held not to inval-
  idate description by reference. (Text 8.19)

### 8.22 Addenda to the description

*Gordon* v. *Grant* (1851) 13 D 1. Parts and pertinents.
*Jamieson* v. *Welsh* (1900) 3 F 176. Fixtures and fittings.

**Chapter 9.   Reservations**

**9.1   The implication of reservation: minerals**

*Bain* v. *Hamilton* (1865) 3 M 821. Coal; constitution of title by reservation to superior.

*Hamilton* v. *Graham* (1871) 9 M (HL) 98. Reservation of coal and limestone with right to sink pits.

*Hamilton* v. *Dunlop* (1885) 12 R (HL) 65. Reservation of right to work.

*Cadell* v. *Allan* (1905) 7 F 606. Minerals under foreshore; charter of novodamus; not reserving minerals, sufficient title to vassal.

*Lord Advocate* v. *Wemyss* (1899) 2 F (HL) 1. Minerals under sea.

*Millar* v. *Marquess of Landsdowne* 1910 SC 618. Competing titles; possession of surface.

*Fleeming* v *Howden* (1868) 6 M 782. Disposition of a bare superiority does not carry minerals previously reserved to, and owned by, disponing superior.

**9.2   Definition of minerals**

*Caledonian Railway* v. *Glenboig Union Fireclay Co. Ltd.* 1910 SC 951. Fireclay a mineral in 1856.

*Magistrates of Glasgow* v. *Farie* (1887) 15 R (HL) 94. Clay forming ordinary subsoil two or three feet below surface is not a mineral.

*Linlithgow* v. *N.B. Ry. Co.* 1914 SC (HL) 38. Shale not a recognised mineral in 1818 but would be now.

*North British Railway* v. *Budhill* 1910 SC (HL) 1. Sandstone not a mineral in 1845.

*Caledonian Railway* v. *Symington* 1912 SC (HL) 9. Whether freestone is a mineral is a question of fact; relevant factors discussed.

*Borthwick-Norton* v. *Gavin Paul & Sons* 1947 SC 659. Whether sand a mineral.

**9.4   Rights of parties: support**

*Buchanan* v. *Andrew* (1873) 11 M (HL) 13. Right of surface owner to prevent mineral working.

*White* v. *Dixon* (1883) 10 R (HL) 45. Normal right of support may be excluded by express provision.

*North British Railway Co.* v. *Turners Ltd.* (1904) 6 F 900. Nature of obligation to support.

*Hamilton* v. *Turner* (1867) 5 M 1086. Support of buildings.

*Bain* v. *Hamilton* (1867) 6 M 1. Support of buildings.

*Dryburgh* v. *Fife Coal Co. Ltd.* (1905) 7 F 1083. Support of buildings.

*Barr* v. *Baird & Co.* (1904) 6 F 524. Support of existing buildings

*Neill's Trs.* v. *Wm. Dixon Ltd.* (1880) 7 R 741. Support of building later erected.

*British Coal Corporation* v. *Netherlee Trust Trs* 1995 SLT 1038. Corporation was liable to carry out remedial action where damage was caused by the shifting of infill rather than true subsidence.

*Osborne* v. *British Coal Property* 1996 SLT 736. The Lands Tribunal now has jurisdiction in compensation claims, but jurisdiction of Court of Session is not wholly excluded.

Other reserved rights

*Scottish Temperance Life Assurance Co. Ltd.* v. *Law Union & Rock Insurance Co. Ltd.* 1917 SC 175. Reservation of power to build on ground disponed held ineffective against singular successors.

*Wemyss Water Trs.* v. *Lawson* 1924 SLT 162. Reservation of trout fishings. (See also cases under 8.10).

**Chapter 10.   Burdens**

**10.3   Real and personal conditions**

*Tailors of Aberdeen* v. *Coutts* (1840) 1 Rob. App. 296. Definition of real conditions and requirements for their creation.

*Corbett* v. *Robertson* (1872) 10 M 329. Restriction imposed for ten years only.

*Magistrates of Glasgow* v. *Hay* (1883) 10 R 635. Obligation to build by a certain date binding singular successors.

*Peter Walker & Son (Edinburgh) Ltd.* v. *Church of Scotland General Trs.* 1967 SLT 297. Obligation to build by a certain date binding original vassal only.

*Marshall's Trs.* v. *Macneill & Co.* (1888) 15 R 762. Obligation to build contained in a contract of ground annual not personally binding on singular successor.

*Rodger (Builders) Ltd.* v. *Fawdry* 1950 SC 483. Effect of personal contract on singular successor. (Text 28.94, 28.97, 28.98, 33.59, 33.61, 33.78, 35.10)

*Wallace* v. *Simmers* 1960 SC 255. Effect of personal contract on singular successor. (Text 33.60)

*Beckett* v. *Bissett* (1921) 2 SLT 33. Shooting rights cannot be constituted by way of a real burden.

*Harper* v. *Flaws* 1940 SLT 150. Fishing rights cannot be constituted by way of a real burden.

*Inverlochy Castle Ltd.* v. *Lochaber Power Co.* 1987 SLT 466. Benefit of a personal obligation was held to run with the lands.

**10.4 Distinction between real conditions and real burdens**

*Marquis of Tweeddale's Trs.* v. *Earl of Haddington* (1880) 7 R 620. Nature of personal liability of sub-vassal to over-superior for payment of over-feuduty. (Text 10.7)

*Wells* v. *New House Purchasers Ltd.* 1964 SLT (Sh Ct) 2. Personal liability of singular successor to implement real condition imposed by disposition. (Text 10.5, 10.6, 10.7, 29.12, 29.18, 29.19)

*Magistrates of Edinburgh* v. *Begg* (1883) 11 R 352. Circumstances in which an obligation to pay road money was neither a real condition nor a real burden. (Text 10.7)

**10.6 Mode of enforcement of real conditions**

See Ch. 17 – Enforcement of Burdens

**10.9 Constitution of real conditions: the inherent characteristics**

*Tailors of Aberdeen* v. *Coutts* (1840) 1 Rob. App. 296. Definition of fundamental characteristics.

*Marquis of Tweeddale's Trs.* v. *Earl of Haddington* (1880) 7 R 620. Discussion of fundamental characteristics. (Text 10.7)

*Corbett* v. *Robertson* (1872) 10 M 329. Restriction not permanent.

*Magistrates of Edinburgh* v. *Begg* (1883) 11 R 352. No element of permanency. (Text 10.7)

*Stewart* v. *Duke of Montrose* (1860) 22 D 755. An obligation undertaken by a superior transmitted against his singular successors, although not duly constituted as a real burden on the superiority title.

*Hope* v. *Hope* (1864) 2 M 670. The same as *Stewart* above.

*Hislop* v. *MacRitchie's Trs.* (1881) 8 R (HL) 95. General discussion on real conditions and the *jus quaesitum tertio*. (Text 17.4, 29.21, 29.35)

**10.10 Essential intrinsic qualities**

*Aberdeen Varieties Ltd.* v. *Jas. F. Donald (Aberdeen Cinemas) Ltd.* 1940 SC (HL) 52. Condition contrary to public policy cannot bind a singular successor.

*Phillips* v. *Lavery* 1962 SLT (Sh Ct) 57. Condition contrary to public policy does not bind original disponee.

*Co-operative Wholesale Society* v. *Ushers Brewery* 1975 SLT (Lands Tr.) 9. Whether a restriction on use contrary to public policy. (Text 17.21, 17.30)

*Giblin* v. *Murdoch* 1979 SLT (Sh Ct) 5. Restrictive condition imposed on purchaser void as being in restraint of trade.

**10.11 Qualification of an infeftment**

Obligations undertaken by the vassal

*Morier* v. *Brownlie & Watson* (1895) 23 R 67. Conditions not entering the title.

*Magistrates of Edinburgh* v. *MacFarlane* (1857) 20 D 156. Conditions not recorded. (Text 10.9)

*Robertson* v. *NB Ry. Co.* (1874) 1 R 1213. Conditions not recorded. (Text 10.9)

*Liddall* v. *Duncan* (1898) 25 R 1119. Condition not recorded. (Text 10.9)

*Campbell's Trs.* v. *Glasgow Corporation* (1902) 4 F 752. Recorded agreement, 1874 Act s. 32 not applicable. (Text 33.57, 33.61)

*Gorrie & Banks Ltd.* v. *Mussleburgh Burgh* 1973 SC 33. Reference to recorded agreement; 1874 Act s. 32 applied.

Obligations undertaken by superior

*Duke of Montrose* v. *Stewart* (1863) 1 M (HL) 25. Obligation of relief undertaken by superior in a feu charter may bind successors in superiority.

*Hope* v. *Hope* (1864) 2 M 670. Obligation of relief undertaken by superior. (Text 10.9)

*Leith School Board* v. *Rattray's Trs.* 1918 SC 94. Superior undertaking to insert conditions in subsequent feu charters may incur liability in damages for breach of contract for failing to do so.

*Duncan* v. *Church of Scotland General Trs.* 1941 SC 145. Implied obligation on superior to relieve vassal of cost of repairs.

*Jolly's Exx.* v. *Viscount Stonehaven* 1958 SC 635. Circumstances where failure by superior to insert conditions in subsequent titles did not infer liability on superior. (Text 33.77)

*Rutherford* v. *Virtue* 1993 SCLR 886. In a disposition the developer undertook to form a road giving access over his adjoining ground. He then sold the adjoining ground without having formed the road.

## 10.12 The subjects affected must be clearly identified

*Anderson* v. *Dickie* 1915 SC (HL) 79. Description of subjects affected too indefinite.

*Scottish Temperance Life Insurance Co. Ltd.* v. *Law Union & Rock Insurance Co. Ltd.* 1917 SC 175. Insufficient specification.

## 10.13 The presumption for freedom

*Anderson* v. *Dickie* 1915 SC (HL) 79. Burden not expressly imposed.

*Walker Trs.* v. *Haldane* (1902) 4 F 594. Restriction not expressly imposed.

*Kemp* v. *Largs Magistrates* 1939 SC (HL) 6. Particular use not expressly prohibited.

*Russell* v. *Cowper* (1882) 9 R 660. Building not expressly prohibited.

*Cowan* v. *Edinburgh Magistrates* (1887) 14 R 682. Further buildings not expressly prohibited; vassal not restricted.

*Carswell* v. *Goldie* 1967 SLT 339. Particular building not expressly prohibited.

*Murray's Trs.* v. *St. Margaret's Convent Trs.* 1907 SC (HL) 8. 'Unseemly building'.

*Mannofield Residents Pty. Co. Ltd.* v. *Thomson* 1983 SLT (Sh Ct) 71. Whether a prohibition against acts injurious to amenity too vague to be enforceable.

*Lothian RC* v. *Rennie* 1991 SC 212. Obligation to maintain the supply of water in a mill lade and to cleanse the remaining parts of the lade 'to the reasonable satisfaction' of the grantor held void from uncertainty.

*Lawson* v. *Hay* 1989 GWD 24–1049. Requirement that dwellinghouse must be 'conventional' too vague for a real burden.

*David Watson Property Management* v. *Woolwich Equitable BS* 1992 SLT 430. View expressed that an obligation of maintenance would not be enforceable if in the form of an obligation to pay an indefinite sum of money. (Text 10.5, 10.6, 22.43, 29.19)

*Dunedin Property Management Services Ltd* v. *Glamis Property Ltd.* 1993 GWD 31–2006. Meaning of the term 'roof' in relation to a tenement comprising two single-storey shops and an adjacent tenement. Extrinsic evidence rejected. (Text 10.12)

*Southwark Project Services Ltd.* v. *Granada Leisure Ltd.* 1993 GWD 2–126. The construction of a deed of conditions; effect of alleged omission of a comma.

*Meriton Ltd.* v. *Winning* 1995 SLT 76. *Held* that the word 'objectionable' was not so indefinite as to be incapable of enforcement.

*Porter* v. *Campbell's Trs.* 1923 SC (HL) 94. Distinction between construction and use.

*Mathieson* v. *Allan's Trs.* 1914 SC 464. Restrictions as to structure do not restrict subsequent change of use.

*Hunter* v. *Fox* 1964 SC (HL) 95. Surplus words, if not ambiguous, treated as *pro non scripto*.

*Arnold* v. *Davidson Trust Ltd.* 1987 SCLR 213. Discussion on the powers of *proprietors* in applying the provisions of a deed of conditions.

### 10.14 The intention to burden
*Duke of Montrose* v. *Stewart* (1863) 1 M (HL) 25. General observations.
*Magistrates of Arbroath* v. *Dickson* (1872) 10 M 630. Annual money payments not declared real burdens.
*Cowie* v. *Muirden* (1893) 20 R (HL) 81. Residue bequeathed explicitly under burden of an annuity. (Text 32.26, 32.36)
*Geary* v. *Tellwright* 1994 GWD 17–1077. Respective liability of upper and lower proprietors for common repairs.
*Buchanan* v. *Eaton* 1911 SC (HL) 40. A general bequest of residue, under burden of an annuity, held not sufficient to imply a real burden.

### 10.18 Subsequent reference to burdens
*King* v. *Johnston* 1908 SC 684. Burdens imposed by disposition may possibly be extinguished by failure to refer to for twenty years.

### Chapter 11.   Servitudes

### 11.1 Servitudes and burdens compared
*Patrick* v. *Napier* (1867) 5 M 683. Servitude a real right, not a personal right.
*Cowan* v. *Stewart* (1872) 10 M 735. Whether obligation personal or real.
*Allan* v. *MacLachlan* (1900) 2 F 699. Whether obligation to repair personal or real; no duty on servient owner to maintain
*McLean* v. *Marwhirn Developments Ltd.* 1976 SLT (Notes) 47. Distinction between servitude and real burden. (Text 11.3)
*Crichton* v. *Turnbull* 1946 SC 52. Servitude or right of property.
*Taylor's Trs.* v. *McGavigan* (1896) 23 R 945. Prohibition on building to preserve light; servitude or burden.
*Safeway Foods Stores Ltd.* v. *Wellington Motor Co. Ayr Ltd.* 1976 SLT 53. Servitude cannot be created in favour of tenant of dominant tenement.

### 11.3 Salient characteristics of servitude
*Hamilton* v. *Elder* 1968 SLT (Sh Ct) 53. Servitude cannot be created where same person owns both tenements.
*Irvine Knitters* v. *N. Ayrshire Co-op. Society Ltd.* 1978 SC 109. Servitude is for benefit of dominant tenement only.
*Hunter* v. *Fox* 1964 SC (HL) 95. Presumption for freedom.
*Clark & Sons* v. *Perth School Board* (1898) 25 R 919. If ambiguous, least onerous construction is preferred.
*Lanarkshire Water Board* v. *Gilchrist* 1973 SLT (Sh Ct) 58. Owner of dangerous bull may be interdicted from grazing it on land adjoining right of access.
*Walker's Exx.* v. *Carr* 1973 SLT (Sh Ct) 77. Occasional access or regular daily use.
*Fraser* v. *Secretary of State for Scotland* 1959 SLT (Notes) 36. Whether planting trees interference with right of pasturage.
*Drury* v. *McGarvie* 1993 SC 95. Circumstances in which held that erection of unlocked gates by servient proprietor not interference with servitude of access.
*Central Regional Council* v. *Ferns* 1979 SC 136. Aqueductus; interference by overburdening by servient owner.
*Inverness Farmers' Dairy* v. *Kinlochdamph Ltd.* 1989 GWD 25–1106. Right of access for purposes connected with boat house could be used for lorries carrying food to fish farm.
*Mendelssohn* v. *The Wee Pub Co. Ltd.* 1991 GWD 26–1518. Right to hang shop sign not one of known servitudes.

*Alvis* v. *Harrison* 1991 SLT 64. Discussion of extent of use permitted and of right of dominant proprietor to repair servient tenement.

*Alba Homes Ltd.* v. *Duell* 1993 SLT (Sh Ct) 49. If dominant tenement subdivided, both parts can exercise servitude provided no increase in burden. (Text 11.12)

*Baillie* v. *Mackay* 1994 GWD 25–1516. Road which had ceased to be public right of way held to be still subject to servitude rights of access.

*Viewpoint Housing Association Ltd.* v. *Lothian Regional Council* 1993 SLT 921. *Held* that the fact that street had acquired character of a road, as defined in 1984 Act s. 59, did not *per se* make it public.

*Oliver* v. *Cameron* 1994 GWD 8–505. Only dominant owner has title to enforce servitude right.

### 11.5  Constitution of positive servitudes: express grant or express reservation

*Cowan* v. *Stewart* (1872) 10 M 735. Agreement in missives.

*Campbell's Trs.* v. *Glasgow Corporation* (1902) 4 F 752. Unfeudalised grant not followed by possession. (Text 33.57, 33.61)

*Millar* v. *McRobbie* 1949 SC 1. Meaning and extent of express grant of access. (Text 24.1, 24.4)

*Stansfield* v. *Findlay* 1996 GWD 37–2170. *Held* that access route included verge. Access could be taken of route across verge at any one or more points.

*Ross* v. *Beck* 1992 GWD 16–930. Original line of servitude constituted by express provision not affected by subsequent widening and other alterations to route.

*Hermiston Securities Ltd.* v. *Kirkcaldy District Council* 1994 GWD 39–2317. Agreement as to access by planning officer acting in that capacity did not bind council as owners. (Text 11.3)

*Mackay* v. *Burton* 1994 SLT (Lands Tr.) 35. Servitude not a right capable of being held as separate interest by dominant proprietor who cannot therefore qualify as burdened proprietor. (Text 11.3)

*Brennan* v. *Roberton's Exrs.* 1997 GWD 1–32. There was nothing indefinite or uncertain in the undertaking as to servitude rights contracted for in missives, which were sufficient as a general obligation to render them enforceable. *Callander* v. *Midlothian District Council* 1996 SCLR 955, involving a similar obligation, approved. (Text 11.3)

*Callander* v. *Midlothian District Council* 1996 SCLR 955. In a contract for sale, purchasers of heritage were bound to permit owners and occupiers of adjoining land access over subjects of sale. Obligation in original missives was collateral and therefore not superseded, and language used was sufficient to determine intention. (Text 28.53)

*Munro* v. *Mclintock* 1996 SLT (Sh Ct) 97. Dominant owner in servitude right of access sought interdict to prevent encroachment. *Held* that right having been precisely defined by express grant, it could not be altered, and decree in favour of the pursuer granted. (Text 11.3)

*McEachen* v. *Lister* 1976 SLT (Sh Ct) 38. Express grant excludes alternative implied grant. (Text 11.6, 11.8).

*Balfour* v. *Kinsey* 1987 SLT 144. Possession is unnecessary if servitude enters titles of servient or dominant tenement. (Text 33.62)

*Turner* v. *Macmillan Douglas* 1989 SLT 292. Question whether right of access stipulated for in missives was personal or servitude right.

*Norcott* v. *Sanderson* 1990 SCLR 622. Right of access granted in favour of a named individual, and without reference to a dominant tenement, held not sufficient to constitute a servitude.

*Robertson* v. *Hossack* 1995 SLT 291. Right of access granted in favour of named individual without reference to successors held not sufficient to constitute servitude.

*Douglas* v. *Crossflags (Motors) Ltd.* 1989 GWD 22–941. Servitude cannot be acquired by tenant in his own name.

*Fearnan Partnership* v. *Grindlay* 1990 SLT 704. If proposed servient tenement is owned in common, all co-owners must concur in the grant. (Text 11.3)

*Love-Lee* v. *Cameron of Locheil* 1991 SCLR 61. Obligation on owner of land to maintain road giving access to that land cannot be read as conferring servitude right of access in respect of road.

*Grant* v. *Cameron* 1991 GWD 6–328. Servitude of access 'for all purposes' held to include right to invite the public to use road.

### 11.6  Implied grant or implied reservation

*Cochrane* v. *Ewart* (1860) 22 D 358. Implied grant of servitude of necessity for drainage. (Text 11.8).

*Walton Brothers* v. *Glasgow Magistrates* (1876) 3 R 1130. Implied grant of servitude of necessity; access.

*Fergusson* v. *Campbell* 1913 1 SLT 241. Implied reservation of servitude of necessity; aqueduct. (Text 11.7)

*Shearer* v. *Peddie* (1899) 1 F 1201. Circumstances where right of access held not necessary for reasonable enjoyment.

*Fraser* v. *Cox* 1938 SC 506. Circumstances where right of access held not to have been granted expressly or by implication. (Text 11.8)

*Alexander* v. *Butchart* (1875) 3 R 156. No implied grant of servitude for shop sign.

*Murray* v. *Medley* 1973 SLT (Sh Ct) 75. No implied reservation of servitude of necessity; water pipe. (Text 11.8, 28.49)

*Central Regional Council* v. *Ferns* 1979 SC 136. Grant of servitude of acqueductus created by statute, by implication.

*Moffat* v. *Milne* 1993 GWD 8–572. On subdivision and sale of part, it does not necessarily follow that remainder is landlocked. (Text 11.7)

*Midlothian District Council* v. *McCulloch* 1993 SCLR 152. Two properties separated by road. Owner of half the road held entitled to access over other half.

*King* v. *Brodt* 1993 GWD 13–886. Circumstances where conveyance held to carry by implication right of access to disponee, formerly tenant.

*Neill* v. *Scobie* 1993 GWD 13–887. For servitude by implication there must be presumption that granter intended it.

*Harris* v. *Wishart* 1996 SLT 12. See *Harris* v. *Wishart* (8.13), where claim to ownership rejected. Question then arose whether servitude right of access had been created. (Text 11.9)

### 11.9  Prescription

*Scotland* v. *Wallace* 1964 SLT (Sh Ct) 9. Constitution of right of access by prescription.

*Kerr* v. *Brown* 1939 SC 140. *Tantum praescriptum quantum possessum.*

*Carstairs* v. *Spence* 1924 SC 380. *Tantum praescriptum quantum possessum.*

*McLellan* v. *Hunter* 1987 GWD 21–803. Possession without title under 1973 Act s. 3. (Text 14.14)

*Middletweed Ltd.* v. *Murray* 1989 SLT 11. Discussion on constitution and extent of servitude right of access as accessory to right of salmon fishings.

*Kennedy* v. *MacDonald* 1988 GWD 40–1653. Discussion on extent of right of access established by prescriptive possession; comments on incidental rights of parking, unloading *etc.*

*Harris* v. *Wishart* 1996 SLT 12. See 11.6 above.

*Wilson* v. *Ross* 1993 GWD 31–2007. Claim to access by prescriptive use failed.

*Lord Burton* v. *Mackay* 1995 SLT 507. See 11.15 below.

*Landward Securities (Edinburgh) Ltd.* v. *Inhouse (Edinburgh) Ltd.* 1996 GWD 16–962. Conveyance of heritable property 'but only so far as I have right thereto' held habile to acquisition by prescription. (Text 8.22, 14.7)

*Hogg* v. *Campbell* 1993 GWD 27–1712. Circumstances where servitude right of access held to have been abandoned. (Text 11.14, 14.11)

### 11.10  Acquiescence

*Macgregor* v. *Balfour* (1899) 2 F 345. Estate factor no implied authority to create servitude by express grant or acquiescence.

*Robson* v. *Chalmers Property Investment Co. Ltd.* 1965 SLT 381. Laying of water pipes, known to servient owner.

*More* v. *Boyle* 1967 SLT (Sh Ct) 38. Common water pipe. (Text 28.49)

### 11.11  Constitution of negative servitudes

*Hunter* v. *Fox* 1964 SC (HL) 95. Constitution in disposition of servient tenement.

*Cowan* v. *Stewart* (1872) 10 M 735. Constitution by agreement.

*Inglis* v. *Clark* (1901) 4 F 288. Cannot be constituted by implication.

## 11.12  Transmission of the right

*Royal Exchange, etc.* v. *Cotton* 1912 SC 1151. Whether singular successor entitled to enforce. (Text 11.13)

*Braid Hills Hotel Co. Ltd.* v. *Manuels* 1909 SC 120. Whether singular successor entitled to enforce. (Text 10.7, 29.23)

*Watson* v. *Sinclair* 1966 SLT (Sh Ct) 77. Communicating the right to tenant.

*Keith* v. *Texaco Ltd.* 1977 SLT (Lands Tr.) 16. Communicating the right, increasing the burden.

## 11.14  Extinction of the right

*Millar* v. *Christie* 1961 SC 1. Acquiescence.

*Walker's Exx.* v. *Carr* 1973 SLT (Sh Ct) 77. Negative prescription; *non utendo.*

*Largs Hydropathic Ltd.* v. *Largs Town Council* 1967 SC 1. Acquisition for statutory purposes may render servitude unenforceable.

*Devlin* v. *Conn* 1972 SLT (Lands Tr.) 11. By the Lands Tribunal under the 1970 Act s. 1(3)(a).

*Gray* v. *MacLeod* 1979 SLT (Sh Ct) 17. Limited right of access suspended when purpose ccases.

## 11.15  Public rights of way

*Richardson* v. *Cromarty Petroleum Co. Ltd.* 1982 SLT 237. Quality of possession required to constitute public right of way. (Text 14.14)

*Sutherland* v. *Thomson* (1876) 3 R 485. Erecting gate on public footpath.

*Midlothian District Council* v. *McKenzie* 1985 SLT 36. Servient owner may not encroach unjustifiably on public right of way.

*Love-Lee* v. *Cameron of Lochiel* 1991 SCLR 61. Sub-post office, part of a private house, held not to be public place in sense required for terminus of public right of way.

*Cumbernauld & Kilsyth District Council* v. *Dollar Land (Cumbernauld) Ltd.* 1993 SLT 1318. Cumbernauld Development Corporation constructed the new town with a public walkway through town centre. Defenders subsequently acquired new town and closed walkway to public at night. *Held* that nature of past use was not by mere tolerance but continuous and plain assertion of a public right of way. (Text 14.14)

*Lauder* v. *MacColl* 1993 SCLR 753. Public right of way between two public places established by past use over long period.

*Viewpoint Housing Association Ltd* v. *Lothian Regional Council* 1993 SLT 921. Road of a public character, used for less than prescriptive period, held not to have become public right of way.

*Lord Burton* v. *Mackay* 1995 SLT 507. (Follow-up to *Mackay* v. *Burton*, noted at 11.5 above.) Mackay failed to establish ownership of *solum* of road. Lord Burton then sought to interdict him from taking access over that route. *Held* that, a public right of way having been established, proprietors along its route could continue to use it as access. (Text 14.14)

*Renfrew District Council* v. *Russell* 1994 GWD 34 2032. Local authority obtained interdict against two persons who had attempted to deter public from exercising public right of way.

## Chapter 12.   Subordinate Clauses

## 12.4  Entry

*Thomas* v. *Lord Advocate* 1953 SC 151. Significance of date of entry.

## 12.5  Assignation of writs

*Porteous* v. *Henderson* (1898) 25 R 563. Effect of assignation of writs.

## 12.6  Assignation of rents

*Butter* v. *Foster* 1912 SC 1218. Interpretation of statutory clause.

**12.7 Obligation of relief**

*Spottiswoode* v. *Seymer* (1853) 15 D 458. Special obligation of relief in disposition requires special assignation.

*Duke of Montrose* v. *Stewart* (1863) 1 M (HL) 25. But not if undertaken by superior in feu charter.

*North British Railway* v. *Edinburgh Magistrates* 1920 SC 409. Extent of obligation.

**12.8 Warrandice**

*Cairns* v. *Howden* (1870) 9 M 284. Extent of claim.

*Leith Heritages* v. *Edinburgh & Leith Glass Co.* (1876) 3 R 789. Warrandice of 'all right, title and interest'.

*Brownlie* v. *Miller* (1880) 7 R (HL) 66. Warrandice guarantees only against eviction and does not warrant the particular tenure. (Text 12.17)

*Horsburgh's Trs.* v. *Welch* (1886) 14 R 67. Warrandice from fact and deed guarantees only against acts of grantor himself.

*Duchess of Montrose* v. *Stuart* (1887) 15 R (HL) 19. Warrandice obligation strictly construed according to its terms. Express absolute warrandice in gratuitous deed so construed.

*Welsh* v. *Russell* (1894) 21 R 769. Partial eviction. Nature of remedy. (Text 12.19, 28.43)

*Clark* v. *Lindale Homes Ltd.* 1994 SLT 1053. To establish eviction under warrandice, competing proprietor must actually have challenged the title.

*Watson* v. *Swift & Co's JF* 1986 SC 55. Claim under warrandice is competent without ejection, if unquestionable burden on subjects can be proved.

*Palmer* v. *Beck* 1993 SLT 485. No remedy in warrandice without judicial eviction. (Text 11.10, 28.95)

*Lothian & Border Farmers Ltd.* v. *McCutchion* 1952 SLT 450. Existing lease not breach of warrandice. (Text 12.9, 28.41)

*Christie* v. *Cameron* (1898) 25 R 824. Liability under warrandice persists and continues to bind original warrantor after grantee has sold subjects.

*Cobham* v. *Minter* 1986 SLT 336. Claim by subsequent purchaser against earlier purchaser; transmission discussed. (Text 12.20)

*Young* v. *McKellar Ltd.* 1909 SC 1340. Warrandice following articles of roup.

*Fraser* v. *Cox* 1938 SC 506. Warrandice not reflecting prior agreement. (Text 11.8)

*Kildrummy (Jersey) Ltd.* v. *IRC* 1991 SC 1. Warrandice clause in disposition referred to lease. Lease void and held not to be capable of being validated by adoption by disposition. (Text 12.9, 14.7, 26.3)

**Chapter 13. Registration**

**13.5 Registration**

*Ceres School Board* v. *McFarlane* (1895) 23 R 279. In a competition between recorded titles, priority of infeftment determines preference. (Text 29.38, 29.40, 32.1, 33.57, 33.58)

**13.6 Register of Sasines**

*Johnston* v. *Fairfowl* (1901) 8 SLT 480. Possession without title.

*Cameron's Trs.* v. *Cameron* 1907 SC 407. Effect of recording. (Text 4.7)

*Macdonald* v. *Keeper of the General Register of Sasines* 1914 SC 854. Need for adequate description. (Text 8.11)

*Brown* v. *NB Ry. Co.* (1906) 8 F 534. Indefinite conveyance not mandate for infeftment.

*Swans* v. *Western Bank* (1866) 4 M 663. Superior must be infeft; accretion. (Text 7.3)

**13.28 Content of the title sheet**

*McCarthy & Stone (Developments) Ltd.* v. *Smith* 1995 SLT (Lands Tr.) 19. Owner of *dominium utile* acquired superiority and consolidated. His title was then registered in Land Register. Burdens section of title sheet disclosed burdens in *dominium utile* title as still subsisting. *Held,* in application to Tribunal for discharge thereof, that no *jus quaesitum* having been created, there were no longer enforceable burdens falling to be discharged, and application dismissed. (Text 13.35)

### 13.33 Rectification of the Register
*Brookfield Developments Ltd.* v. *Keeper of the Registers of Scotland* 1989 SLT (Lands Tr.) 105. Keeper included burdens which were no longer subsisting; rectification allowed. (Text 13.35, 17.35)

*Short's Trs.* v. *Keeper of the Registers of Scotland* 1996 SLT 166. Decree of reduction not registrable under 1979 Act s. 2(4) and will not normally justify rectification of Register. (Text 13.13, 13.35, 29.9, 30.10, 33.67, 33.99)

*Scottish Enterprise* v. *Ferguson* 1996 GWD 26–1522. Disposition by registered proprietor immune from challenge based on an unregistered prohibition and Register would not be rectified. (Text 13.13, 13.35)

## Chapter 14. The Effects of Possession: Prescription

### 14.5 Positive prescription
*Scott* v. *Bruce-Stewart* (1779) 3 RLC 334. Purpose of positive prescription. (Text 14.6)

*Lord Advocate* v. *Graham* (1844) 7 D 183. Working of positive prescription.

*Edmonstone* v. *Jeffray* (1886) 13 R 1038. Possession without title cannot create proprietory rights by prescription.

*McLellan* v. *Hunter* 1987 GWD 21–803. Constitution of servitude right by possession for twenty years without title under 1973 Act s. 3. (Text 14.14)

*Johnston* v. *Fairfowl* (1901) 8 SLT 480. Possession without title.

*Grant* v. *Henry* (1894) 21 R 358. Rights such as trout fishing cannot be acquired by prescriptive use.

### 14.7 The result of title and possession
*Ex facie* invalidity

*Cooper Scott* v. *Gill Scott* 1924 SC 309. Discussion on *ex facie* invalidity. (Text 33.4)

*Lock* v. *Taylor* 1976 SLT 238. Was title express grant, or merely title habile to found prescription?

*Fraser* v. *Lord Lovat* (1898) 25 R 603. Possesssion on Crown grant disconform to enabling Act.

*Hilson* v. *Scott* (1895) 23 R 241. Title *a non domino.*

*Glen* v. *Scales's Tr. & Others* (1881) 9 R 317. Title *a non habente potestatem.*

*Ramsay* v. *Spence* 1909 SC 1441. Which register, county or burgh?

*Troup* v. *Aberdeen Heritable Securities Co. Ltd.* 1916 SC 918. Not competent to refer to earlier titles in order to make title bounding.

*Meacher* v. *Blair-Oliphant* 1913 SC 417. Not competent to refer to earlier titles in order to qualify foundation writ.

*Watson* v. *Shields* 1996 SCLR 81. If person in possession is challenged by alleged competitor, he cannot interdict that competitor to prevent challenge unless the competitor totally unable to demonstrate colourable title. (Text 14.2)

*Love-Lee* v. *Cameron of Lochiel* 1991 SCLR 61. Even after granting a conveyance, grantor has, in original title, title which is habile for purposes of prescription. Hence if he retains possession for ten years after the grant, land reverts to his ownership.

Ambiguity of description

*Auld* v. *Hay* (1880) 7 R 663. Ambiguity; title to *pro indiviso* shares; possession of whole.

*Suttie* v. *Baird* 1992 SLT 133. Ambiguous boundary sufficient title for prescription. (Text 8.15)

*Nisbet* v. *Hogg* 1950 SLT 289. 'All rights in any way competent to' disponers.

*Robertson's Trs.* v. *Bruce* (1905) 7 F 580. Right of property or right of servitude.

*Fleeming* v. *Howden* (1868) 6 M 782. Title to 'superiority' not habile to acquisition of *dominium utile.*

*Agnew* v. *Lord Advocate* (1873) 11 M 309. No presumption that foreshore is a pertinent without express grant; prescriptive possession is necessary. (Text 18.2)

*Young* v. *NB Ry. Co.* (1887) 14 R (HL) 53. Possession of foreshore on title from subject superior sufficient.

*Luss Estates Co.* v. *BP Oil Grangemouth Refinery Ltd.* 1987 SLT 201. Foreshore – barony title with bounding description excludes acquisition by possession. (Text 18.2)

*Stuart* v. *McBarnett* (1868) 6 M (HL) 123. Crown grant of 'fishings'; possession of salmon fishings established title.

*Zetland* v. *Glover Incorporation of Perth* (1870) 8 M (HL) 144. Salmon fishings; consolidated title. (Text 29.43)

*Zetland* v. *Tennent's Trs.* (1873) 11 M 469. Possession of salmon fishings beyond boundaries of associated land may create title thereto.

*Farquharson* v. *Lord Advocate* 1932 SN 28. Possession of salmon fishings on base title may establish right. (Text 18.2)

*Millar* v. *Marquess Landsdowne* 1910 SC 618. Minerals, competing titles, both claimants averring possession.

*Lord Advocate* v. *Wemyss* (1899) 2 F (HL) 1. Barony title, minerals under foreshore and sea.

*Borthwick-Norton* v. *Gavin Paul & Sons* 1947 SC 659. Construction; minerals; sand.

*Meacher* v. *Blair-Oliphant* 1913 SC 417. Whether rights in lochs exclusive or common.

*Stewart's Trs.* v. *Robertson* (1874) 1 R 334. Whether rights in lochs rights of property or servitude.

Parts and pertinents

*Magistrates of Perth* v. *Earl of Wemyss* (1829) 8 S 82. Possession of island as a pertinent prevailed over express infeftment therein.

*Gordon* v. *Grant* (1851) 13 D 1. Corporeal property cannot be acquired outwith bounding title.

*Cooper's Trs.* v. *Stark's Trs.* (1898) 25 R 1160. Saloon as pertinent of house.

*Mead* v. *Melville* 1915 1 SLT 107. Title to basement flat habile to acquisition, by prescriptive possession, of cellar as a pertinent.

*McArly* v. *French's Trs.* (1883) 10 R 574. Right to retain signboard on a building established by prescriptive possession.

Bounding title

*Cooper's Trs.* v. *Stark's Trs.* (1898) 25 R 1160. Bounding title prevents acquisition of corporeal property outwith boundary.

*Zetland* v. *Tennent's Trs.* (1873) 11 M 469. Bounding title does not prevent acquisition of salmon fishings beyond boundaries.

*North British Railway* v. *Moon's Trs.* (1879) 6 R 640. Title bounding; conflict between written description and plan.

*Anderson* v. *Harrold* 1991 SCLR 135. Title bounding; conflict between written description and plan.

*Brown* v. *NB Ry. Co.* (1906) 8 F 534. Title bounding; identification by reference to extrinsic evidence; separate plan.

*Reid* v. *McColl* (1879) 7 R 84. Identification by reference to extrinsic evidence; adjoining title.

*North British Railway* v. *Hutton* (1896) 23 R 522. Particular description with exception; bounding so as to exclude exception.

*Houstoun* v. *Barr* 1911 SC 134. Title bounding; 'bounded by Quarrelton Street'. (Text 8.13)

*Watt* v. *Burgess's Trs.* (1891) 18 R 766. Title bounding; conveyance of attic storey.

*Lord Advocate* v. *Wemyss* (1899) 2 F (HL) 1. Title bounding; statement of county.

*Gordon* v. *Grant* (1851) 13 D 1. Title bounding; statement of parish.

*Nisbet* v. *Hogg* 1950 SLT 289. Title not bounding.

*Troup* v. *Aberdeen Heritable Securities Co. Ltd.* 1916 SC 918. Title not bounding; not competent to make it so by referring to earlier titles.

## 14.8 The quality of title and nature of possession

Generally

*Robertson's Trs.* v. *Bruce* (1905) 7 F 580. Title must support possession.

*Argyll* v. *Campbell* 1912 SC 458. Title must support possession; competent to refer to earlier titles to explain possession.

*Houstoun* v. *Barr* 1911 SC 134. Title must support possession; competent to refer to earlier titles to explain possession. (Text 8.13)

*Warrand's Trs.* v. *McIntosh* (1890) 17 R (HL) 13. Salmon fishings; possession relied on to construe express grant.

*McLellan* v. *Hunter* 1987 GWD 21–803. Constitution of a servitude right by possession for twenty years without title under the 1973 Act s. 3. (Text 14.14)

*Fothringham* v. *Passmore* 1984 SC (HL) 96. Salmon fishings; possession not referable to title.

*Luss Estates Co.* v. *B.P. Oil Grangemouth Refinery Ltd.* 1987 SLT 201. Barony title; bounding title expressly excluding foreshore; possession did not create title. (Text 18.2)

*Landward Securities (Edinburgh) Ltd.* v. *Inhouse (Edinburgh) Ltd.* 1996 GWD 16–962. Qualification 'so far as I have right thereto' no bar to prescription. (Text 8.22, 11.9, 14.7)

Quality of possession

*Millar* v. *Marquess of Landsdowne* 1910 SC 618. Possession must be exclusive.

*Young* v. *NB Ry. Co* (1887) 14 R (HL) 53. Whether possession sufficient to create title; foreshore.

*Meacher* v. *Blair-Oliphant* 1913 SC 417. Whether possession sufficient to create title; salmon fishings.

*Maxwell* v. *Lamont* (1903) 6 F 245. Possession must be lawful and by legal methods; salmon fishings.

*Warrand's Trs.* v. *Mackintosh* (1890) 17 R (HL) 13. Salmon fishing; barony title; possession by rod and line.

*Richardson* v. *Cromarty Petroleum Co. Ltd.* 1982 SLT 237. Quality of possession required to constitute public right of way. (Text 14.14)

*Strathclyde (Hyndland) Housing Society Ltd.* v. *Cowie* 1983 SLT (Sh Ct) 61. Quality of possession required to constitute public right of way.

*Cumbernauld & Kilsyth District Council* v. *Dollar Land Ltd.* 1993 SC (HL) 44. Quality of possession required to constitute public right of way. (Text 11.15, 14.14)

*Middletweed Ltd.* v. *Murray* 1989 SLT 11. Quality of possession required to constitute servitude right of way.

*Bain* v. *Carrick* 1983 SLT 675. Competing titles; use by one party; extent of use necessary.

*Hamilton* v. *McIntosh Donald Ltd.* 1994 SLT 793. Detailed analysis of requisites for prescriptive possession. (Text 14.11)

*Tantum praescriptum quantum possessum*

*Kerr* v. *Brown* 1939 SC 140. Limitation on right of drainage.

*Carstairs* v. *Spence* 1924 SC 380. Whether access for all, or limited, purposes.

Interruption

*Barratt* v. *Keith* 1993 SCLR 120. An obligation to deliver a disposition is an obligation in relation to land to which twenty-year prescription is appropriate.

*Lauder* v. *MacColl* 1993 SCLR 753. What acts of interruption are sufficient to break continuity of possession of a public right of way?

*Renfrew District Council* v. *Russell* 1994 GWD 34–2035. What evidence of possession is necessary for declarator that there was a public right of way?

*Hogg* v. *Campbell* 1993 GWD 27–1712. Discussion on adverse actings and effect on continuity of peaceful possession. (Text 11.14, 14.11)

## 14.14  Public rights of way

See cases under 11.15 above.

## 14.15  The long negative prescription

*Porteous's Exrs* v. *Ferguson* 1995 SLT 649. Effect of negative prescription on personal unfeudalised rights. (Text 14.7, 32.49)

## Chapter 16.  Feuduty

### 16.2  Remedies for recovery

*Sandeman* v. *Scottish Property Investment Co. Building Society* (1881) 8 R 790. Discussion of general principles. (Text 16.3)

*Marquis of Tweeddale's Trs.* v. *Earl of Haddington* (1880) 7 R 620. Right of personal action against subvassals; interest on arrears. (Text 10.7)

*Nelson's Trs.* v. *Tod* (1904) 6 F 475. Poinding of ground. (Text 16.9)

*Scottish Heritages Co. Ltd.* v. *North British Investment Co.* (1885) 12 R 550. Superior previously divested cannot poind ground.

### 16.3  Irritation of the feu

*Sandeman* v. *Scottish Property Investment Co. Building Society Ltd.* (1881) 8 R 790. Discussion of general principles.

*Fothringham* v. *Anderson* 1950 SLT (Sh Ct) 25. Superior must irritate whole feu, not part only.

### 16.4  Effect of irritancy

*Pickard* v. *Glasgow Corporation* 1970 SLT (Sh Ct) 63. Irritancy does not extinguish statutory burden for cost of repairs. (Text 16.3)

*Sandeman* v. *Scottish Property Investment Co. Building Society Ltd.* (1881) 12 R (HL) 67. Effect of irritancy. (Text 16.3)

*Cassells* v. *Lamb* (1885) 12 R 722. Irritation of feu annuls right of vassal and subvassals without creating any right to recompense for improvement.

*Ardgowan Estates Ltd.* v. *Lawson* 1948 SLT 186. Use by Crown for prohibited purpose incurred irritancy.

### 16.5  Purging the irritancy

*Anderson* v. *Valentine* 1957 SLT 57. Obligation to build without time-limit; purging irritancy.

*Glasgow Corporation* v. *Regent Oil Co. Ltd.* 1971 SLT (Sh Ct) 61. Whether irritancy purgeable.

*Precision Relays Ltd.* v. *Beaton* 1980 SC 220. Obligation to build; whether irritancy purgeable as of right or in discretion of court.

*James Miller & Partners Ltd.* v. *Hunt* 1974 SLT (Lands Tr.) 9. Failure to implement condition within time-limit incurred irritancy which could be purged.

*Maxwell's Trs.* v. *Bothwell School Board* (1893) 20 R 958. Purging irritancy.

*Duncanson* v. *Giffen* (1878) 15 SLR 356. Court will normally allow time to implement a breached condition. (Text 16.5)

*Ross & Cromarty District Council* v. *Ullapool Property Co. Ltd.* 1983 SLT (Lands Tr.) 9. Tribunal granted application for variation while superior's action for irritancy pending.

### 16.7  Allocation of feuduty

*Nelson's Trs.* v. *Tod* (1904) 6 F 475. Effect of allocation. (Text 16.9)

*Pall Mall Trust* v. *Wilson* 1948 SC 232. Allocation under power contained in charter. (Text 16.9)

*Mitchell's Trs.* v. *Galloway's Trs.* (1903) 5 F 612. Whether superior bound by informal agreement to allocate feuduty.

*Moray Estates Development Co.* 1971 SC 306. 1970 Act; objection to amount allocated. (Text 16.12, 16.13)

*Barr* v. *Bass Ltd.* 1972 SLT (Lands Tr.) 5. 1970 Act; allocation on partly demolished building. (Text 16.13)

## Chapter 17.  Enforcement of Burdens

(Enforcement by a disponer, and his successors, of real conditions created by a disposition, and the *jus quaesitum tertio* of co-disponees of part of a feu to enforce the charter conditions *inter se*, are dealt with in Ch. 29)

**17.2  Title to enforce**

*Hislop* v. *MacRitchie's Trs.* (1881) 8 R (HL) 95. Title of superior and co-feuar compared. No *jus quaesitum tertio* created. (Text 10.9, 17.4, 29.21, 29.35)

*Nicholson* v. *Glasgow Blind Asylum* 1911 SC 391. The requirements for the *jus quaesitum tertio*. Conditions in titles indicating community of interest. (Text 17.3)

*Johnston* v. *Walker's Trs.* (1897) 24 R 1061. Reference to common feuing plan indicating community. (Text 17.11)

*Stevenson* v. *Steel Co. of Scotland Ltd.* (1896) 23 R 1079. Constitution of *jus quaesitum tertio* by agreement. (Text 17.6, 29.23)

*Lees* v. *North East Fife District Council* 1987 SC 265. Real conditions affecting area later subdivided held enforceable as between proprietors of parts thereof on basis of *jus quaesitum tertio*. Lands Tribunal subsequently discharged condition. See 17.28 below  (Text 17.23, 29.21, 29.22, 29.23)

*Botanic Gardens Picture House* v. *Adamson* 1924 SC 549. No *jus quaesitum tertio* created. (Text 29.23)

*Gray* v. *MacLeod* 1979 SLT (Sh Ct) 17. No *jus quaesitum tertio* created.

*Turner* v. *Hamilton* (1890) 17 R 494. Right reserved to superior to vary conditions excludes implied *jus quaesitum tertio*. (Text 17.6)

*Lawrence* v. *Scott* 1965 SC 403. Express *jus quaesitum tertio* not invalidated by superior's reserved right to vary. (Text 17.6, 17.12)

*Smith* v. *Taylor* 1972 SC 258. Power of Lands Tribunal to adjudicate on *jus quaesitum tertio*. (Text 17.21, 17.28, 17.30, 29.21)

*Crombie* v. *George Heriot's Trust* 1972 SLT (Lands Tr.) 40. Objection by benefited proprietor having *jus quaesitum tertio* to application for variation of feuing conditions.

*Eagle Lodge Ltd.* v. *Keir & Cawdor Estates Ltd.* 1964 SC 30. Tenant of vassal has no standing in question with superior to insist on title conditions. (Text 17.9)

*Inverlochy Castle Ltd.* v. *Lochaber Power Co.* 1987 SLT 466. Personal agreement to supply electricity held to run with the lands, or main part thereof, for benefit of singular successors even though not feudalised. (Text 10.3)

*Fraser* v. *Church of Scotland General Trustees* 1986 SC 279. Discharge of real conditions by the Lands Tribunal excluded possibility of subsequent irritancy by superior.

**17.7  Interest to enforce**

*Zetland* v. *Hislop* (1882) 9 R (HL) 40. Nature of superior's interest.

*Maguire* v. *Burges* 1909 SC 1283. Nature of co-feuar's interest.

**17.8  Loss of interest to enforce: superior**

*Ewing* v. *Campbells* (1877) 5 R 230. Circumstances in which actings of superior did not infer acquiescence. (Text 17.12)

*Macdonald* v. *Douglas* 1963 SC 374. Actings by superior not inferring acquiescence. (Text 17.10)

*Howard de Walden Estates Ltd.* v. *Bowmaker Ltd.* 1965 SC 163. Actings by superior not inferring acquiescence. (Text 17.9, 17.10)

*Campbell* v. *Clydesdale Banking Co.* (1868) 6 M 943. Interest of superior extinguished by acquiescence. (Text 17.10)

*Ben Challum Ltd.* v. *Buchanan* 1955 SC 348. Substantial and costly breach of condition of tenure, known to superior, implied acquiescence. (Text 17.11)

**17.12  Loss of interest to enforce: co-feuars**

*Stewart* v. *Bunten* (1878) 5 R 1108. Circumstances in which actings of co-feuar having *jus quaesitum tertio* did not infer acquiescence. (Text 17.11)

*MacTaggart* v. *Roemmele* 1907 SC 1318. Acquiescence by co-feuar. Effect. (Text 17.11)

*Gray* v. *MacLeod* 1979 SLT (Sh Ct) 17. Initial objections not persisted in.

### 17.19   Statutory variation or discharge: definition of land obligations

*George T. Fraser* v. *Aberdeen Harbour Board* 1985 SC 127. Exclusion of assignees in lease not land obligation. (Text 17.23)

*Macdonald, Applicant* 1973 SLT (Lands Tr.) 26. Right of pre-emption is land obligation but Lands Tribunal has no jurisdiction to vary same if imposed by statute; but see *Banff & Buchan D.C.*, under s. 1(3)(c), at 17.27 below (Text 17.23, 17.27)

*Ross & Cromarty District Council* v. *Ullapool Property Co. Ltd.* 1983 SLT (Lands Tr.) 9. Tribunal may vary land obligation notwithstanding pending irritancy proceedings. (Text 16.5)

*Fraser* v. *Church of Scotland General Trustees* 1986 SC 279. Discharge of real conditions by Lands Tribunal excluded possibility of subsequent irritancy by superior.

*Watters* v. *Motherwell District Council* 1991 SLT (Lands Tr.) 2. Date of creation of obligation is date of delivery of deed, not date of recording.

*Mackay* v. *Lord Burton* 1994 SLT (Lands Tr.) 35. Proprietor of dominant tenement in servitude is not burdened proprietor. (Text 11.3)

*McCarthy & Stone (Developments) Ltd.* v. *Smith* 1995 SLT (Lands Tr.) 19. Where no *jus quaesitum tertio* created, adjacent proprietors are not benefited proprietors. (Text 13.35)

### 17.24   Who may apply?

*Walker* v. *Strathclyde Regional Council* 1990 SLT (Lands Tr.) 17. Tribunal cannot vary landlord's title in application by secure tenant.

### 17.26   Circumstances justifying variation or discharge: 'by reason of' (s. 1(3) (a))

Change in character of land

*Bolton* v. *Aberdeen Corporation* 1972 SLT (Lands Tr.) 26. Decline in trade is not.

*Clarebrooke Holdings Ltd.* v. *Glentanar's Trs.* 1975 SLT (Lands Tr.) 8. Overgrown garden is not.

Change in character of neighbourhood

*Manz* v. *Butter's Trs.* 1973 SLT (Lands Tr.) 2. 'Neighbourhood'. Pitlochry, not merely its High Street. (Text 17.31)

*Pickford* v. *Young* 1975 SLT (Lands Tr.) 17. More restricted interpretation.

*Stoddart* v. *Glendinning* 1993 SLT (Lands Tr.) 12. Alterations to other properties in same street had not changed character of neighbourhood.

Other circumstances

*Murrayfield Ice Rink Ltd.* v. *Scottish Rugby Union (Trs.)* 1973 SC 21. Decline in skating as recreation, *etc.* (Text 17.28, 17.32)

*James Miller & Partners Ltd.* v. *Hunt* 1974 SLT (Lands Tr.) 9. Drainage problems not amounting to. (Text 16.5)

*Manz* v. *Butter's Trs.* 1973 SLT (Lands Tr.) 2. Change in local habits in Pitlochry amounting to.

*Owen* v. *Mackenzie* 1974 SLT (Lands Tr.) 11. Change in social habits due to tourism, *etc.*, amounting to.

*Morris & Another* v. *Feuars of Waverley Park* 1973 SLT (Lands Tr.) 6. Disappearance of domestic staff amounting to.

*Pickford* v. *Young* 1975 SLT (Lands Tr.) 17. Change not sufficient to justify use of house as hotel.

*Stoddart* v. *Glendinning* 1993 SLT (Lands Tr.) 12. Alterations to other properties in same street had not changed character of neighbourhood.

'The obligation is or has become unreasonable or inappropriate'

*Bolton* v. *Aberdeen Corporation* 1972 SLT (Lands Tr.) 26. Reasonableness not related to profitability.

*McArthur* v. *Mahoney* 1975 SLT (Lands Tr.) 2. Tribunal's discretion to protect 'affected proprietor'.

*United Auctions (Scotland) Ltd.* v. *British Railways Board* 1991 SLT (Lands Tr.) 71. Change of use from livestock auction mart to shopping development not unreasonable.

**17.27   The obligation is unduly burdensome (s. 1(3)(b))**

*Murrayfield Ice Rink Ltd.* v. *Scottish Rugby Union (Trs.)* 1973 SC 21. Applies both to positive and negative obligations. (Text 17.28, 17.32)

*McQuiban & Another* v. *Eagle Star Insurance Co.* 1972 SLT (Lands Tr.) 39. Circumstances in which restriction against assigning a lease, except as *unum quid*, unduly burdensome.

*West Lothian Co-operative Society Ltd.* v. *Ashdale Land Property Co. Ltd.* 1972 SLT (Lands Tr.) 30. Circumstances in which obligation to maintain ruinous building, requiring pointless and expensive maintenance, unduly burdensome.

*Nicolson* v. *Campbell's Trs.* 1981 SLT (Lands Tr.) 10. Time-limit for reinstatement; application for extension of time under 1970 Act s. 1(3)(b) refused.

*Miller Group Ltd.* v. *Gardner's Exrs.* 1992 SLT (Lands Tr.) 62. Inability to build flats not unduly burdensome compared with benefit of *status quo*

*Stoddart* v. *Glendinning* 1993 SLT (Lands Tr.) 12. Alterations to other properties in same street had not changed character of neighbourhood.

*Murray* v. *Farquharson* 1996 GWD 3–162. Application to make structural alterations granted; superior had previously given consent.

*Cumbernauld Development Corporation* v. *County Properties & Developments Ltd.* 1996 SLT 1106. Property purchased as ice rink, but that did not proceed; change to bingo hall permitted; compensation awarded.

**17.28   The obligation impedes some reasonable use (s. 1(3)(c) )**

*Solway Cedar Ltd.* v. *Hendry* 1972 SLT (Lands Tr.) 42. Squeezing in one extra house in small development not reasonable use. (Text 17.21)

*Main* v. *Lord Doune* 1972 SLT (Lands Tr.) 14. Proposed use as nursery. (Text 17.25, 17.30)

*Devlin* v. *Conn* 1972 SLT (Lands Tr.) 11. Circumstances justifying discharge of servitude of access.

*Campbell* v. *Edinburgh Corporation* 1972 SLT (Lands Tr.) 38. Subdivision into flats; application withdrawn after objection by superior.

*Murrayfield Ice Rink Ltd.* v. *Scottish Rugby Union (Trs.)* 1973 SC 21. Applicant must specify particular proposed use which land obligation impedes. (Text 17.32)

*Gorrie & Banks Ltd.* v. *Musselburgh Town Council* 1974 SLT (Lands Tr.) 5. Planning permission not conclusive of reasonableness, but application granted. (Text 17.31)

*Bachoo* v. *George Wimpey & Co. Ltd.* 1977 SLT (Lands Tr.) 2. Grant of planning permission not conclusive of reasonableness; application refused.

*Scott* v. *Fulton* 1982 SLT (Lands Tr.) 18. Application for discharge of restriction on building in garden of subdivided house refused; refusal of planning permission indicating that proposed use is not reasonable.

*Cameron* v. *Stirling* 1988 SLT (Lands Tr.) 18. Observations on interrelationship between planning permission and Tribunal orders.

*British Bakeries (Scotland) Ltd.* v. *Edinburgh District Council* 1990 SLT (Lands Tr.) 33. Grant of planning permission normally implies that proposed use is reasonable.

*Tully* v. *Armstrong* 1990 SLT (Lands Tr.) 42. Erection of house in garden ground not unreasonable.

*Lees* v. *North East Fife District Council* 1989 SLT (Lands Tr.) 30. Neighbouring proprietors held by Court of Session to have valid title to enforce land obligation very recently imposed on adjoining land, but Lands Tribunal nonetheless discharged it. See 17.2 above.

*Macdonald* v. *Stornoway Trust* 1988 SC 299. Refusal to vary prohibition on sale of liquor in croft upheld as not impeding some reasonable use.

*Banff & Buchan District Council* v. *Earl of Seafield's Estate* 1988 SLT (Lands Tr.) 21. Observations on effect of right of pre-emption. (Text 17.27)

*Spafford* v. *Brydon* 1991 SLT (Lands Tr.) 49. Servitude right not discharged because still used.

*British Steel plc.* v. *Kaye* 1991 SLT (Lands Tr.) 7. Antecedent breach ignored; courts to decide result if irritancy incurred following discharge by Tribunal.

*Miller Group Ltd.* v. *Gardner's Exrs.* 1992 SLT (Lands Tr.) 62. See 17.27 above.

*Ramsay* v. *Holmes* 1992 SLT (Lands Tr.) 53. Obligation to obtain consent can be waived or discharged; existence of obligation impeded proposed use; *British Bakeries*, 17.28, above, not followed.

*Murray* v. *Farquharson* 1996 GWD 3–162. See 17.27 above.

*Stoddart* v. *Glendinning* 1993 SLT (Lands Tr.) 12. See 17.26 above.

*Harris* v. *Douglass* 1993 SLT (Lands Tr.) 56. Alterations required superior's consent; superior sought compensation for giving consent; condition discharged; expenses against superior.

*Irvine* v. *John Dickie & Son Ltd*. 1996 GWD 3–163. Application for further access granted, subject to conditions.

### 17.29 Compensation

*McVey* v. *Glasgow Corporation* 1973 SLT (Lands Tr.) 15. Compensation claimed by superior refused under s. 1(4)(i).

*Robertson* v. *Church of Scotland General Trustees* 1976 SLT (Lands Tr.) 11. Compensation refused under s. 1(4)(i).

*Blythswood Friendly Society* v. *Glasgow District Council* 1979 SC (HL) 1. Compensation refused under s. 1(4)(i).

*Keith* v. *Texaco Ltd*. 1977 SLT (Lands Tr.) 16. Compensation refused under s. 1(4)(i) and (ii). (Text 11.12)

*Sinclair* v. *Gillon & Another* 1974 SLT (Lands Tr.) 18. Application for change of use from dwellinghouse to coffee-house; compensation claimed by adjoining proprietor refused.

*Co-operative Wholesale Society* v. *Ushers Brewery* 1975 SLT (Lands Tr.) 9. Compensation granted under s. 1(4)(i) for economic loss. (Text 17.21, 17.30)

*Smith* v. *Taylor* 1972 SC 258. Compensation granted under s. 1(4)(i) for loss of amenity. (Text 17.21, 17.28, 17.30, 29.21)

*Gorrie & Banks Ltd*. v. *Musselburgh Town Council* 1974 SLT (Lands Tr.) 5. Compensation granted under s. 1(4)(ii). (Text 17.31)

*Manz* v. *Butter's Trs*. 1973 SLT (Lands Tr.) 2. 'Affected proprietor' has no claim. (Text 17.31)

*Campbell* v. *Edinburgh Corporation* 1972 SLT (Lands Tr.) 38. Expenses awarded against applicant on withdrawal of application.

*McArthur* v. *Mahoney* 1975 SLT (Lands Tr.) 2. Expenses awarded to successful objector.

*Co-operative Wholesale Society* v. *Ushers Brewery*, above. Compensation awarded but no expenses to either party. (Text 17.21, 17.30)

*Lees* v. *North East Fife District Council* 1989 SLT (Lands Tr.) 30. Compensation refused.

*United Auctions (Scotland) Ltd*. v. *British Railways Board* 1991 SLT (Lands Tr.) 71. Compensation refused.

*Harris* v. *Douglass* 1993 SLT (Lands Tr.) 56. See 17.28 above.

*Cumbernauld Development Corporation* v. *County Properties & Developments Ltd*. 1996 SLT 1106. Appeal from decision of Lands Tribunal to award £206,000 refused.

### 17.32 Variation or discharge

*Crombie* v. *George Heriot's Trust* 1972 SLT (Lands Tr.) 40. Restrictions on type of buildings and screening by trees.

*Co-operative Wholesale Society* v. *Ushers Brewery* 1975 SLT (Lands Tr.) 9. Limitation on use. (Text 17.21, 17.30)

*Brookfield Developments Ltd*. v. *Keeper of the Registers of Scotland* 1989 SLT (Lands Tr.) 105. Role of Keeper in registration of title. (Text 13.35, 17.35).

### 17.34 Procedure

*Scott* v. *Wilson* 1993 SLT (Lands Tr.) 52. Tribunal cannot consider only written submissions from objectors who did not appear at hearing.

*Rowan Property Investments Ltd*. v. *Jack* 1996 GWD 16–946. Tribunal decision to refuse application for a discharge of right of access upheld; observed that applicant might have been better to have raised ordinary court action because of uncertainty about title provisions.

**Chapter 18. The Estate of the Vassal**
(See also Chs. 7 and 8 for a summary of the vassal's rights under the feu charter, especially joint and common property, common interest, tenements, water rights and game. Cases on these topics are included under those chapter headings)

**18.2 Barony privileges**
(See also Ch. 8.10 – Fishings and game)
*Lord Advocate* v. *Cathcart* (1871) 9 M 744. General principles; salmon fishings.
*Lord Advocate* v. *Wemyss* (1900) 2 F (HL) 1. Minerals under foreshore and sea; various titles.
*Magistrates of Perth* v. *Earl of Wemyss* (1829) 8 S 82. Prescriptive possession of pertinent on barony title.
*Newell, Petitioner* 1985 SLT (Lyon Ct) 26. Creation of barony title by prescription.
*Spencer-Thomas of Buquhollie* v. *Newell* 1992 SLT 973. A competing title case. Lord Clyde discussed in some depth the nature, quality and effect of a barony title.

Foreshore and sea
*Keiller* v. *Dundee Magistrates* (1886) 14 R 191. Express title to foreshore, subject to overriding public rights for recreation by possession from time immemorial.
*Luss Estates Co.* v. *BP Oil Grangemouth Refinery Ltd.* 1987 SLT 201. Whether a barony title habile to include foreshore.
*Smith* v. *Lerwick Harbour Trustees* (1903) 5 F 680. Udal tenure extends to and includes foreshore, where applicable; general discussion on udal tenure.
*Agnew* v. *Lord Advocate* (1873) 11 M 309. Foreshore; prescriptive possession.
*Young* v. *NB Railway Co.* (1887) 14 R (HL) 53. Foreshore, 'bounded by the sea'.
*Crown Estate Commissioners* v. *Fairlie Yacht Slip Ltd.* 1979 SC 156. Public right of navigation in tidal territorial waters does not permit laying down of moorings on seabed.
*Walford* v. *Crown Estate Commissioners* 1988 SLT 377. Lease of seabed for salmon farming; interference with navigation.

**18.3 Parts and pertinents**
(See Ch. 14)

**18.4 Possession of heritage**
(See Ch. 14 – Possession – *passim*)
Rights of exclusive occupation
*Halkerson* v. *Wedderburn* (1781) M 10495. Overhanging trees.
*Thom* v. *Hetherington* 1988 SLT 724. Tree on boundary, roots encroaching into neighbouring property; resulting damage.
*Brown* v. *Lee Construction Ltd.* 1977 SLT (Notes) 61. Intrusion of crane into air space.
*Houston* v. *McLaren* (1894) 21 R 923. Overhanging building
*Alexander* v. *Butchart* (1875) 3 R 156. Shop sign.
*Anderson* v. *Brattisani's* 1978 SLT (Notes) 42. Outside flue affixed to gable; equitable power of court to refuse enforcement of proprietor's right to object.
*Leith Buchanan* v. *Hogg* 1931 SC 204. Beaching boats on loch shore.
*Brown* v. *Baty* 1957 SC 351. Wall encroaching on adjoining land
*Griffin* v. *Watson* 1962 SLT (Sh Ct) 74. Wall encroaching on adjoining land.
*Girdwood* v. *Paterson* (1873) 11 M 647. Encroachment; no acquiescence; restoration.
*More* v. *Boyle* 1967 SLT (Sh Ct) 38. Underground waterpipe. (Text 11.10, 28.49)
*Brown* v. *Lord Advocate* 1973 SLT 205. Straying animals, remedy available to aggrieved proprietor under the Winter Herding Act 1686, now repealed; see Animals (Scotland) Act 1987.
*Farquharson* v. *Walker* 1977 SLT (Sh Ct) 22. Straying animals; but see Animals (Scotland) Act 1987.
*Paterson* v. *Robertson* 1944 JC 166. Squatters; remedy available to aggrieved proprietor under Trespass (Scotland) Act 1865.
*GTW Holdings Ltd.* v. *Toet* 1994 SLT (Sh Ct) 16. Person in possession of land without title or lease liable for real worth and annual value.

*Strathclyde Regional Council* v. *Persimmon Homes (Scotland) Ltd.* 1996 SLT 176. Grant of planning permission did not imply consent for construction of access road on to land claimed to be owned by pursuers.

*Watson* v. *Shields* 1996 SCLR 81. Defender had not failed totally to establish title; pursuers not entitled to interdict preventing him from entering subjects. (Text 14.2, 14.7)

*Stevenson* v. *A. & J. Stephen (Builders) Ltd.* 1996 SLT 140. Proof before answer allowed of averments that builders, who were also superiors, were liable as superiors for damage to property caused by faulty construction.

## Chapter 19.   Restrictions on the Use of Land
(See cases under Ch. 10 – Burdens – and Ch. 17 – Enforcement of Burdens)

## Chapter 20.   Securities

### 20.1   The concept of security
*Mumford* v. *Bank of Scotland* 1996 SLT 392. Lender does not owe any duty of care to wife in connection with transaction being entered into by husband with her consent. Reversed on appeal to House of Lords.

*Bank of East Asia Ltd.* v. *Shepherd & Wedderburn* 1995 SC 255. Solicitors may owe duty to lender to disclose information which could affect decision whether or not to lend.

## Chapter 21.   Heritable Securities Before 1970

### 21.4   The bond and disposition in security: effect
*Bell's Trustees* v. *Bell* (1884) 12 R 85. Effect on bond of 1696 Act.

*Smith Sligo* v. *James Dunlop & Co.* (1885) 12 R 907. Whether disposition expressly in security for future liability struck at by the 1696 Act.

*Alston* v. *Nellfield Manure & Chemical Co.* 1915 SC 912. Need for precision, interest rate not specified.

*Edmonstone* v. *Seton* (1888) 16 R 1. Security for obligation *ad factum praestandum.*

*Church of Scotland Endowment Committee* v. *Provident Association of London Ltd.* 1914 SC 165. No one can be debtor and creditor in same capacity in the same obligation.

### 21.5   Ranking of loans *inter se*
*King* v. *Johnston* 1908 SC 684. Whether bond extinguished *confusione*; ranking.

*Ashburton* v. *Escombe* (1892) 20 R 187. Effect on postponed bondholder.

### 21.7   Reserved powers
*Cumming* v. *Stewart* 1928 SC 296. Power to feu (Text 21.9)

*Morier* v. *Brownlie & Watson* (1895) 23 R 67. Power to feu, effect on bondholder.

### 21.10   Creditor's rights
*Gatty* v. *Maclaine* 1921 SC (HL) 1. Whether debtor in default.

*Arnott's Trustees* v. *Forbes* (1881) 9 R 89. Bond on superiority; failure by debtor-superior to implement superior's obligations.

*McNab* v. *Clarke* (1889) 16 R 610. Creditor may exercise various powers concurrently.

### 21.12   Creditor's remedies: summary diligence
*Taylor, Petitioner* 1931 SLT 260. Effect of registered bond.

### 21.13   Entering into possession
*Baillie* v. *Shearer's JF* (1894) 21 R 498. Liabilities of creditor in possession.

*Campbell* v. *Deans* (1880) 17 R 661. Creditor in possession is not a singular successor of debtor.

*Inglis' Trustees* v. *Macpherson* 1910 SC 46. Ejection of debtor.

### 21.15 Sale

*Stewart's Trs.* v. *Brown* (1882) 10 R 192. Improper procedure invalidating sale; effect of sale on postponed bondholder.

*Nicholson's Trs.* v. *McLaughlin* (1891) 19 R 49. Sale by *pari passu* bondholder.

*Reis* v. *Mackay* (1899) 6 SLT 331. Sale by postponed bondholder; right to assignation of prior bond on repayment.

*Morier* v. *Brownlie & Watson* (1895) 23 R 67. Whether deeds granted by debtor affect purchaser from bondholder.

*Cumming* v. *Stewart* 1928 SC 296. Whether deeds granted by debtor affect purchaser from bondholder. (Text 21.9)

### 21.20 Re-exposure and foreclosure

*Sutherland* v. *Stoddard Assurance Co.* (1905) 8 F (HL) 1. Effect of irregularity in procedure on title of purchaser.

*Gatty* v. *Maclaine* 1922 SLT (Sh Ct) 141. Discussion on alleged irregularities in foreclosure procedure.

### 21.22 Pecuniary real burden

*Tailors of Aberdeen* v. *Coutts* (1840) 1 Rob. App. 296. General principles.

*Cowie* v. *Muirden* (1893) 20 R (HL) 81. Created by notarial instrument. (Text 32.26, 32.36)

*Buchanan* v. *Eaton* 1911 SC (HL) 40. Circumstances where directions in will did not indicate intention to create pecuniary real burden.

*Magistrates of Arbroath* v. *Dickson* (1872) 10 M 630. Intention to burden.

*Ewing's Trs.* v. *Crum Ewing* 1923 SC 569. Condition too indefinite to qualify

*Macrae* v. *Mackenzie's Trs.* (1891) 19 R 138. Transmission of personal obligation.

### 21.23 Contract of ground annual

*Church of Scotland Endowment Committee* v. *Provident Association of London Ltd.* 1914 SC 165. Debtor and creditor same person.

*Royal Bank of Scotland* v. *Gardyne* (1853) 1 Macq. 358. Singular successor not personally liable. (Text 29.12, 29.18)

*Marshall's Tr.* v. *Macnelll & Co.* (1888) 15 R 762. Personal liability of singular successor.

*Murray* v. *Parlane's Trs.* (1890) 18 R 287. Bond held to be extinguished *confusione*, but not a ground annual.

*Healy & Young's Trs.* v. *Mair's Trs.* 1914 SC 893. Ground annual not extinguished *confusione*.

### 21.26 Transmission

*Fenton Livingstone* v. *Crichton's Trs.* 1908 SC 1208. Transmission on death of debtor.

*Carrick* v. *Roger, Watt & Paul* (1881) 9 R 242. Obligation of relief by purchaser does not *per se* imply transmission of personal obligations against him.

*University of Glasgow* v. *Yuill's Tr.* (1882) 9 R 643. Creditor may enforce personal obligations against original debtor, notwithstanding transmission thereof to disponee under 1874 Act s. 47.

### 21.33 Discharge

*North Albion Pty. Investment* v. *McBean's CB* (1893) 21 R 90. Debtor entitled to assignation on repayment.

*Fleming* v. *Black* (1913) 1 SLT 386. Circumstances where debtor, repaying, not entitled to assignation.

*Bruce* v. *Scottish Amicable Life Assurance Society* 1907 SC 637. Creditor not obliged to grant assignation to debtor subject to qualifications

*Cameron* v. *Williamson* (1895) 22 R 293. Implied discharge, marketable title. (Text 22.60)

*Bowie's Trustees* v. *Watson* 1913 SC 326. Fraudulent discharge; effect on title.

### 21.35 Future and fluctuating debt
*Devaynes* v. *Noble* (Clayton's Case) (1816) 1 Merivale 529. On running account, sums credited are part repayments, sums drawn are new lendings.

### 21.37 The *ex facie* absolute disposition
*Union Bank of Scotland Ltd.* v. *National Bank of Scotland Ltd.* (1886) 14 R (HL) 1. General principles. (Text 21.44, 21.47)
*Heritable Reversionary Co. Ltd.* v. *Millar* (1892) 19 R (HL) 43. Effect of sequestration of creditor. (Text 4.1, 21.42).
*Ritchie* v. *Scott* (1899) 1 F 728. Effect on debtor's title. (Text 21.47)

### 21.40 Creditor's rights and liabilities
*Clydesdale Bank Ltd.* v. *McIntyre* 1909 SC 1405. Creditor may require debtor to accept reconveyance.
*Duncan* v. *Mitchell & Co.* (1893) 21 R 37. Power of sale; consent of debtor not necessary to fortify title.
*Aberdeen Trades Council* v. *Ship Constructors & Shipwrights Association* 1949 SC (HL) 45. Power of sale, recorded back letter. (Text 21.41)
*Rimmer* v. *Thomas Usher & Son Ltd.* 1967 SLT 7. Power of sale; duty to debtor. (Text 21.43, 22.23)
*Lucas* v. *Gardner* (1876) 4 R 194. Circumstances in which debtor held entitled to interdict proposed sale by creditor.
*Scottish Property Investment Co.* v. *Horne* (1881) 8 R 737. Right to eject debtor.
*Macintyre* v. *Cleveland Petroleum Co. Ltd.* 1967 SLT 95. Conditions of loan; restraint of trade.
*Marshall's Tr.* v. *Macneill & Co.* (1888) 15 R 762. Liability of creditor; reconveyance.
*Liquidators of City of Glasgow Bank* v. *Nicholson's Trs.* (1882) 9 R 689. Prior bondholder in possession; liability for feuduty.

### 21.44 The extent of the security
*Union Bank of Scotland Ltd.* v. *National Bank of Scotland Ltd.* (1886) 14 R (HL) 1. Effect of intimation of second security. (Text 21.47)
*Campbell's JF* v. *National Bank of Scotland Ltd.* 1944 SC 495. Continuing security for interest; bankruptcy of debtor; but see now 1970 Act s. 42.
*Nelson* v. *Gordon* (1874) 1 R 1093. Security for all indebtedness, stated limit in back letter.
*Scottish & Newcastle Breweries Ltd.* v. *Liquidator of Rathburne Hotel Co. Ltd.* 1970 SC 215. Stated limit in back letter.

### 21.47 The nature of the debtor's right
*Union Bank of Scotland Ltd.* v. *National Bank of Scotland* (1886) 14 R (HL) 1. Nature of debtor's reversionary right; second security. (Text 21.44)
*Ritchie* v. *Scott* (1899) 1 F 728. Nature of debtor's reversionary right; lease by debtor.
*Edinburgh Entertainments Ltd.* v. *Stevenson* 1926 SC 363. Nature of debtor's reversionary right; lease by debtor.
*McBride* v. *Caledonian Ry.* (1894) 21 R 620. Title of debtor to sue and defend actions.
*Scobie* v. *Wm. Lind & Co. Ltd.* 1967 SLT 9. Title of debtor to sue and defend actions. *Red Court Hotel Ltd.* v. *Burgh of Largs* 1955 SLT (Sh Ct) 2 disapproved.

### Chapter 22.  Standard Securities

### 22.6 Style of deed
*Bank of Scotland* v. *Graham's Tr.* 1992 SC 79. Debtors signed as debtors, but not as proprietors; rectification allowed. (Text 30.14)

*Spowart* v. *Wylie* 1995 GWD 23–1257. Standard security in respect of sums set out in missives; held that obligation to pay was clear. (Text 28.56)

*Bennett* v. *Beneficial Bank plc*. 1995 SLT 1105. Description of whole tenement is not sufficient where security is over one flat. (Text 8.11, 31.21, 33.88)

*Beneficial Bank plc*. v. *McConnachie* 1996 SC 119. Postal address not a particular description. (Text 8.11, 8.13, 8.18, 8.21, 22.6, 33.88)

*Beneficial Bank plc*. v. *Wardle* 1996 GWD 30–1825. Rectification of description in standard security which did not meet test as set out in *McConnachie*. (Text 8.11)

### 22.7 Statutory effect of new form of security

*Trade Development Bank* v. *Warriner & Mason* 1980 SC 74. Creditor entitled to set aside unauthorised lease. Standard conditions; whether recording of standard security form B constituted notice of conditions in unrecorded minute of agreement; duty of enquiry. (Text 24.22, 25.4, 33.60).

*Trade Development Bank* v. *D.W. Haig (Bellshill) Ltd*. 1983 SLT 510. Standard conditions; heritable creditor not affected by personal obligations undertaken by debtor relating to security subjects.

*David Watson Property Management* v. *Woolwich Equitable Building Society* 1992 SC (HL) 21. Heritable creditor in possession not liable for personal obligations entered into by debtor in relation to property. (Text 10.5, 10.6, 22.43, 29.19).

*Trade Development Bank* v. *Crittall Windows Ltd*. 1983 SLT 510. Effect of knowledge of prior personal right on subsequent real security. (Text 33.60)

*Bank of Scotland* v. *T.A. Neilson & Co*. 1990 SC 284. Whether registration *de novo* validated standard security by company. (Text 33.67)

*Sanderson's Trs.* v. *Ambion Scotland Ltd*. 1994 SLT 645. Assignation must follow statutory form, but need not be identical; assignation covers original and further advances, if these are covered by agreement.

*Alliance & Leicester Building Society* v. *Murray's Tr*. 1994 SCLR 19. Warrant to cite purchaser granted prior to recording of disposition in his favour and standard security; *held* to be *acquirenda*. (Text 3.20, 30.7, 33.32)

*McCabe* v. *Skipton Building Society* 1994 SC 467. H and W granted standard security; H obtained further advance by fraud; W's action for reduction dismissed. (See also 30.10)

*Mumford* v. *Bank of Scotland* 1995 SCLR 839. Lender does not owe duty to explain nature of loan transaction to wife, who signs documentation at request of husband involved in a fraud. Reversed on appeal to House of Lords. (Text 20.1)

*Johnston* v. *Robson* 1995 SLT (Sh Ct) 26. House purchased in joint names of J and R; R contributed part of price in cash; balance obtained by loan in joint name; later, on division and sale, R sought to recover his cash contribution, based on recompense; proof before answer allowed.

*Christie's Exr.* v. *Armstrong* 1996 SLT 948. Endowment policy by H and W assigned in security; on death, proceeds paid to lender; executor sought to recover one half of proceeds from surviving W, based on recompense; proof before answer allowed.

*Tamroui* v. *Clydesdale Bank plc*. 1996 SCLR 732. T took lease from debtor under B's standard security, unaware of security; B obtained decree against debtor and sought to eject T; interim interdict granted.

### 22.11 Ranking of loans *inter se*

*Sowman* v. *Glasgow District Council* 1984 SC 91. Ranking; statutory burden in favour of local authority. (Text 19.49)

*Skipton Building Society* v. *Wain* 1986 SLT 96. Where there are two or more heritable securities on same property, creditor who first obtains decree under 1970 Act s. 24 is entitled to retain possession to exclusion of other(s). (Text 22.43)

*Alloa Brewery Co. Ltd.* v. *Investors in Industry plc* 1992 SLT 21. Meaning of 'charge' in ranking agreement. (Text 22.17, 35.36)

**22.17 Ranking clauses**

*AIB Finance Ltd* v. *Bank of Scotland* 1993 SC 538. See 23.6. (Text 35.7)

*Scotlife Home Loans (No. 2)* v. *Muir* 1994 SCLR 791. Debtor granted two securities, first was recorded second; *held* that intended first creditor had postponed ranking.

**22.23 Calling-up notice**

*Bank of Scotland* v. *Flett* 1995 SCLR 591. Request by debtor for statement of amount due must comply with s. 19(9); in any event, no prejudice to the debtor.

*Clydesdale Bank plc* v. *Davidson* 1996 SLT 437. Calling-up notice served, but no obtempered; action of removal raised, but no notice requiring debtor to vacate; creditors not required to serve such a notice. (Text 25.7, 26.3)

**22.24 Form of notice**

*Clydesdale Bank plc* v. *R. Findlay & Co.* 1989 SLT (Sh Ct) 77. Calling up notice held not to be invalidated by statement in notice under s. 19(9), to which debtor replied calling for amendment.

*Royal Bank of Scotland plc* v. *Shanks* 1996 GWD 36–2124. No need for final determination of amount due when calling-up notice served.

**22.30 Application to the court**

*Halifax Building Society* v. *Gupta* 1994 SC 13. If sheriff is satisfied about creditor's entitlement to remedy, he has no discretion to refuse. (Text 22.33)

**22.31 Procedure: petition under 1970 Act s. 24**

*Bradford & Bingley Building Society* v. *Roddy* 1987 SLT (Sh Ct) 109. Discussion on procedure on application by heritable creditor under 1970 Act s. 24.

*Hill Samuel & Co. Ltd.* v. *Haas* 1989 SLT (Sh Ct) 68. Discussion on procedure in petition under 1970 Act s. 24.

*Clydesdale Bank plc* v. *R. Findlay & Co.* 1989 SLT (Sh Ct) 77. Discussion on correct procedure under 1970 Act s. 24 and interaction of ss. 20–24 and standard condition 9. (Text 22.24)

*Cedar Holdings Ltd* v. *Iyyaz* 1989 SLT (Sh Ct) 71. Discussion on procedure under 1970 Act s. 24; not followed in *Clydesdale Bank plc* above.

*Clydesdale Bank plc* v. *Mowbray* 1991 GWD 28–1686. Interdict of debtor trying to prevent sale.

**22.32 The creditor's powers on default**

*Armstrong, Petitioner* 1988 SLT 255. Duty of creditor to exercise his power of sale and other powers *civiliter*. (Text 22.33)

*Associated Displays* v. *Turnbean Ltd.* 1988 SCLR 220. Circumstances in which debtor held not entitled to prevent creditor exercising power of sale by interdict, on grounds that best price not being obtained. (Text 22.33)

*Bank of Credit* v. *Thomson* 1987 GWD 10–341. Discussion on obtaining best price on exercise of power of sale. (Text 22.33)

*UDT Ltd.* v. *Site Preparations Ltd. (No. 1)* 1978 SLT (Sh Ct) 14. Default; application to court.

*Dick* v. *Clydesdale Bank plc.* 1991 SC 365. Duties of creditor in obtaining best price. (Text 22.33)

*Dunlop & Son's JF* v. *Armstrong* 1994 SLT 199. Creditor's right to sell and debtor's right to redeem can co-exist; if debtor tenders amount which is refused, that stops interest running on debt.

*Halifax Building Society* v. *Gupta* 1994 SC 13. Creditor has discretion about which remedy to choose, but sheriff has no discretion to refuse. (Text 22.33)

*Gordaviran* v. *Clydesdale Bank plc* 1994 SCLR 248. Creditor not obliged to demonstrate to debtor that terms of Act complied with. (Text 22.33)

*Thomson* v. *Yorkshire Building Society* 1994 SCLR 1014. *Held* incompetent for debtor to try to prevent creditor from exercising power of ejection. (Text 22.33)

**22.36 Sale**

*Gordaviran* v. *Clydesdale Bank plc* (See 22.32).

*Dunlop & Son's JF* v. *Armstrong* 1995 SLT 645. Judicial factor is officer of court to which he has given undertaking protecting the interests of heritable creditor; so heritable creditor not entitled to interdict proposed sale by JF. (See also 22.33)

**22.38 Clearing the record**

*Halifax Building Society* v. *Smith* 1985 SLT (Sh Ct) 25. Sale by heritable creditor; debtor inhibited; effect of inhibition on rights of unsecured creditors to surplus on sale. (Text 22.40)

*Newcastle Building Society* v. *White* 1987 SLT (Sh Ct) 81. Inhibition registered against debtor after recording standard security does not prevent selling creditor, on default, from providing clear search. (Text 33.43)

*Abbey National Building Society* v. *Barclays Bank plc*. 1990 SCLR 639. Sale by heritable creditor; effect on free proceeds of inhibitions and arrestments.

**22.39 Application of proceeds of sale**

*Bass Brewers Ltd.* v. *Humberclyde Finance Group Ltd.* 1996 GWD 19–1076. Challenge of various deductions made by prior-ranking creditor.

**22.42 Entering into possession**

*Northern Rock Building Society* v. *Wood* 1990 SLT (Sh Ct) 109. Heritable creditor in possession not liable for community charge. (Text 22.43)

*Skipton Building Society* v. *Wain* 1986 SLT 96. Creditor holding earlier of two competing decrees entitled to possession. (Text 22.43)

*David Watson Property Management Ltd.* v. *Woolwich Equitable Building Society* 1992 SC (HL) 21. Real conditions about repairs transmit against creditor in possession; but obligation to pay particular amount is personal to debtor and does not transmit against creditor (Text 10.5, 10.6, 22.43, 29.19)

*Clydesdale Bank plc* v. *Davidson*. (See 22.23)

*Halifax Building Society* v *Gupta*. (See 22.30)

*Bank of Scotland* v. *Guardian Royal Exchange plc*. 1995 SLT 763. Where creditor's interest is endorsed on insurance policy, creditor has separate right thereunder.

*Bass Brewers Ltd.* v. *Humberclyde Finance Group Ltd.* 1996 GWD 19–1076. Discussion of computing entitlements of creditors in ranking agreement.

*Holt Leisure Parks Ltd.* v. *Scottish & Newcastle Breweries* 1996 GWD 22–1284. Heritable creditor who has not entered into possession of lease has no liability thereunder.

*Ascot Inns Ltd. (In receivership)* v. *Braidwood Estates Ltd.* 1995 SCLR 390. If creditor does not enter into possession, no entitlement to rents.

**22.48 Transmission**

*Sanderson's Trs.* v. *Ambion Scotland Ltd.* (See 22.7)

**22.55 Discharge**

*Cameron* v. *Williamson* (1895) 22 R 293. Infeftment in security may be extinguished by payment or discharge of debt. (Text 22.60)

*Security Pacific Finance Ltd.* v. *Graham* 1995 GWD 29–1545. Extrinsic evidence admissible to prove that discharge granted by mistake.

**22.57 Redemption**

*Dunlop & Son's JF* v. *Armstrong* 1995 SLT 645. Debtor has unfettered right to redeem, no matter whether creditor proceeding to sale; comments on calling up. (See 22.36)

**Chapter 23. Floating Charges**

**23.3 Effect of the charge**

*Forth & Clyde Construction Co. Ltd.* v. *Trinity Timber & Plywood Co. Ltd.* 1984 SC 1. Nature of fixed security on appointment of receiver.

*Scottish & Newcastle Breweries* v. *Liquidator of Rathburne Hotel Co. Ltd.* 1970 SC 215. Extent of security; stated limit in back letter. (Text 21.44)

*National Commercial Bank Ltd.* v. *Liquidators of Telford, Grier, Mackay & Co. Ltd.* 1969 SC 181. Extent of security; interest due from date of liquidation.

*Libertas-Kommerz* v. *Johnson* 1977 SC 191. Whether bond and floating charge assignable by creditor.

*Hill Samuel & Co. Ltd.* v. *Laing* 1989 SC 301. Discussion on personal liability of receiver for debt incurred on behalf of company.

*Shanks* v. *Central Regional Council* 1988 SC 14. Appointment of receiver does not necessarily exclude powers of directors of company to take action in certain circumstances.

### 23.4 Property affected

*Sharp* v. *Thomson* 1995 SC 455. Company which had granted a floating charge sold the property; before recording of disposition receiver was appointed; *held* in Inner House that property still subject to charge; reversed on appeal to House of Lords. See also *Sharp* v. *Woolwich Building Society* 1997 SLT 636 and comment at 4.1 above. (Text 4.1, 12.4, 29.33, 33.51, 35.7, 35.12, 35.15, 35.18)

### 23.5 Registration

*Prior, Petitioner* 1989 SLT 840. Petition to extend time for registration refused. (Text 23.10)

### 23.6 Ranking

*AIB Finance Ltd.* v. *Bank of Scotland* 1993 SC 538. A discussion of 'creation' in competition between floating charge and standard security. (See also 22.17.) (Text 35.7)

*Ascot Inns Ltd. (In receivership)* v. *Scottish & Newcastle Breweries plc* 1994 SLT 1140. Certain subjects held to have been released from floating charge.

*Grampian Regional Council* v. *Drill Stem (Inspection Services) Ltd* 1994 SCLR 36. Landlord's hypothec has priority over rights of receiver.

### 23.10 Petition for rectification

*Allan, Black & McCaskie, Petitioners* 1987 GWD 19–709. Application by a company to extend twenty-one-day period for registration of floating charge granted, subject to certain provisos.

## Chapter 24. Leases

### 24.1 The creation of a lease

*Millar* v. *McRobbie* 1949 SC 1. Possession by tenant in advance of date of entry does not bind a singular successor of landlord under 1449 Act. (Text 24.4)

*Brador Properties Ltd.* v. *British Telecommunications plc* 1992 SC 12. Description of a lease. (Text 25.72)

*Goldston* v. *Young* (1868) 7 M 188. Lease perfected by *rei interventus.*

*Ferryhill Property Investment Ltd.* v. *Technical Video Productions* 1992 SCLR 282. Lease perfected by *rei interventus.*

*Gray* v. *Edinburgh University* 1962 SC 157. The four cardinal elements in a lease are essential to bind singular successors under 1449 Act.

*Kildrummy (Jersey) Ltd.* v. *Inland Revenue Commissioners* 1991 SCLR 498. Lease by proprietor to company preceded by deed of trust by company which declared that it would hold subjects in trust for proprietor; lease a nullity. (Text 12.19, 14.7, 26.3)

### 24.2 Lease as a real right

Formal requirements

*Morrison Low* v. *Paterson* 1985 SC (HL) 49. Discussion on necessary requirements to establish a lease.

*Buchanan* v. *Harris & Sheldon* (1900) 2 F 935. Effect of possession following on improbative missives of let.

*Shetlands Islands Council* v. *BP Petroleum Ltd.* 1989 SCLR 48. Whether possession by the tenant without specific agreement as to rent was sufficient to create a lease.

*Trade Development Bank* v. *Haig; Trade Development Bank* v. *Crittall* 1983 SLT 510. Effect of registration. (Text 33.60)

*Andert Ltd.* v. *J. & J. Johnston* 1987 SLT 268. Question whether, in the circumstances, the subjects of lease were sufficiently described.

*Mann* v. *Houston* 1957 SLT 89. Lease must specify continuing rent to bind singular successors under 1449 Act.

*Johnson* v. *Cullen* (1676) M 15231. Tenant must take possession to qualify for protection under 1449 Act.

*BP Oil Ltd.* v. *Caledonian Heritable Estates Ltd.* 1990 SLT 114. Discussion on documentation required validly to vary formal lease.

*Thomson* v. *Thomas Muir (Waste Management) Ltd.* 1995 SLT 404. Implication of lease term.

The need for consensus

*Andert Ltd.* v. *J. & J. Johnston* 1987 SLT 268. Necessity for *consensus in idem.*

*Dickson Cameras (Glasgow) Ltd* v. *Scotfilm Laboratories Ltd* 1987 GWD 31–1152. Need for *consensus.*

*McKenzie & Sons* v. *Sutherland D.C.* 1987 GWD 16–611. Need for *consensus* – method of determining rent not precisely stated.

*Smyth* v. *Caledonian Racing (1984) Ltd.* 1987 GWD 16–612. Need for *consensus* – miscalculation in method of determining rent.

*Pickard* v. *Ritchie* 1986 SLT 466. Need for *consensus* – whether lease constituted by *rei inter ventus.* Land originally leased to an individual but later farmed by partnership in succession. Rent accepted by landlord.

*Dickson* v. *MacGregor* 1992 SLT (Land Ct) 83. Lease of farm to partnership, where landlord was the limited partner, held not to be illegal *per se.* (Text 26.29)

Pro indiviso proprietors

*Bell's Executors* v. *IRC* 1986 SC 252. Lease by several *pro indiviso* proprietors to one of their own number held to be competent and valid under 1449 Act in the circumstances; but with a caveat by the Lord President and Lord Grieve.

*Pinkerton* v. *Pinkerton* 1986 SLT 672. Held, *inter alia*, that it was consistent with the definition of a lease that the landlord might also be one of a group of tenants in a joint tenancy. (Text 26.3)

*Dickson* v. *MacGregor* 1992 SLT (Land Ct) 83. See above. (Text 26.29)

*Clydesdale Bank plc* v. *Davidson* 1996 SLT 437. *Pro indiviso* proprietors granting lease of subjects to one of their number held to be a nullity. (Text 25.7, 26.3)

### 24.3 Assignability by tenant

*Elliot* v. *Duke of Buccleuch* (1747) M 10329. Assignability of lease of exceptional duration.

*Lousada & Co. Ltd.* v. *J.E. Lesser (Properties) Ltd.* 1990 SC 178. Where lease requires landlord's consent to assignation, that consent must be clearly given. (Text 25.71)

*Continvest Ltd.* v. *Dean Property Partnership* 1993 GWD 40–2675. Reasonableness of landlord's refusal of consent. (Text 25.71)

### 24.4 Transmission

*Donald Storrie (Estate Agency) Ltd. Petitioners* 1987 GWD 20–774. Clause in assignation of lease restricting user by assignee held to be truly a provision in restraint of trade.

*Bisset* v. *Aberdeen Mags* (1898) 1 F 87. Real and personal conditions; enforceability against singular successor of landlord. (Text 24.23)

*Davidson* v. *Zani* 1992 SCLR 1001. Option to purchase; enforceable against singular successor of landlord; personal bar. (Text 24.23)

*Waydale Ltd.* v. *DHL Holdings (UK) Ltd.* 1996 SCLR 391. Transmissibility of guarantee to the benefit of singular successor of landlord. (Text 25.8)

### 24.6 Possession

*Jalota* v. *Salvation Army Trustee Co.* 1994 GWD 12 – 770. Renewal of lease could cause hardship to landlord.

*Dollar Land (Cumbernauld) Ltd.* v. *CIN Properties Ltd.* 1992 SLT 211 and 669 (HL). Highlights dangers which may rise from interposed leases. (Text 24.20)

### 24.7 Registration

*Roger* v. *Crawfords* (1867) 6 M 24. Registration not the only method of creating real right; but see now 1979 Act for leases in operational areas. (Text 24.8)

*Palmer's Trs.* v. *Brown* 1989 SLT 128. Lease of shootings, if registered under 1857 Act, binds singular successors. (Text 8.10, 24.8)

### 24.20 Interposed leases

*Dollar Land (Cumbernauld) Ltd.* v. *CIN Properties Ltd.* 1992 SLT 211 and 669. Highlights dangers which may arise from interposed leases. (Text 24.6)

*Kildrummy (Jersey) Ltd.* v. *Calder* 1994 SLT 888. See s. 17 of Land Tenure Reform (Scotland) Act 1974 and para. 24.1 above. Notwithstanding decision in *Kildrummy (Jersey) Ltd* v. *IRC*, Kildrummy Ltd. ostensibly as landlords, served notice on a subtenant in possession of part of a farm, which was held invalid. (Text 26.26)

### 24.22 Examination of the landlord's title

*Trade Development Bank Ltd.* v. *Warriner & Mason (Scotland) Ltd.* Nature of obligation on tenant's agent to examine title of landlord. (Text 25.4, 33.60).

*Cumming* v. *Stewart* 1928 SC 296. Need for obtaining consent of existing heritable creditor to granting of lease. (Text 21.9)

*Armia Ltd.* v. *Daejan Developments Ltd.* 1979 SC (HL) 56. Examination of landlord's title. (Text 28.43, 28.76)

*Hand* v. *Hall* (1877) 2 ExD 355. Stamp duty on lease. (Text 25.10)

### 24.24 Notices to quit

*Campbell's Trs.* v. *O'Neill* 1911 SC 18. Lease: removing by warrant for summary ejection through procedure laid down by Sheriff Courts (Scotland) Act 1907. (Text 24.26)

### 24.27 Periods of notice

*Esson Properties Ltd.* v. *Dresser UK Ltd.* 1996 SCLR 1041. Timeous service of notice.

### 24.28 Service of notice

*Capital Land Holdings Ltd.* v. *Secretary of State for the Environment* 1996 SLT 1379. Lease stated means of service by which notice of termination was to be served: any other way was invalid.

*Netherfield Visual Productions* v. *Caledonian Land Properties Ltd.* 1996 GWD 19–1107. When serving a notice of termination there is a presumption in favour of delivery.

Miscellaneous

*Life Association of Scotland Ltd.* v. *Black's Leisure Group plc* 1989 SC 166. Whether singular successor has the benefit of notice of irritancy previously served by seller on tenant.

*Walford* v. *Crown Estate Commissioners* 1988 SLT 377. Whether lease by Crown Commissioners of rights to fish farming interferes with inalienable right of public navigation.

*Chevron Petroleum (UK) Ltd.* v. *Post Office* 1987 SLT 588. Landlord not entitled to derogate from his lease by actings or otherwise.

## Chapter 25. Commercial Leases

### 25.4 Title

*Trade Development Bank* v. *Warriner & Mason (Scotland) Ltd.* 1980 SC 74. Consent of heritable creditor (Text 24.22, 33.60)

**25.7 Designations of parties to the lease**

*Clydesdale Bank plc* v. *Davidson* 1994 SCLR 828. Parties to a lease must be distinct from one another. (Text 26.3)

**25.8 Guarantors**

*Waydale Limited* v. *DHL Holdings (UK) Ltd.* 1996 SCLR 391. Transferability of guarantee.

**25.9 Description of the leased subjects**

*Marfield Properties* v. *Secretary of State for the Environment* 1996 SLT 1744. What is a common part in a lease of part of multi-occupancy building? (Text 8.7, 25.9)

*Hand* v. *Hall* [1877] 2 Ex D 355. Calculation of stamp duty. (Text 25.10)

**25.10 Duration**

*MacDougall* v. *Guidi* 1992 SCLR 167. Recovery of possession; tacit relocation; form of notice to quit.

**25.11 Use and keep-open clauses**

*Whitelaw* v. *Fulton* (1871) 10 M 27. Obligation to keep premises plenished.

*Grosvenor Developments (Scotland) plc* v. *Argyll Stores Ltd.* 1987 SLT 738. Enforcement of keep-open obligation by interdict.

*Postel Properties Ltd.* v. *Miller & Santhouse plc* 1993 SLT 353. Enforcement of keep-open obligation.

*Church Commissioners for England* v. *Nationwide Anglia Building Society* 1994 SLT 897. Keep-open obligation.

*Church Commissioners for England* v. *Abbey National plc.* 1994 SLT 959. Keep-open obligation.

*Retail Parks Investments Ltd.* v. *Our Price Music Ltd.* 1995 SLT 1161. Interdict obtained by landlords to enforce keep-open clause recalled in part only.

*Overgate Centre Ltd.* v. *Wm. Low Supermarkets Ltd.* 1995 SLT 1181. Keep-open obligation.

*Retail Parks Investments Ltd.* v. *The Royal Bank of Scotland plc (No. 2)* 1996 SLT 669. Keep-open obligation.

*Highland & Universal Properties Ltd.* v. *Safeway Properties Ltd.* 1996 SLT 559. Keep-open obligation. Interim interdict granted.

*Co-operative Insurance Society Ltd.* v. *Argyll Stores (Holdings) Ltd.* [1997] 1 WLR 898. Keep-open obligation.

**25.12 Monetary obligations of tenant**

*Kleinwort Benson Ltd.* v. *Barbrak* [1987] AC 597. Use of back letters. (Text 25.13)

*Provincial Insurance plc* v. *Valtos Ltd.* 1992 SCLR 203. Quarter days for payment .(Text 25.13)

**25.21 Rent review**

*Montleigh Northern Developments Ltd.* v. *Ghai* 1992 GWD 24–1381. Purchaser from landlord entitled to claim arrears of rent due to seller.

*Pacitti* v. *Manganiello* 1995 SCLR 557. Withholding of rent.

*Ravenseft Properties Ltd.* v. *Aberdeen District Council* 1996 GWD 22–1285. Determination of fair market rent.

*Visionhire Ltd.* v. *Britel Fund Trs. Ltd.* 1992 SCLR 236. Time of the essence. (Text 25.25, 28.20, 28.94)

*Dunedin Property Investment Co. Ltd.* v. *Wesleyan & General Assurance Society* 1992 SCLR 159. Counter notice; time of the essence. (Text 25.25)

*United Scientific Holdings Ltd.* v. *Burnley Borough Council* [1978] AC 904. Time of the essence. (Text 25.25)

*Banks* v. *Mecca Bookmakers (Scotland) Ltd.* 1982 SC 7. Waiver by landlord; time of the essence. (Text 25.25)

*Waydale Ltd.* v. *MRM Engineering* 1996 SLT (Sh Ct) 6. *Falkirk District Council* v. *Falkirk Taverns Ltd.* 1993 SLT 1097. Waiver by landlord-personal bar; waiver by landlord. (Text 25.25)

*Scottish Development Agency* v. *Morrisons Holdings Ltd.* 1986 SLT 59. Rent review procedure effective beyond review date.

*Yates, Petitioner* 1987 SLT 86. Landlord's notice of intention to review.

*Leeds Permanent Pension Scheme Trustees Ltd.* v. *William Timpson Ltd.* 1987 SCLR 51. Time of the essence.

*Legal and Commercial Properties Ltd.* v. *Lothian Regional Council* 1988 SLT 463. Tenant's counter notice.

*Crawford* v. *Bruce* 1992 SLT 524. Basis for review. (Text 25.28)

*Beard* v. *Beveridge, Herd & Sandilands.* 1990 SLT 609. Absence of basis for review. (Text 25.28)

*Scottish Mutual Assurance Society* v. *Secretary of State for the Environment* 1992 SLT 617. Basis of review. (Text 25.28)

*Stylo Shoes Ltd.* v. *Manchester Royal Exchange Ltd.* [1967] 204 EG 803. Upwards-only review. (Text 25.29)

*Plinth Property Investment Ltd.* v. *Mott, Hay & Anderson* [1978] 249 EG 1167. Effect of restrictive user at rent reviews. (Text 25.33)

*Campbell* v. *Edwards* [1976] 1 WLR 403. No appeal against decision of expert.

*National Westminster Bank* v. *Arthur Young McLelland Moores & Co.* [1985] 2 All ER 817. Disregard of future rent reviews. (Text 25.37)

*Pugh* v. *Smiths Industries Ltd.* [1982] 264 EG 823. Effect of provision for disregards.

*British Gas Corporation* v. *U.S.S. Ltd.* [1986] 1 All ER 978. Effect of exclusion of provisions as to rent. (Text 25.37)

*F.R. Evans (Leeds) Ltd.* v. *English Electric Co. Ltd.* (1977) 245 EG 657. Willing Landlord/Willing Tenant assumption. (Text 25.32)

*Prudential Assurance Co. Ltd.* v. *Smiths Foods* 1995 SLT 369. Notice by tenant whether validly served. (Text 25.25)

*Co-operative Wholesale Society Ltd.* v. *National Westminster Bank plc, Broadgate Square plc* v. *Lehmann Brothers Ltd.; Scottish Amicable Life Assurance Society* v. *Middleton; Prudential Nominees Ltd.* v. *Greenham Trading Ltd.* [1995] 01 EG 111. Headline rents. (Text 25.28)

*Church Commissioners for England and Sears Property Glasgow Ltd.* v. *Etam plc* 1995 SCLR 947. Headline rents v. open market rents. (Text 25.28)

*Colonial Mutual Group (UK Holdings) Ltd.* v. *National Industrial Fuel Efficiency Services Ltd.* 1994 GWD 29–1761. Basis of review. (Text 25.28)

*Ponsford* v. *HMAerosols Ltd.* [1979] AC 63. Effect of tenant's improvements. (Text 25.41)

*Standard Life Assurance Co.* v. *Debenhams plc* 1995 GWD 9–514. Tenant's improvements. (Text 25.41)

*Witan Properties Ltd.* v. *Lord Advocate* 1993 GWD 29–1846. Disagreement with finding of arbiter.

*EAE (RT) Ltd.* v. *EAE Property Ltd.* 1994 SLT 627. Fax transmission and delivery of copy to solicitors held to be sufficient service of notice of intention to review.

**25.49 Tenant's repairing obligation**

*Turner's Trs.* v. *Steel* (1900) 2 F 363. Exclusion of common law. (Text 25.50)

*Allan* v. *Robertson's Trustees* (1891) 18 R 932. Extent of repairing obligation. (Text 25.52)

*Dickie* v. *Amicable Property Investment Society* 1911 SC 1079. Wind and watertight obligation. (Text 25.50)

*Gunn* v. *NCB* 1982 SLT 526. Landlord's duty as to repair.

*House of Clydesdale Ltd.* v. *Universities Superannuation Scheme Ltd.* 1992 GWD 23–1330. Landlord's duty as to repair.

*Duff* v. *Flemming* (1870) 8 M 769. Damage to premises by *damnum fatale.*

*Lurcott* v. *Wakely & Wheeler* [1911] 1 KB 905. Effect of obligation to repair. (Text 25.52)

*Cantors Properties (Scotland) Ltd.* v. *Swears & Wells Ltd.* 1978 SC 310. *Rei interitus.* (Text 25.65)

*Ravenseft Properties Ltd.* v. *Davstone (Holdings) Ltd.* [1980] 1 QB 12. Examination of concept of 'repair'. (Text 25.52)

*Blackwell* v. *Farmfoods (Aberdeen) Ltd.* 1991 GWD 4–219. Exclusion of common law. (Text 25.50)

*House of Fraser plc* v. *Prudential Assurance Co. Ltd.* 1992 SCLR 884. Wording wide enough to cover ordinary and extra-ordinary repairs. (Text 25.52)

*Taylor Woodrow Property Co. Ltd.* v. *Strathclyde Regional Council* 1996 GWD 7–397. Implication of reasonableness. (Text 25.52)

*Mothercare UK Ltd.* v. *City Wall (Holdings) Ltd.* 1994 GWD 28–1712. Extent of premises for repairing obligation. (Text 25.55)

*Lord Advocate* v. *Shipbreaking Industries Ltd. (No. 2)* 1993 SLT 995. Dispute re acceptance of site in good and tenantable condition.

## 25.56 Insurance

*Muir* v. *McIntyres* (1887) 14 R 470. Rent abatement. (Text 25.63)

*Allan* v. *Markland* (1881) 10 R 383. *Rei interitus*. (Text 25.65)

*Fehilly* v. *General Accident Fire & Life Assurance Corp.* 1983 SC 163. Tenant's insurable interest in building.

*Beacon Carpets Limited* v. *Kirby & Another* [1984] 2 All ER 726. Destruction to leased subjects; interest of tenant.

*Mark Rowlands Ltd.* v. *Berni Inns Ltd.* [1985] QB 211. Insurer's right of subrogation.

*Cantors Properties Ltd.* v. *Swears & Wells Ltd.* 1978 SC 310. *Rei interitus*. (Text 25.65)

*Barras* v. *Hamilton* 1993 SLT 1301. Where landlord agrees to insure whole and the tenant pays the premium for his part only, he remains liable for negligence if other parts are damaged. (Text 25.62)

## 25.67 Alienation

*Skene* v. *Greenhill* (1825) 4 S 25. Termination of tenant's liability on assignation.

*Burns* v. *Martin* (1887) 14 R (HL) 20. Joint and several liability of tenant.

*Duke of Portland* v. *Baird & Co.* (1865) 4 M 10. Landlord's power to refuse consent. (Text 25.71)

*Walker* v. *McKnights* (1886) 13 R 599. Effect of exclusion of assignees and sub-tenants.

*Renfrew District Council* v. *AB Leisure (Renfrew) Ltd.* 1988 SLT 635. Landlord's consent not to be unreasonably withheld. (Text 25.71)

*International Drilling Fluids Ltd.* v. *Louisville International Ltd.* [1986] 1 All ER 321. Refusal of consent by landlord. (Text 25.71)

*Lousada & Co. Ltd.* v. *J.E. Lesser (Properties) Ltd.* 1990 SLT 823. Landlord's consent subject to conditions. (Text 25.71)

*John E. Harrison Ltd.* v. *Sun Life Assurance Society plc (No. 1)* 1991 GWD 29–1761, 1992 GWD 38 226. Landlord's consent. (Text 25.71)

*Brador Properties Ltd.* v. *British Telecommunications plc* 1992 SLT 490. Constitution of sub-lease. (Text 24.1, 25.72)

*Continvest Ltd.* v. *Dean Property Partnership* 1993 GWD 40–2675. Assessment of financial strength of assignee. (Text 25.71)

*Scotmore Developments Ltd.* v. *Anderton* 1996 SLT 1304. Conditions on consent. (Text 25.71)

## 25.77 Irritancy

*Dorchester Studios (Glasgow) Ltd.* v. *Stone* 1975 SC (HL) 56. Effect of strict irritancy clause; but see now 1985 Act. (Text 25.78)

*HMV Fields Properties* v. *Bracken Self Selection Fabrics Ltd.* 1991 SLT 31. Acceptance of rent after notice of irritancy served. (Text 25.78)

*Mountleigh Northern Developments Ltd.* v. *Ghai* 1992 GWD 24–1381. Appeal against declarator of irritancy refused.

*CIN Properties Ltd.* v. *Dollar Land (Cumbernauld) Ltd.* 1992 SLT 669. Oppression. (Text , 25.78)

*Dollar Land (Cumbernauld) Ltd.* v. *CIN Properties Ltd.* 1996 SLT 186. Claim for unjust enrichment. (Text 24.6, 25.82)

*Bellevue Cash and Carry Ltd.* v. *Singh* 1996 GWD 4–220. Form of irritancy notice (Text 25.79)

*Blythswood Investments (Scotland) Ltd.* v. *Clydesdale Electrical Stores Ltd. (In receivership)* 1995 SLT 150. 'Fair and reasonable landlord'. (Text 25.79)

*Auditglen Ltd.* v. *Scotec Industries Ltd.* 1996 SLT 493. Strict interpretation of irritancy clause.

*Scottish Exhibition Centre* v. *Mirestop Ltd.* 1996 SLT 8. Entitlement to irritate lease.

*Holt Leisure Parks Ltd.* v. *Scottish & Newcastle plc* 1996 GWD 22–1284. Liability of heritable creditor following upon irritancy.

## 25.83 Hypothec

*Macpherson* v. *Macpherson's Trustees* 1905 8F 191. *Invecta et illata.* (Text 25.85)

*Steuart* v. *Stables* (1878) 5 R 1025. Goods of sub-tenant. (Text 25.85)

*Grampian Regional Council* v. *Drill Stem (Inspection Services) Ltd.* 1994 SCLR 36. Procedure of hypothec.

## Chapter 26.   Agricultural Leases

*Fothringham* v. *Fotheringham* 1987 SLT (Land Ct) 10. Proposed resumption of the majority of a hill farm by a landlord for planting was held to be in bad faith and not contemplated by the parties at time lease was entered into. (Text 26.8)

*Baird's Exrs.* v. *Inland Revenue Commissioners* 1991 SLT (Lands Tr.) 9. Tenant's interest in an agricultural tenancy can have a value for tax purposes. (Text 26.37)

*Dickson* v. *MacGregor* 1992 SLT (Land Ct) 83. Letting to a limited partnership in which landlord is a partner is not *per se* illegal. (Text 26.3)

*Kennedy* v. *Johnstone* 1956 SC 39. Discussion on whether exclusion of successors effectively brings tenancy to an end on death of tenant. (Text 26.4)

*Edinburgh Corporation* v. *Gray* 1948 SC 538. Power of resumption under agricultural lease contested. (Text 26.8)

*Turner* v. *Wilson* 1948 SC 296. Power of resumption under agricultural lease contested. (Text 26.8)

*Glencruitten Trs.* v. *Love* 1966 SLT (Land Ct) 5. Power of resumption under agricultural lease contested. (Text 26.8)

*Lady Auckland* v. *Dowie* 1964 SLT (Land Ct) 20. To avoid risk of claim for compensation for deer damage on arable land, it is necessary to allow tenant to kill and take deer. (Text 26.9)

*Morrison's Exr.* v. *Rendall* 1986 SLT 227. Informal undertakings to remove are invalid. (Text 26.26)

*Johnston* v. *Moreton* [1980] AC 37. Public policy in regard to security of tenure reviewed. (Text 26.29)

*Macfarlane* v *Falfield Investments Ltd.* 1996 SCLR 826. Position of a limited partnership as tenant. Intention of parties. (Text 26.29)

*Pinkerton* v *Pinkerton* 1986 SLT 376. Landlord can let to group of which he is a member.

*Clydesdale Bank plc* v. *Davidson* 1006 SLT 437. Several *pro indiviso* proprietors cannot let to one of their number.

## Chapter 27.   Residential Leases

## 27.2   Public sector tenancies

(Cases on the right to buy are dealt with generally in Ch. 28.79)

*Midlothian District Council* v. *Tweedie* 1993 GWD 16–1068. Circumstances in which decree for recovery of possession was upheld on appeal.

*Edinburgh District Council* v. *Stirling* 1993 SCLR 587. Sheriff Principal, on appeal, reversed Sheriff's dismissal of three actions for recovery of heritable property on grounds that he had moved too quickly in reaching his decision.

*Glasgow District Council* v. *Erhaiganoma* 1993 SCLR 592. Inner House, on appeal, dismissed appeal against decision of Sheriff granting possession to landlords on grounds of arrears of rent.

*Midlothian District Council* v. *Kerr* 1995 GWD 30–1586. Local authority obtained decree for recovery of possession against troublesome tenant.

*Edinburgh District Council* v. *Lamb* 1993 SCLR 587. Recovery of possession sought by a council where the landlord could not deal with the question of reasonableness; Housing (Scotland) Act 1987 s. 48.

### 27.5 Protected tenancies

*Margaret Blackwood Housing Association Ltd., Appellants* 1994 GWD 22–1368. Appeal against a decision of Rent Assessment Committee determining fair rent on grounds involving housing association service charge.

*Milnbank Housing Association Ltd.* v *Murdoch* 1995 SLT (Sh Ct) 11. *Held* that secure tenancy which had purportedly been converted into an assured tenancy had not in fact been converted.

*Quinn* v. *Monklands District Council* 1995 SCLR 393. Local authority tenant took occupation and house seemed to be in a satisfactory state of repair. Within two months black mould appeared caused by condensation; she claimed and was awarded damages.

*Western Heritable Investment Co. Ltd.* v. *Johnstone* 1995 GWD 30–1584. Landlord appealed against decision of Rent Assessment Committee who assessed a fair rent for a substantial number of regulated tenancies. Landlord claimed that, since there was no substantial level of scarcity, comparable rents for regulated tenancies were no longer valid. Appeal refused.

*Tamroui* v. *Clydesdale Bank plc* 1996 GWD 23–1340. Heritable creditor sought to eject short assured tenant. Landlord had granted lease without creditor's knowledge and should not have done so, given the standard conditions. Tenant argued that creditor would have to make application to Court to dispense with requirement for notice of possible repossession under s. 18 of Schedule 5 ground (2) of 1988 Act, and was upheld in that argument.

*Midlothian District Council* v. *Kerr* 1995 GWD 30–1586. See above at 27.2.

*Edinburgh District Council* v. *Lamb* 1993 SCLR 587. See above at 27.2.

*McKay* v. *Leask* 1996 GWD 30–1828. Unlawful eviction of assured tenant while on holiday; damages awarded.

### Chapter 28. Contracts of Sale and Purchase of Heritage

(With the passing of the Contract (Scotland) Act 1997 the problems caused by the rule excluding extrinsic evidence, the non-supersession rule and the rejection of the *actio quanti minoris* ceased to have any significance in contracts concluded on or after 21 June 1997, but cases on these problems have been retained in the Digest for reference where appropriate)

### 28.1 Constitution and essential content of the contract

*Rockcliffe Estates plc* v. *Co-operative Wholesale Society Ltd.* 1994 SLT 592. In a contract of sale and purchase for a portfolio of properties for a single global price, the purchasers were entitled to withdraw certain properties, and elected to do so, at prices fixed by them. The sellers declined to complete the sale on the footing that the purchasers had allocated artificially high prices on the withdrawn properties. *Held* that the purchasers must act reasonably and not capriciously. Proof allowed. (Text 28.28, 28.37, 28.59)

*Hopkinson* v. *Williams* 1993 SLT 907. Circumstances in which an agent was held to have ostensible authority to contract. (Text 28.4)

### 28.2 Form and authentication

*Davidson* v. *Gregory* 1988 GWD 25–1076. An alleged prior verbal agreement, referred to indirectly in a formal contract, is nonetheless extrinsic and cannot be considered in construing the formal document. (Text 28.5)

*Caithness Flagstone* v. *Sinclair* (1880) 7 R 1117. Unsigned offer accepted in writing; no resulting contract.

*McGinn* v. *Shearer* 1947 SC 334. Improbative acceptance; covering letter holograph. (Text 28.5)

*Gavine's Tr.* v. *Lee* (1883) 10 R 448. 'Adopted as holograph' below signature effective to constitute binding offer.

*Harvey* v. *Smith* (1904) 6 F 511. Circumstances where an individual, illiterate and without separate advice, held not bound by offer signed by him 'adopted as holograph'.

*Maclaine* v. *Murphy* 1958 SLT (Sh Ct) 49. 'Adopted as holograph'; effect.

*Whyte* v. *Lee* (1879) 6 R 699. Acceptance by agents, in proper form, binds the principal.

*Findlater* v. *Maan* 1990 SC 150. When an offer for heritable property is met by qualified acceptance which rejects its terms, it is then too late subsequently to accept offer *de plano*. (Text 28.8, 28.29)

*Scott* v. *J.B. Livingstone & Nicol* 1990 SLT 305. Where a firm makes an offer purportedly on behalf of named but non-existent principal, firm is delictually liable in damages for breach of warranty of its authority to contract.

*Heron* v. *Thomson* 1989 GWD 11–469. Discussion on scope of agent's authority to conclude missives.

*Inglis* v. *Lowrie* 1990 SLT (Sh Ct) 60. Formal, concluded missives of sale and purchase of heritage cannot be discharged or rescinded by oral agreement.

*McMillan* v. *Caldwell* 1991 SLT 325. Formal written offer to purchase or sell heritage can be withdrawn verbally, provided withdrawal is intimated before acceptance. (Text 28.5).

*Clyde Shopping Hall Ltd.* v. *Canning* 1990 SLT (Sh Ct) 10. Agreement provided that either party must serve notice of termination in writing on other party to bring agreement to an end. Such a notice was posted by one party but not received by the other. *Held* that a proper construction of wording of the agreement required that the notice be actually received.

*Edinburgh Property and Investment Co. Ltd.* v. *Norfolk Capital Hotels Ltd.* 1988 GWD 27–1161. Proof allowed on averments of subsequent improbative variation of concluded missives. Question of personal bar considered but not decided.

*Hamilton* v. *Wakefield* 1992 SCLR 740. Validity of contract made in England. (Text 2.39, 28.5)

*Stewart's Exrs* v. *Stewart* 1993 SCLR 641. *Held*, that informal contract for sale and purchase of heritage cannot be proved simply by actings alone.

*Abegg Ltd.* v. *Ladbrook Retail Parks Ltd* 1993 GWD 14–947. Two separate contracts for sale and purchase of separate lots amended by subsequent missives. *Held* that terms of missives were not sufficient to overcome the presumption against novation and accordingly the two contracts remained separate and distinct.

*Stewart Milne Group Ltd.* v. *Skateraw Development Co. Ltd.* 1995 GWD 32–1650. Where a contract clearly assumed a knowledge of surrounding facts and circumstances not disclosed in the missives, it would be hazardous to attempt to interpret provisions therein without further evidence.

*Littlejohn* v. *Mackay* 1974 SLT (Sh Ct) 82. A partner, not merely an assistant, must sign for a firm. But see now 1995 Act Schedule 2.2. (Text 2.52, 3.22, 28.5)

### 28.4 Form and authentication – agents
*Hopkinson* v. *Williams* 1993 SLT 907. See Ch. 1.3.

### 28.7 Consensus in idem
*Haldane & Another* v. *Watson* 1972 SLT (Sh Ct) 8. Unilateral undertaking. (Text 28.2)

*Dickson* v. *Blair* (1871) 10 M 41. No *consensus*; qualified acceptance. (Text 28.8)

*Heiton* v. *Waverly Hydropathic Co.* (1877) 4 R 830. No *consensus*; all conditions not agreed.

*Stobo Ltd.* v. *Morrison's (Gowns) Ltd.* 1949 SC 184. No *consensus*; 'subject to contract'. (Text 28.9)

*Westren* v. *Millar* (1879) 7 R 173. *Consensus*; purchaser taking possession and making alterations. (Text 28.9)

*McCallum* v. *Soudan* 1989 SLT 522. Circumstances where, following general principle, uninduced error *held* not sufficient to avoid contract

*Angus* v. *Bryden* 1992 SLT 884. Disposition ostensibly implemented missives but disponer alleged error. Lord Cameron expressed opinion that unintentional essential error known to and taken advantage of by other party implied bad faith for which the law provided a remedy. *Stewart's Trs.*, above, applied and *Spook Erection (Northern) Ltd.* 1990 SLT 676 not followed. (Text 28.33)

*McLeod's Exr.* v. *Barr's Trs.* 1989 SC 72. Where price is not stated and no basis is given for fixing it in contract, there is no *consensus* and no contract. (Text 28.37)

*Grant* v. *Peter G. Gauld & Co.* 1985 SC 251. Provision that 'the actual boundaries would be agreed between the parties' not sufficiently precise to create *consensus*. (Text 28.33)

*Coomber* v. *Ross* 1987 SLT 266. Single contract for sale and purchase of two separate heritable properties *held* to be severable and individually enforceable.

*Chapelcroft Ltd.* v. *Inverdon Egg Producers Ltd.* 1973 SLT (Notes) 37. Knowledge of agent imputed to principal.

*Turner* v. *Macmillan Douglas* 1989 SLT 293. Subsequent writings can be taken into account in construing ambiguity in antecedent contract.

*Barratt (Scotland) Ltd.* v. *Keith* 1993 SC 142. Circumstances where lack of precision in defining subjects of offer in missives *held* not necessarily to exclude evidence of prior communings. But see *Angus* above. (Text 33.51, 33.79)

*Martone* v. *Zani* 1992 GWD 32–1903. Extrinsic evidence admitted to determine the extent of the property subject to an option to purchase. (Text 28.33, 28.97)

*Aberdeen Rubber Ltd.* v. *Knowles & Sons (Fruiterers) Ltd.* 1995 SLT (HL) 870. A offered to purchase four areas of ground; disposition in implement conveyed five areas by mistake. Purchaser failed to satisfy Court that the fifth area had been properly included in disposition, which was accordingly reduced. (Text 28.33)

*McClymont* v. *McCubbin* 1995 SLT 1248. *Held* that where missives did not contain everything agreed, and which had to be agreed on, in order to constitute a contract, it was competent to prove that agreement had been reached by reference to prior communings taken together with missives themselves.

*Tweedie* v. *Ritchie* 1992 GWD 34–2008. *Held* that there had been no *consensus* in relation to division and sale and alleged agreement as to unequal division of proceeds.

*Colgan* v. *Mooney* 1992 GWD 34–2009. Seller and purchaser in dispute as to *consensus* on terms of contract, in particular provisions as to whether fire certificate required. (Text 28.95)

**28.8    The effect of a qualified acceptance**

*Rutterford Ltd.* v. *Allied Breweries Ltd.* 1990 SLT 249. *Held*, following *Wolf & Wolf* v. *Forfar Potato Co.* 1984 SLT 100, that latest qualified acceptance, in series of letters of offer and subsequent qualifications, represented a fresh counter-offer which supplanted and cancelled out previous counter-offer represented by original offer and earlier qualified acceptances which were therefore no longer open for *de plano* acceptance.

*Findlater* v. *Maan* 1990 SC 150. When offer to purchase is met by a qualified acceptance, that is, in effect, a counter-offer. If purchaser accepted those qualifications but subject to a further qualification, that is, again, a new counter-offer. (Text 28.29)

**28.10    *Rei interventus* and homologation**

*Colquhoun* v. *Wilson Trs.* (1860) 22 D 1035. All conditions not explicitly agreed, but purchaser carrying out alterations to property.

*Secretary of State* v. *Ravenstone Securities* 1976 SC 171. Whether actings unequivocally referable to informal agreement.

*Mitchell* v. *Stornoway Trs.* 1936 SC (HL) 56. Homologation of improbative agreement by actings. (Text 28.15)

*East Kilbride Development Corporation* v. *Pollock* 1953 SC 370. Contract lacking essentials cannot be completed by *rei interventus*.

*Errol* v. *Walker* 1966 SC 93. Proof of agreement to found *rei interventus*. (Text 28.13)

*Mulhern* v. *Mulhern* 1987 SLT (Sh Ct) 62. Oral agreement to sell and purchase heritage can be proved only by writ or oath. *Errol* v. *Walker* considered. (Text 28.13)

*Law* v. *Thomson* 1978 SC 343. Circumstances insufficient to warrant *rei interventus* or homologation.

*Clark's Exr.* v. *Cameron* 1982 SLT 68. Delivery of improbative writ to grantor's agent does not normally constitute homologation; nor would the agent's actings constitute *rei interventus*.

*Rutterford Ltd.* v. *Allied Breweries Ltd.* 1990 SLT 249. See para. 28.8 above. Following exchange of missives, the sellers replied to the final but invalid acceptance in terms indicating that they were proceeding with the contract. This was held not sufficient to constitute homologation, there being no *consensus*. Fact that purchasers in turn embarked on examination of title and drafted a disposition and incidental documents *held* insufficient to constitute *rei interventus*, as not constituting proceedings not unimportant. (Text 28.8)

*Ferryhill Property Investments Ltd.* v. *Technical Video Productions* 1992 SCLR 282. Circumstances in which actings of defenders *held* sufficient as evidence of consent to written lease, following *Errol* v. *Walker*. (Text 24.1)

*Shetlands Islands Council* v. *BP Petroleum Ltd.* 1990 SLT 82. Discussion on actings sufficient to constitute *rei interventus*.

*Stewart's Exrs.* v. *Stewart* 1994 SLT 466. In an *obligatio literis*, pursuer must prove informal agreement by writ or oath before he can attempt to prove homologation. (Text 33.79)

*Ferryhill Property Investments Ltd* v. *Technical Video Productions* 1992 SCLR 282. *Held* that actings of the defender following on a written offer of lease were sufficient evidence of consent for *rei interventus* and proof before answer allowed.

*Tomorrow's World* v. *Burgess* 1993 GWD 29–1845. In the case of a draft lease followed by actings, Court admitted evidence *habili modo* on footing that the tenant claimed entitlement by *rei interventus*.

*Barratt (Scotland) Ltd.* v. *Keith* 1994 SLT 1343. See para. 28.7 above.

*Nelson* v. *Gerrard* 1994 SCLR 1052. Binding contract (here, lease) could be constituted by actings following prior informal communings.

*Hamilton* v. *Wakefield* 1992 SCLR 740. See text at para. 28.5 above. (Text 2.39, 28.5)

## 28.18 Survey reports

*Martin* v. *Bell-Ingram* 1986 SLT 575. Discussion on duty owed by surveyor when inspecting a property for building society in anticipation of purchase.

*Crouches* v. *Murray & Muir* 1987 GWD 12–428. Discussion on measure of damages in claim against surveyor.

*UCB Bank plc* v. *Dundas & Wilson* 1990 SC 377. Liability of solicitors and surveyors for depreciation in land value due to subsidence.

*Robbie* v. *Graham & Sibbald* 1989 SLT 870. Liability for negligent survey.

*Melrose* v. *Davidson & Robertson* 1993 SLT 611. Validity of disclaimer of liability on survey report discussed.

*Hunter* v. *J. & E. Shepherd* 1991 GWD 17–1043. Discussion on the basis of assessment of damages arising out of negligent survey.

*Peach* v. *Iain G. Chalmers* 1992 SCLR 423. Discussion on basis of assessment of damages arising out of negligent survey.

*Smith* v. *Carter* 1994 SCLR 539. Discussion on duty of care owed by a surveyor to undisclosed co-purchaser.

*Alliance & Leicester BS* v. *J. & E. Shepherd* 1995 GWD 11–608. Firm of surveyors stated that they had not seen any evidence of flood damage and that property had no unusual hazard. In following year and in two subsequent years property was seriously flooded and the owner abandoned property to building society, who sold it for half the amount of their loan. They sued surveyors in contract and delict for failing to take reasonable care. On evidence produced by surveyors, they were exonerated.

*Mortgage Express Ltd.* v. *Dunsmore Reid & Smith* 1996 GWD 10–590. Claim for negligence in two mortgage valuations, and dispute as to persons liable in negligence claim, given that surveyors operated in Scotland and in England and there was a question whether one of surveyor group was to be treated as partner.

## 28.22 Winston v. Patrick

(See also cases under 28.53 and 29.99)

*Meek* v. *Bell* 1993 GWD 20–1238. Question as to how far missives were superseded by delivery of lease. See under 28.53 for further detail.

*Aberdeen Rubber Ltd.* v. *Knowles & Sons (Fruiterers) Ltd.* 1995 SLT 870. Delivery of disposition totally supersedes antecedent missives but only on matters which it is intended to implement. (Text 28.33)

*McClymont* v. *McCubbin* 1995 SLT 1248. See 28.7 above. (Text 28.7)

### 28.24 The *actio quanti minoris* and collateral obligations
(See also cases under 28.53, 28.64 and 28.96)

*King* v. *Gebbie* 1993 SLT 512. Under missives, a house was still uncompleted at date of entry. After settlement, defects were discovered in structure. Obligations to perform building work held collateral, following *McKillop* v. *Mutual Securities Ltd.* 1945 SC 166; and the missives were not superseded. (Text 28.23)

*Hardwick* v. *Gebbie* 1991 SLT 258. Circumstances where obligation to build house *held* to be intended as continuing obligation, notwithstanding delivery of disposition but only *quoad* matters not reasonably discoverable on inspection. Remedy was damages for breach of contract, not *actio quanti minoris*. (Text 28.25, 28.101)

*Black* v. *Gibson* 1992 SLT 1076. Obligation to build house *held* to be a single complete collateral obligation. Building partly completed before missives concluded; but held not appropriate to apportion collateral obligation with reference to that part of building already completed, and the remaining part not completed until after conclusion of missives.

*Fortune* v. *Fraser* 1996 SLT 878. Purchasers contracted to acquire a business. Sellers warranted, *inter alia*, correctness of accounts, which were materially inaccurate. Full discussion in Inner House on *actio quanti minoris* and effect of misrepresentation. See also article by Professor Thomson at 1994 SLT (News) 29. (Text 28.23, 28.64)

*Tomorrow's World* v. *Burgess* 1993 GWD 29–1845. See 28.10 above.

*Colgan* v. *Mooney* 1994 GWD 1–43. M sold a guest house with certain assurances as to fire certificate. M qualified a condition as to fire certificate 'to the extent that the subjects are too small to require a full fire certificate' and disclosed fire officer's letter confirming that safety standards were met. *Held* on appeal that M not liable under *quanti minoris* clause. Lord Clyde doubted whether, in any event, claim properly fell within scope of that clause. (Text 28.95)

*Adams* v. *Whatlings plc* 1995 SCLR 185. See 28.27 below. (Text 28.101)

### 28.27 The need for express provision
*Fortune* v. *Fraser* 1996 SLT 878. See 28.24 above. Standing this decision, it may not be sufficient simply to include warranty in missives without declaration that clause is material and breach thereof will entitle purchaser to certain remedies by express provision. (Text 28.23, 28.64)

*Rockcliffe Estates plc* v. *Co-operative Wholesale Society Ltd.* 1994 SLT 592. See 28.1. Parties presumed by implication to act reasonably, not capriciously, in relation to contract conditions. (Text 28.28, 28.37, 28.59)

*Adams* v. *Whatlings plc* 1995 SCLR 185. Contract to purchase land incorporated obligation to erect a house thereon. After completion, defects developed and purchaser claimed damages for defective workmanship. Seller was *held* liable on footing that condition as to good workmanship, though not express, was necessarily implied and not extinguished by delivery of the disposition. (Text 28.101)

### 28.28 Effect of conditions in contracts
*Burnside* v. *James Harrison (Developers) Ltd.* 1989 GWD 11–468. Provision in contract that either party may resile if completion certificate not obtained by specified date binding and enforceable even if certificate later obtained. Specific provisions in missives as to notice superseded and excluded normal ultimatum rule. (Text 28.30, 28.94)

*Park* v. *Morrison Developments Ltd* 1993 GWD 8–571. Missives included suspensive conditions to be implemented by successive stated dates. Purchaser was *held* entitled to resile, when first fixed date had passed, without implement of that condition. Both sides having been legally advised on complicated missives, *contra proferentem* rule inapplicable.

*Manheath Ltd.* v. *H.J. Banks & Co. Ltd.* 1996 SLT 1006. Purchaser was to apply for planning permission on which the contract was conditional and, unless purchaser intimated within five years that permission had been granted, missives would fall. Planning permission not granted. Purchaser intimated that suspensive condition as to planning permission had been purified although permission had not been granted. *Held* that condition was not conceived solely in favour of purchaser and therefore not capable of unilateral waiver. (Text 28.30)

*Khazaka* v. *Drysdale* 1995 GWD 23–1258. Contract conditional upon the purchaser obtaining planning permission. Time-limit for lodging application specified. Seller qualified missives to effect that purchaser would have four weeks in which to make application. Seller purportedly resiled when the purchaser's application was lodged six days late, on the footing that suspensive condition required strict adherence to time limit specified. *Held* that time-limit fixed for lodging application was not of same character; and ultimatum procedure was appropriate. (Text 28.51)

### 28.29 Effect of conditions inserted for the benefit of one party
(See also para. 28.75)

*Dewar & Finlay Ltd.* v. *Blackwood* 1968 SLT 196. Condition as to planning permission.

*Ellis & Sons Ltd.* v. *Pringle* 1974 SC 200. Condition as to planning permission. (Text 28.30)

*Imry Property Holdings Ltd.* v. *Glasgow YMCA* 1979 SLT 262. Whether seller entitled to waive condition.

*Gilchrist* v. *Payton* 1979 SC 380, 1979 SLT 135. Whether purchaser entitled to waive condition. (Text 28.28)

*Zebmoon Ltd.* v. *Akinbrook Investment Dev. Ltd.* 1988 SLT 146. Condition in missives may be waived by one party unilaterally if it satisfies two tests: (i) that it is in the interests of that party only; (ii) that it is not inextricably connected with other parts of contract. (Text 28.30)

*Manheath Ltd.* v. *H.J. Banks & Co. Ltd.* 1996 SLT 1006. See 28.28 above. (Text 28.28)

### 28.32 Identification of the subjects sold

*Macdonald* v. *Newall* (1898) 1 F 68. 'Property known as the Royal Hotel.' (Text 28.33, 33.50)

*Houldsworth* v. *Gordon Cumming* 1910 SC (HL) 49. 'The Estate of Dallas.' Prior negotiations. (Text 28.33)

*McKendrick* v. *Wilson* 1970 SLT (Sh Ct) 39. Whether salmon fishing included in sale. (Text 8.3, 28.34)

*Davidson* v. *Gregory* 1988 GWD 25–1076. Alleged prior verbal agreement, referred to indirectly in formal contract, is nonetheless extrinsic and cannot be considered in construing formal document. (Text 28.5)

*Grant* v. *Peter G. Gauld & Co.* 1985 SC 251. Provision to the effect that 'the actual boundaries would be agreed between the parties' not sufficiently precise to create *consensus*. (Text 28.7, 28.33)

*Anderson* v. *Lambie* 1954 SC (HL) 43. Farm and other subjects; prior communings. (Text 28.98)

*Murray* v. *Cherry* 1980 SLT (Sh Ct) 131. Not legitimate to refer to prior negotiations to contradict terms of missives, unless ambiguous. (Text 28.33)

*Turner* v. *Macmillan Douglas* 1989 SLT 293. Subsequent writings can be taken into account in construing ambiguity in antecedent contract.

*Russell's Exr.* v. *Russell's Exrs.* 1983 SLT 385. Discussion of rule in *Anderson* v. *Lambie* above.

*Martone* v. *Zani* 1992 GWD 32–1903. Extrinsic evidence admitted to determine extent of property subject to option to purchase. (Text 28.33, 28.97)

*Angus* v. *Bryden* 1992 SLT 884. Discussion on proper construction of contract of sale or purchase where parties took different views as to what was included. (Text 28.33)

### 28.35 Fixtures and fittings

*Nisbet* v. *Mitchell-Innes* (1880) 7 R 575. Vegetables, grapes *etc.*

*Cochrane* v. *Stevenson* (1891) 18 R 1208. Picture in panel.

*Christie* v. *Smith's Exrx.* 1949 SC 572. Summerhouse.

*Assessor for Fife* v. *Hodgson* 1966 SC 30. Storage heaters.

*Assessor for Lothian Region* v. *Blue Circle Industries plc* 1986 SLT 537. Discussion on whether semi-mobile plant heritable or moveable.

*Scottish Discount Co. Ltd.* v. *Blin* 1985 SC 216. Whether plant, on hire purchase and affixed to hirer's yard, heritable or moveable.

*Jamieson* v. *Welsh* (1900) 3 F 176. Passing of moveables.

## 28.36 Price

*Stirling* v. *Honyman* (1824) 2 S 765. No binding contract if price not fixed.

*McLeod's Exr.* v. *Barr's Trs.* 1989 SC 72. Price must be stated or precise method prescribed for ascertaining it. (Text 28.7, 28.37)

*Zemhunt (Holdings) Ltd.* v. *Control Securities Ltd.* 1992 SLT 151. Where deposit paid in terms of a contract of sale and purchase of heritage, the term will normally be construed as meaning that purchaser guarantees he will complete, and that deposit will be forfeited if he is in breach. (Text 28.38)

*Inverkip Building Co. Ltd.* v. *City Ploy Ltd.* 1992 GWD 8–433. Purchaser can insist on recovering deposit if he is not in default, in cases where contract cannot be implemented. (Text 28.38)

*Singh* v. *Cross Entertainments Ltd.* 1990 SLT 77. Purchaser may be entitled to recover deposit if justified, on principle *causa data causa non secuta*. (Text 28.38)

*Scottish Wholefoods Collective Warehouse Ltd* v. *Raye Investments* 1994 SCLR 60. Clause in a lease giving option to purchase to tenant at 'the current open market price pertaining at the time ... as between a willing buyer or a willing seller ... and as the said price shall be mutually agreed between the parties ...' held to be sufficiently precise and therefore enforceable according to its terms, on footing that, if parties failed to agree, Court would determine price. (Text 28.37)

*Rockcliffe Estates plc* v. *Co-operative Wholesale Society Ltd* 1994 SLT 592. In contract of sale and purchase for a portfolio of properties for a single global price, purchasers were to intimate individual prices for dispositions, with right to withdraw properties at their discretion. Purchasers elected to withdraw certain properties and sellers declined to complete sale, on footing that purchasers had allocated artificially high prices on withdrawn properties. *Held* that there could be no implication that the purchasers would allocate prices on reasonable basis, having regard to market values because contract otherwise provided, but that it was implied that purchasers would act reasonably and not capriciously and proof before answer allowed with certain limitations. (Text 28.28, 28.37, 28.59)

*Stewart Milne Group Ltd.* v. *Skateraw Development Co. Ltd.* 1995 GWD 32–1650. Purchasers of land sued sellers for cost of constructing part of road. Whether sellers were liable depended on meaning of obscure provision in contract. Court declined to interpret provision without further information as to background to purchase, since it would be 'hazardous' to do so.

## 28.41 Entry

*Sloan's Dairies Ltd.* v. *Glasgow Corporation* 1977 SC 223. Agreed date of entry not essential. (Text 28.52)

*Law* v. *Thomson* 1978 SC 343. Date of entry essential.

*Secretary of State* v. *Ravenstone Securities* 1976 SC 171. Question whether date of entry would always be implied.

*Gordon District Council* v. *Wimpey Homes Holdings Ltd.* 1988 SLT 481. Entry 'not earlier than ...' sufficient to create valid contract; exact date of entry not necessary. (Text 28.78)

*Speevak* v. *Robson* 1949 SLT (Notes) 39. 'Entry' and 'settlement' contemporaneous.

*Heys* v. *Kimball & Morton* (1890) 17 R 381. 'Immediate entry' means such early possession as is possible and practicable. (Text 28.90)

*Bosal Scotland Ltd.* v. *Anderson* 1988 GWD 30–1275. Seller of property may have implied duty to take reasonable care to maintain property until entry, notwithstanding that risk may pass to purchaser. (Text 28.52)

## 28.42 Title

*Christie* v. *Cameron* (1898) 25 R 824. Seller bound to clear title.

*McConnell* v. *Chassels* (1903) 10 SLT 790. Long lease not a marketable title. (Text 28.43)

*Bruce* v. *Stewart* (1900) 2 F 948. Decree of irritancy in absence.

*Dryburgh* v. *Gordon* (1896) 24 R 1. Undischarged inhibitions. (Text 33.43)

*Hamilton* v. *Western Bank of Scotland* (1861) 23 D 1033. Title defective; buildings erected in part on adjoining feu.

### 28.43  Title to whole and identical property – reservation of minerals
*Whyte* v. *Lee* (1879) 6 R 699. Purchaser entitled to resile.

*Campbell* v. *McCutcheon* 1963 SC 505. Purchaser entitled to resile. (Text 28.68, 28.97)

*Macdonald* v. *Newall* (1898) 1 F 68. Purchaser's knowledge; personal bar. (Text 28.33, 33.50)

*Mossend Theatre Co.* v. *Livingstone* 1930 SC 90. Whether knowledge to be imputed to purchaser. (Text 28.46)

### 28.44  Burdens and conditions
*Corbett* v. *Robertson* (1872) 10 M 329. Personal, not real, condition.

*Smith* v. *Soeder* (1895) 23 R 60. Undisclosed burden. (Text 28.43)

*Welsh* v. *Russell* (1894) 21 R 769. Undisclosed servitude. (Text 12.9, 28.43).

*Cameron* v. *Williamson* (1895) 22 R 293. Undischarged security. (Text 22.60)

*Bremner* v. *Dick* 1911 SC 887. Unallocated feuduty renders title unmarketable.

*Armia* v. *Deajan Developments Ltd.* 1979 SC (HL) 56. Purchaser not bound to accept undisclosed burdens. (Text 28.43, 28.76)

*Umar* v. *Murtaza* 1983 SLT (Sh Ct) 79. Seller bound to disclose all restrictions on title. (Text 28.43)

*Morris* v. *Ritchie* 1992 GWD 33–1950. In contract of sale and purchase, seller bound to disclose all burdens, existing or proposed, if material. (Text 28.43, 28.46)

### 28.45  Variation of the obligation as to marketable title – 'title as it stands'
*Morton* v. *Smith* (1877) 5 R 83. Observations on effect of this clause.

*Young* v. *McKellar Ltd.* 1909 SC 1340. No title to 25 sq. yds. out of 383 sq. yds. Purchaser bound to accept title.

*Wood* v. *Magistrates of Edinburgh* (1886) 13 R 1006. Purchaser must accept real conditions in title.

*Davidson* v. *Dalziel* (1881) 8 R 990. Purchaser must accept real undischarged burdens.

*Carter* v. *Lornie* (1890) 18 R 353. Purchaser not bound to accept incurable defects.

*Leith Heritages Co.* v. *Edinburgh & Leith Glass Co.* (1876) 3 R 789. Effect of obligation 'to put purchaser in the sellers' place'.

*Mackenzie* v. *Clark* (1895) 3 SLT 128. Provision that purchaser not entitled to search does not deprive him of right to marketable title.

*Morris* v. *Ritchie* 1992 GWD 33–1950. *Held* that purchaser entitled to resile on account of burden restricting parking places substantially below total originally contracted for. (Text 28.43, 28.46)

*MacDougall* v. *MacDougall's Exrs.* 1994 SLT 1178. Sellers' title unmarketable, but they pleaded, *inter alia*, that as *bona fide* purchasers for value without notice, recorded disposition in their favour was exempt from challenge by way of reduction. *Held*, on this point, that, when purchasing subjects, sellers had been put on notice by narrative in earlier writ and had failed to make due enquiry as to facts. (Text 28.46, 31.26)

*Watson* v. *Gillespie MacAndrew* 1995 GWD 13–750. Purchaser sought damages from his solicitors for failing to disclose existence over part of estate which he had purchased of servitude right of access and wayleave agreement for electricity pylons. (Text 28.49)

### 28.46  Personal bar
*Ceres School Board* v. *McFarlane* (1895) 23 R 279. Unrecorded charter granted by seller. (Text 13.5, 29.38, 29.40, 32.1, 33.57, 33.58)

*Davidson* v. *Dalziel* (1881) 8 R 990. Burden in a will not made real.

*Stodart* v. *Dalzell* (1876) 4 R 236. Purchaser barred by knowledge from objecting to right of occupancy. (Text 33.58)

*Rodger (Builders) Ltd.* v. *Fawdry* 1950 SC 483. Second purchaser having notice of prior sale.

*Trade Development Bank* v. *Crittal Windows Ltd.* 1983 SLT 510. Creditor taking real security with knowledge of prior personal obligation; whether affected thereby. (Text 33.60)

*Campbell's Trs.* v. *Glasgow Corporation* (1902) 4 F 752. Personal contract not binding on singular successor. (Text 33.57, 33.61)

### 28.51 Planning and other statutory matters
(And see paras. 28.29 and 28.78)

*Bradley* v. *Scott* 1966 SLT (Sh Ct) 25. Closing order an 'outstanding notice'. (Text 28.21, 28.22)

*Kelly* v. *A. & J. Clark Ltd.* 1968 SLT 141. 'Notices *etc.* under Town and Country Planning Acts.'

*Murray* v. *Hillhouse Estates Ltd.* 1960 SLT (Notes) 48. Meaning and effect of condition as to 'unqualified planning permission'.

*Hood* v. *Clarkson* 1995 SLT 98. Offer contained standard clause to effect that there were no existing applications, orders, notices *etc.* and seller had no knowledge that any such were intended. Qualified acceptance modified that provision, stating that, with regard thereto, the usual local authority letter would be exhibited and, if letter disclosed any materially prejudicial matter, purchaser could resile. After settlement, disponee discovered that seller had negotiated with local authority for sale of the land for roadworks, which did not show up in local authority letter. Purchaser maintained that seller had misrepresented position and claimed damages. There was a non-supersession clause. Claim rejected, court holding that seller obliged to provide local authority letter and nothing more. He had not made any misrepresentations as to his knowledge at date of sale.

*Khazaka* v. *Drysdale* 1995 SLT 1108. See 28.28 above. (Text 28.28)

### 28.52 Structure and passing of the risk
Structure
(See also para. 28.18)

*Martin* v. *Bell-Ingram* 1986 SLT 575. Discussion on duty owed by surveyor when inspecting property for building society in anticipation of purchase. (Text 28.18)

*Crouches* v. *Murray & Muir* 1987 GWD 12–428. Discussion on measure of damages in claim against surveyor.

*UCB Bank plc* v. *Dundas & Wilson* 1990 SC 377. Liability of solicitors and surveyors for depreciation in land value due to subsidence.

*McKay* v. *Leigh Estates (Scotland) Ltd.* 1987 GWD 16–609. Missives contained condition that purchaser should receive a satisfactory report on suitability of ground for development. Purchaser did not adequately investigate ground and then purportedly resiled. Purchaser was ordained to lead proof to establish that decision to resile reasonable. (Text 28.28, 28.78)

Passing of the risk

*Sloan's Dairies Ltd.* v. *Glasgow Corporation* 1972 SC 223. Risk of damage to subjects of purchase passes from seller to purchaser at date of completion of contract. (Text 28.41)

*Bosal Scotland Ltd.* v. *Anderson* 1988 GWD 30–1275. Notwithstanding rule as to risk, seller may have duty to take reasonable care to maintain property until entry.

*Hall* v. *McWilliam* 1993 GWD 23–1457. Missives included standard clause that subjects would be in substantially same condition at date of entry. After conclusion of missives and before entry, house flooded. Seller undertook remedial work, which was completed by date of entry, and purchaser *held* bound to proceed.

### 28.53 Contract to remain in full force and effect – non-supersession clause
(See also cases under paras. 28.24, 28.64 and 28.96)

*Lee* v. *Alexander* (1883) 10 R (HL) 91. General principles. (Text 28.22, 28.58, 28.59).

*Orr* v. *Mitchell* (1893) 20 R (HL) 27. General principles. (Text 29.35, 29.39)

*Butter* v. *Foster* 1912 SC 1218. General principles.

*Winston* v. *Patrick* 1980 SC 246. General principles. (Text 28.22, 28.23, 28.53, 28.54, 28.58, 28.59, 28.90, 28.100, 28.101, 29.31, 33.84).

*Hayes* v. *Robinson* 1984 SLT 300. General rule excluded by specific clause in missives to that effect. (Text 28.101)

*Pena* v. *Ray* 1987 SLT 609. Non-supersession clause in missives competent and will keep contract open, notwithstanding delivery of a disposition in implement which does not refer to it. (Text 28.56)

*Ferguson* v. *McIntyre* 1993 SLT 1269. Time-limit in non-supersession clause not invalidated by Prescription and Limitation Act 1973 s. 13. (Text 28.56)

*Sinclair-MacDonald* v. *Haitt* 1987 GWD 7–232. Agreement in missives, supported by non-supersession clause, that seller would remain in occupation beyond date of entry *held* not to be superseded by delivery of disposition as being personal right affecting the parties within exception (c) in *Winston* v. *Patrick*. (Text 28.41)

*Jamieson* v. *Stewart* 1989 SLT (Sh Ct) 13. Non-supersession clause need not be included in disposition to be effective after delivery thereof, under exception (c) to rule in *Winston* v. *Patrick*.

*Finlayson* v. *McRobb* 1987 SLT (Sh Ct) 150. Non-supersession clause not effective unless incorporated in disposition. Observed that *actio quanti minoris* incompetent in sale and purchase of heritage. (Text 28.25, 28.54, 28.64, 29.31)

*Jones* v. *Stewart* 1988 SLT (Sh Ct) 13. Obligation in missives as to condition of swimming pool *held* to be collateral. Several earlier cases reviewed and discussed in the context of *Winston* v. *Patrick*. (Text 28.24, 29.31)

*Wood* v. *Edwards* 1988 SLT (Sh Ct) 17. Condition as to planning permission *etc. held* not to be collateral; but condition as to state of repair of central heating system at date of entry might be so. (Text 28.25)

*Fetherston* v. *McDonald (No. 1)* 1988 SLT (Sh Ct) 16. Where non-supersession clause effective and contains time-limit, it is sufficient to raise action within time-limit, even though action not disposed of until later. See also *Pena* v. *Ray* above. (Text 28.56)

*Fetherston* v. *McDonald (No. 2)* 1988 SLT (Sh Ct) 39. Provision in missives as to condition of central heating system at date of entry *held* collateral and so not superseded by disposition.

*Hardwick* v. *Gebbie* 1991 SLT 258. Circumstances where obligation to build house *held* to be intended as continuing obligation, notwithstanding delivery of disposition, but only *quoad* matters not reasonably discoverable on inspection. Remedy was damages for breach of contract, not *actio quanti minoris*. (Text 28.24, 28.25, 28.101)

*Black* v. *Gibson* 1992 SLT 1076. Obligation to build house *held* to be single complete collateral obligation. Building partly completed before missives were concluded; but, on this basis, *held* not appropriate to apportion collateral obligation with reference to part already implemented prior to missives and part not implemented until after conclusion of missives.

*King* v. *Gebbie* 1993 SLT 512. Under missives, house to be completed before date of entry. After settlement, defects discovered in structure. *Held* that missives not superseded. Obligations to perform building work *held* collateral, following *McKillop* v. *Mutual Securities Ltd.* 1945 SC 166. (Text 28.23)

*Porch* v. *MacLeod* 1992 SLT 661. Contract of sale and purchase of heritage contained warranty that all consents and warrants had been obtained for work carried out or for change of use; and undertaking to exhibit evidence thereof. There was also a non-supersession clause, limited to two years. *Held* that undertaking to exhibit evidence was a personal obligation collateral to the warranty; but it fell on delivery of disposition because it did not come within one or other of three express exceptions in *Winston* v. *Patrick* 1980 SC 246 which are exhaustive. (Text 28.59, 28.99, 28.101, 29.31)

*Parker* v. *O'Brien* 1992 SLT (Sh Ct) 31. Contract of sale and purchase of heritage contained phrase 'the seller will warrant' condition of fitments and appliances. *Held* that wording implied a future promise or warranty and thus did not fall within collateral obligation exception in *Winston* v. *Patrick* 1980 SC 246. (Text 29.31)

*Taylor* v. *McLeod* 1990 SLT 194. Undertaking in missives by seller of heritage to put machinery thereon in working order *held* to be both collateral obligation and personal obligation covered by a non-supersession clause included in missives but not in disposition. On both grounds, undertaking survived delivery of disposition. Authorities discussed. (Text 28.99, 28.101)

*Bourton* v. *Claydon* 1990 SLT (Sh Ct) 7. Undertaking by seller to bear cost of repairs to any defect in central heating system *held* to survive delivery of disposition on footing that it was a collateral obligation which had nothing to do with conveyance. *Wood* v. *Edwards* 1988 SLT (Sh Ct) 17 and *Finlayson* v. *McRobb* 1987 SLT (Sh Ct) 150 not followed. No non-supersession clause in contract and the Sheriff proceeded on footing that, since this was a collateral obligation, it automatically survived delivery of disposition.

*Robson* v. *Inglis* 1990 GWD 2–92. In special circumstances, involving obligations clearly intended to remain enforceable beyond a contractual time-limit, time-limit *held* inapplicable and *Pena* v. *Ray* 1987 SLT 607 distinguished. (Text 28.56, 28.93).

*University of Strathclyde (Properties) Ltd.* v. *Fleeting Organisation Ltd.* 1992 GWD 14–822. Parties free to contract for time-limit different from statutory period laid down in 1973 Act, or elsewhere. (Text 28.56, 28.59)

*Meek* v. *Bell* 1993 GWD 20–1238. Missives for sale of business included benefit of a lease. In addition, missives provided that purchaser should have option to purchase. Purchaser exercised right, which seller disputed, basing his argument on fact that contract had been implemented by delivery, in this case, of lease which superseded whole missives. *Held* that delivery of lease had superseded only that clause in missives which provided that lease should be entered into. All other provisions in missives collateral and therefore survived *proprio vigore*.

*Rae* v. *Middleton* 1995 SLT (Sh Ct) 60. Offer for sale provided that, where subjects had been altered, consents and certificates should wherever applicable be exhibited prior to settlement and delivered with titles. Purchaser maintained that this was collateral obligation which survived delivery of disposition. *Held* that clause was operative only up to the date of settlement and not beyond and was not saved by non-supersession clause. *Greaves* v. *Abercromby* 1989 SCLR 11 and *Porch* v. *MacLeod* 1992 SLT 661 followed.

*Spowart* v. *Wylie* 1995 GWD 23–1257. Purchaser maintained that he had no liability under a clause in the missives in terms of which, if planning permission was obtained, he would pay additional sum. He granted a standard security covering the additional sum. Missives also contained a two-year non-supersession clause which had expired. *Held* that standard security contained obligation to pay the additional sum in clear terms and was in substance self-contained. Purpose of standard security was to protect seller's position; and in terms of the missives it was clear that parties intended liability to survive beyond two-year period. (Text 28.56)

*Glazick* v. *Iyer* 1996 SCLR 270. Missives contained usual clause as to planning permission, building warrants *etc.* and non-supersession clause with two-year time-limit. Transaction settled and disposition delivered. It then turned out that building alterations had previously been carried out without building warrant which was clearly in breach of consents clause. *Held* that, since disposition in its terms incorporated antecedent contract by specific reference, it then formed part of the conveyance and as such became 'sole measure of the rights and liabilities'. (Text 28.23, 28.53)

*Callander* v. *Midlothian District Council* 1996 SCLR 955. Missives of sale and purchase provided, *inter alia*, for right of access. Seller argued that missives provision as to access, not repeated in disposition, was superseded thereby. *Held* that access provision remained enforceable and was not too unspecific to be implemented. Not superseded by disposition, being collateral; and it was not an obligation personal to the parties but in the nature of a servitude. (Text 11.5, 28.53)

*Aberdeen Rubber Ltd.* v. *Knowles & Sons (Fruiterers) Ltd.* 1995 SLT 870. *Held*, in House of Lords on the non-supersession point, that additional area of land was conveyed patently by mistake and formed no part of antecedent contract. Accordingly, non-supersession not in point. (Text 28.33)

### 28.60  Matrimonial Homes (Family Protection) (Scotland) Act 1981

*Verity* v. *Fenner* 1993 SCLR 223. In the case of cohabiting couples under s.18 of 1981 Act, primary condition to establish is that cohabitation existed at date when Court considered the case.

*Armour* v. *Anderson* 1994 SLT 1127. Discussion on Matrimonial Homes (Family Protection) (Scotland) Act 1981 s. 18 (3) as it applies to cohabiting couples. By the time action raised parties no longer cohabiting and *held* by the Sheriff Principal to be outwith provisions of Act. On appeal, decision of Sheriff Principal reversed, holding that, since parties were cohabiting when relevant events occurred, application was competent.

### 28.63 Time of the essence

*Toynar Ltd.* v. *R & A Properties (Fife) Ltd* 1989 GWD 2–92. Discussion on effect of making time of essence of contract, and then giving time to pay. (Text 28.94)

*Ford Sellar Morris Properties plc* v. *E. W. Hutchison Ltd.* 1990 SC 34. Where time-limit is specified for implement of contractual condition, whether suspensive or resolutive, and is made of essence of contract, time-limit must be adhered to, failing which either party may resile. (Text 28.94)

*Ahmed* v. *Akhtar* 1995 GWD 24–1287. Contract for sale of business included provision for assignation of lease of premises from which business conducted. 'Material condition' that landlords gave consent to assignation. When landlords had failed to give consent by date of entry, purchaser withdrew from bargain. Seller argued that withdrawal unlawful. Action dismissed. Rule that time is not of essence is a rule of sale of heritable property. This was sale of business conducted from leased premises, and rule did not apply. Thus it was not necessary for contract to provide in terms that obtaining of consent by date of entry was of essence. Words of contract supported view that time ought to be of essence. Hence purchaser justified in rescinding.

### 28.64 The *actio quanti minoris* clause

(See also cases under paras. 28.24 and 28.96)

*Hayes* v. *Robinson* 1984 SLT 300. Purchaser, after completion, sought to retain subjects and claim damages for breach of collateral obligation. *Held* premature to consider whether claim *quanti minoris*. (Text 28.101)

*Neilson* v. *Barratt* 1987 GWD 13–467. Discussion as to whether claim for damages in circumstances amounted to *actio quanti minoris*.

*McKillop* v. *Mutual Securities Ltd.* 1945 SC 166. Combined sale and building contract; distinguished in *Winston* v. *Patrick*. (Text 28.21, 28.22, 28.25, 28.99, 28.101)

*Fallis* v. *Brown* 1987 GWD 13–466. Discussion on claim arising out of damage between completion of contract and date of settlement, where missives contained clause requiring seller to maintain non-supersession clause. (Text 28.52)

*Fortune* v. *Fraser* 1996 SLT 878. See 28.24 above. (Text 28.23, 28.64)

*Colgan* v. *Mooney* 1994 GWD 1–43. See 28.24 above.

### 28.65 Time-limit for acceptance

*Effold Properties Ltd.* v. *Sprot* 1979 SLT (Notes) 84. Condition as to time-limit in qualified acceptance did not prevent withdrawal of acceptance within the time-limit.

### 28.67 Let property – vacant possession

*Lothian & Border Farmers* v. *McCutcheon* 1952 SLT 450. Tenant in occupation under lease. (Text 12.9, 28.41)

*Stuart* v. *Lort-Phillips* 1977 SC 244. Provision for 'actual occupation' entitles purchaser to insist on vacant possession of whole subjects. (Text 28.41, 28.90)

### 28.75 Intended development

(See also paras. 28.29 and 28.51 above.)

*Gordon District Council* v. *Wimpey Homes Holdings Ltd.* 1989 SLT 141. Where contract contains suspensive conditions as to planning permission *etc.*, it is normally implied that parties will act reasonably in determining whether or not condition has been implemented. (Text 28.78)

*John H. Wyllie* v. *Ryan Industrial Fuels Ltd.* 1989 SLT 302. In the ordinary case each party to contract entitled to assume that the other will act reasonably with particular reference to suspensive conditions. (Text 26.4, 28.78)

*McKay* v. *Leigh Estates (Scotland) Ltd.* 1987 GWD 16–609. Missives contained condition that purchaser should receive satisfactory report on suitability of ground for development.

Purchaser did not adequately investigate ground and then purportedly resiled. Purchaser ordained to lead proof to establish that decision to resile was reasonable. (Text 28.28, 28.78)

*Burnside* v. *James Harrison (Developers) Ltd.* 1989 GWD 11–468. Provision in contract that either party may resile if completion certificate not obtained by specified date binding and enforceable even if certificate later obtained. (Text 28.30, 28.94)

*Elwood* v. *Ravensele Properties Ltd.* 1991 SLT 44. Sellers in contract undertook to use all reasonable endeavours to obtain consent. *Held* competent for purchaser to seek order from Court ordaining sellers to raise action against landlord seeking to procure consent.

## 28.79 Purchase of public sector houses and the right to buy

*Dundee District Council* v. *Anderson* 1994 SLT 46. Tenants' rights to purchase a dwelling-house provided with facilities specially designed or adapted for persons of pensionable age or disabled persons; call/alarm system installed but not connected. *Held* that correct approach to the 1987 Act s. 61 was to consider whether, at the material date, house satisfied statutory conditions.

*McLoughlin's CB* v. *Motherwell District Council* 1994 SLT (Lands Tr.) 31. Purchase of dwellinghouse; tenant incapax and permanently hospitalised. *Held* that tenancy not abandoned, curator could competently make application.

*Jack's Exx* v. *Falkirk District Council* 1992 SLT 5. Sheriff of opinion that ss. 72 and 73 of 1987 Act in effect incorporated into missives. *Held* further that executrix of deceased tenant who had contracted to buy but died before delivery of disposition entitled to implement of bargain. Discussion of concept of ownership arising under missives as opposed to mere *jus crediti.*

*Glasgow District Council* v. *Doyle* 1993 SLT 604. *Held* on appeal that legislation envisaged the tenants becoming proprietors of the same subjects which they *held* on lease as tenants and that local authority had no discretion to vary extent of the ground in tenancy except in unusual cases where local authority might find themselves incapable of making offer to sell the whole.

*Drummond* v. *Dundee District Council* 1993 GWD 26–1637. Discussion on level of discount where continuous occupation had been interrupted.

*Lamont* v. *Glenrothes Development Corporation* 1993 SLT (Lands Tr.) 2. Onus lies on tenant to show that she has secure tenancy to entitle her to right to buy.

*McLuskey* v. *Scottish Homes* 1993 SLT (Lands Tr.) 17. Tenant maintained that potential liability, under existing deeds of conditions, to contribute towards maintenance of common parts unreasonable. *Held* that, in circumstances, conditions reasonable and tenant's contention rejected. Tribunal made observations on disapplying 1979 Act s. 17 in case of houses built for letting, some of which were being sold.

*Henderson* v. *Glasgow District Council* 1994 SLT 263. Under earlier procedure, Lands Tribunal had found that tenant had right to purchase and ordered local authority to issue appropriate papers. Offer duly made subject to right of pre-emption but no bargain concluded. Thereafter, Lands Tribunal served on tenant offer to sell under s. 63 (2) without reference to pre-emption. Offer accepted. On appeal, Inner House *held* Tribunal correct in issuing offer without reference to right of pre-emption.

*Ross & Cromarty District Council* v. *Patience* 1995 SLT 1292. *Held* by Lord Marnoch that superior entitled to right of pre-emption on right-to-buy offer. Decision reversed in House of Lords – see 1997 1997 SLT (HL) 463. (Text 33.13)

*Clydebank District Council* v. *The Keeper* 1994 SLT (Lands Tr.) 2. *Held* that sale of dwelling-house purchased under right-to-buy legislation by executors of deceased purchaser discharged obligations of deceased to repay discount. (Text 28.85)

*Cumbernauld & Kilsyth District Council* 1993 SLT (Lands Tr.) 51. Dispute arose between adjoining proprietors as to how much should be included in the offer to sell.

*Fernie* v. *Strathclyde Regional Council* 1994 SLT (Lands Tr.) 11. *Held* that in application under s. 68(4) Tribunal not restricted to deciding whether ground of refusal valid, but could competently consider other reasons why tenant had no right to purchase.

*Dundee District Council* v. *Kelly* 1994 SLT 1268. Discussion on meaning of the term 'succession' under 1987 Act s. 61(5). *Held* that 'succession' not limited to succession on death. But occupation by child of tenant during tenancy which ended before 1980 did not count for continuous occupation.

*Beggs* v. *Kilmarnock & Loudoun District Council* 1995 GWD 12–687. Local authority tenant opted to purchase his house but Lands Tribunal refused his application to find that he had been a secure tenant since 1990. Immediately prior to his application in 1992, tenant given six years' imprisonment. His furniture and personal effects, however, remained in house, and he continued to pay rent. He received housing benefit. His aunt occupied the house in 1992 and removed at the request of council. On release from prison tenant returned to house and argued that he had been only temporarily absent and was technically 'in occupation'. Council argued that, to qualify as secure tenant, the house should have been his only or principal home. Case referred to Lands Tribunal. See further proceedings below.

*Beggs* v. *Kilmarnock & Loudoun District Council* 1996 SLT 461. Follow up to preceding case. Lands Tribunal refused tenant's application on the basis that occupation for this purpose required physical presence in house. Tenant appealed to Court of Session, arguing that, in all the circumstances, he was 'in possession' and intended to return as soon as released, which meant he was in possession. Court of Session upheld appeal.

*Waverley Housing Trust Ltd.* v. *Roxburgh District Council* 1995 SLT (Lands Tr.) 2. Trust applied to purchase two houses owned by the district council with no change of tenancy. Council offered to sell on condition that, subject to statutory rights of occupying tenants, houses were not to be sold with vacant possession until they had first been offered to council at equivalent value of tenanted property. *Held* that, in absence of evidence that pre-emption clause depressed value placed on the two houses, Lands Tribunal could not assume that this was so and condition did not prevent giving good and marketable title, but right of pre-emption in this form would contravene 1988 Act s. 63 and so should be struck out. (Text 33.13)

*McKay* v. *Dundee District Council* 1996 SLT (Lands Tr.) 9. Tenant of local authority, being undoubtedly a secure tenant, sought to purchase her house. Landlords failed to issue offer to sell or a refusal in good time. Accordingly, the tenant referred to Lands Tribunal. While case was before Tribunal, local authority obtained order for ejection and then argued that tenant was no longer entitled to purchase, not being secure tenant any more. *Held* that exercise of right to buy occurred when tenant accepted offer to sell. To exercise that right, tenant had to remain secure until such offer was received and accepted. That was not the position here and accordingly tenant was disqualified.

*McLean* v. *Cunninghame District Council* 1996 SLT (Lands Tr.) 2. Husband and wife, joint secure tenants, applied to purchase. Wife had longer period of occupation as wife of former husband during his tenancy of a public sector house. *Held* that her period of occupancy, being longer, counted in calculating discount.

*Hamilton* v. *Glasgow District Council* 1996 SLT (Lands Tr.) 14. Wife succeeded husband as tenant of public sector house. Later, son became joint tenant along with her. She died and son became sole tenant. He applied to purchase. Local authority offered discount of sum calculated from date when he became joint tenant. Son appealed. *Held* that son not entitled to discount in respect of occupation during the tenancy of his father.

*Kennedy* v. *Hamilton District Council* 1995 SCLR 980. Lands Tribunal rejected application to purchase council house on grounds that, at date of application, house formed one of a group of houses with special facilities. Tenant appealed but was refused.

*Houston* v. *East Kilbride Dev. Corp.* 1995 SLT (Lands Tr.) 12. Lands Tribunal allowed application by tenant to purchase her house. Decided that house had not been provided with facilities specified in s. 61(4)(a) of Housing (Scotland) Act 1987.

**28.89   Resulting obligations of seller and purchaser**

*Inglis* v. *Lowrie* 1990 SLT (Sh Ct) 60. Concluded formal missives for sale and purchase of heritage cannot be discharged by oral agreement.

*Rockcliffe Estates plc* v. *Co-operative Wholesale Society Ltd* 1994 SLT 592. Reminder that parties are presumed by implication to act reasonably, and not capriciously, in relation to contract conditions. Compare *Hutton* v. *Barrett* para. 28.96 below. (Text 28.28, 28.37, 28.59)

**28.90 Seller's obligations – to deliver a valid disposition**
(For title, possession, and searches *etc.*, see above)
*Leith Heritages Co.* v. *Edinburgh & Leith Glass Co.* (1876) 3 R 789. General principles. (Text 28.98)
*Anderson* v. *Lambie* 1954 SC (HL) 43. Reduction of disposition as erroneous; effect on prior contract. (Text 28.98)
*Russell's Exr.* v. *Russell's Exrs.* 1983 SLT 385. If formal contract does not properly reflect intentions of both parties, and that can be proved, Court will correct error.
*Johnston's Trs.* v. *Kinloch* 1925 SLT 124. Terms of description to be inserted in disposition.
*Equitable Loan Co.* v. *Storie* 1972 SLT (Notes) 20. Disposition not conveying whole subjects sold.
*Hay* v. *Aberdeen Corporation* 1909 SC 554. Sale of 'right and interest'; seller bound to dispone land.
*Cowan* v. *Stewart* (1872) 10 M 735. Servitude to be inserted in disposition.
*Mackenzie* v. *Neill* 37 SLR 666. Seller must grant absolute warrandice.
*Young* v. *McKellar Ltd.* 1909 SC 1340. Warrandice following articles of roup.
*Fraser* v. *Cox* 1938 SC 506. Warrandice not reflecting terms of antecedent contract. (Text 11.8)
*Porteous* v. *Henderson* (1898) 25 R 563. Writs.

**28.91 Purchaser's obligations – payment of price**
*Rodger (Builders) Ltd.* v. *Fawdry* 1950 SC 483. Date of payment. (Text 28.94, 28.97, 28.98, 33.59, 33.61, 33.78, 35.10)
*Prestwick Cinema Co.* v. *Gardiner* 1951 SC 98. Interest on unpaid price. (Text 28.39)
*Bowie* v. *Semple's Exrs.* 1978 SLT (Sh Ct) 9. Purchaser not in possession; interest. (Text 28.39, 28.90)
*Chapman's Trs.* v. *Anglo-Scottish Group Services Ltd.* 1980 SLT (Sh Ct) 27. Delay in payment of price; whether sellers entitled to claim damages or merely interest.
*Tiffney* v. *Bachurzewski* 1985 SLT 165. Seller not entitled to interest unless purchaser actually in possession; interest not due *ex mora*. (Text 28.39, 28.63)
*Davidson* v. *Tilburg Ltd.* 1991 GWD 2–115; 1991 GWD 18–1109. Purchaser cannot be required to settle contract of sale and purchase of heritage except in exchange for delivery of disposition. Sellers not entitled to resile on account of purchaser's refusal to settle on this ground unless sellers themselves in position to settle, notwithstanding apparently contradictory provision in missives. (Text 28.90)

**28.92 Breach of contract – both parties in breach**
*Mason* v. *A. & R. Robertson & Black* 1993 SLT 773. Complex case involving breach or alleged breach on both sides and professional negligence. *Held*: that letter of obligation was contract collateral to missives, to be read in context thereof; that pursuer by taking decree had not irrevocably elected because, as a matter of law, missives were not automatically terminated by decree; and accordingly pursuer's averment that letter of obligation became ineffective was irrelevant. Subsequently, decree of dismissal granted. See 1.3 above (Text 28.102)

**28.93 Default by the purchaser – seller's remedies**
*Carter* v. *Lornie* (1890) 18 R 353. Action for implement.
*British Railways Board* v. *Birrell* 1971 SLT (Notes) 17. Action for payment.
*Muir & Black* v. *Nee* 1981 SLT (Sh Ct) 68. Action for payment – whether purchaser's obligations extinguished by the short negative prescription.
*Inveresk Paper Co. Ltd.* v. *Pembury Machinery Co. Ltd.* 1972 SLT (Notes) 63. Rescission. (Text 28.94)
*Rodger (Builders) Ltd.* v. *Fawdry* 1950 SC 483. Circumstances not justifying rescission. Disposition to second purchaser reduced. (Text 28.94, 28.97, 28.98, 33.59, 33.61, 33.78, 35.10)
*Grant* v. *Ullah* 1987 SLT 639. Discussion on quantum of damages on breach by purchaser. (Text 28.95)

*Johnstone* v. *Harris* 1977 SC 365. Rescission; seller's duty to mitigate damages. (Text 29.44, 28.95)

*Commercial Bank* v. *Beal* (1890) 18 R 80. Forfeiture of deposit. (Text 28.38)

*Reid* v. *Campbell* 1958 SLT (Sh Ct) 45. Forfeiture of instalments paid to account of price. (Text 28.40)

*Geo. Packman & Sons* v. *Dunbar's Trs.* 1977 SLT 140. Impossibility, delay; seller entitled to rescind without notice. (Text 28.94)

*Robson* v. *Inglis* 1990 GWD 2–92. Time-limit in non-supersession clause *held* not to apply to recovery of damages by seller following on breach by purchaser. (Text 28.56, 28.93)

*Atlas Assurance Co. Ltd.* v. *Dollar Land Holdings plc,* 1993 SLT 892. Actings of parties, in particular delay in enforcing contract, may imply that right to resile has been waived. (Text 28.94)

*University of Strathclyde (Properties) Ltd.* v. *Fleeting Organisations Ltd* 1992 GWD 14–822. Claim for damages founded on clause in missives but not in disposition; non-supersession clause limited to 18 months after settlement. *Held* that action raised outwith that period was out of time. (Text 28.56, 28.59)

*Mills* v. *Findlay* 1994 SCLR 397. Purchaser defaulted and sellers rescinded and resold, then raised action of damages against defaulting purchaser for, *inter alia*, solatium, and each awarded £1,100. On appeal to Sheriff Principal, solatium reduced to £500 for each pursuer. (Text 28.95)

*Hall* v. *McWilliam* 1993 GWD 23–1457. See 28.52 above. (Text 28.52)

*Cumming* v. *Brown* 1993 SCLR 707. *Held* that, while the seller could have resiled in interval between date of entry and date of tender by purchaser, he had not done so and was therefore bound to proceed with bargain. Decree of specific implement granted. (Text 28.94)

*Charisma Properties Ltd.* v. *Grayling* 1996 SCLR 918. Missives of sale and purchase provided that it was a material condition that price was paid by certain date and time. If price was not paid within 21 days, seller could treat purchaser as in material breach and rescind on giving prior notice to that effect. On stipulated date, no payment had been made. Seller's solicitors sent letter purportedly giving notice that the missives were rescinded with immediate effect. Purchaser's solicitors responded by refusing to accept that intimation on footing that seller not entitled immediately to resile, and prior notice required. *Held* that contract itself declared breach material and no further indulgence beyond stipulated 21-day period was necessary. (Text 28.94)

### 28.95  Default by the purchaser – measure of damages

*Lloyds Bank plc* v. *Bamberger* 1993 SCLR 727. Missives contained standard clause for payment of interest if not paid on date of entry. Purchasers defaulted and sellers resiled. Sellers claimed that purchasers were liable for interest at rate specified in interest clause over period from due date of payment to date of resiling. Sellers *held* not entitled to interest. There was a total failure to pay the price, following on which sellers had rescinded and resulting entitlement was damages, not contractually stipulated rate. (Text 28.39, 28.59)

*Palmer* v. *Beck* 1993 SLT 485. *Held* that (a) if there is no actual eviction, there is no claim under warrandice; (b) if claim is for fraudulent misrepresentation, solatium is element in damages; (c) not so if claim is under warrandice. (Text 11.10, 12.8, 28.95)

*Colgan* v. *Mooney* 1994 GWD 1–43. See 28.24 above.

*King* v. *Moore* 1993 SLT 1117. Award of damages for purchasers' failure to implement contract based on difference between (a) the contract price of two years ago and (b) present value of subjects about £100,000 less plus interest.

### 28.96  Default by the seller
Time for implement

*Gilfillan* v. *Cadell & Grant* (1893) 21 R 269. Valid title tendered too late.

*Kelman* v. *Barr's Tr.* (1878) 5 R 816. Valid title tendered too late.

*Campbell* v. *McCutcheon* 1963 SC 505. Where defect fundamental, purchaser not obliged to give time. (Text 28.43, 28.68, 28.97)

*Carter* v. *Lornie* (1890) 18 R 353. Circumstances in which purchaser bound to take title tendered late.

*Kinnear* v. *Young* 1936 SLT 574. Defect incurable; purchaser having taken possession and given time still entitled to resile.

*Rodger (Builders) Ltd.* v. *Fawdry* 1950 SC 483. Price not tendered at date of entry. (Text 28.94, 28.97, 28.98, 33.59, 33.61, 33.78, 35.10)

*Burns* v. *Garscadden* (1901) 8 SLT 321. Circumstances in which seller *held* not to have given sufficient notice to defaulting purchaser of intention to rescind and resell.

*Macdonald* v. *Newall* (1898) 1 F 68. Purchaser's objection to title made too late. (Text 28.33, 33.50)

*Crofts* v. *Stewart's Trs.* 1927 SC (HL) 65. Instalment purchase; no objection to title until after instalment paid.

*Morrison* v. *Gray* 1932 SC 712. Purchaser *held* not barred from objecting until disposition delivered.

*Speevak* v. *Robson* 1949 SLT (Notes) 39. Seller contractually bound to effect alterations to subjects by date of entry; alterations not completed. Seller *held* to be in breach and liable in damages; but purchaser not entitled to resile. (Text 28.41)

*Boland & Co. Ltd.* v. *Dundas Trs.* 1975 SLT (Notes) 80. Suspensive condition not within power of contracting party to purify. (Text 28.94)

*Macdonald* v. *Scott* 1981 SC 75. Obligation to deliver conveyance of heritable property not imprescriptible. (Text 33.79)

*Burnside* v. *James Harrison (Developers) Ltd.* 1989 GWD 11–468. Provision in contract that either party may resile if completion certificate not obtained by specified date is binding and enforceable even if certificate later obtained. (Text 28.30, 28.94)

*Ford Sellar Morris Properties plc* v. *E. W. Hutchison Ltd.* 1990 SC 34. Where date is fixed in contract for purification of condition, that date must be strictly adhered to. *Boland & Co. Ltd.*, above followed. (Text 28.94)

*Stewart's Exrs.* v. *Stewart* 1993 SLT 440. Opinion that mere contractual obligation to grant disposition not imprescriptible under 1973 Act Schedule 3(h). Schedule 3(h) applies to personal titles which are imprescriptible. (Text 33.79)

*Burrull Scotland Ltd.* v. *Keith* 1994 SLT 1343. Obligations of seller under missives are obligations relating to land, as such are subject to 20-year prescription, not five year prescription. (Text 33.51, 33.79)

*Wright* v. *Frame* 1992 GWD 8–447. Obligation relating to land, for the purposes of Prescription Act 1973, falls under the long negative prescription, not five-year prescription, following *Burrull* above. (Text 33.51, 33.79)

Purchaser's remedies
(See also 28.64 above)

*Smith* v. *Soeder* (1895) 23 R 60. Title not marketable; rescission. (Text 28.43)

*Campbell* v. *McCutcheon* 1963 SC 505. Undisclosed mineral reservation; rescission. (Text 28.47)

*Louttit's Trs.* v. *Highland Ry. Co.* (1892) 19 R 791. Remedies of purchaser after settlement. (Text 28.43, 28.98)

*Welsh* v. *Russell* (1894) 21 R 769. Remedies of purchaser after settlement. (Text 12.9, 28.43)

*Fielding* v. *Newell* 1987 SLT 530. Discussion on quantum of damages on breach by seller.

*McKillop* v. *Mutual Securities Ltd.* 1945 SC 166. Retention and damages. (Text 28.21, 28.22, 28.25, 28.99, 28.101)

*Bradley* v. *Scott* 1966 SLT (Sh Ct) 25. Retention and damages. (Text 28.21, 28.22)

*Hayes* v. *Robinson* 1984 SLT 300. Retention and damages; whether *quanti minoris*. (Text 28.101)

*Neilson* v. *Barratt* 1987 GWD 13–467. Discussion as to whether a claim for damages amounted to *actio quanti minoris*.

*Steuart's Trs.* v. *Hart* (1875) 3 R 192. Circumstances justifying *restitutio* after settlement.

*Angus* v. *Bryden* 1992 SLT 884. Disposition ostensibly implemented missives but disponer alleged error. Lord Cameron expressed opinion that unintentional essential error known to and taken advantage of by other party implied bad faith for which law provided remedy.

*Steuart's Trs.*, above, applied; *Spook Erection (Northern) Ltd.* v. *Kaye* 1990 SLT 676 not followed. (Text 28.33)

*Hamilton* v. *Western Bank of Scotland* (1861) 23 D 1033. Circumstances justifying *restitutio* after settlement.

*Stewart* v. *Kennedy* (1890) 17 R (HL) 1. Specific implement; general observations.

*McKellar* v. *Dallors Ltd.* 1928 SC 503. Specific implement.

*Mackay* v. *Campbell* 1967 SC (HL) 53. Specific implement.

*Hoey* v. *Butler* 1975 SC 87. Specific implement and damages.

*Speevak* v. *Robson* 1949 SLT (Notes) 39. Purchaser *held* not entitled to resile on breach by seller but awarded damages.

*Plato* v. *Newman* 1950 SLT (Notes) 30. Specific implement, seller claiming implement impossible.

*Boag Petitioner* 1967 SC 322. Seller disappeared; clerk of court empowered to execute disposition. (Text 28.97)

*Mowbray* v. *Mathieson* 1989 GWD 6–267. Purchaser had been in possession for over two years and had already sued for implement; no longer open to him to rescind. (Text 28.98)

*Tainsh* v. *McLaughlin* 1990 SLT (Sh Ct) 102. Discussion on measure of damages. (Text 28.95, 29.31)

*Caledonian Property Group Ltd.* v. *Queensferry Property Group Ltd.* 1992 SLT 738. Discussion on quantum of damages (anticipated capital loss and interest) on default by the seller after settlement. (Text 28.98)

*Martone* v. *Zani* 1992 GWD 32–1903. Decree in an action of implement; clerk of court authorised to sign disposition. (Text, 28.33, 28.97)

*Parker* v. *O'Brien* 1992 SLT (Sh Ct) 31. *Held* that (a) condition in missives fell to be construed as future promise to grant warranty and was not a collateral obligation; and (b) mere warranty is nothing more than that, whether present or future, and in particular does not oblige warrantor to do anything. In the result, any claim for damages based on such warranty is illegitimate attempt to use *actio quanti minoris* in circumstances which do not support it. (Text 29.31)

*Hutton* v. *Barrett* 1994 GWD 37–2188. Following on concluded missives, which provided for preliminary variation of seller's title, seller then produced title duly varied, but purchaser demurred at new burdens imposed, on footing that they materially diminished value and prevented parking, which in turn rendered planning permission valueless. *Held* that purchaser entitled to resile without proof and that question of his acting reasonably did not arise since seller clearly could not perform his obligation.

*MacDougall* v. *MacDougall's Exrs.* 1994 SLT 1178. See 28.46 above. (Text 28.46, 31.26)

*McLennan* v. *Warner & Co.* 1996 GWD 22–1281. In terms of titles, right of access provided for limited purposes by path to be made, six feet wide, stretching from back of building. Owner of upper flat subsequently built garage over access without consent. *Held* that seller in breach; that purchaser could not be required to implement bargain and take entry pending resolution of title problem; and, when title problem later resolved, seller not entitled unilaterally to seek to revive contract already earlier validly terminated on this ground. (Text 28.97)

## 28.99  Collateral obligations
(See also cases under 28.24, 28.53 and 28.96)

*Taylor* v. *McLeod* 1990 SLT 194. Obligation to repair defects in lift *held* collateral. (Text 28.101)

*Bourton* v. *Claydon* 1990 SLT (Sh Ct) 7. Obligation on seller to bear cost of repairs to central heating *held* collateral.

*Hardwick* v. *Gebbie* 1991 SLT 258. Circumstances where obligation to build house *held* to be intended as continuing obligation, notwithstanding delivery of disposition but only *quoad* matters not reasonably discoverable on inspection. Remedy was damages for breach of contract, not *actio quanti minoris*. (Text 28.24, 28.25, 28.101)

*Porch* v. *MacLeod* 1992 SLT 661. Missives provided that all necessary consents *etc.* had been obtained for any work on subjects, 'and satisfactory evidence to substantiate this will be exhibited ... and delivered at ... entry'. Missives also contained non-supersession clause, not repeated in subsequent disposition. *Held* that the warranty clause contained warranty as to condition at date of missives and 'a personal and collateral obligation on the sellers' to produce satisfactory evidence, but that warranty and obligation ancillary thereto (*i.e.* the obligation to produce evidence) had both terminated on delivery of disposition in implement. (Text 28.59, 28.90, 28.101, 29.31)

*University of Strathclyde (Properties) Ltd.* v. *Fleeting Organisations Ltd* 1992 GWD 14–822. Where claim for damages founded on clause in missives but not in disposition and non-supersession clause was limited to 18 months after settlement, *held* that action raised outwith that period was out of time. (Text 28.56, 28.59)

*Meek* v. *Bell* 1993 GWD 20–1238. Following on concluded missives for sale and purchase of business, which involved *inter alia* lease and option to purchase, *held* that delivery of lease superseded missives only to extent that missives provided for lease being entered into in terms of agreed draft; and that all other provisions in missives were collateral and so excluded from rule in *Winston* v. *Patrick*.

*King* v. *Gebbie* 1993 SLT 512. Composite contract for sale and purchase of ground including an obligation on the seller to construct a dwellinghouse according to certain specifications. *Held* that obligation imposed in missives to give entry to house according to certain specifications *etc.* covered works carried out before and after conclusion of missives; that obligation to build *etc.* was collateral; and that missives could not be so construed as to prevent purchaser claiming damages for reasonably discoverable defects. Observed that condition in missives obliging seller to produce planning permission, building warrants and completion certificates not collateral and would be superseded by delivery of disposition. (Text 28.23)

*Rae* v. *Middleton* 1995 SLT (Sh Ct) 60. Offer for sale provided that, where subjects had been altered, consents and certificates should wherever applicable be exhibited prior to settlement and delivered with titles. Purchaser maintained that this was a collateral obligation which survived delivery of disposition. *Held* that clause operative only up to date of settlement, not beyond, and not saved by non-supersession clause. *Greaves* v. *Abercromby* and *Porch* v. *MacLeod* followed.

*Adams* v. *Whatlings plc* 1995 SCLR 185. On purchase of building plot from builder who undertook to build dwellinghouse thereon, builder, by implication, was *held* to have warranted quality of building. See 28.24 above. (Text 28.101)

## Chapter 29. The Special Disposition

### 29.1 Transmission of the feu
*Hyslop* v. *Shaw* (1863) 1 M 535. General principles.
*Morris* v. *Brisbane* (1877) 4 R 515. Effect of 1874 Act s. 4.

### 29.5 Entry with the superior
Feu disponed to singular successor
*Dundee Police Commissioners* v. *Straton* (1884) 11 R 586. Vassal and heirs bound jointly and severally; old vassal liable for future prestations.
*Marshall* v. *Callander & Trossachs Hydropathic Co. Ltd.* (1895) 22 R 954. Obligations prestable before disposition granted; continuing liability of old vassal. (Text 29.11, 29.12)
*Rankine* v. *Logie Den Land Co. Ltd.* (1902) 4 F 1074. Obligations prestable before disposition granted; continuing liability of old vassal. (Text 29.12)

Death of vassal
*Aiton* v. *Russell's Exrs.* (1889) 16 R 625. Executors renouncing succession not liable for future prestations.
*Macrae* v. *Mackenzie's Trs.* (1891) 19 R 138. Trustee renouncing succession not liable to implement conditions *ad factum praestandum*.

### 29.17 Operative clause
*George Thompson Services Ltd.* v *Moore* 1993 SLT 634. Disposition allegedly conveyed less

ground than intended. *Held* that there being no averments establishing some common intention, petition was irrelevant and there was nothing to rectify.

*Dunedin Property Management Services Ltd.* v *Glamis Property Co. Ltd.* 1993 GWD 31–2006. Argument as to meaning of 'Whytehouse Mansions' in title, with reference to common repairs. *Held* that no ambiguity in disposition, which clearly referred to tenement building alone as forming designated subjects. (Text 10.12)

*Rutherford* v *Virtue* 1993 SCLR 886. Developer failed to implement obligation to form a road but took his successor bound. Original purchaser sued developer for failing to implement the obligation but, in his action, failed correctly to specify amount of his claim for damages and action failed on procedural grounds.

### 29.18    Enforcement of conditions imposed by disposition

*Braid Hills Hotel Co.* v. *Manuels* 1909 SC 120. Condition in disposition; title of co-disponee to enforce. (Text 10.7, 29.23)

*SCWS* v. *Finnie* 1937 SC 835. Disponer must show interest to enforce.

*Dalrymple* v. *Herdman* (1878) 5 R 847. Original conditions in single feu charter held to be mutually enforceable by purchasers of parts of feu, *inter se.*

*Hill* v. *Millar* (1900) 2 F 799. Charter conditions held mutually enforceable.

*Hislop* v. *MacRitchie's Trs.* (1881) 8 R (HL) 95. Observations on mutual enforceability. (Text 10.9, 17.4, 29.21, 29.35)

*Girls School Co.* v. *Buchanan* 1958 SLT (Notes) 2. Charter conditions held not mutually enforceable. (Text 29.21)

*Williamson & Hubbard* v. *Harrison* 1970 SLT 346. Charter conditions held not mutually enforceable. (Text 29.21)

*Fergusson* v. *McCulloch* 1953 SLT (Sh Ct) 113. Charter conditions held mutually enforceable. (Text 29.21)

*Smith* v. *Taylor* 1972 SC 258. Charter conditions held mutually enforceable. (Text 17.21, 17.28, 17.30, 29.21)

*Lees* v. *North East Fife D.C.* 1987 SC 265. A plot of ground disponed for building development was subject to real conditions affecting the whole area. On subsequent subdivision on sale of the dwellinghouses, each purchaser held to have *jus quaesitum tertio* to insist on conditions. Lands Tribunal subsequently discharged a condition without compensation – 1989 SLT (Lands Tr.) 30. (Text 17.23, 29.21, 29.22, 29.23).

### 29.31    (b) Non-supersession clause

*Aberdeen Rubber Ltd.* v. *Knowles & Sons (Fruiterers) Ltd.* 1995 SLT (HL) 870 – see 28.7. (Text 28.33)

*Note*: Several other decisions on the effect of a disposition on the antecedent contract are dealt with already at 28.53 above and reference is made thereto.

### 29.34    Transmission of superiority

Form and effect of disposition

*Orr* v. *Mitchell* (1893) 20 R (HL) 27. May carry *dominium utile* of reserved minerals. (Text 29.35, 29.39)

*Ceres School Board* v. *McFarlane* (1895) 23 R 279. Carries *dominium utile* of parts previously sub-feued if prior feu charter remains unrecorded. (Text 13.5, 29.38, 29.40, 32.1, 33.57, 33.58).

*Gardner* v. *Trinity House of Leith* (1841) 3 D 534. Effect of conveyance of a bare superiority.

*Fleeming* v. *Howden* (1868) 6 M 782. Disposition of bare superiority does not carry *dominium utile* of reserved minerals.

Transmission of obligations undertaken by superior

*Durie's Trs.* v. *Earl of Elgin* (1889) 16 R 1104. Personal obligations undertaken in mere personal contract to grant charter do not transmit.

*Leith School Board* v. *Rattray's Trs.* 1918 SC 94. Failure to insert conditions.

*Jolly's Exrx.* v. *Viscount Stonehaven* 1958 SC 635. Failure to insert conditions. (Text 33.77)
*Duncan* v. *Church of Scotland General Trs.* 1941 SC 145. Obligation to repair.
*Montrose, Duke of* v. *Stewart* (1863) 1 M (HL) 25. Obligation of relief.
*Hope* v. *Hope* (1864) 2 M 670. Obligation of relief. (Text 10.9)

### 29.43  Consolidation
*Bald* v. *Buchanan* (1787) 2 RLC 210. Consolidation is not effected *confusione*. (Text 29.43, 29.46)
*Hay* v. *Paterson* 1910 SC 509. Consolidation by prescription; destination in superiority title rules.
*Park's Curator* v. *Black* (1870) 8 M 671. Effect on *dominium utile* title and destination therein. (Text 29.43)
*Glasgow* v. *Boyle* (1887) 14 R 419. Effect on *dominium utile* title and destination therein.
*Zetland* v. *Glover Incorporation of Perth* (1870) 8 M (HL) 144. Effect on pertinents of *dominium utile* title. (Text 14.7, 29.43)

### Chapter 30.  Statutory Titles

### 30.2  Adjudication in implement
*Boag, Petitioner* 1967 SC 322. Seller disappeared. Clerk of court authorised to sign disposition. (Text 28.97)
*Martone* v. *Zuni* 1992 GWD 32–1903. Decree in action of implement. Clerk of court authorised to sign disposition. (Text 28.33, 28.97)

### 30.4  Adjudication for debt
*Watson* v. *Swift & Co.'s JF* 1986 SC 55. Effect on title of decree of redeemable adjudication within the ten-year period of the legal.

### 30.5  Bankruptcy and sequestration
*Boyle's Tr.* v. *Boyle* 1988 SLT 581. Discussion on gratuitous alienations as between husband and wife in a sequestration. (Text 30.9)
*Bank of Scotland, Petitioners* 1988 SLT 690. A creditor is entitled, at common law, to challenge actings of a debtor company in making a gratuitous alienation and that right not excluded by Insolvency Act 1906, s. 242.
*Matheson's Tr.* v. *Matheson* 1992 SLT 685. A husband conveyed a dwellinghouse to his wife and claimed he was solvent, notwithstanding his subsequent sequestration. This was held to be a suitable question for proof.
*Clark's Tr., Noter* 1993 SLT 667. In special circumstances power of sale may be conferred on interim trustee.

### 30.7  Completion of title by trustee
*Alliance and Leicester Building Society* v. *Murray's Trs* 1995 SLT (Sh Ct) 77. Bankrupt acquired heritable property after the date of sequestration. The bankrupt granted a standard security in favour of the building society, and both deeds were recorded in the Register of Sasines. The court held that the property vested in the trustee in sequestration notwithstanding that the conveyance in favour of the bankrupt was granted after the date of sequestration. If the property had formed part of the bankrupt's estate at the date of sequestration it would have vested automatically in the trustee at that date. The bankrupt could not therefore grant a valid standard security. (Text 3.20, 30.7, 33.32)

### 30.9  Gratuitous alienation and unfair preferences
*Short's Tr.* v. *Chung* 1991 SLT 472. Sale at undervalue is gratuitous alienation for purposes of Bankruptcy (Scotland) Act 1985, s. 34; and reduction of the offending disposition is the appropriate remedy. (Text 13.33).

*Bank of Scotland* v. *T.A. Neilson & Co.* 1988 SCLR 487. Common law rule against gratuitous alienation applies to companies. (Text 33.67)

*Latif's Tr.* v. *Latif* 1992 GWD 14–784. Disposition granted gratuitously by husband to his wife reduced on subsequent sequestration.

*McLuckie Brothers Ltd.* v. *Newhouse Contracts Ltd.* 1993 SLT 641. Price paid for a property prior to sequestration inadequate and reduction granted.

*Stuart Eves Ltd. (In liquidation)* v. *Smiths Gore* 1993 SLT 1274. In the circumstances liquidator sufficiently averred gratuitous alienation at common law.

*MacFadyen's Tr.* v. *MacFadyen* 1994 SLT 1245. The owner of a dwellinghouse conveyed half to his mother. He was then sequestrated within the relevant period. The trustee in sequestration sought to have the disposition of the one half share reduced, not having been made for adequate consideration. The mother argued that there had been consideration – she had paid the purchase price, the running costs, and the title was in joint names of herself and her son because the bank had insisted. The arguments were rejected on the grounds that consideration, in the Bankruptcy (Scotland) Act 1985, implied something which had patrimonial worth at the time at which it was given. The disposition was reduced.

*Ashraf's Tr.* v. *Ashraf* 1994 GWD 24–1440. Argument that property had been purchased and held in trust rejected.

*Thomson* v. *MB Trustees Ltd.* 1994 GWD 32–1894. Liquidator raised action against trustees of a pension fund and a bank seeking reduction of a disposition granted by the company in favour of the pension fund. The company acquired the property by disposition dated August 1988 and recorded in March 1989. The company conveyed the subjects to the pension fund in August 1988, recorded October 1988. The liquidator averred that the company was insolvent, or the granting of the disposition rendered it insolvent, and persons associated with the company benefited as a result. The pension fund trustees argued they paid full consideration. Proof before answer was allowed. The onus of establishing consideration was with the pension fund trustees.

*Rankin* v. *Meek* 1995 SLT 526. On the winding up of a company, if a claim against a company has been discharged by an alienation made by the company within two years prior to the winding up, the alienation can be challenged and can only be upheld if made for adequate consideration.

### 30.10 Reduction

*Mulhearn* v. *Dunlop* 1929 SLT 59. Extent of protection of s. 46 of 1924 Act. (Text 30.12, 33.56)

*Grant's Tr.* v. *Grant* 1986 SC 51. Disposition granted in 1978 but not recorded in Sasines until March 1980. In August 1980, the disponer went bankrupt. Held that relevant date was date of recording, not delivery; and disposition was accordingly reduced. (Text 30.9)

*McLeod* v. *Cedar Holdings Ltd.* 1989 SLT 620. When a husband forged his wife's signature on a standard security over a dwellinghouse held in joint names, partial reduction of the security was held appropriate in order to maintain the obligation against the grantor but to release his wife therefrom. (Text 2.8, 30.11)

*Sereshky* v. *Sereshky* 1988 SLT 426. Where a signature on a power of attorney was alleged to have been forged, the onus lay on the challenger; but expert evidence was admitted to disprove authenticity and, on the basis of that and other evidence, the power of attorney was reduced as a forgery. (Text 2.8)

*Hughes* v. *McCluskie* 1991 GWD 3–177. In an action for reduction of a disposition, the principal deed must be produced.

*Leslie* v. *Leslie* 1987 SLT 232. Illustration of reduction of disposition under the Divorce (Scotland) Act 1976 (now the Family Law (Scotland) Act 1985).

*Stockton Park (Leisure) Ltd.* v. *Border Oats Ltd.* 1991 SLT 333. In special circumstances and in the exercise of its equitable jurisdiction, the court may refuse to reduce a disposition although *ex facie* reducible, but compensation is payable.

*Broadley* v. *Wilson* 1991 SLT 69. In appropriate circumstances, partial reduction only of a disposition held to be appropriate remedy. (Text 30.11)

*Matheson's Tr.* v. *Matheson* 1992 SLT 685. A husband conveyed a dwellinghouse to his wife and claimed he was solvent notwithstanding his subsequent sequestration. This was held to be a suitable question for proof.

*Angus* v. *Bryden* 1992 SLT 884. Missives included sea fishings in subjects of sale, but Lord Cameron held that as a matter of construction, it was intended that the river fishings only be included. (Text 28.33)

*Aberdeen Rubber Ltd.* v. *Knowles & Sons (Fruiterers) Ltd.* 1995 SLT (HL) 870. An offer was made to purchase four areas of ground. Subsequently informal letters passed between the agents, one referring to the fact that it was intended that a fifth area be included. The offer was met by a qualified acceptance which was accepted *de plano*. Disposition conveyed all five areas. Sellers sought reduction on ground that the fifth area not mentioned in missives. House of Lords found no element of common error had been established. (Text 28.33)

*Stirling* v. *Bartlett* 1992 SC 523. Partial reduction of a disposition which exceeded the extent of the subjects sold was appropriate. (Text 8.9)

*Dougherty* v. *MacLeod* 1993 GWD 39–2599. Disposition in favour of mother and daughter contained a special disposition in favour of the survivor. Another daughter sought to have disposition reduced on ground that the mother had not intended there to be a survivorship destination. The action failed.

*MacDougall* v. *MacDougall's Exrs.* 1994 SLT 1178. This case involved a challenge to the validity of a will; the granting of a Charter of Novodamus in favour of the alleged heir-at-law; and completion of title. Could the disponee from the wrong heir defend this title against an action of reduction brought by the true heir within the prescriptive period? The court held that completion of title by someone not the true heir is worthless in defence of a challenge by the true heir, however the mistake arose. This applies against the wrong heir as against *bona fide* third parties. The Charter of Novodamus fell to be reduced together with a disposition in favour of a purchaser for value. (Text 28.46, 31.26)

*Bain* v. *Bain* 1994 GWD 7–410. A proprietor who had personal right, but no title to heritable property sold it to a purchaser but died before making up title and conveying it to the purchaser. A heritable creditor sought to make up title and obtained a disposition from two members of the family which he recorded. At the time of recording the disposition, the disponee was aware of the previous sale by the beneficial owner and the subsequent proceedings by which the purchaser sought to implement the missives. *Held* that in these circumstances the recorded disposition fell to be reduced under the offside goal rule in *Rodger Builders Ltd.* v. *Fawdry* 1950 SC 483.

*Gordaviran Ltd.* v. *Clydesdale Bank plc* 1994 SCLR 248. A debtor challenged the sufficiency of the advertisement by the creditor on the exercise of a power of sale. *Held* that s. 25 of the 1970 Act confers no right on the debtor to require the creditor to demonstrate that he has fulfilled his duties, and so interim interdict of the proposed sale was refused. (Text 22 33)

*Dunlop & Son's JF* v. *Armstrong* 1995 SLT 645. The judicial factor appointed to the sequestrated estate of a firm sought to sell its heritable property which was subject to a standard security. Members of the family manipulated the standard security by clearing an assignation immediately prior to the appointment. They then sought to block the sale. Held that the judicial factor, as an officer of the court, had given an undertaking which fully secured the interests of the holder of the standard security, and on a balance of convenience he should be entitled to sell.

*Johnstone & Clark (Engineers) Ltd.* v. *Graham* 1994 SCLR 1100. Discharge of a standard security wrongly granted on a misunderstanding on the part of the solicitors. There was a subsequent sequestration and the discharge was challenged by the trustees. Proof before answer was allowed on the basis that, in a reduction, proof of error could be led by parole, and in this case the error was essential.

*McCabe* v. *Skipton Building Society* 1994 SC 467. A standard security was granted by a husband and wife. The husband acted fraudulently in obtaining a further advance. The wife's action for reduction was dismissed.

*Mumford* v. *Bank of Scotland; Smith* v. *Bank of Scotland* 1996 SLT 392. Two partners in the same firm fraudulently obtained loans on security from the bank. In one case the property was in joint names and the wife signed at the request of the husband. In the other case the wife signed a consent under the Matrimonial Homes (Family Protection) (Scotland) Act 1981. Both wives argued they had been induced to sign by their husbands on fraudulent misrepresentations. Neither wife had been separately advised. *Held*, except in the case of agency, the law of Scotland did not confer constructive notice simply because of surrounding circumstances; and so, in the absence of actual knowledge on the part of the bank, the bank had no implied duty to explain to each wife the nature of the transaction or the consequences. Reversed on appeal to the House of Lords. (Text 20.1)

*Sanderson's Trs.* v. *Ambion Scotland Ltd.* 1994 SLT 645. Where a standard security is assigned the form of assignation must conform as nearly as may be to the statutory form but not necessarily verbatim, and the standard security so assigned may secure both original and further advances by the assignee if that is covered by the agreement.

*Cameron* v. *Lightheart* 1996 SLT 1038. An application for reduction of a disposition granted 10 years previously by L in favour of C's husband, H, and subsequent disposition from H to X. The first title was a disposition in favour of C and L as trustees for a firm in which C and L were the partners. C argued that this disposition had been granted without her consent. The disposition contained the proviso that L and C and their successors in office were entitled to sell the subjects without limitation of anything contained in it, or otherwise dispose of the subjects in whole or in part by themselves or herself alone as if they or she were absolute beneficial owners and without consent of the other partners. The court refused to reduce the disposition. (Text 3.22)

*Short's Tr.* v. *Keeper of the Registers of Scotland* 1996 SLT (HL) 166. A trustee in sequestration obtained a decree of reduction of a disposition as a gratuitous alienation. The subjects had, however, been registered as being in an operational area, and the gratuitous disponee had registered title. While that title, in Sasines, would have been open to reduction under the 1985 Act and the decree of reduction could have been recorded under the 1924 Act, the Court of Session (upheld by the House of Lords in this reference) held that a decree of reduction was not registrable in the Land Register. For more details see 13.16 above. (Text 13.13, 13.35, 29.9, 30.10, 33.67)

*Frost* v. *Unity Trust Bank plc* 1996 GWD 14–813. This case, involving allegations of misrepresentation, concerned an attempted reduction of a standard security. The pursuer failed to sustain relevant averments and the action was dismissed.

### 30.14 Rectification

*Shaw* v. *Wm Grant (Minerals) Ltd.* 1989 SLT 121. Requirements of rectification provisions in s. 8 of Law Reform (Miscellaneous Provisions) (Scotland) Act 1985 discussed.

*MAC Electrical & Heating Engineers Ltd.* v. *Calscot Electrical Distributors Ltd.* 1989 SCLR 498. Discussion on relevancy of averments in petition for rectification.

*Oliver* v. *Gaughan* 1990 GWD 22–1247. Circumstances in which an order granted rectifying disposition as disconform to missives.

*Bank of Scotland* v. *Graham's Tr.* 1993 SLT 252. A standard security, imperfectly completed, can nonetheless be rectified under the 1985 Act, s. 8, even although the defects were *in substantialibus.*

*Rehman* v. *Ahmad* 1993 SLT 741. A dispute between two partners. Lord Penrose, in a lengthy judgment, held that there had to be proof of agreement and of consensus independent of and prior to the document intended to give effect to it; and there had to be proof that the document failed to express accurately the common intention.

*George Thompson Services Ltd.* v. *Moore* 1993 SLT 634. Following the conclusion of missives, a disposition was delivered which the purchaser later maintained to be incorrect. He sued for rectification. The action was dismissed on the basis that, to rectify a disposition, a prior agreement had to be founded on disclosing the common intention which it was alleged the disposition did not reflect.

*Angus* v. *Bryden* 1992 SLT 884. Held that missives of sale and purchase of salmon fishings were intended to be, as a matter of construction, restricted to river fishings only and not to include sea fishings, although these were included in the express terms of the missives. Reduction and rectification under the 1985 Act were discussed. (Text 28.33)

*Aberdeen Rubber Ltd.* v. *Knowles & Sons (Fruiterers) Ltd.* 1995 SLT 870 (HL). A offered to purchase four areas of ground. Informal letters passed between the agents. One mentioned that the offer had been intended to cover a fifth area of ground not mentioned. The offer was met by a qualified acceptance and the purchasers concluded the bargain *de plano*. The disposition conveyed all five areas. The seller sought reduction on the basis that a fifth area was conveyed which was not referred to in the missives. The court held that the disposition was the ruling document, and on the face of it there was no apparent error. Accordingly the onus on the sellers to show that it did not accurately implement the missives. The purchasers were not obliged to establish the terms of the prior agreement, but were entitled to lead evidence to support their claim that the fifth area was intended to be included and that reflected the common intention. Furthermore, the provision for non-supersession did not prevent or render invalid the conveyance of the fifth area if that was the common intention, and proof allowed. (Text 28.33)

*McClymont* v. *McCubbin* 1995 SLT 1248. In a boundary dispute, a petition for rectification was dismissed. On appeal, proof before answer allowed. (Text 28.7)

*Huewind Ltd.* v. *Clydesdale Bank plc* 1996 SLT 369. A question of the construction of a guarantee. The points involved patent and latent defects and ambiguity as to interest. On appeal the petition relating to rectification refused and proof before answer allowed on the question of interest only.

*Bank of Scotland* v. *Brunswick Developments (1987) Ltd.* 1995 SLT 689. On a petition for rectification of instructions to a bank in relation to a transfer of funds, it was held that the letter of instruction was in fact an assignation and therefore within the Law Reform (Miscellaneous Provisions) (Scotland) Act 1985, s. 8(1)(b). Rectification competent even where mistake related to identity of grantor.

## 30.16 Compulsory purchase

*Argyll* v. *LMS Railway Co.* 1931 SC 309. Statutory and common law title compared; authorities reviewed.

*Magistrates of Elgin* v. *Highland Railway Co.* (1884) 11 R 950. Effect of statutory title.

*Campbell's Trs.* v. *L & NE Railway Co.* 1930 SC 182. Effect of statutory title.

*Barr* v. *Glasgow Corporation* 1972 SLT (Sh Ct) 63. Statutory title; effect on superior's right to feuduty.

*Heriot's Trust* v. *Caledonian Railway Co.* 1915 SC (HL) 52. Discussion on nature and effect of statutory conveyance. (Text 30.19)

*Rush* v. *Fife Regional Council* 1994 SCLR 231. Notices to treat: some observations on the implications of a notice to treat with substantial citation of authority. (Text 30.19)

*JDP Investments Ltd* v. *Strathclyde Regional Council* 1996 SCLR 243. Sale of surplus land which had previously been acquired by a local authority. Subjects had not been compulsorily acquired. *Held* that Crichel Down rules inapplicable. (Text 30.19)

## Chapter 31. Transmission on Death

### 31.3 Position before the Succession (Scotland) Act 1964 – Intestacy

*MacRae* v. *MacDonald* 1980 SC 337. Special service; effect of decree.

*Stobie* v. *Smith* 1921 SC 894. Special service. Wrong heir served; effect of decree. (Text 31.26)

*Mackay's Exx.* v. *Schonbach and Another* 1933 SC 747. General service; validity and effect of decree.

*Sibbald's Heirs* v. *Harris* 1947 SC 601. General service. (Text 31.26, 33.55, 33.106)

*McAdam* v. *McAdam* (1879) 6 R 1256. 1874 Act, s. 9. Vesting in the heir.

*Robertson, Petitioner* 1978 SLT (Sh Ct) 30. 1874 Act, s.10. Petition for authority to complete title may be presented by an executor.

*Fraser, Petitioner* 1978 SLT (Sh Ct) 5. 1874 Act, s. 10. Petition for authority to complete title may be presented by a surviving spouse entitled to prior rights.

*McKenzie, Applicant* 1979 SLT (Sh Ct) 68. 1874 Act, s. 10. Petition for authority to complete title not competent where the property was last vested in an *ex facie* absolute disponee.

*Robertson, Petitioner* 1980 SLT (Sh Ct) 73. The heir of a deceased heir at law cannot serve as heir in trust under the 1874 Act, s. 43.

*MacMillan, Petitioner* 1987 SLT (Sh Ct) 50. In determining the identity of an heir of provision in trust where the deceased in question died after 10 September 1964, the new statutory code of succession must be applied and not the old rule operating prior to that date. (Text 32.11)

*MacDougall* v. *MacDougall's Exrs.* 1994 SLT 1178. The validity of a will was questioned. The heir-at-law obtained a Charter of Novodamus which was used as a link in title by apparently *bona fide* purchasers for value. *Held* that completion of title by service or otherwise by one who is not the heir is valueless if challenged by the true proprietor. (Text 28.46, 31.26)

## 31.10   Special destinations
(See also cases under 7.13 and 7.15 above)

*Haddow's Exrs.* v. *Haddow* 1943 SC 44. A destination to A and B in conjunct fee and liferent, for A's liferent and for B in fee, is not a special destination.

*Cormack* v. *McIldowie's Exrs.* 1975 SC 161. Definition of special destination.

*Hay's Tr.* v. *Hay's Trs.* 1951 SC 329. Whether destination revocable. (Text 7.17, 31.13).

*Gordon-Rogers* v. *Thomson's Trs.* 1988 SC 145. Extrinsic evidence not admissible to contradict plain terms of the narrative clause in a disposition; and, in the instant case, there was sufficient in the deed to infer that the destination was contractual and therefore irrevocable. (Text 31.13)

*Shand's Trs.* v. *Shand's Trs.* 1966 SC 178. Whether destination revocable; price jointly contributed. (Text 31.13)

*Brown's Tr.* v. *Brown* 1943 SC 488. Whether destination revocable; condition of gift. (Text 31.13)

*Munro* v. *Munro* 1972 SLT (Sh Ct) 6. Whether destination revocable; joint or common property. (Text 31.14)

*Perrett's Trs.* v. *Perrett* 1909 SC 522. Revocation; destination created by testator.

*Campbell* v. *Campbell* (1880) 7 R (HL) 100. Revocation; destination created by another.

*Stirling's Trs.* v. *Stirling* 1977 SC 139. Revocation; 1964 Act, s. 30. (Text 18.7, 31.15)

*Steele* v. *Caldwell* 1979 SLT 228. Effect of survivorship destination on *inter vivos* deed.

*Smith* v. *Mackintosh* 1988 SC 453. A special destination in the title, even if contractual, cannot prevent *inter vivos* disposal; nor is it legitimate to look behind the disposition to determine whether or not the destination is contractual. (Text 31.13)

*Marshall* v. *Marshall's Exr.* 1987 SLT 49. A contractual special destination is irrevocable by *mortis causa* deed; and, in any event, even if revocable, the revocation must comply with 1964 Act, s. 30. If a special destination is claimed to be contractual, that must appear *ex facie* of the deed. (Text 31.15)

*Barclays Bank Ltd.* v. *McGreish* 1983 SLT 344. Property passing on a special destination is not subject to personal debts of deceased institute.

*Gardner's Exrs.* v. *Raeburn* 1996 SLT 745. Title to matrimonial home taken in name of husband and wife and survivor. The parties then divorced. The wife conveyed to her husband her one half *pro indiviso* share. The husband then died. *Held* that the disposition was restricted in its terms to the wife's one half *pro indiviso* share only. As a result the wife was entitled to succeed to the husband's original share. (Text 31.17)

*Redfern's Exrs.* v. *Redfern* 1996 SLT 900. Following a separation, the parties entered into an agreement regulating *inter alia* sale of the matrimonial home. The title stood in joint names of both parties and the survivor. Under the agreement, both relinquished any rights of succession in the estate of the other. *Held* that the agreement in its terms impliedly waived normal prohibition against evacuation. (Text 31.17)

## 31.18   Testate succession
*Smith* v. *Wallace* (1869) 8 M 204. Effect of general disposition at common law.

*Thoms* v. *Thoms* (1864) 6 M 704 and 174. Effect of general disposition *mortis causa* at common law.

*Studd* v. *Cook* (1883) 10 R (HL) 53. Effect of general disposition under 1868 Act, s. 20.

*Grant* v. *Morren* (1893) 20 R 404. Effect of general disposition under 1868 Act, s. 20.
*Lawson's Exr.* v. *Lawson & Others* 1958 SLT (Notes) 38. Estate carried by the will. 'Money'.
*Crozier's Tr.* v. *Underwood* 1963 SLT 69. Estate carried by the will. 'All my other affect'.

## Chapter 32.  Completion of Title

### 32.8  Lapsed trusts
*Browning, Petitioner* 1976 SLT (Sh Ct) 87. Service as heir in trust. (Text 32.11)
*MacMillan, Petitioner* 1987 SLT (Sh Ct) 50. Service as heir in trust and the Law Reform Act
  1980, s. 6. (Text 32.11)

### 32.26  Notarial instrument
*Kerr's Tr.* v. *Yeaman's Tr.* (1888) 15 R 520. Effect of notice of title. (Text 32.26)
*Sutherland* v. *Garrity* 1941 SC 146. Effect of notice of title. (Text 32.26)
*Cowie* v. *Muirden* (1893) 20 R (HL) 81. Real burden in favour of third party can be duly
  constituted by recording notice of title, if general disposition on which it proceeds so
  warrants. (Text 32.26, 32.36)
*MacKenzie* v. *Clark* (1903) 11 SLT 428. *Cowie* v. *Muirden* (above) not followed because
  burden not set out in the notice. (Text 32.26)

## Chapter 33.  Examination of Title

### 33.2  Conditions in the contract
*Hood* v. *Clarkson* 1995 SLT 98. Standard clause that there are no existing applications, orders,
  notices etc modified to effect that the usual local authority letter would be exhibited. After
  settlement, the disponee discovered that the seller had previously received notice of
  proposed roadworks. Purchaser's claim rejected. (Text 28.51)
*Hawke* v. *W. D. Mathers* 1995 3CLR 1004. Sellers, prior to settlement, offered purchasers a
  letter of comfort instead of a completion certificate. Purchasers held entitled to resile. (Text
  28.51)

### 33.3  Proprietary title
Prescriptive progress of titles
*Scott* v. *Bruce-Stewart* (1779) Mor 13519. General principle of positive prescription. (Text
  14.6)
*Lord Advocate* v. *Graham* (1844) 7 D 183. General principle of positive prescription.
*Wallace* v. *St. Andrews University* (1904) 6 F 1093. Title.
*Fraser* v. *Lord Lovat* (1898) 25 R 603. Title.
*Meacher* v. *Blair-Oliphant* 1913 SC 417. *Ex facie* validity.
*Cooper Scott* v. *Gill Scott* 1924 SC 309. *Ex facie* validity. (Text 14.7, 33.4)
*Troup* v. *Aberdeen Heritable Securities Co. Ltd.* 1916 SC 918. *Ex facie* validity.
*Hilson* v. *Scott* (1895) 23 R 241. *Ex facie* validity.
*Glen* v. *Scales' Tr. and Others* (1881) 9 R 317. *Ex facie* validity.
*Ramsay* v. *Spence* 1909 SC 1441. Recording in 'appropriate register' – BRS or GRS? (See now
  1979 Act, s. 15(1) – 'Recording' means recording in GRS).
*Auld* v. *Hay* (1880) 7 R 663. Title need not be unambiguous.
*Troup* v. *Aberdeen Heritable Securities Co. Ltd.* 1916 SC 918. Title need not be unambiguous.
*Hay* v. *Aberdeen Corporation* 1909 SC 554. Title must be definite. (Text 6.10)
*Brown* v. *N.B. Ry. Co.* (1906) 8 F 534. Title must be definite.
*MacDougall* v. *MacDougall's Exrs* 1994 SLT 1178. See 31.3 above. (Text 28.46, 31.26)
*Stewart* v. *J. M. Hodge & Son* 1995 GWD 12–691 (OH). Partnership bought property in 1974.
  In 1990 it was found that part of the property lay outwith the title boundary.

### 33.6 Burdens

*Campbell* v. *McCutcheon* 1963 SC 505,. Where the contract made no mention of minerals, which were reserved, purchaser was entitled to resile. (Text 28.43, 28.68, 28.97)

*Bremner* v. *Dick* 1911 SC 887. Unallocated feuduty entitles purchaser to resile.

*Armia* v. *Daejan Developments Ltd.* 1979 SC (HL) 56. Material undisclosed burdens entitle purchaser to resile. (Text 28.43, 28.76)

*Umar* v. *Murtaza* 1983 SLT (Sh Ct) 79. Unless seller discloses all restrictions on title, purchaser may resile. (Text 28.43)

*Spurway, Petitioner* 1987 GWD 2–65. Title may contain right of pre-emption which overrides contract. (Text 33.8, 33.12, 33.13)

*Welsh* v. *Russell* (1894) 21 R 769. Undisclosed servitude, if material, may entitle purchaser to resile. (Text 12.9, 28.43)

*Cameron* v. *Williamson* (1895) 22 R 293. Purchaser not obliged to take a title subject to outstanding heritable securities; but something less than a formal discharge may suffice. (Text 22.60)

*Watson* v. *Gillespie MacAndrew* 1995 GWD 13–750. Solicitors for purchaser of landed estate failed to advise purchaser of existence of servitude right of access. Solicitors held negligent. (Text 28.49)

### 33.13 Pre-emption

*Matheson* v. *Tinney* 1989 SLT 535. Right of pre-emption in feudal writ not struck at as a prohibition against alienation under Tenures Abolition Act 1746

*Spurway, Petitioner* 1987 GWD 2–65. Where title contains right of pre-emption, seller must make formal offer to creditor in the pre-emption. (Text 33.8, 33.12)

*Roebuck* v. *Edmonds* 1992 SLT 1055. Disposition granted in contravention of clause of pre-emption may be reduced; but the clause is strictly construed and reduction will not necessarily entitle the creditor to take up the right.

*Ross & Cromarty DC* v. *Patience* 1997 SLT (HL) 463. Effect of right of pre-emption.

*Waverley Housing Trust Ltd.* v. *Roxburgh DC* 1995 SLT (Lands Tr.) 2. Local authority inserted pre-emption clause in two offers with no change of tenancy. *Held* condition unreasonable in terms of Housing (Scotland) Act 1988, s. 58 and pre-emption clause conditions should be struck out from each offer.

*Henderson* v. *City of Glasgow DC* 1994 SLT 263. Prior titles contained right of pre-emption which was not brought to the attention of the Tribunal when they made their order effectively conferring title on the purchasing tenant. Tribunal satisfied that they were correct in issuing an offer to the tenant which took no account of the right of pre-emption, and were upheld.

*Roberts* v. *Tait & Peterson* 1995 GWD 10–548. R bought a cottage. On later sale a pre-emption clause was discovered. Superior could not be traced and purchasers rescinded. R sued his agents. Proof before answer allowed.

### 33.14 Redemption and reversion

*Hamilton* v. *Grampian Regional Council* 1996 GWD 5–277. Purchaser of large landed estate successfully sought declarator that ground conveyed in 1858 to trustees under the School Sites Act 1841 belonged to him on ceasing to be so used.

### 33.18 Possession in support of the title

(See also generally Chapter 14 – The effects of possession.)

*Robertson's Trs.* v. *Bruce* (1905) 7 F 580. The title must support the possession.

*Meacher* v. *Blair-Oliphant* 1913 SC 417. Discussion on quality of possession required to support title.

*Houstoun* v. *Barr* 1911 SC 134. Possession must be directly referable to title it allegedly supports. (Text 8.13)

### 33.22 The Property Register

*Cameron* v. *Williamson* (1895) 22 R 293. Purchaser entitled to clear search in Property Register. (Text 22.60)

*Rodger (Builders) Ltd.* v. *Fawdry* 1950 SC 483. Purchaser may be personally barred from relying on title as disclosed by search. (Text 28.94, 28.97, 28.98, 33.59, 33.61, 33.78, 35.10).

*Robson* v. *Chalmers Property Investment Co. Ltd.* 1965 SLT 381. Purchaser, as singular successor, may be affected by actings or acquiescence on the part of a predecessor in title although nothing is disclosed on Record. (Compare overriding interests in Registration of Title.) (Text 11.10)

## 33.29 The Register of Inhibitions

General effect

*Menzies* v. *Murdoch* (1841) 4 D 257. Preference created by inhibition over other creditors.

*Murphy's Trs.* v. *Aitken* 1983 SLT 78. Effect of inhibition in English bankruptcy.

*Dryburgh* v. *Gordon* (1896) 24 R 1. Inhibition effective even where no feudal title. (Text 33.43)

*Leeds Permanent Building Society* v. *Aitken, Malone and Mackay* 1986 SLT 338. Right of purchaser under missives not heritable and so not caught by inhibition until a disposition in implement thereof has been delivered in his favour.

*Scottish Wagon Co. Ltd.* v. *James Hamilton's Tr.* 1906 13 SLT 779. Inhibition is negative in nature.

*McInally* v. *Kildonan Homes Ltd.* 1979 SLT (Notes) 89. Partial recall of inhibition competent.

*Murray* v. *Long* 1992 SLT 292. Pursuer claimed that inhibition on the dependence was effectually executed diligence in a question with a receiver but the point was not decided.

*Commissioners of Customs & Excise, Applicants* 1992 SLT 11. Inhibition in security (a rare bird) competent only to cover future or contingent debts.

*Murray* v. *Long* 1992 SLT 292. Opinion that interdict may be a competent remedy to support an inhibition but only on cause shown.

*Rhodes* v. *Boswell* 1994 SLT 371. Circumstances in which recall of inhibition granted.

*M T Group* v. *Howden Group plc* 1993 SLT 345. Danish company, seeking performance of obligations undertaken by a Scottish company had obtained inhibition on the dependence which the inhibited debtor moved to recall. They argued, *inter alia*, *forum non conveniens*. Motion for recall refused.

*Hogg* v. *Prentice* 1994 SCLR 426. Held that service and registration of letters of inhibition on the dependence of an action constituted a relevant claim for purposes of Prescription etc. Act 1973, s. 6(1) and so interrupted running of prescription. Prescription starts running again from that date.

Effect on heritable creditors

*McGowan* v. *A. Middlemass and Sons Ltd.* 1977 SLT (Sh Ct) 41. Inhibition does not prevent sale by bondholder but creates no preference for inhibitor.

*Newcastle Building Society* v. *White* 1987 SLT (Sh Ct) 81. In view of provisions of Act, s. 26, it was clear *ex facie* of the Record that the property was disencumbered and the search was therefore clear for purposes of marketable title as provided for in the missives. (Text 22.38, 33.43)

*Bank of Scotland* v. *Lord Advocate* 1977 SLT 24. Inhibition does not prevent sale by holder of standard security, but creates a preference for inhibitor on any surplus as against other creditors

*Abbey National Building Society* v. *Sheik Aziz* 1981 SLT (Sh Ct) 29. Inhibition creates preference for inhibiting creditor on free proceeds of sale over posterior arresting creditors.

*Ferguson & Forster* v. *Dalbeattie Finance Co.* 1981 SLT (Sh Ct) 53. Subjects sold by secured creditors. Inhibiting creditor not to be preferred to free proceeds over unsecured creditors. *Cf. Abbey National Building Society* v. *Sheik Aziz* above, and *Halifax Building Society* v. *Smith* below.

*Halifax Building Society* v. *Smith* 1985 SLT (Sh Ct) 25. Nature of preference created by inhibition. (Text 22.40)

*Mackintosh's Trs.* v. *Davidson and Garden* (1898) 25 R 554. Inhibition does not prevent debtor discharging heritable security.

*Henderson* v. *Dawson* (1895) 22 R 895. A creditor, who had inhibited, agreed to a discharge on receiving an assurance as to payment; and was held entitled to enforce that assurance.

*Atlas Appointments Ltd.* v. *Tinsley* 1995 SLT 635. Accurate information needed when instructing inhibitions.

*Allied Irish Bank plc* v. *GPT Sales & Service Ltd*. 1995 SLT 163. Owner of a hotel subjected to an inhibition by a company GS, formerly known as GR. GR and GS exchanged names. There was a confusion of dates. Heritable creditors successfully petitioned for the recall of inhibition.

### 33.32   Sequestration

*Alliance & Leicester Building Society* v. *Murray's Trs* 1995 SLT (Sh Ct) 77. Heritable property acquired by bankrupt, by disposition in his favour granted after date of sequestration. The bankrupt then immediately granted a standard security in favour of the building society and both deeds were recorded in Sasines. *Held* that the property vested in the trustee notwithstanding the conveyance in favour of the bankrupt. Since the bankrupt had no right to the subjects, he could not have granted a valid standard security.

*Sharp* v. *Thomson* 1995 SC 45, 1997 SLT(HL) 636. See 4.1 above. (Text 4.1, 12.4, 23.4, 29.33, 33.51, 35.7, 35.12, 35.15, 35.18)

### 33.44   Settlement obligations

*Johnston* v. *Little* 1960 SLT 129. Letter of obligation is personally binding on the solicitor who grants it. (Text 33.44)

*Gibson* v. *Hunter Home Designs Ltd*. 1976 SC 23. Effect of payment of price in exchange for letter of obligation only but no title. (Text 4.1, 33.51).

*Richardson* v. *MacGeoch's Trs*. (1898) 1 F 145. Obligation by agent to deliver discharge of a loan does not bind principal creditor if the agent embezzles the money.

*McGillivary* v. *Davidson* 1993 SLT 693. Seller's solicitors gave a letter of obligation undertaking to deliver planning permission, building warrant and completion certificates. After settlement, the purchasers discovered that the local authority had served an enforcement notice. *Held* that the seller and his solicitors were jointly and severally liable. Purchaser entitled to sue both the solicitors granting a letter of obligation at settlement and their client jointly, if obligation not implemented.

*Emslie* v. *James Thomson & Sons* 1991 JLS 349 (unreported). Where solicitors have granted a letter of obligation which is not implemented, the purchaser can sue them in his own name although the obligation was granted to his own agents.

*Mason* v. *A. & R. Robertson & Black* 1993 SLT 773. Seller's solicitors granted a letter of obligation giving certain undertakings which they were not able to implement. The solicitors were exonerated but the case underlines the danger of giving such letters. (Text 28.102)

*Warners* v. *Beveridge & Kellas* 1994 SLT (Sh Ct) 29. Solicitors granted an obligation to deliver within a specified time-limit a search brought down in terms of an agreed memorandum showing clear records 'which search will disclose your client's title, provided your client's title is recorded within 21 days from this date'. The purchaser's solicitors failed to record within the 21-day time-limit. The selling solicitors, having granted an obligation in these terms, argued that they escaped liability because of the failure of the purchaser's solicitors. *Held* that, since the primary obligation was to give a clear search and this did not depend on recording within 21 days, there was no reason why an alternative construction should not be adopted limiting the proviso to the phrase immediately preceding it. The decision underlines the need for care in drafting letters of obligation. (Text 33.46) See also Caveat, referred to in the Reading List.

*Digby Brown & Co.* v. *Lyall & Others* 1995 SLT 932. Solicitors granted letter of obligation 'on behalf of their clients' which was signed by them without any reference to their agency. Lord Cullen held the letter of obligation was not personally binding on the firm who granted it.

### 33.67   Gratuitous alienations

*Leslie* v. *Leslie* 1987 SLT 232. Reduction of a disposition under Divorce (Scotland) Act 1976, s. 6 does not necessarily imply that a standard security over the property will also fall, looking to the proviso to s. 6(2). (See now the Family Law (Scotland) Act 1985, s. 18 for equivalent provisions now in force.)

*Bank of Scotland, Petitioners* 1988 SLT 690. Common law rule against gratuitous alienation applies to companies.

### 33.69 Occupancy rights of non-entitled spouses
*Murphy* v. *Murphy* 1992 SCLR (Sh Ct) 62. A dwellinghouse was purchased in joint names of A and B. B then married C who moved into the house and it became their matrimonial home. The marriage broke up and B moved out leaving C in occupation. *Held* that, since A had never occupied the house and allowed B to occupy it with his wife C, A had waived her rights of occupation in favour of B under s. 1(2) of the 1981 Act. (Text 33.70)

### 33.79 Negative prescription
*Barratt (Scotland) Ltd* v. *Keith* 1993 SC 1420. Seller's obligation to grant a disposition is an obligation relating to land, not imprescriptible but subject to the 20-year prescription. (Text 33.51)
*Wright* v. *Frame* 1992 GWD 8–447. Discussion on interaction of Prescription and Limitation (Scotland) Act 1973, Sched. 1, para 1(g) – obligations arising from contract; and para 2(e) – obligations relating to land. (Text 33.51)
*Stewart's Exrs.* v. *Stewart* 1993 SLT 440. Obligation to grant a disposition not imprescriptible. Exclusion in Prescription and Limitation (Scotland) Act 1973, Sched. 3, para (h) applies only where a disponee holds an unrecorded disposition. Sched. 3(h) allows completion of title thereon indefinitely.
*Hogg* v. *Prentice* 1994 SCLR 426. See 33.29 above.
*Porteous' Exrs* v. *Ferguson* 1995 SLT 649. The defender granted a disposition in his own favour *a non domino* recorded 17 January 1992. Executors took out Confirmation as representing the reputed owner of the same ground and then recorded a Notice of Title on 5 August 1992. Executors then sought to reduce the *a non domino* disposition but failed on the footing that the personal right of the deceased who died in 1952 had been extinguished by the long negative prescription before 25 July 1976 when the 1973 Act came into force, since no action and no infeftment was taken following her death. (Text 14.7, 32.49)
*MRS Hamilton Ltd.* v. *Arlott* 1995 GWD 25–1355. Short negative prescription of five years did not apply to arrears of leasehold casualties which were not, in terms of the 1973 Act, periodical payments. (Text 33.16)

## Chapter 34.   A Typical Sasines Conveyancing Transaction

### 34.37   Surveys and valuation inspection
*Stevenson* v. *A. & J. Stephen (Builders) Ltd.* 1996 SLT 140. Purchaser sued builders (who were also the feudal superiors) for losses due to fire damage, alleging defective design.

### 34.71   Loan – second stage
*Bank of East Asia Ltd.* v. *Shepherd and Wedderburn* 1995 SC 255. Bank as secured lenders claimed conflict of interest and failure to advise the possibility of set-off. (Text 20.1)

## Chapter 35.   Transactions with Companies

### 35.1   General
*Weir* v. *Rees* 1991 SLT 345. Circumstances where it was held appropriate to appoint an interim judicial factor to a company without directors.

### 35.3   Company name
*Banque de l'Indochine etc.* v. *Euroseas Group Finance Co. Ltd.* [1981] 3 All ER 198. The abbreviation of the word 'Company' to 'Co.' has been held in England not to invalidate the document at common law.

### 35.4 Capacity

*James Finlay Corporation Ltd.* v. *R. & R. S. Mearns* 1988 SLT 302. Discussion on *ultra vires* actings.

*Re Introductions Ltd.* v. *National Provincial Bank Ltd.* [1969] 1 All ER 887. Discussion on actings.

*Piggins & Rix Ltd.* v. *Montrose Port Authority* 1995 SLT 418. Montrose Port Authority wished to sell some land that was surplus to its requirements. A special case was presented to the Court to ascertain whether it had the capacity to do so. The Court concluded that it did not, and to do so would be *ultra vires*. The Court did however consider, *obiter dictum*, that the Port Authority may have power to enter into long leases. (Text 3.2, 3.15)

### 35.5 Execution of deeds

*Liquidator of Style and Mantle Ltd.* v. *Prices Tailors Ltd.* 1934 SC 548. Discussion on form of disposition granted by a company in liquidation.

### 35.7 Floating charges

*Forth & Clyde Construction Co. Ltd.* v. *Trinity Timber & Plywood Co. Ltd.* 1984 SC 1. Nature of fixed security on appointment of receiver.

*Lord Advocate* v. *Aero Technologies Ltd.* 1991 SLT 134. No reason in principle why a company and its receivers should not be regarded as joint occupiers for various statutory and other purposes.

*Iona Hotels Ltd., Petitioners* 1990 SC 330. *Held*, distinguishing *Lord Advocate* v. *Royal Bank of Scotland Ltd.* 1977 SC 155, that if a security is prior in date to registration of a charge, it takes priority.

*National Commercial Bank Ltd.* v. *Liquidators of Telford, Grier, Mackay & Co. Ltd.* 1969 SC 181. Extent of security; interest due from date of liquidation.

*Libertas-Kommerz* v. *Johnson* 1977 SC 191. Bond and floating charge is assignable by creditor.

*Hill Samuel & Co. Ltd.* v. *Laing* 1989 SC 301. Discussion on personal liability of receiver for debt incurred on behalf of the company.

*Shanks* v. *Central RC* 1988 SC 14. Appointment of receiver does not necessarily exclude powers of directors of company to take action in certain circumstances.

*Taymech Ltd.* v. *Rush and Tompkins Ltd.* 1990 SLT 681. Conceded by counsel that an inhibition, registered after creation of the charge, was ineffective in a question with a receiver subsequently appointed.

*Myles J. Callaghan Ltd.* v. *Glasgow DC* 1987 SC 171. Discussion on nature of crystallisation of a charge on appointment of a receiver.

*Bank of Scotland, Petitioners* 1988 SLT 690. *Held*, notwithstanding provisions of Insolvency Act 1986, creditors still retained the right to challenge transactions as gratuitous alienations at common law.

*Bank of Scotland* v. *T. A. Neilson & Co.* 1990 SC 284. Standard security by a company, recorded in Sasines, was not registered in the Register of Charges. Second security recorded simultaneously was duly registered. There was a ranking agreement in terms of which the unregistered security was intended to have prior ranking. Held that the ranking agreement could not alter the effect of the statutory ranking provisions then in force. (Text 22.7)

*Prior, Petitioner* 1989 SLT 840. Application for extension of time to register a floating charge, with or without conditions attached, was refused. (Text 23.5, 23.10)

*Scottish and Newcastle plc* v. *Ascot Inns Ltd.* 1994 SLT 1140. Informal letter from creditor in a floating charge to solicitors for the company amounted to a release of the properties specified in the letter. The letter did not require to be registered to be valid. (Text 35.12, 35.18)

*AIB Finance Ltd.* v. *Bank of Scotland* 1993 SC 538. Dispute as to ranking between heritable creditor holding a fixed security and creditor holding a floating charge.

*Sharp* v. *Thomson* 1995 SC 45, 1997 SLT (HL) 636. A company as a going concern executed and delivered a disposition of property to a *bona fide* purchaser for value. The company had already granted a floating charge which included that property. On the day after settlement, a receiver was appointed to the disponer before the purchaser had recorded the disposition. Held, the property was caught by the floating charge. This decision was reversed in the House of Lords. (Text 4.1, 12.4, 23.4, 29.33, 33.51, 35.7, 35.12, 35.15, 35.18)

*Bass Brewers Ltd.* v. *Humberclyde Finance Group Ltd.* 1996 GWD 1076. Bass objected to certain payments made to Humberclyde, prior security holders. Humberclyde's security was ranked and preferred to that of Bass. Discussion on the payments permitted on construction of the ranking agreement.

### 35.18 Alternative methods of protecting the purchaser
*Bank of Scotland, Petitioner* 1988 SLT 690. Common law rule against gratuitous alienations applies to companies.

### 35.19 Purchase of heritage from an administrator
*Scottish Exhibition Centre Ltd.* v. *Mirestop Ltd.* 1996 SLT 8. Landlord can serve an irritancy notice on a tenant in administration notwithstanding Insolvency Act 1986, s. 11.

### 35.24 Purchase of heritage from a receiver
*Norfolk House plc* v. *Repsol Petroleum Ltd. (In receivership)* 1992 SLT 235. S. 72 of the Insolvency Act 1986 is designed to operate as a bridge from creation of floating charge to the receiver's appointment, in order to ensure that a receiver can exercise his powers under Sched. 1 to the 1986 Act in relation to Scottish property untrammelled by Scottish conveyancing and property law. (Text 35.7, 35.12)
*Independent Pension Trustee Ltd.* v. *LAW Construction Co.* 1996 GWD 33–1956. On attachment of floating charge, directors are implicitly divested of their powers.

### 35.28 Title
*Iona Hotels Ltd., Petitioners* 1990 SC 330. Arrestment, not followed by furthcoming, nonetheless constituted effectually executed diligence in a question with a receiver.
*Taymech Ltd.* v. *Rush & Tompkins Ltd.* 1990 SLT 681. Inhibition against a company, not followed by adjudication, is of no effect in a question with a receiver subsequently appointed and has nuisance value only, which justifies recall of the inhibition; but *cf. Iona Hotels Ltd.* above.
*Murray* v. *Long* 1992 SLT 292. Question raised, but not resolved as to whether or not an inhibition registered before receivership was effective against the receiver.
*Allou Brewery Co. Ltd.* v. *Investors in Industry plc.* 1992 SLT 121. Discussion on the meaning of 'charge'. (Text 22.17, 35.36)
*Grampian RC* v. *Drill Stem (Inspection Services) Ltd.* 1994 SCLR 36. In a competition between landlord and tenant in receivership, landlord's hypothec takes precedence.
*Scottish and Newcastle Breweries plc.* v. *Ascot Inns Ltd.* 1994 SLT 1140. Informal letter from creditor in a floating charge to solicitors for the company amounted to release of the properties specified in the letter. Letter did not require to be registered to be valid. (Text 35.12, 35.18)

### 35.30 Consent of creditor or application to the court
*Murray* v. *Long* 1992 SLT 292. Discussion on effect of inhibition on powers of receiver to sell heritable property.

### 35.32 Liquidation
*McLuckie Brothers Ltd.* v. *Newhouse Contracts Ltd.* 1993 SLT 641. Gratuitous alienation by a company reduced. Onus on the disponee seeking to uphold the transaction to prove that it was not either gratuitous or a sale at under value.
*Stuart Eves Ltd. (In liquidation)* v. *Smiths Gore* 1993 SLT 1274. In the circumstances of the case, the liquidator had sufficiently averred a gratuitous alienation at common law.
*John E. Rae (Electrical Services) Linlithgow Ltd.* v. *Lord Advocate* 1994 SLT 788. Bond granted to Inland Revenue was an alienation for adequate consideration.
*Thomson* v. *MB Trustees Ltd.* 1994 GWD 32–1894. Liquidator raised action against trustees of a pension fund and a bank seeking reduction of a disposition granted by the company in favour of the pension fund. The company acquired the property by disposition dated August 1988 and recorded in March 1989. The company conveyed the subjects to the

pension fund in August 1988, recorded October 1988. The liquidator averred that the company was insolvent, or the granting of the disposition rendered it insolvent, and persons associated with the company benefited as a result. The pension fund trustees argued they paid full consideration. Proof before answer was allowed. Onus of establishing consideration was with the pension fund trustees.

*Rankin* v. *Meek* 1995 SLT 526. Gratuitous alienation by a company in liquidation, and a question as to whether valuable consideration had been given in exchange for a grant by the company.

### 35.36   Second securities by companies

*Armour and Mycroft, Petitioners* 1983 SLT 453. Affirmation of general rule that, where there is competition between creditors with equal security rights, preference is given according to the dates of the securities.

# TABLE OF CASES

NOTE:
Cases for which there are paragraph numbers in bold type are referred to in the text. All other paragraph numbers refer to the Digest of Cases.

# TABLE OF STATUTES

# TABLE OF STATUTORY INSTRUMENTS

# Part 1

# PRELIMINARY MATTERS

# Chapter 1

# GENERAL INTRODUCTION

## 1.1 General

The *Manual* is intended primarily for students following the degree and diploma classes of conveyancing, although it is hoped that it will also be of assistance to practitioners. It deals only with conveyancing in the narrow sense, and those seeking information on the wider aspects of the law of heritable property are directed to works such as W. M. Gordon's *Scottish Land Law* and Volume 18 of the Stair Encyclopaedia – Property paras. 1–718. (See also Professor K. G. C. Reid, *The Law of Property in Scotland*.)

An extensive Reading List is included at the front of the volume. Further and more detailed information on the Reading List is contained later in this Chapter.

## 1.2 Content and scope

As a general indication of the content and scope of this subject, for the degree and diploma student, I do not think I can do better than quote directly from the Law Society's submission to the Royal Commission on Legal Services in Scotland Volume 1, published in 1977.

'Conveyancing has been defined as "the art which deals with the transfer of property in writing" (Wood's Lectures). The essence of the definition is some form of writing or deed. Wood uses the word "property" in its widest sense as meaning everything which can be possessed. The expression "transfer" includes every kind of right relating to such property which can be created, conveyed or extinguished in writing. Such a transfer may be an absolute one of ownership as from seller to purchaser or donor to donee, it may be redeemable *i.e.* subject to extinction at a future date such as a security or a lease. It includes the preparation of those documents which are preliminary to the actual deed of transfer, such as missives of sale. Conveyancing therefore embraces the preparation of contracts, writs and deeds of every kind, and is not confined to the transfer of heritable property or rights therein. Settlements, trusts, wills, contracts for the purchase or sale of businesses or shares, debentures and loan agreements, leases, leasing or hire purchase agreements, building contracts, contracts of employment, partnership, patent, licence and "know-how" agreements and indeed every contract or writing of any kind which is preliminary to or in itself creates, transfers, modifies or extinguishes a right or obligation, falls within the work of a conveyancer.

It is of course true that the greater part of the conveyancer's work is concerned with heritable property. This work covers not only the buying

3

and selling of such properties and the preparation of conveyances and securities, but also the preparation of tenancy agreements and leases, deeds granting limited rights such as servitudes or wayleaves, and deeds extinguishing or varying rights or obligations. Further, the conveyancer's duty is not limited to the mere preparation of the deed giving effect to the transaction in question. He must be able to advise his client on the effect of the transaction generally, as to the ways of achieving the desired result, the financing of the transaction and its effect on his client's affairs, for example, in relation to taxation, insurances, succession, etc. When acting for a seller of property or the grantor of a right, discharge or waiver, he must ensure that his client can give a good title and does not contract to do something which he cannot fulfil or, if the consents of other persons are required, that these can be obtained. When acting for a purchaser or for the person in whose favour the right, discharge or waiver is being granted he must ensure that any preliminary contract is correctly and sufficiently drawn and, by examination of the grantor's title, that the grantor can grant and that his client will obtain a valid and enforceable title good against all parties and free from any burdens or restrictions prejudicial to his client's interests. He must also ensure that all necessary permissions for the transaction have been obtained from any third party who may have rights in the matter such as the feudal superior, heritable creditor, landlord or over-landlord, or in respect of any statutory requirements or regulations such as planning permission, building regulations, fire certificates, or licensing requirements. Where there are title restrictions the conveyancer may also be involved in an application to the Lands Tribunal to have the restrictions discharged or modified.

**1.3 The role of solicitors in heritable property transactions.** In relation to heritable property transactions, the work of the solicitor in Scotland is not confined to carrying out the conveyancing, as the solicitor in Scotland, unlike his English counterpart, is also engaged in the negotiations leading up to the purchase and sale which in England are, with few exceptions, handled by the estate agent. Indeed, the majority of properties in Scotland are bought and sold by solicitors. This fact is undoubtedly to the advantage of the public for, of all the advisers who may or should be involved at one stage or another in the sale of the house such as a surveyor, estate agent, insurance broker, banker, building society or accountant, only the solicitor has the overall knowledge and training to co-ordinate all the various steps and carry through the transaction from the point when the seller first decides to put his property on the market to the point where the purchaser completes the purchase by settling the price, taking possession of the property and recording his title in the Sasine Register. Furthermore, it has already been shown that the solicitor's duty does not stop at the transaction in question. He is also expected to advise his client on the effect which it may have on that client's other affairs and it is only the legal profession which is trained to look at and appreciate the overall picture. This is not to say that the profession is blind to the considerable specialist expertise which other advisers can offer and in many cases the solicitor will advise his client to make use of these services. For example, when selling commercial or in-

4

dustrial property, the client may well be advised to put the sale in the hands of a firm of estate agents specialising in the sale of this kind of property. If this is to be done, the solicitor will consider the client's title and the other aspects of the transaction before instructing the estate agents. On the other hand, the profession is only too well aware of the dangers to the client who instructs someone who has only a limited sphere of activity and is unable to take a broad view of the subject, for example, the client who is persuaded to take out a large endowment policy on the explanation that he will not obtain a building society loan unless he does, or where the policy is not suitable for his needs or he cannot really afford the premiums or where the client incurs heavy and unnecessary advertising costs because he has been advised to advertise on four successive days each week, every fourth advertisement being free.

Heritable property ranges from the small tenement flat on the one hand to the large housing development, on the other, from the small shop to the large shopping development, from the single factory to the industrial estate and from the country cottage or smallholding to the large landed estate. The work can, and does, vary enormously from one type of property to another but the difference can be said to be one of degree, for the steps which the solicitor has to take and the considerations which he has to have in mind are normally much the same.'

The monopoly previously enjoyed by solicitors in the provision of conveyancing services for money was ended by Part II of the Law Reform (Miscellaneous Provisions) (Scotland) Act 1990. The 1990 Act established the Conveyancing and Executry Services Board which is charged with the regulation of a new profession of non-solicitor conveyancers, to be known as qualified conveyancers. The reference in the final paragraph of the foregoing quotation should therefore now be to the conveyancer, rather than the solicitor.

As an illustration of the great variety of situations where a solicitor may be held liable for negligence, see Digest of Cases 1.3.

## 1.4 Heritable and moveable

As the foregoing summary indicates, heritable property includes primarily land and everything affixed to or growing on land such as buildings and trees. It also includes rights directly connected with land such as servitudes.

In contrast, moveable property, which includes both corporeal and incorporeal assets, has no direct connection with land.

This Manual is confined exclusively to heritable property, heritable rights and heritable titles.

## 1.5 Heritable property

There are two main aspects to the law of heritable property:

(i) the substantive law, which is dealt with in some textbooks under such headings as 'Landownership', 'Rights in Security', 'Leases', etc. The substantive law regulates the rights and liabilities of the owner or occupant, on the assumption that his right as such has been properly constituted by the appropriate title;

(ii) conveyancing, which is primarily concerned with the constitution and transmission of the right of property (or occupancy) in the form appropriate to the type of property being dealt with. The conveyance is the traditional document of title by which a right of property in land is transferred from one person to another – hence the term.

As indicated above, all rights to land in Scotland generally require a written title to constitute and to transmit the right. In many cases, rights and liabilities of the proprietor of land are implied at common law but these rights may be varied to a greater or lesser extent by the terms of his particular title; that is, by 'conventional provision'. Therefore, although the substantive law of landownership is concerned with rights and liabilities of owners and occupiers generally, it is also necessary in each individual case to examine the individual title to the property concerned and consider the particular terms of that title and the extent to which, if any, the title modifies what the common law would otherwise imply. This, in turn, involves the application of conveyancing principles in construing the terms of the documents constituting the title.

So, under the common law of the tenement, as applied to tenement property generally, the proprietor of the top flat is by implication responsible for the whole cost of maintaining the roof. In many cases, however, this common law liability is modified by the terms of the titles to the individual flats in that tenement.

Similarly, the owner of a vacant piece of land has, at common law, an unqualified right to build on or use that land as he pleases. In his particular title, however, he may be prevented from building altogether; or at least limited in his freedom to use land for building or other purposes.

### 1.6 Reading and references

This is a big subject and there is a good deal of material in statutes, decisions, institutional writers and textbooks. A detailed Reading List will be found at the beginning of the book, divided up to correspond to the different chapters. The Reading List for the present chapter sets out the principal texts and statutory provisions which deal with conveyancing and related areas of law. Note that some of the abbreviations used there are used hereafter in the text. The Reading List for each subsequent chapter relates only to the content of that chapter and is divided into separate sections for books, statutes and for articles. No individual cases are listed in the Reading List but a Digest of Cases is also included at the beginning of this work, divided once again according to chapters.

All the matters dealt with in this Manual are treated much more fully and exhaustively, and with ample citation of authority in Halliday's *Practice* (1985–1990) to which reference should be made on any point of difficulty.

### 1.7 Recording and registration

Since the first edition of this Manual was published, registration of title has been introduced; and there are now several operational areas – see Chapter 13.

To avoid unnecessary repetition, the reader should assume that, whenever the expression 'Sasines' or 'Register of Sasines' or 'GRS' or the term 'recording' is used, this includes registration of the appropriate writ in the Land Register unless the context otherwise requires.

# Chapter 2

# AUTHENTICATION

## 2.1 The significance of written documents

Conveyancing involves the preparation of written evidence in competent form to constitute rights or obligations. Is writing essential for this purpose?

The general principle is that, in a court action to establish or enforce a right or obligation, every kind of evidence is admissible to prove the facts and circumstances out of which the action arose. Apart from special cases, the intention of the parties, in any transaction, can be proved without recourse to writing as evidence. But that general principle is subject to a considerable number of exceptions and qualifications.

Obviously, written documents form an important category of evidence; and, in this context, may be classed as public or private.

(a) *Public writings.* These are documents and records specially prepared by duly authorised officials for the express purpose of preserving evidence in matters of public interest, *e.g.* Acts of Parliament, rules of court, court records, public registers, such as the Registers of Births, Deaths and Marriages, and so on. See Walker *Evidence*, Chapter 18.

(b) *Private writings.* These are documents prepared by individuals either:

(i) because writing is an essential to the constitution of the right or obligation; or
(ii) because the parties simply wish to preserve evidence of the terms of a transaction, although a written document may not be an essential to the constitution of the right.

The foregoing general principles still apply but, in the case of private writings executed on or after 1 August 1995, the whole of the previous law governing the authentication of documents of various kinds, both at common law and under a number of earlier statutory provisions, is replaced by a new statutory code introduced under the Requirements of Writing (Scotland) Act 1995. The main provisions of this new and important statute are discussed at para. 2.40 onwards.

The new Act does not, however, have any effect whatever on the law of authentication as it applied prior to 1 August 1995 in the case of any document executed before that date. In the result, for several decades, it will remain essential for the practitioner to be familiar with the rules of authentication as they applied prior to this Act. This is particularly so in the following instances.

(a) *Heritable titles* where, inevitably, as will later emerge, titles normally have to be examined for at least 10 years prior to the current transaction and, in many cases, deeds of a very much earlier date also have to be examined for various purposes. One important point which has to be considered when examining such titles is whether or not they were duly executed, that is according to the law as it applied prior to the 1995 Act.

(*b*) In the case of *testamentary writings*, again, notwithstanding that the death occurs after the 1995 Act came into operation, if the testamentary writings were executed prior to 1 August 1995, the validity of the document so far as authentication is concerned will be tested according to the rules in force prior to the 1995 Act.

(*c*) In a great variety of *other writs*, the old rules will be applied to determine whether or not a deed was validly executed according to the rules in force before the 1995 Act.

That being the position, the first part of this chapter down to 2.39 is devoted exclusively to an explanation of the rules in force prior to 1 August 1995, and the same treatment is applied to the Digest of Cases and other references at the beginning of the volume.

For ease of reference, the rules which applied to the authentication of documents executed prior to 1 August 1995 are referred to simply as 'the old rules', and for documents executed on or after that date the provisions of the 1995 Act are referred to as 'the new rules'.

## 2.2 The authentification requirements under the old rules
There were two types of private writing. The distinction between them depended on the form which the writing took and the manner in which it was executed.

(*a*) *Formal writs.* These are often referred to (not strictly correctly) as 'probative writings'. A formal writ had to comply with strict rules as to form and authentication.

It might be either:

(i) a solemnly attested deed, which implies subscription of the deed by the grantor(s) and by two subscribing witnesses; or

(ii) a holograph deed, which means written and subscribed by the grantor but not attested; or a deed 'adopted as holograph'.

(*b*) *Informal writings.* These include anything whatever in documentary form (written, printed, etc., signed and unsigned), which failed to conform to the rules for a formal writ.

The distinction was important and relevant when considering whether or not writing was an essential, or was merely desirable as evidence, in any given transaction.

## 2.3 Transactions where writing is obligatory (*obligationes literis*)
In a number of transactions, the law required some written document (formal or informal), as a prerequisite to the creation of a right or the constitution of an obligation. If there was no written document, no right was created, whatever the intention of the parties may have been. For most but not all such transactions, a formal writ was necessary; but there were some

special types of transaction, by statute and at common law, where the necessary document did not need to be a formal writ.

(*a*) *Transactions requiring formal writ.* The principal cases, where a formal writ was essential included:

(i) Testamentary writings and *mortis causa* dispositions generally.

(ii) Titles to heritable property, and any contract or unilateral deed intended to create rights or obligations of whatever kind affecting land, including leases, except leases of one year's duration or less.

(iii) Contracts of service of more than one year's duration.

(iv) Assignations of incorporeal moveable rights.

(v) Contracts where the parties have agreed that they would not be bound at all, unless and until a formal written contract had been entered into.

(*b*) *Transactions where informal writings sufficed.* In such cases, writing was still an essential to create the right or to constitute the obligation, but it did not need to be a formal writ. In other words, there must still be a written document but the strict rules which apply to the form and authentication of formal writings were relaxed. In this class were:

(i) At common law, writings *in re mercatoria* generally, *e.g.* bills of exchange, promissory notes, etc.

(ii) Writings statutorily privileged, *e.g.* the memorandum and articles of association of a company, where certain formalities are required, but falling short of the Scottish requirements of probativity.

### 2.4 *Rei interventus*, homologation and adoption
In transactions where a formal writ was obligatory, the rule (above stated) was that, if there was no formal writ, no right or obligation was created. That rule was subject to two qualifications:

**2.5** (*a*) *Rei interventus and homologation.* This applied only in contracts. The general principle was that, where the parties to a contract have reached agreement but the requisite (formal) document is wanting, the subsequent actings of one or both parties might create a binding contract. There must be:

(i) Proof of the agreement, probably limited to writ or oath; and

(ii) Subsequent actings. *Rei interventus* meant actings by the party seeking to enforce the contract, which proceeded upon the supposed contract, which were material, and which materially altered the position of the party so acting. Homologation implied actings by the party seeking to escape from the contract.

In the 1995 Act s. 11 (1) and (2), proof by writ or oath is abolished and, in s. 1 (5), *rei interventus* is replaced. See 2.41 below.

**2.6** (*b*) *Adoption.* Adoption implies the existence of an informal writing (in a case where formal writ is required) coupled with a second, formal document (earlier or later in date), referring to and 'adopting' the informal writing, either expressly or by implication.

Adoption is not referred to in the 1995 Act. In s. 14 (3), however, nothing in the 1995 Act applies to any document executed or anything done before the commencement of the Act. Likewise, the 1995 Act is not to affect the operation, in relation to a document executed under the old rules, of any procedure for establishing the authenticity thereof.

In the context of adoption, the implications of this provision are not clear. Is adoption of a pre-1995 document by a document validly executed under the new rules still effective, as being a 'procedure for establishing authenticity' under s. 14(3)(b)?

## 2.7 Proof by writ or oath

In certain special types of contract, writing, as such, was not an essential to the constitution of the contract; but the fact of constitution could be proved in court only by production of a written document (formal or informal); or, if no writ was available, then the matter might be referred to the oath of the defender.

If there is no writ, and if, on oath, the defender admits the existence of the contract, his admission supplies the want of writ. If, on oath, he successfully denies it, the pursuer's case fails.

If, in such cases, the alternative of writ (as opposed to oath) is relied on, then it is relied on purely as a matter of evidence or proof. The written document, as such, is not an essential to the constitution of the contract. Examples of this limited class of case, where proof is thus restricted to writ or oath, are:

(*a*)  Agreements involving loan.

(*b*)  Agreements implying trust. See the Blank Bonds and Trusts Act 1696.

(*c*)  Innominate and unusual contracts.

Under the 1995 Act s. 11, the need for proof by writ or oath and the relevant procedure are abolished but not in relation to proceedings already commenced before 1 August 1995.

## 2.8 Probativity and authentication

Probativity as such disappears under the new rules but an analogous concept is introduced under s. 1 although the detailed requirements are different. With that in mind, the old rules can be stated as follows, using the term 'probative' as it applied under the old rules.

Probativity implies that a writing bears *prima facie* evidence of authorship and that no further enquiry is necessary as to the genuine quality of the probative writing. A deed cannot be probative unless it complies with strict rules as to form and authentication. The formal rules are designed to ensure that writings which, in point of form, comply therewith, are genuine. They are, necessarily, a balance of convenience; on the one hand, not so strict or exacting as to make compliance difficult or burdensome; on the other, not so undemanding as to make forgery easy.

Forgery is rare. Two recent reported cases involve forged signatures. In *McLeod* 1989 SLT 620 the title was in joint names. The husband himself signed, and forged his wife's signature on a standard security. The court declined to reduce the deed entire. Instead, it preferred to adopt a device of partial reduction so as to allow the husband's obligation to remain intact but to relieve the wife of the obligations purportedly undertaken by her on her forged signature. See also *Sereshky* 1988 SLT 426 where the signature on a power of attorney was forged and the deed was reduced entire. Forgery can take other forms. See 'Execution of Deeds' 1987 JLS 148.

Every probative deed is divided into two main parts – the body of the deed which contains all the operative clauses (*i.e.* clauses which in themselves give rise to legal consequences); and the authentication of the deed which cannot, in law, add anything to the substance of the operative clauses, but is concerned solely to establish that the deed is the genuine, voluntary and intended act of the grantor.

If a writing is probative it is accepted by the court as the genuine and authentic act of the purported grantor, without any supporting or corroborative evidence. But probativity is only a *prima facie* presumption; and probative writings are not beyond challenge. If, however, the authenticity of a writing, *ex facie* probative, is challenged, the whole onus of proof lies on the challenger, and it is a very heavy onus to discharge. Unless and until a probative document is successfully challenged (the appropriate process being an action of reduction), the deed must be accepted as genuine and must receive effect. Therefore, no other evidence is required of the rights or obligations which the probative document purports to create or confer, *i.e.* it proves its own terms. A writing, which is not probative, is competent evidence but will only be admitted in proof if it is supported, and spoken to, by the oral evidence of a witness on oath; and it can only be treated as an adminicle of evidence. A writing which is not probative cannot, of itself, and unsupported, prove rights or obligations, nor is it conclusive as to its terms.

### 2.9 Formalities of execution
The essentials required by law for probative authentication of documents executed prior to 1 August 1995 are:

(1) Subscription by the parties on the last page of the deed, and on the last page of the inventory, schedule, etc., appended thereto; except in the case of testamentary writings which must be subscribed on each page.

(2) Subscription by two witnesses on the last page of the deed but not on the addenda.

(3) Designations of the witnesses, either in the testing clause (Subscription of Deeds Act 1681) or appended to their signatures (Conveyancing (Scotland) Act 1874 s. 38).

(4) A reference, in the testing clause, to all alterations in the deed.

### 2.10 Form of probative deed
A probative deed may be written, typed, or printed by any person (grantor or otherwise) in any permanent medium, or it may be a photographic representation of any of these. Further, a deed may be partly in one medium and partly in another, *e.g.* partly printed and partly typewritten.

Today, most deeds are engrossed bookwise, when on more than one sheet, in terms of the Deeds Act 1696. Under that Act, sheets may be single (written on the front only or front and back), or double, folded quarto; each page had to be numbered (abolished by the Form of Deeds (Scotland) Act

1856), and the total number of pages had to be mentioned in the testing clause (abolished 1874 Act s. 38). Further, the parties to the deed had to subscribe each page but this was altered by the Conveyancing and Feudal Reform (Scotland) Act 1970 s. 44, which provides that where:

(*a*) a deed;

(*b*) an inventory, appendix, schedule, plan or other document annexed to a deed,

is subscribed and (where appropriate) sealed on the last page (*i.e.* of the deed and of the inventory and of the schedule and of the plan, etc.) the fact that it is not subscribed on every page is unobjectionable.

But s. 44 does not apply to wills or other testamentary writings.

Witnesses subscribe on the last page only.

### 2.11 Additions and alterations (vitiations)

It occasionally happened that, due to an error in engrossing or because of later alterations, additional words or phrases had to be added to a deed or were substituted for other words which had been erased. Occasionally, certain words or phrases in a deed had to be deleted. Any such additions or alterations on the face of a probative deed raise an immediate presumption in law that they have been made after execution, and so are not authenticated by the grantor. In law, no person is presumed to have signed an altered document if intended to be probative. If such additions or alterations are to receive effect, they must be properly authenticated.

### 2.12 (1) Marginal additions.
In a probative deed, if a substantial addition is made before execution, it will normally be added separately in the margin. This is known technically as a 'marginal addition'. The marginal addition will be signed by the party or parties, but not the witnesses. The practice is to sidescribe in the margin, with the initials or pre-name below the marginal addition and the surname above it; and the marginal addition receives a special mention in the testing clause, the purpose being to show *ex facie* of the deed that the witnesses to the signature on the deed itself also witnessed the signing of the marginal addition. This practice is not affected by the 1970 Act s. 44.

### 2.13 (2) Interlineations.
Minor additions of a word or two can simply be interlined at the appropriate place. Interlineations in a probative deed are not normally signed or initialled, but they must be specially mentioned in the testing clause.

### 2.14 (3) Erasures.
In the same way, alterations, erasures and deletions are not in practice signed or initialled, but must be specially mentioned in the testing clause.

### 2.15 Effect of vitiations on validity

An addition to a probative deed, whether marginal or as an interlineation, if not authenticated, is held *pro non scripto*; but normally it has no effect on the validity of the deed as a whole. Thus, if a deed contains an unauthenticated marginal addition, the marginal addition is ignored. The same rule applies to words written on erasure, where the words on erasure are not *inter essentialia*; and also to words deleted, if the deleted words still remain legible. Thus, a word interlined which is not duly authenticated is simply ignored; the deed receives effect excluding the interlined word(s). Words deleted, if the deletion is not authenticated, are read back into the deed. But if the words written on erasure, or deleted, are *inter essentialia*, or if any deleted words are illegible, then the whole deed may be reduced. If there is any suggestion of fraud, any alteration, however trivial, may result in the reduction of the whole deed.

For a recent case involving an unauthenticated deletion and interlineation in a will see *Syme's Executors* 1986 SLT 161 where these rules are discussed and the principles laid down in the earlier case of *Pattison's Trs.* (1888) 16 R 73 were applied. But for a criticism of this decision, see 'Execution or revocation', 1986 SLT (News) 129.

### 2.16 Blanks in deeds
Under the Blank Bonds and Trusts Act 1696 (now repealed by the 1995 Act), a document of debt (except *in re mercatoria*) is void unless the name of the creditor has been inserted, at latest, before delivery. In other cases, the effect of a blank in a deed depends on the nature of the omission. Thus, if the description is omitted from a disposition, the deed is patently void. Lesser omissions normally have no effect and are simply ignored; but of course they may cause problems of construction.

### 2.17 Addenda
A probative deed is normally in two connected parts, the body of the deed and the testing clause. The testing clause follows immediately upon the last word of the deed on the final page, and on that page the party or parties, and the witnesses, sign. In practice, for convenience, matter appropriate to the deed itself is frequently relegated to a schedule or schedules annexed to the deed on separate sheets following on the last page of the deed proper. If the schedules are to receive effect as part of a probative deed (which is of course the intention), they must also be properly authenticated. In practice, schedules are specially referred to in the body of the deed so as to incorporate them in the deed by adoption; they are signed (on the last page only – 1970 Act s. 44) by the parties (but not the witnesses); and they are referred to in the testing clause to show that the signatures to the addenda have been properly attested. Each separate schedule or other addendum must be signed on its last page by the party(ies).

According to Professor K.G.C. Reid in 1987 JLS at pp. 148 and 149, the common law rule is that addenda to a probative deed need not be signed at all and may be effectively adopted without subscription. While that may be so, this is never relied on in practice in formal writs, because the schedule or other addendum is referred to specifically in the deed in some such terms as 'the schedule annexed and executed as relative hereto'. Where such a formula is used, subscription of the addendum, on the last page only under the 1970 Act, is thought to be necessary by express provision.

### 2.18 Endorsation
Titles to Land Consolidation (Scotland) Act s. 140. Where a writ is permitted or directed by statute to be endorsed upon any probative deed, additional sheets may be used, but the engrossment of the endorsement must commence on part of the original deed.

**2.19 Execution by parties of a deed intended to be probative**
In formal writs by individuals, subscription is essential. Some further points to note on subscriptions:

(1) By the Lyon King of Arms Act 1672, superseding earlier Scottish practice, noblemen (and bishops; but these are 'obsolete' – *Drummond* 6th July, 1809 FC) may subscribe using their title; all others may subscribe their Christian name, or the initial letters thereof, and their proper surname. But subscription in terms of the 1672 Act is good practice rather than a mandatory requirement of the law, and in the case of the parties to the deed less may be accepted. It is thought, however, not altogether logically, that witnesses must sign in accordance with the Act.

(2) A party to a deed may sign by surname only: *American Express Europe Ltd. (No. 2)* 1989 SLT 650.

(3) Married women in Scotland may sign, using their maiden surname or their married surname; but, if a married woman uses her maiden surname, that should be specially mentioned in the testing clause: *Dunlop* (1863) 2 M 1.

(4) Subscription by initials has been recognised as sufficient, where this was the usual method of signature: *Gardner* (1878) 5 R (HL) 105, and *Lowrie's Judicial Factor* 1972 SC 105. In other special cases, deviation from the strict statutory essentials has been recognised; *e.g.* a holograph will in letter form signed 'Connie' – *Draper* 1954 SC 136 and 'lots of love, Mum' – *Rhodes* 1971 SC 56. See Lord Hunter: 'I see no reason to reject ... the signature by a familiar or pet name, provided it is proved the writer used to sign letters by that name.'
Note that any such abbreviated mode of signature requires proof; and a deed so signed is not *ex facie* probative.
For an extraordinary case where a solicitor whose surname was Wilson subscribed 'D.C.R. Williamson', see *Williamson* 1996 SLT 92. The other witness signed correctly. It was not disputed that the witness was indeed named Wilson but it was not suggested that this was his normal mode of signature. The name of the testator, whose will he attested, was 'Williamson', which presumably accounts for the error. Lord Cullen referred to the decision in *Walker*, below, and the view of Lord Dunedin in that case in the House of Lords that subscription by a witness was a matter of solemnity, not merely of evidence. Accordingly, to lead evidence that Mr Wilson had inadvertently signed with the wrong name was held by Lord Cullen to be irrelevant.
This disposed of the validity of the signature of the witness, which was clearly invalid but, in turn, raised a subordinate question. On the face of it, the will bore to be subscribed by the testator and to be attested by two witnesses subscribing. Was this a mere informality of execution curable under the 1874 Act s. 39 (for which again see below) or was it a fundamental lack of a solemnity of execution? Clearly, based on the dictum of Lord Dunedin, the signature of the witness in this case fell into the latter category and accordingly the will could not be validated under s. 39.
The position is very much more clearly provided for under the new rules.

(5) Subscription by mark is wholly invalid for formal deeds, though poss-

ibly it may suffice on a writing *in re mercatoria*: *Morton* 1908 SC 171. The same applies to stamps and cyclostyles. See 1993 JLS 270.

(6) A signature of a party on erasure is unobjectionable (*Brown* (1888) 15 R 511), but very undesirable.

(7) The signature must be the voluntary, spontaneous act of the grantor. Thus, if the writer's hand is guided when he signs his name, that is fatal, *Moncrieff* (1710) M 15,936. Similarly, if the signatory inks in a pencilled signature written by another, *Crosbie* (1749) M 16,814. The hand may be supported, if held above the wrist, *Noble* (1875) 3 R 74, but this is to be avoided except in extreme emergency, because the witnesses may not remember exactly what was done; and there is a serious risk that the deed may be reduced. If a person is physically incapable of signing, then the alternative of notarial execution is always available.

(8) Blindness does not *per se* prevent a person from validly executing a deed as a party, provided he can sign his name; and, if he does himself sign the deed, it need not have been read over to him. Obviously, it is always better to adopt notarial execution on behalf of a blind person, *Ker* (1837) 15 S 983.

### 2.20 Attestation under the old rules
The rule for subscription by witnesses (attestation) is statutory, under the Subscription of Deeds Act 1681 which, with the Deeds Act 1696, forms the foundation of the modern testing clause.

The 1681 Act, as judicially interpreted, and brought up to date by later legislation, applies thus:

### 2.21 (1) Execution by various types of person. The 1681 Act applied
generally to all writs and to all parties; but its requirements were modified by statute in a variety of special cases.

The undernoted provisions applied under the old rules to the execution of documents by special parties. The 1995 Act makes a new and comprehensive provision for the execution by various special parties in Schedule 2, for which see below. Prior to 1 August 1995 the position was as undernoted.

*Companies incorporated under the Companies Acts.* By s. 36B of the Companies Act 1985 (inserted by the Law Reform (Miscellaneous Provisions) (Scotland) Act 1990 s. 72) a probative deed is validly executed by a company if it is subscribed on behalf of the company (a) by two directors or (b) by a director and the secretary or (c) by two persons authorised by the company to execute deeds. The addition of the company's seal is competent but unnecessary. There is no need for witnesses. The three methods of execution are alternatives and cannot be mixed: thus a deed signed by a director and an authorised person is not validly executed unless the director also happens to be an authorised person.

A deed executed under s. 36B is probative as to the fact of execution but not as to authority to sign, and it remains necessary to check that the signatories are indeed directors, secretaries, or authorised persons, as the case may be.

Section 36B came into force on 1 December 1990 but applies to deeds executed on or after 31 July 1990. It replaced an earlier version of s. 36B which applied to deeds executed between 31 July and 30 November 1990 but which was withdrawn following criticism of its drafting. Deeds executed prior to 31 July 1990 were regulated by s. 36(3) of the Companies Act 1985 (now repealed) and were usually signed by two directors (or a director and the secretary) with the addition of the common seal.

A company is not bound to use one of the methods set out in s. 36B. Companies also fall under the general law of execution of deeds contained in the authentication statutes and may execute by the signature of an authorised person attested by the signature of two witnesses.

Section 36B applies only to a company which is a going concern. Where a company is in receivership, administration or liquidation, deeds are subscribed by the liquidator (or as the case may be) with two witnesses, in conformity with the authentication statutes. The common seal is not required but in practice is often used.

The previous statutory provision contained in the Companies Act 1989 s. 130 (3) was repealed by the 1990 Act Schedule 9.

*Chartered companies.* If a company is incorporated by a special Act of Parliament or by Royal Charter, such Act or Charter may prescribe the mode of execution and should be referred to.

*Regional and district councils* (formerly cities, burghs and county councils). Execution by these bodies is now governed by the Local Government (Scotland) Act 1973 s. 194. Any deed sealed with the common seal of the Council and subscribed by two members of the Council and the proper officer of the Council is validly executed, whether attested by witnesses or not. Every Council has the option of adopting the provisions of this Act or of adopting special administrative provisions in its own local Act.

Regional and District Councils were abolished by the Local Government etc. (Scotland) Act 1994 and their respective functions were transferred to new Unitary Councils as from 1 April 1996 under the Local Government etc. (Scotland) Act 1994. Provision is made for the transfer of property to the new Unitary Authorities from and after that date. The new Unitary Authorities therefore fall under the new rules for the execution of documents and are dealt with below.

**2.22 (2) Number of witnesses.** 'Witnesses' means two witnesses. See *Ferguson* 1959 SC 56 – the ordinary rule of Scots law applies, requiring corroboration of any fact by two witnesses.

**2.23 (3) Qualification of witness.** Any person of or over the age of 16 and *compos mentis* is a competent witness to a probative deed. See Age of Legal Capacity (Scotland) Act 1991 ss. 1(1) and 9. There are certain exceptions, *viz.*:

(*a*) A blind person is never a competent witness (*cf.* subscription by parties); and

(*b*) A party to a deed cannot competently witness the signature of another party to the same deed.

On the other hand, there can be no competent objection in Scotland to an instrumentary witness on the ground of interest, undue influence or bad character; although the oral testimony of a witness in court may be discounted or rejected on such grounds. Thus, one spouse may witness the other's signature; and a beneficiary named in a will may act as a witness, although in neither case is this recommended.

In terms of the 1681 Act, the witnesses must then know the grantor of the deed but this is reasonably interpreted. Introduction at the time by a mutual acquaintance suffices. The essential test is that the witness shall have credible information as to the identity of the grantor.

Only subscribing witnesses shall be probative, *i.e.* each witness must sign his proper signature. See *Williamson* above. Where a deed is written book-wise, then under the 1696 Act each witness signs on the last page on which the deed ends and the testing clause begins. This still applies, even if there are addenda to the deed.

**2.24 (4) Signatures of witnesses.** The rules which apply to the signature of a party apply generally to signature by witnesses, but with witnesses mere initials or mark can never suffice.

It was normal practice, although not strictly necessary, for a witness to add the word 'witness' after his signature; or it could be added in another hand. The purpose was, firstly, to show that the witness knew why he was signing; and, secondly, to protect the witness against any possible risk that his signature might involve him as a party to the deed and to the obligations contained in it.

**2.25 (5) Designations of witnesses**. Witnesses must be designed in the deed. This is an additional precaution against fraud as well as preserving a permanent record in the body of the deed of the identity of the witnesses, should they require to be traced. The designation of the witness must be sufficient to identify him beyond reasonable doubt. Thus in 1696 'Indweller in Edinburgh' was deemed a sufficient designation but would not suffice now – *Grant* (1694) M 16,913.

Under the 1681 Act, the designations of the witnesses had to appear in the body of the writ. For the purpose of this and other Acts, information in the testing clause is taken as information in the body of the deed, but subject to this qualification that the testing clause cannot legitimately contain anything which purports to add to or qualify the operative clauses in the body of the deed – *Blair* (1896) 23 R (HL) 36.

By the 1874 Act s. 38, it is no objection to the probative character of the deed that the witnesses are not named or designed in the body thereof (or in the testing clause thereof – note the distinction between body and testing clause now recognised by statute) provided always that, where the witnesses are not so named and designed, their designations 'shall be appended to or follow' their signatures. The witnesses must still be designed, under s. 38; but the effect is to render a formal testing clause unnecessary. The designation need not be written by the witnesses themselves.

**2.26 (6) Function of witnesses.** On the function of witnesses, the statutes are silent. In the ordinary case, their true function is merely to attest, *i.e.* to provide evidence by their signature to the deed that the signature of the party which they attest is the genuine, voluntary signature of that party.

Thus, a witness need have no knowledge of the nature or content of the deed which he attests, because he speaks only to authentication. But the witness must know why he signed, *i.e.* that he is 'attesting' a signature, and

17

the grantor of the deed must know that the witness is present, as a witness, for the express purpose of attesting his signature.

Grantor and witnesses perform their respective functions of mutual consent. On the one hand, a witness otherwise competent cannot be compelled to sign as such; on the other hand, a witness otherwise competent cannot properly sign unless, at the time, he has the consent of the party whose signature he attests. If the witness does not have such consent, and if he signs notwithstanding, then (although the deed is *ex facie* probative) it is open to reduction, although the grantor of the deed may be personally barred from reducing it on that ground, as explained below.

The witnesses must know the grantor, but that is not enough in itself; they must be satisfied that the signature on the document which they attest is the authentic signature of the grantor. On this last point, the 1681 Act is express. Two situations are envisaged. Either:

(*a*) the witnesses must see the grantor adhibit his signature. If so, there is apparently no express statutory time limit within which the witnesses must sign; or

(*b*) at the time when the witnesses subscribe, the grantor must acknowledge his signature. This is reasonably interpreted and does not necessarily mean that, as the witness actually signs, the grantor must acknowledge; but in practice, in either case, no interval of time should elapse between signature or acknowledgement by party and signature by witness.

One witness may see the grantor sign and another hear him acknowledge. Or the grantor may acknowledge his signature separately to two witnesses at different times. The acknowledgement need not be verbal.

The same two witnesses may attest several signatures to a deed. If all the parties sign together, the same two witnesses require to sign once only; if several parties sign at different times, the same two witnesses should sign again on each occasion.

**2.27 (7) Time limits.** It is certainly fatal to a deed if one, or both, of the witnesses fail to sign before the deed is registered for preservation, or is founded on in court. The same rule applies where a witness signs after the consent or mandate from the grantor of the writ has been withdrawn. See *Walker* 1916 SC (HL) 75.

**2.28 The testing clause**
Prior to 1874, a testing clause was essential in order to incorporate in the writ certain information then required by statute. Since 1874, the only information statutorily necessary is the designation of witnesses; and this may be appended to their signatures. If, therefore, there are no vitiations in a deed, a testing clause is not obligatory. But, in practice, certain information over and above the strict statutory requirements was invariably inserted; and, even if the s. 38 alternative was followed, a shortened form of testing clause was almost always used.

**2.29 Some points on testing clauses**
The testing clause must commence on the deed, *i.e.* the words 'in witness whereof' which introduce the testing clause must appear on a page which also contains part of the operative clauses of the deed, however short that

part may be. Parties and witnesses must all subscribe on that page; otherwise the subscription of witnesses is not on the last page of the deed, and fails to comply with the 1696 Act. But this only applies to deeds written bookwise, not to deeds on one sheet. See *Ferguson* 1959 SC 56.

The pages of the deed and all addenda are normally numbered (not essential since 1856); and the number of pages is mentioned in the testing clause (not essential since 1874).

Addenda and marginal additions are always mentioned in the testing clause; and the same applies to all vitiations.

Sometimes a party signs a deed in two or more capacities, *e.g.* as trustee and as an individual. If so, then arguably he ought to sign the deed twice. If he signs once only, that is accepted in practice as sufficient if his dual capacity is specifically referred to in the testing clause, *e.g.* 'subscribed by me, the said AB as trustee foresaid and as an individual'. But, if a party to a deed signs it once only and there is no such reference in the testing clause, he would find it extremely difficult later to maintain that he had signed in one capacity but not in the other.

Where (as often happens) there is a discrepancy between the name of a party (or witness) and the signature of that party (or witness), this should be mentioned in the testing clause. So, if a witness Alan Bell Smith signs simply 'A. Smith', his full name should be given in the testing clause, adding 'subscribing with his usual signature "A. Smith"'.

Date and place of execution are not essential by statute or common law, but both are always included. The place of execution may be relevant, *e.g.* in wills – see the Wills Act 1963. The date of execution is often necessary for stamp duty purposes, and may otherwise be relevant.

If an error is made in the testing clause, *e.g.* erasure, interlineation, etc., the error should be declared at the end of that clause.

**2.30 Completion of testing clause.** In practice, a deed was engrossed down to and including the words 'in witness whereof'. These words indicate that the operative clauses have ended and that what follows is the testing clause only; that is a precaution to prevent the risk of additional clauses being added to the deed after it has been signed. Bell in his *Lectures*, and Burns in Green's *Encyclopaedia*, Vol. 2 s. 660, 'Blanks in Deeds', recommend that the deed should be taken further, and that, before it is signed, the testing clause should be partially completed so as to include the number of pages and all vitiations, etc., leaving only the date and place of execution and the names of the witnesses to be filled in after signature. This prevents the possibility of spurious alterations being made after execution and being apparently duly authenticated by declaration in the testing clause, also added after execution. But this suggestion, though excellent, is rarely adopted in practice. In any event, that part of the testing clause dealing with place and date of execution and the designations of the witnesses cannot be filled in until after execution. Some interval must therefore elapse; it may be only an hour or two or it may be some weeks if a deed is to be signed by several parties, but the interval should always be kept to the minimum, because completion of the testing clause is part of the solemnity of authentication. This is stressed in *Walker*, although it is recognised that, by long custom, the strict rules in this respect are not applied above. Thus, in *Blair* (1827) 6 S 51, a 32-year interval did not invalidate the deed.

Under the 1874 Act s. 38, witnesses' designations may be added at any time before the deed is founded on in any action or is registered for preservation. The same rules apply to completion of the testing clause. Death is no bar to adding designations or completing the testing clause – see opinion of Lord Dunedin in *Walker* which does not support the view that the testing clause may not be completed after death. Even where a deed has been registered, or has been founded on, uncompleted, there is a remedy and the defect need not be fatal – 1874 Act s. 39 and *Thomson's Trs.* (1878) 6 R 141; but, of course, the deed is not *ex facie* probative.

### 2.31 Notarial execution or vicarious subscription

At common law, a writ was sufficiently authenticated if the seal of the grantor was affixed, without subscription; and the grantor himself was not required to affix his own seal. This could be done for him. Therefore, questions of personal capacity or incapacity presented no problem in the authentication of a document. The presence of the seal on a document sufficiently authenticated it, and it did not matter by whose hand the seal was affixed. Subscription is a personal matter, and it must be the voluntary spontaneous act of the grantor himself. The Subscription of Deeds Act 1540, which first introduced subscription as an essential solemnity, also made provision for the execution of documents vicariously by a notary public on behalf of a person who could not sign his own name. The requirements of that and later Acts were wholly superseded by the 1924 Act s. 18 and Schedule I for any deed executed after 31 December 1924.

The 1924 Act s. 18 and Schedule I are now in turn superseded by new provisions in the 1995 Act, explained below. Accordingly, the comments which follow on notarial execution apply only to a deed vicariously executed prior to 1 August 1995. Bearing that in mind, the points to note on deeds notarially executed under the old rules are as follows.

(1) The 1924 Act referred to any deed of whatever nature.

(2) The section is permissive ('any deed, etc., may'). In other words, in the case of blind persons, this procedure is optional and the section does not alter the rule that a blind person may validly execute at his own hand; but in the case of physical incapacity there is no effective alternative.

(3) The official who signs vicariously may be:

(*a*) As regards any writ a law agent, notary public, or justice of the peace. Law agent is defined in the 1924 Act s. 2 (6), thus 'law agent shall mean and include writers to the signet, solicitors in the supreme courts, procurators in any sheriff court and every person entitled to practise as an agent in a court of law in Scotland' (for the latter, see the Solicitors (Scotland) Act 1980). Notary public is defined in the 1868 Act s. 2 as a notary public duly admitted to practise in Scotland. Justice of the peace is not defined and presumably covers a Justice anywhere in the United Kingdom.

(*b*) As regards testamentary writings only, in addition to the foregoing, the parish minister acting in his own parish or his assistant and successor so acting. (See Church of Scotland (Property and Endowments) Amendment Act 1933, s. 13, for some slight modifications.)

(4) The official must know the grantor or have credible evidence of his identity.

(5) The grantor must be blind or unable to write.

(6) He must declare his disability.

(7) The deed must be read over to him.

(8) He must give authority, visible or audible, to the signing of the deed on his behalf.

(9) At that point, the official signs the deed using his own, ordinary signature. In testamentary deeds, he signs each page; for other deeds, the 1970 Act s. 44 applies, and signature on each page is strictly unnecessary, but certainly desirable. In all cases, he must write a holograph docquet in his own handwriting on the last page of the deed, which he subscribes, adding his qualification and designation. Note that, on the last page, the official's signature to the docquet authenticates the whole page, *i.e.*, he does not require to sign the last page twice. (See note to Schedule I.)

(10) The whole of the foregoing procedure must be carried out entire, as a single continuous process, in the presence of the grantor and of the two witnesses, who then sign the deed, in the ordinary way, on the last page only. For a cautionary case, see *Hynd's Trustee* 1955 SC (HL) 1. A solicitor read over a will to the testator and signed it in his presence and in the presence of two witnesses, employees of the solicitor. He did not add his docquet at the time nor did the witnesses then sign. The solicitor and the two witnesses then all returned to his office, and one and a half hours later the solicitor added the docquet and the witnesses then signed. The will was held invalidly executed.

**2.32 The docquet.** The form of docquet to be written on the deed by the official is prescribed in Schedule I to the 1924 Act, thus:
'*Docquet where grantor of deed is blind or cannot write*
Read over to, and signed by me, for and by authority of the above named AB (without designation) who declares that he is blind (or is unable to write) all in his presence, and in presence of the witnesses hereto subscribing.'

    CD, law agent, Edinburgh,
    MN, witness
    PQ, witness

The docquet must be holograph; a typewritten docquet or one written in some other hand was not sufficient.
    There are some notes to Schedule I which give directions as to signatures, etc.

**2.33 Interest of the notary.** Although there is no reference to this in the 1924 Act s. 18, the official, who signs vicariously, is not permitted to have any patrimonial interest whatever, actual or potential, in the provisions of the deed. That rule is absolute and is most strictly applied. If ignored, the deed is invalid and reducible. The leading (modern) case is *Finlay* 1948 SC 16.

## 2.34 Informality of execution

Prior to 1874, the standard rule was that, if any of the strict requirements for probativity was not complied with, then the deed was inevitably invalid.

If the transaction was one of the *obligationes literis*, this carried the inevitable consequence that the whole transaction was invalidated. Thus, prior to 1856, it was a statutory requirement that each page of a deed should be numbered and that the number of pages should be mentioned in the testing clause. Failure to number any one page of a deed, or to mention the number of pages, totally invalidated the whole document.

The common law rule was modified by statute in two ways:

(*a*) Under the 1874 Act s. 38, and earlier provisions, certain of the old meticulous requirements were abolished *e.g.* numbering of pages etc.; and

(*b*) By the 1874 Act s. 39, even if a deed did not comply in all respects with the remaining statutory requirements, under the old rules, it was, and for a deed executed under the old rules it still is, possible to petition the court under this section for a declarator that the deed was subscribed by the grantor and two witnesses, notwithstanding some 'informality of execution'. Note, however, that the 1874 Act s. 39 applies only to 'informalities'. The section cannot be used to cure serious defects in the solemnity of execution. Thus, it is an essential statutory requirement that a subscribing witness must either see the grantor sign the deed or hear him acknowledge his signature. If a witness signs without having done either of these, the deed is invalid; and that invalidity is more than a mere 'informality'. Therefore, the deed cannot be declared probative under this section. If a witness subscribes using the wrong name, that is not a mere 'informality' – see *Williamson* above – and is not curable.

In the case of notarial execution, the 1924 Act s. 18(2) applied the provisions of s. 39 to any deed notarially executed in accordance with s. 18(1) as if it were a deed actually subscribed by the grantor.

## 2.35 The effect of *ex facie* probativity

A deed is *ex facie* probative under the old rules if it bears to be subscribed by the grantor and by the necessary two witnesses, and the testing clause has been properly completed. Nonetheless, the deed may be a nullity because there has been some radical defect in the solemnity of execution which is not a mere informality and is thus not curable under s. 39, *e.g.* where one witness has neither seen the grantor subscribe nor heard him acknowledge the signature. That is the standard rule. It is subject to two qualifications:

(*a*) A deed which is *ex facie* probative must receive effect unless and until it is set aside by a decree of reduction. The onus always lies on the challenger to prove the want of due authentication, and very clear proof will be required. It is not sufficient, in an action of reduction on this ground, to produce one of the witnesses to the signature who merely says he cannot remember, *e.g.* seeing the grantor sign. Very convincing evidence from the witnesses will be required. Nonetheless, if it can be shown conclusively that a witness did not properly subscribe as a witness, the deed, although *ex facie* probative, may be set aside and invalidated by a decree of reduction.

(*b*) Even although the challenger may prove that the deed was not properly signed and should therefore be invalidated under the previous rule, the challenger may himself be personally barred from founding on that invalidity. Thus, if A signed a loan document and handed it to the creditor apparently duly attested by two witnesses, and obtained a loan in exchange, A cannot then turn round and say that the deed is improperly executed, with a view to invalidating the loan document. A is personally barred from founding on such latent defects in authentication.

### 2.36 Privileged writings

The old rules for probative writings summarised above applied generally to all situations and all types of deed; but there were certain circumstances, and certain types of deed, to which, at common law, the statutory provisions have been held not to apply.

Such writings are termed 'privileged writings'. The commonest illustrations of privileged writings are:

**2.37 (1) Holograph writings.** A writing which is wholly in the handwriting of and is subscribed by the grantor is holograph. It is privileged to this extent, that attestation of the signature is unnecessary at common law, and so the statutory provisions summarised above do not apply to it. Holograph writings differ from solemnly attested deeds in this important respect, that the onus of proving a holograph writ to be genuine lies on the party founding on it, and not on the party who challenges its authenticity.

In contrast, where a writing is solemnly attested according to the statutory rules, the onus always lies on the challenger to prove that the deed is not in fact probative although *ex facie* it appears to be so; and that is a heavy onus to discharge.

However, if a holograph writ can be proved to be written in the handwriting of and subscribed by the grantor or is admitted so to be in a court action, then it does have all the qualities of a probative writ, in that it proves its own terms and serves as formal writ for the purposes of the *obligationes literis*.

The privilege extended to deeds which were not written in the grantor's own hand but which he 'adopted as holograph'. If these words were written by the grantor in his own hand at the end of the document and if he then also subscribed, the document is deemed to be wholly holograph.

Similarly, documents in themselves improbative can be given the qualities of probativity by being 'adopted' in another probative writing.

For specialties which arise with documents partly handwritten and partly printed, see *Campbell* 1963 SLT (Sh Ct) 10.

**2.38 (2) Writings *in re mercatoria*.** This covered a wide variety of documents in everyday commercial use. If signed before 1 August 1995, they are privileged in that they might receive effect although they did not comply with the statutory requirements for solemn execution.

The concept of privileged writings has no place under the new rules and accordingly, under the 1995 Act s. 11(3), the privilege previously enjoyed by writs holograph or adopted as such is abolished for any writ executed on or after 1 August 1995. That, of course, has no effect whatever on any documents executed prior to that date under the old rules. They will continue to enjoy whatever privilege they had prior to 1 August 1995, with whatever benefit that may carry with it, depending on the nature of the writ and of the transaction to which it relates.

There is still a lingering trace of the privilege accorded to writings *in re mercatoria*, however, in s. 1(2)(a)(ii) which exempts gratuitous unilateral business obligations from the statutory requirement prescribing a written document. That exemption would not apply to any such obligation if not in the course of business.

**2.39 (3) Writs executed abroad.** The general rule of private international law, applied in Scotland, is that any deed executed abroad will receive effect here if executed in accordance with the required formalities in the place of execution.

The rule is most commonly applied in the case of wills, and powers of attorney.

In the case of wills, the common law rule has been reinforced with modifications under the Wills Act 1963 which continues to apply under the new rules.

Some authors treat this exception for writs executed abroad as falling under the general heading of privileged writings and they are so treated here. See Burns' *Practice*, 4th edn. p. 14 and also Rennie and Cusine on *The Requirements of Writing* p. 40. For a recent illustration of the application of the rule in practice, see *Hamilton* 1992 SCLR 740 where it was held in the Scottish Courts that a contract for the sale and purchase of a superiority, being heritable property, had been validly created under the English rule which provides that, where a person bids at an auction, he incurs a binding legal obligation, even where the subject-matter is heritable.

The only mention in the 1995 Act of documents executed abroad is in s. 6 (3)(c)(iii) which authorises registration in the Books of Council and Session or Sheriff Court Books if the Keeper or Sheriff Clerk is satisfied that the document is formally valid according to the law governing its validity. This is a statutory exception to the provision under the new rules.

The 1995 Act abolishes the first two categories of privileged writing mentioned above. Except for the speciality of registration, however, writs executed abroad are not otherwise referred to in the Act. It is presumed by this author that the privilege accorded to a deed executed abroad under the old rules will continue to apply, but no express provision seems to be made in the 1995 Act.

Under the old rules, titles to heritable property in Scotland form an exception; they must conform to the Scottish requirements of authentication, regardless of other factors. It is assumed that this will continue to apply.

Professor Reid in *The Requirements of Writing (Scotland) Act 1995*, when dealing with the express provision in s. 11(3), states without qualification that ss. 1 and 2 of the Act abolished 'the types of privileged formal writing recognised by the common law'. He makes a clear distinction between common law rules and statutory provisions. The privilege for foreign writs under the old rules was a common law rule and not a statutory one. For reasons stated below, the practical result may not be of any significance. In the result, it is uncertain whether the common law privilege for writs executed abroad continues to apply generally as before.

## 2.40 The new rules under the 1995 Act

In the 5th edition of the Manual at para. 2.40 reference was made to proposed reforms recommended by the Scottish Law Commission in their Report No. 112 on 'The Requirements of Writing'. These recommendations have now in large part been implemented by the 1995 Act which introduces the 'new rules'. The Act in itself is a complete, self-contained statutory code governing the execution of documents in Scotland. At the same time, the Act repeals the whole body of earlier statutory provisions relating to such execution as well as abolishing certain common law rules and some outdated and unnecessary rules of evidence which, under the old rules, in certain transactions, restricted proof to the writ or oath of the grantor.

In summary, this is achieved, under the 1995 Act, thus:

(1) In s. 1 (1), a written document is generally not required to constitute a contract, an obligation or a trust; but there are certain important specified exceptions where a formal document is still required under s. 1(2).

(2) The old rules under which the lack of the required formality might be supplied by *rei interventus* or homologation are abolished, but under s. 1(3) to (6) comparable provision is made; and so the general principle at least of *rei interventus* still continues to apply although in a modified form.

(3) In those cases where, under s. 1 (2) above, a formal document is still required, the only formality is subscription of the document by the grantor. Attestation, although it still has an important function under s. 3 below, ceases to be an essential to the required formality. Further, in those cases where attestation is appropriate, only one witness is now required instead of two.

Attestation is thus now segregated from subscription. Under the old rules, subscription and attestation were, taken together, essential solemnities and both were therefore necessary for the validity of the document. Under the new rules, in contrast, subscription alone suffices to validate a document in cases where a formal writing is required. For that purpose, attestation is unnecessary but it still remains essential if the subscribed document is to achieve the same quality which a probative writing acquired under the old rules in the sense that, by attestation, a subscribed document, which under the new rules is formally valid, is made self-proving both as to subscription and as to content.

Clearly, these are major and important reforms. In particular, the old solemnities of execution are fundamentally changed; the function of attestation is fundamentally altered; the *obligationes literis* disappear; the procedure of proof by writ or oath is abolished; and the privilege accorded under the old rules to certain types of document, dealt with above, is no longer of any significance and is done away with. At least, that applies in the case of holograph writs and writings *in re mercatoria*; but some exceptions to the statutory provisions required for certain writs under s. 1(2) may still continue to apply, including in particular deeds executed abroad. They are dealt with indirectly under s. 6(3)(iii) but only in the context of registration, not validity. For the continuing importance of this privilege, see *Hamilton* above. Opinion on this point differs.

As already mentioned, the 1995 Act contains in itself a complete coherent self-contained code setting out the rules for the execution of formal documents in Scotland, the requirements for formal validity and for self-proving status. The Act is reproduced *in extenso* in *Greens Property Statutes*. It is also reproduced, with extensive annotations by Professor Reid, in *Current Law Statutes*; and Greens have produced the annotated Act as a separate publication by Professor Reid in their Annotated Acts series. In addition, the old rules, the new rules and the significance of these fundamental changes in the requirements for formal validity are also dealt with at length and in detail by Professors Rennie and Cusine in their book on the Act above referred to, and in Halliday, *Conveyancing Law and Practice*, 2nd edn. Vol. I. Given this wealth of up-to-date detailed information on the provisions of the Act, it is not proposed to deal with the new rules at great length or in meticulous detail in this Chapter; instead the salient features of the Act and the changes which it introduces are dealt with *seriatim*, section by section as they appear in the Act itself and in its Schedules.

### Examination of the salient features of the new rules

**2.41 When is a written document obligatory?** The general provision under s. 1(1) is that, with certain exceptions, a written document is not required for the constitution of any contract, unilateral obligation or trust.

The principal qualification to that rule is then set out in s. 1(2) in terms of which a formal written document is required, speaking generally, for any writ relating to land; for any gratuitous unilateral obligation except in the course of business; to establish any trust by which the truster declares himself to be the sole trustee of his own property including acquirenda; and for any testamentary writing in any form.

Section 1(3) to (6) then provide a qualification to the new rule requiring formal writing for the various transactions referred to in s. 1(2)(a) where there has been what, under the old rules, would have amounted to *rei interventus* or possibly homologation. So, under these sections, lacking the necessary formal written document, if a creditor in an obligation which was intended to be constituted thereby or a beneficiary under such a trust as is referred to above has acted in reliance thereon to the knowledge and with the acquiescence of the other party, that other party, notwithstanding the lack of the required formal writing, is personally barred from withdrawing from the contractual obligation or trust which, as a result, is not to be treated as invalid if the conditions of s. 1(4) are satisfied. Under that subsection, the requirement is that the aggrieved party, by so acting or refraining from so acting, has been, and would be, materially and adversely affected if the transaction was not implemented. By express provision in s. 1(5) these rules replace *rei interventus* and homologation under the old rules.

The same principles are then applied with the like effect under s. 1(6) to a variation of any such transaction where the variation itself lacks the necessary formal documentation.

Under s. 1(7) and (8) 'interest in land' is then defined for the purposes of s. 1(2). As Professor Reid points out in his book, the use of the term 'interest in land' may raise some ambiguity as to exactly what is required by way of formal documentation. His comment on the use of the term 'interest in land' is not, perhaps, entirely justified. It has, admittedly, come to be used in recent statutes in place of the term land or estate or real right in land; but its use dates back to the 1874 Act s. 3 where an estate in land is said to be an 'interest in land' and is clearly distinguished from land itself by the two separate definitions in that section. It seems fairly clear from that definition of 'estate in land' in the 1874 Act that its meaning is not confined, as Professor Reid suggests, to real rights in land, or at least not to real rights in land vested directly by infeftment in the party to the relevant contract or grantor of the relevant deed. Accordingly, the only safe assumption here is that any contract or deed where the subject-matter is directly or indirectly land, whatever the state of the infeftment, should be treated as falling within s. 1(2). The trust liferent is typical. The trustees may have a real right in land by infeftment; the trust liferenter certainly has not, but equally certainly has an 'interest in land'.

Note that all the new rules for execution by parties and witnesses are subject to any other special statutory provision which takes precedence. See s. 1(1), s. 7(1) and s. 8(1)

**2.42  Requirements for formal validity.**  Under s. 2(1), formality of execution as required by s. 1(2) means subscription on the last page by the grantor of the relevant document or by each grantor where there is more than one. Nothing other than such subscription is required to validate the document. Under s. 2(2), two or more contractual documents taken together satisfy these requirements if each is so subscribed. Section 2(3) permits the use of an informal document as evidence in cases where a formal document is strictly required.

Subject to detailed and elaborate provisions in s. 3(2) to (7), s. 3(1) provides that, where a document bears to be subscribed by the grantor, bears to have been signed by a witness, bears to state therein or in the testing clause the name and address of the witness; and where there is no contra-indication in the document, then that document is presumed to have been subscribed by that grantor.

A document which is thus on the face of it presumed to have been so subscribed is self-proving in the sense that the authenticity of the grantor's subscription and of the content of the deed requires no further corroborative evidence to establish its terms and the formality of its execution. In old rule terminology, it is therefore probative. Note particularly that attestation, although necessary for this purpose, is no longer a necessary element in the solemnity of execution. Compare the effect of this provision with the resulting situation in *Walker*, above, where a witness, otherwise competent to act as such, failed to sign the deed as a witness before the death of the testator. That was treated unhesitatingly by the Court as a fundamental defect in the solemnities of execution which inevitably rendered the codicil in that case invalid even although it had been duly subscribed and indeed duly attested by one subscribing witness. If the other witness had also then signed, the codicil would have been valid and would have received effect. His failure to sign could not, however, be treated as a mere informality of execution. The codicil was therefore worthless and could not receive effect to any extent.

The qualifications to the main provision in s. 3(1) can be summarised briefly thus:

27

s. 3(2)  Testamentary writings must be subscribed on every sheet.

s. 3(3)  The name and address of the witness may be added at any time before the document is founded on or registered, and need not be written by the witness himself.

Under s. 3(4) if a question arises as to formality of subscription and if it is proved that the signature of the witness is false, or is the signature of another party to the deed, or if the witness did not know the grantor, was under 16 years of age, or incapax, or if the witness failed properly to attest, *unico contextu,* or if the name and address of the witness were added after the time limit in s. 3(3) above, then there is no presumption that the document was subscribed by the grantor. The same result follows in the case of a testamentary writing on more than one sheet if a signature on any of the sheets is proved not to be the signature of the testator.

Under s. 3(5), knowing the grantor merely means having credible information as to his identity.

Under s. 3(6), where there is more than one party to a deed and the same witness attests two or more signatures, the fact that an interval occurs between the signature of the parties and the subscription by the witness does not disqualify the attestation as failing to satisfy the *unico contextu* rule.

Under s. 3(7), the witness must see the grantor subscribe or the grantor must acknowledge his subscription to the witness.

Under s. 3(8), if the document is so authenticated and bears to state, *in gremio* thereof or in a testing clause, the date or place of subscription, that statement is presumed to be correct in the absence of any contra-indication, except in the case of a testamentary writing, under s. 3(9). But, under s. 3(10), an equivalent rule applies to testamentary writings, even if not self-proving. This avoids problems of the relative dates of several codicils which may be valid but not self-proving.

**2.43  Presumptions in Court proceedings – s. 4.**  The provisions of this section arise out of the alteration in the rules by virtue of which a subscribed document is formally valid although, if not attested, it is not self-proving. Normally, that is not important. But it can be where the writ is to be registered or used to obtain confirmation. In such cases, if not self-proving as to signature, date or place, application can be made to the Court for certification of all or any of these facts. Procedure is regulated by Act of Sederunt of 1 July 1996 (SI 1534).

**2.44  Alterations to documents – s. 5.**  The general effect of this section is to validate any alteration to a document:

(*a*) if made before the document is subscribed by the first or the only grantor, in which case the alteration forms part of the document; or

(*b*) if made after subscription and if the alteration is then signed by the grantor, or by all grantors when there is more than one.

Otherwise, alterations are not valid, unless so declared on application to the Court. The facts may be established by any evidence, for which detailed provision is made in Schedule 1.

An alteration to a document subscribed by the grantor or all the grantors is presumed to have been made before subscription and therefore to form part of the document:

(i) where the document is self-proving, the alteration is declared, and there is no contra-indication in the document; or

(ii) if (i) is not applicable, the same result is achieved if application is made to the Court, if the facts are established and if the document is suitably endorsed.

The provisions of s.4 apply generally to any such application.

Where the alteration is made after subscription, certain presumptions apply as set out in Schedule 1 to the Act, for which see below.

**2.45 Registration – s. 6.** Under the statutory rules covering registration in the Books of Council and Session or Sheriff Court Books, a deed will normally only be accepted for such registration if, under the old rules, it is probative. Where executed under the new rules, the position is now regulated by this section. Generally speaking, to be registerable, the document must be self-proving except in the case of a testamentary document or a deed executed abroad. No consent to registration is required.

**2.46 Subscription and signing – s. 7.** (1) Under s. 7(1), subscription means signing the document at the end of the last page.

(2) Signing as grantor means:

(*a*) signing with the full name as stated in the document; or

(*b*) with the surname preceded by at least one forename or initial or abbreviation; or

(*c*) in the case of subscribed but not self-proving documents, other modes of signature are permitted to take account of such situations as *Rhodes* 1971 SC 56 see above. These include initials or mark; but in all such cases it must be established that this was the usual mode of executing that type of writing and was intended as a signature.

(3) Where there is more than one grantor, signing at the end of the last page is achieved if at least one grantor so signs; but the others must also sign on that page or on an additional page or pages.

(4) One signature covers all capacities in which a party signs.

(5) An attesting witness must sign with the full name as in the document, or testing clause or at least with the surname preceded by one forename or an initial or abbreviation. A witness need not sign more than once when attesting several signatures.

The rule which permits members of the Royal family, peers and other privileged persons to sign in a special manner remains unaltered.

The foregoing rules apply to subscription and signing by individual natural persons. Schedule 2 to the Act contains a number of provisions for execution of documents by various non-natural persons, for which see below.

**2.47 Annexations – s. 8.** These have always caused problems.

Under the 1970 Act s. 44 the old rules were changed as noted above. The grantor, except in the case of testamentary writings, was required to subscribe on the last page of the deed only, but not preceding pages, and any inventory, appendix, schedule, plan or other document annexed required subscription by the party or parties on the last page of each such annexation. Prior to the 1970 Act, in any probative document, every page required subscription by the grantor, which applied both to the pages of the deed itself and to all annexations. At least that was the accepted rule although Professor Reid considers that annexations to a probative deed did not require subscription. It is doubtful whether that would apply in any case where the deed itself expressly states that the annexation is annexed and signed or subscribed as relative thereto.

These rules are changed again under s. 8.

Under the new rules, any annexation is regarded as incorporated in a document if the document refers to it and if the annexation is on the face of it identified as being the annexation so referred to. The identification should be in particular, not merely general, terms. If these conditions are observed, no signature or subscription is required. The annexation, unsigned, is regarded as incorporated in the document.

Under s. 8(2), however, there is a special provision, applicable only to a document relating to land, which incorporates an annexation and only where that annexation describes or shows all or part of the land to which the document relates. In that case, but in that case only, the annexation is regarded as incorporated in the document if, in addition to the above requirements, it is signed on the last page or, where the annexation takes the form of a plan, drawing, photograph or other representation, on every page thereof.

The Keeper takes the view that some schedules, *e.g.* a schedule of condition or dilapidations annexed to a lease, must be signed on every page, being annexed to a document relating to land and, arguably, containing a plan, drawing, photograph or 'other representation'. It would be unsafe not to adopt the same view until the point is clarified.

Under s. 8(3), if an annexation requires a signature and bears to have been signed by the grantor, it is presumed to have been signed by the person who subscribed the deed as that grantor. Accordingly, if so signed, the annexation is self-proving. The provisions of s. 7(2) apply to the signing of any annexation, and under s. 8(6), if any one of several grantors signs on the last page of an annexation, the other grantor or grantors must also all sign, but may competently do so on an additional page. It is not clear how this applies (if at all) where an annexation must be signed on every page under s. 8(2)(c)(i).

Section 8(5) alters the old *unico contextu* rule to the extent that an annexation to a self-proving document need not be signed at the same time as the document itself. It must, however, be signed before the document itself is founded on, registered for preservation, or recorded or registered in the GRS or Land Register. No doubt this is a convenient relaxation but it may produce unexpected problems.

**2.48 Vicarious subscription – s. 9.** The old rules for 'notarial execution' are abolished and a new set of rules are introduced in a simplified form but with substantially the same effect under s. 9 and Schedule 3. The requirements under the new rules can be summarised thus:

(1) The grantor must declare to 'a relevant person' that he is blind or cannot write. Notwithstanding this provision, blind persons may themselves still competently sign a document as before.

(2) The relevant person means a solicitor with a practising certificate, an advocate, a JP or a Sheriff Clerk. Where the document is executed outwith Scotland, it also includes a Notary Public or anyone else who, in the place of execution, has official authority so to execute documents.

(3) The relevant person must read the document to the grantor unless the grantor otherwise declares this to be unnecessary. If then authorised by the grantor, he may then subscribe the document on the grantor's behalf. In the case of testamentary writings only, the relevant person must subscribe each sheet as in s. 3(2). In all cases, the signature must be in the presence of the grantor.

The same provisions apply, generally, to vicarious execution of annexations and alterations as apply in the case of personal subscription by the grantor but with the special qualification that the reference above to reading the document to the grantor includes, where appropriate, describing a plan, photograph or other representation, however best that can be achieved.

In contrast to the position under the old rules, s. 9(4) now provides that, under the new rules, a document vicariously subscribed which confers a benefit on the subscriber or his or her spouse, son or daughter is invalidated only to the extent that it confers such a benefit. This is a welcome improvement on the position under the old rules, where any interest of the notary invalidated the whole deed.

The intention of these new provisions in s. 9 was clearly to simplify the old rules for notarial execution. No doubt the procedure under s. 9 is a move in the right direction. Unfortunately, however, the simplified provisions are subject to extensive minor amendments in Schedule 3 to the Act which runs to nearly three pages of print. The amendments are not substantial in their effect. The general result, however, is that, for practical purposes, in the case of vicarious subscription, the provisions in the 1995 Act s. 3 and 4 with parts of Schedule 1 are, to a greater or lesser extent, repeated. This is unfortunate but probably inevitable in order to ensure precision.

The main amendments made for vicarious execution can be summarised thus:

(1) On the face of the document it must be evident:

(*a*) that the grantor gave authority; and

(*b*) that the document was either read over or that requirement was dispensed with.

These two elements can conveniently be set out in the testing clause.

(2) Additional requirements are superimposed on the new rules for attestation. The witness must attest the giving of authority, the reading of the document or dispensation thereof and the subscription by the relevant person. As Professor Reid points out in his annotation of this Schedule, the resulting position is not entirely clear. To avoid any possibility of challenge, the testing clause should therefore confirm that the attestation satisfied these three additional requirements.

Equivalent provision is then made for application to the Court for certification of a document vicariously subscribed.

It is clear from these modifications in Schedule 3 that the old rule requiring that the whole procedure should be *unico contextu* in the presence of grantor and witness still applies. On the other hand, the old rule is relaxed to the extent that the holograph docquet of the relevant person is no longer an essential requirement. Accordingly, if care is taken to observe the *unico contextu* rule and if a standard testing clause is adopted to incorporate the special requirements for vicarious execution, this elaborate modification of the terms of the Act should cause no serious problems.

As mentioned above, a blind person does not require to adopt vicarious execution but may himself validly subscribe. As under the old rules, however, this is not to be recommended in practice. Likewise, under the new rules, the document may either be read over to the grantor or the grantor may dispense of that requirement. In practice, while that may be convenient, it is almost certainly not advisable to encourage dispensation but instead it is better, if practicable, to read the document over to the grantor.

If there is any likelihood that vicarious execution may have to be resorted to in individual cases, the alternative of a power of attorney, or, better, an enduring power, should always be seriously considered.

**2.49 Testing clauses – s. 10.**   Reference has been made above to the testing clause, which is a standard feature of formal deeds under the old rules.

Under s. 10, information required under the new rules for creating a self-proving document can be incorporated in the deed itself but, more conveniently, may be incorporated in a testing clause. The Secretary of State is to prescribe a form. At the time of writing, however, no such form has been forthcoming. That does not, of course, prevent the use of a testing clause in conventional form which, subject to the specialities required in the case of vicarious execution, would normally contain all the necessary information for self-proving status.

**2.50 Amendments, repeals and transitional provisions.**   These are dealt with in s. 14. As already mentioned, a substantial number of archaic and more recent statutory provisions on the execution of deeds are all repealed entire, except special provisions under other enactments not primarily concerned with execution, which, generally speaking, are preserved and take precedence over the provisions of the 1995 Act. Even in these cases, however, there are a substantial number of minor amendments in Schedules 4 and 5.

Under s. 14(3), generally speaking, nothing in the Act applies to any document executed under the old rules nor affects the operation of any procedure for establishing the authenticity of any such document, *e.g.* under the 1874 Act s. 39. That is, however, subject to an exception in the case of proof by writ or oath which is abolished under s. 11 as noted above. In that special case, unless proceedings have been commenced before the commencement of the Act, proof by writ or oath is no longer applicable. Instead, any evidence, including parole evidence will be competent from and after 1 August 1995 to establish transactions or obligations already entered into or undertaken prior to 1 August 1995 which, under the old rules, could only have been proved by writ or oath.

It remains to mention only two of the Schedules to the Act.

**2.51 Alterations after subscription – Schedule 1.** Schedule 1 deals with alterations made to a document after it has been subscribed. There are two main paragraphs. The first deals with the presumption in such circumstances as to the signature of the grantor or date or place of signing.

Contemporaneous alterations to documents have been dealt with above. The provisions of Schedule 1 apparently envisage later additions or alterations to a document previously executed. The provisions are lengthy and cumbersome.

Broadly speaking, Schedule 1, para. 1 deals with a subsequent alteration to a self-proving deed previously executed as such and involves substantially the same formalities as apply in the case of the execution of the self-proving deed itself.

Paragraph 2 deals with alterations to a document not in form self-proving for which an application to the Court is required. No doubt it will be useful to have these provisions in place as a fall back in unusual and unexpected circumstances but normally they will not be used.

Alterations to testamentary writings using these provisions are particularly undesirable.

**2.52 Special persons – Schedule 2.** Schedule 2 to the Act sets out in detail special provisions which apply where the deed is subscribed or signed by or on behalf of various special categories of persons other than individuals.

*(a) Partnerships*
Under the old rules, there was no statutory provision for execution of deeds by partnerships and this occasionally caused problems. See *Littlejohn* 1974 SLT (Sh Ct) 82. Provision is now made in Schedule 2.

Where the grantor of a document is a partnership, it is duly executed if signed on its behalf by a partner or by a duly authorised person. The person signing will sign in his own name, or in the partnership name. Where the firm name is used, there seems to be no need for the signatory to declare his personal identity or authority.

Alterations are similarly dealt with.

No special provision is made for the self-proving quality of a deed so signed but since, in every case, the signature required is the signature of an individual, it is assumed that, if attested, a document so signed on behalf of a partnership will have self-proving status, as signed by the firm.

This does not, however, in addition imply that a partner or an authorised person was, or is presumed to be, duly authorised to sign; nor does the self-proving quality carry with it a guarantee that the signatory was in fact a partner. Some investigation may therefore be required, even in the case of *ex facie* self-proving documents.

*(b) Companies*
Between 1985 and 1995, the rules for the execution of deeds by companies were confused. The new provisions under the 1995 Act will, it is hoped, clarify and stabilise the position. To some extent, the new rules echo the latest provisions for company execution in the amendments to the Companies Act 1985 prior to 1995.

Under the new rules, alternative provisions for the execution of deeds by companies are made thus:

*Self-proving status:*

(i) *Attested documents.* Where a document appears to have been subscribed on behalf of a company by a director, or the secretary, or a duly authorised person, and, in addition, it bears to be signed by a witness whose name and address are given, then, in the absence of any contrary indication on the face of the document, a document so subscribed is formally valid and is self-proving.

(ii) *Unattested documents.* If the document is not attested but is subscribed on behalf of the company by two directors, or by a director and the secretary, or by two duly authorised persons but is otherwise unattested, and in the absence of any contrary indication on the face of the document, then, in this alternative form, the document is formally valid and is self-proving.

*Formal validity*

If self-proving status is not required, a document is validly executed on behalf of a company if signed by one director, or the secretary, or one duly authorised person.

A company no longer requires to have a common seal and so, in any of the foregoing alternatives, the seal is unnecessary.

Note that, as in the case of partnerships, the foregoing provisions as to execution are restricted to authentication only and in no circumstances imply that any person so signing is in fact a director, or the secretary, or an authorised person.

Equivalent provision is then made for subsequent alterations of any writings so executed on behalf of a company.

*(c) Local authorities*

Again there have been changes over the years in the mode of execution of documents by local authorities. Under the old rules, the latest of these was in the Local Government (Scotland) Act 1973 s. 194.

Until 1 April 1996, local authority meant a Regional or District Council. As from that date, it means a new Unitary Council established under the Local Government etc. (Scotland) Act 1994. There is no equivalent provision for execution of deeds in that Act and instead execution is dealt with under the 1995 Act new rules. These apply to the old local authorities for the very short period between 1 August 1995 and 1 April 1996. Thereafter they apply to the new Unitary Councils.

The requirements in Schedule 2 for execution by a local authority are as follows.

Where the grantor of the document is a local authority, it is signed by the authority if signed on its behalf by the proper officer of the authority. That, by itself, creates formal validity. No additional signatures of members of the authority or witnesses and no corporate seal are required.

For the purpose above stated, however, a person purporting to sign on behalf of a local authority as the proper officer of the authority is presumed to be the proper officer. Note the difference between other juristic persons and local authorities. Here, there is a presumption that the signatory is authorised to sign. Accordingly, no further enquiry is necessary in such cases.

Consistent with the other provisions in the Act, such a signature creates formal validity. If the document is to be self-proving, then either the signature must be witnessed by one witness and the attestation details must be incorporated in the deed or, if not witnessed, the deed must also carry the common seal.

Again there is the usual provision that there is no contra-indication on the face of the deed.

Provisions similar to those noted above apply to contemporaneous and subsequent alterations.

### (d) Bodies corporate

There is an infinite number of bodies corporate, whether under statute or Royal Charter, each of which has its own special provision for authentication of documents. This is clearly troublesome and the new provision in Schedule 2 for bodies corporate generally is to be welcomed. The provision applies to any body corporate except a company or local authority which have been dealt with above.

Where the grantor of a document is a body corporate, it is to be signed by either:

(i) a member of the governing board or a member of the body if there is no board; or

(ii) the secretary of the body by whatever name he is called; or

(iii) a duly authorised person.

Such signature confers formal validity.

For self-proving status, consistent with the other provisions in the Act, attestation of the signature by one witness is required, with the inclusion of the name and address of the witness; or in the absence of attestation, the document must carry the common seal.

Again, there is the standard provision that there is no contra-indication in the document itself.

When so executed, it is self-proving.

As with companies, so with bodies corporate, the presumptions referred to above relate only to authentication. There is no additional presumption that the subscriber satisfies the statutory requirement.

### (e) Ministers of the Crown and office holders

Where the grantor of a document is a Minister or office holder, it is signed by him if signed:

(i) personally; or

(ii) if authorised by statute, by an officer of the Minister or some other authorised person; or

(iii) in the case of an office holder who is duly authorised to delegate, it may be signed by the authorised person; or

(iv) in any case, by any other person who is duly authorised to sign.

Such signature satisfies the formality validity rule. If in addition the document is to have self-proving status, there must be attestation and the document must disclose the name and address of the witness.

There is the usual provision that the deed contains no contra-indication.

## Caveat

As stated in para. 2.40, the foregoing paragraphs indicate, in broad outline, the statutory requirements under the new rules for formal validity and self-proving status. For the reasons stated above, however, all the provisions in the Act and, more particularly, in the Schedules are not set out in full here. The reader should refer to the sources mentioned in para. 2.40 for the full details.

Chapter 3

# CAPACITY

## 3.1 Capacity

On the general question of capacity, and its effect on the ability of a person to contract see Gloag & Henderson, 9th edn., Chapter 6.

Broadly speaking, the same general principles apply to the ownership of, title to, and disposal of, heritable property.

## 3.2 Power

In addition to capacity, the party must also have power to make contracts. In the case of individuals acting for their own beneficial interest, if such an individual has capacity, he also has, by necessary implication, power to deal with his proprietary rights in any way. If, however, a person acts in a representative capacity, such as a trustee, or as an agent, the trustee or agent may have capacity but may lack power. If so, any deed granted by him may be voidable or even void. In *Piggins & Rix Ltd.* 1995 SLT 418 a port authority acquired heritable property under statutory powers which also conferred on the authority a number of other powers but not power of sale. In a special case presented to the Court of Session to determine whether or not power of sale could be implied, the Court held that the reasonable inference to be drawn from the omission of this power in the relevant statutory provisions was that Parliament did not intend that the authority should have power of sale, and that power was not considered to be reasonably incidental to the main purposes of the corporation.

## 3.3 Domicile

In relation to capacity, the question of domicile may be significant. The general rule, which applies to Scottish heritage, is that the *lex situs* determines whether or not a person has capacity to deal with his heritable property in Scotland. See Anton *Private International Law*, 2nd edn., p. 604. But that general principle is hedged about with certain limitations and qualifications. So, in the case of children, there is some support for the view that the *lex domicilii* may determine the capacity of a foreign child to deal with Scottish heritage.

Clearly, in such cases, the ideal rule is to ascertain the position under both systems of law, *lex situs* and *lex domicilii*; and only to act in reliance on a deed by a person domiciled abroad if that deed is valid under both systems.

Further, where a person acts in a representative capacity in reliance on statutory powers, *e.g.* trustees, corporations, etc., their powers are necessarily limited by the relevant statutory authority in their own jurisdiction.

Scottish Acts, in particular the Trusts (Scotland) Acts, have no application in such cases.

## 3.4 Title

The question of title is distinct and separate from the question of capacity and power. The case of trustees is typical. The constituent deed, *i.e.* the deed of trust, must itself be valid before the trustees can act. But, in addition, the trustees must themselves be capable of acting, which does not depend on the terms of the deed, but on personal factors; and they must also have power to act with reference to the trust assets which, again, involves different considerations. The technicalities of title will be dealt with later.

## 3.5 Trustees

The case of Scottish trustees is taken first because some of the rules applicable to trustees apply also in other comparable cases, *e.g.* guardians and children, etc.

**3.6 Capacity**. The individual trustee is generally subject to the same rules as to capacity as is any individual. So, a person who is insane cannot effectively deal with his own property; and although he may validly be appointed as a trustee, he cannot effectively deal with trust assets.

**3.7 Title**. Normally, there is a deed of trust (or its equivalent, *e.g.* confirmation-dative) which constitutes the trustees' title. That deed must, of course, be intrinsically valid in itself. It may take various forms, and, in relation to *mortis causa* trusts, there are now special rules, supplementing the common law position, under the Succession (Scotland) Act 1964. In *inter vivos* trusts, assets of various kinds may pass to the trustee under the constituent deed or by separate conveyance or transfer; *mortis causa*, assets pass to the trustees either directly under the constituent deed, or, since 1964, indirectly by virtue of confirmation. In certain circumstances, with both *inter vivos* and *mortis causa* trusts, the trustees may later acquire assets during the course of administration of the trust. In all cases, they may also come to dispose of trust assets. In addition, during the course of administration, there may be supplementary trust titles in the form of deeds of assumption and conveyance and minutes of resignation of trustees, and decrees of appointment of new trustees by the court, etc. In any given trust, there may therefore be a whole series of formal deeds which, together, make up the title of the trustees for the time being to a particular asset in the estate.

**3.8 Sale of heritage**. At common law, trustees had no implied power to dispose of heritage conveyed to them by the truster. Instead, the necessary implication was that any such heritable estate was to be retained by the trustees for the ultimate benefit of the beneficiaries. Thus, if A died leaving a will conveying his whole estate to trustees, including heritage, the trustees had a title to that heritage and capacity to deal with it; but they had no power to sell or dispose of it, except in terms of the will. This rule could, and can, be displaced in the following ways:

(*a*) *Express power of sale*. The truster might competently confer on his trustees an express power of sale; and this express power is still regularly met with in practice in deeds of trust. For a typical illustration, see Burns' *Practice*, p. 802, and Elder's *Forms of Wills*, p. 165.

'My trustees ... shall have power ... to sell or otherwise realise the trust estate or any part or parts thereof, heritable and moveable.'

(*b*) *Implied power.* The Trusts (Scotland) Act 1921 s. 4 provides that, in all trusts, the trustees have power to do certain acts, provided that the act is not at variance with the terms or the purposes of the trust; and any such act, when done, is as effectual as if the trust deed had contained an express power to that effect. These powers in s. 4, include:

(i) to sell the trust estate or any part thereof, heritable as well as moveable;

(ii) to grant feus of heritage;

(iii) to grant leases;

(iv) to borrow money on security;

(v) to excamb (or exchange) land;

(vi) to grant all deeds necessary for carrying into effect the powers vested in the trustees.

Section 6 prescribes the method of sale, which may be by public roup or private bargain.

Prior to the Trusts (Scotland) Act 1961, in all cases when dealing with trustees, a purchaser had to examine not only the trustees' title to satisfy himself as to its intrinsic validity, but, in addition, he had to consider the purposes of the deed, and the powers of the trustees thereunder, to see whether or not they had power of sale. Otherwise, he might find himself with an invalid title.

The 1961 Act s. 2 has improved the position of the purchaser, although it does not in any way alter the strict rules as to trustees' power of sale. The sole purpose of the section is to protect the purchaser and to spare him the necessity of enquiring into trustees' powers. Note the following features of this section:

(i) It applies to any of the powers in the 1921 Act s. 4, not merely sale of heritage.

(ii) If, after 27 August 1961, the trustees exercise one of the implied powers in s. 4, *e.g.* sale, the validity of the sale, and of the purchaser's title, cannot be challenged by any person merely on the grounds that the sale is at variance with the terms or purposes of the trust. Good faith on the part of the purchaser is not required.

(iii) If trustees are acting under the supervision of the accountant of court s. 2 only applies if the accountant of court consents. This applies only in special cases, *e.g.*, a *curator bonis* selling heritage for an *incapax* ward.

(iv) The section does not in any way affect the relationship between trustees and beneficiaries. Thus, trustees who sell, *ultra vires*, may now confer a valid title and the purchaser is no longer concerned with their powers; but, in so doing, they lay themselves open to an action for breach of trust at the instance of an aggrieved beneficiary.

(*c*) *Power granted by the court.* If the deed of trust contains no express power, and if no effective power is implied under s. 4, trustees may not sell unless specially authorised by the court under the 1921 Act, s. 5. Prior to the 1961 Act, such petitions to the court were commonplace, and are still competent and not unusual. Undoubtedly, however, petitions under s. 5 are less frequent than they were before 1961, when purchasers were scrutinising trustees' titles, and challenging their powers. Note that the petition in this case is not concerned with matters of title, but only with power of sale. Provided the trustees have power (express, implied or from the court), the purchaser is not further concerned to consider whether or not the power is being properly exercised. An improper exercise of the power would not in any way invalidate the purchaser's title.

**3.9 Purchase or acquisition of assets.** The same problem does not here arise, in that a person selling any asset, heritable or moveable, to trustees has no duty whatever to consider, or enquire into, the powers of the purchasing trustees. If, having sold to trustees, it turns out that the trustees do not have power to purchase, the trustees cannot rescind the contract nor retract in a question with the seller. Contrast the position of a purchaser from trustees without power of sale, prior to 1961; his title was open to reduction, and, if reduced, he lost the property. If trustees do make an unauthorised purchase, they have implied power to resell – see Mackenzie Stuart *The Law of Trusts*, p. 237.

On the other hand, as between trustees and a beneficiary, the trustees cannot properly purchase any asset, heritable or moveable, unless they are duly authorised by:

(i) Express powers of purchase, or investment, in the deed of trust, which often are expressly conferred.

(ii) Implied powers under the Trusts (Scotland) Act 1921, now substantially supplemented by the Trustee Investments Act 1961.

(iii) The Trusts (Scotland) Act 1961 s. 4 which empowers trustees to acquire an interest in residential accommodation in Scotland or elsewhere, if it is reasonably required as a residence for a beneficiary. This power to purchase under the 1961 Act is added as one of the implied powers in the 1921 Act s. 4, now s. 4(1)(*ee*). It is, therefore, still competent to petition the court, under the 1921 Act s. 5, for authority to purchase heritage in cases not within the new s. 4(1)(*ee*) – see *Bristow* 1965 SLT 225 where, in special circumstances, a *curator bonis* applied for special powers to purchase under this section. The petition was dismissed as unnecessary on the basis that the curator did have implied power; but, as in other similar cases, Lord Cameron stated 'It may well be that curators will decide to err on the side of caution in determining whether to seek the Court's authority for the exercise of such a power as is sought here, or to act at their own hands.'

**3.10 Foreign trusts**
The foreign trust most commonly encountered in practice is an English trust. Trust law in England differs radically from trust law in Scotland. In particular, the Trusts (Scotland) Acts 1921 and 1961 have no application whatsoever in an English trust. But, on the basis of international comity, the Court of Session in Scotland will exercise its *nobile officium* to make an

order in a foreign trust, if required. Therefore, English trustees may petition the Scottish court under the *nobile officium*, but not under the 1921 Act s. 5, for, *inter alia*, power of sale. The Scottish court must then consider how English law views the powers of trustees in relation to the sale of immoveable property.

For a typical case see *Campbell, Petitioner* 1958 SC 275, where the court granted power of sale to English trustees, but declined to include in the order an English provision regulating the exercise of the power. Lord President Clyde said: 'It is clear that, as this is an English trust, the Trusts (Scotland) Act 1921 does not apply ... and it is equally clear that, as the English Court does not operate in Scotland, an application to this Court is necessary to enable the trustees to give the purchaser of Scottish subjects a good marketable title.'

Note, particularly, that the 1961 Act s. 2 applies only to Scottish trusts. It does not protect a purchaser from e.g. English trustees; and so a purchaser must still satisfy himself that English (or other foreign) trustees do have the requisite power to deal with Scottish heritage under the proper law of jurisdiction of the trust.

The same considerations apply where English trustees purchase Scottish heritage, but again, with this difference, that, in such cases, the seller is not concerned with the powers of a purchasing trustee after the transaction has settled. In all such cases, it is as well to take advice from a lawyer practising in the country having jurisdiction over the trust.

### 3.11 Children

The common law rules relating to capacity of children were substantially recast by the Age of Legal Capacity (Scotland) Act 1991, which came into force on 25 September 1991.

The common law distinguished between pupil children and minor children. A pupil was a girl under 12 or a boy under 14, while a minor was a child above these ages but who had not yet attained the age of 18. Pupils had no legal capacity and their property was administered by a tutor or tutors, in practice usually a parent. Minors had full legal capacity subject to the need to obtain the consent of a curator if there was one, which there usually was.

Under the 1991 Act, which replaces the common law rules, a dividing line is set at the age of 16. Children under that age have no active legal capacity except in certain limited circumstances which do not usually affect rights to heritage. Children aged 16 or over have full legal capacity and there is no equivalent, in the new law, to the minor's curator at common law.

### 3.12 Children under 16.

Subject to a small number of exceptions, a child under the age of 16 has no legal capacity to enter into any transaction. Thus a child cannot buy or sell a house, or burden it with a standard security. But a child aged 12 or over has testamentary capacity and may bequeath heritable property by will.

Juristic acts are performed on behalf of a child by the child's guardian or guardians. The appointment of guardians is regulated by the Law Reform (Parent and Child) (Scotland) Act 1986 ss. 2–4 (as amended). In the normal case the guardian is the mother of the child and, provided that he was married to the mother at the time of conception or subsequently, the father also. Where there are two guardians, each may exercise guardianship rights without the consent of the other.

Guardians are trustees within the meaning of the Trusts (Scotland) Acts 1921 and 1961. Thus purchasers are protected by s. 2 of the 1961 Act (see above) and may take title from a guardian without inquiry into his powers. But a guardian who sells beyond his powers is liable in damages in a question with his ward. The question of power of sale was considered in *Cunningham's Tutrix* 1949 SC 275, where a distinction was made between heritage held as an investment and heritage in the nature of a family estate or residence. It was suggested that a guardian was empowered to sell the former but not the latter.

The position of a guardian differs from that of a trustee, in that the property of the child is held, and title is taken, in the name of the child. The guardian merely acts as an administrator and will make up title in name of the child and not in his own name as guardian. In practice, purchase of heritage by a guardian is unusual, although it is authorised under s. 4 of the 1961 Act where its purpose is to provide a residence for the child – see *Bristow* above. Further, a child may, *e.g.*, inherit heritage by will.

As pointed out in para. 3.8 (iv) above, the 1961 Act s. 2 only operates to protect parties transacting onerously with trustees. It does not prevent a beneficiary from suing for breach of trust.

**3.13 Children aged 16–18**.  A child aged 16 or over has full legal capacity and may buy and sell heritable property in his own name. However, it is provided by the Age of Legal Capacity (Scotland) Act 1991 s. 3 that a child between the ages of 16 and 18 who enters into a prejudicial transaction may apply to the court at any time before attaining the age of 21 to have the transaction set aside. This replaces the common law rule that transactions could be reduced for enorm lesion within the *quadriennium utile*.

A transaction is prejudicial within the 1991 Act if (a) an adult, exercising reasonable prudence, would not have entered into it, and (b) it has caused, or is likely to cause, substantial prejudice to the child. Obviously, sales and purchases of heritable property will not ordinarily be prejudicial within this definition. Nonetheless a seller to or a purchaser from a child between 16 and 18 will need to be cautious. There are various ways in which his position might be protected. First, s. 3(3) of the Act lists a number of transactions which cannot be set aside. These include transactions in the course of the child's trade and transactions induced by fraudulent misrepresentation on the part of the child. Secondly, a projected transaction can be ratified by the court in advance under s. 4 of the Act. Thereafter it cannot be set aside. Thirdly, the child can himself ratify a transaction if he is over the age of 18. Finally, care can be taken to ensure that the transaction is not in fact prejudicial. Thus in the case of a sale by a child there should be sufficient advertising of the property and, preferably, an independent valuation. See Halliday's *Practice*, 2–27 to 2–32 (2nd edn. 2–04 to 2–40).

The position of children under the age of 18 has recently been affected further by the Children (Scotland) Act 1995. This Act is primarily concerned with family relationships and parental responsibilities, and also deals at considerable length with promotion of the welfare of children by local authorities. In large measure, therefore, the Act is outwith the scope of this Manual. There are, however, two provisions to which attention should be given in this context. First, in the 1995 Act ss. 1 and 2, certain parental responsibilities are imposed on a parent which include, *inter alia*, power to act as the child's legal representative and, under s. 2, a variety of parental rights which are less relevant in this context are conferred on a parent. For the purposes of these two sections, child means a person under 16 years of age. Further elaborate provisions deal with these responsibilities and rights and with the appointment of guardians.

Sections 9 and 10 of the Act deal with the safeguarding of the property of a child and with its administration by the legal representatives.

Section 9 imposes quite onerous provisions on persons who hold property to which a child (again under 16 years of age) has an absolute indefeasible and vested right and would therefore be entitled to call for immediate payment and delivery, were the child not under 16 years of age. Section 9 applies *inter alia* both to trustees and to executors holding such property for a child under the age. A trustee or executor in that position comes under certain obligations as to how to deal with the property of the child, which in turn depends on the value of the property.

Section 10 is perhaps the most important section in the context of this chapter. In terms of that section, a person acting as a child's legal representative in relation to administration of assets comes under a statutory duty to act reasonably and prudently, but, with that qualification, is generally entitled to do anything which the child could do in relation to the child's property if that child were of full age. The child, in this provision, apparently means a child under 18 years of age, although the ability so to act ceases at age 16.

These new provisions are supplementary to the provisions in the 1991 Act referred to above which continues to apply as summarised under this sub-head.

The foregoing provisions came into force on 1 November 1996.

### 3.14 Curators and judicial factors
A curator or judicial factor ('JF') may be appointed by the court in various circumstances to safeguard and administer an estate, both heritable and moveable.

The decree or act and warrant appointing the JF operates as his title to the estate coming under his control but with this specialty that, if there is a known and living ward, the act and warrant does not operate as a title to divest the ward and invest the JF instead, the title remains vested in the ward, but the JF has power to administer and deal with the asset in the ward's name.

As to powers, a JF is a trustee for the purposes of the Trusts Acts; and the 1961 Act s. 2 applies to protect a purchaser in dealings with a JF. See above. But a JF acts under the supervision of the court and the accountant of court must consent to the exercise of the statutory power *e.g.* of sale. Failing that consent, a purchaser is not protected under the 1961 Act s. 2.

### 3.15 Corporations
A corporation is a separate legal person and may hold property in its own name. Of necessity, however, all contracts and deeds relating to the corporation's assets must be entered into and granted by the directors or other officer. The mode of execution of a deed by a corporation is discussed in

Chapter 2. The execution of documents by companies under the new rules in the Requirements of Writing (Scotland) Act 1995 is dealt with in Chapter 2.

Every statutory and chartered corporation enjoys powers conferred on it by the relevant statute or charter, and these should be consulted in all cases. *Piggins & Rix*, referred to above, para. 3.2, serves as a warning.

The commonest corporation met with in practice is the company incorporated under the Companies Acts. Every such company must have a memorandum and articles of association. In the objects clause of the memorandum, the company's powers and the limits of those powers are defined; and the articles prescribe the mode in which those powers may be exercised. Thus, the memorandum of every incorporated company will, in practice, include a power to the company to acquire and to dispose of property of all kinds, and to borrow on the security thereof.

Typical objects clauses in a memorandum of association of a company, taken from Palmer's *Precedents* read:

'To purchase, take on lease or in exchange, hire or otherwise acquire, any real and personal property and any rights or privileges which the company may think necessary or convenient for the purposes of its business.'

'To sell, lease, mortgage or otherwise dispose of the property, assets, or undertaking of the company or any part thereof for such consideration as the company may think fit.'

For the exercise of these powers, a typical clause in articles of association might read:

The business of the company shall be managed by the directors who ... may exercise all such powers of the company as are not, by the Act or by these regulations, required to be exercised by the company in general meeting ...'

The power to borrow is often limited by the articles to a stated maximum. Often there is no power in the memorandum to guarantee borrowing by some other person and to grant security therefor. In recent years, this created problems in the case of groups of companies where the parent company borrows for the benefit of the whole group on the footing that the subsidiary companies will guarantee the parent company's borrowing.

At common law a transaction was void if it was beyond the powers of the company as set out in its memorandum, but this *ultra vires* rule has been displaced by statute. The current provision is s. 35 of the Companies Act 1985 (inserted by Companies Act 1989 s. 108 with effect from 4 February 1991). This provides that the validity of an act done by a company shall not be called into question on the ground of lack of capacity by reason of anything in the company's memorandum. Thus, where A purchases property from a company, the company is able to confer a good title even although there is no express power of sale in its memorandum. Unlike the original version of s. 35, which was in force until 4 February 1991, there is now no requirement that the purchaser be in good faith. Section 35 does not alter the rule that directors are liable to the members of the company in respect of any breach of the memorandum or articles, but a party transacting with the company is unaffected.

**3.16 Liquidation**.   A company may be wound up voluntarily, either in a members' or in a creditors' liquidation; or it may be wound up compulsorily by the court. In all cases, a liquidator, or joint liquidators, is or are appointed. In contrast to the sequestration of an individual (see below), liquidation does not divest the company of its assets; but an order or resolution for the winding-up of the company has the effect of suspending the powers of the directors and, by statute, the liquidator is invested with comparable powers. In particular, the liquidator may, without the sanction of the court, sell both heritable and moveable property belonging to the company by public roup or private bargain. A deed granted by a company in liquidation runs in name of the company, but the fact of liquidation is referred to; and the deed is executed by the liquidator in place of the directors.

**3.17 Administrators**.   Under the Insolvency Act 1986 Part II, the court has power, in specified circumstances, to make an order appointing an administrator as an alternative procedure to liquidation in the case of a potentially or actually insolvent company which, it is thought, may be rescued by competent administration.

In terms of the 1986 Act s. 11, during the period of administration, the company cannot be wound up; no creditor can take steps to enforce any security; and no other proceedings, and no diligence, are competent against the company or its assets except with the leave of the court.

Further, on the making of the order, any petition for the winding-up of the company is automatically dismissed.

Under s. 15(7), the administrator is required, within fourteen days of his appointment, to notify the Registrar of Companies.

Wide powers are conferred on the administrator under ss. 14 and 15. In particular under s. 15, the administrator is empowered to deal with and dispose of any asset of the company which is subject to any form of security or diligence; but the preference of the secured creditor is preserved in the net proceeds of such disposal. In terms of s. 14(6), a person dealing with an administrator in good faith and for value is not under any obligation to enquire whether he is acting within his powers.

In terms of s. 16(1), when the administrator disposes of an asset in Scotland, the recording, intimation or registration of the document of transfer (as appropriate), has the effect of disencumbering the property from the security thereon.

During the period of administration, the assets of the company remain vested in the company; and deeds relating thereto will run in name of, and be granted by, the company. For this purpose, the administrator is given power to use the company's seal and to do all acts and execute in name and on behalf of the company any deed, receipt or other document.

As with the case of the liquidator, so with the administrator it is safest to assume that, in executing deeds intended to be self-proving, the signature of the administrator should be attested.

The execution of documents on behalf of a company by a liquidator or administrator is dealt with in the Insolvency Act 1986 – see now the 1995 Act Schedule 23(2).

### 3.18 Sequestration

Where an individual becomes apparently insolvent and is sequestrated, a trustee in sequestration is appointed by the court. His position is analogous to that of a judicial factor, but he is appointed under special procedure, and with special powers, under the Bankruptcy (Scotland) Act 1985.

No attempt is made here to deal in detail with the provisions of the Bankruptcy (Scotland) Act 1985 but attention is drawn to certain sections which apply with particular reference to title to heritable property.

### 3.19 Procedure.

Firstly, in a sequestration, various steps in procedure are laid down in the Act leading to the election and confirmation by the court of a permanent trustee. The primary responsibility of the trustee is to ingather and safeguard the estate of the sequestrated debtor for the benefit generally of his creditors. The decree confirming the appointment of the permanent trustee in office is termed the act and warrant.

### 3.20 Vesting.

Sections 31–33 deal with the vesting of the estate of the debtor in the permanent trustee as at the date of sequestration. Under s. 31, the whole estate of the debtor vests at the date of sequestration in the permanent trustee for the benefit of the creditors by virtue of the act and warrant. The act and warrant has the same effect on the heritable estate of the debtor by statute as if a decree of adjudication in implement of a sale as well as a decree of adjudication for payment and in security of a debt, subject to no legal reversion, had been pronounced in favour of the permanent trustee. For adjudication and its effect, see Chapter 30.

Under s. 31(2), the exercise by the permanent trustee of any power conferred on him by the Act in respect of any heritable estate vesting in him under the act and warrant is not subject to challenge on the ground of any prior inhibition.

In cases where the debtor has an incomplete title to heritable estate in Scotland, the permanent trustee is empowered under s. 31(3) to complete title to that estate either in his own name or in the name of the debtor but completion of title in the name of the debtor is not permitted, under the Act, to validate by accretion any unperfected right in favour of any person other than the permanent trustee. For the effect of accretion in ordinary cases see Chapter 7.

By s. 33(1), property held in trust by the debtor for any other person is expressly excluded from the sequestration and does not vest in the permanent trustee. Further, the vesting of the heritable estate in the permanent trustee is without prejudice to the rights of any secured creditor preferable to the right of the permanent trustee.

Under s. 32(6), assets subsequently acquired by the debtor after the date of sequestration also vest in the permanent trustee who is entitled, by virtue of that provision, to require a conveyance of that estate from any person holding the same. So if, after sequestration, the debtor succeeds to a heritable estate under the will of his father, the executors of the father would be obliged to convey that heritable estate to the permanent trustee for the benefit of the general body of creditors.

For a discussion on the position of the bankrupt after sequestration, see *Alliance & Leicester Building Society* 1994 SCLR 19. In that case, a debtor, although sequestrated, succeeded in acquiring title to a heritable property by way of a feu disposition in his favour and he then granted a standard security in favour of the building society. Both documents post-dated the registration of the sequestration order. The argument for the debtor, that both deeds were interlinked and together constituted *acquirenda*, was rejected by the Sheriff who held, instead, that the subjects conveyed by the feu disposition vested in the trustee as *acquirenda*, not in the debtor; and accordingly that the standard security granted in favour of the building society was a separate transaction, struck at by the deemed inhibition on the debtor created by the sequestration.

The argument of the bankrupt and the significance of *acquirenda* derive from the Titles to Land Consolidation (Scotland) Act 1868 Act s. 157 in terms of which no inhibition is effective against any heritable property acquired by the inhibited debtor after the date when the inhibition was laid on. The flaw in the argument in this case was that, under the Bankruptcy Act 1985 s. 32(6), the subjects conveyed to the debtor by the feu disposition vested immediately and directly in the trustee in sequestration, not in the debtor, and accordingly the 1868 Act s. 157 had no application.

**3.21 Sequestration and liquidation contrasted.** Note the significant difference between sequestration and liquidation. As already mentioned, in liquidation, the title to heritable property remains vested in the company although the directors are stripped of their powers. In contrast, in sequestration, all the assets of the debtor, both heritable and moveable, are transferred as if by conveyance from the debtor to the trustee who thereby acquires a title to these assets in his own person as trustee and thereafter deals with them as such. The act and warrant is the link in title.

The equivalent vesting provisions under the Bankruptcy (Scotland) Act 1913 created certain problems as between the trustee in sequestration and third parties in certain situations. The vesting provisions in the 1985 Act do not seem to have resolved all of these problems, some of which, and some related problems in liquidations, are discussed in the articles in the Reading List, to which reference is made.

## 3.22 Partnerships

In Scotland, a firm has a distinct legal *persona*, in contrast to an English firm which is simply a number of individuals trading together. But the legal status of a Scottish firm is not equivalent to a corporation. A Scottish firm may own, hold and deal with moveable property *socio nomine*. It may also be the beneficial owner of heritage, but it is not feudally possible to take the title to land in name of a firm. Instead, title must be taken in name of trustees acting on behalf of the firm. The partners normally (but not necessarily) act as trustees. Prior to the Trusts (Scotland) Act 1961, this could cause problems in partnership titles; but, by s. 2 of that Act, a purchaser has no concern with beneficial ownership and can safely take a title from the trustees for a firm. Nonetheless, problems can still arise. In particular, if heritage was purchased many years ago by a firm and the title taken in name of the then partners as trustees, all the original partners may now be dead, with a resulting lapsed trust, which produces a technical difficulty in the title.

*Cameron* 1996 SLT 1038 is a most unusual case. Heritable property was acquired by a partnership and, following the rule stated above, the title was taken, as is standard practice, in name of the two partners as trustees for the firm. Trustees are empowered to act by majority and quorum and of course this cannot apply where there are only two trustees. Presumably, with that in view, the conveyance to the partners as trustees contained an additional clause in which, by express provision, each partner as such trustee had power to sell the subjects without the consent of her co-trustee or any other present or future partner. The intervening transactions are not relevant here. Ultimately, however, purportedly exercising the express power so conferred, one partner then conveyed the subjects to a disponee who in turn sold them to *bona fide* purchasers for value. The other partner, some years later, having disappeared in the interim, then raised an action of re-duction to set aside the disposition by her former partner. Her argument, however, was rejected on appeal on the footing that, in the circumstances, reduction of that disposition would achieve no useful purpose. On the mer-its of the clause itself, Lord McCluskey took the view that any such unusual power would have to be created in words which were absolutely unam-biguous; but, subject to that proviso, he seemed clearly of the view that such a provision was in principle competent. In his opinion, however, the clause in this case did not meet the strict test which he applied and so in terms of that clause alone, a valid title could only be granted by both trustees conjoined together.

However, for other reasons indicated above, the Court considered that no useful purpose could be achieved by reducing the disposition in question and so the title remained valid. It would therefore clearly be inadvisable in such circumstances to attempt to achieve the desired result by the insertion of such a clause. Other means should always be used.

Under the Requirements of Writing (Scotland) Act 1995 Schedule 2, special provision is now made for the execution of documents by a part-nership. These are discussed in Chapter 2.52(*a*). While this removes some uncertainties illustrated in *Littlejohn* referred to in that paragraph, the pro-visions in the 1995 Act as to execution will not normally be relevant in the context of title to heritage, because such titles are invariably taken in name of trustees.

### 3.23 Unincorporated associations
Any association which is not incorporated may beneficially own heritable property but cannot take the title in its own name. It must always act through the medium of trustees. Since 1961, this does not normally present any significant problem not already mentioned; but again lapsed trusts are not unusual.

In appropriate cases, the 1868 Act s. 26 and, less commonly, the 1874 Act s. 45 may be used when taking a title in name of trustees for the association to ensure continuity of infeftment.

### 3.24 Bodies corporate
The Requirements of Writing (Scotland) Act 1995 Schedule 2 also makes elaborate provision for the execution of documents by any body corporate other than a company or local authority which are separately dealt with in the same Schedule. Again, this has been referred to in more detail in Chapter 2.52(*d*).

Chapter 4

# DELIVERY

## 4.1 The need for delivery

In a number of important transactions, the law requires a formal written document to effect that transaction. But the mere fact that a party has executed a formal written document does not automatically bind the party in terms of that deed. In most cases, something more is required to make the writing obligatory on the grantor; and that further requirement is delivery of the deed into the hands of the grantee, or its equivalent. So, with limited exceptions dealt with below, the standard rule is that any deed, whether onerous or gratuitous, becomes effective, irrevocable, and binding on the grantor only if it is delivered; and, similarly, that the grantee thereunder cannot enforce that writ against the grantor unless and until he has taken delivery thereof.

It follows that, particularly in the case of gifts and other gratuitous transactions, delivery is a vital element in completing the rights and obligations of the parties. Perhaps rather surprisingly, no formal legal act or procedure is required to effect delivery. In all cases, delivery is a question of fact and intention.

In practice, difficulties do not often arise. A deed is normally delivered simply by handing it over physically to the grantee or his agent, either gratuitously, or, in the case of onerous deeds, in exchange for the consideration thereunder. The fact of physical handing over, coupled with intention to make the deed operative, is of itself sufficient delivery. Similarly, a deed is not delivered by physical handing over of a deed if accompanied by a covering letter, which says: 'You are to hold the accompanying deed as undelivered'. This is quite a commonplace qualification when physically parting with a deed.

In the context of heritable titles, delivery of the appropriate deed to a vassal, disponee or heritable creditor is an essential first step towards establishing the real right by infeftment. The requirements for infeftment are dealt with in greater detail in Chapter 13. This proposition was always generally accepted in the past but some difficulties could arise. In a competition between two parties claiming the same property, whether as proprietors or heritable creditors, each having taken a delivered deed from the same granter, priority of infeftment determined the beneficial right. In a question between a disponee or creditor on the one hand and a trustee in sequestration or the equivalent on the liquidation of a company on the other, doubts had been expressed as to the effect of delivery. These doubts at least in part date back to the decision in *Heritable Reversionary Company* (1892) 19 R (HL) 43. In that case, a bankrupt was infeft in certain heritable property *ex facie* absolutely, but truly in trust for a beneficiary. No indication of the existence of the trust was disclosed on the record. Accordingly, on the face of it, since he was infeft and had the real right in his own person apparently as beneficial owner, then, applying the strict rule, the trust property so held by him but truly as trustee should have passed to the trustee in sequestration of the bankrupt to the exclusion of the person beneficially entitled thereto under the undisclosed trust. This, of course, was manifestly inequitable and was so held in the House of Lords, reversing the judgment of the First Division and holding that a heritable property to which the bankrupt had an unqualified feudal title but which did not belong to him was not his property in the sense of the Bankruptcy Act then in force and so did not vest in his trustee.

Extrapolating on that argument, it was possible then to argue that in other comparable situations, but where there was no established trust, the strict rule should not be applied and, in comparable cases, property should not pass to a trustee in sequestration, or the equivalent when a company went into liquidation. This in turn involved an argument as to the proper construction of the language used in the insolvency legislation, both with reference to individuals and companies, to determine what was the property of the bankrupt, or of the company, which was affected by insolvency in the context of that legislation. In the Bankruptcy (Scotland) Act 1913 s. 97, which was the vesting section in that Act, it was provided that, at the date of sequestration, the act and warrant should *ipso jure* transfer to and vest in the trustee in sequestration 'the whole property of the debtor'. Notwithstanding the earlier decision in *Heritable Reversionary Company*, however, no special exception was made in the 1913 Act to exclude trust property from the sequestration but the rule already established in that case continued to be applied nonetheless. That apparent omission has now been corrected by statute in the Bankruptcy (Scotland) Act 1985 s. 33(1)(b) which expressly provides that property held on trust by the debtor shall not vest in the permanent trustee.

In the case of companies, a comparable question of construction arose particularly in relation to the floating charge. Under the Companies Act 1985 s. 462 and earlier legislation which originally introduced the floating charge into Scotland in 1961, it is competent for a company in Scotland to create a floating charge in favour of a creditor over all or any part of 'the property which may from time to time be comprised in the property and undertaking of the company'. Again, there is no special exclusion of property held in trust.

This failure to make specific provision to exclude trust property in the situations envisaged above and instead to rely on the common law rule in *Heritable Reversionary Company* left the way open for an argument that if, at common law, trust property was not the property of the debtor vesting in his trustee in sequestration, then there might be other situations where, on an application of the *tantum et tale* rule or of the rule in *Heritable Reversionary Company*, property in which the debtor was still feudally infeft at the date of sequestration but truly had no beneficial interest should be excluded from vesting in the trustee in sequestration on the same argument as succeeded in *Heritable Reversionary Company*. A typical situation where this argument could be most persuasively applied is the case where a disposition of heritable property has been delivered to a *bona fide* purchaser for value by the infeft disponer who, in exchange, has received the price, but where, for whatever reason, on insolvency or on the appointment of a receiver, a real right has been created for the benefit of the trustee in sequestration or the receiver before the disponee has recorded his title. Applying the strict rule referred to above in that situation, where the property has been ostensibly transferred to the purchaser on a delivered but unrecorded disposition, it nonetheless still remained vulnerable to the acts and deeds of the infeft disponer until he was feudally divested, and the disponee was feudally invested in the real right by the recording of his disposition.

The decision in *Gibson* 1976 SC 23 apparently added some support for the foregoing argument. In that case, there was a binding contract for sale and purchase of heritable property. On the strength of that contract but without taking delivery of a disposition, the purchaser took possession and paid the price, assuming he would then get a delivered title which he could record to perfect his real right. Unfortunately, before the relevant title was delivered and recorded, the company which sold the subjects went into liquidation and a debate then arose as to whether, in these circumstances, the property had already passed to the purchaser by virtue of the missives, the taking of possession and payment of the price, or whether it fell under the liquidation. Given that, at the date of liquidation, no title had been delivered, and the purchaser's right rested simply on missives and nothing more, his position was fairly hopeless and the argument that he had acquired a right preferable to the liquidator was scarcely tenable. However, in the course of his judgment, the Lord President, admittedly in an *obiter dictum*, states:

> '[I]n the law of Scotland, no right of property vests in a purchaser until there has been delivered to him the relevant disposition. On delivery of the disposition the purchaser becomes vested in a personal right to the subjects in question and his acquisition of a real right to the subjects is dependent upon the recording of the disposition in the appropriate Register of Sasines. Putting the matter in another way, the seller of subjects under the missives is not, in a question with the purchaser, divested of any part of his right of property in the subjects until, in implement of his contractual obligation to do so, he delivers to the purchaser the appropriate disposition.'

He then observes that the purchaser in this position has no more than a *jus crediti* until delivery of the disposition. It is really quite clear from the language used by the Lord President that, when he refers to the vesting of the personal right in the purchaser and the divesting of the seller by delivery of a disposition, he was looking at the resulting position merely as between seller and purchaser. However, in the way in which the judgment was phrased, it did add force to the argument that a delivered disposition might be said to have divested the disponer at least to the extent of taking the subjects out of the property of the insolvent or out of the property and undertaking of the company for the purposes of the insolvency legislation referred to above.

In the result, as the Reading List discloses, this question was debated in a number of articles in the journals between 1981 and 1986. The matter rested there until the recent case of *Sharp* v. *Thomson* 1997 SLT (HL) 636. In that case, a company had granted a floating charge in the statutory terms.

Several years later they then sold a heritable property to a *bona fide* purchaser for value who, in due course, took delivery of a disposition of the subjects in proper form in exchange for the purchase price. On the day after the disposition was delivered, a receiver was appointed, so creating an immediate real right in security. The disposition in favour of the purchaser was subsequently recorded. The essential question therefore was whether, at the date of delivery of the disposition to the purchaser, the subjects conveyed by that disposition had ceased to be part of the property and undertaking of the company or whether the subjects remained part of that property and as such were subject to a real right created for the benefit of the creditor under the floating charge on the date when the receiver was appointed. In the Outer House, Lord Penrose found in favour of the receiver and, on appeal, reported in 1995 SLT 837, following on exhaustive argument by both sides with an extensive citation of authorities, his decision was unanimously upheld. The Lord President delivered a lengthy, learned and detailed judgment in which the competing arguments are closely examined in the context of property law and the law of contract. At the same time, he considered and rejected arguments founded on the wording of the relevant insolvency legislation, and he dismissed the idea of a resulting constructive trust. He was supported in his views by Lord Sutherland and Lord Coulsfield, each of whom delivered equally conclusive opinions. All four judgments, in the Outer House and in the Inner House, merit careful study. The decision was, however, appealed to the House of Lords by the Woolwich Building Society who financed the purchase, and the appeal was allowed. See 1997 SLT (HL) 636.

It should be emphasised that, in allowing the appeal, the House of Lords did not in any way depart from or qualify the general principles so carefully analysed by the Lord President in his judgment and summarised above, and, for that reason, the summary of his judgment has not been modified in the light of the appeal. As noted above, he reached his conclusion on a strict application of what is undoubtedly a general principle of the law of property, namely that the infeft proprietor of a heritable property is not divested of his real right until a disponee from him of that property has taken delivery of and recorded or registered the relevant conveyance in the appropriate register, so taking infeftment and perfecting his real right in the subjects so conveyed in place of the disponer. As Lord Jauncey observes in his opinion in the House of Lords, 'property' is not a technical legal expression; in the Companies Act 1985 and in the Insolvency Act 1986 there is no exhaustive definition of that word. Accordingly, in his view, it was appropriate to construe 'property and undertaking' in a practical and realistic way. Having regard to the context in which the expression occurs in *Sharp* v. *Thomson*, the expression fell to be construed in the context of a floating charge, and, as Lord Jauncey later points out when summarising the position in this case, at the time when the floating charge crystallised by the appointment of the receiver the disponer still held the recorded title to the subjects and therefore the real right but, by delivery of the disposition, the disponer had divested himself of all beneficial interest in the property. Accordingly, although the real right still remained vested in the disponer at that date, that residual infeftment did not amount to a right of property in this context, and any deed granted by that infeft proprietor in these circumstances would necessarily be a deed granted in fraud of the delivered disposition. The effect of the Insolvency Act 1986 s. 53(7) is to make available as security to the holder of the floating charge all property in which the company had a beneficial interest at the date of crystallisation. By delivery of the disposition, the company in this case had no remaining beneficial interest in the property and accordingly the charge did not attach thereto. As Lord Jauncey points out, however, the position of a receiver appointed under a floating charge differs from that of a trustee in bankruptcy or a liquidator because his appointment automatically creates an immediate real right in security over heritable property belonging to the company. In the result, the decision in the House of Lords is special to its own particular facts and does not on the face of it have any wider application.

The implications of the decision are discussed at greater length in articles by Professor Reid in 1997 SLT (News) 79 and Professor Rennie in 1997 JLS 130, to which the reader is referred. Professor Reid clearly prefers the judgment in the First Division which proceeded on a strict application of the law of property and does not appear to favour the equitable approach to the question adopted by all the judges in the House of Lords. 'In the House of Lords, property law was eschewed. Instead, the issue is said to be one merely of statutory interpretation' of the expression 'property and undertaking' used in the Companies Act 1985 and in the Insolvency Act 1986, as noticed above. 'The only question before the Court was what meaning could be given to these words.' But, as he says later in that same article, now that the House of Lords has pronounced, this particular issue on its merits is closed; but he underlines, as Lord Jauncey and Lord Clyde emphasised in their respective judgments, that the decision is a decision on floating charges only and in the special circumstances of this case only. Clearly, therefore, it would be unsafe to assume that the Court would be prepared to adopt a comparable approach in construing the term 'property' in different circumstances. As Professor Rennie observes in his article, 'It remains to be seen how far the judgment can be interpreted; for the moment, I think it should be restricted to the insolvency context.'

In *Russo's Trustee* 1996 GWD 21–1245 parties attempted to escape from the consequences of the insolvency legislation by way of a declaration of trust. Following on the decision in *Heritable Reversionary Company*, and now, in the case of sequestration, by statutory provision under the 1985 Act, if it can be shown that a bankrupt or a company in liquidation or to which a receiver has been appointed was, in any such case, infeft in heritable property apparently *ex facie* absolutely for the beneficial interest of the insolvent but if the property is truly held under an existing trust, then there is no real doubt that any such asset held in trust will not be caught under any of the foregoing insolvency provisions.

In *Russo's Trustee*, B was infeft in heritable property but had granted a probative letter delivered to A stating that, notwithstanding the terms of the title, B (who was himself also sequestrated) held the property in trust for A. On the basis of that letter, A's trustee in sequestration claimed the property. A's wife maintained, on the strength of certain documents produced, that she was the true purchaser and that she had paid the price. She produced holograph letters from A which she maintained were declarations of trust. The evidence seems to have been unreliable and there was a suggestion that the letters, claimed to be declarations of trust, had been prepared after the event. In the result, the Sheriff and the First Division on appeal rejected the arguments put forward by A's wife. The property was therefore dealt with as part of A's estate for the purposes of his sequestration. This decision does not in any way affect the principles established in *Sharp* v. *Thomson* but turns entirely on the suspect nature of the evidence produced.

**4.2 Presumptions arising from the custody of the deed**
Occasionally, a doubt arises as to whether or not a deed is to be treated as delivered in particular circumstances. In these cases, there are certain presumptions, arising out of the surrounding circumstances, but in all cases these are rebuttable. The presumptions may be summarised thus:

**4.3 Deed held by grantee.** Where a deed, gratuitous or onerous, is held by the disponee or grantee thereunder, this raises a strong presumption that the deed was delivered and is, therefore, operative. But mere possession of the deed alone does not *per se* imply delivery; in doubtful cases, it is necessary to establish *animus* or intention.

**4.4 Deed in the hands of an agent.** Frequently, in practice, deeds are delivered and accepted, and held, by solicitors or other agents. The rule is that the agent is equivalent to the party whom he represents.

**4.5 Deed in hands of common agent.** If, as often happens, a common agent acts for grantor and grantee (*e.g.* the family solicitor acting for father and son as donor and donee) the fact that the common agent holds a deed, which apparently effects donation, raises no presumption one way or the other. In such cases, therefore, it is very important to establish delivery by other means; *e.g.* a separate letter confirming the fact of delivery and a signed acknowledgement thereof.

**4.6 Equivalents to delivery**
Certain acts by the grantor may imply delivery.

**4.7 Registration.** There are two main types of registration which may or may not raise presumptions, according to circumstances. These are:

(i) *Registration for publication in Sasines.* Registration of a deed in Sasines is the final step in perfecting the real right of a disponee of heritage. It follows that if A, as owner of a heritable property, dispones that property to B, and thereafter the disposition is recorded in Sasines on behalf of B, the disponee, this necessarily raises an almost irrebuttable presumption that the deed has been delivered. See *Carmichael* 1920 SC (HL) 195 for the ordinary case. But compare *Cameron's Trustees* 1907 SC 407 for a specialty, where title was taken in name of A as trustee for his daughter B, and was recorded on A's behalf; recording was not sufficient to establish delivery as between A and B.

The same principles would apply on registration of a title under the Land Registration (Scotland) Act 1979.

(ii) *Registration for preservation in the Books of Council and Session.* In this case, registration does not create rights. The only purpose is to avoid the loss of the principal deed. As a result, registration for preservation is less significant than registration for publication. See *Tennent* ((1869) 7 M 936.

**4.8 Intimation to the debtor in an obligation.** When an incorporeal moveable right is assigned, the assignee completes his title by intimating the assignation to the debtor in the obligation. Intimation here is equivalent to registration in the Register of Sasines in the case of heritage. In exactly the same way as with heritage, intimation will normally infer delivery.

**4.9 Intimation to donee.** This too may imply delivery. This question has been considered in a number of modern cases, which are listed in the Digest of Cases.

**4.10 Deeds not requiring delivery**
Contrary to the general rule, certain deeds do not require to be delivered in order to become effective. The principal cases are:

(i) *Testamentary writings.* Delivery is never necessary; and, even if a testamentary deed is delivered to the beneficiary, that does not make it irrevocable nor confer any enforceable rights on the beneficiary *inter vivos*. See *Clark's Executor* 1943 SC 216.

(ii) *Bilateral contracts.* A contract becomes immediately binding, once executed by all parties. This is an important point to consider when dealing with leases.

**4.11 Acceptance of delivery**
The grantee is not normally obliged to accept delivery; he has the option to accept or reject it. But apparently, a deed may be delivered so as to bind the grantor even although the grantee may be unaware of its existence. Therefore, although delivery is conditional upon acceptance by the grantee, that condition is resolutive and not suspensive. See *Dowie & Co.* (1891) 18 R 986 and *Allan's Trustee* 1971 SC (HL) 45.

# Chapter 5

# STAMP DUTIES AND VAT

### 5.1 Liability to stamp duty
Stamp duty is simply one form of taxation. You will find in Wood's *Lectures*, at p. 103, a short account of the origins and development of this particular tax. All the older taxing provisions have been consolidated and re-enacted in two principal Acts – the Stamp Act of 1891, which imposes the duties, and the Stamp Duties Management Act 1891 which deals with administration. It is the former Act, as subsequently amended, with which we are chiefly concerned.

As with other forms of tax, the law relating to stamp duties is *positivi juris*; and the relevant Acts are always strictly construed in favour of the taxpayer. This principle has been frequently explained and applied in other spheres of taxation. So, in applying the Stamp Act (or amending Finance Acts), there can be no room for ideas of principle or equity. The Act may operate as a hardship in some cases and not in others; but that is irrelevant. The sole question is 'Does the strict wording of the Act impose a liability or not?'

This leads to a further point. Stamp duty is only payable when expressly imposed in terms of the relevant Act. Sometimes it is possible, by framing a document in one way, to avoid paying stamp duty which would be chargeable on that document were it framed in another way. Provided that the writ as framed achieves its purpose, and that there is no concealment or distortion of the facts, it is perfectly legitimate so to frame it that stamp duty is altogether avoided or perhaps is payable at a lesser rate. But, of course, there must never be any attempt to evade the tax by mis-statement. The Inland Revenue have power to request sight of all antecedent relevant documents.

In the Budget on 2 July 1997 the Chancellor announced substantial changes to stamp duty, both on rate of duty and on thresholds. These are not detailed in the text of this chapter.

### 5.2 The Stamp Act 1891
This is the principal charging Act. It has been frequently and extensively altered by subsequent Finance Acts. It is divided into three parts. Part I contains the charging section, which imposes the duty on certain specified documents arranged alphabetically in the First Schedule, and also contains some general regulations. Part II amplifies the First Schedule. Part III contains miscellaneous provisions.

### 5.3 Scope of the Act.
The Act imposes duties on documents; no document, no duty. 'The thing which is made liable to duty is the instrument'.

**5.4 Method of payment**. The duty is paid by way of impressed stamps, which involves the lodging of the document with the Revenue for stamping, together with the duty itself, and the relevant Form – Stamps 61 (Scotland), duly completed. The use of adhesive postage stamps for small fixed duties was abolished many years ago.

**5.5 Time limits**. As a precaution against evasion, every document (if liable) must have the stamp duty impressed thereon within thirty days after execution. In practice, where there are several parties to a deed, the time limit runs from the date on which the last party signed.

**5.6 Sanctions**. To ensure that in every case the duty is paid when due, two separate sanctions are imposed:

(i) that a document which is not duly stamped is not admissible as evidence in any civil action; and

(ii) that any document not timeously stamped incurs a penalty over and above the duty due, when eventually presented. The penalty can be up to £10, plus the amount of the duty, plus interest. But this potentially large amount will normally be remitted in whole or in part.

These two provisions are essentially complementary. The effect, with certain limited exceptions, is not to render an unstamped document invalid, because (with few exceptions) any document may be presented out of time for stamping. But if so, then the second proviso operates, and a penalty is payable in addition to the duty. The result is that, if you ever have to found on an unstamped document in any action, the court will not reject it out of hand, but will insist that it be properly stamped, before considering its terms; and that of course means payment of duty, plus penalty.

Fines are imposed:

(i) For intent to defraud.

(ii) On persons who execute or issue or negotiate unstamped documents.

(iii) For refusal to stamp.

(iv) On persons who give effect to unstamped documents, e.g. registrars, official and private, bankers, etc.

It follows that a writ which is insufficiently stamped will not be accepted for registration, nor as a link in title by any agent. Nor will the Revenue, for income tax and other purposes, accept a writ as effective unless it is stamped. This, in practice, is sufficient to ensure, in a great number of cases, that stamping is timeously effected.

**5.7 Basis of assessment**

Two methods are used to arrive at the actual duty payable on any particular document. The method to be adopted in any case may depend purely on the nature of the document, or on the nature of the document and the purpose for which (or the circumstances in which) it is intended to be used. The methods are either a fixed duty of a stated amount for the particular document regardless of the value of the property to which it relates; or *ad valorem* duty, calculated as a percentage on the amount involved. A disposition (a conveyance) may carry either fixed duty of 50p, or *ad val-*

*orem* duty calculated by reference to the price paid for, or the value of, the property conveyed; it will depend on circumstances which mode of fixing the duty applies.

To deal now with particular instances, being cases which you will meet commonly in practice.

**5.8 (1) Fixed duties**. The old fixed duties of 2d. and 6d. (pre-decimalisation) were abolished by the Finance Act 1970.

Many other fixed duties have been abolished by the Finance Act 1985. Until 1987, the fixed duty of 50p applied in a variety of cases, *e.g.* a conveyance or transfer, other than those expressly charged with duty under the Act. A conveyance is usually charged *ad valorem*. The fixed duty applied to tranfers vesting property in new trustees, transfers of assets to residuary legatees under a will and other like conveyances which were exempt from *ad valorem* duty.

Under the Stamp Duty (Exempt Instruments) Regulations 1987, a substantial number of documents which previously attracted the fixed duty of 50p are now exempt from duty, provided the document contains a certificate in appropriate form to the effect that the instrument falls within one of several categories listed in those regulations. In that event, not only is the document exempt from stamp duty, but it is unnecessary to submit the document to the Stamp Office for adjudication or franking in any way. These regulations are reproduced in the Diploma Styles.

As a result, the fixed duty of 50p which at one time was chargeable on almost every formal document of any kind not subject to *ad valorem* duty, is now much less frequently required.

**5.9 (2) Ad valorem duties.** *Ad valorem* duties are (as a general rule) fixed, not according to the type of document, but according to the nature of the transaction. And there are different scales of duty for different kinds of transaction. Thus the standard rate of *ad valorem* duty on sale and purchase approximates to 1% (until recently 2%). The amount of duty depends on the amount involved in a particular transaction, or the value of the property dealt with. The principal cases are:

**5.10** (*a*) *Conveyance on sale duty.* This includes every instrument and every decree of court whereby any property is, on sale, transferred to a purchaser. 'Property' includes not only land and heritable property generally but also any interest in land and all incorporeal moveable property and rights, e.g. stocks and shares, vested interests in trust estates, goodwill of a business, book debts, and incorporeal rights generally.

'Sale' necessarily involves some element of consideration, and it is the value of the consideration on which (as a rule) the amount (and the rate – see later) of duty is based. In the ordinary case, where the consideration is a lump sum in cash, no difficulty arises. But consideration need not be in one single payment, nor need it be in cash.

So, property may be transferred in exchange for an allotment of shares; the consideration is then the actual value of the shares at that time.

Again, pre-1974, the consideration on the sale of land could be represented by annual or periodical payments. If the total period did not exceed 20 years, the consideration was the whole amount which was or might have been payable during that period. Where it exceeded 20 years, it was the whole amount which would or might become due in the first 20 years. Thus, in the ordinary case of a feu charter before the Land Tenure Reform (Scotland) Act 1974, the consideration was normally an annual feuduty in perpetuity; so 20 years' feuduty was taken as the consideration. Feuduty can no longer be charged since 1 September 1974, so this no longer applies to Scottish land titles. Where there is a lump sum payment, plus annual payments – as often happened – the two must be aggregated.

The deed on which the duty is charged is normally the conventional document whereby the actual transfer is effected, *e.g.*, on sale of land, the disposition; on sale of stock, the transfer. But, in many cases, other documents are found liable under this head because they in fact effect a conveyance on sale, though not in conventional form. The emphasis is on the nature of the transaction, not on the nature of the deed.

Partnership agreements and dissolution agreements, where one partner buys or sells a share in a business, often in fact operate as conveyances on sale, and are chargeable accordingly; but this does not apply in every case. Again, receipts may operate in the same way, *e.g.* a receipt for purchase price of goodwill, no document being required to vest the goodwill in the purchaser. A contract for sale of goodwill may also be so liable – see below. But if there is no written contract and no receipt, there is no duty payable.

Agreements for sale are normally charged as agreements and not as conveyances on sale, if by law some formal document must follow thereon to vest the property in the purchaser. So, in the simple case of the purchase of a house, missives of sale cannot give the purchaser a valid title – a disposition is also required. The missives are exempt from duty, and the disposition attracts *ad valorem* conveyance on sale duty.

But if the agreement covers other property for which no vesting document is required, it may be liable to *ad valorem* duty *quoad* that other property. This is expressly provided, under s. 59 of the Stamp Act as amended, which renders such agreements liable in respect of any equitable estate or interest, or any interest in property except land; goods; stocks and shares; and ships. So, in the sale of a business, it may be necessary to allocate the price between the various items acquired, *e.g.* land, goodwill, stock-in-trade, etc., and to pay duty on the missives in respect of certain of these items, *e.g.* goodwill, fixed plant and machinery (where not heritable, since heritable plant passes under the disposition); benefit of contracts; book debts; cash on deposit (not cash in bank, by concession, nor cash in hand); patents, etc.

**5.11** Rate of duty.   The rate of duty in the original Stamp Act 1891 for all conveyances on sale was 10 shillings per £100 of consideration. There have been frequent alterations to the basic rate in subsequent Finance Acts. Although of no significance now from the point of view of stamping a deed, it may be important to know the various rates of duty from time to time in force in the past when examining a heritable title, because one of the things you have to check is that each writ in the title is properly stamped.

When the rate of duty was first increased in 1910, there was a special exemption in respect of conveyances (other than transfers of stock or marketable securities) where the consideration did not exceed £500; provided always that the conveyance contained a clause certifying that the transaction thereby effected did not form part of a larger transaction or of a series of transactions in respect of which the total consideration exceeded £500. In such a case (*i.e.* under £500), the stamp duty remained at 10 shillings per £100; above that, and for transfers of stock £1 per £100.

This system of exemptions has been repeated in subsequent Finance Acts. The current rate of duty and all earlier rates in force under previous Finance Acts are given in the Diploma Styles, together with the style of the certificate of value with one temporary exception, noted below. In all such cases, to qualify for the exemption or for the reduced rates from time to time in force, the deed must contain the certificate of value. If the clause is not included, the full rate is exigible, no matter how small the consideration. If omitted by mistake, the Revenue will accept an endorsed certificate signed by the parties to the deed. The exception referred to above relates to the period from and after 20 December 1991 to 19 August 1992 where the threshold above which stamp duty was payable was raised from £30,000 to £250,000, but purely as a temporary measure. The limit was raised in the 1993 Budget to £60,000.

The clause certifies that 'the transaction hereby effected does not form part of a larger transaction or of a series of transactions in respect of which the amount or value or the aggregate amount or value of the consideration exceeds (a stated limit)'. This is designed to prevent evasion of duty by breaking down a single large transaction into a number or series of smaller transactions, *e.g.*, on a purchase of heritable property for £100,000, two conveyances, each at a consideration of £50,000, would each be *prima facie* exempt. But in such a case the certificate could not truly be signed.

On the sale of a business, cash and stock-in-trade can be left out of account; see the Finance Act 1958 s. 34(4).

What constitutes a larger transaction or a series of transactions, in terms of the certificate? Clearly, any single sale at a single price constitutes a single transaction for the purpose of the Finance Acts; that single price cannot be broken down in order to benefit from a reduced rate. The same would apply to a single contract for the purchase of several heritable properties each at a separate stated price.

A series of transactions is more difficult to define. There is no Scottish authority but there is an English case, *Cohen* [1937] 1 KB 478. The facts were that a purchaser acquired several separate lots of real estate at an auction; this was held not to constitute a larger transaction or a series of transactions under the Acts. The test seems to be whether the transactions in question were inter-related and inter-dependent; and, if not, each transaction qualifies for exemption.

Note, also, that the exemption and reduced rates do not apply to transfers of stocks and shares or other marketable securities, but do apply to other transfers and assignations, *e.g.* partnership, reversions, etc.

**5.12** Excambion.   Where two properties are exchanged, whether by contract of excambion or by two separate conveyances, the stamp duty was formerly 50p regardless of value. However, this was changed by s. 241 of the Finance Act 1994 in respect of deeds executed after 7 December 1993 in implement of contracts made on or after 30 November 1993. The new rule is that *ad valorem* duty is charged on the consideration for each part of the exchange, represented by the market value of the property exchanged. The £60,000 exemption limit applies separately to each part of the exchange. If one party makes an additional cash payment to the other in order to equalise values, this amount will be deducted from the value of the more expensive property. If the transaction is structured as a sale rather than an exchange, the transaction will attract duty only on the value of the more expensive property. (On this, see the notes at 1996 JLS 75 and 232.)

**5.13** Charities. Conveyances or transfers to charities were made exempt from stamp duty under the Finance Act 1982.

**5.14** (*b*) *Mortgage duty* Abolished under the Finance Act 1971 from 1 August 1971.

Duty was chargeable under this head in every transaction involving the loan of money, present or future, where there was some formal document containing an obligation on the part of the debtor to repay a capital sum.

**5.15** (c) *Lease duty.* There are special *ad valorem* scales of duty for leases, depending on the duration of the lease and the rent. Note that frequently an agreement for lease, which effectively creates the relationship of landlord and tenant and is often not followed by a formal lease, is liable to duty on the appropriate lease scale. The lease itself (if one follows) is exempt. If the term of lease is more than seven but less than twenty years, a Form L.V.(Λ.) must be completed and signed by the tenant or his agent; and the top copy thereof is then lodged with the lease for stamping. The lease will then be impressed with a produced stamp.

Following s. 240 of the Finance Act 1994, both the formal lease and any prior agreement should be submitted together; but in terms of a guidance note issued on 30 June 1994, the Revenue will accept either an agreement for lease or a formal lease, as long as it contains a certificate in the following terms:

> 'I/we certify that this lease is not a lease which gives effect to an agreement for lease as interpreted by the Inland Revenue in terms of the guidance note dated 30 June 1994 referring to section 240 of the Finance Act 1994.'

For a general discussion of the instances where VAT may be payable on rent and stamp duty will be due on the VAT inclusive sum, see para. 5.34.

An agreement to lease is charged to duty as if it were an actual lease made for the same term and consideration (s. 75(1) Stamp Act 1891). If a lease is subsequently granted, substantially conform to the agreement to lease, the lease is also chargeable to duty; however, credit is given for duty paid on the agreement (s. 75(2) Stamp Act 1891). There is no provision, however, for repaying any excess stamp duty that may have been paid under the agreement to lease.

**5.16** (*d*) *Miscellaneous.* Certain other transactions attract special scales of *ad valorem* duty, *e.g.* issues of bearer instruments.

**5.17 Voluntary dispositions.** There was no provision in the Stamp Act for *ad valorem* duty on gratuitous dispositions and transfers of property by way of gift. But by the Finance Act 1910 s. 74, duty was imposed on any conveyance or transfer operating as a voluntary disposition *inter vivos*, as if it were a conveyance on sale, the value of the property conveyed being taken as 'consideration' in assessing the duty. In other words, a voluntary disposition became a hypothetical sale, and all the provisions as to duty on 'conveyance on sale' applied, including the recent amendments in the rates of duty referred to above, and the exemptions and reliefs on values under the relevant limits.

The scope of this provision extended not only to simple gifts *inter vivos*, but also to voluntary settlements, to the exercise of a power of appointment, to release of life interests, etc.

It also covered any conveyance (other than a conveyance to a purchaser or other person in good faith and for valuable consideration) where, in the opinion of the Revenue, the consideration was inadequate, and the conveyance conferred substantial benefit on the transferee. This prevented evasion of duty by spurious sales to donees at 'give away' prices. The value of the property was the basis of the charge to duty.

Except in the case of marketable securities, the conveyance or transfer qualified for the exemption from duty and for the reduced rates of duty, provided the deed included the appropriate certificate of value.

The Finance Act 1910 s. 74 is repealed and *ad valorem* duty is no longer payable on *inter vivos* gifts, under the Finance Act 1985, as from 26 March 1985.

### 5.18 Exemptions

The Stamp Act 1891 (First Schedule – end) lists certain documents as wholly exempt from any stamp duty. The principals are:

(i) Transfers of government stock. This extends even to voluntary conveyances; and

(ii) testamentary and *mortis causa* dispositions and settlements.

The Finance Act 1949 created certain further exemptions.

Again, the various heads in the First Schedule to the Stamp Act confer specific exemptions in certain cases under that head, and this practice is followed in the various Finance Acts amending it or imposing new duties.

Certain special exemptions from existing duties have been introduced by Finance Acts to relieve inequities, *e.g.* Finance Act 1949 exempting certain documents from 6d. duty and FA 1970 abolishing certain duties, *e.g.* 2d., 6d. on agreements, etc. FA 1971 also abolished several *ad valorem* duties; *e.g.* bond or covenant; mortgage etc.; and FA 1985 which abolished most of the remaining fixed duties. The 1987 Regulations, introducing further exemptions, have already been referred to above.

Finally, quite apart from the Stamp Act and Finance Acts, there are a large number of miscellaneous Acts which confer special exemptions from stamp duty in special cases.

Apart from these special exemptions, certain documents require no stamp duty because there is no head of duty to bring them into charge. Thus, stock and share certificates are not liable, nor a simple IOU.

### 5.19 Miscellaneous and general

Before leaving this subject, there are certain general and miscellaneous matters which I wish to touch on briefly.

Firstly, some general points as to assessment of duty in certain cases.

### 5.20 (1) Double operation of a deed.   Where two separate and unrelated

deeds or instruments are both embodied in a single document, two stamps are obviously required, and in any event this is covered by the Stamp Act 1891 s. 3, *e.g.* a disposition (conveyance on sale) with minute of consolidation (deed) endorsed. Two stamps were required until 1985 when deed duty of 50p was abolished.

Under s. 4, if a single deed effects two or more principal (though related) purposes each of which would, independently, attract duty, it must be separately stamped for each separate matter, or purpose. So, until 25 March 1985, a deed of assumption and conveyance appointing new trustees was stamped £1, being 50p as an appointment and 50p as a conveyance. The 50p fixed duty on appointments was abolished by the Finance Act 1985; the fixed duty of 50p on the conveyance was abolished under the 1987 Regulations. Accordingly, a deed of assumption and conveyance is now wholly exempt from stamp duty. But it has been observed judicially that 'all that is required is that the instrument should be stamped for its principal object, and that stamp covers everything accessory to this object'.

**5.21 (2) Deed answering more than one description**. This applies in a variety of cases, *e.g.* an assignation of a bond might also be a voluntary conveyance *inter vivos*, and, if so, attracted conveyance on sale duty. This still applied post-1971 until 25 March 1985, when duty on voluntary dispositions was abolished, although the head of charge 'mortgage duty – assignations' was abolished by FA 1971. In all such cases, the Revenue can claim duty under one head only, and as a rule will always claim the larger duty. But where a deed is specifically chargeable under one specific head, that duty is exacted, though the deed might be liable to greater duty under some more general head. So, until 25 March 1985, the duty on a charter of novodamus was always 25p under its specific head, though it is also a deed (50p); and a conveyance (50p). All of these duties are now abolished.

**5.22 (3) One transaction effected by several deeds**. It often happens that, for the completion of a single transaction, several deeds are necessary. *Ad valorem* duty is paid on one deed only; the others are stamped with fixed duty, usually 50p as a conveyance.

### 5.23 Adjudication

The Revenue, if required, will adjudicate the stamp duty on any document, and in certain cases adjudication is obligatory. If adjudicated and duly stamped, the document is impressed with a further stamp, in addition to the duty, called an adjudication stamp. That is then conclusive evidence that the proper duty has been paid. This has two distinct advantages in that it settles the question of duty with the Revenue once and for all, and any person to whom the deed is subsequently produced is bound to accept it as properly stamped.

There is a general obligation under the Stamp Act 1891 s. 5 to set out all material facts relevant to stamping in the body of the deed, and where this is done, adjudication is normally unnecessary. But if the case is complicated, or if there is any doubt as to the head under which the deed is chargeable, then adjudication is appropriate. The normal method of initiating an appeal against an adjudged duty is by stated case in the Court of Session.

Despite the general obligation of disclosure, however, it is permissible to omit relevant facts provided there is no intent to defraud. But in that case, adjudication is almost always essential; and all the relevant facts must then be placed before the Revenue.

Adjudication was obligatory in the case of voluntary conveyances until 1985 and is still required in certain other special instances.

The deed is lodged for adjudication with a completed Form 188 and a duly certified abstract or full copy within the time limit for stamping, together with such documents and information as may be relevant.

### 5.24 Denoting stamps
There are two common examples.

### 5.25 (1) Duplicate denoting stamp. Where a deed is executed in duplicate, the principal is stamped with the appropriate duty.

If this is 50p the duplicate is also stamped with that duty and no denoting stamp is required – each deed being *ex facie* sufficiently stamped. Where the duty on the principal deed exceeds 50p, the duplicate may be stamped 50p only; in addition, to show *ex facie* that it is sufficiently stamped, it is impressed with a duplicate denoting stamp.

As from 1 August 1976 the practice has been altered by omitting from the counterpart deed stamps showing the amount impressed on the original. Instead, the duplicate denoting stamp will simply say:

'Duplicate or counterpart – original fully and properly stamped.'

### 5.26 (2) Duty paid denoting stamp. A deed may, on the face of it, appear liable to a larger duty than that actually impressed, but in fact the principal duty has been stamped on some other deed, *e.g.* a formal lease following an agreement for lease, the latter bearing the *ad valorem* duty; the lease is exempt (formerly a fixed stamp of 6d. only) but, as *ex facie* evidence that this is sufficient, it is also impressed with this stamp to show the duty paid on the agreement. In neither case does the denoting stamp act as an adjudication stamp and is not conclusive evidence that the stamp duty impressed on the other document is in fact the correct duty.

### 5.27 VAT – General
The rules relating to VAT in the UK are complex. It is not the intention here to give detailed information as to the applicability of VAT, but rather to provide a general outline of some of the more common areas when a professional adviser acting for a commercial client will require to consider VAT implications.

VAT was introduced into the UK in 1973 as a result of joining the European Community. It has its origins in Art. 99 of the 1957 Treaty establishing the European Economic Community which requires a 'harmonized system of indirect taxes' to prevail throughout the Community.

The VAT rules applicable to land and property transactions were changed in the Finance Act 1989, as a result of a judgment of the European Court handed down on 21 June 1988 which decided that the UK had not implemented its obligations under an EEC directive with regard to VAT provisions. Introduction of these new rules has led to numerous anomalies, which consequently make it difficult for advisers to extract general principles.

VAT will not be applicable on the normal domestic conveyancing transaction. However, when considering the sale or purchase of land and/or property by a commercial client, or a leasehold transaction, VAT will be an element that will require to be considered.

If a commercial client buys, sells, leases, licenses, rents or hires out land or buildings or parts of a building on a regular basis, then he will be seen as acting in the course or furtherance of a business, and the VAT liability of the supply will require to be considered. Property development or redevelment on a 'one off' basis is also seen as carrying on a business for the purpose of VAT.

### 5.28 Types of supply

Supplies are categorised for VAT purposes into taxable and exempt supplies. Taxable supplies fall into two categories: (a) zero rated supplies; (b) standard rated supplies, which are those on which VAT is paid at the current rate of 17.5%.

The difference between taxable and exempt supplies is that input VAT (VAT on expenses for the business) related to taxable supplies may be recovered whereas input VAT related to exempt supplies is in principle not recoverable.

Prior to 1 April 1989 the supply of an interest in land and buildings (sale or lease) was exempt with certain exceptions. The supply of a major interest in a building by the person constructing the same was zero rated. 'Major interest' meant an outright transfer of ownership or lease for more than twenty one years. The provision of construction services for the construction of a new building was also zero rated. After 1 April 1989 the position changed substantially.

### 5.29 (a) Zero rated supplies.

Zero rating is now restricted to prescribed instances in which a supply has as its subject a 'qualifying' building. 'Qualifying' buildings include a dwelling or group of dwellings, but excludes those which cannot be occupied throughout the year by the person to whom the grant is made – for example timeshare accommodation. The sale of timeshare accommodation is standard rated where the property involved was completed less than three years before the sale, and is otherwise exempt. 'Qualifying' buildings also include a building or part of a building to be used for charitable purposes; and a residential building or residential part of a building which will be used as *inter alia* a children's home or a home for old or disabled persons. The person constructing such a qualifying building can zero rate the supply of such a building provided that the undernoted conditions are met.

The conditions are that:

(i) The building must 'qualify' as explained above.

(ii) A certificate of proposed use must be obtained from the purchaser or grantee where the intended use is for relevant residential or relevant charitable purposes.

(iii) A major interest in all or part of the building must be granted.

(iv) The supplier must qualify as the person constructing the building and, with effect from 1 March 1995, the supply must be the first grant of a major interest.

(v) The building formerly required to be new but, since 1 March 1995, a non-residential building converted for a residential or other qualifying purpose would also generally attract zero-rating.

A major interest includes a grant of the *dominium utile* or a long lease – one which is capable of exceeding twenty one years.

Any supply of a qualifying building which does not meet these criteria will be exempt.

Note that, if within ten years of its completion, a zero rated qualifying building (other than a dwelling) is used for non-qualifying purposes, VAT must be accounted for.

**5.30 (b) Standard rated supplies**. Any sale of a new 'non-qualifying' building will be standard rated for VAT. 'New' is defined as up to three years old from the date of first occupation or the date of practical completion (whichever is the earlier).

**5.31 (c) Exempt supplies**. All supplies of buildings or land which do not meet the criteria to be zero rated, as discussed above, and which do not fall to be standard rated will be exempt with the option to tax.

### 5.32 The election to waive exemption

The election to waive exemption (or option to tax) for a supply which is otherwise exempt, is now to be found in Schedule 10, paras. 2–4 of the Value Added Tax Act 1994. Subject to the rules, the option to tax means that, if it is exercised by the supplier, supplies which would otherwise be exempt will become taxable at the standard rate. Thus, a landlord of non-residential property, any supply of which is exempt, can waive this exemption and opt to tax the rental income received by him, whereupon VAT will become payable on rents. Similarly the seller of used non-residential property which does not 'qualify' for zero rating and is not mandatorily standard rated can opt to tax the property whereupon VAT will become payable on the sale price. However, the Finance Act 1997 contains provisions restricting the option. Its effects are removed where the developer of property which falls within the Capital Goods Scheme makes a grant in relation to the property, with the intention or expectation that the property would be occupied other than mainly for taxable business purposes by the grantor, or a person funding the development, or a person connected with either of them. This is a much more limited restriction of the option than originally proposed in the Finance Bill.

This option is virtually irrevocable, although provisions were introduced in 1995 allowing an option to be revoked in certain circumstances within less than three months, or after more than 20 years, of its exercise. Subject to this, once the option has been exercised for a given building or area of land, the choice is binding for all future supplies by the person exercising the option; after a change of ownership the new owner has the right to exercise the option or not as he chooses. Therefore while a property remains in the ownership of the person who has exercised the option the rents cannot be taxed without taxing any subsequent sale. Furthermore, if the option is exercised, it must be exercised for a building as a whole. Customs and Excise treat buildings linked internally or by a covered walkway as single buildings for the purposes of the option to tax. Certain buildings, including private dwellings, and all other 'qualifying' buildings cannot be the subject of the option to tax. Further, supplies of land to D.I.Y. homebuilders or to housing associations for the construction of dwellings cannot be subject to the option.

The option takes effect from the beginning of the day on which it is exercised, or at a later date if specified. The option can be exercised without prior consultation with tenants or a purchaser, no matter what the stage of the transaction. If negotiations have proceeded on the basis that the building is exempt, then a binding undertaking must be obtained by the purchasers from the seller not to exercise the option. If a seller exercises the option, VAT becomes payable on the purchase price. If an agreement has been entered into which is silent on VAT, the VAT payable as a result of the exercise of the option will be payable in addition to the agreed price. Given that the option can be exercised at any time, these issues should be resolved prior to conclusion of missives: see *Jaymarke Development Ltd.* 1992 SLT 1193.

### 5.33 The advantages and disadvantages of opting to tax
If an option to tax is exercised, input tax relating to the supply, such as VAT on land purchases and construction costs, can be recovered. However, disadvantages include the indirect effect on the residual value of the property together with the irrevocable nature of the option. Furthermore, opting to tax when dealing with a building that will subsequently be leased will mean that subsequent rents will be subject to VAT. Potential tenants may include those not subject to the VAT regime who would thus be unable to reclaim their input VAT.

### 5.34 Recent amendments
The Value Added Tax (Buildings and Land) Order 1991 which came into effect on 1 January 1992 made a number of minor changes to liability for VAT. For example, if a personal right is granted to acquire an interest in land in Scotland, the supply of that personal right will be exempt, unless it is of a type which is specifically taxed at the standard rate or unless the client has opted to tax the land.

Furthermore, if an option to purchase or lease land or buildings is granted which in itself will be taxed at the standard rate of VAT, the grant of the option is also standard rated.

Most of the law (with the exception of Orders) relating to value added tax has now been consolidated in the Value Added Tax Act 1994 and the Value Added Tax Regulations 1995.

The Value Added Tax Act (Buildings and Land) Order 1995 made a number of important changes to the option to tax, including providing for its possible revocation as noted above. It also effectively abolished a very complex part of the law in this field, called the 'developer's self-supply' charge.

The Value Added Tax (Land) Order 1995 brought the treatment of surrenders or renunciations of leases into line with other grants of land, notably with regard to exemption from VAT being available, subject to the option to tax.

The Value Added Tax (Construction of Buildings) Order 1995 dealt with a number of matters in relation to zero-rating, providing a number of definitions and allowing certain converted buildings to qualify for zero-rating.

Further changes are expected in the 1997 Finance Act, in relation to the option to tax, as noted above.

### 5.35 Interaction between VAT and stamp duty

The Inland Revenue issued a Statement of Practice on 12 September 1991 highlighting the interaction between stamp duty and VAT. A number of points arise from this Statement of Practice which should be borne in mind:

(1) For stamp duty purposes, on sale of a new non-domestic building, the amount or value of the consideration is the gross amount inclusive of VAT. Therefore, where VAT is payable on the sale of new, non-residential property, stamp duty is calculated on the VAT inclusive consideration. This point was confirmed in *Glenrothes Development Corporation* v. *IRC* 1994 SLT 1310.

(2) As discussed above, certain transactions with non-residential property other than the sales of new buildings are exempt from VAT. However, where the seller or lessor opts to tax, then:

(i) where the election has already been exercised at the time of the transaction, stamp duty is chargeable on the purchase price, premium or rent (depending on the transaction) including VAT;

(ii) where the election has not been exercised at the time of the transaction, VAT should be included in any payments to which an election could still apply. This will include a VAT element in the stamp duty charge in cases where an election to waive the exemption has not been exercised but it is still possible to exercise it;

(iii) where VAT is charged on the rent under a lease, subject to certain considerations, stamp duty at the appropriate rate according to the length of the term will be charged on the VAT inclusive figures. The rate of VAT in force at the date of execution of the lease will be used in the calculation;

(iv) where there is a formal Deed of Variation varying the terms of a lease so as to provide payment of VAT by way of additional rent, further stamp duty may be payable (s. 77(5) Stamp Act 1891).

# Part 2

# FEUS

# Chapter 6

# CREATION OF THE NEW FEUDAL ESTATE

### 6.1 The historical background
In common with other European countries in the medieval period, land in Scotland came to be held on feudal tenure, although feudalism was probably not a significant force until the twelfth century, which is late by comparison with other countries. Feudalism became and remained the dominant form of land tenure throughout Western Europe from the late medieval period until the early modern period. The feudal system was abolished in France with the Revolution of 1789, and in most other countries in the 50 years which followed. England had effectively dismantled its feudal system a century earlier. By about 1850 Scotland was the only country in Europe to retain a feudal system of land tenure. The position remains unchanged today, although it now seems unlikely that feudalism will survive for many years longer.

### 6.2 Characteristics of feudal land tenure
Feudal land tenure is difficult to characterise succinctly. Partly this is because of the vast historical time span which it has occupied. Partly it is because feudalism seems to have been in a state of almost constant evolution, a process which has accelerated in modern times. Partly also it is because legal theory, perhaps necessarily, pays little regard to the evidence as uncovered by historians, so that feudal theory in the form in which it is usually expressed by lawyers is profoundly unhistorical.

Legal theory holds that all land in Scotland belonged, and indeed, in a sense which is explained below, belongs still, to the Crown. Much of that land was then feued out to the Crown's supporters in return for a periodic rendering of services or, in the later period, of money, known as reddendo. A number of different feudal tenures existed, and the nature of the reddendo depended on the type of tenure. The person to whom the land was feued was known as the vassal or feuar, and the Crown was referred to as his feudal superior. The vassal was entitled to the use of the land but only in exchange for payment of the reddendo. If he failed to pay the reddendo he could lose the feu by the process known as irritancy. In effect therefore, a feu was, and still is today, much like a perpetual lease, and indeed in analysing feudalism the institutional writers drew parallels with the *emphyteusis* of Roman law.

### 6.3 The feudal tenures
Land could be held on a number of different tenures. Apart from mortification, which was granted to religious houses and which did not survive the Reformation, the available tenures were the following:

(1) *Wardholding.* This was the paradigm feudal tenure. In exchange for his land the vassal was subject to the *reddendo* of hunting and hosting,

71

which was the rendering of military services to the superior by the provision of men and equipment.

(2) *Feu-farm.* 'Farm' means rent, and in feu-farm tenure the reddendo was the payment of feuduty, whether in coin or in kind. A variant of feu-farm was, and is, the tenure of the kindly tenants of Lochmaben, which is found in four villages in the parish of Lochmaben. 'Kindly' in this context means hereditary, and in origin kindly tenancies appear to have been perpetual leases. The reddendo is rent rather than feuduty and is payable to the hereditary Keeper, who is the Earl of Mansfield.

(3) *Blench.* In blench tenure the reddendo was purely nominal, so that the vassal took the land for nothing. A typical blench reddendo was one penny Scots a year, if asked only.

(4) *Burgage.* Burgage was the only tenure permissible within the royal burghs. No reddendo was payable other than watching and warding, which meant assisting in the keeping of the peace within the burgh. Subinfeudation was prohibited and it seems likely that the vassals held directly from the Crown, although the precise position is obscure.

Of these four traditional tenures, only two now survive. Wardholding was converted to blench tenure by the Tenures Abolition Act 1746, following the 1745 Rebellion, and burgage tenure was converted to feu-farm by the 1874 Act s. 25. Today almost all land is held on feu-farm tenure, although blench holdings are found occasionally. The 1974 Act ss. 4–6 contains provisions for the redemption of feuduty by a single payment to the superior of its capitalised value, and many feuduties have now disappeared. No new feuduty may be imposed after 1974. Where feuduty remains payable today, it is payable in coin and not in kind.

### 6.4 Casualties
Unlike reddendo, which was a regular payment due periodically, a casualty was a single payment which was due on the occurrence of a certain event. Casualties often involved substantial liability and were of considerable importance, but they were abolished by the Feudal Casualties (Scotland) Act of 1914 and are now of historical interest only. The casualties payable depended on the tenure on which the land was held and no casualties at all were due in burgage tenure. Typical were the casualties of composition and relief, payable when a new vassal entered with the superior, respectively by *inter vivos* transfer and by inheritance.

### 6.5 Heritable jurisdictions
As part of a feu of land the Crown could confer upon favoured vassals the right of heritable jurisdiction. The technical means by which this was done was by a grant of barony, the grantee being known as a baron. A baron was entitled to hold baron's courts. Jurisdiction was determined by the terms of the grant and usually included both civil and criminal jurisdiction. For all practical purposes, baron courts were abolished by the Heritable Jurisdictions (Scotland) Act of 1746, but barony grants remain in existence, giving rise to certain conveyancing peculiarities and conferring on the holder the right to use the title of baron. In recent years there has been a growing market for barony titles.

## 6.6 Allodial land

Not absolutely all land in Scotland is held on feudal tenure. There is also a small amount of allodial land, that is to say, land which is owned outright and without reference to a feudal superior. The main example of allodial land is udal land in Orkney and Shetland, which is Scandinavian in origin. In udal land the owner (or 'udaller') holds the land absolutely, subject to the payment of land tax known as skat. But over the centuries a considerable quantity of udal land has become feudalised and is now indistinguishable from ordinary feudal land.

Other examples of allodial land are land which has not been feued by the Crown, and certain churchyards in the ownership of the Church of Scotland. It is sometimes said that land which has been acquired by compulsory purchase is allodial, but the case law is inconclusive.

## 6.7 Substitution and subinfeudation

In the modern law a vassal is free to transfer his interest in the land, either by substitution or by subinfeudation. This was not always so, and in earlier times transfer could be restricted or prevented altogether by the terms of the original feudal grant or by the refusal of the superior to give entry to the new vassal. Restrictions of this kind cannot now receive effect: see Tenures Abolition Act 1746 s. 20, 1874 Act s. 22, and 1938 Act s. 8.

The distinction between substitution and subinfeudation is simple, but of fundamental importance to an understanding of feudal law. In substitution the vassal transfers his entire interest in the land to someone else. In subinfeudation he replicates the original act of the Crown by feuing the land to another party, who then holds of him and, until 1974, when new feuduties ceased to be possible, was bound to pay him reddendo. An example illustrates the difference. Suppose that A holds land directly from the Crown. If A then transfers to B by substitution, the effect is that B takes A's place as vassal of the Crown, with the same rights and liabilities as were formerly held by A. A then has no further interest in the land. By contrast, if A subfeus to B, B becomes the vassal of A (and not of the Crown), and A remains as the vassal of the Crown. In principle, B must pay reddendo to A, and A must pay to the Crown. Only B is entitled to possession of the land, and historically the main value to A of subfeuing was where the reddendo paid to him exceeded the reddendo which he required to pay to his superior. There is no direct relationship between B and the Crown, but the Crown is said to be the over-superior of B, and B the subvassal of the Crown.

In this chapter we are concerned with subinfeudation only, and treatment of substitution is postponed until Chapter 29.

## 6.8 Divided dominium

There is no restriction on the number of times the same piece of land may be subfeued. Thus A, who holds of the Crown, may subfeu to B, who subfeus to C, who subfeus in turn to D. The result is five different parties holding simultaneous interests in the same property. How are these interests to be classified? The answer to this question puzzled Continental jurists in the early modern period. Roman law taught that there could only be one right of ownership in respect of any one thing at any one time. But in the case of feudal land it was difficult to identify which one of the various parties was

73

the owner. The solution ultimately adopted was to say that each had *dominium* (ownership), but *dominium* of a different kind. Thus the ultimate vassal (D in our example) had *dominium utile*, the intermediate or 'subject' superiors (A, B, and C) had *dominium directum* and the Crown had *dominium eminens*. There was no single owner of the land. Each party had ownership of a different and distinctive type; and the totality of these different kinds of ownership was full ownership of the land.

In Scotland this idea of divided ownership was adopted, first by Craig, in his *Jus Feudale*, and then later by Stair. It remains the accepted view in the modern law. But it is necessary to emphasise that legal theory is here utterly remote from economic reality. Thus Mr Smith buys a house and moves into it. He believes that he owns it, and so he does, at least in the sense that he has *dominium utile*. But Mr Smith would be surprised to learn that he is not the only owner of the house, and that *dominium* is held also by his superior, by his over-superior, by the Crown, and possibly by other subject superiors as well. Of course the economic reality is otherwise. Mr Smith is entitled to live in the house and no one else is. Probably no feu-duty is now payable. In practice the interest of the superiors is likely to be almost valueless. Nonetheless the full feudal hierarchy remains in place. As this example shows, in modern times feudalism is often complex without actually being useful, and this is the most powerful argument in favour of its abolition.

In our example the sequence of subfeus occurred in rapid succession. In practice the timescale is much more likely to involve several centuries. So the Crown might have feued to A in 1600 whereupon for the next hundred years the feu might have been transferred only by substitution. Then in 1700 A(5), a successor (by substitution) of A and, like A, holding directly from the Crown, might have subfeued to B. Another 100 years might have passed before B(5), B's successor by substitution, subfeued to C. And so on. Once a new interest in land is created, by subinfeudation, that interest remains in existence unless or until it is extinguished either by irritancy or by consolidation. Both are relatively rare. Further, a superiority interest (*dominium directum*) is perpetual in precisely the same manner as the *dominium utile* and may likewise be transferred by substitution.

### 6.9 Subinfeudation before the 19th century reforms
As might be expected, the precise method by which subinfeudation was carried out was not constant through time. In recent years legal historians have done much to revise and to clarify our view of early conveyancing practice, for example by casting doubt on the existence of the *breve testatum*, which was once thought to be a precursor of the modern feu charter. This is not, however, the place to trace the evolution of the different feudal forms. For present purposes it is sufficient to examine feuing practice as it existed in the years between the establishment of the Register of Sasines in 1617 and the sequence of major statutory reforms which began in 1845.

If, between 1617 and 1845, A wished to subfeu his land to B, the following steps were required to be taken:

(1) A executed and delivered to B a charter granting the lands in feu. The charter described the land, stipulated the tenure and fixed the reddendo.

(2) An agent ('bailie') of A and an agent of B proceeded to the land itself.

A's agent derived his authority to act from a precept of sasine contained in the charter. At the land A's agent 'gave sasine' (*i.e.* possession) to B's agent by delivery of the appropriate symbol for the land. The choice of symbol was regulated by feudal law, and in the case of land with a building on it was earth and stone. This symbolical delivery took place in the presence of a notary public and two witnesses.

(3) Subsequently, the notary public drew up an instrument of sasine which summarised the terms of the charter and narrated the ceremony of giving of sasine. The witnesses signed.

(4) Finally, the instrument of sasine was recorded on B's behalf in the Register of Sasines. This had to be done within 60 days of its date. Only the instrument could be recorded, which explains the name of the Register. On registration, the instrument of sasine was minuted, engrossed in the Register, and returned to the presenter duly certified as registered.

All four steps were mandatory, and only on completion of registration, the fourth and final step, was B infeft, that is to say, entered with A as his vassal. Until infeftment B did not have *dominium* and his right was personal and not real.

## 6.10 Subinfeudation after 1845
Between 1845 and 1858, an initial series of conveyancing statutes simplified and modernised the system of land tenure. These were consolidated in 1868. Further reforms were introduced in 1874 and 1924, but by and large, the fundamental feudal principles of tenure remained unimpaired. The new simplified procedures and writs 'merely introduced shorthand means of expressing what was formerly stated at length, but made no difference in the import of the clauses or the true principles on which our feudal system is based'. *Hay* 1909 SC 554, *per* Lord Dunedin.

Since 1964, however, we have been gradually moving away from the original common law forms and procedures, thus:

(1) The Succession (Scotland) Act 1964 completely altered transmission of heritage on death.

(2) The Reid Committee report on Registration of Title to Land of 1963 (Cmnd. 2032) followed by a further report on Registration of Title by the Henry Committee in 1969 (Cmnd. 4137) recommended, and made detailed provision for, legislation completely altering the old land registration system, now implemented by the Land Registration (Scotland) Act 1979.

(3) The Halliday Committee report on Conveyancing Legislation and Practice of 1968 (Cmnd. 3118), recommended a large number of reforms. The report has been substantially implemented by the Conveyancing and Feudal Reform (Scotland) Act 1970, which completely altered the law of heritable securities and made other major changes to the law of land tenure; and by the Land Tenure Reform (Scotland) Act 1974, mainly relating to feuduty but introducing certain further reforms.

(4) In a White Paper produced by the Labour Government in 1969 'Land Tenure in Scotland – a Plan for Reform' (Cmnd. 4099), and in a Green Paper produced by the Conservative Government in 1972 'Land Tenure

Reform in Scotland', further major reforms are discussed; and these were in part implemented by the Land Tenure Reform (Scotland) Act 1974, altering the law on subinfeudation and on feuduty.

(5) A Discussion Paper by the Scottish Law Commission issued in 1991 (No. 93: 'Abolition of the Feudal System') recommends the abolition of the feudal system and explores some of the technical means by which this might be achieved. It is expected that the Discussion Paper will be followed in due course by a report, and that ultimately there will be legislation. So far, however, no report has appeared. Feudalism enjoyed something of a revival in 19th century Scotland as a means of imposing conditions on the use and development of land, and today it is the existence of these real conditions which forms the main technical obstacle to outright abolition.

### 6.11 The Conveyancing Acts
The main purpose of the series of Conveyancing Acts, commencing with the Infeftment Act 1845, was simplification, in part by providing short clauses with a long statutory interpretation which would serve for practically all situations; and in part by eliminating unnecessary steps in the procedure. But all this was achieved within the framework of the feudal system and hitherto the fundamental principles of tenure have remained unaltered.

**6.12** The Conveyancing Acts fall conveniently into two parts:

(1) The initial series. Between 1845 and 1868 there were a number of statutes, each making further amendments to the system. All of these are now consolidated and re-enacted in an Act of 1868 called Titles to Land Consolidation (Scotland) Act 1868. Such consolidation, while convenient for the practitioner, is confusing for the student because it blurs the process of gradual statutory development.

(2) Since 1868, the 1868 Act itself has been radically amended by a number of subsequent statutes, principally the Conveyancing (Scotland) Acts 1874, 1924 and 1938; the Succession (Scotland) Act 1964; the Conveyancing and Feudal Reform (Scotland) Act 1970; the Land Tenure Reform (Scotland) Act 1974; and the Land Registration (Scotland) Act 1979. But there has been no subsequent consolidating statute.

The main simplifications in the Acts 1845–1868 were:

(i) Abolition of symbolic delivery on the ground.

(ii) Direct recording of charters and other conveyances in the Register of Sasines in place of the recording of the instrument of sasine, which, as a result, disappears.

(iii) The introduction of the warrant of registration.

(iv) The reorganisation, in 1868, of the registration system by abolishing the old particular registers of sasines maintained in each of the separate county districts and by centralising all registration for publication in the General Register of Sasines in Edinburgh except the Burgh Registers. The General Register is now divided into County Divisions.

**6.13** The Titles to Land Consolidation (Scotland) Act 1868 ('the 1868 Act') consolidates all the foregoing provisions other than (iv) and a number of other earlier ones as well. Originally, it formed a comprehensive statutory conveyancing code but was fairly quickly amended and has now been largely superseded by later legislation.

It suffices to mention at this stage the following sections of this Act:

(i) Sections 5 and 8 with Schedule B, which authorised short clauses for conveyances.

(ii) Sections 141 to 143 which deal with direct recording of conveyances and the warrant of registration.

(iii) Note, particularly, a provision in s. 15 to the effect that a conveyance, when recorded, has the same legal effect as if a conveyance in the old form had been followed by the recording of an instrument of sasine. This is termed 'the system of equivalents', often adopted in this and other conveyancing statutes. The general effect is that a new or shorthand method or formula introduced in a later Act is equated to the position under the earlier rules.

### 6.14 Specific reforms
The later Conveyancing Acts made various changes on particular matters affecting subinfeudation, dealt with under the following subject headings. These matters include:

**6.15 Burgage.** Burgage was originally a distinct and separate tenure within the feudal system applicable to lands within the Royal Burghs, and was always separately treated in the Conveyancing Acts. Thus, Burgh Registers were introduced separately for burgage under an Act of 1681; and the 1868 Act makes separate provision for burgage and non-burgage property.

Since 1874, however, burgage has been assimilated with feu farm tenure by:

(a) The 1874 Act s. 25 which provides for the abolition of the distinction between burgage and feu farm; and

(b) The Burgh Registers (Scotland) Act 1926, under which, by a gradual process, Burgh Registers have all been absorbed into the Register of Sasines. The last such separate register closed in 1963.

**6.16 Subinfeudation.** Subinfeudation was often expressly prohibited in a feu charter and any such prohibition was binding on the vassal. But such prohibitions can no longer be enforced; and can therefore be ignored in any title. 1938 Act s. 8.

**6.17 Casualties.** Casualties were due *ex lege*, the actual casualties exigible depending on the nature of the tenure. But the nature of the casualty might be (and often was) varied by the express terms of a feu charter. This was known as taxing the casualty. The point of taxing casualties was to substitute casualties definite in amount, or in point of time (or both), in place of the indefinite casualties due *ex lege*.

All casualties, *ex lege* and taxed, have ceased to be exigible as a result of:

(a) the 1874 Act ss. 4, 15, 16, 18, and 23; and

(*b*) the Feudal Casualties (Scotland) Act 1914.

From a practical point of view, the result is that in examining a title, the question of casualties can be ignored altogether, except in so far as the parties have agreed to commute the casualty by payment of additional feuduty, in which case there had to be an agreement setting out the amount of the additional feuduty payable, recorded in the General Register of Sasines under the Acts above cited. Particular care should still be taken with leasehold casualties, however.

**6.18** *Reddendo*. Historically the *reddendo* to be rendered by a vassal to his superior might take various forms, including military services, watching and warding, hunting and hosting, agricultural non-military services, known as carriages and services, and feuduty which might be payable in cash or in kind. All services have disappeared and all feuduties are now expressed in money sterling under:

(*a*) the 1874 Act ss. 20 and 21;

(*b*) the Feudal Casualties (Scotland) Act 1914 s. 18;

(*c*) the 1924 Act s. 12.

Until 1974, it was still competent to provide for a permanent increase or permanent reduction in the amount of feuduty payable, such increase or reduction to take effect on a definite date or on the happening of a definite event. Any such provision in a pre-1974 deed is still effective.

Finally, the 1974 Act provides:

s. 1(1). No deed executed after 1 September 1974 shall impose any feuduty. But otherwise subinfeudation remains competent.

s. 1(2). If a deed so executed does impose feuduty, that does not invalidate the deed; but the feuduty clause is unenforceable.

s. 2. Makes a similar prohibition on other perpetual outgoings, *e.g.* ground annual, in respect of tenure or use of land, excluding rent and repairs provisions.

Further, under ss. 4–6, feuduties generally other than unallocated feuduties are redeemable, voluntarily, on sale or on compulsory purchase; and this applies to other like annual payments. For details, see Chapter 15, Superiorities.

s. 21. There is no contracting-out of these provisions.

**6.19 Warrants of registration.** The 1924 Act made some technical changes in the form of warrant, simplifying the provisions of the 1868 Act. There is no change in principle.

**6.20 Summary of position at the present day**
What we have so far done is to consider the historical origins and common law development, and later the statutory development, in the process of subinfeudation. The position as we now find it to-day, resulting from the developments above referred to, is:

(1) Agreement by the parties which is incorporated in the formal vesting

document, *viz.*, the feu charter. The content and terms of the feu charter are dealt with in Chapter 7. Note at this stage that no precept or mandate for infeftment is now required.

(2) The charter is (i) duly executed, (ii) delivered to the vassal, (iii) stamped with the Inland Revenue stamp.

(3) The warrant of registration in the modern form is then endorsed in the name of the vassal, and is signed by him or his agent.

(4) The charter, duly stamped, is then presented to the Keeper of the Registers either:

(*a*) with warrant of registration endorsed thereon, for recording in the appropriate Division of the General Register of Sasines, together with a completed application form C.P.B. 2 for recording in the Sasine Register and the recording dues; or

(*b*) with the appropriate Land Registration Application Form for registration of the title in the Land Register, if the land lies in an 'operational area'– see Chapter 13.

In either case, the Keeper now requires the recording or registration dues to be paid on presentment. See a note from the Keeper in 1995 JLS 482.

No further procedure is required. Assuming that the charter itself is intrinsically valid, then registration of the charter in name of the vassal completes the infeftment of the vassal and perfects his real right of ownership (*dominium*).

As a result, infeftment and sasine have lost their old meaning. An infeft proprietor now means a proprietor who has perfected his real right in the subjects by the recording in the Register of Sasines or Land Register of an appropriate written title. Nonetheless, by his charter, the vassal obtains his grant of land and establishes his right of tenure to which the basic feudal rules still apply. He is the vassal holding of and under the grantor, his superior, subject to the conditions in the charter, termed the 'incidents of tenure'.

## 6.21 Registration of title

Logically, it would obviously have been better to reorganise the land registers as part and parcel of a major land tenure reform. Originally, it was proposed first to complete the tenure reform and thereafter to introduce the new system of registration of title. But land tenure reform is a controversial matter and will take a considerable time to work out and agree. Registration of title, on the other hand, is not controversial and a scheme was already worked out for this in detail in the Henry Committee Report. In the result, registration of title has been introduced, before the major final reforms to land tenure, by the Land Registration (Scotland) Act 1979. In outline only at this stage, the new registration of title system involves the guaranteeing of each individual property title by the state on the same general lines as the English system of registration of title. In contrast, under the present system of registration, deeds are recorded in Sasines; but the Keeper accepts no responsibility whatsoever for the accuracy or validity thereof.

**6.22.** In registration of title a new register is used, known as the Land Register, and ultimately this will replace the Register of Sasines. It was originally hoped that the Land Register would be fully operational throughout Scotland by 1990, but this ambitious timetable has not been realised and the date currently projected is 2003. At the time of writing 14 of the 33 registration counties are operational for the purposes of registration of title, and in the remaining counties deeds continue to be recorded in the Register of Sasines.

Once a county or district has been declared a registration of title district, each property is converted from the Sasine to the Land Register, generally speaking, only on sale; so that, inevitably, within each district, properties only gradually convert to registration of title.

In the result, although we now have a registration of title Act on the statute book, it may be 20 or 30 years before 90 per cent of the properties in Scotland have been converted from the present registration system.

As mentioned above, the final stage in the reform of land tenure is still under consideration; but the ultimate form of the revised tenure is still undetermined. Several of the more important points have already been legislated for piecemeal in the 1970 Act and the 1974 Act. Future progress inevitably depends on parliamentary time available.

# Chapter 7

# THE FEU CHARTER

## 7.1 General form

A feu charter, in its standard form, is unilateral. A typical example will be found in the Appendix of Styles. The charter runs in name of and is executed by the superior alone. It contains, in essence, the identification of the parties; the consideration; the identification of the subjects; the tenure; and some subordinate matter such as the right to title deeds, etc., rents, relief and warranties as to title. Originally, this subordinate matter was incorporated in the deed itself by the inclusion of express clauses. Under the Land Registration (Scotland) Act 1979, a number of the old traditional clauses are now implied, and the statutory effect of a conveyance omitting such clauses is provided by the 1979 Act.

The feu charter may be sub-divided into:

(1) the narrative, or inductive, clause or clauses;

(2) the operative clauses, which may again be sub-divided into the dispositive clause, which rules, and subordinate clauses, conferring rights ancillary to the main or dispositive clause; and

(3) the testing clause (see Chapter 2).

## 7.2 Narrative clause

The standard content of the narrative clause is:

**7.3 Grantor.** The name and designation of the grantor will be given followed by a description of his status, normally 'heritable proprietor of the subjects and others hereinafter disponed' which implies that the grantor is infeft. There are a number of variants to meet special cases.

If the feu charter is to be effective as a title to the vassal, then the grantor of the feu charter (the superior) must have title and capacity to grant it.

(*a*) *Title.* It is not necessary that he is the beneficial owner; he may, for example, hold the property as trustee or in some other representative capacity. If so, it may be relevant to consider his powers (*e.g.* if he is a trustee). But he must have the legal title, to enable him effectively to convey; and, whatever his capacity, he must be infeft. Deduction of title is not possible in a feu charter.

Absence of title at the time of making a grant is cured if the grantor comes subsequently to own the property. This is by virtue of the doctrine of accretion. Accretion applies to all conveyancing deeds and not just to feu charters; but the deed must contain either a grant of absolute warrandice or a conveyance by the grantor of his whole right, title and interest, present and future, in the property. Feu charters in practice usually contain both. Accretion is not restricted to the case of uninfeft grantors but applies even where there was no shadow of a title at the time of making the grant. See *Swans* (1866) 4 M 663. Initially a grant by a non-owner is ineffective, because no one can convey that which he does not have. But if, after registration of the ineffective grant, the grantor comes to own the property, the title of the grantee is immediately and automatically perfected by accretion. If there are competing grantees, priority is determined by applying the fiction that accretion is retrospective, so that the grantee who registered first prevails.

(*b*) *Capacity*. Mere title and infeftment are not enough, standing alone. The grantor of the charter must also be capax. See Chapter 3.

**7.4 Consentors.** In addition, for various reasons, it may be appropriate, although not very usual, for a party or parties to consent to the charter in which case they are also named and designed in the narrative clause and the reason for their consent is there stated. Consents in other writs (*e.g.* dispositions) are more common.

**7.5 Consideration.** It is usual but not essential for a conveyance to set out explicitly the consideration. In the case of a feu charter executed on or before 1 September 1974, the consideration was normally feuduty 'and other prestations afterwritten' which includes *e.g.* implement of various obligations by the vassal. The feuduty had to be in sterling money, but it might be of any amount, with a provision for a permanent increase or decrease. There might be, in addition, a grassum or lump sum payment. No feuduty may now be created under the Land Tenure Reform (Scotland) Act 1974 s. 1, if the charter was executed after 1 September 1974, subject to limited transitional provisions.

**7.6 Operative clauses**
These include:

**7.7 The dispositive clause.** This is the main or ruling clause in the conveyance. The remaining operative clauses are subordinate to it. Its essential elements are:

**7.8** (*a*) *Words of conveyance.* To be effective, every conveyance, including feu charters and dispositions, must contain clear words expressing an immediate present transfer (or conveyance) of the right to the disponee. Thus, a mere agreement to convey was not (and is not) a valid title to heritage. It merely creates a personal obligation on one contracting party to convey property to the other contracting party; but the word 'dispone' has ceased to be a *verbum solemne* (1874 Act s. 27) although it is invariably used in practice.

**7.9** (*b*) *Identity of the grantee and the destination.*

**7.10 Capacity of disponee.** Subject in certain cases to the consent of some other person (*e.g.* guardians for children under 16), there is now no legal bar arising out of nationality, domicile, residence, age, sex or capacity to prevent or disable anyone from owning heritage in Scotland. This includes both natural and legal persons; but partnerships and other unincorporated associations are excluded from this general rule. They cannot sustain the feudal relationship, and may hold heritage only through the medium of trustees.

**7.11 Plural disponees.** In Scotland, heritage may competently be conveyed to, and held by, several persons. There is no legal limit on the total number. If there are two or more co-proprietors, then they hold either as joint proprietors or as proprietors in common.

**7.12** *Joint property.* Joint property vests as a single undivided unit in two (or more) persons, no one of whom has any absolute beneficial or exclusive right to an aliquot or severable share of the subjects. Instead, each has a joint right in the whole subjects along with all his co-proprietors 'not merely *pro indiviso* in respect of possession, but altogether *pro indiviso* in respect of the right,' *per* Lord Moncreiff in *Cargill* (1837) 15 S 408. Joint property arises automatically wherever title to land is taken by trustees. This includes property taken by trustees for behoof of a partnership. Although the authorities are not entirely clear, it is thought that joint property cannot be created, even by express words, except where the grantees are trustees.

One of several joint proprietors cannot separately dispose of his joint interest in the property to a third party; and, on his death or resignation as trustee, his right and interest in the joint property automatically accresces to the survivor(s). No deed or other procedure is required to vest the joint property exclusively in the survivor(s).

**7.13** *Common property.* Here, each of the several proprietors has an absolute, unrestricted right to a fractional or aliquot share of the whole property so long as it remains undivided. The relative size of his share (*i.e.* the amount of the fraction) may be stated expressly in terms of the titles. The shares of owners in common are not necessarily equal; but, failing any express statement in the title, the implication is that all co-proprietors own equal *pro indiviso* shares. One of several co-proprietors, owning a *pro indiviso* share, may dispose of that *pro indiviso* share without consulting his co-owners or may burden it with debt; and on his death, the *pro indiviso* share passes to his representatives and does not accresce by implication to the remaining co-proprietors. There is a right to have the property divided at any time or, where physical division is impractical, as it usually is, to have the property sold and the proceeds divided. The appropriate court action is an action of division or of division and sale.

A right of common property may arise simply because several separate persons come to be interested in the same undivided property, whether by joint purchase, succession or otherwise. It also often arises in special cases, *e.g.* tenements where certain parts of the building are owned in common.

In the ordinary case, any one or more owners in common can insist on an action of division and sale; but, in special circumstances, the Court may intervene and grant interdict to maintain the *status quo* while other problems are resolved.

The Court also has a discretion in special circumstances to refuse to grant decree. This occurs mainly in matrimonial cases, and several illustrations are given in the Digest of Cases at 7.13.

While in the ordinary way any one proprietor in common can insist on division and sale, it was emphasised in *Miller Group Ltd* 1993 SLT 207 that applications to the Court in actions of this kind involve the exercise by the Court of an equitable jurisdiction. The point at issue in this case involved a question as to whether the property should be sold by public roup or private bargain. Apparently, at one time, there was a strong presumption in favour of public roup but, more recently, opinion seems to have swung the other way. However, in *Miller Group Ltd*, the Court were firmly of the view that there was no presumption one way or the other; and the true test was which of the two methods would produce the best price. In dealing with the equitable jurisdiction in such cases, Lord Weir referred to the opinion of the Lord President in *Upper Crathes Fishings Ltd* 1991 SC 30. In the present case, since neither party would alter its position, the action was simply dismissed.

*Gray* 1996 SCLR 331 is unusual in that, instead of an action of division and sale, one of two joint proprietors sought an order from the Court ordaining the other to sell his share to her. Division of the property was impossible. Again, in the exercise of the equitable jurisdiction, the Sheriff held in all the circumstances that such an order could be made, subject to payment of appropriate compensation to the other party. There was then a debate as to how that compensation should be calculated. In certain other cases summarised in the Digest at 7.13, the Court has exercised its jurisdiction in one way or the other on such applications. There is, of course, nothing to prevent the parties simply agreeing between themselves on a sale by one to the other at an agreed price.

Two unusual recent cases are worth mentioning here.

In *Riddell* 1994 GWD 38–2238 two proprietors separately acquired two adjoining plots and each built a house on his own plot. Prior to taking occupation, the two parties had together negotiated for the acquisition of an additional area of ground to improve their access and the disposition of the *solum* of the access ground was granted in favour of both of them. There was no agreement as to how the ground should be divided. In his original title, one proprietor enjoyed a servitude right of access over a route quite close to the plot of his neighbour through the garden. The facts here are special and involve what is really no more than a neighbours' dispute. No real question of principle emerges but the case underlines the need for care and of ensuring prior agreement before committing parties to a purchase which may then turn out not to be as one or both of them expected.

*Langstane Housing Association Ltd* 1994 SCLR 158 involves a point of principle and highlights a serious difficulty. The pursuers were a housing association whose policy was to encourage shared ownership of individual houses in the association's complex. In this case, the individual occupier owned one half and was 'tenant' of the association in the other half. But of course this was a half *pro indiviso*, not a physical one half of a divisible property. Accordingly, the owner/tenant occupied the whole house on the foregoing basis. He then defaulted on his loan arrangements and the creditor, who had a standard security over the defaulter's one half *pro indiviso* share sought to recover possession. The association also sought to take possession and raised an action for that purpose. The action was undefended. In giving judgment, the Sheriff underlined the difficulties which such a socially desirable arrangement might produce in law, but concluded that, in the circumstances, an action of eviction or for recovery of possession was not competent. In the result, the crave by the housing association for eviction was dismissed. In so doing, the Sheriff emphasised that the only competent legal remedy was division and sale.

**7.14** *Common interest.* In certain special situations, separate proprietors owning separate properties are united by a common interest which entitles each of them to object to certain acts by any other proprietor which may interfere with the comfortable enjoyment of his property.

This body of rules is known generally as the law of common interest. The significant difference between the restrictions arising out of property owned in common, and arising out of common interest, is that, in the first case, the individual has, at most, a right to a share only, and not the whole, of a particular property; whereas, with common interest, each individual owns the full and exclusive right of property in his own land, subject only to special restrictions for the benefit of his neighbours. These restrictions need not appear in his title, but are implied by law.

**7.15 Destinations.** There are two forms:

**7.16** (a) *A general destination.* In this case, the property is conveyed to the named vassal 'to his executors [or successors, formerly heirs] and assignees whomsoever'. A general destination adds nothing, and, if omitted, would have no adverse effect. In fact, it is normally included in any conveyance or other common law deed. In contrast, the statutory form of standard security contains no destination; and under the Conveyancing and Feudal Reform (Scotland) Act 1970 s. 11(1), a standard security operates to vest the interest in the grantee. There is no reference to executors or successors, since that is inevitably implied.

**7.17** (b) *The special destination.* This was a device, of ancient origin, frequently adopted to circumvent feudal limitations on the free power of *mortis causa* disposal. Typically, and in its simplest form, the feu was disponed on a special destination 'to A (designed) whom failing' (or 'on his death') 'to B (designed)'; or, commonly, 'to A and B (both designed) and to the survivor of them and to the heirs and assignees whomsoever of the survivor'. In considering the rights of the parties to a destination (*e.g.* in the illustrations A and/or B) a number of technical and complex rules may have to be taken into account. For some problems which the special destination creates, see Chapter 31.

All valid reasons for resorting to the special destination in a conveyance of land disappeared under the 1868 Act s. 20; but the device still continues to be used as one method of controlling the devolution of a heritable property on the death of the proprietor for the time being. A much more common method (and a preferable one) is to arrange for the devolution of the property through a will or other general *mortis causa* deed; and the use of the special destination is now generally discouraged. See Lord President Cooper in *Hay's Trustee* 1951 SC 329. Notwithstanding the foregoing comments and criticisms, the special destination continues to be used regularly, particularly in the title to matrimonial homes and, as further cases dealt with in Chapter 31 indicate, problems still continue to arise.

**7.18 Nature of conveyance.** Finally, the feu is disponed 'heritably and irredeemably', which establishes:

(*a*) that the vassal's right is inheritable (*i.e.* transmissible *mortis causa*) as of right in perpetuity. But this has always been so in Scotland; and

(*b*) that the vassal's right is an absolute and irredeemable one. *Cf.* heritable securities in the forms used before the 1970 Act, where the debtor as proprietor, having pledged his land in security by conveyance to the creditor, may nonetheless redeem his land on payment of the secured debt.

Both elements are implied, if not express, and the phrase, though invariably included in any conveyance, is strictly redundant.

### 7.19 Specimen style
To illustrate these various points by a practical example, a typical narrative clause in a feu charter may read:

'I AB (design) heritable proprietor of the subjects and others hereinafter disponed (who and my successors as proprietors of the *dominium directum* of the said subjects are hereinafter referred to as "the Superiors") in consideration of the sum of £      paid to me by CD (design) and of other feudal prestations hereinafter contained have sold and do hereby, at the request and with the consent and concurrence of the said CD as is testified by his signature hereto, in feu farm dispone to and in favour of the said CD and his wife Mrs. XY or D residing with the said CD and the survivor of them and the successors and assignees whomsoever of the survivor heritably and irredeemably ALL and WHOLE...'

The description, reservations (if any), burdens and subordinate clauses then follow.

For the content of these clauses see Chapters 8 to 12.

Chapter 8

# DESCRIPTIONS

## 8.1 Identification of subjects

A conveyance of land, to be valid, must properly and distinctively identify the subjects conveyed. This applies alike to charters and to any other special conveyance, including the disposition. Complete lack of identification completely invalidates the conveyance; this occasionally occurs, for technical reasons, in a blundered description by reference.

The part of the dispositive clause which so identifies the subjects conveyed is termed the description. There are two aspects to descriptions:

(1) Given that a heritable property is to be conveyed, how do you set about identifying it in the charter?

(2) Assuming that land has been conveyed in a charter containing a description, what is carried to the vassal under that description?

The vast majority of titles in Scotland deal primarily with land as the subject of the conveyance, other rights being carried to the grantee as incidental thereto. But this is not necessarily so in every case, since a variety of incorporeal heritable rights are capable of separate infeftment. Such rights include, generally, all the *regalia minora*, teinds, and certain other rights. By contrast, certain rights associated with heritable property can never be severed from land and can never be held separately on a separate infeftment. Contrast salmon fishings which can be separately held on a separate title, and trout fishings which cannot be so held.

Further, land or buildings may be divided both in the vertical and in the horizontal planes. Therefore, any given surface area of land can be sub-divided into any number of smaller separate surface areas, each held on a separate title; and in the horizontal plane, land can be divided into layers or strata, each layer or stratum being held on a separate title by separate infeftment. The same applies to buildings, both vertical and horizontal division being permitted within a building. But there are practical limits. So, the Keeper using his common law discretion refused to record souvenir plot titles, on the footing, *inter alia*, that each plot was not 'separately identifiable by description or plan' (Keeper's Report 1969); and, for registration of title, this is now statutory by the Land Registration (Scotland) Act 1979 s. 4(2)(*b*).

Whatever the nature of the property (or right) to be conveyed, the general rule in all cases is that, in a conveyance, any words which are sufficient to identify the subject matter of the conveyance are in themselves an adequate description. There are no *verba solemnia*, there are no statutory formulae for an identifying description and no hard and fast rules at common law. But that general principle falls to be applied in accordance with the following general rules:

**8.2 (1) The extent of the grant**. Land is described in a conveyance in terms of two dimensions only *i.e.* in the horizontal plane, by reference to surface features only; it is nonetheless normally implied that this carries to the disponee everything *a coelo ad centrum i.e.*, all sub-adjacent minerals and sub-strata to the centre of the earth and everything above the surface, including air space indefinitely upwards.

**8.3 (2) Separate tenements**. As explained, land and buildings can be divided vertically and horizontally, the resulting divisions each being capable of separate infeftment and known as separate tenements. Some, but not all, heritable rights are also capable of separate infeftment as separate tenements, *e.g.* salmon fishings. The rule is that each separate tenement must be separately and specifically described (or properly referred to) in a conveyance. Otherwise, it will not pass to a disponee. Thus, a conveyance of land, described as such, will not carry automatically to the disponee the right of salmon fishings – see *McKendrick* 1970 SLT (Sh Ct) 39. A farm was conveyed 'with parts and pertinents', but no reference was made to salmon fishings to which the disponee laid claim. Held that, as the title did not expressly include salmon fishings, the action by the disponee must be dismissed.

As a result of this rule, a separate lease of salmon fishings has always been regarded as competent and as binding a singular successor of the landlord. On the other hand, a lease of trout fishings has always been regarded as purely a personal contract, not running with the land. This rule is altered by the Freshwater and Salmon Fisheries (Scotland) Act 1976 s. 4, in terms of which a lease of freshwater fish (*i.e.* trout) in inland waters for more than one year will bind a singular successor of the landlord and thus, for this limited purpose, is created a *quasi* separate tenement.

So also with discontiguous areas of ground. Suppose A owns a plot of ground with a house on it. He also owns an allotment, 50 yards away on the other side of the public road. These are separate tenements. A conveyance which describes the house and garden would not normally carry the allotment as well; special reference to the allotment is required. Similarly, a conveyance of land will automatically carry to the disponee all sub-adjacent minerals, unless and until the minerals are severed from the surface and held on a separate title. Thereafter, the minerals having become a separate tenement, they must be separately conveyed.

**8.4 (3) Fixtures**. Corporeal things are heritable or moveable according to their physical state. The general rule is that, when moveable things are affixed to land, they lose their moveable character and become heritable by accession. This is summed up in the Latin brocard, *inaedificatum aut plantatum solo, solo cedit*. When moveables have become heritable in this way by physical annexation, then on a conveyance of land, described as such, fixtures pass to the disponee without express reference thereto. Thus a conveyance of land automatically carries to the disponee all buildings thereon, all fixtures within the buildings, growing timber and the like. In practice this is an area, both on contracts and on subsequent conveyances, where disputes frequently arise; and the question of fixtures should always be carefully considered.

**8.5 (4) Implied or inherent rights**.  A conveyance of land, described as such, automatically carries to the disponee certain natural and ancillary rights. It is, therefore, unnecessary in any description of land expressly to define, describe or refer to rights in this category. The implied rights, which are carried automatically to the disponee with a conveyance of land, are summarised here for convenience in the context of the description in the charter. They are referred to again in Chapter 18 – The estate of the vassal. This class of right includes, typically, but not exhaustively:

(a) *Exclusive possession.*  This entitles the disponee to prevent trespass or encroachment by the superior or third parties within his boundaries.

(b) *Unrestricted user.*  In practice, the theoretical unrestricted right of user is now severely limited by a variety of statutory provisions of general application, and by conventional provisions in particular cases.

(c) *Support.*  The disponee is entitled to require his neighbours, laterally and vertically, to support his land, unless that right is expressly varied in the titles.

Certain of these rights may be varied or negatived by the express terms of the conveyance. But, in the absence of any express provision, they pass automatically on a conveyance of the land.

**Special cases**

**8.6 (1) Tenements.**  The ownership of heritable property in Scotland, including buildings, may be split laterally in strata and vertically within a single building. This longstanding rule has tended to encourage, in Scotland, the development of flatted tenements within burghs in which several flats on several floors are owned outright (not merely held on lease) by several independent heritable proprietors. Clearly, this is a situation in which each owner is peculiarly vulnerable to prejudice from the actings of his neighbour.

Very often (but not by any means universally, especially in older titles), the rights and obligations of the owners of individual flats in a tenement are regulated, *inter se*, in great detail in their respective titles. But, where no provision is so made (or where the provision so made is not exhaustive), then (or to that extent at any rate) the law in Scotland implies certain rights and obligations based on common interest and in this context known as the law of the tenement.

**8.7** *The law of the tenement.*  Very briefly, and in outline, the rules are:

(1) Each flat-owner has an exclusive right of property in the air space within his flat; and may use it as he pleases, subject to the common interest of other owners in the tenement.

(2) The owner of a ground-floor flat has an exclusive right of property in the *solum* of the tenement below his flat and in the front area and the back ground *ex adverso* thereof; but subject to the common interest of other proprietors which allows any one of them to prevent the use of the *solum* or

front and back ground in a manner injurious to the amenity of the objector's property, *e.g.* building thereon in such a way as to exclude light.

(3) In each individual flat, each proprietor owns the enclosing walls, except where these separate him from an adjoining property in which case they are mutual. This applies both to gables and to internal division walls. But each such proprietor must uphold his main walls in order to afford support to proprietors above him. Note particularly the positive obligation to maintain. In the case of common gables, there are cross rights of common interest between the whole proprietors of all houses in each tenement on either side of the gable, to prevent interference with the gable so as to render the building unstable.

(4) As between upper and lower flat, the floor/ceiling are notionally divided along an imaginary line drawn along the centre of the joists. But again, neither party may interfere with or weaken the joists to the detriment of the other.

(5) The roof and the space between the ceiling and the roof beams belongs to the top floor proprietor (or severally to two or more top floor proprietors); but again, they are bound to maintain the roof (so far as it covers their individual houses) in order to afford protection to the floors below them. This is the most serious burden, as a rule, short of demolition.

(6) The common passage and stair in the tenement, the *solum* of such passage, etc., and the enclosing walls thereof, are common property vested in the whole proprietors of the several flats in the tenement served by that passage and stair (but no others) as *pro indiviso* owners.

(7) The cost of repairs to common parts and the cost of demolition of the whole tenement will be divided equally amongst all proprietors. In *Marfield Properties* 1996 SLT 1244, a leasehold case, subjects were described in the lease as comprising certain parts of the building including a right in common with the landlords and other occupiers of the building to certain subjects and services referred to thereafter in the lease as 'the common parts'. These common parts are then listed. It is emphasised, however, that this is a special case, first, because the term is included in a lease, not in a title and accordingly the law of the tenement is probably not applicable; and, secondly, because the so-called 'common parts' may have been common to the tenants in that building but that does not necessarily imply that they would be treated as common parts in proprietary tenement titles, if there is no specific definition therein.

(8) It is said that one proprietor may insist that the others conjoin with him in rebuilding a destroyed or demolished tenement. In such rebuilding, the rights originally enjoyed must be preserved, but there seems to be no reported case in which this rule has been applied; and according to Professor K. G. C. Reid in 1983 JLS 472 at p. 477, it can no longer be relied on, following *Thomson* 1958 SC 380, unless there is a specific provision in the title. In *Taylor* 1996 SCLR 937 a double top flat in a tenement block was conveyed together with a joint right with the other proprietors to, *inter alia*, electric wiring, with access thereto when required. In a technical argument for the defender based on *Jamieson* 1952 SC (HL) 44 counsel maintained that the wiring to which the pursuer sought access was not among the com-

mon parts. On the wording used in the relevant clause, access was conferred but only to wiring 'connected therewith'. This was held to mean wiring connected with the tenement. The wiring in question was not wiring connected with the tenement but was the exclusive property of the individual owner. There was nothing to support that a servitude of necessity had been created.

**8.8** *Distinction between common property and common interest.* Note particularly a very important difference in effect between a right of common property in *e.g.* a main wall where no operation can be carried out without the consent of all proprietors; and a main wall owned by a particular flat owner, and not owned in common, where any operations may be carried out on that main wall (*e.g.* converting it into a shop front) provided other proprietors are not endangered by these operations. The law of the tenement does not impose absolute liability. Proof of negligence, in commission or omission, is required.

In the Digest of Cases 8.6 a number of cases are listed under the heading 'Liability for damage caused by alterations and reconstruction' which confirm the foregoing rule that no liability arises *ex dominio*. Therefore, no claim for damages is available to the proprietor of any flat in a tenement arising out of operations in some other flat, or from the failure in the structure in some other flat, unless it can be shown that an operation was carried out negligently, or negligence can otherwise be proved, as the direct cause of the damage.

In a recent case, *Macnab* 1971 SLT (Sh Ct) 41, an attempt was made to escape from the strict rule of liability requiring evidence of *culpa* by relying instead on the law of nuisance as the basis of the claim for damages. In that case, the tenant of a ground floor shop, with the necessary building warrant, carried out certain alterations on the shop which included the removal of a timber standard partition. The pursuer owned the flat immediately above the shop which she had purchased some years earlier. Immediately following on the alterations made by the tenant on the ground floor, the floor of the flat above sagged to a depth of about $1\frac{1}{4}$ inches, and there was resultant cracking in the walls of the flat and other minor damage. The owner of the upper flat claimed that this was caused by the alterations in the shop below, but this was not admitted. At the same time, however, the tenant of the shop installed various machines to allow her to use the premises for the purposes of dry cleaning with the result that vibration, noise and fumes penetrated into the flat above, which in turn resulted in the service of a statutory notice. There was no doubt whatever that the latter feature did constitute a nuisance and in the circumstances was sufficient to sound in damages. The Sheriff also held that the removal of the partition in itself constituted a nuisance and therefore, without proof of *culpa*, would likewise give rise to a claim for damages *proprio vigore*. In an article in 1973 SLT (News) 68 the implications of this novel application of the rule of nuisance to structural alterations in a tenement are discussed.

In *RHM Bakeries (Scotland) Ltd* 1985 SC (HL) 17 bakery premises were flooded as the result of the collapse of a sewer maintained by the local authority. The bakery company sued for damages on the grounds of nuisance at common law. On that point, the House of Lords held that the case as so pleaded was irrelevant because there was no averment of fault on the part of the defenders. According to Professor Reid in the *Stair Encyclopaedia*, Vol. 18, para. 233, note 8, this decision closes the door which appeared to be opened by the decision in *Macnab*; and on that basis the point was not specifically referred to in the previous edition of this work. However, in *Kennedy* 1996 SLT 1186 the point was raised again in comparable circumstances. The tenants of the basement in that case, against the advice of the consulting engineers, removed a wall which was known to be load bearing, and the removal caused cracking and settlement. The owner of the basement was advised by the consulting engineers that this was a probable outcome but nonetheless proceeded with the work. On appeal, the Inner House held that a case of nuisance was appropriate in these circumstances where the consulting engineers knew that the work constituted a positive interference with support and that the proposed works would probably result in damage to the upper floor proprietors, but observed that averments of fault were irrelevant in a claim for damages without supporting averments of negligence.

In practice, in modern titles, the law of the tenement is substantially excluded by express provision in the title to each separate flat, as follows.

The conveyance to the disponee includes a right, in common with the other proprietors:

(i) to the *solum* on which the tenement is erected, the front ground and back green, and boundary walls thereof, the roof, main walls and gables, rhones, and down pipes, and all pipes, drains and cables serving the tenement in common;

(ii) of access for repairs.

It then imposes on each proprietor a real burden for payment of:

(i) a share (equal, or calculated on some equitable basis) of repair to all items held in common;

(ii) (where this has not already been redeemed) a share of the feuduty, unallocated.

It will usually contain:

(i) a declaration that a majority of proprietors (how determined?) may carry out repairs, often through a common factor; and

(ii) a declaration that the back green, washhouse, etc., shall be used, in common, only for washing and drying clothes and for no other purpose.

For a typical style, see Burns' *Practice*, p. 351, and Halliday's *Practice*, 19–37.

At the time of writing, the Law Commission are still considering proposals for the amendment of the law of property, both heritable and moveable. They have published two discussion papers, No. 91 'The Law of the Tenement', and No. 93, 'Proposals for the Abolition of Feudal Tenure'. So far, however, no report has been issued on either of these papers.

### 8.9 (2) Water rights

(*a*) *Surface water.* Surface water, and water percolating underground, which, in each case, is not confined in a definite bed or channel, may be appropriated by the owner of the land. This rule operates even if, by such appropriation, the owner interferes with the legitimate enjoyment of his neighbours, so there is no common interest in this case. Further, each neighbouring proprietor is bound to accept the natural flow of water from an adjoining property in its natural state; and the neighbour cannot complain if the natural flow is artificially interrupted by some other proprietor on whose land the water falls or flows.

The decision in *RHM Bakeries* was referred to in para. 8.8. It was cited in *GA Estates Ltd* 1993 SLT 1037. In that case, in the construction of a new development, a stream which flowed across the site was diverted through a culvert. Subsequently, after completion of the works, the development flooded as a result of heavy rainfall which the culvert was inadequate to cope with. In the course of his judgment, Lord Coulsfield referred to a *dictum* of Lord Jauncey in the earlier case of *Noble's Trs.* referred to below, where Lord Jauncey states that, if the owner knows that an operation on his land will or will probably cause damage, however much care is exercised, that amounts to *culpa*. This is also the case where the owner knows that certain steps are necessary to prevent damage to a neighbour and, notwithstanding, proceeds with his operations without taking those precautions. This still, however, necessitates proof of *culpa*, although possibly in a special form.

(b) *Rights in rivers and streams.* The ownership of waters depends upon whether they are tidal or non-tidal. The *alveus* (bed) of the sea and other tidal waters belongs to the Crown. Non-tidal streams, rivers and lochs are in private ownership and are presumed the property of the owner or owners of the banks. Thus, if land being conveyed extends across both banks, so that the river (or as the case may be) runs through the land, the *alveus* of the river is carried by the conveyance. Conversely, if the river forms a boundary, there is a presumption that the *alveus* is carried *ad medium filum* (to the mid-point). If the river permanently alters its course because of extraordinary flooding or other natural cause, then the boundary line may shift to coincide with the new *medium filum*. See *Stirling* 1993 SLT 763.

Unless it is very short, a non-tidal river or stream is likely to be owned in sections by a number of different people. In such a case all proprietors of land through (or along) which the stream flows, from its source to its mouth, are united together in a common interest, to preserve their individual rights in the flow of water in its usual channel, undiminished in quantity and without any deterioration in its quality. Any one riparian proprietor may object if any of these rights is imperilled through the operation of any other riparian proprietor; but he must show actual or probable interference with his rights, arising from some such operation. If his rights are not interfered with in any way, then he has no cause to object. Subject to that common interest, each individual riparian proprietor is entitled as of right, and without express provision in his title, to appropriate the water in the stream (a) for primary purposes, *i.e.* for domestic use and for animals; and (b) for secondary uses, but only if he does not interfere with the enjoyment of others.

There is no presumption as to the ownership of the foreshore, which is sometimes owned privately and sometimes by the Crown.

A number of public rights exist in respect of waters and the foreshore. These are quite extensive in the case of tidal waters and the foreshore, and include a right of navigation and a right of fishing (other than for salmon). There is also a public right of navigation in non-tidal waters, but only where the waters are 'navigable' in the sense of having been used for navigation for a period of at least 40 years. See *Wills' Trs.* 1976 SC (HL) 30.

**8.10 (3) Fishing and game**. Every riparian proprietor enjoys an absolute right to fish, as a natural incident of ownership, for any fish except salmon. Salmon fishings are a separate heritable right and require a separate conveyance. But the methods of fishing are controlled by statute, under the Trout Acts 1902 and 1933 and the Salmon, etc., Acts 1828 to 1986. The right to fish for trout, etc. ('white fish') cannot vest as a separate and independent heritable right, in someone who is not the owner of land adjacent to the stream (or loch).

Recent provisions have been made, under the Freshwater and Salmon Fisheries (Scotland) Act 1976 and the Salmon Act 1986, for the preservation of freshwater and salmon fisheries in Scotland by means of protection orders to be made by the Secretary of State if he is satisfied that this will increase the availability of fishing in inland waters, and provision is made for policing by wardens, etc., with fines for contravention.

Game, like fish, are *ferae naturae* and, therefore, *res nullius.* The term 'game' includes a variety of animals, variously defined in various statutes. Nonetheless, mere ownership of land carries with it by implication the right to take or kill all kinds of game on that land as a natural incident of the right of property. It is a right personal to the landowner, as landowner, and not inherent in or necessarily associated with the use or occupancy of land. Therefore, where land is let to an agricultural tenant or for other purposes, there is no implication that the tenant has the right to take or kill game.

Under the Ground Game (Scotland) Act 1880, an agricultural tenant has the right to kill rabbits and hares on the subjects of lease; and there is no contracting out of the provisions of this Act. The same applies to vermin unless protected by statute as an endangered species.

The right to take game may be the subject matter of a valid lease; and, possibly, particularly where the lease is a lease of land with right to shoot thereover, it may come within the provisions of the Leases Act 1449 and so transmit against a singular successor. Until recently, it was not considered possible legally to constitute a lease of shooting over land as a separate and independent heritable right transmissible against, and binding on, singular successors of the landlord. A right of shooting cannot, by decision, be made a burden on land. See Paton and Cameron *Leases,* p. 106, and the authorities there cited.

In *Palmer's Trs.* 1989 SLT 128, however, the court held that an ordinary game lease, if otherwise in appropriate terms, is registrable under the Registration of Leases (Scotland) Act 1857 and, if so registered, transmits against and is binding on singular successors. It was unnecessary in that case to decide whether or not such a lease, without registration, would transmit against singular successors under the Leases Act 1449; and that question is therefore not yet finally decided, but the indications in this decision are that a game lease is protected by the 1449 Act. The justification for this decision lies in the wording of the 1857 Act s. 2. A lease which is binding on the grantor and which is registered is effectual against any singular successor in the land subsequently infeft therein.

## 8.11 Infeftment

In the ordinary way, a feu charter or other special conveyance operates of itself as a mandate for infeftment by *de plano* recording. This is only so if the conveyance contains a description 'recognised in Scots conveyancing, *e.g.* general or particular description or a description in statutory form'. See *Macdonald* 1914 SC 854. But want of such a description does not render a conveyance invalid, provided the subjects are identifiable, *e.g.* by description in general terms. Such a conveyance cannot, however, be recorded of itself; a notice of title is needed to supply the want of description if the grantee is to become infeft. Typically, before the Succession (Scotland) Act 1964, heritage passed to trustees under a will which described the property in general terms, thus, 'the whole means and estate, heritable and moveable, real and personal which shall belong to me at my death'. A will in this form was a valid general disposition and, as such, operated of itself as a title to the trustees but it was not recordable in the GRS. Since 1964, heritage vests in executors by confirmation thereto; and confirmation is also for practical purposes a general disposition, not recordable *de plano*.

While these rules apply generally in the case of a conveyance of any kind – although possibly not in the case of notarial instruments and notices of title – very much stricter rules are applied in the case of standard securities, as the series of *Beneficial Bank* cases show. These cases are noted in the Digest of Cases and are dealt with in Chapter 22, Standard Securities. The difference in treatment between conveyances and standard securities in relation to description is, in the view of the writer, almost certainly unintentional but nonetheless undoubtedly applies, as the *Benefical Bank* decisions clearly show. Contrary to the writer's view, the Lord President in *Beneficial Bank plc* v. *McConnachie* 1996 SLT 413 takes the view that Parliament made a deliberate choice when prescribing the type of description required for a standard security in Note 1 of Schedule 2 to the 1970 Act. The requirements for a bond and disposition security, where exactly the same considerations would seem to apply, were not nearly so specific. In Schedule F to the 1868 Act, which prescribed the new form, the requirement simply is 'here describe or refer ... to the lands'.

The qualities of a description 'recognised in Scots conveyancing' for the purpose of securing infeftment by the recording of a title are not laid down by statute. They have evolved under common law rules explained below. One type of such description is the particular description, the requirements for which are set out in para. 8.13. A speciality which arises in relation to the standard security but which does not apply to a conveyance is created by the 1970 Act s. 9, which introduces and authorises the use of the form of standard security. The security must be in conformity with one of the forms prescribed in Schedule 2. No other form will suffice. Schedule 2 in turn describes two forms of security, Form A and Form B. Note 1 to Schedule 2 applies to both forms. In terms of that note, the security subjects, in either form, shall be described by means of a particular description, or by a statutory description by reference – dealt with below at para. 8.18. No further definition of a particular description is given. In *Bennett* v. *Beneficial Bank plc* 1995 SLT 1105, the first of the *Beneficial Bank* cases, a flat in a tenement was described simply by the postal address of the tenement, without locating the flat itself within the tenement, which, even in a conveyance, would have been invalid. See *Macdonald*, above. In *Beneficial Bank plc* v.

*McConnachie*, the subjects comprised a mid-terraced villa with ground at the back and at the front. The subjects were described in the standard security as the heritable subjects known as 57 Longdykes Road, Prestonpans in the County of East Lothian. Such a description would undoubtedly have been valid in a conveyance and would have been accepted by the Keeper as a mandate for infeftment by recording in the Sasines Register. The question at issue here was whether that brief description could be accepted as a particular description for the purposes of Note 1. In one sense it was particular, to the extent that it distinguished the subjects from all other subjects in the ownership of the debtor. In contrast, where property is described as 'my whole means and estate heritable or moveable' in a will, there is no attempt to identify individual properties, and that is clearly a description in general terms, but nonetheless effective as a conveyance although it would not be accepted by the Keeper as a mandate for infeftment by direct recording.

The actual requirements for a particular description are discussed at length by the Lord President in that last decision. Notwithstanding that careful and detailed consideration, no definitive conclusion emerges as to the requirements of a particular description in every case. It could hardly be otherwise, given the great range of possibilities. But at p. 417K he states that it may be going too far to assert that a postal address will never constitute a particular description, because the postal address of the subjects may contain all that is needed to identify the boundaries. He illustrates that proposition by reference to an entire island in the sea, the name of which is its postal address. Professor Wood in his *Lectures* at p. 203 uses the same illustration: 'All and Whole the island of A lying in the County of B.' He then adds the caustic comment that the words 'bounded on all sides by the sea' were then superfluously added. In *Beneficial Bank plc* v. *McConnachie*, however, it could not be said that the description there used did in fact contain all that was necessary to identify the boundaries because, along with that mid-terraced villa, there was also included ground at the back and front, and no attempt was made to describe such ground.

Halliday, *Conveyancing Law and Practice*, para. 18–10, seems to indicate that, to constitute a particular description, it must be in its terms bounding. It seems to the writer that this is going too far and that a particular description can be achieved within the meaning of that term, although it may not be bounding. However, the Court in *Beneficial Bank plc* v. *McConnachie* would seem to follow Professor Halliday's view.

The only concession which the Court was prepared to make is in the case of flats in a tenement; and this in turn introduces an illogical anomaly. In *Beneficial Bank plc* v. *McConnachie* the postal address of a mid-terraced villa was held insufficient as a particular description. In contrast, however, in the case of an upper flat in a tenement, the Court held that a description which identifies the flat by reference to its individual location within the tenement and 'gives the postal address of the tenement' will be sufficient to define the extent of the security subjects. But this implies that, although the flat itself is located within the tenement and so to that extent is particularly described, the description of the tenement itself is left to rely on its postal address alone, without reference to the ground at the front or rear of the tenement or its physical size or location. If the postal address is sufficient to identify a block of flats comprising a tenement building, without any further particulars included, why should the postal address of a mid-terraced villa not suffice as a particular description?

Understandably, the decision in *Bennett* v. *Beneficial Bank plc* caused considerable dismay in the profession. In a great number of cases, while the subjects might be adequately described in a standard security in terms which would suffice for a proprietary title as a mandate for infeftment, that description would not in its terms qualify either as a particular description or a statutory description by reference according to the tests laid down in *Bennett*. In all such cases, such a recorded security is invalid, and inevitably complications will arise *inter alia* on subsequent repossession and sale on default of the debtor. These and associated problems are discussed in the articles on this point referred to in the reading list under Chapters 8 and 22, but the difficulty has not yet been resolved.

In the third *Beneficial Bank* case, *Beneficial Bank plc* v. *Wardle* 1996 GWD 30–1825, the bank applied to the Court for rectification of the standard security to incorporate the required form of description, using the rectification facilities provided by the Law Reform (Miscellaneous Provisions) (Scotland) Act 1985 s. 8. However, while rectification may generally be available in such cases, it will not always be so. For example, if the debtor is subsequently sequestrated, the trustee in sequestration would not consent to rectification of the standard security since that would adversely affect the value of the debtor's estate for his general creditors – likewise in the case of a company which goes into liquidation or where a receiver is appointed. Further, rectification may prove impossible where there are second secured creditors who would not agree to a rectification and who might justifiably found on the provisions in the 1985 Act s. 9(1), which is designed to protect the interests of persons who might be adversely affected by the rectification, as a postponed heritable creditor undoubtedly would be. The only satisfactory solution is statutory modification of the requirement of Schedule 2, Note 1, or some equivalent, and there is no suggestion at the moment that such legislation is in contemplation.

In the discussion on methods of description which follows, this distinction between the requirements for a conveyance and the requirements for a standard security must be borne in mind.

## Methods of description

**8.12 (1) General description.** This is not to be confused with a description in general terms, nor with a general disposition. Under this method, the subjects are identified simply by name, and no attempt is made to define the property by reference to physical features on the ground. Such descriptions are common in older titles, but are not now normally employed in a conveyance of new except in conjunction with a particular description. The identification of the property so conveyed, and its limits, are determined by possession following on the title, and by the operation of the positive prescription. But, clearly, it may often be extremely difficult to identify precisely on the ground the extent of the subjects conveyed under this form of description, and this is often a major problem when examining older titles. In practice, these difficulties are in most cases resolved by reliance on the Prescription and Limitation (Scotland) Act 1973 s. 1, taken together with occupation of the subjects within defined physical boundaries on the ground for the prescriptive period. This is dealt with at greater length in Chapter 14.

**8.13 (2) Particular description**. Under this method, the subjects conveyed are identified by actual physical features on the ground, whether these features be natural or artificial. This is the method now normally used in practice where land is first conveyed as a separate tenement. Obviously, the variety of possible circumstances is almost infinite and there are no hard and fast rules. There is still, however, some difference of opinion as to what amount of detail is required to constitute a particular description. Halliday, *Conveyancing Law and Practice*, para. 18–09, appears to equate a particular description with a bounding title. The Court would appear to adopt that view in *Beneficial Bank plc* v. *McConnachie* at p. 417G, where the Lord President says that a particular description is one which makes it unnecessary to refer to any extraneous material to define the extent of the subjects, such as the state of possession or the title of the debtor to grant the security. Extraneous material of that kind will be an uncertain guide to the security holder, if only because it will not otherwise be clear whether the whole of the debtor's property or part only is subject to the heritable security. In the view of the writer, as already stated, that seems to be an unnecessarily stringent requirement. A particular description can, it is thought, quite easily be achieved with sufficient precision without creating a bounding title and without incorporating every individual boundary in the description itself. However, given the dictum of the Lord President in *Beneficial Bank plc* v. *McConnachie*, the only safe rule, when framing a description for a standard security, is to incorporate every such detail, and so to constitute a bounding description. Subject to these comments, any particular description will, or may, contain the following elements:

(*a*) The name or postal address of the property, with a reference to the parish and county; but none of this is necessary, provided the location of the property is clear.

(*b*) Identification of the boundary line or boundary feature on each side of the property; but very often only some of the boundaries are so described. For this purpose, natural or artificial features are used where appropriate, *e.g.* walls, streams, roads, etc., and the length of each such boundary is normally given. This may raise difficulties as to the actual extent of the property conveyed in relation to that boundary feature. Thus, where property is described as bounded, on one side, by a wall, it is assumed that the whole wall is excluded altogether on that particular wording. *Contra*, where the words used are 'enclosed by a wall'; the presumption is that the whole wall is included. Where the boundary is a public road, the presumption is *medium filum*; but 'bounded by a road' excludes the whole road, at least if supported by plan and/or measurements. *Houston* 1911 SC 134 and Burns' *Practice*, p. 328; but *cf. Magistrates of Hamilton* 1929 SC 686 at p. 694 where 'bounded by a public road' includes it to *medium filum*.

'Bounded by the Water off Leith', a non-tidal stream, included the stream to the *medium filum*, even in the face of measurements, which were held not to be taxative, in *Gibson* (1869) 7 M 394.

For the presumptions which apply for various other features on the ground, see Burns' *Practice*, pp. 327 to 329, and Halliday's *Practice*, para. 18–11. Any such presumption can be altered by express provision in the deed, *e.g.* bounded, on the north, 'by the southern face of a wall' or 'by the northern edge of the road', or 'by the mid-line'.

More recent examples of individual boundary features are given in the Digest of Cases, 8.13.

(*c*) Often the length of the boundaries is given, and there may also be a statement of the superficial area. Until 30 September 1995 measurements could be given either in imperial or in metric measure, but as from 1 October 1995 new descriptions require to use metric measure. This new requirement derives from the Units of Measurement Regulations 1995, taking effect as from 1 October 1995. The requirements of this Directive are discussed in detail in an article by the Keeper in *Greens Property Bulletin*, issue 19, p. 4, to which the reader is referred. Briefly, for conveyancing and registration purposes, the rule is that as from 1 October 1995, in any description, every measurement of length, depth, height or area must be in metric and not Imperial measure. There is one exception in that it remains permissible to use the acre as an indicator of area, although the use of the hectare in lieu is common-place and recommended. The Directive has no effect on descriptions in existing documents prior to that date.

The article referred to above gives convenient conversions. The more important can be summarised thus:

One yard equals 0.9144 metres
One foot equals 0.3048 metres
One inch equals 0.0254 metres
One acre equals 0.4047 hectares.

Reversing the measurements:

One metre equals 3.2808 feet.
One hectare equals 10,000 sq. metres or 2.471 acres
One sq. foot equals .0929 sq. metre.
One sq. metre equals 10.764 sq. feet.

If an acre is used as an indicator of area, the old sub-divisions of the acre cannot also be used, *i.e.* roods, poles etc. Instead any sub-division of an acre must be in decimal terms. So 'one acre, one rood' or 'one acre, 40 poles' will each become '1.25 acres'.

The use of Imperial measure in addition to metric units of measurement is permitted, provided the metric unit is given first, which seems unnecessarily pedantic. How can this be complied with on a plan?

Scales on plans are similarly affected. A plan can no longer be described as to the scale of one inch to eight feet and instead must be represented by the ratio equivalent, *e.g.* 1:500.

The article in *Greens Property Bulletin* also contains detailed information on the Keeper's requirements for the preparation of plans, and it merits close study.

The effect of failure to observe the new requirements is not entirely clear. The Keeper indicated that he would almost certainly refuse to accept for recording or registration any description, written or by plan, which fails to conform to the new requirements. That is not to say, however, that a conveyance which uses old measurements of length or area is in itself invalid. It may not operate as a mandate for infeftment, but it would almost certainly operate effectively as a link in title for the creation of infeftment either by the recording of a notice of title or in a subsequent conveyance for deduction of title. The Keeper's bar on accepting deeds for registration would appear to apply only to the Sasines and Land Register. So, such a deed could be recorded for preservation in the Books of Council and Session or Sheriff Court Books. Thus, any such link in title can be effectively preserved.

(*d*) A plan is not essential to supplement a written particular description; but, even in the simplest case, it is always desirable. Normally, the plan is not embodied in the deed but is appended as a schedule, being referred to and adopted as part of the deed by a reference in the description; and as such it is signed and referred to in the testing clause.

It is perfectly competent, and increasingly common, to describe properties simply by reference to a plan, without incorporating any written description in the deed. See article 1971 JLS 62. But, normally, the conveyance contains both a written description and a reference to the plan in support of it. The disadvantages of relying solely on a plan are:

(a) that it is comparatively easy to alter a plan fraudulently, but difficult so to alter a written description. See 1959 JLS 144, letter from the Keeper. This comment dates back to the original edition of this work and has lost much of its force by the introduction, in 1970, of modifications to the rules for probativity, repeated in the 1995 Act, under which each page of a deed no longer requires to be subscribed by the granter. While the writer would hesitate to suggest that this occurs in practice, it is perfectly possible, given the flexibility of the production of documents by word processor, to substitute pages other than the last page without detection, at least prior to registration or recording.

(b) that, until 1934, no record of plans appended to deeds was kept at the Register House. Since 1934, plans up to a certain size (28″ × 22″) are photographed and appear on the Record volumes, but, even so, the photographed plan does not show colourings. This means that, if a description depends solely on a plan (or on colours on a plan), and the principal deed is then lost (as may happen), the title might well be rendered invalid. To get over this difficulty, statutory provision was made in the Conveyancing (Scotland) Act 1924 s. 48 for the lodging of duplicate plans in the Sasines Register which are then permanently retained there. The duplicate plan is signed in the same way as the deed and docquetted with reference to it, *viz.*, 'This is a duplicate of the plan annexed to a feu charter by ... etc.'; and it is referred to in the testing clause. The deed itself with principal plan annexed is, of course, returned to the ingiver. This provision has not been very much used. For a lost plan case, see *Maclachlan* (1887) 25 SLR 734. For some details as to plans in Register House practice, see a note from the Keeper at 1968 SLT (News) 22, and the Keeper's article referred to above. No additional application for recording in the Sasine Register is required; but the number of plans lodged should be mentioned in Box 11 of the form. See further under para. 13.10. It must be borne in mind that principal and duplicate plans inevitably fall within the provisions of the 1995 Act s. 8(2) as being documents relating to land and describing it; and the authentication requirements of that sub-section must therefore be observed.

**8.14** *Part and portion clause.* Any piece of ground which, on a sub-division, is conveyed for the first time as a separate heritable unit, and particularly described as such, necessarily forms part of a larger area of ground already held on its own title in name of the disponer. It is customary, although not essential, to link up the new particular description with the previous titles by a 'part and portion' clause. This simply repeats, in the most convenient form (normally a description by reference) the description of the larger property of which the subjects (now described for the first time as a separate unit) form part.

**8.15** *Repugnancies and ambiguities.* Information in a particular description may be duplicated, *e.g.* written boundaries and plan, or measurement, which carries with it the possibility of some conflict or discrepancy. Thus, property may be described as 'bounded on the north by an existing stone wall along which it extends for one hundred feet or thereby'; but it turns out on inspection that the wall is only eighty feet long. Or again, property may be described in a written description by reference to physical features 'all as delineated and coloured pink on the plan annexed'; but, when the written description is related to physical features on the ground, it may turn out that the area delineated and coloured pink on the plan is not the same area. In the ordinary way, discrepancies of this type will not invalidate the deed. Instead, rules have been developed in the reported cases for reconciling such discrepancies. These you will find discussed in Rankine, *Landownership*, Chapter 6, Halliday's *Conveyancing Law and Practice*, para. 18–13, and Gordon's *Scottish Land Law*, para 4–08.

Everything depends on the particular title and particular circumstances but some general rules emerge from the cases:

(1) If, in the deed, there are written boundaries with stated measurements, and these conflict with a plan annexed, the plan will normally be treated as demonstrative and the written boundaries rule.

(2) If, in the deed, there are written boundaries without measurements, and these conflict with a plan containing measurements, the plan will normally be preferred. But the deed may declare expressly that the plan is 'demonstrative only and not taxative', in which case the written boundaries normally prevail.

(3) The deed may contain written boundaries with stated measurements which cannot be reconciled on the ground, *e.g.* 'bounded by a wall along which it extends 25m'. and, on checking the wall, it is found to be 20m. only. If the written description of the boundary feature is clear and specific, the measurement will be rejected, and the written description is taxative. For a recent case involving an ambiguous written description and a plan annexed, see *Suttie* 1992 SLT 133.

(4) In the converse case where the written boundary is clearly stated and is greater than the stated measurement, the written boundary again will rule, and the smaller measurement will not be held to limit the grant, *e.g.* 'bounded by a wall running from the road to the southeast corner of the

tenement at 5 King Street a distance of 100m.' which turns out to be 200m. on the ground.

**8.16** (*3*) *Description by reference.* In this method of description, there is no specific identification of the property conveyed. Instead, to identify the subjects, a previous recorded deed containing either a general or a particular description is referred to. Therefore, with limited exceptions, this form of description is only suitable for a conveyance which transmits to the disponee an entire separate tenement which is already held on a separate title and is already separately described as such in a prior title. There are three types of description by reference (though not always so referred to in the textbooks) which are:

**8.17** (*a*) *Description by reference at common law.* In older conveyances, it was normal to find the description of the property repeated in each successive conveyance of that property. But it is now accepted that, at common law, it never was necessary to repeat, word for word, the previous description of the property conveyed. Instead, the property could be identified (or described) in a conveyance simply by reference to some prior writ which itself contained an identifying description. For a description by reference at common law (as opposed to a statutory description by reference, see below), there are no settled rules except the over-riding principle that the words used must be sufficient to identify the property. This means that the writ referred to for description must be identifiable. In practice, however, this method of description is seldom relied on and, instead, the next method should always be employed.

**8.18** (*b*) *Statutory description by reference.* The relevant statutory provisions are the 1874 Act s. 61, the 1924 Act s. 8 and 1924 Act Schedule D. Under these sections and Schedule, the requirements for a valid statutory description by reference can be summarised thus:

(i) The deed referred to may be a deed of any type, provided it contains a particular description and has been recorded in the Register of Sasines. Note the requirement that the deed referred to in a statutory description by reference must itself contain a particular description. In the *Beneficial Bank* cases, the requirements for a particular description are discussed and are, it is thought, a great deal more stringent than had previously been imagined. Apart from the case of the tenement flat, in the *Beneficial Bank plc* v. *McConnachie* the Court appear to lay down that a particular description must be complete and self-contained and in itself constitute a bounding title. Admittedly, that case was concerned with a particular description as required for a standard security. But the term 'particular description' has been used for more than a century in other contexts, especially in the context of the notarial instrument and notice of title, and there seems to be no reason to suppose that the requirement that a statutory description by reference should refer to a deed which itself contains a particular description would be any less rigorously construed than the requirement for particular descriptions in standard securities.

There are almost certainly a considerable number of what were thought to be statutory descriptions by reference which refer back to a deed containing a fairly specific description but not one which satisfies the stringent rules which now apparently have to be applied in determining whether a description, in whatever form of deed, constitutes a particular description or not.

In the case of proprietary titles, and given the very lenient rules applied to determine whether or not a description meets the requirements for a description by reference at common law, this will probably not create any serious problems in practice, at least where the prescriptive period has run on such a description. In the case of a standard security, however, the requirement in the 1970 Act Schedule 2, Note 1, is specific as to the type of description to be used. It may well turn out that a standard security which, on the face of it, contains a statutory description by reference in fact does not contain such a description because the prior deed referred to does not itself contain a particular description as that term is now understood for security purposes post *Beneficial Bank*. Whether or not that defect is curable in cases where the creditor has a title recorded more than 10 years previously is open to question; and so, again, in the case of standard securities, descriptions by reference apparently valid may turn out not to satisfy the requirements of Note 1. Again, while rectification may be available, there clearly are situations where the facilities for rectification cannot be used and where, as a result, no real security has been created although the personal obligation will be duly constituted by such a security, notwithstanding the defect in description.

There seems to be no solution to this problem for standard securities, nor indeed for the statutory requirements for a description by reference, except legislation relaxing the rules as to the form of description required in such cases.

(ii) The description by reference must:

(a) state the County (for burgage, the burgh and county) in which the property is situate – 1874 Act s. 61. This has not been altered by the introduction of regions and districts; nor by the further recent replacement of Regional and District Councils by the new Unitary Councils under the 1994 Act.

(b) specify the prior deed referred to for description in terms of the 1924 Act Schedule D. The basic requirements of such specification are not itemised in the Acts or Schedule; but normally a description by reference should specify:

The type of deed referred to, *e.g.* feu charter.
The parties, without designations.
The date of the deed – but is this necessary?
The Division of the GRS.
The date of recording.
The Book and Folio, or, for recent deeds which are held on microfiche, the fiche and frame number – if otherwise there would be ambiguity which is rare.

See 1924 Act s. 8(3), and see especially notes 1 and 4 to Schedule D for further detail.

Nothing more is required; but it is normal to preface the statutory description by reference with a short identifying description (usually the postal address). See 1924 Act Schedule D, note 2.

By the 1874 Act s. 61, such specification and reference to the prior recorded deed in any conveyance, etc., are equivalent to the full insertion in that conveyance of the particular description contained in the prior deed referred to.

**8.19** These are the rules for a statutory description by reference and in practice they should always be strictly followed, when framing new descriptions. But you will sometimes find, when examining a title, that a description by reference in one of the existing deeds does not comply in some respect with the statutory rules. The question then is whether the deed is valid or not, and in deciding this question there are three main considerations to keep in view:

(1) The strict statutory essentials are a particular description in the prior deed, specification of the county, the Register, the date of recording and a reference to the prior deed in such terms as shall be sufficient to identify it on record. Omission of county, which is common, or of Register Division is probably fatal. But an error in the date of recording, *e.g.* wrong day of month, may not be, if the deed can be clearly identified notwithstanding. The same applies to minor errors, *e.g.* in the names of parties. An error in or omission of the date(s) of the deed (not the date of recording) is never fatal, except in very exceptional cases (*e.g.* two deeds, same parties, same recording date, no Book and Folio number, and different dates).

(2) Even if the error is sufficiently serious to disqualify the description under statute, it may nevertheless be a valid description by reference at common law; such a description has always been competent, and in the past was not infrequently employed for 'eking out a generalised or incomplete description'. The statutory facilities do not exclude it, or render it invalid in any way; they merely provide a convenient alternative with statutory sanction. As stated above, the exact requirements for a valid common law description by reference are not defined. See *Murray's Trs.* (1887) 14 R 856, *Matheson* (1903) 5 F 448, and *Cattanach's Trs.* (1884) 11 R 972. While this may be sufficient to rescue and validate a proprietary deed such as a feu charter or disposition, it will not do, for reasons stated above, in the case of a standard security where a statutory description by reference is prescribed and where that must be adhered to.

(3) Even if the description by reference has been so hopelessly bungled that it is invalid as such both under statute and at common law, it may still contain sufficient in itself to constitute a general description, in terms sufficient to identify the subjects. Here, very little will suffice. The normal short introductory words will certainly serve in most cases, *e.g.* 'All and Whole that dwellinghouse and pertinents No. 10 Glebe Road, Dundee' standing alone are an adequate general description of a detached dwellinghouse. Again, if a deed contains only a bare reference, without identifying words, to a deed itself containing a description by reference, that is not a valid statutory description. But if the deed referred to contains anything which could amount to an identifying description, that will be valid at common law. In the case of a bungled statutory description by reference in a standard security, however, that is fatal and it will not be competent in such cases to fall back on a general description which may suffice in the case of

proprietary title, at least if fortified by possession for the prescriptive period.

**8.20** (*c*) *Description by general name.* This is simply another method of description by reference, although not usually so described. In view of the statutory provisions for description by reference later introduced (as above), it is now virtually obsolete. In the case of Barony or Regality titles, one general name, at common law, sufficed to describe several separate subjects. The same effect could be achieved at common law in any Crown grant by including a clause of union. A statutory equivalent was introduced for any estate by the Titles to Land (Scotland) Act 1858, re-enacted and consolidated in the Titles to Land Consolidation (Scotland) Act 1868 s. 13. But the essential requirements for a description by general name are more onerous than the requirements for a description by reference; and the latter is, therefore, now almost invariably used in preference.

**8.21 (4) Illustrative style.** In practice, with a modern description, there is often a combination of two or even all three of the foregoing methods of description, *e.g.*:

> 'ALL and WHOLE the farm and lands of Nether Mains in the Parish of Strathmartine and County of Angus' (a general description) 'being the subjects delineated and enclosed within the red line on the plan annexed and signed as relative hereto' (a particular description) 'which subjects hereinbefore disponed form part and portion of all and whole the subjects in said Parish and County particularly described in and disponed by a disposition by John Smith in my favour dated seventh and recorded in the Division of the General Register of Sasines for the County of Angus twelfth both days of August, Nineteen hundred and Fifty-nine',

If the prior deed so referred to itself contains a particular description which meets the requirements laid down in the *Beneficial Bank plc* v. *McConnachie*, that is a statutory description by reference. If not, it is still a description by reference at common law, which suffices for a proprietory title but not for a standard security.

**8.22 (5) Addenda to the description.** In any heritable conveyance, in practice, it is normal to find (appended at the end of the description of the property) certain additional incidentals, varying in number and nature according to the nature of the property conveyed. Sometimes, such addenda do materially add to the main description, *e.g.* in the case of separate tenements in the form of incorporeal rights such as salmon fishings where, following on a description of a landed estate, you may find some such right as:

> 'Together with the salmon fishings in the River Isla, bounding the said subjects hereinbefore disponed on the north and west sides, but only up to the *medium filum* thereof *ex adverso* of the said subjects hereinbefore disponed;'

For reasons already examined ('Separate tenements') if salmon fishings are to pass with a conveyance of land, they must be expressly described; accordingly, this addendum to the description forms a material addition to the subjects conveyed. So also new servitude rights and privileges, typically free ish and entry, or access, drainage and other like rights materially add to the description of the land. In other cases, standard and typical addenda in fact add little or nothing to the description of the subjects. Thus, in practice, you will often find in a conveyance four typical addenda, which are:

(i) 'The teinds of the said subjects, so far as I have right thereto.' Teinds are a separate tenement and, strictly, require a separate conveyance. Therefore, in feudal theory, this addendum is necessary if teinds are to pass under the conveyance to the disponee. But, in fact, teind and stipend have ceased to be of any practical significance and no practical harm is done if, as is increasingly common, the reference to teinds is omitted. In any event, they probably would now be held to pass by implication.

(ii) 'The whole parts, privileges and pertinents of and effeiring to the said subjects hereinbefore disponed.' The exact implication of the term 'parts, privileges and pertinents' is nowhere clearly defined. The general principle has already been mentioned above, *viz.*: that all implied rights inherent in the ownership of the land pass automatically on a conveyance of the same; *per contra*, separate tenements must be separately identified and conveyed. It is, therefore, unnecessary, and adds nothing, to itemise or list implied rights in a charter or disposition. The term 'parts, privileges and pertinents' is a general phrase wide enough to embrace all the normal implied rights. Any right not ordinarily implied must be distinctly specified; otherwise, the disponee could not lay claim to it. Therefore, the parts and pertinents clause normally adds nothing but is nonetheless normally included as an addendum. In rare cases, some weight may be placed on the presence of a 'parts and pertinents' clause; for this, see Chapter 14 – Prescription.

(iii) 'The whole fittings and fixtures in and upon the said subjects hereinbefore disponed.' Again it is doubtful whether this can ever add anything. If the fittings, etc., are heritable in law they pass *sub silentio*; if moveable, they pass under the Sale of Goods Act 1979 and not by virtue of the conveyance. See Lord Kinnear in *Jamieson* (1900) 3 F 176.

(iv) 'My whole right, title and interest, present and future, in the subjects disponed.' This is probably implied, at least in onerous conveyances. But the express clause has the advantage of enabling the operation of accretion, should that prove necessary. See Chapter 7. Occasionally, where the title of the grantor is in doubt and it is uncertain whether or not he owns the whole or certain parts of the subjects conveyed, this last addendum may be modified to the effect that the subjects, or a specified part thereof, are conveyed but only in so far as the disponer has right thereto. It seems settled that this does allow the grantee to found on that conveyance as a title habile to the running of the positive prescription. In addition, it will of course be necessary to protect the disponer by excepting the title or that part thereof which is in doubt, at least from absolute warrandice and possibly to restrict it to simple warrandice only *quoad* the parts in doubt. For a recent illustration of a comparable case, see *Landward Securities (Edinburgh) Ltd.* 1996 GWD 16–962.

**8.23 (6) Description by exception.** As a general rule, in practice, you always use the most convenient method of describing any particular subjects. Suppose that you acquire an acre of ground, area X, by feu charter containing a detailed particular description; later you dispone one-half acre, area Y, by disposition containing a particular description. You are left with the remaining half acre, X–Y. The whole area X is already particularly described, and so is the lesser area Y, the remaining area X–Y is nowhere particularly described as such. Supposing you sell it; there are two alternatives:

(*a*) to describe the area X–Y using a particular description incorporating boundaries, measurements, etc., and plan; or

(*b*) much more simply by describing it as the whole area X by reference under exception of subjects Y, also by reference. The form is suggested in 1924 Act Schedule D, note 3. This is one example of ground first conveyed as a separate entity where a new particular description is not necessary.

There is no doubt that a description by exception as outlined in (*b*) above would be a perfectly valid way of describing the area X–Y in a conveyance on a proprietary title. But, following the decisions in the *Beneficial Bank* cases, a description by exception in the foregoing form is certainly not a particular description. Is it a description by reference thereof 'as in Schedule D ...' in the 1924 Act which is necessary to satisfy the requirements of the 1970 Act Schedule 2, Note 1?

**8.24 Descriptions in registration of title**
As you know, registration of title is map based. With limited exceptions, every title sheet (and therefore every land certificate) will include a plan which is an excerpt from the Ordnance Survey Map of an appropriate scale coloured to indicate the registered property. Therefore, every description, at the date of first registration, whatever its form has been in the past progress of titles, must at that point be translated onto the Ordnance Survey Map. Obviously this will to some extent affect conveyancing practice both before and after registration of each individual title.

For an instructive article on Ordnance Survey plans, see 1981 JLS (Workshop) 245.

**8.25 (1) Pre-registration practice.** In an operational area, the deed which induces registration of title in each case is the first sale by way of disposition, feu charter or lease of the property after the commencement date. The statutory requirement is that the purchaser, vassal or lessee under such a writ must apply for registration of title; and is barred from recording his disposition, charter or lease in the Register of Sasines to procure a real right.

So far as registration practice is concerned, the deed inducing registration need not itself contain a particular description, need not constitute a bounding title, and need not contain a plan. Further, if the deed does contain a plan, it need not be exact and to scale nor on the Ordnance Survey, nor on one of the Ordnance Survey recognised scales of 1:1,250, 1:2,500, 1:10,000. Notwithstanding the foregoing, however, if a standard security is presented for registration at the same time as the deed inducing registration, care must be taken to ensure that the description in the standard security complies with the strict rules which emerge from the *Beneficial Bank* decisions. Thereafter, the notorious Schedule 2, Note 1, ceases to apply to standard securities over registered interests.

Nonetheless, at the time of application for registration, the applicant

107

must provide the Keeper with sufficient information on the property to be registered to allow him to translate that information on to an Ordnance Survey Map. But the information required for this purpose can be given separately from the title deed itself.

Accordingly, prior to first registration of the title, there is unlikely to be any significant change in conveyancing practice except that, as a matter of convenience, parties may tend increasingly to use Ordnance Survey Maps of appropriate scale to identify the property conveyed.

**8.26** *Boundaries.*   Registration of title produces a new problem in that, on the 1:1,250 scale (the largest scale normally used), boundary features such as walls are represented by a single black line, and it is impossible to represent such features diagrammatically on the Ordnance Survey so as to show whether the boundary lies on one or other side thereof or on the midline. To get over this difficulty, the Land Certificate provides for the use of arrows to indicate where the boundary line lies in relation to particular boundary features. An arrow across the boundary line indicates the midline thereof. An arrow pointing at one or other face of the boundary feature indicates that the boundary line is on that side of the feature. See note on Land Certificate. In practice, however, the Keeper seems to prefer in most cases to indicate the exact position of the boundary in the written description in the property section of the title sheet rather than to resort to arrows.

It is unlikely that the practice of using arrows will commend itself to the profession when preparing individual title plans. Conveyancers will probably still continue, where appropriate, to draw plans on a sufficiently large scale to show the boundary line of any individual feature; or rely on a verbal description for that purpose.

One standard exception to the rule that registration of title is map based is the tenement flat or part of a building separately conveyed. In this case, the postal address and a verbal description of the location of the flat in the tenement will suffice. In addition, where appropriate, the Keeper will plot the *solum* of the tenement and the front and back ground, if any, on an Ordnance Survey Map incorporated in the title sheet and Land Certificate.

Again, this is unlikely to produce any change in current conveyancing practice.

If no visible feature exists on a particular boundary, the Keeper indicates this by a dotted line on the plan; and the plan will carry a legend, thus:

'The boundary shown by dotted lines has been plotted from the Deeds. Physical boundaries will be indicated after their delineation on the Ordnance Map'.

At a later date, when the boundary features, such as fences, have been constructed on the ground, and then plotted on the Ordnance Survey Map, they will then find their way on to the title sheet.

**8.27  (2) Registered land**.   This implies that the title has already been registered in the Land Register. Therefore:

(i) the property will already appear on the Master Index Map in the Land Register and will have an individual title plan in its title sheet, all on the appropriate Ordnance Survey scale; and

(ii) a title number will have been allocated to that property on the title sheet. Therefore, any subsequent transfer of the whole of the property can be simply and precisely effected by reference to the title number. The position is regulated by the 1979 Act s. 15(1) and the Land Registration (Scotland) Rules 1980 Sch. B. An example which complies with the statutory guidelines is 'ALL and WHOLE the dwellinghouse known as One Graham Road, Dundee, being the subjects registered under Title Number ANG 1697.'

Nothing more is required. In particular, note:

(i) No reference is required to any prior recorded deed (1979 Act s. 15(1)) – *cf.* description by reference.

(ii) No addenda are necessary – they are all set out in the title sheet. See 1979 Act s. 3(1)(a).

(iii) No part and portion clause is necessary – the part and portion element is all dealt with by reference to the Index Map.

(iv) There is no need to refer to burdens, as these are already set out at full length in the burdens section of the title sheet. See 1979 Act s. 15(2).

If, alternatively, part only of One Graham Road was to be disponed, a particular description would be required in the disposition in implement of that part sale, in order to identify separately the part of the property being given off for the first time as a separate heritable unit. The practice has still to develop, but one assumes that, in a disposition of part of the registered title, the disposition will proceed substantially as at present, with a written description of the boundaries and a reference to a plan. But, bearing in mind that there will already be in existence in the title sheet an accurate Ordnance Survey plan, the particular description may be much more simply accomplished than at present, by reference to that Ordnance Survey Map.

In any event, whatever method is adopted to identify the separate part, it will have to be followed with some such short reference as:

'being part of the subjects registered under Title No. ANG 1697'.

Chapter 9

# RESERVATIONS

## 9.1 The implication of reservations

Where a conveyance contains a reservation, this implies that a right which, under the description, would ordinarily be conveyed to the disponee, is by express reservation excluded from the conveyance, and retained by the grantor/disponer.

This is always competent, subject to the proviso that a right can only be thus reserved to the disponer if it is capable of separate infeftment as a separate heritable right on a separate heritable title, *i.e.* as a separate tenement.

A clause of reservation is, therefore, strictly speaking, part of the description since it defines some thing or right which is to be excluded from the major or larger thing conveyed. In practice, however, reservations tend to be treated in the same category as burdens, because by far the commonest reservation in a conveyance in practice is a reservation of minerals which usually contains elaborate burdens clauses regulating the working of the minerals for the protection of the surface owner.

As a matter of standard practice, reservations of minerals to the disponer, which in the past were very common in feu charters, define the thing reserved by reference to its physical substance; and do not attempt to describe the reserved minerals in the same way in which land is described. Accordingly, a typical clause of reservation of minerals qualifying a conveyance of land reads (Burns' *Practice*, p. 243):

> 'Reserving always to the superiors all stone, iron stone, shale, and all metals, mineral substances and things in or under the subjects hereby feued with full power by themselves or through lessees or others to work and carry away the same ...'

*Cf.* Halliday's *Practice*, para. 17–81.

Where a conveyance contains a clause of this kind, it qualifies the implied rule that a conveyance of land carries to the disponee everything *a coelo ad centrum* and excludes from the conveyance everything falling within the categories of things defined in the reservation; in this case, that would include stone, iron stone, shale and 'minerals'. In other typical clauses, the thing reserved is 'minerals' alone, without any specific narration of particular types of minerals; or again other types of mineral may be separately specified and identified by name.

Note that, while minerals are often severed from the surface by way of reservation in a charter, it is equally competent for the owner of surface and sub-strata to convey the minerals on a separate feudal title as a separate heritable right, or 'separate tenement'.

Once minerals have been severed from the surface, they will not pass in any future conveyance of the surface. But because ownership is deemed to be *a coelo ad centrum*, the granter must exclude the minerals from the dispositive clause if he is not to be liable to the grantee in warrandice. In practice this is usually done by making reference to the deed in which the minerals were reserved or conveyed.

## 9.2 Definition of minerals

Clearly, since the accepted method of defining minerals in a reservation or conveyance thereof, is by reference to their physical substance and by using such terms as 'minerals' (or 'mines and minerals'; or 'quarries, mines and minerals', etc.) rather than describing their geographical location, it becomes necessary to consider (for the purpose of defining the thing conveyed or reserved) what the terms mean.

Note, first, three specialities:

(1) Mines of gold and silver are *regalia minora*, and a conveyance of land does not by implication carry such minerals. By the Royal Mines Act 1424, they remain vested in the Crown; but the Crown is bound to make a grant of such minerals to the owner for the time being of the *dominium utile* of the surface, on payment of 1/10th royalties—the Mines and Metals Act 1592. Professor Reid in the *Stair Encyclopaedia*, Vol. 18, para. 210, note 15, considers that lead, which was stated, in the previous edition of this work, to be among the *regalia minora* is not in fact within the terms of the two Acts mentioned in the foregoing paragraph, and that the Crown rights are restricted to gold and silver only.

(2) Coal and associated minerals. Under the Coal Industry Nationalisation Act 1946, all coal and certain associated minerals, wherever situated, and whether being worked or not, vested in and were managed by the National Coal Board. Under the Coal Industry Act 1987 the name was changed to the British Coal Corporation. Under the Coal Industry Act 1994, a new regulatory body was established known as the Coal Authority. The Act creates a new structure for the ownership and control of the industry, provides for the transfer from the Corporation of its assets and liabilities and for the dissolution of the Corporation, and sets out the regime for the licensing of coal-mining operations. More generally, it amends the law relating to coal-mining operations (including the legislation relating to liability for subsidence damage) mainly to take account of restructuring and makes clear that the ownership of coal-bed methane existing in its natural condition in strata is vested in the Crown. See *Green's Annotated Statutes* for comment. Accordingly, a conveyance of land no longer carries coal. This has made a good deal of the law regarding minerals in Scotland of academic interest only.

It is now possible to obtain from the Coal Authority an improved search on any given area to determine whether or not, and if so to what extent, the area is or may have been affected by coal mining and therefore may be liable to subsidence. Details are contained in the note of guidance referred to in the Reading List and there is a comment thereon in 1995 JLS 326. This will be referred to again in the context of missives and examination of title in Chapters 28 and 33. The introduction of this new facility, which has operated successfully in England and Wales for a number of years, has been criticised. See 1995 JLS 259.

(3) Petroleum and natural gas are vested in the Crown under the Petroleum (Production) Act 1934. Provision is made in the Act for the issuing of licences to work onshore and offshore.

It follows that the term 'minerals' or 'mines and minerals' cannot include the above substances. As to what else the terms include depends, to some extent, on surrounding circumstances.

The word 'mineral' 'is of flexible meaning, to be construed very generally if there be nothing in the deed or in the surrounding circumstances to control this construction' (Rankine *Landownership*, p. 171).

## 9.3 Rights of parties

Normally (but not necessarily) the rights and obligations of the surface owner and of the mineral owner or lessee who is to work the sub-adjacent minerals under reservation, are set out in detail in the relevant title. These clauses normally cover three main points, *viz*:

(1) The nature of the reserved right. There are two possibilities, *viz*: that the right reserved is:–

(*a*) an express right of property in the minerals, which carries with it by implication the right to work them and carry them away; or

(*b*) a privilege or servitude of working the minerals.

It is recommended that in every case a right of property should be reserved rather than a mere servitude or privilege of working, since under the latter right the person working the minerals may not enjoy the right to use the resulting shaft or gallery as a pipe-line for transporting minerals extracted from adjoining properties.

(2) The right to work. The method of working is normally laid down in the title.

(3) Right of support. A landowner is inherently entitled to support, both lateral and vertical, from adjoining proprietors of land abutting his boundaries and from the owner of sub-adjacent minerals. The mere fact that minerals have passed into the ownership of another person does not of itself in any way limit or derogate from the surface owner's right. So far as mineral reservations are concerned, the right of support extends to and includes land in its natural state and (subject to possible qualifications) buildings erected on the land.

## 9.4 Support

The right of support of land is often expressed as being a natural right consequent on ownership. In English law the natural right ceases if land is built upon, support thereafter depending on whether or not a servitude (easement) right can be established. The rule in Scotland is sometimes said to be the same, but the balance of authority favours the view that the natural right of support continues even in respect of buildings. See the *Stair Encyclopaedia*, Vol. 18, para. 260.

The term 'right of support' is, perhaps, misleading. There is no positive obligation on the mineral owner to provide support. Rather he is bound to avoid acts which interfere with the existing support, however adequate or inadequate that support might be. Further, the mineral owner is not under any duty to refrain from excavations altogether, leaving the whole sub-strata in the original state; if this were so, then severance of minerals from the surface would be of no practical importance. Instead, his duty is to re-frain from carrying on his mineral operations in such a way that the surface is (or will probably be) damaged thereby. Admittedly, this may result in an absolute bar on mineral working in certain circumstances, *e.g.* where the top and sub-soil is of such a kind and the mineral operations are of such a kind, that, taken together, the surface is bound to come down. But this will be a question of facts and circumstances to be considered in each individ-ual case. As a result, if the surface owner has reason to believe that the op-erations of the mineral owner will inevitably bring down the surface, he has the right, by interdict, to prevent the mineral owner from carrying out any such operations. In any other case, his remedy is damages for injury caused, each recurrent subsidence creating a fresh ground of action.

This is only a very brief summary of some of the complex rules which control the relationship between surface and mineral owners. All or any of these general rules may be expressly varied in terms of the respective titles and in practically all cases there is some degree of variation. For typical clauses, see Burns' *Practice*, pp. 243-244, the Styles and Halliday's *Practice*, 17–81. Further, in certain special cases, the ordinary rules have been varied by statute, *e.g.* the Coal Authority under the Coal Mining Subsidence Act 1991, must execute remedial works (or pay for the cost thereof) in respect of any damage caused to land or buildings due to the lawful working of coal.

In cases where the right is not available at common law or under the titles, a mineral owner may apply to the Court for power to bring down the surface under the Mines (Working Facilities and Support) Act 1966, but subject in all such cases to payment of compensation. The Coal Authority likewise enjoys comparable powers under the Coal Industry Act 1994, and that also applies to any licensed operator under s. 38.

In *British Coal Corporation* 1995 SLT 1038 a question arose as to the meaning of subsidence. In the ordinary way, subsidence implies that a va-cant space left behind in the empty gallery or shaft from which coal has been extracted simply implodes on itself and so brings down the surface. In *British Coal Corporation*, however, the empty shaft had been filled in and the argument was that the Coal Corporation (as it then was) was not liable for damage caused by a shifting of the material used for in-filling. The ar-gument was rejected and the Corporation was held liable to carry out re-medial works.

# Chapter 10

# BURDENS

## 10.1 The nature of real burdens and real conditions

A conveyance of land (by charter or disposition) carries with it to the disponee certain implied rights, which include, *inter alia*, the right to make what use the proprietor pleases of his land, including the right to exhaust, convert or destroy the substance of his ground, surface, subsoil, minerals, etc., in any way, but subject always to certain implied restrictions which are imposed on the proprietor at common law or by statute, either for the benefit of adjoining proprietors or of the public generally; and possibly, but not necessarily, subject also to such restrictions as have effectively been imposed on the proprietor by agreement, either as conditions in his title or as conditions in the nature of servitudes.

What we are concerned with here are the obligations and restrictions imposed on the vassal by express provision in the feu charter, as conditions of his tenure, which limit and qualify the vassal's right in individual cases, for the benefit of his superior, and in certain cases his neighbours.

Commonly, such conditions are prescribed, as conditions of the tenure, in a feu charter; but may also competently be imposed in a disposition as real burdens or real conditions; or by a deed of conditions.

In the charter, such conditions are normally imposed on and bind the vassal; but occasionally a charter includes a condition binding on the superior and his successors.

## 10.2 Standard classification of conventional conditions

According to Erskine, following Craig, the conditions in a feu charter ('conditions of tenure') fall into one of three categories.

*(1) Essentials of the feu.* These are conditions without which the feudal relationship cannot exist and include:

*(a)* the *tenendas*, by virtue of which the tenure is created, and the superior's radical right to the *dominium directum* is preserved. According to Halliday, *Conveyancing Law and Practice*, para. 17–15 the *tenendas* clause, although almost invariably inserted in practice, is strictly superfluous if, in the dispositive clause, the subjects are expressly conveyed 'in feu farm'.

*(b)* reddendo or feuduty, the annual return or consideration for the grant; but, by the Land Tenure Reform (Scotland) Act 1974 s. 1(1), no deed may now impose a feuduty. Any deed executed after 1 September 1974, which contains a grant of land in feu, takes effect otherwise as if there were a feuduty therein. The point of this provision is to negative the common law feudal principle by virtue of which a feudal grant, to be valid, must contain

some return by vassal to superior as consideration for the grant, whether it be a money feuduty or, in older charters, a return in kind.

(2) *Natural obligations.* These are conditions implied by law; and include casualties (pre-1914) and warrandice. No express provision need be made, in which event the law implies a certain legal result. But, by express provision, the implied legal result may be expressly varied in terms of the charter.

(3) *Accidental or conventional obligations.* These include a wide variety of conditions and restrictions which may be imposed on the vassal by charter. They are not essential to the relationship of superior and vassal, nor to the tenure; and they are never in any circumstances legally presumed or implied. Therefore, if any such condition is to be effective, it must be expressly set out in the charter. In modern times such conditions are often referred to under the general heading of 'Building Conditions'; and they are indexed in the *Faculty Digest* 1868–1922 under the heading of 'Building Restrictions'. In practice, such conditions include conditions of other types as well, *e.g.* pre-emption which have nothing to do with building.

Such conditions are normally imposed by the superior on his vassal:

(a) to secure the feuduty; obviously, a plot of land with a house on it is better security for feuduty than a bare plot of land. For charters after 1 September 1974 this no longer applies. But also,

(b) to preserve amenity. This serves a double purpose, *viz*:
(i) to maintain the value of the feu as security for feuduty (again no longer applicable for post 1 September 1974 charters); and
(ii) to maintain the general amenity of the neighbourhood in order to maintain the value of adjoining land still belonging to the superior for future feuing or for the benefit of neighbouring proprietors.

### 10.3 Real and personal conditions
As between superior and vassal, the feu charter is a contract. Any conditions which it contains are enforceable, on the basis of the contractual relationship which the charter establishes between original superior and original vassal. But any vassal may now freely alienate his feu without the consent of the superior. Accordingly, if building conditions are to be of any practical value to the superior, he must be able to enforce them not only against the original vassal but also against successors of the vassal, singular and universal, as future proprietors of the feu in perpetuity; and the right of enforcement must be available not only to the original superior but also to his successors, singular and universal, in the estate of superiority. In other words, such conditions must attach to the land rather than to the original vassal personally, and must run with the land. But, if a condition in the charter is to run with the land in this way, then it must satisfy certain fundamental requirements. A condition in a charter which fails to satisfy these requirements may, and probably will, bind the original vassal personally and his universal successors; but it will not run with the land, so as to bind singular successors. For a general discussion on the distinction between real and personal conditions and the implications of that distinction, see *Peter Walker & Son (Edinburgh) Ltd.* 1967 SLT 297; and, for an unusual case, see *Inverlochy Castle Ltd.* 1987 SLT 466 where the North of Scotland

115

Hydro-Electric Board, a public corporation, personally undertook to supply electricity to a particular heritable property. It was held that the benefit of the original obligation to supply electricity ran with the lands and that an assignation thereof was not required to transmit the right to a singular successor.

Broadly speaking, a condition is valid as a personal condition if it is enforceable under the ordinary rules of contract. But any condition in a feu charter or other title is not normally intended merely as a personal condition. It is intended to operate as a permanent condition, running with the land, and effectively binding on, and enforceable against, a singular successor in perpetuity, regardless of changes in ownership.

### 10.4 Distinction between real conditions and real burdens
Conditions or burdens running with the land must be further sub-divided into two separate categories.

(1) *Real conditions.* Such conditions may occur either in a feu charter, where they are commonly referred to as conditions of tenure, or in a disposition as conditions of the grant. There cannot be 'conditions of tenure' in a disposition because no new tenure is created. To qualify as a real condition, a number of strict rules must be complied with, detailed later.

Further, if the condition occurs in a disposition, then to qualify as a real condition it must be imposed for the benefit of adjacent property.

(2) *Real burdens.* Any condition imposed in a title which does not qualify as a real condition may qualify as a real burden and as such may run with land. In the strict sense, a real burden involves payment of a fixed sum, whether capital or recurring, secured on the land. See the *Stair Encyclopaedia*, Vol. 18, paras. 382 *et seq.* for a detailed analysis of the development of feudal conditions and variations in the terms used.

### 10.5 Importance of distinction.
Both real conditions and real burdens may be positive, *ad factum praestandum* or for payment of a sum of money; or negative in the form of prohibitions, normally against the use of the property for specified purposes.

The importance of the distinction between real conditions and real burdens lies in the manner of enforcement and the resulting liability of the proprietor for the time being of the burdened subjects. The importance of this distinction is not always fully appreciated; and has tended to become blurred because of the habit of referring to all conditions running with land (whether real conditions or real burdens) as 'real burdens'.

For a general discussion, see *Wells* 1964 SLT (Sh Ct) 2 and cases there cited. For a discussion of the rules which apply to a real burden in the strict sense, see the decision of the Lord Chancellor in *Watson Property Management* 1992 SC (HL) 21.

### 10.6 Mode of enforcement of real conditions
Here again, there is a distinction between real actions (including real diligence) and personal actions (including personal diligence) as the vehicle for enforcement of such conditions. This distinction is not always clearly stated in earlier texts; but is underlined in Halliday's *Conveyancing Law and Practice*, para. 19–16, and in *Watson Property Management.*

Broadly speaking, a personal action in this sense is an action founded on a particular or personal obligation undertaken by a particular person and therefore normally involves a contractual undertaking.

A personal action is directed against the obligant himself and no other person.

Ignoring land altogether for a moment, take the case of a simple contractual obligation by A to pay a sum of money to B on a particular date. A is the debtor, B the creditor. If A fails to pay, B can enforce by personal action against A. The procedure is a summons at the instance of B served on A narrating the terms of the obligation and concluding for payment. If decree is granted, A the debtor is personally liable to B the creditor for the whole sum contained in the decree; and his whole estate, heritable or moveable, can be attached by B (through the process of diligence) in satisfaction of the debt.

A real action, on the other hand, is an action founded on a real right in property; the element of contract does not enter into it at all. There is no question of personal obligation. But any action, real or personal, must have a defender; it is not possible in Scotland to raise actions against inanimate objects. Therefore, any real action is personal in this sense, that it is directed against a particular person, being, in the case of real conditions, the proprietor for the time being of the subjects burdened or affected by the pursuer's right. But, in setting out the averments in a real action, it is unnecessary and irrelevant to aver a contractual relationship between pursuer and defender; the important averments are the pursuer's real right of action and the defender's real right in the property. Typical real actions are adjudication and poinding of the ground. Decree in such a real action entitles the pursuer to recourse against the particular property affected by the decree; but he has no recourse by diligence or otherwise against any other assets of the defender.

## 10.7 The distinction between real and personal actions
It was this distinction between real and personal actions which was the essence of the dispute in *Wells*, above. In certain circumstances, a condition in a title may involve substantial liability; and possibly this liability may exceed the value of the property. If the condition gives rise to a personal action against the proprietor for the time being, the value of the property *vis-à-vis* the limit of liability is irrelevant. The debtor's whole estate, including the property affected, can be attached. If, however, the condition gives rise to a real action only, then the value of the property is relevant, since, in effect, this is the limit of the pursuer's claim.

A real condition (or condition of tenure), occurring in a feu charter, is enforceable as between the original superior and the original vassal on the basis of contract. Further, in feudal theory, there is a recurring personal contract between successive proprietors in the superiority on the one hand and successive vassals in the *dominium utile* on the other hand. This originates from the feudal method of transmitting the vassal's right in the *dominium utile* by renewal of investiture and public entry with the superior involving direct participation on his part.

The principle of entry with the superior still applies. The result is that, in any feu, the superior for the time being is deemed to be in direct contractual relationship with the vassal for the time being, just as though both of

117

them were original parties to the feu charter. On this basis, the superior always has a right of personal action against his vassal for the time being to implement any condition of tenure in the original charter but only if the condition has become real. Further, in certain circumstances, a condition of tenure may also be enforced by real action. This always applies in the case of feuduty; it may apply in the case of other burdens as well.

Where a real condition occurs in a disposition, then as between disponer and disponee any such condition is enforceable on the grounds of contract. But a disposition creates no new tenure between disponer and disponee. When the original disponee transmits his right of property to a singular successor, the theory of recurring personal contract has no application as between the original disponer on the one part and the singular successor of the disponee on the other part.

So, A dispones to B by disposition containing real conditions; A and B are in contractual relationship; the disposition is their contract; and on the basis of that contract, A can enforce the conditions in the disposition by personal action against B. Suppose B dispones to C; there is no actual or notional contractual relationship between A and C. Nonetheless, such conditions, if duly constituted as real conditions in the disposition, may be enforced by personal action in a question between the original disponer and singular successors of the disponer as creditors in the burden on the one hand, and singular successors of the original disponee as debtors in the burden on the other.

In *Wells*, above, the resulting relationship is described as 'a continuing reciprocal relationship between the creditor and the debtor' or 'a continuing relationship associated with the property between the creditor and the debtor in the obligation'; and in such cases, where there is 'a direct proprietary interest in the property in the persons seeking to enforce the obligation', the person in right of the obligation may enforce it by personal action. According to Halliday, *Conveyancing Law and Practice*, para. 19–62, a real condition in a disposition can be enforced by personal action at the instance of the original disponer, or an assignee from him, or by any person on whom the right of enforcement has been expressly conferred in terms of the disposition which imposed the condition. In justification of that last proposition, he refers to the *Braid Hills Hotel Co. Ltd.* 1909 SC 120 where the burden was declared to be a burden affecting the ground conveyed for the benefit of the disponer and his successors as proprietors of the ground on the east and west side of the subjects disponed. In a subsequent conveyance of the east and west ground there was no specific assignation of the benefit of this burden, but the disponees were held to have a title personally to enforce the condition as against the burdened proprietors. The Court appears to have decided that personal enforcement was available on the basis of *jus quaesitum tertio*. This decision and the principle of *jus quaesitum tertio* does not appear to have been mentioned in *Wells*.

Professor Reid in the *Stair Encyclopaedia*, Vol. 18, paras. 376 *et seq.* traces the development of the real condition as opposed to the pecuniary real burden as an obligation running with the lands and analyses both the nature of the distinction between these two types of burden and the methods of enforcement. In dealing with the decision in *Wells*, he comments that, by 1964, it was far too late to seek to argue that real conditions imposed by disposition could be enforced only by real remedies. Instead he considers that such real conditions are clearly personally enforceable by singular successors of the original disponer against singular successors in the burdened property. He does not restrict enforceability by personal action in the same way as Professor Halliday in the passage above cited. Professor Reid goes further back and refers to *Tweeddale's Trs.* (1880) 7 R 620 and in particular the judgment of Lord Deas at pp. 630–634. In that passage, Lord Deas contrasts pecuniary real burdens on the one hand and what he there terms inherent conditions of the right on the other. That term would seem apt to include a real condition imposed by disposition, running with the lands, and binding singular successors in the burdened property. This distinguishes it from the pecuniary real burden in the strict sense which is enforceable by real remedies only. Such inherent conditions, he states, have the advantage of being enforceable by personal action against the proprietor for the time being at the instance of whoever has an interest to enforce it, whether named in the deed or not. This is, again, a different basis for enforcement from that suggested by Professor Halliday. This decision and the later decision in the *Magistrates of Edinburgh* (1883) 11 R 352 are relied on by Professor Reid and seem clearly to have been relied on by the Sheriff in *Wells* as authority for the view that such real conditions are personally enforceable. Accordingly, the argument in *Wells* had already been settled on the basis of these decisions in the latter part of the last century. Nonetheless, the juridical basis of this right of personal action is not really satisfactorily explained.

Where a condition in a title (charter or disposition) is a real burden as opposed to a real condition, this will normally imply personal liability on the original vassal or original disponee; but, with limited statutory exceptions, no personal liability will transmit against singular successors. Therefore, where the property has transmitted, the creditor in the real burden (superior or original disponer) can enforce the burden against the singular successor by real action only, or by real diligence only. He can never, in such circumstances, sustain a personal action against a singular successor. But he has this advantage, that a properly constituted real burden for money gives an absolute and indefeasible preference to the creditor. A real burden of a negative character, *e.g.* prohibition against certain uses, can always be enforced by interdict. A real burden *ad factum praestandum* may be more difficult to enforce.

## 10.8 Constitution of real conditions

Real conditions and real burdens, whether constituted by a charter or by a disposition, must satisfy several strict requirements. These have to be kept firmly in mind when drafting real conditions or real burdens in a heritable title. Otherwise, the condition may effectively bind the original vassal or original disponee personally, but will not transmit against a singular successor. For practical purposes, this is virtually useless in the majority of cases. It is of cardinal importance, when drafting conditions for a charter or disposition, to ensure that the conditions do qualify as real conditions or real burdens.

A simple illustration serves to underline the point.

A grants a disposition to B containing conditions by which he hopes to regulate construction of buildings on the subjects and the use thereof. By an oversight on the part of the draftsman, he fails to make them effective as real conditions or real burdens. On delivery of the disposition from A to B, B is contractually bound to observe the conditions. Therefore, initially, the conditions are immediately effective in that, if B is to build on the subjects, he must comply therewith by virtue of his contract.

Suppose B wants to build on the property but wants to breach the conditions. He forms a small private company at nominal cost and conveys the property to the company which is, in feudal terms, a singular successor of B. If the conditions of the disposition from A to B are personal only and not real, the company is not bound in any way by mere personal conditions and could build as it pleased on the property. Further, depending on the terms of the disposition, there will rarely be any comeback by way of an action of damages or otherwise against B for disponing the property to a company without imposing burdens thereon. So far as the writer is aware, no attempt has ever been made to apply the off-side goal rule in such a situation. Rectification of the original disposition to create an effective real burden may, however, be a possibility.

Since private companies are easily, quickly and cheaply formed and very flexible in practice, any personal condition could be avoided by this sort of device with great ease.

Hence the emphasis on making conditions and burdens real.

**10.9 (1) The inherent characteristics.** In order to constitute a valid real condition there are certain essential prerequisites which do not apply in the case of real burdens. For a valid real condition:

(*a*) There must be an element of permanency.

(*b*) There must be an inherent connection with the subjects disponed.

(*c*) There must be a natural connection between the condition and the purpose of the deed.

It has been suggested that a condition in a charter which satisfies these three prerequisites falls to be classified as an inherent condition and binds singular successors of the vassal; and this is said to be so even where the condition did not enter the vassal's infeftment. See Halliday's *Conveyancing Law and Practice*, para. 19–14, and Gordon's *Scottish Land Law*, paras. 22–33 and 22–34.

Undoubtedly, a condition which is genuinely an inherent condition, including in particular feuduty, binds the vassal in perpetuity even although it may not enter the record and may not qualify his infeftment. So, in practice, many older instruments of sasine, although repeating all the conventional conditions at full length, do not repeat the feuduty, which therefore does not find its way into the Register. But it seems doubtful whether this principle extends to ordinary real conditions.

The only reported case in which a condition not entering a vassal's infeftment was held to be enforceable against successors is *Magistrates of Edinburgh* (1857) 20 D 156. But in that case the successor had accepted a charter of confirmation which incorporated the conditions by reference and the real basis of the decision appears to have been contract. It was not followed in *Liddall* (1898) 25 R 1119, where the successor acquired title after 1874, and there was no charter of confirmation; and it is thought that the earlier decision has not survived the introduction of implied feudal entry effected by s. 4 of the 1874 Act. In *Robertson* (1874) 1 R 1213 a majority of the court was prepared to overlook the absence of conditions in the infeftment of a party who wished to enforce the same conditions against a neighbour, but Lord President Inglis dissented and the decision is doubted by Lord Watson in *Hislop* (1881) 8 R (HL) 95 at p. 102.

Thus it seems unlikely that the modern law accepts that a real condition can bind successors without entering the infeftment; and indeed under registration of title a proprietor is not affected by burdens which are not entered on his title sheet (1979 Act s. 3(1)(a)). The rule may be different in respect of burdens binding superiors, at least for Sasine titles, but this is no longer a matter of any practical importance. See, on this subject, *Stewart* (1860) 22 D 755 and *Hope* (1864) 2 M 670.

In the case of both real conditions and real burdens, there are a number of strict rules which must also be observed if the condition or burden is to be duly constituted as such. These requirements include the following.

## 10.10 (2) Essential intrinsic qualities

(*a*) The condition must not be illegal, *contra bonos mores* nor contrary to public policy.

(*b*) The condition must not be vexatious or useless.

(*c*) The condition must not be inconsistent with the nature of the property conveyed.

## 10.11 (3) Qualification of an infeftment

(*a*) Deeds executed before 5 April 1979.

(i) The condition must appear at full length in the dispositive clause of a conveyance *e.g.* feu charter, disposition, etc.; or there must be a valid reference, in the dispositive clause of a conveyance, to a deed of conditions already recorded under the Conveyancing (Scotland) Act 1874 s. 32.

(ii) That conveyance, containing the burden or the reference, must itself be recorded in the Register of Sasines, or registered in the Land Register; and in Land Register titles the burden must also enter the burdens section of the title sheet.

(*b*) Deeds executed after 4 April 1979 – see the Land Registration (Scotland) Act 1979 s. 17.

(i) the condition must appear at full length in the dispositive clause of a conveyance duly recorded or registered as in (*a*) above; or

(ii) a deed of conditions must be recorded in the Sasines Register or in the Land Register, where appropriate. Such a deed, so recorded or registered, of itself immediately constitutes a real condition or real burden, unless that deed itself expressly otherwise provides.

## 10.12 (4) The subjects affected must be clearly identified.
For a recent illustration of the working of this rule, see *Dunedin Property Management Services Ltd.* 1993 GWD 31–2006.

## 10.13 (5) The presumption for freedom.
This implies that the condition must be expressed in clear and unambiguous terms, emphasising the familiar rule requiring precision for the proper constitution of real conditions and real burdens.

As a particular application of this rule in the case of real burdens, the creditor in a real burden must be clearly identified.

The most recent illustration of the application of this rule is *Meriton Ltd.* 1995 SLT 76. In terms of a charter, the vassals were prohibited from carrying out any operations which the superiors might deem objectionable. On previous authority, in particular *Murray's Trs.* 1907 SC (HL) 8, it might have been thought that such a prohibition would have been held unenforceable. Given the context in which the term was used, however, the Court came to the view that it was sufficiently precise to allow enforcement.

**10.14 (6) The intention to burden.** There must be an evident intention to burden the property, not merely to burden the disponee personally.

Of the above rules, the most important from the point of view of drafting is paragraph (5) above – the need for precision. This is the rule in relation to which most difficulties arise in practice and on which there is most argument as to whether or not a condition in a title is effective in a question with a singular successor. On this question, see further Halliday's *Conveyancing Law and Practice*, paras. 19–30 to 19–33, Gordon's *Scottish Land Law*, paras. 22–41 to 22–50, and Part 1 of the *Stair Encyclopaedia*, Vol. 18, paras. 415–422. The first two works contain substantial lists of cases illustrating various aspects of the rule requiring precision in the drafting of real conditions. Some of these cases are summarised in the Digest of Cases at the start of this volume under headings 10 and 17.

In Burns' *Practice*, p. 230, under the heading of 'Substance and Expression of the Restrictions', the author formulates three rules, *viz.*:

(1) the presumption for freedom;

(2) precision;

(3) the difference, in the case of buildings, between restrictions on what may be built and restrictions on the use of the buildings after they are built.

In fact, although Burns then deals with each of these rules in turn and cites different cases in support of each, they all amount to the same thing, *viz.*: if you want to create a condition which binds singular successors, it must be couched in clear and wholly unambiguous terms.

As these cases show, some of the more important points, on which such conditions come to grief, include:

the identification of the subjects to be affected by the burden;

the identification of the subjects having the benefit of the burden;

the exact nature of the burden imposed on the vassal and in particular how his obligation is to be determined;

the absence of time limits which, in some cases, can be fatal;

the distinction between clauses relating to structure and clauses relating to subsequent use; and

a reference to extrinsic material which is not incorporated at full length within the four corners of the deed.

Any ambiguity will be construed in the least onerous manner and for the benefit of the proprietor. If there is any area of the law in which a 'strict construction' is favoured, it is in this field, as the reported cases show.

### 10.15 Enforcement clauses
Various provisions are inserted in the charter to ensure that the conditions in the charter are duly constituted as real burdens on the feu and that, if they are breached, the superior can take punitive action against the vassal. The enforcement clauses typically include:

**10.16 (1) Provision for registration of the charter.** This may occur in the destination, or as a burden in the dispositive clause. The effect is to limit the validity of the charter as a warrant for infeftment to a stated time, say six months from the date of delivery. If not recorded within that period, then the vassal is denied his real right. The objective is to ensure that the charter is recorded, so that the burdens become real burdens on the feu. In one way, this is less important than might at first appear, in that, if a charter remains unrecorded and if the benefit thereof is transmitted, as an unrecorded personal title, to an assignee or general disponee, he is bound (even although he is a singular successor) by all the conditions in that unrecorded charter. 'So long as the title remains personal, an heir or assignee must take it subject to the burdens which were binding on the original disponee in respect that he cannot both plead the personal title and repudiate its conditions.' Craigie *Elements*, p. 50. But it is undesirable that the title should be left in that state. Hence this clause.

**10.17 (2) Further special provision for registration of burdens.** The vassal normally takes infeftment by recording the charter and, under the preceding clause, he must do this within six months.

Under normal registration practice, the charter when presented for registration will be recorded entire unless it contains a clause of direction; and the superior can ensure that it does not. But the vassal may, if he prefers, complete his title by recording, not the charter but a notarial instrument or notice of title. If he does so, then it is possible for him to omit the burdens in the charter from the notice of title, and thus to exclude them from his infeftment. In that case, they do not become real burdens on the feu for reasons stated above. Clearly, this is undesirable, and the charter therefore normally contains a provision designed to ensure that the burdens will enter the record at full length as a qualification of the vassal's infeftment.

**10.18 (3) Subsequent reference to burdens.** The practical rule is that a burden created as a condition of tenure in a charter, which has become real by registration in Sasines, continues in perpetuity until discharged, even although the charter and its burdens have not been referred to in subsequent transmissions of the feu. Nonetheless it is customary both in the charter and in a disposition to require the vassal for the time being, when disposing of his feu, to repeat or at least refer to the deed for its burdens in terms of the 1874 Act s. 32. Notwithstanding the obligation normally imposed on a vassal requiring him to refer to the original feu charter for burdens in any subsequent transmission of the subjects, there are certain express statutory modifications to this obligation in the 1924 Act s. 9.

First, notwithstanding an obligation on the vassal to refer to burdens, such a reference to burdens is unnecessary in any heritable security.

Secondly, if a required reference to burdens has, inadvertently, been omitted from a particular title, that omission can be cured, and any resulting irritancy avoided, if:

(i)  a reference is now made in the current title to the omitted writ; or

(ii) failing that, if a special memorandum is recorded in Sasines, expressly referring to the omitted writ. 1924 Act, Schedule E provides the form.

**10.19 (4) Declaration of real burdens**.  No *voces signatae* are required to constitute real conditions or real burdens; but there must be an evident intention that the subjects should be burdened rather than the vassal personally. This can best be achieved by an express provision that all burdens and conditions are to be real burdens upon and affecting the feu in perpetuity; and an express provision of this kind is commonplace.

**10.20 (5) Irritant and resolutive clauses.**  If the vassal fails to observe a condition of the charter, he may, by express provision therein, forfeit the feu to the superior – a very stringent penalty for non-compliance. Express provision is required except for non-payment of feuduty.

The enforcement, variation and discharge of feuing conditions is dealt with in Chapter 17.

# Chapter 11

# SERVITUDES

## 11.1 Servitudes and burdens compared

Real conditions and real burdens can be imposed only *in gremio* of a conveyance (charter or disposition) to a disponee, or by a deed of conditions under the Land Registration (Scotland) Act 1979 s. 17. Otherwise, the proprietor of land cannot, by agreement or unilateral grant, impose a real burden on his own land for the benefit of his superior or a neighbour. But servitudes can be so created; and for this reason servitudes are often treated as a separate heritable right. But, in practice, servitudes are normally created *in gremio* of a charter or disposition and are dealt with here, in the context of the charter, with particular emphasis on the similarities and points of difference between servitudes and real conditions.

A servitude is a conventional condition running with lands. It is created for the benefit of a proprietor of land – the dominant tenement – and entitles the dominant owner to exercise certain rights on or over an adjoining piece of land – the servient tenement. From the point of view of the landowner, there is little difference in practical effect between a real condition in the title, and a servitude. Both derogate from the absolute quality of his ownership; both entitle some other party to exercise a right or enforce a restriction affecting the landowner as such. But in law, there are certain important distinctions, both as to constitution of the respective rights and as to their nature.

## 11.2 Classification – positive and negative servitudes

The distinction is important because the mode of constitution differs for each type of right. Positive servitudes entitle the dominant owner to enter on the servient tenement and exercise the servitude right actively thereon or thereunder. Negative servitudes (principally light and prospect) merely entitle the dominant owner to restrict the use of the servient tenement. So, a positive servitude may be actively possessed or enjoyed; a negative servitude cannot be.

## 11.3 Salient characteristics of servitudes

(1) There must be two separate tenements, the dominant and the servient, in separate ownership, and they must be adjacent, though not necessarily actually contiguous. Where a servitude is so created, it is created exclusively for the benefit of the dominant tenement and cannot be held as a separate right on a separate title – *MacKay* 1994 SLT (Lands Tr.) 35.

(2) The person entitled to exercise the servitude is so entitled, not personally as an individual, but as owner of the dominant tenement. The servitude

may not be separated from the dominant tenement; and so the benefit thereof may not be communicated to someone other than the owner (or occupier) of the dominant tenement. Only the dominant owner has a title to enforce – *Oliver* 1994 GWD 8–505.

(3) While a servitude necessarily infringes on, and derogates from, the absolute freedom of the servient owner, it must nonetheless be consistent with his right of property; in other words, it cannot be so extensive or so burdensome that the servient owner is entirely precluded from using his land.

(4) The presumption for freedom operates here, as with real conditions. But the strict rules applied in construing real conditions do not apply so rigorously when the right created is a servitude of a well known kind. See *McLean* 1976 SLT (Notes) 47 and Halliday's *Practice*, 20–08. The rules for servitudes are:

(*a*) that the servitude must be duly constituted. In the case of common property, owned by two or more proprietors, all proprietors must concur together to create a servitude right. See *Fearnan Partnership* 1992 SC (HL) 38.

The planning officer or other person duly authorised to act in that capacity by the local authority who agrees, in the context of planning permission, to access by a particular route does so in his capacity as planning officer only and cannot bind his local authority as proprietors by way of servitude. See *Hermiston Securities Ltd.* 1994 GWD 39–2317;

(*b*) that, in cases of ambiguity, the least onerous result is preferred;

(*c*) that the dominant owner must exercise the right *civiliter*, in the least burdensome manner. In *Alba Homes Ltd.* 1993 SLT (Sh Ct) 49 a servitude right of access was created for the benefit of a plot of land and of a neighbouring plot. The owner of the first plot built a dwellinghouse thereon and intended to build a second dwellinghouse, to which the owner of the neighbouring plot objected on a curious argument that the purchaser of part only, but not the whole, of the dominant tenement was not entitled to the benefit of the right. The argument was rejected. 'The dominant tenement in favour of which the servitude is constituted is the whole of the land conveyed to the defenders by the disposition in their favour and not any particular part of that land.' This is the standard rule in such cases. The decision in this case would, of course, be subject to the standard proviso that there must be no overburdening of the right; but there was no element of overburdening in this case. See also *Irvine Knitters* 1978 SC 109.

(*d*) that the servient owner is limited in his freedom of use only to the extent necessary to allow the proper exercise of the servitude. So, with a servitude of way, the servient owner may use it himself, may erect unlocked gates, or, in rural areas, if the exact line is not defined precisely, may alter the line to another route equally convenient. A servitude of access constituted by express grant along a defined line cannot be altered unilaterally by the dominant owner; nor may the servitude owner encroach thereon. See *Munro* 1996 SLT (Sh Ct) 97 – a case of encroachment.

In *Brennan* 1995 GWD 19–1087 missives for the sale and purchase of an area of ground contained a provision that servitude rights of wayleave for services, including drainage, existed or would be granted as far as necessary. A plan was incorporated in the missives to define boundaries and the access road. It was not incorporated in the provision above referred to although it did apparently show the line of the drainage and the position of a septic tank in an adjoining plot. The seller then sold the adjoining plot to another purchaser without reserving any servitude rights for the benefit of the first purchaser.

In the subsequent debate, Lord Gill held that the plan was not incorporated in the servitude provision and in any event, given a condition in the missives that the drainage and septic tank were subject to local authority approval, the purchaser could not have obtained a decree to enforce the terms of the obligation in the missives. The averments on the servitude provision itself failed to disclose any agreement between seller and purchaser as to the location of the drainage or the site of the septic tank, since the plan was not incorporated in the drainage provision. Lord Gill did not accept, however, that this inevitably produced an ambiguity but rather that it rendered the whole provision meaningless. Even assuming that this was a servitude of a well-known kind and that less demanding standards of specification were required than for a real burden, the specification in the servitude provision was, in his view, inadequate and could not create an enforceable obligation.

On appeal, however, reported at 1997 GWD 1–32, Lord Gill's decision was reversed and proof before answer allowed. Note, however, that the basis of this decision in the Inner House proceeded on the footing that the question at issue was whether or not a contractual obligation was sufficiently specific to allow it to be implemented, because the obligation occurred in a contract of sale and purchase, not in a formal deed. In that context, there was nothing indefinite or uncertain about the seller's intention in his undertaking to secure certain servitude rights for the benefit of the purchaser, and the purchaser was founding on this general obligation in the contract. It was unnecessary for the contract itself to specify the exact route, or the precise content, of the servitude to be granted. Lord Gill was held to have confused a general obligation in the contract to create servitude rights generally with a specific obligation to create particular servitude rights. It seems doubtful whether the same approach would be adopted in construing a servitude or burden created by deed or conveyance where the strict rule of precision and strict construction has always been applied. This, in turn, underlines the danger of inserting clauses in a formal deed or conveyance either conferring on a disponee or reserving to a disponer respectively, in general terms, all, if any, existing servitudes and wayleaves presently enjoyed by, or serving, the dominant property and passing through the servient property, or vice versa. In the light of Lord Gill's comments above, is such a general description of services sufficiently definite to constitute servitude rights, as is apparently intended? Reid and Gretton in 'What Changed in 1995', p. 52, comment on this case and point out the resulting dangers. They limit their observations to a grant of new servitudes, where clearly this decision would have adverse implications. But the same must also apply, it is thought, to servitudes already granted in such terms in existing titles created within the last 20 years until the servitude can be claimed to have been established by prescriptive possession over the 20-year period.

(5) The servient owner must suffer or permit a restriction on his freedom of use of his property at the instance of the dominant owner. But (with possibly one exception, *oneris ferendi*) there can be no positive obligation on him to do or execute any act or thing. His role is purely passive.

The various types of servitude right are all of long standing, well defined and well established, and are natural incidents to the proper enjoyment of heritable property. The same, or counterpart, rights exist in other systems (*cf.* English 'easements' and 'profits à prendre'). But, nonetheless, they are a feudal anomaly, inconsistent with the established principles of tenure in that, in some cases, written title is not necessary for their constitution, and sasine (or infeftment) is never necessary. Nothing need enter the GRS, and servitudes are overriding interests for the purposes of registration of title. In contrast, at common law, real conditions run with lands only if they occur in a conveyance or deed of conditions, qualify an infeftment, and enter the record.

As a result, the class of negative servitudes is now closed and will not be further extended; and the court is very slow to recognise as a positive servitude any right not already so categorised. But new positive servitudes remain a possibility; and the quality of existing servitudes may be extended, *e.g.* a servitude of carriageway now normally includes use by motor vehicles.

### 11.4 Constitution of positive servitudes
They may be constituted in three, or possibly, four, ways:

**11.5 (1) Express grant or express reservation.** Such express provision may occur in the titles of the persons acquiring the dominant or servient tenement respectively; or there may be a separate minute of agreement or deed of servitude. So, in a feu charter, the superior may expressly confer on the vassal a right of access over other land of the superior or he may reserve a right of access to himself, or to a third party, over the vassal's property. Alternatively, positive servitudes may be constituted by mere written agreement (not a title) between the servient owner and dominant owner; or by a unilateral deed of servitude granted by the servient owner. Any deed creating a servitude and executed prior to 1 August 1995 must be in formal writing (probative, holograph or adopted as holograph); or, if in informal writing, be followed by *rei interventus*. Any such deed, executed on or after 1 August 1995, must be a formal document in terms of the 1995 Act s. 2 and, for practical purposes, should always be self-proving, as it must be if the deed is to be recorded or registered. In no case need any deed enter the record (although in fact it is always desirable to record it).

Where the deed containing the servitude is a recorded title to the dominant or the servient tenement, nothing further is required. The dominant owner may exercise the right, or not, as he pleases; and only the operation of the negative prescription can (as a rule) deprive him of his right. But, where the servitude is not contained in a recorded title, then the dominant owner must in addition enter into possession of the servitude right (*i.e.* he must commence, and continue, to exercise his right) in order to make it effective against singular successors in the servient tenement. In *Balfour* 1987 SLT 144 Lord Sutherland held that publication in the title of either dominant or servient tenement sufficed, without possession following thereon.

He was not prepared to take the logical further step of holding possession unnecessary provided the servitude was published by recording in any form. Accordingly, if the servitude is created by a recorded deed of servitude or minute of agreement, possession following thereon is apparently still necessary to establish the right.

It is said that possession is required as an alternative to publication in the General Register of Sasines to ensure that, by possession and public enjoyment, the existence of the servitude is made known openly, and can be ascertained, from inspection of the property; in this way, a purchaser of the servient tenement is protected. According to Lord Sutherland in *Balfour*, the servitude must 'qualify the recorded sasine'. Publication in other forms, *e.g.* by recorded deed or recorded agreement, does not satisfy the rule, and possession is therefore still required. Possession is, in practice, a haphazard and uncertain method of discovering burdens which may be very onerous and can altogether frustrate the intentions of a purchaser.

Where the right is not contained in a feudalised title, then probably it must be a known servitude. But, where the deed is a feudalised title, then the right, if not in an exact category of known servitude, may yet be recognised as a servitude right, provided it has all the salient characteristics of a servitude right and qualifies the recorded sasine by entering one or other title – see *Balfour* above.

An express grant or reservation of servitudes, as with reservations and burdens in titles generally, will be strictly construed in favour of the servient tenement. The terms of the grant must be definite and there must be a definite intention to create a servitude running with the lands. But there are no statutory forms or any necessary words of style. *Robertson* 1995 SLT 291 is an illustration of a case where almost certainly the intention was to create a permanent servitude right but, on the wording of the deed, the right was held to be personal only to the original grantee.

Notwithstanding the foregoing rules as to precision, however, it would seem that these are applied only to the formal deed creating the servitude, not necessarily to an antecedent contract. See *Brennan* above and *Callander*, noted in the Digest of Cases, where general expressions of intention in missives were held sufficient to justify the creation of a formal right. Whether or not the same would apply in the case of burdens is an open question.

**11.6 (2) Implied grant or implied reservation.** An implied servitude can only be created when the two tenements, dominant and servient, have previously been owned by the same proprietor who has disposed of one (or both) of them, and in so doing has omitted to express such servitude rights as are either absolutely necessary or, in certain circumstances, reasonably necessary for the proper enjoyment of the subjects disponed. As with express grant, so where an implied grant or reservation is claimed, the dominant owner must be able to demonstrate a deemed intention to create the right. See *Neill* 1993 GWD 13–887. See also *McEachen* , para. 11.8 below, where express provision of access by one route was held to exclude any presumption that access by a second, alternative route had been intended by implication.

**11.7** *(a) Rights absolutely necessary to the use or enjoyment of the dominant tenement (servitude of necessity).*   Suppose, for example, A sells to B land completely surrounded by other land of A, but gives B no express right of access; a grant of servitude of way will be implied. Likewise, if A disponed the other land to B, retaining the landlocked subjects without reserving to himself access in B's disposition, a reservation of a servitude of access is implied for A's benefit. Note that the mere fact of sub-division and sale of part does not by itself imply that the part sold or retained is necessarily landlocked. See *Moffat* 1993 GWD 8–572. It is easier to establish such a servitude, by constitution (or grant) in a conveyance over the retained remainder of the subjects, than by implied reservation in a conveyance of the 'servient' part. *Fergusson* 1913 1 SLT 241.

**11.8** *(b) Rights necessary for the proper, comfortable enjoyment of the dominant tenement.* The extent and limits within which servitudes may be constituted in these circumstances are less certain.

The general principle seems firmly established in *Cochrane* (1861) 23 D (HL) 3. This case involved the continued use, following sub-division of a property, of a pre-existing drain serving the dominant and passing through the servient tenement. 'Where two properties are possessed by the same owner, and there has been a severance, anything which was used and which was necessary for the comfortable enjoyment of that part of the property which is granted' (*i.e.* the part sold and disponed) 'shall be considered to follow from the grant.'

In contrast, in *Murray* 1973 SLT (Sh Ct) 75, the owner of a group of buildings sold one of them, together with a small area of ground. Unknown to the purchaser, a water pipe ran under the subjects of sale, supplying mains water to the remaining buildings retained by the seller. In the disposition in favour of the purchaser, there was no reserved right to continue using this pipe. The sheriff rejected an argument that an existing mains water supply was necessary for the reasonable enjoyment of a dwellinghouse on the footing that plenty of dwellinghouses in Scotland have no mains water; and that the property in question was capable of being used as a house without a mains supply. A servitude right for this mains supply pipe would clearly derogate from the grant in favour of the purchaser and so requires an express reservation, except in cases of necessity. Since there was no 'necessity' in this instance, there could be no implied reservation of the necessary servitude right. In the result, by failing to reserve an express servitude right, the seller was deprived of his existing mains water supply. For a comparable case where the omission to make express provision for an electricity supply was held to be deliberate and did not justify an implied grant, see *Neill* above.

These cases confirm the general statement of principle, in Green's *Encyclopaedia* 13.1236, that a servitude under this head (necessary for comfortable enjoyment) can only be created by implied grant for the benefit of the disponee; but can never be created by implied reservation for the benefit of the disponer. According to Halliday's *Conveyancing Law and Practice*, para. 20–16, a servitude can be implied, by reservation, only if absolutely necessary for the property to be used at all, *e.g.* in the case of landlocked subjects.

If, in *Murray*, the facts had been reversed, and if the water mains serving the sold property had passed through the retained property, it might have been possible to establish a servitude by implication for the benefit of the disponee.

In *McEachen* 1976 SLT (Sh Ct) 38, A owned and occupied a dwelling-house with land attached. He sold and disponed the dwellinghouse and part of his land to B. In the disposition, A conveyed to B the benefit of all rights of way, etc., in general terms; and specifically conferred on B a servitude right of access to the house by a road leading thereto from the public road across the remainder of A's land, the route being coloured blue on the attached plan. It later transpired that, when A himself had occupied the house, he had also taken access thereto by a second route over the retained land, but in the disposition no right was conferred on B to use this second route. Following on the sale, A closed the second route, leaving the first route open. B objected, claiming access to the dwellinghouse by both routes. It was held that, since a right of access had been specifically conferred in the purchaser's title by the first route, this by itself automatically excluded the possibility of any implied right of access by the second route.

There is a discussion in this case on the requisites for a servitude of access necessary for convenient and comfortable enjoyment. Clearly, there could be no question here of a servitude of absolute necessity, since there was an alternative access route in the title. The sheriff principal reviewed the authorities at p. 41 and concluded: 'I find it difficult to presume an intention to create by implication a right of way in a case where the proprietor took pains to provide for access to the property disponed by making an express grant of a right of way.' He then distinguished *Cochrane* on the grounds that, in that case, the title was silent as to the mode of access; and followed *Fraser* 1938 SC 506.

The wording in *McEachen* also discloses a common trap for the draftsman which frequently passes unnoticed and on which the Sheriff Principal made comment in his decision in this case. The subjects conveyed were part of a larger estate. As stated in para. 11.1 above, for the existence of a servitude there must be two separate tenements in separate ownership. Accordingly, on a sub-division, if the intention is to create servitude rights as between the sub-divided parts, it must be borne in mind that there are at that date no existing 'servitudes' serving the disponed part over the retained part or vice versa. This is a contradiction in terms. No such servitude can exist until there has been actual sub-division.

**11.9 (3) Prescription.** Until 1976, the period of possession required was forty years, with added years for non-age and disability. By s. 3(1) and (2) of the Prescription and Limitation (Scotland) Act 1973, which came into force on 25 July 1976, the period is now twenty years in all cases. Possession before the commencement of the Act may be counted towards the twenty years provided that it continued at least for a time, however short, after the Act came into force. See s. 14(1)(a).

The person claiming the right must be the proprietor (infeft or, probably, uninfeft) of the dominant tenement; and he must show possession of the right, as of right, throughout the full period. Possession is not only proof that the right exists but also proof of the measure and extent of the right; it defines the dominant tenement, and probably the servient tenement affected by the right and the degree, and way, in which the right may be exercised. *Tantum praescriptum quantum possessum.* In a recent case the pursuer claimed to have established a right of access by prescriptive use but failed on the grounds that there had been no possession as of right but only by mere tolerance for limited purposes. See *Wilson* 1993 GWD 31 –2007.

In *Harris* 1996 SLT 12 the pursuer claimed to have established ownership by prescriptive possession but the claim was rejected because the possession was not proved to be exclusive. A subordinate point then arose as to whether or not, and if so to what extent, a servitude right of access had been created either by implied grant or prescriptive possession or a combination of the two.

See also *Landward Securities (Edinburgh) Ltd.* 1996 GWD 16–962. This last case is discussed again in the context of a title habile to acquisition of a servitude by possession in para. 14.10

The acquisition of heritable rights by prescription generally is dealt with again in Chapter 14.

**11.10 (4) Acquiescence.** 'It does appear that, in certain circumstances, a servitude or some similar right' (*sic*) 'may be created by acquiescence' – Bell's *Principles*, 947; and there is authority for the view that in some cases singular successors in lands will be bound by the acquiescence of their predecessors; *Macgregor* (1899) 2 F 345. This has been stated to occur when the thing acquiesced in is visible and obvious, especially where it is of such a character or cost as to be inconsistent with its having been allowed merely during pleasure. See also Rankine *Personal Bar* Chapter IV.

In *More* 1967 SLT (Sh Ct) 38, four cottages in a row were served by a common water main running through each garden at the rear of each house. The main burst and was repaired by A, the first proprietor in the row of four. The other three owners declined to pay a share of the cost. So A cut off their water. It then transpired that none of the titles contained any reference to the common pipe, which had been 38 years *in situ*; and there was no right of servitude in the titles, by implication or by prescription. The sheriff seemed inclined to the view that a servitude right to maintain the pipe had been established by acquiescence.

Note, however, that in this case the common pipe was laid by the original builder while all four plots were in his ownership. By the time each plot was sold, the common pipe was covered and invisible; and it is very doubtful if any of the four original purchasers knew of its existence. If they did, they may have acquiesced. If not, where was the 'acquiescence'?

Possibly, in this case, the right may, alternatively, have been constituted by implication in the four original dispositions; but compare *Murray* referred to in para. 11.8 above.

In *Robson* 1965 SLT 381, there clearly was acquiescence, and nothing else. The owner of the allegedly dominant tenement, apparently with the agreement of the servient owner, laid pipes through the servient property for drawing water. The right to lay pipes was not contained in the titles nor established by any formal deed of servitude. Later, the servient owner requested the dominant owner to remove the pipes. *Held* that the servient owner, having acquiesced in the laying of the pipes, was personally barred from requiring their removal. Note in particular the comments of Lord Kissen at pp. 386–387 on the effect of acquiescence in such circumstances.

## 11.11 Constitution of negative servitudes
These may only be constituted by title, or by express grant or by agreement in writing. The writing must be probative or, if executed on or after 1 August 1995, formal and, if recorded or registered, self-proving. But the writing need not enter the record.

With a negative servitude, there cannot be any active exercise or enjoyment of the right until the servient owner actually contravenes his servitude obligation. So, with negative servitudes, there cannot be any possession; writing alone is therefore sufficient, whether recorded or not, to establish the right. So nothing may show, on record or from inspection of the property, that a negative servitude exists.

## 11.12 Transmission of the right
It is inherent in the nature of a servitude that, once properly constituted in any of the ways indicated above, it runs with the lands so far as the servient tenement is concerned and will continue to affect it no matter into whose ownership it may pass. A servitude is, therefore, effective not only against the original owner of the servient tenement but against singular successors whether they have prior notice of the right or not, and whether they acquire the whole, or part only, of the servient tenement. For example, a servient tenement subject to a right of way is later sold in fifty lots as a building estate; all fifty lots remain servient if the right of way is through each lot.

So far as the dominant owner is concerned, the right subsists for the benefit of the dominant tenement. Two results follow:

(*a*) singular successors, as owners of the dominant tenement, require no express assignation of the servitude; mere title to the dominant tenement entitles them to exercise or enforce it; and

(*b*) the servitude cannot be divorced from the dominant tenement so as to benefit someone other than the owner of the dominant tenement. So the dominant owner cannot assign the right to a third party. In fact it is doubtful whether, in certain cases, the dominant owner can communicate the benefit of the servitude right to feuars and tenants, and if so to what extent. Clearly, to communicate a servitude of taking peat to several purchasers on the break-up of an estate materially increases the burden and would be objectionable; less so, in the case of access or way; not so at all in, *e.g.*, stillicide from a tenement roof when flats are sold individually, with a common right or interest in the roof.

See *Watson* 1966 SLT (Sh Ct) 77; *Keith* 1977 SLT (Lands Tr.) 16 and *Alba Homes Ltd.* 1993 SLT (Sh Ct) 49.

## 11.13 Interest to enforce
With real conditions generally there must be interest to enforce – the superior's is assumed, a co-feuar must aver it. Similarly, with servitudes, the dominant owner must have an interest, but the rule now seems to be, logically, that the dominant owner need not prove or aver his interest; it is up to the servient owner to show that the dominant owner has no interest to enforce – *Royal Exchange* 1912 SC 1151.

### 11.14 Extinction

A servitude, once constituted, will subsist until extinguished. The following are methods of extinction:

(*a*) *Express discharge* by the dominant owner in formal writing. If recorded it binds the singular successors of both parties: 1979 Act s. 18.

(*b*) *Confusio*. See 1995 SLT (News) 228 for an article on this point.

(*c*) *Prescription*. Under the Prescription and Limitation (Scotland) Act 1973 from 25 July 1976, the period has become 20 years absolute without any addition for non-age or disability. With positive servitudes, the period runs from the last active exercise of the right by the dominant owner; with negative servitudes, it runs from the date when the servient owner first does some act inconsistent with the servitude right.

(*d*) *Acquiescence, etc.* Acquiescence or other evidence of abandonment by the dominant owner may operate to extinguish servitudes within the prescriptive period; the same applies on such a change of circumstances that the servitude becomes redundant. In *Hogg* 1993 GWD 27–1712 a servitude right of access was held to have been abandoned.

(*e*) *Compulsory acquisition* of the servient tenement. See under 'Compulsory Purchase', Chapter 30.

(*f*) *Discharge*. By the Lands Tribunal under the Conveyancing and Feudal Reform (Scotland) Act 1970, Part I – see below, Chapter 17.

(*g*) *Expiry of purpose.*

### 11.15 Public rights of way

A servitude exists for the benefit of an adjoining dominant tenement. A public right of way exists for the benefit of the public, between and connecting two public places. It may be of the same degree as the servitude right of way, *i.e.* footpath, horse road, drove road or carriage road. It may be constituted by express grant, but in the great majority of cases public rights of way exist by virtue of prescriptive possession for the full prescriptive period of 20 years in terms of s. 3(3) of the 1973 Prescription and Limitation (Scotland) Act. It may be lost by disuse for the full prescriptive period; or by disuse coupled with actings by the servient proprietor which are inconsistent with the existence of the right and which are unchallenged over a period of time of lesser duration than the prescriptive period.

Public rights of way may be vindicated by the general public, or by public bodies such as local authorities and Rights of Way societies.

Two recent cases illustrate the distinctive features of this right.

In *Cumbernauld and Kilsyth District Council* 1993 SC (HL) 44 it was held in the House of Lords, affirming earlier decisions in the lower courts, that a public right of way had been constituted by a continuous and plain assertion of a public right. The Development Corporation originally constructed the new town of Cumbernauld which incorporated a public walkway through the town centre. The defenders purchased the whole development in 1987 and, shortly after completion, locked the doors on this walkway at night to prevent vandalism.

They argued principally that, even although there had apparently been prescriptive possession, there was no evidence that the public use was an assertion of a public right. It could equally be ascribed to tolerance on the part of the then proprietors. But that argument was rejected in the First Division. Lord President Hope stated that 'where the use is of such amount and in such manner as would reasonably be regarded as being the assertion of a public right, the owner cannot stand by and ask that his inaction be ascribed to his good nature, or to tolerance'.

In *Burton* 1995 SLT 507 the pursuer sought to interdict a neighbouring proprietor from using an old road as a means of access to his property. The road had ceased to qualify as a public right of way. The Court held that, given that a public right of way had been established, it necessarily followed that proprietors along that route remained entitled to use it for access to their individual properties although the road itself had ceased to be public because it no longer led from one public place to another. Accordingly, the higher right of public right of way would seem to carry with it by implication the lesser right of private servitude of access.

It is, of course, obviously difficult to disentangle and distinguish between use by the public in the assertion of a public right of way concurrently with private use by individual proprietors of the public right of way as a means of access to their own individual properties. But, as Lord Coulsfield observed, although the point was without authority, it would be extraordinary if an established right of use along a public right of way enjoyed by intermediate proprietors was to be lost when the road ceased to be public. He stated that the defenders must at least continue to enjoy a private right of access to their own property, and for that purpose he considered that there was sufficient evidence of material use as of right without interruption to sustain a servitude right of access to the property in question. Notwithstanding this decision, however, there clearly could be cases where the distinction between the use of a public right of way and an assertion of a public right would not, of itself, be sufficient to satisfy the requirements for the creation of a private servitude right of access although, on the evidence in this case, Lord Coulsfield did not consider that point significant.

Chapter 12

# SUBORDINATE CLAUSES

## 12.1 Function
In a charter, the subordinate clauses include (*a*) clauses peculiar to the charter or other feudal grant; and (*b*) subordinate or executory clauses common to any conveyance of land, including a disposition which creates no tenure.

## 12.2 Clauses peculiar to a feudal grant
(1) *Tenendas.* This is the clause which, reflecting the phrase 'in feu farm dispone' in the dispositive clause, indicates the manner of holding, and clearly stamps this writ as a conveyance on tenure. In its standard form, it reads 'to be holden the said subjects of and under me and my foresaids as immediate lawful superiors thereof in feu farm fee and heritage forever'.

(2) *Reddendo.* This clause is essential for a proper feudal grant, and is peculiar to feudal grants. It sets out the *reddendo* or return to be made by the vassal to his superior as the consideration for the grant. As explained above, under the Conveyancing (Scotland) Act 1924 feuduty had to be stated as a fixed amount of sterling money payable at fixed terms. But, in older charters, the *reddendo* might take various forms, and in addition the clause normally set out the taxed casualties or duplicands.

Now, under the Land Tenure Reform (Scotland) Act 1974 s. 1, no feuduty may competently be created in a deed executed after 1 September 1974. But:

(*a*) Tenure may be validly created without any *reddendo* – not even 1p. is required.

(*b*) A purported *reddendo* does not invalidate the whole charter – it is simply unenforceable.

(*c*) If a binding contract to feu was entered into before 8 November 1973 (Green Paper Date) and the charter is executed by 8 November 1975, a feuduty may validly be constituted; 1974 Act s. 7. But the deed must contain, *in gremio* or endorsed, a memo to that effect, in the form of Schedule 4.

## 12.3 Subordinate clauses
The remaining subordinate clauses are not peculiar to feudal grants but are common to all types of conveyance, although in a feu charter the clauses take a special form.

In the original form of feu charter, all these clauses were set out at great length. In the modern form they are considerably abbreviated. The abbreviated forms now in use are statutory, first introduced by the Lands Transference Act 1847 and re-enacted in the Titles to Land Consolidation (Scotland) Act 1868 ss. 5, 8 and Schedule B.1. Each short clause authorised in s. 5 receives a lengthy and detailed interpretation in s. 8.

In fact, the forms in Schedule B.1 are primarily designed for use in a disposition, not a charter; and in the feu charter some adaptation of the statutory clauses is normal.

**12.4 (1) Entry.** Schedule B.1 reads: 'With entry at the term of Whitsunday 19 '. This clause determines the date at which the grantee is entitled to possession (which may either be civil possession or, more usually, natural possession). See 1874 Act s. 28 for implied dates, if this clause is omitted. If the grantee himself intends to occupy the subjects it is essential to stipulate in the missives for 'entry and actual occupation (or vacant possession)'. This is because the existence of a lease may not give rise to a claim in warrandice (see below), and, if not, the grantee would be left without a remedy against the grantor.

For a discussion on the inter-relationship of date of execution, date of delivery, date of entry and date of registration in Sasines, see *Thomas* 1953 SC 151. Disposition of land as a gift *inter vivos*; signed, 4 May, delivered 6 May, date of entry 15 May 1945; donor died 12 May 1950, more than five years (the estate duty gift period) after delivery, less than five years after entry. Was estate duty payable under F.A. 1894 s. 2(1)(c)? *Held* (Lord Mackintosh dissenting, *q.v.*) that, by delivery, the deceased had completed the gift outwith the period. It should be emphasised that this decision turned on the wording of the relevant Finance Act in the context of what was then estate duty. No doubt in that narrow compass the decision may have been correct, but it does not in any way detract from the validity of the decision in *Sharp* v. *Thomson* in the Inner House, referred to in Chapter 4 above. On the general principles expounded by the Lord President in that case, it would have been the date of recording of the disposition by the donee which was the critical date, not the date of delivery. The *dicta* in *Thomas* were expressly not followed in the Inner House. As explained in Chapter 4, the Inner House decision was reversed in the House of Lords on narrow grounds of statutory interpretation, which probably would not extend to the facts in *Thomas*. See also articles in the Reading List – Chapter 4 Delivery.

**12.5 (2) Assignation of writs.** Under the Sasine system, recording of the appropriate writ is the final, mandatory step in the acquisition of the real right of ownership. By recording the appropriate title, the disponee thereunder establishes his real right if, but only if, the recorded title is itself valid and proceeds upon a valid prior progress of titles. The mere fact that A holds land on a recorded title is not, *per se*, conclusive evidence of his right; some enquiry into (*a*) the antecedents of that recorded title and/or (*b*) possession for the prescriptive period, is always necessary. Therefore, every disponee, whether under a feu charter or under a disposition, normally has an interest in the prior titles in order to maintain his own right. If these titles are not delivered to him (as they may not be), then he should have the right to call for production or exhibition of the prior titles when required; but, since 1970, this right has become of less importance because, under the 1970 Act, s. 45, an extract of a deed from Sasines must be accepted for all purposes as sufficient evidence of the contents of the original. In other words, a Sasines extract is now equivalent to the principal writ; and so the want of missing principal deeds can be made good by producing Sasines extracts.

On subinfeudation, the superior is not wholly divested; he retains the *dominium directum* which is, in law, ownership of land, albeit burdened with the vassal's right under the charter. The superior, therefore, in practice, retains all prior titles; and the only writ delivered to the vassal is his charter. The purpose of this clause in the charter is to confer on the vassal a right to call for production of the superior's titles, when need arises.

Schedule B.1 states: 'And I assign the writs and have delivered the same according to Inventory'. For the reason stated above, this is unsuitable for a charter, and the charter clause reads, instead: 'And I assign the writs, but to the effect only of maintaining and defending the right hereby granted'.

For deeds executed after 4 April 1979 – the date of the passing of the Land Registration (Scotland) Act 1979 – the assignation of writs clause need no longer be included in a feu charter and, if omitted, as invariably it is, the charter implies:

(i) an assignation to the vassal of all prior title deeds and searches, to the effect of maintaining and defending him in the feu; and

(ii) that the superior is obliged for that purpose to make the title deeds and searches furthcoming to him on all necessary occasions at the vassal's expense.

**12.6 (3) Assignation of rents.** Schedule B.1 reads: 'And I assign the rents'. The vassal under the charter may himself enter into personal possession and occupation of the subjects conveyed to him and usually does so. Alternatively, having acquired the right of property under the charter, he may part with possession of the property for a term of years to a tenant under a temporary arrangement known as a lease, in virtue of which, *inter alia*, the proprietor becomes entitled to an annual rent from the tenant. If the lease is to be valid, the proprietor as landlord must himself be infeft. If the feu is sold and disponed to a disponee, that does not automatically bring the lease to an end; but the disponee becomes entitled to the rents in place of the disponer. It is the person infeft for the time being who is entitled to rent; and rents follow infeftment. Accordingly, the assignation of rents clause in a conveyance is not necessary to confer a title on the disponee to collect rents; but it does serve to determine the basis of apportionment of the rent payable by the tenant, as between disponer and disponee with reference to the date of entry.

In deeds executed after 4 April 1979, the assignation of rents clause need no longer be included and, if omitted, the charter itself implies an assignation to the vassal of the rent payable in respect of the feu, if any.

**12.7 (4) Obligation of relief.** Schedule B.1 reads: 'And I bind myself to free and relieve the said disponee and his foresaids of all feuduties and public burdens'. By s. 8, this imports an obligation to relieve of all feuduties due to the superior and all public, parochial and local burdens due from or on account of the lands conveyed, prior to the date of entry. In other words, as between grantor and grantee all outgoings are apportioned at entry. The clause is not suitable as it stands for a charter, because so far as feuduty is concerned, the grantor/superior will remain liable for the feuduty due by him to his superior (the over-feuduty) in all time coming.

If he feus his whole property, he may have to redeem the over-feuduty, if allocated. 1974 Act s. 5. 'Obligation to grant a conveyance' includes a feu charter.

In deeds executed after 4 April 1979, no express clause of obligation of relief is necessary and, if omitted, the charter itself implies an obligation on the superior to relieve the vassal of feuduty payable by the superior to his own superiors in perpetuity; and of all other ground burdens up to the date of entry.

**12.8 (5) Warrandice.** In any transaction for sale and purchase of heritage, there are two stages; first, completion of the contract, and second, delivery of the conveyance to the purchaser against payment of the price when the purchaser takes actual possession. The rights and obligations of the parties differ at each stage. On completion of the contract, the seller's obligations are briefly to give a good title, possession, and a clear search. If at that stage the purchaser finds that the seller cannot fulfil any of these obligations, his remedy is rescission of the contract and an action of damages for breach thereof. But once the conveyance has been delivered and the transaction completed, the seller's only remaining obligation, in the absence of special provisions in the missives, is warrandice against eviction; it is then normally too late for rescission. If, after completion, the purchaser then discovers some defect in the title or some impingement on his possession, he cannot normally then reduce the contract, and return the property to the seller. His only action is for damages *quanti minoris*, and it is on the seller's warrandice that this action is based. This is dealt with again in more detail in Chapter 28.

In its absolute form, the warrandice obligation represents a personal guarantee by the disponer that he will indemnify the disponee against any loss or damage which the disponee may suffer owing to a diminution in the value of his real right arising out of:

(i) complete eviction of the disponee from the whole subjects, or partial eviction from part, owing to a defect in the title; or

(ii) a real burden, or other adverse real right, affecting the subjects, actually made effective against the disponee, which he was unaware of at date of delivery of the disposition – 'constructive partial eviction'.

It is important to be clear on the fairly narrow scope of the warrandice obligation. So in *Palmer* 1993 SLT 485 a purchaser, having taken delivery of a disposition with the usual warrandice clause, then sought to claim damages from the seller on the grounds of alleged misrepresentation, basing her claim on the warrandice obligation in the disposition in her favour. The claim was rejected on the grounds that there had been no actual eviction or even a threat thereof although there may have been an undeniable absence of title. Lord Kirkwood took the view that, if there had been a claim under warrandice, damages would have been limited to indemnity only and not solatium as well.

In *Clark* 1994 SLT 1053, the pursuer purchased a flat and occupied it for two years. She then resold it. The purchaser declined to take the title. The defect was eventually cured, but only after long delay. Consistent with previous authority, the court held that indemnity under absolute warrandice extended only to eviction or threatened eviction and that nothing less than actual physical ejection or at least a challenge from a competing title holder would be deemed to be eviction for this purpose. Her claim therefore failed.

For a comment on the decision in *Palmer*, see an article by Professor Robert Rennie in *Greens Property Law Bulletin*, No. 5, p. 6.

**12.9 (a)** *Nature of obligation.* Warrandice is necessarily, and of its nature, a personal guarantee only; and of course, as with any personal obligation, the value of the indemnity to the purchaser depends entirely on the financial stability of the seller and his ability to pay. Thus warrandice by a disponer who later has become bankrupt, although it infers an obligation to indemnify the purchaser to the extent of his loss, may well in fact be worthless. That, however, is a risk which the purchaser must take. He cannot ask for more than the seller's warrandice, and he cannot insist that the obligation be fortified either by security or by a third party's guarantee, except by express provision in the contract of sale and purchase, which is rare.

The warrandice obligation does not indemnify against loss or damage which the grantee may suffer from any cause, other than actual or constructive eviction by an adverse real right.

The existence of a feu right would found a claim in warrandice, since the disponee would be excluded from *dominium utile*. Similarly, servitudes will found a claim, if patrimonial loss can be demonstrated. Leases, on the other hand, may not found a claim. See *Lothian and Border Farmers Ltd.* 1952 SLT 450, and compare Halliday's *Practice*, 15–73 and the article in 1988 JLS at p. 164.

In every case, the disponer's obligation is to indemnify. He is not obliged to take any steps to put the title right, nor can the disponee claim *restitutio in integrum*. This is most strongly emphasised in *Welsh* (1894) 21 R 769. In that case, after completion of the purchase of a house and garden, a right of way was later established across the garden by an adjoining owner. Founding on warrandice, the disponee sued for the present value of the whole subjects, offering to reconvey them as they stood to the seller; in other words, he sought restitution, not indemnity. *Held* that in cases of partial eviction, the purchaser's right under warrandice was limited to indemnification for the loss sustained.

**12.10** *(b) Extent of claim.* Warrandice is indemnity and the quantum of any claim must therefore be calculated on the basis of the actual pecuniary loss suffered by the purchaser. In cases of total eviction, it is settled that, if the value at the time of eviction is greater than the price paid, then warrandice covers the excess and is not limited to the original price. Thus, if A buys land for £10,000 and builds to the value of £100,000 on it, A can (if evicted) claim £110,000, not merely the original £10,000. The converse case, where the value at eviction is less than the original price, is not settled; but presumably, only that value could be recovered. In cases of partial eviction, the quantum of the claim is the amount in money terms by which the adverse right diminishes the value of the property. If the adverse right is, *e.g.* a standard security for an exact amount, no question arises; the sum in the standard security is the amount claimed. In other circumstances, it is a question of valuation.

**12.11** (*c*) *Degrees of warrandice.* The extent or degree of warrandice to be undertaken by the grantor of a deed varies according to circumstances. In every heritable conveyance, warrandice is almost invariably expressed. But, if no warrandice is expressed, then in every case some degree of warrandice will be implied. To omit the clause of warrandice altogether does not therefore mean that the grantor gives no warrandice; in the result, a higher degree of warrandice may be implied against him than that which he would have undertaken or been obliged to undertake had the clause been expressed in the deed. The nature of the transaction and the capacity of the grantor will normally determine what degree of warrandice is appropriate in any particular case. But, of course, it is always open to the parties to agree to specialties to meet special circumstances.

**12.12** (i) Absolute warrandice, the highest degree, indemnifies against loss arising from any defect in the title or any adverse right, not attributable to the act or neglect of the grantee. Absolute warrandice is implied in onerous transactions, *e.g.* sale for adequate price.

**12.13** (ii) Warrandice from fact and deed. Here the grantor is bound to indemnify the grantee against loss arising from any act or deed, past, present or future of the grantor himself. He is not liable for any defects not personally attributable to him. This degree is implied where the consideration is not a full one; and probably also where the grantor acts in a representative capacity only. Certainly, in the last case, this is the degree of warrandice always expressed by trustees, thus – 'I as trustee foresaid grant warrandice from my own facts and deeds only'. It would be unfair if a trustee were personally liable to indemnify for all defects, because he has no patrimonial or beneficial interest in the price, but, in onerous transactions, the trust beneficiaries are also taken bound in absolute warrandice.

**12.14** (iii) Simple warrandice. Here the grantor is liable only for future voluntary deeds adverse to the grantee's right. It carries no indemnity against past acts of the grantor, nor against future acts in implement of a prior binding obligation. It is implied in all gratuitous transactions; if expressed, the term used is 'I grant simple warrandice', or 'I grant warrandice, but only against all voluntary acts and deeds hereinafter to be executed or done by me', and this, or fact and deed warrandice, is normally expressed in any gratuitous deed.

**12.15** (*d*) *Combined degrees.* It is quite common for two separate degrees of warrandice to be combined expressly in a deed. The normal clause in an onerous deed by trustees exemplifies: 'And I as trustee foresaid grant warrandice from my own facts and deeds only and I bind the trust estate under my charge and the beneficiaries interested therein in absolute warrandice'.

**12.16** (*e*) *Consenters.* Pure consent alone will not normally imply warrandice in any degree against the consenter; but, where the consenter is conjoined in the operative clause, some warrandice will probably be inferred, at least simple warrandice, possibly more according to the nature of the consent; consenter's warrandice should always be express. Usually fact and deed will serve, sometimes absolute is required. It depends on the circumstances in which consent is required.

**12.17** *(f) The statutory clause.* 1868 Act, s. 5 and Schedule B.1. This clause in the Schedule reads 'I grant warrandice'. The interpretation of that clause in s. 8 implies '... unless especially qualified ... absolute warrandice as regards the lands and writs and evidents, and warrandice from fact and deed as regards the rents ...'. This means:

(1) Absolute warrandice as to title, discussed above.

(2) The same for the title deeds. In other words, the grantor warrants that the whole progress of titles is good and sufficient to maintain the grantee in possession in terms of the dispositive clause of his conveyance. It is not necessarily an absolute warranty that each individual writ is wholly valid according to its terms. This distinction is drawn in *Brownlie* (1880) 7 R (HL) 66 (and see (1880) 5 R 1076).

(3) The rents are warranted from fact and deed only. The rents are assigned, as noted above. In any assignation of a debt the degree of warrandice implied is fact and deed only and *debitum subesse* – that the debt subsists and is owing. There is no guarantee that the debtor is solvent or that he will pay; if that were inferred, the grantor would be in the position of guarantor to all the tenants. In practice, it means that the leases are valid and are effectually assigned, for what they are worth. *Debitum subesse* is implied; Menzies *Lectures* 179.

**12.18** *(g) Implied warrandice.* If no warrandice is expressed, it will be implied in one degree or another, according to the nature of the transaction and capacity. The converse also holds, *viz.*: that where warrandice is express, it will entirely supersede whatever obligation would otherwise have been implied by law. Further, any express warrandice is strictly interpreted according to its terms. This may have unfortunate results. Thus, the use of the statutory clause 'I grant warrandice' is not appropriate in a gratuitous conveyance; fact and deed is the most that should be given, more often simple warrandice only; but if 'I grant warrandice' is so used, it will receive full effect. On the other hand, where fact and deed warrandice only is given in an onerous disposition, that is all that the grantee can later found on, although, had no warrandice been expressed, then absolute warrandice would have been implied.

**12.19** *(h) Qualifications of warrandice.* In an onerous conveyance, the statutory clause is almost always used but it may require qualification. One example – trustees – has already been given; a similar qualification is appropriate in any conveyance granted by someone not the true beneficial owner.

Where there are adverse rights subsisting at the date of conveyance of which the purchaser is aware and which he is to accept (*e.g.* servitudes, leases, bonds, etc.), all such rights must be excepted from warrandice to prevent any possibility of future claims against the grantor.

As already noted, where property is sold subject to a lease, it is usual and possibly necessary, in order to protect the seller, to except leases from warrandice, so limiting the seller's liability by excluding any possible claim on that ground. But that is the only effect of such a qualification. In *Kildrummy (Jersey) Ltd.* 1992 SLT 787, as part of a tax-minimisation exercise, title to a heritable property was taken in name of a Jersey company, subject to a lease. For technical reasons, the lease was held to be void. In the disposition in favour of the company, however, the lease was excepted from warrandice under a general exclusion of all current leases. The company then argued that, having accepted a disposition with that exclusion, it had effectively adopted the lease and thus had validated it. The argument was rejected on the footing that, since the lease was a nullity *ab initio*, it could not be so validated; and in any event the warrandice clause in the disposition was, according to its own terms, merely an obligation of relief and nothing more.

**12.20** (*j*) *Transmission.* It is settled that the assignation of writs clause in a conveyance passes on the benefit of existing warrandice obligations to the grantee under a conveyance. Probably, this passed by implication on a disposition alone without assignation of writs before the Land Registration (Scotland) Act 1979; but this is now implied by the 1979 Act s. 16(1).

This in turn, however, creates a trap for the unwary. Suppose that A dispones heritable property to B with absolute warrandice. B then dispones the same property to C with absolute warrandice. Having taken delivery of the disposition B to C, suppose that C is then physically evicted and claims damages against B under the warrandice obligation in the disposition by B to C. The claim would almost certainly succeed. That same defect in title, however, was warranted by A in the warrandice obligation in the disposition A to B. On the face of it, B has in turn a claim for damages against A under that warrandice obligation. In theory, this is undoubtedly correct. But the disposition by B to C impliedly assigned to C the benefit of the warrandice obligation in the disposition by A to B. B was therefore divested of the benefit of that obligation by A in his favour. Accordingly, if B is to claim effectively against A, he requires a retrocession or a reassignation in his own favour by C of the transmitted warrandice obligation in the disposition A to B. In *Cobham* 1986 SLT 336 a situation along these lines occurred. Using the same scenario, C, the ultimate disponee, after recording his disposition, was evicted. He claimed damages against B under the warrandice obligation in the disposition B to C and recovered damages from B. B in turn sought to recover damages from A, the original disponer under the warrandice obligation in the disposition A to B. However, that warrandice obligation had passed to C under the implied assignation of writs clause in the disposition B to C and B had not obtained a retrocession or reassignation before A was conjoined as a third party when B sought relief against A in the claim by C against B. C's claim was settled. B pursued his claim against the third party, A, but, because B had not obtained a reassignation before A was conjoined as a third party, his claim was rejected and he recovered nothing from A. No doubt on strictly technical grounds that decision was correct. However, Lord Kincraig stated his view that, since B himself had not actually been evicted, he had no grounds of claim against A. It was conceded that there was no authority on this point. If that view is correct, however, it produces a very inequitable result. Professor Reid, in his article on warrandice in a *Scots Conveyancing Miscellany*, considers this *dictum* by Lord Kincraig to be unsound. 'It is manifestly unjust that B should be unable to recover from A' – a view which this writer certainly shares.

For a comment on the decision in *Palmer*, see the article by Professor Robert Rennie in *Greens Property Law Bulletin*, No. 5, p. 6.

**12.21 (6) Certificate of value for stamp duty.** See Chapter 5.

**12.22 (7) Consent to registration for execution.** A deed may be registered for publication, for preservation, or for execution; and the same deed may be registered for all three purposes. Registration for publication means registration in the Register of Sasines. Registration for preservation or for execution means registration in the court books, either the Books of Council and Session in Edinburgh or the books of the local sheriff court.

Each type of registration has a different purpose. Registration for publication is the means of obtaining a real right in land. A copy of the deed (now a microcopy) is held by the Register of Sasines and the original is returned.

By contrast, no rights are conferred on the grantee by registration for preservation, the sole purpose of which is the physical preservation of the deed, which is retained in the court books. Registration for preservation is routinely used for deeds such as trust dispositions and settlement and powers of attorney; but it is not normally used for deeds which have already been registered in the Register of Sasines because, even if Sasine deeds are lost, an extract copy from the Register is as good as the original (1970 Act s. 45).

Finally, registration for execution enables the creditor in a deed to use the expedited procedure of summary diligence against the debtor. The debtor's consent is required for registration for execution, and, if forthcoming, a short clause of consent is included in the deed, normally at the end. A clause of consent is appropriate only for deeds which impose a pecuniary obligation on one of the parties, and in normal conveyancing practice they are found mainly in standard securities and in leases.

**12.23 (8) Testing clause.** See Chapter 2.

# Chapter 13

# REGISTRATION

## 13.1 The requirements for infeftment

The mere fact that a charter is prepared containing all the requisite clauses does not, of itself, operate to confer any right on the vassal and imposes no obligations on the grantor thereof. Before the vassal can perfect his real right and become infeft, a number of further steps are necessary. The further elements involve:

## 13.2 1. Authentication

See Chapter 2 and relevant Reading List references.

A feu charter is a formal writ relating to land. If executed before 1 August 1995, it must be probative, and proper authentication will involve:

(*a*) Execution of the charter by the superior on each page, or on the last page under the Conveyancing and Feudal Reform (Scotland) Act 1970.

(*b*) Subscription by two witnesses to the superior's signature on the last page of the deed.

(*c*) The insertion in the deed (normally in the testing clause) of the names and addresses of the witnesses.

(*d*) In addition, although this is not all legally necessary, the testing clause contains some further information including the number of pages of the deed, schedules, plans, etc., a reference to any alterations, marginal additions, etc., in the deed in order properly to authenticate them, and the date and place of execution.

Writs executed on or after 1 August 1995 must be formally valid in terms of the 1995 Act s. 2. See Chapter 2.

## 13.3 2. Delivery

See Chapter 4 and relevant Reading List references.

The mere execution of the deed by the grantor does not, of itself, immediately create binding rights and obligations. So long as the deed remains in the possession of the grantor or under his control, it is inoperative; to make it operative, it must be delivered to the vassal who must accept delivery.

## 13.4 3. Stamp duty and VAT

See Chapter 5 and relevant Reading List references.

The feu charter is, for stamp duty, a conveyance on sale by superior to vassal and is liable to *ad valorem* conveyance on sale duty. With appropriate certificate of value, it qualifies for exemption.

Special provision applied before the Land Tenure Reform (Scotland) Act 1974 to the feu charter, where the consideration took the form of or included a feuduty. The consideration for stamp duty was the total sum of feuduties which would become payable within the 20 years following the date of the deed, plus the capital cash payment (if any), termed *grassum*.

### 13.5 4. Registration

Mere delivery of a feu charter, although essential to the vassal's right, does not of itself operate to divest the superior nor to perfect the vassal's real right in the subjects. Instead, delivery of the charter merely confers upon the vassal a valid personal title to the *dominium utile* only, which is of itself a mandate for infeftment and assignable as such by disposition (and pre-1970 also by special assignation). To convert his personal title into a real right, good against the world, the vassal must complete his infeftment by registration. See *Ceres School Board* (1895) 23 R 279, for an illustration of the general principle 'that a singular successor takes the lands free from the personal obligations of his predecessor and unaffected by burdens not appearing on the Records', and *Sharp* v. *Thomson* noted in Chapter 4.

Even on registration of the charter, the superior is not totally divested; and still retains his title to the *dominium directum* – see Chapter 15. In contrast, the granting and registration of a disposition fully divests the grantor thereof who has no remaining or continuing interest in the subjects disponed; and no tenure, nor any equivalent relationship, is created as between disponer and disponee.

Two separate registers for land are currently in operation. If the feu charter or other deed relates to land in an area which is operational for registration of title, registration is usually (but not always) in the new Land Register. Otherwise registration is in the Register of Sasines. These registers are dealt with in turn, beginning with the Register of Sasines.

### 13.6 5. Register of Sasines

When the Register of Sasines was first set up, in 1617, feu charters and dispositions could not be recorded and infeftment was obtained by recording an instrument of sasine, which summarised the content of the charter or disposition. But direct recording has been possible since 1858, and instruments of sasine are no longer used. Before a writ can be recorded, it must satisfy certain requirements – see *Macdonald* 1914 SC 854. Briefly, these are:

(*a*) that the writ is self-proving, formerly probative;

(*b*) that it is properly stamped;

(*c*) that it is appropriate to the Register of Sasines, *i.e.*, that it deals with an estate in land;

(*d*) that it contains an identifying description. See generally, *Macdonald* above;

(*e*) that it carries the statutory warrant of registration;

(*f*) that the deed is presented along with the relevant application form CPB2, and the recording dues, for recording in the Sasine Register.

On grounds of public policy the Keeper of the Register also feels constrained to refuse to record deeds of a frivolous or vexatious nature. Thus conveyances of souvenir plots are not accepted for recording; and in recent years a number of dispositions *a non domino* presented for registration in competition with the true owners have been refused registration. The Keeper's stance against recording souvenir plots in Sasines is similar to the statutory position in s. 4(2)(c) of the 1979 Act in relation to the Land Register. See the article on the subject in 1997 JLS 72.

Refusal to record or register an *a non domino* disposition is certainly consistent with the Keeper's discretion referred to in *Macdonald* above. In that case, the pursuer, who sought to record a deed which did not contain a sufficient description, argued that the Keeper had no duty, and therefore no right, to question the sufficiency of the description and that he had no discretionary power in the matter but was bound, without question, to record the deed as presented to him. Exactly the same argument can be put forward in the case of the *a non domino* disposition. However, that view was roundly rejected by the Court. The Lord President stated in unqualified terms that the Court were wholly unable to accede to that view. The Keeper was a highly placed official in charge of the Register, and was bound, in the faithful discharge of his statutory duty, to exercise due care and control over the Register in order to secure its efficiency for the purpose for which it was created.

Prepayment of recording and registration dues in the Register of Sasines or Land Register, effective from 1 April 1996, was introduced by the Land Register (Scotland) Act 1995. For a note explaining this new provision, see 1995 JLS 482.

**13.7 Warrants of registration.** The Titles to Land (Scotland) Act 1858, when abolishing the instrument of sasine, also introduced as a new requirement that the conveyance when presented for registration should carry a warrant of registration endorsed thereon, authorising the Keeper to record the writ. In terms of the 1858 Act, the warrant must identify the person taking infeftment and must be signed by him or his authorised agent.

When, in 1868, all land registers were centralised in Edinburgh, a further statutory requirement was added to the warrant of registration, in that from 1868 onwards the warrant must also direct the division of the Register in which the writ is to be recorded.

**13.8 Requirements of warrants.** The Titles to Land Consolidation (Scotland) Act 1868 s. 141 provides, as to warrants, as follows:

(1) All deeds and writs of every sort must have a warrant; and this applies both to writs to be registered in the General Register of Sasines and in the Burgh Registers.

(2) All warrants must specify (which meant in 1868 name and design) the person on whose behalf the writ is to be recorded and the Division of the General Register of Sasines or the Burgh Register.

(3) The warrant must be signed by the person requiring registration or by his agent.

The section then referred to four forms of warrant adapted to meet various circumstances; but these forms are in turn superseded by the 1924 Act

s. 10 and Schedule F which supplies a single new composite form of warrant capable of being adapted to a variety of circumstances. The principal amendments in the 1924 Act are:

(1) It is no longer necessary to design a party in a warrant; he is referred to simply as 'within-named' provided he is designed in the writ itself.

(2) Where the conveyance being recorded contains a destination to several persons and the survivors, or to trustees *ex officiis* and to their successors as trustees, the effect of that destination is impliedly imported into the warrant, without any express reference thereto. Thus, in a disposition in favour of 'A and B and the survivor of them', the warrant of registration simply refers to 'A and B' without reference to survivorship; but the survivorship element is impliedly imported into the warrant for the purposes of their infeftment.

The form of warrant in Schedule F now reads:

'Register on behalf of the within-named A.B. [or on behalf of A.B. (designation)] in the Register of the County of G (or in the Registers of the Counties of G, H, and J).

A.B.
W.S., Edinburgh,
Agent.'

**13.9 Notes on Schedule D**. The Schedule has five notes for guidance in particular cases. The subject matter of these notes is:

(1) A variation on the standard form of warrant referring to a clause of direction.

(2) A variation on the standard form of warrant dealing with combined registration in Sasines and Books of Council and Session.

(3) A simplification in the case of trustees, who no longer need set out at full length their fiduciary capacity; but instead insert, in the warrant, the words 'as trustees within mentioned'.

(4) A variation on the standard form of warrant to meet one special case, where a writ is recorded along with certain other writs endorsed on it. We will come to this later.

(5) A variation on the standard form of warrant to meet the case where several related writs are recorded together; but this no longer applies, assignations of unrecorded conveyances having been abolished by the 1970 Act s. 48.

Note that, as a necessary result of statutory provisions relating to warrants, the warrant is the limit of the infeftment. Thus, where a feu charter is granted in favour of 'A and B' and is recorded with warrant of registration 'on behalf of the within-named A', without reference to B, A is infeft but B is not, even although the charter in favour of B appears on the record.

**13.10 Presentation for registration.** Following on delivery and stamping of the feu charter or disposition, and the signing of the warrant of registration, the deed is ready to be presented for registration. The deed is delivered, by hand or by post, to the Register of Sasines at Meadowbank House in Edinburgh. On presentation, brief details of the deed are entered in the Presentment Book, and the date of this entry is the date of infeftment. The Presentment Book has been computerised since 1 April 1992, and all applications for registration must now be accompanied by a special application form (form CPB2) which is machine-readable. Note particularly that form CPB2, recently introduced as an additional requirement for recording, does not render the warrant of registration unnecessary.

A number of further registration processes then follow. First the deed is minuted, *i.e.*, a short summary of its terms is prepared for the Minute Book. A copy of the minute is entered on the search sheet for the property in question. Next, a microcopy is made of the deed. (Previously this was a photocopy, and earlier still a copy written out by hand.) Finally, the deed is stamped with the Keeper's certificate showing that it has been recorded in the Register of Sasines and is then returned to the ingiver. The whole registration process takes several months.

The certificate of registration endorsed by the Keeper on the deed merely certifies that the deed has been recorded on a given date, but goes no further than that. In particular, the certificate does not guarantee the validity or sufficiency of the deed. At the date of recording, the disponee may or may not be in possession, and he may or may not be the person properly entitled to the land, in that the deed may or may not be valid; but, unless the deed is grossly inept, the Keeper will accept and record it, although he may raise matters of substance or of detail with the ingiver, as a matter of Register House practice. As noted, the Keeper does have discretion to refuse to accept a writ in special circumstances: see para. 13.6 above.

### 13.11 6. Disadvantages of the Sasines system

The Register of Sasines has proved remarkably efficient and effective over a period of more than 300 years. In modern times, however, it was seen as suffering from a number of disadvantages, which, viewed cumulatively, were deemed sufficient to justify the introduction of registration of title. Once registration of title is fully operational, the Register of Sasines will be closed down and all registration will take place in the Land Register.

The perceived disadvantages of the Register of Sasines were, and are, the following.

### 13.12 Identification.

Until, perhaps, 100 years ago, it was commonplace to describe properties, particularly rural properties, simply by their name alone, without any attempt to define area or boundaries on a plan. Detailed particular descriptions, usually supported by plans, are now the accepted norm for 'new' properties, but modernisation or redrafting of an inadequate description in an existing title is relatively unusual. Even the modern particular description is very often inadequate and does not precisely define and delimit the subject matter of the grant. Further, deed plans are not always accurate; and Register House has never been in a position to correlate plans of adjoining properties in order to make sure that boundaries coincide.

One remedy would be to improve the standard of conveyancing and, in particular, to make it obligatory, in any description of old or new properties, to refer to a plan prepared by a person properly qualified. Normally, a simple two-dimensional plan on one sheet would suffice. For more complex subjects, plans on several sheets, possibly in three dimensions, or showing different elevations, might be required, *e.g.* for mineral strata, parts of buildings, etc. To a limited extent, more rigorous rules have been imposed on the profession by the recent decisions in the *Beneficial Bank* cases dealt with in Chapter 8.

Accurate mapping of individual properties on Ordnance Survey maps, and correlation of individual properties and their boundaries *inter se* on index or master plans, is one of the cardinal features of any system of registration of title; and the introduction of registration of title will cure this weakness in the existing system.

The same criticism applies to the identification of ancillary rights, *e.g.* servitudes, fishings, the right to enforce burdens, etc. Here, precision, in the nature of things, is much more difficult to attain, and registration of title is not such a certain solution.

**13.13 Conditions of tenure.** Another criticism of the existing system is that the burdens and conditions affecting the title (and to some extent reservations, although this is perhaps a criticism of the identification system) are difficult to discover and may be uncertain. But at least with our system of registration for publication, any condition of tenure, to be effective, must be recorded in the Register of Sasines; and to this standard rule there are only very limited exceptions, *e.g.* in the case of servitudes and leases, where there are other means of discovering the adverse right.

Apart from these limited exceptions, all conditions of tenure are ascertainable by searching in the Register of Sasines. Again, registration of title is not the only and necessary cure for this weakness in the system and other solutions are possible. But registration of title will virtually eliminate this weakness, again subject to certain standard exceptions and qualifications.

**13.14 Heritable securities.** The same principles apply to heritable securities as apply to conditions of tenure, although, in practice, it is usually easier to ascertain whether or not securities are outstanding than to ascertain the position as to old burdens. Again, registration of title will eliminate all difficulties.

**13.15 Proof of ownership.** Finally, and most importantly, the mere recording of a title in the Register of Sasines is never in any circumstances a guarantee of the validity of that title nor of the right of the party on whose behalf the title was recorded. The grantee has an indefeasible real right if, but only if, his deed derives from a grantor whose own title is in turn valid and unchallengeable. But a defect in the title of the grantor is not cured by the recording of the grantee's deed and the deed may later be reduced, notwithstanding that it has been recorded, if it turns out that the grantor's title was invalid.

The consequence is that in practice proof of title depends upon the operation of positive prescription (for which see Chapter 14). Therefore, in every title, some examination of the titles for at least 10 years back is always necessary. Often, such examination is time-consuming, repetitive and uncertain. The reduction in 1970 of the period of positive prescription from 20 years to 10 years (with certain exceptions) cut down the necessary period over which the title must be examined but did not eliminate examination, nor did it eliminate the risks inherent in the Sasines system.

The only true cure for this defect is a system of registration of title. Under registration of title, the state assumes responsibility for registering the ownership of every individual heritable property throughout the country or in defined areas; and, on such registration, issues a certificate to reputed owners which, when issued, becomes conclusive evidence of title and, therefore, bars all questions as to, and investigation of, antecedent titles. In the process, this eliminates all earlier invalidities or doubtful points and defects in the earlier titles on which the right depends.

### 13.16  7. Registration of title and the Land Register

After protracted delays, registration of title was introduced to Scotland by the Land Registration (Scotland) Act 1979; but, although the Act has come into operation, the process of registration itself is gradual. As at May 1997, the system is operating in the counties of Renfrew, Dumbarton, Lanark, Glasgow, Clackmannan, Stirling, West Lothian, Fife, Aberdeen, Kincardine, Ayr, Dumfries, Wigtown and Kirkudbright.

The new Scottish registration system follows, fairly closely, the system of registration of title which has been operating in England on a compulsory basis for over 70 years. But there are significant differences between the two systems, in part reflecting differences in the land tenure systems; and in part reflecting ideas which emerged in the preparation of the Reid and Henry Committee Reports. In the result, the Scottish system is a good deal simpler than the English one.

Note, in contrast to the Sasines system that, in registration of title, the role of the registrar is an active one, in that the Keeper, as registrar, must scrutinise the individual title, must satisfy himself that the reputed owner has a valid title, and must satisfy himself as to identity and burdens affecting the property which he is registering. He must then positively certify that the individual proprietor is indeed the proprietor of that particular property. By so certifying, he makes unchallengeable what was possibly an invalid or vulnerable title.

Note also, in contrast to certain other forms of registration, that the state here intervenes, in the public interest, to certify ownership. Compare, in particular, motor vehicle registration where, for fiscal purposes, and also for the purpose of control and law enforcement in traffic offences, every vehicle operating on the public roads in Britain must be registered. But the certificate issued under statutory authority has no effect whatsoever *quoad* title.

### 13.17  The Register and the Registrar

Obviously, a new register of title was required. But, in Scotland, this was a relatively simple problem. A comprehensive system of registration already exists, with a central Register House in Edinburgh fully and efficiently staffed with sophisticated techniques for the existing system of registration. The Sasines Register contains, in readily accessible form, a great deal of information which will be translated onto the title sheet on registration of title. Logically, under the 1979 Act, the new Land Register is placed under the control of the Keeper of the Registers. It is housed partly in the same premises (Meadowbank House in Edinburgh) and partly at Cowglen in

Glasgow, and the two registers work in parallel and are closely co-ordinated. But, in registration of title, the role of the Keeper alters from a mere passive role in the controlling of intake of deeds for publication to the much more important and active role of examining and adjudicating upon titles presented for registration. In the new system of registration of title, he is given a great deal of discretion as to what he registers and more importantly as to what he guarantees.

### 13.18 Registration

For practical reasons, the process of registration of title can only be introduced gradually. It would be quite impossible to introduce it instantaneously for every title throughout the whole of the country.

The original intention was to introduce the new system, area by area throughout Scotland, on a nine-year programme starting in April 1981 with the county of Renfrew. For some years previously, the Keeper had been operating a pilot scheme for this county and a good deal of practical experience had thus been gained. However, the original programme has now fallen badly behind.

The counties which are currently operational for registration of title are: Renfrew (6 April 1981); Dumbarton (4 October 1982); Lanark (3 January 1984); Glasgow (30 September 1985); Clackmannan (1 October 1992); Stirling (1 April 1993); West Lothian (1 October 1993); Fife (1 April 1995); Aberdeen and Kincardine (1 April 1996); and Ayr, Dumfries, Wigtown and Kirkudbright (1 April 1997). The projected future timetable is now:

| | |
|---|---|
| 1 April 1998 | Angus, Perth and Kinross |
| 1 April 1999 | Berwick, East Lothian, Peebles, Roxburgh and Selkirk. |
| 1 April 2000 | Midlothian |
| 1 April 2002 | Argyll, Bute |
| 1 April 2003 | Banff, Caithness, Inverness, Moray, Nairn, Orkney and Zetland, Ross and Cromarty, and Sutherland. |

Once an area has been declared a compulsory registration area in terms of s. 30 of the 1979 Act ('an operational area'), then broadly speaking (for details see later) on any sale of heritage within that area after it has been declared an operational area, the title of the purchaser must be registered in the new Land Register.

In urban areas, properties change hands about once every seven or eight years on average, and much less frequently in rural areas. On that average, it will therefore be at least a further ten years from the date when the area is declared operational until a majority of the titles in that area have been registered.

By way of comparison, registration of title has been compulsory in England on the same sort of basis since 1925, and it has proceeded district by district, although on a much slower programme than ours. By 1978, in England, more than 50 years after registration became compulsory, about 75% of the whole of the country was within compulsory registration areas; and about 50% of all properties in England had found their way onto the Register. See 1978 NLJ 131.

Registration of title is therefore a very gradual remedy for the imperfections which it eventually will cure.

152

## 13.19 Certificate of title

On receiving an application for registration of a title to a particular property the Keeper examines the whole progress of titles, satisfies himself as to its validity, and then certifies that the applicant is the owner of the property, which he identifies on an official certificate known as a land certificate. The extent and particulars of the property are similarly certified, subject to the burdens and conditions specified in the certificate; and subject also to certain inherent qualifications which apply to every certificate.

Therefore, the system of registration embodies machinery for the identification of:

(1) the property and its ancillary rights, with plan;

(2) the burdens affecting the title which include:

    (*a*) the conditions of tenure;
    (*b*) heritable securities;

(3) the owner of the property, with a specification of the nature of his right therein.

All this is contained in the land certificate issued to the owner; and the certificate exactly reproduces the entries in the title sheet maintained in the Register itself.

Again, under the Sasines system, this machinery exists in embryo in the search sheets maintained in Register House; but, of course, a new format is required and substantial additional information appears on the certificate of title. But, in Scotland, we are a good deal further ahead than, say, in England, where registration of title is superimposed on unregistered titles.

The land certificate almost wholly replaces and supersedes the title deeds; but a reference back to the earlier titles may still be necessary in limited and unusual cases. Therefore, the owner may still have an interest to retain his title deeds.

## 13.20 Overriding interests

Some interests are too ill defined or indeterminate to register on individual certificates; and certain interests are too insignificant to register. In any system of registration of title, this is inevitable. In the result, the legislature has the choice either:

(1) of eliminating all such interests in land, so that the certificate of title can be a complete and exhaustive record of every single minute item in or affecting that title; or

(2) of permitting these minor and indeterminate adverse rights to co-exist along with the registered title and to affect the registered land, although they may not appear in the certificate of title.

In Scotland, as in England, we have adopted the second alternative, and these adverse interests are termed 'overriding interests'.

Obviously, and ideally, overriding interests should be kept to the minimum; and the 1979 Act has gone further than the English system in curtailing these adverse rights which affect or 'override' every certificate of title, although not explicitly mentioned therein.

We are already familiar with the general principle of 'overriding interests' in Scotland in the sense that certain rights prevail against the infeft proprietor holding on a recorded title without these rights themselves entering the Register of Sasines. Thus, servitudes, although normally constituted by recorded deed, do not require to enter the Register of Sasines; and the same applies to public rights of way. Nonetheless, these rights prevail against singular successors in perpetuity. So also leases, under the Leases Act 1449, bind singular successors although not disclosed on the Record.

### 13.21 Rectification and indemnification

The Sasines system is negative in this sense that, unless a title is recorded, no real right is obtained. But it does not necessarily follow that recording automatically creates a real right; a recorded title is not beyond challenge. Suppose that A, improperly and without having right or title to do so, dispones land to B who in good faith and for value accepts the disposition and records it. Suppose the property really belongs to C who has an unchallengeable right and title thereto. The fact that B, in good faith, has recorded a title does not prevent C from attacking that title by an action of reduction. If he successfully attacks B's title and if that title is reduced, then C acquires a title to the property in place of B whose only remedy is an action of damages against A. If A cannot pay, B is the loser. C, the true owner, emerges virtually unscathed.

In contrast, in a system of registration of title, if B has become the proprietor on a fully indemnified registered title, and has taken possession, his registered title is beyond challenge. Even although C may be able to demonstrate beyond doubt that he had a valid right and title to the property registered in B's name, C cannot, as of right, reduce B's title. On the other hand, in certain circumstances a discretion is vested in the Keeper to amend or rectify the Register where it appears to him that a mistake has been made. But in any such case, whether the Register is rectified or not, if anyone can show that, as a result of registration or rectification, he has suffered loss, then he may be able to claim compensation from the state. The provision of state indemnification is discussed more fully below. Thus in the A–B–C case above, in a system of registration of title, where A wrongly and without any power to do so transfers his registered title to B (if that were possible), C cannot challenge B's title as of right, unless of course B's title is subject to a relevant exclusion of indemnity. He may, however, make representations to the Keeper; and the Keeper in certain circumstances may at his own hand rectify the Register by removing B from the Register and putting C in his place. If he does so, then he may have to compensate B for his loss; if he does not rectify the Register in this way but if C can satisfy him as to the rights which he has lost, then the Keeper would normally be bound to indemnify C.

Further, under the 1979 Act, the Keeper is not allowed to rectify the Register to the disadvantage of the proprietor in possession; and the court cannot so require the Keeper, except in certain specified situations. See below.

### 13.22 The Land Registration (Scotland) Act 1979

Section 1. This is the formal section under which the new Register is created known as 'The Land Register of Scotland'. The Register is public, and is placed under the management of the Keeper of the Registers.

Throughout the 1979 Act, the word 'register', 'registered', etc., mean the new Land Register and registration of title therein.

**13.23 (1) Commencement.** Section 1 of the Act, setting up the Register, came into operation on 4 April 1979 under s. 30. The remaining sections in Parts I and II of the Act, dealing with the mechanics of registration, have been and are to be introduced for particular defined areas of Scotland on the phased programme above referred to. This is to be achieved by Statutory Instrument; and different days have been and are to be appointed under s. 30 for different areas, as indicated in the timetable outlined above.

It follows that everything provided for in the Act and referred to in this Manual as regards the mechanics of registration, etc., apply only within an area which has been so declared to be an operational area.

'The commencement of the Act' in ss. 2–14 therefore means, in relation to each operational area only, the date on which it became operational.

**13.24 (2) Compulsory registration.** Within each operational area, and from and after the operational date as fixed in the Statutory Instrument, broadly speaking, every title must be registered in the Land Register when the property is feued, sold or leased on a long lease.

In addition, in limited circumstances, the Keeper may be willing to accept a title on a voluntary registration, but this facility will be sparingly used in Scotland, although more common in England.

Once a title to a property has been so registered under this section, thereafter (but only thereafter) every subsequent transaction relating to that property also becomes registrable, *e.g.* the transfer of the registered interest, a heritable security over the registered interest, a liferent of the registered interest, and generally any other transaction which affects the registered title.

Further, under s. 2(5) the Secretary of State may, at some future date, require certain interests in land, not then registered, to be brought onto the Register, so as to complete registration in a particular area. It is thought that this power will not be used for a very long time to come. According to Halliday: 'Ultimately, in each area, a stage will be reached when a substantial majority of interests in land within the area will have been registered in the Land Register, and it will be desirable to enable the Division of the Register of Sasines for that area to be closed. This subsection empowers the Secretary of State to require that interests in land in that area ... be registered'.

**13.25 (3) The effect of registration.** The effect of registration is defined in s. 3 as having the following effects.

(*a*) Under s. 3(1)(*a*) it vests in the registered proprietor a real right in the registered interest as also in any right, pertinent or servitude, express or implied, forming part of that registered interest. The right so vests subject only to:

(i) any adverse entries in the title sheet itself, *e.g.* heritable securities, conditions of tenure, notices of improvement grants, etc., actually entered in the title sheet and land certificate; and

(ii) any overriding interest, whether entered in the title sheet or not.

(*b*) Under s. 3(1)(*b*), on registration, all rights and obligations entered in the title sheet are similarly made real.

(*c*) Under s. 3(1)(*c*) registration also 'affects' any registered real right or obligation relating to the registered interest in land.

These three subsections, however, are qualified by a proviso to the effect that registration only has these effects insofar as the right or obligation in question is capable, under existing law, of being made real.

Further, under s. 3(3), from the date when a particular area becomes an operational area, certain transactions have to be registered in the Land Register which, at the moment, do not require to be recorded in the Register of Sasines. In these cases, registration is obligatory in the sense of being the only means of making the right or obligation real. These cases, where registration is obligatory, are:

the right of the lessee under a long lease;
the right of the udal proprietor; and
the right of a kindly tenant of Lochmaben.

In contrast, in any other case, rights can be made real by any other means which are effective at present. Thus under the existing law in non-operational areas a short lease is made real, under the Leases Act of 1449, by the granting of a lease in certain terms, followed by possession by the tenant. If the lease is a long lease, recording is an alternative to possession.

But once an area has been declared operational by the Secretary of State, then, on the granting of a long lease (*i.e.* a lease for more than 20 years), possession ceases to be available as a method of making the right real. The long lease must be registered, whether or not the landlord's title has been registered. In contrast, under a short lease, possession still makes the right of the tenant real, and indeed registration is incompetent.

**13.26 (4) Mechanics of registration.** The mechanics of registration are controlled by ss. 4–6 of the 1979 Act and are considered more fully in Chapter 33. They differ in some important respects from the procedure applicable to the Register or Sasines. Thus:

(*a*) A formal deed in normal form is still required to vest the right in the disponee, although the Keeper may be prepared to allow some shortcuts in the completion of the required formalities.

(*b*) No warrant of registration is required. Instead, under s. 4(1), the vesting deed is sent to the Keeper along with an application for registration of the title. If it is a first registration, *i.e.*, if the interest in land is held on a Sasines title and is being presented to the Land Register for the first time, the applicant sends all relevant Sasines deeds with the application. The Keeper examines the title, just as a purchaser would examine it, for validity, burdens, etc.; and may require the applicant to furnish further information, *e.g.* as to identification of the property, boundaries, servitudes, possession, etc.

(*c*) The Keeper must reject the application if:

(i) the property is not sufficiently described to allow him to identify it on the Ordnance Survey map;

(ii)  it relates to a souvenir plot;

(iii)  it is frivolous or vexatious; or

(iv)  the title is already registered, and the deed omits to mention the title number.

In addition, the Keeper has discretion to reject an application which is not accompanied by such documents and other evidence as he may require. On this principle the Keeper could, if he wished, reject a conveyance which was granted *a non domino*.

(*d*)  On receipt of that application for registration, the Keeper notes the date of receipt thereof which is deemed to be the date of registration, *i.e.* the date of infeftment, unless the application is rejected by the Keeper or is withdrawn.

**13.27 (5) The title sheet.**  Under s. 5, the process of first registration of a title involves, in the case of proprietary rights, *i.e.* resulting from a disposition, a feu charter, etc., the preparation, by the Keeper, of a title sheet to the property (or rather, to the interest being registered). The title sheet is a summary of all the salient features in the title to that interest and is dealt with in detail in s. 6. The essential content of the title sheet comprises:

(*a*)  a description of the property by reference to an Ordnance Survey plan;

(*b*)  the name of the proprietor;

(*c*)  any adverse entries in the Personal Register;

(*d*)  any heritable securities;

(*e*)  any enforceable real right or subsisting real burden;

(*f*)  any exclusion of indemnity;

(*g*)  such other information as the Keeper may think fit to enter.

Further, in terms of s. 6(2), the Keeper is empowered either to repeat verbatim rights or burdens, or to summarise these, or to refer to them in the title sheet by reference to a previous recorded deed, a copy of which is put up with the title sheet for completeness.

Under s. 5(4), overriding interests will also be registered by the Keeper in most cases, if drawn to his notice.

**13.28 (6)  Content of title sheet.**  The content of the title sheet is set out in detail in Part II of the Land Registration (Scotland) Rules 1980. The title sheet contains four parts, *viz*:

The property section – the description of the property
The proprietorship section – the identity of the owner
The charges section – heritable securities, etc.
The burdens section – conditions of tenure, etc.

Every title sheet will be given a distinguishing number (the 'title number'); and, in any future transaction relating to that title, the number must be quoted.

The title sheet is part of the Land Register and is retained permanently by the Keeper. It will be updated from time to time whenever information reaches the Keeper relating to any individual property in the Register.

**13.29 (7) Land and charge certificates.** For each individual owner, a formal copy of the title sheet, containing all the same information, will be issued on registration, and it will be updated from time to time as required. In the case of proprietary interests, the copy of the title sheet issued to the owner takes the form of a land certificate which certifies that he is the owner of the land described in the property section.

Lesser interests, such as heritable securities, liferents, etc., are also registrable; but only after the title to the property itself has been registered. Thus, if the infeft proprietor of heritable property in Renfrew holding on a Sasines title sells and dispones it to a purchaser, the purchaser must apply for the registration of his title as purchaser (s. 2(1)(a)(ii)).

If that same owner of property in Renfrew, instead of selling it, grants a standard security in favour of a creditor, the standard security will be recorded in the Register of Sasines. Registration in the Land Register is not required, and indeed not competent, merely on the granting of securities, etc.

If, however, the property in Renfrew has been sold and the purchaser has registered his title as purchaser, a title sheet will have been prepared in the Land Register and a land certificate will have been issued to him. If he then grants a standard security, the creditor must register that standard security in the Land Register and it is then noted on the title sheet of that proprietor (s. 2(3)(i)). In other words, once the title of the proprietor has been registered, every subsequent transaction is registrable in the Land Register; and nothing can subsequently be recorded in the Register of Sasines to affect that title.

As will be later explained, the land certificate issued to the registered proprietor, and any other writ issued or updated by the Keeper of the Registers, is guaranteed by the Keeper, with certain exceptions.

Because the Keeper guarantees every registered title, and every subsequent transaction relating thereto, he has to examine the title on first registration, as indicated above, in exactly the same way as the purchaser's solicitor examines the title at the present time in the Sasines system, in order to satisfy himself as to the validity of the proprietary title and the burdens and heritable securities thereon.

If he is not satisfied with the validity of the title, then he will normally register it, but will exclude indemnity either generally or on certain aspects of that title. If there is any exclusion of indemnity, this must be explicitly expressed on the title sheet and on the land certificate. See below.

**13.30 (8) The land certificate.** The form of land certificate, which mirrors the title sheet, is prescribed in Sch. A. Form 6 of the Land Registration (Scotland) Rules 1980 (as amended). An example is given in the Appendix of Styles. The land certificate consists of at least eight separate pages and, in addition, there may be incorporated in, or annexed to it, schedules of burdens, or copies of whole writs. Minor amendments have been made to the form of land certificate and certain other forms by the Land Registration (Scotland) (Amendment) Rules 1988 with effect from 1 October 1988. Further minor amendments to the form of land certificate and significant changes to the layout and content of some other forms were introduced by the Land Registration (Scotland) Amendment Rules 1995 with effect from 1 April 1995.

The salient features of the land certificate are as follows:

*Page 1* contains:

(a) the title number;

(b) the postal address;

(c) standard information about the indemnity.

*Page 2* contains a series of boxes for inserting the date to which the land certificate has been updated. As indicated above, the land certificate is a document issued to the individual registered proprietor. With limited exceptions, the land certificate will have to be produced to the Keeper by the registered proprietor on any subsequent transaction affecting the registered interest. The land certificate is then made to correspond with the title sheet by adding whatever additional information is required.

The successive dates to which the land certificate is thus updated will be shown in the boxes on page 2.

*Page 3* reproduces the plan of the individual property, an essential feature of the system of registration of title. It is simply a copy of the relevant section of the Ordnance Survey map and the property in question is outlined with a heavy red line or tinted or otherwise delineated. The title number appears again at the top right-hand corner.

Three scales of Ordnance Survey plan are used:

1:1,250 which will be used for all normal urban property. In exceptional cases, however, the Keeper may produce a special plan on a larger scale, *e.g.* 1:500, if that is necessary to show details.

1:2,500 which is the scale to be used for rural properties, farms, etc.

1:10,000 – a much smaller scale for use in hill and moorland properties.

One weakness of the plan system is that, because of limitations of scale, it is impossible in many cases exactly to define the boundary line in relation to the boundary feature, *e.g.* the centre line of a wall, etc.; but the Keeper overcomes this difficulty either by verbal description or by a system of arrows, mentioned below. Differing colours will be used in appropriate cases to distinguish different areas or rights.

The next pages of the land certificate reproduce the four sections above referred to, with the individual information for each of these four sections in the standard form.

A. *The property section.* The property section gives the title number, the County, the nature of the interest, the nature of the tenure, and a description of the property, primarily by reference to the plan. The verbal description is cut to the minimum.

Ancillary rights, *e.g.* servitudes of access for the benefit of the property will be added to the description, as additional proprietorial rights.

B. *The proprietorship section* gives the name and address of the proprietor, the date of his registration as such, and a note of the price paid.

C. *The charges section* lists the outstanding heritable securities on the property. Sections B and C may be updated by deletion of spent items and the addition of new entries, without reframing the entire land certificate afresh on each registration.

*D. The burdens section.* This is the final section of the land certificate and will normally be the longest one. For this reason, it is put as the last section of the land certificate to allow for additional pages and for the annexing of copy deeds, etc.

In general there are three ways in which conditions of tenure, etc., will be introduced into the title sheet, thus:

(*a*) Feu charter by ... etc. 'Note: Copy in certificate'. This means that a full and complete copy of the feu charter referred to in this entry will be attached to the land certificate.

(*b*) Feu charter etc. ... 'Contains the following burdens'. In this case, the terms of the burdens are reproduced verbatim, so that the full original text thereof is copied in the land certificate.

(*c*) Minute of waiver, etc. The import of the minute of waiver is then summarised by the Keeper in the entry itself, but is not reproduced at full length. The Keeper guarantees the accuracy of this summary.

In the amended form of land certificate introduced under the 1988 Rules general information appears on the last page and covers the following matters:

(*a*) Overriding interests. The full definition of overriding interests is contained in the interpretation section, s. 28(1). The land certificate details overriding interests, thus:

(i) short leases (*i.e.* leases not exceeding 20 years);

(ii) long leases where the lessee acquired the real right (by recording in Sasines or by possession) prior to the area becoming operational;

(iii) the right of crofters or cottars under statute;

(iv) servitudes – although in many cases servitudes will in fact be disclosed on the land certificate;

(v) public interests generally, except those which, on the Sasines system, require the recording of a deed in the Register of Sasines. This includes, *e.g.* matter affecting property under the Planning Acts, Housing Acts, Health and Safety at Work Acts, Fire Precaution Acts, etc. But a notice of improvement grant which, under the present housing legislation, requires to be recorded in the Register of Sasines will, under the new system, have to be registered in the Land Register as a burden on the title sheet of the property concerned and these will not override;

(vi) rights created by the Telecommunications Act 1984;

(vii) certain rights of licence holders under the Electricity Act 1989;

(viii) an interest vesting in the Coal Authority by virtue of s. 7(3) of the Coal Industry Act 1994;

(ix) floating charges (whether fixed or not);

(x) public rights of way;

(xi) the rights of the non-entitled spouse under the Matrimonial Homes (Family Protection) (Scotland) Act 1981;

(xii) real rights which have become real otherwise than by recording of a deed in the Register of Sasines, *e.g.* terce;

(xiii) rights of common interest and common property generally, excluding such rights as have been constituted by recorded or registered deed. Therefore, only the common law rights override under this head.

(*b*) The use of arrows on title plans. This has already been referred to above. The intention is to indicate the actual boundary line as defined in the title with reference to a boundary feature by the use of arrows. As already mentioned, because of limitations of scaling, the plan itself cannot accurately show whether the boundary line is, say, to the east or west of an existing wall or along the middle of the line of it. This may be important. To get over the limitations of scaling, the Keeper may indicate by the use of arrows (or, in the case of some irregular areas, a combination of arrows and letters) whether, according to the titles, the boundary line lies on one side or other of the physical features on the ground, or along the mid line thereof, as indicated in this note, but the information so given is not guaranteed. Alternatively, this information may be incorporated in the property section as a verbal addendum to the written description.

(*c*) Measurements. All measurements on title plans are subject to the qualification 'or thereby'; and indemnity is excluded in respect of such measurements.

(*d*) The land certificate must be produced on any application to the Keeper.

(*e*) Finally, there is a warning that no unauthorised alteration should be made to the land certificate.

**13.31 (9) Charge certificate.** The charge certificate is the equivalent document issued to the creditor in a heritable security and contains similar entries to those in the land certificate. The security document itself is attached to it.

**13.32 (10) Ranking.** Section 7 of the 1979 Act preserves the general principle which applies to recording in the Register of Sasines, *viz.*, that, subject to the terms of any ranking agreement, titles to land rank according to the date of registration. Thus if A grants a standard security to B and a second standard security to C, priority of ranking is determined by the order in which the securities are registered and not by the order in which they were granted.

As between the two Registers, Sasines and Land Registers, again, priority of infeftment determines priority of right (s. 7(3)), but with qualifications. Thus, A, infeft, grants a standard security to B which B records in Sasines under the present rule; and, at the same time, A dispones the property to C who applies for registration of the title. If B records the heritable security before C applies for registration, B is preferred. If not, B acquires no real right by his security but has a personal right of action against A under warrandice.

If, however, in the same situation, A sells land in an operational area to B and, simultaneously, sells the same land to C; and B and C are both *bona fide* purchasers for value without notice of each other's claim, the two dispositions to B and C are each registrable in the Land Register. The first to apply for registration will obtain a fully indemnified title; the latecomer will also obtain a registered title but under exclusion of indemnity in the respect of the prior title of the first party. In the event that both applications for registration are lodged on the same day, indemnity will be excluded from both titles.

Under s. 3(2) and s. 8(4), the Keeper should refuse to record either of these two dispositions if presented for recording in the Register of Sasines in the traditional way. Suppose, however, that, by oversight, the disposition A to B entered the Register of Sasines and, later, C applied for registration of his title. In this case, even although B has the first recorded title, the title has been wrongly recorded; and C would prevail over B.

**13.33 (11) Rectification of the Register.** In contrast to the present system, under registration of title the document of title issued to the registered proprietor is the land certificate which in turn exactly reflects the content of the title sheet. The title sheet and land certificate are the creation of the Keeper of the Registers and absolutely determine the rights and obligations of the individual proprietor to the exclusion of the contents of the earlier titles. That being so, there must clearly be, and under s. 9 there is, provision for correcting errors or mistakes in the title sheet and land certificate in relation to individual properties.

Thus, under s. 9(1), the Keeper in certain circumstances may, and if so required by the court or the Lands Tribunal shall, rectify any inaccuracy in a title sheet which is brought to his notice. But this power to rectify the register is very severely restricted by s. 9(3). Under that section, the Keeper may not rectify the Register to the prejudice of the proprietor in possession of the registered interest except in very limited circumstances; and so, with these limited exceptions, the proprietor in possession on a registered title is now immune from the challenge of that title on any grounds whatever.

The Keeper cannot rectify the title sheet and land certificate to the prejudice of the proprietor in possession except in the following circumstances:

(1) to note an overriding interest; but the overriding interest would, of course, override in any event, whether noted or not. This, therefore, does not truly prejudice the registered proprietor;

(2) where everyone concerned has consented;

(3) where the error was caused by the fraud or carelessness of the proprietor in possession – and therefore he has only himself to blame;

(4) where rectification relates to something against which the Keeper has previously declined to indemnify the proprietor in possession, by an express exclusion of indemnity on the title sheet and land certificate.

Similarly, on the application of an interested party to the Lands Tribunal or to the court, rectification may be ordered; but the Lands Tribunal and court are similarly restricted in ordering rectification to the prejudice of a proprietor in possession.

So, under registration of title, if a *bona fide* grantee registers a title and enters into possession of the registered land, then, assuming that indemnity has not been excluded, his title is immediately put beyond challenge and he does not require to possess on that title for ten years in order to validate it. This is a very considerable improvement on the present law of positive prescription, so far as the owner in possession is concerned.

This point is emphasised and underlined in the recent decision in *Short's Tr.* v. *The Keeper and Others* 1996 SLT (HL) 166.

In 1986, Short conveyed two properties by separate dispositions, both at under-value, to a purchaser who in turn, in May 1987, by two separate dispositions conveyed them gratuitously to his wife. All four dispositions were duly registered in the Land Register. When Short was subsequently sequestrated, his permanent trustee successfully applied for a decree of reduction of all four dispositions, on the footing that the two original dispositions at under-value were gratuitous alienations struck at by the Bankruptcy (Scotland) Act 1985 s. 34(4). See *Short's Tr.* v. *Chung* 1991 SLT 472. Having reduced the dispositions, he then applied to the court for an order requiring the Keeper to register the decrees of reduction under the 1979 Act s. 2(4)(c) as a transaction or event which is capable, under any enactment or rule of law, of affecting the title to a registered interest in land. There was clearly some force in the permanent trustee's argument in that a decree of reduction, in a Sasines title, is recordable by express statutory provision in the 1924 Act s. 46 and, if so recorded, subject to the qualifications in that section, has the effect of restoring the title to the state it would have been in if the reduced deed(s) had never been granted. In other words, in this particular case, the properties would have reverted to the debtor's estate for the benefit of his general creditors.

Notwithstanding a vigorous argument along these lines by the permanent trustee, however, the Inner House rejected the application as being incompatible with the provisions of the 1979 Act and the clear underlying purpose and principles of registration of title.

The trustee appealed to the House of Lords unsuccessfully. His arguments were again rejected, but on somewhat different grounds. According to the rubric in the SLT report, the House of Lords considered that Parliament could not have intended that reduction should be an event capable of affecting a registered interest. Accordingly, the decree could not be registered; instead, the trustee was entitled to claim compensation under 1979 Act s. 12(1)(b).

This decision is important in emphasising the difference in effect between the recording of a deed in Sasines, which creates a real right but is open to reduction in certain events, and registration of title, which, at least in a question with a registered proprietor in such circumstances as in *Short's Tr.*, produces an unchallengeable title unless the Keeper has qualified his indemnity. If, in the foregoing circumstances, the properties had lain in a non-operational area, the same result would not have followed and the properties would in fact have reverted to the permanent trustee for the benefit of the general creditors.

For a comment on and criticism of this decision, see Professor K. G. C. Reid 1993 SLT 97.

In the recent case of *Scottish Enterprise* 1996 GWD 26–1522 a member of the public maintained that the public had a right of access to and use of the waterfront, based on the provisions of an old feu charter on which, however, no infeftment had followed. The pursuers had acquired title to the area, which was registered in the Land Register. The entry in the Register made no reference to the original charter or its terms. The pursuers were granted interdict against protestors on the footing that, to challenge the validity of the title, the disposition in favour of the pursuers would require to be reduced and the Register rectified. As the decision in *Short's Tr.* demonstrates, this would not have been competent.

**13.34 (12) Indemnity.** Closely linked with the question of rectification is the matter of indemnity. Not only does the Keeper guarantee the validity of every title which is registered, subject only to those cases where he excludes indemnity. In addition, where the registered proprietor or a third party can demonstrate that, because of entries made in the Register by the Keeper, he has suffered loss, then he normally has a claim for compensation against the Keeper. This right to indemnity is expressly conferred by s. 12 in terms of which any person who suffers loss as a result of:

(1) rectification of the Register;

(2) refusal of the Keeper to rectify the Register;

(3) any error or omission in a land or charge certificate or in other information given by the Keeper in writing, *e.g.* in a search;

is entitled to be indemnified by the Keeper.

Clearly, there will be quite a number of cases where, because of known or suspected defects, the title is not marketable; and in these cases it clearly would be impracticable for the Keeper to guarantee the title absolutely. In exactly the same way, where a seller under the present system knows that there is a defect in his title, he is at risk if he grants absolute warrandice. In any such case, the Keeper is empowered by s. 12(2), on registration, to exclude the right of the registered proprietor to indemnity in respect of anything appearing in, or omitted from, the title sheet of that interest, by an express exclusion of indemnity endorsed on and appearing in the title sheet and land certificate.

Thus, A is the reputed owner of 100 acres. He has an *ex facie* valid title to 95 acres, supported by possession, but not to the remaining 5 acres. He sells and dispones the whole property to B. B applies for registration of the title. The Keeper will register the title to the whole 100 acres; but would exclude indemnity in respect of the 5 doubtful acres. The title to those 5 acres will be cured in the end of the day by the operation of the normal rules of positive prescription, *i.e.* possession following on a recorded or registered title for the relevant period; and, on application, the exclusion of indemnity is then deleted. For prescription, see Chapter 14.

**13.35 The implications of rectification of the Register**
In the case of *Short's Tr.* referred to at para. 13.33, Lord Jauncey commented: 'Nobody could accuse the Act of being well drafted.' That comment is supported in the note by Professor Gretton, reporting on the House of Lords' decision in 1996 SCLR 571 at p. 585. The drafting of the Act has been criticised in several other sources, many of which are listed as articles

under this chapter heading in the Reading List at the beginning of this volume. The criticisms seem well justified, even on the basis of the very few cases which have come to the Courts since 1979. On the other hand, while that is so, critics of the drafting must perhaps keep in mind that the Act was drafted hurriedly and under considerable pressure. It only just clawed its way on to the statute book in the very last days of the Labour government in 1979. If it had not then received the Royal Assent, registration of title would certainly have been delayed, possibly for a considerable time, and that would undoubtedly have been unfortunate. Nonetheless, the drafting does present problems.

One of these problems is highlighted in the decision in *Short's Tr.* Another more recent difficulty is discussed in *McCarthy & Stone (Developments) Ltd.* 1995 SLT (Lands Tr.) 19, where the owner of *dominium utile* on a Sasines title also acquired its own superiority. On the recording of that superiority title the *dominium utile* was consolidated with the superiority thereof, and as between superior and vassal, the feuing conditions originally imposed on the *dominium utile* in the original charter were extinguished. The title then came to be registered and the Keeper felt obliged to insert the burdens originally imposed on the now-consolidated title as subsisting burdens in the burdens section of the land certificate. The Keeper's view presumably was that, while the conditions were no doubt extinguished as between superior and vassal, there was a possibility that third parties had a *jus quaesitum tertio* to enforce them, and that *jus quaesitum* would not have been extinguished by consolidation. *McCarthy & Stone* applied to the Lands Tribunal for a discharge, but this in turn created a problem in that the Tribunal can only discharge an enforceable burden in which there is both a benefited and a burdened proprietor. Given consolidation in this case and the resulting extinction of the conditions as between superior and vassal, there could only be a benefited and a burdened proprietor if the applicant could show that there was a *jus quaesitum tertio* vested in an identifiable *tertius*. The Tribunal held that the original feu contract did not create a *jus quaesitum tertio*, and accordingly there were no benefited proprietors. That being so, it was not within their jurisdiction to discharge the conditions, which in their view no longer subsisted. Armed with this decision from the Tribunal, the applicants sought and obtained rectification, by deletion of all the original conditions except those involving joint maintenance obligations in respect of boundary walls.

A similar difficulty with subsisting restrictions arose earlier in the case of *Brookfield Developments Ltd.* 1989 SLT (Lands Tr.) 105, with a comparable outcome. See and contrast *Scottish Enterprise* 1996 GWD 26 1522 at para. 13.33, where in somewhat different circumstances the Keeper had registered a title notwithstanding a prohibition against alienation in the original deed relating to the same subjects. The case was dismissed, which underlines the creative element in registration although arguably, in this case, the prohibition against alienation had never been effectively made a real condition of the title. Whether or not that point was considered as relevant, the condition was overridden and extinguished by registration of the title and exclusion of the conditions from the title sheet.

Chapter 14

# THE EFFECTS OF POSSESSION: PRESCRIPTION

## 14.1 Sasine
'Sasine' in its original sense involved physical symbolic delivery on the ground. The last traces of sasine in this sense disappeared in 1858; and, since then, the real right of ownership of land has come to depend solely on title. Delivery (other than delivery of the appropriate title, which is not the same thing) and subsequent possession of heritage are no longer relevant factors. Thus, A, infeft in the lands of X on a valid progress of titles, has delivered by post to B, then resident in Hong Kong, a feu charter by A to B of the lands of X, in usual form. Delivery of the charter confers a valid personal title on B. By posting the feu charter from Hong Kong to the General Register of Sasines in Edinburgh, with warrant of registration thereon, B is able to convert his personal title into a real right; and, at the moment of recording, his real right is perfected, notwithstanding that B still remains in Hong Kong and that the property remains unoccupied for the next 30 years. At the end of that period, B still has the real right unimpaired, subject only to one possible qualification explained below.

But possession of heritage may be significant in three ways.

## 14.2 (1) Possessory remedies.
A person in possession of land has the right not to be dispossessed against his will except by judicial order. This right arises from possession alone and no title is required. Wrongful dispossession founds an action of ejection, allowing recovery of the land. But if the possessor does not have a title to the land, he is vulnerable to subsequent dispossession by judicial process.

Further rights arise where possession has subsisted for a period of 7 years, and where the possession was based on a *prima facie* title to the land, such as a recorded disposition. In this case the possessor is entitled to remain in possession of the land unless or until his *prima facie* title is reduced; and to protect his possession against an action of ejection or trespass. This rule was of considerable importance when the period of positive prescription was 40 years, but today it is of historical interest only and the 7-year possessory judgment is unknown in modern practice. Thus the reduction in the period of the positive prescription to 10 years has rendered these remedies largely academic.

For a recent case where two parties claimed ownership on competing titles, see *Watson* 1996 SCLR 81. The outcome was that the person in actual possession of heritable property was held not to be entitled to obtain interdict against anyone challenging his possession unless the challenger in turn is unable to show any right whatsoever to support his claim. On the other hand, if the possessor has *prima facie* evidence of title, that title must first be reduced before the challenger can succeed. Commenting on the case in SCLR, Professor Gordon refers to the possessory remedies and the quality of title required for prescriptive possession, although that last point was not at issue here.

**14.3 (2) *Bona fide* possession.** Where a person possesses land in the reasonable but mistaken belief that he is the owner, or is otherwise entitled to possession, he is said to be a *bona fide* possessor. As such he has certain privileges in the event of ultimate dispossession by the true owner. In particular, a *bona fide* possessor is not required to account to the owner for the fruits of his period of possession.

**14.4 (3) Prescription.** The general principle is that mere lapse of time, of itself, may operate to create, modify or extinguish rights or obligations in land. Two applications of the rule apply to heritable titles, namely, the positive prescription which applies only in the case of heritage, and the long negative prescription (formerly the negative prescription) which applies generally to all rights, including rights relating to heritable property.

The positive and long negative prescriptions now rest wholly on statutory provision, as interpreted by judicial decision.

All earlier statutory provisions were repealed entire by the Prescription and Limitation (Scotland) Act 1973, with effect from 25 July 1976. The 1973 Act therefore now provides a complete and self-contained statutory code for both the positive and the long negative prescriptions. However, the old law is to a large extent re-enacted in the 1973 Act, albeit with some significant modifications; and, in the result, the basic underlying principles of earlier legislation on both prescriptions are substantially preserved. Therefore, many of the cases decided under previous statutory provisions still remain relevant to the new code.

Under the 1973 Act, the period of the positive prescription in most cases is now ten years, but remains at 20 years in certain special cases dealt with below. The period of the long negative prescription is 20 years in all cases.

**14.5 Positive prescription**
The positive prescription operates actively to create, enlarge, or fortify rights in land which did not previously exist or which, previously, were at least open to challenge.

In feudal theory, all land belongs to the Crown. Therefore, at common law, in order to establish a good title to land, it is essential to trace back the title to an original Crown grant and to produce all the links in title intervening between the original Crown grant and the present proprietor. These links must, in themselves, be valid and sufficient to transmit the right. In almost every case, this would involve enormous labour; and the result might well be inconclusive. The original object of the Prescription Act 1617 was to secure a proprietor in possession against spurious challenge; but the emphasis has shifted and the main object of the modern legislation on the positive prescription is to limit the period of research and enquiry, in any particular case, to the title, in the progress, last recorded more than 10 years ago; and to declare that such title, so recorded, is absolute in the person of the possessor, no matter what other competing titles may be produced against him. The implications of this for examination of title are considered in Chapter 33. Note the two separate elements. There must be, firstly, a title; and, following thereon, possession for a period. In the result, the rule stated above that title alone, without possession, confers real rights, suffers a qualification to this extent that, in a competition, where two competing parties can both produce titles and infeftment in the same subjects, the one who can prove possession, in addition, for the ten-year period will be preferred.

Certain specialties arise in the case of land registered in the Land Register, and these are discussed later in the chapter.

### 14.6 The result of title and possession

If title and possession for the prescriptive period do coincide, all enquiry into the *initium possessionis*, and into the validity of prior titles, is altogether barred. It does not matter that the basic title originated from someone who had no right to grant it *i.e. a non domino*, or *a non habente potestatem*. It does not matter that the original title was granted in bad faith. Indeed, the basic title may have been granted *a non domino*, with the sole purpose of possessing thereon for the prescriptive period in order to create a real right in the subjects to which, prior to the granting of the disposition, the possessor had no colourable right or title.

One of the leading early cases on prescription contains the frequently quoted statement: 'It is the great purpose of prescription to support bad titles. Good titles stand in no need of prescription' *Scott* (1779) 3 RLC 334. This proposition is perfectly correct, so far as it goes. But, since a bad title can be validated by prescription, a bad title may prevail in a question with a title originally good on which possession has not followed. Accordingly, a good title may require possession following thereon to maintain it if, or to the extent to which, it conflicts with another competing title.

### 14.7 Practical consequences

The positive prescription has two important practical consequences:

**(1) *Ex facie* invalidity.** Prescription cannot cure a title which is itself *ex facie* invalid or which is forged. With these two exceptions, a recorded title initially defective from whatever other cause is validated and put completely beyond challenge by possession for the necessary period. So, if A occupies land without any right or title thereto, he can grant a disposition of that land in favour of himself and record it in the Register of Sasines. If he continues to occupy that land for ten years thereafter, then, on the expiry of the ten-year period, the disposition, which he granted in favour of himself and which was originally totally invalid, becomes valid and unchallengeable; and the true owner of the land, whoever he may be, is no longer able to reduce the disposition, as he could have done initially, and so loses his right of property altogether.

The meaning of *ex facie* invalidity is discussed in para. 14.2. It has caused some difficulty and has been discussed in a number of reported cases. It appears that a deed is *ex facie* invalid if, and only if, its invalidity is clearly apparent on its face and without recourse to extrinsic evidence. So a deed which is neither clearly valid nor clearly invalid is not considered to be *ex facie* invalid in the sense meant by the law of prescription and is capable of founding a prescriptive title.

The case of *Watson* is referred to above, para. 14.2, in the context of mere possession and the possessory remedies. In relation to prescription and the question of *ex facie* invalidity, the same case raises two further points.

Firstly, in an attempt to create a title for themselves, the parties in actual possession granted a disposition in their own favour *a non domino* since they had no prior colourable disposition. Presumably, the intention was to continue in possession on that title and in the fullness of time to validate it by prescription. However, at the date of the raising of the action, the prescriptive period had not run. The Prescription and Limitation (Scotland) Act 1973 s. 1(1)(b) requires that possession should follow on the recording of a deed sufficient in its terms to constitute a title. Further, under s. 1(1A) that does not apply if the deed is invalid *ex facie*. This echoes the earlier provision in the 1924 Act s. 16 which required possession following on an *ex facie* valid irredeemable title to an estate in land duly recorded. Given the similarity of the wording, it was not thought in the previous edition of the Manual that this represented any change in the law; and the preceding paragraph dealing with invalidity was written on that assumption.

In his decision in *Watson*, however, the Sheriff seems to have taken the view that, because the narrative of the *a non domino* disposition expressly stated that it was granted *a non domino*, that constituted an *ex facie* invalidity. Professor Gordon in commenting on the case in SCLR does not really deal with the point, being more concerned with the possessory elements of the decision. He does not, however, apparently disagree with the Sheriff.

Professors Reid and Gretton, in 'What Changed in 1994' and 'What Changed in 1995', positively expressed the view that to state in the narrative that the disponers had no title was an elementary blunder and automatically rendered the deed *ex facie* invalid. Professor Halliday in *Conveyancing Law and Practice*, para. 18–88, expresses the view that the disposition must contain nothing which indicates the defect, because the deed must be sufficient in respect of its terms to constitute a title. He seems to contradict himself, however, in para. 21–07, where he emphasises that the foundation deed must be free from intrinsic defects but extrinsic defects have no effect. In support of that latter view, he then cites the familiar case of *Cooper Scott* 1924 SC 309. The decision in that case would seem to support the view expressed in the preceding paragraphs, especially since the addition of s. 1(1A), referring to invalidity *ex facie*. But according to Professors Reid and Gretton in the 1994 edition of 'What Changed', there must be nothing on the face of the deed which discloses its invalidity. That is certainly what the 1973 Act now states. The question is what is meant by 'invalid *ex facie*'. In the writer's view, this necessarily means that, if a deed is invalid *ex facie*, the defect must be such that no external enquiry is necessary and that the Court, without requiring proof of the facts, would accept that the deed was invalid. So, if a disposition is not subscribed by the grantor, it is undoubtedly *ex facie* invalid. Likewise, if a disposition omits altogether a description of the subjects purportedly conveyed it is ex facie invalid. If, however, the deed contains statements which indicate that the grantor may have no title or that the grantor, although having a title, is not conveying the property conform to specific instructions in an earlier link in title, then that must be in all cases an extrinsic invalidity and so the deed is not invalid *ex facie*.

In *Cooper Scott*, which was a seven-judge case, a deed of entail was challenged as being *ex facie* invalid because, in the narrative of the deed, the disponers, who were trustees acting under a trust disposition and settlement, expressly narrated the terms of their instructions thereunder in the narrative of the deed of entail and then proceeded to convey the subjects on a destination which was patently disconform to the testator's instructions as earlier narrated. So, on the face of the deed, it was clearly invalid. But to establish the fact of its invalidity, it was necessary to go outside the four corners of the deed and to check the correctness or otherwise of the narrative by reference to the terms of the trust disposition. That was held by the Court to be extrinsic and therefore not a legitimate ground of challenge to the *ex facie* validity of the deed of entail as a foundation writ. As the Lord Justice-Clerk states, the sole question debated was 'Does the deed of entail suffer from an intrinsic nullity or does it not?' In considering the question, he then proceeds: 'The deed must *per se* afford complete and exclusive proof of its nullity. It must be, in short, a self-destructive title.' So, in this case, the deed of entail was not probative evidence of the instructions in the testator's will. Accordingly, the Court could not assume that the narrative correctly reproduced those instructions, and that could only be ascertained by extrinsic evidence, that is, by looking outside the deed of entail and referring to the trust disposition and settlement itself. Therefore, there was no *ex facie* or intrinsic nullity and on that footing such a deed can effectively operate as a valid foundation writ for the running of prescription as being sufficient in its terms to constitute a title. In considering such potential ambiguities, the dispositive clause rules, and in *Watson* that clause was clear and unambiguous. Lord Skerrington in *Cooper Scott* quotes Bell's *Principles* 2010, where Bell states that an infeftment is good as a title of prescription even where the title bore evidence *in gremio* of the objection, but the ground of that objection had to be collected extraneously. In the light of the judgments in that case and the Sheriff's criticism of the *a non domino* disposition in *Watson*, the comments of the two professors would seem unwarrantable.

Professors Reid and Gretton suggest in the publications above referred to that where the grantor of an *a non domino* disposition conveys the subjects to himself, as in *Watson*, that deed is a nullity. There is certainly some force in this argument, looking to the case which they cite, *Kildrummy (Jersey) Ltd.* 1992 SLT 787. The facts are simply stated. With a view to minimising stamp duty, the owners of a landed estate first set up a Jersey company. They then entered into an agreement with the company which took the form of a declaration by the company, delivered to and accepted by the estate owners, that the company would enter into a lease with the estate owners and would hold the lease in trust and as nominees for the estate owners as beneficial proprietors. Having entered into that arrangement, the estate owners then granted a lease to the company. A month later, the estate owners conveyed the estate to the company. A further month elapsed and the company then assigned their rights as tenants under the lease to the true proprietors. The Court held that the lease was a nullity because it was a contract entered into between the estate owners as the proprietors of the *dominium utile* and their own nominees, under the earlier deed of trust. They held the tenants' interest under the lease for the benefit of the true proprietors. In the view of the Court, in so doing, the true proprietors were in effect contracting with themselves and so the lease was null. Note, however, that there is no suggestion in any of the judgments in this case that the disposition by the estate owners as true proprietors in favour of their own nominees was void on the footing that they were contracting with themselves, which would seem to destroy the argument that a disposition by A in his own favour is intrinsically null.

That point apart, however, there is ample precedent for the view that a disposition by the true proprietor *a non domino* in his own favour is perfectly valid. Indeed, this device with modifications was regularly used, in the 19th century and before, in the setting up of entails. In any number of such cases a disposition by the proprietor in fee simple in favour of himself as institute and his heirs male, or whatever, as substitutes was treated, without question, as a perfectly valid disposition. Likewise, in the context of tenure in the feudal system, A as proprietor of the *plenum dominium* may grant a feu charter in favour of B. There is nothing to prevent A, later, from acquiring the *dominium utile* of the feu by disposition in his own favour. That does not automatically produce consolidation or *confusio* for which some further action on the part of the superior as owner of the two estates, *dominium directum* and *dominium utile*, is required. This may take a variety of forms; but whatever form it takes it inevitably involves a grant by conveyance or resignation by the same person as the proprietor of the *dominium utile* in favour of himself as his own superior which, subject to certain procedure, then produces consolidation. This is a familiar feature of the feudal system and is illustrated in *Zetland* (1870) 8 M (HL) 144. Lord Westbury at p. 154 deals with the point. There is no suggestion by him or any of the other judges in the House of Lords that a resignation *ad remanentiam* by the proprietor of the *dominium utile* as vassal in favour of himself as superior was in any way objectionable on these grounds. But any such grant is in essence a conveyance by A to A.

See also *Porteous's Exrs.* 1995 SLT 649. This was a case of competing claimants, one of whom, within the prescriptive period, recorded a disposition *a non domino* in favour of himself. Since prescription had not run on that disposition for the benefit of the disponee thereunder and since that was his only title, it was challenged by the pursuers on the basis that the disponer and disponee had no personal right or title to the property. The case was dismissed on other grounds, dealt with in Chapter 32, but, so far as the report discloses, there was no attempt on the part of counsel for the pursuers to challenge the validity of a disposition *a non domino* by the disponer in favour of himself as disponee, although it was attacked on other grounds.

**(2) Ambiguity of description.** In many cases, the description in a title is indefinite or ambiguous, in that the description is not precisely bounding on all sides. In such cases, the extent of the land contained in that title is defined by possession for the necessary period. In order for prescription to operate, the land as possessed must be capable of being reconciled with the land as described; but in the application of this rule an ambiguous description need not be given its most natural interpretation provided that it is given a possible interpretation, and prescriptive possession may produce a result which might not be anticipated from a first reading of the deed. For a recent and instructive example, see *Suttie* 1992 SLT 133.

If, however, a description is precise and bounding, possession of land beyond those precise boundaries cannot be founded on or referred to that title, in that the possession on the face of it contradicts the title. Hence the importance of the distinction between bounding titles and titles which are not bounding.

A bounding title in this context is one where the description so precisely defines all the boundaries of the land that the exact extent of it can be ascertained from the title itself.

Where the title is so bounding, corporeal property, *e.g.* land and buildings, etc., cannot be acquired by prescriptive possession beyond those boundaries; but incorporeal rights, *e.g.* a servitude right of access, or a right of fishings, may be acquired beyond the boundaries. The rule is the same even where the property sought to be acquired is being claimed as a part and pertinent.

Not infrequently, there may be some doubt as to the extent of the subjects conveyed or as to the nature of the title in relation to, for example, a particular pertinent. In such cases, to limit the liability of the disponer, but to allow for prescription to operate for the benefit of the disponee, it is common practice for the subjects or the pertinents conveyed to be qualified by some such terms as 'but only insofar as I have right thereto'. This then raises a doubt as to whether or not that is a title sufficient in its terms for the positive prescription to run thereon in terms of the 1973 Act s. 1.

It is generally accepted that a title so qualified will operate as a valid foundation title for the running of prescription, and that view is confirmed in the recent decision in *Landward Securities (Edinburgh) Ltd.* 1996 GWD 16–962, where a title in these terms was held habile to the running of prescription. The words 'but only insofar as I have right thereto' did not detract from or qualify the description which preceded them.

### 14.8 The quality of title and nature of possession
**(1) Earlier provisions**. Until 1976, the basic Act was the Prescription Act of 1617 (c. 12) which provided, in outline, that possession of land, following on infeftment therein, for 40 years, continually and together, peaceably and without lawful interruption, secured the right and title of such possessor beyond challenge, whatever the nature of any competing title may be, unless the title on which he possessed was a forgery. The infeft proprietor in possession had to produce, as the basis of his prescriptive right, a charter on which infeftment had followed, or an instrument of sasine following on a retour of service or a writ of *clare constat*. The period (or periods) of minority of the person(s), against whom prescription was pleaded, were not counted in computing the 40-year period.

The nature of the title on which the prescription proceeds, and the period of possession, were redefined in the 1874 Act s. 34; but that, in turn, was repealed and re-enacted by the 1924 Act s. 16. The 1924 Act provided that any *ex facie* valid, irredeemable title to an estate in land, recorded in the appropriate Register of Sasines, was to be sufficient foundation for prescription under the 1617 Act; and, further, that possession following on such recorded title for the space of 20 years, continually and together and peaceably, without any lawful interruption, should be equivalent to possession for 40 years under the 1617 Act. Further, no deduction or allowance was to be made on account of years of minority. This period was further reduced to ten years by the 1970 Act s. 8, except *quoad* foreshore and fishings vested in the Crown. The 1924 Act and 1970 Act had no application to servitudes or public rights of way or other public rights, for which the prescriptive period remained 40 years.

In *Hamilton* 1994 SLT 793 there were two competing titles, one *a non domino* and the other unchallengeable as a title to the subjects in question but on which the proprietor could not claim to have possessed. The proprietor holding the title *a non domino* maintained that he had had possession for the prescriptive period commencing before the coming into operation of the 1973 Act but continuing thereafter. Since the nature and quality of possession are thought to be the same both before and after the passing of this Act, the case is dealt with again in para. 14.11.

**14.9 (2) The 1973 Act**. Three distinct but parallel provisions are made in the 1973 Act for three separate cases dealt with in ss. 1, 2 and 3.

Section 1. This applies to interests in land generally, and covers, *inter alia*, ownership of land (both *dominium utile* and *dominium directum*) and recorded leases, but not servitudes.

Section 2. This deals with unusual special cases where, for technical reasons, the title has not been recorded, *e.g.* allodial land, unrecorded leases, etc. as in s. 2(2)(*b*) and (*a*) respectively.

Section 3. This deals exclusively with servitudes and public rights of way.

The general principle of each of the three sections is the same, *viz.*: if in any given case the owner (and his predecessors in title, if any) have possessed a heritable property or exercised a heritable right for the appropriate period following on the appropriate title, then on the expiry of the period, the validity of the title or right is put beyond challenge. But the detail differs in each of the three sections to take account of the different nature of the title, and of the property or interest in each case.

**14.10** *(a) Section 1. Interests in land: general.* So far as Sasines titles are concerned the provision takes this form:

Section 1(1). If:

(i) an interest in land has been possessed by the reputed owner (and his predecessors in title, if any), for a continuous period of ten years, openly and peaceably; and

(ii) that possession was founded on, and followed, the recording in the GRS of a deed sufficient in its terms to constitute a title to that interest;

then, on the expiry of that ten-year period, the validity of that title so far as relating to that interest is exempt from challenge except on the grounds that the deed is *ex facie* invalid; or was forged.

Section 1(2). The section applies to any interest in land, the title to which can competently be recorded. Obviously, this covers *dominium utile*, *dominium directum* and recorded leases as stated above; but, by virtue of the definition in s. 15, interest in land here specifically excludes servitudes, which are specially dealt with in s. 3.

**14.11** *Possession.* In terms of s. 1(1)(*a*) there must have been possession

173

for a continuous period of ten years (or 20 years under s. 1(4)), which has been held: 'openly, peaceably and without any judicial interruption.'

In one special case, under s. 1(4), possession must be for 20 years, not 10 years. This is where the right claimed by possession is a right to the foreshore or to salmon fishings as against the Crown, as owner of the regalia. This only applies as between the proprietor claiming the right and the Crown. Thus, if the Crown has granted salmon fishings on a Crown charter to a Crown vassal who in turn sub-feus on a charter which refers to fishings but not 'salmon fishings', and if the sub-vassal possesses the salmon fishings on that title for 10 years, he has a good claim to the salmon fishings as against his superior. The superior's right as against the Crown is established by the plain terms of the title and requires no possession to validate it.

This requirement as to possession is then further amplified by s. 4 dealing with interruption, by s. 14 dealing with the computation of the period, and by the definitions in s. 15.

The possession may be natural, by actual physical occupation on the part of the proprietor claiming the right; or it may be civil, by actual occupation on behalf of the owner by his tenants or some other person: s. 15(1).

In either case, 'possession' implies *animus*, *i.e.* it must be either in the belief that the occupant is in possession as of right, or with the intention of establishing a right. Possession in *mala fide* counts. But none of this is statutory.

The possession must be in support of and consistent with, the title, not 'in the teeth of the title'. See above, with particular reference to bounding titles.

The possession must be exclusive, and sufficient in extent to support the right claimed by it. The extent and nature of possession vary according to circumstances.

Under s. 1(1)(*a*) the possession must be for a continuous period of 10 years (or, under s. 1(4), 20 years) 'openly, peaceably and without any judicial interruption'. As to continuity, the term 'continuous' is interpreted *secundum materiam*. Thus, it is not necessary, in order to establish a right to salmon fishing by prescription, to show that the claimant has fished continuously, 24 hours a day throughout the ten-year period (or 20-year period in a question with the Crown); nor, in the case of a right of way, that someone has walked continuously over it throughout the 20-year period. On the other hand, mere occasional acts of apparent possession will not serve. There must be regular and continuing acts throughout the period.

Further, the possession must be open and peaceable, not clandestine or in the face of opposition.

*Hamilton* has been referred to already. This is an important case, hinging almost exclusively on the question of the nature, extent and quality of possession required to establish a prescriptive title. The reasons are summarised above – that the pursuer had an unchallengeable title to the subjects, but had never had possession; the defenders had a title recorded in 1950 but *a non domino* which was habile to acquisition by prescriptive possession. A number of acts of possession were alleged by the defenders and the critical question was whether, in the circumstances and looking to the nature of the subjects, these acts of possession, some of which were proved, were sufficient to establish possession of the whole subjects for a 10-year period openly, peaceably and without any judicial interruption. There had been no judicial interruption and the question therefore was whether there had been open and peaceable possession sufficient to constitute a valid title.

The Lord Justice-Clerk, in his judgment commencing at p. 796, lays down nine requirements which the alleged possessor must satisfy in order to establish title. These can be summarised briefly.

(1) There must be a habile title. In this case, although *a non domino*, the title was otherwise habile and was not significantly challenged.

(2) Possession must be continuous, open and peaceable without judicial interruption.

(3) It may be natural or civil which was important here because most of the acts of possession were acts arguably in the latter category.

(4) The required acts of possession depend on the nature of the subjects. Again, that was important here because the subjects were of an unusual nature, being largely a marsh or peat bog which, arguably, was largely unusable for any reasonable purpose.

(5) Possession must be directly referable to the title. That did not cause any problem in this case.

(6) It must be continuous. This did cause problems in this case, because the continuity was arguably insufficient to justify the defender's claims.

(7) *Tantum prescriptum quantum possessum*. Again, that was important here in that, arguably, such possession as could be established might be said to have been localised to very small areas, and might not justify treating that limited possession as possession of the whole. A distinction falls to be made between the cases where prescription is relied on to constitute a new right and cases where it is relied on for the purpose of establishing the extent of the right. That distinction has been criticised.

(8) In appropriate cases, circumstantial evidence is acceptable, with the proviso that the claimant must nonetheless establish whether there has in fact been requisite possession.

(9) The onus of establishing possession lies on the party claiming to have acquired by prescriptive possession.

This is undoubtedly a useful and exhaustive survey of the law of possession. It was particularly important in the case in question and the decision was very evenly balanced. One of the judges in the Inner House dissented, and in a subsequent article in 1994 SLT 261 Professor Rennie concludes that the defenders had not in fact made out a sufficient case.

If the possession is physically interrupted either because, for a definite period, the possessor excludes himself from possession or is excluded by another, that will interrupt the prescription and the period would have to start to run again entire from the date when possession was resumed. The same effect follows on judicial interruption, *i.e.* where a competing claimant has raised an action to exclude the possessor from his possession.

*Interruption.* For a discussion of acts of interruption and whether or not they can be treated as excluding a claim to continuous peaceable possession, see *Hogg* 1993 GWD 27–1712.

**14.12** (*b*) *Section 1. Interests in land under registration of title.* For titles registered in the Land Register, certain modifications are made to s. 1 by s. 10 of the 1979 Act. This is in recognition of the fact that, on registration in the Land Register without exclusion of indemnity, an immediate and unchallengeable title is conferred on the *bona fide* applicant, provided that he enters into and continues in possession. Hence in the normal case there is no need for positive prescription.

However, where an applicant for registration of title presents to the Keeper a title which is clearly defective, the Keeper may exclude indemnity, in which case, under the rectification rules, if the invalidity is later established by appropriate action by a competing proprietor, this is one of the cases where the Keeper can rectify the Register to the disadvantage of the proprietor in possession. Therefore, if a title is registered with exclusion of indemnity, it still requires the ten-year prescription to cure that defect. On the expiry of the ten-year period, the proprietor with a registered title excluding indemnity simply applies to the Keeper for the removal of that exclusion, whereupon his title immediately becomes virtually unchallengeable.

The detailed rules for positive prescription are set out in s. 1 (as amended), and follow closely the equivalent rules for Sasines titles. There are three requirements. First, the interest in land in question must be registered in the Land Register in the name of the person founding on prescription. Secondly, indemnity must be excluded by the Keeper. Thirdly, the land must be possessed in precisely the same way and for precisely the same period as for Sasines land (for which see above). Prescription is excluded if the registration proceeded on a forged deed and the applicant was aware of the forgery at the time of registration.

Contrary to what might at first sight appear, a title recorded in the Register of Sasines can still effectively compete with a registered title.

Suppose that, in an operational area, A is already in possession of one acre of ground on a title recorded in Sasines, which either expressly includes, or is habile to include, that acre; but the title to that acre is defective.

Under the present rule, possession on that title for ten years will cure the defect, and give A an absolute right thereto.

Suppose that B acquires an adjoining estate by disposition which expressly includes A's one acre. B registers the title in the Land Register, and so becomes the registered proprietor of A's acre. If, in that situation, A continues in possession for the ten-year period and so validates his right by prescription, A could then apply to the Keeper for a rectification of the Register so as to exclude A's acre from B's registered title. This is not one of the cases where B could object to rectification because, since A is in possession, B, the registered proprietor, is not the proprietor in possession. On rectification, B might have a claim against the Keeper, but he could not insist on retaining his title to the one acre because, lacking possession, the Register will be rectified against B, to exclude that one acre from B's earlier registration.

In the converse situation, where B registers a title to 100 acres in the

Land Register and where, after the date of that registration, A then records a title habile to include the one acre in the Register of Sasines, A can never prevail against B on a title recorded in the Register of Sasines because, the 100-acre title having first been registered, it is no longer competent to record a title in Sasines which includes any part of that 100 acres under s. 8(4) of the 1979 Act. If A is to compete with B, whose title is already registered, A himself must apply for registration of a title to the one acre. In normal circumstances, the Keeper will be prepared to accept that application and register A as proprietor to the one acre only, even although B is already shown as the proprietor of that acre and 99 more; but, when registering A's title, the Keeper will exclude indemnity.

If A then possesses the one acre on that registered title, excluding indemnity, for the period of positive prescription, he can then prevail against B, and require rectification of the Register in his favour in respect of that one acre because B is not in possession.

**14.13** (c) *Section 2. Interests in land: special cases.* Almost identical provision is made in this section for special and very unusual cases where, for technical reasons, the title is not recorded or is not recordable.

In contrast to s. 1, under s. 2 possession is founded on and follows the execution of a deed (whether recorded or not) which is sufficient to constitute a title to that interest. Note particularly that the initial title need not be recorded. But, in all these cases, the necessary period of possession is, under s. 2(1)(a), 20 years, not ten years as in s. 1.

**14.14** (d) *Section 3. Positive servitudes and public rights of way.* Under this section, alternative provisions are made for the establishing of servitude rights by prescription, taking account of the special nature of a servitude right.

Thus, under s. 3(1), possession of a servitude for 20 years following on the execution of a deed will establish the right beyond challenge, subject to the same exceptions as are provided in s. 1. The deed must be sufficient in its terms to constitute the servitude either by express provision therein or by necessary implication.

Alternatively, under s. 3(2), if a positive servitude has been possessed for 20 years, without reference to any written deed, the existence of the servitude as so possessed is exempt from challenge. This simply re-enacts, in a modified form, the former rule that positive servitudes can be created either by deed followed by possession or by mere possession. It underlines the peculiar feature of servitudes with particular reference to prescription in that a written title is not necessary, and nothing need appear on the record. In contrast, under s. 1, possession must follow on a written recorded title; and under s. 2, a written, though unrecorded, title. For an illustration of a case where the right was based on 20 years' possession alone, without title under s. 3(2), see *McLellan* 1987 GWD 21–803.

A similar provision is made in s. 3(3) under which a public right of way is established by 20-year possession. See *Richardson* 1982 SLT 237.

Further, under s. 3(4), possession of servitudes means possession of the servitude right by any person in possession of the dominant tenement.

There have been a number of recent cases – see the Digest of Cases at the beginning of this volume – on the establishing, or loss, of public rights of way, whether by active exercise for the prescriptive period or by disuse or abandonment.

*Cumbernauld & Kilsyth DC* 1993 SC (HL) 44 has been referred to in the context of public right of way in Chapter 11. It is an unusual case, probably without direct precedent. The case of *Burton* 1995 SLT 507 is dealt with under servitudes in the same chapter. This case, again, is probably without direct precedent. The question at issue involved a public right of way of ancient origin which was finally extinguished because it ceased to lead from one public place to another. The question was whether the individual owners of properties along the route of the right of way could continue to use it. It was held that the proprietors were so entitled, but the basis of the decision was not satisfactorily explored or explained. The continuing right is attributed to prescriptive possession, but the evidence of possession as establishing a servitude could hardly be said to be directly referable to the right claimed, since the right previously exercised had been exercised as a public right of way.

### 14.15 The long negative prescription
This is dealt with in the context of Examination of Title in Chapter 33.

### 14.16 Evidence of possession
In all the foregoing situations, whether in seeking to establish that a servitude right has been created or has been extinguished, the critical question frequently turns on possession over a period of years. In practice, possession is normally taken for granted unless there is something in the title to create a reasonable doubt. If so, it may be necessary to obtain a declarator of ownership.

In certain situations, to avoid expense and unnecessary delay, the parties may be content to rely on affidavit evidence by two or more parties as to possession or lack of possession over the relevant period; and it may be useful to obtain this coupled with indemnity to protect the interests of one party or the other. It is unlikely, however, that affidavit evidence alone would be accepted by the Court.

Similar situations arise in other contexts, *e.g.* under the Matrimonial Homes Act where affidavits have been lost. Again, facts reinforced by affidavit evidence with a statement of indemnity may serve the purpose. There is no situation, however, in the absence of any positive provision in the missives, in which a purchaser could be compelled to accept a title where there is any genuine possibility that the position is not in fact as it seems to be.

Part 3

# RESULTING RIGHTS OF SUPERIOR AND VASSAL

# Chapter 15

# THE ESTATE OF SUPERIORITY

## 15.1 Infeudation and subinfeudation

Immediately before the feu charter is granted, the grantor (the superior) stands at the foot of the feudal ladder, which reaches up, rung by rung, through his superior and his over-superior, each holding on tenure of and under the Crown as ultimate or paramount superior. In his position at the foot of the feudal ladder, the superior, immediately prior to the granting of the charter, owns the *plenum dominium*, and is in physical occupation of the *dominium utile* of, *inter alia*, the subjects which are now to be feued to the new vassal under the feu charter. In practice, the superior normally owns a good deal more land besides. By the granting of the charter, the superior is not divested. Instead, retaining his title to the land, he grants certain rights therein for the benefit of his vassal; but his title is now burdened with the subaltern rights of his vassal which he has created for the vassal under the charter. The superior's title is, and remains, essentially a title to land – his own original title to the *dominium utile* – with the same characteristics *quoad* transmissions, securities, etc., as any ordinary *dominium utile* title. So, where there have been successive sub-feus of the same land since the original Crown grant, the resulting position is that several separate persons in law own the same land, on separate titles, each for his own separate interest of vassal in the *dominium utile* at the bottom of the ladder, superior, over-superior, etc., upwards to the Crown.

Immediately after the feu charter is granted, as a result of which the vassal acquires his right to the *dominium utile*, a new and additional feudal estate has been created. The superior, granting the charter, remains within the feudal framework. Thus, the Crown feus to A who thus becomes a vassal of the Crown, holding land of and under the Crown as paramount superior. If A sub-feus to B, a new feudal estate is created of and under A. In the result, the Crown now has as its immediate vassal, A, and as its sub-vassal B. In other words, there are now sub-adjacent feudal estates of and under the Crown in the same land. Thereafter, if B then feus to C, a third feudal estate is created of and under B holding under A, holding under the Crown. And so on downwards *ad infinitum*. However, for practical purposes, B when sub-feuing, is divested in this sense, that, having feued and thus parted with the *dominium utile*, he can no longer enjoy physical occupation of the land itself. That right has passed to his vassal C as owner of the *dominium utile*. In lieu of his right to physical enjoyment of the land itself, however, B, as superior, acquires certain new rights by virtue of the charter B to C which he did not previously enjoy. It is these new rights which in sum make up the *dominium directum* and comprise in substance

181

the estate of the superior, although in form that estate remains a right and title to land.

## 15.2 Resulting rights of the superior

These remaining and emergent rights of the superior, which arise as a result of the granting of the charter, in essence comprise:

(i) a right to enforce conditions of tenure as against the vassal for the time being, in perpetuity, but subject to variation or discharge by the Lands Tribunal under the Conveyancing and Feudal Reform (Scotland) Act 1970; and

(ii) a right to collect feuduty in perpetuity, but subject to redemption under the Land Tenure Reform (Scotland) Act 1974.

In practice, the superior may also retain other rights, *e.g.* salmon fishings in or related to the land conveyed, and minerals thereunder, etc. Rights of this kind, so retained, are not properly speaking rights of the superiority at all. They are, instead, elements in the original *dominium utile* which have been separated from the *dominium utile* feued to the vassal and retained. The superior thus retains the actual physical enjoyment of these retained elements for his own benefit. To illustrate:

A owns four acres. He may sub-feu one acre to B, retaining his right of *dominium utile* in the remaining three acres. That retained right in the three acres is not one of the rights of superiority in any sense. Instead, A has simply split his *plenum dominium* into two parts, one acre and three acres; and of these two components, has sub-feued the one-acre part, but not the three-acre part.

In exactly the same way, if A owns four acres, he may sub-feu all four acres to B, but reserve to himself the minerals. In that illustration, the minerals are not one of the rights of the superiority, as such. Instead, the superior has split the *plenum dominium* into two components, surface and sub-adjacent minerals, and has sub-feued the surface only, retaining the *dominium utile* of the minerals.

Therefore, to treat reservations of this kind as part of the resulting estate of the superior, is not strictly accurate. However, in practice, minerals are often so regarded, because they are so frequently reserved in the feu charter.

## 15.3 Reform

In July 1991 the Scottish Law Commission issued a Discussion Paper, 'Property Law: Abolition of the Feudal System' (No. 93), which has far-reaching proposals for the abolition of the feudal system and its replacement by a system of absolute ownership. Under these proposals, feuduties would eventually cease to be exigible, the system of creating, enforcing and discharging land conditions would be altered and the paramount superiority of the Crown would disappear.

# Chapter 16

# FEUDUTY

## 16.1 The need for *reddendo*

Until 1 September 1974 feuduty was *inter essentialia*, a necessary element in any feudal grant, and had all the qualities of a real condition and of a pecuniary real burden. It affected the whole feu and every portion of it. The superior must be infeft when granting the feu; he requires no further or additional infeftment, beyond his original title to the lands, in order to secure for himself the benefit of this real burden. His right is reserved out of the grant to the vassal, and to the extent of that reservation he remains infeft on his original title. Accordingly, his right to feuduty necessarily antedates, and is preferable to, any rights, absolute or in security, created by or deriving from the vassal.

Again, a feudal grant constitutes a recurring personal contract between successive superiors and successive vassals in the respective estates of *dominium directum* and *dominium utile*. The contract is completed by the vassal's acceptance of the charter; he and his successors in the feu thereby become personally liable, by way of personal action at the instance of the superior, for implement of the feudal prestations. Once the contract is so constituted, the vassal cannot escape from or renounce it.

On the death of the vassal before the Succession (Scotland) Act 1964, the heir-at-law became personally liable though not bound to take up succession. Post-1964 Act, the executors, on confirming to the feu, become similarly bound.

On sale to a singular successor, the obligation to pay feuduty passes to him, and, when the original vassal serves a notice of change of ownership on the superior (1874 Act s. 4(3)) and the new vassal becomes infeft, he ceases to be liable for feuduty subsequent to the date of transfer.

## 16.2 Remedies for recovery

Arising out of these two distinct elements – personal contract and real burden – the superior has a variety of remedies for recovery of feuduty if the vassal fails to pay on the due date.

(1) *Personal action.* This is the ordinary action for payment of a debt arising *ex contractu.* The action lies against:

    (*a*) the original vassal and/or his successors, subject as above;

    (*b*) the sub-vassals of the vassal himself, *i.e.* where the vassal has in turn made sub-feus. Each sub-vassal is personally liable to the over-superior but only to the amount of the feuduty due to his own superior (the debtor vassal); and

(c) the tenants of the vassal, to the amount of their rents.

Where a sub-vassal or tenant is, by personal action, forced to pay feuduty to the superior in this way, he has a right of relief against the vassal.

(2) *Hypothec.* This is for last and current feuduty, preferable to the landlord's hypothec, over moveables on the feu. This remedy is very rarely used by superiors, because other remedies are available.

(3) *Poinding of the ground.* This is a real diligence available to the creditor in any real burden. Under it, he can attach all the vassal's moveables on the feu and those of tenants to the extent of unpaid rents. It covers all arrears, unless the vassal is sequestrated. The superior is, in that event, entitled to recover by this process only the current feuduty and one year's arrears. Like hypothec, this remedy is rarely used and the Scottish Law Commission has recommended that the remedy of poinding of the ground should be abolished (Discussion Paper No. 78, Vol. 2, Proposition 8.1).

(4) *Adjudication.* See Chapter 30 for detail.

All these remedies are alternative; the superior may select whichever suits him best. The whole feu is burdened; so the superior may proceed, as above, against the whole, or he can select any particular part of it which best suits his purpose. Suppose A feus 10 acres to B; B builds a house on one acre and sells the house and one acre to C. B retains the 9 acres, which remain unbuilt upon. Both B and C are each personally liable for the whole feuduty; and C's property (possibly the only part of any worthwhile value for a real action by the superior because it is the only plot built on) is liable (*e.g.* by poinding of the ground) for the whole feuduty.

The superior is entitled to exercise all or any of these remedies *ex lege*; there is no need to make express provision for them in the charter.

### 16.3 Irritation of the feu
#### (1) Non-payment of feu duty – *ob non solutum canonem*
This is not a remedy for recovery of unpaid feuduty; but it is the superior's ultimate sanction. The modern feu charter in practice always contains building conditions and restrictions which transmit, as real conditions, against singular successors, and, until 1 September 1974, had to include a provision for *reddendo*, which is also a real burden on the feu.

The superior is always entitled to enforce building conditions, and to recover feuduty, by way of the remedies already mentioned.

In support of, and as an alternative to, these remedies, the modern feu charter also invariably contains clauses known as the irritant and resolutive clauses which provide that, on failure to observe any of the building or other conditions, or on failure to pay feuduty, the vassal's right created by the charter is rendered void and becomes forfeit; whereupon the *dominium utile* is to revert to the superior, as if the charter had never been granted.

In addition to the conventional irritancy, but for non-payment of feuduty only, the superior has a statutory right to irritate the feu under an old Scots Act, the Feuduty Act 1597 (c. 250), even although the charter contains no conventional irritancy clause. This statutory remedy became available when the feuduty had fallen two years in arrears. The conventional irritancy clause normally (but not necessarily) repeats this statutory two-year-arrears provision.

By the Land Tenure Reform (Scotland) Act 1974 s. 15, no action of declarator may be raised, after 1 September 1974, unless at the time the feuduty is five years in arrears. This applies both to the statutory irritancy and to conventional clauses, whatever their terms.

On irritation of the feu, the right which the vassal acquired under the feu charter, and the relationship of superior and vassal thereby created, is extinguished. The *dominium utile*, which passed to the vassal under the charter, reverts to the superior just as if the charter had never been granted. Further, any real rights deriving from the vassal are extinguished along with the vassal's right; and this includes the rights granted by the vassal to his own sub-feuars, heritable creditors, and tenants. The *dominium utile* reverts into the hands of the superior as it stands at the date of irritation. Accordingly, the superior on irritation becomes entitled to all buildings and other erections on the feu and all heritable plant and machinery. No compensation is payable by the superior to the vassal, regardless of the value of the feu, buildings, etc. See *Sandeman* (1885) 12 R (HL) 67; and *cf. Pickard* 1970 SLT (Sh Ct) 63.

**16.4 Restraints on the right to irritate.** Clearly, this is a very stringent remedy. There are various statutory provisions designed to prevent oppression of the vassal himself, of his sub-feuars, creditors and others deriving right from him.

In the first place, under the Feuduty Act 1597, and also under any conventional irritancy clause (notwithstanding provision in that clause to the contrary), the superior cannot irritate the feu except after judicial process, taking the form of an action of declarator *ob non solutum canonem*.

To protect the interests of persons deriving right from the vassal, it is provided by statute that such an action of declarator must be served not only on the last entered vassal, but also on sub-feuars, heritable creditors, and others who, at the date of the raising of an action, appear to have some real right in, or security over, the *dominium utile* as disclosed in a 20-year search.

Special provisions also apply to the finality of the decree – see the Conveyancing Acts Amendment Act 1887 s. 4 and the Conveyancing Amendment (Scotland) Act 1938 s. 6.

**16.5 Purging the irritancy.** By virtue of the 1887 Act s. 4, it is competent in all cases to purge the irritancy, and to escape from the effect of irritation, by payment or performance at any time before the extract decree is recorded. Further, in the case of failure by the vassal to observe an obligation *ad factum praestandum*, the court (on cause shown) will normally allow the vassal a reasonable period within which to implement the breached condition – *Duncanson* (1878) 15 SLR 356.

In practice, irritation of the feu is rare because the effect, on the vassal, is so severe. But nonetheless, it is the ultimate sanction *in terrorem* which must always be taken into the reckoning.

For a case involving irritancy for failure to complete buildings within a time limit and a parallel application to the Lands Tribunal for a variation of that condition, see *Miller & Partners Ltd.* 1974 SLT (Lands Tr.) 9. The application was refused and so, presumably, decree of irritancy was duly granted in the sheriff court; but that is not reported.

Compare *Ross & Cromarty District Council* 1983 SLT (Lands Tr.) 9.

Superiors raised an action of irritancy for breach of feuing conditions. The vassal applied to the Lands Tribunal for a variation; and the superiors moved the Tribunal to sist the application. The Tribunal refused the superiors' request, and granted the application, leaving it to the Court of Session to determine whether or not an impurgeable irritancy had meantime been incurred.

### 16.6 (2) Conventional irritancies – for other than non-payment of feu duty

The statutory provisions mentioned above apply only to irritancy for non-payment of feuduty. Irritancy following upon a failure to comply with an obligation other than to pay feuduty is not automatically purgeable; rather it is within the court's discretion whether to allow purgation or not. Although the statutory provisions apply only to irritancy on the ground of non payment of feuduty, a superior would probably be able to rely on a decree in an action of irritancy only where an extract had been recorded or registered.

Irritancy is not available where the feuing condition has been discharged.

### 16.7 Allocation of feuduty

This involves some specialties. Feuduty is a *debitum fundi*. It is a real burden secured upon the whole of the feu and every part thereof. Suppose that A feued 10 acres to B for a feuduty of £100 per annum. That feuduty is a real burden on the whole 10 acres; and A, as superior, can proceed against the whole 10 acres, or any part thereof, if the feuduty is not paid. Suppose that B builds 10 houses, each with one acre of ground and sells off each house to a separate purchaser. Each such house remains liable to the superior, A, for payment of the whole feuduty of £100 per annum. If the whole feuduty is not paid, A can proceed against the individual owner of one particular house for recovery of the whole amount due. In particular, the superior is not affected by, and has no concern with, the apportionment of the *cumulo* feuduty of £100 in the respective dispositions of the 10 individual houses.

The same general principles apply to building conditions and restrictions. Such conditions are real burdens on the whole feu and every part thereof. Suppose, in the previous illustration, that the feu charter in favour of B contained a condition under which the vassal had to maintain 10 houses on the feu in all time coming. Suppose one house burns down. The proprietor thereof collects his insurance money, leaves the country and makes no effort to rebuild it. In the last resort, refusal by a vassal to observe feuing conditions involves irritation of the feu. In this illustration, refusal by one proprietor to rebuild his house involves the other 9 proprietors in the risk of forfeiture.

### 16.8 Statutory right of vassal to allocate.
Until the 1970 Act, the liability of a proprietor of part of a feu could not be limited except with the sanction or consent of the superior. The appropriate process is allocation of feuduty. When a proportion of the original *cumulo* feuduty has been validly allocated on a portion of the original feu, the proprietor of that portion is, thereafter, liable only for the proportion of feuduty so allocated; and, so far as conditions are concerned, while his portion remains subject to the orig-

inal feuing conditions in the charter, he is no longer affected by failure to observe those conditions on other portions of the feu. The resulting position is, substantially, as if the portion of the feu on which feuduty has been allocated had been the subject of a separate feu charter. Clearly, the superior's position is adversely affected by allocation, in that the burden of collection is increased and his remedies are restricted. A superior would, therefore, normally only agree to an allocation of feuduty subject to augmentation.

If the feuduty is not allocated, and if one of the proprietors of a portion of the feu has paid the whole feuduty to the superior, he has a right of relief against the proprietors of the other portions and may call on the superior to assign his remedies for recovery (Burns' *Practice*, p. 266); but this is never satisfactory.

**16.9 Allocation by the superior.** Prior to the 1970 Act, there were three ways in which an allocation of feuduty might be obtained by agreement of the superior.

(*a*) *Express provision in the original charter.* Where, at the time of the granting of the charter, a split-up of the feu was envisaged, as on a building estate, it was quite common for the parties to agree, by express provision in the *reddendo* clause, that the vassal, at his own hand, might subsequently allocate portions of the *cumulo* feuduty on parts of the feu. To avoid prejudice to the superior, this power was conferred on the vassal subject to certain restrictive conditions which normally included (i) the permitted amounts of feuduty, and permitted areas on which the same might be allocated; and (ii) conditions which must first be satisfied before the allocation can be made – normally completion of buildings on the portion of the feu on which feuduty is to be allocated, followed by sale of that portion to a purchaser.

Any allocation made by the vassal which complies with these conditions is a valid allocation and binds the superior. Any purported allocation by the vassal which does not comply with these conditions is not binding on the superior. See *Pall Mall Trust* 1948 SC 232.

(*b*) *Charter of novodamus.* This is perfectly competent but not now normally used for allocations.

(*c*) *Memorandum of allocation.* This is a simple statutory method of obtaining an allocation, and may take one of two forms:

(i) Endorsed memorandum. By the 1874 Act s. 8, the vassal may obtain a memorandum in the form of 1874 Act Schedule B endorsed on his own title, whether before or after the recording thereof, signed by the superior or his agent but not requiring to be formal or tested.

(ii) Separate memorandum. By the 1924 Act s. 13, the same result can be achieved by the recording of a separate, formal, memorandum signed by the superior himself.

Either memorandum is, by statute, binding on 'all others having interest', presumably all future proprietors of *dominium directum* and *dominium utile* and others having a real right therein; but not on existing heritable creditors who do not consent to it.

*(d) Implied allocation.* These are the formal methods by which an allocation may be obtained; but an allocation may be inferred from the actings of the superior. See *Nelson's Trustees* (1906) 6 F 475 and *Pall Mall Trust* 1948 SC 232.

### 16.10 Statutory allocation by the vassal under the 1970 Act
In practice, feus and buildings are very often split without any formal allocation of feuduty being obtained; but liability for the *cumulo* feuduty is informally apportioned (the term 'allocated' is often used, misleadingly), in the respective dispositions, amongst the owners of the individual parts, *e.g.* a tenement of 6 flats subject to a feuduty of £30. The flats are all sold separately; and each disponee is taken bound, in his disposition, to pay £5 of the *cumulo* feuduty. But this is no concern of the superior and is not of his doing. He continues to collect £30 in one sum from the original owner of the whole tenement and his successors – usually, the purchaser of the last flat to be sold. He in turn collects £5 per annum from the other 5 flat-owners.

The superior plays no part in these arrangements. He is usually quite unaware that individual flats have been sold, and knows nothing of the purchasers of individual flats nor of the apportioned feuduty.

Note also that, in the illustration, $6 \times £5 = £30$ which exactly equals the *cumulo* feuduty. Often, in practice, the sum of the apportioned feuduty exceeds the *cumulo*.

### 16.11 The salient points of the 1970 provisions
(1) The procedure is alternative to existing procedures, by minute, etc.

(2) Any proprietor, whose feuduty is not allocated, may serve a notice on the superior or his agent three months before the next term of payment (usually Whitsunday or Martinmas).

(3) The form of notice has been prescribed by the Allocation of Feuduty etc. (Form of Notice) Regulations 1971. It is very brief, and simply states:

    the name of the superior;
    the amount to be allocated;
    the part of the feu on which allocation is made – but no formal description is required;
    the name of the owner thereof.

### 16.12 Objection by superior.
Allocation may prejudice the superior for reasons already stated. The Act protects his position by providing that, if the superior objects to the amount proposed to be allocated on the portion of the feu, he has the right to apply to the Lands Tribunal. In *Moray Estates Development* 1971 SC 306 a superior objected to a notice on the grounds that 'it was not known that the amount of the portion of feuduty specified in the notice of allocation has been apportioned', etc. The Inner House, on a stated case from the Lands Tribunal, held that, since the superior could not check the validity of the amount, without investigation, he was entitled to object.

### 16.13 Proceedings before the Tribunal.
Note the following points.

(1) Only the superior can apply to the Lands Tribunal, never the vassal;

s. 4(1). Any objection must be lodged within 28 days of receipt of the notice.

(2) The only ground of application is objection to the amount to be allocated; s. 4(1). (But see *Moray Estates Development* above.)

(3) On application to the Tribunal, notice must be given by the Tribunal to all interested proprietors, and may be given to others at the discretion of the Tribunal; s. 4(2).

(4) The Tribunal must then allocate a portion of the feuduty on every portion of the feu; s. 4(1). The onus lies on the Tribunal to investigate the title in order to determine how the *cumulo* feuduty may be fairly allocated on the whole.

(5) The Tribunal will not normally disturb the existing basis of apportionment, and there will normally be no rearrangement of apportioned feuduties under this procedure. But:

(*a*) under s. 5(2), the total of the allocated feuduties must not exceed the *cumulo*; and

(*b*) under s. 4(1), the Tribunal is to allocate in such manner as they consider reasonable. This may produce different amounts on allocation compared with the informal apportionment, *e.g.* in a tenement, if the apportioned feuduties add up to more than the *cumulo*. For a curious case, where the Tribunal did reallocate apportioned feuduties on what they considered to be a more equitable basis, see *Barr* 1972 SLT (Lands Tr.) 5. A tenement had been partially demolished. It comprised a public house, a betting shop, and 15 houses. The Tribunal were pressed by the objecting superior to ignore the actual apportionment in the titles, and to allocate substantially the whole on the pub and shop, and nominal amounts only on the demolished houses. They refused to do so, but did not stick to the apportioned amounts in the title either. The interesting concept emerges of a feuduty allocated on a cube of air without surrounding walls or roof. 'The interests of co-feuars whose dwellinghouses have been demolished will still subsist under feudal tenure.' But the Tribunal's President concedes that 'if the Tribunal allocates feuduty on non-existent houses' (some of whose owners had disappeared) 'the superior is likely to incur loss on those allocations'.

(6) An order, when given by the Tribunal, supersedes all existing informal apportionments and invalidates any notice of allocation given under the Act, however long before; s. 5(3) and (4). But any prior formal allocation by the superior is unaffected.

(7) An order by the Tribunal need not be, but normally is, recorded in the Register of Sasines. In a registered transaction, the Keeper will enter the amount of the allocated feuduty in the title sheet.

(8) An order by the Tribunal takes effect at the next term occurring not less than three months after the date of the order.

**16.14 Effect of allocation by notice or order.** In all cases, the allocation effected by notice or order is as if there had been a duly recorded memorandum of allocation under the law in force prior to the Act; s. 5(5). In addition, under s. 5(1), when feuduty has been allocated, that portion of the feu on which allocation is effected 'shall, in relation to the rights and obligations of the proprietors of the remainder of the feu, be treated as if it had never formed part of the *cumulo*'.

### 16.15 Ground annuals
The same provisions, *mutatis mutandis*, are applied to ground annuals under s. 6.

### 16.16 Contracting out
By s. 7, any agreement or other provision, however constituted, is void, in so far as it purports to exclude or limit the operation of any of the provisions of ss. 3 to 6.

### 16.17 Redemption of feuduty
This was originally always a matter for agreement; and the superior could refuse to redeem without reason assigned. The common law rule has been altered by statute.

### 16.18 (1) Voluntary redemption
Under the 1974 Act s. 4, every vassal is entitled to redeem an allocated feuduty by giving notice to the superior and paying the redemption price at or before any term of Whitsunday or Martinmas; s. 4(1) and (2). The redemption price is the cash amount required to purchase a holding of 2½% Consols. sufficient to yield the annual amount of feuduty. The figures are published each month in the *Journal of the Law Society of Scotland*.

### 16.19 Unallocated feuduty.
Under s. 4(7), feuduty includes any *cumulo* feuduty which is unallocated and any part of a *cumulo* feuduty which has been allocated. Suppose A owns a flat in a tenement and, in the titles, £5 of the *cumulo* feuduty of £30 is apportioned on the flat, but not allocated. A may redeem the *cumulo* feuduty of £30 voluntarily but not his own apportioned £5 alone. This is no great hardship, in that any proprietor can now serve a notice of allocation three months prior to the term and allocate the £5 on his flat, which he can then redeem. On the other hand, if A sells his flat subject to an unallocated feuduty, there is no obligation whatever on him to redeem; and that feuduty will continue to subsist indefinitely.

Professor Love, in an article in 1976 JLS 364, takes the view that, on a correct construction of the Act, unallocated feuduty may be redeemed voluntarily, but not compulsorily. This view is not, however, generally held.

### 16.20 Effect of redemption.
The only effect of redemption is to extinguish future liability for payment of the annual sum. Otherwise, the tenure is totally unaffected. So, voluntary redemption is not equivalent to the purchase of the *dominium directum*, and the same applies to compulsory redemption. There is no actual or deemed consolidation of *dominium directum* and *dominium utile*; and all the conditions of tenure, including irritant and resolutive clauses, other than the *reddendo* clause, continue to be enforceable in perpetuity. Therefore, if the object of redeeming feuduty is to extinguish the conditions of tenure rather than to get rid of the annual payment, then a contract to purchase the superiority and a disposition thereof under the old rules is the appropriate method, followed by consoli-

dation; and for that purpose a somewhat higher price may have to be paid than the current going price of Consols. See later under Consolidation – Chapter 29.

**16.21 Heritable creditors on the superiority**. Redemption of feuduty (voluntary or compulsory) has no adverse effect on heritable creditors on the *dominium utile* and they need not be consulted.

On the other hand, it does have a very adverse effect on heritable creditors on the superiority in that, by redemption, the total value of the superiority can disappear without the creditor being paid anything. So, by these provisions, heritable creditors on superiorities might be seriously prejudiced. To prevent this, s. 4(5) provides that redemption is not to prejudice the rights of existing heritable creditors who are not parties thereto. In other words, in a question with heritable creditors, unless they consent, redemption is ineffective.

With voluntary redemption, the result seems to be that the feuduty would revive for the benefit of non-consenting creditors, but the Act is silent on this point.

The practical effect is that no one should redeem a feuduty without being satisfied that there are no securities on the superiority. Admittedly, the superior is bound to indemnify, and this is made explicit in the Act; but if the superior meantime has gone bankrupt, or disappeared, then the vassal is bound to be prejudiced.

**16.22 (2) Compulsory redemption of feuduty**
When a feu is conveyed for valuable consideration (*i.e.* on sale), the feuduty is automatically redeemed under the 1974 Act s. 5. This does not apply, however, on any other type of disposal, *e.g.* on gift, on death, or in security; none of these events trigger off compulsory redemption; s. 5(1).

Compulsory redemption applies:

(i) where the contract of sale was completed on or after 1 September 1974; or

(ii) if there was no contract of sale (which is rare), then on the date of entry on or after 1 September 1974.

The redemption date in all these cases will normally be the actual date of entry, whether, at that date, a disposition has been delivered or not; but by s. 5(2), if entry is given before the date of the contract, which is rare, then the redemption date is the subsequent date of the contract (or disposition if there is no contract).

**16.23 Unallocated feuduty**. There is no compulsory redemption under s. 5 on the sale of part of a feu on which no part of the *cumulo* feuduty has been allocated.

Suppose there is a tenement of six flats which has a *cumulo* feuduty of £30 payable thereon. Before 1 September 1974, a flat (or more than one) has already been sold on a separate title to a separate purchaser without allocation of feuduty but with £5 of feuduty apportioned on that flat. The same flat is later sold by its owner after 1 September 1974. Since the feuduty is not allocated, there is no obligation on the seller to redeem, and the feuduty continues in perpetuity.

Suppose there is a single feu, subject to a single feuduty, which is sold entire after 1974. Feuduty is compulsorily redeemable. But if the same property is sold in parts, under separate contracts (even although to the same person) with an apportionment of feuduty on each portion, there would seem to be no obligation to redeem; and, instead, the apportioned feuduty would continue in perpetuity. So also if, prior to sale, A, the seller, conveys part of the feu to a nominee, with an apportionment on that part.

If, on 1 September 1974, a flat in a tenement had already been sold, and if feuduty had been allocated on that flat; and if the flat is later sold, feuduty on that flat is compulsorily redeemable. In the same situation, however, if the proprietor of the remainder of the tenement later sold a further flat, apportioning part of the remaining *cumulo* feuduty on the flat so sold, there would be no obligation on him to redeem the whole or that part of the feuduty. Remember, however, in relation to these illustrations, that allocation of feuduty may arise by implication. Suppose, again, there is a tenement of six flats with a *cumulo* feuduty of £30. One flat is sold, and feuduty of £5 apportioned thereon in the disposition. The owner of that flat can now give notice and obtain an allocation of feuduty on that flat under the 1970 Act; and in many cases has done so. By implication, the remaining £25 of feuduty would be allocated on the remaining 5 flats as a whole. Therefore, if the whole remaining 5 flats in the tenement were sold on a single contract to a single purchaser, a feuduty of £25 has been allocated by implication, and is therefore compulsorily redeemable.

**16.24 Procedure on redemption.** Section 5(6). Where compulsory redemption takes place, the feuduty is automatically deemed to have been redeemed on the redemption date; s. 5(1). That applies, whether or not notice has been given to the superior and whether or not payment has been made. (Contrast voluntary redemption under s. 4, where feuduty is redeemed only if due notice and payment has been made.)

However, to avoid prejudice to the superior, the redemption money, and arrears of feuduty, remain a real burden on the feu until notice is given. To release the feu from that real burden, the seller or purchaser must give notice to the superior under s. 5(6) and Schedule 2. The notice runs:

Take notice that, in terms of s. 5 of the 1974 Act, the feuduty of £  per annum exigible in respect of (here describe) as at        , will be deemed to have been redeemed at that date by reason of entry having been taken to the said subjects under an obligation to convey by (the name of the seller) dated        .'

When two months have elapsed from the date of the giving of that notice (or from the date of entry if later), the feu is then automatically disburdened of the real burden for redemption money and arrears of feuduty; and the superior automatically loses his real security therefor. Obviously, this is a serious matter for the superior; and he can only prevent it happening and retain his real security, if:

(i) he raises an action against the seller for payment of the redemption money and arrears of feuduty;

(ii) having obtained warrant to cite the seller, he then applies to the court for an order continuing the real burden for such additional period as is reasonable to enable the superior to recover the amount due to him;

(iii) he records that order in the General Register of Sasines, or has it entered in the title sheet.

The whole of the foregoing must be completed within the two-months' post-redemption period; s. 5(8). If so, then the real security for redemption money may continue beyond the two-months' period; if not, real security is lost altogether.

Even if the real security is so continued, the superior may not recover the amount due from the purchaser unless the court is satisfied that he cannot reasonably practicably recover from the seller; s. 5(7).

**16.25 Heritable creditors**. The same rules apply here as on voluntary redemption; and heritable creditors of the superiority are not to be prejudiced by compulsory redemption. But the effect is not expressed and is not clear. Arguably, under s. 4, payment to the superior of redemption money without a creditor's consent is not 'due payment' for the purposes of s. 4(3) and so there is no effective redemption. But under s. 5(1), on sale, redemption is immediate, automatic and unconditional. What rights have non-consenting creditors under s. 5(10)? Does the redemption money remain as a real burden for their benefit, under s. 5(5)? The Act is wholly silent.

### 16.26 (3) Apportionment
Nothing is said in the 1974 Act about apportionment, but the Apportionment Act 1870 applies. The current feuduty running from the last term to the redemption date is deemed to accrue from day to day and is apportionable accordingly.

### 16.27 (4) Superior's receipt
With voluntary redemption, notice and payment are both necessary elements in redeeming the feuduty; and there is a statutory form of receipt. With compulsory redemption, the feuduty is redeemed whether or not notice is given or payment made, and, as a result, there is no provision for a statutory receipt. But, looking to the terms of s. 5(6), evidence of payment is desirable. Note, again, the different effect. With voluntary redemption, feuduty itself continues as a real burden until the redemption money is paid; with compulsory redemption feuduty itself is at once extinguished on sale, regardless of payment.

### 16.28 (5) Acquisition by local authorities etc.
Special provision is made in s. 6 for compulsory acquisition of land by *e.g.* a local authority. The same general principle applies as on sale. Feuduty is automatically redeemed. But, in this case, the acquiring authority as purchaser, not the seller, is responsible for payment to the superior of the redemption money.

Further, if part of a feu is acquired, the feuduty in relation to that part is redeemed, although no formal allocation had previously been made thereon. Contrast private sale of an unallocated portion which does not bring about redemption.

The same rules apply to ordinary voluntary acquisition, without a compulsory purchase order, by an authority possessing compulsory powers.

The acquiring authority, not the seller, has the duty to give notice to the superior; and the acquiring authority, not the seller, is personally liable for payment of the redemption money.

But s. 5(5) to (9) do not apply. So the redemption money in this case never becomes a real burden and the superior need not take any action against the authority to protect his position. Instead, under s. 6(5), in all cases the authority:

(*a*) must give notice before the redemption date, which is the date when the authority takes entry by agreement or under notice to treat, or the vesting date under a general vesting declaration; and

(*b*) is personally liable for the redemption money and interest.

### 16.29 (6) Over-feuduties

Over-feuduties are totally ignored in the Act. There seems to be no doubt that they are redeemable, voluntarily; or compulsorily on a sale of the superiority. So, on sale of a superiority, you must now redeem the over-feuduty; and you may redeem voluntarily at any time.

But what effect does redemption of feuduty by a vassal have on the over-superior? Since tenure continues after redemption, the over-superior's rights in a question with his vassal (the mid-superior) and the sub-vassals are unimpaired.

Suppose A feus three acres to B for £50. B in turn sub-feus three separate acres to each of X, Y and Z, each for £25. B then has a surplus of income over outgoings of £25. So long as this continues, there is no risk to X, Y and Z, in that if B defaults, X, Y and Z pay £50 to A direct; and their combined feuduties are more than enough to cover the total due to A.

But suppose X, Y and Z all redeem their respective feuduties of £25 each, paying the redemption money to B. B is not obliged to pass on the redemption monies to A, nor to redeem his £50 feuduty to A in whole or in part. So B must continue to pay £50 to A, though now drawing no income from X, Y and Z.

Suppose B stops paying A. Under the existing law, A has two remedies against the sub-feuars:

(i) Recover from X, Y and Z to the extent of their unpaid feuduties. But their feuduties have been validly redeemed, and so they have no liability.

(ii) Irritancy. When B is five years in arrears with his feuduty to A, A may irritate the feu. B would then forfeit his title and the titles of X, Y and Z would fall as well. So sub-feuars are indirectly liable to over-superiors in this way, even after redemption.

# Chapter 17

# ENFORCEMENT OF BURDENS

## 17.1 Title and interest to enforce

If the superior wishes to enforce a condition of tenure against the vassal for the time being, there are two essential elements, namely, (*a*) he must have a title to enforce the condition, and (*b*) he must, if challenged, be able to demonstrate interest to enforce the condition. The same principles apply to any other person (*e.g.* co-feuars with the *jus quaesitum*) seeking to enforce a real condition as against the owner of the burdened subjects.

## 17.2 Title to enforce

As between superior and vassal, title causes no problem. The original charter is a contract between the original superior and the original vassal, constantly renewed between successors in the superiority and *dominium utile*, on the feudal theory of recurring personal contract. Accordingly, the superior's title to enforce feuing conditions is his title to the *dominium directum*, which is in form a title to land and carries with it, *sub silentio*, the title to enforce conditions in the vassal's charter generally, whether as real conditions or real burdens. See Lord Dunedin in *Nicholson* 1911 SC 391:

> 'The title of the superior to enforce a restriction contained in a vassal's title is always to be found in that title, because it begins as a contract between the original superior and the vassal and continues as between succeeding superiors and succeeding vassals by virtue of the tenure which, in the case of each succeeding vassal, binds him by the contract.'

Again, as between superior and vassal, the general rule is:

(1) that conditions in a feu charter are strictly a private matter between the superior and the vassal for the time being. No one can compel the superior to insist on feuing conditions in a question with his own vassal, if the superior himself does not so choose; and

(2) no one other than the superior can so enforce feuing conditions.

## 17.3 The *jus quaesitum tertio*.

In certain special circumstances, however, a situation may be created as a result of which adjoining feuars who derive their title from the same superior may acquire a title to enforce conditions in the charter of a neighbouring co-feuar. The right of enforcement, when so acquired by a co-feuar, is based on the contractual principle of *jus quaesitum tertio*, viz: 'An obligation imposed by a contract is *jus tertii* to third parties, and they have no right to enforce it' ... but the rule 'suffers an exception where it is shown that their object was to advance the interests of a third party. That may create a *jus quaesitum tertio*, which will give the third party, or *tertius*, a title to sue'. Gloag & Henderson, 10th edn. para. 11–04. Since the charter is fundamentally a contract, the rule has been applied to conditions of tenure.

The title of a co-feuar, as a third party, to enforce feuing conditions in the charter of his neighbour can only arise if superior and vassal have actively agreed to this in that original charter, 'and therefore there must be some evidence in the deed itself,' (*i.e.* the charter) 'that it is intended that the restriction shall be enforceable by a *tertius*': Nicholson.

**17.4** *Illustration.* To illustrate this by an example, suppose that A grants a feu charter to B; A then grants a second feu charter of an adjoining feu to C. A, the superior, is in direct contractual relationship with B, and with C, both being his vassals. But there is no relationship, contractual, feudal or otherwise between B and C *inter se*. A, as superior, can enforce feuing conditions against B and against C. But B has no title on the grounds of direct contract to enforce the conditions in C's charter against C; there is no contractual relationship between B and C. If B is to have the right to enforce the conditions in C's charter, this can only be on the basis of *jus quaesitum tertio*; and that *jus quaesitum tertio* must arise out of, and be based on, the terms of the feu charter by A to C. There is nothing else on which it can be based. Further, the feu charter by A to C must, by express provision, or by clear implication, confer the *jus quaesitum tertio* on B. This means that A, the superior, and C, the vassal, when adjusting the terms of the charter, must have agreed, expressly or by implication, that B, a *tertius*, is to be entitled at any time in the future to step in and enforce the charter conditions in a question with C, although at the time B was not a party to the charter.

If, however, B in the illustration can establish his *jus quaesitum tertio*, on the basis of the feu charter A to C, B's title to enforce feuing conditions against C, once so constituted, is a separate and distinct title, independent of the title of the superior to enforce the feuing conditions.

Thus, Lord Watson in *Hislop* (1881) 8 R (HL) 95 states:

> '[I]t is necessary to keep in view that, when the feuar has a *jus quaesitum tertio*, his title and that of the superior to enforce common feuing conditions are independent and substantially different rights. The title of the superior rests upon contract, a contract running with the estate of superiority and burdening the subaltern estate of the vassal. The right of the feuar, though arising *ex contractu*, is of the nature of a proper servitude, his feu being the dominant tenement.'

**17.5 Importance of the title to enforce**. Clearly, the right or absence of right in one proprietor to enforce conditions in the other's title may be very material to his enjoyment of that property. Similarly, it is very material, from the point of view of a proprietor whose title contains burdens, to know whether the superior alone can enforce those burdens against him or whether not only the superior but also neighbouring feuars on the basis of *jus quaesitum* have a right to enforce those conditions against him. There have been a number of reported cases.

**17.6 Creation of a *jus quaesitum***. In what circumstances, then, is a *jus quaesitum tertio* conferred upon a *tertius*? Firstly, certain conditions precedent must be satisfied which are:

(*a*) the feuars must both or all hold of the same superior; and

(*b*) the condition, which a *tertius* seeks to enforce, must be properly constituted as a real condition.

Given these conditions precedent, there are two ways in which it is said the *jus quaesitum tertio* may be created. These are:

(*a*) By express provision in the respective charters. Typically 'the feuars and the superior's other feuars shall be entitled to enforce against each other the conditions and restrictions expressed in their respective feu charters for the protection of the amenity of the neighbourhood'. Such clauses are common. See *Lawrence* 1965 SC 403, for a typical illustration.

(*b*) 'When the whole titles of the co-feuars manifest an intention that a *jus quaesitum tertio* will be created, by a mutuality of title inferred from an undertaking by the superiors to insert similar restrictions in each feu, or by reference to a common plan', *per* Lord Guthrie in *Lawrence, supra*, and cases there cited. This is always a difficult question and, if the *jus quaesitum tertio* is to be created by implication in this way, there must be a very clear inference in the titles that this was the intention. Thus, it is not enough that neighbouring feuars hold of the same superior on titles containing similar or even identical conditions. Again, a *jus quaesitum tertio* cannot be created by implication if there is a power reserved to the superior to alter the conditions of the charter. See *Turner* (1890) 17 R 494; but this does not apply to those cases where the right is expressly conferred by express provisions in the charters. See *Lawrence, supra*. On the other hand, a reference to a common feuing plan in several charters as containing (common) restrictions generally implies mutuality; similarly, where the superior undertakes to insert identical conditions in other future charters, and where this has been done. A *jus quaesitum tertio* would normally, in these circumstances, be inferred.

A third method is suggested by some authorities, *viz*. an agreement between co-feuars that each may enforce the other's title conditions. See Burns' *Practice*, p. 228, and *Stevenson* (1896) 23 R 1079, at p. 1090 *per* Lord Kinnear. But is this truly a case of *jus quaesitum* rather than a direct contractual relationship? In any event, such agreements were not often used because it was doubtful whether such an agreement could effectively bind singular successors. But this doubt is removed in appropriate cases by the Land Registration (Scotland) Act 1979 s. 17.

## 17.7 Interest to enforce
A title to enforce charter conditions (whether by the superior or by a co-feuar based on the *jus quaesitum tertio*) is an essential pre-requisite; but mere title alone is not enough. In addition, the superior or co-feuar must have an interest to enforce the condition. In relation to interest, there is a significant difference between the position of the superior and the position of a co-vassal.

The superior's title to sue is contractual; and the general rule of contract is that one party to the contract cannot successfully sue for implement of contractual conditions if his motive is vexatious and if he has no legitimate interest to sue. But he need not aver his interest, which is presumed; and the onus lies on the defender to prove (if he can) that the legitimate interest (which presumably the superior originally had to enforce the charter conditions) now no longer exists. See *Zetland* (1882) 9 R (HL) 40:

> '*[P]rima facie*, the vassal in consenting to be bound concedes the interest of the superior; and the onus is upon the vassal to allege and prove that owing to some change in circumstances any legitimate interest which the superior may have had in maintaining the restriction has ceased to exist.'

The nature of the superior's interest is not defined; but it is settled that his interest need not be patrimonial, involving financial loss.

In contrast, a co-feuar seeking to enforce a charter condition on the basis of *jus quaesitum tertio*, must aver his interest; and his interest must be patrimonial. See *Maguire* 1909 SC 1283. The defender established a *jus quaesitum tertio* to enforce a restriction in a neighbouring title which limited the buildings thereon to dwellinghouses only. The owner of the neighbouring feu proposed to erect a Roman Catholic church. In the proceedings the defender failed to aver and could not prove patrimonial interest; and on that ground failed. But the superior could probably have insisted that a condition of this kind be observed.

**17.8 Loss of interest to enforce**.   Since interest to enforce is an essential element in the enforcement of conditions of tenure, it follows that a superior or co-feuar who lacks or has lost his interest to enforce is barred from compelling compliance. Loss of interest occurs in three typical situations.

**17.9** *(a) Mala fides*.   Where, in withholding consent to a variation or discharge of a condition of tenure, it can be shown that the superior is acting *in mala fide* or oppressively, or capriciously. So in *Eagle Lodge Ltd*. 1964 SC 30 the superior withheld his consent to a variation in charter conditions, except upon payment of £1,000. The vassal argued that, by suggesting a monetary consideration for a waiver, he had either demonstrated his lack of interest or put himself *in mala fide*; but the point was not decided. In similar circumstances in the later case *Howard de Walden Estates Ltd*. 1965 SC 163 the superior asked for a payment of £1,250 as consideration for his consent; the defender did not press the argument that in so doing he was *in mala fide*. In any event, see Lord Guthrie: 'The fact that the superior demanded a sum of £1,250 in consideration of their consent ... does not indicate a change of circumstances showing a loss of interest.'

**17.10** *(b) Change of circumstances*.   Where, owing to change of circumstances in the neighbourhood, it can be shown that restrictions in the title have ceased to have any content or meaning and accordingly the superior has lost all interest to enforce a condition which is useless to him or to anyone else. This may occur where there has been a general abandonment of the whole plan of development owing to supervening circumstances; where, for example, 'the superior had permitted a continuous and systematic departure from the conditions of feu' as in *Campbell* (1868) 6 M 943. Contrast *Macdonald* 1963 SC 374, where a feuar proposed to convert a private house into a licensed hotel in the face of a charter condition prohibiting use for any purpose other than as self-contained villas. The charter expressly conferred a *jus quaesitum tertio* on co-feuars. On the grounds of certain other minor departures from that condition in other charters, the vassal argued that the character of the area had so changed as to extinguish the interest to enforce it; but the court refused to accept that argument. Similarly, in *Howard de Walden Estates Ltd.*, above, the point is expressed thus: 'The court has always required, in the absence of acquiescence, clear evidence of a loss of all residential character before it will regard the conditions imposed in the titles as devoid of any content. In my opinion, the present case is very far from any such situation.'

**17.11** *(c) Acquiescence.* Where a superior, otherwise entitled to enforce a feuing condition, has acquiesced in encroachments on or deviations from the feuing conditions, he may become personally barred from seeking, any longer, to enforce them. His interest is thus extinguished. As to the nature and quality of acquiescence, see Rankine, *Personal Bar*, Chapter 4. And note particularly:

(i) The superior's acquiescence must be deliberate, in the full knowledge that the feuar is in breach and that he as superior has a right and title to object. Mere silence, looking on, without objection, is not enough; the superior's acting must amount to positive tacit consent. See *Ben Challum Ltd.* 1955 SC 348.

(ii) Acquiescence to the breach of a particular condition in a charter does not *per se* imply loss of interest to enforce any other condition in the charter. See *Stewart* (1878) 5 R 1108.

(iii) Acquiescence by the superior in a prohibited use in the past may not prevent him from objecting to the continued future use for that purpose by the feuar, unless the feuar has with the superior's acquiescence expended large sums of money. See *Johnston* (1897) 24 R 1061:

> 'Structural alterations made in breach of building conditions, in the knowledge of and without objection by those having right to object, cannot after completion be pulled down. But the mere use of a dwelling-house in a manner contrary to the title, however long permitted in the past, cannot have any efficacy as to the future.'

(iv) 'A singular successor, with express or plainly implied notice, is fixed with the consequence of his author's acquiescence' Rankine, *Personal Bar*, p. 62, and *MacTaggart* 1907 SC 1318. But the singular successor will be no further bound than his author; and may be less so.

**17.12 Co-feuars**

All the foregoing rules as to loss of interest apply equally to a co-feuar who has a *jus quaesitum tertio* to enforce conditions in his neighbour's title. He, too, may be personally barred from insisting on conditions, by loss of interest. But on the final point *(c)* above, Acquiescence, there is a distinction between the effect, on a superior, of past acquiescence and the effect thereof on a co-feuar. Acquiescence by the superior in a breach, by one feuar, of a feuing condition does not necessarily imply loss of interest to enforce the same condition in the charter of other feuars in the area. See *Ewing* (1877) 5 R 230 and *Lawrence* 1965 SC 403. But 'generally speaking, if the superior allows the act of the first offender to pass, he must either have willingly allowed it or he must have conceded that all legitimate interest to stop such acts has gone': *MacTaggart*. Whereas a co-feuar, having acquiesced in a breach by one co-feuar, may still object, later, to the same act of contravention by another co-feuar if, in the circumstances, it is more damaging to his own amenity. See again *MacTaggart*: '[I]t is much more difficult to affirm that the quality of the superior's interest differs as regards each instance' (of contravention) 'than it is to do so in the case of a co-feuar', *per* Lord Dunedin at p. 1323.

The title of the vassal, based on *jus quaesitum tertio*, is independent of the superior's title. Therefore, acquiescence by the superior in a breach of charter conditions cannot bar the vassal from objection; and vice versa. See *Lawrence, supra.*

### 17.13 Voluntary variation of feuing and other conditions

Feus are perpetual. The rights created for the vassal, and the obligations undertaken by the vassal, in the original charter continue in perpetuity. At common law, neither superior nor vassal may, unilaterally, alter or vary these rights or obligations. But, fundamentally, the relationship of superior and vassal is contractual. It is, therefore, open to the parties to agree together to a variation of the terms of the charter. Further, in certain circumstances, the estate of superiority and (more commonly) the estate of *dominium utile* may be extinguished and cease to exist.

### 17.14 The superior's consent.

There are two necessary elements to the enforcement of feuing conditions by superior against the vassal, namely, title and interest.

The superior's title to enforce certain categories of feuing condition can be, and in the past has been in certain cases, altered by statute, *e.g.* as to carriages and services, and as to prohibitions against subinfeudation.

By the Housing (Scotland) Act 1966 s. 189, and earlier enactments, the vassal might, unilaterally, apply to the sheriff for a variation of a building restriction which prevented sub-division of a dwellinghouse. This was repealed on 29 November 1970 by the Conveyancing and Feudal Reform (Scotland) Act 1970 s. 52(3) and Schedule 11.

Otherwise, broadly speaking, a variation in the superior's title to enforce feuing conditions was, until 1970, always a matter of active agreement by the superior. But, under the 1970 Act Part I, the vassal may now apply to the Lands Tribunal for a variation of a feuing condition. The Tribunal may discharge the condition *de plano* or vary the charter by substituting a new condition in its place.

The superior may however also lose his interest to enforce a feuing condition owing to change of circumstances in the neighbourhood; owing to his acquiescence; or where the vassal can demonstrate that the superior's consent to a variation in a feuing condition is withheld oppressively or capriciously. This still applies, post-1970, rendering the condition unenforceable so that application for variation under the 1970 Act may be unnecessary. But the superior's interest to enforce need not be patrimonial and it could, and can, be difficult to prove loss of interest, thus often impeding development.

### 17.15 The consent of third parties.

The superior may have agreed to a variation of a feuing condition; or he may be personally barred, through loss of interest, from objecting to a breach, by a vassal, of a particular building condition or restriction; or the estate of *dominium utile*, with its rights and its feuing conditions, may by merger have ceased to exist. But the *jus quaesitum tertio* to enforce feuing conditions is not in any way affected by subsequent actings of the superior. Thus, an adjoining feuar, with the *jus quaesitum*, can continue to insist on a feuing condition notwithstanding that the superior has agreed to waive it. The existence of the *jus quaesitum* (where it exists) usually means that, even if the superior is willing, a variation by agreement – of superior and of neighbouring feuars – is a practical impossibility.

**17.16 Charter of novodamus.** Where the superior does agree to an alteration in the building conditions or restrictions, or to an alteration in the feuduty, the appropriate feudal process is for the vassal to surrender his feu into the hands of the superior. The *dominium utile* having then merged with the *dominium directum*, all existing feuing conditions are extinguished. Originally this operated *confusione*, although it has more recently been held that *confusio* does not apply. Technically, as a preliminary to the granting of a novodamus, the superior should be reinvested; but by statute this is made unnecessary: 1887 Act s. 3. The superior is then in a position to make a new grant of the original feu to the vassal, on new conditions. This new grant differs from an original feu charter in that it represents the renewal of an existing investiture. The writ is therefore called a charter of novodamus; and proceeds, in outline, in the following form:

'I, AB (design), immediate lawful superior of the subjects hereinafter disponed, considering that (here narrate the reason for the granting of the charter) Do hereby of new give, grant, dispone and forever confirm to CD (design) and his executors and assignees whomsoever, heritably and irredeemably, ALL and WHOLE....'

The charter then proceeds with a description of the subjects, the burdens, as contained in the original charter with such variations as have been agreed, and the usual formal feudal clauses. Some adaptation of these clauses, in particular the warrandice clause, will be necessary to take account of the special circumstances under which this charter is granted. The superior will normally grant warrandice from fact and deed, or simple warrandice only.

The provisions of the Land Tenure Reform (Scotland) Act 1974 s. 1, which prohibit future feuduties after 1 September 1974 cannot be circumvented by using a novodamus to increase or create new feuduty, and any purported increase is unenforceable.

Further, if a novodamus is granted with reference to two or more feuduties, the effect must not be to increase the total amount payable. Otherwise, the purported increase is unenforceable. See 1974 Act s. 3.

**17.17 Minute of waiver.** The charter of novodamus, although the correct and recommended feudal method for varying conditions (and indeed the only competent method for imposing new conditions or for effectively altering *reddendo*) is elaborate and expensive. In practice, where no new or varied condition is to be imposed upon the vassal but where the parties have simply agreed that the superior will not insist on a particular feuing condition, it is common to incorporate such a variation in a minute of waiver. This is shorter and cheaper than a charter of novodamus. But, at common law, it is a mere personal agreement between superior and vassal which does not affect the title or real right of either of them.

In the result, the minute of waiver was, at best, positive evidence that the superior had acquiesced; but went no further than that. It was therefore not suitable for effecting a variation of certain kinds of conditions; nor for imposing new conditions or additional feuduty. Sometimes, rather than pay the cost of a minute of waiver, the vassal obtains a 'letter of comfort' from the superior which purports to waive the condition. Such a letter, while binding on the superior who grants it, may not be enforceable against singular successors.

However, by the 1979 Act s. 18, the minute of waiver has acquired a new significance.

Under that section, the terms of any deed recorded in the Register of Sasines, whether before or after the passing of the Act, by which a 'land obligation' is varied or discharged, shall be binding on the singular successors of the person entitled to enforce that land obligation, and on the singular successors of the person burdened by that land obligation. But new conditions cannot competently be imposed by this device.

For this purpose, 'land obligation' has the same meaning as in the 1970 Act.

### 17.18 Statutory variation and discharge of land obligations
Under the 1970 Act ss. 1 and 2 a new judicial body, the Lands Tribunal, was established and given powers to vary or discharge feuing conditions and servitudes, which have either become obsolete, or which frustrate development, because:

(1) the superior refuses to agree to variation, or will only agree at a price; and/or

(2) in some cases (not all), adjoining feuars have the *jus quaesitum tertio*. To obtain agreement from a large number of co-feuars (and indeed even tracing them, in some cases) may prove impossible, even although the superior may be willing to co-operate.

**17.19 Definition of land obligations** The Act provides for the judicial variation of 'land obligations' which are defined in s. 1(2). To qualify for variation, the obligation must satisfy the following requirements.

**17.20** (*a*) It must be an obligation 'relating to land'.

**17.21** (*b*) It must be enforceable by a proprietor of an 'interest in land', *qua* proprietor. He is referred to in these sections as the 'benefited proprietor' – s. 2(6). Under that section, an interest in land means any estate or interest in land capable of being owned or held as a separate interest, and to which a title may be recorded in the General Register of Sasines.

The definition clearly includes:

(i) the superior or landlord;

(ii) a neighbouring feuar, if he has the *jus quaesitum tertio*, but not a neighbouring feuar without that right;

(iii) the owner of the dominant tenement in relation to servitudes.

The Tribunal probably do not have power to determine whether or not a 'land obligation' was originally validly created; nor to grant an order which is purely declaratory of subsisting rights and obligations. See *Solway Cedar* 1972 SLT (Lands Tr.) 42 and *Co-operative Wholesale Society Ltd.* 1975 SLT (Lands Tr.) 9.

The Tribunal have power to determine who is a benefited proprietor in this sense: *Smith* 1972 SLT (Lands Tr.) 34 and *Co-operative Wholesale Society Ltd*. If an application is made for variation of a burden which is conceded to be a 'land obligation', then all subsidiary questions of entitlement to enforce fall within the Tribunal's jurisdiction.

In very many cases, neighbouring proprietors are materially affected by a proposed variation of feuing conditions, but do not qualify as benefited proprietors within the meaning of the Act. The significance of this is that a benefited proprietor always has a right to be heard before the Tribunal and to state his objection – s. 2(2) – and to claim compensation. A proprietor who does not qualify as a benefited proprietor may be heard, in the discretion of the Tribunal, as an affected proprietor; but cannot appear as of right, and cannot claim compensation.

**17.22** (*c*) Under s. 1(2) the obligation must be one which is binding on a proprietor *qua* proprietor of:

(i) another interest in the same land, *e.g.* as between superior and vassal, or

(ii) an interest in other land, *e.g.* as between adjoining proprietors.

Such a proprietor is referred to in these sections as the 'burdened proprietor'; where property is held on an *ex facie* absolute disposition, the expression includes both the creditor and the debtor in that obligation – s. 2(6).

The second paragraph of s. 1(2) further defines a land obligation as including certain familiar categories of burden, *e.g.* future and contingent burdens, obligations to contribute towards or defray some expense, negative restrictions on use, and servitudes. But this really adds nothing to the substance of the section.

**17.23** Clearly, s. 1(2) embraces:

(i) all ordinary building conditions and restrictions in a feu charter, disposition, or contract of ground annual;

(ii) all leasehold conditions, if the lease is recordable (whether or not recorded); but see below for some exceptions;

(iii) servitudes, but not wayleaves or other similar agreements for the benefit of some person (*e.g.* British Gas) who is not an adjoining proprietor.

Certain special obligations set out in Schedule 1, are expressly excluded and cannot be varied under s. 1:

(i) feuduty and similar annual ground burdens;

(ii) mineral obligations generally;

(iii) certain Crown benefits;

(iv) leasehold conditions in agricultural leases and tenancies of crofts, even although recordable.

Further, by decision in *Macdonald* 1973 SLT (Lands Tr.) 26 conditions imposed directly by Act of Parliament cannot be varied.

Under s. 2(5), any condition (otherwise variable) which was created within two years immediately preceding the application, cannot be varied. Further, the Tribunal are unlikely to agree to vary relatively recent conditions of longer duration, except for compelling reasons. At least until recently, this was thought to be a reasonable assumption; but in the case of *Lees* 1987 SC 265 the pursuer obtained interdict to prevent the breach of a prohibition imposed as recently as 1983; and, arguably, the presence of this prohibition in the title was a material factor in the selling of a number of houses in a development. Nonetheless, shortly thereafter, the condition was varied by the Lands Tribunal. In the result, the somewhat surprisingly short period of two years in s. 2(5) renders new title conditions of little value, in many cases.

For a discussion on the definition of a 'land obligation' for the purposes of the Act, see *Fraser* 1985 SC 127.

**17.24 Who may apply?**   The only person who can apply for a discharge or variation of a land obligation is 'the burdened proprietor'.

No application can be entertained until the expiry of two years after the date of creation of the condition, the operative date being delivery of the disposition or deed creating the condition.

**17.25 Circumstances justifying variation or discharge.**   The Tribunal is empowered to vary or discharge a land obligation, on being satisfied that, in all the circumstances, one of three alternative situations has arisen as provided for in s. 1(3).

These three situations are strictly alternatives, and are not mutually exclusive *inter se*. It is up to the applicant to demonstrate that he comes within one or other of the three alternatives; and he may set about it by picking one of the alternatives which suits his case or, if he prefers, he can bring his application under two, or all three, heads in this section. If so, then the application may well be refused under one or two of the three alternative heads, but granted under the third. See, typically, *Main* 1972 SLT (Lands Tr.) 14.

The three alternative provisions in s. 1(3) are as follows.

**17.26** *Section 1(3)(a)*:   That, by reason of changes in the character of the burdened land, or in the neighbourhood, or other material circumstances, the obligation is or has become unreasonable or inappropriate. See Halliday's *Practice*, Chapter 19, Part C, for an analysis of cases. A typical case under this head would be a restriction limiting the use of a building in a town centre to a dwellinghouse only, where, with the passage of time, surrounding properties generally have been converted to commercial uses as offices and shops.

**17.27** *Section 1(3)(b)*:   That the obligation is unduly burdensome compared with any benefit which would result from its performance, *e.g.* a positive obligation to build (or, more likely, rebuild) a stone wall 10ft. high, where a brick wall 6ft. high would serve equally well. A right of pre-emption is a land obligation as defined in the Act; and, as such, may be varied by the Tribunal unless it has been directly conferred by statute. See *Macdonald* 1973 SLT (Lands Tr.) 26. But, since the law on rights of - pre-emption has recently been clarified by statute, the existence of such a right will not normally be considered as unduly burdensome by the Tribunal for the purposes of s. 1(3)(*b*), nor as impeding a reasonable use of land under s. 1(3)(*c*). See *Banff & Buchan District Council* 1988 SLT (Lands Tr.) 21.

**17.28** *Section 1(3)(c)*: That the existence of the obligation impedes some reasonable use of the land. This is the commonest ground of application, either alone or in conjunction with (*a*) and/or (*b*). From the reported decisions of the Tribunal, the following points emerge under this head.

(i) The Tribunal will not consider whether the obligation impedes some abstract or hypothetical use. The applicant must put forward, and found on, a specific, proposed use which is impeded: *Murrayfield Ice Rink* 1973 SC 21.

(ii) It is not enough for the objector to show that the land can be used for some reasonable use, *e.g.* the existing use. If an alternative, prohibited, use is proposed by the applicant, the Tribunal must consider it under s. 1(3)(*c*): *Smith, supra*, and in the Inner House, unreported; and *Main, supra*.

(iii) The fact that planning permission has been granted is persuasive, but not conclusive. Logically, the fact that planning permission has not been applied for, while adverse, is not necessarily fatal. If, however, planning permission has been refused, this 'is probably conclusive evidence that the relevant land obligation does not of itself impede the proposed new use of the land'. See *Cameron* 1988 SLT (Lands Tr.) 18. For a detailed discussion of the interrelationship between planning permission and the variation of land obligations, see an article in 1988 JLS 434.

(iv) The grant or refusal of other forms of permission or licence, *e.g.* liquor licences under the licensing Acts will also be taken into account on a similar basis.

(v) It is not enough for the applicant merely to show that a particular proposed use is reasonable in relation to the property in question. The whole circumstances, and in particular the effect on adjoining properties, whether they be benefited or not, should be taken into account. *Main, supra.* For recent cases demonstrating what the Tribunal considered to be unreasonable use, see *MacDonald* 1988 SC 299 and *Lothian Regional Council* 1985 SLT (Lands Tr.) 2.

There is a fairly large area of overlap between the three alternative grounds of application in s. 1(3)(*a*), (*b*) and (*c*). As indicated above, many of the reported applications have been brought under all three heads or under two of them.

**17.29 Compensation.** Compensation may be awarded to a benefited proprietor under s. 1(4) in one of two alternative cases; but not under both heads. Only a benefited proprietor may claim; an affected proprietor has no entitlement to compensation. The grounds of claim are:

**17.30** (i) Compensation for any substantial loss or disadvantage resulting from the variation or discharge. This covers:

(*a*) Loss of amenity – see *Smith* 1972 SLT (Lands Tr.) 34, where the Tribunal granted an application to vary tenure conditions so as to permit a dwellinghouse to be used as a licensed hotel, with an extension of the building for that purpose. There was resulting loss of amenity to neighbouring feuars who had the *jus quaesitum tertio* and were therefore benefited proprietors. Compensation was awarded for depreciation in the market value of the adjoining houses. *Contra, Main* where, again, benefited proprietors claimed for loss of amenity but, in the circumstances, the Tribunal held that there was no loss in permitting a sub-basement to be used as a nursery school; and

(*b*) Economic loss, *e.g.* loss in trading receipts to a public house resulting from the discharge of a restriction against sale of liquor in the title of an adjoining shop, so as to allow for an off-sales certificate there: *Co-operative Wholesale Society Ltd*. 1975 SLT (Lands Tr.) 9.

If the Tribunal discharges a restrictive condition, the superior, obviously, can no longer expect to be paid for granting a waiver of the discharged condition. There is thus a potential loss of revenue to a superior when applications are granted by the Tribunal. The superior is not, however, entitled to compensation for this loss of potential revenue under s. 1(4)(i).

Note, particularly, that the Tribunal may refuse to vary or discharge a land obligation on the grounds specified in s. 1(3)(*c*) if, in their opinion, 'due to exceptional circumstances related to amenity or otherwise, money would not be an adequate compensation for any loss or disadvantage which a benefited proprietor would suffer from the variation or discharge'.

**17.31** (ii) Compensation to make good the reduced consideration originally payable for a feu because of the presence in the title of restrictive conditions. In other words, where the superior insists on, *e.g.*, a prohibition against sale of liquor, he may get a lesser feuduty for his feu in the first place, because of insisting on that condition. In that situation, if the condition is removed, it is equitable that the superior should get compensation. The onus lies on the superior to establish that the feuduty was originally fixed below the free market value. In *Manz* 1973 SLT (Lands Tr.) 2, the superior failed to demonstrate this and so no compensation was awarded. Compare *Gorrie & Banks* 1974 SLT (Lands Tr.) 5, where the superior satisfied the Tribunal that a reduced feuduty had been charged in the original charter and so was awarded compensation which was calculated by capitalising at the date of variation the difference between the original feuduty and what the feuduty would originally have been, at full market rate, assuming no restriction in the title.

**17.32 Variation or discharge.** In addition to their powers to award compensation, the Tribunal have some discretion in relation to variation or discharge. They may either discharge the condition *simpliciter*, or in their discretion, under any of the alternative grounds of application, they may prescribe a substituted provision; but the applicant then has the opportunity of rejecting the proposed variation and continuing the *status quo*. This facility has frequently been used, as reported cases show.

When the order takes effect (see below), any substituted condition can be enforced as if it were an original condition in the original deed.

The Tribunal's power under the Act is limited to varying land obligations; they cannot, in the process of variation, impose a new or extended burden on adjoining land in which the burdened proprietor has an interest, *e.g.* by removing a restriction on the burdened land and in the same process creating or enlarging a servitude right of access over other land not owned by the burdened proprietor, in order to facilitate a new use of the burdened land. 'Only the burdened proprietor may apply, and only ... to have burdens varied or discharged; he may not apply, directly or indirectly, ... to have any additional burden on any (other) land': *Murrayfield Ice Rink* 1973 SC 21.

**17.33 Effect of the order**. The order will be recorded; and, when recorded, 'it shall be binding on all persons having interest'. Even if not recorded, it presumably binds any party to the proceedings; but not singular successors.

**17.34 Procedure**. The procedure is outlined in s. 2 and supplemented in detail by the Lands Tribunal for Scotland Rules 1971, as amended by the Lands Tribunal for Scotland (Amendment) Rules 1977.

**17.35 Registration of title**
In a Sasine transaction, the Keeper is not concerned with the question whether the conditions still subsist or are enforceable. However it has been held that in the context of registration of title, the Keeper is obliged to form a view and not put burdens in the burdens section if they are not in his opinion still subsisting. He is not, however, obliged to form a view as to whether they are still enforceable, *e.g.* by those who might have a *jus quaesitum tertio*. See *Brookfield Developments Ltd.* 1989 SLT (Lands Tr.) 105.

Chapter 18

# THE ESTATE OF THE VASSAL

## 18.1 Implied rights

The whole of this topic is treated systematically in Gordon's *Scottish Land Law*, Chapters 2, 10, 15, 17 and 18, and most of the ground has been covered already in outline in Chapters 7 and 8 above, to which reference is made. See also the Digest of Cases for these two chapters.

When dealing with descriptions in the feu charter in Chapter 8, the rights and benefits, which pass to the vassal *sub silentio* by virtue of the conveyance of the land alone, are summarised. The purpose of the chapters in Gordon, noted above, is to amplify that summary, and to spell out in detail the nature of these implied and inherent rights. In particular, it is important to keep in mind the rule as to separate tenements, explained in the context of descriptions, namely, that certain, but not all, heritable rights are capable of separate infeftment as separate tenements on a separate title, *e.g.* salmon fishings; and that each separate tenement must be separately and specifically conveyed to a disponee in a charter or disposition. Otherwise, such separate tenements do not pass to the disponee. In contrast, rights which are implied or inherent in landownership do pass automatically and require no separate or specific reference in the conveyance.

The following points are selected for special comment here.

## 18.2 (1) Barony privileges.

See Green's *Encyclopaedia* Vol. 2, p. 155 *et seq.* for a detailed treatment, and *Spencer-Thomas* 1992 SLT 973, a competing title case, where Lord Clyde examines in some depth the nature, quality and effect of a barony title. See also 1992 JLS 306 for the historical background.

The significant feature of a barony title in this context is in relation to the acquisition, by prescription, of rights not specifically conveyed by the Crown charter creating the barony.

In the ordinary case, salmon fishings, being a separate tenement, must be separately conveyed; and the complementary rule is that, to acquire a right to salmon fishings, you must either have:

(*a*) an express conveyance in a Crown charter of salmon fishing (*cum piscationibus salmonium*) with or without an attendant grant of land; or

(*b*) a conveyance (charter or disposition) either from the Crown or from a subject superior 'with fishings' ('*cum piscationibus*') followed by possession of the necessary quality for the prescriptive period, which still remains at 20 years under the Prescription and Limitation (Scotland) Act 1973 s. 1(4) in a competition with the Crown. See Chapter 14.

Note particularly that, in such cases, a specific reference to 'fishings' in the title is essential; and, if absent, possession for however long a time is of no avail, because it is possession without a title. See generally *Farquharson* 1932 SN 28. But the barony title is specially favoured in that possession of salmon fishings on a barony title alone, without reference therein to 'fishings', is sufficient to establish a title by prescription.

The same special privilege applies in other like cases, *e.g.* the foreshore. See *Agnew* (1873) 11 M 309; *Luss Estates Co.* 1987 SLT 201.

**18.3 (2) Parts and pertinents**. These are covered already in Chapter 8, Descriptions.

**18.4 (3) Possession of heritage**. There are two aspects of possession:

(*a*) *The effect of possession on title.* This is already dealt with, in the context of the infeftment of the vassal in Chapter 14 where it more naturally belongs.

(*b*) *The right of exclusive occupation and use.* This inherent right implies an absolute right to prevent trespass or encroachment by any person or any thing, *e.g.* buildings, trees and animals, but with the following general exceptions:

(i) Mineral and other reservations, whether by statute (*e.g.* coal, petroleum, etc.) or in the titles.

(ii) Burdens and servitudes in the title, *e.g.* rights of access, aqueduct, grazing, fuel, feal and divot.

(iii) Public rights of way.

(iv) In certain situations (*e.g.* emergency), trespass may be justified; and, in certain instances, persons are entitled to enter upon land with statutory sanctions.

**18.5 (4) Support**. This inherent right of ownership has been dealt with briefly when dealing with mineral reservations, in Chapter 9.

**18.6 (5) Rights in buildings, minerals, and timber**. These are all components of land which pass *sub silentio* as *partes soli* with the exception, of course, of matters reserved and excepted in earlier titles and by statutory provision. This has been dealt with under Descriptions and Reservations in Chapters 8 and 9.

**18.7 Entails**
The entail was a device for securing the devolution of heritage on a predetermined line of succession in perpetuity. The aim was to preserve the family estate intact. The entail was created by a charter or disposition containing an elaborate special destination which, under the statutory sanction in the Entail Act of 1685, was made irrevocable by the use of special further clauses in the deed, known as the cardinal prohibitions of entail, and by recording the deed in the Entail Register in addition to registration in Sasines.

The cardinal prohibitions provided, in essence:

(i) a prohibition against disposing of the entailed estate in whole or in part;

(ii) a prohibition against creating any heritable security on the entailed estate; and

(iii) a prohibition against altering the destination in the original deed of entail.

These three prohibitions were supported by irritant and resolutive clauses, the effect of which was, in brief, that, if the heir of entail in possession attempted to breach any of the cardinal prohibitions, he immediately forfeited his right to the entailed estate for the benefit of the next heir.

The strict application of these prohibitions was gradually relaxed by the Entail Amendment Acts during the eighteenth and nineteenth centuries. Finally, by the Entail (Scotland) Act of 1914, no new entails may now be created and for this purpose the Entail Register is closed. The Register remains open, however, for other purposes, in particular for the registration of instruments of disentail.

Any entail validly created prior to the 1914 Act is still effective as an entail, and the cardinal prohibitions still receive effect, unless and until the heir of entail in possession disentails, which he can now do, under the 1914 Act, in any circumstances if he is major and capax but possibly subject to the obtaining of certain consents. The entail destination continues to control succession, even after disentail. See, for illustration *Stirling's Trs.* 1977 SC 139.

Almost all entailed estates have now been disentailed and the entail is rapidly becoming of historical interest only. See Gordon, Chapter 18.

### 18.8 Liferents

Liferent and fee are recognised in Scots law as two distinct and separate rights which can co-exist concurrently in the same property. Liferents take two distinct forms. The proper liferent is created by direct conveyance of heritage; and the improper liferent is created through the medium of a trust, whereby the liferented property, heritable or moveable, is conveyed to trustees, and held by them for the liferenter's use and enjoyment. We are concerned here, briefly, with the proper liferent only.

Heritable property can competently be conveyed to A in liferent and to B in fee. Under that conveyance, A takes an immediate vested right of liferent and is entitled to the beneficial enjoyment of the property during his lifetime, to the total exclusion of B. But B also takes an immediate vested right of fee in the property, as absolute proprietor, subject only to the overriding interest of the liferenter. On the older view and for practical purposes his proprietary right of fee can be regarded as burdened with the liferent. Accordingly, B takes the property as disponee and institute; and takes infeftment as such. But his possession and enjoyment is postponed until the liferenter's death. A, as direct or proper liferenter under the same conveyance, also takes infeftment in liferent, since a proper liferent of heritage is regarded in Scotland as a heritable right capable of separate infeftment. So, in effect, this conveyance is a mandate for two simultaneous and concurrent infeftments, the one in liferent and the other in fee; and it may be and usually is recorded with warrant of registration on behalf of A and B for their respective interests.

Where there is a conveyance in this form, infeftment of A, the liferenter, is essential if the right of the liferenter is to be properly constituted as a burden on the property, and to be enforceable against singular successors of B as the proprietor in fee. But the liferent infeftment goes no further than that, and confers no higher right on the liferenter. Accordingly, a liferenter, infeft, is not in the position of vassal or absolute owner. Instead, his right is very similar to that of a tenant under a recorded lease, occupying the property free of rent but with certain obligations as to outlays and repairs.

## 18.9 Teinds, church, manse and glebe

Before the Reformation (1560), teinds formed a standard and substantial inherent burden on land for the benefit of the church, equivalent to tithes in England. After the Reformation, teinds in the great majority of cases passed into the ownership of the landowner on whose property they had formerly been a burden; but soon became subject to a new, but lesser, burden known as stipend, a fluctuating annual monetary charge based on the price of corn.

The present position is now regulated by the Church of Scotland (Property and Endowments) Act 1925. The purpose of the Act is to remove old anomalies and to standardise stipend payments. Under the Act, the standardised stipend has become automatically a real burden on the lands (not on the teinds) in favour of the Church of Scotland General Trustees and is called standard charge. It is preferred to all other real burdens except the incidents of tenure, and is recoverable by the Church of Scotland General Trustees in the same way as if it were feuduty. Where the teinds are held on a separate title from the lands by a third party titular, which occurs very occasionally, the heritor is empowered (s. 17) to deduct the standard charge in accounting to the titular for free teind.

Where the standardised stipend is under £1, it is compulsorily redeemed under the 1925 Act.

Standard charge (not stipend) is redeemable on sale under the Land Tenure Reform (Scotland) Act 1974 s. 5; or voluntarily under the 1925 Act.

There are also various administrative provisions in the 1925 Act, including provisions for allocation of standard charge between various parts of the subjects burdened with it, e.g. on the breakup of a large estate.

Broadly speaking, standard charge can be ignored in urban properties; in rural properties it may form a substantial impost.

As to title, the technical rule (with qualifications) was that teinds, being a separate tenement, required a separate express conveyance. So, one of the standard addenda to a conveyance was, and to some extent still is, 'together with the teinds'.

Probably in all cases, this conveyance of teinds would now be held to be implied; and in any event, with standardisation of stipend, teinds have no value and no relevance.

Stipend and standard charge are inherent burdens on land; and nothing appears in the title to disclose the burden, except in cases where, on the breakup of an estate, stipend or standard charge is apportioned in the dispositions to purchasers of parts. See Gordon, paras. 10–50 to 10–77.

# Chapter 19

# RESTRICTIONS ON THE USE OF LAND

## 19.1 Common law restrictions
The limitations imposed on individual owners by conditions in or affecting their individual titles have been dealt with already in Chapters 10 and 11; but landowners generally are also subject to restraints at common law and, increasingly comprehensively, by statute in their implied right of unrestricted user.

**19.2 (1) Liability for injury to person or property – *culpa*.**   Certain acts, or omissions, by a proprietor of land, are regarded by the law as innocuous in themselves; but if the landowner (or occupier) in the doing of such an act or in such an omission is negligent or reckless, and as a result damage is caused to some other person or property, then he is liable in damages. But in the absence of negligence or *culpa*, there is no liability on the landowner (or occupier) who is free to act as he pleases, and in particular no one can prevent him from carrying out, on his land, any such innocuous act. See *Noble's Trs*. 1988 SLT 662.

**19.3 (2) Nuisance.**   In certain circumstances, however, the law regards certain acts by the heritable proprietor as noxious in themselves, in that an act in this category inevitably interferes with the legitimate enjoyment by a proprietor of neighbouring property or inevitably causes inconvenience or injury to the public at large. In these cases, generally grouped under the heading of 'nuisance', the doing of the act itself is illegal, whether or not there is negligence or fault in the actual execution of it; and the heritable proprietor can be restrained or prevented from any such act by his neighbours or, possibly, by the public at large. He will also incur liability for any demonstrable damage caused to a neighbour or the public. See *Noble's Trs*. above. There are a number of such acts which are nuisances at common law; and a large number of further acts have become statutory nuisances.

**19.4 (3) *Aemulatio vicini*.**   Actings of a kind which in the ordinary way are lawful and unobjectionable, may nonetheless be validly objected to, and the proprietor so acting may be interdicted, if his sole or primary motive is malice or spite towards his neighbour.

The three foregoing principles are all applications of the law of delict, and as such, are not further dealt with in this Manual.

## 19.5 Statutory controls
With increasing frequency and comprehensiveness, in recent years, statutory controls of various types have been introduced affecting land, some of which may affect a purchaser. The following are some of the more import-

ant areas where such controls exist and in regard to which investigation on behalf of a purchaser is, or may be, required. The rule of *caveat emptor* will apply, unless suitable provision has been made in the antecedent contract. This underlines the need either for prior enquiry before a contract is concluded; or for the making of suitable provisions as to statutory controls in the contract of sale and purchase. See Chapter 28.

**19.6 (1) Town and country planning**. This is just a reminder of some of the more important points in relation to town and country planning which may affect a purchaser of heritable property. No attempt is made here to deal in detail with the law of town and country planning.

The previous edition of the Manual sketched in outline some of the more important provisions in the town and country planning legislation then in force.

On 27 May 1997, when this edition was in proof, the Town and Country Planning (Scotland) Act 1997 came into force, and some time thereafter the print of the Act itself became available. The 1997 Act and an associate Act, the Planning (Listed Buildings and Conservation Areas) (Scotland) Act 1997, are substantially consolidating statutes but introduce a number of new provisions as recommended by the Scottish Law Commission. In the time available before going to press, it has not been possible to attempt to recast the material on town and country planning and related matters to give effect to and identify the equivalent provisions in the new legislation. Thus, the text remains substantially as it was in the 5th edition and contains references to the 1972 Act although that Act is now repealed. Equivalent provisions were introduced in the 1997 Act.

In addition, parts of the 1972 Act have been segregated and embodied in the Planning (Listed Buildings and Conservation Areas) (Scotland) Act 1997 which, again, substantially reproduces earlier provisions with some additional amendments.

The repeal of the 1972 Act is in fact enacted by the Consequential Provisions Act, 1997, referred to below. That last Act contains several other repeals and a substantial number of amendments to earlier statutes consequent upon the consolidation of planning in the principal statute.

**19.7** *(a) Background.*

**19.8** (i) Statutes. The main statutes at present governing town and country planning in Scotland are the Town and Country Planning (Scotland) Act 1997 (henceforth 'the principal statute' or 'the Act'), the Planning (Listed Buildings and Conservation Areas) (Scotland) Act 1997, the Planning (Hazardous Substances) (Scotland) Act 1997, and the Planning (Consequential Provisions) (Scotland) Act 1997, which consolidated the law as at 27 May 1997. Planning law is however in a practically continuous state of change. Legislation covering related areas (*e.g.* housing, roads) may also be relevant in dealing with planning matters. But the above statutes, together with regulations made thereunder, form the legislative framework of planning in Scotland.

**19.9** (ii) Regulations. The principal regulations include the Town and Country Planning (General Permitted Development) (Scotland) Order 1992 (S.I. 1992 No. 223), referred to as 'the Permitted Development Order'; the Town and Country Planning (General Development Procedure)

(Scotland) Order 1992 (S.I. 1992 No. 224), referred to as 'the Procedure Order' which both came into effect on 13 March 1992, and the Town and Country Planning (Use Classes) (Scotland) Order 1989 (S.I. 1989 No. 147), referred to as 'the Use Classes Order', which came into effect on 27 March 1989. There are numerous other regulations and orders covering in detail specific aspects of planning procedure.

Most procedural matters are dealt with by regulation. Thus, for example, s. 32 of the Act provides: 'Any application ... for planning permission shall be made in such manner as may be prescribed by regulations under this Act or by a development order.'

**19.10** (*b*) *History.* Town and country planning in Scotland goes back to 1919; but, for practical purposes, the origin of the modern system was the Town and Country Planning (Scotland) Act 1947. While the provisions of that Act have been largely superseded, the development control aspects may be of relevance in the conveyancing of older property.

The consolidating Town and Country Planning (Scotland) Act 1972 provided for a two-tier system of development planning based on the Regional and District Councils established by the Local Government (Scotland) Act 1973. This in turn was replaced by the provisions of the Local Government etc. (Scotland) Act 1994 establishing a single-tier system of local authorities.

Development planning is only one of the two main roles of planning authorities. The other is development control, which forms the more negative and detailed side of land use planning. This has developed similarly over the years, and the 1997 Acts contain the basic provisions.

**19.11** (*c*) *Post-1972 Act planning authorities.* The Secretary of State for Scotland has overall responsibility for town and country planning in Scotland, exercised principally through The Scottish Office Development Department, while the actual administration is carried out by the planning authority as defined in the principal statute. Between 1975 and 1996, in terms of the Local Government (Scotland) Act 1973, the planning functions were divided between regional and district councils – in Central, Fife, Grampian, Lothian, Strathclyde and Tayside regions. In these regions the Regional Council was the regional planning authority responsible for regional planning functions and the District Councils were the district planning authorities with the responsibility for district planning functions. In these regions, there was a concurrent two-tier system of planning. The Regional Councils in the Highland, Borders, and Dumfries and Galloway regions and the councils of the three Island areas (Orkney, Shetland and Western Isles) were general planning authorities with responsibility for all planning functions in their areas.

The basic division of functions between the two tiers of planning authority derived from the areas they respectively served. The interest of the regional planning authority was more general and less detailed (at least in theory) than that of the district planning authority in respect of the latter's area. In general, the regional planning authority was responsible for survey and structure plans covering its area and had certain reserve powers in respect of district planning authorities in its area. The district planning authority had responsibility for the preparation of local plans and development control (*i.e.* the granting of planning permission and the enforcement of planning control) amongst other matters, subject to the call-in powers of the Secretary of State for Scotland and the regional planning authority.

With the reorganisation of local government in 1996 the planning authority for the purposes of the 1997 Act is the local authority for the area. However, s. 33 of the 1994 Act provides that the Secretary of State may by order provide for structure plan areas overlapping local authority boundaries and that where a structure plan area extends to the district of more than one planning authority, the planning authorities concerned shall jointly carry out certain structure planning functions under the principal statute. The precise arrangements for carrying out these functions jointly are to be such as the authorities concerned may agree.

Such an order, namely the Designation of Structure Plan Areas (Scotland) Order 1995 (S.I. 1995 No. 3002) came into effect on 1 April 1996 and the former structure plan area of Tayside was divided into two structure plan areas – (1) Perth and Kinross and (2) Dundee and Angus.

**19.12** *(d) Pre-1972 Act development plans.* Under the 1947 Act every planning authority (which, by and large, meant every large burgh and county authority in Scotland) was charged with the duty of preparing a development plan for its planning area. That plan, once prepared, then had to be reviewed every five years.

The development plan was to comprise:

(i) a map of the area;
(ii) a policy statement and survey report in support of the map; and
(iii) a series of detailed plans for each individual area.

It would disclose, *inter alia*, the manner in which, or purposes for which, particular areas were to be used, *e.g.* for housing, commercial, education, etc.; and the stages by which development was to proceed.

For this purpose, the development plan was to include sufficient maps and statements to illustrate all the proposals for the future development within a 20-year period. It would normally:

(i) define the sites or proposed sites of roads, buildings, and public open space;
(ii) allocate (or 'zone') areas for particular types of development;
(iii) define comprehensive redevelopment areas for special, and usually urgent, reconstruction.

For example, in Dundee there were two stages, 1964 to 1969, and 1970 to 1984 followed by a third unspecific stage beyond 1984.

Designations under the old style development plans clearly may still be of concern to a greater or lesser extent to a purchaser and enquiry should always be made of the planning authority, although in most cases the old style development plans will by now be superseded by those made under the 1972 Act. As a precaution, a purchaser will normally make his offer conditional upon there being no adverse planning implications in the development plan (which will refer to either the old style or the new development plan), by the inclusion of a clause such as 'There is no existing designation ... order or notice or other matter ... affecting the subjects of sale or amenity thereof under ... any enactment.'

**19.13** (*e*) *1972 to 1996 development planning.*

**19.14** (i) Structure plans. The intention of the system introduced by the 1972 Act was to separate policy planning from the detailed land use planning of an area. (The old-style development plans comprised very detailed land use direction.) The regional planning authority set up under the 1973 Act considered the policy implications for its whole area and might have produced, first, a regional report (which set out policies, programmes and proposals, and indicated development planning priorities), and thereafter and more importantly, a structure plan for its area. The structure plan comprised a written statement supplemented by diagrams setting out policies for development and land use. Considerable preparatory study and discussion was required before the structure plan could be prepared; and the approval of the Secretary of State was then required. The majority of structure plans are now under review for at least the second time.

**19.15** (ii) Local plans. Detailed land use planning was contained in the local plans, which were the responsibility of the district planning authorities. They consisted of a written statement and a map or maps. They either covered a specified, and usually a fairly restricted, area (such as a village or part of a town) or they could take the form of a subject plan (such as recreational uses of land). They were not to be inconsistent with relevant provisions of the relevant structure plan, though they did not need to await approval of the latter. Once approved (and normally the approval of the Secretary of State was unnecessary) local plans offered detailed guidance to developers and purchasers.

The development plan for an area therefore comprised the structure plan and one or more local plans.

**19.16** (iii) Advisory plans. These do not have statutory effect and may consist of a statement of policy (perhaps to be found in the planning authority's minutes) or a more formal document (such as a proposed local plan which has not yet entered the consultation process). Such advisory plans do, however, offer guidance to a planning authority's views, and should be given consideration.

**19.17** (*f*) *Post-1996 development planning*

**19.18** (i) Structure plans. The plan prepared for a structure plan area follows very closely the procedure under regional planning authorities, but there is now no longer any provision for a regional report. Schedule 4 to the 1994 Act makes further and transitional provisions particularly where the new structure plan area differs from the previous one. Since new structure plans will be in the majority of cases prepared by several authorities acting together, the Schedule provides for dealing with disagreements through each authority setting out its own reasoned alternative proposals and powers to the Secretary of State to issue directions. Also with the new structure plan areas being generally smaller than the previous ones, consultation is required with any other planning authority which is likely to be affected, before submission of a structure plan to the Secretary of State, or before its alteration.

**19.19** (ii) Local plans. Under the 1994 Act the provisions as to local plans are virtually identical to those described at para. 19.15, but every planning authority is now required to prepare local plans for all parts of its area and it is now competent for two or more planning authorities to make a joint local plan extending to parts of each of their districts.

Section 24 of the Act makes it explicit that structure and local plans made prior to 1 April 1996 remain in force until replaced by new plans.

**19.20** (iii) *Advisory plans.* The information given at para. 19.16 remains unchanged.

**19.21** (*g*) *Development plans and control.* It should not be assumed that an individual application for planning permission will receive automatic approval simply because the application appears to fall within the guidelines set out in a development plan. Each application requires to be considered on its own merits. The development plan simply outlines the planning authority's considered view and offers guidance. There may be many reasons why an application for planning permission is refused. Normally, however, an application which lies within development plan guidelines should not be refused on policy grounds, *e.g.* a planning authority should not refuse an application for a house in an area which has been indicated in an approved local plan as suitable for residential development on the grounds, for example, that this use is not appropriate.

**19.22** (*h*) *Development and development control.* The principal statute operates by imposing a statutory control on all development of land. Development is defined in the Act s. 26(1) as:

(i) '... the carrying out of building, engineering, mining, or other operations in, on, over or under land, or

(ii) ... the making of any material change in the use of any buildings or other land.'

Certain of these expressions are defined in the Act, which also provides for modification in certain cases, both as to what constitutes development and as to certain categories of development which do not require planning permission. Generally speaking, however, before land (which includes buildings or structures and land covered by water) may be developed, planning permission for that development must be obtained from the appropriate planning authority.

Unless and until planning permission is obtained, it is unlawful to carry out any proposed development on land, unless, by statute, permission for that development is not required.

**19.23** (*j*) *Permitted development.* In terms of the principal statute and relevant regulations (particularly the Permitted Development Order), certain minor developments do not require planning permission.

Examples of types of permitted development which commonly occur in practice, and which are authorised under the Act s. 26(2) include:

(i) the maintenance, improvement or other alteration of a building, affecting only the interior and not materially affecting the external appearance (this does not however avoid the need for listed building consent where applicable nor building warrant);

(ii) the use of any building or land within the 'curtilage' of a dwelling-house for any purpose incidental to the enjoyment of that dwellinghouse as such;

(iii) the use of land, or buildings thereon, for agriculture or forestry;

(iv) a change of use of land or building which is authorised by or falls within any of the use classes specified by the Use Classes Order.

The Permitted Development Order in Schedule 1 (relating to article 3 of the Order) sets out in various 'parts' general types of permitted development and these are further divided into a number of 'classes'. Many of these are generally of little relevance to the individual purchaser or developer, but Part 1, classes 1 to 6, Part 2, classes 7 to 9 and Part 3, classes 10 to 13 are important to the practitioner. Thus, under the Permitted Development Order, Part 1, classes 1–6, development within the curtilage of a dwellinghouse (not including a flat) is permitted within certain tolerances without planning permission being required. But see Part 1, class 6, and Part 21, classes 6–8 as to satellite dishes.

Part 2, classes 7–9 – sundry minor operations are permitted without permission, *e.g.* erecting fences within certain prescribed dimensions.

Part 3, classes 10–13 – certain changes of use are permitted; see below.

In terms of the Act ss. 49 to 54 and Schedule 5, planning authorities have a duty to consider whether it would be desirable to establish simplified planning zones in their area. The effect of a simplified planning zone scheme, if adopted, is to grant planning permission for the types of development specified therein.

**19.24** (*k*) *The Use Classes Order.* This order came into operation on 27 March 1989. There are 16 separate classes of use, which include:

Class 1 – Use as shop (with special exclusions) but including a number of uses previously excluded, *e.g.* launderettes and dry cleaners and pet shops (use as a shop for the sale of motor vehicles is excluded by Article 3(5)(*d*) of the Order and motor fuel by Article (3)(5)(*c*)).

Class 2 – Use for the provision of financial services, professional services or any other service including use as a betting office where such provision is appropriate in a shopping area and the services are provided principally to visiting members of the public.

Class 3 – Use for the sale of food or drink for consumption on the premises or of hot food for consumption off the premises (public houses are expressly excluded by Article 3(5)(*h*) of the Order and the sale of cold food for consumption off the premises is permitted by Class 1).

Class 4 – Use (*a*) as an office other than a use within Class 2; (*b*) for research and development of products or processes; or (*c*) for any industrial process being a use which can be carried on in any residential area without detriment to the amenity of the area.

Class 5 – Use for an industrial process other than one falling within Class 4 and special industrial groups Classes 6–10.

The Use Classes Order is not a comprehensive listing of all possible uses of land but merely catalogues certain types of use. Some uses are expressly excluded, *e.g.* use as an amusement arcade.

Within any one of the classes so specified in the Use Classes Order a change of use is not considered as development and therefore does not require planning permission. For example if a shop (Class 1) is used as a butcher shop, the owner (or a purchaser) may change its use to a grocer shop or even a Post Office or launderette but may not change its use to a chip shop nor to a bank or a building society without obtaining planning permission.

In some cases planning permission is not required for a change of use between classes; there are cases where in effect the proposed use is less detrimental than the previous use, for example, a hot food shop can be changed to a shop for the sale of other types of goods, but not vice versa – see Part 3 of Schedule 1 to the Permitted Development Order. In general however any change of use between classes constitutes development.

The 1989 Order retains effective control over changes of use which, because of environmental consequences or relationship with other uses, need to be subject to specific planning permission but the scope of each class is wide enough to take in changes of use which generally do not need to be subject to specific planning control.

**19.25** (*l*) *Application for planning permission.* An application for planning permission can be made by anyone, but if the applicant is not the owner, notification of the application must be given to the owner (s. 35 of the Act). The application is made to the planning authority on a form obtained from that authority. An environmental statement must be lodged with an application for certain types of development and may be requested in others (Environmental Assessment (Scotland) Regulations 1988, S.I. 1988 No. 1221). The authority may seek additional information from the applicant about the proposed development. A fee is payable at the time of submission of the application. Notice must have been given of the application and the correct certificates duly completed. The certificates are normally printed on or accompany the form.

Intimation of every application (with very limited exceptions) must be given either to neighbouring proprietors or to the public in general. Every application must be notified to 'persons having a notifiable interest in neighbouring land' (article 9 Procedure Order) unless notification has been made in terms of the Act s. 34 or s. 35. Due to the fact that domestic property is no longer entered in the valuation roll, article 9 of the Procedure Order requires notices to 'the owner' and 'the occupier' in respect of each address of premises comprising neighbouring land.

Applications under the 1972 Act s. 23 – the so-called 'bad neighbour' applications (Act s. 34 and Schedule 7 Procedure Order) must be advertised in the press and notified to neighbouring proprietors in terms of article 12 before the planning authority may entertain them.

Planning authorities may also give public notice of certain other applications (*e.g.* in conservation areas or of public interest) and seek representations before dealing with the application. It should be noted, however, that, while a planning authority must 'take into account' representations made to it, neither these, nor an objector's strongly held views, can derogate from the right and duty of the planning authority to take whatever decision it feels correct in all the circumstances.

**19.26** (*m*) *Consideration of an application.* Under s. 36 of the Act every planning authority is obliged to maintain a register of applications for, and grants of, planning permission, which is public and may be consulted at any time during working hours. Planning authorities will, by the nature of the size of their area or their organisation, have adopted different procedures for dealing with planning applications. Section 56(1) of the Local Government (Scotland) Act 1973 provides for powers to be delegated by the authority to a committee, a sub-committee or an official and the majority of straightforward planning applications will be dealt with under delegated powers. Certain authorities may hear representations in respect of particular applications; certain may only be prepared to consider written representations.

**19.27** (*n*) *Determination of application for planning permission.* A planning authority must issue its decision on a planning application within (normally) two months of submission of the application. It may, however, if necessary consultations are numerous or if the application is of more than ordinary importance, seek the applicant's consent for an extension of this period. If no timeous decision is issued, the applicant has a right of appeal on the grounds of a 'deemed refusal'. A determination must be issued in respect of each application.

The planning authority may refuse an application, or may grant it unconditionally, or subject to stated conditions which must be observed in carrying out the development. A grant of permission may, depending on the application, be for outline permission (*i.e.* a decision in principle, leaving the reserved matters as defined in article 2 of the Procedure Order for later approval) or for detailed permission (allowing the development to be commenced without further planning approval being required).

**19.28** (*o*) *Appeal.* If no timeous decision is issued, if the application is refused, or if the application is granted subject to conditions which the applicant considers to be unacceptable, the applicant has a right of appeal to the Secretary of State for Scotland which must be exercised within six months. The applicant has the right to have his appeal heard at a public local inquiry but the vast majority of appeals are dealt with on the basis of the written submission procedure. This procedure allows each side to present a written statement of its position and avoids the delay and expense inherent in the public local inquiry. Following the 'closing of the record' in the written submissions procedure, or the completion of the report following upon the public local inquiry, the decision on the appeal is then taken, in the vast majority of cases by a reporter (a Scottish Office official) who has the necessary power delegated to him. The principal parties (usually the applicant/appellant and the planning authority) must agree to adopt the written submissions procedure, otherwise a public local inquiry will be held. In the case of a major application, or one which has generated considerable local concern, a public local inquiry will almost certainly be held.

No one, other than the principal parties, is entitled to make oral representation at the public local inquiry as of right; but normally all relevant and non-repetitive evidence will be heard, and there is nothing to prevent written representations being made by any interested party.

**19.29** (*p*) *Planning permission.* Under the Act s. 44, any planning permission which has been granted enures for the benefit of the land irrespective of who is the owner for the time being.

The Act ss. 58 and 59 require any development normally to commence within five years from the date of the granting of permission. Where outline permission has been granted, application for detailed permission (or for approval of reserved matters) must be made within three years of the outline permission; and the development must normally commence within five years of the outline permission being granted.

**19.30** (*q*) *Outline planning permission.* If an applicant intends to build a house on a particular plot of land, he lodges an application for planning permission and, with it, detailed plans showing the layout of the house and details of the building itself. Permission may be granted with or without modification. If the applicant intends to develop a housing estate with, say, 200 houses, it would obviously be a very laborious job to lodge detailed layout and building plans for each plot, which in the end of the day might prove to be abortive in that the planning authority might not approve what was proposed. It is, therefore, competent, under s. 59 of the Act to apply for 'outline planning permission' (often referred to as planning permission in principle) indicating the general intention without specifying all the detail of the proposals for which planning permission is, ultimately, required. Outline planning permission implies that the developer has approval in principle for his proposals but must submit detailed applications for each phase of the development, all of which requires permission in detail.

**19.31** (*r*) *Enforcement of planning control.* The corollary of a system of controlling land use is the means of enforcing that control. This is provided principally by the enforcement notice procedure contained in the Act Part VI and regulated by the Town and Country Planning (Enforcement of Control) (Scotland) Regulations 1992 (S.I. 1992 No. 477) which came into effect on 26 March 1992.

Where a proprietor or occupier of the land either:

(i) carries out development without permission; or
(ii) fails to comply with the conditions subject to which planning permission was granted,

a breach of planning control has occurred. The Act provides for the following remedies:

(1) The power to serve an enforcement notice where it appears there has been a breach of planning control and it is expedient to issue a notice having regard to the development plan and other material considerations (ss. 127–129).

(2) The power to serve a 'planning contravention notice' where it appears that there may have been a breach of planning control and the planning authority require information about activities on the land, or the nature of the recipient's interest in the land (s. 125).

(3) The power to serve a 'breach of condition notice' where there is failure to comply with any condition or limitation imposed on a grant of planning permission (s. 145).

(4) The ability to seek an interdict to restrain any actual or apprehended breach of planning control (s. 146).

(5) The power to serve a stop notice where a planning authority considers it expedient that any relevant activity should cease before the expiry of the compliance period in an enforcement notice (s. 140).

An enforcement notice must state the matters which constitute the breach of planning control and specify the steps required to remedy this. The planning authority has discretion as to whether or not to serve an enforcement notice and cannot be compelled to do so by, for example, an affected neighbour.

The procedure is statutory and detailed. In Scotland there is no prescribed form of notice, although a specimen form is now given in SOED Circular 8/1992. A right of appeal lies within 28 days to the Secretary of State for Scotland and the grounds of appeal are specified in the 1997 Act s. 130.

A planning contravention notice does not constitute taking enforcement action (as defined in s. 123 of the 1997 Act). Recipients of a notice are required to provide such information as the notice specifies regarding any operations being carried out on the land, any use of the land, and any conditions or limitations which apply to any planning permission that has been granted in respect of the land. Failure to comply with a notice within 21 days of it being served is an offence.

A breach of condition notice can be served on any person carrying out a development on ground or the person having control of the ground. The notice must specify the steps which the planning authority consider ought to be taken, or the activities which the authority consider ought to cease, to secure compliance with the conditions specified in the notice. The recipient of the notice has 28 days from service of the notice to comply and failure to do so constitutes an offence.

The application to either the Court of Session or the sheriff court for interdict is not dependent on the exercise of any other powers under the Act. Whether an interdict should be used as opposed to other powers may depend on the seriousness of the breach of control and the particular circumstances of the persons against whom proceedings are initiated.

A stop notice comes into effect immediately on service but cannot be used to prohibit the use of any building as a dwellinghouse.

The planning authority's powers to take enforcement action are subject to time limits in terms of s. 124 of the 1997 Act. Thus, where there has been a breach of planning control consisting of the carrying out without planning permission of operational developments, enforcement action must be taken within 4 years of the date on which the operations were substantially completed. The 4-year period also extends to the situation where the use of a building has been changed to that of a single dwellinghouse without planning permission. For any other breach of planning control, there is a limitation period of 10 years for enforcement action to be taken though there are a number of exceptions to this. See *e.g.* s. 124(4).

This immunity from enforcement is important; but unauthorised development which has become immune from enforcement as a result of the statutory provisions is not equivalent to an authorised development for which planning permission has previously been obtained. Therefore, any purchaser should always confirm very carefully that the current use of the property is the authorised use. For this purpose, it may be prudent to check the original use of the property on 1 July 1948 (the date of commencement of the current planning system). The permitted use of any given property is clearly critical to a purchaser. In many cases, no problem arises and there is no need to make special enquiry, *e.g.* dwellinghouse clearly used as such for 60 years; or factory recently erected after planning permission obtained. But it is always prudent to make the necessary enquiries.

**19.32** (*s*) *Certificate of lawful use or development.*   In any case of serious doubt until 25 September 1992 the matter could be resolved by obtaining from the planning authority a certificate of established use, in terms of s. 90 of the 1972 Act. If the planning authority refused to grant the certificate applied for, their refusal could be appealed to the Secretary of State for Scotland.

As from 25 September 1992, a new system was introduced for certifying the lawfulness of proposed or existing operations, uses or activities, in, on, over or under land, by applying to the planning authority for a certificate of lawful use or development, and providing a mechanism for obtaining from the planning authority a statutory document certifying the lawfulness, for planning purposes, of existing operational development, or use as a single dwellinghouse (see the Act ss. 150 to 154). There is also provision for appeal to the Secretary of State for Scotland.

**19.33** (*t*) *Additional controls*

**19.34** (i) Section 75 agreement.   A planning authority may enter into agreement with any person having an interest in land, such as would allow him to bind the land for the purpose of restricting or regulating development or use of that land. The agreement is normally recorded in the Register of Sasines and can then be enforced by the planning authority against the owner for the time being. The principal benefit of such an agreement (from the point of view of the planning authority) is that it enables binding conditions to be enforced regulating the development of land which may be of a financial nature or which may not be conditions which could be attached to a grant of planning permission with any certainty of their being enforceable. Unlike feudal conditions, the Lands Tribunal has no jurisdiction to review such conditions, and they can only be varied by agreement with the planning authority.

Some local authorities are prepared to enter into personal agreements under the Local Government (Scotland) Act 1973 s. 69, usually in relation to minor or temporary matters, but such an agreement is not recorded and the conditions thereof do not attach to the land.

**19.35** (ii) Orders under the Act ss. 65 and 71.   The planning authority may, in terms of ss. 65 to 67, revoke or modify a planning permission previously given; and, under s. 71 may require a proprietor to discontinue an existing use or to alter or remove any existing buildings or works. These powers are infrequently used.

**19.36** (*u*) *Special controls*.

**19.37** (i) Listed buildings. (Planning (Listed Buildings and Conservation Areas) (Scotland) Act 1997 ss. 1–60). The Secretary of State is required to compile a list of buildings of special architectural or historic interest – listed buildings – throughout Scotland, and may amend the list from time to time. Generally speaking, a listed building cannot be demolished or altered without consent of the planning authority or the Secretary of State for Scotland and, in addition, in the case of demolition, until notice has been given to the Royal Commission on the Ancient and Historical Monuments of Scotland. The Permitted Development Order does not apply to listed buildings.

The primary control which the planning authority has over unauthorised development affecting listed buildings is by means of the listed building enforcement procedure (s. 34) but there is a power of prosecution in s. 8. Essentially the form of a listed building enforcement notice is as for the normal enforcement notice although the statutory references etc. are different. Further controls are available to a planning authority in the form of a repairs notice (s. 43) and, in the case of a building which is not actually listed but which is considered to be of special architectural or historic interest, a building preservation notice (s. 3).

**19.38** (ii) Trees. The planning authority are empowered to make tree preservation orders on a single tree or group of trees, or woodlands, prohibiting without consent the cutting down of listed trees and for securing replanting. Provisional orders are competent. The order is recorded in the Register of Sasines (the Act ss. 160, 167, 168, 171).

The Farm Land and Rural Development Act 1988 provides for the payment of grants for the conversion of agricultural land into woodlands to the owners or lessees of that land by the Secretary of State. The scheme under which this is done may impose requirements to be complied with by those applying for such grants.

**19.39** (iii) Advertisements. (the Act ss. 182–187). The control of advertisements is dealt with by the Town and Country Planning (Control of Advertisements) (Scotland) Regulations 1984 (S.I. 1984 No. 467).

**19.40** (iv) Waste land. (the Act s. 179). The planning authority may require the owner to take steps to improve the amenity of waste land.

**19.41** (v) *Compulsory purchase*. Under Part VIII of the 1997 Act there is an elaborate code for the compulsory acquisition and appropriation of land for various planning purposes, subject, of course, to payment of compensation to the expropriated proprietor. Power is given elsewhere also to various authorities and utilities to acquire land compulsorily for the purposes of their functions. This is discussed below in Chapter 30.16–30.20.

Although it has not been possible to overhaul the foregoing summary of town and country planning in Scotland, the above comments do in fact represent a fairly accurate summary of the planning legislation in general under the 1997 Act.

**19.42** **(2) Building control**. In terms of the Building (Scotland) Acts 1959 and 1970, and regulations made thereunder virtually all building operations anywhere in Scotland come under the supervision and control of the local authority and require a building warrant. The authority also has power to deal with dangerous buildings thereunder.

### 19.43 (3) The countryside.

**19.44** (*a*) *The Countryside (Scotland) Acts 1967 and 1981.* Rights of way and access to the countryside generally are dealt with under an elaborate statutory code. In particular, an agreement or order, describing the property affected, may be recorded in the Register of Sasines and, when so recorded, is effective against singular successors in that land. It is possible, under this code, that public rights of way may be imposed on the landowner when none previously existed in which case compensation is payable.

**19.45** (*b*) *National Parks and Access to the Countryside Act 1949.* A planning authority has power to provide or secure the provision of nature reserves on land in their area and may enter into agreement with owners with regard to the management of land, carrying out of works or doing of other things, defrayal of cost and payment of compensation. It may acquire land compulsorily and make byelaws for the protection of the Reserve. Scottish Natural Heritage constituted under the Natural Heritage (Scotland) Act 1991 has similar powers.

**19.46 (4) Ancient (Scheduled) Monuments.** The Ancient Monuments and Archaeological Areas Act 1979 has superseded the provisions of earlier legislation, such as the Field Monuments Act 1972, in dealing with the preservation of 'monuments'. Section 17 provides for agreements to be made between the Secretary of State or the local authority and the owners or occupiers of any monument to ensure preservation, and allows the possibility of compensatory payments. Such agreements may be recorded in the Register of Sasines and can accordingly be enforced against singular successors. Sections 1 and 2 of the Conveyancing and Feudal Reform (Scotland) Act 1970 do not apply to such agreements.

**19.47 (5) Fire precautions.** The Factories Act 1961, the Offices, Shops and Railway Premises Act 1963, the Fire Precautions Act 1971 and the Health and Safety at Work etc. Act 1974 impose obligations on owners and occupiers of buildings used as factories, shops, hotels and boarding houses, and for public entertainment to comply with fire regulations, and if necessary to adapt their premises. This can be a very awkward and expensive matter for any builder or developer. Often, when applying for a building warrant for very minor adaptations, onerous fire precautions are required. This frequently happens following on the purchase of a property and may be a major deterrent to a purchaser. Fire certificate requirements are independent of building warrant and depend on use.

In all these cases, it is illegal to use the premises unless a valid fire certificate has been issued and is still in force, or an exemption has been granted. The local authority are given the necessary powers of inspection. If the owner (or occupier) fails to comply with any remedial action prescribed by the local authority, the fire certificate may be cancelled.

**19.48 (6) Public Health, Housing, Civic Government and Roads Acts.** These Acts make detailed and elaborate provisions for numerous matters relating to sanitary conditions, housing, streets and drainage, and ruinous and dangerous properties and nuisance.

To some extent, they are superseded by more recent statutory codes on, *e.g.*, pollution, waste disposal, sewage, etc.

In the context of examination of title, it is relevant to mention the undernoted items especially, since these are occasionally encountered on a sale and purchase of heritage, and may cause problems.

**19.49** (*a*) *Repairs to houses.*

Civic Government (Scotland) Act 1982.
Housing (Scotland) Act 1987.
Housing (Scotland) Act 1988.

Under the 1987 Act s. 108, if the local authority are satisfied that any house is in a state of serious disrepair, they may serve notice on the person having control of that house, requiring him, within a reasonable time, to execute works specified in the notice in order to bring the house up to a standard of reasonable repair. If the property is purchased subject to such a notice, the onus lies on the purchaser to carry out the work. The rule of *caveat emptor* applies. The person having control of the house is defined in s. 338(2) of the Act.

Under the 1987 Act ss. 108(3), (5) and 109 the local authority may themselves carry out the necessary work, if the owner fails or refuses; and recover the cost from the owners.

In terms of the 1987 Act s. 109 and Schedule 9, the local authority may make a charging order burdening the property with the cost. The order is recorded in the Register of Sasines and transmits as a real burden, preferred to almost all other charges. It takes the form of a 30-year annuity of an amount calculated to repay the cost incurred over that period. It should be noted that a charging order has priority over all future and practically all existing burdens and incumbrances, including heritable securities recorded prior to it. The amount of the annuity can be recovered by the same means, and in the like manner, as if it were a feuduty. See *Sowman* v. *Glasgow District Council* 1985 SLT 65, at p. 67, where reference is made to similar wording in the Building (Scotland) Act 1959 in this respect.

**19.50** Under the repairs notice procedure each person having control of premises (including non-residential premises) in a building should receive a notice referring to defects for which that owner would have some responsibility, even if this is only a partial responsibility. Failing collective action by the recipients, if that is necessary, for example, to secure common repairs, and subject to appeal to the sheriff, the local authority may themselves undertake the necessary repairs after the expiry of the specified period which must not be less than 21 days. The expenses incurred by the local authority may be apportioned amongst the persons having control of premises in the building concerned, and retrieved (by charging order if appropriate) from such persons following service of a demand for payment. In a building containing a number of houses, or houses and other premises, expenses will be apportioned for recovery from the owners responsible. This apportionment extends to owners of commercial premises in a tenement building where a due share of repairs falls to be allocated against such premises. In terms of the 1987 Act s. 248, repair grants are available, including to owners of commercial premises, subject to certain provisos if a repairs notice has been served under s. 108(1) of the 1987 Act. A local authority must, under s. 218 of the 1987 Act, offer a loan towards the cost of repair works provided *inter alia* an application is made within 21 days of service of the repair notice, and the authority are satisfied that the applicant could meet the expense of a loan.

**19.51** The 1982 Act ss. 87–98 give local authorities a number of functions in respect of the safe and efficient upkeep of private property. Such functions are in most cases exercised by the issue of notices requiring the carrying out of repairs, etc., within a certain time. Notice powers would clearly be ineffectual unless the local authority had reserved enforcement powers enabling them to step in and take action where notices were ignored. Sections 99–109, therefore, provide enforcement powers enabling the execution of works in the owner's default and the recovery of expenses incurred in so doing. Section 106 provides for appeals against any requirement of any notice served under any provisions of this Part, or against the amount of any associated expenses. Such expenses are recoverable from the owner at the time the local authority are in a position to make their claim, perhaps long after the default of the owner on whom the notice was served – see *Purves* 1987 SLT 366. It is accordingly essential to make checks with the local authority before a property is purchased and to provide for relief in the missives where appropriate.

**19.52** (*b*) *Closing orders and demolition orders.*   Housing (Scotland) Act 1987 Part VI.

If the local authority are satisfied that a house or houses do not meet what is termed the tolerable standard and ought to be closed, demolished, or improved, then they make either a closing order or a demolition order or an improvement order.

The tolerable standard is defined in s. 86 of the 1987 Act. To meet this standard, the house or houses must satisfy a number of conditions, *e.g.*:

(i) they must be structurally stable;
(ii) they must be free from rising or penetrating damp;
(iii) they must have satisfactory lighting, ventilation and heating, piped hot and cold water and a toilet etc.

Under the 1987 Act, the appropriate order is:

(i) where the house not meeting the tolerable standard forms part only of a building, a closing order. The effect of this is to prohibit the use of the house for human habitation as from a date specified in the order; and any occupier must remove by that date; or

(ii) where the building in question comprises only the house in question or a number of houses, but no other accommodation (*e.g.* shop), all of which fail to meet the tolerable standard, the local authority make a demolition order requiring the building to be vacated within not less than 28 days, and further requiring that the building be demolished within six weeks of the date on which it is vacated.

In practice, these periods are often extended, sometimes for a considerable time, until the occupiers find alternative accommodation.

The owner of a house then has the option either of carrying out repairs necessary to bring the house up to the tolerable standard in which case the closing order or demolition order can then be removed; or of leaving the property as it is in the case of a closing order or demolishing in the case of a demolition order. In many of these cases, the local authority take over the tenement from the owner at a nominal figure and carry out the work themselves; but the local authority have no obligation so to do.

Under the 1987 Act s. 123, if a demolition order is not complied with, the local authority may themselves demolish and recover the cost from the owner. Under s. 131 they may then make a charging order for a 30-year annuity on the property, to secure payment of the cost of any works over the 30-year period. The 1987 Act Schedule 9 regulates the form and recording of the order.

If property is purchased subject to a closing order or a demolition order, the effect transmits against a purchaser.

In terms of ss. 125 and 126 of the 1987 Act, a local authority may serve upon the owner or owners of an obstructive building, being one which, by reason only of its contact with, or proximity to, other buildings, is injurious and dangerous to health, a notice requiring the demolition of the building but the local authority must purchase the building if the owners offer to sell the building to them or otherwise pay compensation to the owner if they proceed with the demolition themselves in the absence of such an offer.

In terms of s. 119 of the 1987 Act, it is only possible to make a closing order in respect of a listed building, and not a demolition order.

**19.53** (*c*) *Improvement orders.* A local authority may require a sub-tolerable house not situated in a housing action area to be brought up to the tolerable standard and put into a good state of repair by an improvement order where the house has a future life of not less than 10 years (1987 Act s. 88). Such an order requires the owner to carry out works within 180 days to bring the house up to standard. The owner has a right of appeal against the order to the sheriff. The house may be acquired by the authority by agreement or, if necessary, by compulsion to secure enforcement.

There is no requirement, under the provisions referred to above relating to orders, for repairs or closing or demolition orders, or improvement orders, which makes it obligatory to record any writ in the Register of Sasines as a necessary prerequisite of liability. So, a purchaser will not be put on his guard by a search over the property. He has to make enquiry of the local authority direct to see whether or not any such order has been issued or is pending.

**19.54** (*d*) *Local authority grants.* (Part XIII of the 1987 Act as amended by the Housing (Scotland) Act 1988.)

**19.55** (i) Improvement grants. Local authorities operate a scheme under which grants are available to individual owners and certain tenants for improving the standard of houses generally, though it is now possible to obtain grants from Scottish Homes as aftermentioned.

Standard grants are obliged to be given by the local authority for the provision of standard amenities including a bath or shower, wash basin, sink, W.C., and hot and cold water supply (s. 244 of the 1987 Act) but the local authority must be satisfied:

(*a*) that the house will be provided with *all* the standard amenities for the exclusive use of the occupier;

(*b*) that the house will meet the tolerable standard (s. 86 of the 1987 Act);

(*c*) that the house will be available for use as a house for 10 years; and

(*d*) that the works to be carried out on the house will not prevent the improvement of any other house in the building.

Discretionary improvement grants for improving existing dwellinghouses to a high standard or for converting properties into flats are payable only in the discretion of the council who may refuse to make a grant 'on any grounds that seem to them sufficient'.

The local authority must be satisfied that the house, when improved, will provide satisfactory housing for such period and conform to such requirements as to construction, condition and services and amenities as may be specified from time to time by the Secretary of State; and the valuation band for council tax must not exceed the prescribed limit which at present is Band E (see the Housing (Valuation Bands for Improvement and Repair Grants) (Scotland) Order 1996 (S.I. 1996 No. 741).

**19.56** (ii) Conditions. The following conditions are generally applied to grants:

(*a*) the house must not be used for any purpose other than a dwelling-house;

(*b*) the house must not be occupied by the owner or a member of his family except as his main residence;

(*c*) all steps must be taken to secure the maintenance of the house in good repair.

The local authority are required to record Notices of Payment of Improvement Grant in the Register of Sasines (1987 Act s. 246) in the prescribed form specifying:

(i) the conditions attaching to the grant;

(ii) the period for which the conditions are to be observed; and

(iii) the provisions of Schedule 19 regarding repayment on breach of the conditions.

**19.57** (iii) Housing Action Areas. Local authorities are empowered to declare certain areas 'Housing Action Areas'. In such areas, the council have power to secure that work is carried out to bring the houses in that area up to a specified standard, being not less than the tolerable standard (1987 Act ss. 89–107). But in all such cases, improvement grants can be obtained up to 75% of approved expenditure.

The Housing (Forms) (Scotland) Regulations 1974 (S.I. 1974 No. 1982) contain the prescribed statutory forms for use in connection with improvement/repairs grants, housing action areas etc. but they must be read with Schedule 22 to the 1987 Act until such time as new regulations are issued.

**19.58** Type and amount of grant. The 1987 Act s. 242 and orders thereunder provide for the various amounts of grants in different categories, as shown below.

**19.59** (i) Improvement grant.

| Type | Percentage | Maximum approved expenditure | Maximum grant |
|---|---|---|---|
| Outwith Housing Action Area – house meets tolerable standard and conversion grants. | 50% | £12,600 | £6,300 |
| Outwith Housing Action Area, below tolerable standard, without all standard amenities or disabled facilities | 75% | £12,600 | £9,450 |
| In H.A.A. | 75% | £12,600 | £9,450 |
| In H.A.A., hardship case | 76% to 90% | £12,600 | £11,340 |
| In H.A.A. Pre-1914 tenement | 75% | £17,100 | £12,825 |
| Ditto – hardship case | 76% to 90% | £17,100 | £15,390 |
| In H.A.A., Housing Association acting on applicants' behalf | 75% | £19,700 | £14,775 |
| Ditto – hardship case | 76% to 90% | £19,700 | £17,730 |
| Standard Grant based on fixed amount for each missing amenity | 50% | £3,010 | £1,505 |

**19.60** (ii) Repairs grants. For repair works which if neglected would threaten the future useful life of the house. Normal repair and maintenance does not qualify. The prescribed amounts thereof are:

| Type | Percentage | Maximum approved expenditure | Maximum grant |
|---|---|---|---|
| Outwith H.A.A. | 50% | £5,500 | £2,750 |
| Outwith H.A.A., in pre-1914 tenement subject to common repairs scheme | 50% | £7,800 | £3,900 |
| In H.A.A. | 75% | £5,500 | £4,125 |
| In H.A.A. pre-1914 tenement as above | 75% | £7,800 | £5,850 |
| In H.A.A. – hardship case | 76% to 90% | £5,500 | £4,950 |
| In H.A.A. – hardship case, pre-1914 tenement as above | 76% to 90% | £7,800 | £7,020 |

But there is a financial means test unless the grant:

(1)  is for renewal of lead piping (see below), or

(2) the works are regarded by the council as substantial and structural and

(3) the works are required under a repairs notice order under the 1987 Act s. 108(1).

The council tax band limit is also applied.

**19.61** (iii) Lead piping renewal and radon gas works. These are dealt with as a type of repairs grant.

The grant for lead piping covers the cost of providing a lead free supply at the drinking tap provided the council is satisfied there is a health risk.

The grant to reduce the levels of radon gas can be applied for where the annual verage level of radon gas in a house exceed 200 becquerels per cubic metre.

The maximum grant is 90% of £5,500, *i.e.* £4,950.

There is no financial means test and no council tax band limit.

The sample should be arranged first by the Environmental Health Department. The house must otherwise be up to standard.

**19.62** (iv) Loft insulation. This covers loft insulation and also the insulation of water tanks and pipes in lofts, and uninsulated hot water tanks wherever they are located.

The grant is for 90% of the cost or £144, whichever is the less.

To qualify for a grant the applicant or his spouse or partner must be eligible for

(i) housing benefit, or

(ii) income support, or

(iii) family credit.

The house must be built before 1976 and have no insulation or insulation less than 30mm.

**19.63** (*e*) *Scottish Homes grants.* Scottish Homes was established by the Housing (Scotland) Act 1988. It has amongst its functions the provision, and assisting in the provision, of finance to persons and bodies intending to provide, improve, repair, maintain or manage housing. It may do anything which is calculated to facilitate or is incidental or conducive to the discharge of its general functions including making grants and loans. In terms of s. 239A of the 1987 Act, the Secretary of State may however give directions to local authorities and/or Scottish Homes to prevent the duplication of the making of grants.

**19.64** (*f*) *Proposals for reform of the home improvement system.* There were Government proposals for the reform of the home improvement system contained in the White Paper 'Housing: The Government's Proposals for Scotland' (Cm. 242) published in November 1987.

In terms of these proposals, a 'rehabilitation grant', which would be generally subject to an eligibility test based on an applicant's resources, would replace improvement and repairs grants and similar grants such as those for home insulation. There would also be 'adaptation grants', 'grants to developers' and 'block repair grants'. Notices of payment of grant setting out the conditions attached to grants would no longer be recorded in the General Register of Sasines, making it essential to obtain an appropriate certificate from the local authority. Grants would become liable to repayment in whole or part if the property is sold within 3 years or in whole if sold with vacant possession within 5 years by a landlord.

It was also proposed to replace the various statutory notices with two notices, namely a rehabilitation notice and a demolition notice. These proposals have not been implemented.

Section 170 of the Local Government and Housing Act 1989 makes provision for a local authority to provide services of any description for owners or occupiers of housing in arranging or carrying out works of maintenance, repair or improvement or to encourage or facilitate such works. See also the Housing (Relevant Works) (Scotland) Regulations 1992 (S.I. 1992 No. 1653).

**19.65** (g) *Roads, pavements and sewers.* Roads may be public or private, in the sense that they are either open to the public or under private control. Roads may however also be public or private in relation to the liability to maintain, in that a road which is open to the public as a public thoroughfare may nonetheless be maintainable by private individuals, normally the frontagers on that road. A road does not pass automatically to the council unless and until on application by an interested party the council has agreed to take over the road. It will probably do so if and when the owner or frontagers make up the road to the required standard at their own expense. Thereafter, the council will assume liability for maintenance.

The same applies, generally speaking, to foot pavements adjacent to public streets. The liability to make up and maintain rests with the individual frontagers according to the length of their frontage. This is, therefore, a relevant point of enquiry when examining title to see whether there is any liability on the purchaser for making up or maintenance.

The burden of making up a public road can be very heavy, particularly with corner properties having a road on two sides.

Under the Roads (Scotland) Act 1984 the council have power to require frontagers to make up a road, failing which the council themselves make it up and charge the frontagers with the due proportion of the cost. Normally, this would coincide with the liability in the title; but, if not, title liability is ignored and overridden by this provision.

In dealing with the acquisition of a house in a new housing development, it should be established with the local authority whether the developer has deposited with the local authority, or secured to the authority's satisfaction, a sum of money sufficient to meet the cost of constructing the road in accordance with construction consent, and to the standard required by the authority under s. 17 of the Roads (Scotland) Act 1984 and the Security for Private Road Works (Scotland) Order 1985 (S.I. 1985 No. 2080).

Failure by the builder to lodge such security is a criminal offence, but the regulations do not provide a mechanism for preventing the construction of the houses prior to lodging a security. Accordingly, in the event of a security not having been lodged, a purchaser's agent should consider the desirability of retaining an appropriate part of the price until either a security is lodged, or the road has actually been constructed to an appropriate standard.

**19.66 (7) Health and Safety at Work etc. Act 1974**. Under s. 4 of this Act, a person in control of premises is statutorily bound to take such measures as are reasonable to ensure that the premises, and means of access thereto, are safe.

Under s. 5, any person having control of premises is statutorily obliged to use the best practicable means to prevent emission of noxious or offensive substances.

Under the Act, a Health and Safety Commission is set up, whose principal function is to carry out the general purposes of the Act; and there is power to make regulations on various matters.

### 19.67 (8) Environmental controls

**19.68** (*a*) *The Clean Air Act 1993 and orders made thereunder.* This Act deals with air pollution and imposes controls on emission of smoke, dust, grit and fumes, and other forms of air pollution. In particular, local authorities are empowered under the Act to declare areas within their districts to be 'smoke control areas' in which, subject to certain exemptions and limitations, the emission of smoke, or of smoke of certain qualities, from chimneys is an offence. Such smoke control orders require the consent of the Secretary of State.

**19.69** (*b*) *Noise.* The Control of Pollution Act 1974 Part III makes provision for controlling noise from construction and other works. Noise abatement zones may be designated; the local authority must then record in a register noise levels which are not to be exceeded, and may serve noise reduction notices. The Secretary of State may make regulations regarding noise from plant or machinery, and approve codes of practice for minimising noise.

**19.70** (*c*) *The Rivers (Prevention of Pollution) (Scotland) Acts 1951 and 1965 and Control of Pollution Act 1974.* The 1951 Act set up River Purification Boards but their powers were from 1 April 1996 passed to the Scottish Environment Protection Agency (SEPA), established in terms of the Environment Act 1995. SEPA was set up to unify pollution controls previously administered by a variety of different agencies. The Control of Pollution Act 1974 Part II replaced most of the provisions of the earlier Acts and provides the modern statutory code relating to river pollution and largely supersedes the common law code. This Act also extended controls to nearly all inland and coastal waters. The Secretary of State is given wide powers to make regulations for the protection of water, as to precautions by persons having custody or control of poisonous, noxious or polluting matter, and for prohibiting or restricting the carrying on of activities in particular areas. Registers of consents, analyses etc. are to be kept for public inspection, with provision for public notice. There are provisions about pollution from vessels and on-shore sanitary facilities. Care is required, and enquiry should be made, when any existing drainage or sewage is not direct into a public sewer, as the consent of SEPA is required where discharges would affect any watercourse.

Special consideration must also be given to private water supplies for human consumption. The Water (Scotland) Act 1980 s. 76G, inserted by Schedule 22 to the Water Act 1989, makes provision for periodical testing of such supplies, and non-conforming supplies may require to be discontinued and an alternative supply provided by the proprietor. Since the water authority is not obliged to provide a public supply unless this can be done at reasonable expense, compliance with a s. 76G Notice may involve the proprietor in a considerable outlay. It is therefore prudent to obtain a warranty from the seller as to the wholesomeness of any private water supply.

**19.71** (*d*) *The Environmental Protection Act 1990.* Part I of this Act requires anyone wishing to have authorisation to carry out any emissions as specified in regulations, namely the Environmental Protection (Prescribed Processes and Substances) Regulations 1991 (S.I. 1991 No. 472), as amended by the Environmental Protection (Precribed Processes and Substances) (Amendment) Regulations 1995 (S.I. 1995 No. 3247), to seek the necessary authorisation from SEPA in relation to release of substances into the air or into the water.

There are powers to serve enforcement notices on anyone contravening their authorisation, and prohibition notices where any emission is likely to involve an immediate risk of air pollution.

Sections 29 to 78 deal with the collection, recycling, deposit and other forms of disposal of waste. They replace Part I of the Control of Pollution Act 1974. Waste Regulation Authorities, which in Scotland are the local authorities, have power under s. 35 of the Act to grant waste management licences for the treating, keeping or disposal of controlled waste in, or on, land. In terms of s. 34 of the Act, there is a duty of care imposed on all persons *inter alia* keeping, treating or disposing of controlled waste (as defined in s. 75 of the Act) to take all necessary measures to prevent unlawful deposit of such waste, and to prevent the escape of the waste from their control, or that of any other persons, and to ensure, in transferring waste, that it is only passed to an authorised person. Any person wishing to treat, keep or dispose of controlled waste is obliged to apply for a waste management licence to the local authority. Such licences will only be granted to fit and proper persons, and the local authority will have extensive powers of supervision and investigation to ensure persons holding such licences comply with the provisions of the Act.

In terms of s. 90 of the Act, local authorities have power to designate, by order, any area of land in their district as a litter control area. Persons affected by the order must be notified of the intention to make the order, but once in force, the occupiers of such an area have a duty imposed by s. 89 to ensure that the land is, so far as practicable, kept clear of litter. There is power to serve litter abatement notices, and failure to comply constitutes an offence.

Section 57 of the Environment Act 1995 inserts a new Part II A into the Environment Protection Act 1990 to deal with contaminated land and abandoned mines. This requires local authorities to cause their areas to be inspected for the purpose of identifying contaminated land as defined in the Act. If they identify any contaminated land they have to give notice to SEPA and to the occupier of the land and to the 'appropriate person', who in terms of s. 78F of the 1990 Act has responsibility for carrying out 'remediation', *i.e.* restoring the land to its former state or mitigating the effects of the contamination. In terms of s. 78E, the local authority has to serve a remediation notice on the appropriate person specifying what remediation work is required and the period within which the works are to be effected.

A remediation notice in terms of s. 78G may require an appropriate person to do works by way of remediation, notwithstanding that he is not entitled to. Accordingly, s. 78G(2) provides that any person whose consent is necessary before anything required by a remediation notice may be done shall grant such rights as necessary to allow compliance with the notice. These provisions will have important consequences for conveyancers as it will be necessary to check whether any such notice has been served. Regulations may prescribe the style of notice and the procedural steps to be taken in connection with it. The provisions are only partly in force to allow the Secretary of State to issue regulations. No regulations have yet been made.

**19.72** (e) *Miscellaneous.* For various other controls see *inter alia*:
Radioactive Substances Act 1993 – *re* keeping and disposing of radioactive substances.

Prevention of Damage by Pests Act 1949 and Pests Act 1954 – *re* control of vermin and creation of clearance areas.

The Weeds Act 1959 – *re* control of some noxious weeds.

Hazardous substances – new controls introduced under the Planning (Hazardous Substances) (Scotland) Act 1997.

**19.73 (9) Local Acts.** Under earlier legislation, now repealed, local authorities were entitled, if they wished, to introduce their own statutory code, imposing a variety of environmental controls by private Act of Parliament. Such local Acts replaced, in the individual local authority area, equivalent general legislation dealing with the same matters under a variety of earlier Acts.

Several of the larger local authorities took advantage of this facility. Such legislation covered, typically, streets, buildings, sewers and drains; and a variety of licensing matters. Under the Civic Government (Scotland) Act 1982, these private local Acts of Parliament have already been or will shortly be wholly repealed. The total repeal has however been postponed on several occasions by statutory instrument.

It is, however, always open to a local authority to promote fresh local legislation to cover items not dealt with by general legislation by utilising the Private Legislation Procedure (Scotland) Act 1936. Thus the former City of Dundee District Council had enacted the City of Dundee District Council Order Confirmation Act 1990.

The Civic Government (Scotland) Act 1982 entitles local authorities to make management rules in respect of land owned by them, *e.g.* parks; and there is power also to make byelaws for the good rule and better government of the area.

Part 4

# SUBORDINATE RIGHTS IN THE FEU –
# SECURITIES AND LEASES

# Chapter 20

# SECURITIES

## 20.1 The concept of security

The normal rule in Scotland is that a debtor's whole estate, both heritable and moveable, is liable for payment of his whole debts. If, therefore, A lends £1,000 to B, the debtor, without security, A can enforce repayment of his loan by the appropriate diligence out of any of the assets, heritable or moveable, belonging to B at the time of enforcement. But, when A calls for repayment, B may have no assets; and so, in the result, A gets nothing. Or B's assets may prove insufficient to repay the debts of A and others in full; and in insolvency no one ordinary creditor has any preference over another. A creditor may however acquire a preference by taking security under which, as a matter of contractual arrangement, the creditor annexes a specified asset of the debtor, in advance, at the date when the debt is contracted, and retains his nexus on that asset until such time as the debt has been paid.

The nature of the property determines the method by which an effective voluntary security can be created. So far as heritage is concerned, the cardinal common law principle of an effective voluntary security is that a real right in security in a particular heritable property must vest in the creditor. Written title, followed by infeftment, is essential to create a real right in land; and this rule applies to heritable securities as it applies to proprietary rights. Accordingly, to create an effective security on heritage at common law, it is necessary either (*a*) that the sum secured should be properly constituted as a real burden on a particular heritable property, as a qualification of an infeftment in name of the debtor; or (*b*) that a real right in the security subjects should be conveyed to, and vest in, the creditor, by the recording in Sasines of a title in name of the creditor. Such a conveyance to the creditor may take one of two general forms, *viz.*, (*a*) a conveyance to the creditor expressly for the purpose of securing payment or repayment of a debt (an *ex facie* security deed); or (*b*) a conveyance to the creditor which is ostensibly (*ex facie*) an absolute conveyance of the right of property without reference to the security element, thus apparently vesting the property in the creditor as owner. For a general discussion on the theory and practice of securities, both over heritage and over moveables, see Gretton 'The Concept of Security', in the *Conveyancing Miscellany*.

There has been some interesting discussion in two cases about duties of lenders to borrowers and the duties of disclosure by solicitors to lenders. In *Smith*, the House of Lords reversed the decision of the First Division (1996 SLT 392) and held that if a creditor reasonably believes that owing to the personal relationship between the debtor and the proposed cautioner (in this case husband and wife) the cautioner's consent may not be fully informed, or freely given, the creditor is under an obligation to ensure that the cautioner is fully advised of the nature of the transaction. It may be that this decision will give rise to the practice of husbands and wives, and others in similar situations, having to be separately advised in order to avoid, or minimise, the possibility of any suggestion of misrepresentation or undue influence. In *Bank of East Asia* 1995 SC 255 the court held that a solicitor may owe a duty of care to advise a lender of something which might be a determining factor in whether or not to lend on security.

### 20.2 Methods of creating heritable security

Broadly speaking, then, the creditor at common law has a choice of three available methods for securing his indebtedness:

(1) by creating a real burden in the debtor's title for the benefit of the creditor; typical illustrations are the pecuniary real burden and the ground annual in the older form;

(2) by infeftment of the creditor expressly in security, typically by a bond and disposition in security; and

(3) by infeftment of the creditor on an *ex facie* absolute title as though he were owner, typically by an *ex facie* absolute disposition.

All these methods were in common use up to 29 November 1970; and each had certain advantages and certain disadvantages. Under the 1970 Act, securities can no longer be created by methods (2) or (3) (and possibly (1)); and a new form of security, the standard security, is introduced in this Act to replace the older forms of deed. But any such security effectively created in the old form before 29 November 1970 remains valid until discharged. Although it is in the context of a discharge of one of these securities that a solicitor will encounter these in practice, it is necessary to be familiar with them as they can appear in titles for examination.

### 20.3 The effect of the Consumer Credit Act 1974

Under this Act, loans below the statutory limit (presently £15,000) are 'regulated agreements' which have to comply with certain statutory requirements. This applies whether or not the loan is secured. For a discussion on the provisions of the Act and the requirements of the current regulations, see an article in 1985 JLS 130.

### 20.4 Factors affecting the common law forms

When considering the forms of security used before 1970 and their effects, two main points must be kept in mind.

(1) A real burden securing payment of a sum of money is of its nature a mere burden on, and a qualification of, the debtor's infeftment. It is, therefore, affected by the rule, already examined, under which such burdens, to be effective, must be precisely stated. This means that the sum secured must be definite and ascertainable on the face of the title. Under a bond and disposition in security and equivalents, the creditor takes infeftment but expressly in security; and, for the application of this rule, a bond is treated as a burden. Accordingly, only precise and definite amounts could be secured by bond and disposition in security. But an *ex facie* absolute disposition, being in form a proprietary title and not a mere burden or security, was not affected by this rule, and was not treated as a burden for this purpose.

(2) The Bankruptcy Act 1696 (c. 5) (now repealed by the Bankruptcy (Scotland) Act 1985) provided that a heritable security was ineffective to secure a preference for the creditor for any debt contracted after the date of the creditor's infeftment. This Act applied generally to pecuniary real burdens and to the bond and disposition in security, and other comparable deeds under which the creditor was expressly infeft in security. It had no application to the *ex facie* absolute disposition since, under that form of security, an absolute right of property is apparently conferred on the creditor, not merely a security. As a result, the bond and disposition in security was not available to secure future and fluctuating debt although, by special statutory provision, a cash credit bond which is akin to a bond and disposition in security could secure future indebtedness, up to definite limits.

# Chapter 21

# HERITABLE SECURITIES BEFORE 1970

### 21.1 The bond and disposition in security
In this form of security, the relationship of debtor and creditor and the form of security document are largely statutory. The relevant provisions are as follows:

Titles to Land Consolidation (Scotland) Act 1868 s. 118 which authorised the use of a statutory form, supplied in Schedule FF 1 and laid down the statutory effect.

1868 Act s. 119, containing an elaborate interpretation of the Schedule FF clauses, s. 119 being in turn substantially amended, and supplemented, by:

Conveyancing (Scotland) Act 1874 ss. 47 to 49;

Heritable Securities (Scotland) Act 1894 – the whole Act;

Conveyancing (Scotland) Act 1924 ss. 25 to 43;

Conveyancing and Feudal Reform (Scotland) Act 1970 Part III ss. 33 to 43;

### 21.2 The statutory form
The statutory form (1868 Act, Schedule FF 1) contains two separate and distinct elements, namely the personal bond which operates to constitute the debt and establish the debtor's personal obligation and the disposition in security, which operates as a conveyance of the security subjects, in security, in favour of the creditor.

### 21.3 Content of statutory form
**(1) The personal bond**.   This follows the standard form of personal bond, often used without security to establish indebtedness. The personal bond is dealt with in Halliday's *Practice*, paras. 6.02 – 6.27.

**(2) The disposition in security**.   The statutory form runs on as follows:
'And in security of the personal obligation before written, I dispone to and in favour of the said CD and his foresaids heritably, but redeemably as aftermentioned, yet irredeemably in the event of a sale by virtue hereof, ALL and WHOLE (here follows the description) and that in real security to the said CD and his foresaids of the whole sums of money above written, principal, interest and penalties; and I assign the rents; and I assign the writs; and I grant warrandice; and I reserve power of redemption; and I oblige myself for the expenses of assigning and discharging this security; and on default in payment I grant power of sale; and I consent to registration for preservation and execution. In witness whereof'.

## 21.4 Effect

The conveyance to the creditor is expressly redeemable except on the happening of one event, namely, sale, in which event, only, the conveyance to the creditor becomes irredeemable.

The conveyance is expressly in security of the obligations set out in the personal bond.

The security subjects are described exactly as in a special disposition but no reference to burdens is necessary: 1924 Act s. 9(1).

By virtue of the disposition in security in this form, the deed was recordable in Sasines; but the creditor's infeftment following thereon was not an absolute, but a limited, infeftment in that the debtor can compel the creditor to reinvest him, on repayment of the sums due under the bond.

If however the debtor defaults and the creditor sells under his power of sale, then the conveyance to the creditor becomes irredeemable and the bond and disposition in security becomes in effect equivalent to an absolute disposition to the creditor, on the strength of which he is then in a position to convey the security subjects to the purchaser.

## 21.5 Ranking of loans *inter se*

The bond is a mandate for the creditor's infeftment. Infeftment is essential to constitute the creditor's real right and, unless and until the creditor has perfected his real right (*i.e.* until the bond is recorded), he has no effective security.

Because of the limitations in the dispositive clause and because the creditor's infeftment is initially redeemable, the recording of the bond does not divest the debtor. Instead, the bond is treated merely as creating a real burden on the debtor's title, and accordingly he can subsequently deal with the security subjects as infeft proprietor, either by way of a subsequent real security in favour of the same or a second creditor or by absolute disposition of the proprietary right to a singular successor from him. But the creditor under the bond having taken infeftment, the subsequent actings of the debtor cannot adversely affect the rights secured to the creditor by his infeftment. Therefore, any subsequent conveyance by the debtor, insecurity or absolutely, is necessarily subject to the infeft creditor's prior rights.

For the general principles which govern the ranking of heritable securities *inter se*, see Chapter 22, Standard Securities, dealing with the 1970 Act s. 13. Exactly the same principles apply to the ranking of the bond and disposition in security.

## 21.6 Ranking clauses.

The ordinary rules of ranking may be varied by express ranking clauses in one or several (contemporaneous) bonds. But, if a bond to A has been recorded and contains no express reference to ranking, a clause in a bond in favour of B, recorded later, purportedly ranking B's bond prior to A's, is ineffective. Priority of infeftment rules. Again, the same principles apply to the bond as apply to the standard security. See Chapter 22.

## 21.7 Reserved powers

It was perfectly competent, in a bond, and common, for the debtor to reserve to himself certain powers which, otherwise, he would not or might not be entitled to exercise. There are two typical cases.

**21.8 (1) The power of redemption.** The right to redeem is implied but the mechanics are statutory. The statutory short clause reads: 'And I reserve power of redemption', which is interpreted in the 1924 Act s. 25(1)(*c*) and s. 32, entirely superseding equivalent provisions in the 1868 Act s. 119. The object of the statutory clause is to protect the debtor who, in the ordinary way, duly and punctually pays interest and, when required, tenders repayment of the principal sum and expenses. This provides machinery for discharging the bond and clearing the record if the debtor tenders repayment and the creditor cannot or will not grant the appropriate formal discharge. See s. 32 and Schedule L.

**21.9 (2) The power to feu, etc.** The debtor, by granting the bond, has not divested himself; he has merely burdened his title. Accordingly, he can thereafter competently feu, dispone, etc. But any feu charter or other deed which he may grant is necessarily subject to the prior preference established by the creditor on the recording of his bond unless the debtor has expressly reserved to himself in the bond an express power to the effect that, on granting a feu charter, the *dominium utile* of the ground thereby feued will be released from the creditor's security. Normally, the creditor will agree to the insertion of such a reserved power in a bond only subject to certain conditions which qualify the power, and which must be strictly observed. If not, then feu charters purportedly granted by the debtor in exercise of this power will not in fact release the feu from the security. See *Cumming* 1928 SC 296.

On such feuing, the *dominium directum* remained vested in the creditor and subject to the security. He thus acquired the superiority right in lieu of *dominium utile* and, at normal feuing rates, this was at least of some substituted value for the creditor. Now, under the 1974 Act, feuing remains competent but there cannot be a feuduty. Therefore, future superiorities will have no security value. So, presumably, this device will die out.

### 21.10 Creditor's rights

The creditor's principal right under the bond and disposition in security is to receive repayment of the principal sum in loan when he calls for it in terms of the bond (or in terms of some collateral agreement or 'back letter' qualifying the terms of the bond); and, in the meantime, so long as the principal remains unpaid, he is entitled to regular half-yearly payments of interest at Whitsunday and Martinmas. The debtor is under corresponding obligations.

The only concurrent right of the creditor, while interest is being regularly paid and payment of the principal has not been demanded, is to insure the security subjects against loss by fire to an amount necessary to cover his interest therein and to recover the premiums from the debtor. This is competent under the statutory interpretation of the assignation of rents clause in the 1924 Act s. 25(1)(*a*).

He has no other powers except on the debtor's default. In particular, since the debtor retains his title and is left in possession, the creditor has no right to interfere with the management of the property or to transact with tenants where the property is let; nor, being a mere security holder, has he any liability to the superior or others in respect of the security subjects.

**21.11 Creditor's remedies**

If the debtor defaults, *i.e.* fails to pay interest when required or to repay the principal sum when required, or is sequestrated or grants a trust deed, the creditor is then entitled to exercise a variety of remedies (some available at common law, others by virtue of the security) against the debtor which include the following.

**21.12 (1) Personal action and summary diligence**. As we have seen, the debtor's personal obligation is distinct from the security element. Under the personal bond, the creditor can sue the debtor in an ordinary personal action for payment of principal and interest; and, by virtue of the clause of consent to registration for preservation and execution, he can do summary diligence against the original debtor. (For successors, see below.)

**21.13 (2) Entering into possession**. Notwithstanding the apparent effect of the creditor's infeftment following on the dispositive clause and the assignation of rents clause, the creditor is not entitled to physical possession of the security subjects nor to deal with tenants and collect their rents unless and until the debtor has defaulted. Thereafter, unless the debtor consents, the creditor must establish his title to rents and to possession by judicial process, which is known as an action of maills and duties. Procedure is regulated by the 1894 Act s. 3 and Schedules.

When in possession (either by decree or by consent) the creditor then acquires additional powers, but also incurs certain new liabilities. His powers are contained in the 1924 Act s. 25 and the 1894 Act ss. 6 and 7.

In a question with third parties, the creditor in possession incurs the liabilities of the proprietor and is, therefore, personally liable to implement feudal prestations and may be liable in damages for injury resulting from defective premises.

**21.14 (3) Poinding of the ground**. This is a real diligence which entitles the creditor in any real security to attach and sell corporeal moveables on the ground belonging to the debtor or his tenants or vassals, but not goods of third parties, with a view to satisfaction of the indebtedness out of the proceeds of sale.

**21.15 (4) Sale**. The statutory clause in the 1868 Act Schedule FF1 reads 'and on default in payment, I grant power of sale'; and this receives an elaborate interpretation, now, in the 1924 Act s. 25(1)(*d*) and ss. 33 to 42 as amended extensively by the 1970 Act ss. 33 to 38.

This being an express *ex facie* security document, there is no implied power. If the creditor is to have power of sale, this must be expressly conferred as it is under this clause, and the power can only be exercised in accordance with strict statutory rules contained in the 1924 Act, as amended. If these rules are not observed, then there is no valid sale and the purchaser cannot be given a good title.

The statutory procedure is elaborate and detailed, and the detail has been altered substantially by the 1970 Act Part III.

For the detail of this procedure see Halliday *1970 Act*, Chapter 5. Only the salient features are mentioned here.

**21.16 (*a*) *Procedure on sale*.** As a preliminary point, power of sale is available to any bondholder, whether his bond be prior or postponed; but with this qualification, that a postponed bondholder exercising the power of sale must have regard to the rights of the prior bondholder, and the sale is subject to, and cannot in any way prejudice or over-ride, those rights. *Pari passu* bondholders as a rule must concur; otherwise, they fall to be treated as prior bondholders by the selling bondholder, subject to a statutory exception which will be noted later. But the selling bondholder need have no regard to postponed bondholders or to other postponed rights, subject to a general overriding duty to act reasonably. The essential features of the sale procedure are as follows.

(i) Notice. To initiate the sale procedure, and put the debtor in default, the creditor must serve a notice (1924 Act Schedule M) requiring payment of the capital sum with interest and expenses within three months of its date (1924 Act s. 33).

(ii) Expiry of notice. The three-month period of notice must elapse before any further step is taken, unless with the agreement of the debtor under s. 35. The notice itself is effective for five years.

(iii) Mode of sale. 1924 Act ss. 36 to 40 and 1970 Act ss. 35 to 37. The object of the 1924 Act (and its predecessors) was to prevent oppression of the debtor. Detailed provisions are therefore made in these sections regulating the procedure to be followed by the creditor after the three-month period of notice has expired. These strict rules have been to some extent relaxed by the 1970 Act, and in particular the creditor may now sell either by public auction or by private negotiation, 'at the best price that can be reasonably obtained'. But he must still advertise in specified newspapers, for specified periods, and adhere to a specified timetable, all prescribed in detail in ss. 36-39. As will be seen in Chapter 22, the procedure under the standard security is much simpler.

**21.17** (*b*) *Purchaser's title.* Assuming the subjects to have been duly sold, by roup or privately, by the selling creditor, he is then required to furnish a marketable title to the purchaser. This involves two elements, namely, giving the purchaser a valid and irredeemable proprietary title and ensuring that the property is disburdened of all subsisting heritable securities.

**21.18** (i) Proprietary title. In terms of the dispositive clause of the bond itself, sale having taken place, the selling creditor's title has *ipso facto* become absolute and irredeemable. Accordingly, *quoad* title, the bondholder is in the same position as if the bond had been a special disposition in his favour, and accordingly the bond becomes a proprietary writ. The next step is for the selling creditor to dispone the security subjects to the purchaser by ordinary special disposition, narrating the circumstances.

In addition, the purchaser will, of course, have to be satisfied that the sale procedure was carried through strictly in accordance with the statutory formulae and, in particular, he will require:

(1) Evidence of service of the notice. 1924 Act s. 34 makes suitable provision for such evidence.

(2) Evidence of advertisement. The substituted 1924 Act s. 38(4) (formerly 1924 Act s. 38(5)) again makes provision for suitable evidence, being a

copy of the advertisement, certified by the publisher as having duly appeared.

Strictly speaking, if the purchaser is satisfied with the validity of the prior title and with the sale procedure, the disposition by the selling creditor in his favour is all that he requires to validate his title. But this is a statutory procedure and any defect, however trivial, may invalidate the sale, whereupon the purchaser's title becomes reducible by an aggrieved debtor or postponed creditor, etc. As a further protection to the *bona fide* purchaser for value from a selling bondholder, special statutory provision is made under the 1924 Act s. 41 as amended by the 1970 Act, which excludes any challenge of the purchaser's recorded title on the grounds that the debt had ceased to exist (unless the purchaser knew that) or on the ground of any irregularity in the sale procedure. Under the 1868 Act s. 119 the selling creditor is empowered to bind the debtor in absolute warrandice in the disposition in favour of the purchaser, and to oblige the debtor to corroborate the same.

**21.19** (ii) Disburdening the subjects sold. The purchaser is entitled to a clear record. The seller must clear it of all subsisting securities. Prior bondholders are not affected by the sale. Therefore, prior bondholders must be paid in full by the selling creditor out of the sale price, against which they grant discharges. These discharges clear the record of these securities. But there still remains the selling creditor's own bond; and possibly also, (a) *pari passu* and (b) postponed securities.

(1) *Pari passu* bonds. Where there is a *pari passu* bond, the selling bondholder must obtain the consent of the *pari passu* bondholder to the sale. Otherwise, he will have to treat the *pari passu* bondholder as ranking prior to him. The selling bondholder can now compel the co-operation of an unco-operative *pari passu* bondholder under statutory procedure in the 1894 Act s. 11.

(2) Postponed bonds. The selling creditor prepares an account of his intromissions and produces it to a law agent; and the law agent then prepares a certificate of surplus (or of no surplus) in the form of Schedule N of the 1924 Act. The certificate is then recorded in the Register of Sasines; and such recording, together with the recording of the disposition in favour of the purchaser, of itself disburdens the record of the seller's bond (unless assigned to the purchaser in corroboration) and of all postponed bonds.

The assignation of the bond in corroboration and fortification of the purchaser's title is another device to protect a *bona fide* purchaser against the possibility of challenge of his disposition. If that disposition is reduced because of some technical defect in the procedure (now improbable, looking to the terms of the 1924 Act s. 41 but still a possibility) the purchaser loses his title. As some compensation, the debtor's bond is assigned in corroboration; and the creditor at least has the benefit of the heritable security. He would, of course, probably also be entitled to claim against the selling creditor under warrandice.

**21.20 (5) Re-exposure and foreclosure.** In dealing with sale procedure, I have assumed that the property was duly sold. That may not happen. The selling creditor then has three possible courses to follow.

(1) Re-exposure. There were special provisions for periods of advertisement etc. on re-exposure in the 1924 Act s. 38(4); but now, under the new s. 38, all periods are the same.

(2) He may abandon the sale and continue as he was, probably in possession drawing the rents. This is always unsatisfactory but may continue indefinitely.

(3) Foreclosure. This is a statutory remedy introduced under the 1894 Act s. 8, but again with strict limitations and restrictions to prevent oppression. The purpose is to allow the creditor to take over the security subjects as his own property in part satisfaction of the debt. The prerequisites which must first be satisfied are:

(a) That the property has been exposed for sale by public roup, and no purchaser has been found.

(b) That the last upset price did not exceed the combined total of all prior and *pari passu* securities; and the seller's own security excluding expenses.

Subject to these prerequisites, the selling creditor may then petition the sheriff for a decree finding that the debtor's right of redemption is forfeit. The extract decree may be recorded in Sasines, and on being so recorded the bond is converted into an absolute title for the benefit of the creditor, as from the date of recording. Recording automatically disencumbers the land of all postponed securities; but prior and *pari passu* securities are wholly unaffected by foreclosure. They therefore remain enforceable against the foreclosing creditor. A *bona fide* purchaser for value taking a title from the foreclosing creditor is protected, and his title made indefeasible by the 1894 Act s. 10, comparably with the provision in the 1924 Act s. 41(2).

**21.21 Collateral effects of exercise of power of sale.** Sale is one of the creditor's remedies. It is an alternative to any other remedy. Accordingly, even although sale procedure may have been initiated, the creditor may take any other action open to him under any of his other available remedies. In particular, sale does not exhaust or limit the personal obligation; so, if the proceeds of sale are insufficient to repay the selling creditor in full, he can still proceed by personal action against the debtor for the balance of the indebtedness. There is no question in Scotland of the debtor's liability under a heritable security being limited to the value, or proceeds of sale, of the security subjects.

**21.22 Pecuniary real burden**
See Halliday's *Practice*, paras. 35.02–35.07.
Under a bond and disposition in security, the creditor obtained his real right by active infeftment following on a special disposition in his favour operating as his mandate for infeftment. The real right created for the benefit of the creditor under a pecuniary real burden is secured in a different way, and is based on the principle that any conveyance of land may create real burdens as a qualification of the disponee's infeftment. Such burdens may be *ad factum praestandum* or for payment of a sum of money.
Note, in particular, that the creditor in a pecuniary real burden has no separate infeftment in his own person; and indeed there is no writ on which

he could take an infeftment. He therefore has no separate title to the security.

The pecuniary real burden suffered from serious disadvantages compared with the bond and disposition in security. It operates as a *debitum fundi*, and as such entitles the creditor to poind the ground or to adjudication; but he has no power of sale; he cannot enter into possession; and he has no personal obligation from the debtor.

For these reasons, this form of security was rarely employed.

### 21.23 Contract of ground annual

See Halliday's *Practice*, paras. 35.08 to 35.24.

This is another method by which a pecuniary real burden could be created and secured on land prior to 1 September 1974. It has this distinctive feature, that the cash payments secured are annual payments in perpetuity (subject now to the statutory redemption provisions in the 1974 Act) with which the land becomes burdened instead of capital sums, which produced a result very similar to feuduty under a feu charter. The fundamental difference between feuduty and ground annual is that, under a contract of ground annual, no feudal tenure is created, and therefore there is no equivalent to the relationship of superior and vassal between the parties to it.

Primarily, a contract of ground annual is a conveyance on sale by seller to purchaser, the purchase price being fixed as an annual sum instead of a capital payment. As a secondary element, the contract of ground annual creates a *debitum fundi* on the land conveyed, firstly by way of a reserved real burden *in gremio* of the dispositive clause; and secondly by way of a reconveyance to the seller in security. It thereby secures to the seller, as disponer, and to his successors, payment in perpetuity of the agreed annual sum. The writ is bilateral in form, as is the feu contract. The selling proprietor is the disponer and creditor thereunder; the purchaser as disponee acquires the beneficial right but, as consideration therefor, becomes debtor in the ground annual payments.

Ground annuals cannot be created after 1 September 1974 by the 1974 Act s. 2. Nor can existing ground annuals be varied so as to increase the annual burden – 1974 Act s. 3. For practical purposes, the contract of ground annual is therefore now obsolete and will never again be used. But existing pre-1974 ground annuals continue in perpetuity until redeemed by agreement or under the 1974 Act ss. 4 to 6. In contrast, subinfeudation continues, albeit for no feuduty.

### 21.24 (1) Modern form of ground annual. The distinctive feature of the contract of ground annual in its modern form is the inclusion of certain further clauses designed to improve the security of the creditor and the creditor's remedies in the event of default. These further clauses include:

(*a*) The debtor's personal obligation. Merely to constitute a real burden does not, of itself, constitute a personal obligation on the debtor. In terms of this clause, the debtor/disponee expressly undertakes the personal obligation of payment of the annual sums, and so becomes personally liable.

(*b*) A disposition in security. Under this clause, the debtor/disponee, to whom the subjects are conveyed in the main dispositive clause, reconveys the security subjects to the original disponer/creditor, but in security only for payment of the annual sums. This reconveyance by the debtor/proprietor in favour of the disponer/creditor is similar in form to the form of conveyance in a bond and disposition in security. The effect is to re-invest the disponer/creditor in the subjects conveyed, but in security only, with the attendant advantages of such reinvestiture which are conferred by the subordinate clauses appropriate to a conveyance in security.

On completion of the writ, both disponer and disponee take infeftment with two separate warrants of registration. The debtor/proprietor takes infeftment as disponee, in order to perfect his real right of property in the subjects conveyed to him; the disponer/creditor takes infeftment on the reconveyance in his favour in security, in order to perfect his security right.

**21.25 (2) Remedies of creditor under ground annual.** In the result, the remedies available to a creditor under a contract of ground annual in the modern form are as follows.

(*a*) Poinding of the ground.

(*b*) Maills and duties, in virtue of the assignation of rents clause in the reconveyance in favour of the creditor.

(*c*) Personal action and summary diligence. Note, however, that the personal action is available only against the original debtor and his universal successors. It will not transmit against singular successors in the property.

(*d*) Adjudication.

(*e*) Irritancy, under the conventional clause and under a statutory provision in the 1924 Act s. 23(5). In the case of the ground annual, the irritancy takes the place of power of sale.

While no new ground annuals may now be created, there are any number of existing ground annuals still subsisting; and these will only gradually disappear on redemption under the 1974 Act.

**21.26 Transmission**
As we have seen, there are two elements in the ordinary heritable security, *viz*.:

(a) *Real security*. The creditor's preference is established at the date of creation of the real right. But the debtor is not divested and can deal with the property subsequent to that date, or the security subjects may transmit on his death or on sequestration. But any such transmission of the debtor's right is subject to, and does not in any way adversely affect, the creditor's real remedies, *e.g.* sale.

(b) *The personal obligation*. It is usual, in addition to real security, to obtain the debtor's personal obligation for payment or repayment of the indebtedness. The personal obligation binds the original debtor for payment thereof, without reference to the value of the security subjects; and subsists so long as the sum secured remains unpaid, notwithstanding that the original debtor may have parted with the subjects in the meantime.

**21.27 Change of debtor/proprietor**. A singular successor who acquires heritable property subject to a heritable security does not, at common law, incur any element of personal liability, although he cannot prevent the creditor from exercising his real remedies on the property.

It is unusual in practice for the personal obligation to transmit against a singular successor but this may occur occasionally. If so, the common law bond of corroboration may be used; and the statutory provisions in the 1874 Act s. 47 and the 1924 Act s. 15 apply as they apply to a standard security. For further details see Chapter 22, para. 22.47.

The mere fact that a singular successor undertakes the personal obligation in a bond does not, of itself, release the original debtor from his personal liability. A separate personal discharge is required. Any such discharge is without prejudice to the transmitted personal obligation; 1874 Act s. 47. It is not recordable in Sasines.

**21.28 Change of creditor *inter vivos*.** The creditor's right in a heritable security is, primarily, a right to payment of the debt with, secondarily, certain additional real remedies for enforcing payment. As such, it is, of course, an asset of commercial value and, like any debt, it may be transferred to a purchaser or donee *inter vivos*; and on the death of the creditor it transmits, as an asset in the estate, to his successors. There are some special features here which distinguish transfer *inter vivos* of a heritable security from transfer of an ordinary debt, because, in addition to his right to payment, the creditor has real security over the lands constituted by infeftment. The actual method of transfer varies in detail according to the nature of the security.

**21.29** (a) *Bond and disposition in security.* The old common law disposition and assignation has been replaced by a short and simple statutory form of assignation under the 1924 Act s. 28 and Schedule K, as amended by the 1970 Act Schedule 10, by which the sum in loan and the benefit of the security is transmitted to an assignee.

The statutory assignation (1924 Act Schedule K1) is a mandate for the infeftment of the assignee by *de plano* recording of the assignation with warrant of registration thereon on his behalf. On such recording, although the assignation contains no description of the security subjects, and no *de praesenti* conveyance thereof, nonetheless the assignee is then infeft in the security subjects; and is otherwise in all respects in the same position as the original creditor under the original bond *quoad* real remedies and the personal obligation of the debtor.

**21.30** (b) *Contract of ground annual.* Again, there are simplified statutory forms, here under the 1924 Act s. 23(1). And again a simple assignation is appropriate in the form of Schedule K2; but with this difference that it is necessary in the case of an assignation of a contract of ground annual to describe the lands. The effect of the assignation is set out in the 1924 Act s. 23, in terms of which, briefly, the assignee is in exactly the same position *quoad* debtors in the ground annual as was the original creditor under the contract.

**21.31** (c) *Pecuniary real burdens.* Prior to 1874, the benefit of a real burden was transferred by simple assignation, coupled with intimation to the debtor; and recording of the assignation in the Register of Sasines was not appropriate. This is because, with pecuniary real burdens, the creditor has no infeftment. But the rule was altered by the 1874 Act s. 30 which provides that the recording in Sasines of an assignation is to take the place of intimation to the debtor as the criterion of preference. This produces a curious anomaly. The original creditor has no infeftment and no recorded title in his own person; but the assignee can record his title, although by such recording he does not become infeft. For transmission of pecuniary real burdens, the 1924 Act provisions for the bond and disposition apply, as modified by the 1924 Act s. 43 and Schedule K, Note 4.

**21.32 Death of creditor.** See Chapter 31 – Transmission on Death.

**21.33 Discharge**

(*a*) *Bond and disposition in security.* A modern form of discharge is now prescribed by the 1924 Act s. 29, which provides that any bond may be effectually renounced and discharged and the land therein effectually disburdened of the same, in whole or in part, by a discharge in the form of Schedule K3 to the Act, duly recorded in Sasines.

In practice a formal discharge is almost invariably employed to disburden the security subjects. But very much less in fact will serve, and there are other circumstances in which property may be disburdened of a subsisting security. The various alternative methods by which the security subjects may be disburdened apply, *mutatis mutandis*, to the standard security and are dealt with in Chapter 22.54.

(*b*) *Pecuniary real burden.* The same applies as for bonds under the 1924 Act s. 43 and Schedule K, Note 4.

(*c*) *Ground annual.* At common law, a ground annual is perpetual and does not fall to be discharged. But, occasionally, ground annuals are expressly made redeemable; and, of course, debtor and creditor may agree at any time to capital redemption of the annual sum. In that case, the ground annual may be discharged by a similar form under the 1924 Act s. 23(2) and Schedule K, Note 4. The same general principles apply as apply to the discharge of a bond.

Exactly the same provisions are made, under the 1974 Act ss. 4 to 6, for the voluntary and compulsory redemption of ground annuals as are made for feuduties; and the earlier comments on feuduty redemption apply here also*, mutatis mutandis.* So the formal discharge is now rare.

**21.34 Restriction.** A heritable security creates a real burden on the whole of the security subjects and on every individual part thereof. As a result, where part only but not the whole of the security subjects is sold, the purchaser will not take the title unless the heritable security is either discharged or restricted so as to release the part sold. Again, exactly the same principles apply to the standard security and the question of restriction is dealt with in Chapter 22.60.

**21.35 Future and fluctuating debt**
Before the 1970 Act and in terms of the Bankruptcy Act 1696 (now repealed by the Bankruptcy (Scotland) Act 1985), a heritable security was effective only to secure sums advanced prior to the creditor's infeftment thereunder. In simple cases, this provided no problem. But, clearly, cases arise in practice where the parties find it very convenient to have a heritable

security covering future and fluctuating debt. This is typically and obviously necessary in any ordinary business, running on overdraft, particularly in view of the rule in (*Clayton's Case*) *Devaynes* (1816) 1 Merivale 529. You will remember that, under that rule, if A has an overdraft of £2,000 which he secures by bond and disposition in security; and if he then operates on that account by paying in £100 each month and drawing out £100 each month, each payment-in is ascribed as a partial repayment of the original £2,000 overdrawn, and each drawing-out of £100 is a new loan. So that after 20 months, although his overdraft is still £2,000, the whole of it is represented by drawings since the date of the security. If, therefore, the security was by way of bond and disposition in security, these drawings would have been struck at by the Bankruptcy Act 1696 as new indebtedness, and would not have been secured. Yet in substance, there has been a continuing security for a continuing loan of £2,000.

Prior to 1970, there were two standard ways in which the provisions of the 1696 Act could be avoided, to secure future and fluctuating debt, namely, by cash credit bond and by *ex facie* absolute disposition. Both methods are now incompetent and have been replaced by the standard security, under the Conveyancing and Feudal Reform (Scotland) Act 1970. In the case of companies, a third method was made available by way of floating charge, under the Companies (Floating Charges) (Scotland) Act 1961 and the Companies (Floating Charges and Receivers) (Scotland) Act 1972. These provisions are now repealed and re-enacted in the Companies Act 1985 ss. 410–424 and 462–466. These provisions have in turn been amended by provisions in the Companies Act 1989, not in force at the date of going to press. See Chapter 23.

### 21.36 Cash credit bonds
Halliday's *Practice*, paras. 33.72 to 33.76.

Under the Debt Securities (Scotland) Act 1856, a bond and disposition in security might be given as security for cash credit (*i.e.* a running account), provided that the principal sum in loan, and interest, was limited to a definite sum; such definite sum took the form of a stated amount of principal plus 15 per cent, (representing three years' interest at 5 per cent). The infeftment on any such security is declared, by this Act, to be equally valid and effectual as if the whole sums advanced on cash credit had actually been advanced by creditor to debtor prior to the date of the creditor's infeftment.

The only special features of the bond for cash credit and disposition in security were:

(*a*) that, in the personal bond, it was normal (but not necessary) to provide expressly for a method of fixing the balance due at any given date on the running cash account, and the personal obligation is adapted accordingly, *e.g.*:

'Declaring that a stated account, with a certificate thereon signed by the secretary of the company, shall be sufficient to ascertain and constitute a balance and charge against me and that such a stated account shall sufficiently ascertain and fix the amount of interest chargeable on the said advances which shall have been made on the said cash account as aforesaid';

(*b*) that the disposition in security, and in particular the clause declaring that the conveyance is in real security, was adapted to meet the limitations imposed by this Act.

Apart from these specialties, the cash credit bond is in essence a bond and disposition in security and the same rules for assignation, restriction and discharge apply as apply to an ordinary bond.

The bond of cash credit is, of its nature, specially adapted for use by banks or finance companies who keep running accounts with clients. It is not suitable for private lenders. In practice, it was not commonly used.

### 21.37 The *ex facie* absolute disposition
Halliday's *Practice*, paras. 34.01 to 34.27.

The security document on which the creditor took his real right in security, in this case, was a special disposition granted by the debtor in favour of the creditor by which, on the face of it, the debtor conveyed to the creditor the absolute and unqualified right of property (not merely a right in security), in the subjects thereby conveyed, just as if the transaction were a conveyance on sale. In particular, there is nothing in the disposition to disclose the security element; in terms of the narrative, it bears to be 'for good and onerous causes and considerations'; the dispositive clause is 'heritably and irredeemably'; and there is no power of redemption reserved to the debtor, nor anything equivalent to it. The creditor perfected his security by recording the disposition, with warrant of registration, in the Register of Sasines; and no other writ (as a rule) entered the record to qualify or explain the true relationship between the parties.

As a result, the immediate effect of the recording of the disposition was feudally to divest the debtor, and invest the creditor, with the *plenum dominium* in the subjects thereby conveyed.

**21.38 Back letters**. Notwithstanding the resulting feudal position, the transaction remained in substance, as between debtor and creditor, a security transaction and it was, therefore, standard practice, and in the interests of both parties, to establish that relationship, and regulate the terms thereof, by a collateral agreement or 'back letter', qualifying the terms of the *ex facie* absolute disposition.

From the point of view of the creditor, the collateral agreement was desirable in order:

(i) to establish the personal obligation of the debtor (the disposition itself creates only real security);

(ii) to establish the terms of loan, including interest and repayment of capital; and

(iii) to a lesser extent, to constitute certain other obligations of the debtor.

From the point of view of the debtor, he has parted with his property on an absolute title which empowers the creditor to act as if he were the absolute proprietor. The resulting relationship between debtor and creditor is in its nature fiduciary, with the result that, under the Blank Bonds and Trusts Act 1696 (c. 25), the presumption is that the *ex facie* absolute disposition is what it appears to be. Accordingly, the debtor can only establish the true relationship by reference to the creditor's writ or oath.

The collateral agreement serves to establish this relationship in the appropriate form.

**21.39 Terms of back letters**.   Naturally, the terms of back letters varied substantially, depending on circumstances. They might be relatively short and brief; or they might be very lengthy, as in the case of most building societies. Whatever form the back letter took, its salient features normally included:

(i) an express acknowledgement by the creditor that he holds the subjects in security, either for advances to a stated limit, or for all future advances without limit, plus interest and expenses, and any other indebtedness to be incurred by debtor to creditor;

(ii) a personal obligation by the debtor to pay, or repay, the indebtedness, including the rate of interest and term(s) of payment, etc.;

(iii) a time bargain, binding one or both parties not to call for repayment, or to repay, for a fixed period;

(iv) express undertakings by the debtor:

  (a) to pay all outgoings;
  (b) to keep the property in repair;
  (c) to observe the conditions of tenure;
  (d) not to let the security subjects;
  (e) to insure;
  (f) to pay all expenses;

(v) express powers for the creditor, which include power of sale (although this is unnecessary) and power to insure (again unnecessary);

(vi) a reserved power of redemption to the debtor, on payment in full of the indebtedness; and

(vii) a consent to registration for preservation and execution.

Such agreements are normally bilateral, formal and tested. For reasons which we will shortly examine, the back letter was not normally recorded, although it might be.

**21.40 Creditor's rights and liabilities**
Because the terms of the security document conceal the true nature of the transaction, the creditor's position *vis-à-vis* third parties not deriving right through the debtor is significantly different from his position *vis à vis* the debtor.

**21.41 In a question with third parties**.   The debtor, by the *ex facie* absolute disposition, has clothed the creditor with the *indicia* of ownership. He must take the consequences of that act. This implies that third parties are entitled to transact with the creditor as if he were in fact the beneficial owner, with the result that the creditor can, without the debtor's consent, sell the subjects and confer a valid and unchallengeable title on a purchaser who is acting in *bona fide* for value without notice of the debtor's rights. Since the back letter is not normally recorded, a purchaser relying on the record does not normally have such notice.

If the back letter is recorded, which is rare, then some authorities state that this imports a real limitation on the creditor's infeftment. Certainly, recording of the back letter gives notice to anyone dealing with the creditor that his title is a security title only. But it is now settled by *Aberdeen Trades Council* 1949 SC (HL) 45 that the recording of the back letter does not deprive the creditor of his implied power of sale and will only affect the purchaser to the extent, if any, to which the back letter prescribes restrictions on the creditor's rights to sell, *e.g.* requiring the giving of notice and advertising the property for sale as if the security were a bond and disposition in security, under the relevant statutory provisions. This was occasionally incorporated.

Since the back letter is rarely recorded, and since, in any event, the creditor's power of sale is almost always unrestricted, a purchaser is very unlikely to be affected thereby.

But the creditor, having agreed to accept a title which, in form, conveys the right of property to him, with the attendant advantages of such a title, must also accept the liabilities inherent in ownership. Accordingly, third parties are entitled to rely on the form of title; and, in particular, the *ex facie* absolute disponee becomes liable for all feudal prestations, including payment of feuduty and obligations *ad factum praestandum* in the title. He may also incur liability, as owner, to third parties having claims arising out of the defective state of property, etc. (in so far as these fall on the owner rather than the occupier). He has a right of relief against the debtor for any liability so incurred.

**21.42 In a question with the debtor.** The creditor's rights and obligations *vis-à-vis* the debtor, and parties deriving right from the debtor, are regulated, not by the nature of the title, but by reference to the substance of the transaction. For practical purposes, the creditor is regarded as a trustee for the debtor and, subject to the preference established for the creditor by the recording of the *ex facie* absolute disposition and to payment or repayment of the indebtedness thereby secured, he must account to the debtor or his representatives for his intromissions with the security subjects and must, on repayment, denude in favour of the debtor or his representatives.

This inherent qualification of the creditor's absolute right in a question with the debtor and those deriving right from the debtor will transmit against the personal representatives of the creditor, *e.g.* in bankruptcy or on his death; the trustee in sequestration or testamentary trustee acquires right to the security subjects, but on the same terms, *vis-à-vis* the debtor, as the creditor himself enjoyed. See *Heritable Reversionary Co. Ltd.* (1892) 19 R (HL) 43.

**21.43** *Creditor must act reasonably.* It follows that, in a question with the debtor, the creditor is bound to act reasonably. Therefore, although he has an absolute power of sale, and can confer a valid title on a purchaser, he is not entitled, as between himself and the debtor, to exercise that power unreasonably and will be liable in damages if he does so. Further, although the debtor cannot challenge the purchaser's title, he may, if he acts in time, prevent the creditor from proceeding to a sale, by interdict.

These equitable principles which control the relationship of debtor and creditor may be modified or supplemented by the terms of the back letter. *Rimmer* 1967 SLT 7 is typical and illustrative. 'The creditor is entitled to sell and in recovering the amount due to him he acts *in rem suam*, but he is also *quasi* trustee for his debtor ...' He must not in exercising his power of sale 'do so unfairly and without due regard to the interests of the debtor'. A provision in the back letter allowing 'sale by private bargain, with or without advertisement at such price and on such conditions as the creditor thinks proper' (a usual clause) does not relieve the creditor of his common law duty.

If the debtor defaults, he can be removed and the creditor may enter into possession, simply on the strength of his *ex facie* absolute title; and on the strength of that title can deal with tenants as if he were owner.

**21.44 The extent of the security.** It is well settled that an *ex facie* absolute disposition is not a 'heritable security'. As a result, the Bankruptcy Act 1696 (c. 5) (now repealed) and the Debt Securities (Scotland) Act 1856 had no application. Further, since the creditor's title does not create an encumbrance or burden, but is in form a proprietary title, the rule as to precision in regard to real burdens is inapplicable. An *ex facie* absolute disposition is, accordingly, an effective security for future and fluctuating debt; and will afford effective security to the creditor for all indebtedness however incurred unless (as is rare) the terms of the back letter are taxative and limit the security to certain specific sums only. For a recent case where the back letter was considered by Lord Fraser to be taxative see *Scottish & Newcastle Breweries* 1970 SC 215. In the back letter, the security was stated as covering an advance up to the maximum limit of £1,800. Lord Fraser thought this taxative. See also Burns' *Practice*, p. 482: 'If the back letter declared that property was to be held in security of present and future advances up to ... a certain limit, it might more readily be held that anything beyond that limit ... was not secured.'

The creditor, therefore, has a continuing and covering security, for all indebtedness, present and future, either to the stated limit or without limit. That is the normal rule. It is subject to the following qualifications:

(i) If the back letter is recorded. The precise effect of the recording of the back letter is not settled; but it is probably the case (and safest to assume) that the recording of the back letter limits the amount secured to the lesser of either:
(*a*) The amount actually advanced at the date of recording of the back letter; or
(*b*) The stated limit in the back letter (this may be the limit anyway. See *Scottish & Newcastle Breweries* above).

(ii) Where the debtor has transferred his reversionary right, absolutely or as further security, and the transfer by the debtor is intimated to the creditor, this then limits the security of the creditor to the amount actually advanced at the time when intimation was made, without reference to any limitations in the back letter. If, therefore, the creditor subsequently makes any further advance, such further advance is unsecured. See *Union Bank* (1886) 14 R (HL) 1, below.

**21.45** *Statutory restriction on amount secured.* From 29 November 1970 this became statutory. The 1970 Act ss. 13 and 42 provide that, where the creditor in an ex facie disposition has received notice of the creation of a subsequent security over, or of the subsequent assignation or conveyance of, the same interest in land which is recorded in the General Register of Sasines, the creditor's preference is restricted to present advances, interest and expenses, and future advances which he is bound to make under his loan agreement. Mere recording of the later deed is not, *per se*, notice; but judicial conveyance is notice.

**21.46 Transmission of the creditor's right**. The creditor's right is heritable. It is an estate in land, but it is not a heritable security within the meaning of the Conveyancing Acts. Therefore, the abbreviated statutory forms of assignation, etc., which are available for heritable securities are not appropriate for transmitting the creditor's interest under an *ex facie* absolute disposition.

*Inter vivos*, the creditor may transmit his interest to a new creditor by disposition of the security subjects in favour of the new creditor (not disclosing the security element), coupled with a separate assignation of the debtor's personal obligation in the back letter. It is probably incompetent to attempt a partial transfer of the creditor's interest, and in any event this is unknown.

*Mortis causa*, the interest of the creditor in the security subjects transmitted, pre-1964, as any other heritable estate, being always heritable, although the benefit of the personal obligation might be a moveable asset in the creditor's estate.

Under the Succession (Scotland) Act 1964, the whole benefit of the security and the personal obligation now passes to and vests in the executors of the deceased creditor, if included in the confirmation. See Chapter 31.

**21.47 The nature of the debtor's right**

Prior to *Union Bank*, it was generally accepted that, because of the form of the *ex facie* absolute disposition, the result was to divest the debtor completely and to leave him with no remaining or residual right which he could subsequently deal with. But it is now settled, following on that case, that whatever the state of the original title may have been, whether or not there is a back letter, and whether or not that back letter is recorded, the debtor, notwithstanding the absolute quality of the disposition in favour of the creditor, retains a right to call for a reconveyance analogous to the right of redemption of the debtor under a bond. This right is in the nature of a *jus crediti* only, a *jus ad rem*, but nonetheless a right in the nature of a right of property, heritable by nature, descendable on death, and transmissible *inter vivos* by the debtor either by way of sale to a purchaser or by way of further security to a second creditor. Any such transmission is, of course, subject to the preferable right of the first *ex facie* absolute disponee which he established by the recording of his disposition in Sasines. This remaining right of the debtor is termed, generally, the debtor's radical, or reversionary, right; and it may be a right of considerable value.

In a later case, *Ritchie* (1899) 1 F 728, Lord Kinnear suggested that, in certain circumstances, the debtor, notwithstanding the granting of an *ex facie* absolute disposition, retains a residual real right in the security subjects; and is, therefore, not completely divested, feudally, by the granting of the *ex facie* absolute disposition. This opinion seems to be approved in the subsequent case *Edinburgh Entertainments* 1926 SC 363. For a full discussion, see the article by Professor Halliday in the *Conveyancing Review*, Vol. 1, p. 5. See also *Scobie* 1967 SLT 9 for a discussion on the nature of the debtor's right in a question between the debtor and third parties, where it was held that a debtor, originally infeft, but divested *ex facie* absolutely, retained a title to sue in an action by him to prevent infringement by a third party. The decision in *Red Court Hotel* 1955 SLT (Sh Ct) 2 was distinguished, but in fact disapproved.

**21.48 Factors affecting the reversionary right**. In considering the nature of the debtor's reversionary right, in the light of these decisions, it is necessary to bear in mind two factors which affect the position:

(*a*) The state of the original title. In the simplest case, the debtor, when granting the *ex facie* absolute disposition, was already infeft. In other words, he started off with a real right, and then conveyed the property to the creditor. But very often in practice the security was constituted at the time when the debtor acquired his right of property; and, to save expense and to eliminate unnecessary writs, the practice was that the selling proprietor, with consent of the debtor, conveyed the property directly to the *ex facie* absolute disponee. In such cases, the debtor had no title at all; and was never infeft. There is an intermediate case where the debtor, without infeftment, but holding on, *e.g.*, a general disposition, conveyed to the *ex facie* absolute disponee, deducing his title. Here, he had title but no infeftment.

(*b*) Recording of the back letter in Sasines. Normally, as has been stated, the back letter is not recorded, but it is recordable in the majority of cases and occasionally is recorded. It is generally accepted that the recording of the back letter imports real limitations into the creditor's title; and this in turn may affect the quality of the debtor's right.

**21.49 Sale or second security by debtor**. Whatever the nature of the debtor's reversionary right may be, it is transmissible. If the debtor sells his reversionary interest, he grants a special disposition of the property in favour of the purchaser in normal form, and, in addition, the disposition incorporates a clause assigning to the disponee the debtor's radical (or reversionary) right, and his right to call for a reconveyance from the *ex facie* absolute disponee. If the debtor grants a second security, he may do so either by a second *ex facie* absolute disposition, in similar form to the foregoing; or by bond and disposition in security (at least Burns so maintains, irrespective of the state of the debtor's title: *Practice*: p. 484) or by a standard security.

The disponee from the debtor, in order to complete his title, will in practice:

(*a*) record the disposition in the General Register of Sasines; and

(*b*) intimate the disposition to the first *ex facie* absolute disponee. Intimation is the appropriate method of perfecting a real right to any incorporeal right which has been assigned – in this case, to the debtor's reversionary right. Intimation creates a preference for the assignee at the date of intimation, just as registration creates a preference at the date of recording in Sasines. 1970 Act, s. 13.

The same principles apply to a second creditor's security.

The effect of an intimated assignation on the extent of the security has already been noticed above, at para. 21.44.

**21.50 Leases by the debtor**.   The validity of a lease depends on the validity of the landlord's title and the landlord must be infeft. Clearly, an infeft *ex facie* absolute disponee can grant a valid lease. Clearly, also, if the granting of the *ex facie* absolute disposition does not feudally divest the debtor, who remains infeft, then the debtor on the strength of his original title can grant valid leases. But the courts have held, in several cases, where the debtor is left in possession, that he has an implied mandate from the creditor to grant effective leases, which will be valid whether or not the debtor retains an infeftment in his own person. This principle seems well settled, although of very doubtful logic.

**21.51 Death of the debtor**.   On the death of the debtor, his right is heritable and transmits as such. This now creates no problem following on the Succession (Scotland) Act 1964. The executors confirm to the reversionary right.

**21.52 Discharge**
Since the *ex facie* absolute disposition is not a 'heritable security', the statutory form of discharge appropriate to heritable securities is not suitable to discharge this form of security. Instead, at common law, nothing less than a full formal conveyance (or reconveyance) served to divest the creditor and reinvest the debtor with the security subjects. The reconveyance is, in form, a special disposition, with all the normal clauses.

In addition, the debtor is entitled to a discharge of the personal obligation constituted by the back letter.

The debtor is always entitled to a reconveyance, on payment of all indebtedness. Further, the debtor is bound to accept a reconveyance when required by the creditor; and if he refuses to do so the creditor may invoke the assistance of the courts in order to complete his divestiture, normally with a view to avoiding continuing liabilities.

Clearly, a short form of discharge, rather than a full reconveyance would save time and effort, in drafting and revising, although *quoad* title the reconveyance is entirely effective.

So, the 1970 Act, s. 40(1) provides that a discharge, in a form provided in Schedule 9, separate or endorsed on the *ex facie* absolute disposition, shall, from the date of recording, disburden the subjects 'to the extent that it is the subject of the security, and vest the land in the person entitled thereto,' as if there had been a reconveyance.

But who is the person entitled thereto? This may be clear from the titles, but some further investigation will normally be required. There is no provision in the form for indicating the identity of the 'person entitled'.

Under s. 40(2), the old procedure remains competent.

The form provided in the 1970 Act Schedule 9 runs:

'I, AB (designed) hereby acknowledge that the disposition granted by CD (design) (or by EF (design) with consent of CD (design)) in my favour recorded G.R.S. on    , although in its terms *ex facie* absolute, was truly in security of an advance of £    ; and that all moneys intended to be secured thereby have been fully paid. In Witness Whereof:'.

By Note 3 to the Schedule, deduction of title is competent where the grantor is uninfeft. No deduction of title is envisaged for the grantee.

There is no reported case in which a discharge has caused problems in a title; but, nonetheless, because of potential difficulties in determining the person entitled, many agents prefer to use the more cumbersome but arguably more reliable reconveyance.

# Chapter 22

# STANDARD SECURITIES

## 22.1 Reforms under the 1970 Act

Under the Conveyancing and Feudal Reform (Scotland) Act 1970 Part II (ss. 9 to 32 and Schedules 2 to 7), the whole law of heritable securities in Scotland was fundamentally changed from and after 29 November 1970. It is now no longer competent to use the traditional forms of heritable security (including the bond and the *ex facie* absolute disposition), and, in lieu, the Act provides a new form of heritable security, known as the standard security, which must now be used for all types of security transaction, and which replaces all existing traditional forms.

The background to this major innovation on the law of securities is set out in Halliday *Report*, Chapter 8, paras. 102–106.

Only the main points of this legislation are dealt with in this Manual because:

(1) The 1970 Act Part II and Schedules 2–7 contain a comprehensive, intelligible and more or less self-contained code.

(2) Halliday *1970 Act*, in Chapters 6, 8 and 10, deals extensively with all the new legislation, and some resulting problems; and in Chapters 7 and 9, Halliday deals with practice and procedure in relation to the new standard security. These chapters also include a wide range of styles.

(3) Halliday's *Practice*, Chapters 36–42, bring Halliday *1970 Act* up to date.

## 22.2 The new forms of security

Section 9 authorises the use of the new forms of standard security; styles are provided – Form A and Form B in Schedule 2. Section 9 further provides that the standard security is now to be the only competent medium for securing any 'debt' by way of heritable security over any 'interest in land'.

The new standard security in either form can be used for any other purpose for which a heritable security could have been used pre-1970. The Bankruptcy Act 1696 (now repealed by the Bankruptcy (Scotland) Act 1985), which rendered heritable securities of no effect for future debt and also the common law rule which requires that a real burden for money must precisely state the sum due, are not to apply to a standard security. This released the standard security from the two limiting factors which effectively prevented a bond and disposition in security from being used to secure future or fluctuating debt. Therefore, in contrast to the bond and disposition, the standard security (although *ex facie* a security deed) is an all-purpose security, covering fixed or fluctuating, present or future, monetary or other obligations.

## 22.3 Exclusion of other forms of security
The use of the new form of security is made obligatory by s. 9(4). If a deed is granted to secure a debt over an interest in land which is not in the form of a standard security but which contains a disposition or assignation, then it is void as a security. If such a deed has been recorded, then the grantee is bound to clear the record. But, under s. 31, this does not apply to, nor affect, the validity of any heritable security (including the *ex facie* absolute disposition) recorded before 29 November 1970.

The word 'debt' in the 1970 Act covers payments of every kind, other than feuduties and ground annuals or other periodical sums payable in respect of land; and also obligations *ad factum praestandum* (s. 9(8)(*b*)). So, until 1 September 1974 feuduty and ground annuals could be 'secured' by charter, etc., being excluded from the restrictive terms of s. 9(3). It is, of course, no longer competent to create such annual charges on land under the 1974 Act; and accordingly the exception for periodical sums is no longer relevant.

## 22.4 The pattern of the new legislation
The standard security, in both its forms, and the supporting legislation, is clearly modelled on the bond and disposition in security and on the legislation authorising the use of the statutory form of bond. So, the 1970 Act s. 32 provides that any earlier statutory provisions relating to a bond and disposition in security, unless excluded in Schedule 8, shall apply to a standard security. Most of the earlier bond provisions are so excluded; and new separate provision is made in Part II of the Act for the comparable position under a standard security. But there are still some important provisions carried over from bonds to standard securities which are not so excluded and which therefore apply to standard securities. This applies particularly to the creditor's powers. Further, by s. 20(1), a creditor's powers on default at common law are preserved. In the result, some of the powers of the creditor are set out explicitly in Part II of the 1970 Act; some are set out in the standard conditions in Schedule 3; and some are carried over, by implication from the common law and from the 1868 Act, 1874 Act, 1894 Act, and 1924 Act. Further, certain of the powers in the standard conditions apparently conflict with the Act. Thus, standard condition 10(4) provides that a creditor in possession 'may let the security subjects or any part thereof'. But this apparently unfettered power is restricted by s. 20(3), on the same lines as existing powers under a bond and disposition in security. The result is somewhat confusing.

## 22.5 Earlier statutory provisions not excluded
The principal provisions which are carried forward and which continue to apply to the standard security include:

1868 Act s. 117. So the standard security is moveable in the succession of the creditor, except for legal rights.

1868 Act ss. 120, 126 and 127 – Completion of Title. Thus, the title of the creditor under a standard security may be completed during his lifetime by recording *de plano* in Sasines with warrant of registration; and is available to his successors, if he dies before the standard security has been recorded.

1874 Act s. 47 and 1924 Act s. 15. These two sections deal with the transmission of the personal obligation of the debtor on sale by the debtor or on his death and are dealt with later.

1894 Act ss. 3 and 4, dealing with procedure for entering into possession by action of maills and duties; and the 1924 Act s. 26, dealing with the comparable position where the security includes a superiority.

1894 Act s. 5, which entitles the creditor to eject a debtor in actual occupation.

1924 Act s. 40. Sale of the security subjects in lots.

1924 Act s. 41. Protection of purchasers; but a new subsection (2) is added by the 1970 Act s. 38, which applies to the bond and the standard security alike.

Notwithstanding this extensive carry-over of earlier statutory provisions, however, the new legislation on the standard security does represent a substantial innovation on the law of heritable securities in Scotland; and the Act introduces a number of improvements on the old law and on the old forms previously used.

### 22.6 Style of deed
Both forms provided in the 1970 Act, Form A and Form B, are *ex facie* security documents and therefore more closely resemble the bond and disposition in security than the *ex facie* absolute disposition.

Form A closely follows the form of the bond and disposition in security, in that it contains an undertaking to pay; but with this significant difference that, in Form A, the obligation may cover not merely fixed advances already made, but also future or fluctuating advances, to a stated limit or advances of indefinite amount without limit.

Section 10(1) provides an elaborate interpretation for the short form of undertaking incorporated in Form A; it does not apply to Form B.

Form B, in contrast, although *ex facie* a security document, does not contain *in gremio* any personal obligation or undertaking whatsoever. Instead, it simply refers to the debt or obligation constituted in a collateral document, equivalent to the minute of agreement qualifying an *ex facie* disposition, which itself constitutes the personal obligation and defines the undertaking to repay. There is no implied personal obligation in Form B.

The Act requires that in a standard security, the security subjects should be described by a particular description, or a statutory description by reference. It has been held that a postal address of a tenement building is not a sufficient description where the security is over one property in the building. (*Bennett* v. *Beneficial Bank plc* 1995 SLT 1105) and further that a postal address is not a particular description. To be a particular description, the boundaries must be identified and extrinsic evidence is incompetent (*Beneficial Bank plc* v. *McConnachie* 1996 SC 119).

For the execution of standard securities, the Requirements of Writing (Scotland) Act 1995 s. 3(1) provides that a deed which bears to be subscribed by the granter and attested by the signature of one witness is presumed to have been subscribed by the granter. Similarly, if the deed or testing clause contains information as to the date and place of execution, the deed is presumed to have been executed on that date and at that place (s. 3(8)). There is continuity here with the previous law which conferred similar presumptions in relation to attested writings (although under that law two witnesses were required).

**22.7 Statutory effect of new forms.** Under s. 11(1), when recorded, the standard security operates to vest the security subjects in the creditor as security for the performance of the contract to which the security relates. Feudally, the effect is the same as if, under former law, the debtor had granted a bond and disposition in security. So, the debtor is not divested, retains his real right, if infeft, and can deal with the subjects as *ex facie* proprietor. The creditor is a mere *ex facie* creditor and, unless in possession, incurs no personal liability for feudal prestations.

A standard security must be recorded in the Register of Sasines or registered in the Land Register. In the case of a standard security granted by a limited company, the security, being a charge, must also be registered in the Register of Charges within 21 days of the date of recording or registration. A failure so to register means that the charge is void against the liquidator or administrator and any creditor of the company (Companies Act 1985 s. 410). It is not competent to re-register the security as of new, if it is otherwise valid – see *Bank of Scotland* 1990 SC 284. The Companies Act 1989 s. 95 amends the provisions of the 1985 Companies Act so that a failure to register a charge at all will mean that the charge is void against a liquidator or administrator and any person who for value acquires an interest in or right over the property subject to the charge. In the case of late registration of the charge, the charge will be void where the company is insolvent and goes into liquidation within a prescribed period. It is still to be decided whether the provisions are to come into force (DTI Companies Act 1989 Commencement Summary Table as at 3 July 1995).

**22.8 Deduction of title.** The 1924 Act s. 3 introduced an innovation for the disposition but not for any other form of writ by permitting a person having right to land by a title not recorded in Sasines to grant that disposition uninfeft, provided that, in the disposition, a clause of deduction of title was introduced in a statutory form. This facility was not available to the grantor of a bond and disposition in security and is still not available to the grantor of a feu charter or of a lease.

Under the 1970 Act s. 12, however, the deduction of title facility has been extended, on very similar lines to the facility provided for the disposition under the 1924 Act s. 3, which permits a proprietor, uninfeft, to grant a standard security over his interest in heritable property. A statutory form of deduction of title is provided on very similar lines to the 1924 Act form; and s. 12(2) further provides that, on the recording of a standard security containing the statutory clause of deduction of title, the title of the grantee shall, for the purpose of the standard security but for no other purpose, be of the same effect as if the grantor thereof had been infeft. For the purposes of this deduction, mid-couples are as defined in the 1924 Act. See again on this topic under Chapter 32.

**22.9 Standard conditions.** This is an innovation. Every standard security embodies, by statutory implication under s. 11(2), the standard conditions contained in Schedule 3, with or without such variation as the parties may agree. These conditions operate both in relation to Form A and Form B. Note, particularly, that those conditions in Schedule 3 which relate to power of sale or foreclosure, and to the exercise of those powers, cannot be varied. The power of redemption may only be varied to the limited extent prescribed in the Redemption of Standard Securities (Scotland) Act 1971. The effect of the 1971 Act is that, while the parties may validly agree on certain matters, including in particular the duration of the loan and the period of notice, the actual procedure on redemption specified in standard condition 11 may not be altered. This is referred to again below.

## 22.10 Variation

Except as noted above, the terms of a standard security including a standard condition may be varied by agreement, either at the time when the standard security is granted in which case the variation is embodied in the loan documents or at any subsequent date, under the 1970 Act s. 16. This applies even where the condition to be varied (*e.g.* rate of interest in Form A) appears in the security itself, and so on the record; but in that case the deed of variation must itself be recorded.

In practice, it is unusual to find a standard security in which the variable standard conditions have not been altered. The variations which are commonly encountered deal with the insurance of the subjects, prohibitions against parting with possession or transferring the security subjects, alterations in use, improvement grants, power to deal with any moveables left on the premises, the creation of other securities and expanding the circumstances in which the debtor will be in default. Many building societies and other lenders produce booklets with the standard conditions in their original form and the standard conditions in the altered form and some of these have been registered in the Books of Council and Session.

## 22.11 Ranking of loans *inter se*

The general principles of ranking have already been referred to in the context of the bond and disposition in security above. As was there explained, in order to create a real security, the bond had to be recorded in Sasines, thereby creating an infeftment in security for the creditor as at the date of recording. But the bond, although so recorded and although it contained a dispositive clause conveying the security subjects to the creditor, did not divest the debtor absolutely. Instead, in feudal theory, the bond so recorded merely created a burden on the debtor's title unless and until the creditor under that bond exercised his power of sale, whereupon the creditor's title became absolute. As a result, the debtor could effectively deal with his property, whether on sale or in further security, unless and until the creditor exercised his powers because the debtor remained beneficial owner and infeft proprietor.

Under the 1970 Act, the standard security has become the only competent form of heritable security; and other forms are abolished for the future. In terms of s. 9(2), it is competent to record the standard security in the Register of Sasines or now, of course, in the Land Register in operational areas. Under s. 11, where a standard security is duly recorded, it operates to vest the interest over which it is granted in the grantee as security for performance of the contract to which that security relates.

Although the Act does not specifically so provide, it is generally accepted that, for the purposes of determining preference, the recording of a standard security has exactly the same effect as the recording of a bond and disposition in security had prior to 29 November 1970. In other words, as with the bond so with the standard security, notwithstanding the vesting of the heritable property in the creditor, that vesting is initially for the purpose of security only. The debtor remains the beneficial owner and the infeft proprietor, not wholly divested by the recording of the standard security in Sasines or in the Land Register.

The question of ranking is dealt with in the 1970 Act s. 13 but only to a limited extent. Except in so far as that section provides, therefore, common law rules and statutory provisions operating prior to 1970 continue to apply, to determine the order of preference as between competing rights in land, including the rights secured for the creditor under a recorded standard security.

**22.12 (1) Priority of infeftment determines preference.** By the combined effect of the Registration Act 1617 and the Real Rights Act 1693, real rights in land are preferred strictly according to priority of infeftment. This rule applies to security rights as it applies to proprietary rights. Suppose A, as infeft proprietor grants a standard security to X recorded in 1975; a second standard security to Y recorded in 1980 and a third standard security to Z recorded in 1985. X has the first infeftment in security, and takes an absolute priority over Y and Z; similarly Y is preferred to Z. If the property is sold on A's default, X is therefore entitled to payment in full of his principal, interest and penalties before Y can take anything; and similarly Y is paid in full before Z can take anything. This order of preference amongst heritable creditors *inter se* is termed ranking; and their ranking *inter se* is prior or postponed, strictly according to the respective dates of infeftment or recording.

**22.13 (2) *Pari passu* ranking.** But, in certain cases, two or more creditors fall to be ranked not prior and postponed *inter se*, but equally *pro rata* in proportion to the respective amounts of their several loans. This is termed *pari passu* ranking. Where two or more creditors rank *pari passu*, they share *pro rata* in the proceeds of any sale. *Pari passu* ranking may be constituted in the following ways.

**22.14** (*a*) *The 1868 Act s. 142 and the 1979 Act.* If two or more standard securities are received by the Keeper of the Registers on the same day they are deemed to be recorded simultaneously and, therefore, rank *pari passu*.

**22.15** (*b*) *Two or more lenders.* Normally, the personal obligation to pay is in favour of a single creditor; but it is equally competent in a single standard security to incorporate several obligations to pay in favour of several creditors. If this is done, and if the standard security is then recorded on behalf of the several creditors at the same time, they all rank *pari passu*.

Note, however that to achieve *pari passu* ranking by this method, the standard security must be recorded on behalf of all the creditors. This means that there must be a warrant of registration on behalf of each creditor, duly signed, before the standard security is presented for registration.

If, in such a case, the standard security was presented for registration with a warrant on behalf of one creditor only and not on behalf of the other creditor or creditors thereunder, that one creditor named in the warrant would have a prior ranking unless there was a special ranking clause in the standard security itself. The same applies to registration in the Land Register.

**22.16** (*c*) *Subsequent partial assignation.* The priority of a standard security is established as at the date of its recording. If the original creditor later assigns the whole security to an assignee, the assignee completes his right by recording the assignation – see below. If the creditor, fraudulently, grants two or more assignations of the same security, in whole, to different assignees, then as between these competing assignees the preference *inter se* would normally be determined strictly according to the order of recording of the respective assignations. But, as between any such assignee and a third party deriving right from the debtor, the assignee has the benefit of the preference established by the original recording of the standard security, and ranks accordingly.

A single standard security may competently be assigned in part, or in several parts to several assignees. If so, such assignees rank *pari passu inter se*; but again, in a question with third parties deriving right from the debtor, each several assignee enjoys the benefit of the preference established by the recording of the original standard security, *quoad* his portion thereof.

**22.17 (3) Ranking clauses.** The ordinary rules of ranking may be varied by express ranking clauses in one or several (contemporaneous) standard securities. But, if a standard security to A has been recorded and contains no express reference to ranking, a clause in a standard security in favour of B, recorded later, purportedly ranking B's standard security prior to A's, is ineffective. Because the first recorded security contains no contrary express ranking provision, priority of recording determines the order of ranking and the preference.

In many instances, where there is more than one security, it is common for the parties to enter into a ranking agreement rather than have ranking clauses in the security deeds. This device is adopted, particularly where the ranking arrangement is complex. See *Alloa Brewery Company Ltd.* 1992 SLT 121. To be fully effective, such agreements should always be recorded or registered on behalf of all the creditors thereto.

### 22.18 Statutory limitation on amount secured

The 1970 Act s. 13 is headed 'Ranking of standard securities', but that section is in fact restricted in scope. Contrast the much more detailed statutory provision for the ranking of floating charges, dealt with in the next chapter.

Ranking, therefore, still depends on priority of infeftment; and is determined by the date of recording of the standard security as explained above. Section 13 merely provides that the security thereby created is restricted to existing advances already made (with interest and expenses) at the date on which the creditor receives notice of the recording of a subsequent security or conveyance; but his security also covers any future advances, not yet made, but which the creditor is bound to make in terms of the security documents. For the comparable provision referred to above in the context of the *ex facie* absolute disposition, see s. 42.

## 22.19  Reserved powers

As with the bond, it is competent for the creditor not merely to vary the terms of the standard security or standard conditions as referred to above, with the limitations also above referred to; but, in addition, it is competent for the creditor to reserve to himself certain powers or certain rights not provided for in either of the forms in Schedule 2 nor in the standard conditions in Schedule 3, provided that such reservation does not contravene the restrictions on variation prescribed in the 1970 Act s. 11(3) or s. 16.

In the case of a standard security, apart from the power of redemption which is statutory and is dealt with below, it would be competent, as in a bond and disposition in security, for the debtor to reserve to himself power to feu. But, as is noted under the bond and disposition in security above, feuing for an annual feuduty is now no longer competent. As a result, superiorities cannot be created having any commercial value, and creditors will be very reluctant, except in special circumstances, to allow the debtor a reserved power to feu because, by so doing, his security is eroded without any compensating advantage in the form of an emerging feuduty. As a result, this particular reserved power is dying out, although occasionally it is still used in appropriate circumstances.

## 22.20  Creditor's rights and remedies

As with the bond, the creditor's primary right is to receive payment or re-payment of the principal sum in loan; or, since the standard security is wider in effect than the bond and disposition in security, to insist on implement of the obligation or performance of the contract to which the security relates. He has no other interest, and in particular no true proprietary right, in the security subjects, notwithstanding the recording of the standard security in the Register of Sasines except as security for the secured debt or obligation.

In contrast to the position under the bond, however, where the creditor's only concurrent right by statute was to insure the subjects for a limited sum to cover his own interest, standard conditions 1 to 7 in Schedule 3 impose a variety of obligations on the debtor which, under the older forms of security, were normally provided for by back letter or collateral agreement, but which are now statutory. All these standard conditions 1 to 7, which impose a variety of obligations on the debtor and give the creditor standard rights, are capable of variation and may be supplemented in any way which the parties agree upon, subject only to the restrictions referred to above which are unlikely to affect a variation of any of the standard conditions 1 to 7.

## 22.21  Import of standard conditions 1 to 7.

Without going into full detail, standard conditions 1 to 7 impose the following obligations on the debtor:

(1)  To maintain the security subjects.

(2)  To complete any uncompleted buildings.

(3)  To observe all the conditions in the title.

(4)  To inform the creditor as soon as the debtor receives any notice or order under the Town and Country Planning Acts.

(5)  To insure the security subjects or, if the creditor prefers, to allow the creditor to insure in which case the debtor pays the premium; and, in this

case, in contrast to the position under the bond and disposition in security, the amount insurable is the market value of the subjects. The insurable risks are fire and such other risks as the creditor may reasonably require. The debtor must also intimate any claim and give the creditor the opportunity to negotiate a settlement thereof.

(6) The debtor is prohibited from letting the security subjects which, by virtue of his proprietary title, he would otherwise have power to do.

(7) The creditor is authorised at his own hand to carry out any obligation imposed on the debtor under standard conditions 1 to 6, if the debtor himself fails to implement that obligation and to recover the costs thereof from the debtor. Such costs, if so incurred, are deemed to be secured by the standard security and therefore have a preference over other creditors.

### 22.22 Default by the debtor – standard conditions 8 to 10
Standard conditions 8 to 10 deal with default by the debtor but with this major caveat that the provisions of these three standard conditions, and in particular the rights of the creditor under standard condition 10, are very substantially restricted by the provisions of ss. 19 to 28 of the 1970 Act; and these standard conditions must be read along with these provisions in the Act, all of which must be strictly observed. Otherwise, any purported action by the creditor in the exercise of the powers conferred on him under the standard conditions may be void and, in addition, the creditor runs the risk of an action for damages for failure to observe his statutory obligations in these sections.

Broadly speaking, under a bond and disposition in security, there is only one default, namely, failure to pay principal and interest when demanded. So, as a preliminary to the exercise of the creditor's powers of sale, the creditor must serve notice requiring payment, to put the debtor in default. On the expiry of the three months' period of notice without payment, the creditor can exercise his power of sale; and, meantime, can exercise certain other remedies, including entering into possession.

With the standard security, in contrast, there are three alternative default situations, which are outlined in standard condition 9, and amplified in detail in ss. 19 to 24 of the 1970 Act.

### 22.23 Calling-up notice – standard condition 9(1)(a)
Failure to comply with a calling-up notice entitles the creditor, on the expiry of the two-month period of notice, to exercise all or any of the powers in standard condition 10 which include sale; entering into possession; carrying out repairs; foreclosure. See s. 20.

Section 19 contains the statutory provisions as to the form, service and effect of the notice, which substantially re-enact, with some important differences in detail, the comparable provisions for the notice calling up a bond and disposition in security.

**22.24 Form of notice.** The form of notice calling up the sum in loan secured by a standard security is prescribed in Schedule 6 Form A. It is designed primarily for monetary obligations but can be used for obligations *ad factum praestandum* with appropriate adaptation.

Section 19(9) deals with the case where the sum in loan is not a definite ascertained amount. This position could not normally arise with the bond and disposition in security for reasons already explained. The standard security, being more flexible, may be used to secure future and fluctuating debt and provision is made for this in the calling-up notice Form A. In such cases, it is competent to include in that notice a proviso to the effect that the amount required to redeem the loan is subject to adjustment. In *Clydesdale Bank plc* 1989 SLT (Sh Ct) 77, the debtor sought unsuccessfully to take advantage of this provision to prevent the creditor from entering into possession and proceeding to sell the security subjects, founding on a letter by him to the creditor calling for amendment/adjustment of the sum in loan. Failure by the creditor to comply with the provisions of this section invalidates the calling-up notice; and this underlines the importance of meticulously observing all the statutory requirements on the exercise of these powers.

**22.25 Service of the notice.** The statutory procedure should invariably be followed to the letter and it is prudent, before serving the notice, to study in detail the provisions of ss. 19 and 20 to ensure that all the statutory requirements have been meticulously complied with. In brief, these statutory requirements include:

Section 19(2) requires notice to be served on the person last infeft or his representatives.

Section 19(3) makes detailed provision for situations where there is difficulty in determining on whom to serve the notice. Thus, where a company has been removed from the Register of Companies, or where the person last infeft is deceased and has left no representatives, the notice is served on the Lord Advocate.

Section 19(4) and (5) amplify these provisions.

Section 19(6), (7) and (8) contain detailed provision for the method of service of the notice and for preserving evidence of such service, for which purpose Forms C or D of Schedule 6 should be used.

**22.26 Period of notice.** Section 19(10) deals with the period of notice which, in contrast to a notice calling up a bond, is two months, not three months. In terms of the statutory Form A Schedule 6, failing payment of the sum in loan with interest and expenses within that two-month period, the security subjects may then be sold. The notice is normally valid for a period of five years from the date thereof.

As with the bond, the period of notice may be dispensed with, given the appropriate consents of the debtor and *pari passu* or postponed creditors.

**22.27 Default notice – standard condition 9(1)(b)**
Where there has been a failure to comply with any other requirement arising out of the security, for example, if the debtor had failed to pay interest on the due date or had failed to maintain the security subjects in good repair, the creditor may alternatively serve a default notice under standard condition 9(1)(*b*), to which ss. 21 to 23 apply.

This provision is entirely new. There is nothing comparable in the 1924 Act for the bond and disposition in security. Note that under 9(1)(*a*), service of the notice is required to create default. Under 9(1)(*b*), the debtor is in default automatically by mere failure to comply. This would normally entitle the creditor to serve a calling-up notice. But he may, as an alternative to calling-up, where appropriate, serve on the debtor a notice of default, calling upon the debtor to remedy his default (*e.g.* failure to repair, etc.) within a period of one month. Failure to comply with an effective notice of default entitles the creditor to exercise the powers of sale, of carrying out repairs and of foreclosure; but it does not entitle him to enter into possession.

There is a different form of notice, Form B of Schedule 6, for a 9(1)(*b*) default as opposed to a calling-up Notice Form A; but otherwise the provisions of s. 19 apply generally to the service of the notice Form B, for which see above.

**22.28 Objection by debtor**. The notice of default may be objected to under s. 22(1) by application to the sheriff who adjudicates thereon. In contrast, the notice calling up the security under 9(1)(*a*) is not open to objection in this way. Therefore, although the calling-up notice requires a two-month period following thereon in contrast to the one-month period following on the notice of default, the calling-up notice may prove a quicker remedy in the long run because it is not open to objection.

Probably the best advice in many cases, where appropriate, is to serve both notices, calling-up and default. See Halliday's *Practice*, 39–20.

**22.29  Insolvency – standard condition 9(1)(c)**
Where the proprietor of the security subjects has become insolvent, default is automatic. But the creditor acquires no powers unless and until he applies to the court under s. 24; or, alternatively, serves a calling-up notice or a default notice.

There is a detailed definition of 'insolvency' in standard condition 9(2).

**22.30  Application to the court**
In terms of s. 24, where the debtor is in default under 9(1)(*b*) or 9(1)(*c*), the creditor may apply to the court for a warrant to exercise any of the powers available to the creditor under 9(1)(*a*).

Many agents take decree in every case as a precautionary policy.

Under s. 24(2), where an application is made to the court on default under 9(1)(*b*), a certificate in terms of Schedule 7 may be lodged in court which is *prima facie* evidence of the facts therein stated.

**22.31  Procedure**
Section 29 of the Act deals with procedure. The appropriate court for all actions under Part II of the Act is the sheriff court in whose jurisdiction any part of the security subjects is situate. Any application to the court, in terms of this section, is by way of summary application. This has given rise to a number of recent cases where a creditor has applied to the court by summary action under s. 24 and has incorporated, in that summary application, a crave for ejection of the debtor-proprietor and for a warrant to enter into possession of the security subjects. There is no doubt as to the creditor's right to eject the debtor in such circumstances; but that right is conferred by the 1894 Act s. 5. It is not therefore a right arising under Part II of the

1970 Act. The doubts about the correct procedure have now been resolved by the passing of an Act of Sederunt (S.I. 1990 No. 661) which provides that if a creditor is seeking only the remedies in standard condition 10, this must be done by summary application. If on the other hand, an additional remedy is sought, for example ejection, an ordinary action must be raised.

### 22.32 The creditor's powers on default
Standard condition 10 outlines the creditor's remedies on default as defined above in standard condition 9.

### 22.33 Creditor must act reasonably.
Reference has already been made to the obligation on a creditor to exercise his powers reasonably. See the *ex facie* absolute disposition above in Chapter 21.43 and in particular the case of *Rimmer* 1967 SLT 7, there referred to. In the context of the *ex facie* disposition, the rule is particularly relevant because the *ex facie* absolute disposition is not regarded as a heritable security in the strict sense, and so none of the statutory controls imposed on the creditor under a bond and disposition in security apply to the creditor under the *ex facie* absolute disposition. Accordingly, were it not for this common law rule, the creditor might take advantage of his position to the prejudice of the debtor, as illustrated in the case of *Rimmer*.

The standard security legislation imposes strict controls on the creditor, under the Act itself and under the standard conditions. Nonetheless, there is scope for abuse to the prejudice of the debtor. For a recent discussion on the duties of a creditor exercising his powers under a standard security and in particular under standard condition 10, see *Armstrong, Petitioner* 1988 SLT 255. This case involved a competition between a heritable creditor and a judicial factor on a partnership estate. A calling-up notice had already been served before the judicial factor was appointed and in the circumstances the court held that the subsequent appointment of the factor did not disable the creditor from exercising rights which he already possessed. But Lord Jauncey comments that the creditor must exercise these rights *civiliter* and with proper regard for the interests of the debtor. The creditor's primary interest is recovery of the debt and on that basis Lord Jauncey did not consider that the creditor has unlimited discretion as to which one or more of the powers he should exercise. Accordingly, if the creditor elects to exercise his powers under condition 10 in a manner which does not produce the best result for the debtor, then he might very well be restrained from so acting; or be liable in damages if he acted in such a way. 'A heritable creditor cannot use his powers for the primary purpose of advancing his own interest at the expense of the debtor when he has the alternative of proceeding in a more equitable manner.' However, in *Halifax Building Society* 1994 SC 13, *Armstrong* was regarded as a decision limited to its peculiar facts and the normal position is that the Court has no discretion but to allow the creditor to exercise the powers under the Act.

A similar question arose in *Associated Displays* 1988 SCLR 220 where a heritable creditor, acting under his power of sale, concluded missives for the sale of the security subjects. The debtor then sought to prevent the sale going through until such time as the creditor satisfied the court that he had taken all reasonable steps to ensure that he had obtained the best price.

The sheriff held that the debtor's application was incompetent on two grounds. First, the creditor was under no duty to satisfy the court about anything; and, secondly, it was in any event too late, after missives had been concluded, to seek to prevent the creditor from proceeding with the sale. In the light of the decisions in *Rimmer* and *Armstrong* referred to above, this is a somewhat surprising decision. When exercising the power of sale, as will be noticed shortly, 'it shall be the duty of the creditor ... to take all reasonable steps to ensure that the price ... is the best that can be reasonably obtained'. One would have thought that, if the debtor had serious grounds for maintaining that the creditor was not implementing his duty, the court might have intervened. See also, on the same point, *Bank of Credit* 1987 GWD 10–341, *Gordaviran* 1994 SCLR 248 and *Thomson* 1994 SCLR 1014 which have followed the approach in *Associated Displays*. If these decisions are correct, it would follow that even if the debtor sees the property being advertised at a very low figure, he must wait until after the sale before taking any action.

The creditor's obligation to obtain 'the best price' was discussed in *Dick* 1991 SC 365. The Clydesdale Bank had a standard security over two areas of ground, one of which was used for commercial purposes and a larger area for agricultural. The bank called up their standard security and instructed professional advisers to market the property. The debtor wrote to the bank asking them to consider a number of matters before they proceeded with the sale and he suggested that the land would become more valuable as soon as the route for a new by-pass had been announced. He clearly wanted the bank to delay until the circumstances were more favourable. The bank, however, advertised the subjects and an offer for both areas of ground was accepted. The debtor then raised an action against the bank for damages for the loss which he claimed he had sustained because the agricultural ground had not been sold having regard to the expected rise in value. While the Inner House dismissed the debtor's averments of loss as irrelevant, they did go on to discuss the creditor's obligations. In that connection, they made four points (a) the creditor has a duty to the debtor as well as to himself; (b) the creditor is entitled to sell the security subjects at a time of his own choosing, provided he has taken all reasonable steps to ensure that the price at which he sells is the best that can reasonably be obtained at that time (in the *Bank of Credit* case, the sheriff thought that, because any further delay in the marketing of the property would have resulted in interest running against the debtor, that factor had to be weighed against the requirement that the creditor must try to get the best available price); (c) in the ordinary case, the creditor will be regarded as having fulfilled the duties imposed upon him if he takes and acts upon appropriate professional advice. The implication may be that in an unusual case the creditor has to do more than just take professional advice; (d) what matters is the reality of the market place in which the property is exposed for sale at the time when the creditor decides to sell. As long as the creditor takes all reasonable steps to attract competition in that market, he will not be criticised for not taking further steps to attract an appropriate purchaser, unless there is evidence to show that a better bargain would have been achieved. It follows from that case that great care has to be taken in the marketing of security subjects and if the property is unusual in some way, it may be prudent for the heritable creditor to take advice, other than from his solicitor, about the most appropriate method of marketing the property.

**22.34 Interrelationship between standard conditions and statutory provisions in the Act.** Standard condition 10 outlines the various remedies which the creditor may resort to on default by the debtor. Note, firstly, that these remedies are without prejudice to the exercise by the creditor of any other remedy arising out of the contract to which the security relates. Accordingly, depending on the nature of the obligations secured by the standard security, there may be other and more appropriate remedies than those listed in standard condition 10.

The remedies there listed include:

(*a*) sale of the security subjects;

(*b*) entering into possession and, when in possession, granting leases etc.;

(*c*) carrying out repairs;

(*d*) foreclosure.

As stated above, however, the standard conditions have to be read along with the provisions of the Act itself; and there are now three default situations involving either a calling-up notice, a default notice, or insolvency. Different provisions apply to each of the three alternative default situations.

Under s. 20, when the debtor fails to implement a calling-up notice and is therefore in default under 9(1)(*a*), the creditor can exercise all or any of the powers in standard condition 10. His power to grant leases, however, which is unqualified in standard condition 10(4), is restricted by the statutory provisions of s. 20.

In contrast, where the debtor fails to implement a default notice and has not effectively objected to it under s. 22, then, under s. 23, the creditor is given power to sell under standard condition 10(2), to carry out repairs under 10(6), and to foreclose under 10(7). But he is not entitled to enter into possession, to grant leases etc. If he wants to have these powers under standard condition 10(3) to 10(5), then he must apply to the court under s. 24.

In the third default situation under 9(1)(*c*), namely insolvency, the creditor does not acquire any powers. Instead, he must always apply to the court for power to exercise any of these powers under s. 24.

**22.35 Particular powers**
Turning now to the particular powers conferred by standard condition 10, and keeping in mind that the powers there conferred are a summary only and must be read along with the statutory provisions in the Act itself, there are four main powers.

**22.36 (1) Sale.** The statutory provisions for sale under a standard security are commendably simple and brief. Instead of the elaborate detail in the 1924 Act, which still applies to the bond and disposition in security and still remains elaborate, notwithstanding the amendments in Part III of this Act, the 1970 Act s. 25 simply provides that the creditor may sell either by private bargain or by public roup. In either event, it is his duty to advertise the sale and to take all reasonable steps to ensure that the price at which the security subjects are ultimately sold is the best price that can be reasonably obtained. This requirement, and some recent cases thereon, are referred to above. Nothing more is required. In particular, there are no provisions prescribing the period or number of advertisements, newspapers, place of sale, or upset price, as in the 1924 Act provisions. The word 'advertise' as used in s. 25 is not defined. Looking to the elaborate provisions in the 1924 Act, and the general duty of the creditor, referred to above, to take reasonable steps to protect the debtor's interests, it was originally assumed, without question, that advertisement implied public advertisement in the public press. See Halliday *1970 Act*, Chapter 10.38, and in particular his reference to certificates of advertisement from the publishers. Three separate instances have been brought to the notice of the Keeper of the Registers in relation to the Keeper's indemnity in registration of the title. In each of these three instances, the property was sold by the creditor in the exercise of the power of sale but not by advertisement in the public press. The Keeper is believed to take the view, however, that s. 25 does not prescribe the mode of advertisement and indeed, in this context, it is significant that, in the 1970 Act, no provision whatever is made for preservation of evidence of advertisement as in the earlier legislation regulating the power of sale under a bond and disposition in security. If the view is accepted, then anything which lets it be known to the public by whatever medium that the property is for sale could be construed as advertising. But it would certainly be safer to follow the advice of Professor Halliday referred to above.

The missives for the sale of subjects which are being sold by a heritable creditor may differ in some respects from the norm. For example, because the property may have been vacant for some time and, in any event, the heritable creditor will not have been in occupation, it is unlikely that the heritable creditor will grant some of the warranties which are customarily asked of sellers, particularly in the sale of domestic property. The heritable creditor is unlikely to be willing to warrant the ownership of the moveables, or that the central heating system and electrical appliances are in good order. In addition, the heritable creditor may put the onus on the purchaser to ascertain whether the erection of the building and any alterations complied with local authority requirements and that all other consents have been obtained. The heritable creditor is unlikely to be willing to clear the Personal Registers of any inhibitions which post-date the granting of the standard security and any letter of obligation will be qualified to that extent.

**22.37** *Procedure on sale under ss. 26 and 27.*   The procedure following on sale differs from the procedure on sale under a bond and disposition in security in certain important respects.

**22.38** *Clearing the record.*   Prior creditors are not affected in any way by a sale by a postponed creditor; are entitled to be paid, in full, the principal sum in loan due to them with interest and expenses; and, unless and until so paid, are not obliged to grant the necessary discharge which will clear the record. Accordingly, if a postponed creditor sells under the power of sale and there is a shortfall, he may find himself personally liable to make good the difference in order to clear the record.

As to other securities, the creditor is still bound to account to the debtor

for his intromissions but, with the standard security, there is no requirement to produce a formal certificate of surplus or no surplus. Instead, the
record is cleared of the selling creditor's own security, all *pari passu* and
postponed securities and diligences, merely by the recording of the disposition in favour of the purchaser, which in its terms bears to be in implement of the sale. The old rule which required the consent of *pari passu*
creditors is abolished for the standard security by the 1970 Act ss. 26(1) and
27(1).

In *Newcastle Building Society* 1987 SLT (Sh Ct) 81 the building society,
on default of the debtor, duly exercised their power of sale and, in the customary form, undertook in the contract of sale and purchase to deliver a
clear search. It then emerged that, after the recording of the standard security but before the sale, an inhibition had been registered against the debtor
proprietor. The purchaser maintained that, in these circumstances, the
search was not clear; but the Sheriff Principal held that, in view of the provisions of s. 26(1) referring to diligences postponed to the security of the
selling creditor, it was clear *ex facie* of the record that the property had
been disencumbered and accordingly no further action was required on the
part of the building society.

**22.39** *Application of proceeds of sale.*   Under a bond and disposition in
security, the creditor is obliged to pay off prior securities and, possibly, securities ranking pari passu with his own; but there his duty ends, beyond accounting to the debtor for the surplus or no surplus as the case may be. In
the case of the standard security, however, the debtor is given what may be
a more onerous role in that under s. 27(1) the proceeds of sale are to be
held by the selling creditor in trust and applied thus:

(*a*) to pay the expenses properly incurred in connection with the sale;

(*b*) to pay the whole amount due under prior securities;

(*c*) to pay the whole amount due under his own security and *pari passu*
securities, *pro rata* if the proceeds are insufficient;

(*d*) to pay the amounts due to any heritable creditors with postponed ranking, according to their ranking;

(*e*) finally, any residue remaining is to be paid to the person entitled to the
security subjects at the time of sale.

**22.40** *Problems of accounting.*   Clearly, this may cause problems to the
selling creditor and so, under s. 27(2), if the creditor cannot obtain a receipt
or discharge for any of the foregoing payments, he is obliged to account for
his intromissions but may consign the amount due in the sheriff court for
the benefit of the persons having best right thereto.

The decision in *Halifax Building Society* 1985 SLT (Sh Ct) 25 illustrates
the difficulties which may confront the selling creditor. In that case, the
Halifax Building Society properly exercised its power of sale and there was
a resulting surplus. After the standard security had been recorded but
before the sale was concluded, a number of inhibitions were registered
against the debtor. There was no doubt that, in the circumstances, these inhibitions did not interfere with the sale and that the record was cleared
under s. 26(1); but the question was whether, for the purposes of s. 27(1),

inhibiting creditors held securities with a ranking postponed to that of the selling creditor. If so, then they were entitled to share in the distribution of the surplus. The Sheriff Principal held that, for the purposes of s. 27(1)(*d*), inhibitions were securities.

**22.41** *Protection of the purchaser.* This has already been referred to under the bond and disposition in security. The same provision applies to a purchaser under a standard security. By way of reminder, the provision is contained in the 1924 Act s. 41(2), in the form substituted by the 1970 Act s. 38. The effect of that section is that, where a disposition bearing to be in implement of a power of sale has been duly recorded and where the exercise of the power of sale was *ex facie* regular, the title of a *bona fide* purchaser for value is not open to challenge either:

(*a*) on the grounds that the debt had ceased to exist; or

(*b*) on the grounds of any irregularity in the sale procedure.

The protection afforded to the purchaser, however, does not exclude a claim for damages at the instance of an aggrieved debtor against a selling creditor who has abused his powers.

It is not clear exactly what enquiry the *bona fide* purchaser must make to establish his *bona fides*; but the prudent agent will at least investigate the sale procedure to ensure that the same was *ex facie* regular.

**22.42 (2) Entering into possession.** Standard condition 10(3) empowers the creditor, on default, to enter into possession and receive the rents and feuduties. This power is not available to a creditor under standard condition 9(1)(*b*) without authority from the court. In any event, even if the creditor is proceeding under a calling-up notice and standard condition 9(1)(*a*), a decree of maills and duties or its equivalent is required unless the debtor consents.

Once in possession, whether by decree or of consent, the creditor may let the security subjects. The power to let is, however, restricted by the 1970 Act s. 20(3) to leases for a term not exceeding seven years, except with the consent of the sheriff. This is similar to the provisions of the 1894 Act s. 7; but, for the standard security, there is no maximum term.

The creditor in possession also has the same rights as the debtor in relation to management and maintenance if the property is already let.

**22.43** *Implications for creditor in possession.* The exact implications of 'entering into possession' are not clear. On the one hand, where a default notice has been served under 9(1)(*b*) and not complied with, the creditor has power of sale but does not automatically have power to enter into possession unless he applies to the court for that power. It is a little difficult to see how a creditor can sell the security subjects without being in possession thereof, but that seems to be the implication of s. 23(2).

Whatever the meaning of the term, entering into possession is not something to be undertaken lightly and without some prior investigation. For one thing, a creditor in possession undoubtedly becomes liable for feudal prestations and for the liabilities of the proprietor in a question with the public which, as a mere security holder, he would not incur. In *David Watson Property Management Ltd.* 1992 SC (HL) 21 the question of what additional liabilities might be imposed upon the heritable creditor was raised. A building society repossessed security subjects with a view to sale. At the time they entered into possession, there were arrears of common charges which had been incurred by the debtor. The House of Lords *held* that an obligation in the title to maintain was enforceable against singular successors. However, when a resulting obligation to pay a specific amount arose, that was a debt which was personal to the owner at the time the work was done and did not transmit against a heritable creditor in possession.

In this connection it is worth noting that there are various statutes which impose obligations on the 'owner', for example, the Housing (Scotland) Act 1987 which deals with statutory repairs notices. It remains to be decided whether a heritable creditor in possession is the 'owner' for such purposes. It is submitted that he is not and it has been decided that he is not liable for the community charge. See *Northern Rock Building Society* 1990 SLT (Sh Ct) 109.

As a general rule, a postponed creditor can exercise his statutory powers notwithstanding subsisting prior securities. Thus, a postponed creditor can sell the security subjects although he must then pay off the prior security in full in order to obtain a discharge thereof and to clear the record. However, that rule does not apply to entering into possession – see *Skipton Building Society* 1986 SLT 96, where Lord Stewart held that the creditor holding the earlier of two competing decrees was the creditor entitled to possession.

**22.44 (3) Carrying out repairs, etc.** Standard condition 10(6) empowers the creditor, when the debtor is in default, to effect necessary repairs, reconstruction or improvement, and to enter on the subjects for this purpose. This is wider than the equivalent power of the bondholder under the 1924 Act s. 25(1)(*a*). There are no statutory limitations on this right; and, in particular, the creditor need not, first, be lawfully in possession.

**22.45 (4) Foreclosure.** The whole foreclosure code applicable to a bond and disposition in security is excluded, but, in substance re-enacted, for standard securities under the 1970 Act s. 28. The statutory requirements are:

(1) Exposure for sale by public roup at a price not exceeding the amount due under the security, and all prior and *pari passu* securities.

(2) The expiry of 2 months from first exposure.

(3) An application to the sheriff served on the debtor, the proprietor and any other heritable creditor disclosed by a 20-year search.

(4) On such application, the sheriff may either:

(*a*) allow time to pay not exceeding 3 months; or

(*b*) order re-exposure, with power to the creditor to bid; or

(*c*) grant decree of foreclosure, declaring the right of redemption extinguished.

On recording that decree, then:

(1) the right of redemption is extinguished;

(2) the subjects are disburdened of the foreclosing creditor's security and

all postponed securities. But prior and *pari passu* securities are unaffected. The creditor may redeem these as the debtor might have done;

(3) the creditor's title is unchallengeable on grounds of irregularity in procedure; but

(4) the debtor's personal obligation to the foreclosing creditor is not discharged.

**22.46 (5) Poinding of the ground**. This common law remedy is also available, but rarely used.

**22.47 (6) Adjudication**. This is also a common law remedy which is rarely used because the creditor will not acquire a real right until the expiry of 10 years ('the legal'). The Scottish Law Commission has produced a Discussion Paper (No. 78) with proposals for reforming the law to make adjudication a more attractive remedy.

**22.48 Transmission**

As already explained in relation to the bond and disposition in security, there are two elements in a heritable security such as a bond and a standard security.

(*a*) Real security. The creditor's preference is established at the date of creation of the real right by the recording of the standard security; but the debtor is not divested. Accordingly, the debtor can still deal with the property by way of sale or second security; and, on his death or on sequestration the security subjects will transmit to his representatives, or trustee. Any such dealing with the debtor's proprietary right is subject to, and cannot affect, the preference created for the creditor by the recording of the standard security.

(*b*) The personal obligation. In contrast to the bond and disposition in security, two different forms of standard security are provided in the 1970 Act, Form A and Form B, the detail of which has already been referred to above. The principal difference between the two forms is that in Form A the personal obligation appears on the face of the deed; whereas, with Form B, the security is granted by the debtor for the purpose of securing a separate obligation contained in a collateral agreement, which is referred to and detailed in Form B. With the bond and disposition in security, the personal obligation was restricted to payment, or repayment, of a specified capital sum. With the standard security, there are wider possibilities but the same general principles apply. In particular, the personal obligation, whether contained in Form A or in a separate collateral agreement secured by Form B, subsists until the debtor fully implements his obligations therein; that obligation, (unless otherwise expressly so provided which is virtually unknown) is not restricted to the value of the security subjects; and the personal obligation subsists and remains enforceable against the original debtor as a personal debt even although he may have parted with the security subjects.

**22.49 (1) Change of debtor; liability of singular successor**. A singular successor acquiring heritable property subject to a standard security does not, at common law, incur any element of personal liability although, notwithstanding his proprietary right, he cannot prevent the creditor from exercising any of his real remedies as against the security subjects which the singular successor has acquired from the original debtor. Suppose, then, that A owns heritage subject to a loan secured by a standard security. He sells the property to B on the footing that B will take over responsibility for the outstanding loan. Some years elapse. B then defaults. The creditor can still sue A on the personal obligation, but cannot sue B by way of personal action; alternatively the creditor can exercise his power of sale and recoup himself out of the proceeds, which does not directly affect A, the original debtor. If B has to pay, he may have a right of relief against A, the original debtor; but this does not affect the creditor.

This is unsatisfactory, and in practice it is unusual for a purchaser or disponee to take over a loan in this way. Instead, the loan is normally paid off and the disponee borrows of new. But, if taking over the loan is the arrangement between the parties, then the disponer, A, would normally wish to be relieved of personal liability; and the creditor would not normally release him unless he got a personal obligation from B in lieu. The creditor is not, in any event, bound to release A, the original debtor.

**22.50** *Modes of transferring personal liability.* The personal obligation can be made to transmit against B, as singular successor in two ways:

(a) Bond of corroboration. This is a separate deed in terms of which the disponee expressly undertakes personal liability.

(*b*) The 1874 Act s. 47, as amended by the 1924 Act s. 15 and Schedule A2. The object of this provision is to render the bond of corroboration unnecessary. These sections are not excluded by the 1970 Act and continue to apply to the standard security. The combined effect of the sections is:

(i) Where the disponee takes by succession, gift, or bequest, he incurs personal liability up to the value of the subjects taken by him.

(ii) Where the disponee takes by conveyance, other than on succession, gift or bequest, the disposition in his favour may contain an express undertaking by the disponee of personal liability in lieu of obtaining a separate bond of corroboration. A statutory form is provided in the 1924 Act Schedule A2 which is equally applicable to the taking over of personal liability for a standard security.

As with the bond and disposition in security, so with the standard security, the mere fact that a singular successor undertakes the personal obligation in a standard security does not, of itself, release the original debtor from personal liability; and a separate personal discharge is required. Being purely personal, such a discharge is not recordable in Sasines.

**22.51 (2) Change of creditor.** The same general principles apply here as apply to the bond and disposition in security. The benefit of the personal obligation undertaken by the debtor is an asset in the estate of the creditor. This applies whether the personal obligation is undertaken *in gremio* of the standard security Form A or in a collateral obligation secured by Form B. It would be theoretically possible to exclude transmission of the debtor's obligation in this way to a new creditor but this is virtually unknown in practice.

The right of the creditor under a standard security, accordingly, involves both the benefit of the personal obligation of the debtor and the real security granted by the debtor in support of that personal obligation. If the benefit of the personal obligation is to transmit as it may, by *inter vivos* or *mortis causa* deed, then it is essential that the person succeeding to the debtor's obligation should take over both the benefit of the personal obligation of the debtor and the real security created for the benefit of the original creditor.

**22.52** *Transmission inter vivos.*  Looking to the special features of this form of asset involving, as it does, both the personal obligation of the debtor and the real security, transmission *inter vivos* involves some specialties as does transmission of a bond and disposition in security. In particular, the transferee or assignee will require an effective transfer of the personal obligation so that the assignee in turn can enforce it directly against the debtor; and he will also require a transfer of the security subjects in a form which will allow him to exercise all the powers enjoyed by the original creditor under the standard security when originally granted in his favour by the debtor.

Special provision is duly made for the transfer of both elements in the standard security, the personal obligation and the real security, by way of a statutory form of assignation authorised by the 1970 Act s. 14(1) and Schedule 4 Form A. In appropriate cases, a partial assignation is competent. On such assignation being duly recorded, the security or the part thereof assigned, vests in the assignee as if the security or that part thereof had originally been granted in his favour.

In addition, under s. 14(2), the assignation carries with it to the assignee the benefit of all corroborative obligations; the right to recover from the debtor all expenses properly incurred by the creditor; and the benefit of any notices served by the creditor before the assignation.

There are a number of notes to Schedule 4 dealing with various specialties. In particular:

Note 1.  If the assignor does not himself have a recorded title, deduction of title is necessary in the assignation.

Note 2.  This deals with securities for uncertain amounts and prescribes the method of defining what is assigned.

**22.53** *Transmission mortis causa.*  See Chapter 31, Transmission on Death.

#### 22.54 Extinguishing the debtor's obligation
As already explained, the standard security is granted to secure performance by the debtor of a pecuniary obligation or an obligation *ad factum praestandum.* If the debtor fails to implement his obligations, then the creditor has remedies, both personal and real, which have already been dealt with. But, in the great majority of cases, the debtor does fulfill his obligations in the fullness of time either by payment or performance; and, when the obligations are thus fully implemented, the debtor is entitled to a discharge.

**22.55  (1)  Discharge.**  The purpose of the discharge is two-fold:

(*a*) to release the debtor from his continuing personal obligation to the creditor; and

(*b*) to release the security subjects from the burden of the standard security as a real security thereon.

A short statutory form is provided in the 1970 Act s. 17 which achieves both objectives by the granting of a discharge, following Form F of Schedule 4 to the Act.

Notes 1 and 2 to Schedule 4, referred to above in para. 22.52, likewise apply to the discharge Form F. Section 17 further provides that, on the recording of the discharge in the statutory form, the security subjects are disburdened thereof.

**22.56 (2) Alternative modes of disburdenment.** The form provided and its effect are very similar to the equivalent form for the discharge of a bond and disposition in security; and, as mentioned in that context, a discharge is normally used to release the debtor and clear the record. But in fact very much less will serve to achieve the same purpose although not normally relied on in practice. So, the security subjects may be disburdened of a subsisting security not merely by discharge but also in one or other of the following ways.

**22.57** (*a*) *Redemption.* Under the debtor's power of redemption and related procedure, without the intervention of the creditor, the record is cleared. 1970 Act s. 18(3).

**22.58** (*b*) *Confusio.* This is a rule of general application to obligations in Scots law and applies where the same person in the same capacity becomes both the debtor and the creditor in an obligation. The effect, *quoad* heritable securities, is that the security is absolutely extinguished and cannot be revived.

**22.59** (*c*) *Prescription.* A bond and disposition in security, being essentially an obligation for payment of a sum of money, is extinguished by the running of the long negative prescription, notwithstanding the infeftment of the creditor. In practice, payment of interest by the debtor normally regularly interrupts the running of prescription, which rarely runs its full course.

In the case of the standard security, however, the obligation secured may be, and usually is, payment or repayment of a sum of money in which case the same principle applies; but the standard security may also be used to secure other obligations. It is difficult to see how a standard security could be used to secure an imprescriptible obligation as defined in Schedule 1 to the Prescription and Limitation (Scotland) Act 1973; but that possibility, at least in theory, cannot be altogether dismissed.

**22.60** (*d*) *Payment.* 'An infeftment in security may be extinguished by payment or discharge of the debt' *per* Lord Kinnear in *Cameron* (1895) 22 R 293, where part of a sum in loan was repaid but no formal discharge was granted. The remaining balance of the loan was later discharged by a formal partial discharge which referred expressly to the earlier partial repayment; held that the record was clear of the whole bond.

## 22.61 Restriction

As already explained in the context of the bond and disposition in security, a standard security creates a real burden on the whole of the security subjects and on every individual part thereof. Thus, if the owner of a tenement of flats grants a standard security thereon for £20,000 and one flat is later sold, the sold flat remains liable as real security for payment of the whole debt. The creditor, following on such sale, may then in his option exercise his power of sale over the sold flat alone and satisfy his debt out of the proceeds; or he may proceed against the whole, or other parts, of the tenement.

As a result, no purchaser will take a title to heritable subjects forming part of a larger whole where the larger whole is subject to a subsisting security. In such a case, the debtor may pay off the whole loan and have the standard security discharged, which undoubtedly clears the record and renders the title marketable. But this may be inconvenient to the debtor on a sale of a small portion only of the larger whole. So, as an alternative, a debtor frequently bargains with the creditor in such circumstances for the release by the creditor of the sold portion, on such terms and conditions as the debtor and creditor mutually agree. Where such a release is arranged, it would be inappropriate for the standard security to be discharged; if that were done, the creditor would lose his security for the remaining outstanding loan. Instead, the sold portion can be taken out of the creditor's security by three methods.

**22.62 (1) Deed of restriction**. This is a separate formal deed granted by the creditor. The 1970 Act s. 15(1) provides that the security constituted by a standard security may be restricted as regards any part of the subjects burdened thereby by a deed of restriction following Form C of Schedule 4 and on such deed being recorded, the security shall be restricted to those subjects under exception of the land disburdened by the deed; and the part so disburdened is cleared from the security. Again, Notes 1 and 2 to Schedule 4 apply.

**22.63 (2) Consent *in gremio*.** Instead of using the separate deed of restriction, it is competent and effective for the creditor to consent to the disposition in favour of the purchaser of the portion sold. A clause is inserted in the narrative of the disposition to the effect that the creditor agrees to release the subjects disponed from his security. The disposition is then executed by the creditor and recording thereof disburdens the part so disponed.

**22.64 (3) Reserved power to feu.** This has already been referred to. The debtor, when granting the standard security, may reserve to himself power to feu. At one time this was a popular device to avoid the need for separate deeds of restriction on the occasion of the sale of each plot in a development but, with the abolition of feuduty, it is now only used in very special circumstances. If there is such a power in the standard security, however, and if any conditions attaching thereto are properly observed, then the reservation of the power to feu or, possibly, to dispone, will effectively release any part of the security subjects feued or disponed in terms thereof.

# Chapter 23

# FLOATING CHARGES

## 23.1 The principle of heritable security

The fundamental principle of a heritable security is that a real right in the security subjects vests in the creditor. Such real rights are created by either:

(*a*) an active infeftment in the person of the creditor, *e.g.* by the recording in Sasines of a bond and disposition in security, a standard security or an *ex facie* absolute disposition; or

(*b*) the effective creation of a real burden, as a qualification of a simultaneous infeftment in the security subjects.

Every such heritable security necessarily affects a particular heritable property. It becomes effective only when a writ relating to that particular property enters the Register of Sasines; the date of recording is the criterion of preference and of ranking; and the security subsists on the security subjects until it is later actively discharged. The result is that, as with proprietary rights, the Register of Sasines is the measure of, and the index to, all security rights affecting heritable property in Scotland.

In the case of companies only this fundamental principle has been radically altered by the Companies (Floating Charges) (Scotland) Act 1961, later repealed and re-enacted by the Companies (Floating Charges and Receivers) (Scotland) Act 1972, now consolidated in the Companies Act 1985 and the Insolvency Act 1986.

The Companies Act 1985 ss. 462–466 deal with the creation, effect, ranking and alteration of floating charges in Scotland, and ss. 410–424 deal in detail with the registration of charges, both fixed and floating.

The Insolvency Act 1986 ss. 50–71, superseding the Companies Act 1985 ss. 467–485, deal in detail with the appointment and powers of receivers in Scotland; and s. 72 deals with the cross-border operation of receivership provisions in Great Britain as a whole. The system will change again when Part IV of the Companies Act 1989 is brought into force. The changes are dealt with in para. 23.13 below.

Under the 1961 Act (now the 1985 Act), following English precedent, a new type of security known as a floating charge was introduced into Scotland.

## 23.2 Creation of the charge

The 1985 Act applies only to 'an incorporated company (whether a company within the meaning of this Act or not)'. 'Incorporated' excludes partnerships, etc., but guarantee and unlimited companies are included, and also companies registered outside the UK. Any such company may create an effective security for any debt or obligation, including guarantees. The method is to grant a floating charge over all or any part of the property, which may from time to time belong to the company ('be comprised in its property and undertaking'). This includes, *inter alia*, heritable property in Scotland. In the case of Scottish companies, under the 1961 Act, a floating charge could only competently be created by an instrument of charge in statutory form, as set out in a Schedule to that Act. But the statutory form was dispensed with in the 1972 Act, and there is now no prescribed form of charge.

### 23.3 Effect of the charge
The benefit to the creditor of the security effected by the floating charge is limited, under the Act, in the following ways.

### 23.4 (1) Property affected.
Under the 1985 Act a charge may be created either:

(*a*)  on the whole property; or

(*b*)  on a specified part of the property (*e.g.* 'all heritable property in Scotland').

In contrast, under the 1961 Act, the charge affected all property other than assets specifically excluded from the charge, which proved cumbersome. Note that, in either case (notwithstanding the reference to 'property from time to time comprised in the property and undertaking of the company'), the floating charge in fact only attaches to those assets actually owned by the company at one or other of:

(*a*)  the date of commencement of winding up; or

(*b*)  the date when a receiver is appointed.

In the case of a partial charge, only those assets comprised in the specified part of the property at such date are attached.

Thus any asset owned by the company but disposed of before such date escapes from the charge; and any such asset not owned by the company at the date of creation of the charge but subsequently acquired and still owned at such date comes within the charge.

The landmark decision of the First Division in *Sharp* v. *Thomson* 1995 SLT 837 created considerable problems in practice. The decision arose out of a very simple factual situation in which a company sold a property which was subject to a floating charge. After delivery of the disposition, but before it could be recorded, a receiver was appointed. Although the Courts in Scotland had held that title and hence a real right did not pass on delivery, but only on recording or registration, that decision was reversed by the House of Lords (1997 SLT 636). The reasoning of the judges there, which was expressly restricted to cases of receivers, was that on delivery of the disposition, the purchaser acquires a beneficial interest, and accordingly the property no longer forms part of the property and undertaking of the company to which the charge applied. That leaves the purchaser of a property which is subject to a floating charge in a stronger position than a purchaser from a liquidator, or trustee in bankruptcy, where there could still be a race to the Register. While the decision removes the inequity which followed from the decisions in the courts below, the problems it raises would be best dealt with by legislation. It remains to be seen whether the practice of obtaining confirmation from the floating charge holder that the property will be regarded as free of the charge upon delivery will continue, but in the light of the decision, such confirmation is unnecessary, as are clauses providing that, upon delivery of the disposition, the seller will hold the subjects in trust for the purchaser until recording.

**23.5 (2) Registration**.   A floating charge has no effect unless and until the instrument creating it has been registered in the Register of Charges. This was a new Register set up in Scotland under the 1961 Act and is kept by the Registrar of Companies. Detailed provision is made in the 1985 Act ss. 410–424, for registration of charges in this Register; and, in particular, time limits are prescribed to meet various circumstances.

In the case of a Scottish company the floating charge must be registered within 21 days of its date. If not so registered, it is void as against the liquidator or administrator and any other creditor; the only remedy is to petition the court to allow late registration, but such petitions will not necessarily be granted. See *Prior, Petitioner*. 1989 SLT 840. The same rule applies to any company incorporated outside Great Britain which creates a charge on property in Scotland.

Until 22 December 1981 companies registered in Scotland, having a place of business in England, were treated exactly as if they were companies registered outside Great Britain and had to register floating charges over their assets in both the Scottish and English Registers. Since that date, the registration requirement has been altered so that floating charges have to be registered only once in the Register of Charges appropriate to the situation of the registered office of the company concerned (which was the rule for English companies prior to that date). See Companies Act 1985 s. 410 and s. 396.

It is further provided in the 1985 Act s. 462(5) that a floating charge, although registrable in the Register of Charges, does not require to be registered in the Register of Sasines nor in the Land Register, even if heritable property in Scotland is included in the property affected by the charge.

**23.6 (3) Ranking**.   The property is attached by the floating charge subject to certain preferential claims, including the rights of any person who has effectually executed diligence on the property, and any person holding a fixed or floating charge ranking prior to the charge in question.

Three possibilities are covered in the 1985 Act s. 464(1):

(*a*) A floating charge in competition with a fixed security arising by operation of law, *e.g.* hypothec. In this case, the fixed security always has priority.

(*b*) When there are express ranking clauses. Ranking as between a floating charge and a voluntary fixed security not arising by operation of law and between two or more floating charges may be regulated by express ranking clauses. Thus the instrument of charge may, and usually now does, prohibit the creation by the debtor company of (i) any fixed security; or (ii) any floating charge having priority over, or ranking *pari passu* with, the floating charge which the instrument creates.

The instrument of charge may, by such express provision therein, regulate the order of ranking, *inter se*, of the floating charge and any other specific charge, fixed or floating, present or future. But a pre-existing charge is not affected by such a provision, unless it also contains a corresponding clause.

(*c*) Where there is no operative ranking clause, then:

(i) a fixed security which has become real by recording in Sasines or the Land Register before the floating charge attaches to the property (*i.e.* on the commencement of a winding up or the appointment of a receiver) ranks before a floating charge, even although the latter is first registered;

(ii) two or more floating charges, if and when they attach to property of the company, rank according to their respective dates of registration.

Note that, under this provision, future fixed securities with prior ranking can validly be prohibited. So, on taking security from a company, always search the Register of Charges. But a subsequent fixed security, so prohibited, is not voided, merely postponed. It is thought that the charge cannot validly prohibit outright disposal by the company to a *bona fide* purchaser. So a search in the Register of Charges is not in theory necessary on sale except for the purpose of disclosing whether or not a receiver has been appointed. But the appointment of a receiver instantly converts a floating charge into a fixed security, the effect of which will transmit against a purchaser of any heritable property of the company. Since sale may trigger off the appointment of a receiver and crystallise the charge, a search is for practical purposes required. This is dealt with again in Chapter 35.

**23.7 (4) Variation.** A new provision in the 1985 Act s. 466 (formerly the 1972 Act s. 7) allows for alteration of the terms of a floating charge, once granted. This was not competent under the 1961 Act with unfortunate results on additional lending. For a comparable difficulty in relation to fixed securities and its solution see above para. 22.10.

Variation requires a deed executed by the company, the creditor and any other fixed or floating creditors affected by the variation; and the deed must be registered if it makes certain alterations, *e.g.* by ranking clauses, or by releasing property or increasing or decreasing the amount secured.

### 23.8 Effect of floating charges on property

If, in accordance with the foregoing requirements, a floating charge does effectively attach to property at the date of winding up, or of appointment of a receiver, then it has effect as if the charge had become, at such date, a fixed security over the property to which it has attached in respect of the principal sum in loan and interest due and to become due thereon – the 1985 Act s. 463(1) and the 1986 Act s. 53(7) and s. 54(6).

### 23.9 Special provisions as to fixed securities

Floating charges represent a substantial innovation in the law of heritable securities in Scotland. In particular, nothing need enter the Register of Sasines or Land Register; and the charge attaches to future-acquired property not in the ownership of the company at the date of creation of the charge. Further, property is automatically released from the charge if disposed of prior to liquidation, or the appointment of a receiver.

But the 1961 Act also made an important and unexpected innovation with regard to conventional heritable securities in Scotland. Under the new Companies Act provisions introduced by the 1961 Act (now the Companies Act 1985 s. 410), a fixed charge created after the date of passing of the Act must also be registered in the Register of Charges, failing which it is void in a question with the liquidator. In this context, fixed charges include any charge on land, wherever situate, or any interest therein, including a charge created by bond and disposition in security or by *ex facie* absolute disposition, and, now, standard security, but excluding a charge for rent, ground annual or other periodical sum payable in respect of land. If, therefore, a company grants a standard security, it is not now sufficient simply to record that standard security in Sasines, although this still remains necessary. In addition, the standard security, to be effective, must be registered in the Register of Charges; and must be so registered within 21 days following on the date of recording in Sasines. Special forms are provided, and the procedure is regulated under the Companies Act 1985.

The *ex facie* absolute disposition created special problems. The essence of this form of security was non-disclosure of the security element; and publication of that element (*e.g.* by recording a back letter in Sasines) might limit the security to sums advanced at date of recording. Nonetheless, the *ex facie* absolute disposition was a 'fixed security' and, as such, registrable, thus disclosing the security element. So the 1985 Act s. 414 specially provides that, in the case of *ex facie* absolute dispositions, registration thereof in the Register of Charges as a charge shall not, of itself, 'render the charge unavailable as security for indebtedness incurred after the date of compliance'. In other words, to register the *ex facie* absolute disposition (which was obligatory under the Act) did not give notice of the security element. The same difficulty could not arise with a standard security because it is *ex facie* a security; and the security thereby created is only limited by subsequent recorded deed 1970 Act s. 13.

If property is acquired by a company and if that property is already subject to a charge, *e.g.* a standard security, particulars of that charge must be registered by the acquiring company within 21 days after the date of acquisition. Failure to register, however, does not render the charge void in this case.

### 23.10 Petition for rectification

If a charge (fixed or floating) is not registered in the Register of Charges within the 21-day time limit, then an application to the Court of Session is competent and necessary for a rectification of the Register. The court may allow the 21-day limit to be extended. See *Allan Black & McCaskie, Petitioners* 1987 GWD 19–709; *Prior, Petitioner* 1989 SLT 840.

### 23.11 Miscellaneous

Special provision is also made (now in the Companies Act 1985) for various miscellaneous matters including:

(1) time limits for registration of charges created out of the UK. See s. 411(1);

(2) time limits for registration of charges created in the UK but which include property situate outwith the UK. See s. 411(2);

(3) an obligation on every company to make up and maintain its own private register of charges, in which are to be entered copies of instruments creating charges. This is in addition to, and separate from, the requirement to register in the Register of Charges maintained by the Registrar of Companies. The register of charges of each individual company is available for public inspection. See s. 422;

(4) suitable entries will be registered in the Register of Charges when property is released from a charge, by restriction or discharge. The appropriate entry is by memorandum of satisfaction, or partial satisfaction as appropriate. See s. 419.

Special forms are provided for these various registration requirements under the Companies (Forms) Regulations.

### 23.12 Appointment of a receiver, and liquidation
This chapter is concerned exclusively with the constitution of the charge and its effect as a fixed security on heritable property on the happening of certain events including, in particular, the appointment of a receiver and liquidation. Some of the problems which these events create are touched on in Chapter 35.

### 23.13 Companies Act 1989
As has been said earlier, Part IV of the Companies Act 1989 contains provisions to alter the system for registration of charges. The Government has indicated that it is unlikely that the provisions will come into force without amendment. The reader should therefore check the up-to-date position.

### 23.14 Particulars for registration.
Although there are changes to the list of charges requiring registration, these are not of significance in the context of heritable property. Under the new scheme a company will still be required to deliver to the Registrar the particulars of any charge and that must be done within 21 days of its creation (*i.e.* the date of execution) or in the case of heritable property 21 days from the date of recording. As will be noted later, the Registrar will be sent particulars of the charge and not the charge itself or a copy.

The Registrar must note the date of receipt of the particulars and send both the company and the chargee a copy of them. The chargee will then have proof of the particulars and the date of receipt by the Registrar (s. 398(1)(4)(5)).

### 23.15 Consequences of registration.
There will no longer be any need to register a certified copy of the charge. The important consequence of this is that any certificate issued by the Registrar (and there will not be a requirement to issue one although any person may require the Registrar to provide one (s. 397(3))) will no longer be conclusive evidence that the provisions of the Act have been complied with. Only where the actual charge or a certified copy is sent could the Registrar give this assurance. Any certificate issued by the Registrar will be conclusive evidence only of the fact that the particulars were delivered no later than the date on the certificate. The

company must still keep a copy of the charge and creditors may inspect the company's own register free of charge (s. 411).

**23.16 Late registration**.   While it will still be possible to register a charge late, a charge so registered will be void against an administrator or liquidator, as before, but, in addition, it will also be void against any purchaser. However, this protection will relate only to an unregistered charge in respect of the period prior to registration. Accordingly, once a charge is registered, it will be valid against any persons subsequently acquiring an interest in or right over the property (s. 399).

Where a charge is registered late and insolvency proceedings are commenced against the company before the end of the relevant period beginning with the date of delivery of the particulars to the Registrar, the charge will be void as against the administrator or liquidator. The relevant period is two years in the case of a floating charge created in favour of a person connected with a company (within the meaning of s. 249 of the Insolvency Act 1986) or one year if not so connected; and six months in the case of a fixed charge (s. 400(3)).

However an administrator or liquidator appointed after the expiry of the relevant period is prevented from treating a late charge as void (s. 400(2)(b)). The charge will also be void against an administrator or liquidator if the company is unable to pay its debts at the date of delivery of the particulars or becomes unable to pay them as a result of the transaction relating to the charge. If a charge is void, the whole sum secured is payable on demand (s. 407(1)).

**23.17 Omissions and inaccuracies**.   Where the particulars of the charge which are delivered for registration contain omissions or inaccuracies, the charge can be relied on only in relation to the information disclosed in the actual particulars and is void *quoad* undisclosed or inaccurate matters. That said, however, the court has power on the application of the chargee to order that the charge will not be void if a 'relevant event' occurs at the time when the particulars are either incomplete or inaccurate. A relevant event, in relation to either an administrator or a liquidator means the commencement of insolvency proceedings and in relation to a purchaser, it means the acquisition of that purchaser's right or interest (s. 399(2)). Before a court orders that such a charge is effective it must be satisfied that the omission or error is unlikely to prejudice an unsecured creditor to a material extent, or that no person became an unsecured creditor at the time when the error or omission existed. So far as a purchaser is concerned, the court must be satisfied that the purchaser did not rely on the incomplete or inaccurate particulars in connection with the acquisition (s. 402(4)).

**23.18 Memorandum of charge**.   There is no longer a requirement to submit a statutory declaration with the memorandum of satisfaction or release, but both the company and the chargee will be required to sign or authorise the signature of a memorandum of charge, formerly known as a memorandum of satisfaction or release (s. 403). The court may dispense with one signature if one of the signatories refuses to sign or is not available. Once the memorandum has been registered, the Registrar will send a copy of the memorandum and a note of the date of delivery to both the company and the chargee (s. 417). The significant alteration here is that the Act requires the chargee to sign the memorandum of charge in respect of all charges. Formerly this applied only to the holders of floating charges in Scotland.

**23.19 Exercise of the power of sale**.   Where a charge has become void to any extent as against an administrator or a liquidator or a purchaser, the chargee may sell the property free of that charge. The proceeds of sale are to be held by the chargee in trust and are to be applied firstly, to discharge any prior incumbrances, secondly, to pay the chargee's expenses of sale, and of any previous sale, thirdly, to discharge the sum secured by the charge and other incumbrances ranking *pari passu* and fourthly, to discharge any sum effectively secured by incumbrances which are postponed to the charge. The residue is to be paid to the company or any other person authorised to give a receipt for the proceeds of the sale. Where a chargee in Scotland is unable to obtain a discharge for any payment which he is required to make under the above provisions, he may consign the amount due in court and that consignation will have the effect of the discharge. A certificate from the sheriff clerk will be sufficient evidence of that discharge (s. 406).

**23.20 Floating charges**.   The 1989 Act makes changes to ss. 463, 464 and 466 of the Companies Act 1985. The amendment to s. 463, which relates to the effect of a floating charge on a winding up, is no more than a tidying up arrangement, and in place of the words 'on the commencement of the winding up of the company' the provision will read 'where a company goes into liquidation within the meaning of s. 247(2) of the Insolvency Act 1986'.

The amendments to s. 464 are more significant. In the first place, the right of the holder of a floating charge to create a ranking order by his charge with other subsisting or future charges is now limited by the need to obtain the consent of the holder of any existing fixed or floating charge which would be adversely affected by the arrangement. Furthermore, the right of the chargee to restrict the creation of subsequent fixed or floating charges taking priority over his own floating charge, is now expressly effective to give his charge priority over any later charge. Lastly, where there is no ranking clause the order of ranking remains the same, but the amended wording is more accurate.

**23.21 Crystallisation**.   The Secretary of State may make regulations to require notice to be given to the Registrar of (a) the occurrence of any prescribed event affecting the nature of the security; and (b) the exercise of powers conferred by the charge, or by order of the court (s. 410).

# Chapter 24

# LEASES

## 24.1 The creation of a lease

At one time, leases in Scotland were used for residential property and for small commercial and industrial premises, for example, shops, but it has been common for many years for leases to be used in larger properties, for example, shopping developments, where the rent paid for any one unit may be fairly considerable. Such leases will usually be for lengthy periods and will almost certainly be registered. The whole topic is therefore of greater practical significance than was the case say 20 years ago. However, it is important to bear in mind that something which may be described as a lease may not be one (see *Millar* 1949 SC 1) and something which is not described as a lease may be one (see *Brador Properties Ltd.* 1992 SC 12). Furthermore, in many leases, the tenant may have security of tenure, for example, in an agricultural holding (see Chapter 26 for more detail), but there is a great deal of legislation dealing with such matters and although the precise detail is outwith the scope of this Manual it is worth noting, in passing, that strict adherence to the time limits is very often a feature of this legislation.

It is assumed that the reader is already familiar with the general law of landlord and tenant; and no attempt is made in this Manual to rehearse the general principles which apply to that relationship. All we are concerned with here is, briefly, some points to note on the practical aspects of leases in everyday practice.

Under the new rules laid down by the Requirements of Writing (Scotland) Act 1995, a lease for more than one year falls under the category of a contract relating to an interest in land. Such a contract is one of the exceptions to the basic principle laid down by the Act: that writing is not required for the constitution of a contract. However, it is no longer the case that the writing need be probative; a subscribed document is valid (although it may be witnessed to establish self-proving status if desired). The new statutory personal bar, which closely resembles its common law counterpart, will apply to a purported lease which falls short of these requirements. If the lease is for less than a year the Act does not apply and *rei interventus* and homologation may apply. See *Goldston* (1868) 7 M 188; *Ferryhill Property Investment Ltd.* 1992 SCLR 282. There must, of course, be consensus on the subjects to be let, the rent or other consideration, and the term, and without that, there will not be a lease (see *Gray* 1962 SC 157).

## 24.2 Lease as a real right

At common law, a lease is essentially a personal contract between the infeft proprietor, in this context 'the landlord', and a temporary occupant, in this context 'the tenant', who is permitted by the landlord, for a limited period of time and for payment of a rent, to enjoy the benefit of the property to the temporary exclusion of the landlord throughout the duration of the lease.

This fundamental characteristic of the lease as a personal contract carries with it two consequences.

**24.3 (1) Assignability by tenant.** The selection of the tenant in most cases involves some element of *delectus personae*. In the result, in the great majority of cases, either by implication or by express provision in the lease, the tenant is prohibited from parting with possession of the whole or any part of the subjects of let either by way of assignation of his interest, in whole or in part, or by subletting. This is one feature which distingushes occupation of property under a lease from occupation on tenure where, generally speaking, there is freedom of disposal.

**24.4 (2) Transmission against landlord's successor.** Since a lease is essentially a personal contract, the common law rule was (and is) that the lease is not binding in a question with a singular successor of the landlord because the tenant has no real right. That common law rule has been excluded, in the great majority of cases, by the Leases Act 1449 (c. 6).

The principal purpose of this Act was, originally, to give some security of tenure to tenant farmers; but it has since been extended to include leases of almost every kind of property with very limited exceptions.

The main result of the Act is to create for the tenant a right to maintain himself in possession in terms of his lease, when the landlord dispones the property to a singular successor who takes infeftment as proprietor in his place. As a result of the provisions of this Act, the tenant is equally entitled to insist on the terms of the lease in a question with a singular successor as he was with the original landlord on the basis of contract; and so the tenant acquires, under this Act, a *quasi* real right which transmits against singular successors for the duration of the original lease.

As an extension of this principle, by later statutes, tenants of particular types of property are given much more extensive security of tenure, and certain other rights as well, including, in some cases, the right to continue in occupation at a controlled rent. Two particular cases where statute further controls the relationship of a landlord and tenant in this way are agricultural property under the Agricultural Holdings Acts, and dwelling-houses under the Rent (Scotland) Act 1984 and the Housing (Scotland) Act 1988. These statutory provisions are referred to later in Chapters 26 and 27 respectively.

The 1449 Act, in contrast, protects the tenant strictly according to the terms of the original contract and not beyond. To produce this result, however, the lease must first satisfy certain basic requirements.

(*a*) It must be in writing in compliance with the Requirements of Writing (Scotland) Act 1995, except for leases of less than one year's duration.

(*b*) There must be a definite and continuing rent and the rent must not be illusory.

(*c*) There must be a definite termination date, however far into the future.

(*d*) The tenant must have entered into possession. In the case of leases, taking possession on the part of the tenant is equivalent to the taking of sasine by the vassal under the feudal system. The tenant is not protected during any period of possession prior to the date of entry specified in the lease. Without possession, the tenant is merely the personal creditor of the landlord (see *Millar* 1949 SC 1 at p. 6).

If a lease is entered into which fails to satisfy these requirements, it may be binding, on the basis of contractual agreement, between the original landlord and his universal successors on the one hand and the tenant and his successors on the other; but it will not bind a singular successor of the landlord. The same applies to a lease which complies with the above requirements but where the subjects of let are not within the scope of the Act, *e.g.* fishings. That particular exception has, however, largely been negatived by the Freshwater and Salmon Fisheries (Scotland) Act 1976 s. 4 in relation to leases of fishings in inland waters.

### 24.5 Rent
As with feus in earlier days, so with leases the contractual arrangement between landlord and tenant starts off, in the ordinary way, on a strictly commercial basis with the tenant paying to the landlord an annual rent of full commercial value. In other words, the landlord as proprietor receives by way of rent a return on his property equivalent to what he might expect to receive as a return on any other form of investment. But, taking into account improvements to the premises carried out by the tenant, and the steady increase in property values particularly in periods of inflation, rents tend to diminish in real value to the landlord with the passage of years, which has two results.

(1) As time passes, the lease becomes an asset of increasing value to the tenant, particularly in commercial premises with the build up of goodwill; and

(2) In modern leases, this tendency for the rent to get out of line with current rental values is counteracted by the introduction into the lease of a rent review clause, the effect of which is that, at regular intervals throughout the period of the lease, the rent is reviewed and may be increased in line with increases in real values.

### 24.6 Possession
So far as the tenant is concerned, the lease has two substantial disadvantages compared with ownership of property on tenure.

(1) Sooner or later, the lease comes to an end, whereupon at common law, and in the absence of contrary provision in the lease, the property, with all buildings, fixtures and improvements generally, even although these have been provided at the expense of the tenant, reverts to the landlord without any compensation to the tenant. This, in effect, means that the value of the tenant's asset is written down to nil at the termination of the lease.

To some extent this disadvantage can be counteracted either:

(*a*) by entering into a lease for a long initial term or by providing in the lease for an option to the tenant to renew his lease for successive terms; or

(*b*) by providing expressly for compensation for tenant's improvements.

Note, however, the terms of the Tenancy of Shops (Scotland) Act 1949 which provides that a shop tenant can, within 21 days of receipt of the landlord's notice to quit, and in circumstances where a renewal of the tenancy cannot be negotiated on satisfactory terms, make application to the sheriff for renewal of the lease for a period of up to one year on such terms and conditions as the sheriff thinks reasonable. Such an application is made by way of summary cause.

(2) Because of the requirement that, to qualify for the protection of the 1449 Act, the tenant must enter into possession, a lease could not be used as security for borrowed money because the essence of any heritable security is that the borrower is left in possession to enjoy the benefits of the property, while the lender has security without actual occupation. Given the requirements of the 1449 Act, a creditor of a tenant could not obtain security over the lease except by taking possession of the subjects of let; and in any event that would probably be prohibited either by implication or by the express terms of the lease itself.

In many cases, the tenant takes land on a long lease with the intention of building. If the lease is for a long enough term, the tenant may find it economically viable to put buildings on the land even although, at the end of the lease, the buildings pass to the landlord without payment. Such leases were and are commonplace in England. Until recently, in Scotland, building leases were much less commonly encountered, but, for technical reasons, did regularly occur. In recent urban redevelopments they are now frequently used, particularly in commercial and industrial precincts.

One consequence of this type of lease is that the tenant invests substantial sums of money in building, or in improving and fitting out buildings on land, although he is not the owner thereof. Inevitably, in many such cases, the tenant has to borrow the money required for such development; but, under the 1449 Act, he is not in a position to grant security. Borrowing for development on leasehold land was therefore impracticable, notwithstanding the protection of the 1449 Act. For an example of the dangers facing tenants in such leases, see *Dollar Land (Cumbernauld) Ltd.* 1992 SLT 211; 1992 SLT (HL) 669 and 1997 SLT 260.

### 24.7 Registration

These difficulties, which the tenant on a long lease encountered, were removed by the Registration of Leases (Scotland) Act 1857. The main purpose of the Act was to permit publication of the tenant's right by recording of the lease in the Register of Sasines in place of, or as an alternative to, the publication of that right by the taking of possession.

When registration was first introduced for feudal titles under the Registration Act 1617 and the Real Rights Act 1693, the essential feature of the registration legislation was that recording of a deed in Sasines became an essential element in the obtaining of the real right. In contrast, under the Registration of Leases Act, registration is optional in this sense that the tenant may still secure his real right under his lease simply by entering into possession, without recording any deed in the Register of Sasines. As an alternative, but strictly as an alternative, he may, if he prefers, record the lease in the Register of Sasines, in which case he is not obliged to take possession in order to establish his real right under the 1449 Act. In practice, he may, and often will, do both. Once an area is made operational for registration of title under the Land Registration (Scotland) Act 1979, however, the tenant no longer has this option; and registration of a long lease and of writs relating thereto is, in all cases, obligatory – see Chapter 13.25 and paras 24.10 and 11 below.

**24.8 (1) Benefit of registration.** The principal benefit to the tenant of this legislation is that it allows the tenant, while taking possession, at the same time to grant security on his lease and to borrow money on that security so as to allow him to develop his leasehold property.

A further effect of the 1857 Act is that, if a lease is recorded before the landlord has disposed of the subjects to a singular successor, then no rent is necessary and no definite termination date is required, in contrast to the position where the 1449 Act alone is relied on. This is because the 1857 Act does not define the term 'lease'; and, in particular, does not incorporate the statutory prerequisites laid down in the 1449 Act. For a recent discussion on this aspect of a registration of a lease, see *Palmer's Trs.* 1989 SLT 128.

Even though leases and transmissions thereof may be recorded in Sasines or registered in the Land Register, the recording or registration of the lease, or of an assignation thereof, does not create infeftment. Therefore, a lessee with a recorded/registered title is still a tenant holding on a lease. He is in no sense infeft as tenant, in contrast to the position of a proper liferenter or of an heir of entail in possession; and the recording or registration of his lease does not to any extent divest the landlord nor exclude the landlord from his full proprietary title.

**24.9 (2) Short-term leases.** Leases of short duration are commonplace. To allow every lease to be recorded in the Register of Sasines, regardless of its duration, would have vastly increased the volume of writs entering the Sasines Register and created a major administrative problem there. Therefore, to prevent overloading of the system, the 1857 Act originally restricted the recording of leases to those leases:

(*a*) where the term of the lease was not less than 31 years; and

(*b*) where the subjects of let did not exceed 50 acres in extent.

**24.10 (3) Amendments to the 1857 Act.** The Act has been amended by two later provisions, namely:

(*a*) The Land Tenure Reform (Scotland) Act 1974 Schedule 6 reduced the necessary term for a recordable lease to a term of more than 20 years, and abolished the 50-acre limit. At the same time, the 1974 Act introduced a prohibition against the granting of a long lease of property intended to be used as a dwellinghouse.

The reason behind the prohibition is also to be found in the 1974 Act which prohibited the imposition of new feuduties. It was thought that developers might move to leasing residential property and thus recover, by way of rent, what they previously would have been paid as feuduty.

There are, however, some long leases of residential property which pre-date the 1974 Act and they are unaffected by its provisions. Indeed, they may be renewed for a period in excess of 20 years (see Law Reform (Miscellaneous Provisions) (Scotland) Act 1985 s. 1). Other long leases (*i.e.* for more than 20 years) are not affected by the 1974 Act, but, if there is an obligation on the landlord in these leases to renew the lease at its expiry, the sheriff has power to grant a renewal if the landlord is unknown or his consent is otherwise not forthcoming (see the 1979 Act s. 22A).

(*b*) Under the 1979 Act, when an area has been declared operational for the purposes of registration of title, then the tenant under a long lease no longer has the option either to take possession or to register the lease. Instead, after the area becomes operational, registration of the lease in the land register is an essential requirement to the obtaining of a real right; and to that extent the 1449 Act is excluded and repealed.

**24.11 (4) Procedure under the 1857 Act**. The provisions and effect of the 1857 Act as amended can be summarised thus:

(*a*) Any self-proving lease of more than 20 years duration may be recorded in the Register of Sasines, either by the original tenant or by any subsequent assignee. Provision is also made for the recording of a certified copy lease where the principal is lost – Long Leases (Scotland) Act 1954 s. 26; and of extracts in certain circumstances – 1857 Act s. 19 as amended by the 1974 Act Schedule 6(6).

(*b*) In operational areas, any such lease, or transmission thereof, taking effect after the date when the area became operational must be registered in the Land Register to secure the real right. But this does not apply to securities on leases already validly recorded in the G.R.S.

(*c*) The acreage of the subjects let is now irrelevant – 1974 Act Schedule 6(5).

**24.12 (5) Forms.** No statutory form of lease is provided by the 1857 Act; and any normal conventional form of lease will serve for the purposes of registration. The 1857 Act does, however, provide statutory forms of assignation and of renunciation of a lease; and also provides forms of heritable security over leases with appropriate forms for assignation and discharge of such securities. The forms have been amended and adapted by the following provisions.

**24.13** (*a*) *The Conveyancing (Scotland) Act 1924 s. 24.* The general purpose of this section is to assimilate lease forms with the forms in use for proprietary rights; and, in particular, for the purposes of any assignation or security writ, the subjects of let are to be described in terms of Schedule J to the 1924 Act.

Further, by s. 24, all the powers, rights and forms applicable to feudal property are, with necessary adjustments, made applicable to leases and securities over leases as if the right of the tenant thereunder were a proprietary right.

**24.14** (*b*) *The Long Leases (Scotland) Act 1954 s. 27.* This section removed certain earlier requirements for the description of the subjects of let, and simplified the forms of writ above referred to.

**24.15** (*c*) *The Conveyancing and Feudal Reform (Scotland) Act 1970 s. 32 and Schedule 8.* The statutory modifications introduced by the 1970 Act in relation to heritable securities were applied, by these provisions, to registered leases in the same way as to proprietary rights; and, in consequence, certain provisions in the 1857 Act dealing with assignations in security etc. were abolished.

As a result of the 1970 Act provisions, heritable securities over leases can be constituted by standard security in either Form A or Form B, using the 1924 Act provisions for description; and otherwise with the same general results as apply to a standard security over proprietary rights.

**24.16** (*d*) *The Land Tenure Reform (Scotland) Act 1974 ss. 8–10 and Schedule 6.* The principal modifications in this Act are, as above noted:

(i) the reduction in the required period of a registrable lease to 20 years; and

(ii) the prohibition on the granting of long leases of dwellinghouses.

The 1974 Act also abolished casualties in leases granted after the passing of that Act; but casualties in pre-existing leases continue to be exigible. See below at para. 24.19.

Finally, Schedule 6 amends the 1857 Act s. 16 in such a way that a registrable lease should always be registered; and possession alone should not be relied on. See Halliday's *Practice* Chapter 26–06.

### 24.17 Procedure and effect of recording/registration
Where the lease itself has not been recorded by the original tenant, it can be recorded/registered by any subsequent tenant in right thereof for the time being as assignee, by the recording/registration of the lease together with a notice of title, using the notice of title Form 2 of Schedule B to the 1924 Act, and specifying the links in title connecting him with the original tenant. As with the use of that form in other situations, the notice of title carries the warrant of registration and the lease carries a docquet referring to that notice.

Once the lease has been recorded/registered, whether by the original tenant or by a successor in the manner above referred to, it can then be transmitted by the tenant in right thereof for the time being, whether or not he himself has a recorded/registered title, using the form of assignation provided by the 1857 Act as amended by the later enactments above referred to.

Similarly, the tenant in right of the lease for the time being can grant a standard security thereon.

### 24.18 Real right without possession
The combined effect of the enactments above referred to is that a lease, on recording or registration, effectively secures a real right for the tenant thereunder as at the date of recording or registration in a competition with all other recorded titles which enter the Register of Sasines or Land Register subsequent to the date of the recording or registration of that lease.

### 24.19 Transmission by the tenant
In the case of unrecorded/unregistered leases, where the right transmits by assignation as it may do, subject possibly to the prior consent of the landlord, the title of the assignee is completed by intimation of the assignation to the landlord.

In the case of recorded/registered leases, consistently with the provisions for the recording/registration thereof, the title of an assignee of a recorded/registered lease is completed by the recording/registration of the assignation in the Register of Sasines or Land Register; and the recording/registration of the assignation effectively vests the lease in the assignee to the extent to which the lease is assigned.

In relation to all the foregoing forms, whether of assignation of the lease itself or securities thereon, and of renunciation of leases, the whole lease may be dealt with, using the forms provided by the 1857 Act as amended in terms of the enactments above referred to.

In that case, it is unnecessary to describe the subjects of let; and all that is required is to assign the lease itself thus:

'I AB (design) in consideration of the sum of pounds (£ ) now paid to me by CD (design) hereby assign to the said CD a lease granted by EF (design) in my favour of the subjects therein described lying in the County of dated and recorded in the Division of the General Register of Sasines for the County of on ; With entry as at .'

Where part only of the subjects of the lease is to transmit, then a description is required to indicate the part assigned. In that case, the foregoing form is used but with a description of the lease modified on the following lines:

'but in so far only as regards the following portion of the subjects of lease, viz. ...'

The portion assigned is then described or referred to as in Schedule D to the 1924 Act for proprietary writs.

Transmission by assignation of a lease, whether registered or not, creates a special problem. In the case of long leases, it was commonplace for the landlord to provide that, on transmission of the lease, whether on death or by *inter vivos* assignation, a casualty was payable. In the case of transmission on death, the casualty was normally double the rent, and in the case of older leases, the rent is not normally a significant amount.

The casualty payable on an *inter vivos* transmission, however, was frequently fixed by a reference to the current rental value of the subjects at the date of transfer, which, of course, would be very much more substantial than the original rent.

The same position formerly applied on transmission of proprietary feudal interests, but all such casualties in the case of feudal property were abolished by the Feudal Casualties (Scotland) Act 1914, which did not, however, abolish leasehold casualties. In recent years, this has created a problem because it would be fair to say that the liability for leasehold casualties on transmission was frequently overlooked. Unfortunately, the liability for payment of the casualty persists in a question with singular successors in perpetuity. Liability for payment of each individual casualty is extinguished by the 20-year long negative prescription, not the five-year prescription. See *MRS Hamilton Ltd.* 1995 GWD 25–1355. In the result, a purchaser of a leasehold interest may find himself unexpectedly confronted with a demand for one or more casualty payments fixed by reference to current rental value. See the Scottish Law Commission Discussion Paper (No. 102, May 1997) on the question of leasehold casualties, with recommendations for their abolition.

Instead of assigning the lease, the tenant may wish to sub-let the leased subjects in whole or in part. The tenant then becomes the landlord in the sub-lease but, as with an assignation, the original lease may prohibit sub-leases or impose restrictions on the circumstances in which they are permissible.

While there may be restrictions on the tenant's ability to assign or sub-let, there is no such restriction on the landlord who is the proprietor, and the tenant may find himself with a new landlord without being able to object. If the conditions under the Leases Act 1449 have not been met, the tenant will not have a real right against successors of the original landlord and so the new owner would not be bound to recognise the lease at all.

The same provisions apply, modified as appropriate, if the subjects lie in an operational area for registration.

## 24.20 Interposed leases
As an alternative to selling his interest outright, the landlord may interpose the lease which creates a sub-tenancy at his instance. The landlord grants the lease of his interest to a new tenant who then becomes the landlord of the existing tenant. The 1974 Act recognises interposed leases and gives effect to those which were created prior to the Act (s. 17). One of the common reasons for interposing a lease is where a developer has leased out various units in the completed development but, rather than sell the interest, wishes to retain it but without having the day-to-day management responsibility. That responsibility can be passed on to the interposed tenant/landlord. For two cases illustrating the potential dangers which may arise as a result of such an arrangement, see *Dollar Land (Cumbernauld) Ltd.* 1992 SLT 211 and 1992 SLT (HL) 669 and *Kildrummy (Jersey) Ltd.* 1996 SCLR 727.

## 24.21 Succession to the tenant
On the death of the tenant, the lease vests in his executors (1964 Act ss. 14, 36(2)) and the executor is given power to assign the lease where the tenant has not made any valid provision in his will or other testamentary document. In such a case, the executor may transfer the lease to one of the persons entitled to succeed on intestacy, or in satisfaction or partial satisfaction of claims with prior or legal rights. This power must be exercised within one year, otherwise the lease will terminate (s. 16(4)). (See also the Rent (Scotland) Act 1984 s. 1(1) and the Housing (Scotland) Act 1987 s. 52.)

However, the tenant may make a testamentary disposal of the lease in favour of any one of the persons who would be entitled to succeed on intestacy (1964 Act s. 29(1)).

Special conditions apply to agricultural leases (see Chapter 26).

## 24.22 Examination of the landlord's title
It is an essential feudal requirement that, for the granting of an effective lease, the landlord must be infeft, subject only to the rules of accretion which apply to leases as they apply to the granting of the feu charter. The facility for deduction of title which applies to the granting of a disposition and, now, to the granting of a standard security, has not yet been extended to the granting of leases.

Further, not only must the landlord be infeft as a preliminary to the granting of an effective lease but he must also have a valid and marketable title.

This is a point which is frequently overlooked by the tenant's agent when revising the lease. But it is just as important to a tenant as it is to a purchaser to ensure that the landlord granting the lease has a valid title so to do.

Therefore, the solicitor for the tenant should insist, in the preliminary contract, that the landlord has a valid and marketable title; and, as part of the procedure of revising the lease produced by the landlord's solicitor, the tenant's solicitor should insist on examining the landlord's title to assure himself of its validity. Such an examination should consider such things as the description of the subjects, rights of access, use of services and conditions of title.

The tenant's solicitor must also bear in mind that there may be conditions in the title, *e.g.* restricting the use of the property etc. which apply not only to the ownership of the property by the landlord but to the use to be made of the property by the tenant. All writs referred to for burdens must therefore be carefully examined just as in the case of sale and purchase.

The tenant's solicitor should also insist on production of searches in exactly the same way in which a purchaser's solicitor insists on searches before completing a transaction of sale and purchase.

Further enquiry may be necessary, *e.g.* where there is a heritable security, in which case the consent of the heritable creditor may be necessary (see *Trade Development Bank* 1980 SC 74); or a floating charge, where the same applies.

Finally, exactly the same principles apply to settlement obligations on completion of a lease as apply to settlement obligations on completion of sale and purchase.

## 24.23 Real and personal conditions

Even though a lease is binding on a singular successor of the landlord, it is still necessary to ascertain which of its conditions are real and bind singular successors and which of its conditions are personal and, as such, are not binding. The general rule is that only those conditions which are *inter naturalia* of a lease run with the lands. See *Bisset* (1898) 1 F 87. The class of conditions which have been held to bind singular successors is quite restricted. For example, an obligation to grant renewals has sometimes been held to bind singular successors. Each case must be considered according to its circumstances. As a result, care should be taken when framing conditions which are designed by the contracting parties to be permanent. Of particular importance to a tenant is the question of how best to draft an option to purchase so as to ensure its enforceability against singular successors of the landlord. Unfortunately there are no *voces signatae* – a declaration that such a provision is deemed to be *inter naturalia* of the lease will not suffice. For a conflicting decision, however, see the case of *Davidson* 1992 SCLR 1001 where the element of personal bar and knowledge was deemed to play a significant part in the decision as to whether such a provision was binding.

## 24.24 Notices to quit

## 24.25 Common law

At common law, the rules on removing from urban subjects depended on local custom. For example, the practice of 'chalking' involved the burgh officer chalking the most prominent door of the building in the presence of a witness, 40 days before the appropriate term of removing, either Whitsunday or Martinmas.

### 24.26 Sheriff Courts (Scotland) Act 1907
Most current requirements are now derived from the Sheriff Courts (Scotland) Act 1907, ss. 34 to 38, although it has been said that this Act has 'thrown the whole matter, which was by no means devoid of confusion at any rate, into still greater confusion': *Campbell's Trs.* 1911 SC 188 at p. 192.

### 24.27 Periods of notice
The 1907 Act provides that notices to quit must be in writing. The Schedule to the Act also lays down the form of notice. The periods of notice required vary according to circumstances. It is of course open to the landlord and the tenant to agree a longer period of notice to be specified in a lease. It is questionable whether or not the parties can agree to a shorter period. When calculating the last date by which notice must be served, it is advisable to disregard both the date of service and the date of receipt. It is essential that 28 or 40 (as the case may be) clear days' notice is given. See *Esson Properties Ltd.* 1996 SCLR 1041.

### 24.28 Service of notice
All notices should be served in terms of the lease. It is also advisable to serve all notices by recorded delivery post. In *Capital Land Holdings Ltd.* 1996 SLT 1379 the Court held that the notice ought to have been served on the landlord at his registered office, as the parties, having made specific provision for the places to which notices had to be sent, were entitled to hold each other to them.

The importance of serving termination notices by recorded delivery post was confirmed in the case of *Netherfield Visual Productions* 1996 GWD 19–1107, where the landlords claimed never to have received the tenants' notice of termination of the lease which the tenants contended had been posted to the landlords. In that case, however, the Court held that the presumption of delivery had not been rebutted by the landlords. Notwithstanding this decision, however, service by recorded delivery post is strongly recommended in order to avoid potential dispute. Care should also be taken when the term of removing is either Whitsunday or Martinmas. See the Term and Quarter Days (Scotland) Act 1990 and the re-definition of the terms of Whitsunday and Martinmas and the inherent conflict with the Removal Terms (Scotland) Act 1886.

A notice to quit, served timeously, may prevent tacit relocation from applying, but it should be borne in mind that the actual removal of the tenant is regulated by the Sheriff Courts (Scotland) Act 1907 and it may take some time to recover the property from a tenant who refuses to remove from the premises on the expiry date.

The need for clarification or simplification of the law has been recognised and certain recommendations were made by the Scottish Law Commission in its report on 'The Recovery and Possession of Heritable Property' (No. 118). These recommendations are yet to be implemented, however, and the current statutory requirements continue to be complicated and unsatisfactory.

Chapter 25

# COMMERCIAL LEASES

## 25.1 Introduction

The approach to leasehold tenure in general in Scots law and English law is fundamentally different. In the law of Scotland reference is often required to the general law of contract. In England a lease confers an estate in land on the tenant; and the position is largely governed by a number of Landlord and Tenant Acts. In Scotland, there is no equivalent legislation to the Law of Property and the Landlord and Tenant Acts. As mentioned above, the main Scottish statute is the Leases Act 1449 (c. 18). Naturally, linked to this statutory intervention in England, there is a vast amount of case law on all aspects of the law from both the viewpoint of the landlord and of the tenant. These English cases and articles thereon must be read with caution by the Scottish practitioner who should always remember the different principles applied in Scots law. However, within the last two decades, investment leases on a full repairing and insuring basis have been introduced into Scotland, closely following the English pattern.

It can now be fairly said that this is an established area of the law of landlord and tenant in Scotland. The principal Scottish text on the subject is Ross and McKichan (2nd edn., 1993). Reference is also made to McAllister, *The Law of Leases in Scotland* (2nd edn., 1995) for a good general view of the subject.

As a matter of professional practice in Scotland, the lease is normally drafted by the landlord who therefore inserts all the clauses in the form which will best protect his interests; and the purpose of this chapter is to discuss briefly some of the clauses which regularly occur in commercial leases in Scotland and to suggest possible revisals on behalf of the tenant. Only the major points in a commercial lease will be dealt with here but the whole document should always be considered when acting on behalf of a tenant. It must always be kept in mind that a lease is a contract and, as such, may well be strictly enforced according to its terms.

There are many different types of commercial lease, *e.g.* offices, shopping centre developments, industrial units etc. Each lease has its own characteristics and every clause must therefore be considered fully and carefully revised so as to take account of each tenant's individual circumstances. Care should be taken to avoid using a style of lease that is not suitable for the property to be let.

The tenant's solicitor should first carefully read all the documents received from the landlord before commencing to revise the draft lease. Under no circumstances should the bargain be concluded prior to the terms of the draft lease being agreed by the landlord and the tenant. The tenant's solicitor should first take a copy of the draft lease and use this as a working draft. This draft should then be revised and sent to the client with a report outlining the salient terms thereof. After a meeting with the client, alterations can be made to the fresh draft and forwarded to the landlord with a qualified acceptance to his offer to lease. If then the landlord refuses to accept certain revisals made by the tenant's solicitor, the tenant can be advised of the consequences of such rejections.

In revising the draft, it is suggested that the tenant's solicitor should read it through from beginning to end before making any form of detailed revisal. This is important as many related clauses are often separated by a number of pages in the deed. Use of a checklist highlighting the salient points to look for could be helpful. If there is a definition/interpretation section in the lease document, it should be studied carefully. The lease should then be revised where applicable to safeguard the tenant's interests. At all times, keep your client advised as to the state of negotiations and request instructions on all points of principle.

Once the terms of the lease have been agreed and an engrossment executed and delivered to the landlord's solicitor, it is recommended that a synopsis of the lease be prepared summarising the salient dates and important clauses. Such lease summaries can be of great benefit to the tenant during the lease and especially prior to rent review. The best time to prepare such a summary is when the terms of the revised draft are clearly in one's mind.

The foregoing is a very brief outline of the general steps to be followed by a tenant's solicitor in revising a commercial lease. There are a number of important areas which require specific mention. These are:

1. Landlord's title to lease, parties, the description of the subjects and duration.
2. Use and keep-open clauses.
3. Monetary obligations of the tenant.
4. Rent review.
5. Tenant's repairing obligation.
6. Insurance.
7. Alienation.
8. Irritancy.
9. Hypothec.

## 25.2 1. Landlord's title to lease, parties, the description of the subjects and duration

### 25.3 (1) Title.
*(a) Sub-leases.* The landlord may himself hold the subjects on lease as principal or sub-tenant. In this case, the head lease should be examined in addition to the head landlord's title. An important consequence of the landlord holding title by virtue of a lease is that, if the landlord's lease is forfeited, any derivative rights will fall with it. Unlike the situation in England, sub-tenants under commercial leases in Scotland are not protected under statute. The tenant should seek to obtain an undertaking from the head landlord (*i.e.* the infeft proprietor), that, if the immediate landlord's lease falls, the head landlord will grant a new lease on the same terms

for the remaining duration of the original lease. (This is dealt with further under 'Irritancies'). Such an undertaking will not be enforceable against singular successors of the infeft proprietor as head landlord. The landlord may be taken bound to transmit the obligation under penalty of damages.

**25.4** *(b) Heritable creditors.* The premises may be subject to a standard security. In this event, it is essential that the tenant sees a letter of consent to the lease from the heritable creditors in order to satisfy standard condition 6. Failure to comply with this procedure could be fatal for the tenant: see *Trade Development Bank* 1980 SC 74.

**25.5** *(c) Planning permission, etc.* Exhibition of all planning permissions, building warrants, certificates of completion and other necessary permissions and consents should be requested to satisfy the tenant that the landlord has complied with all relevant legislation etc. In addition, the usual enquiries should be made of the local authorities regarding roads, footpaths, and planning, drainage, water supply, and of the statutory undertakers (electricity, gas, British Telecom) as applicable. A valid fire certificate should also be exhibited, if applicable. Environmental issues must also be borne in mind. See the Environmental Protection Act 1990 and related legislation. More than ever before, careful checks require to be made so as to avoid incurring responsibility for pollution on the site.

### 25.6 (2) Designations of parties to the lease.

**25.7** *(a) The tenant.* Privity of contract, as known in English law, is not implied in Scots law. Indeed, such a continuing obligation requires to be expressly provided for in the lease before it will be effective. Accordingly, any attempt to provide that the original tenant continues to be bound along with assignees should be resisted. It is still common to find this continuing obligation or privity of contract inserted in several different places in the lease. Every such reference should be deleted. The privity of contract rule in English law has been amended by the Landlord and Tenant (Leasehold Covenants) Act 1995.

Where the tenant is an individual or a limited company, the position is relatively straightforward. However, the case of a firm or a partnership deserves separate treatment. Partnerships cannot own heritage in Scotland, *socio nomine*, but a partnership as such may become a tenant. Landlords usually insist that the individual partners must act as trustees for the firm. Frequently, however, the obligations are deemed to extend to existing partners at the date of commencement of the lease and to all persons who may subsequently become partners at any time during the period of the lease. Effectively, the landlord is trying to bind future partners of the firm before they even become partners. Such a clause should be strongly resisted.

It is essential that the parties to a lease are distinct from one another. See *Clydesdale Bank plc* 1996 SLT 437.

**25.8** *(b) Guarantors.* A landlord may well request that the tenant's obligations be guaranteed by a third party. Such a request should be resisted if possible by the tenant. If it is agreed that a guarantee be given, the landlord will obviously wish to ensure that it is a worthwhile one. Therefore, in the case of a limited company, only a director being a major shareholder with a certain proportion of the issued share capital will be accepted by the landlord, with an obligation that, if he leaves the company, then another similar guarantor, approved by the landlord, should be obtained. If the guarantor is a company, the landlord may request confirmation that it can competently give guarantees in terms of its memorandum and articles. If the guarantee is given, the guarantor's solicitor should read the definition of 'guarantor' carefully so as to ensure that there is no possibility of the guarantee continuing once the original tenant assigns his interest in the lease. This is a common fault. From the landlord's point of view, care should be taken to ensure that the benefit of the guarantee is transferable to singular successors of the landlord. See *Waydale Ltd.* 1996 SCLR 391.

The landlord may also request that a rent deposit agreement be entered into whereby rental for, say, six months is placed on deposit as a form of security against the tenant failing to meet his obligation to pay rent in terms of the lease.

**25.9 (3) Description of the leased subjects.** It is essential that the tenant obtains the subjects which he thought he was to obtain together with all necessary pertinent rights for their proper use and enjoyment. Careful investigation of plans and the landlord's title is therefore essential. If possible, a site visit should be made. The tenant's solicitor should also obtain a copy of the prospective tenant's survey report and plans.

There is no reason why a description in a lease should be any different from a description in any feudal grant. This is often not the case in practice, however. In complex office blocks or shopping centres, great care will have been taken when drawing the description of the subjects, indeed, it is advisable to incorporate an adequate conveyancing description in the lease, whether or not the lease is to be registered. Reference ought also to be made to a plan – Ordnance Survey if suitable. As well as the subjects themselves, the tenant will require all necessary pertinent rights such as access, use of services, etc. Revise this into the lease if omitted by the landlord. The exceptions and reservations made by the landlord should also be noted carefully by the tenant's solicitors, as their import can often be far reaching. Such reservations will normally take the form of reservations to the landlord of various rights such as the right to lay and maintain services, etc. It is not uncommon for such reservations to be scattered throughout the lease. It is advisable therefore that a summary be given to the tenant of all the rights which he has in the subjects whether exclusive or common; and what exceptions or reservations have been made in favour of the landlord. Ensure that the landlord is obliged to make good any damage caused to the subjects by reason of the exercise of such reserved rights.

In many office block or shopping centre leases, one often finds that the tenant is leasing no more than the airspace within the unit. In such cases, the landlord will retain responsibility for the main walls and roof, etc., but will recover the cost of repairing and renewing such items by way of a service charge. It is therefore essential that when investigating the description of the subjects, the tenant's solicitor should consider the whole lease so that he may report to his client on the extent of his holding and the restrictions on it, if any.

Questions may arise as to what constitutes a 'common part' in a multi-occupancy situation. See *Marfield Properties* 1996 SLT 1744.

**25.10 (4) Duration.** The date of entry in the lease should be a definite stated date not earlier than the actual date of entry – howsoever it may be determined. The term of a lease may vary depending on a number of factors such as the individual characteristics of the landlord and the tenant and perhaps the state of the commercial market in the area. The period of lease may be prolonged by the operation of tacit relocation if the contractual term of the lease expires without either party having given notice to the other of his intention to terminate it and there is nothing in the conduct of the parties which might rebut the presumption that renewal of the lease was intended. For a review of the common law principle, see *MacDougall* 1992 SCLR 167. Note also the limited protection afforded to shop tenants in Scotland in terms of the Tenancy of Shops (Scotland) Acts 1949 and 1964.

If a lease is to be recorded in Sasines it must be for a duration of more than 20 years; 20 years and one day will suffice. In operational areas, all such long leases must be registered in the Land Register in order to have effect against singular successors of the landlord. Registration, unlike the recording of a lease in Sasines, is not optional in such circumstances.

The rates of stamp duty increase by reference to the term of the lease at seven years, 35 years and 100 years (Finance Act 1974 Schedule 11). Therefore, if the desired term is to be for longer than 35 years, it may be desirable to prescribe an initial term of less than 35 years, with an option to renew, so as to minimise the stamp duty implications for the tenant. It should however be borne in mind that (i) a lease for 30 years with an option to renew for a period of 25 years is chargeable as a lease for 30 years and not 55 years; *Hand* (1877) 2 Ex D 355 and Sergeant on *Stamp Duties*; (ii) when the option is exercised, the instrument used to evidence the renewal will attract *ad valorem* duty at that time – Rankine on *Leases*, p. 106; and (iii) the possibility that the option may not be binding on a singular successor of the landlord should be considered – Paton and Cameron on *Landlord and Tenant*, pp. 95–97.

### 25.11 2. Use and keep-open clauses

(1) *Permitted user*
The use to which the premises may be put will be regulated in the lease. This is usually done by specifying a type of use with provision that no other use is permitted without the consent of the landlord – such consent not to be unreasonably withheld. If the permitted use is tightly controlled, this is likely to have a detrimental effect on the rent obtainable at review. It is not uncommon to find use defined by reference to the appropriate class in the Schedule to the Town and Country Planning (Use Classes) (Scotland) Order 1989. The lease is also likely to prohibit certain types of use that might be a nuisance to adjoining proprietors.

(2) *Keep-open clauses*
Most recent commercial leases have imposed an obligation on the tenant to trade from the premises for the duration of the lease. Such obligations are commonly known as 'continuous trading' or 'keep-open' clauses.

An example of such a clause is as follows:

'The Tenant shall take possession of and use and occupy and trade from the premises for the aforementioned purposes within one calendar month from the date of entry and shall thereafter continue so to do throughout the whole period of this Lease. The Tenant shall not keep the premises nor shall it allow the premises to be kept closed for any period longer than twenty-one consecutive days in any one year.'

Landlords argue that such an obligation is essential for the benefit of the development of which the premises forms part. A tenant, on the other hand, will always try to resist such an obligation, arguing that while it is prepared to continue to pay rental until a suitable assignee or sub-tenant is found it is not prepared to trade from the premises at a loss.

### (3) Common law
In cases where there is no continuous trading obligation in the lease but where a use is prescribed and other uses are prohibited, there is nonetheless an obligation at common law to keep the premises plenished. There is ample authority for this in both commercial and agricultural leases. Accordingly, even without a continuous trading clause or an obligation to trade in whatever fashion, the premises will have to be stocked.

In the case of a shop, the tenant cannot be compelled to carry on business from the premises. He must, however, furnish the shop, keep fires in it and air it: *Whitelaw* (1871) 10 M 27. The landlord enforces his right by a plenishing order in the Sheriff Court.

### (4) Recent case-law
There was, for some time, little case-law on the subject of 'keep-open' clauses in Scotland. Then came the case of *Grosvenor Developments (Scotland) plc* 1987 SLT 738, which was followed by the decision in *Postel Properties Ltd.* 1993 SLT 353. There have been a number of recent cases on this subject, however, both north and south of the border. See *Church Commissioners for England* 1994 SLT 897; *Church Commissioners for England* 1994 SLT 959; *Overgate Centre Ltd.* 1995 SLT 1181; *Retail Parks Investments Ltd. (No. 2)* 1996 SLT 669; *Highland & Universal Properties Ltd.* 1996 SLT 559; and, perhaps most importantly, *Co-operative Insurance Society Ltd.* [1997] 1 WLR 898. See also two recent cases: *Co-operative Insurance Society Ltd.* [1996] 9 EG 128; *Co-operative Insurance Society Ltd.* 1997 GWD 17–798.

### (5) Summary
The above cases demonstrate the problems which can occur with the enforcement of keep-open clauses. It would appear to be the case that the Courts north and south of the border are interpreting the provisions in a similar manner. Much will depend on the wording in each lease and the individual circumstances of each case, however.

Many tenants refuse to accept such obligations in new leases and the logic of their argument can often be difficult to resist. In addition, it is possible that the existence of the clause may lead to there being a discount at review.

## 25.12 3. Monetary obligations of tenant

**25.13 (1) Rent.** The amount of rent to be charged by the landlord may well have already been agreed by the tenant before a solicitor is consulted. The annual rental may be fixed for the initial period of the lease, say five years, or it may be staged over this period. Depending on the state of the market, there may be a rent-free period available to the tenant which should, if possible, cover his initial fitting out works. The period granted will vary depending on the type of unit involved. An alternative to a rent-free period is for the tenant to commence payment of rental at the date of entry but at a reduced rate for a certain period. Frequently, such rent-free periods are documented by way of back letter and are not incorporated in the lease itself, in an effort not to weaken the position of the landlord on rent review. The landlord's agent should exercise care in the granting of such back letters since the court might hold them to be binding in this context. See *Kleinwort Benson Ltd.* [1987] AC 597.

Rent is usually payable quarterly or half-yearly in advance. Indeed it is not uncommon to find rent being paid monthly in advance. Payment half-yearly in advance is onerous and should be resisted. The landlord may also provide for rent to be payable by banker's order. Quarterly payments are generally made on the Scottish quarter days of Candlemas, Whitsunday, Lammas and Martinmas. In terms of the Term and Quarter Days (Scotland) Act 1990, these quarter days are, in the absence of provision to the contrary, deemed to be the Twenty eighth days of February, May, August and November respectively. Note the 'old' quarter days of Second February, Fifteenth May, First August and Eleventh November, however, which are still commonly found in leases. See *Provincial Insurance plc* 1992 SCLR 203.

The tenant should not, if possible, agree to forego his common law right of retention of rent. Such a right can be useful to the tenant in attempting to secure performance of the landlord's obligations under the lease. If however there is a head lease and the sub-tenant retains rent, the head lease could well be irritated, thus causing derivative rights (*e.g.* the sub-lease) also to fall. Therefore in such circumstances, the tenant's revisal may be refused. In practice, landlords do not wish anything to interfere with the regular payment of rent on the due date.

**(2) Turnover rent**. The concept of turnover rent is common in America and is often found in the UK in shopping centre developments. An additional sum over a flat-rate rent (which itself is subject to review) is usually paid. This additional sum is a percentage of gross sales over a minimum figure of sales. In most cases, a base rent is set between 75% and 80% of the estimated open market rental value, thus guaranteeing the landlord a minimum return. Turnover rent is therefore only payable when the percentage (less agreed deductions) exceeds the base rent. Turnover rent, unlike normal rental payments, is normally paid in arrears. The machinery for calculating this form of rent should be examined carefully.

**25.14 (3) Interest**. There will undoubtedly be an interest provision either in the rent clause or in a separate clause to which reference is made throughout the lease. Generally, the rate provided for by landlords is high and should be reduced if possible. The reason for a high interest rate is to prevent the landlord becoming the 'unofficial and unpaid banker' of the tenant. If at all possible, the tenant should not be committed to paying a penal rate of interest and a period of grace before interest becomes due should be requested. Many leases have a clause providing for payment of a fifth part more by way of liquidate penalty for failure to pay rent when due. This is certainly penal and should be deleted. There will probably also be other clauses throughout the lease which contain interest provisions. Interest at the rate applicable for non-payment of rent should not be accepted in respect of any payment due by the tenant to the landlord of any balance between the rent previously payable and the new rent payable following on a rent review.

**25.15 (4) Insurance premiums.** If the landlord insures, the tenant will be required to pay the premiums on demand. The tenant will also have to pay any premiums for risks against which he himself must insure, *e.g.* plate glass, public liability, etc.

**25.16 (5) Rates and other charges.** Rates will be the responsibility of the tenant. The other charges should however be restricted, if possible, to those of an annual or recurring nature. Taxes arising out of the landlord's dealing or deemed dealing with the subjects should be excluded along with any rents payable to a head landlord. If possible, the tenant should also try to avoid paying commission or factorial charges to the managing agents. Such a provision should always be deleted in the lease of a single free-standing building; but deletion is less likely to be acceptable to the landlord in a multi-occupancy complex. It is common to find a provision to the effect that such a charge is to relate to the work done by the landlord or its agents but not to the collection of rent.

**25.17 (6) Service charge.** Many leases contain a clause obliging the landlord to carry out certain services for which he then charges the tenant(s). Such clauses can be very onerous. There are a number of essential points to be considered in the service charge clause. Briefly, however, the most important items to be excluded from the cost of the services are:

(i) damage caused by the insured risks:

(ii) damage caused by latent or inherent defects – see *infra*; and

(iii) the cost of the initial provision of the subjects or any part thereof.

The basis of apportionment should also be investigated, especially if there are unlet units in the development. Provision is sometimes made for a sinking fund to ensure regular payments from the tenants towards the ultimate cost of repair, renewal, etc. If there is a sinking fund, however, the tenant must ensure that it is placed outwith the control of the landlord in order to safeguard the tenant's position in the event of insolvency of the landlord. The services to be performed by the landlord for which the service charge is to be levied must be carefully considered so as to ensure that the landlord is not, in essence, given a 'blank cheque' to carry out whatever repairs, refurbishment or other services the landlord may think desirable. The terms of a service charge clause or schedule should be considered carefully and, in the case of a new letting, details of previous years' service expenditure and accounts should be inspected.

**25.18 (7) Common charges, etc.** These will be ascertainable following upon an examination of the title deeds. The tenant's potential liability should thus be calculated prior to conclusion of missives. Note in particular the provisions of the title deeds of a tenement or other multi-occupancy building in respect of the liability for roof and other common repairs especially where liability is shared on a rateable value basis and you are acting for a prospective tenant of the ground-floor shop premises.

**25.19 (8) Expenses**. It is suggested that it is an outdated feature of the practice of landlord and tenant that the tenant must pay the landlord's legal fees in respect of the preparation of the lease. Resist this if at all possible, especially in recessionary times. At the very least, the tenant should seek to impose an upper limit on legal costs. If the tenant must pay these fees, ensure that they are reasonable and properly incurred. Most certainly refuse to pay the landlord's surveyors' and other professional advisers' costs. There may also be expenses throughout the lease in respect of the service of schedules of repair and applications for consent etc. These are unavoidable. However, the tenant should provide that these charges must be reasonable and properly incurred.

**25.20 (9) VAT**. Changes in the UK VAT legislation were made in the 1989 Finance Act, in the main taking effect from 1 April 1989. As a result, many leases expressly state whether the rent is inclusive or exclusive of VAT. Since the effective date, landlords have had the choice of obtaining exempt rental income or of charging VAT on rent. Many landlords reserve the option to elect to tax at some time in the future. Note in particular however the position of certain types of tenant who may be unable to recover VAT on rental payments. Such tenants will often attempt to insert a provision in the lease to the effect that the rent is VAT inclusive or that the landlord is prohibited from electing to charge VAT. Such provisions are rarely acceptable. For further comment on VAT, see Chapter 5.

### 25.21 4. Rent review

**25.22 (1) Object of review**. The object of a rent review clause is to minimise the consequence of inflation on the landlord's investment. Such a clause allows the landlord to take account of fluctuations in market value so that the tenant is paying throughout the duration of the lease a rent which equates in real terms with the market rental value of the subjects. Therefore, the rent review clause will have been drafted carefully by the landlord's solicitor – possibly in conjunction with the landlord's surveyor. Essentially, a rent review clause provides for the rent to be reviewed after a set period following agreement between the parties. If there is no agreement, the matter will be decided by some independent third party. Clauses are not so straightforward in practice however and there are a number of elements of a rent review clause which require further comment. In this area of the law, comparisons are often made with English precedents, of which there are many. For a detailed discussion on rent review clauses in general, reference is made to the series of articles in the 'Workshop' of the JLS, commencing April 1983 by E. D. Buchanan.

The following is a summary of some of the major elements in the rent review clause, which merit consideration.

**25.23 (2) Rent review dates**. The frequency of reviews will vary with location, the norm presently being three/five years. It is essential for a land-lord that these dates are clearly and unambiguously expressed in the lease. Phrases such as 'in the fifth year of the lease' are not recommended.

Older leases tend to provide for longer periods between reviews. In such cases, the landlord may well attempt to obtain a premium rent, *i.e.* a higher rent than that which would have been the case had the review interval been less. In other words, the tenant would be paying a premium rent for the advantage of infrequent rent reviews. Even if accepted, such a clause has the disadvantage however that the market rent may rise dramatically, in which event, the premium would not adequately compensate the landlord.

In leases of a longer duration than say 25 years, it is common to see procedure for a review of reviews. This will probably take the form of an option exerciseable by the landlord entitling him to review the frequency of reviews or redraft the rent review clause so as to produce a new clause which conforms to the prevailing market practice. Such a clause is really another attempt to protect the landlord's investment.

### 25.24 (3) Timetable for review

**25.25** *(a) Notice.* Certain leases provide that the rent will be reviewed without the necessity of any form of notice from the landlord to the tenant. Many leases however provide for some form of notice to trigger the operation of the review machinery. As a result, these leases are drafted to ensure that, even if the landlord fails or omits to serve notice, he may do so at a later term without penalty. There have been a number of decisions on this point in England, where the general rule now is that time is not of the essence in relation to rent review procedure unless the parties expressly so stipulate or it could be inferred from the circumstances that the parties so intended – *United Scientific Holdings Ltd. and Cheapside Land Development Co. Ltd.* [1978] AC 904.

The law in Scotland on this matter is now settled following the judgment of the Inner House in *Visionhire Ltd.* 1992 SCLR 236, where Lord President Hope undertook a comprehensive review of both English and Scottish cases on the whole subject of whether or not time is of the essence in contracts. To avoid any possible argument, the landlord's clause may well dispense with the requirement of notice altogether and specify that time is not of the essence.

The question, whether time is of the essence in a particular case, is very important to the parties. Every case must be considered on its own merits. This involves a consideration not merely of the rent review clause but also the import of that clause in the context of other clauses in the lease as a whole.

Any notice of the landlord's intention to review the rent should be clear and unequivocal; and should be served in accordance with the provisions of the lease. See *Dunedin Property Investment Co. Ltd.* 1992 SCLR 159. But see also *Prudential Assurance Co. Ltd.* 1995 SLT 369.

Acceptance of rent at the old rate by the landlord after the stipulated re-view date may amount to acquiescence in the situation. The result would therefore be that the landlord would be barred from insisting on the missed rent review. See *Banks* 1982 SC 7 and *Waydale Ltd.* 1996 SLT (Sh Ct) 6. In light of these decisions therefore, landlords often insert a provision to the effect that demand for and/or acceptance of rent at the old rate by the land-lord after a review date shall not constitute a waiver of the landlord's right to review.

**25.26** *(b) Counter-notice.* Some leases are drafted so that once the landlord serves notice of review the tenant only has a specified period within which he can object or else be deemed to have accepted the reviewed rental. This can be beneficial for a landlord but should be avoided by the tenant who could be faced with an inflated reviewed rental with only a short period to object. If the tenant omits to serve such notice due to error or administrative failure he will pay the penalty. The 'time of the essence' cases are of direct significance when considering the effect of such counter-notice provisions.

**25.27** (c) *Postponed reviews*. Failure on the part of a landlord to initiate the rent review procedure will result in back rent being due. If such a late rent review takes place, it is only equitable for the tenant that the level of the market rent should reflect the level that would have applied at the original rent review date. In addition, the tenant should not suffer a penalty when he has not been in a position to pay the increased rent which was unknown. Therefore, the increased rent should be payable only from the postponed date and not backdated to the original rent review date. The tenant must also ensure that he is not required to pay interest on any balancing payment at the rate chargeable in the event of non-payment of rent.

**25.28 (4) Basis for review**.   By necessity, the world of rent review is a hypothetical one. At each rent review date, the premises must be valued and the rent assessed on the basis of a hypothetical letting involving a hypothetical landlord and a hypothetical tenant. In determining the reviewed rental, the parties will have regard to certain valuation guidelines (assumptions and disregards) as provided for in the lease. For a long time, these valuation guidelines were relatively straightforward. This is often not the case now, however.

One of the valuation guidelines which has recently been under the judicial microscope has been that relating to rent-free periods. The whole point at issue has been whether or not the hypothetical letting should take account of rent-free periods.  The landlord's argument is that a rent-free period, if applicable at all, should apply only at the commencement of the lease – not at each review date throughout the term. A tenant, on the other hand, may argue that if rent-free periods are being granted to potential new tenants of similar premises at the review date, then a similar concession should be assumed in the hypothetical letting. Alternatively, the tenant may seek a discounted rent to reflect the fact that, unlike a tenant in an open market letting, he will not have the benefit of a rent-free period.

In an effort to avoid such disputes, landlords have commonly inserted additional valuation guidelines into the rent review clause. These take the form of either (a) an assumption that any rent-free period or concessionary rent or other inducement which may be offered in the open market at the review date in question shall have expired immediately prior to the review date or (b) a disregard of the rent-free period or other such inducement. Indeed, it is often common to find a combination of both. Such attempts to minimise the effect of rent-free periods at review are found in many forms and few, if any, provisions can be said to be totally free from possible ambiguity.

Whether or not a rent-free period is given at the commencement of a lease depends on (*a*) market conditions at the time and (*b*) the strength of the parties' bargaining power. A rent-free period is essentially a concession to the tenant to encourage him to take a lease at the then open-market rental.

If such inducements have been the norm, however, where does that leave the parties to a review (or in default, the arbiter/expert) in seeking to establish the true open-market rental value of neighbouring premises in the same centre? Are the rental levels of the comparable premises truly passing rentals in the open market, or are they headline rents?

For an illustration of the sometimes complex issues debated when seeking to interpret such provisions on the occasion of rent review, see *Co-operative Wholesale Society Ltd., Broadgate Square plc, Scottish Amicable Life Assurance Society and Prudential Nominees Ltd.* [1995] 01 EG 111. The matter has also been judicially considered in Scotland. See *Church Commissioners for England and Sears Property Glasgow Ltd.* 1995 SCLR 947.

One lesson which can be learned from case-law is that artificial assumptions and disregards in rent-review clauses can produce unexpected and often quite costly results. Indeed, it is now often argued that an effective disregard of a rent-free period will itself be viewed as an onerous term in a lease which should have a discounting effect on review. The various assumptions to be made and the facts to be taken into account in establishing the current market rental value of the subjects are an essential part of the review process. Indeed, without such a basis for review being specified, the whole rent review may be void by reason of uncertainty. See *Beard* 1990 SLT 609, *Crawford* 1992 SCLR 565 and *Colonial Mutual Group (UK Holdings) Ltd.* 1994 GWD 29–1761. It is essential therefore that the lease contains details as to the basis on which the rent is to be reviewed. These details should be clear and unambiguous to avoid dispute. Accordingly, both the landlord and the tenant must ensure that the lease, as agreed, enables their surveyors (and in default of agreement the arbiter or expert) to establish clearly the market rent of the hypothetical letting of the subjects. See *Scottish Mutual Assurance Society* 1992 SLT 617. The salient matters are:

**25.29** (*a*) *Upwards only review.* Most leases provide for the rent to be reviewed in an upwards only direction. However, this may not be commercially viable, from the tenant's point of view, especially in poor market conditions. This has been commented on in England in the case of *Stylo Shoes Ltd.* [1967] 204 EG 803. Notwithstanding these comments, it is extremely unlikely that landlords will even countenance the possibility of a 'downwards' review. From time to time there is pressure for reform of upwards only reviews.

**25.30** (*b*) *Valuation.* There are a number of important definitions and assumptions built into a rent review clause – especially as regards the definition of 'the current market rental value' of the subjects. The most important of these are:

**25.31** (i) *Best rent.* It is suggested that the existence of this phrase in a rent review clause might allow a special rental to be considered for the purposes of comparison. A tenant's solicitor will normally seek alternative wording akin to 'fair' or the omission altogether of a descriptive word.

**25.32** (ii) Willing landlord and willing tenant. These hypothetical characters are assumed as they may not be present in the negotiation. This assumption is consistent with the hypothetical open market assumption. The implication of this assumption was clearly dealt with in the English case of *F.R. Evans (Leeds) Ltd.* [1977] 245 EG 657. The willing landlord assumption prevents the actual landlord from arguing that he would not in fact let the property to the tenant at the review date, *e.g.* because the market was depressed at that date. The term was initially introduced in England in s. 34 of the 1954 Act, presumably for this reason. It also prevents the landlord arguing that, due to personal difficulties, he could only accept a certain level of rent. The term thus recognises the fact that, with a rent review, a settlement must at some stage and by some means be reached, *e.g.* a notional letting must be effected and there is a rent on which a willing landlord and willing tenant would agree.

**25.33** (iii) User. It is a fact that a restrictive user clause will result in the rent available at a review date being less than what would otherwise have been available. This was demonstrated by the English case of *Plinth Property Investment Ltd.* [1978] 249 EG 1167, CA. To counter this fact, many landlords attempt to introduce an assumption that notwithstanding the actual use, the use at the review date will be any use within a certain use class order under the Town and Country Planning Acts. This should be resisted by the tenant who should insist upon the review being in the context of the user clause in the lease. A landlord should not be entitled to unilaterally consent to uses not specifically requested by the tenant solely in order to benefit his case on a rent review. The existence of an enforceable keep-open or continuous trading obligation is also likely to have a restrictive effect on the rent obtainable at review.

**25.34** (iv) Duration. The assumed duration of the hypothetical letting may either be for a period equal to the original term of the lease or for a period equal to the unexpired term. The former is better for the landlord in most cases and the latter for the tenant. Many leases are now drafted with a compromise based on an assumed duration of either the unexpired residue or ten/fifteen years whichever is the greater.

**25.35** (v) Lease whether as a whole or in parts. Most landlords require such a provision in the rent review clause in order that account may be taken of the possibility of the sub-letting of the whole or part of the premises as individual units. Its omission may not, however, be detrimental; and regard must be had to the terms of the alienation clause in the lease in that the hypothetical letting is usually deemed to be on terms and conditions similar to those in the existing lease.

**25.36** (vi) Vacant possession/rent-free periods. Where a rent review clause provides for the yearly rental value to be assessed on the basis of a letting with vacant possession, a discount may be applied to the rent to compensate for the fact that no rent-free period will occur at the rent review. Tenants should beware of the vacant possession assumption where there are sub-tenants. Furthermore, the assumption may also negate the effect on rent of a restrictive user clause as the courts may hold that, if vacant possession is to be assumed at a review date, it is illogical also to assume that only the existing tenant can occupy the subjects.

The whole question of whether a rent-free period is to be assumed or disregarded can have significant valuation implications and much depends on the wording in individual leases. The recent economic recession has also produced a spate of preventive drafting on the part of landlords' agents, to such an extent that many of the valuation guidelines commonly found in leases bear little resemblance to the reality of the circumstances of the actual letting or open-market conditions at the review date. One thing is certain, however, and that is that over-complicated drafting may well backfire at the end of the day.

**25.37** (vii) 'Lease on the same terms and conditions as the existing lease – other than the amount of rent and the provisions of the rent review clause.' The latter part of this assumption is often referred to as the 'overage factor'. Taken literally, the landlord is entitled to assume that the hypothetical letting does not contain any provisions as to rent review. As a result, a higher rent would be payable by the 'willing tenant'. There have been several English decisions on this point; and, in particular, the principles laid down in *National Westminster Bank plc* [1985] 2 All ER 817 have been debated in a series of subsequent cases. Reference is made in particular to the decisions in *Pugh* [1982] 264 EG 823 and *British Gas Corporation* [1986] 1 All ER 978, particularly the opinion of the Vice-Chancellor in the latter case.

The point has not yet been judicially decided in Scotland but it is suggested that, where the lease contains clear words which require the rent review provision (as opposed to all provisions as to rent) to be disregarded, then, as was the case in *Pugh* and as was envisaged by the Vice-Chancellor in *British Gas Corporation*, effect must be given to this direction. Faced with such possible difficulties in interpretation, the tenant should amend the clause so as to specify expressly that the review provisions are to be taken into account.

**25.38** (viii) Rent to be without premium. This is designed to ensure that, on each rent review, any premium or inducement offered to the tenant at the commencement of the lease is not to be taken into account on reviewing the rent. This is to avoid the possibility of such a payment or inducement distorting the annual rental to be paid.

**25.39** (*c*) *Assumptions and disregards.* In practice, it is now increasingly common for detailed lists of 'assumptions' and 'disregards' to be specified in the rent review clause. In such circumstances, it is essential that these provisions are considered and the rent review clause read as a whole so as to ascertain the exact intention of the parties. The following are typical 'assumptions':

**25.40** (i) Compliance with tenant's obligations. The rent review clause may also provide for the valuation to be on the assumption that the tenant has performed all his obligations under the lease. This is not unreasonable. What is objectionable, however, is an assumption that the landlord has complied with all his obligations under the lease.

(ii) Damage to premises repaired.
(iii) Fully fitted-out unit – see above.
(iv) VAT.

(v) 'Artificial' assumptions such as it being assumed that the landlord will grant consent to a change of use or assignation is unreasonable if the terms of the lease in this regard are restrictive.

**25.41** (*d*) *Disregards for valuation.* The tenant's agent should ensure that the effect (if any) on rent of certain matters is not to be taken into account when the landlord reviews the rent. Express provision of these disregards is essential as, unlike the position in England, on a renewal of a lease (Landlord and Tenant Act 1954 s. 34) they will not be implied in a Scottish lease. These 'usual' disregards are as follows:

(i) Occupation by the tenant or any predecessor in title or permitted sub-tenant of the tenant;
(ii) Goodwill attached to the subjects by reason of the trade of the tenant or his foresaids;
(iii) Initial shop-fitting works – especially in a shop unit; and
(iv) Alterations or improvements carried out by the tenant otherwise than in pursuance of any obligation to the landlord. This is an important disregard as failure by the tenant to include this in the rent review clause will result in all his improvements being taken into account by the landlord at the review date. This was demonstrated in the case of *Ponsford* [1979] AC 63. See also *Standard Life Assurance Co.* 1995 GWD 9–514. If the lease is a ground lease where the tenant has paid for and erected buildings on the ground, then the landlord ought to be entitled only to a revised rent based on his interest in the subjects, *i.e.* the ground alone. In light of the problems which can be associated with improvements on the occasion of rent review, it is recommended that both landlord and tenant should keep a comprehensive record of works undertaken and by whom. The tenant's solicitor should also attempt to revise the clause so as to provide that all work done pursuant to any statutory obligation on the tenant is also to be disregarded.
(v) The landlord may also add that the fact that the subjects have been damaged or destroyed is to be disregarded.

The list of 'disregards' and indeed 'assumptions' appears to grow with each new lease produced on the word processor! Is there not a risk that the drafting may simply become unnecessarily over-complicated?

**25.42 (5) Determination of reviewed rental in the event of dispute**. If there is no agreement between the parties by a given date, the lease usually provides for the matter to be referred to the decision of some independent person to be agreed between the parties or failing agreement, to be appointed by a third party. The usual procedure is by way of a reference to arbitration. However, many landlords prefer that the matter be referred to an expert, *i.e.* a surveyor having specialised knowledge of the area. The referral to an expert is designed to accelerate the process of determining the new rent. It is arguable, however, exactly how valid the distinction between the arbiter and the expert is. The essential distinction is that the arbiter, unlike the expert, can only decide on the basis of the facts as presented to him in the parties' submissions. Many leases expressly state that the third party is to act as an 'expert and not an arbiter'. Note that an expert, unlike an arbiter, may be sued for negligence. For a detailed review of this matter, reference is again made to the articles in 1983 JLS (Workshop) April *et seq.*

Some landlords attempt to exclude s. 3 of the Administration of Justice (Scotland) Act 1972 where the determination is by an arbiter (right of appeal to the courts on a point of law). The tenant should also resist any provision that he pays for the independent determination of rent. Each party should pay their own costs unless the award of the arbiter or expert, as the case may be, declares otherwise.

### 25.43 (6) Miscellaneous matters

**25.44** (*a*) *Rent pending determination of review.* If the reviewed rental has not been ascertained by the review date, the landlord may be entitled to assess a provisional rent. The tenant will therefore pay this new rent, which may be high. Such a clause ought to be resisted by the tenant. If it is to be accepted, there should be an accounting between the parties upon the determination of the reviewed rental with interest at a high rate if possible. However, many leases provide that the existing rental will continue to be chargeable in such circumstances with the increased sum due by the tenant as a debt to the landlords. If interest is to be chargeable on this debt, then the tenant should attempt to reduce the interest rate as much as possible.

**25.45** (*b*) *Counter inflation legislation.* Many leases contain clauses dealing with the possibility of rent increases being prohibited or restricted in the future by statutory control. These clauses are a result of controls imposed in s. 11 of the Counter Inflation Act 1973. It is suggested that these clauses may not be necessary. The regulations, if reimposed, will probably only restrict or prohibit collection of increased rentals. Therefore, it will still be competent for the rent to be reviewed on the normal dates in the normal way. Any increase will be payable in whole or in part as soon as the relevant regulations permit. The tenant should avoid clauses providing for interim reviews, but, if such a clause must be accepted, the tenant should ensure that any such review or reviews will contain a valuation based on market values at the original review date and not at any later date.

**25.46** (*c*) *Memoranda.* Once the review has been agreed, that agreement will be incorporated into a formal addendum to the lease. Try to ensure that the tenant does not have to meet all the expenses of this. In particular, the tenant should not meet the landlord's surveyor's costs. Note also the increasing use of 'privacy' or 'confidentiality' agreements whereby a landlord, having made some form of inducement, insists that the tenant enters into an agreement whereby the information may be suppressed. This is seen by many as a rather regrettable development.

**25.47** (*d*) *Retail prices index.* Review clauses often provide for the rent to be increased in accordance with the appropriate increase in the retail price index between the date of entry and the review date. The use of indexed rents which provide for automatic increases in line with the retail price index may seem an attractive proposition in times of difficult open market rent reviews and falling rental values. However, landlords and tenants generally prefer the revised rent to be fixed by real people rather than by an anonymous index. A major problem with this procedure is that all the indices measure rises in prices and no official index is related to property. The use of such review provisions can be a gamble for both parties. If the matter is non-negotiable, resist the tendency to panic at the sight of a mathematical formulation.

**25.48** *(e) English law.* As mentioned previously, English law has had a major influence on the development of the law of commercial leases. There are numerous English cases on each of the salient points of the review clause and there are a number of excellent English publications such as the *Estates Gazette* which provide useful up-to-date commentary and case reports. In recent years in England, however, there has been a tendency to seek to adopt a 'presumption in favour of reality'. It is important to remember that such a presumption is only an aid to the determination of the commercial purpose of the rent review in question. If a lesson is to be learned from these English cases, it is that landlords' solicitors should draft their review clauses with care and attention so as to avoid litigation, if possible. Although the English cases may not always be followed in Scotland, they cannot be ignored.

### 25.49 5. Tenant's repairing obligation

**25.50 (1) The common law position.** The institutional writers state that once a tenant is in possession under an urban lease, the landlord is bound to repair any defect which makes the subjects less than wind and water tight and not in a tenantable condition. Such an obligation is very rarely found in a modern commercial lease. The position at common law in Scotland is that there is an implied warranty by the landlord that the subjects are reasonably fit for the purpose for which they are to be let, and that the landlord has a duty to keep the subjects in tenantable repair and wind and water tight throughout the period of the lease: see *Dickie* 1911 SC 1079 and the more recent case of *Blackwell* 1991 GWD 4–219. It is now invariably qualified to some extent, if not altogether excluded. The wording of such an exclusion from liability at common law must be carefully drafted however. See *Turner's Trs.* (1900) 2 F 363.

Without proper repair, the landlord's investment is put in jeopardy. However, the fact that the property is held on lease, so that the maintenance responsibility can be divided between the two parties involved, seems to give scope for endless disputes. In recent years, the clear trend has been for the landlord to transfer all the responsibilities on to the tenant. The aim is, from the landlord's point of view, to ensure that the landlord incurs no financial liability whatsoever and so receives the rent in full without any deduction. Many landlords have taken the view that an undivided repairing obligation reduces the scope for argument. However, there are always situations where a building is or may be converted into multi-occupation and where significant structural work and even external decoration can only be appropriately done by someone with an interest in the whole property. In such circumstances, the cost of these works will undoubtedly be recovered by the landlord by way of a service charge payable by all the tenants.

Each lease will differ according to circumstances. Therefore, a tenant's agent must read the entire lease carefully, especially the link between the repairs and the insurance clauses. Indeed, a major problem arises where damage is caused to the subjects by a risk for which there is no insurance cover. Accordingly, it is essential to the tenant that his liabilities should be mitigated wherever possible.

The two main areas where such qualification can be made are as follows:

**25.51 (2) Damage by insured risks**. Generally, the landlord will insure the subjects and recover the premium from the tenant. Therefore, there will be a specified list of risks against which the landlord is obliged to insure. The tenant should insist on seeing the insurance policy or an extract thereof. To cover the situation where damage is caused by an insured risk, the tenant's agent will require to make an exception to the repairing obligation on the tenant so as to provide that reinstatement of such damage should not be the responsibility of the tenant, because it is the landlord who will recover the cost thereof from the insurance company. Any such qualification will, however, normally be further qualified by the landlord to the effect that the cost of such reinstatement will remain with the tenant if the insurance policy has been vitiated, or payment of the insurance monies has been withheld in whole or in part, by reason of the act or default of the tenant himself.

**25.52 (3) Extent of tenant's repairing obligation**. One of the most common sources of argument, when revising a lease, is the extent of the repairing obligation of the tenant. In England, the word 'repair' has a different interpretation – see *Lurcott* [1911] 1 KB 905. There are a number of English precedents on the same point. The position in England appears to be that it is always a question of degree whether that which the tenant is asked to do can properly be described as a repair, or whether it would involve giving back to the landlord a wholly different thing from that initially let. In other words, the approach in England is to look at the particular subjects, consider the state which they are in at the date of the lease, consider the terms of the lease and then come to a decision as to whether the requisite work can be fairly called repairs. However onerous the obligation, it is not to be looked at *in vacuo*.

The whole question of what constitutes a 'repair' was dealt with *inter alia* in the English case of *Ravenseft Properties Ltd.* [1980] 1 QB 12, where it was established that the tenant's repairing obligation did extend to repairs caused by inherent defects and to the work required to remedy that defect. Furthermore, that result would have ensued, even if the obligation had merely been 'to repair' as opposed to 'repair, renew, rebuild, uphold ... and keep the premises ...'.

The critical test in England seems to be whether or not, if the tenant carries out the reinstatement, he would be giving back to the landlord something totally different from what was originally leased to him.

It has been suggested however that there is no such test in Scots law which would take works of repair, no matter how extensive, out of the tenant's repairing obligation in the lease. In other words, in Scots law, regard should be had to the scope of the rebuilding obligation against the background of the common law doctrine of *rei interitus*. See 1985 JLS 99. See also *House of Fraser* 1994 SLT 416. In that case, the tenant contended that works to a retaining wall in the premises amounted to extraordinary repairs for which the landlord had responsibility at common law. Accordingly, reimbursement did not arise. The Court held that the landlord was indeed responsible for both ordinary and extraordinary repairs to the building as the common law would have imposed, but that the tenant was liable to reimburse the landlord for the cost of these works, given the terms of the lease.

The important point which distinguishes this case from the type of case which might be encountered in practice, however, is that it was the landlord who was responsible for carrying out all such repairs and charging the tenant therefor by way of a service charge. It would certainly be a different result altogether if it was the tenant who had responsibility for repairs to the leased subjects and there was no reference to renewal or rebuilding in the event of damage to or destruction thereof. It is now common for a lease to impose an obligation on the tenant to repair, renew and rebuild the subjects irrespective of the cause of damage to or destruction thereof and notwithstanding the age or state of repair of the subjects. Such obligations will be interpreted strictly according to their terms. See *Taylor Woodrow Property Co. Ltd*. 1996 GWD 7–397, however, for an illustration of circumstances where reasonableness will be implied. The onus is, however, on the landlord to transfer the obligations to repair, rebuild, renew and reinstate the subjects to the tenant. A simple obligation to repair does not amount to an undertaking to restore the subjects if they are accidentally destroyed. See *Allan* (1891) 18 R 932.

In each instance, it is still a matter for construction of the relevant lease. If the lease is silent on the question of extraordinary repairs, it is clear that the matter has to be regulated at common law.

**25.53 (4) Limiting tenant's liability for latent defects**. A lease, being a contract, will be interpreted strictly according to its terms. To avoid argument, landlords always seek to incorporate a clear and unambiguous obligation on the tenant to rebuild, reinstate and renew. The more explicit the provision, the better from the landlord's point of view. It is clear, from recent cases in Scotland, that the doctrine of *rei interitus*, and the common law obligations and warranties of the landlord, can competently be excluded by express provision. Accordingly, the tenant must always attempt to amend the wording used in the repairing clause. However, landlords generally resist such revisals, taking the view that it is the tenant who is in possession of the subjects on a full repairing lease.

Generally speaking, in every case, the landlord will insist on expressly excluding the implied common law duty on the landlord. Such defects may, however, have been caused by some negligent design or bad workmanship on the part of the landlord or his contractors or architects in the initial design or construction of the subjects. Accordingly, the defect may have been inherent in the structure of the subjects. If the repairing and rebuilding obligation of the tenant is not qualified, the landlord will invariably require the tenant to repair and make good all such defects occurring at any time throughout the lease, provided the terms of the repairing obligation on the tenant so permit. Some landlords may agree to carry out such reinstatement but this should not be regarded as a general rule. Indeed, the clause in the Styles Committee Lease (1980 JLS (Workshop) 117) on this point is not standard. The landlord will have his own contractual rights against his contractors, etc., whereas the tenant has no such right of recourse. It is therefore recommended that the tenant attempt to revise this clause by excepting liability for reinstatement necessitated by latent or inherent defects. Care should be taken to ensure that such liability is also excepted from the service charge provisions in the lease if any, so as to avoid the possibility of the landlord still being able to charge the tenant under this provision.

If the landlord accepts this revisal (which it must be said is often unlikely), the tenant should also seek to provide for compensation for any loss or damage to the tenant during the execution of such reinstatement by the landlord; and reference should also be made in the insurance clause to the exclusion of the tenant's liability for inherent defects etc. In addition, if the subjects are of recent construction, the tenant should, if possible, require an assignation from the landlord of his rights against contractors, architects and others. If this is not possible, then a back letter should be obtained from the landlord to the effect that the landlord will enforce his rights against the contractors and others at the expense of the tenant if so required. It may also be possible to obtain either a warranty or a 'duty of care' agreement from the professional team responsible for the design and construction of the building. In the case of recently constructed property, enquiries should also be made to see if there is a decennial insurance policy in place in respect of the subjects. Such insurance policies, which are more common in the United States and mainland Europe, are a means of insuring the building against design fault etc. and tend to be very costly. All of these possibilities should be explored, so as to minimise as far as possible the tenant's liability to reinstate under the repairing and rebuilding provisions.

Basically, all tenants should be advised before taking a lease of subjects, whether new or old, that they should have the subjects surveyed. The survey should be carried out prior to the bargain being concluded. The surveyor can also be asked to comment on the level of rent being sought and the rent review patterns. On obtaining the survey, the prospective tenant can either refuse to take a lease or negotiate for a reduced rent or reduced liability to reinstate if the subjects are not in good tenantable condition, *e.g.* internal repairing only.

The tenant's solicitors should also attempt to reduce the tenant's obligation to repair and reinstate by introducing an exception in respect of 'fair wear and tear'. This could be a useful protection for a tenant of an old building in that it would absolve him of liability to carry out major repairs or reinstatement due to the age or dilapidated state of the building.

If a survey discloses wants of repair, there are a number of possible scenarios: (1) the prospective tenant chooses not to proceed with the lease; (2) all wants of repair are remedied by the landlord prior to the date of entry and the tenant's assumption of a full repairing obligation; or (3) the tenant takes the lease subject to it not being liable for any works of repair or renewal as a result of the premises not being in perfect condition at the date of entry. In the third case, it is essential for the lease to be carefully revised, otherwise the tenant may find itself still being liable for major works of repair or renewal as a result of the wording in the lease or its acceptance of the premises and the common parts as being in good, tenantable condition and repair.

The only safe way of limiting the tenant's potential liability in such circumstances is for the parties to agree a record of the condition of the premises at the date of entry and for that record to be referred to in the lease. It is unfortunately only too common for the parties to go to the expense of preparing such a record, but then to fail to make any reference to it in the

323

lease document itself. To be fully effective, the record or schedule of condition should be referred to wherever there is any possibility of the tenant directly or indirectly being liable for works of repair or renewal. It is essential that there is no room for ambiguity in this regard.

In addition, it is recommended that such records of condition contain a photographic schedule. The photographs should be numbered by reference to the content of the schedule itself. If a photographic record of condition is to be used, it should be prepared in duplicate so that each party has a copy. Indeed, if the lease is to be registered in the Books of Council and Session, for example, the parties might consider having three copies prepared. This saves problems once the lease is registered and the colour photographs are reproduced in black and white in the extract registered copy of the lease.

Quite commonly, the parties are uncertain as to the respective repairing liability of landlord and tenant. Most leases nowadays contain a full repairing and rebuilding obligation on the tenant; and the tenant should consider the whole lease carefully to establish the extent of his liability, the meaning of the repairing obligations in the lease, and whether or not this obligation is reasonable, given the nature and state of repair of the subjects. From the tenant's point of view, much depends on the age and state of repair of a property at the date of entry. This should be taken into account before a lease is issued to a prospective tenant. Unfortunately, however, this is not often the case. The tenant should therefore be aware of the extent of the obligations which it may be about to assume and the alternatives available to it before the lease is signed. Blind acceptance of the landlord's solicitors' style lease without regard to the state of repair of the premises could have serious consequences.

**25.54 (5) Back letters.** It is quite common for back letters to be prepared to the effect that, notwithstanding the terms of the lease, certain items will not require to be repaired by the tenant. Such important matters ought perhaps to be regulated in the lease itself, however, in order to avoid any problem with transmission against singular successors of the landlords.

**25.55 (6) Effect of description on repairing obligations**. The definition of the subjects, perhaps elsewhere in the lease, should also be considered carefully in order to discover whether the tenant is directly liable for repairs to external walls, roof, drains and other services, etc. For a case in point, see *Mothercare UK Ltd.* 1994 GWD 28–1712. As previously stated, many leases provide the tenant with no more than a right to the air space within the internal walls, with the landlord maintaining the external walls, etc. and recovering the cost by way of a service charge. In practice, the tenant cannot argue against carrying out day-to-day maintenance or repairs of a decorative nature. However, arguments arise where there are major repairs. In such cases, the definition of the subjects can be critical. If the title to the subjects in question includes a right of common property or common interest in the roof, such right of ownership forms part of the subjects so that, if the obligation merely says that the tenant must repair the subjects, the tenant is liable for the repair of the relevant material parts. However, if part of the subjects or the building of which the subjects form part remains in the landlord's control or if the landlord has retained a contractual duty of repair, then he has an implied contractual duty to take reasonable care that his tenant shall not suffer damage. What constitutes 'reasonable care' in this context has however to be determined by reference *inter alia* to the landlord's knowledge of the defect or potential defect which gives rise to a risk of damage.

### 25.56 6. Insurance

**25.57 (1) Object of insurance provision**. As has been previously stated, the insuring obligation is the complement of the repairing obligation. Basically, the insuring obligation is designed to secure that financial resources will be available to restore insured damage and to reinstate the subjects when destroyed by an insured risk. Insurance will either be carried out by the landlord, with the tenant normally repaying the premiums or by the tenant under the supervision of the landlord who will request sight of the policy and premium receipts, etc. Most leases contain an obligation of the former type since landlords prefer to keep reinstatement under their control. Therefore, the usual arrangement is that the landlord insures the subjects and the tenant refunds the premium or an allocated portion thereof, often as '*quasi* rent'.

There are two supplementary reasons for this common arrangement:

(*a*) the tenant automatically bears the full cost of increased premiums; and

(*b*) a refund of premium is not rent, and so attracts no stamp duty.

The main points to be noted in this very broad area are as set out below.

**25.58 (2) Choice of insurance company**. Normally, the landlord decides the amount of cover and selects the appropriate insurance company. It is therefore essential for the tenant to have the right at any reasonable time to have sight of the insurance policy, or an extract thereof and the premium receipts. This will enable the tenant to check the sufficiency of cover and that the policy is in force. The landlord is not likely to accept a revisal allowing the tenant to alter the insurance company if he can find a better quotation. The insurance company should be an office of repute. The tenant's agent should investigate this matter fully, and refer a copy of the relevant provision in the lease to the tenant's insurance broker for comment if necessary.

**25.59 (3) Extent of cover**. The tenant should consider the definition of 'the insured risks' carefully. The definition may be in a totally separate place in the lease from the insurance clause itself. This definition ought at least to list the minimum risks to be covered. Any discretion in the landlord's favour to insure against other risks should be limited to other 'normal commercial' risks if possible. If the risk of terrorism is to be insured against, this should be expressly stated in the lease. It is suggested that it is not sufficient for such insurance to be imposed on a tenant by implication. The value insured should be no greater and no less than the full reinstatement value with associated fees and loss of rent. This will require constant reappraisal however in order to keep it in line with inflation and building costs generally. Loss of rent insurance is designed to provide cover for the landlord when the subjects are destroyed, in whole or in part, and he is receiving no rent or at the most partial rent. The period of cover is linked to the likely period of reinstatement, this presently being for a minimum of three years. The tenant will pay the premium on such insurance.

**25.60 (4) Liability in the event of shortfall in insurance monies.** If the landlord insures, the tenant should always revise the lease so as to provide that the landlord is liable for any such deficiency out of his own resources. It is the landlord after all who is in control. Although it would be better to express this in the lease, the common law may in fact provide a remedy for the tenant where the landlord has not fully insured. It is not uncommon for landlords (for reasons perhaps best known to themselves) to resist this revisal.

**25.61 (5) Damage by insured risks.** If the landlord has sole control of insurance, it is essential that the tenant qualifies his repairing obligation with regard to the restoration of insured damage. This emphasises the point made previously when discussing the reinstatement obligation of the tenant. If damage from an insured risk occurs, the insurance company may, except where the tenant is one of the insured (*infra*), have the right to enforce the contractual obligation of the tenant to reinstate the subjects, if this is so provided. Therefore, as previously stated, it is essential to exclude from the tenant's repairing obligation the restoration of insured risks damage unless the policy or claim has been invalidated because of some act or default of the tenant.

**25.62 (6) Insurance in joint names of landlord and tenant.** Fire insurance is a contract of indemnity against loss or damage by fire. Therefore, the insurance company will have a right of subrogation entitling them, on indemnifying the insured, to be put into the position of the insured and to exercise all rights competent to the insured against third parties in respect of the fire damage. Accordingly, if the tenant is one of the insured and was responsible for the damage to the subjects, then the insurers would have no such claim because it is generally no answer to a fire policy claim that the damage resulted from the negligence (without fraud) on the part of the insured or one of them. See *Barras* 1994 SLT 949.

Some insurance companies now waive their subrogation rights and such a waiver should always be requested by the tenant. In addition, the tenant's agent should also seek to introduce into the lease a provision for the insurance policy being endorsed with the interest of the tenant. It has been argued that this may be recognition of the tenant's interest in the insurance monies. The position is by no means clear; and the terms of this clause in each lease should be carefully considered. One result of such an endorsement may be that the insurance company, in the event of damage or destruction, might issue their cheque in settlement in the joint names of the landlord and tenant. Many leases now provide that, in the event of reinstatement being impossible or unacceptably costly, the insurance monies belong exclusively to the landlord who at his option may terminate the lease. For a full discussion, see an article in 1985 JLS 99.

**25.63 (7) Rent abatement.** The provision that a lease endures notwithstanding damage will be dealt with *infra*. However, if there is such a provision, the tenant may well be liable to continue paying rent for a period during which he may not be able to obtain access to the subjects. This is unacceptable. In practice, the landlord insures against loss of rent in addition to the usual perils as aforementioned. Accordingly, in the event of damage to or destruction of the subjects, and the landlord's insurance policy not being vitiated in whole or in part or insurance monies being withheld due to the actions of the tenant, the 'loss-of-rent' insurance monies (designed also to cover any provisions for rent review) will compensate the landlord during the period when the tenant's obligation to pay rent is suspended. It is now common for a lease to provide that the rent is suspended until reinstatement is effected or until the expiry of the period of cover for loss of rent insurance monies, whichever is the earlier. The common law provides that in circumstances where the damage caused does not amount to *rei interitus*, actual or constructive, and is the fault of neither party to the lease, the tenant will be entitled to an abatement of rent according to the nature and extent of the damage and loss suffered. See *Muir* (1887) 14 R 470. This is unlike the position in England where express provision must be made before there is an abatement of rent.

A rent abatement provision is designed to protect a tenant so that he is not obliged to pay rent in the circumstances previously described. It would also be advisable to ensure that service and other common charges are abated with rent. Abatement may be for a period during which the whole or any part of the subjects are destroyed. Therefore, it may be that only a proportion of the rent, etc., payable will be abated. It may also be worth considering whether the tenant ought to attempt to introduce a 'long stop provision' into the lease which would enable the tenant to bring the contract to an end if the subjects are not restored within a specified period. Landlords do not generally accept this revisal however (see (9) below).

**25.64 (8) Reinstatement.** There is no general rule as to who should reinstate subjects damaged or destroyed by an insured risk. In theory, under a full repairing and insuring lease, the reinstatement obligations should rest with the tenant. However, many landlords prefer to undertake reinstatement works. Indeed, some landlords declare that it shall be in their option whether or not to rebuild the subjects at all! If the landlord reinstates, the lease will normally provide that he shall apply the proceeds of the insurance monies towards reinstatement within a definite period. It is preferable that a set period of say three years is laid down in the lease within which the landlord must complete the reinstatement works.

If the tenant reinstates, the landlord will wish to retain some control, *e.g.* over the type of building/plans to be submitted and approved, etc. The landlord may also provide for the insurance monies to be consigned in joint names in a bank and only released upon receipt of the tenant's architect's certificate of completion.

While it is quite proper, when dealing with a lease in Scotland, to take into account the implications of the rules at common law, it is suggested that some agents are over-anxious on this question. If the reinstatement period is of sufficiently long duration, taking into account the nature of the subjects and the type of damage sustained, the landlord should not object to a provision in the lease that the lease be terminated if reinstatement is not completed within, say, five years of the damage occurring, or such longer period as may be agreed, assuming both parties to be acting reasonably.

**25.65 (9) *Rei interitus*.** At common law, if subjects are destroyed or can be regarded as constructively destroyed through the fault of neither the landlord nor the tenant, the lease comes to an end and the loss is divided equally between the landlord, who will lose rent, and the tenant, who will lose possession. Indeed, the circumstances of each individual case must be decided on the respective merits. Destruction of a part of the subjects may be enough if the part in question was essential for the purposes for which the subjects were let. See *Allan* (1882) 10 R 383, *per* Lord Shand at pp. 389–390. An institutional investor in the landlord's interest will not accept this. Accordingly, it has become common for leases to contain a contractual provision to the effect that, the lease will remain in full force and effect notwithstanding damage or destruction of the subjects. Such a provision will often be found in various places in the lease, most notably in the repairing and insurance clauses.

A landlord's solicitor is likely to try to avoid the application of the doctrine of *rei interitus*. Indeed, one often finds that as well as stating that the lease will continue as aforesaid, the landlord is often successful in stating that the tenant will be fully liable for repairing, renewing and, if necessary, rebuilding the subjects if damaged or destroyed by any defect latent or patent.

The common law recognises that, while it is possible for parties to bind themselves to perform some particular act no matter what may happen, it is rarely their intention to do so, and that to enforce performance after a material change in circumstances would often be to bind the parties to a contract which they did not intend to make. In other words, the common law principle rests on the basic 'frustration of contract' rule.

The landlord's solicitor may therefore seek to combat the application of these principles in whatever way possible – especially if there is an investor involved. Therefore, the lease will be drafted so as to transfer all obligations onto the tenant so as to give him little room to plead frustration. However, it becomes increasingly difficult to avoid the operation of *rei interitus* in respect of a lease of premises within a larger building, control of the remaining units of which does not lie with the landlord.

It is suggested that it is now settled that since the case of *Cantors (Properties) (Scotland) Ltd.* 1980 SLT 165, in the absence of express or necessarily implied stipulations to the contrary, the effect of total and accidental destruction by fire of the whole leased subjects is that the contract is terminated. It is always, however, open to the contracting parties to provide otherwise. If they do not, then the contract will terminate if the subject matter is totally destroyed so that neither party is bound and neither party can compel performance of any of the stipulations to the contract. Such provisions are not unreasonable.

**25.66 (10) Other insurances**. The tenant may also be liable to insure against a selection of other risks such as public liability, plate glass insurance, loss of licence (if applicable), etc. Exhibition of the policies and/or premium receipts will be required by the landlord.

Always check that there is no possibility of double insurance occurring.

**25.67 7. Alienation**

**25.68 (1) Common law freedom**. At common law, a tenant has freedom to assign and sub-let unfurnished urban subjects (which will, of course, include all normal commercial properties). This right however is severely curtailed in most, if not all, modern commercial leases. Modern clauses are drafted so as to provide the landlord with a degree of control over the tenant. Privity of contract, in the sense that the term is understood in English law, has not really been a feature of the law of landlord and tenant in Scotland. Accordingly, a provision in a Scottish lease that the original tenant guarantees the whole terms of the lease throughout its endurance should be rejected. This is essentially an attempt to import into Scottish leases what was until recently an implied term of similar leases in England. See the Landlord and Tenant (Leasehold Covenants) Act 1995.

A landlord will have investigated the financial standing of his original tenant thoroughly and may well be reluctant to release him for a substitute who may not be as acceptable. A feature of the landlord's control over the identity of his new tenant may be that he will insist upon the new tenant being of 'sound financial standing'. In practice, landlords' agents use a wide variety of phrases to attempt to obtain such control (see *infra*). If there is any doubt as to the financial standing of the proposed assignee, the landlord may request that the original tenant stand as guarantor for his successor throughout the unexpired period of the lease. Such a request should be resisted if possible.

**25.69 (2) Alienation of part only of the subjects.** Alienation of part of the subjects whether by assignation or sub-lease, is generally prohibited. There are sound reasons supporting such a prohibition unless the subjects are of such proportions that a dealing with part only would be beneficial.

**25.70 (3) Alienation of the whole**

**25.71** *(a) Assignation.* Assignation of the tenant's interest in the whole of the subjects will almost always, by express provision, require the landlord's consent. If there is an element of *delectus personae* in the lease, consent may well be required notwithstanding the absence of express provision. The matter of consent, and any other restriction on the right of the tenant to assign the lease or indeed to sub-let the subjects, will be read according to its terms. A simple provision for the landlord's consent, for example 'but excluding assignees, legal or conventional, without the previous written consent of the landlord' may give the landlord an absolute discretion as to whether to grant or withhold his consent. Questions may arise as to an implication of reasonableness in such circumstances however. The most common revisal to such a clause and in fact elsewhere in the lease is to add the phrase 'which consent shall not be unreasonably withheld'. Without such a revisal being made, the basic Scottish common law position as stated in the case of *Portland* (1865) 4 M 10 would prevail, namely that the landlord's power to refuse consent is absolute. Indeed, apart from the provisions of common law mentioned above and statutory provisions of general application (such as s. 31 of the Sex Discrimination Act 1975 and s. 24 of the Race Relations Act 1976 which make it unlawful for the landlord to discriminate on grounds of sex or race against a person by withholding consent for disposal of premises to him or her), there is little control over the absolute discretion of the landlord to withhold or grant consent save such as may be contained in the lease itself. The landlord may have good reasons as to why he should have full power to decide whether a prospective substitute tenant is acceptable to him. Basically, however, each case will be decided on its own merits with the onus of proof being firmly on the tenant. Such a revisal may in fact do no more than provide for the possibility of the question being referred to the objective consideration of a neutral arbiter as a control on the subjective view taken by the landlord. For examples of cases involving conditions imposed on a grant of landlord's consent to assignation, see *Lousada & Co. Ltd*. 1990 SC 178; *John E. Harrison Ltd. (No. 1)* 1991 GWD 29–1761; *(No. 2)* 1992 GWD 38–226; and *Scotmore Developments Ltd*. 1996 SLT 1304.

Many clauses also lay down detailed qualifications as to the financial standing and suitability, etc., of the prospective tenant. It has been argued, however, that such phrases may possibly weaken the landlord's power to withhold consent if the assignee fulfills these additional qualifications. Such a provision may run, *e.g.*, 'not without the written consent of the landlord, which consent shall not be unreasonably withheld in the case of a respectable and responsible assignee'.

From the tenant's point of view, such a clause will fall to be considered in two stages. If the assignee is not a 'respectable and responsible person' as evidenced by bank and trade references, then the landlord will have an unqualified right to withhold consent. It would only be if the proposed assignee complied with this provision that the landlord's power to withhold consent would be fettered and could only be exercised if it was reasonable to do so.

The case of *Renfrew District Council* 1988 SLT 635 dealt with the right of the landlord to grant or withhold consent. The same question has also been considered by the English courts: see *International Drilling Fluids Ltd*. [1986] 1 All ER 321. An assessment of the financial strength of the proposed assignee is critical: see *Continvest Ltd*. 1993 GWD 40–2675.

Notwithstanding the guidance given by recent case-law in Scotland as to when consent may be reasonably withheld, there are still likely to be a number of instances where landlords may appear to act capriciously in order to take advantage of the position in which the tenant and potential assignee find themselves. An understanding of what in many instances may be the landlord's quite justifiable concerns, however, may go a long way towards ensuring the ultimate grant of consent within the preferred timescale. As is often the case, negotiation is likely to be more successful than confrontation.

**25.72** (*b*) *Sub-letting*. The landlord may not *per se* object to the tenant sub-letting the whole subjects as he will retain his rights against the original tenant. This right is still likely to be regulated in the lease however. He will insist upon the rent in the sub-lease not being less than the open market rent. Indeed, he may insist on the rent not being less than the rent in the head lease. This should be resisted, if possible, by the tenant especially in a recessionary economic climate where rents are actually falling. The landlord may prohibit the sub-tenant from granting further sub-leases so that he does not become too distant from the actual tenant in occupation. However, this is not a valid objection as he does retain his rights against the original tenant, and, if that lease falls, all derivative rights from it also terminate in the absence of express provision to the contrary. As mentioned earlier however, landlords will usually expressly prohibit sub-letting of parts. See also the case of *Brador Properties Ltd.* 1992 SC 12, where agreements entered into by a tenant with third parties were regarded as being sub-leases. The court held that the definition in Scots law of a lease is different from the definition in English law and is wide enough to include contracts which would not be regarded as leases in England. In *Brador*, it was held that the agreements with third parties amounted to a device to circumvent the express provisions of the lease.

**25.73 (4) Assignation to related or associated companies**. If a tenant is a large multiple company, it may be desirable to obtain the landlord's consent to an assignation to another company within the same group. Landlords will generally refuse permission unless the original tenant company or the parent company continues to guarantee the lease. Otherwise, the tenant could assign the lease to an associated company, liquidate that company and thus walk away from its responsibilities under the lease. The landlord may also be approached for his consent to the occupation of the subjects by an associated company of the tenant company as defined in the Companies Act 1985 s. 538. Once again, however, this may be permitted only subject to the landlord having prior notification and on the strict understanding that no rights of landlord and tenant are thereby created.

**25.74 (5) Franchises/concessions**. It is common to find franchises/concessions being offered in large leased subjects such as superstores. Franchisees/concessionaires do not have security of tenure as their exact pitch within the subjects may be uncertain. They thus lack particular subjects of let. Landlords usually allow franchises but often impose an upper limit on their number and the maximum amount of retail floor space which may be so occupied.

**25.75 (6) Pre-emption**. Beware of a lease containing a right for the landlord to buy back the lease on the occasion of an assignation. This can delay the sale of the tenant's interest quite substantially. In general, this clause should be read carefully in order to advise the tenant of the restriction on his ability to deal with his interest in the lease at some time in the future. The clause may also restrict the tenant from dealing in any manner of way with his interest or the subjects themselves. Such a comprehensive prohibition could also exclude the tenant's right to create a security over the subjects.

**25.76 (7) Miscellaneous**. If the alienation clause provides for a rent review on the occasion of an assignation or sub-letting, then it should be deleted. It has been suggested that such a provision is contrary to s. 16 of the Land Tenure Reform (Scotland) Act 1974 which prohibited the creation of casualties in leases. If a lease contains such a provision, it is suggested that it will have a restrictive effect on the marketability of the tenant's interest in the lease and, as such, would have a detrimental effect on the rent obtainable on rent review.

**25.77 8. Irritancy**

**25.78 (1) Legal or conventional**. An irritancy may be legal, imposed by law, or conventional, agreed upon by the parties to a particular contract. The parties to a lease are free to make any lawful stipulation for the conventional irritancy of that lease and consequently irritancy clauses vary in form from lease to lease. Their stipulations, however, must be lawful.

The only legal irritancy in a lease is for non-payment of two successive years' rent. Such irritancies are purgeable.

At common law, conventional irritancies, unless they merely expressed what the law implied, were not purgeable once incurred, notwithstanding questions of hardship. A tender of payment after irritancy has been incurred but before declarator came too late. The court could grant relief if the landlord's exercise of his right to terminate the lease amounted to oppression. See the decision of the House of Lords in *CIN Properties Ltd.* 1992 SLT (HL) 669 where the claim of oppression was made but rejected. If however, rent is accepted by the landlord after notice of irritancy has been served and the tenant remains in occupation of the subjects, the landlord may lose his right to irritate the lease. See *HMV Fields Properties Ltd.* 1991 SLT 31. This will be a question of fact in each case.

At common law, the tenant was always at risk of losing his lease, possibly by mere oversight or inadvertence, for non-payment of rent on the due date or some other quite minor infringement; and heritable creditors and sub-tenants were similarly affected. See *Dorchester Studios (Glasgow) Ltd.* 1975 SC (HL) 56.

**25.79 (2) The Law Reform (Miscellaneous Provisions) (Scotland) Act 1985 ss. 4–7.** This statute implemented the recommendations of the Scottish Law Commission and resulted in a measure of statutory protection for tenants in certain circumstances.

In general, the Act makes provision for two forms of protection for a tenant against the penal enforcement of irritancies in leases. The first is a notice procedure in s. 4 applicable where a landlord seeks to terminate a lease on the basis of the tenant's failure to make any monetary payment due under the lease. The second, which is applicable to all other conventional irritancies in leases, is a development of the equitable power of the court to grant relief from abuse or oppressive use of irritancies. Both forms of protection also cover the possibility of breach of a contractual term which is, or which is deemed to be, material as well as a reliance by the landlord on a conventional irritancy clause. The Act does not apply to leases of land used wholly or mainly for residential purposes or to crofts, cottars, and other holdings to which the Small Landholders (Scotland) Acts 1886 to 1931 apply.

Section 4(3) stipulates a minimum period of fourteen days for payment of arrears by a tenant. This must be specified in the notice. Account is taken of the possibility of 'days of grace' being permitted. The notice must be served by recorded delivery at an address in the United Kingdom. For comment on the form of the notice, see *Bellevue Cash and Carry Ltd.* 1996 GWD 4–220.

Section 5 is designed to restrict a landlord's powers of termination in circumstances other than those covered in s. 4 by reference to the test of the 'fair and reasonable landlord'. This test is based on the proviso to s. 26(1) of the Agricultural Holdings (Scotland) Act 1949. All the material facts will be looked at in each particular case. The onus of proof is on the tenant. The test is applicable only to the particular circumstances in which a landlord seeks to rely on the irritancy clause. It is not intended to exclude the possibility that in certain circumstances it may be fair and reasonable for a landlord to resort to irritancy without offering the tenant an opportunity to remedy the relevant breach. Furthermore, in considering the circumstances of a case, regard will be had as to whether a reasonable opportunity has been afforded to the tenant to enable the breach to be remedied. The test is how a 'fair and reasonable landlord' would act. See *Blythswood Investments (Scotland) Ltd*. 1995 SLT 150.

Section 6 provides that the parties to a lease cannot contract out of any provisions of ss. 4 or 5.

**25.80** The 1985 Act undoubtedly provides a degree of protection for tenants, but only to a limited extent. No protection is provided for third parties having an interest in the lease whether as heritable creditors, sub-tenants or otherwise.

In the result, no heritable creditor will lend to the tenant on the security of his lease unless the lease contains an express provision to the effect that the creditor is to receive notification of any impending action of irritancy, including the possibility of purging the irritancy.

Sub-tenants would be advised to insist upon similar protection.

**25.81** Finally, if the tenant is a company, and a liquidator, administrator or receiver is appointed, the tenant's interest in the subjects may have substantial value, which the liquidator, administrator or receiver may wish to realise for the benefit of the tenant's creditors by finding an assignee acceptable to the landlord. The tenant's agent should therefore ensure that a period of time is given to the liquidator, administrator or receiver so as to enable him so to do, provided always that he undertakes liability for performance of all the obligations of the lease which may include payment of the rent in arrears as well as rent accruing during the period itself.

**25.82** The general aim in revising the irritancy clause in a lease has been to produce a clause which effectively acts as a compulsitor to performance of the relevant contractual obligations rather than as a means by which a landlord can rid himself of an unsatisfactory tenant. While the 1985 Act ss. 4–7 go a long way towards protecting a tenant from the rigours of irritancy clauses, it is suggested that the tenant's solicitor should, whenever possible, carefully revise the irritancy clause, so as to procure the maximum protection for the tenant. It is still quite difficult to prove a claim for unjust enrichment following an action being raised for irritancy. See *Dollar Land (Cumbernauld) Ltd*. 1997 SLT 260.

### 25.83 9. Hypothec

**25.84** In addition to his ordinary remedies as a creditor, a landlord has a special remedy for the recovery of rent due to him, in the form of a right in security without possession of the subjects over which it extends. This right is implied by law and is called a right of hypothec.

**25.85** Hypothec has been described as being 'a real right in security', implied by law as between landlord and tenant over subjects allowed to remain in the tenant's possession. Essentially, it represents a right to have retained upon the subjects and to recover from those in whose possession they are, if they have been removed in breach of the right, the produce of the subjects or other articles and effects which are upon them. The property covered is known as the *invecta et illata*. Money, bonds, bills, the tenant's clothes and the tenant's tools of trade are not included: *Macpherson* (1905) 8 F 191. While hypothec may cover goods brought onto the subjects although they do not belong to the tenant, as in the case of hired furniture, it does not cover goods which are on the subjects for a purpose which is merely temporary, such as goods sent to be repaired or for exhibition. Nor does it cover goods which are the property of a member of the tenant's family. Goods of a sub-tenant, however, may be sequestrated for the rent due by the principal tenant, and also for the rent due by the sub-tenant himself: *Steuart* (1878) 5 R 1024.

**25.86** Hypothec secures one year's rent but not prior arrears. The process whereby the right of hypothec is converted into a real right is known as sequestration for rent. The right of hypothec falls if not put into force by sequestration within three months of the last term for payment. It is standard practice to sequestrate for the rent actually due and in security for that to become due at the next term. The right of a landlord to sequestrate for rent is not affected by the insolvency of the tenant. Such right is, however, subject to certain preferential claims, insofar as is possible, from the proceeds of the sale of the *invecta et illata*.

**25.87** Sequestration for rent is exclusively a sheriff court process. The ordinary course of procedure is that a warrant to sequestrate is granted on an *ex parte* statement, the goods are inventoried and valued by a sheriff officer and ultimately sold under a separate warrant from the sheriff by auction. After they have been inventoried, the goods cannot be removed unless the person who removes them, if in good faith, accounts for their value. If in bad faith, he is liable for the rent. Without applying for sequestration, a landlord may interdict the removal of the *invecta et illata* and, if they have been removed, may obtain a warrant to have them brought back. It should be noted however that interdict and recovery of goods, being exceptional remedies, will render the landlord liable in damages, if either the statement on which he obtains authority proves untrue or if there is a genuine dispute as to the rent and the circumstances render extreme measures unnecessary.

**25.88** After obtaining warrant to sequestrate and having the goods inventoried, the landlord may proceed with their sale. For this, a separate warrant is required from the sheriff and it must be executed by an officer of the court or another person appointed by the sheriff. The sale is by public roup or auction and has to be reported to the court within 14 days. The sheriff may order the gross proceeds of the sale to be consigned whereupon the accounts are taxed and the sale approved; and the landlord is then paid in full or *pro tanto* if not enough is realised. Where the landlord is paid in full, the balance, if any, is paid to the tenant less commissions and expenses. This balance can be attached by ordinary diligence by creditors of the tenant, including the landlord for any arrears of rent.

**25.89** While the landlord's right of hypothec has several advantages over other remedies for collection of rent arrears, it should be remembered that a landlord's claim is postponed to those of certain other creditors.

Hypothec is, however, a useful deterrent although, given the preferential claims which it may be subject to, it is a remedy which is often used only as a last resort.

# Chapter 26

# AGRICULTURAL LEASES

## 26.1 Introduction

Three decades of high agricultural prosperity followed the passing of the Agricultural Holdings (Scotland) Act 1949. That Act and subsequent legislation affecting agricultural holdings has now been consolidated in the Agricultural Holdings (Scotland) Act 1991 ('the 1991 Act'). These Acts have consolidated and strengthened the security of tenure afforded by earlier measures. As a result, farm lettings were rarely encountered except by solicitors specialising in agricultural matters. The very significant reduction in the level of price support operated by the EEC Common Agricultural Policy has altered the position substantially. 'Investment farming' by estate owners and institutional landowners has become unprofitable and a consequence of this has been that many more farms are being placed on the letting market. This trend has accelerated over the last few years. While the drawing of leases will doubtless largely remain in the hands of those who specialise in agricultural work, the equally important task of revising will inevitably be entrusted to a much wider range of practitioners. Although the number of lettings has increased for the reasons given and will probably continue to do so, only a small percentage of these have been or will be effected by way of a lease bringing the landlord and the *de facto* tenant into contractual relationship. The vast majority of lettings will incorporate one of the arrangements designed to avoid the security of tenure afforded by ss. 21 and 22 of the 1991 Act and thus enable the lease to be terminated at the end of some predetermined period. The most widely used arrangement is for the tenant applicant to be required to enter into a contract of co-partnery (usually limited) with a nominee of the landlord; for this contract to have a guaranteed duration; and for the partnership to be adopted as the tenant.

## 26.2 Terms of lease

So far as the lease itself is concerned, there are numerous styles available to the practitioner ranging from the abbreviated form set out in *Connell on the Agricultural Holdings (Scotland) Acts* (7th edn.), p. 306, to the more detailed and comprehensive style provided by the Law Society's Workshop series (1980 JLS 135), reproduced as Appendix B to this Manual. The purchase of agricultural land on a comparatively large scale during the 1970s by institutional investors whose advisers are more accustomed to the detailed and very stringent provisions of commercial leases, has given rise to numerous agricultural styles of inordinate length and varying degrees of stringency bordering, in some cases, on oppressiveness. During the period of prosperity when the demand for tenanted farms far exceeded the supply to the extent that there were frequently 40 or 50 offers for each holding, the scope for revising out repugnant conditions was invariably limited as offers which did not adopt the style of lease offered by the landlord were simply rejected out of hand. With the decline in agricultural prosperity and a consequent awareness on the part of landlords of the need to obtain tenants who are both technically sound and financially secure, the situation has arisen where it is now possible to have conditions modified which were, until recently, regarded as non-negotiable. The probable consequence of this is that the solicitor acting for a prospective tenant is under a somewhat greater obligation to scrutinise a landlord's draft and to attempt to have revised out at an early stage any unduly oppressive or repugnant conditions.

**26.3 Parties.** The parties to the lease must be correctly named and designed. For the reasons stated above, the *persona* of the tenant will seldom be that of the applicant for the tenancy and is more likely to be a partnership or a company in which the applicant tenant has the predominant financial stake and the landlord's nominee an interest such as to ensure that the tenancy can be brought to an end after a predetermined period. It goes without saying that it is essential to ensure that the 'tenant' is properly constituted by a contract of co-partnery or other instrument before the lease is executed, and any limited partnership agreement must be properly registered at Companies House. It was generally accepted that a landlord can let property to a group of which he is a member, following *Pinkerton* 1986 SLT 672. But it is now also accepted that several *pro indiviso* proprietors cannot competently grant a valid lease to one of their number. See *Clydesdale Bank plc* 1996 SLT 437. While it may be possible to reconcile these two decisions as consistent *inter se*, which the Lord Justice-Clerk seems content to do in *Clydesdale Bank* at p. 441 H-K, the decision in *Pinkerton* should now be treated with caution. Leases to a company which is merely a nominee of the true proprietors in favour of those same proprietors will be treated as a nullity, on the view that this is equivalent to trying to contract with oneself. See *Kildrummy (Jersey) Ltd.* 1992 SLT 787.

**26.4 Destination.** The Workshop Style excludes not only assignees and sub-tenants which, in any event is implied at common law, but also successors. Notwithstanding the terms of s. 14 of the Succession (Scotland) Act 1964, there is warrant for the view that an exclusion of successors effectively brings the tenancy to an end on the death of the tenant (*Kennedy* 1956 SC 39), although this point has not been conclusively established.

**26.5 Description of subjects.** Measurements should be given in hectares and there should always be a carefully prepared detailed plan showing the Ordnance Survey parcels and their respective areas expressed in hectares. A schedule of measurement detailing the Ordnance Survey number, area and land category (*i.e.* arable, permanent pasture, rough grazings) should be annexed and executed as relative to the lease. Such a schedule may prove invaluable during future rent negotiations or arbitration, particularly if, as frequently happens, a record of holding is not prepared.

**26.6 Duration.** In view of the provisions of ss. 21 and 22 of the 1991 Act, it is now common practice to provide that the lease itself will be for a period of one year only and for the duration of the letting to be effectively regulated by the contract of co-partnery or whatever vehicle has been used to create the *persona* of the tenant. If, however, the lease is to be granted for a period of years, it is usual to provide breaks to coincide with the statutory rent review period, at present three years. Notice of intention to invoke the break normally mirrors the statutory provision of not less than one and no more than two years.

**26.7 Rent**. The traditional practice of providing for payments of rent on a forehand or backhand basis is becoming much less frequent and the normal practice is for the rent to be referable to the period of possession and payable either half-yearly, quarterly, or even monthly in arrears.

**26.8 Reservations**. Minerals are invariably reserved as are powers to alter marches and very often powers of entry.

The style gives a power of resumption for any purpose except agriculture. In contested resumption cases, *e.g. Edinburgh Corporation* 1948 SC 538, *Turner* 1954 SC 296, and *Glencruitten Trs.* 1966 SLT (Land Ct.) 5, the question of what was contemplated by the parties at the commencement of the lease was considered by the court. Accordingly, and notwithstanding the wide power expressed in the style, it is good practice to refer to specific purposes, particularly if these are unusual, *i.e.* resumption of ground for game cover. *Fothringham* 1987 SLT (Land Ct.) 10 should also be borne in mind when considering the conditions of a hill sheep farm lease.

**26.9 Game**. This is the normal reservation and the substitution of 31 October for the end of the calendar year, as provided under the 1991 Act, is now regarded as sensible practice. Notwithstanding the tenant's powers under the Deer (Scotland) Act 1959, and subsequent legislation, it is necessary, in order to avoid the risk of a claim for compensation for deer damage on arable land and enclosed pasture, to modify the reservation and allow the tenant to kill and take deer: *Auckland* 1964 SLT (Land Ct.) 20.

**26.10 Woods, plantations, wayleaves and roads**. These provisions are normal.

**26.11 Access by the landlord**. It is probably unnecessary to include this in the style as it is implied at common law and made the subject of a special power under s. 10 of the 1991 Act.

**26.12 Landlord's obligation to reinstate and insure**. Section 4 of the 1991 Act enables the landlord or tenant to secure a written lease and, in the circumstances narrated in the section, to require a revision of existing leases in order to bring the lease in line with the provisions contained in Schedule I of the 1991 Act. Paragraph 5 of the Schedule embodies an undertaking by the landlord to apply insurance monies received in the event of damage by fire towards the replacement of fixed equipment in accordance with the requirement of the paragraph.

**26.13 Tenant's obligation to insure crops, etc**. This is the corresponding obligation on the tenant to that referred to immediately above.

**26.14 Landlord's obligation for fixed equipment**. The style narrates the statutory provisions which are almost invariably made the subject of a contracting-out agreement as contemplated by s. 5(3) of the 1991 Act. Such an agreement, or post-lease agreement as it is commonly called, stipulates in detail the contractual as opposed to the statutory obligations of the parties.

It is now the standard, but not universal practice, for tenancies to be placed on a tenant's full repairing and renewing basis, including such repairs and renewals as may be occasioned by fair wear and tear. The initial rent offered and any subsequent rent review, whether negotiated or arbitrated will require to take this into account, under s. 13 of the 1991 Act.

It is customary practice in farm lettings to require the prospective tenant to enter into a post-lease agreement and it is therefore essential, to ensure compliance with s. 5(3) of the 1991 Act, that the contracting-out agreement post-dates the lease. The usual procedure is to provide a preamble to the agreement stating that the lease has previously been executed and that the parties have agreed to vary it in accordance with the stipulations contained in the agreement.

**26.15 Record**.   As already stated, it is common practice to dispense with a record of holding. A number of potential claims by either party to a lease are dependent upon a record at the commencement of the tenancy having been made. So far as the landlord is concerned, compensation for dilapidation and deterioration of the holding under s. 45 of the 1991 Act, will not be enforceable in regard to new leases unless a record of the holding has been made under s. 8 of the 1991 Act. The converse applies in regard to a claim by the tenant under s. 44 of the 1991 Act for the continuous adoption of a special standard of farming.

**26.16 Alterations to fixed equipment**.   Notwithstanding the compensation provisions under Schedule II to the 1991 Act, this provision in the style is contractual.

**26.17 Tenant's fixtures**.   Although this strikes at the tenant's right to remove fixtures and buildings under s. 18 of the 1991 Act, the question as to whether or not it is competent to contract out of this section has not been decided by the court.

**26.18 Stock**.   The restriction in the style is enforceable as is the prohibition against the breaking up of permanent pasture.

**26.19 Use of the holding**.   The restriction on the use of the holding to an arable and/or livestock rearing unit is enforceable as is the prohibition against the breaking up of permanent pasture unless the tenant succeeds in having the provisions varied by invoking s. 9 of the 1991 Act.

**26.20 Muirburn**.   The provisions of any lease in regard to muirburn are overridden by ss. 23 to 27 of the Hill Farming Act 1946, the effect of which is to set time limits within which muirburn is lawful and to entitle tenants to carry out muirburn in certain circumstances regardless of the terms of the lease. The safeguard for the landlord, so far as overburning is concerned, is contained in s. 24(1) of the Act which enables the landlord to refer any dispute on muirburning to the Secretary of State.

**26.21 Camping or caravanning**.   This is a contractual provision and there are frequently prohibitions of a similar nature which are commonly incorporated in leases.

**26.22 Market gardening and dairy farming**.   This clause ensures that the landlord will not be required to provide for the alteration or provision of or pay compensation for specialised fixed equipment as may be required for market gardening, commercial flower or vegetable cultivation, dairy farming, pig or poultry production. The tenant, however, is entitled under the freedom of cropping provisions (1991 Act s. 7) to use the farm for these purposes.

**26.23 Waygoing year**. Freedom of cropping and disposal of produce does not extend to the year before the expiration of the lease (1991 Act s. 7(5)(*b*)) and it is therefore customary, in order to ensure the continuity of husbandry, to stipulate the cropping to which the tenant will be bound to adhere in the year immediately preceding his waygo. Provision is also made for the landlord or incoming tenant to take over certain crops which will still be in the ground at the outgoing tenant's waygo.

**26.24 Residence**. This is contractual and enforceable.

**26.25 Irritancy**. The clause in the style is drawn in the usual terms but more draconian clauses are commonplace. The clause gives the landlord the option to terminate the lease on the occurrence of a forbidden event and, being a conventional irritancy, cannot be purged. Great care should be taken when revising an irritancy clause and solicitors acting for tenants should endeavour wherever possible to have the terms watered down. It should be noted that the defences to an action of removal following a conventional irritancy are limited and that the provisions of the Law Reform (Miscellaneous Provisions) (Scotland) Act 1985 ss. 4 and 5 do not apply to agricultural leases.

**26.26 Removing**. This clause is standard but may be rendered unenforceable by the operation of tacit relocation and the provisions of ss. 21 and 22 of the 1991 Act. A tenant of an agricultural holding cannot be compelled to remove otherwise than by an order of the court following either a notice to quit or a finding by an arbiter that a conventional irritancy has been incurred. Informal undertakings to remove are of less certain effect, following the decision in *Morrison's Exrs.* 1986 SLT 227. The parties can, however, waive strict compliance with the statutory provisions: *Kildrummy (Jersey) Ltd.* 1994 SLT 888.

**26.27 Registration for preservation and execution**. This is invariably provided.

### 26.28 Taking instructions

It is largely the case that whereas a landlord contemplating the letting of a farm seeks advice from his factor or land agent who will deal with the practical matters involved, advising on the overall terms and conditions upon which the farm should be let, and referring only matters of law to the estate solicitor, a prospective tenant will very often depend on his solicitor for the whole spectrum of advice required in connection with the letting.

**26.29 Security of tenure**. Turning first to the landlord's position, he must first be advised of the general rules concerning security of tenure and that, having leased a farm to a tenant, there is no guarantee that it will revert to vacant possession at the end of the stipulated period. The arrangements referred to earlier and designed to frustrate security of tenure have been tested in the Scottish courts. Lettings to a limited partnership have been recognised by the court: *Dickson* 1992 SLT (Land Ct.) 83. Informality in the conduct of a limited partnership has been disregarded: *Macfarlane* 1996 SCLR 826. Best practice, however, is for the terms of the limited partnership contract to be adhered to by the parties, with separately identifiable accounting information, whether or not part or a larger account. In the English case of *Johnston* [1980] AC 37, the theory of public policy in regard to security of tenure was reviewed by the House of Lords and this, and the decisions in subsequent English cases, notably *Gisbourne* [1988] 3 All ER 760, may be regarded as warning shots that, if necessary, the English courts at least may be prepared to consider the substance rather than the form of leasing arrangements; but see *Macfarlane, supra*. Consequently, it should be made clear to a landlord seeking to lease a holding that, whatever form the arrangements may take, unless the lease is approved by the Secretary of State for Scotland under the 1991 Act s. 2 provisions – and approval is given only in limited cases – the possibility of being unable to recover vacant possession must be taken into account.

**26.30 Rent review**. The landlord should also be informed of the statutory provisions with regard to the variation of rent and that scarcity value must be discounted by an arbiter when reviewing a rent. Accordingly, it is possible, and indeed likely in the present climate, that a rent tendered at the commencement of the tenancy may be reduced at the first review. The landlord client should have the review procedure explained to him, namely that an arbiter appointed to the panel of agricultural arbiters by the Secretary of State for Scotland will determine the matter unless the landlord and tenant agree to refer to the Scottish Land Court by way of a joint application, or agree the rent privately.

**26.31 Consents**. If the property is subject to a heritable security, the consent of the creditor is required in terms of Standard Condition 6 of Schedule 3 of the Conveyancing and Feudal Reform (Scotland) Act 1970, before a lease is entered into.

If there is a heritable creditor, his consent to the letting should be sought at an early stage.

**26.32 Expenses**. The landlord should also be informed of the cost of preparing and agreeing a lease and whatever other charges are to be made for managing the property or collecting the rents and so forth.

**26.33 Quotas and premium schemes**. Following the reforms in the Common Agricultural Policy of the EU in 1992/93, the number and complexity of subsidy schemes for many types of agricultural 'produce' have increased. These include Milk Quota introduced in 1984; Sheep Premium Scheme; Suckler Cow Premium Scheme; Arable Aid; Beef Special Premium Scheme, and Setaside. The complex rules have altered markedly in the few years during which the schemes have been in operation and are beyond the scope of this Manual. The sums payable under the schemes frequently form a considerable part of the total income which can be derived from farming a holding, and entitlement to them in the case of livestock premiums, or whether or not the holding qualifies for them in the case of arable schemes, is of great practical significance.

Landlords will often seek to ensure that entitlements under the livestock schemes remain with the holding on the waygo of the tenant, sometimes without payment to the tenant. While this may be acceptable in part where the tenant was allocated a Quota at no cost, the opposite applies where the rights were bought in by the tenant. Such provisions must be scrutinised carefully and specialist advice taken where appropriate.

**26.34 Record of holding.** The necessity or otherwise to have a record of holding prepared should be discussed. If the fixed equipment on the holding is in good condition and the lease is to be drawn on a traditional basis, the landlord would be well advised to meet the expenses involved in having a record prepared. On the other hand, if the fixed equipment is in poor condition, it is more than likely that the tenant, if he is properly advised, will insist on a record being prepared.

### 26.35 Selecting a tenant

Although most new lettings are now conducted by a firm of chartered surveyors or resident factors, there are occasions when solicitors are instructed to carry out this work. The usual procedure is to prepare detailed particulars, to draft the lease, and then to advertise the farm to let, outlining briefly the terms and conditions which the landlord has in mind. The letting particulars should require prospective tenants to provide the landlord with details of their experience, financial standing and probably details of the working capital required, model cashflows and profit and loss accounts. In the event of tenders being sought, it is usual to find a fairly wide variation in the range of rents offered and care requires to be taken to select a tender where the rent is such that the tenant is able to make a reasonable profit.

**26.36 Particulars and advertisement.** The particulars of the farm should include matters such as:

(i) Description and situation.

(ii) Type of land, including whether or not it is classed as in the Less Favoured Area (LFA) of the country, whether Disadvantaged or Severely Disadvantaged.

(iii) Area.

(iv) Plan.

(v) Number of houses and steading accommodation.

(vi) Services such as water, electricity, telephone, gas and drainage.

(vii) Detail of waygoing valuations and the method by which these will require to be determined.

(viii) Viewing arrangements.

(ix) Nature of the tenancy agreement, *i.e.* whether it is to be a straightforward tenancy or a contract of limited co-partnery.

(x) Whether any Quota or similar rights are available with the holding under any Livestock Premium Scheme, and how such rights are to be dealt with.

Following advertisement, it is customary to set a closing date for the submission of offers and it is normal for a number of offers to be received.

Very often, some of the most suitable candidates will be local farmers or their sons known to the landlord and probably to the solicitor or other letting agent. In such cases, enquiries as to competence and financial standing may be very straightforward. In the case of applicants from another locality, it may be wise to inspect the applicant's existing holding and, if he is a tenant, to make enquiries of his landlord or landlord's factor. The proceedings will usually end in the form of a short leet of say three applicants and it may almost be immaterial which candidate is eventually chosen. Formal missives should then be entered into and the draft lease and plan of the farm incorporated in these missives.

### 26.37 Inheritance tax (formerly capital transfer tax)

Agricultural property relief is available on a death or on a lifetime transfer for both owner/occupiers and landlords. It takes the form of a reduction for tax purposes in the value of the property which is liable to tax. Since 10 March 1981, in order to qualify for relief, the agricultural property must have been owned for seven years prior to the death or transfer, or the deceased or transferor must have occupied the property for two years prior to the death or transfer. The rules are relaxed where one agricultural property replaces another or where the property has been inherited within these periods.

The relief is a 100% reduction in the value for tax if the deceased or the transferor has the right to or can obtain vacant possession within twelve months or the property was let by a lease commencing after 1 September 1995. In other cases, relief is 50% except, in some circumstances, in the case of property let before 10 March 1981.

Agricultural property relief may be lost wholly or partly if the property has been the subject of a potentially exempt transfer (PET) for inheritance tax (usually a gift) and is sold or disposed of by the recipient within seven years of the date of transfer followed by the death within the seven-year period of the donor. This can seriously affect the *original* transferor's tax liability. The grant of an agricultural tenancy for full consideration is not a transfer of value for inheritance tax purposes. Following the case of *Baird's Exrs*. 1991 SLT (Lands Tr.) 9 a tenant's interest in an agricultural tenancy can have a value for tax purposes. However, following the Finance (No. 2) Act 1992, the value of that interest can obtain 100% relief for inheritance tax purposes, if it can be classed as business property, as will usually be the case.

# Chapter 27

# RESIDENTIAL LEASES

## 27.1 Public and private sectors

The letting of houses is divided broadly between houses in the public sector where the landlord is a local authority, New Town Development Corporation or Scottish Homes; and houses leased by private landlords. Scottish Homes was a new body established under the Housing (Scotland) Act 1988 to take over the rights and liabilities of the Scottish Special Housing Association, which was dissolved on 1 April 1989, and of the Housing Corporation. Its principal functions include the provision of housing, the maintaining of housing, assisting with finance, promoting owner-occupation and assisting in the development of housing associations.

## 27.2 Public sector tenancies

The letting of public sector houses is regulated by an elaborate code, contained in the Tenants' Rights etc. (Scotland) Act 1980 Part II, which introduced secure tenancies, as amended by the Housing (Scotland) Acts 1987 and 1988 and further amended by the Leasehold Reform, Housing and Urban Development Act 1993. Most local authority tenants other than those in job-related accommodation or who have been housed under the Housing (Homeless Persons) Act 1977, qualify as secure tenants. A secure tenant has a right to a written lease, and to a degree of security of tenure, and there are provisions for succession to the tenancy on the death of the tenant.

The statutory right of secure tenants to purchase public sector houses is dealt with in Chapter 28.79.

## 27.3 Private sector tenancies

The private sector covers all residential leases not in the public sector. There are two main statutes: (*a*) the Rent (Scotland) Act 1984 which consolidates all previous Rent Act legislation, and (*b*) the Housing (Scotland) Act 1988 which came into force on 2 January 1989. In practice, almost all future private sector residential leases will be governed by the 1988 Act; but many of the provisions of the 1984 Act have been left intact and still apply to existing leases. Both Acts contain lengthy and detailed provisions, particularly in relation to security of tenure, recovery of possession and control of rents. What follows is a brief outline only of these provisions and no attempt is made to deal with them exhaustively.

## 27.4 The 1984 Act

The principal features of this Act are security of tenure, statutory transmission of tenancy on the death of the tenant and a system of rent control.

**27.5 Protected tenancies.**   Section 1 of the 1984 Act provides that a tenancy is a protected tenancy where a house is let as a dwellinghouse, unless the rateable value exceeded £200 on 23 March 1965. If the house was not completed until after that date, then a lease thereof created a protected tenancy if the rateable value first assigned to the dwellinghouse on completion did not exceed £600; or, from and after 1 April 1985, £1,600. The 1984 Act covered both unfurnished and furnished tenancies; but the provisions relating to furnished tenancy contracts falling under Part VII have now been repealed by the 1988 Act.

In order to establish a protected tenancy under the 1984 Act, there must have been a lease of a house or part of a house as a separate unit with exclusive possession. During the currency of the lease, the tenant of a protected tenancy is known as the contractual tenant. On expiry of the contractual term, the tenant becomes a statutory tenant by virtue of s. 3 of the Act.

A statutory tenant cannot be removed by the landlord except on one of the grounds specified in Schedule 2 to the 1984 Act. There are 21 possible grounds. Part I of Schedule 2 contains those grounds on which a court may grant an order for possession (the discretionary grounds); Part II states those grounds on which the court must grant an order for possession (the mandatory grounds). Additionally, the court may grant an order for possession if it is satisfied that suitable alternative accommodation is available and it is reasonable to grant an order for possession (s. 11(1)(a)).

**27.6 Notice to quit.**   To entitle the landlord to recover possession, a notice to quit must first have been served on the tenant. The style of notice is contained in the Sheriff Courts (Scotland) Act 1907; and certain prescribed information must also be appended to the notice advising the tenant of his or her right to remain in possession after expiry of the notice, and that possession may only be recovered on the grounds set out in the 1984 Act. Failure to include the prescribed information renders the notice invalid.

**27.7 Protection of statutory successors.**   The 1984 Act provides statutory security of tenure not only for the original contractual tenant, but also for successors. These rights of succession have since been restricted by the 1988 Act s. 46 for deaths occurring after that section comes into operation. The resulting position is that, on the death of the original tenant, the spouse or cohabitee is automatically entitled as of right to remain in possession as a statutory tenant. Failing such spouse or cohabitee, any other member of the family of the original tenant, or of his or her spouse, may in certain circumstances be entitled to succeed to the tenancy either on the first or on the second death; but this is subject to complex residential requirements which are now contained in the 1988 Act s. 46 and Schedule 6, amending the original provisions in the 1984 Act.

**27.8 Short tenancies.**   The 1984 Act s. 9 also introduced the concept of the short tenancy. To qualify, the tenancy must be for a fixed period of between one and five years, at a registered fair rent. The fair rent must have been registered before the commencement of the lease and the tenant must have received notice in the prescribed form before the commencement of the lease that the tenancy was to be a short tenancy in terms of the Act. Compliance with these conditions entitles the landlord to recover possession at the end of the period of lease; provided he serves the appropriate notices timeously, the tenant has no statutory right to remain in possession as tenant.

**27.9 Rent control**. The 1984 Act effectively controlled the level of rent payable in the private sector by providing for a system of rent registration. Either or both parties jointly may apply to the rent officer for the registration of a fair rent. Such fair rents are generally substantially below open market value because, in determining the level of rent, the rent officer takes into account the age, character, location and state of repair of a dwellinghouse as well as the quality and quantity of furniture provided, but must disregard the element of scarcity value and any circumstances personal to the landlord and tenant in question. Appeal from the decision of the rent officer is to the Rent Assessment Committee. Once a fair rent has been established, it cannot be reviewed or increased for a period of three years unless there is a material change of circumstances. Further, even although the tenant may have agreed to pay a higher rent in terms of the lease, any excess above the fair rent is irrecoverable by the landlord.

### 27.10 The 1988 Act

The principal purpose of this Act is to relax the statutory controls on private sector leases and to widen the scope for open market negotiation on rent between the landlord and tenant. Two new types of tenancy are introduced, the assured tenancy and the short assured tenancy; Part VII of the 1984 Act, which previously governed certain furnished lettings, is repealed. The provisions relating to the new types of tenancy are contained in Part II of the 1988 Act (ss. 12–55).

**27.11 Assured tenancies**. An assured tenancy is defined in s. 12 as a tenancy under which a house is let as a separate dwellinghouse and the tenant, or one of the joint tenants, is an individual who occupies the dwellinghouse as his or her only or principal home. A tenancy which falls within any paragraph in Schedule 4 to the Act cannot qualify as an assured tenancy. These exclusions embrace, *inter alia*, tenancies rent-free or at very low rents, lettings to students by educational institutions, some tenancies by resident landlords and other special cases.

Section 14(1) then extends the definition of assured tenancy to those tenants who have exclusive occupation of accommodation forming part of a dwellinghouse, with shared accommodation of other parts of the same dwellinghouse where that accommodation is shared with persons other than the landlord.

**27.12 Termination of assured tenancies**. A contractual assured tenancy will not come to an end unless and until the landlord has served the appropriate notice to quit in the prescribed form. The purpose of the notice is intended primarily to bring the contractual tenancy to an end. It is not necessarily an indication that the landlord is to take steps to recover possession. If, following on that notice, the tenant remains in possession, a statutory assured tenancy is created which cannot be terminated unless the landlord obtains an order for possession from the sheriff in accordance with the provisions of the Act. The grounds of removal are set out in Schedule 5 to the Act, 17 in all, of which 1 to 8 are mandatory (Part I of Schedule 5) and 9 to 17 are discretionary (Part II of Schedule 5). In seeking to remove the tenant by court action, the landlord must first have served notice of his intention to raise such court action on the tenant in terms of s. 19 of the Act.

On the death of an assured tenant, the tenancy passes, under the 1988 Act s. 31, to the spouse or cohabitee living with the tenant at the time of the tenant's death as a statutory assured tenant. There are no further rights of succession to an assured tenancy.

**27.13 Rent control.** Under the 1988 Act, the landlord and his tenant are free to negotiate the initial rent at the commencement of the tenancy and there is no statutory restriction on the level of rent so agreed for the assured tenancy. Thereafter, however, the landlord cannot increase the rent of an assured tenant except by serving notice on the tenant proposing an increase in the rent. The tenant may then refer the notice to the Rent Assessment Committee who will, in terms of s. 25 of the 1988 Act, determine a market rent for the property. The committee may take into account scarcity factors. The rent fixed by the committee will be effective from the date specified by them; but will not apply if the landlord and tenant have in the meantime reached agreement on the variation of the terms of the tenancy.

**27.14 The short assured tenancy.** A short assured tenancy is defined in s. 32 as an assured tenancy for a term of not less than six months, in respect of which a notice in a prescribed form has been served on the tenant by the landlord before the creation of the tenancy. The short assured tenant has no statutory security of tenure whatsoever when the contractual term comes to an end. Instead, if the landlord so requires, the sheriff must make an order for possession provided he is satisfied that the ish has been reached, that tacit relocation is not operating, that no further contractual tenancy is in existence and that the landlord has given the prescribed notice to the tenant stating that he wishes to obtain possession. Certain of the grounds of removal, for example, grounds 1 and 2 of Schedule 5 to the Act, require notice in writing to be given to the tenant prior to the commencement of the lease that the landlord may seek to recover possession on these grounds.

**27.15 Rent control.** In contrast to the assured tenancy, where the tenant cannot apply for a review of the rent unless the landlord serves notice proposing an increase, the short assured tenant may, subject to certain qualifications in s. 34 of the Act, apply to the Rent Assessment Committee at any time on his own initiative for a determination of the rent which the landlord might reasonably obtain.

**27.16 Provisions which apply under both Acts**
A number of provisions apply both to tenancies under the 1984 Act and under the 1988 Act with minor differences. The more important of these can be summarised as follows.

**27.17 Written lease.** In every case, the tenant is entitled to require the landlord to provide him with a written lease setting out the full terms of the tenancy. If the landlord refuses or delays in providing the tenant with a written lease, the tenant can, under s. 30(2) of the Act, by summary application to the sheriff, request that the sheriff draw up a lease reflecting the agreement between the parties, or adjust the terms of the same.

**27.18 Rent books.**   Where the rent is collected weekly (but not rent collected at longer periods) the landlord is required by statute to provide the tenant with a rent book or alternatively to give a rent receipt, which, in either case, must also contain additional information setting out explicitly the tenant's rights under the relevant Act.

**27.19 Notices.**   Notice has always been required in Scotland to terminate a lease, failing which it will continue by tacit relocation. The same general principle applies to residential leases controlled under the 1984 and 1988 Acts but with this difference that, in addition to the normal notice to quit, further notices are or may be required prior to the commencement of the lease, or to convert the lease from a contractual to a statutory tenancy, or to allow the landlord to take proceedings. In each case, statutory forms are prescribed and additional information must be provided to the tenant. Otherwise the notice and subsequent proceedings are invalid.

**27.20 Minimum periods for rent increases.**   Under the 1988 Act ss. 24(4) and 34(4) no further new rent fixed by the committee for an assured, or a short assured, tenancy can take effect until after the first anniversary of the previous determination. Under the 1984 Act, the comparable period is three years and there are provisions phasing any increase over that period.

**27.21 Premiums.**   Part VIII of the 1984 Act prohibits the taking of premiums. A premium includes any payment made for the grant or for the assignation of a lease, and the Act contains special deeming provisions to prevent evasion. So, an obligation on a tenant to acquire furniture at an inflated price is to be regarded as a premium. Where a premium has been paid, it is recoverable by the party who paid it. The same prohibition applies to assured and short assured tenancies under the 1988 Act s. 27.

   With furnished leases, it is common practice to take a deposit as security for damages, often amounting to one or two months' rent. Such a deposit, not exceeding two months' rent, is not to be regarded as a premium; 1984 Act s. 90.

**27.22 Harassment and unlawful eviction.**   Under s. 22 of the 1984 Act, it is a criminal offence to remove a tenant without a court order or to harass him. In practice, however, the police are reluctant to interfere in such cases because they consider these to be matters of civil rather than criminal jurisdiction. Additional provisions are also made for unlawful eviction and harassment in the 1988 Act ss. 36 to 38. These provisions apply generally to all types of tenancy.

### 27.23 Phasing out of the 1984 Act
The 1984 Act meantime continues to apply to tenancies protected by that Act. But, under the 1988 Act s. 42, no tenancy commencing after the appointed day will be a protected tenancy under the 1984 Act except in the limited situations specified in s. 42. As a result, the 1984 Act provisions will gradually cease to apply, as pre-1989 tenancies come to an end and new ones are created.

**27.24 Health and safety**
It is appropriate to make specific reference to two recent sets of regulations which may affect landlords and/or agents who let out residential property.

**27.25 Gas Safety (Installation and Use) Regulations 1994.** These regulations came into force, mainly on 31 October 1994 and also on 1 January 1996 and 1 January 1997. The important regulation is reg. 35(2) which states: 'It shall be the duty of any person who owns a gas appliance or installation pipe-work installed in premises or any part of premises let by him to ensure that such appliance or installation of pipe work is maintained in a safe condition so as to prevent risk of injury to any person.'

The regulations go on to state that the person should 'ensure that each appliance to which that duty extends is checked for safety at intervals of not more than 12 months by an employee of a member of a class of persons approved for the time being'.

**27.26 The Furniture and Furnishings (Fire) (Safety) (Amendment) Regulations 1993.** These regulations amend the Furniture and Furnishings (Fire)(Safety) Regulations 1988 and are aimed at improving safety by requiring all furniture and furnishings to pass certain flammability tests. From 1 January 1997 any furniture or furnishings provided in let furnished accommodation must comply with the regulations. At present, there is some doubt whether the regulations affect the private individual landlord who lets out his property – for example, if he is going abroad – as they apply only to furniture or furnishings which are 'supplied' in terms of the Consumer Protection Act 1987. Section 46(5) of the Act defines 'supply' as 'supply . . . in the course of a business'.

349

Part 5

# TRANSMISSION OF THE FEU

# Chapter 28

# CONTRACTS OF SALE AND PURCHASE

### 28.1 Constitution and essential content of the contract

'It is remarkable that there has been no attempt to formulate, in an Act of Parliament, the law on the general subject of sale of Scottish heritable property as has been done in the case of land in England and the sale of goods both in Scotland and in England.' Green's *Encyclopaedia*, Vol. 13 s. 318. More than 60 years later this remains the position.

The Contracts (Applicable Law) Act 1990, implementing the Rome Convention, allows parties to select the law applicable to a particular contract or part thereof. It is unlikely, however, that this Act will be used, other than in exceptional circumstances, in any contract relating to the sale and purchase of heritage in Scotland. Subject thereto, contracts for the sale and purchase of heritage are, therefore, governed by the ordinary common law rules of contract. Only the special features of such contracts are dealt with here.

There are three basic requirements.

### 28.2 (1) Form and authentication.
Since these are contracts relating to land, they must, under the general rule, be in writing; and they must be bilateral. There are three recognised forms:

(*a*) A formal, bilateral contract of sale and purchase executed by the parties.

(*b*) Articles of roup, being the appropriate document for sales by auction and constituting a formal offer which is completed by endorsation of a minute of preference and enactment, binding the purchaser to the purchase. See Halliday's *Practice*, Chapter 15–141.

(*c*) An exchange of missive letters between seller and purchaser or their respective agents.

Exchange of letters between agents is by far the commonest method.

The foregoing references to formal contracts are, of course, to be read in the context of the Requirements of Writing (Scotland) Act 1995, for which see Chapter 2. Very briefly, the implications are that:

(*a*) Under the 'old rules', where the contract, in whatever form, was entered into prior to 1 August 1995, it had to be probative or privileged, normally adopted as holograph.

(*b*) Under the 'new rules', where the contract is entered into on or after 1 August 1995, there must be a written document subscribed by a party or agent but without any further formality of execution. See s. 1(2) and s. 2. Under s. 2(2), in the case of missives, several such documents taken together may form the contract. The provisions of s. 8, Annexations, may also apply.

A unilateral undertaking to convey land may bind the grantor, but will normally be construed merely as an offer, requiring acceptance. See *Haldane* 1972 SLT (Sh Ct) 8: 'I ... undertake to sell to X the flat occupied by me at (address) for £625, when I vacate the flat.' It was held that this was a mere offer; there was no acceptance, and hence no binding obligation.

**28.3** *(a) Missives.* In the ordinary case, the purchaser's agent submits an offer to purchase, in letter form addressed to the seller's agent and, under the old rules, adopted as holograph, which is accepted by the seller's agent, again by letter addressed to the purchaser's agent and again adopted as holograph under the old rules. But an offer to sell, followed by an acceptance thereof, is equally competent.

Under the new rules in the 1995 Act, a formal contractual document must be subscribed but does not require attestation unless it is intended to be self-proving. In the case of missive letters, all that is now required is the subscription of each letter by the party or agent; and, as stated above, two or more such missive letters can together constitute the contract.

Under the old rules, such missive letters had to be actually holograph of the writer, or, much more commonly, adopted as holograph. Not only was that an essential for due formality under the old rules but it also served a distinct and useful purpose of identifying those letters which were intended to form part of the contract of sale and purchase. With the relaxation of the requirements for formality in the 1995 Act, any signed letter may serve as part of the missives, whether adopted as holograph, attested or merely signed. This then raises the possibility that a letter, not intended to form part of the contract but signed, might in fact operate as a part of the contract in an exchange of missive letters.

Practice has still to stabilise but various methods are at the moment being adopted to make sure that only those letters which were intended to form part of the contract do in fact so operate. This difficulty did not, of course, arise with missive letters under the old rules.

**28.4** *(b) Agents.* Normally, missive letters pass between agents who may bind the principal, whether purchaser or seller, if the agent has special authority. Under the ordinary rule of agency, a contract by an agent duly authorised on behalf of a disclosed principal binds the principal only, and not the agent; otherwise, the agent is personally bound.

The agent's special authority need not be in writing; it may be verbal. It is presumed that this rule still applies for contracts signed by an agent on or after 1 August 1995, notwithstanding the provisions of the 1995 Act s. 1(2) (a)(i). But note that the agent, when making an offer on behalf of a named principal, warrants his authority, although he does not warrant that his principal is solvent nor that his principal will duly carry out the contract. Accordingly, if an agent makes an offer without due authority, he is personally liable in damages to the offeree; and, of course, cannot recover from his alleged principal. Verbal authority, at a meeting or on the telephone, though competent, is often hard to prove; the agent should normally insist on having authority in writing, from his principal, to avoid incurring personal liability. For a recent case involving, *inter alia*, a disagreement as to whether or not the agents purportedly acting had due authority to do so, see *Hopkinson* 1993 SLT 907: see Digest of Cases 1.3. Particular care should be taken in accepting a fax either as constituting agency or as forming part of a series of contractual missives; or, in other situations, where intimation is made by this method. The position is unclear, but it is unsafe to rely on a fax as an alternative to a delivered written document.

If the agent is duly authorised to act generally for either party to the contract, he does not require to seek specific authority in relation to every individual clause therein.

**28.5** *(c) Probative contract.* Under the old rules before the Requirements of Writing (Scotland) Act 1995, as referred to above, the whole of the contract must be probative of the respective parties. In the case of an exchange of missive letters, the contract comprises at least two letters, usually more in practice. Each separate missive must be probative of the party who signs it, by being holograph, adopted or tested. Thus, if a holograph offer is met by a non-holograph acceptance, the contract is not probative as a whole, and neither party is bound. *A fortiori*, a holograph offer, which is accepted verbally or by telegram, telex or fax, does not create a contract. For a general discussion, see *McGinn* 1947 SC 334 where an acceptance (not holograph or adopted) of a probative offer was held to be adopted by a holograph covering letter, thus completing the contract. *Cf. Davidson* 1988 GWD 25–1076, where an alleged prior verbal collateral agreement was held not to bind the purchaser although it was referred to indirectly in the formal contract.

The foregoing requirements as to probativity no longer apply, of course, for any contractual document executed on or after 1 August 1995. In the context of sale and purchase of heritage, however, there must still be a written document under s. 1(2) and, since the document inevitably relates to land, that document must be subscribed. It must also be remembered that, under the 1995 Act, mere signature of a document does not make it self-proving. The dispensation provided by the 1995 Act s. 2(3), which permits an unsigned document to be used in evidence, should not be relied on. On the other hand, this dispensation increases the risk that a document which at least one party did not intend to form part of the contract may be produced nonetheless in evidence, which would not have been permissible in the ordinary way under the old authentication rules.

A letter by a firm, adopted as holograph, must be so adopted and signed by a partner – an assistant, even although duly authorised, will not do: *Littlejohn* 1974 SLT (Sh Ct) 82. The reference to adoption as holograph in this paragraph applies only to documents signed before 1 August 1995. Where a document is signed on or after that date, the special provisions for partnerships in Schedule 2 to the 1995 Act will apply; and these, in particular, permit an authorised person to sign on behalf of a partnership under para. 1.

A contract made by one or both parties furth of Scotland does not require to comply with the strict Scottish formalities provided that it is valid, in point of form, as a contract for sale and purchase of land, according to the law of the place of execution. For a recent illustration, see *Hamilton* 1992 SCLR 740. There is no express provision in the 1995 Act which allows for this relaxation in formalities under the new rules. The only reference to deeds executed validly under some other jurisdiction is in the context of registration and does not advance matters one way or another. It is presumed, but only presumed, that the courts would apply the old common law privilege accorded to foreign documents but there is as yet no authority for this proposition. Halliday, *Conveyancing Law and Practice* (2nd edn.), 3–169, takes the opposite view.

Any defect in point of form may be cured by *rei interventus* or homologation, for which see below. The references in this paragraph to *rei interventus* or homologation apply only to formalities in documents executed prior to 1 August 1995. There is, as noticed in Chapter 2, a comparable provision in the 1995 Act s. 1 which expressly abolishes the rules of *rei interventus* and homologation as they applied before 1 August 1995 but introduces a statutory equivalent to *rei interventus* with comparable rules. For more detail, see Chapter 2.

A formal contract, once duly concluded, cannot subsequently be rescinded or discharged by mere verbal agreement. But a formal written offer, whether to sell or to purchase, may be withdrawn if intimation of the withdrawal is made to the other party before the offer is formally accepted, and, unexpectedly, a mere verbal withdrawal suffices if so made. See *McMillan* 1990 SC 389. As a general rule, any informal agreement, verbal or written, which purportedly adds to or modifies the formal contract, whether entered into before or after conclusion thereof, is normally ineffective and unenforceable. But this may introduce elements of error, lack of consensus, personal bar, innocent or fraudulent misrepresentation, *rei interventus* and homologation for some of which see below.

The preceding paragraph must be read in the context of the old rules which applied to documents executed prior to 1 August 1995. For documents executed on or after that date, it is thought that the same general principles will apply but with necessary modifications as to formality and *rei interventus*, but, at the time of writing, there is no guidance as to how these modifications will apply in practical situations.

**28.6 (2) Content**.   In addition to the formal requirements, the contract must contain two essentials, namely, proper identification of the subjects of sale and a statement of the price. Given these two essentials, the law will supply by implication all the remaining conditions and obligations of seller and purchaser; in practice, many of these conditions and obligations are expressed in the contract in a number of standard supplementary clauses, for which see below.

In an endeavour to achieve some element of standardisation in the content of such contracts, and to speed up and simplify the process of completion thereof, the Law Society of Scotland in 1991 suggested standard missive clauses which were revised in a second edition issued in 1992. No further edition is contemplated. The indications seem to be that the standard missives clauses are not generally being used.

As an alternative, there are indications that, in certain areas, local agents are seeking to adjust a common formula for missive clauses with the same general objective. For an illustration of such an alternative, see an article in 1995 JLS 142, discussing the equivalent local position in Tayside.

**28.7 (3) *Consensus in idem***.   The third requirement, as in any contract, is that the parties should be at one, at least on the main essentials of the contract. Thus, an offer (valid in point of form and content) to purchase heritable property can never be binding on either party if not accepted because, until accepted, there is no competent evidence of *consensus* and hence no contract. In *Grant* 1985 SC 251, a provision in missives to the effect that 'the actual boundaries will be agreed ...' between the parties was held not sufficiently precise to establish *consensus*. Similarly, an offer to purchase identified heritage but without fixing the price, which is accepted, would not be binding, again, because of want of evident *consensus*. So, in *MacLeod's Exr.* 1989 SC 72, no price was stated and there was no agreed basis for determining the same in the contract. Since there was no evident *consensus*, the contract was invalid.

The principal application of the rule as to *consensus* in practice involves the qualified acceptance of an offer. An offer to purchase heritage normally lays down conditions; and others are implied (see below). An unqualified acceptance completes the contract on those conditions. If the acceptor does not agree *de plano* with the whole conditions, express and implied in the offer, he may accept, but subject to qualifying conditions. That acceptance, in turn, binds neither party, unless and until those qualifications are in turn accepted, in proper form, by the original offeror. The acceptance may, in its turn, lay down further qualifying conditions. If so, then again neither party is bound unless and until those qualifications are accepted *de plano*. In practice, a contract of sale and purchase often comprises several missive letters from seller and purchaser (or agents) each qualifying to some extent the previous missive letter. It is only when the final qualification has been accepted *de plano* that the contract is complete; and, to indicate that this point has been reached in a series of missive letters, it is commonplace (although unnecessary) to embody in the final letter a statement that the party 'holds the bargain as concluded'.

In the light of the relaxation under the 1995 Act in the formal rules for authentication of contracts of sale and purchase of heritage referred to above, it is probably now increasingly desirable, in the final letter concluding the bargain, to specify precisely those letters which, taken together, form the complete contract and expressly to exclude all other communications between the parties or their agents. This was less necessary before because of the requirement that any such communication intended to form part of the contract should be adopted as holograph or otherwise formalised.

Even the old rule as to *consensus* and formality of documentation seems to have suffered some measure of relaxation in the decision in *McClymont* 1995 SLT 1248, where it was held that, if the missives did not contain all the matters agreed on between the parties and necessary to a sale and purchase of heritage, the additional omitted matters could be proved and the documentation rectified under the Law Reform (Miscellaneous Provisions) (Scotland) Act 1985 s. 8. This, of course, still continues to apply after 1 August 1995, although less likely to do so given the relaxation in formalities under the 1995 Act.

As an illustration of the dangers and difficulties which may thus be caused, see *Merrick Homes Ltd.* 1996 SLT 932, where missives were initially constituted by fax although the actual signed letters adopted as holograph were then delivered. It was argued that, as *obligationes literis*, the contract could not be competently concluded by fax. That argument is presumably still available because writing requires actual subscription although the formalities required are less onerous. The pursuers appealed but failed: 1997 SLT 570. Opinions were reserved as to whether *obligationes literis* could be duly constituted by fax alone.

### 28.8 The effect of a qualified acceptance

In the ordinary case, any qualified acceptance of a previous offer or acceptance falls to be treated, in turn, as a fresh offer. It is then in the option of the other party to accept or reject those conditions. See *Dickson* (1871) 10 M 41, where an acceptance of an offer contained an additional condition that the seller would not give a search, and that additional condition was never explicitly accepted by the purchaser. It was held that there was no *consensus*.

The effect of a qualified acceptance on the preceding offer is discussed by Lord Caplan in *Rutterford Ltd.* 1990 SLT 249. Lord Caplan held, following the decision in *Wolf & Wolf* 1984 SLT 100, that the effect of a qualified acceptance was to set up a counter-offer. In *Rutterford*, the purchasers' initial offer was met by a qualified acceptance. The qualifications therein were accepted by the purchaser but subject to further qualifications; and these in turn were subsequently qualified in an exchange of successive formal missive letters culminating in a qualified acceptance by the purchasers of the previous qualifications made by the sellers dated 11 October 1988. Thereafter, an interval occurred during which the parties continued to negotiate by informal correspondence but without any formal modification to the contract. This is just one illustration of the risks above referred to created by the relaxation in the required formalities under the 1995 Act and underlines the need for distinguishing between formal contractual documentation and informal negotiation. Finally, in January 1989, the purchasers, in an endeavour to conclude the bargain which had not yet been finalised, purportedly withdrew the qualifications in their letter of 11 October 1988, accepted the prior qualifications made by the sellers in their immediately preceding missive letter and purportedly held the bargain as concluded. Lord Caplan held that this purported acceptance was ineffective. He supports the views expressed by Lord Robertson in the earlier case of *Wolf & Wolf* to the effect that, when an offeree replies by qualified acceptance, he is in effect saying that this is his response to the offer. The focus then shifts to the original offeror who has to consider whether or not he will accept the counter proposals. In the result, on Lord Caplan's view of the matter, supported by earlier authority, every qualified acceptance in effect represents a new offer and the party who made that qualified acceptance is not then free to withdraw it in order to accept the bargain on the terms previously proposed.

The same point was again considered by the Second Division in *Findlater* 1990 SC 150. Although the facts in that case are more complex, the decision in *Findlater* clearly supports the view above expressed that, in the ordinary way, if a party to a contract makes a qualified acceptance, that is a counter-offer, and the original offer is no longer open to *de plano* acceptance. Because of the unusual circumstances in *Findlater*, the court held that a valid bargain had been concluded. But it would seem that, in the ordinary case, every qualified acceptance represents a new offer; and, as a result, it is no longer competent for the maker of the qualified acceptance subsequently to withdraw it, and to revert to and accept the original offer.

McBryde's *Contract* 5–90 takes a somewhat different view of the decision in *Wolf & Wolf*; and certainly the decision in *Rutterford* runs counter to the view previously held within the profession that, if an offer is met by a qualified acceptance, the acceptor is free at a later stage to withdraw the qualification and substitute an unqualified acceptance, thus concluding the bargain. But clearly this can no longer be relied on.

Finally, where an offer is accepted apparently subject to qualifications but where the qualifications simply state explicitly what, in any event, the law would imply, that will be treated as an unqualified acceptance and will conclude the bargain. It is assumed that this rule continues to apply notwithstanding the recent decisions as to qualified acceptance.

**28.9 'Subject to contract'.**   This precautionary phrase is commonplace in England but is not much used in Scotland. The object is to prevent the parties being bound unless and until a formal contract is entered into following on a concluded agreement not intended to be irrevocably binding. The effect in Scotland is not settled:

> 'The only rules of Scots law which it appears to me to be possible to extract from past decisions and general principles are that it is perfectly possible for the parties to an apparent contract to provide that there shall be *locus poenitentiae* until the terms of their agreement have been reduced to a formal contract; but that the bare fact that the parties to a completed agreement stipulate that it shall be embodied in a formal contract does not necessarily import that they are still in the stage of negotiation. In each instance, it is a matter of the construction of the correspondence in the light of the facts proved, or averred, on which side of the borderline the case lies'. Lord President Cooper in *Stobo Ltd.* 1949 SC 184.

For a comparable case, see *Westren* (1879) 7 R 173 where a purchaser introduced an element of doubt into an otherwise completed contract by writing 'I will finally arrange it on my return'.

For a discussion of the English situation, see Law Commission Memorandum No. 65 'Transfer of Land'. This is a report on 'subject to contract' agreements, where the English practice is discussed in detail and commented on. But the Law Commission concluded that, while the existing procedure had drawbacks, it was based on the sound concept that the buyer should not be bound until he has had full opportunity to obtain legal and other advice, to arrange finance, and to make the necessary inspections, searches, and enquiries.

In Scotland, this is all incorporated in the initial contract by appropriate suspensive or resolutive conditions; and, therefore, 'subject to contract' agreements are not generally used.

While the foregoing general principles still apply, the above quotation from the opinion of Lord President Cooper and the reference to a formal contract must, again, be read in the light of the 1995 amendments. In the case of contracts entered into on or after 1 August 1995, there is a greater risk that, possibly inadvertently, a contract may apparently include a letter not intended to form part of the contract, or indeed may appear to be concluded although that may not have been intended. This is because it is no longer necessary to formalise missive letters by adoption as holograph. Care must be taken to exclude that possibility.

**28.10 *Rei interventus* and homologation**

The comments in this and the succeeding paragraphs dealing with *rei interventus* or homologation apply only to contracts entered into and concluded prior to 1 August 1995. In such cases, the following rules still apply as before.

In the case of contracts concluded on or after 1 August 1995, the new alternative provisions introduced by the 1995 Act s. 1(3) and (4) replace the rules of *rei interventus* or homologation and will accordingly be applied where appropriate to any such contract. The comments which follow are subject to that important qualification.

*Rei interventus* and homologation are two applications of the rule of personal bar. Neither is peculiar to sale and purchase of heritage; both apply to contracts in general. In practice, however, cases of *rei interventus* and homologation commonly arise out of contracts relating to heritage, in particular sale and purchase and lease, because of the essential requirement that, properly to constitute such a contract, there must be a probative writing.

Suppose that two parties have reached *consensus in idem* for the sale and purchase of heritage but have not embodied that *consensus* in the necessary probative form; or, alternatively, suppose that two parties have negotiated for the sale and purchase of heritage and have reached agreement on the main essentials, although they have not reached *consensus* on every minute particular. In the latter case, the parties may have embodied their imperfect agreement in probative form, or they may not. In any of such cases, the normal rule is that because of want of form, or because of want of *consensus*, neither party is bound and either party can refuse to proceed. The motive of the party so repudiating the contract is quite irrelevant. The other party has no remedy, no right to enforce the alleged contract and no right to claim damages.

But if, in any of the circumstances outlined above, one of the two parties to the contract, in good faith and in the belief that a binding agreement has been reached, acts on the supposed contract in such a way that his position is materially altered, and if the other party knows of these actings and acquiesces therein (or if such actings are the natural consequence of the supposed contract), the contract then becomes binding and enforceable by *rei interventus*.

To illustrate: Suppose that A, by holograph letter addressed to B, offers to purchase a house, which he identifies, at a stated price on a stated date of entry. B accepts the offer in unqualified terms, but the acceptance is not probative, being typed and signed but not adopted as holograph. There is no contract and neither party is bound. But if, thereafter, A pays the whole of the purchase price to B who accepts payment and gives possession, this at once creates a binding contract on both A and B by *rei interventus*, from which neither party can thereafter escape.

It is too early yet to say how the rules in the 1995 Act s. 1(3) and (4) will apply compared with the operation of *rei interventus* under the old rules. Generally speaking, however, the position would not seem to be significantly altered except, of course, that the new provisions apply to writings which fail to comply with the new rules as opposed to probative or privileged writings which were previously required in order to constitute such contracts. So, Professor Reid, in his book on the Act referred to above, states that the new provisions re-enact the common law rules of *rei interventus* but in a simplified form. Under the new rules, a contract will not fail for lack of formal validity if followed by significant actings. A party is personally barred from withdrawing from an informal contract if the other party has acted or refrained from acting in reliance thereon to the knowledge of and with the acquiescence of the party seeking to withdraw, if the consequences are material. *Rei interventus* is thus preserved more or less in its old form. For a discussion of 'old' and 'new' *rei interventus*, see Rennie and Cusine, *Requirements of Writing* paras. 3.03–3.07.

On the other hand, there seems to have been no intention to re-enact provisions comparable to homologation and, according to Professor Reid, it thus disappears as a legal doctrine. While he may be right in this, it does seem possible to figure a case, on the wording of s. 1, which would, for practical purposes, fall to be treated as equivalent to homologation under the old rules. Compare Rennie and Cusine para. 3.08.

**28.11 (1) The need for *consensus*.** In the ordinary case of sale and purchase, both parties must be at one on every smallest particular; and, if not, neither party is bound. But if actings have followed on an incomplete contract, *rei interventus* may operate to overcome the lack of *consensus* on minor particulars; or, put another way, such *consensus* may be presumed from the actings. *Rei interventus* cannot, however, operate to overcome lack of *consensus* on any major, material matter. Thus, A, by holograph letter, offers to purchase the westmost first floor flat at 6 Park Avenue, Dundee, for £35,000 with entry at Martinmas next, with a condition that the property is subject to a feuduty of £10.50, unallocated. B, the offeree, accepts by holograph letter to A, and in his acceptance states 'the unallocated feuduty apportioned on the flat is in fact £10.60'. A does not reply. While matters remain in that state, and if no actings have followed, there is no contract, and neither A nor B is bound. But if A takes possession and pays the price, his actings would constitute *rei interventus* which would overcome the apparent lack of *consensus* on the minor discrepancy in feuduty. In other words, by *rei interventus* an incomplete contract has been made binding. But suppose that B, when replying to A's offer, says 'with reference to your offer of £35,000 for the dwellinghouse 6 Park Avenue, I would accept £36,000 for it', A does not reply. Here, there is clearly lack of consent on an essential fundamental of the contract, namely price, which normally *rei interventus* cannot cure. But, again, if A took possession and paid £36,000 not £35,000 to B, his acceptance of B's qualification would be implied and, by *rei interventus*, the contract, with that variation, would become binding on both parties.

**28.12 (2) The quality of actings.** In order to constitute *rei interventus*, one of the parties to the contract must act:

(i) in the genuine belief that agreement has been reached and in reliance on the supposed contract;

(ii) to the knowledge (actual or presumed) of the other party; and

(iii) in a way which materially alters the position of the party so acting, or produces some change of circumstances, or loss, or inconvenience, although not necessarily irretrievable.

**28.13 (3) Proof.** If *rei interventus* is to operate, there are two essentials: firstly, a contract involving *consensus* on the main essentials, and secondly, actings which follow the contract. Both these elements require to be proved.

It is settled that actings alleged to constitute *rei interventus* can be proved *prout de jure*. Thus, any evidence may be led to demonstrate the nature of the actings and to relate them to the antecedent contract.

The rules as to proof of the contract itself are less certain. Thus, Walker on *Evidence* at p. 310 indicates that, in every case, the agreement must first be established by writ, or oath, or by judicial admission on record (or by a combination of these), although the writ so founded on need not, of course, be probative. But Gloag on *Contract* at p. 46 makes an apparent exception to the rule in the case of incomplete contracts, followed by actings; the same actings (proved *prout de jure*) may be founded on to establish *rei interventus* and to prove that agreement has been reached. This exception is apparently supported in *Errol* 1966 SC 93. But the decision in *Errol* is expressly disapproved by Walker's *Contract*, 13.36, 'the decision ... is irreconcilable with principle and precedent ... Facts cannot both create agreement and be actings on the faith of that agreement'.

In *Mulhern* 1987 SLT (Sh Ct) 62, the sheriff principal followed the decision in *Walker* (1863) 1 M 417 and held that the alleged agreement must be proved by writ or oath. He rejected an argument, based mainly on *Errol*, that the alleged agreement might be proved by parole evidence. In McBryde's *Contract* at p. 649 the author states, in relation to *Errol*, 'this remarkable decision has been criticised' and refers to an article in 1986 SLT (News) 137 where the decision is again considered and discussed. The Scottish Law Commission were clearly unhappy with the decision on grounds of principle. They recommend, on equitable grounds, that the rule restricting proof to writ or oath should be abolished. See Chapter 2.

There seems to be no doubt that the new rules of personal bar replacing *rei interventus*, based on actings, under contracts entered into after the relevant date, resolve a number of the complex and controversial points referred to in the foregoing paragraph.

Proof by writ or oath is now abolished; further, the comparable provisions in the 1995 Act proceed on the footing that a formal contract has not been constituted in a written document which complies with s. 2 but that one of the parties to the informal contract has acted or refrained from acting in certain ways. Nothing more is said as to the method of establishing *consensus* or the terms of that informal contract; but clearly the existence of a contract, however informally arrived at, is a prerequisite to the application of the new provisions. On the other hand, equally clearly, the contract and the actings can be proved by any evidence, which substantially simplifies the position compared with the earlier rules.

In principle this may be desirable, but it does carry hidden dangers where seller and purchaser personally agree on a verbal and informal basis to the proposed conditions of a contract of sale and purchase, and one of the parties then acts in reliance on that verbal agreement. This in turn raises a further question as to the effect and extent of the 1995 provisions. The point is discussed at greater length by Rennie and Cusine para. 3.09. The question is, as there stated, whether or not the new legislation, in abolishing *rei interventus* for the purposes of formality of documentation, has also overridden the decision in *Errol* as to the method of constituting an informal agreement. In other words, is *rei interventus* replaced for all purposes, or only for the purposes with which the 1995 Act is concerned directly, namely solemnities and formalities in the execution of documents? Clearly, under the new provisions, there must be a pre-existing contract, however informal, before the new rules of personal bar can apply. What evidence is then required to establish the constitution of that informal agreement?

**28.14 (4) *Locus poenitentiae*.** Once again, the content of this paragraph is relevant only to contracts concluded prior to 1 August 1995 and must be read subject to that major qualification. But the new rules in the 1995 Act may produce a very similar result in practice. If a contract for sale and purchase of heritage is constituted by informal writings, or is incomplete under the old rules or constituted by oral agreement under the new rules, it is said that there is *locus poenitentiae*, which means that neither party is bound to proceed; or that either party may resile. *Rei interventus* excludes the plea of *locus poenitentiae*, and effectively prevented either party from resiling. But these terms, '*locus poenitentiae*' and 'resile' are also used in a different context as implying the power to escape from a contract, which was previously or otherwise binding, because of some suspensive or resolutive condition which has not been purified, or on account of breach of contract by the other party. In the context of an informal or incomplete contract for sale and purchase of heritage, the parties may have reached agreement. But there is no binding legal contract whatsoever, and neither party is bound, unless and until there are relevant actings.

The same general principles apply to contracts concluded on or after 1 August 1995, but such contracts will be much more easily validated because of the relaxation in the documentary requirements and, as a result, the situation envisaged in the preceding paragraph is less likely to occur, as noted above.

**28.15 (5) Homologation.** For practical purposes, this paragraph applies only to contracts entered into before 1 August 1995 although something akin to homologation may possibly be achieved under the statutory provisions in the 1995 Act s. 1. In cases of *rei interventus*, the party who has acted binds the other party by his actings. In cases of homologation, a party commits himself to a contract by his own actings, which, accordingly, do not, in this case, require to produce a loss or change of circumstances. Rather, such actings are evidence that the party so acting has agreed to be bound by the contract, *i.e.* they are evidence of acquiescence. Thus A, by holograph letter, offers to purchase heritage, which he identifies, at a stated price on a stated date. B accepts by improbative letter. Later B, the seller, intimates notice of change of ownership, redeems the feuduty on the footing that the subjects have been sold, and tells the tenant to pay his rent to A, since A is now the owner. By these actings, he has homologated the contract. Homologation is less common than *rei interventus*, although not infrequently both *rei interventus* and homologation may be pleaded in the same case, *e.g.* A pays the price, which is *rei interventus*; B accepts it and gives a receipt, which is homologation by B. Both could be founded on in a subsequent litigation. For a typical illustration, see *Mitchell* 1936 SC (HL) 56.

**28.16 Factors which affect the normal content of missives**
In addition to the matters which are essential to the constitution of a valid

contract, it is commonplace to include a number of conditions, many of which are in more or less standard form, in order to protect the interest either of the purchaser or of the seller, as the case may be. The reason for inclusion of certain clauses is fairly obvious. Thus, although a date of entry is not strictly necessary, it is clearly desirable that a date of entry should be expressly specified. Reference has already been made above to the standard form of missives proposed by the Law Society of Scotland.

Before discussing various factors which give rise to the inclusion of additional special clauses to protect seller or purchaser, it is appropriate to draw the reader's attention to the Scottish Law Commission Report No. 152 on 'Three Bad Rules in Contract Law', issued at the beginning of 1996. The bad rules referred to can be summarised thus:

(i) As a general rule, extrinsic evidence is not admissible in Scotland to prove the terms of a formal contract which are not expressed therein. Accordingly, the Court will not permit one party to seek to introduce extrinsic evidence to prove additional terms of a contract not therein expressed if the other party denies that such additional terms were ever agreed to. A major general exception to the rule is that matters which are collateral to an agreement can be proved by extrinsic evidence. Otherwise the standard rule is as above stated.

(ii) As an extension of the first general rule, there is a further rule that the execution and delivery of a formal conveyance purportedly implementing a prior contract entirely supersedes that contract; and the conveyance thereafter becomes the sole measure of the rights and liabilities of the parties to the antecedent contract. In this case, there are special exceptions to the standard rule:

(a) Since the contract and conveyance are concerned with heritage, the supersession rule does not apply to moveables dealt with in the antecedent contract. So, in the case of moveables, notwithstanding delivery of the disposition, it is still competent to refer to the antecedent contract to determine what was agreed.

(b) Collateral obligations. The scope of this exception and the meaning of the collateral obligations in this context will be discussed in the succeeding paragraphs. A typical illustration of such an obligation is, however, where the owner of land agrees to sell it to a purchaser and, in the same contract, undertakes to erect a building on it. The subsequent disposition of the land itself will not normally supersede any of the provisions in the antecedent contract which deal with the construction of the building.

(iii) The rejection in Scots law of the *actio quanti minoris* applies generally both to heritage and moveables but, under the Sale of Goods Act 1979 s. 11, a statutory provision in substance introduces the *actio quanti minoris* in the case of sale and purchase of moveables. It has never been admitted in the case of heritage without express provision in the relevant documentation.

The effect of this is that, where a purchaser has taken delivery of a disposition in exchange for the price and then finds that the subjects thereby conveyed are disconform to the antecedent contract, he cannot proceed with the contract and claim an abatement in the price on that account, nor can he claim damages in lieu since this would in effect amount to allowing an *actio quanti minoris* under a different name.

Again, there are quite a number of exceptions which are discussed at length in the Law Commission Report and will be referred to in the succeeding paragraphs.

The Law Commission recommends that the three rules of contract be abolished or modified, as described in the Report. It has a bill attached as an annexation to give effect to the proposals.

The proposals have now been enacted in the Contract (Scotland) Act 1997. The enactment of proposal (i) applies only to proceedings commenced on or after 21 June 1997. The enactment of proposals (ii) and (iii) apply to missives concluded on or after that date.

These factors and several others gave rise to additional conditions commonly included in contracts with appropriate variation or modification in special cases. Some comments on the more important of these factors follow.

**28.17 (1) The rule of** *caveat emptor.* As mentioned below, the law implies, in a contract of sale and purchase of heritage, that the seller will provide a marketable title. To that extent, the purchaser is therefore protected by implication. Beyond that, it is up to the purchaser to satisfy himself on such matters as the fitness of the subjects for his purpose; the structural condition of all buildings on the property; planning and other statutory matters which may affect the property, its use and its amenity; and the possibility of future developments in the area which may have an adverse effect. There are two ways in which this problem can be dealt with, with a view to protecting the purchaser:

(*a*) By the inclusion of appropriate conditions in the contract relating to such matters which, if not satisfied, will allow the purchaser to escape from the bargain. The seller may be reluctant to accept clauses of this type, and may reject or qualify the purchaser's offer accordingly. But in practice such clauses are often accepted.

(*b*) In advance of submitting the offer, to obtain a survey report and to make other relevant enquiries so that, before the purchaser makes his offer, he is satisfied on some or all of the foregoing matters and can therefore make his offer without reference to these items in the contract, relying on the survey report and his own preliminary enquiries.

In the majority of cases, the seller will not accept an offer which is subject to a survey report satisfactory to the purchaser, although this condition is occasionally agreed to in missives. That being so, Halliday's *Practice* at 15–60 suggests that a solicitor, if consulted, should always advise that an independent professional survey be obtained in advance of conclusion of the contract. The purchaser, on the other hand, is often reluctant to incur the expense of an independent survey and may prefer to rely on the survey report of his lending institution if he is obtaining a loan to assist in the purchase.

As Halliday points out in the passage above quoted, an independent survey will found a claim for damages against the surveyor but only in respect of defects which should have been disclosed and in respect of which no disclaimer is included in the surveyor's report. A report provided for the purchaser's lending institution and relied on by the purchaser may not provide the same degree of protection.

**28.18 (2) Survey reports.** For a useful article explaining the three general types of survey report commonly available and the implications of each of these three reports see 1988 JLS 89 'House Valuations and Surveys'. For a comment on the liability of a surveyor for negligence in the preparation of a report and on the assessment of damages, see 1986 JLS 484 'Surveyors' Negligence', discussing the decision in *Martin* 1986 SC 208. See also an article in 1986 SLT (News) 293 'Disclaiming liability for negligence in property surveys', which discusses the same decision. Note, however, that the Law Reform (Miscellaneous Provisions) (Scotland) Act 1990 s. 68 has amended the Unfair Contract Terms Act 1977. The right of a surveyor to exclude or limit liability for negligence by way of a non-contractual notice of disclaimer is now as a result severely restricted and the foregoing references must be read with this amendment in mind. See J. M. Thomson and others, in their commentary on the 1990 Act, for further details of this amendment.

Apart from the question of structural defects, other matters which may affect the property under various statutory controls will be disclosed by enquiries to appropriate authorities, in particular, local councils who issue property certificates on such matters as town and country planning and roads. It is not normal for the purchaser to make enquiries on certain of these matters prior to contract. Instead, protective clauses are normally included in the contract which the seller may or may not accept, with or without qualification.

A number of further cases of negligence by surveyors, actual or alleged, are included in the Digest of Cases under this sub-head. As the decision in *Alliance & Leicester Building Society* 1995 GWD 11–608 discloses, liability in such cases is by no means automatic.

**28.19 (3) The passing of the risk.** Contrary to popular expectation, the risk of damage or destruction to the property passes to the purchaser immediately on conclusion of the bargain unless the contract contains suspensive conditions which are never purified so that, in the result, there is no contract. See Scottish Law Commission Discussion Paper No. 81, 'Passing of Risk' (March 1989) and the Report No. 127 (1990), commented on at para. 28.52 below.

But the seller has a duty to take reasonable care of the property and appropriate precautions to ensure, as far as possible, that damage does not occur. See *Meehan* 1972 SLT (Sh Ct) 70.

**28.20 (4) Time of the essence.** In contracts of sale and purchase of heritage, time is not of the essence by implication, but can be made of the essence by express provision. It is now increasingly common for the seller's solicitor to insist on making time of the essence in relation to payment of the price on, or within a short period following, the date of entry. There are circumstances, however, where it is also in the interests of the purchaser that time should be of the essence of the contract; and his solicitor should carefully consider whether or not to make such an express provision. For comment on such express provision, see Lord President Hope in *Visionhire Ltd.* 1992 SCLR 236.

**28.21 (5) Prior communings**. Prior to the coming into force of the 1997 Act, the disposition when delivered supersede the antecedent formal missives. This fundamental rule was firmly established in the House of Lords in *Lee* (1883) 10 R (HL) 91; and the *dictum* of Lord Watson in that case has subsequently been referred to and approved on numerous occasions. The rule was subject to certain exceptions, particularly in the case of what may be termed collateral obligations as illustrated in *McKillop* 1945 SC 166. Notwithstanding the decision in *Lee*, it would be fair to say that the profession had come to regard any obligation in the contract of sale and purchase which did not relate directly to the transfer of title to the purchaser as in its nature a collateral obligation and therefore that such conditions were not superseded by the subsequent disposition. In the *McKillop* case there was a contract for the sale and purchase of a shop in course of construction which contained, *inter alia*, an obligation to complete the erection of the shop with proper skill and materials. The contract was implemented by delivery of a disposition in favour of the purchaser in exchange for the price but the building subsequently proved to be defective. The purchaser sued the seller for damages for breach of contract for not completing the building according to the original specifications. The builder in turn, relying on the rule in *Lee* above quoted, maintained that, on delivery of the disposition, all the conditions of the antecedent missives were superseded and the disposition became the sole measure of the rights and obligations of the parties. The court rejected the builder's argument on the footing that, in the missives, there was not only an agreement for sale and purchase of the land and buildings, but also a second independent, though collateral, agreement for the doing of supplementary work and doing that work to a proper standard. That separate and independent agreement was not superseded by the granting of the formal disposition.

This trend, stemming from *McKillop*, is well illustrated in the case of *Bradley* 1966 SLT (Sh Ct) 25, where the missives contained a condition to the effect that there were no outstanding notices for repairs, etc, issued by the local authority. Following on delivery of the disposition to the purchaser, it was discovered that part of the property was in fact subject to a closing order. The sheriff rejected an argument that the missives had been superseded by the delivery of the disposition on the footing that the disposition is confined to a description and conveyance in the usual manner, and does not reproduce and exhaust every term in the missives and is not intended so to do. As a result, he was prepared to treat the provision in the missives in this case as collateral in the sense in which that term had been applied in *McKillop* 1945 SC 166.

**28.22** *Winston v. Patrick*. That general view, as illustrated in *Bradley*, had to be substantially modified following on the decision in *Winston* 1980 SC 246.

In that case, the seller of a heritable property had previously constructed an extension, purportedly in accordance with a building warrant granted by the local authority. On a subsequent sale, the offer contained the following clause: 'The seller warrants that all statutory and local authority requirements in connection with the erection of the subjects of sale and any additions, extensions or alterations thereto have been fulfilled'. After settlement of the transaction, the purchaser discovered that the extension did not comply with the building warrant. In accordance with standard conveyancing practice at that time, the clause in the missives above quoted was not repeated in the disposition; and the missives themselves did not contain a non-supersession clause. The purchaser argued that the condition was collateral, as in *McKillop*; but that argument was rejected by the court in this case, primarily on the footing that, as worded, the clause was simply a statement of fact and imposed no personal obligation on the seller to do anything in the future. Accordingly, the general rule in *Lee*, referred to above, applied. It was clear from the cases decided since *Winston*, that a mere warranty in the terms used in *Bradley* above would not be treated as a personal or collateral obligation and would certainly not survive the missives, apparently even where the missives contain a non-supersession clause.

The inclusion and effect of the non-supersession clause in missives and in the subsequent disposition, and the question of collateral conditions generally are dealt with below at paras. 28.24 and 28.53; and the resulting position, on a breach of a clause in the missives which survives delivery of the disposition either *proprio vigore* or under a non-supersession clause, is dealt with at 28.99.

**28.23 (6) The exclusion of the *actio quanti minoris*.** As explained above in para. 28.16, at common law, a purchaser, whether of moveables or of heritage, did not have the right to retain the subject-matter of the purchase and at the same time claim damages if it proved to be defective or disconform to contract. The statutory modification of the Sale of Goods Act 1979 s. 11 is restricted to moveables only and had no application in the case of sale and purchase of heritage, for which there was no equivalent legislation, until the passing of the Contract (Scotland) Act 1997. In the case of heritage, the position prior to 21 June 1997 can be summarised thus:

(*a*) *Before delivery of the disposition. Restitutio in integrum* in this situation is always possible, except in very unusual circumstances. If the seller simply refuses to proceed with the bargain, or if there is a condition in the contract which is capable of being purified but which the seller, for whatever reason, declines to implement or purify, then in the ordinary way the remedy of the purchaser is an action of implement.

Alternatively, faced with an absolute repudiation by the seller or unreasonable delay on his part, the purchaser, after due notice, is entitled to rescind and claim damages.

In cases where the seller cannot implement his contract by the date of entry but where there is a curable defect in the title or a condition in the missives which can be purified, the purchaser is obliged to give the seller time to implement his obligations; and the ultimatum procedure is appropriate. If time is expressly of the essence, the purchaser has the alternative remedies of implement or immediate rescission and damages. No ultimatum is required.

In cases where the seller is unable to perform his part of the contract and the defect is not of its nature curable, the remedy of the purchaser is to rescind and claim damages.

It is never competent for the purchaser in any such case to seek to proceed with the bargain, but at a reduced price, because this is simply one application of the rule which excludes the *actio quanti minoris*.

It may be possible, however, for the purchaser to insist on implement of the principal contract of sale and purchase but to claim damages, in addition, for failure to implement a collateral obligation therein. Such a claim is not strictly *quanti minoris*. Such a situation is unlikely to occur before settlement and does not seem to have been considered in any reported case.

(*b*) *After delivery of the disposition*. Founding on the contract, the purchaser may or may not be able:

(i)  to sue for implement;

(ii)  to rescind and claim damages; or

(iii)  without rescinding, to claim damages for breach of a collateral obligation. See para. 28.99.

Prior to 21 June 1997, this depends, in part, on whether or not the missives have been kept alive by express provision following delivery of the disposition, thus excluding the rule in *Winston* above; in part, on whether or not *restitutio in integrum* is possible; and in part, on the nature of the condition which has not been implemented.

For a typical recent case, see *King* 1993 SLT 512. In that case, there was a contract for the sale and purchase of a house in course of construction, and in terms of the contract, it was to be completed according to certain specifications. The purchaser took entry and then discovered defects in construction. The seller maintained that, by accepting the disposition in his favour, the purchaser had barred himself from making any claim; that the obligation to build was not collateral in the circumstances; but in any event, if there was any element of collateral obligation, it related solely to that part of the house still unfinished at the date of the contract. Given that the missives prescribed specifications for the dwellinghouse, it was also clear from the missives that any obligation imposed on the seller thereunder would cease to apply at settlement.

The seller's arguments were rejected and in particular Lord Caplan held that an obligation in the missives to build was collateral and, as a result, conditions in the missives could not be so interpreted as to prevent the purchaser from claiming damages for defects in construction. In the course of his judgment, Lord Caplan refers to a number of earlier cases which underline the difficulties raised by the decision in *Winston*.

In a more recent case, *Glazik* 1996 SCLR 270, there was, again, a contract for the sale and purchase of a dwellinghouse which contained certain provisions as to local authority approval, and a non-supersession clause with a two-year time limit which was in substance repeated in the disposition. In this case, the Sheriff held it unnecessary to apply the rules laid down in *Winston* because the missives were expressly incorporated in the disposition itself, which therefore, with that inclusion, became the sole measure of the rights and liabilities of the parties; and damages were awarded accordingly. In the course of his judgment, however, the Sheriff took into account and considered some 16 earlier cases, most of them following on *Winston*. This is a useful decision to refer to as it contains a fairly comprehensive review of previous cases which have caused problems under this head. Many of these are summarised in the Digest of Cases.

For a recent illustration of the problems raised by the lack of the remedy *quanti minoris*, see *Fortune* 1995 SCLR 121. The owner of heritable property in that case accepted an offer to purchase the business carried on in the premises and to grant a lease of the premises to the purchasers. The offer contained, *inter alia*, a warranty by the seller that a financial account annexed to the offer was accurate. The offer also contained a non-supersession clause with a two-year time limit. The transaction settled and the purchasers of the business took entry under the lease. Some six months later, they concluded that the financial statement referred to in the offer was seriously inaccurate and that the turnover and profits of the business were not as shown in the accounts. They further alleged that the seller, who had warranted the accounts, was aware that they were inaccurate. The purchasers accordingly averred that the warranty had been fraudulently made and that the seller was in breach of contract, and claimed damages. The missives did not contain an *actio quanti minoris* clause, but the purchasers were able to found on fraudulent misrepresentation as justifying retention of the premises, and to claim damages based on delict. After substantial amendments to the original pleadings, the purchasers succeeded in their claim to the extent that proof before answer was allowed. Again, the reports of the case contain a useful index of earlier decisions under this head.

In cases of eviction, actual or constructive, a claim is always competent under warrandice, and is in effect a claim *quanti minoris*.

**28.24** (*a*) *Collateral obligations and the basis of damages.* Prior to 21 June 1997 where a claim is based on a breach of a condition in the missives which is a collateral obligation, then, depending on the circumstances, it may still be possible for the purchaser to raise an action of specific implement after settlement; and, in any event, a claim for damages is usually competent. The basis of the claim for damages is not altogether clear, but the accepted view now seems to be that, where a collateral obligation is breached, whether or not there is a non-supersession clause in the contract, it remains enforceable *proprio vigore.* The seller must therefore implement it or incur liability in damages in lieu. The basis of assessment is not *quanti minoris* but on a true damages basis by ascertaining the actual cost to the purchaser of putting matters right. This is because collateral obligations are an acknowledged exception to the rule in *Winston* on the footing that, being collateral, the obligation is a distinct and separate contract from the main contract of sale and purchase. Accordingly, it stands on its own feet and, even although delivery of the disposition may supersede the main contract, it does not supersede the collateral contract because it is separate and independent in itself. See *Hardwick* 1991 SLT 258, where the question is discussed in considerable depth with substantial citation of authority, *Jones* 1988 SLT (Sh Ct) 53, and the more recent cases cited under the preceding subhead.

**28.25** (*b*) *The basis of damages quanti minoris.* In the ordinary way, the basis of a claim for damages *quanti minoris* is the difference in the value of the subjects arising out of the failure of the seller to implement his obligation: *Finlayson* 1987 SLT (Sh Ct) 150. This may or may not be the same as the amount required to put matters right. *McKillop*, *supra*, is a clear-cut case of a collateral obligation surviving delivery of a disposition in favour of the purchaser. The seller failed to implement that collateral obligation. On the question of damages Lord Moncrieff comments that there was no question of claiming damages for failure to transfer the contracted value of the subjects conveyed by the disposition. Instead, the purchaser was simply seeking implement of an independent and separate agreement. He comments 'that is not a case of claiming damages on the doctrine of *quanti minoris*, but is an assertion of a separate contractual right having a separate contractual origin'. See also *Hardwick*, *supra*. But in *Finlayson* the sheriff's view of the decision in *McKillop* is that the collateral obligation which survived delivery of the disposition 'opened up the *actio quanti minoris* to the pursuer for the failure in the collateral obligation'.

In *Wood* 1988 SLT (Sh Ct) 17 the actual method of assessing the *quantum* of damages was provided for expressly in the missives; and it may be prudent to include such a provision in the contract.

The point is important because there may be a very substantial difference in the amount of damages awarded, depending on whether the basis of damages is *quanti minoris* or is separately and independently assessed as damages for failure to implement the collateral obligation.

**28.26** (*c*) *Express provision for the actio quanti minoris.* In an article in 1988 JLS 285 Professor K. G. C. Reid discusses the implications of the rule which excludes the *actio quanti minoris* and suggests a clause for insertion in the missives with a view to creating, contractually, the right of the purchaser to retain the subjects but claim damages *quanti minoris* in appropriate cases. If some such provision is not made, it may be competent for the purchaser to hold the seller in breach of contract even after delivery of the disposition if the obligation is collateral; but otherwise the strict rule is applied. The purchaser's remedy is either to rescind or to keep the subjects as he finds them without any redress against the seller by way of damages, unless the seller is in breach of a collateral condition which generates its own separate entitlement to damages. Alternatively, depending on circumstances, an action of specific implement may still be available to the purchaser.

It will be evident from what has been said in the preceding paragraphs, and from the numerous cases in the Digest of Cases under these heads, that the comments and criticisms of the Scottish Law Commission on the three bad rules of contract are more than justified and that the 1997 Act will certainly be welcomed by the profession.

**28.27 (7) The need for express provision.** All the foregoing rules apply by implication to a contract of sale and purchase of heritage, in the absence of an express provision in the contract varying or excluding any one or more of these rules which would otherwise apply. Such a provision is normally competent and, as indicated below, fairly standard clauses have become commonplace to modify or avoid the effect of some or all of the foregoing rules in the great majority of contracts. After 21 June 1997 such clauses will not be required.

**28.28 Effect of conditions in contracts whether suspensive or resolutive**
This distinction is not normally significant in contracts of sale and purchase

of heritage in that, whether a condition in a contract of sale and purchase is suspensive or resolutive, neither party is bound to proceed with the contract, nor to settle the transaction, unless and until all the conditions have either been implemented or, by agreement, departed from.

For a discussion as to whether a particular condition in a contract is suspensive or resolutive, see *McKay* 1987 GWD 16–609. It is clear from the decision in that case and other cases mentioned in the Digest of Cases at para. 28.75 that, whatever the nature of the condition, each party is entitled to expect that the other will act reasonably.

For a recent case reaffirming this proposition, see *Rockcliffe Estates plc* 1994 SLT 592. Lord McLean at p. 595L quotes with approval an earlier decision of Lord Clyde, who states: 'Each party must have intended that the other would act reasonably and I do not consider that it could have been the intention that the purchasers would have been enabled to act arbitrarily or unreasonably in the operation of' a certain condition. The condition in the contract in *Rockcliffe Estates* provided that payment would only be made after the purchasers were satisfied with the terms of a lease. The terms 'satisfaction' and 'reasonable satisfaction' and other comparable expressions cause difficulties in a variety of contexts including, in particular, sale and purchase and in construing title conditions and are to be avoided. It is, however, often impossible to avoid such subjective tests.

For an unusual case of a resolutive condition still operative after settlement see *Gilchrist* 1979 SC 380 where the property was purchased subject to a condition to the effect that the contract was subject to the seller obtaining approval, for dedication of part of the property, from the Forestry Commission. The application for dedication was then rejected. The purchaser then sought to waive the condition in order to proceed with the bargain, tendering the price in full in exchange for a disposition already delivered. That in itself is very unusual. It was held that the condition relating to dedication was resolutive and the bargain accordingly came to an end automatically when the application for dedication was refused. Therefore, the purchaser was not in a position to waive that condition and to proceed.

In *Park* 1993 GWD 8–571 there were in effect two suspensive conditions. One of these made the contract subject to the acquisition of an adjoining property by a stated date; the other contained a condition as to obtaining planning permission, again by a specified date. Neither condition was purified by the respective dates. Despite arguments on the part of the seller that the conditions had been purified or withdrawn, her claim failed. This case illustrates the general rule and underlines the importance of following up such conditions with formal evidence of purification or failure to purify by the date or dates specified.

In *Khazaka* 1995 SLT 1108 the contract was again conditional upon the obtaining of planning permission by the purchaser who was required to lodge his planning application by a stated date. In addition, if permission was not granted by a later stated date, the purchaser was free to resile or to appeal. The purchaser failed to lodge his application within the period specified and the seller purportedly resiled on that account, arguing that time limits specified in a suspensive condition must be strictly adhered to. That argument was, however, rejected on the footing that the date for lodging the application was not suspensive and was not in itself material. What mattered was whether or not permission was obtained within the stated time. The time limit for lodging the application could, of course, have been made a material condition and of the essence by express provision, and this is usually advisable. Failing such provision, the ultimatum procedure must be adopted if the condition is truly material to the interests of either party.

**28.29 Effect of conditions inserted for the benefit of one party.** The rule above stated, that neither party is bound to proceed until all conditions are satisfied, suffers this qualification, that a condition inserted in a contract exclusively for the protection or benefit of one of the parties may be waived, unilaterally, by that party even if not purified. If so waived, the contract is then immediately binding on both parties. Clearly, it may be very important to determine which, if any, conditions in a contract can be said to be for the exclusive benefit of the seller or of the purchaser, and therefore capable of being unilaterally waived in this way.

For a discussion and analysis of this problem, see *Ellis & Sons Ltd.* 1975 SLT 10. The facts in that case were, briefly, that an offer to purchase heritage contained *inter alia* the following condition:

> 'This offer is conditional on our clients obtaining planning permission for the use of the subjects as office premises. Our clients undertake to apply for this as soon as possible'.

The seller accepted the offer, but subject to a qualification allowing the seller to resile from the bargain if planning permission had not been obtained by 6 October 1973.

Before that date arrived, the purchaser unilaterally purported to withdraw the condition in his offer as to planning permission and sought settlement of the contract at the stated date of entry, tendering the price in full. Thereafter, planning permission which had been applied for was refused; and the seller then refused to complete the bargain. The purchaser sued for implement, claiming that the condition as to planning permission was inserted solely for the protection of the purchaser and accordingly that the purchaser was entitled unilaterally to waive that condition and had effectively done so. In argument, the purchaser founded on the earlier case of *Dewar & Finlay Ltd.* 1968 SLT 196, where, on a similar set of facts, the court had found in favour of the purchasers.

In *Ellis*, however, the court took the opposite view holding that, in this contract, there was no implied right allowing the purchaser unilaterally to waive the planning condition which could, therefore, only be waived with joint consent. Therefore, the seller was entitled to resile. This view is confirmed indirectly in the decision in *Findlater* 1990 SLT 465 at p. 469.

**28.30 Categories of condition.** In the course of his opinion in *Ellis*, Lord Dunpark classifies contractual conditions in three categories.

(*a*) Conditions which can be waived unilaterally. These are principally conditions which cannot in any circumstances be construed as having been inserted for the benefit of both parties. Examples of these are the normal conditions requiring the seller to provide a good title, which can only be for the benefit of the purchaser. Similarly, an offer made 'subject to surveyor's report on structure' can only be for the benefit and protection of the purchaser. Such conditions can clearly be waived unilaterally by the purchaser. In *Zebmoon Ltd.* 1988 SLT 146, it was held that a condition can be waived unilaterally if (i) it is conceived solely in the interests of one party; and (ii) it is severable and not inextricably connected with other parts of the contract.

(*b*) Conditions which cannot be so waived. These include conditions which, although *ex facie* inserted by one party in his own interests, may also operate incidentally for the benefit of the other. Thus, if one party makes an offer 'subject to formal contract' and this is accepted, the condition as to formal contract affects both parties and cannot be unilaterally waived. A condition of this kind is illustrated in *Manheath Ltd.* 1996 SCLR 100. The condition in that case required planning permission to be obtained within five years. Two days before the five-year period expired, the purchaser intimated to the seller that this suspensive condition had been purified although planning permission had not in fact been granted. The seller rejected these arguments and was upheld.

(*c*) Borderline cases which include conditions of such a kind that only one of the parties normally would have an interest in that condition but in which the other party may exceptionally have an interest. According to Lord Dunpark, on the facts in *Ellis*, the planning condition fell into this third category and in the circumstances could not be waived by one party. Of course, as he later pointed out in his judgment, it is open to the parties to provide expressly in the contract that a condition may be waived unilaterally by one or other of them; and this is often done. It was not done in this case with the result above stated.

In appropriate cases, both parties should therefore carefully consider whether to include or exclude an express provision permitting one or other party unilaterally to withdraw or waive a particular condition.

In *Burnside* 1989 GWD 11–468, it was held that a provision in a contract, which entitled either party to resile if a certain certificate was not obtained by a specified date, was enforceable strictly according to its terms even although the certificate was in fact later obtained; and that the terms of the missives rendered the ordinary common law ultimatum procedure inapplicable.

### 28.31 Normal content of a contract of sale and purchase of heritage

For examples, see Halliday's *Practice* 15–136 to 15–140, Diploma Styles and the standard missive clauses proposed by the Law Society of Scotland for house purchase and sale which have already been referred to and give a general indication of the normal content of such contracts, although open to criticism on several points. For convenience the offer and acceptance incorporated in the specimen styles in Appendix A to this Manual are based on these standard clauses. See also several articles on special matters listed in the reading list under Chapter 28.

### 28.32 (1) Identification of the subjects sold.

A formal 'conveyancing' description is unnecessary, and the barest specification or identification is usual. But care is required here, and a full description, possibly with a plan, is often desirable and sometimes essential. In a great number of cases, particularly in the case of the purchase of a dwellinghouse, postal address alone is used to identify the subject-matter of the purchase. There is no objection to this common practice subject to the undernoted comments.

**28.33** (*a*) *Doubt as to identity.* Where a short description of this kind is used, as is usual, and when a dispute then arises as to what was intended to be sold and purchased, it is competent to refer to prior communings in order to determine the extent and nature of the subjects sold. See *Macdonald* (1898) 1 F 68, where the subjects were simply described in the contract as 'the property known as The Royal Hotel at Portmahomack ... belonging to Peter Macdonald ...'. The parties subsequently disagreed as to the subject-matter of the sale; and extrinsic evidence was admitted to prove the facts.

The true question, where a doubt arises as to the nature and extent of the subjects of sale, is not what the contract says, but rather what the parties thought was being sold and purchased. 'In my view, these negotiations are crucial, and all that passed, either orally or in writing, is admissible in evidence to prove what was in fact the subject of the sale; not to alter the contract, but to identify its subject': Lord Chancellor Loreburn in *Houldsworth* 1910 SC (HL) 49. See also *Martone* 1992 GWD 32 1903.

This rule, however, cannot be invoked to alter or modify the plain terms of the contract. See *Murray* 1980 SLT (Sh Ct) 131.

Even if the subjects are not described by particular description in the contract, which is commonplace, there must be *consensus in idem* between seller and purchaser as to what is being sold and purchased. So, in *Grant* 1985 SC 251, where the missives provided that 'the actual boundaries will be agreed between the parties', this was held not to be sufficiently precise; and so there was no *consensus* and therefore no valid contract.

*Angus* 1992 SLT 884 is clearly a borderline case. An offer was made for certain salmon fishings which were described in the offer in fairly detailed terms. The seller in a qualified acceptance deleted the description in the offer entire and, instead, introduced into the missives a description by reference to the titles which clearly, in their terms, included not only fishings in a river but fishings in the sea at the river mouth. The disposition in implement followed that description. Some two years later the seller challenged the terms of the disposition and sought to rectify it on the footing that the sea fishings were included by error. The matter was disposed of at procedure role without hearing evidence as a matter of plain construction gleaned from the terms of the missives themselves. In the course of his judgment, Lord Cameron usefully reviews the authorities and concludes:

(1) that an unintentional essential error known to and taken advantage of by the other party necessarily implies bad faith; and

(2) that, in the result, the missives and the disposition were not capable of rectification since the purchasers appreciated the error made by the seller in the missives and so could not have intended, when concluding those missives, to agree to purchase the subjects as plainly defined in the missives.

In *Aberdeen Rubber Ltd.* 1995 SLT (HL) 870, there was a dispute between seller and purchaser as to what was actually intended to be sold. The missives referred to four areas of ground. The disposition purportedly in implement thereof actually conveyed a fifth area. The sellers then raised an action of declarator that the fifth area had never been included in the missives and that the disposition accordingly failed to implement the agreement of the parties. It was held in the Inner House that, since the missives were not challenged by the purchasers, they must prevail over prior communings and accordingly the disposition fell to be reduced to the extent of excluding the fifth area. Again, in the decision in this case, there is a useful review of the earlier authorities on error *in consensus*. The appeal to the House of Lords was dismissed.

**28.34** (*b*) *Separate tenements.* Subject to the observations in the preceding paragraph, the rules which apply in interpreting a description in a conveyance, and which make it obligatory to incorporate, expressly, all separate tenements, also apply to contracts for sale and purchase. Therefore, if separate tenements are the subject of sale and purchase, each tenement should be separately specified; this applies, typically, to such rights as salmon fishing. See *McKendrick* 1970 SLT (Sh Ct) 39.

**28.35** (*c*) *Fixtures and fittings.* In the absence of special provision, it is implied in a sale and purchase of heritage, as in a conveyance, that all corporeal heritable property is included in the subjects of sale and all corporeal moveable property is excluded; therefore, the character of a fixture or fitting, whether heritable or moveable, determines whether or not it is included in the price. But of course parties may (and almost always do) make special contractual provision as to fixtures and fittings.

In practice, under this clause, certain items which in any event are heritable fixtures are often included in the contract by express provision (unnecessarily); and, in addition, a large number of other items, principally in the category of fittings, not being heritable by nature and therefore by implication excluded, are by express provision included in the price. For an exhaustive list of items which may or may not be included in the sale by implication under this general head, see Green's *Encyclopaedia* 7.361–385 – Fixtures, and Halliday's *Practice* 15–37 and 38.

Items which may require special provision in the ordinary case include television aerials, washing machines, refrigerators, electric and gas fires, and other electric fittings, floor coverings, summerhouse and garden sheds.

Further, in the case of sale and purchase of business premises, such as hotels, public houses, shops, etc., or agricultural property, an elaborate clause may be necessary, with a long inventory of items. See Burns' *Practice*, p. 87 and Halliday's *Practice* 15–138 and 15–140. It is commonplace, in sale and purchase of business premises, to provide, in addition that certain corporeal moveables, typically furniture, stock, machinery, etc., shall pass from seller to purchaser at date of entry at a price to be agreed or fixed by valuation. If so, then it should be made clear whether or not the provision is binding on both parties, or optional to both or either of them. The date of take-over should be specified, with a proviso that it is only such items as then exist which are to be purchased, but subject to a proviso that the seller should not unduly increase, nor unduly run down, the stock, etc., prior to that date.

If the items are to pass at valuation, then additional provisions will have to be made appointing the valuer and providing for payment of his fees.

**28.36** **(2) Price.** This is the second essential of the contract. It is normally payable in one sum at the date of entry, in cash; but payment of the price by instalments is not uncommon; and sometimes the price is represented in whole or in part by shares or by some other consideration such as an exchange; and occasionally no price is payable.

Some special points to note in regard to price are as follows.

**28.37** *(a) Precision.* If the price is not expressly stated, the contract must contain a precise provision for the fixing of the price. Otherwise, on this ground, there will be no *consensus* and therefore no valid contract. See *McLeod's Exr.* 1989 SLT 392. Compare *Scottish Wholefoods Collective Warehouse Ltd.* 1994 SCLR 60. In an option to purchase contained in a lease, 'the current open market price pertaining . . .' on a specified date was held to be an adequate formula to enable the price to be ascertained.

In *Rockcliffe Estates plc* 1991 SLT 592 there was a contract of sale and purchase for a whole portfolio of properties at a single global price. The purchasers were to intimate the individual prices allocated on each individual property for inclusion in the relevant disposition. The contract also permitted the purchasers to withdraw any property from the portfolio if they were not satisfied with the lease or leases relative thereto, in which case the purchase price was to be reduced by the amount so allocated by the purchasers. The purchasers exercised this right by intimating a list of properties which they wished to withdraw from the portfolio; but the sellers refused to complete the sale of the remaining properties on the footing that the price allocated by the purchasers on the properties to be withdrawn was too high. In the subsequent action, it was held that there could be no inference in such a contract that the purchasers would allocate individual prices on a reasonable basis, having regard to market values, since this would be contrary to the express terms of the contract, but that it was an implied term of the contract that the purchasers should act reasonably and not capriciously or arbitrarily in exercising their discretion to withdraw properties. While there may no doubt have been special circumstances in this case and good reasons for conferring these options on the purchasers, greater precision in the method of fixing individual prices and a much more strictly drawn option would normally be desirable.

**28.38** *(b) Deposits.* In Scotland it is unusual, but nevertheless competent, to stipulate for a deposit, except in articles of roup, or in the sale of higher-value country properties. If there is to be a deposit, then the clause should be carefully framed and should make it clear whether or not the deposit is forfeit absolutely if the purchaser fails to complete: *Commercial Bank* (1890) 18 R 80.

In *Zemhunt (Holdings) Ltd.* 1992 SC 58 it was held that a deposit will normally be construed as a pledge or guarantee of performance by the purchasers, not simply an advance of part of the purchase price, and accordingly the deposit in this case was forfeited, the purchasers being in material breach of contract. In contrast, in *Inverkip Building Co. Ltd.* 1992 GWD 8–433 a purchaser was held entitled to recover a deposit where the contract could not be implemented but the fault was not his. See also *Singh* 1990 SLT 77.

**28.39** *(c) Interest on the price.* Interest is due *ex lege* from the date of entry if the purchaser is in possession and if the price is not then paid. This rule applies, even where the delay is mainly or solely due to the fault of the seller.

There is no legal rate of interest; 5% used to be usual, but, while higher interest rates prevail generally, a higher rate is charged, often linked to bank or building society rates.

This rule as to interest can be avoided if the purchaser, at the date of taking possession, deposits the whole purchase price in joint names of himself and the seller (or their respective agents). Following on such consignation, the seller is entitled to the deposit receipt interest only. See *Prestwick Cinema* Co. 1951 SC 98. As a result, missives now almost invariably include express provision for payment of interest by the purchaser if there is delay in settlement not attributable to the fault of the seller. As to whether or not this interest clause can operate where the seller repudiates the contract because of the purchaser's default, see *infra* at para. 28.95.

In *Bowie* 1978 SLT (Sh Ct) 9, the sheriff principal held that a purchaser is not obliged to agree to take entry, and to pay the price or interest thereon, unless and until the seller is in a position to fulfil his part of the bargain by delivering a valid disposition. In such circumstances, if the purchaser in his option prefers to wait until the title is ready, no interest runs between the date of entry and the date of actual settlement. If the purchaser fails to pay the price on the due date through no fault of the seller, the seller's ultimate remedy is to rescind the contract and claim damages. See para. 28.95 – Default by purchaser.

If, however, the transaction proceeds and the price is ultimately paid some time after the due date; and if, in the interim, the seller has retained possession, he cannot claim interest on the unpaid price unless there is an express provision in the missives to that effect. Such a provision is now commonplace. The rule is based on equitable grounds; the seller cannot, in equity, claim to have both the benefit of the property and interest as well. See *Tiffney* 1985 SLT 165.

While this rule operates logically enough in a landed estate or commercial property which is let and earning rent, it operates harshly in the case of the ordinary sale and purchase of a dwellinghouse; and, as a result, counterprovision is regularly now made in the acceptance of an offer to purchase, for the protection of the seller.

In *Lloyds Bank plc* 1993 SCLR 727 the purchaser defaulted and the seller sought to recover interest under this clause. The claim failed on the footing that the provision for interest was clearly intended to apply only where the contract was actually to be performed and the price would eventually be paid. The decision is therefore dealt with below in the context of default by the purchaser in a subsequent claim for what was in effect damages. Their claim under this head was rejected on the footing that the interest provision was intended to apply only where the contract was being performed and was therefore inapplicable where the contract had been repudiated. For a comparable case, see *Field* 1995 SCLR 1146. The full text of a typical interest clause is included in the rubric of this case and is a useful reference. It differs in its terms from the clause in *Lloyds Bank* and was clearly intended to circumvent the limitations of the *Lloyds Bank* clause. In contrast to the *Lloyds Bank* decision, however, the purchasers in this case did in fact pay the price although several months after the due date; and the sellers were clearly entitled to interest for that period under this provision since the contract here was in fact implemented. The speciality in this case is that, in addition, the sellers claimed further damages resulting from the delay in payment and were held entitled so to do by the Sheriff Principal on appeal.

**28.40** *(d) Price by instalments.* Contracts involving payment of the price by instalments over a period of years are now almost unknown. For further information on this now obsolete form of transaction, see the article in 1968 JLS 46, and *Reid* 1958 SLT (Sh Ct) 45.

**28.41 (3) Entry**. A date of entry is not essential to the constitution of a valid contract: *Sloan's Dairies* 1977 SC 223, followed in *Gordon District Council* 1988 SLT 481. But in practice a date of entry is almost invariably specified. Failing express provision, the 1874 Act s. 28 applies; or possibly immediate entry would be implied.

Does 'entry' imply 'vacant possession'? Walker states that the seller must give actual possession of the subjects, unless this is excluded by the contract, citing *Heys* (1890) 17 R 381. Admittedly, in that case, 'immediate entry' was so construed; but from the outset, actual possession had been a known and accepted requirement of the purchasers. Elsewhere, he states that 'a title tendered is good notwithstanding ... leases usual in such a property'. Burns' *Practice* at p. 343 suggests that leases are unexceptionable failing express provision. Both refer to *Lothian & Border Farmers* 1952 SLT 450 as authority (lease not a breach of warrandice). Certainly, express provision in the contract for actual occupation is desirable, if not necessary. For a commentary on the terms 'vacant possession' and 'actual occupation' and their implication when used in missives, see *Stuart* 1976 SLT (Notes) 39. In *Sinclair-MacDonald* 1987 GWD 7–232 warrandice was held not to warrant vacant possession. In the article referred to below on marketable title at p. 164, however, Professor K. G. C. Reid takes the view that a purchaser is entitled to resile if he finds that the property is let, even although there may be no express provision in the contract as to vacant possession. He refers to his article in the *Scots Conveyancing Miscellany* where the point is further discussed.

If the property is being purchased subject to tenant's rights, it is normal so to stipulate, and to make further provision – see below.

For an article, comparing date of entry and date of settlement, see 1988 JLS 431 and compare *Speevak* 1949 SLT (Notes) 39.

**28.42 (4) Title**. The contractual position as to title, whether by express provision or by implication at common law, differs depending on whether or not the subjects of sale lie in an operational area for registration of title; and, if in an operational area, whether or not the title has actually been registered. As a result, different provision as to title is made in the missives depending on which of the three possibilities applies. These are dealt with separately in the following paragraphs, which deal with the traditional view of marketable title. Attention is drawn, however, to some important recent statutory developments referred to below under para. 28.51, which deals with planning and other statutory matters generally; but particularly, in this context, with the recent Construction (Design and Management) Regulations 1994 and the statutory provisions for environmental control. Likewise, the recent innovation of coal-mining searches is referred to in Chapter 9 in the context of mineral reservations.

In the ordinary case, missives will make specific provision where appropriate to protect the purchaser against unexpected or undisclosed adverse matter in these and other comparable circumstances. Whether or not, in the absence of specific protective provision for that purpose, a title might be treated as unmarketable by implication where any of the requirements under statutory provisions of this kind are not complied with is a point which has not been decided. That being so, the only safe assumption is that express provision is necessary. The general catch-all clause referred to above should normally suffice, although some standard clauses may not be wide enough in their terms to cover the most recent statutory requirements.

**28.43 (i) Sasines titles in non-operational areas.** It is implied in any contract of sale and purchase of property held on a Sasines title in a non-operational area that the seller will deliver a valid disposition in favour of the purchaser, and will deliver or exhibit a valid marketable title and clear searches. This implied obligation is normally the subject of express provision in the contract of sale and purchase, usually with a further provision specifying the period of search. See generally an article in 1988 JLS 162. The question of 'clear' searches is also dealt with in Chapter 33.

By far the most important question arising under this express or implied obligation on the seller is as to marketable title. A marketable title means a title so clear as to protect the purchaser, not only from actual eviction, but also from the risk of any reasonable challenge; a title which is so regular in form and so correct in all particulars that no one, later dealing with the purchaser on sale or for security, will take any exception to it on any ground. The points summarised under this head are dealt with in an article on 'Marketable Title' by Professor K. G. C. Reid in 1988 JLS 162.

This obligation may, of course, be varied by express provision in the contract, of a general or a particular nature. See below for examples. In the absence of any such provision, the rule carries the following implications:

(a) *Exclusive and absolute right of property.* A feudal title satisfies this requirement; but not a leasehold title, even for a term of 999 years. See *McConnell* (1903) 10 SLT 790.

(b) *Title to whole and identical property.* It will not suffice to tender a title to practically the whole of the property; and the title tendered must cover the identical property referred to in the missives. On this, the purchaser is absolutely entitled to insist, and his motives are irrelevant. The best illustration is in the case of minerals. In the ordinary way, a conveyance of, or contract to purchase, an area of ground, carries by implication sub-adjacent minerals. But, of course, if minerals have already been severed from the surface, before a sale, the seller's title to the surface does not carry them. In that event, in the absence of special provision in the missives, the title is not marketable and the purchaser is not bound to accept it; and this applies even to urban properties where minerals are not being worked. This long-standing rule was reaffirmed in *Campbell* 1963 SC 505. Lord President Clyde: 'In such circumstances, in my opinion, the purchaser is not obliged to take something less than he purported to buy and is entitled to withdraw his offer, as he did.'

(c) *Burdens and conditions.* The purchaser is entitled to the property freed from all burdens and incumbrances affecting the subjects; but subject to this qualification that he must accept a reasonable feuduty (provided that it is allocated). But, of course, since 1 September 1974, if the feuduty is allocated, it is automatically redeemed on sale and the question does not arise. If the feuduty is unallocated, the title is not marketable and the purchaser cannot be compelled to accept it. This rule has become somewhat unrealistic in view of the provision in the 1970 Act allowing for unilateral allocation by the vassal but, nonetheless, can still cause problems. The purchaser must also, it is thought, accept normal and reasonable conditions of tenure. But much will depend on circumstances. Thus, in the purchase of a vacant lot of ground, an absolute prohibition in the title against building would render it unmarketable. See *Louttit's Trustees* (1892) 19 R 791 and *Urquhart* (1835) 13 S 844.

In *Smith* (1895) 23 R 60, a foreign purchaser, acting without legal advice, was held entitled to resile from a contract to purchase a two-storeyed cottage, when he discovered that the titles contained the typical restriction limiting the use of the land to the building of one house only, but also requiring the proprietor thereof not to open up windows in the rear of the house and to leave part of the ground unbuilt on. 'But it can hardly be the law that the purchaser of a house is entitled to resile because the title contains a provision that it shall be used as a private dwellinghouse only': Burns' *Practice*, p. 211.

Similarly, in the purchase of a shop, a prohibition against sale of liquor may render the title unmarketable – at least so says Burns' *Practice*, p. 211, referring to *McConnell* (1903) 10 SLT 790; but in that case, the purchaser explicitly stated his intention to apply for a licence, and the seller stipulated for a further payment on his obtaining it.

In *Umar* 1983 SLT (Sh Ct) 79, following on the sale of a shop, the purchasers discovered, on examining the title, that there was a prohibition against the sale of alcohol on the premises. They objected to the title on that ground. The sheriff, quoting from *McConnell*, and following Lord Keith in *Armia Ltd.* 1979 SLT 147, held that the seller was bound to disclose all restrictions which might materially diminish the value of the property, except where the purchaser knew or must be deemed to have known of the restrictions. This decision has been severely criticised: see the article in 1988 JLS at p. 163.

Servitudes affecting the subjects of sale are a narrower case; and it may depend, to some extent, on how burdensome the servitude is. See, typically, *Welsh* (1894) 21 R 769, where the indications are that a purchaser can object to any adverse servitude right, if it detracts from the value of the subjects and if he was not aware of it when making his offer. See also *Armia Ltd.*, where a servitude right of access, 10 feet wide, across the property rendered the title unmarketable.

In *Morris* 1991 GWD 12–712 and 1992 GWD 33–1950, following on a contract of sale and purchase in which no reference was made to a proposed right of access across the subjects of sale, the seller tried to introduce such a right into the disposition in favour of the purchaser who objected thereto, and sought to resile. Lord Clyde held that the objection was properly taken, in that the seller was obliged to disclose any burdens, existing or proposed; and that the purchaser was entitled to rely on the missives and his examination of the titles. On a subsequent proof as to the materiality of the proposed servitude, Lord Kirkwood held that the test to be applied was whether it materially diminished the market value of the subjects, and on the facts held that the purchaser was entitled to resile. In assessing value, it was legitimate to take into account the purchaser's intention to develop the subjects.

This point should, of course, have been specifically provided for in the missives, for which see below.

**28.44 Variation of the obligation as to marketable title.** There are two ways in which this general rule, whether arising by implication or by express provision in a contract, may be varied or qualified, either by the seller or the purchaser.

**28.45** (*a*) *Express modification in the contract.* This is commonplace and may take various forms. For a more detailed discussion on the implied obligation and express modification thereof, see 1988 JLS 162, referred to *supra*.

(i) Express partial qualification on a particular point, *e.g.* that the feu-duty is unallocated; or that minerals are excluded; or are included in the sale, only in so far as the seller has right and title thereto.

(ii) A more general qualification, *e.g.* that the property is sold subject to the burdens and conditions in the title deeds. This throws the onus on the purchaser to examine the title for himself and to satisfy himself as to the nature, extent and effect of the burdens therein contained. But it does not protect the seller against adverse rights not disclosed on examination of the title, *e.g.* a positive servitude constituted by prescription or by an undisclosed and unrecorded agreement.

(iii) A general provision that the purchaser must take the title as it stands; commonly called the *tantum et tale* clause. Such a clause is standard in articles of roup, but may be used in missives, although less commonly. It may or may not be coupled with a clause to the effect that the purchaser has satisfied himself as to the identity, extent and particulars generally and to the burdens and conditions affecting the property in the hands of the seller. The language varies. In its ordinary form, it is implied that the beneficial right of property in the subjects of sale (or at least a substantial portion of them) is vested in the seller; but that any curable defect in the title must be put right at the expense of the purchaser, and that the purchaser must suffer any burdens on the property. If, however, the title proves to be incurably bad, or if the seller is unable to show that he has the substantial beneficial right, the purchaser is entitled to resile. 'But, under some present day contracts, the conditions are wide enough and strict enough to compel the purchaser to proceed, even in the second case.' Burns' *Handbook* p. 180. This proposition is, at best, doubtful, on equitable grounds.

For a typical clause, see Burns' *Practice* p. 192.

Whatever form the clause may take, a purchaser cannot be barred from objecting to defective stamp duty; Stamp Act 1891 s. 117.

**28.46** (*b*) *Personal bar.* The purchaser may have private knowledge, when making the offer, of a subsisting adverse right. If so, and even if there is no reference to this in the contract, the purchaser is not entitled to require of the seller, when the bargain has been closed, something which the purchaser knew, *ab initio*, that the seller could not give him. See *Mossend Theatre Co.* 1930 SC 90, where a purchaser, discovering that minerals were not included in the sale, although this was not referred to in the contract, was held entitled to resile. The main ground of argument between the parties was as to whether the purchaser knew, or could be presumed from circumstances to have known, that minerals were excluded from the sale, because in the district all minerals generally were reserved to the superiors in all previous titles. In this case, the facts and circumstances were not sufficient to impute knowledge to the purchaser. But it is implicit in the decision that, had he known in fact of the mineral reservation, he could not later have taken advantage of that fact after completion of the bargain, but would have been personally barred from resiling.

In *Morris, supra*, the purchaser's right to object to a proposed burden not provided for in the missives was challenged on the footing that the purchaser already knew that the seller was under obligation to impose a servitude right of access in the purchaser's title; but, in allowing proof before answer, Lord Clyde excluded the seller's averments on this point, presumably being satisfied that the purchaser had no such knowledge and was not therefore personally barred from raising this objection. The point was not further pursued at the proof in 1992.

For a case involving a complex series of successive transmissions, see *MacDougall* 1994 SLT 1178. The significant point of that decision is that a purchaser was put on his enquiry by the plain terms of the titles and failed to discharge his obligation to enquire, thereby denying himself the protection afforded to a *bona fide* purchaser for value without notice.

**28.47 (ii) Property in an operational area where the title is not yet registered, but the transaction will induce first registration.** The position as to title is substantially the same in this situation as in the case of a Sasines transaction dealt with in the preceding paragraphs. But there is one significant point of difference. Not only must the purchaser's solicitor be satisfied as to the validity of the seller's title but, in addition, he must satisfy the Keeper thereon when applying for registration of the purchaser's title. He must therefore make appropriate provisions in the missives and in the settlement obligation to ensure that the Keeper will not take exception to the title; and, in particular, that he will not seek to qualify his indemnity.

In the result, in lieu of the title clause normally incorporated in the missives in a Sasines transaction and illustrated in the offer included in the titles in the Appendix, the title clause in a transaction of this type will require the seller to deliver a valid disposition and a valid marketable title; and, in addition, the seller will be taken bound to produce such documents and evidence, including a plan, as the Keeper may require to enable him to issue a land certificate containing no exclusion of indemnity and disclosing no entry, deed or diligence prejudicial to the interests of the purchaser other than those for which the purchaser himself is responsible, *e.g.* a standard security granted by the purchaser to finance the purchase. See R.T.P.B. G.2.08.

There are also different provisions as to searches; but this point is dealt with in detail in Chapter 33.

**28.48 (iii) Property already registered.** The sale of property held on a registered title is technically referred to as a dealing. The same general rules apply to a contract for sale and purchase of property on a dealing; but there is of course this significant difference that the seller's title is now represented by a land certificate which, within itself, contains all the information on title including in particular the identification of the property, the ownership thereof, securities affecting the same other than floating charges, and burdens; and all of this information is guaranteed. The title is, nonetheless, subject to overriding interests, some of which may materially affect the interest of the purchaser.

Bearing these differences in mind, the seller, in the title clause, will be taken bound to deliver a duly executed disposition in favour of the purchaser and to exhibit or deliver to the purchaser the land certificate containing no exclusion of indemnity; any necessary links in title between the registered proprietor and the seller; and such documents and evidence as the Keeper may require to enable the interest of the purchaser to be registered in place of the seller, again without exclusion of indemnity. As on first registration, it should also be provided expressly that the land certificate to be issued to the purchaser will disclose no entry, deed or diligence prejudicial to the purchaser's interest except such adverse interests as may have been created by the purchaser himself. See R.T.P.B. G.3.05.

As in the case of first registration, so also on a dealing, the title clause will also make different provisions in relation to searches. Again, these are dealt with in Chapter 33.

The sale and purchase of heritable property in operational areas, both in the case where the transaction induces first registration and in the case of a dealing, is dealt with in detail in Chapters 15 and 16 respectively in the *Registration of Title Manual*.

**28.49 (6) Servitudes and wayleaves serving the property**.   In urban property, mains services normally enter the subjects of sale directly from the public road, which requires no special provision. But occasionally, as in *More* 1967 SLT (Sh Ct) 38, services pass through adjoining property. If so, it is important that any such services are adequately supported by servitude rights, and express provision may be necessary. See *Murray* 1973 SLT (Sh Ct) 75. A mains water supply to the part of the property retained by the seller, and passing through the part sold, did not justify a servitude of necessity. So the purchaser was free to remove the pipe and the seller lost his mains water. Without appropriate provision in the contract, a purchaser of the remaining property from the seller might have found himself without mains water and without redress against the seller.

In the case of registered titles, all servitude rights serving the registered property will appear in the property section of the land certificate; but remember that, while the Keeper guarantees that rights so entered were originally duly constituted, he does not guarantee that they still remain enforceable.

In cases where a servitude was constituted by an unrecorded agreement or by mere prescriptive possession, it may by inadvertence have failed to enter the title sheet on first registration. If the registered proprietor can satisfy the Keeper that any such servitude right has been duly constituted, then the Keeper has power to rectify the title sheets both of the dominant and servient tenements to give effect to the omitted right.

For a cautionary case, see *Watson* 1995 GWD 13–750 where a purchaser claimed damages from his solicitor for failing to warn him of the existence over part of the subjects of purchase of servitude rights of access and wayleaves for electricity and pylons which the purchaser maintained had diminished the value and the development potential of the property.

**28.50 (7) Feuduty and other liabilities**. A reasonable feuduty does not render the title unmarketable. Probably, the same would apply to stipend and standard charge. But again, since 1 September 1974, where feuduties, etc., are allocated, they are automatically redeemed and do not affect the purchaser. Unallocated burdens must be disclosed to render the title marketable.

Apart from these, the occupier of heritage (except dwellinghouses after 31 March 1989) is subject to occupier's rates and in appropriate cases there may also be various other liabilities, not of their nature rendering the title unmarketable. These include, in the case of frontagers within a burgh, liability for the cost of making up and maintaining roads and foot pavements under statutory provision; in the case of tenement property, a proportionate share of the cost of maintaining the roof, main walls and other common items in the tenement; and, in certain cases, a service charge for maintaining common access and parking areas and the like.

The making-up of roads and foot pavements presents particular difficulties. In new residential and other developments, completion certificates for buildings are not withheld by the local authority pending completion of roads and certain other works, *e.g.* boundary walls. The buildings are usually completed, and completion certificates therefore issued, some time before the roads and foot pavements have been made up. Normally, the developer will have undertaken to make up the roads in terms of the building contract. Having so undertaken, the developer then sells and dispones the houses, receives the price, and then fails to make up the road and/or becomes bankrupt, leaving individual frontagers directly liable for the cost of making-up, when the local authority issues the relevant statutory notice. So, in the result, the purchasers of individual dwellinghouses in effect pay for the road twice. Under the Roads (Scotland) Act 1984 s. 17 the local authority have power to require private developers to provide security, usually in the form of a road bond, to ensure that the roads and foot pavements will be duly completed by the developer. It is important, however, to insist on this in the contract of sale and purchase and to check, on examination of title, that a road bond has in fact been lodged with the local authority under that section. See further Chapter 19.65.

It is usual, but of course not essential, to specify the exact amount of feuduty payable, if not redeemable; to provide that, apart from the stated feuduty, there are no other charges, annual or otherwise; and to make express provision that the road and foot pavement have been made up and are taken over. If this is done, all these matters become, by express provision, conditions in the contract, and any discrepancy between the contractual and the actual liability entitles the purchaser to resile.

It is also normal (although probably unnecessary, at least in urban properties) to provide expressly in the contract for the apportionment, between seller and purchaser, of feuduty and other outgoings at the date of entry.

**28.51 (8) Planning and other statutory matters.** Heritable property may be adversely affected, in a variety of ways, under the Town and Country Planning Acts, Housing Acts, Public Health Acts, and various other Acts dealing with or restraining statutory nuisances. See Chapter 19. None of these things affects the title, as such, and the existence of any of them does not, therefore, render a title unmarketable. Further, except in the case of marketability of title, where certain obligations are implied, a contract of sale and purchase of heritage is not a contract *uberrimae fidei*; and there is no obligation on the seller to disclose any such adverse matter to the purchaser, except under express provision in the contract. Thus, if an offer is made without reference to such statutory matter, the purchaser may later find, after the bargain is closed, that the property is adversely affected by some statutory control.

The maxim *caveat emptor* applies; he is bound to proceed, even although he knew nothing of the existence of any of these matters.

Special clauses may be necessary in special circumstances. A general catch-all clause is generally incorporated to protect the purchaser against most known forms of adverse statutory matter.

In *Hawke* 1995 SCLR 1004 the contract contained a typical catch-all clause relating to building warrants and the like. On conclusion of the bargain, the sellers then found themselves unable to produce a completion certificate which, as was later discovered, had never in fact been obtained. They tendered, instead, a letter of comfort from the local authority. The purchasers were held entitled to resile, on the footing that a letter of comfort was not sufficient compliance with the terms of this clause. See, for illustration, clause 12 of the offer in Appendix A.

In the case of new buildings, dealt with below, and, equally importantly, in the case of existing buildings where there have been additions, improvements or alterations, planning permission will usually be required as well as a building warrant under the Building (Scotland) Acts 1959 and 1970. In addition, where a building warrant has been issued, a completion certificate is required to certify that the work has been carried out in accordance with the warrant. Again, a general catch-all clause is now usually included in an offer to ensure that the purchaser is not adversely affected by some undisclosed matter of this kind. See 1989 JLS 206.

For another cautionary case on the terms of missives, see *Hood* 1995 SLT 98 where the offer contained the normal catch-all clause to the effect that the seller had no knowledge of any intended applications or other notices, etc., and requiring a certificate from the local authority to that effect. The seller modified that clause to the effect that 'the usual local authority letter will be exhibited prior to the date of entry'. If that letter disclosed any matter materially prejudicial to the purchaser's full enjoyment of the subjects as a dwellinghouse, the purchaser would be entitled to resile. A letter from the local authority in normal terms was duly delivered. Subsequently, it emerged that the Regional Council had previously applied for planning permission to construct a road which would directly affect the subjects of purchase of which the seller was aware. The purchaser sought damages from the seller on the grounds of fraudulent or negligent misrepresentation. His claim failed on the footing that, while the clause in the offer, if unqualified, might have sufficed to support a claim for damages, the qualification of that clause limited the liability of the seller to delivery of 'the usual letter' from the local authority and nothing more. That was held to exclude any question of misrepresentation. While this may seem harsh, it underlines the need for extreme caution in framing protective clauses in the purchaser's offer and in accepting qualifications thereof in the seller's acceptance.

Any such development may also have required the prior consent of the superior or neighbouring proprietors; and it is as well to provide for this expressly in the offer although probably this risk is covered by the marketable title provision, whether express or implied.

Environmental protection and the possibility of contamination of land (past and future) by environmentally unfriendly uses is assuming increasing importance to potential purchasers. See the Planning (Hazardous Substances) (Scotland) Act 1997. A new register is to be set up by every planning authority containing information on hazardous substances (s. 27), and under s. 26 the Secretary of State is given wide powers of control.

Where the purchaser proposes to develop, he must include appropriate clauses in his offer, making it conditional upon the obtaining of planning permission and the necessary consents. The case of *Khazaka, supra*, underlines the risks. Again, extreme care is required in the drafting of these clauses, as that case shows. Depending on circumstances and location, further enquiries may be necessary. The question of contaminated land is dealt with in more detail in Chapter 19.71, to which the reader is referred. For subsidence risks, see Chapter 9.4 above. See also recent references, statutes and articles listed in the preliminary section of this Manual.

The reader's attention is also drawn to the Construction (Design and Management) Regulations 1994 and to the articles thereon in *Greens Property Bulletin*, issues 20 and 21: see the Reading List. As the authors of these two articles observe, the regulations will require, in some cases, a change of attitude to health and safety issues on the part of those undertaking projects involving construction work; and this in turn may require special provision in the missives.

**28.52 (9) Structure and passing of the risk.** The question of surveys has already been dealt with, in para. 28.18. The offer may be made subject to the obtaining of a survey report in terms satisfactory to the purchaser but this is not normally acceptable to the seller.

In addition and separately, the purchaser, in his offer, now commonly makes a number of provisions to protect himself against unexpected or undisclosed matters. Such provisions vary widely from one solicitor's office to another; and from one offer to another, but may include:

(*a*) a provision that, so far as the seller is aware, the subjects are not affected by any structural defect, including wet or dry rot, rising damp or woodworm;

(*b*) a provision that, if there has been any specialist treatment to the building, *e.g.* for woodworm or dry rot, and if this is supported by guarantees, that the guarantees with all relevant particulars will be delivered, and the rights thereunder assigned, to the purchaser, and that the guarantees are still valid;

(*c*) a provision that all services, including drainage, plumbing, gas and electric supply, and the central heating system will be in good working order at the date of entry;

(*d*) a provision that the seller will be responsible for maintaining the property in good condition and repair until the date of entry, with a right to the purchaser to resile if the subjects are seriously damaged in the interval. For an illustration of resulting difficulties, see *Fallis* 1987 GWD 13–466.

(*e*) a provision as to passing of the risk. 'The risk passes with the making of the contract, though the seller remains liable for fault till delivery of possession': Green's *Encyclopaedia* following the Latin brocard *periculum rei venditae nondum traditae est emptoris*. See *Sloan's Dairies Ltd*. The purchaser acquires a *jus ad rem specificam* at the date of completion of the contract; his right of action is an action for delivery, or *ad factum praestandum*, and so the risk of damage passes from seller to purchaser at the date of the contract. The purchaser should therefore insure the subjects of sale immediately on the completion of the bargain. Alternatively, the purchaser may require his interest to be endorsed on the seller's insurance policy as 'purchaser, price unpaid', but this is not always satisfactory.

Notwithstanding this common law rule, however, it is also implied at common law that the seller is personally liable for any damage caused by him to the subjects prior to the date of entry; and he must take reasonable precautions against any such damage occurring. Although not directly in point, see *Bosal Scotland Ltd.* 1988 GWD 30–1275 and *Meehan* 1972 SLT (Sh Ct) 70. The Scottish Law Commission, in its Report on 'Passing of Risk' (No. 127, 1990) makes various recommendations for the alteration of the common law rules. First, they recommend that, if property is destroyed or substantially damaged, the contract should be regarded as frustrated. Secondly, if property is damaged but not substantially, the contract should continue in force but the seller should be under obligation to repair the damage and pass the subjects over to the purchaser in the same condition in which they were when the contract was concluded. Failure by the seller would allow the purchaser certain remedies. Finally, the Commission recommend that parties should be free to contract out of the suggested new rules. See the article in 1990 SLT (News) 308.

The case of *Hall* 1993 GWD 23–1457 underlines the serious risks arising from the foregoing rules. Following on a contract of sale and purchase of a dwellinghouse and before the date of entry, the house was flooded. The missives contained a precautionary clause to the effect that the dwellinghouse would remain in substantially the same condition as it was at the date of conclusion of the contract. Following the flood, the seller undertook remedial work which was completed by the date of entry but the purchaser then maintained that the house was, nonetheless, no longer in the same condition in terms of the missives, and purportedly resiled. Lord Marnoch held that the provision in the missives was ambiguous but that the ambiguity could be resolved by reference to subsequent correspondence between the parties and on that footing found in favour of the seller. Otherwise, on the missives alone, he would have found for the purchaser.

**28.53 (10) Contract to remain in full force and effect**. The rule in *Lee*, affirmed in *Winston*, has already been referred to. Following on *Winston*, there have been several articles in the journals and a substantial number of reported cases as a result of which some confusion prevails as noted below.

The best recent article is in 1988 JLS 102, with some comments on the position in a subsequent article in 1988 JLS 285 on the *actio quanti minoris*.

The report of the Scottish Law Commission on 'Three Bad Rules of Contract Law' has already been referred to, and the draft Bill is now enacted in the Contract (Scotland) Act 1997, taking effect on 21 June 1997. Problems which currently arise out of the rules which require contractual provision for non-supersession and for the application of the *actio quanti minoris* will thereafter cease to have any significance. Until 21 June, the law remains as already stated on these matters and, accordingly, a non-supersession clause and an *actio quanti minoris* clause will still be standard clauses in missives concluded before that date.

To keep the missives alive, it has become standard practice to incorporate in an offer an express provision, commonly termed a non-supersession clause, to the effect that, notwithstanding delivery of the disposition, the contract will remain in full force and effect, possibly for a limited period of time after the date of entry or possibly without limit.

In practice, in many cases, it does not significantly matter to the purchaser or to the seller whether the missives remain operative after delivery of the disposition or not because, during the period between completion of the missives and the date of entry, the purchaser's agents will have satisfied themselves that all the conditions of the contract have been or will be duly implemented.

In recent years, however, purchasers have become more impatient to obtain entry within a shorter period from conclusion of the bargain; and the making of the necessary enquiries, and in particular, answers to the property enquiry letters from local authorities are taking longer to obtain. In the result, it is often not within the power of the purchaser's solicitor to complete all the necessary enquiries by the date when the purchaser wishes to take possession. But, from the point of view of the purchaser, it is critically important that the undertakings given by the seller on such matters as planning, roads, etc., should remain enforceable, notwithstanding the taking of entry and delivery of the disposition. Hence the need for the non-supersession clause.

The introduction of non-supersession clauses, however, did not solve all the problems and has, in turn, raised further questions.

Since the Contract (Scotland) Act became law with effect from 21 June 1997, the cases which have occurred since the previous edition of the Manual are noted in the Digest of Cases but are only briefly dealt with here; some of them have already been mentioned above.

The most recent is *Glazick* 1996 SCLR 270. That case was unusual in that the disposition itself in its terms incorporated the antecedent contract by specific reference so that the contract entire formed part of the final ruling document. This allowed all the clauses in the missives to be founded on within the time limit of two years prescribed. In the course of considering the problem, however, the Sheriff Principal made a survey of the relevant cases – 16 in number – and the report is a useful source of reference to cases falling under this head.

A further case merits mention. In *Callander* 1996 SCLR 955 missives entered into in 1978 provided that the purchasers would permit the owners and occupiers of the adjoining land suitable access over the subjects of purchase along a route to be determined at the purchasers' discretion. The

County Council resisted on three grounds: (1) that the provision in the missives for access was not a positive agreement, but a vague and indefinite promise, not sufficiently precise to be enforceable; (2) that even if it was enforceable, the obligation was superseded by subsequent delivery of the disposition which made no reference whatsoever to the question of access; and (3) in any event the obligation in the missives was purely personal to the original purchaser. These arguments were rejected. In particular, Lord Osborne held that a provision for access was a collateral obligation and was therefore not superseded by delivery of the disposition.

**28.54 Import of clause.**   Before 21 June 1997, was it sufficient to incorporate a non-supersession clause in the formal contract without going further; or did that clause have to be repeated either in the disposition itself, as being the document which implements the contract, or in a separate collateral contract or obligation delivered at settlement? As early as 1981, in an article in 1981 JLS 414, Professor K. G. C. Reid suggested that a non-supersession clause, standing alone, was ineffective and, in order to bind the parties after settlement, the clause would have to be incorporated in the disposition; and he suggested a suitable form of clause for that purpose. That has turned out to be wise advice which, nonetheless, seems to have been largely ignored by the profession until the decision in *Finlayson* 1987 SLT (Sh Ct) 150. Since that decision, it has become more or less standard practice to incorporate a non-supersession clause in the disposition itself in order to carry forward and keep alive the obligations of both seller and purchaser in the antecedent missives. In the interim between the decision in *Winston* and the time of writing, there have been several reported cases in which the decision in *Winston* is referred to. In some of these, a non-supersession clause in the missives was not repeated in the disposition, but was held nonetheless to be effective in keeping the missives open; in others, the opposite result was arrived at. See the Digest of Cases 28.53.

**28.55 Repeating the clause in the disposition.**   On balance, the view of the courts would now seem to be that it is not necessary to repeat the non-supersession clause in the disposition; provided the clause appears in the missives, that will suffice. The position still remains uncertain and there seems to be no good reason why the non-supersession clause should not be repeated in the disposition. The Conveyancing Committee of the Law Society, in 1988, recommended that the matter be dealt with by a separate letter granted at settlement and delivered immediately after delivery of the disposition. They have provided suitable styles of letter. After 21 June 1997 the non-supersession clause and the exclusion of the *actio quanti minoris* will cease to be significant. In the meantime, however, the recommendation in this sub-head should be followed to avoid any possible argument that, by omitting the non-supersession clause in the disposition, the missives cease to have effect on delivery thereof.

**28.56 Time-limits.**   Some non-supersession clauses impose no time-limit. Others impose time-limits varying from 28 days to two or three years, depending on the whim of the conveyancer involved. In most cases, the time-limit applies by express provision to the whole missives; but in some cases it applies to certain clauses but no time-limit is prescribed for others. Probably, a period of two years covering all clauses generally is reasonable but there has been some debate as to the appropriate length of period; and of course there may well be special circumstances where a longer period is clearly required. This in turn produces a further problem. If the non-supersession clause provides (as it often does) that, notwithstanding delivery of the disposition, the missives will remain in full force and effect for a period of two years from the date of entry, does this mean that, on the expiry of the two-year period, the missives fall absolutely; or is it sufficient in such cases if a claim is intimated, or if an action is raised, within the period, even although the claim is not determined until after the two-year period has expired? Again, this is a point which can be made clear by suitable drafting of the non-supersession clause. The weight of authority at present seems to lean towards the view that, in the absence of express contrary provision, an action raised within the time-limit specified in the non-supersession clause will be sufficient to keep the contract alive thereafter until the claim is disposed of. See *Fetherston* 1988 SLT (Sh Ct) 16. The point is discussed at some length in an article in 1986 JLS 363, but that, of course, preceded more recent decisions, and in particular *Fetherston*.

In *Robson* 1990 GWD 2–92, in special circumstances, a six-month time-limit was held to be inapplicable.

Note that, since collateral obligations do not require a non-supersession clause to remain enforceable, they may not be covered by a time-limit which applies to other obligations which remain enforceable only by virtue of such a clause. Care must therefore be taken in wording the time-limit.

In *University of Strathclyde (Properties) Ltd.* 1992 GWD 14–822 the sheriff held that there was no difficulty in principle in providing for an agreed modification to the ordinary law of limitation or prescription which would otherwise apply.

Such time-limits are normally enforceable according to their terms: see *Pena* 1987 SLT 609. In *Spowart* 1995 GWD 28–1257 there was a contract of sale and purchase in terms of which, subject to certain conditions, the purchaser was bound to pay a further sum over and above the original price in certain events. The missives contained a non-supersession clause under which the missives, including this provision for the additional payment, were to remain in full force and effect for two years. The two year period expired and, so far as the missives were concerned, the obligations therein ceased to be enforceable. In this case, however, contrary to the usual situation, the purchaser also granted a standard security in favour of the seller to cover the additional sum so payable. In that situation, he argued that, since the two-year time-limit had expired, no additional payments fell due; but that argument was rejected and the purchaser was held liable for the additional payment because it was separately undertaken and secured by the granting of a standard security in favour of the seller for that specific purpose.

Finally, as to duration of a non-supersession clause, the standard practice now is to incorporate a time-limit beyond which the non-supersession will cease to operate. In *Ferguson* 1993 SLT 1269 it was argued that, by virtue of the terms of the Prescription and Limitation (Scotland) Act 1973, any attempt to modify the time-limits specified in that Act was ineffective, looking to the terms of s. 13. The argument was rejected and the contractual time-limit *held* valid. See *Pena*.

**28.57 Form of clause**. In an article in 1986 JLS 316, Professor K. G. C. Reid suggested the following clause:

> 'This offer and the missives following hereon will form a continuing and enforceable contract notwithstanding the delivery of the disposition except in so far as fully implemented thereby, but the missives shall cease to be enforceable after a period of two years from the date of entry except in so far as they are founded on in any court proceedings which have commenced within the said period. A clause to this effect may be included in the disposition at the purchaser's option.'

Since that clause was suggested in 1986, and as a result of subsequent decisions, insertion of the clause in the disposition has become fairly standard practice. A modified version appears in the article by the same author in 1988 JLS 7.

The wording of the non-supersession clause is a matter of adjustment and negotiation between seller and purchaser and may take a variety of forms. Some variations on the form are discussed by D. J. Cusine in 1986 JLS 16. As he there points out, one of the most significant points of difference between the various versions of this clause is the inclusion or omission of the phrase in the clause suggested above to the effect that the missives continue in force except in so far as implemented by the disposition. If that phrase is included, then it would seem that delivery of the disposition closes off any subsequent argument as to matters properly implemented by and dealt with in that disposition, *e.g.* boundaries, burdens, etc. If the phrase is not included, then the whole missives remain open; and this in turn may allow a subsequent argument on matters of title, even after delivery of the disposition.

The land certificate will not disclose whether or not the disposition on which the registration proceeded contained a non-supersession clause; but that does not, of course, prevent the disponee from founding on that clause, using the disposition itself as the basis of his claim in appropriate cases.

The reference to the date of entry in the clause suggested above can also cause problems. See an article in 1988 JLS 431 discussing the distinction between date of entry and date of settlement. To avoid argument, it may be preferable in the suggested non-supersession clause to stipulate a more exact date, *e.g.* the date of conclusion of the missives.

**28.58 The limits of *Winston* v. *Patrick*.** As already noticed above, the decision in *Winston* simply reaffirms the rule established in the House of Lords in *Lee* that a disposition, when delivered, supersedes the antecedent missives in total; and thereafter it becomes the sole measure of the rights and liabilities of the contracting parties.

The clause in *Winston*, which the pursuer sought to enforce after delivery of his disposition, was in the form of a simple warranty to the effect that all statutory and local authority requirements in connection with the erection of a building had been fulfilled as at the date of the missives. It contained no positive obligation on the seller to take any action to put matters right if the warranty was not fully implemented; there was no non-supersession and no *actio quanti minoris* clause in the missives; and the warranty was not repeated in the disposition. In these circumstances, not surprisingly, the court held that the warranty could not survive delivery of the disposition and therefore, although it turned out not to have been implemented, there was no liability on the seller after delivery either to take any action to put matters right or in damages.

In the course of his judgment, however, Lord Wheatley referred to three examples of exceptions to the rule in *Lee*:

(*a*) Obligations in the missives relating to moveables.

(*b*) Collateral obligations in the missives which, of their nature, were distinct from the primary obligation in the missives to convey the subjects to the purchaser.

(*c*) An agreement between the parties in writing, whether in the missives or in the disposition or in a separate back letter, that personal obligations undertaken by the seller in the missives would subsist notwithstanding delivery.

**28.59 The implications of *Porch* on the non-supersession clause.** The decision of Lord Milligan in *Porch* 1992 SLT 661 deals with the decision in *Winston* and comments on the three examples mentioned by Lord Wheatley as exceptions to the rule in *Lee*. He reviews most of the decisions which followed on *Winston* to the date of that report. The facts in *Porch* are not dissimilar to *Winston* in that, in *Porch*, it was a term of the missives that all necessary consents had been obtained and complied with for any work undertaken on the subjects, which is in effect the import of the clause in *Winston*. But in *Porch* the clause also contained a supplementary obligation binding the seller to produce satisfactory evidence prior to settlement that the consents and warrants had been obtained. In addition, and in contrast to *Winston*, the missives in *Porch* did contain a full non-supersession clause although admittedly it was not carried forward into the disposition. Apparently, Lord Milligan did not regard that fact as significant and so presumably was prepared to accept that a clause in the missives, not repeated in the disposition, was nonetheless effective in so far as such clauses can be effective in the light of this decision. However, in the course of his decision, Lord Milligan makes two points of significance in relation to the exceptions in *Winston*:

(1) that the three examples given by Lord Wheatley in his judgment in *Winston* and quoted above are exhaustive of the exceptions to the rule in *Lee*; and that there are no other exceptions whatsoever;

(2) that the supplementary obligation binding the seller to produce evidence that the warrants and consents had been obtained, which was included in the missives clause in *Porch* but not in *Winston*, was a personal and collateral obligation (not 'collateral' in the sense of exception (*b*) in *Winston*) ancillary to the warranty, and as such was not sufficient to bring it within Lord Wheatley's example (*c*) of an agreement in writing that a personal obligation by the seller in the missives would subsist after delivery of the disposition.

This decision has been followed in subsequent cases. So, for example, in *University of Strathclyde (Properties) Ltd.* there was a non-supersession clause with a time-limit of 18 months which was held to be valid; and, as a result, since the action of damages was not raised within that time-limit, it was dismissed.

In the result, the position prior to 21 June 1997 seems to be that, of the three exceptions in *Winston*, exceptions (*a*) moveables, and (*b*) collateral obligations will survive delivery of the disposition *proprio vigore* and require no non-supersession clause to keep them alive. A pure warranty as to the position at the date of the missives, standing alone, cannot come within exception (*c*) as an agreement in writing; and it cannot be brought within exception (*c*) under a non-supersession clause, in the missives or in the disposition, by adjecting thereto an obligation, as in *Porch*, which is merely ancillary to the warranty. So, the obligation in *Porch* to produce evidence that the warranty had been duly implemented did not fall within exception (*c*).

The result of the decisions in *Porch*, and in the earlier cases therein referred to, seems to be to extend significantly the type of obligation in missives which will be treated as collateral and which therefore survive delivery of a disposition, with or without a non-supersession clause; but substantially to restrict the type of obligation which can be kept alive only under exception (*c*), by way of a non-supersession clause, as representing an agreement in writing to that effect. In the result, the scope and efficacy of a non-supersession clause now seems somewhat limited. For practical purposes, however, the clause still continued to be used although some resulting modification to the wording of certain missives clauses would seem to be necessary in an endeavour to bring them within the scope of the non-supersession clause.

The foregoing comments as to the respective obligations of the parties are, of course, subject to the implied qualification referred to *supra* in *Rockcliffe Estates plc* and in a number of other sources that one party to such a contract is entitled to expect that the other will act reasonably.

**28.60 (11) Occupancy rights under the Matrimonial Homes (Family Protection) (Scotland) Act 1981.** Under this Act, which came into operation on 1 September 1982, occupancy rights have been created for the benefit of the 'non-entitled spouse' on the break-up of a marriage. In the ordinary case, a 'non-entitled spouse' is a wife, deserted by her husband, where the title stands in name of the husband alone. Without the protection of the Act, the husband at common law would be in a position to eject her from the matrimonial home. The purpose of the Act is to create overriding rights for the benefit of the non-entitled spouse to allow her to remain in occupation of the matrimonial home; and these 'occupancy rights' transmit against, and are enforceable in a question with, third parties, whether as purchasers or creditors from the entitled spouse who has the title to the property.

Consistent with that general intention, occupancy rights of a non-entitled spouse are overriding interests for the purposes of registration of title.

Whether the title be recorded in Sasines or registered, nothing will appear in the Register of Sasines, in the Land Register or in the Personal Register to give warning to third parties of the existence of such occupancy rights. But, under Rule 5 (as amended) of the Land Registration Rules, the Keeper will endorse a note on the title sheet that there are no subsisting occupancy rights of spouses of persons formerly entitled, if satisfied that this is so. Such endorsements are covered by indemnity. The Keeper, however, gives no assurance as to the current registered proprietor; and anyone dealing with the registered proprietor must make his own enquiries and take the necessary precautions to ensure that there are no subsisting occupancy rights.

In order to protect the *bona fide* purchaser against the possibility of such occupancy rights, any offer to purchase a dwellinghouse or to lend on heritable security thereon should include a clause dealing with potential rights under this Act.

Minor amendments were made to the provisions of the Act by the Law Reform (Miscellaneous Provisions) (Scotland) Acts 1985 and 1990. See Chapter 33.

**28.61 (12) Loan clause**.  In the great majority of cases of house purchase (and in other cases as well), the purchaser requires a loan to allow him to complete his purchase. Normally, the availability of a loan is established prior to making the offer but occasionally this is not possible, in which case it is prudent to make the offer subject to the purchaser obtaining a loan of an amount and on conditions which are acceptable to him. The seller may not be prepared to accept this provision; but it will probably suffice to give the purchaser time to secure his loan before the bargain is concluded.

**28.62 (13) Evidence of compliance**.  It is not sufficient simply to include in the contract provisions on the lines above referred to. All these matters must be followed up and investigated prior to settlement. Otherwise, the purchaser may find himself seriously disadvantaged. To avoid any argument with the seller's solicitors, it is prudent to insert a specific provision, either separately or incorporated in the appropriate clauses, to the effect that, where appropriate, evidence will be produced before settlement to satisfy the purchaser's agents that the relevant provisions have in fact been implemented.

**28.63 (14) Time of the essence.**  It is not normally in the purchaser's interests that time should be of the essence of the contract, although in certain cases it may be; but it certainly is very much in the interests of the seller in most cases to have a provision of this kind in the contract linked to a provision for payment of interest if the price is not paid at date of entry. Recognising this fact, some agents are now incorporating an appropriate clause in the offer to purchase and the standard offer suggested by the Law Society of Scotland includes an appropriate interest clause. If not included, then the seller's agents will normally incorporate a provision to the effect that at least payment of the purchase price on the date of entry is of the essence of the contract. The clause usually includes specific provisions as to the consequences of default and a provision for payment of interest, at a specified penal rate, to exclude the rule in *Tiffney*.

Note that a clause providing that timeous payment of the price is of the essence applies to that clause only. It may be appropriate to make time of the essence in relation to other clauses also, in which case further express provision is required.

**28.64 (15) *Actio quanti minoris* clause.** For reasons referred to above and dealt with again under breach of contract below, the *actio quanti minoris* is not normally available on the sale and purchase of heritage where the contract was concluded before 21 June 1997. In practice, this is often the remedy most acceptable to the purchaser in a case where the seller cannot fully implement all the obligations in the contract, especially in relation to minor matters.

The rule excluding the *actio quanti minoris* from sale and purchase of heritage has always applied and this was stressed in an article by Professor K. G. C. Reid in 1988 JLS 285 following on the decision in *Finlayson*. As he points out, even if the non-supersession clause, which was included in the missives but not in the disposition, had been held to be effective after settlement, the purchaser would still have been in difficulty in seeking to retain the subjects and to claim damages for breach of contract on the part of the seller, because that remedy is not competent at common law. But, as with other common law rules which apply by implication in the case of contracts of sale and purchase of heritage, it is competent for the parties to contract otherwise; and, at the end of his article, he suggests a suitable clause for inclusion in missives, along with a non-supersession clause, to allow the purchaser to have the benefit of the *actio quanti minoris*, whether before or after settlement of the transaction. Since that article appeared, a clause on these lines has now become commonplace.

Even this clause, however, may not give the purchaser the full remedy which he would wish to have in the event of the seller's default. The reason is that, if the seller, in the missives, undertakes obligations which are not collateral, the obligations would normally be superseded by the disposition; but, subject to the limitations discussed in 28.59 above, it may be possible to ensure that such obligations remain enforceable under a non-supersession clause inserted both in the missives and in the disposition, or possibly in the missives alone. By including the additional *quanti minoris* clause, the purchaser can still retain the subjects and claim damages for breach of these obligations. But the measure of damages is, as indicated above at 28.25, the difference in value of the subjects, not the direct cost of putting matters right. In some cases, there may not be much difference; but in other cases the difference can be substantial. It may therefore be desirable to incorporate appropriate provisions in the *actio quanti minoris* clause to allow the purchaser to recover the actual cost of putting matters right.

The case of *Fortune* has been mentioned already, para. 28.23.

After 21 June 1997 there should be no need for the *actio quanti minoris* clause.

**28.65 (16) Time-limit**. An offer, when made, remains open for acceptance for a reasonable time or until withdrawn. It is standard practice to incorporate in an offer a time-limit within which the offer must be accepted, failing which it falls. This would not normally preclude withdrawal of the offer before expiry of the time-limit, but it may be prudent to be specific on this point.

### 28.66 Special clauses

There are any number of special circumstances for which special clauses are necessary. Only five typical specialties are mentioned here.

A number of other special situations are dealt with in Greens *Property Law Bulletin*, most of which are noted in the Reading List for Chapter 28.

**28.67 (1) Let property**. Nowadays the purchaser usually stipulates for vacant possession; but quite often let property changes hands. If so, then special provision in the contract is desirable, specifying:

(*a*) the rent or rents receivable, and the basis of apportionment thereof;

(*b*) whether or not the property is subject to any statutory controls under the Rent Act, the Housing (Scotland) Act 1988, or the Agricultural Holdings Acts;

(*c*) the terms of the lease or leases, including duration and landlord's obligations, which may in certain circumstances be quite onerous.

For a style of offer, see Halliday's *Practice*, 15–139.

**28.68 (2) Flats.** There are two main points here.

(*a*) What is included in the purchase? The starting point is the law of the tenement, which may of course be varied in the titles of each flat. The normal common law rule is that the ground floor flat gets the *solum*, front garden, and the back ground. It is prudent to make this a matter of express stipulation when purchasing a ground floor flat; although on the rule in *Campbell* 1963 SC 505, involving an undisclosed minerals reservation, an offer for a ground floor flat necessarily includes *solum* and ground. *Per contra*, there is no general inference that each upper flat carries with it a joint right to the *solum* or to the use of the back green. Cellars and other pertinents should also be separately identified.

(*b*) Burdens. The roof is the most onerous; and if purchasing a top flat, it is very important to stipulate expressly that the property is burdened with a proportionate share only and not the whole of the cost of maintenance of the roof, in terms of the titles.

**28.69 (3) New houses.** In order to counteract gerry-building in new houses, with consequent loss to innocent purchasers, the National House-Building Council was set up in Scotland on 7 February 1969. The rules of the scheme as originally introduced were substantially altered with effect from 1 January 1980, and again with effect from 1 April 1988 when the current scheme, known as 'Buildmark', was introduced. Since the cover on houses completed before 1 January 1980 has now expired, the rules which operated prior to that date are not dealt with here.

The following points should be noted with reference to the Council.

(*a*) It is a voluntary body, which builders or developers may join; but they are not obliged to do so. In practice, a very large percentage of builders do belong, and 'almost all new houses' for sale or letting 'are built under the NHBC Scheme': Law Commission Report, No. 40, p. 7 ('Civil Liability for Vendors and Lessors for Defective Premises').

(*b*) In Scotland, any house which is less than 10 years old and which does not have NHBC cover may not qualify for a mortgage unless construction was supervised throughout and is certified by an architect.

(*c*) A builder's membership of the Council is conditional upon his implementing certain obligatory conditions which include:

(i) That all new houses must conform to NHBC standards, which are laid down in considerable detail. To ensure this, the Council make regular inspection of buildings in course of construction.

(ii) That the builder, when selling a new house to a purchaser, must deliver the NHBC Scheme documents as soon as missives have been concluded.

(iii) That the builder must complete the house according to standards and requirements laid down by the Council.

**28.70** (*a*) *The risks.*   It is perhaps worth summarising very briefly the main areas of risk which a purchaser runs when purchasing new property.

(i) Purchase of an uncompleted dwellinghouse. There are two possibilities here. Where there is a contract but no title, and deposits or other payments have been made, the purchaser may lose the whole or at least part of these payments because of supervening insolvency of the builder; and will be denied the benefit of the property, which will be disposed of by the liquidator, receiver or trustee in sequestration for the benefit of the creditors. Alternatively, where the purchaser has a title, he will not lose the property; but will be left with an uncompleted building, partly paid for, which, in the nature of things, will cost more to complete (by employing another builder) than on the original contract.

(ii) Condition of dwellinghouse after completion and payment. The building may turn out to be defective in that:

(*a*) minor defects may show up within a short period after completion which were not evident at completion date; and/or

(*b*) major structural defects may develop, possibly a considerable time after completion;

and in either event, for whatever reason (including insolvency) the builder may be unable or unwilling to put matters right.

**28.71** (*b*) *Cover under the NHBC Scheme.*   The principal point which concerns the solicitor in relation to the scheme is whether the purchaser is covered.

The essential conditions are:

(i) The cover extends to new dwellinghouses completed less than 10 years ago. This includes detached, semi-detached and flatted houses; with garage, boundary and retaining walls, internal footpaths and drains.

The Scheme did not originally cover converted or sub-divided dwellinghouses or additions or alterations to houses whether already covered under the Scheme or not; and it does not cover any kind of commercial property. It has, however, since been extended to cover conversions and renewals on comparable terms, but for periods of one and six years respectively, not two and ten years as in the scheme for new dwellinghouses.

The Scheme does not cover roads and footpaths *ex adverso*, and amenity areas, even if the builder is under obligation to complete these as part of the contract. Until comparatively recently, road bonds, in the form of an insurance company guarantee, were commonly used to ensure that the builder did complete the work; or, if not, that money was made available for its completion. Road bonds are now commonly rendered unnecessary by the Roads (Scotland) Act 1984 s. 17, and regulations made thereunder, in terms of which security in the form of a road bond or deposit must be given to the road authority; and work should not start on the construction of a private dwellinghouse until such security has been provided. But the position should be checked with the local authority: see Chapter 19.65.

(ii) Before the introduction of Buildmark, only private purchasers, if acquiring for their own occupation, were covered; but the benefit of the protection transmitted to singular successors of the first purchaser without any special assignation or otherwise. Under the new Buildmark scheme as from 1 April 1988, every purchaser is protected without any exclusions, and 'purchaser' means the first purchaser, each subsequent purchaser and any heritable creditor in possession of the house. In either case, however, the second (and any subsequent) purchaser can only claim for defects which first emerge after the second purchaser acquired the house. The second (or subsequent) purchaser has no rights in respect of patent or known defects which either should have been reported to the NHBC or should have shown up on a survey.

(iii) For houses covered under the pre-1 April 1988 rules, the builder (or the developer) must have been on the NHBC Register at the date when the House Purchaser's Agreement was signed. Under the new rules, the relevant date is the date when the NHBC Scheme documents were delivered to the purchaser.

(iv) The purchaser must have entered into a binding contract with the builder or developer. So, deposits before missives are completed are not covered.

(v) Under the old rules, the purchaser must also have entered into the House Purchaser's Agreement. The 1988 changes in the rules removed this requirement by dispensing with the House Purchaser's Agreement.

(vi) For structural defect claims, the notice of insurance cover/ten year notice must have been issued to the purchaser.

**28.72** (c) *Documentation.*   Under the Buildmark scheme, introduced as from 1 April 1988, the documents comprise:

(i) The offer of cover. This is the offer by the builder and the NHBC to the purchaser of the house of the protection set out in the Buildmark booklet.

(ii) The acceptance. The purchaser accepts the offer of cover by completing the acceptance and returning it to the NHBC.

(iii) The NHBC Guide. This document is issued to the purchaser for information. It is not part of the Buildmark insurance cover, but it does include useful information and advice to the purchaser.

(iv) The ten-year notice of insurance cover. This is issued by the NHBC in duplicate to the purchaser's solicitor once the acceptance of cover has been received by the NHBC and the house has been completed. One copy is intended for the purchaser and one for his lender.

The new documentation is intended to simplify and improve the procedures for obtaining the cover afforded under the scheme.

**28.73** (d) *The cover provided.*   The main cover provided by the policy, against the risks above referred to, includes the following:

(i) Loss before the issue of the notice of insurance cover. This normally means loss to the purchaser before the building is actually completed.
    The purchaser is indemnified against the consequences of the insol-

vency of the builder, to a maximum limit of £10,000 (formerly £5,000) less 10% of the admitted value of the claim.

(ii) Loss after the issue of the notice of insurance cover.

There are two separate provisions.

(*a*) The initial guarantee period, which is two years from the date of the issue of the notice of insurance cover. During this period, the purchaser deals directly with the builder and requires the builder to remedy defects. But if the builder fails to satisfy the purchaser and the dispute goes to court or arbitration, the NHBC undertake to implement any arbitration award, with a 10% discount on the admitted amount of the claim.

(*b*) The structural guarantee period, which is after two years but within ten years of completion of the dwellinghouse. During this period, the NHBC undertake to pay to the purchaser the cost of remedying any major structural defect or subsidence and resulting damage.

Under the new Buildmark scheme, the 10% discount has been excluded and claims are met in full.

The Scheme is subject to certain limits on liability but these are now inflation-proofed automatically and increase as average building costs increase.

No special provisions are required in a contract of sale and purchase either to ensure the issue of the Council's ten-year notice or to ensure its transmission. The only point of enquiry is, prior to the contract, to ascertain whether or not the builder is registered with the Council. If he is, then all the foregoing automatically follows. If he is not, then comparable provisions must be introduced into the contract in lieu. The terms of the NHBC documents can be used as a style for suitable clauses in a contract with an unregistered builder.

**28.74** (*e*) *Earlier arrangements.*  As mentioned above, there are certain limits on the liability incurred by the NHBC. This has always been so. Due to inflation, the cover provided under earlier NHBC certificates got out of line with the cost of repairs. As from 31 March 1979, however, inflation proof cover has been provided as part of the Scheme.

**28.75 (4) Intended development**.  Very often, the purchaser has in mind, at the time of his purchase, some immediate or early development. He may be frustrated in two ways.

**28.76** (*a*) *Restrictions in the title.*  It is normal to stipulate in the offer that the property is free of any conditions and restrictions; or at least any which would effectively prevent the proposed use. Normally, the seller will place the onus on the purchaser by stipulating that, at least *quoad* burdens, the purchaser must take the title as it stands. But at least the purchaser then gets the chance to see what the restrictions are. He may then have to stipulate that the offer is subject to the requisite waivers.

The wording in these clauses requires some care. See *Armia Ltd.*, para. 28.43. In that case there was a condition in an offer in these terms: 'There is nothing in the titles of the said subjects which will prevent demolition and redevelopment'. On subsequent examination of the title, it turned out that the property was burdened by a servitude of access for adjoining subjects, a building restriction, and a right to build an external stair for the benefit of the adjoining property. Lord Wylie in 1977 SLT (Notes) 9 held that the existence of these restrictions on title did not constitute a breach of this condition, because demolition and some redevelopment was possible. Redevelopment of the whole site was excluded by the servitude and conditions; but the clause in the contract did not specify redevelopment of the whole. But, on appeal, the House of Lords held the title to be unmarketable, and the purchaser was free to resile.

**28.77** (*b*) *Planning permission and building committee approval.* Almost all development (including change of use) is subject to planning permission; and any structural work is subject to building regulations. Special restrictions are imposed on listed buildings. There may also be, in special cases, additional special requirements, *e.g.* the fire authorities for various types of property, and special needs under the licensing laws, for public houses. See generally Chapter 19. If planning and other permissions cannot be obtained prior to the making of the offer, then the contract must be subject to the obtaining of these consents. Otherwise, the purchaser runs the risk of finding himself committed to a purchase of property which he cannot use for the proposed development.

The special problem of making up roads and foot pavements is dealt with in para. 28.50, and must not be overlooked.

Any development involving access on to, or an alteration to, a public road or footpath will normally require special permission.

**28.78** *Suggested style.* For a suitable clause, see Halliday's *Practice* 15–106 reproducing a clause recommended by the Styles Committee of the Law Society of Scotland. That clause includes an optional provision that the permission is to be to the purchaser's entire satisfaction. A phrase on these lines is frequently used in such clauses and is often intended by the purchaser as an escape clause which will allow him to resile from the bargain for reasons unconnected with the planning permission but ostensibly on the footing that he is dissatisfied therewith. For a typical illustration of such a situation see *Gordon District Council* 1988 SLT 481, and at 1989 SLT 141, although, in that case, the clause did not include the word 'entire'. The seller sought to hold the purchaser to his bargain on the footing that, although dissatisfied, he was acting unreasonably. Lord Clyde held that, as a matter of construction, each party must have intended that the other would act reasonably; and a decision not to develop for reasons unconnected with the planning permission would not suffice to allow the purchaser to escape from his bargain. But, on the facts in this case, he came to the view that a developer could reasonably declare that he was dissatisfied with the conditions imposed in the planning permission and, on that ground, was not obliged to proceed.

See also *McKay* 1987 GWD 16–609. The missives contained a condition that the purchaser should receive a satisfactory report on the suitability of the ground for development. The purchaser subsequently resiled on the basis that the engineer's report of ground conditions was unsatisfactory; but, in fact, no trial pit investigation had been carried out. Held that the purchaser was under a duty first to obtain a report which justified terminating the contract before he could competently do so.

The question of acting reasonably is again discussed in *Wyllie* 1989 SLT

302. Lord Milligan, in that case, took the view that each party intended that the other would act reasonably.

**28.79 (5) Purchase of public sector houses and the right to buy.** Under the provisions of the Housing (Scotland) Act 1987, principally ss. 61 to 84, almost all secure tenants of public landlords are given the right to buy their homes at varying discounts on the market value thereof, with the power to enforce that right by application to the Lands Tribunal.

The 1987 Act consolidates the previous legislation from the Tenants' Rights, Etc. (Scotland) Act 1980 to the Housing (Scotland) Act 1986, though any reference to the superseded law in any document, etc., is specifically saved by Schedule 22 of the 1987 Act by being construed, except so far as a contrary intention appears, as referring, or (as the context may require) including a reference, to the corresponding provision of the 1987 Act. The 1987 Act has been amended by the Housing (Scotland) Act 1988, the Housing Act 1988, the Local Government and Housing Act 1989 and the Leasehold Reform, Housing and Urban Development Act 1993.

In order to have the right to buy, tenants must be secure tenants of public landlords, *e.g.* local authorities, Scottish Homes, registered housing associations (s. 61(2) of the 1987 Act). They must have a secure tenancy, the house being let as a separate dwelling and the tenant being an individual and having the house as his only and principal home (s. 44 of the 1987 Act).

Such a tenant has the right to buy the house, which must not be one of a group which has been provided with facilities (including a call system and the services of a warden) specially designed and adapted for the needs of persons of pensionable age or disabled persons, or where, if the landlord is a registered housing association, certain types of grant have been received(s. 61(4) of the 1987 Act). The term 'house' (s. 338 of the 1987 Act) includes any part of a building occupied or intended to be occupied as a separate dwelling and any land, outhouses and pertinents let therewith.

**28.80** (*a*) *Application to purchase.* In order to exercise his right to buy, a tenant must complete and serve on his landlord an application to purchase in the prescribed form (s. 63 of the 1987 Act). When the application is served, this becomes 'the relevant date' both for a strict statutory timetable and for valuation of the house. Application forms are available from public landlords, libraries and the Scottish Development Department in Edinburgh.

A secure tenant must have been in occupation of a house or a succession of houses provided by certain public landlords for at least two years prior to the date of service of his application to purchase (s. 61(2), (10) and (11) of the 1987 Act). He may exercise the right to purchase with one or more members of his family acting as joint purchasers if they are at least 18 years of age and have had their only and principal home with the tenant for six months prior to the date of application to purchase.

**28.81** (*b*) *Notice of refusal.* Where a landlord disputes a tenant's right to purchase a house, he must serve a notice of refusal within one month of the relevant date. If the landlord is of the opinion the information in the application is incorrect the tenant must be given reasonable opportunity to amend it, within two months.

**28.82** (*c*) *Valuation.* The house is valued either by a qualified valuer nominated by the landlord, if accepted by the tenant, or the district valuer as the landlord thinks fit, on the basis that the house is available for sale on the open market with vacant possession at the relevant date. In order to ascertain the price, however, a discount is deducted from the valuation. The discount normally represents a minimum of 32% of the valuation rising by 1% per year for each year beyond two of continuous relevant occupation to a maximum of 60%. Where the house is a flat, the minimum discount is 44% rising by 2% for each year as aforesaid to a maximum of 70%. If, however, the discount would reduce the price below the amount of the costs incurred in respect of the house in a five-year period commencing with the beginning of the landlord's financial year prior to the relevant dates, the price is fixed at that amount (s. 62 of the 1987 Act, as amended by the 1988 Act s. 65).

**28.83** (*d*) *Offer to sell.* The landlord must serve on the tenant a notice ('offer to sell') within two months of the relevant date, assuming no notice of refusal has been served. The conditions of sale of the house must ensure that the tenant has as full enjoyment and use of the house as owner as he has had as tenant and must include such additional rights as are necessary for the tenant's reasonable enjoyment and use of the house as owner, *e.g.* common rights (s. 64(1) of the 1987 Act).

If the tenant is unhappy about the terms of the offer he must make a request to the landlord in writing to strike out or vary the conditions or include a new condition within one month of the service of the offer to sell; and, if the landlord agrees, he must serve an amended offer to sell within one month of the service of the request. If the landlord refuses to accede to the request or is dilatory in serving such an amended offer or has not served an offer, the tenant may refer the matter to the Lands Tribunal within one month of the refusal or failure (or two months with the landlord's consent) for determination. The Lands Tribunal has power to order the service of the offer or an amended offer on the tenant if it thinks fit.

If the tenant does not dispute the terms of the offer or such dispute has been resolved, he must serve a notice of acceptance on the landlord within two months of service of the offer to sell or the amended offer as the case may be (s. 66 of the 1987 Act).

**28.84** (*e*) *Title and loans.* The normal conveyancing procedures apply following on the conclusion of missives.

A loan may be obtained from the local authority, housing corporation or Scottish Homes depending on who the landlord is, but an application therefor must be served on the landlord within one month of the offer to sell or amended offer to sell. An offer of loan must be issued, or the loan application refused, within two months of the service of the application. An aggrieved applicant may raise proceedings by way of summary application in the sheriff court for declarator that he is entitled to a loan. If the tenant is unable to obtain a loan of the amount for which he applied, he may within two months of the offer of loan or date of declarator (whichever is the later) serve a notice on the landlord to the effect he wishes a fixed price option, which notice must be accompanied by £100. In that event he is entitled to serve a notice of acceptance on the landlord within two years of the relevant date. The payment is recoverable by the tenant if he purchases the house or on expiry of the two-year period or if the landlord recovers possession of the house.

**28.85** (*f*) *Repayment of discount.* There is a liability to repay the discount in whole or part to the landlord if the house or part thereof is sold before the expiry of three years from the date of service of the notice of acceptance by the tenant.

The exceptions to this are:

(*i*) a disposal from one of the original purchasers to another;

(*ii*) where the remainder of the house continues to be the only or principal home of the seller;

(*iii*) a disposal by the deceased owner's executor acting in that capacity: see *Clydebank DC* 1994 SLT (Lands Tr.) 2. But problems still remain in Sasines titles: see the article at 1991 JLS 186;

(*iv*) a disposal as a result of a compulsory purchase order; and

(*v*) a disposal to a member of the owner's family who has lived with him for twelve months before the disposal and is for no consideration, provided that if the disponee disposes of the house before the end of the three-year period it is treated as a first disposal and he as the original purchaser. The discount repayable in the event of a sale not falling within the exceptions is 100% in the first year, 66% in the second and 33% in the third and nothing thereafter. The landlord can secure the liability to make repayment by a standard security but it is ranked postponed to any security granted for the purchase or improvement of the house, but not a security for any other loan unless the landlord consents.

If the house is sold within the three-year period a discharge will be required but, if it is sold outwith the same, the Law Society of Scotland recommends that provision is made in the re-sale missives to cover the point concerning the discount standard security appearing in the search undischarged. Under the former legislation, the period during which discount was repayable was five years. Therefore if the house was bought before 7 January 1987 the record will show a five-year discount standard security. The Housing (Scotland) Act 1986 s. 23 (not repealed or consolidated) provides that the reduced three-year period will apply retrospectively and therefore no repayment or discharge would be required though it may be a matter of convenience to obtain a suitable discharge from the landlord to clear the record in the circumstances.

**28.86** (*g*) *Transmission on change of landlord.* The right to buy provisions continue to apply notwithstanding the disposal by a local authority of its interest in land resulting in a secure tenant of that authority becoming the tenant of a private landlord unless otherwise prescribed: see s. 81A of the Housing (Scotland) Act 1987, as inserted by s. 128 of the Housing Act 1988, the relative regulations being the Housing (Preservation of Right to Buy) (Scotland) Regulations 1992 (SI 1992 No. 325).

**28.87** (*h*) *Defective houses.* Part XIV of the 1987 Act deals with the assistance for owners of defective housing which must be designated as such by the Secretary of State. A tenant applying to buy his house as aforesaid will receive notice if his house falls into a class of designated defective housing but no assistance by way of repurchase or reinstatement grant is available if the house is bought after the specified cut-off date in the designation. Written application has to be made to the local authority for assistance within the period specified in the designation by those seeking it and the form of that assistance is determined by the local authority though the sheriff has the power to determine questions arising from this Part of the 1987 Act. There has to date been only one scheme and the last date for making application for assistance was 30 November 1994.

**28.88 Purchase of public sector houses and rent to loan scheme**
The Leasehold Reform Housing and Urban Development Act 1993 introduced a statutory rent to loan scheme. There had previously been a pilot scheme, Rent to Mortgage, operated by Scottish Homes which also extended to local authorities, from 1 April 1991 to 20 July 1993.

The rent to loan scheme came into effect on 27 September 1993. The same rules as Right to Buy apply for purchase except that tenants who have been entitled to housing benefit during the period beginning twelve months prior to the application or who have submitted a claim for benefit are disqualified, as are also tenants of defective houses.

The scheme is described in ss. 73A to 73D of the Housing Act 1987, as inserted by s. 142 of the 1993 Act. The price fixed for a house is payable in two elements, namely (*a*) the initial capital payment (ICP) and (*b*) the deferred financial commitments (DFC). The offer to sell must include a provision that the tenant will be entitled to ownership on payment of the ICP, and the DFC is secured by a standard security in favour of the landlord. The purchase price is fixed by reference to tenancy years, but the discount entitlement is 15% less than for Right to Buy, such that the minimum entitlement is 17% for houses and 29% for flats.

The ICP is determined by the tenant but must not be less than the maximum amount of loan which could be repaid at the statutory rate of interest over the loan period by weekly payments equivalent to 90% of the weekly rent payable as at the application date. 'Statutory rate of interest' and 'loan period' are defined in s. 73B(2). The ICP is normally financed by a loan from a bank or building society.

The DFC is calculated by the formula defined in s. 73C of the 1987 Act. It can be reduced at any time by the purchaser making a payment of not less than £1,500, or such sum as prescribed, and is repayable on sale or disposal of the property.

**28.89 Resulting obligations of seller and purchaser**
In the absence of special provision in the contract, or to the extent to which special provision is not made, both parties come under certain obligations.

Note that the comments which follow apply to the position as at 1 January 1997 and may require some modification in the light of the Contract (Scotland) Act 1997.

**28.90 (1) Seller's obligations**
(*a*) To deliver or exhibit a title which complies with the provisions of the missives. In Sasines transactions and in transactions in operational areas where the transaction will induce first registration, the seller is normally under an obligation to provide a good marketable title which implies a valid prescriptive progress of titles to the whole and identical property included in the missives. It also means that the seller must satisfy the purchaser on

all matters expressly, or by implication, dealt with in the contract in relation to title, *e.g.* that feuduty is allocated. If, on examination of the title, the purchaser finds some fault with it, then he is entitled at the seller's expense, to have any such doubt in the title cleared to the extent of an Outer House judgment; but the normal rule as to expenses would apply on appeal. See 1988 JLS 162, 'Good and Marketable Title'.

In transactions in operational areas where the title has already been registered, *i.e.* in the case of a dealing, the seller will normally be under obligation in the missives to produce a land certificate which discloses no exclusion of indemnity. Here, examination of title is substantially simplified in that the land certificate is complete and self-contained and guaranteed; but of course it must still be examined to ensure, in particular, that there are no outstanding securities and that the burdens as set out in the burdens section are all acceptable to the purchaser in terms of the missives. In addition, it has to be borne in mind that every registered title is subject to overriding interests and these, particularly servitudes and public rights of way, may be objectionable as being contrary to provisions in the missives.

(*b*) To give possession. Further, the seller must tender title and possession timeously. This does not mean that, if title or possession is not available on the actual date of entry, the seller is automatically in default. In *Heys* (1890) 17 R 381 the term 'immediate entry' in a contract was held to mean such early possession as is practicable; and possession tendered four days after the contract date did not put the seller in breach. In the ordinary case, the seller must be given reasonable time to implement his obligation, which of course depends on circumstances. But time may be made the essence of the contract, either expressly or by implication, in which case the purchaser is then entitled to insist on title and possession on the due date, failing which the seller is immediately in breach.

In *Stuart* 1976 SLT 39, following on an offer to purchase with actual occupation, failure to give vacant possession timeously to seven acres out of a total of 21 acres purchased under the missives was held to be a material breach of contract, entitling the purchaser to resile, even although the occupant apparently had no legal right or title to be there. The date of entry in the contract was 16 January 1974; and the purchaser intimated his intention to resile on 26 March 1974. There is no suggestion in the report that the seller should have been given time to secure the eviction of the occupant, notwithstanding Lord Stott's comment, on the strength of English authority, that it was for the seller to eject the third party 'before completion'.

(*c*) To deliver a valid disposition in favour of the purchaser or his nominees, containing absolute warrandice. Note, however, that absolute warrandice is not, in any circumstances, an alternative or substitute for marketable title.

(*d*) To deliver or exhibit clear searches (see later under Searches, Chapter 33).

(*e*) To implement any other special obligations in the contract, *e.g.* to exhibit planning permission.

In *Davidson* 1991 GWD 2–115 and 1991 GWD 18–1109 the court held that a purchaser could not be compelled to settle except in exchange for delivery of a valid disposition; and his refusal to settle on this ground did not entitle the sellers to resile, notwithstanding express provisions in the missives which, arguably, gave them the right. This follows *Bowie* 1978 SLT (Sh Ct) 9. If the title is defective, the seller cannot compel the purchaser to settle on the footing that the seller will grant absolute warrandice. Likewise, the seller cannot insist on settlement in such circumstances by providing a property title indemnity unless the purchaser agrees. The defect in title must first be cured unless the purchaser otherwise agrees.

### 28.91 (2) Purchaser's obligations

(*a*) To pay the purchase price on the due date; but see *Bowie* and *Davidson* referred to immediately above.

(*b*) Possibly, to take infeftment and, therefore, implied entry under the 1874 Act s. 4 within a reasonable time so as to relieve the seller of personal liability for feuduty and other feudal prestations.

(*c*) To implement any other special obligations in the contract, *e.g.* to obtain planning permission within a time limit.

### 28.92 Breach of contract

In the remaining paragraphs of this chapter breach of contract is treated as the law stood on 1 January 1997. The reader must remember, however, that, since that date, the Contract (Scotland) Act 1997 has come into operation and applies to any contract concluded on or after 21 June 1997. The main provisions of the Act have been dealt with earlier in this chapter and, as the reader should be aware, the Act abolishes the common law rules which broadly, exclude any reference to prior communings, which will not permit any reliance on the *actio quanti minoris* and which required an express non-supersession clause in the antecedent contract if the contract was not to fall at settlement. To that extent, the discussion which follows on the result of breach of contract in the sale and purchase of heritage falls to be modified to take account of these major statutory innovations; but, subject thereto, the position remains substantially as it was before the Act.

Where the transaction has not yet settled and where, as a result, *restitutio in integrum* is almost always possible, either seller or purchaser have the alternative remedies of an action for implement, or rescission and damages. But the court will not order implement in circumstances where implement is clearly impossible; and, in such cases, the only effective remedy is to rescind and claim damages.

Where *restitutio in integrum* is no longer possible, neither party can rescind because *restitutio* is an essential pre-requisite for rescission. Accordingly, if *restitutio in integrum* has become impossible (for which see below) then the remedy is specific implement, if that is practicable; or damages. The entitlement to damages depends on various factors discussed elsewhere in this Chapter.

### 28.93 (1) Default by the purchaser.

This normally only arises before settlement of the transaction, while *restitutio in integrum* is normally still possible. In almost all such cases, it takes the form of failure or refusal by the purchaser to pay the price. The seller may either:

(*a*) sue for implement, by an action for payment of the purchase price in exchange for which the seller tenders a disposition; or

(*b*) rescind the contract, following on which the seller is free to resell the property at the best price obtainable and thereafter may sue for damages, which will include the difference between the original and the resale price, plus expenses, etc.

In *Robson* 1990 GWD 2–92 it was held that a time limit in a non-supersession clause did not apply to the recovery of damages by the seller following on a breach of contract by the purchaser. The decision here, of course, is clearly distinguishable from the cases mentioned at para. 28.56 in that, in this case, the purchaser was unable to complete. The whole purpose of the non-supersession clause in the ordinary case is to allow a remedy to the purchaser or possibly to the seller within a stated time following on settlement of the transaction.

If the seller decides to rescind the contract and claim damages, he must proceed with caution for two reasons.

**28.94** (*a*) *The ultimatum rule.* Unless the contract otherwise expressly provides, time is not of the essence; and, therefore, failure by the purchaser to pay the purchase price on the due date does not entitle the seller immediately to rescind. Instead, the seller must give notice that, if the price is not paid within the period of notice, then he will hold the purchaser in breach. See *Rodger (Builders) Ltd.* 1950 SC 483. Under missives, the price was payable on 11 November but the purchaser was not ready to settle on that date. On 25 November, the seller's agents gave an ultimatum, requiring payment of the price by the 28th, which was not forthcoming. On 28 November, purporting to rescind, the seller entered into a second contract of sale. (In fact, the purchase price was available on the 29th). *Held* that the seller had acted too precipitately, and was not entitled to rescind on such short notice.

The 'ultimatum rule' applies to any obligation in a contract of sale and purchase, whether that obligation falls to be implemented by the purchaser or by the seller, if the party has it in his own power to implement that condition or not as he chooses, but has unnecessarily, or unjustifiably, delayed or refused to implement it. In such cases, time is not of the essence of the contract unless the contract otherwise expressly provides. So, an ultimatum must be given by the aggrieved party and must expire before he is in a position to rescind. For a discussion on provisions making time expressly of the essence, see Lord President Hope in *Visionhire Ltd.* 1992 SCLR 236.

Not surprisingly, there is no definitive ruling as to the length of notice required under the ultimatum rule. In *Rodger (Builders) Ltd.*, *supra*, three days' notice was held to be too short, but Lord Sorn observed that, provided the time limit is a reasonable one in the circumstances, failure to pay within that time will be treated as entitling the seller to rescind.

In *Johnstone* 1977 SC 365, after a period of several months during which the parties litigated, the sheriff finally fixed a period of six weeks within which the price should be payable. This is at least a guide as to what might be thought by the court to be a reasonable period of notice.

In *Inveresk Paper Co. Ltd.* 1972 SLT (Notes) 63, the purchaser failed to pay the price for a long period after the stipulated date. The seller did not, however, give any formal intimation that failure to pay within a reasonable time would be treated as breach. In the absence of that ultimatum, the seller was held not entitled to rescind the contract.

In *Toynar Ltd.* 1989 GWD 2–82, the missives stipulated that, failing payment on the due date, the seller would have the option 'immediately thereafter' to resile. Six weeks elapsed after the due date without payment; and, after sundry communings, the seller was held entitled to resile. 'Immediately thereafter' qualified the option; it did not require the seller to resile at once. In *Atlas Assurance Co. Ltd.* 1993 SLT 892 the purchaser claimed that, by delay in enforcing the contract, the seller had waived or abandoned his right to resile on account of non-payment; but the claim was rejected in the circumstances.

In contrast, in *Packman & Sons* 1977 SLT 140, where a long period had elapsed since the date of entry, Lord Stott expressed the view that the seller was entitled to resile without notice; and was not bound first to impose on the purchasers a time limit for performance.

If, however, neither party is at fault, and if the fulfilment of a condition in the contract depends not on the seller or purchaser but on a third party or on extraneous circumstances, the ultimatum rule is not appropriate. Instead, the rule seems to be that such conditions must be implemented either: (*a*) before the date specified in the contract by which the condition is to be fulfilled. In that case, the date must be strictly adhered to and time is in effect of the essence of such a condition; or (*b*) where no special date is fixed for fulfilment of a condition, it must be fulfilled before the date for completion of the contract; or (*c*) in the absence of either date, which is very rare indeed, any such condition must be fulfilled within a reasonable time.

See *Boland & Co. Ltd.* 1975 SLT (Notes) 80. That decision was followed in two recent cases.

In *Ford Sellar Morris Properties plc* 1990 SC 34, a leasehold case, it was provided expressly that the contract was conditional upon certain consents being obtained. It was declared a material condition that, if the consents were not obtained by a stated date, either party could resile. Consent was obtained but after the stipulated date; and was intimated to the other side who thereupon resiled. They were held entitled so to do on the footing that, where a date has been set and is of the essence of the contract, it must be adhered to. The party resiling is obliged to exercise his right to do so within a reasonable time but in this case, where eight days had elapsed beyond the stipulated date, that period was held not to be excessive.

The decision in *Ford Sellar Morris Properties plc* was apparently not followed in *Cumming* 1993 SCLR 707 and indeed is not referred to in the report of that case. The purchaser in *Cumming* failed to meet a time-limit where time was of the essence and so, as a result, the seller became entitled to resile. The purchaser thereafter tendered the price and was held entitled so to do, thus holding the seller to the bargain notwithstanding that the time-limit had expired. The reasoning of the Sheriff Principal was that, while the seller was no doubt entitled to resile, he had not actually done so and so could not refuse an offer of performance. But that decision, in turn, seems inconsistent with the later case of *Charisma Properties Ltd.* 1996 SLT 791, where the Inner House rejected a comparable finding by Lord Penrose, based on somewhat special wording in the missives in question, and held that the seller had effectively repudiated the contract and was not bound to proceed with it.

In *Burnside* 1989 GWD 11–468 missives of sale and purchase provided that either party might resile if a completion certificate was not obtained by a specified date, by giving written notice within three days thereof. A completion certificate was in fact obtained but six days after the stipulated date. Within the three-day time-limit provided for, the sellers resiled from the bargain by a written letter to that effect and were held entitled so to do.

**28.95** (*b*) *Measure of damages.*   The seller must make every endeavour to minimise his loss by reselling the property at the best possible price obtainable. See *Johnstone* 1978 SC 365; but he need not anticipate breach by the purchaser before completion date. On the question of *quantum* of damages and the various elements making up the seller's claim, see *Grant* 1987 SLT 639 and *Tainsh* 1990 SLT (Sh Ct) 102.

In *Mills* 1994 SCLR 397 the Sheriff awarded solatium over and above the ordinary elements of damages and was upheld by the Sheriff Principal who, however, reduced the award to £500. In *Palmer* 1993 SLT 485 solatium was held to be an element in a claim for damages if the claim involved fraudulent misrepresentation.

In *Lloyds Bank plc* 1993 SCLR 727, 1994 SLT 424, the missives contained the usual clause providing for payment of interest on the purchase price if not duly paid on the date of entry. The purchasers then defaulted and the sellers repudiated the bargain. In the subsequent action of damages, the sellers claimed that the purchasers were liable for interest at the rate specified in this clause. The Court, however, held that the interest clause, on its wording, restricted the rights of the sellers to interest on the price if duly paid but beyond the due date; but that the clause had no application whatsoever to a case where the purchase price was never paid at all. This did not, of course, exclude a claim for damages but this particular item was disallowed. Following on that decision, Professors Rennie and Cusine put forward some comments on such claims for damages and suggested styles of clause for insertion in the missives to ensure that this particular aspect of a claim was properly covered, along with other elements which go to make up the claim. All this is conveniently summarised in their article in 1993 JLS 450.

Whether or not the Courts will give effect to such clauses is, however, a different matter: see the comments by the Lord Justice-Clerk in particular in the *Lloyds Bank* decision at p. 427L: 'It thus appears to me to be contrary to principle for the pursuers now to be seeking payment of interest on the price when, by rescinding the contract, they for their part are declaring themselves to be unwilling to perform their part of the bargain.'

In *Colgan* 1994 GWD 1–43, in negotiations for a sale of a guest house, it was alleged that the seller advised the purchaser that the guest house could not accommodate a sufficient number of guests to require a fire certificate, which was not correct. In the subsequent missives, the purchaser introduced a condition to the effect that the premises complied with the Fire Precautions Act 1971 and had a fire certificate. The seller qualified this provision to the effect that it applied only to the extent that the subjects were too small to require a fire certificate, and disclosed the fire officer's letter which confirmed that the safety standards were met. His letter was based on the seller's assurance that no more than six guests were ever accommodated. The purchaser claimed damages but, perhaps somewhat surprisingly, the claim failed on a strict application of the terms of the missives on the basis that the seller in fact never took in more than six persons per night, even although more guests could have been accommodated. The missives contained an *actio quanti minoris* clause but Lord Clyde doubted whether or not a claim in this case came within the terms of such a clause.

**28.96 (2) Default by the seller.** This can arise, from various causes, both before and after settlement of the transaction.

**28.97** (*a*) *Before settlement.* *Restitutio in integrum* is still normally possible. The purchaser's remedies are:

(i) An action of implement, to have the seller ordained to deliver a valid disposition, or, failing that, to acquire a title by adjudiction. This remedy is, of course, only appropriate where the seller can implement the contract (*i.e.* he has a title and the beneficial right) but refuses or lacks capacity to implement.

An action of implement is competent either in the Court of Session or in the sheriff court; an action of adjudication can only be raised in the Court of Session. Decree in an action of adjudication operates as an active title to the successful pursuer, for which see Chapter 30.2. A decree in an action of implement does not have the same affect and simply obliges the seller to grant a disposition to obtemper the decree. In an action of implement in the Court of Session, under the *nobile officium*, the court has always had power to authorise the clerk of court to sign a disposition where the seller refuses so to do. See *Boag* 1967 SC 322. The same power is now conferred on the sheriff by the Law Reform (Miscellaneous Provisions) (Scotland) Act 1985 s. 17. In such cases, however, it would seem to be a prerequisite that there should be a disposition in existence ready for signature which, for whatever reason, the seller will not sign; and that it is only in these circumstances that the clerk of court could be authorised to sign in the seller's place. But apparently in *Martone* 1992 GWD 32–1903 the court granted decree, *inter alia* ordaining the defender to execute and deliver a disposition, failing which the clerk of court was authorised to subscribe. The result is not altogether clear; but at least in some cases it would seem that notwithstanding these powers, an action of adjudication may be necessary. Compare the much wider and more explicit powers conferred on the sheriff under the Housing (Scotland) Act 1988 s. 30 to adjust the terms of a lease where the parties cannot agree, and to declare that the resulting document reflects the terms of the tenancy whereupon it is deemed to be duly executed by both parties.

(ii) Rescission and damages. Normally, in an action of implement, there is an alternative conclusion for damages. Where the seller cannot implement the contract, because he lacks title, this is the only competent remedy. Again if time is not expressly of the essence of the contract, notice is appropriate. If the seller fails to implement because of some technical defect in the title which is curable, then the court would normally give him time to put matters right; but not where the defect is complete want of title, even although he may be able and willing to remedy the defect.

See *Campbell* 1963 SC 505, where Lord President Clyde, at p. 294, distinguishes between defects in the title and want of title for this purpose. In that case, property had been sold without reference to a reservation of minerals. The seller offered to acquire the minerals and convey them to the purchaser, but the purchaser insisted on rescinding. The court declined to allow the seller time to acquire the minerals, and held the purchaser entitled to immediate rescission on the grounds of want of title.

In a comparable situation in *McLennan* 1996 SLT 1349, the sellers were unable to produce a marketable title following on conclusion of missives. The purchaser then issued an ultimatum requiring the title to be corrected within a twenty-eight-day time-limit. The seller, for technical reasons, was unable to produce a marketable title within the stipulated time-limit and appeared unlikely to be able to produce such a title within a reasonable time. In these circumstances, the purchaser was held entitled to resile on the authority of *Rodger (Builders) Ltd*. 1950 SC 483.

(iii) At this stage, while *restitutio* is still possible, the *actio quanti minoris* is not competent unless the contract contains a special clause giving the purchaser this remedy; but some agents refuse to agree to its inclusion in the contract. In the absence of such a clause, the purchaser must either accept the subjects and the title as he finds them, subject to the curing of curable defects at the expense of the seller, or he must reject the title and rescind. He cannot insist on proceeding with the transaction, but subject to an abatement of the price *quanti minoris*, although in practice this latter device is a common method of settling minor discrepancies between the contract conditions and the actual state of the property or title. See 1966 JLS 124; and for an article on the *actio quanti minoris*, see 1988 JLS 285.

Accordingly if the missives contain a clause conferring the benefit of the *actio quanti minoris* on the purchaser in appropriate terms, he can insist on proceeding with the bargain but claim damages (in effect a reduction in the price) in respect of any contractual obligation which the seller is unable to implement.

If the contract contains no such provision, then the purchaser's right to proceed with the contract and claim damages may be available where the seller's failure to implement the contract involves breach of a collateral obligation. As to what is and is not a collateral obligation, see below. According to Professor K. G. C. Reid in 1988 JLS at p. 286, this is one of the standard exceptions to the rule excluding the *actio quanti minoris*. Another exception occurs when matters are no longer entire and a latent defect is then discovered. The purchaser may retain and claim damages *quanti minoris,* but this could not normally apply until after settlement of the transaction.

The *actio quanti minoris* will be available in all cases, where missives were concluded on or after 21 June 1997.

**28.98** (*b*) *After settlement.* The remedy of rescission and damages remains available to the purchaser, on breach by the seller of any material obligation in the contract, so long as matters remain entire or, to put it another way, so long as *restitutio in integrum* is still possible. See *Louttit's*

*Trustees* (1892) 19 R 791. In that case, a purchaser, in exchange for the price, took delivery of a disposition of an area of land on which he intended to build and then later discovered a restriction in the titles against building. No work had been carried out when the discovery was made. Notwithstanding this restriction, the purchaser sought to retain the subjects but to claim damages from the seller for breach of contract. The Court was clearly not disposed to grant a remedy on these lines since the purchaser would be retaining the subjects and claiming damages, which is a clear case of the *actio quanti minoris*. But the seller, for special reasons, agreed to settle the claim on this footing; and matters were therefore dealt with on that basis. Surprisingly, there is no subsequent reported Scottish case where a purchaser, having taken delivery of a disposition and paid the price, thereafter exercised his apparent right to rescind and claim damages on the grounds of a subsequently emerging breach of the seller's obligations in the contract. In *Mowbray* 1989 GWD 6–267 a purchaser had taken possession, and the transaction had settled, two years previously. The purchaser then sued for implement. Finally, he sought to rescind but, in the circumstances, was held not entitled so to do.

In contrast, in *Caledonian Property Group Ltd.* 1992 SLT 738 purchasers settled a transaction while the seller's obligation to produce a completion certificate was still outstanding. In anticipation of receiving the certificate within the stipulated time limit, the purchasers then carried out extensive work on the subjects. The certificate was not duly produced and, as a consequence, the purchasers had to abandon plans to sell on the property; and the property market then deteriorated. In the result the purchasers calculated that they would incur a loss on ultimate resale, including loss of interest on the price, and sued for damages accordingly. The report includes a discussion on the claim for interest and the appropriate rate of interest. Given that the transaction was between two property companies, it was held that the seller should have anticipated that the purchaser would borrow at least part of the price and that the interest rate should be fixed with that in mind; and accordingly a proof before answer was allowed on that footing.

There are, of course, other instances where a disposition has been reduced after delivery but not on the grounds of breach of contract by the seller. Such cases involve other elements, *e.g.* error common to both parties as in *Anderson* 1954 SC (HL) 43; or personal bar, as in *Rodger (Builders) Ltd.*

Contrary to clear indications in the decision in *Louttit's Trustees* above, it seems to have been generally accepted in the profession that, after settlement of the transaction, *restitutio in integrum* is no longer possible. To some extent that view may be justified by reference to the nature of the transaction. In *Louttit's Trustees*, the purchaser had acquired a vacant piece of ground with a view to building and, before going further, the restriction on building was discovered. Clearly, in such a case, neither party would be significantly prejudiced if the transaction were reversed, the disposition reduced, and the purchase price repaid to the purchaser.

In ordinary domestic conveyancing, however, it is rather a different matter in that, if the purchaser of a dwellinghouse takes delivery of a disposition in exchange for the price, he will almost certainly, in the process, have sold his own house; will have taken possession, moved in his furniture and taken up residence in the new dwellinghouse. Can it be said in that situation that matters are still entire?

In any event, whatever the correct view of the decision in *Louttit's Trustees* may be, it seems necessarily to follow that, if the contract contains a non-supersession clause which is duly repeated in the disposition or which, even although not so repeated, is held to be effective nonetheless and if the contract also contains a clause conferring the right to the *actio quanti minoris* on the purchaser, then, even after settlement of the transaction, the purchaser will have the right to retain the subjects and to claim damages *quanti minoris* by virtue of express provision in the contract, whether *restitutio* remains possible or not.

Alternatively, whether or not the contract contains a non-supersession clause which is effective, the purchaser may also have the right, after settlement, to retain and claim damages, if he can base his claim on a collateral obligation which the seller will not or cannot implement.

Finally, the purchaser may still be entitled to sue for implement of a particular obligation in the contract, which is capable of being implemented. This would normally imply that there was an effective non-supersession clause in the missives; or that the obligation in the missives was of its nature clearly collateral.

**28.99 Collateral obligations.** The position prior to 21 June 1997 is that, where the condition is collateral to the main contract of sale and purchase, it stands on its own feet. So, even although the primary contract may be implemented by delivery of a disposition in exchange for the price, the secondary and separate collateral obligation still falls to be implemented and, failing implement, will sound in damages. Thus, in *Winston*, which re-affirmed the general proposition that provisions in the missives are superseded by the disposition following thereon, the standard exceptions to that general rule were summarised thus:

(i) provisions in the missives dealing with moveables;

(ii) collateral obligations in the sense referred to above; and

(iii) cases involving an effective non-supersession clause.

In considering the nature of 'collateral obligations' in the above sense, it is necessary to take into account the opinion of Lord Milligan in *Taylor* 1989 SCLR 531, and the cases therein cited, as modified by Lord Milligan's opinion in *Porch* 1992 SLT 661. See para. 28.59.

Accordingly, if the missives contain what is clearly a distinct collateral obligation, and if that obligation has not been implemented at settlement, the purchaser may still insist on it, whether or not the missives contain a non-supersession clause. An illustration of such a collateral condition can be found in *McKillop* 1945 SC 166, where the contract provided both for the construction of a building and for the sale of the completed property to the purchaser. Subsequent to delivery of the disposition in favour of the purchaser, structural defects developed and the purchaser claimed damages as a result. She was held entitled to do so on the footing that, in claiming damages, she was simply asserting a separate contractual right, distinct from her right to a conveyance of the subjects, in terms of which she was entitled to expect that the seller would have provided her with a building of a certain quality which the seller had failed to do. Based on that breach of a separate and independent contract, the purchaser was entitled both to retain the subjects and to claim damages; but, in awarding damages, the court stressed that this was not a case of an action *quanti minoris* because of the two distinct and separate obligations.

**28.100**   In an earlier case, *Wann* 1935 SN 8, there was a contract for the sale and purchase of a piece of ground on which the seller undertook to erect a dwellinghouse in accordance with a certain plan but without any undertaking as to specifications, etc. The purchaser accepted a disposition thereof on completion of the building. Some years later, structural defects developed and the purchaser claimed damages. Apparently, the missives did not contain a non-supersession clause. Nonetheless, the court held that the disposition did not bar enquiry into the antecedent contract and, on that basis, awarded damages. The decision in *Wann* is expressly disapproved in *Winston*.

**28.101**   This same question was raised in the more recent case of *Hayes* 1984 SLT 300. In that case, as noted above, the missives contained the special clause to the effect that the whole terms and conditions of the offer, insofar as not implemented or superseded by delivery of a disposition, were to remain in full force and effect, notwithstanding such delivery.

The particular obligations which the seller had failed to implement were in part representations as to the quality of the subjects at the date of the contract; and in part a failure by the seller to carry out work which he had contracted to carry out in the missives. The first of these obligations would seem to fall squarely within the type of clause referred to in *Winston* and would therefore not constitute a personal or collateral obligation to do anything in the future, being simply a statement of the state of affairs at a certain date. On the authority of *Winston*, *Taylor* and *Porch*, and certainly in the absence of a special clause in the missives, the purchaser could not have founded on that obligation after settlement.

The second obligation, on the other hand, being of a continuing nature, can be properly described as a collateral obligation in the sense of *McKillop* above referred to, but Lord Ross seems to take the view that both obligations could truly be regarded as collateral obligations; and, on that footing, a claim for damages for failure to implement these obligations could be regarded not as an *actio quanti minoris* but as a claim for damages for breach of a distinct collateral obligation. However, in *Hayes*, the purchaser himself was in breach and so not entitled to enforce the contract. In the result, Lord Ross reached the view that it would not be appropriate at that stage to decide whether the action was an *actio quanti minoris* (which would not be relevant) or to enforce a collateral obligation (which would be relevant).

The question of collateral conditions and their enforceability after settlement of the transaction, whether or not the contract and the subsequent disposition contain a non-supersession clause, and the resulting right of the purchaser to claim damages on account of breach of that collateral obligation, have arisen in a number of recent cases both in the Court of Session and in the sheriff court.

In *Taylor* the position is discussed and the authorities reviewed by Lord Milligan. In that case, the missives contained a provision to the effect that the purchaser would be entitled to have the central heating system repaired at the expense of the seller if not in working order at the date of entry; and the missives contained a non-supersession clause. Lord Milligan held that this condition was both a collateral obligation under exception (b) in *Winston* and a personal obligation preserved by the non-supersession clause under exception (c) in *Winston* and so, on both counts, survived delivery of the disposition. The basis of damages was, of course, fixed by the terms of the missives and so is not discussed in this decision but the authorities generally are reviewed. In *Hardwick* 1991 SLT 258 Lord McCluskey seemed disposed to treat the basis of damages in such a situation as being the reasonable cost of remedying the deficiencies, as opposed to *quanti minoris*.

In *Adams* 1995 SCLR 185, the Sheriff held that a contract for the sale of land which included a four apartment dwellinghouse to be erected by the sellers was not simply a contract for the purchase of heritage but incorporated in its terms a separate obligation on the sellers to build the dwellinghouse and that the dwellinghouse should be constructed to reasonable workmanlike standards.

### 28.102 Both parties in breach

For a complex case where both parties were in breach and where, in addition, the pursuers as purchasers under concluded missives maintained that their solicitors had acted negligently, see *Mason* 1993 SLT 773.

Following conclusion of missives for the purchase of a farm, the purchasers paid a substantial sum, over £100,000, towards the purchase price and took possession. The sellers' agents granted a letter of obligation undertaking to deliver a valid disposition in exchange for the remaining balance of the price. Some time later they intimated that they were in a position to deliver that disposition but the purchasers refused to settle on the footing that the acreage of the farm had been misrepresented. This in turn led to an action of implement by the sellers against the purchasers which was defended on these grounds. The purchasers further averred in the course of that action that the sellers' alleged breach of contract amounted to repudiation; that the contract fell to be rescinded; and, on that account, counterclaimed for repayment of the part of the purchase price already paid over. The sellers refused to accept rescission of the contract at which point, apparently, the sellers' solicitors withdrew from the action. The purchasers obtained a decree of dismissal and a decree by default in their counterclaim. They were, however, unsuccessful in enforcing that decree, and so petitioned for the sellers' liquidation. Creditors in a standard security over the farm then entered into possession and resold it.

The basis of the claim for negligence against the purchasers' solicitors was failure on the part of the solicitors to advise the purchasers that obtaining decree in the principal action would probably be worthless and that, in addition, by obtaining that decree, they would render the letter of obligation worthless as well. Lord Cameron of Lochbroom did not accept that the taking of decree amounted to an irrevocable election to terminate the contract and accordingly that the pursuers' averments, that the letter of obligation had become ineffective, were irrelevant.

The case serves as a warning but does not produce any significant matter of principle. Lord Cameron declined to reach a firm conclusion on the averments of the parties beyond what is stated above but put the case out by order and, in the subsequent procedure, decree of dismissal was pronounced.

Chapter 29

# THE SPECIAL DISPOSITION

### 29.1 Transmission of the feu

The creation, by subinfeudation, of a vassal's right to the *dominium utile* and the conversion of the vassal's personal title, represented by the charter duly delivered, into a real right by registration in the General Register of Sasines or in the Land Register are dealt with in Chapter 13. The process of subinfeudation can be repeated indefinitely by successive vassals, each such subinfeudation adding another link, downwards, in the feudal chain. The same general principles apply both to the original act of infeudation by the Crown, and to each act of subinfeudation by each successive vassal.

But instead of subfeuing, the vassal, having acquired a real right in the *dominium utile* of land by recording his feu charter from the superior, may transfer his real right in the *dominium utile inter vivos* not by way of subinfeudation but by way of substitution or delegation, so that the disponee on acquiring the *dominium utile* from the disponing vassal takes the place of the disponing vassal and becomes, in his turn, vassal of the original superior on the original tenure.

The basic principles, and the form of deed, appropriate for transmission of the feu as discussed in this chapter are the same whether the transmission is of a Sasines title and the disposition is to be recorded in Sasines; or, if the property lies in an operational area, the transmission either induces first registration or is a dealing with a registered title.

There are, however, some minor differences in detail which are noted in the appropriate context in this chapter.

**29.2** Such disposal by the vassal may occur in various circumstances, may be effected by various means, and may have a varying result to the transferee. These include *inter vivos* transmission where the property passes from the vassal during his lifetime; or transmission *mortis causa* where the vassal remains proprietor of the property until his death on which event he is necessarily divested. Such transmission may be voluntary, *inter vivos* or *mortis causa*, which implies a positive act of disposal on the part of the vassal, by a deed which may be onerous or gratuitous; or involuntary, by operation of law, *e.g.* on the sequestration of the vassal *inter vivos*, where his property, including heritage, passes to the trustee in sequestration; or, *mortis causa*, where the vassal dies intestate.

**29.3** Property may so transmit, in one or other of these ways, to a singular successor, or to a universal successor. A singular successor is, typically, a purchaser from the vassal of his right to the *dominium utile*. A singular successor is liable only for real burdens and conditions running with the lands. In contrast, where the assets of the vassal transmit to a universal successor as general disponee or in some other equivalent capacity, the disponee acquires the whole assets of the vassal but, in addition, is also normally liable as universal successor, not merely for real burdens and conditions running with the land but generally for all debts and personal liabilities due by the divested vassal. This situation occurs, typically, under a trust deed for creditors granted by an insolvent or where assets and liabilities pass by statutory provision on a statutory vesting order from one public authority to another.

**29.4** In the case of voluntary transmission, written title is essential for reasons already examined, and may take the form of a special disposition or a general disposition. The special disposition is the deed normally used for *inter vivos* transmission, rarely for *mortis causa* transmission; its effect is to convey to the disponee a specific property, described and identified therein. Alternatively, the vassal may grant a general disposition of his whole estate in general terms which embraces, *inter alia*, his right to the *dominium utile* of his feu. This form of deed is commonly used for *mortis causa* transmission but rarely used for *inter vivos* transmission.

With involuntary transmission, the right passes automatically on the happening of a certain event, *e.g.* the appointment of a trustee in sequestration; or on decree of adjudication; or death intestate. But some written evidence in due form is required to vest the right, and constitute the title of the person in right of the property.

Again, with the voluntary disposition, the effect may be to transmit to the disponee the absolute beneficial right of property; or some more limited right, such as a right of liferent or a right in security.

### 29.5 Entry with the superior
Where a new feudal estate is created by feu charter, the disponer as superior retains his title to the land, burdened with the subaltern rights of his vassal. Accordingly, he remains liable to his own superior for all the incidents of tenure inherent in his own title, and becomes, by virtue of the charter to the vassal, entitled to enforce all the conditions of tenure against the new vassal.

Where the vassal transmits his feu to a third party, by delegation or substitution, the disponing vassal is absolutely divested and retains no remaining title or interest in the subjects conveyed. At the same time, he is (normally) relieved of all future liability for incidents of tenure in his own original charter; he continues to be liable for incidents already prestable. The disponee becomes liable directly to the true superior for all such incidents of tenure (past and future) along with, or in lieu of, the disponing vassal; and, on the feudal theory of continuing recurring contract between superior and each new vassal, the relationship of superior and vassal is of new established directly and contractually between the superior and the disponee of the original vassal. As between disponer and disponee, there is no continuing relationship and no new tenure is created, which is relevant when considering the enforcement of conditions created by a disposition.

**29.6** The substitution of a stranger as new vassal of the superior in this way is inherently at variance with fundamental feudal principle. The relationship of superior and vassal involves fidelity and service, and accordingly the selection of the original vassal in mediaeval times involved an element of *delectus personae*. As a result, having personally chosen the original vassal, the superior was not bound later to accept as new vassal someone of whom he had not previously approved. Therefore, where the feu was to transmit by disposition instead of by subinfeudation, the superior personally approved, and agreed to accept, the disponee in place of the disponing vassal. In the result, every special disposition on sale by an existing vassal required the sanction and approval of the superior whose active intervention was essential, if the disponee was to acquire a real right. This active intervention involved the public entry of a new vassal with the superior; and, until publicly entered, the new vassal had a personal title only. Public entry implied that the superior's consent could only effectually be given in the presence of the *pares curiae.*

Originally, the superior had absolute control and could refuse to accept any new vassal. This, of course, created difficulties particularly as to the enforcement of heritable securities and the resulting transmission of the security subjects to the purchaser from the selling creditor. As a result, the rule was gradually relaxed. But it was not until 1747 that the superior could be compelled to accept an outright purchaser as new vassal; and it was not until 1874 that his active participation as consenter was finally dispensed with.

For an excellent account of the origins and historical development of feudal tenure and transmission of the feu, see Halliday's *Practice*, Chapter 16, and the *Stair Encyclopaedia*, vol. 18, paras. 41 *et seq.*

**29.7**    Prior to the 1845 Act, the disponee obtained infeftment either:

(*a*)  by resignation, which involved the surrender of the *dominium utile* by the old vassal directly into the hands of the superior, but for the limited purpose of allowing the superior, thus reinvested, to grant a new charter in favour of the disponee known as a charter of resignation, which was a mandate for the disponee's infeftment as direct new vassal; or

(*b*)  a process of spurious or temporary subinfeudation, following on a conveyance containing the alternative holding, in the form of an obligation to infeft *a me vel de me.* The disponee in the first instance took infeftment as vassal on subinfeudation, holding of and under the disponer (*de me*), thus creating a temporary defeasible mid-superiority in the person of the seller, interposed between himself and the true superior. At a later stage, the disponee then went to the true superior; became publicly entered with him; and had his specious infeftment confirmed by the superior (*a me de superiore meo*), thus eliminating the temporary mid-superiority initially created. The deed confirming was termed a charter of confirmation.

**29.8**    The effect of a disposition in this form was twofold:

(*a*)  Immediate real right. By taking infeftment at once, and ascribing the infeftment to that portion of the obligation to infeft which provided for the holding by the disponee *de me* of the disponer, the disponee obtained an immediate real right, technically as vassal of the disponer on subinfeudation; and accordingly the disponer became mid-superior. No casualty was paid. The true superior could not object, since the disponer still remained his vassal.

(*b*)  Public entry. In virtue of the procuratory of resignation in the disposition, the disponee could, if he preferred, proceed at once to public entry and become infeft on the other leg of the alternative holding *a me de superiore meo*; but this meant that he had to pay a casualty at once, and might be confronted with delays because of defects in the superior's title. If, however, the disponee did proceed in this way, the disponer was immediately and absolutely divested; but the disponee was required immediately to pay the casualty.

Accordingly, in practice, a disponee would normally take immediate infeftment *de me* of the seller; but sooner or later a situation would arise in which it became necessary to enter publicly with the true superior, such public entry being then obtained by confirmation.

This procedure was complicated and cumbersome, and inevitably gave rise to numerous errors and defects in titles. A series of statutory provisions between 1845 and 1874 was enacted in order to simplify the procedure.

### 29.9 The Conveyancing (Scotland) Act 1874 s. 4

This provision represented the final development. It introduced a radical alteration of the whole system of transmission.

Firstly, by s. 4(1), charters and writs by progress generally, including charters and writs of resignation and confirmation, are abolished and can no longer competently be granted by a superior. The effect of this subsection is to render unnecessary the application to the superior for recognition of a disponee as new vassal; and from this point forward the superior's intervention in transmission disappears.

The principle of public entry is, however, preserved by s. 4(2) which provides that every proprietor who is infeft shall be deemed to be, as at the date of registration of his infeftment in the Register of Sasines, duly entered with the nearest superior whose estate of superiority, according to the rules then in force, would not have been defeasible at the instance of the infeft proprietor. Such infeftment is to have the same effect as if the superior had granted a writ of confirmation, irrespective of the state of the superior's title or of his capacity.

In other words, on the recording of the disponee's title, public entry is automatic and, in the process, all temporary mid-superiorities created by the alternative holding have been extinguished, being mid superiorities defeasible at the instance of the infeft proprietor.

In the case of registered titles, registration has substantially the same effect as recording in Sasines under the old system; but the position of the registered proprietor is, in certain situations, more secure, because of the strict limitations on the power of the Keeper to rectify the register against the proprietor in possession – see *Short's Tr.* 1996 SLT (HL) 166 and comment thereon in Chapter 13.33.

**29.10** Clearly, this has important consequences, *viz*:

(1) The alternative holding is redundant and disappears from the disposition.

(2) Defeasible mid-superiorities are abolished and cannot now be created.

(3) Since public entry is implied, the casualty became immediately payable on recording of the disposition. But this is now of no significance since the abolition of feudal casualties. It should be borne in mind that some leasehold casualties remain.

(4)  The state of the superiority title can never affect a disponee's real right.

(5)  The effect of the 1874 Act s. 4 was to eliminate altogether from the disposition the obligation to infeft *a me vel de me* (the alternative holding); the procuratory of resignation; and the precept of sasine. Further, every special disposition has become, of itself, a mandate for infeftment by *de 'plano* recording; and on the recording of such conveyance, without reference to the superior, the disponee perfects his real right and is impliedly publicly entered with the true superior.

**29.11  Effect of implied entry**.  Implied entry was liable to prejudice the superior in two ways.

(1)  Under the old rules, when a superior gave public entry to a disponee as new vassal, he thereby automatically released the old vassal from any continuing liability for feudal prestations. With implied entry, how is the superior to know who is so liable? The 1874 Act s. 4(2) provides that, notwithstanding implied entry, the last entered proprietor remains personally liable for feudal prestations unless and until the disponee has recorded his title; and the disponer has intimated to the superior the change in proprietorship, using a statutory form of notice of change of ownership. See 1874 Act Schedule A. Until both these steps have been taken, the superior may proceed against either the old vassal or the new vassal.

(2)  When a disponee was publicly entered as new vassal, it came to be presumed, in practice, that the disponee was discharged of any liability for arrears of feuduty. See *Marshall* (1895) 22 R 954. The Lord Ordinary, at p. 963, comments that the rule was one of practice only and doubts how far or firmly it was established. Did it apply only *quoad* the new vassal? Did it apply to obligations *ad factum praestandum*? But, before 1874, the superior could reserve his rights against the disponer, when giving entry. By the 1874 Act s. 4(3), the rule is reversed. Implied entry does not prejudice claims for arrears of feuduty against the disponer.

(3)  Certain further provisions in the 1874 Act s. 4(3) and (4) which refer to casualties are now obsolete, and can be ignored.

**29.12  Application of the rule of recurring personal contract**.  The normal rule as between superior and vassal, based on tenure and the recurring personal contract, is that, when the feu transmits by disposition, the original vassal as disponer, parting with the lands, ceases to be liable to the superior for implementing the conditions of the charter; and the disponee, as new vassal of the superior, becomes personally liable in his place. Note that this rule applies only to the feudal relationship. In other comparable situations, the disponer and his universal successors remain personally liable to the creditor in the obligation; whereas the disponee, although he may take the land subject to the real burden, is not personally liable himself in a question with the creditor. See *Wells* 1964 SLT (Sh Ct) 2, and some further comments thereon at Chapter 10.7. For the comparable case of liability under a contract of ground annual, see *Royal Bank of Scotland* (1853) 1 Macq. 358.

Under the 1874 Act s. 4(3) the superior's right to arrears of feuduty exigible prior to the date of entry is preserved. The same principle applies to other obligations and conditions which have already become enforceable before the vassal sells his interest. The selling vassal remains personally liable for these burdens: see *Marshall* above and *Rankine* (1902) 4 F 1074.

**29.13 The continuing need to give notice of change of ownership.** A new situation has arisen with the passing of the 1974 Act, in terms of which feuduty is redeemable, either voluntarily or compulsorily on sale. See Chapter 16. If redeemed, there is no continuing liability on the vassal or his successors to pay feuduty from the date of redemption. But the whole other obligations of the feu continue and remain enforceable against the old vassal and his successors in terms of the 1874 Act. Therefore, notwithstanding that no feuduty is payable, notice of change of ownership should continue to be given, even after feuduty has been redeemed. This applies not only to the sale on which the feuduty is actually redeemed, but also to subsequent sales occurring after that date; but with this difficulty that, as time wears on, it has become more and more difficult to ascertain who the superior is, when no feuduty is being paid. Failure to give notice of change of ownership may involve an owner who has sold his property years previously being held personally liable to implement feuing conditions, *e.g.* rebuilding ruinous buildings, etc. See the article in 1976 JLS 317. Notwithstanding the foregoing theoretical risks, however, notice of change of ownership is now rarely given.

**29.14 Form and content of disposition**
The disposition, like the feu charter, is a unilateral writ, running in name of the grantor alone and is not executed by the grantee. In general form, it closely resembles the feu charter and the principal clauses, with some modifications to suit the altered circumstances, are largely the same. But under the modern form of disposition no new tenure is created, and in the result the *tenendas* and *reddendo* clauses are inappropriate. The modern form of disposition contains nothing equivalent in form or effect.

Under the 1924 Act s. 3, it is now possible for the grantor of a disposition, but not the grantor of a feu charter or a lease, effectively to grant a special disposition on which the disponee can take infeftment even although the disponer is not himself infeft. Prior to 1924, any such disposition would have been invalid. A disposition by an uninfeft proprietor must contain, in addition to its normal content, a clause of deduction of title. This is dealt with again in Chapter 32, Completion of Title.

This principle no longer applies where a title has been registered, by express provision in the 1979 Act s. 3(6) which renders deduction of title unnecessary in any deed granted by the proprietor of a registered interest who is not himself registered. But such proprietor must produce to the Keeper links in title which, under the Sasines system, would operate as links in title, in order to satisfy the Keeper that he is in fact entitled to the registered interest. See *Registration of Title Manual*, Chapter 16.48, and the 1979 Act s. 15(3).

**29.15 Content of feu charter and disposition compared.** First, to contrast briefly the form of disposition with the form of feu charter. The essentials of the deed are: the narrative or inductive clause or clauses; the operative clauses, which again include the dispositive clause, which rules, and subordinate clauses, conferring rights ancillary to the main or dispositive clause; and the testing clause, or the equivalent information now prescribed under the Requirements of Writing (Scotland) Act 1995 in the case of a deed executed on or after 1 August, 1995.

**29.16 (1) Narrative clause.** The normal content here is, as in the charter, grantor, grantee and consideration, the consideration being normally, in a disposition, a lump sum payment. But in the disposition (less often in the charter), there are often circumstances, other than sale, which it may be appropriate to narrate as the reason for the granting of the disposition.

Otherwise, the same considerations apply as to title and capacity of the disponer as apply to the granting of a charter. But, by the special statutory dispensation in the 1924 Act s. 3 referred to above, an uninfeft proprietor may effectively grant a disposition, whereas for an effective feu charter the superior must be infeft. A disposition to two or more parties may or may not require a survivorship destination, for which see Chapter 7.17 and Chapter 31.10 *et seq*. Such destinations should not be inserted without express instructions from both parties. Any consentor will here be named and designed.

**29.17 (2) Dispositive clause.** Again, as in the charter, the dispositive clause is the principal operative clause of which the essential elements are:

(*a*) Words of conveyance. The only difference here is that the property is not 'in feu farm' disponed, since that implies tenure, but is simply 'disponed' to the disponee, with a destination, heritably and irredeemably, as in the charter.

(*b*) Identification of the subjects conveyed. There are no specialties as to description in Sasines titles. In the majority of cases, the disposition transfers the property entire, as it stands in the person of the disponer, in which case a description by reference is usual and appropriate. But it is equally competent to convey, by disposition, part of an original feu; or part of a part, and so on. In that case, a particular description will be necessary and the same rules apply as in the case of the feu charter. In the case of registered titles where the disposition represents a dealing which transfers the whole interest, the traditional form of description is replaced by a very short reference to the name or address of the property and a reference to the title number under which it is registered. On a transfer of part, a particular description of the part transferred or, if appropriate, a description by exception, will be necessary. For more detail, see Chapter 8, Descriptions.

(*c*) Reservations are equally competent in a disposition.

(*d*) Burdens. In Sasines titles, a disposition normally contains a reference to a prior writ for burdens, typically the original feu charter; and there may be several such writs. When the title has been registered and the disposition represents a dealing, a reference to prior writs for burdens is unnecessary. See the 1979 Act s. 15(2). The same applies to a transfer of part, with this qualification that, where a deed of conditions relating to the whole property has previously been recorded or registered and where the 1979 Act s. 17 has been disapplied therein, the deed of conditions must be referred to in the disposition of part, if the burdens therein are to become real burdens on that part. See Chapter 10.11 and 10.18. In addition, it is competent in a disposition to impose real conditions on the disponee, either as real conditions or as real burdens, the effect of which has already been examined when dealing with burdens and conditions in the charter. The same general principles apply to the creation and transmission of real conditions and real burdens in a disposition as apply to real conditions in a by-feu charter. In a disposition, however, such conditions present special additional problems, as follows.

**29.18** *Enforcement.* A condition of tenure is normally enforceable by personal action against the original vassal and all singular successors, on the recurring personal contract principle.

A condition in a disposition is enforceable by personal action against the original disponee and his universal successors on the basis of direct contract. But the disposition creates no tenure. Are such conditions enforceable by personal action in a question with a singular successor of the original disponee?

According to *Wells* 1964 SLT (Sh Ct) 2, the rule in *Royal Bank of Scotland* (1853) 1 Macq. 358 only applies to the contract of ground annual and similar arrangements where the disponer, as creditor in the obligation, is neither feudal superior nor permanently associated with the land which is burdened.

**29.19** Applying that principle:
(*a*) If a burden in a disposition is inserted simply to secure a money payment, *e.g.* a ground annual or the old pecuniary real burden, then the burden is enforceable against singular successors of the original disponee by real action only. But:

(*b*) If a burden in a disposition is inserted to secure the amenity of an adjoining property, it can be enforced against singular successors by personal action. A typical case in this category is a disposition of a flat in a tenement, imposing burdens of maintenance, etc. According to the sheriff in *Wells*, the basis of the right of personal action in this instance is the continuing relationship associated with the property between the creditor and the debtor in the obligation. The right of personal action may, however, equally well be based on *jus quaesitum tertio*. It certainly applies to any obligation *ad factum praestandum*. It may also apply to an obligation on each disponee to contribute a share of the cost of repairs but the decision by Lord Mackay in the House of Lords in *David Watson Property Management* 1992 SLT 430 provides a strong argument to the contrary. It is therefore prudent in all such cases for the whole body of proprietors to conjoin in giving joint instructions for common repairs: see *Wells* and further comments thereon in Chapter 10.13.

**29.20** *Jus quaesitum tertio.* If a superior grants feu charters to several adjoining feuars, and if certain stringent conditions are satisfied, each feuar may acquire a *jus quaesitum tertio* to enforce the conditions in his neighbour's charter. See Chapter 17.

In exactly the same way, if A, by disposition, sells portions of his feu to B, C and D, with the same conditions in each disposition, B, C and D may acquire a *jus quaesitum tertio* to enforce these disposition conditions *inter se.* Exactly the same general principles apply as in the case of charter conditions.

In addition, however, those parts of the feu so disponed are normally subject to the burdens in the original charter which apply to the whole of the feu and every portion thereof. A question then arises whether each of these disponees is entitled to insist on, and enforce, these charter conditions in a question with a disponee of another portion of the same feu.

**29.21** On this point, there is some conflict in the reported cases. Thus, Lord Watson in *Hislop* (1881) 8 R (HL) 95, at p. 104, states: 'A sub-feuar, or disponee, acquiring a building lot, subject to a particular condition, with notice in his title that the common author', *i.e.* the superior when granting the charter, 'has imposed that condition upon the whole area, of which his lot formed part, must be taken', *i.e.* by implication, 'as consenting that the condition shall be for the mutual behoof of all feuars or disponees within the same area, and that all who have an interest shall have a title to enforce it.'

Therefore, according to this dictum, in the ordinary case, every disponee of a portion of a feu can enforce conditions in the original charter, in relation to other parts of the same feu. This principle has been so applied in *Beattie* (1876) 3 R 634 and *Fergusson* 1953 SLT (Sh Ct) 113, where the *jus quaesitum tertio* of co-disponees seems to be taken for granted.

In contrast, in *Campbell* (1897) 24 R 1142, one disponee was held not to have a title to sue in exactly the situation envisaged by Lord Watson in the passage quoted above; and, in somewhat special circumstances, the court so held in *Girls' School Co.* 1958 SLT (Notes) 2.

The point was discussed again more recently in *Williamson & Hubbard* 1970 SLT 346. In that case, the charter of 10 Rothesay Place, Edinburgh (granted in the nineteenth century) restricted the use of that house to a single dwellinghouse only. In 1925, under legislation then in force, the sheriff authorised sub-division; and the house was then converted into three self-contained dwellinghouses. Later again, it was proposed to convert the ground floor and basement to an office. The proprietor on the first floor objected, claiming that she had a title and interest to enforce a condition in the original feu charter in a question with the ground floor proprietor.

The court held that she had no title to object, because, in the charter, there was nothing to create rights as between the owners of individual portions of the original dwellinghouse. This, of course, was necessarily so since, in the original charter, sub-division was prohibited. Lord President Clyde emphasises that the original charter, by prohibiting sub-division, clearly could not have contemplated any mutuality amongst individual owners of portions of the property *inter se*. But that in itself seems quite irrelevant. The question is whether, when the building was originally split up and disponed to the three purchasers from the original single owner, the three purchasers by implication agreed that each of them should be entitled to enforce the charter conditions as between each other. According to Lord Cameron, since there was nothing expressed in the disposition to indicate that there was to be any such mutuality as between the three individual owners, no one owner had a title to enforce these conditions as against any other; but that is certainly contrary to the view of Lord Watson quoted above, where agreement between original disponees is to be inferred by implication in these circumstances.

In contrast, in *Smith* 1972 SC 258 Lord Watson's dictum in *Hislop* is quoted and followed. More recently, in *Lees* 1987 SC 265, a single area of ground was disponed subject to real conditions which applied differently to different parts. It was subsequently sub-divided. A, the owner of one part proposed to breach a condition which applied to that part. *Held* that B, the purchaser of a house on the other part, had a *jus quaesitum* to enforce that condition against A, although the same condition did not apply to B's property.

**29.22** To illustrate these rules, suppose that A, the owner of one acre, dispones one-half of it to B. The disposition in B's favour contains a new burden and an obligation on A, the original disponer, to insert the same burden in any subsequent disposition of the remaining one-half acre. A then dispones the remaining one-half acre to C and in the disposition in C's favour inserts the same burden. Both dispositions enter the Record. In these circumstances, B and C, *inter se*, would each have a *jus quaesitum tertio* to enforce the conditions in each disposition against the other, on the same general principles which apply in relation to co-feuars. Further, if A, when disponing to B and disponing to C, had expressly provided that each disposition was granted subject to the conditions in the original charter and that each of B and C, *inter se*, had the right to compel the other to observe the charter conditions, then again B and C *inter se* would have a *jus quaesitum tertio* to enforce the charter conditions by express provision in each title.

According to Lord Watson's dictum, each would have that right by implication only and without the need for express provision to that effect but not according to Lord Cameron in *Williamson & Hubbard*. But see *contra*, *Lees* above.

**29.23** *Transmission of the title to enforce.* In a feudal grant, this creates no problem. The superior's title to enforce feuing conditions against his vassal automatically transmits with the superiority. Where conditions are created in a disposition, the position is less clear.

Suppose A owns one acre, with a house on it. He dispones one-half acre to B as an amenity feu, retaining the house for himself; and in B's title he prohibits any building on that one-half acre in order to preserve his own amenity. That is a condition imposed on B for the benefit of A's remaining property. A later sells and dispones his house to C. Does C have a title to prevent B from building on B's half-acre? It now seems settled, in a case of this kind, that C can insist on the condition in question with B or with singular successors from B. But does C's right spring from *jus quaesitum tertio*, or is his title to sue based on an assignation from A of A's contractual right to enforce against B, so that C represents A in the contract? If the latter, then C apparently requires no special assignation of A's right of enforcement. It passes *sub silentio* on the disposition by A to C. The difference between these two cases, *jus quaesitum tertio* and implied representation, could be difficult to define in more complex cases, but may be very important.

In *MacTaggart* (1906) 8 F 1101, A disponed an area of ground to B, incorporating in the disposition a real burden restricting buildings on the site to self-contained dwellinghouses. There was no indication as to who would be entitled to enforce that burden and no indication that A, the disponer, owned other land in the vicinity. That was in fact the case and these adjoining portions of A's land were subsequently conveyed to several disponees. Each of the subsequent dispositions contained an express assignation to the disponee thereunder of the right to enforce the restriction in these titles. On a subsequent challenge, the right to enforce thus assigned was upheld on the basis of express assignation, but the Court reserved its opinion as to whether or not, without such express assignation, the disponees would have had a title to enforce. In the subsequent case of *Braid Hills Hotel Co.* 1909 SC 120, A disponed to B part of a larger area of ground, declaring in the disposition that no buildings of any kind should be erected thereon except certain specified types of building below a specified height. That condition was declared to be a real burden and a servitude affecting the ground disponed in favour of the disponer and his successors as proprietors of the remaining parts of the whole area on the east and west sides of the subjects so conveyed. A then conveyed the remaining ground to the east and west sides of these subjects to other proprietors but did not include in their respective dispositions any assignation of the right to enforce the restriction.

The restriction itself, although in part arguably it would qualify as a servitude *altius non tollendi*, went far beyond the limits of that recognised servitude in that it stipulated specified types of building. Clearly, therefore, it could not be enforced in full on the basis of servitude. The Lord President seems inclined to have treated the title to enforce as created by *jus quaesitum tertio*, referring to Lord Watson in *Hislop*. But, in that decision, the title to enforce by *jus quaesitum tertio* was created by implication. In this case, as the Lord President correctly states, there was no need to look for any element of implication because the burden in the title expressly stated that it was imposed not only for the benefit of the disponer but also for his successors in the adjoining areas. Gloag on *Contract* (2nd edn.) p. 236 treats the right of enforcement in this case as one example of a right created by the *jus quaesitum*. 'The most unequivocal indication of an intention that a third party should have a *jus quaesitum* is an express provision', and of course there was express provision in the title in this case. That express provision, according to Gloag, justified the entitlement to enforce without any special assignation.

More recently, Professor Reid in the *Stair Encyclopaedia*, vol. 18, at para. 397 onwards, makes a detailed analysis of the right to enforce in such circumstances. He seems to favour the concept of dominant and servient tenement which, conventionally, is applied only in the case of servitudes, but extends it to include not merely servitudes and their enforcement but also real burdens and their enforcement in cases of this kind. There is another alternative view referred to by Professor Reid in the same context and derived from the decision in *Stevenson* (1899) 1 F (HL) 91. That case is not directly in point. In the course of his judgement, however, Lord Watson observed that, in a different situation, a disposition would have operated as a conveyance or assignation to the disponees of the disponer's title to enforce real burdens imposed on an adjoining proprietor. In other words, once the burden has been duly constituted, the title to enforce it attaches automatically to the creditor area and passes automatically on a conveyance of the whole or part only of that creditor area without specific assignation, as a part and pertinent of the subjects in that conveyance.

To complicate the matter further, in the *Botanic Gardens Picture House* 1924 SC 549, which is later in date than *McTaggart* and the *Braid Hills Hotel* decisions, the Court reached the opposite conclusion. Clearly, in this difficult area, Professor Reid is amply justified in his comment at para. 405 of the *Stair Encyclopaedia* that 'a well-drawn deed will put enforcement rights beyond doubt by making these the subject of express provision'.

In *Lees*, above, the subjects were disponed as a single whole. Different sets of conditions were imposed on two parts thereof. The owner of a house on one part was held entitled to enforce a condition which applied to the other part, but which did not apply to her property.

**29.24 (3) Deduction of title.** If the grantor of the disposition is not infeft, he is now statutorily enabled to grant a special disposition; but, to be effective, the disposition must contain a clause of deduction of title. The clause is inserted after the clause of entry. For further details see Chapter 32, Completion of Title.

As mentioned in para. 29.14, once the title has been registered, deduction of title ceases to be necessary under the 1979 Act s. 15(3). Instead, all that is required is to satisfy the Keeper that a party dealing with a registered interest, who is not himself the registered proprietor, is in fact entitled; and this will normally involve production to the Keeper of the traditional links in title. However, in the case of feudal grants and leases, where infeftment at common law still remains a prerequisite, the Keeper will normally insist that, before granting such a writ, the unregistered proprietor as owner of the registered interest should first himself become registered by production of the appropriate writs to the Keeper before the feu charter or lease is registered, failing which he may qualify his indemnity of the registered interest of the feuar or lessee.

**29.25 (4) Subordinate clauses.** As already explained, the *tenendas* and *reddendo* clauses which feature in the charter have no place in the modern form of disposition. Otherwise, the subordinate clauses follow the same pattern as in the charter, but with differences in detail.

Again, the statutory clauses introduced in Schedule B1 of the 1868 Act authorised by the 1868 Act s. 5 and interpreted in the 1868 Act s. 8 are appropriate to a disposition rather than a charter and less adaptation of the statutory clauses is here required.

**29.26** *(a) Entry.* No specialty.

**29.27** *(b) Assignation of writs.* The statutory clause is 'I assign the writs' but, by virtue of the 1874 Act s. 4, this clause has lost much of its technical value. At common law, a disponee is entitled to delivery of those writs which are essential to vindicate his right and which relate exclusively to the subjects conveyed. Under this clause, he can call for production of any other writs, should he wish to refer to them, which in any event is probably implied. In practice, this clause was almost always supplemented by detailed provisions dealing with delivery and custody of the writs listed in an inventory of writs appended to the disposition, to which reference was made in this clause.

The assignation of writs clause is dispensed with in two separate provisions, in the 1979 Act s. 16(1) and (2), dealing with the disposition and the feu charter respectively, because the position is somewhat different under each type of writ.

Section 16(1) deals with the disposition; and provides that an assignation of writs is implied in every disposition. Further, under this section:

(i) The disponer must deliver all deeds relating exclusively to the subjects; and must produce any writs which he retains.

(ii) The disponee is entitled to call for production of writs from any other custodier.

(iii) The disponee is similarly bound to produce to anyone else having interest any writs delivered to him which are common.

**29.28** *(c) Assignation of rents.* The statutory clause is 'and I assign the rents'. The clause may require adaptation. But there is no specialty here compared with the feu charter. As with the charter, the clause is no longer necessary under the 1979 Act s. 16(3).

**29.29** *(d) Obligation of relief.* The statutory clause 'and I bind myself to free and relieve the said disponee and his foresaids of all feuduties and public burdens' is normally suitable without adaptation. Again, this clause is no longer necessary under the 1979 Act s. 16(3).

**29.30** *(e) Warrandice.* The same rules apply here as in a feu charter. The statutory clause, 'I grant warrandice' is normally used, but may fall to be adapted according to circumstances.

If a disposition is to induce first registration, a warrandice obligation is included in normal form; but, if the title is registered by the Keeper without exclusion of indemnity, then for practical purposes the disponee will rely, not on the warrandice obligation in the disposition in his favour, but on the Keeper's guarantee. Where the Keeper has excluded indemnity, and eviction results from the defect in title on the basis of which indemnity was excluded, then a claim under warrandice against the grantor of the disposition would still be competent. Where there is no exclusion of indemnity and a claim subsequently emerges which, in Sasines titles, would be covered by the warrandice obligation, then the registered proprietor in the ordinary way will have a claim against the Keeper; and the Keeper in turn can claim against the grantor of the warrandice obligation under the 1979 Act s. 13(2) and (3). Note however that no claim is competent against the Keeper if the adverse right is an overriding interest; but the aggrieved proprietor may have a claim under warrandice. For a fuller discussion see *Registration of Title Manual*, Chapter 17.35.

In the case of dealings with a registered interest, the disposition implementing the dealing will likewise contain a warrandice obligation in traditional form and the same general principles apply as on first registration but with this difference that, where warrandice is granted on a dealing, the interest being dealt with is the registered interest which, by virtue of the 1979 Act s. 3, is subject to overriding interests. In the Sasines system, some of such overriding interests, including in particular servitudes and public rights of way, would give rise to a claim under warrandice. In the case of a dealing, however, and given that such interests automatically, by statute, override, does the grantor of the warrandice obligation impliedly guarantee that there are no such adverse rights? This problem has not yet been resolved. For further discussion see *Registration of Title Manual*, Chapter 17.42, Dealings.

**29.31** (*f*) *Non-supersession clause.*     Where missives were concluded before 21 June 1997, a non-supersession clause is still required. Since the decision in *Finlayson* 1987 SLT (Sh Ct) 150, if the missives contain a non-supersession clause, it is common practice to repeat that clause in the disposition amongst the subordinate clauses although not strictly speaking a subordinate clause in the technical sense. So long as the clause appears somewhere in the body of the disposition, the exact positioning thereof is immaterial.

Under the non-supersession clause normally used in practice in missives, the purchaser has the option of insisting that the clause be repeated in the disposition and normally exercises that option. Following on *Winston*, there were a number of cases where it was held that a non-supersession clause in the missives, if not repeated in the disposition, was ineffective; and that inclusion of the clause in the disposition was essential. The courts now seem inclined to take the opposite view. The point is touched on in the decision in *Tainsh* 1990 SLT (Sh Ct) 102 under reference to earlier authorities and in *Parker* 1992 SLT (Sh Ct) 31. But, in these two cases and in a number of others, the question whether or not the non-supersession clause must appear in the disposition itself was in fact irrelevant to the point at issue, in that the obligation in question was treated as a collateral obligation which survived delivery of the disposition without having to rely on a non-supersession clause at all. In *Jones* 1988 SLT (Sh Ct) 53, however, Sheriff Mowat seemed inclined to hold that inclusion of the clause in the disposition was not necessary, disapproving of earlier decisions to the opposite effect, and Lord Milligan seemed likewise inclined in *Porch* 1992 SLT 661. Obviously, however, the safest course is to include the non-supersession clause in the disposition, and this is regularly done.

In the case of registered titles, a non-supersession clause, even if included in the disposition, will not enter the title sheet or land certificate. The same applies to warrandice. It is therefore clearly desirable to retain the antecedent progress of title for a period, possibly 20 years or even longer, after registration to preserve the disponees' recourse, particularly under warrandice.

No non-supersession clause is required in missives or in dispositions after the coming into force of the Contract (Scotland) Act 1997 on 21 June 1997 unless the parties wish to make provision for certain obligations to have a limited life.

**29.32** (*g*) *Certificate of value for stamp duty.*     Again, there is no specialty here compared with the feu charter.

**29.33 (5) Infeftment of the disponee**.     Since 1874, a special disposition operates of itself as a mandate for the infeftment of the disponee by *de plano* recording. The same general principles apply as apply in the case of infeftment of a vassal and, in particular, there must be delivery of the disposition to the disponee. The disposition will be stamped. In non-operational areas, a warrant of registration will be endorsed and signed, and the disposition presented to the Register of Sasines with the completed application form for recording in the Sasines Register, now required in every case. The deed will then be recorded to complete the infeftment of the disponee. In operational areas, the title will probably have to be registered unless the disposition is not for onerous consideration. For procedure on registration of title, see Chapters 13 and 33.

The decision of the Inner House in *Sharp* 1995 SLT 837, referred to in Chapter 4, came as a salutary reminder to the profession that mere delivery of the disposition, taken by itself, might not be sufficient to divest the disponer and that the real right does not pass finally and irrevocably to the disponee until his title has been recorded. The decision was overturned in the House of Lords (1997 SLT (HL) 636) but only on the facts special to that case; and a decision does not affect the general principles as stated at some length in Chapter 4. See a recent article by Professor Rennie, '*Sharp* v. *Thomson* – The Final Act' in 1997 JLS 130. Current practice is to pay over the price in exchange for delivery, notwithstanding the potential risks of so doing, and that practice still continues despite the above decision. The risks are admittedly now limited by the House of Lords decision but there are other situations where the risk remains. As a further safeguard to protect the purchaser in the short gap between delivery and recording, Professor Rennie, in an article in 1994 SLT (News) 183, suggests that every seller should, at settlement, grant a declaration of trust to the effect that, having received the price in exchange for delivery of the disposition, he thereafter holds the property in trust for the purchaser pending the recording/registration. He further suggests that there is no good reason why such a declaration of trust should not be included as an extra clause in the disposition itself, and this is indeed sound advice. Nonetheless, such a declaration of trust may not, in itself, be a cast-iron guarantee of securing the disponee's real right, as the recent article in 1996 SLT 365 suggests. Notwithstanding the possible defects referred to in that article, however, there really is no other practicable solution at present. The only guaranteed solution is legislation. The Law Society of Scotland has submitted proposals to the Department of Trade and Industry with a view to improving the position.

### 29.34 Transmission of the superiority
On the granting of a feu charter, two interests emerge where one previously existed, in that the *plenum dominium* previously held by the superior is split into two elements – *dominium directum* which the superior retains, and *dominium utile* which passes to the vassal under the charter. When the charter is granted, the superior is already infeft on a title which includes *dominium utile*. So far as the superior is concerned, no new title is created by the granting of a charter. Instead, his existing title to land and his existing infeftment become burdened with the subaltern right of the vassal. To that extent only is he divested in favour of the vassal. On the strength of his own original infeftment, the superior is entitled to enforce, as against the vassal and successors of the vassal in the feu, all the conditions in the feu charter, including payment of the feuduty. In other words, the title to an estate of superiority is in essence a title to land; the beneficial interest of the superior is to insist on the incidents of tenure as against the vassal.

It follows that, for the transmission of an estate of superiority, the same rules apply as apply to transmission of *dominium utile*, because the estate of superiority is in itself a title to land. An estate of superiority may therefore transmit by special disposition which is, in its terms, a conveyance of land, not a conveyance of a mere 'superiority', and in the result, it is virtually indistinguishable from a disposition of *dominium utile*. This can be very confusing, particularly where the titles of the superiority and *dominium utile* of the same piece of land become intermixed.

**29.35** There are two typical, and different, cases where a superiority may transmit.

(1) Where the superiority is sold as a commercial investment. In trust law, a superiority is a narrower-range trustee security, and gives a good return. But because of the changes in the 1970 and 1974 Acts, and because of the trouble and expense of collecting individual feuduties, superiorities are no longer a popular form of investment and are not easy to realise.

(2) Where the vassal purchases his own superiority in order to discharge his liability for feuduty and other obligations in his charter. The two estates of *dominium directum* and *dominium utile* then merge in the same person, which raises some specialties, dealt with under consolidation, below. The principal purpose of acquiring the superiority is normally to discharge unacceptable burdens. Insofar as these burdens are enforceable at the instance of the superior, acquisition of the superiority and consolidation effectively achieves this result. But note particularly that, in cases where a *jus quaesitum tertio* has already been acquired by a neighbouring proprietor to enforce the conditions in the title in addition to the title of the superior to enforce the same, the title to enforce under a *jus quaesitum tertio* is not discharged or extinguished by the acquisition of the superiority. See Lord Watson in *Hislop* (1881) 8 R (HL) 95, at p. 102 'it is necessary to keep in view that, when the feuar has a *jus quaesitum*, his title, and that of the superior, to enforce common feuing conditions are independent and substantially different rights ... The superior's consent to discharge the condition cannot affect the right of the feuar ...'

A superiority may also be acquired to neutralise a prior mineral reservation and reunite the minerals with the surface. If that is the intention, care must be taken to ensure that the minerals are still retained in the superiority title; and the disposition must be carefully drafted to ensure that the *dominium utile* of the minerals is carried to the disponee. See *Orr* (1893) 20 R (HL) 27.

### 29.36 Specialties of superiority disposition

The only points of difference between a superiority and a *dominium utile* disposition are as undernoted. Note that, in the comments which follow on the form and effect of a superiority disposition, the fact that the title has been registered in the Land Register makes no difference except where specially noted.

(1) Narrative. This may (but need not) disclose the true position.

(2) Assignation of rents. The clause, if included, usually reads 'and I assign the rents and feuduties', but it is no longer required – 1979 Act s. 16.

(3) Warrandice. The feu rights previously granted to the vassals are excepted from warrandice; but failure to except feu rights has no effect on the validity of the disposition.

(4) Schedule of feuduties. Commonly, a schedule of feuduties is appended, but is unnecessary.

**29.37 Effect.** Since a disposition of superiority is in form a disposition of land, this may lead to some unexpected results.

**29.38 (1) Priority of infeftment.** Suppose a superior, A, grants a charter of a plot on a landed estate, and the vassal B forgets or omits to record the charter. The superior later sells and conveys his landed estate to C, a *bona fide* purchaser for value without notice of the vassal's right. C records this disposition of the estate in the Register of Sasines. For the reasons stated, the disposition is in form a conveyance of land and will include the superiority of B's feu as if it were *dominium utile.* Since C is first on the record, B, the vassal, loses his right. See *Ceres School Board* (1895) 23 R 279.

**29.39 (2) Minerals.** As we have seen, a conveyance of land carries subadjacent minerals, unless these have previously been severed from the surface. Suppose A, owning *plenum dominium* of surface and minerals, feus the surface, reserving minerals, and the vassal records the charter. The resulting position is that A owns the *dominium directum* only in the surface, but retains the *plenum dominium* in the minerals. If he then sells the superiority, the purchaser's title will take the form of a disposition of land. If A, in conveying the superiority to the disponee, does not again reserve minerals, the disposition will normally carry those minerals to the purchaser of the superiority. See *Orr* (1893) 20 R (HL) 27, although in the result in that case, from other evidence in the deed, the court held that minerals were not carried.

### 29.40 Specialties

(1) Splitting the superiority. The owner of *dominium utile* may divide it into any number of smaller portions and dispose of each separately. But a superior may not dispose of the *dominium directum* in such a way that, in the result, one vassal acquires two or more separate superiors.

(2) Interjection of a superiority. Where a superior has granted a feu charter in favour of a vassal, he cannot so manipulate his estate of superiority as to introduce a mid-superior between himself and his vassal, thus removing the vassal one stage further from the Crown. Compare the position in leasehold titles. It was probably competent at common law, and is now competent by express statutory provision, to interpose a lease between the landlord as infeft proprietor of the *dominium utile* and his immediate tenant. See the 1974 Act s. 17.

The superior in the charter may reserve special power to do either (1) or (2) above, but this is now rare.

(3) Mixed estates. Where the owner of a landed estate has feued off portions of it, he still retains intact his original title to the whole estate on the principles already explained; but his beneficial interest in part of the estate is limited to *dominium directum* only. He can dispose of his whole remaining interest, both *dominium directum* and *dominium utile*, by a single conveyance of the whole landed estate which will effectively transfer both the estate of superiority and the *dominium utile* so far as retained. It is unnecessary in such cases to have a separate disposition of *dominium directum* and

a separate disposition of the remaining *dominium utile*. See *Ceres School Board*, above. In registration of title, where a mixed estate is transferred and the deed either induces first registration or represents a dealing, the Keeper will, where practicable, differentiate between *dominium directum* and *dominium utile*. The Keeper's practice is to disclose the existence of the mixed fee both in the property section and in the burdens section of the title.

In the property section:

(i) Under the heading 'INTEREST', there will be entered 'proprietor and superior' instead of merely 'proprietor'.

(ii) A note will be entered in some such terms as:

'Note: the parts edged and numbered in blue on the title plan have been feued – for particulars see schedule below.'

(iii) A schedule of feus will be incorporated which will vary according to the type of property. The schedule would normally disclose (i) the several subjects feued by reference to plots delineated and numbered on the title plan; (ii) the original grant by feu charter or feu disposition; (iii) the original feuar; and (iv) the date of recording of the original feu writ.

In the burdens section, there will be an entry disclosing that the feu rights so created are burdens on the subjects in this title.

The same general practice would be followed in the case of registered leases.

The foregoing statement of practice is, however, subject to the qualification referred to above that, in the case of mixed estates, especially with older feus, it may be very difficult to identify the actual boundaries of individual feus, in which case the Keeper may have to resort to an exclusion of indemnity as to the actual extent of individual feus.

## 29.41 Infeftment of disponee

There are no specialties. The disponee requires infeftment, his title being a title to land. He obtains it by recording the disposition with warrant of registration and the application form for recording in the Sasines Register, or by registration of the title if appropriate.

## 29.42 Extinction of the feudal relationship

In modern practice, it very rarely happens that a superiority is extinguished. Almost all defeasible mid-superiorities, which were at one time temporarily created by the use of the alternative holding, have now been extinguished by the 1874 Act s. 4. Tinsel, or forfeiture, of the superiority is obsolete, as a result of the 1874 Act s. 4. Relinquishment of a superiority by the superior into the hands of his vassal, authorised by the 1868 Act s. 110, has rarely (if ever) been used in practice. But the estate of *dominium utile* is frequently extinguished, by merger with the superiority title, the effect being, in substance and in feudal theory, to disburden the superiority title thereof. This happens by irritation of the feu – see Chapter 16 – and by consolidation.

### 29.43 Consolidation

When the same person in the same capacity becomes debtor and creditor in the same obligation, the obligation is automatically extinguished *confusione*. Originally, *confusio* applied to the relationship of superior and vassal; so that, if the superior acquired the *dominium utile* on a separate title, that, of itself, disburdened the superiority title of the subaltern right created by the charter in favour of the vassal. But this no longer applies; see *Bald* (1787) 2 RLC 210. Instead, where the two separate estates of superior and vassal vest in the same person, they remain separate and distinct. There is no automatic merging or extinction of the subaltern right; and accordingly the superior, having acquired the *dominium utile*, can later dispose of it on the original title, by disposition; or, retaining the *dominium utile*, can dispose of the superiority as a separate feudal estate.

If the *dominium directum* and the *dominium utile*, as two separate feudal estates, are to merge so as to form a single feudal estate, a further step is required, termed consolidation, which is the legal reunion of two separate, but adjacent, fees in the same land. The effect of consolidation is to restore the estate of *dominium utile* to the superior and to merge it in the superiority title. See and compare *Zetland* (1870) 8 M (HL) 144, *per* Lord Westbury, who maintains that the *dominium utile* is not totally extinguished; and *contra* Lord President Inglis in *Park's Curator* (1870) 8 M 671, at p. 675, who takes the view that the effect is to extinguish and destroy the *dominium utile*. It follows that, on consolidation, there is, thereafter, only one feudal estate and only one title, namely, the superiority title which, including the destination, if any, therein, thereafter controls the subsequent devolution of the estate. As mentioned above, consolidation effectively extinguishes all conditions and burdens affecting the *dominium utile* insofar as enforceable by the superior; but does not extinguish a *jus quaesitum tertio* to enforce the same.

Consolidation can be effected in one of three ways, as undernoted.

### 29.44 (1) Resignation *ad perpetuam remanentiam*, or resignation *ad rem*.

This is the original feudal method, the vassal surrendering, or resigning, the feu into the hands of the superior. In contrast with resignation *in favorem*, which was a temporary and conditional resignation, resignation *ad rem* implies a permanent and unqualified surrender of the *dominium utile* into the hands of the superior. It was effected either by a procuratory of resignation granted by the vassal; or by a disposition granted by the vassal in favour of the superior, containing, in place of the usual feudal clauses, a procuratory of resignation. Since 1858, this clause has been replaced by a short statutory clause 'And I resign the lands and others above disponed *ad perpetuam remanentiam*' which is inserted immediately after the clause of entry in an ordinary form of disposition.

This method is still available (1924 Act s. 11(2)). The superior must be infeft in the *dominium directum*, and the disposition, containing the clause of resignation *ad rem*, must be recorded. There is then immediate consolidation of the two estates.

In operational areas, a special situation may arise where a superior, infeft in the *dominium directum* on a Sasines title, acquires the *dominium utile* thereof, also held on a Sasines title, by a disposition *ad rem* or with minute of consolidation endorsed thereon and duly completed before recording, for which see below. In the ordinary way, a disposition to the superior of the *dominium utile* for consideration would induce first registration and so would fall to be registered in the Land Register, not recorded in Sasines. In this particular illustration, however, where the *dominium utile* is to be immediately absorbed into the *dominium directum*, the disposition, even although granted for consideration, will be recorded in Sasines under a special provision in the 1979 Act s. 2(2) so that the titles to both interests, *dominium directum* and *dominium utile*, are recorded in the same register. If, however, there is no clause of resignation and no endorsed minute, the *dominium utile* would not be immediately absorbed into the superiority; and so the disposition thereof, if for consideration, will induce first registration of the *dominium utile* title. The same proprietor may thus hold the superiority on a Sasines title and the *dominium utile* on a registered title, as two separate interests in the same property.

If the title to the *dominium utile* has been registered, the disposition thereof to the superior would normally be a dealing and as such registrable. But, under the special provisions of s. 2(2), a disposition thereof *ad rem*, or with completed minute of consolidation, will in fact be recorded in Sasines, because absorption is then automatic. The disponee must also apply simultaneously for registration of his title in the Land Register, whereupon the title sheet of the registered interest of the *dominium utile*, thus absorbed into the superiority, will be cancelled. This is one of the few cases where an interest, once registered, is then removed from the Land Register and reverts to Sasines.

**29.45 (2) Minute of consolidation.** This is a statutory simplification, in two forms, under 1874 Act s. 6 and 1924 Act s. 11.

By the 1874 Act s. 6, where one proprietor is infeft in two adjacent feudal estates, he may record a minute of consolidation under the 1874 Act Schedule C. The minute, when recorded, consolidates the two estates, to the same effect as if consolidation had been effected by disposition containing the clause of resignation *ad remanentiam*.

By the 1924 Act s. 11(1) where an infeft superior acquires the *dominium utile*, he may endorse a minute of consolidation on the disposition of the *dominium utile* in his favour before that disposition is recorded; and on the subsequent recording of the disposition, with endorsed minute, the *dominium utile* is consolidated with the superiority, to the same effect as if a separate minute of consolidation had been recorded under the 1874 Act s. 6. The endorsed minute can also be used, with the same effect, where an infeft vassal acquires the *dominium directum*.

The same specialty applies here in operational areas where the title to the superiority is recorded in Sasines and the title to *dominium utile* is registered. Consolidation results in absorption with the same effect as in 29.44 above, and the title sheet to the *dominium utile* will be cancelled. Registration of the disposition both in the Land Register and Sasines Register is required.

**29.46 (3) Prescription.** Since the case of *Bald, supra*, the mere acquisition by the same person of the two feudal estates of superiority and *dominium utile* does not, of itself, operate an immediate consolidation. But, where the same proprietor continues to own both feudal estates for the prescriptive period, it is presumed that he has possessed the two estates on the superiority title and that, by prescription, the *dominium utile* is consolidated with the superiority thereof.

Again, there may be a specialty here where the title to the superiority is recorded in Sasines but the title to the *dominium utile* is registered. If, by consolidation, the *dominium utile* is merged with and absorbed into the title to the *dominium directum*, the title sheet to the registered interest of the *dominium utile* would fall to be cancelled under the special rules which apply to absorption above referred to. But in such cases the Keeper will invite voluntary registration of the superiority title in the Land Register; and the existing title sheet of the *dominium utile* will then embrace both estates, consolidated.

For further details of the complexities of these various possible situations, see Halliday's *Practice*, Chapter 17–118 and R.T.P.B. D.4.27.

**29.47 Midsuperiorities**. The foregoing rules apply not only to consolidation of *dominium utile* with the immediate superiority; but also to consolidation of a mid-superiority with the immediate superiority thereof.

**29.48 Specialties**. The foregoing rules may suffer some qualification where:

(*a*) the superiority title is not (as is normal) a title to land, but is merely a title to a 'superiority' or 'estate of *dominium directum*'; or

(*b*) the superiority title is entailed.

Since both these situations are now extremely rare, they are not further dealt with here. See Burns' *Handbook*, pp. 221 and 222, for more detail.

# Chapter 30

# STATUTORY TITLES

## 30.1 Statutory limitation of the real right

The real right is the foundation of ownership; and it is of the essence of the real right that it is secure against challenge from all comers.

In heritage, the real right depends upon infeftment. As we have seen, infeftment proceeds upon a mandate for infeftment, followed by recording of the appropriate writ in the Register of Sasines, or now, in appropriate cases, by registration of the interest in the Land Register.

At common law, if the real right is to transmit *inter vivos*, it can only do so on a mandate for infeftment actively granted by the infeft proprietor which must take the form of a special conveyance *e.g.* feu charter or disposition, by the infeft proprietor; or, at least, a general disposition by him which satisfies the minimum requirements of the Conveyancing (Scotland) Act 1874 s. 27 in that it contains a word or words importing a conveyance or transference or a present intention to convey. Nothing less will operate as a mandate for infeftment to a transferee.

But this general rule is subject to certain qualifications. In the first place, in certain circumstances, the court will intervene to give effect to personal or equitable claims affecting the real right vested in an infeft proprietor. In the second place, by statute, certain bodies, especially local authorities and certain ministers, are given powers of compulsory expropriation in the national interest, in the exercise of which, failing co-operation by the infeft proprietor, the acquiring authority can obtain a valid title under statutory procedure.

## 30.2 Adjudication in implement

The infeft proprietor may, in various ways, voluntarily undertake obligations which affect his real right in heritage, and may create valid and enforceable personal claims at the instance of some other party. Normally, the infeft proprietor implements such obligations by granting an appropriate title in favour of the grantee; but, if he declines to grant the appropriate title, then the grantee may invoke the assistance of the court to supply, by decree, the want of a voluntary mandate for the infeftment of the grantee without which the infeft proprietor cannot be divested and the grantee cannot perfect his real right.

The appropriate process is adjudication in implement, a form of diligence under which a person in right of land, or for whose benefit a debtor has agreed to grant heritable security, may obtain a title to land or security over land. An action of adjudication is competent only in the Court of Session and cannot be raised in the sheriff court.

**30.3**  Suppose that A, infeft, and beneficially entitled to a heritable property, enters into a contract, valid in point of form and content, to sell his heritage to B. In terms of such a contract, A undertakes to convey the heritage to B, but the contract does not contain 'any other word or words importing conveyance or transference, or present intention to convey or transfer' to satisfy the requirements of the 1874 Act s. 27. Accordingly, while it confers on B a valid and enforceable right to the heritable property, it does not *per se* operate as a title, nor as a mandate for the infeftment of B. In the ordinary way, following on such a contract, A will convey the property to B. But suppose he declines to do so. B may then raise an action of adjudication in implement against A for implement of the contract of sale and purchase.

The decree supplies the want of the conveyance by A to B. The extract operates as a title, and may be recorded direct in Sasines or registered in the Land Register to complete the adjudger's infeftment; or it may be used, unrecorded, as a link in title. In a competition, the date of preference is the date of recording of the extract decree, not the date of the decree itself (Titles to Land Consolidation (Scotland) Act 1868 ss. 62 and 129, as amended by the 1874 Act ss. 62 and 65). The same applies to registered titles.

While an action of adjudication in implement is the recognised formal method of obtaining a title where a title cannot be obtained by voluntary means, it is also competent, both in the Court of Session and in the sheriff court, in appropriate circumstances to raise an action of implement *ad factum praestandum* to ordain the defender to grant the appropriate title in favour of the pursuer which, for whatever reason, the defender fails or refuses to grant. The difficulty here is that, while a decree may be obtained in appropriate terms, it cannot of itself operate as a title in contrast to a decree in an action of adjudication which is itself a title and can be recorded in the Register of Sasines or registered in the Land Register to procure an infeftment for the pursuer in that form of process.

Admittedly, in the Court of Session in such an action the court has power under the *nobile officium* to authorise the Principal Clerk of Session or his deputy to sign a disposition in place of the defender who refuses or is unable to sign. But this would normally presuppose that there is in existence a writ in appropriate and agreed form available for signature; and all that is required is the signature of the defender.

In similar circumstances, now, under the Law Reform (Miscellaneous Provisions) (Scotland) Act 1985 s. 17, in a sheriff court action, the sheriff has the like power to authorise the sheriff clerk to sign a disposition but again this presupposes that there is a disposition in existence available and ready to sign which may not always be the case. Certainly, s. 17 reads as if there were such a deed available for signature and all that the sheriff can do is authorise the execution thereof. If so, he would seem to have no power to authorise the preparation of an appropriate disposition in implement; and the power of the Court of Session under the *nobile officium* may be subject to the same limitation. This can be contrasted with the position under the Housing (Scotland) Act 1988 s. 30(2) which empowers the sheriff in prescribed circumstances to draft a lease or adjust the terms thereof. See Chapter 27.17.

## 30.4 Adjudication for debt

The whole of a man's estate, both heritable and moveable, is liable for payment of his whole debts. As we have seen, a secured debt creates a preference for the creditor at the date of the security; and such creditors obtain, *ab initio*, a nexus on the security subjects and powers of enforcement, such as sale. The unsecured creditor has no equivalent, *ab initio*; but can later acquire rights to some extent equivalent to those enjoyed by the secured creditor through the process of adjudication for debt. This takes two forms, adjudication for payment and adjudication in security. This type of adjudication differs from adjudication in implement in that the intention here is not to confer an absolute title on the creditor, but rather to secure payment for the creditor out of the heritable property adjudged to him.

(*a*) *Adjudication for payment.* This process is competent to a creditor holding a liquid document of debt, *e.g.* a personal bond or a decree for payment.

Decree, when obtained, is recordable in Sasines. It operates as a judicial conveyance to the creditor of the heritable property adjudged, for payment of the debt, but subject to a power of redemption at the instance of the debtor at any time within ten years of decree. This ten-year period is the legal period of redemption, otherwise known as the 'legal'. In the result, the creditor's title under an adjudication for payment is initially a redeemable title, whereas under adjudication in implement the pursuer's title is immediately indefeasible. At any time within the legal, the creditor can be forced to denude in favour of the debtor if he receives payment of his claim in full. In the result, the creditor has a mere security only, which he cannot convert into cash to liquidate his debt for at least ten years. This is because, under a decree of adjudication for payment, recording of the decree provides security, but it does not confer any power of sale in contrast to the powers of a creditor under a standard security.

(*b*) *Adjudication in security.* This is competent, but now virtually unknown, where there is no liquid document of debt, in special circumstances only. It differs from adjudication for payment in that there is no 'legal' and the right of redemption persists indefinitely.

## 30.5 Bankruptcy and sequestration

Adjudication for debt, although still competent, is rare in modern practice. Instead, it is usual for the estate of the debtor to be sequestrated for the general benefit of the whole body of creditors.

Until 1 April 1986 procedure was regulated by the Bankruptcy (Scotland) Act 1913. That Act has now been repealed entire and new provision made for sequestration by the Bankruptcy (Scotland) Act 1985 which came into operation on that date, as amended by the Bankruptcy (Scotland) Act 1993.

For the law and procedure under the 1913 Act, see Green's *Encyclopaedia*, Vol. 13.866 *et seq.*

We are concerned here with the effect of sequestration on heritable titles; and the new procedure introduced by the 1985 Act is touched on by way of introduction to that aspect of the Act only.

Sequestration follows on a petition to the court, by the debtor or by a creditor, for the appointment of a trustee to whom the whole of the debtor's estate is transferred. The trustee holds and administers the estate in trust for the general body of creditors. Under the 1985 Act, the appointment of the trustee proceeds in two stages. Firstly, an interim trustee is appointed under the 1985 Act s. 13 to take immediate control of the debtor's estate. Thereafter, following on a meeting of creditors, a permanent trustee is appointed in his place. The same person may, and normally will, act as both interim and permanent trustee.

**30.6 The act and warrant.** For the purposes of title, the act and warrant of the court, confirming the appointment of the permanent trustee, transfers the whole property of the debtor, heritable and moveable, to the permanent trustee absolutely and irredeemably as at the date of sequestration; but only so far as belonging beneficially to the debtor. The effect of the act and warrant on heritable estate of the debtor in Scotland is as if a decree of adjudication in implement and a decree of adjudication for payment but subject to no legal reversion had been pronounced in favour of the permanent trustee.

In contrast to a decree of adjudication in implement in ordinary form (see above), the act and warrant in a sequestration operates as a general disposition in favour of the trustee on which he may, if he wishes, complete title; but he cannot record the act and warrant *de plano*. He will normally complete title immediately in order to exclude the possibility of some other party acquiring a valid adverse real right. Thus, if the debtor, prior to sequestration, has granted a standard security which has not been recorded at the date of sequestration; and if, thereafter, the creditor records it before the permanent trustee completes title, the creditor will be secured. Completion of title by the permanent trustee before the competing infeftment excludes that possibility.

**30.7 Completion of title by trustee.** Special provision is made in the 1985 Act s. 31(3) to allow the permanent trustee to complete title to heritage to which the debtor's title was not completed at the date of sequestration.

Under s. 32 of the 1985 Act, assets subsequently acquired by the debtor after sequestration, *e.g.* as beneficiary under the will of a person who dies after that date, automatically vest in the permanent trustee; and production by the trustee of the act and warrant is sufficient to compel the custodier of any such asset to make it over to the permanent trustee. This is subject to two provisions:

(1) where someone in good faith and without knowledge of the sequestration has made over after-acquired assets to the debtor, he is not liable to account to the permanent trustee; and

(2) where a third party had acquired an interest in some such after-acquired asset in good faith and for value his title to that asset is beyond challenge. See s. 32(6). In a heritable transaction involving third parties, good faith will be difficult if not impossible to establish, given the customary entries in the Personal Register relating to the sequestration. In contrast to the position prior to the 1985 Act, such vesting of after-acquired assets is automatic and does not now require the intervention of the court nor any further procedure by way of recording of a notice in Sasines as was previously necessary.

In *Alliance & Leicester Building Society* 1995 SLT (Sh Ct) 77 the bankrupt acquired heritable property after the date of sequestration. The bankrupt granted a standard security in favour of the building society, and both deeds were recorded in the Register of Sasines. The Court held that the property vested in the trustee in sequestration, notwithstanding that the conveyance in favour of the bankrupt was granted after the date of the sequestration. If the property had formed part of the bankrupt's estate at the date of sequestration it would have vested automatically in the trustee at that date. The bankrupt could not therefore grant a valid standard security.

Under s. 33, any asset genuinely vested in the debtor as trustee for some other person is excluded from the sequestration and does not vest in the permanent trustee.

Further, under s. 33(3), the vesting provisions in ss. 31 and 32 are without prejudice to the right of any secured creditor which is preferable to the rights of the permanent trustee. A short provision in s. 39(4) replaces an elaborate series of sections in the 1913 Act which regulated the relationship of the trustee in sequestration and heritable creditors. For the effect of this provision, see Chapter 35.35.

Under s. 31(2), however, the powers conferred on the permanent trustee under the act and warrant are immune from challenge by an inhibiting creditor and an inhibition is of no effect in a question with the permanent trustee, except in a question of ranking.

**30.8 Registration.** Under the 1913 Act, it was the duty of the trustee to register a notice in the Personal Register immediately on his appointment, in order to give notice to the public at large of the debtor's sequestration. Under the 1985 Act s. 14(1), that duty now falls on the clerk of court who is required, forthwith after the date of sequestration, to send a certified copy of the relevant court order to the Keeper of the Register, for recording in the Personal Register. Recording of the certified copy has the effect, as from the date of sequestration, of an inhibition and of a citation in an adjudication of the debtor's estate, thereby effectively preventing the bankrupt from disposing or otherwise dealing with his heritable estate.

**30.9 Gratuitous alienation and unfair preferences.** Any gratuitous alienation by the sequestrated debtor can be reduced at common law. In addition, gratuitous alienation is struck at, but with certain qualifications and within certain time limits, under the 1985 Act s. 34 which repeals the earlier statutory provisions in the Bankruptcy Act 1621. Under s. 34(4), however, any third party who has acquired right from the gratuitous transferee in good faith and for value is protected. In practice, however, it would probably be impossible to establish good faith in any heritable transaction under this proviso.

A gratuitous transfer includes not only a transfer for no consideration but also a transfer for inadequate consideration, which is always exceedingly difficult to establish. This can cause serious problems for the seller. If the transferee is an associate of the debtor, which includes husband and wife, relatives, and partners, the effect of this provision lasts for five years. For other transferees, the period is two years. During that period, the gratuitous alienation can be challenged by any creditor or trustee in sequestration or under a trust deed. Admittedly, the effect of this section can be excluded if it can be shown that, at any time after the alienation, the debtor's assets were greater than his liabilities or that the alienation was made for adequate consideration; but these are difficult facts to establish.

Accordingly, if there is any suggestion on the face of the title that there has been a transaction for less than full consideration, the purchaser should proceed only with extreme caution. For an indication of some of the problems involved see 1991 SLT 77. For illustrations of reductions following on gratuitous alienations, see Digest of Cases 30.10.

Similarly, under s. 36, earlier provisions are repealed but effectively re-enacted. The general effect of this section is that any transaction entered into by a debtor which creates a preference for a creditor to the prejudice of the general body of creditors (formerly called a fraudulent preference, now termed an unfair preference), can be challenged under this section if the unfair preference was created within six months prior to the sequestration. As under the earlier rules, transactions in the ordinary course of trade, and payments in cash are exempted unless the cash payment was collusively made.

For a discussion on the effect of a gratuitous alienation at common law, which still also applies, see *Boyle's Trustee* 1988 SLT 581.

Under the fraudulent preference provisions in the Bankruptcy Act 1696 (now repealed) it was held that, in calculating the six-months period to determine whether or not a disposition was struck at by the fraudulent preference rules, the date of recording of the disposition, not the date of delivery, was the critical date: see *Grant's Trustee* 1986 SLT 220.

### 30.10 Reduction

A real right in land is secure from challenge against all comers. But the real right only has this characteristic of invulnerability if it has proceeded on, and been constituted in virtue of, a valid antecedent title, or series of titles. The title or series of titles on which the real right is based must be probative writing(s) (or the equivalent as now provided for in the Requirements of Writing (Scotland) Act 1995), and one characteristic of a probative writ is that it is presumed to be validly executed. This does not mean, however, that a probative writing is automatically exempt from challenge. It may be challenged on a variety of grounds including, *e.g.*, want of capacity, error, fraud, force, or defect in the solemnity of execution; but the onus of establishing any such latent defect in a probative writ lies on the challenger and not on the person acquiring right thereunder, whose interest is to sustain the writ.

Suppose, then, that A is infeft in a heritable property as beneficial owner but is insane. He executes a disposition thereof to B. Any deed by a person, insane, is invalid from want of capacity; but the deed may be *ex facie* valid. Suppose this deed is. B records it in Sasines, apparently perfects his real right thereby, and takes possession. A *curator bonis* is then appointed to A. How does the curator recover the property from B as ostensible owner? He must raise an action of reduction against B, the disponee, seeking to have the disposition to B reduced.

The onus lies on A's curator to establish and prove that A, at the date when the disposition was executed, was insane; but if he satisfies the court on this point, then, notwithstanding the apparent probative quality of the disposition by A, the court will then grant decree of reduction, the effect of which is to avoid and invalidate the disposition. This has the further consequence that all titles following on, and deriving their validity through that disposition are also reduced and rendered wholly invalid. In other words, the title to the heritable property in question is restored, by reduction, to the state it was in immediately prior to the granting of the invalid disposition by A.

This still remains the position in the case of Sasines titles. Where a title has been registered, however, the House of Lords in *Short's Trustee* 1996 SLT (HL) 166 upheld the decision of the Court of Session that a decree of reduction was not registrable in the Land Register. The decision is discussed in greater depth in Chapter 13.

This underlines the fundamental difference between registration and recording of a deed in Sasines which is an essential step in the creation of the real right but carries no guarantee of validity or invulnerability. In contrast, an interest registered in the Land Register under the 1979 Act is guaranteed by the Keeper except to the extent to which he has qualified his indemnity. Rectification of the Register to give effect to any inaccuracy therein can be exercised by the Keeper, or ordered by the court, only in very limited circumstances, if such rectification would prejudice the proprietor in possession. See further Chapter 13.33.

For an illustration of reduction of a power of attorney and a discussion on the standard of proof required, see *Sereshky* 1988 SLT 426.

**30.11 Reduction and adjudication compared.** Note the difference in effect between a decree of reduction and a decree of adjudication; the latter operates as an active title, equivalent to a disposition, in favour of the pursuer. A decree of reduction has a purely negative effect, invalidating existing writs. In the ordinary way, a decree of reduction invalidates the deed entire, but partial reduction seems to be competent in appropriate circumstances: see *McLeod* 1989 SLT 620 and *Broadley* 1991 SLT 69.

It follows from what has been said that every heritable title in Scotland is, theoretically, open to challenge at any time on the grounds that any one of the progress of titles is invalidated by a latent defect of the kind described above. In practice, actions of reduction affecting heritable title are rare; and this risk is one which a person dealing with a heritable proprietor on an *ex facie* valid title must simply accept.

**30.12 Protection of purchasers.** As a further protection to a purchaser dealing with a heritable proprietor on the faith of the record, the 1924 Act s. 46 provides that, where a deed, decree or other writing recorded in Sasines (or forming an unrecorded mid-couple in a recorded title) has been reduced by action of reduction, the extract decree must be recorded in the General Register of Sasines; and further that the decree is not pleadable against a third party who has *bona fide* onerously acquired a right to the heritage in question prior to the recording of the decree in Sasines.

The intention of this section may have been to extend and enhance the security of a recorded title in a question with *bona fide* purchasers for value. But in *Mulhearn* 1929 SLT 59, the court held that the section, in its terms, protected a *bona fide* purchaser acquiring the disputed subjects, but only during the short period between the granting of the decree and the recording of that decree; the section did not protect a purchaser who had acquired the heritage in question prior to the date of granting of the decree.

So, in the A–B case above, B (the disponee of the insane A) sells and

445

dispones the property to X, a *bona fide* purchaser, who believes the disposition A–B is valid. X records the disposition B–X before A's curator is appointed. The curator is thereafter appointed and raises an action of reduction to invalidate the two dispositions and obtains decree. X loses the property; but could claim against B under warrandice.

For a detailed discussion of the 1924 Act s. 46 and the implications of *Mulhearn*, see the article in 1986 SLT (News) 125.

The Family Law (Scotland) Act 1985 s. 18 empowers the court, in a matrimonial dispute, to set aside or vary any transfer of, or transaction involving, property by a party to a marriage made within the preceding five years; but no order can be made under this section which would prejudice the rights of a *bona fide* purchaser for value. This replaces the Divorce (Scotland) Act 1976 s. 6.

**30.13 Discharge of heritable security.** The Conveyancing and Feudal Reform (Scotland) Act 1970 s. 41 introduced a novel provision in regard to discharges of heritable securities. Prior to this Act, if a bond had been discharged at any time within the last 20 years, it was still necessary to examine the bond, its transmissions and discharge(s) for intrinsic and extrinsic validity. When the bond was discharged, say, 18 years ago, this was patently rather a waste of time. Section 41 provides that, where a discharge has been duly recorded more than five years previously, the subsequent reduction of that discharge (because, presumably, it was improperly granted) is not to affect the title of a *bona fide* purchaser for value; and the 1924 Act s. 46 ceases to apply to that decree of reduction.

**30.14 Rectification of defectively expressed documents**

As has already been explained in Chapter 2, under the heading of Probativity and Authentication, the rule at common law was that, unless and until a probative writ had been set aside by an action of reduction, it was bound to receive effect. The common law rule has now been altered by the Law Reform (Miscellaneous Provisions) (Scotland) Act 1985 ss. 8 and 9, in terms of which, as an alternative to an action of reduction, it is now competent to apply to the court for the rectification of a probative document if either party can satisfy the court that the document fails to express accurately the intention of the grantor or, in the case of a contract, the intention of the parties. Under s. 8(4), if a document is so rectified, then it takes effect as if it had always been so rectified; and, under s. 8(5), if the deed was recorded in Sasines, the order rectifying the document should also be recorded, whereupon the deed as originally recorded falls to be treated as having been recorded in its rectified form *ab initio*.

When such an action has been raised, it is competent, under s. 8(7), to record a notice of litigiosity in the Personal Register.

There have been a large number of cases on the subject of rectification under s. 8, and the courts are interpreting the provision widely. Thus in *Bank of Scotland* 1992 SC 79, a standard security was rectified when it had been signed only once, and not twice as was provided for in the deed. In *Bank of Scotland* 1995 SLT 689 the name of the wrong granter was inserted in the deed. Proof before answer was allowed. The Court stressed that the deed must be executed by the right person, and if that person was then misdescribed in the deed, that could be rectified.

Whereas it would appear that many different types of error can now be rectified, if what is required is rectification of a deed that is so extensive that it almost amounts to a rewriting, that will not be permitted: see *Huewind Ltd*. 1996 SLT 369. In addition, for rectification under s. 8(1)(a), some 'common intention' of the parties that has not been expressed in the document must be demonstrated. In *Rehman* 1993 SLT 741 Lord Penrose held that to justify rectification the applicant had to prove that there had been an agreement, made independently of and prior to the date of the document. This could be difficult to show in the case of missives not expressing a common intention of the parties, but easier to prove where a disposition does not implement the terms of the missives.

### 30.15 Appointment of trustees, judicial factors, etc.
This is another case where, on the application of an interested party, the court will intervene to appoint a new trustee on a pre-existing trust, where for some reason or other the existing trust machinery has broken down; or to appoint a judicial factor to take over and/or administer an estate on behalf of an incapax, missing, or unknown, proprietor. In such cases, the decree of the court either operates as a feudal conveyance in favour of the trustee or factor so appointed, in virtue of which he can make up title to the trust heritage; or it operates as a judicial power of attorney, entitling the factor to deal with heritable estate in name of an incapax ward. See Chapter 3.

### 30.16 Compulsory purchase
In any developing industrial society, the individual's right of property in land must yield to the overriding needs and interests of society as a whole. Otherwise, if the individual right of property in land is to be paramount, then any individual owner, by declining to co-operate, can frustrate all manner of developments, typically, railways, canals, trunk roads, water and sewage. Of course, many land owners appreciate this need and are willing to co-operate, when required, in disposing of land to the appropriate authority by agreement. But inevitably there will be cases where, for one reason or another, the landed proprietor cannot or will not co-operate; and to meet these cases it is necessary for the State or certain public bodies to have powers of expropriation, subject always to payment of the appropriate compensation. What we are concerned with here is the effect, in outline, *quoad* title, of the exercise by an appropriate authority of powers of compulsory acquisition of land.

In the exercise of such powers, there are two elements to consider, namely, the conferment, by statute, of the actual power to acquire; and, secondly, the procedure regulating the exercise of the power, to prevent oppression and injustice, including regulations for payment of compensation.

Prior to 1845, both elements were normally conferred together on the acquiring authority by a single Act of Parliament especially passed for the purpose. But in all cases the procedure became more or less standard; and accordingly, to avoid the necessity of repeating at length, in each separate Act of Parliament conferring power to acquire, provisions as to procedure, an Act was passed in 1845 known as the Lands Clauses Consolidation (Scotland) Act 1845, which contained a detailed and elaborate procedural code to be adopted in any future Act of Parliament conferring power of compulsory acquisition on an acquiring authority, where that was considered appropriate. The Lands Clauses Act has been subsequently modified, and the statutory procedure expanded by later Acts, principally the Acquisition of Land (Authorisation Procedure) (Scotland) Act 1947, the Land Compensation (Scotland) Acts 1963 and 1973, the Planning and Compensation Act 1991, and The Town and Country Planning (Scotland) Act 1997. In England the comparable older legislation has been repealed and new statutory provision made. So far, there is no Scottish equivalent; subject to these modifications, the Lands Clauses Consolidation Act (Scotland) 1845 still applies.

From the point of view of heritable title only, compulsory acquisition of land implies, in the final analysis, the divesting of an individual heritable proprietor, infeft or otherwise, and the investing of the acquiring authority on a feudal title, or its equivalent. This, of course, can always be achieved by conventional means where the proprietor is willing and able to co-operate and where, by agreement, he conveys his heritage to the acquiring authority. In practice, this very commonly happens. But in the majority of cases, the acquiring authority urgently requires land for its development and, in practice, it will initiate the compulsory purchase procedure, even although it later acquires land by conventional titles, with a view to the ultimate acquisition, if necessary, of land by compulsory purchase.

The commonest cases of compulsory purchase in modern practice are by a local authority for roads, planning and housing purposes.

There are two different procedures under which the acquiring authority can obtain a statutory title to heritage in Scotland. Initially the procedures are similar and are regulated by the Acquisition of Land (Authorisation Procedure) (Scotland) Act 1947.

In outline (and ignoring altogether specialties of which there are any number), both procedures commence in the following form.

**30.17 Compulsory purchase order**. The acquiring authority makes an order, known as a compulsory purchase order, specifying the land to be acquired, which is published by advertisement and served on owners and lessees. Individual owners are given an opportunity to object, and objections may be followed by a public inquiry. None of this has any effect *quoad* title.

**30.18 Confirmation.** The compulsory purchase order must be confirmed by the Secretary of State (or other confirming authority). Confirmation must be advertised and affected persons notified, and only then does the order become final. This has still no effect, *quoad* title.

Thereafter the procedures differ and are dealt with separately.

**30.19 Ordinary procedure under the Lands Clauses Act, as amended**
(1) Notice to treat. This is a notice, served by the acquiring authority on the individual heritable proprietor, intimating the intention to acquire compulsorily and, when served in accordance with the statutory procedure, has the effect of creating a notional binding contract of sale and purchase of heritage between the owner and the acquiring authority under which the owner has agreed to sell his land to the acquiring authority, and is bound

thereafter to convey it in implement of that agreement, as under any normal contract of sale and purchase. The purchase price is represented by compensation, computed in accordance with statutory formulae. After serving the notice to treat, the acquiring authority may take possession of the subjects, on 14 days' written notice, under the Acquisition of Land (Authorisation Procedure) (Scotland) Act 1947, Second Schedule, para. 3(1).

In *Rush* 1994 SCLR 231 the council served notices to treat under the Lands Clauses Consolidation (Scotland) Act 1845 in respect of various subjects which they wished to acquire. The validity of the notices were challenged by *Rush* on the grounds that the descriptions therein did not conform to his title. His challenge was dismissed and he appealed. It was held that the notices to treat were valid in that they adequately showed the location and extent of the lands to be acquired. There was no requirement in the 1845 Act that the notice to treat should refer to the title. The SCLR report contains some other observations on the requirements for a valid notice and a challenge thereof.

(2) Following on this notice to treat, the proprietor may convey the land to the acquiring authority, in which case the conveyance may take one of two forms, namely, a statutory form, as prescribed in schedules to the Lands Clauses Act, which is known as a schedule conveyance; or a common law (or conventional) conveyance such as any heritable proprietor grants in favour of any ordinary purchaser.

Where the title takes the form of a schedule conveyance, the effect is not altogether clear; but it has been authoritatively stated that, on the recording of the schedule conveyance within the 60-day time-limit stipulated in the Act, the acquiring authority creates for itself a statutory tenure which extinguishes the relationship of superior and vassal, and in effect renders the property allodial. See *Heriot's Trust* 1915 SC (HL) 52. For a detailed discussion of the effect of compulsory acquisition on existing feudal titles and, in particular, on the question as to whether reservations, burdens and servitudes persist after such acquisition or are extinguished thereby, see several articles in 1990 and 1992 JLS listed in the reading list under this chapter.

Where the acquiring authority takes a common law (or conventional) conveyance, it acquires a feudal title just as any individual disponee would do.

(3) If the proprietor, having been served with notice to treat, declines to convey, whether by conventional or schedule conveyance, the acquiring authority is statutorily empowered to record a notarial instrument at its own hand, which, by statute, has the same effect as the recording of a schedule conveyance.

(4) Where the subjects compulsorily acquired, on a schedule conveyance or notarial instrument duly recorded under the foregoing procedure, are subject to servitudes, or other real conditions, such servitudes or conditions are extinguished; or, at least, cease to be enforceable in a question with the acquiring authority. In the case of land acquired under Part VIII of the Town and Country Planning (Scotland) Act 1997, extinction is provided for expressly by s. 194.

(5) Disposal. Provision is made in the 1845 Act, as amended, for the disposal of surplus lands compulsorily acquired but no longer needed for their original purpose. Following on a well-known case in England, the statutory provisions were supplemented by a Government Circular, now Circular 38/1992 issued by the Scottish Office: The Disposal of Surplus Government Land – The Crichel Down Rules. The purpose of these rules, which are non-statutory, is to require a local authority when disposing of surplus land first to make an offer thereof to the original owner. In a recent case, *JDP Investments Ltd.* 1996 SCLR 243, the pursuers entered into missives of sale to the regional council of some six hectares of land through which it was proposed to construct a new road. The road proposal was later abandoned and the regional council decided to dispose of part of the site on the open market. The pursuers applied for a declarator that the Crichel Down Rules were applicable to the disposal but their claim was rejected because the land was originally acquired not by compulsory acquisition or under threat thereof but by a purely voluntary arrangement to which the rules had no application. There is a useful discussion in Lord Hamilton's judgment as to how the rules operate in practice.

### 30.20 General vesting declarations

These are regulated by the Town and Country Planning (Scotland) Act 1997, s. 195 and Schedule 15.

When a compulsory purchase order has come into operation, i.e. after the statutory procedure for compulsory purchase has run its course, the acquiring authority may execute a general vesting declaration. It must contain a particular description or a statutory description by reference of the land to be acquired. The intention to make a general vesting declaration must be published in the press not less than two months before the vesting declaration is actually made and this is usually done in conjunction with the advertisement of the confirmation of the order. Immediately on executing the declaration the acquiring authority must intimate its terms to every owner and occupier (except short term tenants) having an interest in the affected land.

On the expiry of a period to be specified in the declaration (at least 28 days):

(1) the Lands Clauses Consolidation (Scotland) Act 1845 (those parts adopted by Schedule 24 to the 1972 Act, now Schedule 15 to the 1997 Act) and the Land Compensation (Scotland) Acts 1963 and 1973 apply as if notice to treat had been served on each owner and occupier; and

(2) the land described in the declaration, and the right to take possession thereof, vests in the acquiring authority subject only to short tenancies. Notice to short term tenants is required.

The declaration is to be recorded in the General Register of Sasines or registered in the Land Register, as appropriate; and thereupon has the same effect as a schedule conveyance duly recorded under s. 80 of the 1845 Act.

# Chapter 31

# TRANSMISSION ON DEATH

## 31.1 Scope of the chapter

We are not here concerned with the substantive rules which determine the beneficial entitlement to property, heritable or moveable, on the death, testate or intestate, of the proprietor thereof, but with the technical machinery by which the person beneficially entitled, on testacy or intestacy, acquires a title and perfects his real right to heritable property passing to him from his deceased ancestor and to which he has succeeded as a beneficiary on the death of the previous proprietor.

## 31.2 Position before the Succession (Scotland) Act 1964

Prior to the 1964 Act, there was a fundamental difference in procedure, particularly noticeable on intestacy, between the transmission of heritage on death and the transmission of moveables.

At common law, heritage never transmitted to the executor as such. On intestacy, heritage transmitted directly to the heir-at-law as the person beneficially entitled, subject to his pursuing the appropriate procedure and procuring the appropriate title. Under the Titles to Land Consolidation (Scotland) Act 1868 s. 20, if the deceased died testate, heritage passed directly under his will to the beneficiaries or trustees, without any administrative procedure. The will itself operated as their title, as general disponees.

In practice, the trustees appointed by will were normally appointed executors nominate as well, and, as executors, confirmed to and administered the moveable estate; but, *quoad* heritage, confirmation was unnecessary and inappropriate.

The procedure for making up title differed substantially depending on whether the deceased was intestate or testate; on whether or not the title contained a special destination; and in the case of intestacy on whether the deceased was infeft or uninfeft.

## 31.3 Intestacy

This implied that, in the deceased's title, the destination was to the deceased and 'his heirs and assignees whomsoever', being a general destination.

The procedure which the heir-at-law followed depended on various factors which can best be illustrated by an example. Suppose that A, the original ancestor, died intestate. B was A's eldest son and therefore, under the old rules, his heir-at-law. C was B's eldest son, and therefore, also under the old rules, B's heir-at-law. There were then three possible situations.

**31.4 (1) A died infeft.** Three alternative courses were open to B, the heir, in whom, by survivance alone, the right to A's heritable estate vested under the Conveyancing (Scotland) Act 1874 s. 9. These alternatives were:

**31.5** *(a) Special service.* This was available only where the deceased died infeft. B, the heir, presented a petition for special service in the sheriff court, describing the property, referring to the burdens, and averring his relationship to the deceased A, to establish his claim as heir-at-law (1868 Act ss. 26 to 46).

Decree was equivalent to a special disposition granted by A in favour of B (1868 Act s. 46) and, as such, could be recorded direct, with warrant of registration, in the Register of Sasines.

If B died before he had recorded the special service decree, the benefit of the decree transmitted to his representatives; and the decree could be used by them as if it were a special but unrecorded disposition (1868 Act s. 46).

**31.6** *(b) General service.* Again, B petitioned in the sheriff court, but the petition for general service did not describe or refer to any specific property. Hence 'general' as opposed to 'special' service.

Decree was equivalent to a general disposition by A in favour of B (1874 Act s. 31). The decree was not recordable in the Register of Sasines, since it contained no identifying description, and indeed no reference to any heritable estate at all; but, as a general disposition, it was a valid midcouple, allowing B to take infeftment by recording a notice of title, using the general service decree as a link. If B did not take infeftment, the benefit of the decree transmitted to his representatives as if it were a general disposition in his favour (1874 Act s. 31).

**31.7** *(c) Writ of clare constat.* This was the original feudal method – a charter by progress from the superior renewing the investiture for the benefit of the heir. It was available only where the deceased A was infeft. Being in the form of a charter, containing a description, it was a mandate for infeftment by *de plano* recording. But, if B did not take infeftment thereunder, the benefit of the writ died with him and did not transmit to his representatives.

**31.8 (2) A died uninfeft.** The only procedure available to B was general service, decree having the effect already described above (1874 Act s. 31).

**31.9 (3) After A's death, B then died with only a personal right.** By the 1874 Act s. 9, a personal right to A's heritage vested indefeasibly in B the heir, simply by his survivance, without further procedure. If B died without having obtained a decree of service nor having recorded a writ of *clare constat*, he had a personal right but no title. B's personal right transmitted to his representatives automatically on B's death; and they acquired title to A's heritage by a petition for authority to complete title, under the 1874 Act s. 10.

### 31.10 Special destinations

Any conveyance of land, *e.g.* charter, disposition, or heritable security, may contain a special, as opposed to a general, destination directing the devolution of the property on the death of the initial disponee along a particular line of devolution, *e.g.* 'to A, and on his death to B, and on B's death to C'; or 'to A and B and the survivor of them'.

The special destination raises problems, particularly:

(1) as to whether or not it can be revoked (or 'evacuated');

(2) if revocable, as to whether or not it has been revoked by some other testamentary writing, *e.g.* a will; and

(3) as to completion of title thereunder.

Normally, such destinations are revocable, except for:

(1) contractual destinations, and

(2) survivorship destinations in gifts.

Failing revocation, the destination still determines the beneficial succession; but, since the 1964 Act, apart from special cases, it has ceased to have any effect *quoad* title.

In fact, since 1868, the use of such destinations is increasingly less common because of the facilities provided by the 1868 Act s. 20 with reference to wills; and, with the exception of destinations to husband and wife and survivor, they are rarely met with in practice.

**31.11 (1) Terms used in destinations.** A special destination may take the form of a conveyance to a series of named persons, one succeeding to the other, which was rare; or it may restrict the line of devolution by reference to derivative terms, which was common; or it may take the form of a survivorship destination. In the second case, quite a number of terms were used in practice and acquired technical legal meanings, *e.g.* heir male of the body, etc. But, whatever form the destination takes, all destinations have this in common, that they are embodied in a *de praesenti* conveyance of heritage to a series of persons who take in succession. The person first called in this conveyance was known as the institute; any person called to take in succession to the institute was known as a substitute.

**31.12 (2) The effect of destinations on the rights of the parties.** In the ordinary case, where the destination in a disposition takes a simple and typical form, *e.g.* 'to A and on his death to B', both parties being named and being strangers *inter se*, A is the institute, being the disponee first called. When the disposition is delivered to A, he becomes the immediate and absolute proprietor, in fee, of the subjects thereby conveyed. The disposition is a mandate for A's infeftment by direct recording in Sasines. The presence, in his title, of the destination-over to B does not in any way detract from, or affect, his unfettered and unqualified right, as absolute proprietor, to dispose of the property by *inter vivos* or *mortis causa* deed, onerously or gratuitously. Any such *inter vivos* disposal by the institute evacuates the destination and wholly defeats the rights of the substitute B; and B has no subsequent claim either on the property itself, nor on the proceeds of sale if A has disposed of it for a consideration.

A also has unfettered power of *mortis causa* disposal which, again, evacuates the destination and defeats the rights of B, provided:

(*a*) that the destination is revocable; and

(*b*) that A observes certain rules as to revocation of the destination.

But, if A dies without effectively evacuating the destination, then B, the substitute, takes in preference to A's representatives or heirs whomsoever.

**31.13** (*a*) *Revocability*. Where the proprietor of heritage dispones it gratuitously to a disponee or several disponees, the disponer as donor is entitled to dictate the terms of any special destination. Alternatively, in an onerous conveyance, it is the disponee as purchaser who dictates the terms of the destination.

Obviously, where there are two (or more) disponees who are jointly putting up the price, they can, together, dictate the terms of the destination in the conveyance; and where they agree to a special destination (*e.g.* to A and B and the survivor) then, because they are jointly contributing, the element of survivorship introduced into the destination would be held to be a matter of contract between A and B.

Any provision as to devolution of property, taking effect on death, is normally revocable; but a party may competently contract to make a testamentary disposition in certain terms, and such a contract is enforceable. The net result is that, where a special destination is contractual, the parties to the destination are deprived of their right of *mortis causa* disposal; and cannot, by *mortis causa* deed, evacuate the destination. Their power of *inter vivos* disposal, onerously or gratuitously, is not affected. See Lord Mackay in *Brown's Trustee* 1943 SC 488. In *Smith* 1988 SC 453, M conveyed her house to herself and her daughter equally between them and the survivor of them. Later, by a second *inter vivos* disposition, she conveyed her own one-half *pro indiviso* share to her son. The disposition was challenged by the daughter, following on her mother's death, on an averment that her mother had agreed that the daughter should have the whole house on the mother's death for services rendered. Her claim was dismissed on the footing that there was no evidence of this contractual arrangement on the face of the first disposition; and in any event, the second disposition in favour of the son, being an *inter vivos* deed, was not in any way invalidated by the presence of the special destination in the earlier title.

In fact, in modern practice, by far the commonest destination is the 'A and B and the survivor' case; and very often, these are in fact contractual, because the parties have jointly contributed, or have borrowed part or the whole of the price and jointly and severally granted a mortgage on the subjects. In the result, the only question which in the ordinary way now arises in regard to the interpretation of destinations is whether or not, by being contractual, they are revocable at the instance of one or other of the parties to the destination.

Thus, where there is a disposition of heritable property to 'A and B and the survivor of them' recorded in the Register of Sasines with warrant of registration on behalf of A and B, the effect is to vest each of A and B with an immediate and indefeasible right to a one-half *pro indiviso* share of the subjects; and each of A and B is thereupon immediately entitled to dispose of that share *inter vivos*, gratuitously or for onerous consideration.

As to *mortis causa* disposal:

(*i*) Where the price was jointly contributed by A and B, or where A and B have jointly granted security, then neither A nor B can by testamentary writing alter the survivorship destination or prevent the survivor from taking the predeceaser's one-half *pro indiviso* of the property. But this does not in any way interfere with the right to dispose *inter vivos* of the one-half *pro indiviso* share of each party. See *Shand's Trustees* 1966 SC 178.

(*ii*) Where the price was contributed solely by A, then A can alter the survivorship destination *quoad* his own one-half *pro indiviso* share of the property. B cannot, by *mortis causa* deed, alter the survivorship destination *quoad* his one-half *pro indiviso* share of the property. But either A or B may dispose *inter vivos* of his one-half *pro indiviso* share, thus, in effect, evacuating the destination. *Brown's Trustees* 1943 SC 488.

For a full discussion of the effect of such a destination in various circumstances, see *Hay's Trustee* 1951 SC 329. In this case subjects were conveyed to a husband and wife and the survivor of them on the narrative that the price had been contributed equally. It was agreed, in subsequent litigation, that the narrative was incorrect and that in fact the wife had provided the whole price. Lord President Cooper, with some hesitation, admitted extrinsic evidence to prove this fact which was not disputed by the other side. This particular point caused some difficulty in *Gordon-Rogers* 1988 SLT 618, where the circumstances were very similar but the parties failed to agree on the facts. Lord Morison distinguished this case from *Hay's Trustee* on the footing that, in the instant case, the facts were not agreed and so extrinsic evidence was not admissible.

(*iii*) Where the subjects were donated by X to A and B and the survivor, then neither A nor B can alter the survivorship destination by *mortis causa* deed. But again, either can dispose *inter vivos* of his one-half *pro indiviso* share: *Brown's Trustees, supra.*

**31.14** (*b*) *Express additional provisions.* The express terms of the destination or express provisions in the deed containing it may modify these rules and further restrict the rights of co-disponees. See Burns' *Practice* pp. 371 and 372 for some illustrative styles which set out the rights of co-disponees explicitly, and it is thought would receive effect. Burns, however, makes no attempt in these styles to modify or take away the right of the co-owner to dispose of his *pro indiviso* share *inter vivos*. He deals with *mortis causa* disposal only. It is arguable that, on principle, the *pro indiviso* owner must have this *inter vivos* right.

In *Munro* 1972 SLT (Sh Ct) 6 the sheriff goes further. In this case, heritage had been disponed by a father to his three children, under an arrangement between all parties, the full nature of which is not disclosed in the report. The disposition was in favour of the father in liferent, and the three children equally between them and to the survivors and the last survivor of them, and the heirs of the last survivor in fee. This was followed by an express declaration that none of them might revoke, alter or affect the destination to the last survivor. The sheriff held that, in the circumstances, the destination created a right of joint ownership, and not of common or *pro indiviso* property. Hence, apparently, no one of the three children had any *pro indiviso* share which he could deal with *inter vivos* or *mortis causa*. He quotes, with approval, Lord President Cooper in *Magistrates of Banff* 1944 SC 36 to the effect that joint property can only exist where the plural disponees are inter-related by virtue of some trust, or contractual or quasi-contractual bond (*e.g.* partnership), so as to create an independent relationship. The sheriff doubts if this independent relationship is created in this case by the disposition alone; but he finds sufficient in the surrounding circumstances to justify his view. 'It is a reasonable inference that the common thought was that each child ... should, throughout his life, have the opportunity to live in or return to the family home ... There was, on my understanding, a pre-existing agreement to keep the family home open for each of them during their respective lives, and the destination was conceived with this in mind.' If so, why not so provide in the deed; or confer a conjunct fee and liferent? As a result of the terms of the very special arrangement in this case, express and implied, it would seem as if the three children were in effect trustees under a self-imposed trust for themselves and the survivors in conjunct liferent and the last survivor in fee, and this *quasi* trust provided joint, not common, ownership.

For a criticism of the decision in *Munro*, see article in 1985 SLT (News) 57.

**31.15 (3) Evacuation.** As to evacuation of a destination, the old rule was that, where the destination was not created by the deceased himself, any will, earlier or later in date, revoked the destination. Where the deceased himself had been responsible for creating the destination, a will later in date than the destination might revoke it; but only if the two were patently incompatible *inter se*. Otherwise, destination and will both receive effect as the joint testamentary instruction of the deceased.

Now, by the Succession (Scotland) Act 1964 s. 30, any will executed after 10 September 1964, revokes a revocable special destination only if it refers to it and expressly revokes it. Otherwise, the destination stands. See *Stirling's Trustees* 1977 SLT 229, no express clause, no revocation; and likewise *Marshall* 1987 SLT 49.

**31.16 (4) Completion of title under destinations.** Where the deceased's title contained a special destination, not revoked at the death, the property passed, not to the heir-at-law, but to the 'heir of provision' under the special destination.

He in turn acquired a title by serving as heir of provision, in special or in general, to the deceased institute or substitute.

The decree of service, special or general, had exactly the same effect for the heir of provision as a decree of service in favour of the heir-at-law, *i.e.* it operated as his title. If the decree was special, he could record it *de plano*; if general, he could complete title by notice of title.

In either case, the benefit thereof transmitted to his successors if he failed to complete title.

**31.17 (5) Survivorship destinations.** These represent a technical specialty. A disposition to A and B and to the survivor operates as an immediate *de praesenti* conveyance of one-half *pro indiviso* of the property to each of A and B as institutes, coupled with a substitution of the survivor of them to succeed, as substitute, to the one-half *pro indiviso* vested originally in the predeceaser. Therefore, on the recording of a disposition to A and B and the survivor, with the warrant of registration on behalf of A and B, each becomes infeft in one-half of the property *pro indiviso* and the mandate for infeftment is wholly exhausted.

If B predeceases survived by A, then A takes B's original one-half of the property as substitute unless B, the predeceaser, could competently have evacuated the special destination as being non-contractual and effectively did so, bearing in mind the special provision of the 1964 Act s. 30 referred to above at para. 31.15. Logically in that situation A, the survivor and as such substitute in the destination to A and B, should, in feudal theory, make up title to B's one-half share as heir of provision, and obtain a decree of service in that capacity. But, in the case of survivorship destinations, the strict rule was not applied and, in the illustration, A, as survivor, did not require to serve or to carry through any other procedure in order to make up title to B's one-half share. By mere survivance, following on a survivorship destination, A as survivor became infeft in the share of the predeceaser. For the origin of this unexpected rule, see Professor Gretton, 1987 JLS 111 at p. 116.

This rule also creates an unexpected problem on separation or divorce where the title to the matrimonial home has been taken in joint names of A and B and the survivor, which is commonplace in practice. If, as part of the financial settlement, A agrees that B should have the matrimonial home, it is not sufficient simply for A to convey his or her one-half *pro indiviso* share to B. That does effectively vest the whole property in B. But the survivorship destination in the title is almost certainly a contractual one and as such is irrevocable by *mortis causa* deed. So, if B then dies first, B's original one-half *pro indiviso* share would pass back to A under the special destination in the original title, notwithstanding the subsequent conveyance by A to B and irrespective of the terms of B's will. Accordingly, in such situations, A and B should jointly convey the whole subjects to B in order to evacuate the special destination in the original conveyance by an *inter vivos* deed, which is always competent. See 1989 JLS at p. 302.

The cases mentioned in the Digest of Cases in para. 7.13 under 'Division and sale' indicate a number of situations where the presence of a special destination in the title has created problems, particularly on divorce or separation or on the break-up of a relationship where property was jointly owned.

Two further cases should be mentioned briefly in this context as demonstrating the type of problem which can arise and the unexpected results which may follow in such circumstances. In *Gardner's Exrs.* 1996 SLT 745 the title to a matrimonial home was taken in name of husband and wife and survivor. The parties then separated and subsequently divorced. As part of the divorce settlement, the husband paid £40,000 to his wife, in exchange for which she conveyed to him her one-half *pro indiviso* share of the matrimonial home and her whole right, title and interest present and future therein. The purpose of this arrangement was, of course, to give the husband the whole house in exchange for a cash payment and, initially, it worked satisfactorily. The husband then died. Following on his death, his widow claimed to be entitled to succeed to the original one-half *pro indiviso* share which initially vested in the husband on the original acquisition of the matrimonial home then taken in joint names. She based her claim on the survivorship destination in that title. Her claim was resisted on the footing that, under the marriage settlement, she had received £40,000 on the understanding that the husband would become the owner of the whole house, not merely one half. The weakness of the argument by the deceased's executors, however, lay in the fact that the original destination was contractual. A conveyance by the wife to her husband of her half share by *inter vivos* deed was competent and effective to vest him with her original one-half share; but that conveyance left the husband's one-half *pro indiviso* share unaffected. In the result, not only was his original one-half share unaffected but, in addition, the special destination which transferred it to his widow on his death as survivor in the destination had not effectively been evacuated. Further, an argument that, in addition to her one-half share, the wife had conveyed to her husband her whole right, title and interest therein was held to be restricted to the one-half *pro indiviso* share conveyed by the wife and did not represent a disclaimer by her of her contingent or expectant right in the husband's one-half share on his death. In the result, the widow was held entitled to succeed to the husband's one-half share, an outcome which was clearly never intended.

A similar situation occurred in *Redfern's Exrs*. 1996 SLT 900. Again, the title to a matrimonial home was taken in joint names of husband and wife and survivor. Both contributed to the price. Subsequently, the parties separated and raised actions of divorce. They then entered into a minute of agreement providing for the dismissal of both actions and further providing for the disposal of the matrimonial home. It was agreed that the house should be sold and the proceeds divided in certain proportions. Except as otherwise provided, 'neither party shall have any claim of any nature against the other either now or at any time in the future and the parties hereby relinquish all rights of succession to the estate of the other party in the event of the death of either of them'. The house was put on the market but, before it was sold, the husband died. Thereafter, his widow withdrew the instructions to sell the house. As a result, the husband's executors raised an action of declarator against her, craving the Court to hold that the minute of agreement still subsisted and bound the parties notwithstanding the husband's death. The widow argued that the agreement was at an end, and so, as she maintained, the disclaimer provisions ceased to apply, thus allowing her to succeed to her husband's one-half share of the house. Her argument was rejected on the footing that, under the disclaimer clause, each party had voluntarily waived the normal bar to evacuation of the special destination. As a result, the husband's half of the house passed to his executors.

These two cases, and those listed in the Digest of Cases under para. 7.13, underline some unexpected results of such destinations.

## 31.18 Testate succession

The common law rule prior to 1868 was that any disposition, special or general, *inter vivos* or *mortis causa*, to be effective had to take the form of an immediate *de praesenti* conveyance containing appropriate clauses and, in particular, had to include the magic word 'dispone'. Further, every such conveyance, to be effective, had to be probative according to the strict Scottish rule.

So far as *mortis causa* deeds are concerned, this rule was altered by the 1868 Act s. 20, the effect of which was that:

(1)  if the apparent intention was to bequeath heritage;

(2)  if the will, in its form, was appropriate to carry moveables; and

(3)  if the will was validly executed;

it operated as an effective title to heritable property belonging to the deceased, and was equivalent to a general disposition.

Thus, any will which referred to 'estate' or 'property, heritable or moveable' or which used other words indicating an intention to deal both with heritage and moveables, and which carried evidence of testamentary intention, was sufficient to carry heritage, even although it lacked any form of *de praesenti* or *mortis causa* conveyance.

**31.19  Three typical forms of will.**  It was important, however, to distinguish between three different forms of will, *viz*:

(1)  a will containing an express conveyance to trustees which they could use as their title but which did not operate in its terms as a direct conveyance to the beneficiary;

(2)  a conveyance directly to a beneficiary or beneficiaries, with or without appointment of trustees, which could be used by the beneficiaries as a direct title to the heritable property, bypassing (as it were) the trustees or executors; and

(3)  a will containing a conveyance to beneficiaries coupled with an appointment of trustees. In this case, to allow the trustees to take up the heritage and administer the estate in preference to the beneficiary or testamentary disponee, the 1874 Act s. 46 applied; and specially empowered trustees, under this form of will, to make up title and then to deal with the heritable estate as if the will had contained a conveyance in their favour.

The 1874 Act s. 46 is repealed by the 1964 Act; and accordingly cannot be used for any death occurring on or after 10 September 1964. It is therefore probably not competent for trustees or executors to use the will as a link in title in a clause of deduction of title in a disposition on sale, although apparently they may use the will as a link for the purpose of completing title in their own person by virtue of amendments to the 1868 Act s. 20 contained in the 1964 Act. But *contra*, see Professor Gretton 1987 JLS at p. 113.

With that possible qualification, then, in any of these cases, the general disponee (trustee or beneficiary), could use the will as a general disposition in his or their favour and complete title by notice of title regardless of the state of the ancestor's title – infeft or uninfeft. Alternatively, the will could be used as an unrecorded mid-couple or link in title for the purpose of deduction of title under the 1924 Act s. 3.

By the 1874 Act s. 29, any two or more such deeds may validly be used, together, as links in title when deducing title.

**31.20  The Succession (Scotland) Act 1964**
The 1964 Act s. 14 makes two complementary and very important innovations so far as *mortis causa* title to heritage is concerned.

(1) The section extends to heritage rules previously applicable only to a moveable succession. At common law, the only person who can make up title to the moveable estate on the death is the executor duly confirmed; and this rule is now applied to heritable property, with limited qualifications as noted below.

(2) For purposes of administration, heritage vests in the executor, provided always that he has duly confirmed thereto as required by this section but not otherwise.

### 31.21 Confirmation as a title to heritage

In relation to heritage, the 1964 Act ss. 14(2) and 15(1) provide that an executor is not to be taken as having duly confirmed to heritable property unless a description of that heritable property is included in the confirmation in accordance with, now, the provisions of the Act of Sederunt (Confirmation of Executors Amendment) 1966 (SI 1966 No. 593). The requisite description is such a description 'as will be sufficient to identify the property or interest therein as a separate item in the deceased person's estate', *i.e.* (normally) the postal address. In *Bennett* 1995 SLT 1105 a standard security was granted in favour of the bank, secured on a flat in a tenement. As is often the case in second-ranking securities, the description was minimal and referred only to the postal address of the tenement itself without attempting to identify the location of the flat within the tenement. On the wording of the 1970 Act which prescribes the form of standard security, it was held that, for the purposes of a standard security, that description was inadequate. The wording of the Act of Sederunt is not so demanding. A formal 'conveyancing' description is clearly not required; and, not uncommonly, the postal address alone may not suffice. In the case of tenement property, however, the location of the flat within the tenement should also be included properly to identify it as a separate item in the deceased's estate. See Halliday's *Practice*, Chapter 48–03 (2nd edn. 21–04).

Assuming the executor has duly confirmed to heritage belonging to the deceased, the nature and quality of the title conferred on the executor by confirmation is defined in s. 15. This section proceeds by applying to heritage generally the limited provisions of the 1924 Act s. 5 which applied only to heritable securities and only if they were moveable in the succession as they usually were in practice. The necessary amendments to the 1924 Act s. 5 are contained in the 1964 Act s. 15 and Schedule 2. The result is that, under the 1924 Act s. 5(2)(*a*), as amended, where the proprietor of any estate in land, which vests in an executor under the 1964 Act s. 14, has died, whether infeft or uninfeft or with or without a recorded title, whether testate or intestate, confirmation in favour of the executor which includes the appropriate description shall of itself be a valid title to such estate in land. Such confirmation is also a valid mid-couple for any deduction of title, but is not recordable in the General Register of Sasines.

It is not clear from these provisions whether confirmation is intended to be the only effective title to heritage. Provided it includes the appropriate description, confirmation is in itself a valid title, equivalent to a general disposition in favour of the executors; and it is certainly arguable that no other title can competently be used. But the professors of conveyancing, in an opinion delivered in April 1965, took the view that testamentary trustees and executors could use the will as an alternative link in title; and two of them took the view that a legatee could also so use the will where it contained a direct bequest of heritage in his favour. See 1965 JLS 153, and the comments thereon in 1965 JLS 189 and 1966 JLS 84.

**31.22 Probates.** The amendment to the 1924 Act s. 5(2)(*a*) also affects probates and letters of administration. But with this difference, that under the 1924 Act s. 5(2)(*b*), probate or letters of administration were deemed to include heritable securities, without actually containing these items; in fact, a probate cannot 'contain' any items since it carries no inventory. The intention, obviously, is to make probate and letters of administration valid links in title to Scottish heritage vested in a deceased of English domicile; but some doubt arose as to whether the 1964 Act s. 15 in fact accomplished this.

This difficulty is now resolved by the Law Reform (Miscellaneous Provisions) (Scotland) Act 1968 s. 19 which provides that s. 15(1) of the 1964 Act shall have effect, 'and be deemed always to have had effect', as if it had read –

'provided that a confirmation (other than an implied confirmation within the meaning of the said section 5(2)) shall not be deemed, for the purposes of the said section 5(2) to include any such interest unless a description of the property ... is included or referred to in the confirmation'.

This made it perfectly clear that a resealed probate, etc., being an 'implied confirmation' under the 1924 Act s. 5(2)(*b*), operated as a valid link without containing any description or identification of the subjects.

Further, under the Administration of Estates Act 1971, English and Northern Ireland probates, etc., no longer require to be resealed, but operate automatically as titles to Scottish land without resealing.

**31.23 Special destinations.** Special administrative provisions are made by the 1964 Act ss. 18, 30 and 36(2). The effect of s. 30 has been noticed already.

Prior to the 1964 Act, there were two peculiar features of heritable destinations. Firstly, such destinations might or might not be revocable. If revocable, and if effectively revoked, the destination was of no effect *quoad* title and instead the property passed to the trustees or legatee under the will of the deceased. Secondly, if irrevocable or if not in fact revoked, then on the death of the person in right of the property for the time being, the right of property passed under the destination, but the deed containing the destination did not of itself operate as a title to the successor, except in the case of survivorships. With that exception, the substitute required a new mandate for infeftment which he obtained by service as heir of provision.

By the combined effect of the 1964 Act ss. 18 and 36, the administrative position post-1964 is as follows.

(*a*) If a special destination in the title has been effectively revoked by the deceased, the property is part of his estate and vests in his executor as if it had been held on a general destination.

(b) If the special destination has not been effectively revoked, then the heritable property does not form part of the deceased's estate. The beneficial interest in the property passes to the substitute next called in the destination.

As to title:

(a) if the substitute requires a title (as he does in all cases except in the case of survivorship destinations) the heritable property vests in the executor by virtue of confirmation thereto, but only for the limited purpose of enabling the executor to convey the property to the substitute next called in the destination (cf. resignation in favorem);

(b) if the substitute does not require a title, as in the case of survivorship destinations, then the property does not vest in the executor at all, and he cannot competently confirm thereto. Even if he does confirm, the confirmation in this case is not an effective title.

**31.24 Entails.** Similarly, under the 1964 Act s. 18(1), all entailed property vests in the executor by confirmation but only for the purpose of conveying it to the next heir of entail.

### 31.25 Subsequent transactions by the executor with heritable property
There are three possible situations following on a death.

(1) The executor is to retain the heritage to which he has confirmed, typically, in a continuing trust. In this case, the confirmation is his title. He can use the confirmation to expede a notice of title and thereby take infeftment as executor. But he is not obliged to take infeftment; and, instead, can hold the property on the confirmation as uninfeft proprietor in trust.

He cannot record the confirmation *de plano* in the Register of Sasines with a view to completing his title.

(2) The property is to be transferred to a beneficiary. A new and useful shortcut is provided here by the 1964 Act s. 15(2). Under the old rule prior to 1964, where the whole estate was conveyed to trustees with a direction to make over heritage to a particular beneficiary, the will was the trustees' link in title but they then had to grant a formal disposition in favour of the beneficiary. Now, under the 1964 Act, any such transfer can be effected to a testamentary beneficiary, to a statutory successor, or to a surviving spouse or child claiming prior or legal rights by endorsing a short docquet on the confirmation (or on a certificate of confirmation). A short statutory form of docquet is given in Schedule 1 to the Act. Any such docquet, so endorsed, may be specified as a mid-couple or link in title in any deduction of title, but is not recordable in the Register of Sasines with a view to completing the beneficiary's title.

This procedure is optional, in that it still remains competent to transfer heritage to a beneficiary by disposition, etc., as before.

(3) The property is to be sold by the executor. Confirmation is his title. He may complete title using it as a link or he may dispone as uninfeft proprietor, using the 1924 Act s. 3. He cannot use a docquet on the confirmation to give a title to a purchaser.

## 31.26  Protection of purchasers

Under the old rules prior to the 1964 Act, where a man died testate leaving a will dealing with heritage, a purchaser from the trustee under that will, or from a legatee, had to satisfy himself that the will was intrinsically and extrinsically valid and that the seller had a valid title thereunder to sell the property to him. Further, prior to the Trusts (Scotland) Act 1961 in the case of trustees, it was necessary to consider whether trustees had power to sell. If it later turned out that the will, as a title, was defective in any respect, or if the trustees (prior to 1961) did not have the requisite power, then in any of these events the purchaser's title might later be reduced on the grounds of any such defect. Similarly, when a man died intestate and his heir had served as heir-at-law in special or in general, the service decree could nonetheless be reduced within the 20-year period following thereon, on the grounds that the wrong heir had been served.

As a result, a purchaser only took a title from the deceased's representatives, whether testate or intestate, after careful enquiry into the title; but he was bound to accept the risk of reduction on these grounds. See *Sibbald's Heirs* 1947 SC 601.

Under the 1964 Act, confirmation for the first time becomes a title to heritable property. But, as with any other form of title, confirmation is open to reduction on a variety of grounds, *e.g.* that the will was improbative because of latent defect, or otherwise invalid because of want of capacity, fraud, revocation, etc.; or, in the case of a confirmation-dative, on the grounds that the wrong person had been confirmed (*cf.* wrong person served as heir).

Were it not for the provisions of the 1964 Act s. 17 then, where a death occurred on or after 10 September 1964, a purchaser or other person dealing with the title would require to consider the terms of the will, or the terms of the petition on which confirmation proceeded, and the validity and propriety of endorsed docquets, etc., or dispositions to beneficiaries, etc. (s. 17 is not confined to docquets). All such enquiry is rendered unnecessary by the 1964 Act s. 17, in the circumstances therein envisaged. The section provides that, where any person has, in good faith and for value, acquired title to an estate in land which has vested in an executor by confirmation thereto, whether such person takes his title directly from the executor or from a person deriving title directly from the executor, the title so acquired is not open to challenge on the grounds that the confirmation was reducible or has in fact been reduced; nor can the title be challenged on the grounds that the property has been conveyed, by the executor, to the wrong beneficiary (by docquet or disposition).

The decision in *MacDougall* 1994 SLT 1178 illustrates a number of points referred to in the foregoing paragraphs. The facts, however, are complex and are not here narrated. The principal point in the context of succession and completion of title also involves the effect of such completion in a question with a *bona fide* purchaser for value.

In this context, there are two statutory protections to a purchaser:

(i) Under the Trusts (Scotland) Act 1961 s. 2, where the trustees enter into a transaction with another party which falls within the statutory of powers conferred on them under the 1921 Act s. 4, including sale, any title acquired by that other party is exempt from challenge on the grounds that the trustees acted at variance with the terms or purposes of the trust. Accordingly, when purchasing from Scottish trustees, a purchaser is protected to that extent, whether he is acting in good faith or not.

(ii) The Succession (Scotland) Act 1964 s. 17 provides comparable protection as noted above, provided in this case that the purchaser acts in *bona fide* and for value.

(iii) Alternatively, at common law, where one of the writs within the prescriptive progress of titles is voidable as opposed to void *ab initio*, a *bona fide* purchaser for value without notice is likewise protected against a subsequent challenge of the antecedent title. See Gretton and Reid, *Conveyancing* p. 117. As they point out in that passage, however, the common law protection to the purchaser in the circumstances narrated has no application in any case where an antecedent title in the prescription progress is void. Further, even in the case of voidable titles, the purchaser is not exempt from challenge if he had notice or was put on his enquiry by something in the antecedent titles which might raise a suspicion that an earlier title was in some way or other defective.

In *MacDougall*, following on a very unusual and complex series of transmissions of a heritable property, four sisters finally obtained from the superior a charter of *novodamus* on the narrative that the original infeft proprietor had died in 1956 intestate; that, on the facts as there narrated, she was succeeded in the property by her only brother; that the brother died in 1966 intestate and survived by his second wife who took the subjects under her prior rights; and that the second wife died in May 1971 intestate, survived by her four daughters who succeeded her. To allow them to complete their title they requested the superior to grant a charter of *novodamus*.

On the evidence produced, the statement in the narrative of the charter that Alexander MacDougall died intestate was not justified. In fact, as brought out in the case, Alexander MacDougall, who died in 1966, had left a will but it was open to challenge on the grounds of improper attestation. If the will turned out to be validly executed the pursuer took as fiar thereunder on the death of an interposed liferenter who, by the date of the raising of this action, had in fact died. The basis of the pursuer's case was that, unless and until that will was found by the Court to be invalid as improperly attested, it stood and had to receive effect, being otherwise *ex facie* probative. The alleged defect in the will involved a question as to whether one of the attesting witnesses had properly attested; but there was nothing on the face of the will to show one way or another whether that was so, both witnesses having duly subscribed as such.

A charter of *novodamus* has never been one of the recognised methods of making up title following on a death, but undoubtedly, where the facts justify it, it can confer a good title although normally it is open to challenge until the positive prescription has run its course. In the ordinary case, given that in the feudal system a superior is invariably *in titulo* to grant charters by progress and of *novodamus*, such a charter would normally be voidable, but not void if it was granted on insufficient or incorrect facts. In the present case, the charter of *novodamus* was indeed correctly granted in favour of the four sisters if the narrative turned out to be correct and if Alexander MacDougall had indeed failed to leave a valid will. This in turn raised two important points:

(i) On these facts, was the charter of *novodamus* in this case void or was it merely voidable?

(ii) Assuming the purchasers from the four sisters had no knowledge of the true facts were they entitled to the benefit of the protection afforded at common law to the *bona fide* purchaser? Or was their title inevitably bad and open to reduction.

Prescription had not run on the charter to validate it. The will of the late Alexander MacDougall had not at this stage been reduced. Accordingly, completion of title by that charter represented in substance completion of title by the four sisters who were not the true heirs. Thus, the infeftment apparently obtained by the four sisters on recording the charter of *novodamus* was worthless as a defence against a challenge by the true heir; and that principle applied not only against the true heir but also against a *bona fide* onerous third party who took title from the wrong heir on the faith of the records. Note particularly that, on the facts as disclosed in this report, the purchasers were indeed *bona fide* purchasers for value without actual notice of any defect in the antecedent title. But given the narrative in the charter of *novodamus*, the purchasers were on their enquiry and should have sought production of intervening links in title which had not previously been obtained to establish the rights of the four sisters to obtain a charter of *novodamus* in these terms. The purchasers had clearly not attempted to establish the facts and were content to accept what turned out to be a defective progress of titles. Therefore, they were not in a position to plead that they were in *bona fide*.

This presents a real problem for a purchaser in unusual cases of this kind. So, in this particular case, even if the purchasers had made diligent enquiries, that might have been unavailing, simply because the narrative in the charter of *novodamus* concealed one fact which, for practical purposes, may well have been undiscoverable, namely that Alexander MacDougall would not have been intestate if it turned out that his purported will was duly attested.

Further, although this will now very rarely occur in practice, the view expressed in *Stobie* 1921 SC 894 was that a decree of service in favour of the wrong heir was void not merely voidable; and that view is supported by Lord Cameron in this case. But there is no possible way in which the purchaser can discover whether a decree of service is void or not. He must simply accept it at face value and rely on warrandice if the title subsequently turns out to be bad.

From the point of view of purchasers, that clearly is an unsatisfactory position. It is partly corrected by the two statutory protections, referred to above, but neither was applicable in this case. Whether or not the 1924 Act s. 46 was intended to provide protection to the purchaser in such situations is open to question. See an article by Professor Gretton in 1986 SLT (News) 125. If, however, a decree of service or, in this case, the charter of *novodamus*, was void, an action of reduction was presumably unnecessary and so the purchaser could not fall back on the 1924 Act s. 46, whatever its effect or its intention may have been.

## 31.27 Proposed reforms

The Scottish Law Commission, in its Report No. 124 issued in 1990, carried out a general review of the whole law of succession in Scotland following on three consultative memoranda published in 1986. The Commission recommended a complete recasting of the law of intestate succession and legal rights and certain specific changes in relation to testate succession, executries and other matters.

So far as this Chapter is concerned, the relevant recommendations of the Commission are contained in Part VI, Special Destinations, and Part VIII, Executry Questions, in the Report.

## 31.28 Special destinations

After making extensive investigations and consultations, the Commission recommend as follows:

25. In future proprietory titles, destinations should cease to be competent but excluding from that sweeping recommendation, survivorship destinations; destinations in liferent and fee; destinations to a person as a trustee or holder of an office or position and his successors as such; and destinations giving effect to the terms of a will executed prior to the passing of the relevant Act.

26. This recommendation relates only to testamentary writings, not to titles.

27. A special destination should be defined as a destination by which the property in question is to devolve on a named or identified person or persons or on a class of persons, other than 'heirs'.

28. These recommendations deal with administrative machinery only, for which see Chapter 32.

29. A successor under a destination should be personally liable for the debts of the predeceaser up to the limit of the value of the property to which the survivor succeeds.

30. (a) The owner of property subject to a destination in the title should have power to dispose of that property, for value or gratuitously, *inter vivos* or *mortis causa*, whether or not the destination is contractual and regardless of who paid for the property, but

(b) this should apply only to destinations created after the commencement of the relevant legislation.

There are also further recommendations in regard to leases.

## 31.29 Executry questions

A number of recommendations are made by the Commission on executry matters in Part VIII of the Report. The only one which is significant in the context of this chapter is:

'44. It should be competent for an executor or trustee to use the deceased's will as a link in a clause of deduction of title; and the same facility should be extended to legatees or general disponees under the will.'

466

Whether or not this would improve the present position is open to question, but at least it has the merit of clarifying the position and removing the doubts expressed in para. 31.21 above.

# Chapter 32

# COMPLETION OF TITLE

## 32.1 The desirability of taking infeftment

As between two parties acting at arm's length, for example, seller and purchaser of heritage, the purchaser at settlement obtains from the seller a title in the form of a special disposition which contains all the essential elements to allow of its recording *de plano* in the Register of Sasines. In all such cases, it is desirable to record the disposition in Sasines on behalf of the disponee with the minimum of delay to avoid the possibility of some supervening impediment to the title, such as the sequestration of the debtor. Failure to record the disposition immediately may mean that the purchaser's title is defeated by a writ which enters the Record before it. The classic case is the *Ceres School Board* (1895) 23 R 279 where a feuar under a feu charter, delivered but on which infeftment had not followed, occupied the feu for many years undisturbed on that unrecorded title; but, several years later, the landed estate of which the feu formed a small part transmitted as a whole to a *bona fide* purchaser for value who had no warning of the existence of the feuar's rights and himself recorded the disposition of that landed estate. In a subsequent competition between the vassal under the prior but unrecorded feu charter and the purchaser of the landed estate with a recorded title, priority of infeftment determined priority of right and the purchaser of the landed estate, having the real right in the whole property including the *dominium utile* of the feu, was preferred to the feuar in occupation thereof on an unrecorded title.

On the other hand, where A infeft in a particular heritable property dies leaving the property to trustees under his will for the liferent of his wife and to his issue in fee, the position is undoubtedly different, in that the possibility of the trustees' title being defeated by some valid intervening and adverse right is exceedingly remote; and, in any event, the form which the title of the trustees takes, whether it be the will of the deceased or confirmation in their favour as executors, is not of itself recordable *de plano* in Sasines. As a result, in the great majority of cases where property is to be retained in trust or by a beneficiary as absolute proprietor, no title enters the record and the trustees or the beneficiary as the case may be remain as uninfeft proprietors. The risk of any adverse interest defeating their title is so remote that for practical purposes it can be ignored.

There are, however, intermediate cases where the risk may be more significant; and, in any event, even in the case of trustees holding heritable property for the liferent of the beneficiary, it may be desirable to convert their valid personal title into an effective real right by the recording of an appropriate writ in Sasines.

**32.2 The general disposition.** The commonest situation where this occurs is following on a death because, in every such case, the title takes a form which is not suitable for recording *de plano*. But there are a variety of other such cases. In all such situations, the title will take the form of a general disposition or its equivalent, *e.g.* confirmation, a decree of general service, a deed of assumption of new trustees, or the like.

Before considering the methods of completion of title, it is convenient here to deal with various cases where a general disposition may operate as a link in title, otherwise than on death. The following list is illustrative but not by any means exhaustive.

**32.3 Trusts**
We have noticed already the situation both pre- and post-1964 where a will or trust disposition and settlement operates as a direct conveyance of heritage by the deceased to his trustees. Since 1964, confirmation is recommended as the appropriate title in all cases rather than using the will as a link; but, nonetheless, in the opinion of the professors of conveyancing, the will itself can still be used as a valid link, at least by trustees, as being a general disposition. See Chapter 31.21.

In exactly the same way, although less commonly, a heritable proprietor can grant a general disposition of his whole estate to operate *inter vivos, e.g.* a trust deed for creditors, or, possibly, a general disposition of his whole estate for *inter vivos* trust purposes. But, normally, when setting up an *inter vivos* trust, specific assets are conveyed by special conveyance rather than by way of a general disposition of the whole estate.

**32.4 Original deed as a link in title to trustees.** In all these cases, where there is a general disposition conveying heritage, the constituent deed operates as the link in title to the trustees.

**32.5 Original deed as a link in title to beneficiary.** Alternatively, in the case of wills, it was and is possible for the deceased to convey his estate directly to the beneficiary and the view of two of the professors was that, in that situation, the will operates as a valid link. But because of the doubts expressed in the professors' opinion, it is undesirable in any circumstances to use the will as a link for a beneficiary post-1964. Under the Succession (Scotland) Act 1964, notwithstanding the direct conveyance to a beneficiary of heritage in a will, the executors or trustees have power to confirm to that heritage and, if they so confirm, it vests in them and the confirmation is their title.

**32.6 Deed of assumption and conveyance.** The trustees acting under any trust, *inter vivos* or *mortis causa*, normally have power to assume new trustees by virtue of the Trusts (Scotland) Act 1921 s. 3; and, under the Act, executors nominate have the like power. But, in addition to their appointment, the new trustees will require a title to the trust assets. The appropriate deed is, therefore, a combined deed of assumption, operating as an appointment of the new trustees, and conveyance, operating as a general disposition of the trust assets in favour of the new trustees.

It is technically competent, in a deed of assumption and conveyance, to incorporate a special conveyance of heritage, but this is now never done. As a result, the deed of assumption and conveyance operates as a general disposition in favour of the new trustees and can be used as a link in their title.

In *inter vivos* deeds, the truster may reserve, or may have by implication, a power to appoint new trustees. Having divested himself of his assets which are invested in the original trustees, the truster has no power to give a title to new trustees appointed by him. Thus, by *inter vivos* deed of trust, A appoints B and C to act as trustees and conveys certain heritable estate to them. B and C both then die. A, the truster, then appoints X as trustee but cannot give X a title. In that situation, X could obtain a title to the trust assets from the executors of C, the last surviving trustee, if they confirm to the trust estate, under the Executors (Scotland) Act 1900 s. 6 – see below.

The same applies in unusual cases where some third party has the power to nominate new trustees. This does not give him power to confer a title on the new trustees.

**32.7 Resignation or removal of a trustee.** A trustee or executor nominate normally has power to resign office, by a minute of resignation. This effectively divests the trustee of his interest in the trust assets, including heritage, which devolve on the continuing trustees without the necessity of any conveyance or other transfer by the resigning trustee – see the Trusts (Scotland) Act 1921 s. 20. Nonetheless, it is the custom to include a minute of resignation in any narration of links in title in a clause of deduction of title, etc. – see below.

Alternatively, in certain situations, the court may remove a trustee – see 1921 Act s. 23. Removal has exactly the same effect as resignation, and the decree of removal would normally be included in the links in title.

**32.8 Lapsed trusts.** If all trustees on an existing trust have died, new trustees must be appointed to continue the administration; and in all such cases the new trustees will also require a title. The new trustees appointed in a lapsed trust, or the beneficiaries, may derive their title in the following ways, whether the deceased died before or after the 1964 Act.

**32.9** (*a*) *1921 Act s. 22.* Where no one has power to appoint new trustees, *e.g.* typically, in a testamentary case, where all the trustees have died without assuming any new ones, then the court may appoint trustees under the 1921 Act s. 22. In terms of that section, the decree appointing the new trustees had to include a warrant authorising them to complete title; but this requirement as to warrant in the decree has been removed by the Conveyancing Amendment (Scotland) Act 1938 s. 1. In the result, a decree of appointment, standing alone, operates as a general disposition in favour of the new trustees appointed thereunder.

**32.10** (*b*) *1921 Act s. 24.* As an alternative, in the case of certain lapsed trusts, to avoid the necessity of appointing new trustees, it is competent for beneficiaries, where the administration in the trust is complete, to petition the court for authority to allow the beneficiaries to make up title to the trust estate. The situation here envisaged is that A has died leaving a will in favour of a trustee B and directing B to make over the residue of his estate to X, Y and Z. B administers the estate but dies before the assets are actually made over; but, at B's death, nothing remains to be done except to make over the assets. X, Y and Z could then petition the court for authority to complete title thereto. In such cases, under s. 24 of the 1921 Act, the decree in favour of the beneficiaries operates as a general disposition in their favour.

**32.11** (*c*) *Deaths before the 1964 Act – service as heir in trust.* Where the deceased and the last surviving trustee died before 10 September 1964, the Executors (Scotland) Act 1900 ss. 6 and 7 did not apply – see below for the effect of these provisions. Instead, it was competent, pre-1964, for the heir-at-law of the last surviving trustee to serve as heir-in-trust, either by virtue of express provision in the deed of trust itself or under the 1874 Act s. 43. In such cases, the heir so serving did so simply for the purpose of providing a title to heritage in the lapsed trust, which he would then convey to new trustees appointed, by one mode or other, to continue the administration, or directly to the beneficiary absolutely entitled.

This device is still regularly used in cases where the title to property has been taken in name of the partners of, and trustees for, a firm and where all the partners have died before the 1964 Act. To make up title now to that partnership property, the heir-at-law of the last surviving trustee can serve so as to provide a title for the benefit of the present partners.

Service as heir-in-trust was not available where the truster died before, but the last trustee died after, 10 September 1964, simply because the 1964 Act did not so provide – see *Browning, Petitioner* 1976 SLT (Sh Ct) 87. The procedure has been revived for an heir of provision (but not for an heir-at-law under the 1874 Act s. 43) by the Law Reform (Miscellaneous Provisions) (Scotland) Act 1980 s. 6. In *MacMillan, Petitioner* 1987 SLT (Sh Ct) 50, the application of this section is discussed and in particular the method of determining who is the heir for the purposes thereof. The Sheriff of Chancery decided that the heir of provision in trust fell to be identified by applying the new rules of intestate succession under the 1964 Act s. 2.

**32.12** (*d*) *Deaths after the 1964 Act – confirmation of executors* If the deceased died after 10 September 1964, then new trustees may be appointed by the court; or title can be made up through the medium of the executors of the last surviving trustee under the Executors (Scotland) Act 1900 ss. 6 or 7.

To illustrate the working of the rules as to confirmation in a practical situation, assume that A died infeft in a heritable property after 10 September 1964, testate or intestate. B confirms as A's executor and includes A's heritage in the confirmation, which therefore vests in B as executor by virtue of confirmation thereto. Normally, B will deal with A's heritage either by selling it or passing it on to A's successors, by disposition or by a 1964 Act s. 15 docquet. But suppose he fails to do so and then dies. The title to A's heritage lapses on B's death and has to be revived.

**32.13** (i) Executors (Scotland) Act 1900 s. 6. B's executor, nominate or dative, if he is willing so to do, may include A's heritable estate in the inventory of B's estate, and so in B's confirmation, under a special heading of estate held in trust. See Currie on *Confirmation*, 8th edition, Chapter 16, for full details. Such confirmation allows B's executor to transfer A's unadministered heritage either (i) to new trustees appointed in A's estate; or (ii) to A's successors; but does not confer any further power of administration on B's executor.

471

**32.14** (ii) Executors (Scotland) Act 1900 s. 7. If s. 6 procedure is not practicable, anyone interested in A's estate may petition the sheriff for appointment of an executor dative *ad non executa* who, when appointed, may confirm to A's unadministered heritage. The confirmation *ad non executa* is a valid title; and the executor *ad non executa* has full power to administer.

**32.15 Jurisdiction in trust petitions.** In all the foregoing situations, the sheriff court now has jurisdiction to appoint or remove trustees and to give authority to beneficiaries to make up title under the Trusts (Scotland) Act 1921 ss. 22–24 by virtue of the Law Reform (Miscellaneous Provisions) (Scotland) Act 1980 s. 13 which substantially reduces the costs of these procedures.

### 32.16 Judicial factors

The decree appointing a judicial factor, prior to the 1938 Act, had to contain a warrant authorising the judicial factor to complete title to the estate coming under his charge as factor. However, this is no longer necessary by virtue of the 1938 Act s. 1, in terms of which any decree appointing a factor operates as a general disposition in his favour of all heritable estate coming under his charge. It can, therefore, be used as a link in title for the purpose of dealing with that estate.

### 32.17 Sequestration

The decree confirming the appointment of the permanent trustee, termed the act and warrant, vests the whole estate of the bankrupt in the permanent trustee under the Bankruptcy (Scotland) Act 1985 s. 31. Accordingly, the act and warrant is equivalent to a general disposition in his favour, and can be used as such when dealing with the bankrupt's heritage. There is no obligation on him to complete his title by recording a notice of title; but normally he will do so in order to exclude possible competing titles or securities. In that case, he will use the notice of title – see below.

**32.18** *Acquirenda* **in sequestration.** Where, after the date of sequestration, the bankrupt acquires right to other estate, *e.g.* as a beneficiary under the will of a deceased testator, this estate also vests in the permanent trustee automatically under the Bankruptcy (Scotland) Act 1985 s. 32(6). Any such after-acquired estate will, no doubt, be held by a third party, *e.g.* a trustee under the will of the deceased in which the bankrupt is the beneficiary. In terms of the 1985 Act s. 32(6), the trustee under that will, on production to him of the act and warrant of the permanent trustee, is obliged to make over to the permanent trustee any assets falling to the bankrupt as beneficiary. In that event, if assets are made over *in specie*, the conveyance by the executor under the will of the deceased in favour of the permanent trustee will operate as the trustee's title and will probably be in the form of a special disposition, in the case of heritage, which can be recorded *de plano*. Accordingly, in the case of such assets, the question of completion of title presents no problem.

Under the Bankruptcy (Scotland) Act 1913, now repealed, the trustee in sequestration was required to record a memorandum in Sasines in order to make up his title to the after-acquired assets.

## 32.19 Completion of title and infeftment following thereon

No real right in land can be created without infeftment; and infeftment implies:

(1) written title;

(2) entry with the superior (now implied under the 1874 Act s. 4 on the recording of the appropriate title without the necessity for any special feudal clauses); and

(3) registration in the Register of Sasines of an instrument of sasine, under the Registration Act 1617, or, where appropriate, registration of the title under the 1979 Act.

Until 1858, in the case of land (in the case of heritable securities and schedule conveyances on compulsory purchase, the change was made rather earlier), the instrument of sasine was the only writ which could competently be recorded; and, in particular, a feu charter or disposition could not itself be recorded in Sasines. This was because, until 1845, symbolic delivery was an essential element in the creation of the real right; and the only competent evidence that symbolic delivery had taken place was the instrument of sasine. Accordingly, the instrument of sasine, in addition to defining the subjects and the person procuring infeftment therein, also narrated the warrant or warrants on which sasine proceeded and the act of sasine. By the Infeftment Act 1845, symbolic delivery was abolished; but it still remained necessary for the disponee to produce to a notary public the warrant of sasine and relative writs; and these had to be incorporated in an instrument of sasine in a similar form to the form in use before 1845. Accordingly, until 1858, the instrument of sasine remained generally in use.

Under the Titles to Land Act of 1858, the last remaining vestiges of sasine, along with the precept of sasine, were abolished; and the special conveyance (feu charter or disposition) became, for the first time, recordable direct in the Register of Sasines for procuring infeftment in the person of the disponee thereunder. As a result, the instrument of sasine became redundant; and, in any event, in its old form, was no longer appropriate since it narrated, *inter alia*, the precept of sasine and the act of sasine, which had ceased to be legal requirements.

This major change in the procedure for procuring infeftment created no special problem where the title took the form of a special, recordable conveyance (other than problems dealt with by the introduction of the warrant of registration – see Chapter 13). In the great majority of cases before the 1868 Act, the title did take this form. But, even before 1858, a general disposition might, in certain circumstances, form a valid link in title. A conveyance of land may operate as a general (as opposed to a special) disposition where, *inter alia*, it contains no particularised description, but merely a description in general terms; but one of the essential prerequisites for registration of the writ in Sasines is that it must take the form of a special conveyance, containing an identifying description.

The need for the introduction of the warrant of registration resulting from the direct recording of deeds permitted under the 1858 Act has already been dealt with in Chapter 13. In the case of operational areas under the Land Registration (Scotland) Act 1979, most deeds will fall to be registered in the Land Register, not recorded in the Register of Sasines as explained in that Chapter. The same general rules apply to infeftment created by registration in the Land Register as apply in the case of titles recorded in the Sasines Register.

### 32.20 The general disponee
After the 1868 and 1874 Acts, it became very much more common in practice for a person to have a right to land under a general, as opposed to a special, disposition. Such a general disposition was, undoubtedly, a valid title, but was not of itself recordable *de plano* for the procuring of infeftment. Such cases arose in the following, typical, situations.

### 32.21 Wills.
The 1868 Act s. 20 validated wills generally as links in title. Such wills were normally in the form of a general disposition either to trustees or to a beneficiary direct.

### 32.22 General service.
The 1874 Act s. 31 introduced general service (as opposed to special service) as a competent title to the estate of an intestate, who had died infeft; and equated such a decree to a general disposition.

### 32.23 Trusts.
The increasing use of trusts produced a consequent increase in deeds of assumption and conveyance and minutes of resignation, not containing any description of the trust heritage.

### 32.24 Heritable securities and confirmation.
Heritable securities became moveable estate under the 1868 Act (in the great majority of cases), with a consequent increase in the number of cases where confirmation, as a general disposition, operated as a link in title, not of itself recordable.

### 32.25 Procedure for completing title
Clearly, to meet cases of this kind which frequently arise in practice, there must be some machinery whereby a person in right of land under a general disposition (or its equivalent), can put his title on record, and so procure himself infeft.

Such provision was duly made, in an elaborate form, in the 1858 Act by the introduction of a new writ, known as the notarial instrument. These provisions were re-enacted and extended by the 1868 Act. The notarial instrument in turn, and to a large extent the foregoing provisions, have been superseded in practice by the 1924 Act ss. 4–6 and the notice of title, introduced under the 1924 Act. But the effect of the notice of title is equated, under the 1924 Act, to the effect of a notarial instrument; and it is therefore necessary in the first place, to look briefly at the 1868 provisions.

The main provisions, in the 1868 Act, relating to completion of title to land, are ss. 17, 19, 23 and 25. Sections 125 to 128 deal with heritable securities.

### 32.26 Notarial instrument
Speaking generally, the notarial instrument is a semi-official narrative under the hand of a notary public but is a narrative only, simply setting out certain facts, or purported facts, which have been brought to the attention of the notary. It is not an operative deed and does not of itself create or confer rights. It merely serves as a necessary and convenient vehicle for transporting a personal, (or unfeudalised), title to land onto the Record, so as to convert that personal title into a real right, and procure infeftment. On

this aspect of the effect of the notarial instrument, see *Kerr's Trustees* (1888) 15 R 520 (the opinion of Lord Rutherford Clark; ignore the other judgments) and *Sutherland* 1941 SC 196.

In addition to procuring an infeftment for the person on whose behalf the notarial instrument is expede and recorded, the instrument may also have the effect of converting personal and unsecured burdens contained in unrecorded links, such as a will, into a real burden on the subjects to which the notarial instrument relates. See *Cowie* (1893) 20 R (HL) 81, where a testator, in his will, conveyed his whole estate, heritable and moveable, in general terms to his son B, declaring, in the dispositive clause of that general disposition, that it was granted *inter alia* under burden of an annuity in favour of the testator's daughter C; and the annuity was declared to be a real burden on the heritage conveyed to B. B, as general disponee, completed title to his father's heritage by recording a notarial instrument which, *inter alia*, narrated the above declaration as to the real burden in favour of C. The court held that the annuity was validly constituted as a real burden on the land; and accordingly that, on the recording of the notarial instrument in this case, two real rights emerged, namely, B's real right to the land which had belonged to his father, and C's real right in security to the annuity as a real burden thereon. Contrast *Mackenzie* 1903 11 SLT 428 where, in similar circumstances, the notarial instrument failed to refer to the burden, and thus the annuitant was unsecured.

### 32.27 Notice of title

In practice, the notarial instrument has been superseded, although not abolished, by the notice of title, introduced under the 1924 Act. The main purpose of the 1924 Act is simplification. In place of the numerous sections in the 1868 Act dealing, separately, with completion of title to land and to heritable securities, the use of the notice of title for completing title to land and securities in all circumstances is dealt with in one relatively simple section, s. 4; and six forms of notice of title, two for land, two for heritable securities other than ground annuals, and two for ground annuals, are introduced, replacing all the various forms of notarial instrument under the earlier Acts.

Further, the notice of title may be signed by any law agent, not merely a notary public. Hence the change of name.

### 32.28 The right to land.  Section 4 provides:

'Any person having right either to land or to a heritable security by a title which has not been completed by being recorded in the appropriate Register of Sasines, may complete his title in manner following.'

Four separate situations are then dealt with under subsections (1), (2), (3) and (4); and the section then concludes:

'And on such notice of title being recorded, as in this section provided, the title of the person on whose behalf it is recorded shall be, in all respects, in the same position as if his title were completed as at the date of such recording by notarial instrument in the appropriate form duly expede and recorded according to the present law and practice.'

**32.29 Nature of the title**. Generally speaking, there are three distinct categories of person who may be said to have a right to land.

(1) The infeft proprietor, having a recorded title. Clearly, the section has no application in his case, because his title is already completed.

(2) The uninfeft proprietor whose right is constituted by an active but unrecorded title, such as a special but unrecorded disposition or, much more commonly, a general disposition or its equivalent. The notice of title is available for any such disponee.

(3) A purchaser under missives or a beneficiary in a trust, although undoubtedly having right to land, does not have right to land by title. A contract is not a title, since it contains no words of conveyance. The trust deed is a title to the trustees. It is not (normally) a title to the beneficiary, whose right is a *jus crediti* only, a mere *jus ad rem*, which entitles him to call on the trustees to denude.

**32.30 Last infeftment**. The 1924 Act s. 4 makes no distinction between the case where the immediate predecessor in title of the person expeding the notice was infeft, and the case where he was uninfeft. The procedure under this section applies equally to either case. Thus A, infeft on a recorded special disposition, died pre-1964, leaving a will containing a general conveyance to B. B is a person in category (2) above, and might complete title to A's heritable property by notice of title. He is not bound to complete title. Suppose in fact, that he failed to do so. He died uninfeft, leaving a will in favour of C. Again, C is a person in category (2), even although B was uninfeft; and C might complete title to the heritable estate originally belonging to A, again by notice of title under s. 4.

**32.31 Alternative forms of notice**. The 1924 Act s. 4(1) and (2) contain two alternative procedures for completing title to land. 'Land' is defined in the 1924 Act s. 2(1) to exclude securities, but otherwise has the definition assigned to it in the 1868 Act s. 3 and 1874 Act s. 3, which is very wide. Section 4(1) deals with the normal case; s. 4(2) provides an alternative for very special circumstances, and is rarely used. Section 4(3) and (4) make comparable alternative procedures for completing title to heritable securities.

**32.32 Form B1**. Section 4(1) provides:

> 'A person having such right to land may complete a title thereto by recording in the appropriate Register of Sasines a notice of title in or as nearly as may be in the terms of form No. 1 of Schedule B to this Act, in which notice of title such person shall deduce his title from the person last infeft.'

'Deduction of title' is defined in s. 2(3) as implying the specification of the writ or series of writs, without narration of the contents thereof, by which the person expeding the notice has acquired right from the person last infeft. In other words, however many unrecorded midcouples may intervene between the person last infeft and the person now completing the title, the deduction of title starts with the last infeftment and then narrates all the intervening unrecorded links.

**32.33** *Links in title.* Broadly speaking, anything which operates as a title to land, *inter vivos* or *mortis causa*, may be used as a link in title in a deduction of title for this purpose; and even were this not implied, it is express in terms of the 1924 Act s. 5(1) which defines the writs which can be used as links in this context as including any statute, conveyance, decree, or other writing whereby a right to land is vested in, or transmitted to, any person. The definition of 'conveyance' in the 1924 Act s. 2(1)(c) is extremely wide; and the definitions of the same term in the 1868 Act s. 3 and the 1874 Act s. 3 are expressly adopted for the purpose of the 1924 Act by s. 2(1). The definition is extended to include, not only the principal writs themselves, but also extracts and office copies, as defined in the 1924 Act s. 2(2). For an equivalent provision in the case of probates and letters of administration, see 1874 Act s. 51 and 1887 Act s. 5.

**32.34** *Statutory vesting provisions.* For an illustration of a statute operating as a vesting writ for this purpose see the Local Government (Scotland) Act 1973 s. 222 and the Local Authorities (Property, etc.) Order 1975 (S.I. 1975 No. 659). Under that Act and Order, heritable property, vested in the old local authorities, was transferred to and vested in the new regional or district authorities set up under the 1973 Act. But it has been made quite clear by the Law Society Conveyancing Committee and the Scottish Development Department that the combined effect of the Act and order is simply to give the new local authorities a title equivalent to a general disposition. It does not create any infeftment for them. Therefore, when disponing land, the local authority must deduce title through the Act and Order.

Comparable provision is made for the vesting of specified properties in new unitary authorities by order of the Secretary of State under the 1994 Act s. 15. In addition, under s. 18, the Secretary of State is empowered by order to establish one or more residuary bodies to take over property, rights and liabilities as may be transferred under s. 15. Section 18 of and Schedule 3 to the Act prescribe their functions and powers.

Further and detailed provision is made for the transfer of property held in trust by a local authority or any individual councillor and the proper officer of that authority to the appropriate person or persons in the new authority, and like provision is made for educational endowments under ss. 16 and 17.

Compare the Church of Scotland General Trustees Order Confirmation Act 1921 in terms of which property is transferred to the transferees thereunder to the same effect as if dispositions had been granted and recorded in the appropriate division of the General Register of Sasines. Obviously, in the latter case, the transferees are deemed to be infeft although having no recorded title.

The first form of statutory provision is common; the second is rare.

**32.35** *'Conveyance'.* 'Conveyance' includes any general or special disposition, *e.g.* before the 1964 Act, a will, or after it, a confirmation. Suppose A, infeft, grants a feu charter or special disposition to B. Normally, B completes title by recording the charter or disposition *de plano*. He may equally well, if he wishes, record a notice of title using the feu charter or disposition as a link, though there is normally no point in so doing.

**32.36** *Content of Form B1.* The normal form of notice for completing title to land in the 1924 Act Schedule B1 is straightforward. In outline, its content is:

(1) Narrative. This defines the person expeding the notice and having the right to the land.

(2) Description. The subjects to which title is being made up are described in conventional form.

(3) Burdens. It is appropriate to refer to burdens in the usual way.

In addition, however, it may be necessary (although this is extremely rare) to set out at length in the notice of title the terms of any real burden or condition running with the land and contained in one of the unrecorded mid-couples or links in title on which the notice proceeds. Special provision is made for this in Schedule B1, in terms of which, in addition to setting out the burden at full length, it is necessary to specify the writ in which the burden appears. See *Cowie* (1893) 20 R (HL) 81.

(4) Deduction of title. This is the clause which complies with the instruction in 1924 Act s. 4(1) to deduce title. It contains three essential elements:

(*a*) Identification of the person last infeft, by name and designation. Note particularly that he must be designed.

(*b*) A specification of his infeftment. Only the minimum detail is required, normally the division of the Register and the date of the last recorded title. It may be that the date of the last recorded title has been incorrectly specified or omitted, but, if so, provided that the writ can be identified, the error may not be fatal, by analogy with the provision for statutory descriptions by reference. See Chapter 8.19.

(*c*) Deduction of title proper, being the specification of the writ, or writs, by which the person expeding the notice acquired right from the person last infeft. There may be one, or several. Each writ must be separately specified, giving sufficient information to identify the writ, *e.g.* the type of writ, the party or parties without designations, its date, and date of registration; but narration of the content of each writ is unnecessary.

(5) Presentment of writs to the official. As already mentioned, under the 1924 Act, the notice of title may now be signed by any law agent, not merely a notary public. It is generally stated that the agent executing the notice should have no direct interest therein; but it is quite unobjectionable for a solicitor to expede a notice on behalf of a client and this is regular practice. The clause simply states 'Which last recorded title and subsequent writ(s) have been presented to me YZ (designed), law agent'.

The notice is executed by the law agent and the testing clause is added in the usual way. Attestation, by one witness, is still necessary on or after 1 August 1995 since the notice is to be recorded. See 1995 Act s. 6 and Schedule 4.

The writ is then sent to Register House for recording with a warrant of registration thereon endorsed and, on recording, the title of the person expeding the notice is completed in accordance with the statutory formula.

**32.37 Form B2**. As already mentioned, the 1924 Act s. 4(2) provides an alternative to s. 4(1) for completing title to land in one very special set of circumstances, rarely encountered in practice. Before this alternative procedure can be used, the following requirements must be satisfied:

(1) There must be in existence a special, but unrecorded conveyance by the person last infeft. In addition, there may, and usually will, be subsequent unrecorded mid-couples, such as a will.

(2) The special but unrecorded conveyance must be in such a form that it could have been recorded by the disponee thereunder, and, had it been so recorded, would have procured an infeftment for that disponee.

(3) The special but unrecorded conveyance is now to be recorded along with the notice of title.

**32.38** *Special uses of Form B2*. The typical case for which the 1924 Act s. 4(2) makes this special provision arises in this way. A, infeft, granted a feu charter in favour of B who, before the charter is recorded, died in 1963 leaving a will in favour of C. The charter contains building and other conditions of title, including an obligation on the vassal to record the charter *de plano*, which is not uncommon. But the charter has not been recorded in accordance with this clause, and cannot now be recorded *de plano* since the disponee, B, is dead. Under the 1868 Act s. 142 a conveyance can be recorded only during the lifetime of the grantee. How can C comply with the requirement of the charter that it should enter the Record? The 1924 Act s. 4(2) provides suitable machinery.

Under this alternative procedure, a notice of title is prepared in the form of Schedule B2 to the Act, again executed by a law agent, and this is then recorded in the Register of Sasines, with warrant of registration, on behalf of the person expeding the notice; and, along with the notice, there is also recorded in Sasines the special but unrecorded disposition, which is docquetted with reference to the notice of title form B2.

**32.39 Forms B1 and B2 compared**. The form B2 differs radically from form B1 in certain important respects:

(1) Description. All that is required in form B2 by way of description is a reference to the special conveyance in these terms 'All and Whole the subjects disponed by the disposition (or as the case may be) granted by CD (designed) to EF (designed) dated and recorded in the division of the General Register of Sasines for the County of Angus of even date herewith'.

(2) Burdens. No reference to burdens in form B2 is necessary, because that reference is already contained in the special conveyance itself. Any burdens contained in any later, but unrecorded, conveyance operating as a link or mid-couple must, of course, be set out in full. It is very unlikely that this will occur.

(3) The specification of the last infeftment is not necessary, because the special conveyance to be recorded along with this notice is itself granted by, or at least must connect up with, an infeft proprietor.

(4) The deduction of title and presentment of writs to the official are modified accordingly.

Otherwise, the general rules for notice of title form B1 apply.

**32.40 Recording**. As mentioned above, the notice of title form B2 is presented for registration along with the special but unrecorded conveyance. The warrant of registration is endorsed on the notice of title, and is adapted to meet the special circumstances under note 5 to Schedule F, in terms of which the warrant will include a reference to the disposition entering the Record along with this notice. There is no warrant of registration on the special conveyance; instead, the special conveyance carries a docquet, also signed by the recording agent, in terms of Schedule B note 7 which runs:

'Docquetted with reference to notice of title in favour of AB recorded of even date herewith. YZ (designation), agent'.

Only one application form for recording in the Sasine Register is required both for the notice of title and for the accompanying disposition; but in that case a suitable note should be entered in Box 13 of the application form.

**32.41 Heritable securities**. The 1924 Act s. 4(3) and (4) then make equivalent provision for the ordinary, and the special circumstances, procedure for completing title to a heritable security (or part thereof) which includes a bond and disposition in security, pecuniary real burden, ground annual, and standard security.

Section 4(3) applies to any heritable security already recorded; for that case, the form Schedule B3 is the normal form (equivalent to B1) for securities other than ground annuals; form B4 is used for ground annuals and differs from B3 in that (as in the case of other forms dealing with ground annuals) B4 contains a description.

Section 4(4) applies to unrecorded securities. It provides for the recording thereof, along with the special form of notice forms B5 or B6, for securities and ground annuals respectively. B5 and B6 follow the same pattern as form B2 for land.

### 32.42 Effect of recorded notice

Finally, the 1924 Act s. 6 provides that a notice of title expede in terms of the Act is equivalent to a notarial instrument expede according to the pre-1924 law and practice. As a result, for practical purposes, the notarial instrument is superseded, although it can still competently be used.

### 32.43 Registration of title

If the subjects lie in an operational area for registration of title and the title has already been registered, the notice of title is no longer used; and instead the uninfeft proprietor (in category (2) above) simply applies to the Keeper to be registered as proprietor. See the 1979 Act s. 3(6). Under the 1979 Act s. 3(1), registration has the effect of vesting in the registered proprietor a real right in the registered property; and the date at which the real right is so created is the date of registration under s. 3(4). Accordingly, for practical purposes, the registered proprietor is infeft.

**32.44 Deeds by uninfeft proprietors**

As a general feudal principle, a mandate for infeftment can originate only from a proprietor who is himself infeft. It follows that, where the proprietor of heritage holds uninfeft on a sasines title, and wishes to grant a charter, he must still first complete title by the recording of an appropriate notice. The same general rule applied also to dealings with heritable securities, and to the granting of leases.

The old rule has now been altered, but with limitations, under three different provisions.

**32.45 (1) Continuity of trust infeftment.** The 1868 Act s. 26 and 1874 Act s. 45 relate to trusts, and the object is to render unnecessary completion of title of new, in the case of a trust, on the occasion of the assumption of a new trustee. The 1868 provision applies only to religious and educational trusts, where the title to trust heritage has been taken in the name of office bearers or trustees for behoof of the association, and their successors in office. The 1874 provision applies to any trust, but only where the office of trustee is conferred upon the holder of that office *ex officio* and his successors in office, or on the proprietor of a landed estate and his successors as such proprietor.

In these limited circumstances, when the trustees have taken an original infeftment, then, notwithstanding subsequent changes in the body of trustees, there is notionally a deemed continuity of infeftment; and the present trustees for the time being (as successors in the office under the 1868 provision, or as the holder of the office or owner of the estate for the time being under the 1874 provision), are deemed to be infeft, even although there is no title on the Record in their name. This is a useful, but very limited, provision. It is particularly appropriate in the case of churches and other similar associations.

**32.46 (2) Disposition, etc., by person uninfeft.** 1924 Act s. 3. This is a statutory short-cut available in all cases, (not merely in the case of trusts) to any person having right to land or to a heritable security whose title thereto has not been completed by being recorded in the Register of Sasines. Compare s. 4 and note the similarity in wording. In other words, the short-cut is available to a person in category (2) of the three categories referred to in the context of the 1924 Act s. 4 above, who holds an active title in his favour which is of itself a mandate for infeftment by expeding a notice of title.

**32.47 Deduction of title.** In the case of such a person in category (2), the section provides:

(*a*) In the case of land, that the person entitled may grant a disposition (which is interpreted as including a special disposition, but not a feu charter or a bond and disposition in security or lease). If, in such disposition, he deduces his title from the person last infeft, by incorporating, in the disposition, a clause of deduction of title in terms of Schedule A (1) then, on such disposition being recorded, the title of the disponee is in all respects in the same position as if, at the date of recording of the disposition, the disponee had completed title by recording a notarial instrument. Put shortly, an uninfeft proprietor can now dispone provided he deduces title; the disposition then becomes a mandate for the infeftment of the disponee by *de plano* recording.

The only significant difference between a disposition by an uninfeft proprietor and a disposition by an infeft proprietor is the incorporation of the clause of deduction of title in terms of Schedule A (1); and this clause is identical in form to the clause of deduction of title in a notice of title.

(*b*) In the case of a heritable security duly constituted as a real burden on land by having been recorded in the Register of Sasines, the creditor for the time being in right thereof may deal with that security by way of assignation, restriction or discharge, without first completing title, provided, again, that in such assignation, deed of restriction or discharge, the uninfeft creditor deduces title in terms of note 2 to Schedule K to the Act, and two alternative methods of deduction of title were provided for dealings with heritable securities. This provision is further amended by the 1970 Act s. 47 and Schedules 10 and 11. The effect of this amendment is that, where the grantor of the assignation, etc., has a recorded title, no further specification or deduction is necessary. Where the grantor has no recorded title in his own name, he deduces title from the last recorded title to the security.

Again, under the 1924 Act s. 3 when the assignee, etc., records the assignation containing this deduction of title, his title is in all respects in the same position as if he had completed it by notarial instrument under the pre-1924 rules.

The same rules apply to dealings with standard securities under the 1970 Act.

**32.48 (3) Standard securities**. (1970 Act s. 12.) Heritable securities (not being dispositions under the 1924 Act s. 3) could not be granted by the uninfeft proprietor; but the 1970 Act s. 12 (1) allows an uninfeft proprietor to grant a standard security, thus: 'a standard security may be granted over an interest in land by a person having right to that interest but whose title thereto has not been completed by being duly recorded' provided he deduces title; notes 2 and 3 of Schedule 2 to the 1970 Act provide the style of deduction.

Note 2 deals with the normal case where A, as uninfeft proprietor, is granting a standard security. He inserts a clause of deduction of title identical in form to the 1924 Act Schedule A, except that, here, the person last infeft need not be designed.

Note 3 deals with the case where the grantor has right as proprietor to the reversion of the property, subject to a loan which is still outstanding and was created, before 1970, by *ex facie* absolute disposition; and where he is granting a second security over his reversionary interest. Such cases, of course, are now very rare. Two situations are covered under note 3:

(*a*) Where the reversionary proprietor was himself originally infeft when he granted the *ex facie* absolute disposition, no clause of deduction of title is required in the standard security now being granted.

(*b*) Where the reversionary proprietor was not originally infeft, but held on a personal title on which he might have taken infeftment, the standard security now to be granted must contain a clause of deduction of title in terms of note 3.

Note 3 does not expressly deal with the commonest case, where the reversionary proprietor never had a title at all. This regularly occurred before the 1970 Act where a purchaser, under missives, consented to a disposition by the seller directly in favour of a building society. The reversionary proprietor still has a reversionary right in such cases but no form of title. Accordingly, he can still grant a standard security over the reversionary interest. In that case, he does not deduce title, but instead incorporates in the standard security an assignation of the reversionary right. In this case, the standard security must be intimated to the *ex facie* absolute disponee.

In cases where deduction of title is appropriate, the 1924 Act s. 5 (Deduction of title) is applied by s. 12(3) to define mid-couples or links in title.

See Halliday's *Practice*, Chapter 36–21 *et seq.*

**32.49 Continuing need for completion of title.** As a result of these provisions, the notice of title is far less common than its predecessor, the notarial instrument. But completion of title by way of notice of title is still commonplace; for one thing, it is generally accepted that, as stated in para. 32.44, a feu charter or a lease cannot competently be granted by an uninfeft proprietor, notwithstanding the provisions in the 1924 Act for a disposition by the proprietor uninfeft. The same applied to granting heritable security before the 1970 Act s. 12 which first introduced deduction of title for the standard security. For another thing, if property is to be retained indefinitely, it may be prudent to complete title in order to establish the real right and to exclude any possibility of challenge to the title as having been extinguished by the long negative prescription under the rule in *Pettigrew* 1956 SC 67. For a recent illustration, see *Porteous's Exrs.* 1995 SLT 649.

In the case of registered titles, see para. 32.43 above. But completion of title for this purpose would now seem no longer to be necessary. See Chapter 33.79.

Notwithstanding registration, however, it is thought that, in exceptional circumstances, the rule in *Pettigrew* might still apply and the uninfeft proprietor of a registered interest should therefore apply to the Keeper for registration of his title in the manner above described.

**32.50 Assignation of an unrecorded special conveyance**
As an exception to the general rule that, before dealing with land or heritable securities, the person in right thereof had to be infeft, it was always competent at common law for the person in right of a special conveyance (*e.g.* feu charter or disposition) who had not taken infeftment thereunder, to assign the benefit of that unrecorded conveyance to an assignee, without himself becoming infeft. The same applied to a heritable security.

This procedure was still available until 29 November 1970 under statutory sanction. The 1924 Act s. 7 and Schedule C applied both to land and to heritable securities; but were rarely employed.

If the 1924 Act s. 7 was used, then the first prerequisite was that there should be in existence a special conveyance, whether a disposition, or feu charter, or equivalent, in favour of a disponee who might have recorded the same in the Register of Sasines *de plano* to complete his title; but that special conveyance had not been recorded. The disponee thereunder might transmit his rights under that special conveyance by assigning the same to an assignee who then came in place of the assignor as if he, in turn, had been the immediate disponee under the special conveyance itself. Accordingly, this is again transmission of a right to land by way of substitution or delegation, but in the special circumstances outlined above.

The 1924 Act s. 7 introduced a new short form of assignation, superseding the old pre-1858 disposition and assignation, for transmitting the benefit of a special but unrecorded conveyance. The assignation might either be endorsed on the special conveyance which was being assigned; or it might be an entirely separate writ. Suitable forms of assignation, endorsed and separate were provided. This situation rarely arose in practice because a special disposition or heritable security would normally itself be immediately recorded. By recording, it ceased to be available as a mandate for infeftment and therefore could not be assigned as such.

**32.51 Completion of title of assignee**.   Where a special but unrecorded disposition has been assigned under the 1924 Act s. 7, the subsequent infeftment of the assignee presented some complicated variations; see Burns' *Handbook* Chapter 16 for detail.

The 1970 Act s. 48 abolished the use of this simple procedure and repealed the statutory provisions under which the short forms were made available. So the special assignation of an unrecorded disposition is no longer competent. But note that only the special assignation is struck at. So, a special but unrecorded disposition, etc., may still be assigned by a general disposition (*e.g.* a will pre-1964) and often so passes. In that case, the grantee must either take infeftment by notice of title under the 1924 Act s. 4; or use both the general disposition and the special but unrecorded disposition as unrecorded mid-couples, when disponing as uninfeft proprietor under the 1924 Act s. 3.

Chapter 33

# EXAMINATION OF TITLE

### 33.1 Sasines or registered titles
The procedure to be followed on the examination of the title of the seller
or borrower depends on whether or not the subjects lie in an operational
area under the Land Registration (Scotland) Act 1979.

At present, 14 counties have become operational namely Renfrew,
Dumbarton, Lanarkshire, the Barony and Regality of Glasgow,
Clackmannan, Stirling, West Lothian, Fife, Aberdeen, Kincardine and,
with effect from 1 April 1997, Ayr, Dumfries, Wigtown and the Stewarty of
Kirkcudbright: see 1996 SLT (News) 220. In the whole of the rest of
Scotland, there are virtually no registered titles and so examination of title
proceeds, as it has done for centuries past, on the basis of titles recorded in
the General Register of Sasines.

In 'operational areas', as defined in the 1979 Act, it will depend in the
first instance on the nature of the transaction as to whether or not the resulting title will fall to be registered in the Land Register or recorded in the
Sasines Register for that operational area. Thus, under the 1979 Act s. 2(1),
speaking generally, on any conveyance or transfer of heritage for value or
on marriage and on any transfer, regardless of consideration, of an interest
held under a long lease, on udal tenure or on a kindly tenancy, it is obligatory to register the resulting title in the Land Register, and is incompetent
to record the deed in the Register of Sasines. In contrast, the granting of a
heritable security over land in an operational area taken by itself, does not
trigger off compulsory registration and there are certain other transactions
in operational areas with the same result. Again, in such cases, examination
of title will proceed under the old rules based on recording in the Sasines
Register.

In cases where registration of the resulting title is obligatory under the
1979 Act s. 2, typically on sale, the disposition granted to the purchaser in
implement of the contract of sale and purchase induces first registration of
the title and that in turn implies a number of significant differences in procedure on the examination of that title compared with the examination of
title in a non-operational area.

Finally, in operational areas, when a title has once been registered and is
then subsequently dealt with, that again involves significant differences in
procedure on examination of the registered title; and the procedure is in
fact very much simpler than in either of the other two types of transaction
above referred to.

For convenience, following the pattern in Halliday's *Practice*, examination of a title in a non-operational area is dealt with first in this chapter in
paras. 33.2 to 33.79; transactions in an operational area inducing first regis-

485

tration are dealt with in paras. 33.80 to 33.99; and transactions involving a registered title, normally referred to as dealings, are dealt with in paras. 33.100 to 33.120.

Accordingly, depending on the location of the property and the state of the title, one of these three procedures will be followed in the examination of the title of the seller or borrower following on a contract of sale or loan to ensure that the purchaser or lender obtains a valid marketable and unchallengeable title or security as the case may be.

This chapter is therefore divided into three parts to take account of these three procedures. Notwithstanding these differences, however, there are a number of common elements in the examination of a title under all three procedures and this is taken into account when dealing with transactions inducing first registration and with dealings. The first part of this chapter deals with titles in non-operational areas; and the full procedure on examination of title is encompassed. In the subsequent two alternative procedures involving registered titles, some reference back to earlier paragraphs in this chapter will be incorporated for the sake of brevity.

### Property situated outwith operational areas

### Sasines Titles

### 33.2 Conditions in the contract

As already explained at some length in Chapter 28, certain general obligations in the contract of sale and purchase are implied; and several special conditions are now almost invariably expressed. The first step in examining a title is to read the contract through from beginning to end; and to note all the special conditions and points to look for when examining the title, *e.g.* is the feuduty allocated? what is the liability for roof repairs? etc.

In this context, it is particularly important when examining the title to check in addition that any previous alteration to the property, including installation of the double glazing, and any change of use was duly authorised and completion certificates duly obtained under the relevant statutory provisions referred to in Chapter 19. Particular care must be taken in the case of listed buildings.

In the case of new developments, it is also important to check not only that planning permission and a completion certificate have been obtained but that, in addition, if the road and foot pavement have not been made up *ex adverso* of the subjects of purchase, a road bond or its equivalent has been lodged with the local authority under the Roads (Scotland) Act 1984 s. 17. See Chapter 19.65.

On these points, see also Chapter 28.50 and 28.51.

### 33.3 Proprietary title

The main point to establish is the validity and sufficiency of the seller's proprietary title, *i.e.* that he has the legal title and the beneficial right. For this purpose, the whole prescriptive progress of title must be carefully examined, starting with the foundation writ. But, for this purpose, nothing earlier than the foundation writ need be considered. The points to look for are the following.

### 33.4 (1) Foundation writ. The quality of the foundation writ has been

dealt with in Chapter 14. Under the Prescription and Limitation (Scotland) Act 1973, possession must be founded on and follow the recording of a deed sufficient in its terms to constitute a title to the interest in land (here, the proprietary interest). By such possession the validity of the title is put beyond challenge, except for forgery, or *ex facie* invalidity. Therefore, we are only concerned with the intrinsic validity of the foundation writ; extrinsic matters can be ignored. Assuming that the foundation writ is a disposition, then the points to look for are as follows.

*Stamp duty.* The writ must be properly stamped, although insufficiency of stamp duty is not a bar to prescription. Where the foundation writ is a conveyance on sale, this simply involves an arithmetical check. In other cases, *e.g.* a disposition carrying a 50p stamp, the facts may vouch the sufficiency of the duty, but in some cases adjudication may be necessary.

*Narrative.* In a foundation writ, nothing in the narrative can affect the intrinsic validity. See *Cooper Scott* 1924 SC 309 which is still relevant to post-1976 foundation titles.

*Dispositive clause.* The points to check are:

*The disponee and the destination.* Check this information against the next writ in the progress.

*Description.* Does this correspond exactly with the contract; and does it correspond exactly with what the purchaser imagines he has purchased? In all but the simplest case, this requires a physical check on the ground by the client, or possibly by a surveyor. Where the foundation writ contains a description by reference, check the description for intrinsic validity and also check the description in the prior writ referred to.

*Reservations and burdens.* Note, for reference, all writs referred to for burdens, and note the content of any new reservations or burdens in this writ.

*Remaining clauses.* Note any specialties but, in the ordinary case, nothing in the subordinate clauses could affect the intrinsic validity of the foundation writ. When a conveyance is granted on or after 4 April 1979, several of the old traditional subordinate clauses are now implied and will not be repeated expressly in the great majority of cases unless there are specialties requiring special treatment.

*Authentication.* The writ must be probative. The Requirements of Writing (Scotland) Act 1995 s. 6 requires deeds to be self-proving as a precondition of recording in the Sasine Register. See para. 29.25 *et seq.*

The warrant of registration, and infeftment following thereon, must coincide with the dispositive clause. From and after 1 April 1992, a deed to be recorded in Sasines should be accompanied by an application form for such recording instead of the old form of recording slip and from 1 April 1996 remittance of the appropriate recording dues, but the deed must still carry a warrant of registration. Accordingly, the old rule still applies.

**33.5 (2) Subsequent titles**. Each writ following the foundation writ must then be meticulously checked, whether recorded or not. For an illustrative warning, see Chapter 31.26. In the case of each subsequent title, you are concerned with extrinsic as well as intrinsic validity. If the next writ in the progress is, *e.g.* a disposition granted by the disponee under the foundation writ, the points to check are as follows.

*Stamp duty.* As above.

*Grantor.* Does he connect up with the grantee under the prior title?

*Narrative.* This must be scrutinised in detail and any material facts must be checked by reference to extrinsic sources.

*Dispositive clause.* Check the disponee and destination. Check the description, make sure that it coincides with the foundation writ, or, if it differs, whether the differences are in order. Check the burdens clause and note the content of any new burdens. Check all the subordinate clauses, noting any specialties. In particular, check carefully any clause of deduction of title, and vouch it by reference to the links narrated therein.

Authentication, warrant of registration and subsequent infeftment will be checked as in the case of the foundation writ.

In addition, there may well be other points which are material in a writ within the progress, although not material in the case of the foundation writ. Typically, questions of capacity are significant, although they cannot affect the validity of a foundation writ. The same applies to, *e.g.*, powers of sale of trustees.

This meticulous check is then repeated for each subsequent writ in the progress down to and including the seller's own title.

If this examination discloses no defect in the title, then the seller has a valid proprietary legal title and the beneficial right.

### 33.6 Burdens
Establishing proprietary title in this way does not, however, mean that the title is unencumbered. There are two main types of burden which may materially affect the property in the hands of the purchaser.

### 33.7 (1) Real conditions, running with the lands.
If real conditions have been constituted by writs within the progress, their content will already have been noted in the examination of the proprietary title. But, in addition, there may be valid subsisting burdens constituted by writs outwith the progress of titles. These will normally be referred to in the reference to writs for burdens; but a failure to refer to prior writs for burdens, even throughout the prescriptive period, does not extinguish conditions of tenure, although it may possibly extinguish real burdens created by a disposition; nor will it extinguish a *jus quaesitum tertio*.

### 33.8 (i) Building conditions.
All building conditions and restrictions must be read carefully and you must consider whether any of the burdens, being of an unusual or unexpected nature, is objectionable in terms of the contract or is contrary to express contractual provision. For a recent cautionary case see *Spurway, Petitioner* 1987 GWD 2–65.

Normally, building conditions fall into three categories.

### 33.9 (a) Conditions *ad factum praestandum*.
These include, typically, an obligation to build a house, to enclose the site and to make up roads, all within a time limit. Failure to comply incurs an irritancy. In the case of old

feus, it is normally safe to assume that all such conditions have been duly complied with; but, in the case of recent feus, the standard practice is to require the seller to produce a certificate from the superior that all such conditions have been duly carried out and complied with.

**33.10** (*b*) Money payments.   These include, typically, payments to the superior for roads; and payments to neighbouring feuars for one-half of the cost of erecting mutual walls, or fences. Again, in old feus, it is normally safe to assume that all these payments have been duly made; but, in the case of recent feus, the seller should be asked to produce receipts for all such payments in order to vouch the discharge thereof.

**33.11** (*c*) Restrictions on user, etc.   These conditions are, of course, continuing. The question is whether they are still being duly complied with. If not, consider (1) whether the consent of the superior to some deviation has been obtained or whether the superior has acquiesced; and (2); whether there is a *jus quaesitum tertio* for the benefit of neighbouring proprietors and if so whether they have consented.

**33.12** (*ii*) *Other real conditions*.   These include clauses of pre-emption and redemption again normally (but not necessarily) contained in the original charter. See *Spurway, Petitioner* 1987 GWD 2–65.

**33.13** (*a*) Pre-emption.  A clause of pre-emption in a charter or disposition entitles the superior, etc., to the first refusal of the feu on sale. Such a clause, though possibly still operative, may not be enforceable, according to its terms, because of statutory limitations in the 1938 Act s. 9, the 1970 Act s. 46, and the 1974 Act, for dispositions. See *Spurway*, above.
    In the case of feu charters, whatever the terms of the pre-emption clause:

(i) the superior must accept the pre-emption offer within 21 days of such offer being made (or less if so provided in the charter); and

(ii) if at any time since 17 May 1938 (or possibly only since 29 November 1970) a pre-emption offer has been made and not accepted, the right is absolutely extinguished and is never again exerciseable on any later occasion.
    By the 1974 Act s. 13, the same rule is applied to any clause of pre-emption in any other kind of deed, (*e.g.* a disposition), if executed after 1 September 1974. A new subsection (3) is added to the 1938 Act s. 9 to that effect. For an interesting debate on the effect of a right of pre-emption, see *Ross & Cromarty D C* 1997 SLT (HL) 463. The decision of the House of Lords is quite clear but no comment was made on the question as to whether the right of pre-emption continues to operate in a question with a purchaser. It is suggested that the pre-emption is not extinguished by the right-to-buy transaction any more than other conditions of tenure are extinguished and so will continue to operate on the occasion of the next sale. Reference is also made to *Waverley Housing Trust Ltd.* 1995 SLT (Lands Tr.) 2. In that case, the local authority inserted a pre-emption clause in the offers to sell two houses to the trust with no change of tenancy. The Tribunal held that the condition in each offer was unreasonable in terms of s. 58 of the Housing (Scotland) Act 1988 and that the clause of pre-emption should be struck out from the offers.

**33.14** (*b*) Redemption and reversion. A clause of redemption in a charter entitles the superior, normally at any time in his option, to reacquire the *dominium utile*, usually at a fixed price.

Under a right of reversion, the *dominium utile* automatically reverts to the superior on the happening of a certain event.

The 1938 Act s. 9 does not apply to such clauses and there is no equivalent statutory restriction. But by the 1974 Act s. 12, a right of redemption or of reversion created by a deed executed after 1 September 1974, may only be exercised within 20 years of the deed, if it is exerciseable on the happening of a definite event which is bound to occur (*e.g.* death) or in the option of the superior.

Otherwise, there is no restriction. So a provision that, if the feu ceases to be used by a charity for charitable purposes, it will revert to the superior, remains enforceable in perpetuity. Rights of reversion remain very much a live issue. See *Hamilton* 1996 GWD 5–277.

**33.15** (*iii*) *Reservation of minerals.* Normally, the original reservation occurs in the original charter; but this is not necessarily so. As a result, a reservation of minerals can easily be missed.

**33.16** (*iv*) *Feuduty.* A purchaser is entitled, by implication, to an allocated feuduty; and if allocated, redemption is automatic on sale. So no special provision is required in the contract of sale and purchase; but the purchaser is entitled to be satisfied that the redemption price has been paid, and that the property is no longer burdened with a real burden for the redemption price.

Accordingly, the purchaser can require from the seller, at settlement, either (i) evidence of the redemption price having already been paid, at the time of sale or on earlier redemption; or (ii) if the feuduty has not already been redeemed at settlement, an obligation to produce in due course due evidence of redemption.

In either case, evidence of redemption will normally take the form of (i) superior's receipt; or (ii) a copy notice with acknowledgment by the superior thereon and a search continued for a period of two months beyond the date of the notice (or date of entry, if later).

The point of these alternatives is that, if the superior is paid the redemption money (and gives a receipt), then he no longer has a real burden therefor. If he gives no receipt so that there is no evidence of payment (and he is not statutorily obliged to do so on compulsory redemption) but if no order appears in the Register of Sasines within two months after the redemption date, then, again, there can be no continuing real burden and so the purchaser is no longer concerned. But remember that the rights of heritable creditors holding securities on the superiority are not to be adversely affected by redemption. See Chapters 16.21 and 16.28. Such securities are now rarely encountered.

Alternatively, after settlement, the purchaser could give the notice, to start the two-month period running, and continue the search until two months thereafter.

Particular care should be taken when examining a long leasehold title. It is not uncommon for such titles to contain leasehold casualties providing for payment of substantial sums on the entry of each new tenant. These were not affected by the Feudal Casualties (Scotland) Act 1914. There have been a number of problems in practice recently with such casualties. See also the case of *MRS Hamilton* 1995 GWD 25–1355 where it was held that the long negative prescription of 20 years applied to the unimplemented obligations relating to arrears of casualty. See the article in (1996) 1 SLPQ 125. The Scottish Law Commission is currently looking at leasehold casualties with a view to abolition.

**33.17 (2) Heritable securities**. It is, of course, necessary to ensure that the title is disencumbered of all subsisting heritable securities. The positive prescription does not assist in this case, although the negative prescription is of some help.

The general working rule is:

(1) Go back over the title for the past 40 years and take a note of all heritable securities appearing from the titles (or the search) as subsisting within the 40-year period.

(2) Check (from the search or titles) which of these have been finally discharged.

(3) Ignore any security discharged more than five years ago, because under the 1970 Act s. 41, a discharge by the ostensible creditor cannot be challenged, in a question with a *bona fide* purchaser, more than five years after recording.

(4) If the security was finally discharged within the five-year period, then check the original security deed, all transmissions thereof, and the final discharge, all in detail, to ensure a proper and valid discharge.

(5) Any remaining securities are presumably still subsisting, unless they have been effectively restricted. Check the title and search for deeds of restriction or clauses *in gremio* in dispositions disburdening the subjects thereby disponed, and, if there are any such, make sure that the property has been effectively disburdened of these securities. If the subsisting securities have not been so restricted, then the purchaser's agents should see and revise draft discharges of the remaining outstanding securities. These discharges should be delivered at settlement, along with the selling solicitor's cheque for the appropriate recording dues, but most agents are prepared to take an obligation from the seller's agents to deliver valid discharges, in terms of the revised drafts, within three to six months after settlement of the transaction.

### 33.18 Possession
There are two points here.

**33.19 (1) Prescription**. In any examination of title, one relies on the positive prescription. This requires both title and possession. The quality and duration of possession have been dealt with in Chapter 14. Strictly speaking, it is not enough simply to examine the title in isolation; one should also enquire into the extent and quality of possession over the 10 year period since the date of the foundation writ. This can be of particular importance with regard to evidence as to whether or not the property is a matrimonial home. But, in practice, evidence of possession is rarely called for by the purchaser, although the seller would require to satisfy the purchaser on this point, if called upon to do so. There is an interesting discussion of the extent of possession required in an article by Professor Rennie at 1994 SLT 261.

**33.20 (2) Vacant possession or subject to tenant's rights**. This is a point which should be dealt with in the contract. If the property is purchased with vacant possession, then an inspection of the property will normally show whether or not vacant possession can be given.

If the property is purchased subject to tenant's rights, the purchaser's agent should always call for and examine in detail the lease or leases. He does this not only to establish the benefits flowing to the landlord under these leases, but also to satisfy himself as to the obligations incumbent on the landlord, since these benefits and these obligations (unless personal to the original landlord, which they would rarely be) will transmit and be enforceable by and against the purchaser.

### 33.21 Searches

A search for incumbrances is essential for the proper examination of heritable title. In all cases, two registers must be searched, namely the Register of Sasines and the Presentment Book (the Property Register) and the Register of Inhibitions and Adjudications (the Personal Register); and, in the case of companies only, the Register of Charges and company files.

In special circumstances, searches in other registers may be appropriate, *e.g.* the Register of Entails; the Register of Rents under the Rent Act in the case of let properties to establish the registered rent(s), if appropriate; Register of Planning Applications, etc. and the Register of land which may be contaminated under the Environmental Protection Act 1990: see Chapter 19.71.

**33.22 (1) The Property Register**. The purpose of a search in the Property Register is:

(*a*) to disclose the state of the proprietary title at the date of completion of the transaction; and

(*b*) to disclose all incumbrances affecting the property, other than floating charges, in each case as evidenced on the record.

In the Property Register, the search is directed at a particular heritable property; and accordingly the search itself opens with a description of the property searched against, normally a particular description or description by reference. The search is confined to the division(s) of the General Register of Sasines in which those subjects are situate, or, where the property was burgage, to the particular Burgh Register of Sasines and the General Register of Sasines in which the property lies. Searches in the Burgh Register are not now normally of any practical importance.

Over a given period, which is specified in the search, the search discloses all recorded writs appearing in those registers which in any way affect the property. The details of the writs so disclosed are very brief, and, in particular, do not normally disclose conditions and restrictions contained therein. Remember that, in a system of registration of deeds, the property search guarantees that the writs which it discloses are the only writs recorded in the relevant registers which purportedly affect the property during the period of search. It therefore gives notice to anyone dealing with the property that these writs have been recorded and apparently affect the property; but it goes no further. In particular, it is not in any sense a certificate of the sufficiency or validity of the title.

**33.23** (a) *Period of search – proprietary title.* The period which the property search must cover for a proper examination of a title, is closely linked with the positive prescription. Thus, in a purchase of heritage, the purchaser's agent first satisfies himself as to the validity of the proprietary title. For this purpose, he examines the foundation writ and subsequent progress. In addition to that examination, he must also be sure that the writs which he has examined are the only recorded writs affecting the property; and for this he relies on the property search. Accordingly, if the property search is to fulfil its function in this respect, it must go back to the foundation writ; and it must cover a continuous period from the date of recording of the foundation writ to completion of the purchaser's title.

**33.24** (b) *Period of search – heritable securities.* In addition to validity of title, the purchaser's agent is also concerned to ensure that the property is disencumbered. Here, the positive prescription does not assist him. A bond and disposition in security, recorded long before the date of recording of the foundation writ, may still be enforceable. The only way of being absolutely sure that the property is disencumbered is to carry the property search back to the original Crown writ. In fact, on grounds of expediency, a shorter period of search is accepted by the profession; the actual period is arbitrary. A 40-year search is now recommended in all cases; but this is not necessarily foolproof. Thus, a bond may have been recorded 50 years ago, and would not be disclosed by a 40-year search; but the probability is that some writ will have entered the record relating to that bond in the past forty years, *e.g.* notice of title, assignation, partial discharge, etc., so indirectly disclosing it.

**33.25** (c) *Seller's obligation as to search.* As already mentioned, the common law obligation on a seller with regard to period of search in the property register is uncertain. Accordingly, the standard practice is to insert, in the contract of sale and purchase, an express obligation under which the seller is obliged to exhibit a clear search in the property register going back either (a) for at least forty years prior to the present date; or (b) to the date of recording of the foundation writ, if that writ was recorded more than forty years ago.

**33.26 (2) The Register of Inhibitions and Adjudications**. (The Personal Register.) This is a purely diligence register, closely associated with the Register of Sasines, but quite separate and distinct from it and serving quite a different purpose. The General Register of Sasines is a publication register, the object being to make known to the public at large the existence, or purported existence, of real rights affecting, or purporting to affect, the land. Accordingly, the only writs which the Keeper will accept for recording in the Register of Sasines are writs relating to land which identify particular heritable subjects to which they relate. The Register of Inhibitions and Adjudications (commonly known as the Personal Register), is not concerned with land, nor with titles to land as such. It is only concerned with persons and the personal capacity of persons to grant deeds affecting land.

Originally, there were several such registers; but all these have now been amalgamated together into a single register under this name (1924 Act s. 44).

The Personal Register is now the only register for the publication of personal diligence; and, further, interdict apart, a third party cannot create any effective bar on the capacity of a heritable proprietor nor prevent him from dealing with heritage unless an entry appears against that heritable proprietor in the Personal Register. This has no application to natural incapacity. If a heritable proprietor is insane, or is not of full age, he is automatically barred from effectively dealing with his heritable estate, but no entry to that effect appears in the Personal Register.

**33.27 Nature of entries**. The law provides equitable remedies for the benefit of persons having valid claims upon heritable property feudally vested in the infeft proprietor. (See Adjudication, Reduction and Sequestration in Chapter 30.) But these equitable remedies involve delay. Meanwhile, in the period between the raising of the action and the granting of the decree, the infeft proprietor remains ostensibly beneficial owner and may confer an active title on a *bona fide* purchaser for value who is unaware of the pending action, to the prejudice of the person claiming an interest in the heritable property in question. To prevent such prejudice, immediate interim procedures are available to the pursuer in an action (or a creditor) whereby he can effectively prevent the debtor in the obligation from dealing with heritage. These procedures do not, in themselves, provide an active title for the claimant (or creditor). To be effective, an entry must be made against the infeft proprietor in the Personal Register, and it is only by making the appropriate entry in this register that this result can be achieved. There are three common types of entry, each producing a similar effect, dealt with below. For a full list of various possible entries in this register, see Gretton on *Searches*, p. 27.

**33.28** (*a*) *Notice of litigiosity*. Heritable property becomes litigious when it is the subject-matter of a depending real action (*e.g.* adjudication or reduction). When heritage is litigious, this implies a prohibition against alienation of the heritage to the prejudice of the pursuer in the action (or to the prejudice of a creditor who has done real diligence), where the object of that action (or real diligence) is to acquire a title to the heritage, absolutely (or in security). Note that the infeft proprietor is not absolutely barred from dealing with the property, simply because his property has become litigious. He may deal with it, but anyone taking a title from the infeft proprietor has notice of the potential claims upon it; and a title so taken may later be reduced at the instance of the person who has rendered the property litigious.

Originally, the mere calling in court of a real action affecting heritable title was sufficient publication, and of itself rendered the property litigious. But by the 1924 Act s. 44(2)(*a*), no action relating to land shall, *per se*, make property litigious; and, in order to produce a state of litigiosity, a notice in the form of Schedule RR to the 1868 Act must be recorded in the Personal Register. Property only becomes litigious at the date of the recording of such notice.

Since 30 December 1985 every notice of summons of reduction, adjudication etc. must incorporate a description of the lands to which the summons relates; and Schedule RR is amended accordingly. See the Law Reform (Miscellaneous Provisions) (Scotland) Act 1985 s. 59 and Schedule 2 paras. 4 and 5. Likewise, every notice of application to rectify a deed relating to land must contain a description of land to which the application relates. See s. 8(8) of the same Act.

Further, by s. 44(2)(b), decree in an action of adjudication does not, of itself, make property litigious.

The notice of litigiosity has no effect on the proprietor's capacity to deal with other heritage; it affects only the heritable property to which the action relates. It was previously impossible to tell what property was affected by litigiosity because the lands were not described; but this defect in the system has been cured under the amending provision referred to above.

Further, litigiosity strikes only at future, voluntary deeds; and so cannot bar the subsequent granting of a disposition of heritage which has been made litigious if it is in implement of a contract dated prior to registration of the notice.

**33.29** *(b) Inhibition.* In any real action, the *status quo* may be preserved, and prejudice to the pursuer may be avoided, by rendering the property litigious, through the recording in the Personal Register of the appropriate notice. A personal action, *e.g.* for payment of a debt, as opposed to a real action, is not directed at, nor does it directly affect, heritable property belonging to the defender. But the whole estate of the debtor is liable for payment of his whole debts. The pursuer in a personal action for payment is therefore indirectly interested in heritage belonging to the debtor in that, if he succeeds in his action, he may then have recourse, by diligence, against heritage of the debtor.

In order to protect his potential interest in heritable property belonging to the debtor, a creditor may, by the appropriate procedure followed by the appropriate entry in the Personal Register, inhibit the debtor. The effect of an inhibition is similar to litigiosity, in that, by inhibition, the inhibited proprietor is effectively prevented from granting any future voluntary deed affecting any heritable estate or interest belonging to him at the date when the inhibition becomes effective. Again, deeds granted by an inhibited party are not, of themselves, void; but they remain voidable at the instance of the prejudiced creditor. The inhibition now differs from the notice of litigiosity in that the inhibition strikes at all heritable property generally, not merely the property described in the notice.

An inhibition is purely negative. It never operates to confer an active title on the inhibitor; and it only affects heritable estate. But an inhibition may confer a certain preference on the inhibitor in a sequestration. For articles on ranking, and recent cases, see the Reading List. Care should be taken by those instructing inhibitions that they have accurate information about the person who it is proposed to inhibit. For an example of this, see *Atlas Appointments Ltd.* 1996 SCLR 476.

**33.30** There are two alternative procedures.

(i) *Letters of inhibition.* This procedure is competent only in execution, where the creditor holds a liquid document of debt; or in security, where the creditor holds an illiquid document of debt and the debtor is *vergens ad inopiam* or *in meditatione fugae.*

No formal action is necessary; instead, all that is required is to present the document of debt with a bill in the Petition Department of the Court of Session, which is granted by the clerk of court. The form of letters of inhibition is statutory under the 1868 Act s. 156 and Schedule QQ.

The letters are signeted, and served on the debtor and, thereafter, entered in the Register of Inhibitions and Adjudications. They are effective only from the date of such registration.

(ii) *Inhibition on the dependence.* Where a debt is illiquid, it requires formal constitution by action in court. But it is competent to include, in the summons of any Court of Session action concluding for payment, a warrant to inhibit; and where so included, the summons (after service on the debtor) may be registered in the Personal Register. The effect is to inhibit the defender as from the date of such registration, which is in practice a very useful device.

Inhibition on the dependence may also be effected in a sheriff court action. The procedure is to apply to the Petition Department of the Court of Session, producing the initial writ or a certified copy thereof, and other appropriate documents. See Macphail *Sheriff Court Practice* p. 364 for details.

**33.31** *Notice of inhibition.* Where the creditor intends to inhibit the debtor by either method, he may register in the Personal Register a notice of inhibition under the 1868 Act s. 155 and Schedule PP. This is a form of advance warning that an inhibition is on the way; but it has no effect whatever unless letters of inhibition, or a summons containing the warrant to inhibit, are subsequently registered within 21 days following on the registration of the notice. In that event only, the letters, or summons, date back to the date of registration of the notice.

**33.32** (*c*) *Sequestration.* The effect of an act and warrant appointing a trustee in sequestration, as a title to the debtor's heritage, has been noticed already. But, in addition, in every sequestration it was obligatory, within 48 hours of the first deliverance, to register in the Personal Register an abbreviate of the petition and deliverance under the 1913 Act s. 44. This provision has now been repealed by the Bankruptcy (Scotland) Act 1985; but, under the 1985 Act s. 14, the clerk of court is now obliged forthwith to send a certified copy of the relevant court order to the Keeper of the Registers for recording in the Personal Register. Such registration has the force of an inhibition. It, therefore, prevents the bankrupt from disposing of his heritable estate to the prejudice of other creditors, pending completion of title, subsequently, by the trustee in sequestration. Similarly, property acquired by a bankrupt after the date of sequestration vests in the trustee in sequestration. See *Alliance & Leicester Building Society* 1994 SCLR 19.

**33.33** (*d*) *Trust deed for creditors.* Under the 1985 Act s. 59 and Schedule 5 para. 2, the trustee may register a notice in a prescribed form which has the effect of an inhibition. This provision is quite new. Note that it is permissive, not obligatory. But the trustee should be advised to record such a notice at once, if the debtor owns heritage.

## 33.34 Duration of entries in the Personal Register

(i) *Notice of Litigiosity*. The effect of such notice expires five years from the date of registration; or on the expiry of six months from the date of final decree in the action, whichever shall first happen; 1924 Act s. 44(3)(*a*).

(ii) *Inhibition.* An inhibition is of no effect after the expiry of five years from the date on which it first became effective; 1924 Act s. 44(3)(*a*).

(iii) *Abbreviate of sequestration.* The effect of an abbreviate under the Bankruptcy (Scotland) Act 1913 lasted for five years only. It then fell; but, unlike a notice of litigiosity or an inhibition, the effect of the abbreviate could be renewed by the recording of an appropriate memorandum, and could be kept in force by subsequent renewals for 20 years, under the 1913 Act s. 44 and the 1924 Act s. 44(4)(*c*).

Similar provisions were made under the 1985 Act s. 14(4). If the permanent trustee was not discharged within three years of the date of sequestration, he was required to send a memorandum in a prescribed form to the Keeper for registration in the Personal Register before the expiry of the original three-year period. Although this requirement was mandatory it was not always observed, and s. 14(4) was amended by para. 3 of Schedule 1 to the Bankruptcy (Scotland) Act 1993, to the effect that registration of a memorandum in a continuing sequestration is now at the trustee's discretion. The trustee's registration of the memorandum in the Personal Register renews the effect of the original registration of the relevant order, but only for a further period of three years. If still not discharged after six years, the permanent trustee can register further memoranda to keep renewing the order for further periods of three years until finally discharged.

Apart from the statutory prescriptions, the effect of any of these entries in the Personal Register can be removed by discharge at the instance of the creditor or trustee who made the original entry; or may be recalled or restricted by the court. Appropriate entries are then made in the Personal Register.

## 33.35 Effect of statutory prescriptions. 
It is generally accepted that the effect of the statutory prescription under the 1924 Act is two-fold:

(i) That, when five years have expired from the date of registration of a notice of litigiosity or an inhibition, the debtor/proprietor is released from the effect thereof; and he is then absolutely free from any prohibition against alienation.

(ii) That, even if the debtor/proprietor has alienated his heritage during the five-year period, the party in right of the inhibition or notice absolutely forfeits his right to reduce the alienation by the debtor/proprietor immediately on the expiry of the full five-year period. It is not altogether clear whether the 1924 Act s. 44 achieves this second effect. The profession are apparently unanimously of the view that the second result is effectively achieved by the legislation, and act on that view in the instructing of searches. But, as Professor Gretton points out in *The Law of*

*Inhibition* (2nd edn.) p. 69 the practice of the profession is by no means necessarily conclusive.

**33.36 Purpose of personal search.** A search in the Register of Inhibitions and Adjudications is intended to disclose any legal bar which may still be effective against the present proprietor or any predecessor in title within the prescriptive period, in case such a legal bar (*e.g.* an inhibition) might have prevented the proprietor from conveying the property at the date when he conveyed it or might render a title granted by such a person reducible at the instance of a third party. A search in the Personal Register is normally combined with a search in the Property Register, for convenience; but it serves an entirely separate purpose and may be separately instructed.

**33.37 Period of search.** The practical rules governing period of search and persons searched against in the Personal Register take into account three main factors, namely:

(i) that inhibitions and notices of litigiosity prescribe in five years – 1924 Act s. 44; but

(ii) that abbreviates of sequestration under the Bankruptcy (Scotland) Act 1913 although they also prescribed in five years, might be renewed by memorandum. In a very few cases, this rule will continue to apply until all existing orders renewed by memorandum under the Bankruptcy (Scotland) Act 1913 have been discharged. The Bankruptcy (Scotland) Act 1985 s. 14 produces a similar result; but the effect of the registered court order expires in three years, although that effect can be renewed for successive three-year periods;

(iii) that extrinsic invalidity (*i.e.* granting deeds under disability) is cured after 10 years by the positive prescription.

The practical rule is that all persons having the legal title, or any beneficial right, to the property within the past ten years are searched against in the Personal Register, but for a period of five years only prior to the date of completion of the purchaser's title. Further, if any proprietor has been searched against for a period of five years prior to the date on which he was divested (which is normal in any sequence of titles), then it is unnecessary to conduct any further search against that person on any subsequent transaction.

**33.38 (3) Companies.** A search in the Register of Charges is only appropriate in the case of a limited company dealing with heritage. It discloses floating charges. It also discloses all fixed securities, although these would, in any event, be disclosed by a search in the Property Register. Accordingly, when a company is granting a standard security, or a floating charge, a search in the Register of Charges is always required because a floating charge may competently prohibit the company from granting any subsequent fixed security ranking prior to the floating charge. In the absence of such a prohibition, a subsequent fixed charge automatically takes priority. Floating charges rank *inter se* according to their dates of registration.

When heritable property is being sold by a limited company, as a going concern, the property is automatically released from a floating charge on sale, and, strictly speaking, no search is required. But, when the company goes into liquidation, or when a receiver is appointed, the floating charge becomes a fixed security. A search in the Register of Charges would not reveal the liquidation of the company but would reveal the appointment of a receiver which is noted in that register.

In the case of liquidation, there is a time-lag of anything up to 15 days during which, under statute, the resolution putting the company into liquidation may be lodged; for the appointment of a receiver the statutory time limit is seven days. Therefore, a search in the company register is never right up-to-date.

When purchasing from, or lending to, a company, one should accordingly search the company's file in the Register of Companies, not merely the Register of Charges, and take other appropriate action, if necessary, as discussed in detail in Chapter 35.

If a search is required in the Register of Charges, then it will normally be from 27 October 1961, which was the date of commencement of this register; or from the date of incorporation of the company, if later.

For a full discussion on the content and effect of searches, with illustrative styles, see Gretton, *A Guide to Searches*.

### 33.39 Instructions to searchers
In practice, the searchers are normally instructed by way of a memorandum for search, or for continuation of search, framed by the seller or borrower and revised by the purchaser or lender. The seller or borrower instructs the search in terms of the revised memorandum.

**33.40 (1) Property Register.** There are two possible cases. Either there already is a search over the property, brought down to a particular date; in which case that search would normally be continued. Or, where there is no such search available for continuation, a new search must be instructed. But in the latter case, the new search will normally connect up with some previous existing search, and this affects the commencing date.

In the case of a new search, the memorandum for search will contain a short description; where an existing search is to be continued, the memorandum instructs that search to be continued, and so no description is normally necessary, unless the search is to be continued over part only, but not the whole, of the property originally included in the initial search. In addition, the memorandum will also specify:

(*a*) the register, *i.e.* the division of the General Register of Sasines in which the search is to be conducted; and

(*b*) the starting and closing date. The starting date will normally be the day after the closing date of the prior search. Note, however, that, where the previous relevant entry is marked 'grantee's interest not traced' the continuation, or new search, should start from that date, not from the date following. The closing date is not normally known at the time when the memorandum is prepared. Thus, on sale and purchase, the closing date of the search will be the date of recording of the disposition in favour of the purchaser; but the memorandum is adjusted prior to settlement. In practice, therefore, the closing date is stated as 'the date of certificate (to include disposition by AB in favour of CD)'.

**33.41 (2) Personal Register.** The working practice is:

(*a*) Make a list of all the parties having the legal title or a beneficial right to the property at any time within the past 10 years.

(*b*) Check, on the existing search, to see if any of these parties have been searched against for a full five-year period prior to divestiture; and, if they have, delete them from the list.

(*c*) The remaining parties now fall to be searched against on this occasion. For this purpose, the searchers should be given the full name and addresses of individuals.

Specialties.
(*a*) Trustees or executors. The practice is to search against them as a body, naming and designing the truster, but not naming individual trustees. The truster or the deceased, as the case may be, may also fall to be searched against under paragraph (*c*) above.

(*b*) Firms. The practice is to search against all individual partners as individuals and as trustees for their firm; and against the firm *socio nomine*. If, as often happens, the trustees for the firm are not the current individual partners, the trustees as a body should be searched against in their trust capacity.

(*c*) Heritable creditors. Creditors under *ex facie* securities, *e.g.* bond and disposition in security and standard security, are not searched against in practice. But see Burns' *Practice* p. 300; the inhibition of a heritable creditor prevents effective discharge, if notarially intimated to the debtor under the Act of Sederunt of 19 February 1680, which in practice is ignored. In theory it applies to any bond, etc., discharged within the five-year period (1970 Act s. 41). *Ex facie* absolute disponees are searched against as having the legal title; and so is the beneficial owner as debtor proprietor for his beneficial interest.

(*d*) Purchaser(s). As a courtesy, the seller will normally agree to the inclusion of the purchaser(s) in the personal search if they are granting a standard security. Since the searchers include up to 6 names for the same charge, this usually causes no problem; but if the seller refuses, then a separate personal search must be obtained to protect the lender.

In all cases, the period in the personal search is for five years prior to completion of the current transaction.

**33.42 Interim reports on search**
The search in the Property Register is made up from the Minute Book which is normally some weeks (or months) behind. Clearly, it is not possible to deliver, at the settlement of a transaction, a search which has been continued right down to date to disclose the disposition in favour of the purchaser. As a precaution (which in fact protects both sets of agents) an interim report on the search should always be obtained as near as possible to the date of settlement. Subject to the comments below on

computerisation of the Presentment Book, this will show, in the Property Register, the writs which the search will disclose to within a short period prior to settlement; and in the Personal Register any entries to within 24 hours of the date of search.

It is prudent practice for the seller to instruct an interim report at the outset of a transaction, in which case the interim report should be updated immediately prior to settlement.

Until 1 April 1992 there was a significant gap of some months between the closing date of the interim report in the Property Register and the date on which the report was issued because of unavoidable administrative delays in Register House between the receipt of the writ and the making-up of the minute for the Minute Book, from which the searchers work. As from 1 April 1992, however, the Presentment Book has been computerised and accordingly the facility now exists for the searchers, by using both Presentment Book, Minute Book and Search Sheet, to produce an interim report which is up to date to within 24 hours of the date of issue. This facility significantly reduces the risk to solicitors in granting of letters of obligation as noted below. A search in the Presentment Book, if required as it normally will be, must be separately instructed: see below.

### 33.43 Is the search clear?

As mentioned in Chapter 28, it is implied in any contract of sale and purchase, and is in any event normally expressly provided for in the contract, that the seller will deliver or exhibit a 'clear' search. For a fuller discussion of this question, see the article already referred to by Professor Reid in 1988 JLS 162, and Professor Gretton, *A Guide to Searches*, p. 35.

Generally speaking, a search is not clear if it discloses, in the Property or Personal Registers, or in the case of companies in the Register of Charges or Company file, any deed or diligence not previously disclosed to the purchaser and which he has not agreed to accept in terms of the contract, expressly or by implication, if such deed or diligence renders the title unmarketable.

Entries in the Property Register normally present no problem; and it is generally perfectly clear whether or not a writ disclosed in the Property Register does or does not mean that the search is not clear.

Until computerisation of the Presentment Book as from 1 April 1992, it had become increasingly common for solicitors, contracting in their letter of obligation to provide clear searches, to be caught out by the appearance in the search of a second security granted by the seller, of which the solici-tors were unaware. This was caused by what was then a substantial gap in the interim report in the Property Register due to delay in completing the Minute Book from which the searchers then worked. Under their letter of obligation undertaking to give a clear search, the seller's solicitors might then find themselves personally liable to pay off the second security. That should not occur when the 'gap' has been eliminated, as explained in para. 33.42 above, if an interim report is obtained immediately prior to settlement because that will effectively be right up-to-date. Note, however, that a search in the Presentment Book requires to be separately instructed. Furthermore, the search in the Presentment Book is not yet warranted by the searchers. This is because computerisation of the Presentment Book is new and it is not yet clear that the system will be totally effective. It is assumed that, when the computerisation system is working efficiently, the Keeper will then be sufficiently confident of the accuracy of the information provided by the new system to allow him to guarantee it; and that in turn will allow the searchers to guarantee Presentment Book searches. Even without that guarantee, such searches will greatly improve the system and will protect the profession against what had become a serious risk.

Most arguments on whether a search is clear arise in relation to entries in the Personal Register. The point is that an inhibition strikes only at future voluntary deeds granted by the inhibited party. Thus, if a contract of sale and purchase is duly concluded and if, thereafter, the seller is inhibited before delivery of the disposition in favour of the purchaser, that disposition is not struck at by the inhibition and cannot be challenged by the inhibiting creditor; but this does not appear *ex facie* of the Record because, of course, the missives are not recorded. On the strength of the decision in *Dryburgh* (1896) 24 R 1, it is generally accepted in the profession that, in such circumstances, the search is not clear because, *ex facie* of the Record, when the disposition was recorded, the grantor was under inhibition. See Halliday's *Practice*, 21–86 and 23–15.

A similar question can arise in relation to heritable securities. In *Newcastle Building Society* 1987 SLT (Sh Ct) 81, the debtor, in a standard security granted to and recorded by the building society, was subsequently inhibited. Thereafter, the building society exercised its power of sale and the purchaser challenged the title on the footing that the search was not clear. The sheriff principal took the view in that case that, looking to the provisions of the 1970 Act s. 26(1), it was clear *ex facie* of the Record that the property had been disencumbered and accordingly the search was clear. For a more detailed discussion, see Gretton *The Law of Inhibition* p. 143.

The problem of company searches is dealt with in Chapter 35.

### 33.44 Settlement obligations

At the settlement of a transaction, the disposition normally supersedes the contract. See Chapter 28.21. One of the seller's contractual obligations is to deliver or exhibit a search. The seller can never implement this at the date of settlement, and some delay in producing the search is inevitable. In addition to the interim report, it is therefore usual, at settlement, to require the seller's agents to grant an obligation undertaking to deliver or exhibit a clear search; and it is customary to include in such obligations an undertaking implement to any other conditions of the contract which are not fully implemented at settlement, *e.g.* delivery of a discharge of a standard security repaid by the seller out of the purchase price. But a purchaser is not obliged to agree to this.

Note that such obligations are always personally binding on the sellers' solicitors. See *Johnston* 1960 SLT 129 and the article in 1959 JLS 135 'Settlement obligations'. So the purchaser's agent is relying on the personal integrity and standing of the other agent; and the agent granting the obligation guarantees his client to that extent. Again, he should grant such obligations only with circumspection. The obligation is also binding on the seller himself; and the purchaser, or his agents, can sue both the selling solicitor and the seller jointly for implement of the obligation. See *McGillivray* 1993 SLT 693. The purchaser himself also has a title to sue, notwithstanding that the obligation is granted by one solicitor to another: see 1991 JLS 349.

**33.45 Implications of the obligation system.** The conveyancing system in Scotland very largely depends for its efficient working on the use of the letter of obligation granted by the seller's solicitor at settlement. Indeed, letters of obligation have been described as 'the lubricant of the daily settlement of transactions involving the sale and purchase of heritable property': 1959 JLS 135. In terms of the contract, the seller is obliged to produce a clear search in the Property and Personal Registers. Even if this is not provided for expressly, it is implied. In the nature of things, because of inevitable delay in preparation of the Minute Book in Register House, it is impossible to produce an up-to-date search in the Property Register at settlement. This still applies, notwithstanding computerisation of the Presentment Book. The personal search will be virtually up-to-date. Delivery of the disposition in favour of the purchaser traditionally superseded the missives; and so, arguably, the seller's obligation to deliver a clear search, whether express or implied, was superseded by the disposition because in practice there will be no reference therein to delivering clear searches. To keep that obligation alive, therefore, either a non-supersession clause in the disposition was required or, as has been the practice in the past for a century or more, a letter of obligation is granted at settlement by the seller's solicitor. The supersession rule ceases to apply from 21 June 1997 under the Contract (Scotland) Act, but letters of obligation will in practice continue to be required. For the reasons stated above, in granting such a letter of obligation, the seller's solicitor is, in effect, giving his personal guarantee that the search will be clear.

When acting for an individual or a firm, solicitors were usually perfectly willing to grant a letter of obligation at settlement, notwithstanding the risk that some adverse deed, *e.g.* a second security, or some other adverse factor, *e.g.* an inhibition, might be recorded or registered in the period between the close of the interim report and the date of settlement. Until computerisation of the Presentment Book on 1 April 1992, there was an increasing risk that an adverse entry might appear in the Property Register; and the selling solicitor, by granting a letter of obligation to deliver a clear search, was in effect giving his personal guarantee that this would not occur. Past delays in completion of the Minute Book, and the resulting increase in the length of this gap, made some solicitors reluctant to grant letters of obligation; and it was this factor which persuaded the Keeper to introduce a computerised Presentment Book which is, in effect, up to date to within 24 hours prior to the close of search. As a result, the risk of any adverse entry in the Property or Personal Registers between the close of the interim report and the date of settlement is, or will be, remote and, unless the circumstances are very special indeed, there should be no valid reason why the seller's solicitors should not grant a letter of obligation in traditional or 'classic' form. This is subject to the proviso mentioned above in para. 33.43 that the search in the Presentment Book is not warranted. There is, however, no legal obligation on a solicitor acting for a seller to grant a letter of obligation. If a solicitor acting for a seller does not propose to grant a personal letter of obligation covering the normal searches in the Sasines, Land and Personal Registers, then he or she has a professional duty in practical terms to advise the purchaser's solicitor that no obligation will be available at settlement. This must be done at the earliest opportunity and preferably before the conclusion of missives so that an alternative method of settlement can be agreed upon.

From the point of view of the purchaser, notwithstanding that the risk is now very slight, his solicitor should never settle a transaction without such an obligation because, otherwise, the purchaser is virtually unprotected. In such a situation, where the selling solicitor declines to grant a letter of obligation and where there is no special contrary provision in the missives, the seller is not in a position at settlement fully to implement all his obligations in the contract because he is not in a position to produce a clear search, that being for practical purposes an impossibility. In the absence of express provision in the missives, no purchaser is obliged to proceed with a contract unless and until the seller has implemented all his obligations; and no purchaser should ordinarily agree, in the missives, to any such express contrary provision. The Law Society of Scotland's view has consistently been that in a domestic property transaction the purchaser's solicitor is entitled to expect a personal obligation from the seller's solicitor unless otherwise stated: 1991 JLS 171. If the seller's solicitor will not grant a letter of obligation, the purchaser should not agree to pay the price, but instead it should be consigned in joint names until the search, or at least an interim report brought down to disclose the disposition in favour of the purchaser, is produced. If the purchaser's solicitor is satisfied in that situation with such an interim report, and assuming the interim report to be clear, then payment of the price would only be postponed for a matter of days, the 'gap' having been eliminated by computerisation of the Presentment Book. It should be pointed out, however, as mentioned above, that the professional searchers do not warrant their interim report at the current time, in so far as it is based on entries in the Presentment Book. Accordingly, such an interim report, although on the face of it clear, is not foolproof and the purchaser is not fully protected. If, however, the purchaser's solicitor is to insist on retaining the price or consigning it in joint names until the search is finally produced, there will be a delay of some months before a guaranteed search can be produced; and it is very unlikely that this will be acceptable to either party.

In the case of sales by individuals, firms, trustees, etc., the problem has not become serious and is largely resolved by computerisation of the Presentment Book, as explained above. In the case of companies, however, for reasons explained in Chapter 35, solicitors acting for a selling company will not normally grant a letter of obligation to produce a clear search in the company file or Charges Register and this in turn produces serious problems which are dealt with in detail in that Chapter.

**33.46 Matters dealt with in the letter of obligation.** Originally, the letter of obligation dealt with searches and, possibly, certain additional items. It is also common practice to cover production and delivery of, *e.g.*, the discharge of a standard security in the settlement obligation. But the purchaser is not obliged to agree to this, for the reasons given above. In that case there are two alternative procedures; either

(1) the seller repays the loan in advance of settlement of the sale and delivers an executed discharge at settlement; or

(2) if the loan is to be repaid out of the proceeds of sale, the practice is to have a tripartite (or multipartite) settlement with the seller, the purchaser and the agent(s) for the secured creditor(s) all present together. The purchaser passes over a cheque to repay the sum in loan, taking delivery of a discharge in exchange, and a second cheque for the balance to the seller.

In either case, the purchaser thus obtains immediate delivery of both the disposition in favour of the purchaser and the executed discharge of the standard security and there is, therefore, no need for the letter of obligation to cover delivery of the discharge since it is delivered at settlement.

The purchaser is quite entitled to insist that, at settlement, discharges of all outstanding heritable securities are actually delivered. He is not in any circumstances bound to accept the seller's letter of obligation on a matter of that kind, and there are risks in so doing.

In recent years, however, it has become common practice to cover delivery of the discharge of a heritable security, etc., in the letter of obligation, at settlement.

One of the difficulties which has arisen from time to time in relation to sasine letters of obligation is the question of time-limits for recording the disposition. See *Warners* 1994 SLT (Sh Ct) 29. As a result of these difficulties, the Law Society of Scotland's Conveyancing Committee, in conjunction with the Insurance Committee, introduced what has come to be known as the 'classic' letter of obligation. This new style of obligation makes it clear that the obligation to deliver a clear search as such is a separate obligation from the obligation to deliver a search which actually discloses the disposition. In the classic obligation, the undertaking to exhibit or deliver the search is qualified to the effect that it will cover a clear search only up to a date 14 days after the date of the letter of obligation. This is to protect the seller's solicitor from his obligation being extended indefinitely. Insofar as the obligation to deliver a search disclosing the disposition is concerned, again this only applies provided the disposition is recorded within 14 days of the date of the letter of obligation.

**33.47 Risks inherent in the obligation system.** From the purchaser's point of view, his agents should not settle a transaction if the subscribed disposition is not ready for delivery. The only protection in such circumstances is for the price to be consigned in joint names, pending delivery of a disposition; but the seller will normally not agree to that because, once the price is consigned, the pressure by the purchaser ceases, and the purchaser's agent tends then to drag his feet. In the result, there is a delay in the seller obtaining the price. Therefore, the seller's agent will normally only agree to early settlement if the price is paid in full, even although he is not in a position to deliver a disposition to the purchaser in exchange. As a result, the purchaser's agent may agree to hand over the price without title but, as a measure of protection, will then insist on an undertaking by the seller that a disposition will be delivered to the purchaser in due course. Solicitors acting on behalf of a seller are strongly advised against granting a personal obligation in such circumstances. Any personal obligation so granted would be regarded as 'non-classic'. Such a practice can be quite unsatisfactory and does involve serious risks for both agents and parties.

The risks can be summarised as follows.

**33.48 (1) The risk to the purchaser**. The risk here is that, in the end of the day, the seller may prove unwilling or unable to implement the obligation, although contractually bound to do so. If he is merely unwilling to do so, then the purchaser has a remedy through the action of implement; but this may involve him in considerable delay and expense.

However, the seller may be totally disabled from completing the transaction by supervening circumstances, *e.g.* apparent insolvency. In that case, the property, although subject to a contract, will pass to the trustee in sequestration who can repudiate the contract. The purchaser has no real right but merely a contractual claim against the seller; and the trustee in sequestration is not bound to implement that claim. In the result, even although the purchaser has paid over the price and is in possession, and even although he has a binding contract with the seller and a binding obligation by the seller's agent to deliver a disposition, he cannot maintain his position in a question with the trustee in sequestration who can eject him and resell the property to some other purchaser. The purchaser's only remedy against the seller in such a situation is to rank in the sequestration and claim damages for a breach of contract; but if, as often happens, there is nothing for the ordinary creditors, then in the result the purchaser has lost his money.

Alternatively, the property could be subject to a heritable security, or several heritable securities, and the seller may have sold at a price less than sufficient to pay off all the creditors in full. In the ensuing delay, one of the heritable creditors gets tired of waiting and exercises his power of sale which, of course, he is perfectly entitled to do, notwithstanding the binding contract of sale and purchase. Again, as a result, the purchaser may lose his money.

**33.49 (2) The risks to the parties' agents**. If the purchaser's solicitor has explained the position in detail to the purchaser, made the purchaser aware of the risks and has then settled without title on the purchaser's express instructions, the agent will not be liable. But in some cases, the purchaser's agent settles without title against the seller's obligation without putting the purchaser in the picture. In that case, he is almost certainly guilty of professional negligence and would be liable in restitution to the disappointed purchaser.

Every practising solicitor is obliged to carry professional indemnity insurance under a master policy negotiated by the Law Society of Scotland. The liabilities of agents, both for seller and purchaser, are understood to be covered by the master policy, but only within certain limits and subject to possible exceptions.

Clearly, if a 'non-classic' obligation is granted, the seller's solicitor may well not be insured. Non-classic letters of obligation are all types of undertaking, other than an obligation to deliver a search and a discharge and possibly a feuduty redemption receipt, where the solicitor personally undertakes to do something more – typically, for example, to deliver some other deed not available at settlement, or to produce a completion certificate. For an indicative (and sadly non-exhaustive) list of such obligations, see 1993 JLS 431.

Any solicitor who grants an obligation of this type and cannot implement it will suffer a double excess or double deductible on any claim made under the Master Policy. If a firm's normal excess is £12,000, the excess on a claim of this type will be £24,000. In many cases, this will mean that the firm will have to pay the whole cost of the claim.

**33.50 (3) The risk to the seller.** Where the transaction settles in this way, the seller gets the purchase price in full, and his risk is minimal. Nonetheless, there are certain risks. For example, it is possible that, notwithstanding payment of the price, the transaction may not settle in the end of the day, *e.g.* the purchaser may claim that the title is unmarketable.

If the unmarketability in title is of a minor nature, it may be that, by paying over the price and taking possession, the purchaser has barred himself from rescinding the contract on grounds which otherwise would have entitled him to do so. See *Macdonald* (1898) 1 F 68.

But, clearly, there could be certain situations where, because of a major defect in the title, the purchaser is entitled to rescind and claim repayment. Meantime the seller may have paid off heritable securities out of the money paid to him by the purchaser; or he may have purchased another house. In either case, the seller might have difficulty then in finding the money to repay.

**33.51 Illustrations of the risks and summary of insurance provisions.** **(1)** For a cautionary case, which illustrates the dangers of settling without a validly executed title, see *Gibson* 1976 SLT 94. Mr Gibson bought a house from Hunter Homes Ltd. which he paid for on 31 October 1974, and took possession, without getting delivery of his feu disposition. Shortly thereafter, Hunter Homes Ltd. went into liquidation before the feu disposition had been delivered. Mr Gibson then sued for implement but the court held, without difficulty, that the house remained the property of the company, and that Mr Gibson had a mere personal right but no real right therein. As a result, the liquidator was entitled to repudiate the contract of sale to Mr Gibson, as he did, and to resell the property, defeating Mr Gibson's claim in the process. This left Mr Gibson with a claim for damages as an ordinary creditor in the liquidation.

It appears from the report that the solicitors for Hunter Homes Ltd. had granted a letter of obligation undertaking to deliver a validly executed disposition, which of course they could not do. Mr Gibson was encouraged by the judges in that case to institute proceedings against the solicitors who granted that obligation, presumably for damages for failure to implement the same. Obviously, this put the solicitors granting the obligation in a position of some difficulty, and they may well have had to pay Mr Gibson in full, and then claim as ordinary creditors in the liquidation.

This case underlines the risks both to the purchaser, and to the seller's solicitors who granted the obligation.

A letter of obligation falls after five years under the Prescription and Limitation (Scotland) Act 1973 s. 6; *Lieberman* 1987 SLT 585 but, arguably, a letter of obligation contains obligations relating to land under Schedule 1, para. 2(*e*). If so, the relevant period is 20 years, not five years. See *Barratt* 1993 SC 142 and *Wright* 1992 GWD 8–447. This point was not raised in *Lieberman.*

For some further comments, see an article by R. A. Edwards in 1975 JLS 260.

See also the commentaries on the more recent case of *Sharp* v. *Thomson*

1997 SLT (HL) 636, as listed in the Reading List for Chapter 4. Although the judgment in the Inner House was reversed in the House of Lords, on a speciality arising out of the statutory provisions for floating charges, there was no criticism and no qualification of the general principles as carefully analysed by the Lord President. For further comment, see an article by Professor Reid in 1997 SLT (News) 79.

(2) It is perhaps useful to summarise the current position under the Law Society of Scotland's Master Policy in relation to letters of obligation.

(a) If a solicitor grants a classic letter of obligation undertaking only to exhibit or deliver a search, discharge and possibly feuduty redemption receipt after having made due enquiry (which means having obtained a search in the computerised Presentment Book and asked the client to disclose any secured loans), the solicitor will be fully covered by the Master Policy with no excess or deductible whatsoever in the event of a claim arising.

(b) If a solicitor grants a classic letter of obligation without having made due enquiry (as aforesaid), the solicitor will suffer the normal excess or deductible in the event of the claim arising.

(c) In the event of a solicitor granting a non-classic letter of obligation (to deliver a disposition or some other such matter), the solicitor will suffer a double excess or deductible in the event of a claim arising.

(d) In the event of a solicitor recklessly granting a non-classic letter of obligation, knowing that the obligation is unlikely to be implemented, so as to raise an inference of bad faith on the part of the solicitor, there may be no cover at all.

### 33.52 Miscellaneous items

According to circumstances, there may be quite a number of other things which affect the validity of the title to a greater or lesser degree, or which impose some restraint on the proprietor, and which may not emerge from mere scrutiny of the titles and the search. In practice, however, an examination of the title will normally disclose the risk. Some of the more important of these undisclosed items are as follows.

**33.53 (1) Want of capacity.** There is no way of telling from the titles if a deed has been granted by persons under age or insane. Normally the purchaser's agents accept this risk without enquiry; but it does sometimes happen.

**33.54 (2) Forgery.** Again, there is no way of telling, by a scrutiny of the title, whether one of the writs is forged. But again, the purchaser's agents normally accept the risk.

**33.55 (3) Latent defects.** Any writ, or decree, although *ex facie* valid, may be void or voidable and open to reduction on various grounds, as we have seen. A typical case is a decree of general service in favour of an heir who later turns out to have been wrongly served. Again, this is a risk which the purchaser is bound to take. See *Sibbald's Heirs* 1947 SC 601 where Lord President Cooper says:

'The obligation on a seller is to produce an *ex facie* valid prescriptive progress of titles, not to guarantee the purchaser, by policies of insurance or otherwise, against every risk of subsequently emerging latent defect. In so far as these risks are taken into account in our system of conveyancing, they have been left to rest on the classical obligation of warrandice, and warrandice is offered here.'

**33.56** *Statutory protection.*   The 1924 Act s. 46 provides that a decree of reduction is not to have any effect in a question with a *bona fide* purchaser for value who has acquired right prior to the extract of the decree being recorded in the Register of Sasines. Whatever the underlying purpose of this section may have been, it is arguably of very limited application following on the decision in *Mulhearn* 1929 SLT 59, as discussed in Chapter 30.12. Recent commentators, however, seem to discount the effect of this decision.

More positive protection is afforded under other statutory provisions, but only with limited effect:

(*a*)  The Succession (Scotland) Act 1964 s. 17. Where a person has, in good faith and for value, acquired a title to heritage which has vested in an executor, either directly or indirectly, from the executor or from someone deriving title from the executor, then his title is not challengeable on the grounds that the confirmation was reducible; nor on the grounds that the executor should not have transferred the property to a particular beneficiary.

(*b*)  The Trusts (Scotland) Act 1961 s. 2. A sale of heritable property by trustees may be contrary to the terms or the purposes of the trust, in which case the trustees have no implied power of sale under the Trusts (Scotland) Act 1921 s. 4. Until 1961, this meant that, in a question with a *bona fide* purchaser for value, the beneficiary could challenge the title of a disponee who purchased heritage from the trustees without the necessary powers. Under this section, notwithstanding the lack of power, a disposition by trustees to a purchaser is put beyond challenge, and good faith is not required.

The section protects only persons transacting with the trustees in a Scottish trust. It does not apply in English or other trusts. Further it protects only the purchaser from trustees. If the trustees, mistakenly, convey heritable property to the wrong beneficiary and the beneficiary then sells the property, that sale is not covered by the 1961 Act s. 2.

In contrast, if the executor dispones or transfers the heritage to the wrong beneficiary, who then sells the property to a *bona fide* purchaser for value, the purchaser is still protected against that defect in title by the 1964 Act s. 17.

(*c*)  The Companies Act 1985 s. 35, as amended by the Companies Act 1989 s. 108. This affords a measure of protection to persons dealing with a company, with particular reference to the *ultra vires* rule which applied at common law. This is dealt with more fully in Chapter 35.

**33.57  (4) Unrecorded interests**.   As we have seen earlier, the significant feature of a real right is that, in a competition between real right and personal right or title, the real right almost invariably prevails. Similarly, burdens and restrictions imposed on or affecting a heritable proprietor will not transmit or run with the lands against a singular successor unless they are made real. We have seen this general principle illustrated in various cases, typically, *Ceres School Board* (1895) 23 R 279. In that case, A granted a feu disposition in favour of B who entered into possession of the feu but did not take infeftment. Many years later, D, in ignorance of the feu disposition by A to B and acting in good faith, took a conveyance from A of the whole estate, and infeftment followed. The court held, in these circumstances, that D's right to the land was not affected by the prior but unfeudalised feu disposition in favour of B.

Again, in *Campbell's Trustees* (1902) 4 F 752, a heritable proprietor gave certain undertakings to the Corporation of Glasgow, for consideration, which were embodied in a recorded agreement, but did not enter or qualify an infeftment. The property having later transmitted to a singular successor, he declined to implement the undertakings and was held entitled to do so on the grounds, *inter alia*, that the agreement was merely a personal contract which derived no efficacy from being recorded in the Register of Sasines and that the recorded agreement did not create a servitude; accordingly, the obligation did not transmit with or run with the lands.

The general principle is well established, but a singular successor may nonetheless find himself bound by some prior personal obligation undertaken by or affecting a predecessor in title, if he was aware of the existence of this personal obligation when perfecting his real right.

**33.58** *The bona fide purchaser without notice.* The general principle and its qualification is stated by Lord Gifford in *Stodart* (1876) 4 R at p. 236. The facts there were similar to the facts in *Ceres School Board*, in that A agreed, by verbal contract, to feu ground to B who entered into possession, built a house on it, and paid feuduty. A then sold the subjects to C who took a title and infeftment. But the facts in this case differ significantly from the facts in *Ceres School Board* because, in this case, C, the singular successor, was aware of the fact that B was in occupation, that B had built a house, and claimed some sort of right in the feu. In these circumstances and in the light of C's knowledge, the court held that he was personally barred from founding on his infeftment and real right with a view to excluding or defeating the prior personal right of B.

Lord Gifford, in this case, sums up the principle and its qualifications thus:

'The principle is, that a singular successor is entitled to be free from the personal obligations of his predecessor, and to take the subjects unaffected by any burden not appearing on the title or on the Record. But the singular successor only has this right if he was in ignorance of the existence of any obligations or deeds granted by the seller relative to the subjects and if he was in all respects a *bona fide* purchaser, without notice of any right in any third party or of any circumstances imposing a duty of enquiry. In this case, I think the pursuer was bound to make an enquiry.'

**33.59** *Rodger (Builders) Limited and the offside goal.* This qualification of the general principle, involving personal bar on the part of the singular successor, is illustrated in a later case *Rodger (Builders) Ltd.* 1950 SC 483. In that case, A contracted to sell heritage to B. Later, thinking (wrongly) that B was in default, A purported to rescind the contract with B and resold the subjects to C, to whom he then disponed them. C recorded the disposition. But C was aware of the prior contract between A and B. On enquiry, he was assured by A that the previous contract had been legally rescinded and, on the strength of that assurance, he went on and completed his title. The court held that (i) A having unwarrantedly rescinded the contract between himself and B; and (ii) C having notice of B's potential rights as prior purchaser, C was then put on his enquiry; and had not sufficiently discharged his duty of enquiry in taking the seller's word for it that the contract between A and B had been rescinded. Therefore, he was not a *bona fide* purchaser without notice of the prior rights of B and, although he had the first and indeed the only feudal title, he could not prevail in a question with B, the prior purchaser, having a personal right only.

In the result, the disposition by A in favour of C was reduced, leaving C with an action of damages only against A. The Lord Justice-Clerk sums up the principle in rather more fanciful idiom thus:

'C assumed that his title would be safe once the goal of the Register House was reached. But, in this branch of the law as in football, offside goals are disallowed. In certain states of knowledge a purchaser is regarded as not being in good faith and goes to the Register House at his peril. .... C is not allowed to rely on the registration which, in the knowledge which he possessed, he succeeded in obtaining.'

Clearly, from these cases, knowledge creates a personal bar in some circumstances, but not in all. It is difficult to define precisely those cases where prior knowledge will create a personal bar and those cases where it will not.

**33.60** *Attempts to define the exceptions.* Burns attempts the definition in these terms (*Practice*, p. 306) 'the opinion may be ventured that this rule would apply to (1) any deed, whether sale or security, following a prior unfeudalised sale; (2) a sale following an unfeudalised security; but that it would not apply to (3) a security following on another unfeudalised security, assuming at least that there was no undue haste'. See also *Trade Development Bank* 1980 SC 74 and *Trade Development Bank* 1983 SLT 510.

Contrast *Wallace* 1960 SC 255, where heritage was sold, subject to a prior agreement conferring a right of occupancy on a third party, not amounting to a lease, of which the purchaser was aware. Having completed his title, the purchaser was held not to be bound by the prior agreement as to occupancy, notwithstanding his knowledge of it. Lord President Clyde, having emphasised that the right constituted by the agreement was a mere personal right of occupancy only, not a liferent, not a servitude and not a real burden, nor capable of being converted into a real right, deals with the general principle in these terms 'From the decisions, it is clear that the exception' (to the general principle) 'only operates where the right asserted against the singular successor is capable of being made into a real right. If it is nothing but a mere personal obligation not capable of being so converted, then the singular successor is not in any way bound or affected by it.'

**33.61** This attempt to define the limits of the exception is not altogether satisfactory. Clearly, from the decisions, a singular successor is personally barred in circumstances such as in *Rodger (Builders) Ltd.* where there was a prior contract of sale and purchase, known to the singular successor. Certainly, in such cases, the right of the first purchaser is capable of being converted into a real right by the granting of the appropriate disposition. But it is very difficult to distinguish, logically, the facts in *Rodger (Builders) Ltd.* from the facts in *Campbell's Trustees* where, again, there was what amounted to an agreement to convey (for consideration), although admittedly at a future date, which is very close indeed to sale and purchase, since the agreement to convey was granted in exchange for a price. Yet in *Campbell's Trustees* the agreement, although known to the singular successor because it was recorded and published, was held to be personal and not binding on him.

Similarly, it is quite clear, on authority, that a mere personal agreement, although recorded (prior to the 1979 Act), purporting to impose burdens on A's property will not bind a singular successor from A, even although he knows of this obligation; yet the right of the creditor in that intended burden might be made real by the granting of the appropriate title. But now, under the 1979 Act s. 17 (Deed of conditions), s. 18 (Variation and discharge of land obligations) and s. 19 (Boundary agreement) recorded agreements in various terms may bind successors under these special statutory provisions.

**33.62 (5) Servitudes.** Both positive and negative servitudes may be duly constituted by a writ which need not enter the Record. Admittedly, in the case of positive servitudes, there must be publication by possession, but this is a very uncertain protection; and for negative servitudes publication and possession are unnecessary. Further, a servitude right may enter the Record in the dominant, not in the servient, title. See *Balfour* 1987 SLT 144.

**33.63 (6) Heritable securities**. As indicated above, securities recorded more than 40 years ago may not be disclosed by a 40-year search, although the risk is small.

**33.64 (7) Terce and courtesy**. This risk is now minimal, but nonetheless these rights may subsist and are enforceable against singular successors, although nothing may appear on the Record. The titles show the risk, but these rights could emerge, under the old rules, following on divorce, not merely on death and here the title does not show the risk. The practice in the past used to be to ask the seller's agent for an assurance that the title was clear of these burdens; but this is not now done.

**33.65 (8) Death duties**. Until 1975, estate duty formed a charge on land for a period of 12 years from the event giving rise to the charge, normally the death of the proprietor.

Estate duty was replaced by capital transfer tax (now called inheritance tax) under the Finance Act 1975 in respect of deaths occurring on or after 14 March 1975. Inheritance tax may be payable on *inter vivos* transfers and on death. Any tax so payable is a charge on the property transferred or held in trust; but with this important exception that heritable property in Scotland is never subject to a charge for inheritance tax, which cannot therefore affect a purchaser or creditor, nor even a gratuitous disponee. See the Inheritance Tax Act 1984 s. 237(4).

**33.66 (9) Charges on land**. From time to time in the past various pecuniary burdens have been imposed on heritable property in Scotland, which do not show in the titles. Such imposts include:

(a) *Teind and stipend thereon, now converted to standard charge.* For the history of teind and stipend, see Green's *Encyclopaedia* 14.793 to 880 – Teind and Teind Court. The present position is now regulated by the Church of Scotland (Property and Endowments) Act 1925. The purpose of the Act is to remove old anomalies and to standardise stipend payments. Under the Act, the standardised stipend has become automatically a real burden on the lands (not on the teinds) in favour of the Church of Scotland General Trustees and is called a standard charge. It is preferred to all other real burdens, except the incidents of tenure, and is recoverable by the Church of Scotland General Trustees in the same way as if it were feuduty. Where the teinds are held on a separate title from the lands by a third-party titular, which is very rare, the heritor is empowered (s. 17) to deduct the standard charge in accounting to the titular for the free teind.

Where the standardised stipend is under £1, it was compulsorily redeemed under the 1925 Act.

Standard charge (not stipend) is redeemable on sale under the 1974 Act s. 5; or voluntarily under the 1925 Act.

There are also various administrative provisions, including provisions for allocation of standard charge between various parts of the subjects burdened with it, *e.g.* on the breakup of a large estate.

Broadly speaking, standard charge can be ignored in urban properties; in rural properties, it may form quite a substantial burden.

(b) *Land tax (cess).* This ancient tax has long since ceased to apply in urban properties. In rural properties, it was exigible as a fixed tax up to 1949; but has been completely abolished by the Finance Act 1963 s. 68.

(c) *Income tax Schedule A (property tax).* This was a tax chargeable, not strictly as a tax on property but as a personal tax on the owner of heritable property, as owner, whether in occupation or not. It was abolished by F.A. 1963 ss. 16–21.

(d) *Local rates.* Until 1956, the owner of heritage in Scotland paid owner's rates; the occupier paid further rates known as occupier's rates. This system was changed by the Valuation and Rating (Scotland) Act 1956, since which Act there was one rate only, levied by local authorities on occupiers. The owner, as such, no longer paid any rates at all. Until 31 March 1989, domestic rates were divided into regional and district. Rates were not a burden on land, in the accepted sense, but merely the personal liability of the occupier, who appeared as such on the valuation roll.

From 1 April 1989, the rating system in Scotland was changed and rates were no longer levied on owners or occupiers of residential property as such under the Abolition of Domestic Rates etc. (Scotland) Act 1987. A non-domestic rate continued to be levied in respect of other properties, broadly as before.

From 1 April 1993, the council tax introduced under the Local Government (Finance) Act 1992 replaced the poll tax or community charge introduced under the 1987 Act. There is now only one charge for each property, not a charge for each person as before. Under the council tax, a property is placed in one of eight valuation bands in accordance with its valuation as at 1 April 1991; and council tax is graduated according to the relevant banding of each property. See Appendix C for details.

(e) In special cases, the local authority have statutory powers to recover sums expended under statutory notices which bind singular successors, whether or not a notice has been registered. See generally Chapter 19, and in particular 19.52–19.54: demolition orders etc.; and 19.65: roads etc.

**33.67 (10) Gratuitous alienations.** Under the Bankruptcy Act 1621 gratuitous alienation by an insolvent person to a conjunct and confident person is reducible; but the title shows the risk. For a recent illustration, see *Hunt's Trustee* 1984 SLT 169.

A similar but not identical provision has been introduced under the Bankruptcy (Scotland) Act 1985 s. 34 for sequestrations on or after 1 April 1986; and the 1621 Act is repealed. Under the 1985 Act s. 34(4), any gratuitous alienation within a maximum period of five years prior to sequestration may be reduced, subject to certain safeguards. The provisions of this subsection are without prejudice to any right or interest acquired in good faith and for value from or through the transferee in the gratuitous alienation. So a *bona fide* purchaser for value from a donee of the bankrupt is absolutely protected.

Under the 1985 Act s. 36, any unfair preference is similarly open to reduction if created within the six months prior to sequestration or the granting of a trust deed. In the majority of cases, the title will show the risk. Further, if the transaction is the purchase of a property from the creditor in a challengeable security exercising his power of sale, a *bona fide* purchaser for value would normally be protected. There were also rules at common law which differed in certain respects from the statutory rule introduced under the 1621 Act by virtue of which gratuitous alienations could be attacked. These common law rules still apply and may still be used; and in *Bank of Scotland* 1988 SCLR 478 the court further held that these common law rules applied to companies as they applied to individuals.

Perhaps surprisingly, in *Short's Trustee* 1996 SLT (HL) 166, referred to above at Chapter 13.33, although the original dispositions by the bankrupt had been reduced as gratuitous alienations and the subsequent dispositions by the original disponee were in themselves gratuitous, counsel does not appear to have seriously pressed the argument that, in these circumstances, rectification of the Register was appropriate under the 1979 Act s. 9(3)(a)(iii) on the footing that the Register was inaccurate in that it no longer truly represented the position according to the titles on which registration had proceeded; that the inaccuracy was caused initially by the fraud or carelessness of the original disponee who took the titles at under-value; and that the registered proprietor, being a gratuitous alienee from him, was not protected by the 1985 Act s. 34(4). Protection is afforded under s. 34(4) only to a person who has acquired an interest in the subjects in good faith and for value through the original gratuitous alienee. The wife of the original disponee in *Short's Trustee*, having herself received the properties gratuitously, did not qualify for protection under that proviso. In these circumstances, could the registered proprietor properly claim that the inaccuracy had not been caused by her fraud or carelessness? Lord Coulsfield held that she was entitled so to do and was protected by the provisions of the 1979 Act s. 9. Certainly to hold otherwise would produce formidable difficulties and serious defects in the system of registration of title.

**33.68 (11) Unrecorded leases and tenants' rights.** In practically all cases, leases transmit against singular successors under the Leases Act 1449.

Except in the case of registered leases, for which see Chapter 24, nothing appears on the Record, and therefore nothing appears in the search to indicate the existence of such rights. But an examination of the property should disclose the position. See also comments on leasehold casualties at para. 33.16(iv).

**33.69 (12) Occupancy rights of non-entitled spouses.** The Matrimonial Homes (Family Protection) (Scotland) Act 1981 (as amended by the Law Reform (Miscellaneous Provisions) (Scotland) Act 1985) which came into operation on 1 September 1982, creates occupancy rights for the benefit of the non-entitled spouse as described in Chapter 28.60. The 1981 Act was further amended by the Law Reform (Miscellaneous Provisions) (Scotland) Act 1990, Schedule 8, para. 31.

When acting for a purchaser or creditor, it is important to ensure that the property is not affected by any occupancy rights; and to bear in mind that the existence of any such rights will not be disclosed either in the Register of Sasines or the Land Register, nor in the Personal Register. As noted below, if the title is registered, the Keeper will state on the title sheet that there are no subsisting occupancy rights of spouses of persons formerly entitled, if satisfied that this is so. The statement is backed by indemnity. It does not cover the current proprietor, so that enquiry is still necessary as to his/her position.

Under s. 6 of the Act, the 'non-entitled spouse' may consent to the dealing (by sale or by security) with the matrimonial home; and such consent excludes any subsequent claim for occupancy rights in that matrimonial home. The Secretary of State, by statutory instrument (S.I. 1982 No. 972) prescribed two separate forms of consent:

(*a*) a clause of consent to be inserted in the deed effecting the dealing, *e.g.* the disposition in favour of the purchaser from the entitled spouse; and

(*b*) deed of consent as a separate document.

In appropriate cases, either of these prescribed forms should be used, and should comply strictly with the statutory requirements.

Alternatively, the non-entitled spouse may renounce his or her occupancy rights by renunciation under s. 6 of the Act.

If there is no 'non-entitled spouse', then the Act provides for an affidavit which, under ss. 6 and 8, protects a third party dealing with the entitled spouse against the possibility of any subsisting occupancy rights adversely affecting the property. The forms of affidavit and renunciation are not prescribed by statutory instrument. The Law Society provided suitable forms in circulars to members dated 28 July and 5 November 1982, updated in 1986 JLS 214. These forms should be followed in practice. They are reproduced in the Diploma Styles and Halliday's *Practice* 21.29–21.31. Some practical points on the effect of the Act on normal transactions are set out below.

**33.70** *(a) Title in joint names.* Where the title to a dwellinghouse is in joint names, no special action is required, on sale, on purchase, or on granting security because both parties grant the deed(s); but with two qualifications:

(i) Title in joint names, and security granted by one of the spouses only, on his or her one-half *pro indiviso* share. This is a very unusual situation and will only rarely occur; but if it does, consent of the other spouse would seem to be required.

(ii) Title in joint names, followed by a divorce. If, after divorce, one of the parties to the marriage remains in occupation of the original matrimonial home (as may easily happen), and then remarries, the title may remain in the original joint names; but on remarriage the new spouse may acquire a right under the Act and become a 'non-entitled spouse'.

There is an argument that, in this situation, the new spouse may not qualify as a 'non-entitled spouse' because of the provisions of the 1981 Act s. 6(2)(*b*). This is not an argument to rely on in practice if an affidavit can be obtained but can be called in aid if there is no appropriate affidavit.

The safe course would seem to be, when selling property on behalf of husband and wife, where the title is in joint names, to confirm with them that they are still the same husband and wife, and that there has been no intervening divorce. When purchasing property from a husband and wife, confirmation should be obtained from the selling agent that there has been no intervening divorce and no second marriage.

An appropriate case in point is *Murphy* 1992 SCLR 62, where a house was purchased in joint names of A and B. B subsequently married C and moved into the house which became their matrimonial home. The marriage broke up and B moved out leaving C in occupation. The Court held that since A had never occupied the house and had allowed B to occupy it with his wife C, A had waived her rights of occupation in favour of B under s. 1 (2) of the 1981 Act.

**33.71** *(b) Title in one name.*

(i) Sale. When selling a dwellinghouse, and when the title is in the name of one spouse only, or in name of one or more unmarried owners then either:

(*a*) if there is no non-entitled spouse, get an affidavit to that effect (one from each owner if more than one); or

(*b*) if there is a non-entitled spouse, get a renunciation from the non-entitled spouse.

These will be delivered to the purchaser at settlement.

(ii) Security. When arranging heritable security, either at the time of purchase or as an additional advance, if the title is not in joint names of the spouses, then proceed as in a sale.

If the security is granted simultaneously with the purchase, the same affidavit or renunciation will serve. But, if the non-entitled spouse is consenting, and has not granted a renunciation, consent (*in gremio* or separate) is required to the granting by the entitled spouse of a standard security.

In the case of a subsequent advance, a new affidavit must be obtained (from each borrower if more than one); or the non-entitled spouse must either renounce, or consent to the additional security.

**33.72** (*c*) *Protecting the purchaser.* When purchasing a dwellinghouse, in all cases where there is no non-entitled spouse, insist on an affidavit by the seller to be delivered at settlement and then registered in the Books of Council and Session. This was essential before the amendments in the 1990 Act and is still desirable to ensure that the affidavit is delivered; but, under the 1990 amendments, affidavits are effective even if produced after a dealing or after the granting of security. No stamp is required on any affidavit.

In all cases where there is a non-entitled spouse, take a renunciation or the consent (*in gremio* or separate) of the non-entitled spouse. The renunciation (which requires to be stamped at £0.50) should be delivered to the purchaser at settlement, and then registered in the Books of Council and Session.

**33.73** (*d*) *Death.* Occupancy rights automatically terminate on the death of an entitled spouse, and so the surviving non-entitled spouse has no protection. Some agents take an affidavit or renunciation from a sole beneficiary to whom the deceased's heritable property has been bequeathed; and that may be a prudent safeguard in appropriate cases.

### 33.74 Examination of superiority and other titles
If the seller produces, as his title, a charter (and subsequent writs) recorded within the last 10 years, the charter is not a good foundation writ, nor is this a valid progress of titles despite a common misconception that a feu charter, even if granted within the 10-year period, is of itself a valid title. In any such case, it is essential to examine the superiority title (which, prior to the granting of the charter, was of course a title to the *dominium utile*) back to a valid foundation writ recorded more than 10 years ago, to ensure that the superior who granted the original charter had a valid title to do so. This, in addition, involves examination of the superiority search.

There are, of course, in most areas, some large superiority titles, typically in building estates, which are well known to agents from previous examination. In such cases, it may be unnecessary to examine the prior title again on a subsequent occasion, although it is normally necessary to look at the search.

It is not unusual, in larger building estates, for the builders' agents to insert in the contract of sale and purchase an express provision excluding the purchaser's right to examine the superiority title (purely for administrative convenience), but possibly subject to the granting of a certificate by the superior's law agent that the title is valid. Some of the less acceptable clauses in builders' missives are discussed in 1979 JLS 485 and 1980 JLS 17.

Otherwise, the title to the *dominium utile* by itself, coupled with possession, normally suffices to establish the proprietary title and the burdens on it. But in certain limited cases an examination of titles to adjoining properties may be appropriate or necessary. There are four common illustrations.

**33.75 (1) Boundary features**. While the proprietor can normally establish possession of the land within the boundaries, he can rarely establish exclusive possession of the boundary feature itself. Suppose, then, that there was a disposition by A in favour of B in 1970 which disponed the lands of X and described them as bounded 'on the north by the north face of a boundary wall separating the said subjects hereinbefore disponed from other subjects belonging to C, which said wall is erected wholly on the subjects hereinbefore disponed'. On delivery of the disposition, B enters into possession. It would seem from his title that he is the exclusive proprietor of the boundary wall on the north boundary; and therefore can use it as he pleases, *e.g.* for a garage, etc. But suppose that, in a disposition by A in favour of the said C of the adjoining subjects on the north recorded prior to the 1970 disposition, the same boundary in C's disposition is referred to as 'the centre line of the mutual wall separating the said subjects hereinbefore disponed from other subjects belonging to me'. Normally, neither B nor C can establish exclusive possession of the boundary feature itself. Therefore, the titles would be conclusive as to the ownership of the boundary feature; and as C's title was recorded before B's, B could not prevail in a competition with C and, accordingly, the wall would be mutual and not B's property. This might frustrate B in some development.

The same sort of problem can occur in other, less usual circumstances, *e.g.* with fishings, lochs, common property, etc.

The Scottish Law Commission have issued a Discussion Paper dated June 1992 on mutual boundary walls which raises a number of questions but no report has so far been issued. See also the boundary cases referred to in Chapter 8.

**33.76 (2) Tenements**. In the absence of express provision in the titles, the law of the tenement supplies, by implication, certain rights and imposes certain obligations on tenement proprietors *inter se*. This can, and often does, cause difficulties. Suppose that A in 1970 dispones the top flat in a tenement to B and imposes on B the burden of payment of a one-eighth share of the cost of maintaining the roof, chimneyheads, main walls, and other common items in the tenement. *Prima facie*, this supersedes the law of the tenement, (at least *quoad* roof) and limits B's liability for roof repairs to a one-eighth share only.

But suppose that A, when selling off the remaining flats in the tenement, fails to insert any comparable obligation in the dispositions of the other flats. Since the other titles are silent, the law of the tenement will apply in their case; and, *quoad* roof, the law of the tenement provides that the top flat proprietor pays the whole cost of maintaining the roof above his flat. Therefore, contrary to what appears in the title, (which is also the earliest separate title) B is in fact burdened with the payment of the whole, not merely a one-eighth share, of the cost of roof repairs. This may be a very serious liability.

For a cautionary illustration, see the article in 1968 JLS 90. A builder disponed a top flat in a new block of eight flats to a purchaser, inserting a clause restricting the disponee's liability for roof repairs to a one-eighth share only and undertaking to insert a similar burden as to roof repairs in the titles of the seven remaining flats. He then went bankrupt. The trustee in sequestration conveyed the remaining seven flats without any comparable condition. In the result, the purchaser had no right of redress except theoretically against the bankrupt; but that was valueless. She complained to the Scottish Law Commission, but there has been no change in the law of the tenement.

The Scottish Law Commission has issued a Discussion Paper No. 91 dated December 1990 on the Law of the Tenement which is dealt with in Chapter 8. The Commission's Report, based on extensive consultations with the legal profession and others, is awaited.

**33.77 (3) New feus**. Exactly the same problem can arise in new feus, with cross obligations to pay for one-half of the cost of boundary features. *Jolly's Executrix* 1958 SC 635 is typical. In that case, under a feu charter, a feuar was bound to erect, at his own sole expense, a boundary wall which was to be mutual to the feuar and the superior, the superior paying no part of the cost of erection; but in terms of the charter, the feuar was to be entitled to recover one-half of the cost of erecting the boundary wall from the feuar of the adjoining ground when the same came to be 'feued'. This is a very common type of provision in practice. Later, the superiority of the feu was sold; and later still, the adjoining ground was sold and disponed (but not 'feued'). In the disposition of the adjoining ground, no obligation was inserted as to payment of one-half of the cost of erection of the boundary wall. Since the titles were silent, the disponee of the adjoining ground could not be held liable for the cost; and, because at the time of granting the disposition the disponer was no longer superior of the feu, he was held not to be liable in damages. Therefore, the apparent right to recover one-half of the cost of the boundary wall in the feuar's charter was totally ineffective.

**33.78 (4) Part disposals, with restrictions on the part retained**. A owns a house and garden, with half-acre spare amenity ground. He sells the half-acre to B, to build a house on. In the contract, and in B's disposition, A undertakes not to use his own house for any purpose other than as a residence. A then sells his own house to C but without inserting any restriction on use. C converts the house to a licensed hotel. B cannot prevent C from so doing. See *McLean* 1904 11 SLT 719, where a right of pre-emption was conferred on a disponee A of part of a tenement, entitling him to acquire the remainder, *i.e.* it entered the disponee's title in the General Register of Sasines. The disponer then sold the remainder, without first offering it to A under the pre-emption. A then sought to reduce the disposition of the remainder to the disponee thereof but was held not entitled, in that the pre-emption had not effectually created a real burden on the remainder.

Note incidentally that, in this case, the fact that the pre-emption appeared on the Record, in the title to another property, was held not to be public notice thereof, and not equivalent to intimation to the disponee of the remainder, warning him of the right and putting him on his enquiry. Otherwise, the principle in *Rodger (Builders) Ltd. supra* would have applied. But, if C could be shown to have known the whole position, an argument on the *Rodger (Builders) Ltd.* principle might succeed.

Note also that, had the right conferred on A been in the nature of a servitude, *e.g. non altius tollendi*, he could have enforced it against the successor in the remainder. Indeed, the case was argued on the basis of dominant and servient tenement, but Lord Low rightly rejected that argument.

Despite what may be serious risks in some cases, titles of adjoining property, flats in tenements, etc., are rarely examined in practice by purchaser's agents. According to Professor K. G. C. Reid in 1988 JLS at p. 164, the purchaser is not entitled, as of right, to require the seller to produce the title deeds of other properties unless the contract so provides. This should therefore be covered by the 'evidence of compliance' clause in the missives: see Chapter 28.62.

### 33.79 Negative prescription

The long negative prescription reintroduced in its new form by the Prescription and Limitation (Scotland) Act 1973 ss. 7 to 11 may indirectly affect heritable titles. In summary, ss. 7 and 8 provide that:

(1) if any obligation has subsisted unpursued for 20 years and not acknowledged by the obligee; or

(2) a right has become exercisable and has remained unenforced for 20 years;

then the right or obligation is altogether extinguished.

Certain rights and obligations are, however, declared to be 'imprescriptible' and are excluded from the operation of these sections by Schedule 3. The rights which cannot be extinguished by the negative prescription include the following:

(1) Real rights of ownership. This applies only to real rights and does not prevent the extinction of mere personal rights or personal titles, see *Macdonald* 1981 SC 75. The obligation to deliver a disposition under a contract of sale and purchase is personal and will prescribe. In the light of the decision in *Barratt (Scotland) Ltd.*, below, that obligation falls to be treated as an obligation relating to land for the purposes of the Prescription and Limitation (Scotland) Act 1973 and Schedule 1(2)(*e*); and so the 20 year period would apply. The same would seem to apply to a personal but unrecorded title as being imprescriptible under the 1973 Act Schedule 3(*h*). See 1993 JLS 11. A right duly made real by infeftment, however, can never be lost by the negative prescription alone. Of course, such a right so constituted may be lost if the infeft proprietor neglects his rights by permitting adverse possession by a third party who has a title habile to create a right for him by positive prescription. In the case of personal titles, it is now generally thought that these are now imprescriptible under the 1973 Act Schedule 3(h).

Three cases in 1992, *Barratt (Scotland) Ltd.* 1993 SC 142; *Wright* 1992 GWD 8–447; and *Stewart's Executors* 1993 SLT 440 appear to confirm the decision in *Macdonald* above in two respects:

(i) that the long negative prescription, not the short prescription, applies in the case of mere personal rights, *e.g.* the right of a purchaser under missives; but

(ii) once a conveyance has been delivered, although it creates only a personal title, the right thereunder is imprescriptible under the 1973 Act Schedule 3(*h*), which applies to completion of title to the land.

The decision in *Barratt (Scotland) Ltd.* referred to above was affirmed by the Second Division on appeal on 10 December 1992.

(2) Similarly, the rights of a tenant under a recorded lease cannot be lost, under the negative prescription, by failure on the part of the tenant to exercise his rights for however long a period.

(3) *Res merae facultatis* cannot prescribe and are not extinguished by non-use.

(4) The right to serve as an heir, and make up title to a deceased's estate, is imprescriptible, and therefore cannot be lost by lapse of time. In *Stewart's Executors,* above, Lord Kirkwood expressed the opinion that, once a disposition has been delivered, the disponee also qualified under Schedule 3(*h*) and his right to complete title was imprescriptible.

Bearing these exceptions in mind, the main cases where the negative prescription affects heritable title are:

(1) *Heritable securities.* If no action is taken by the creditor to enforce a heritable security, and no interest has been paid throughout the 20-year period, the obligation and the security is then automatically extinguished and cannot in any circumstances revive. Therefore, by implication, the title is disburdened thereof, although this does not disclose itself on the Record.

(2) *Servitudes.* In contrast to *res merae facultatis*, servitudes are extinguished by the long negative prescription. Further, under the 1973 Act, the period is now 20 years in all cases, in contrast to the earlier period of 40 years plus non-age, etc.

In the case of positive servitudes, the period starts to run from the date when the servitude was last exercised. In the case of negative servitudes, the period starts to run from the date when the negative servitude was infringed without objection. In order to exclude the long negative prescription under the 1973 Act, a relevant claim must have been made, which means either by appropriate proceedings in court, by diligence or by arbitration.

Alternatively, in the case of obligations, the long negative prescription is interrupted by 'relevant acknowledgment' which means such performance by the debtor as clearly indicates that the obligation subsists or unequivocal written acknowledgment by the debtor or on his behalf. See ss. 9 and 10. Deeds *ex facie* invalid or forged are not exempted from challenge by the negative prescription; this mirrors the equivalent provision for positive prescription in ss. 1 to 3.

## First registration

### 33.80 General

First registration and subsequent dealings, including the conveyancing procedures and applications for registration, are dealt with in detail in the Practice Book, Sections D and G; reports and searches are dealt with in Section F; and a number of points on plans and descriptions are dealt with in detail in Section E.

First registration is also dealt with in the *Registration of Title Manual*, in particular Chapter 15, which is a useful source of reference, and incorporates illustrative forms. Note, however, that the forms in the *Registration of Title Manual* have been amended, in style and content, since it was first published. The most recent changes were promulgated by the Land Registration (Scotland) Amendment Rules 1995.

### 33.81 Pre-sale procedures – Practice Book G.2.01

Note, firstly, that the following comments on pre-sale procedures apply only to registration matters. Other pre-sale procedures, such as the normal road, building warrant and planning enquiries, survey and valuation, and other similar requirements still apply in exactly the same way as on the sale of property in the Sasines system. These matters are not dealt with here; but, for convenience and ease of reference, the foregoing matters dealt with in Chapter 33 are equally applicable on examining a title preliminary to first registration as they are on examining a title which remains in the Sasines Register.

*33.2 Conditions of contract*
These must still be examined in the context of the current transaction.

*33.3 to 33.17 Title*
This must still be examined from the foundation writ to date, for all purposes, including validity of title, burdens, servitudes, and heritable securities. The same considerations apply here.

*33.18 to 33.20 Possession*
The same considerations apply as in Sasines titles but with one specialty in regard to the Registration of Title Form P16, for which see below.

*33.21 to 33.43 Searches*
These paragraphs of Chapter 33 deal with searches, to which special procedures apply on registration of title. This is the main significant point of difference between examining a Sasines title and dealing with a first registration.

*33.44 to 33.51 Settlement obligations*
The same general considerations apply as in Sasines transactions although the terminology is different, taking into account a difference in the provisions in the antecedent missives and the difference in the Search procedure referred to above. In particular, a letter of obligation will be taken from the seller as in a Sasines transaction; but note that no corresponding obligation requires to be granted by the purchaser to the Keeper. Instead, all matters on which the Keeper requires assurances are dealt with in Form 1, the preliminary application form for registration, for which see below.

*33.52 to 33.79   Miscellaneous items*

In the ordinary way, so far as the purchaser is concerned, all these items must be carefully investigated by the purchaser's solicitor, as appropriate, in order to ensure that there is nothing in the title which will cause problems. Depending on the particular title, it may also be necessary to satisfy the Keeper on some, but certainly not on all, of these miscellaneous items which are dealt with in these paragraphs. In the ordinary case, however, the Keeper will not normally require anything more than a purchaser's solicitor would require from the selling solicitor; and so the purchaser's solicitor should normally be in a position, if asked by the Keeper, to deal with any question which occurs under these heads and which the purchaser's solicitor should already have fully investigated when examining the title himself on behalf of his client.

There are a number of items which have the potential to cause serious problems to a purchaser but with which the Keeper is not concerned because they have no implications whatsoever in relation to title as such. For example, the Keeper is not concerned as to whether or not planning permission has been granted for a particular development; and the same applies to completion certificates, fire certificates, licences etc.

Subject to these preliminary comments, four main points have to be considered:

(i) Is the property wholly or partly in an operational area? Unless the property, or at least part of it, is in an operational area, the transaction is not registrable. Admittedly, in appropriate cases, the Keeper may be prepared to consider an application for voluntary registration; but such cases are strictly limited, and the Keeper will not meantime depart from his declared policy of accepting such registrations only in very special circumstances.

The operational areas on 1 April 1997 were the counties of Renfrew, Lanark, Dumbarton, the Barony and Regality of Glasgow, Clackmannan, Stirling, West Lothian, Fife, Aberdeen, Kincardine, Ayr, Dumfries, Wigtown and the Stewartry of Kirkcudbright: see 1996 SLT (News) 220. These registration districts coincide exactly with the county boundaries as prescribed for recording in the GRS. So, if in doubt, consult the certificate of registration on the last recorded title. If one or other of these counties appears therein, whether alone or along with another county or counties, then the property is, at least in part, in an operational area; and so a feu, lease or sale will induce first registration.

(ii) Is the transaction registrable? Transactions which induce first registration are detailed in the 1979 Act s. 2(1). Broadly speaking, they include:

any feu charter, whether granted for consideration or not;

any long lease, whether granted for consideration or not;

any disposition on sale or in consideration of marriage;

any transfer where the subject or interest transferred is absorbed into an interest already registered;

any transfer of an interest under a long lease, on udal tenure, or a kindly tenancy.

(iii) Has the title already been registered? Normally, the agents instructed in the sale will know, from their general knowledge of the client's affairs, whether or not his particular title has been registered; and, on the strength of that prior knowledge, they may well consider that an official enquiry on this point is unnecessary. If in doubt, an application Form 14 should be submitted to the Keeper to establish the position. In practice, this form is seldom used. Agents rely on Form 10 which provides this information.

(iv) Preliminary searches. In the Sasines system it is always advisable to instruct an interim report on the search prior to concluding missives, to guard against hidden surprises, *e.g.* sale of part of the subjects, the grant of a second security or a deed of servitude since the recording of the seller's title, or an inhibition in the personal register against the seller. Further, since we are now dealing with property in an operational area, it is always possible that the Keeper may already have registered a competing title of an adjoining property which includes part of the subjects of the present sale. Obviously, such a competition between the title already registered and the subjects now being sold, is bound to cause problems if not discovered until after missives have been concluded.

### 33.82 Application Form 10

It is recommended in all cases that the seller's agents should instruct a Form 10 report before completing missives – see Practice Book G.2.03. The application form is submitted in duplicate. The purpose of the Form 10 report is in part to update the search in the Sasines Register and in part to identify the subjects on the index map; it also provides a personal search. Forms 10 and 11 reports can be obtained from the Keeper and their equivalents can be obtained from certain private searchers. See 1992 JLS 500 and 1993 JLS 9. Note particularly for future reference that the Form 10 report will not include, in any circumstances, any report in the Companies Register or Register of Charges. The reports market will change in the near future because the Keeper has decided to withdraw in stages from the provision of Form 10, 11, 12 and 13 reports at dates to be announced.

(a) **Identification of subjects**. The application Form 10 must give the Keeper sufficient information as to the title in the Sasines system. This is normally done by referring to the last recorded title, so that the Keeper can then prepare his report by reference to the search sheet in Meadowbank House. This normally presents no problem. Identification of the subjects on the index map may, however, cause some difficulty: see generally Practice Book C.38.

Firstly, it is useful to include in the application form the postal address of the property. Secondly, if there is, in the last recorded title or in some earlier deed, a deed plan which identifies the subjects, then a copy of that deed plan should accompany the application form. If there is no deed plan, the written description may suffice; but in most such cases a plan will be required which may either be a plan specially prepared for the purpose on the appropriate scale (usually 1:1250), or a photostat copy of the Ordnance Survey sheet with the subjects outlined thereon distinctively to indicate the property. For a warning on possible breach of copyright when a copy Ordnance Survey sheet is used, see Practice Book E.04.

If parts of the subjects have previously been sold off, the Keeper's practice is to agree with the instructing solicitors to exclude those parts from the search, so as to restrict the Form 10 report to those parts thereof which are to be registered. It is understood that the practice of private searchers in such circumstances may differ.

(b) The personal search. The persons to be searched against in the personal register must also be listed. This will normally mean naming and designing the seller; but, in many cases, other parties may have to be included as well.

### 33.83 Application Form P16 – Practice Book E – Appendix 1
As part of the process of registration, the subjects will be plotted on the Ordnance Survey map and a copy of the map will be incorporated in the title sheet as the title plan. In many cases, the boundaries as defined in the titles do not in fact coincide with physical boundary features on the ground which the title is meant to represent. Most practitioners are only too familiar with this problem where, on an accurate survey, it turns out that a boundary wall or fence has been erected on a different line from that on the title plan, so that the terms of the title and the boundaries of the property on the ground are inconsistent *inter se*.

Obviously, in such cases, the title plan prepared by the Keeper for registration of the title will follow the physical boundaries on the ground, because the title plan is taken from the Ordnance Survey sheet and it will, of course, show the actual physical boundaries as they are on the ground, not as they ought to be in terms of the title. If, however, there is a major discrepancy between the Ordnance Survey plan and the theoretical boundaries as shown in the title, then this may cause problems on registration. In particular, the Keeper may exclude indemnity as regards part of the property. If this is not discovered prior to completion of a contract of sale and purchase, this will inevitably cause problems as between seller and purchaser. Accordingly, in addition to the application Form 10, it may be appropriate to submit, along with it, an application Form P16 – see Practice Book E.33 to 35. In quite a number of cases, however, Form P16 is unnecessary and even inappropriate, *e.g.* on the sale of a flat in a tenement where there is no exclusive garden ground.

The main function of the application Form P16 is to request the Keeper to compare the boundaries as they appear in the title with the occupied extent as depicted on Ordnance Survey map, to see whether or not there are any discrepancies. Although an on-site comparison can be made, the comparison is more conveniently made through the medium of a P16 report obtained from the Keeper. The form must give the Keeper sufficient information to allow him to compare the description in the titles with the physical boundaries of the property as they appear on the Ordnance Survey sheet. A deed plan or a detailed particular description with measurements taken from the titles will normally be sufficient. For other methods of providing the required information, see Practice Book E.34.

It should be emphasised that the P16 Report issued by the Keeper is intended simply to deal with the question of boundaries and nothing more. Accordingly, a P16 Report from the Keeper which confirms that the boundary features on the ground coincide with the titles is not an assurance that the title itself will be registered without exclusion of indemnity. It merely clears one area of enquiry at the preliminary stage, which is always desirable.

In response to the application Form 10, the Keeper issues a Form 10 Report; and in response to the application Form P16, the Keeper inserts the appropriate information on the reverse thereof and returns it to the applicant.

**33.84 Missives – Practice Book 5.2.08.** As emphasised in Chapters 13 and 28, notwithstanding the introduction of registration of title, landownership and land tenure remain virtually unchanged; and so a sale of land in an operational area has the same characteristics, and presents the solicitor with the same problems, as the sale and purchase of land in the Sasines system. An ordinary contract of sale and purchase of heritage in the Sasines system normally contains a clause dealing with marketable title and Searches. In registration of title transactions, that clause requires adaptation; and this is dealt with in detail in Chapter 28. That clause apart, the clauses which are appropriate to sale and purchase of property in the Sasines system remain equally appropriate to sale and purchase of property in an operational area. So, in particular, clauses dealing with the liability for repairs in tenement property; clauses protecting the purchaser against onerous or restrictive burdens and servitudes; clauses dealing with roads, planning and other statutory matters; and generally other clauses familiar in Sasines missives are also included, in exactly the same form, in missives for sale and purchase of subjects in an operational area. Some modification of the marketable title clause in the missives is necessary for reasons explained in Chapter 28.

(i) *Marketable title.* In the Sasines system, this means that the purchaser's solicitor has to be satisfied with the title as presented to him. If he is, then recording of the disposition completes the purchaser's right and title, backed by the seller's warrandice. In registration of title, however, the purchaser's solicitor first examines the title and satisfies himself thereon; and, having taken a disposition in favour of the purchaser, he must then in turn satisfy the Keeper that the title as presented to the Keeper, including the disposition in favour of the purchaser, is a title which the Keeper can accept without any exclusion or qualification of indemnity. However, registration in the Land Register can sometimes have a curative effect. If therefore the purchaser's solicitor, having identified a possible defect in title, is unsure whether or not the title will satisfy the Keeper, the Keeper may be requested to undertake not to exclude indemnity in respect of the particular defect in title. Such pre-registration enquiries should be supported by appropriate documentation and addressed to the Pre-Registration Enquiries Section, Registers of Scotland Executive Agency, Meadowbank House, DX 555 300, Edinburgh. The Keeper's willingness to comment on title problems is restricted to operational areas, and to counties which are about to become operational areas.

If and when the matter comes to be tested, the courts will almost certainly hold that, if the Keeper excludes or qualifies indemnity, the title is not marketable in the accepted Sasines sense. On this point, therefore, it is probably sufficient simply to stipulate in the missives that the seller will exhibit a marketable title. But the point is still undecided; and, for the better protection of the purchaser, the standard practice is for the missives expressly to provide that the seller will produce a title of adequate quality to allow the Keeper to issue a land certificate without exclusion of indemnity. It should be kept in mind, however, that, while an exclusion of indemnity may seriously affect marketability in many cases, that is not necessarily always so. In some cases, such an exclusion can be accepted without any material adverse effect on the title as a whole; but the position and the risk should always, of course, be explained to and approved by the purchaser and any heritable creditor. As a subsidiary point, the Keeper's requirements on the examination of the title may go further than the purchaser's agents thought necessary. It is therefore prudent, in the missives, to require the seller to produce whatever documents or evidence the Keeper may require to complete registration.

(ii) *Searches.* Both on first registration and on subsequent dealings, the search for incumbrances is no longer appropriate; and, instead, the seller on first registration must produce a Form 10 A Report and, usually, a Form 11 A Report updating it, or the equivalent forms from a private searching organisation.

With these points in view, the Practice Book at G.2.08 suggests a clause in the following form:

'In exchange for the price, the seller will deliver a duly executed disposition in favour of the purchaser and will deliver or exhibit a valid marketable title together with a Form 10 Report, brought down to a date as near as practicable to the date of settlement and showing no entries adverse to the seller's interest, the cost (if any) of the said report being the responsibility of the seller. In addition, the seller will furnish to the purchaser such documents and evidence, including a plan, as the Keeper may require to enable him to issue a Land Certificate in name of the purchaser as registered proprietor of the whole subjects of offer, and containing no exclusion of indemnity in terms of section 12(2) of the Land Registration (Scotland) Act 1979. The Land Certificate to be issued to the purchaser will disclose no entry, deed or diligence prejudicial to the purchaser's interest other than such as are created by or against the purchaser or have been disclosed to and accepted by the purchaser prior to the date of settlement. Notwithstanding the delivery of the disposition above referred to, this clause shall remain in full force and effect and may be founded upon.'

The last sentence of the suggested clause deals with delivery of the disposition, and maintains the effect of this clause notwithstanding such delivery. In practice, in Sasines missives, agents now normally incorporate a general clause to exclude the rule in *Winston* 1980 SC 246. But, in terms of this general clause, missives are usually preserved in full force and effect, except in so far as implemented by delivery of the disposition. Looking to the specific obligations imposed on the seller in the clause normally used in missives in first registration contracts, it might be held, in the context of that general exclusion, that the disposition had superseded some of the obligations imposed on the seller in this clause. A specific exclusion for the purposes of this clause is therefore desirable and is usually incorporated in the clause itself. Alternatively, if a general exclusion clause is used covering the whole missives, the wording may have to be adapted with particular reference to the obligations in the title clause. Such clauses may not be required after 21 June 1997 with the coming into force of the Contract (Scotland) Act 1997.

**33.85 Examination of title – Practice Book G.2.14.** Examination of title proceeds basically as in a Sasines contract, but with these significant differences.

A search for incumbrances may or may not be produced with the titles exhibited to the purchaser; but there will certainly be no interim report. Instead, the seller should exhibit:

(a) *The Form 10 Report.* If not produced with the titles, then the purchaser should ask for this at once. In contrast to an interim report on a search in a Sasines transaction, the Form 10 Report discloses:

(i) the whole prescriptive progress of titles from the foundation writ to date (not merely from the last date of search), but only back to date of recording of the foundation writ;

(ii) all undischarged heritable securities created within the past 40 years, and any deed or deeds relating thereto;

(iii) all discharges of heritable securities granted within the preceding five years but already fully discharged – see the 1970 Act s. 41 for the significance of this disclosure;

(iv) any other deed within the past 40 years which affects the title, *e.g.* a deed of servitude; a minute of waiver; a notice of improvement grant, etc.

In the result, the Form 10 Report covers all the points which the purchaser's solicitors would normally wish to check on the search and interim report. The search for incumbrances is therefore not normally relevant to the examination of the title and would not normally be examined; but it may be helpful in particular cases. For example, a tenement search will show the sale of individual flats; and it may be relevant to examine each break-off disposition to establish the position regarding common rights and mutual repairing obligations. Similarly, if the presence of a deed outwith the 40-year period is suspected, and if that is material to the title, then a reference to a search going back more than 40 years and/or to the prior titles may be appropriate, *e.g.*:

(i) To establish the position of minerals if that is material. Unless the Keeper expressly states in the title sheet and land certificate that minerals are included in the title, that fact is not guaranteed. Even when minerals are included the Keeper may not grant indemnity.

(ii) In a landed estate, where feus have been granted more than 40 years ago, scrutiny of the prior search and prior titles may be necessary at the examination of title stage in order to establish, exactly, the extent of the *dominium directum* and *dominium utile* in that title. This will, of course, eventually emerge when the title sheet is made up and the land certificate produced; but, since the Form 10 Report is limited to a 40-year period, earlier feuing more than 40 years ago will not show up on that report.

There are other similar, although unusual, situations where further investigation is necessary at the examination of title stage, in order to clarify the position, and where the Form 10 Report is not exhaustive.

(b) *The Form 11 Report.* As already explained, the Form 10 Report should be obtained by the seller before missives are concluded. So, there is bound to be a gap, probably of at least some weeks, between the date when the Form 10 Report was prepared and the date of settlement. Just as in a Sasines transaction, where it is prudent to order an interim report as near as possible to the date of settlement, so in a registration of title transaction it is prudent to cover that gap by updating the Form 10 Report to a date within a day or two prior to the date of settlement. The application Form 11 and the resulting report by the Keeper are used for this purpose. The seller's solicitors will normally produce, with the titles, a draft application Form 11, to be revised by the purchaser in the course of his examination of the title. One revisal which the purchaser's solicitor will normally make is to include the purchaser(s) in the application Form 11, to be searched against in the personal register. Obviously, this will not have been done when the Form 10 Report was obtained, pre-sale. Form 11 is lodged with the Keeper in duplicate.

(c) *Search for incumbrances.* There is no need to continue the search for incumbrances for any purpose, *e.g.* to disclose the discharge of an outstanding security, as in a Sasines title. If the security is discharged at the time of, or prior to, the application for registration of the title, then the security will automatically be excluded from the title sheet as having been discharged, which is all that the purchaser requires.

## 33.86 Plans

In the Sasines system, in many cases, the purchaser satisfies himself as to title and marketability without reference to any plan. This is because, if the title is not bounding, possession of the property within the physical boundaries on the ground for more than 10 years establishes the title to the property within those boundaries by prescriptive possession. But, in registration of title, a plan is essential to the making-up of the title sheet and land certificate. So, the purchaser must ensure that there is sufficient accurate information with the title to allow the property to be identified accurately on the Ordnance Survey map. If not, the seller must produce this information; and is taken bound to do so in the suggested missives clause.

This point may already have been dealt with by the seller if he has instructed a P16 Report as part of his pre-sale preparation. In that case, the purchaser must examine the P16 Report as well. If the Keeper's P16 report does not indicate any discrepancy, the report need merely be enclosed with the application for registration (listing it on inventory Form 4) and an affirmative answer given to the first part of question 2 on the Form 1. If the P16 Report discloses any discrepancies between the boundaries in the title and the physical boundaries on the ground ('the occupational boundaries'),

529

then the implications of these discrepancies must be explored at the examination of title stage because, as a result, the title may not be marketable; and the Keeper may exclude indemnity as to part of the subjects.

The seller's obligation to produce a marketable title in the suggested missives clause covers any such material discrepancy; and the purchaser should insist that the seller puts matters right before settlement. Action of some form will require to be taken before the application is submitted for registration, the nature and extent of such action depending upon circumstances and the nature of the discrepancy. As a first step, an on-site comparison between the legal boundaries and the Ordnance Survey map may be advisable in order to check that features on the ground have not altered since the map was last updated. If the comparison shows that the physical and theoretical boundaries cohere, the presumption arises that the map is erroneous. In this situation the only further action needed is to answer the second part of Question 2 of Form 1 in the affirmative.

If the comparison confirms the accuracy of the P16 report, and the area occupied by the seller includes land outwith the legal boundaries, the Keeper will not include that land in the registered title since there is no legal basis upon which he could do so. If therefore the purchaser wishes to include land outwith the legal boundaries in his registered title, remedial conveyancing will be necessary.

In the reverse situation, where the occupied extent is less than the legal extent, the purchaser can choose to limit his title to the occupied extent, relinquishing such land as lies within the title deed boundaries but outwith the occupied extent. This may be a sensible course of action where the occupied extent corresponds to the purchaser's expectation, based on a visual inspection, of what he is buying. Question 2(b) of Form 1 gives the applicant a convenient opportunity to advise the Keeper accordingly. Conversely, the purchaser may wish to assert title to the full legal extent (where it is larger than the occupied extent), in which case the opposite answer should be given to Question 2(b). The latter course carries the risk that the Keeper will exclude indemnity as regards the ground outwith the occupied extent because of the possibility that a third party has a competing title fortified by possession.

In cases of discrepancies in boundaries, the 1979 Act s. 19 – agreement as to common boundary – provides a convenient method of resolving such difficulties as between adjoining proprietors. In terms of that section, where there is a boundary discrepancy and where the adjoining proprietors, both having registered titles, have agreed to and have executed a plan of the correct boundary as represented by the physical feature on the ground, the plan is then registrable; and, on being so registered, it is binding on singular successors of both parties, even although there is no formal excambion and no formal conveyance by each party to the other of the discrepant areas. If one of the titles is a Sasines title still recorded in the GRS, the s. 19 agreement, with plan annexed, is both recorded and registered to produce the same result. For an illustration of a title with a boundary discrepancy where a s. 19 agreement would be appropriate, see Practice Book E.23. It appears that no consents, discharges or restrictions are required from heritable creditors who have securities over the properties concerned. Section 19 agreements can be used only where the discrepancy is relatively minor. If a larger area is effectively being transferred from one property to another a disposition or, where appropriate, an excambion should be used.

The seller should also be asked at the examination of title stage to produce whatever other information the purchaser's solicitor thinks the Keeper may require and which is not with the titles, *e.g.* death certificates; matrimonial homes documentation, both for the current transaction and for previous transactions; wills and confirmations in appropriate circumstances. But it is not necessarily fatal, at this stage, if the seller is not asked to produce all the information which the Keeper ultimately requires. This point is explicitly covered in the suggested missives clause; and that clause continues to apply after settlement. The seller's solicitors should bear this point in mind and should not be in too great a hurry to close their files immediately after settlement.

### 33.87 Occupancy rights

Occupancy rights under the Matrimonial Homes (Family Protection) (Scotland) Act 1981 as amended have been dealt with already in para. 33.69. In registration of title, they are overriding interests; but they will never be noted on the title sheet or land certificate – see 1979 Act ss. 6(4) and 9(4), as amended by the 1981 Act. Solicitors are already familiar with this aspect of the 1981 Act in Sasines transactions.

In the case of registered titles, however, there is a special problem in that the land certificate discloses the present registered proprietor but does not trace the past history of ownership. In order to exclude the need to enquire behind the land certificate as to earlier ownerships from the earlier title deeds, the Keeper is required, under the rules, to insert on the title sheet, in the proprietorship section, a statement to the effect that there are no subsisting occupancy rights under the Act for the benefit of any spouse of any person who was formerly entitled to the interest, if the Keeper is satisfied that this is so.

On first registration, therefore, the purchaser's solicitors will have to satisfy the Keeper that, in the case of every person having a relevant interest in the property during the preceding five years, no occupancy rights are subsisting. The applicant will have to produce the appropriate documents in relation to each previous proprietor, other than the applicant himself, *e.g.* a consent or a renunciation by a non-entitled spouse or an affidavit, etc. Assuming the Keeper is satisfied, on the evidence produced, that there are no subsisting occupancy rights at the time of first registration, then he will endorse the proprietorship section of the land certificate accordingly.

Note particularly, in relation to subsequent dealings with that registered interest, that the certificate applies only to previous proprietors, not to the present registered proprietor. Accordingly, on each subsequent transaction with a registered title, the purchaser or lender must still obtain from the registered proprietor the appropriate consent, renunciation or affidavit, etc. relating to that sale or loan. See Practice Book Section H.4 for a detailed discussion of these and other related points on the 1981 Act; and 1985 JLS 486 for a note on the effect of the 1985 Act on the evidence to be produced to the Keeper for those purposes. This has, of course, been modified by the 1990 Act, as noted in para. 33.69.

### 33.88 Deeds – Practice Book E.39; G.2.29 to 31

(i) **The disposition**. The disposition is the deed most commonly used to implement a contract of sale and purchase; but the comments here apply with equal force to a feu charter, a feu disposition or lease.

The form of disposition used for first registration does not differ materially from the form of disposition used in a Sasines transaction. Remember, at this stage, notwithstanding the impending registration of the title, that there is, so far, no title number. In particular, applications for Form 10 and Form P16 Reports will not produce a title number for that property. A title number is never allotted until an actual application for registration of the title is received. It is therefore not possible to incorporate in the description in the disposition any reference to the title number of the property; and so the 1979 Act s. 4(2)(*d*) does not yet apply.

*Description and plan.* As already explained, a plan will be essential in most cases to allow the Keeper to identify and map the property on the Ordnance Survey sheet, which is then to be incorporated in the title sheet and land certificate. But this does not mean that the disposition in favour of the purchaser must itself incorporate a plan on the appropriate scale. The plan can be separately provided with the application form and need not be formally executed by the seller. Not infrequently, a plan or a sufficiently detailed particular description will be contained in one of the earlier titles submitted with the application; and if so, a new plan may not be required at all.

It is not necessary for the existing description in the Sasines title to be redrafted in the disposition in favour of the purchaser in different or in bounding terms. The repetition of the existing Sasines description in the disposition in favour of the purchaser will suffice in almost all cases, even although that disposition is then to be the subject of a first registration.

If a new, separate, plan is required, it must accompany the application and must be certified by the applicant as defining the subjects in respect of which registration is sought. With effect from 1 October 1995, primary measurements used in new descriptions or on new plans should be metric in order to comply with the relevant EC Directive on Units of Measurements. Existing (pre-1 October 1995) plans and conveyancing descriptions are unaffected, and the effect of the directive is also mitigated to allow the acre to be used for land registration purposes and imperial measurements to be used as supplementary indicators to metric measurements. See the *Metrication Guide* leaflet issued free by the Keeper.

*Burdens.* The reference to burdens is in exactly the same terms as in a Sasines title.

*Warrandice.* The same applies.

(ii) **Standard securities.** In the great majority of cases in practice, the purchaser will be obtaining a loan to finance the purchase; and will grant a standard security to the lender in security thereof. The standard security will fall to be registered contemporaneously with the disposition in favour of the purchaser.

The purchaser cannot grant an effective security until he himself has title; and, in this case, his title is to be registered. Therefore, strictly speaking, the standard security is a dealing, registrable under s. 2(4); and a separate application Form 2 will in fact be required – see below. Nonetheless, if the standard security is to be lodged for registration along with the disposition (which is standard practice), the description in the standard security, although strictly speaking a dealing, will take the same form as in a Sasines transaction; and so will normally repeat the description in the disposition in favour of the purchaser.

If that is a new description of a new unit of property on a first split, containing a particular description and incorporating a plan, it is probably most convenient, in the majority of cases, to repeat that particular description in the standard security and incorporate a copy of the disposition plan therein.

Alternatively, the standard security may refer to the disposition for that description, *e.g.*:

'ALL and WHOLE the dwellinghouse erected on Plot 16 of the North Building Estate, Southtown, in the County of Renfrew, being the subjects more particularly described in and disponed by the Disposition by Southtown Builders Limited in favour of John Smith dated Tenth September, Nineteen Hundred and Eighty Five which is to be presented for registration in the Land Register along with this Standard Security.'

Otherwise, the standard security is in normal Sasines terms. In particular, since a title number will not yet have been allotted, it cannot be referred to in the standard security description, which must therefore be in compliance with note 1 of Schedule 2 to the 1970 Act. Following upon the cases of *Bennett* 1995 SLT 1105 and *Beneficial Bank plc* 1996 SC 119, there is considerable unease among conveyancers as to how descriptions in standard securities will be interpreted and what does or does not constitute a particular description or statutory description by reference. See the articles in 1990 JLS 98 and 1995 JLS 357. Unfortunately the decision in *Beneficial Bank plc* is not now going to the House of Lords.

(iii) **Warrant of registration and inventory of writs.** Except in the highly unusual event of a deed requiring to be both recorded in Sasine and registered in the Land Register simultaneously (for example, a standard security over disparate subjects lying in both operational and non-operational areas), no warrant of registration is necessary on any deed presented for registration, being replaced by the relevant application form. An inventory of writs, even if one might be included in a Sasines title (unusual, although not unknown, following the 1979 Act s. 16), is certainly never needed in a deed falling to be registered, because the inventory of writs is dealt with separately on Form 4 as later explained.

### 33.89 The letter of obligation – Practice Book G.2.20
A letter of obligation is necessary in registration of title for exactly the same reasons as in a Sasines transaction, but the form is different. A

suggested form of letter is given in the Practice Book at G.2.20 in the following terms:

'Dear Sirs,
With reference to the settlement of the above transaction today we hereby (1) undertake to clear the records of any deed, decree or diligence (other than such as may be created by or against your client) which may be recorded in the Property or Personal Registers or to which effect may be given in the Land Register in the period from (a) to (b) inclusive (or to the earlier date of registration of your client's interest in the above subjects) and which would cause the Keeper to make an entry on or qualify his indemnity in the Land Certificate to be issued in respect of that interest and (2) confirm that to the best of our knowledge and belief as at this date the answers to the questions numbered 1 to 14 in the draft Form 1 adjusted with you (in so far as these answers relate to our client or to our client's interest in the above subjects) are still correct.

Yours faithfully.'

Notes:
(a) Insert date of certification of Form 11 Report or, if only a Form 10 Report has been instructed, the date of certification of that Report.

(b) Insert date 14 days (or such other period as may be agreed) after settlement.

The importance of the undertaking (2) in this suggested letter of obligation, regarding the accuracy of the answers to the questions in the application form, is dealt with below.

The letter of obligation may cover other items which the seller has to produce but which are not available at settlement, for example, a feuduty redemption receipt. Under the Sasine system where an outstanding heritable security is being discharged an undertaking will be included to deliver the recorded discharge within an agreed period. Such an undertaking is no longer appropriate where the purchaser's interest is being registered. In the majority of cases the discharge will no longer be recorded in the Sasine Register at all. Even in those cases where recording is appropriate, the purchaser's concern is not that the discharge has been recorded but that effect is given to the discharge in the Land Register when his interest is registered. There are occasions when a purchase has to be settled before a signed discharge is in the seller's hands. The equivalent position in a Sasines transaction has been commented on in paras. 33.46 *et seq*. Subject to the warning there given, if settlement has to take place on this basis, an appropriate addition to the letter of obligation may be made in some such terms as:

'We further undertake to deliver to you within ( ) days (i) a duly executed Discharge of the Standard Security granted by ( ) in favour of ( ) in terms of the draft Discharge approved by you, (ii) a completed Application for Registration of the said Discharge duly signed and (iii) an Inventory (Form 4) completed in duplicate with reference to that Application.'

A letter of obligation may expire in five years under the Prescription and

Limitation (Scotland) Act 1973, Schedule 1, para. 2(g): see para. 33.51 above. This point should be kept in mind in relation to Letters of Obligation on first registration, looking to the very long delay which may occur in the issue of a land certificate.

**33.90 Applications for registration – Practice Book G.2.33; 2.35; 2.39; 2.45**
The procedure to be followed by the purchasers' solicitor is:

(1) Obtain/encash loan cheque and intimate completion to the building society.

(2) Complete the disposition and standard security with appropriate testing clauses.

(3) Have the disposition stamped with conveyance on sale duty, if appropriate.

(4) For the purpose of registering the disposition, complete the application Form 1 already agreed in draft with the seller's solicitors and revised by them. In registration of title, application forms are essential for every writ presented for registration; and an inventory of writs Form 4 must also accompany every application form, along with a cheque/remittance for the appropriate registration dues. The application form, submitted in duplicate, supersedes and renders unnecessary the warrant of registration.

There are three application forms for registration:

Form 1 for first registration (pink).

Form 2 for a dealing, where the whole property is transferred (blue).

Form 3 for a dealing involving a transfer of part of a registered interest only (yellow).

With each application form, notes for guidance are also issued and these should be consulted when the application form is being completed. Copies of all the forms, including Forms 1, 2, 3 and 4, are reproduced at the end of the Practice Book Section B.2; and copies of the notes for guidance for the four forms are included in Section B.3, to which reference is made. Applications for registration are dealt with in the Practice Book D.2. Some minor modifications have since been made to Forms 1, 2 and 3.

**33.91 Forms – general**
(1) Each of the three application Forms 1, 2 and 3 must always be accompanied by an inventory Form 4; but if, for example, Form 1 and Form 2 are lodged together, only one Form 4 (in duplicate) is required.

(2) A separate application Form 1, 2 or 3, as appropriate, is required for each separate deed presented for registration. There is only one exception to this rule, namely where, on sale and purchase, an existing heritable security is being discharged or restricted and the discharge or deed of restriction of that security is presented for registration along with the application for registration of the purchaser's interest. This applies both on first registration and on a subsequent dealing – see Practice Book D.2.22.

(3) When an application Form 2 is submitted along with application Form

1 on first registration (which is commonplace on a purchase with a standard security) the title number is not yet known, and the box for the title number at the bottom right hand corner of Form 2 may be left blank.

(4) Application Forms 1, 2 and 3 are coloured pink, blue and yellow respectively; and are deliberately colour-coded for administrative convenience in the Land Register. The Keeper will therefore not accept a photostat copy of Forms 1, 2 or 3 reproduced on white paper. It is now possible to generate the forms from computer disc. Obviously such forms are not coloured. They are identified with the appropriate form number and are acceptable to the Keeper.

(5) Every application form, to be acceptable, must be signed and dated otherwise the Keeper will reject it.

**33.92 Form 1 (pink) – Practice Book B.2; D.2.11; D.3.02.** This replaces the warrant of registration, but goes much further. In contrast to the application for recording in Sasines, the applicant is required to provide basic information which the Keeper requires to enable him to complete the registration. Great care must be taken in answering these questions and in formulating the supplementary information, where appropriate. The reason is that, on the basis of the answers to the questions in these forms, the Keeper then decides whether or not he is to exclude or qualify his indemnity. The application form is, in part, an application for a guarantee by the Keeper and all information given in the application form is *uberrimae fidei.* In the result, if there is any inaccuracy in answering the questions this may invalidate the Keeper's indemnity in the land certificate which he then issues.

**33.93 Form 2 (blue) – Practice Book B.2; D.2.14.** If a standard security is to be recorded contemporaneously with the purchaser's disposition, which is commonplace, Form 2 must be completed as well. A separate application form is always required for each separate writ, with very limited exceptions.

**33.94 Form 4 (the inventory of writs) – Practice Book D.2.08.** Form 4 must be lodged with every application form; but one Form 4 will normally suffice if two associated writs, *e.g.* disposition and standard security are presented together by the same agent at the same time. In every case Form 4 must be lodged in duplicate. The Keeper returns one copy of Form 4 to the applicant as his acknowledgement of receipt and, when so doing, enters on the front of Form 4 the following information:

(i) the title number allocated to the particular title;

(ii) the date of receipt, which is the date of registration for infeftment purposes;

(iii) an application number.

In all subsequent correspondence or communications with the Keeper, the title number and the application number must be quoted.

In the case of an application for first registration (Form 1), the relevant deeds and documents to be listed on Form 4 are:

(i) a sufficient progress of titles including the deed inducing registration and unrecorded links in the title;

(ii)  all prior writs containing rights or burdens affecting the subjects;

(iii)  any redemption receipt for feuduty or other annual payments;

(iv)  any existing heritable securities and deeds relating thereto;

(v)  where appropriate, consents to leases and sub-leases and assignations of recorded or registered leases;

(vi)  Form P16, if obtained;

(vii)  matrimonial homes evidence;

(viii)  any other relevant documents.

### 33.95  Drafting and revising as compared with Sasines transaction

As in Sasines practice, the purchaser's solicitor will draft and the seller's solicitor will revise the disposition in favour of the purchaser(s). There will be no search for incumbrances, as such, and therefore no memorandum for search or continuation thereof. Instead, the seller will produce a Form 10 Report obtained pre-sale; and should also produce, for revisal by the purchaser, the draft application Form 11.

The purchaser's solicitor will also draft and submit to the seller's solicitor for revisal the application Form 1 for the registration of the disposition along with the draft Form 4, which is referred to in Form 1. The point of this is that, in terms of the recommended missives clause, the seller undertakes that the purchaser is to obtain a land certificate without exclusion of indemnity, and the seller's solicitors confirm, in their letter of obligation, that the answers to the questions in application Form 1, so far as relating to the seller's interests, are still correct at settlement. The seller therefore has an interest in the information provided in the application Form 1 to this extent.

As in Sasines practice, the seller's solicitor will draft and the purchaser's solicitor will revise any discharge or deed of restriction of subsisting standard securities and the draft letter of obligation.

In the case of other writs required at settlement, e.g. a draft minute of waiver, a draft 1979 Act s. 19 agreement, the draft state for settlement etc., drafting practice follows the practice in a Sasines transaction.

The seller's solicitor is not concerned with, and need not revise, the draft application Form 2 for the registration of the standard security. But, where separate agents are acting for borrower and lender, the Form must be adjusted between them.

### 33.96  Settlement – Practice Book G.2.32

The procedure at settlement is, basically, the same as in a Sasines transaction. In particular, the purchaser's solicitor, in exchange for the price, will take delivery of the disposition in favour of the purchaser, together with the supporting titles, the seller's solicitor's letter of obligation, the Form 10 and Form 11 Reports, the Form P16 Report (if any), and the keys. In practice, the seller's solicitor often retains the Form 10 Report (or a copy) for future reference in later related transactions, e.g. when selling flats in a tenement. But it is probably good practice in multiple sale transactions on a Sasines title, each of which induces first registration, to order a separate Form 10 report for each separate sale. See 1991 JLS 203 for detailed comment.

The only special point to note is that, for first registration, the purchaser's solicitor will usually have to produce to the Keeper, with his application for registration, any earlier writs referred to for description or burdens which may be common to his own and other titles. In tenement or estate titles, however, where the Keeper has already seen, and noted the content of, these earlier writs, production may be unnecessary. In a Sasines transaction, these writs are not delivered at settlement; but are retained by the seller's solicitor or returned by the seller's solicitor to the custodian thereof. In a registration of title transaction, however, the purchaser's solicitor should borrow these at settlement for production to the Keeper. They will later be returned by the Keeper to the purchaser's solicitor; by him to the seller's solicitor; and, by him, to the custodian if different.

### 33.97 Acceptance of application by Keeper – Practice Book D.2.10

In the ordinary way, provided the forms are correctly completed and lodged, the Keeper will normally accept an application even although all the information has not yet been provided when the application is lodged. It is therefore possible to maintain the priority of infeftment, which is the date of receipt of the application, even although certain documents have still to be produced before the Keeper can complete registration. If, however, there is undue delay in producing required additional information, then, under Rule 12, the Keeper may exclude indemnity or reject the application altogether.

Where a security is being discharged at the same time as the purchaser's title is being registered, a separate application form is not required, provided the discharge is submitted with the application Form 1 and is included in the Form 4 relative thereto. The Keeper will then give effect to the discharge without further procedure. In that case, a fixed fee is charged.

If, however, the discharge is submitted separately, a separate application form is required for its registration and the appropriate scale fee is chargeable.

It is not only unnecessary but inappropriate to record the discharge in Sasines unless, exceptionally, the discharge also affects other security subjects which are to remain unregistered. Such a discharge will require to be recorded in Sasines – but only in respect of the unregistered subjects – with an appropriate warrant of registration. The Sasine recording can take place contemporaneously with registration in the Land Register provided the Keeper is specifically instructed that dual recording/registration is required. Alternatively, since the Sasine recording is irrelevant to the interest being registered in the Land Register, it can be effected separately either before or after first registration.

The Keeper will examine the writs during the registration process to ensure that the title is valid and indemnity should not be excluded. The Keeper may issue requisitions during this process requesting deeds or plans or other information. If these requisitions are ignored by the purchaser's solicitor, or not responded to within the appropriate time-limit, the Keeper may reject the application and priority of infeftment will be lost.

**33.98 Procedure after registration – Practice Book G.2.43**
In due course, following on completion of first registration, the Keeper will issue to the applicant a land certificate and a charge certificate.

On receiving the land and charge certificates, the purchaser's solicitors should then:

(i) check the land certificate to make sure that the details are correct;

(ii) check the charge certificate. Note that, where the standard security was granted by a limited company, the certificate of registration thereof in the Register of Charges must be produced to the Keeper in due course before he issues the charge certificate. Otherwise, he will exclude indemnity;

(iii) mark the selling solicitor's letter of obligation as implemented and return it, if fully discharged;

(iv) return common titles to the seller's solicitor;

(v) send the land certificate and charge certificate to the building society for retention, along with additional relevant documents not covered by these certificates, *e.g.* feuduty redemption receipts, NHBC documentation, building completion certificates, etc.

(vi) dispose of the title deeds.

**33.99 Disposal of prior title deeds – Practice Book G.2.46 and G.2.47**
In the ordinary way, following on first registration, the title deeds cease to have any relevance. In practice, except for some older titles prior to 1858, the whole progress of titles will have been recorded in the GRS or in the Books of Council and Session and extracts can always be obtained if required. The only cases where a reference to the actual prior title deeds may be required would normally be:

(a) where a deed, with a plan, was recorded prior to 1934. No copy of the plan will normally be held in the GRS and it may be relevant to determine boundaries;

(b) where a deed with a plan was recorded after 1934 but the plan exceeds the maximum size 28" × 22", the plan will not have been photocopied;

(c) in the case of plans which have been copied in the record volume, colouring on the plan may be material to the rights conferred on the disponee and may not show up effectively on the photocopy.

In any of these cases, however, a duplicate plan may have been lodged under the facility provided by the 1924 Act s. 48; but it is probably desirable in such cases to retain the principal deed.

Finally, prescription does not run on a forged deed; and it may be easier to establish authenticity from the original than from a photocopy. Speaking generally, forged titles are virtually unknown, and the risk is negligible.

In cases where the Keeper has qualified or excluded his indemnity, it may be prudent to retain the whole title deeds, until prescription has run.

Otherwise, with the exception of common writs which are returned to the seller or custodian following on registration, the title deeds, subject to the foregoing considerations, could be consigned to the wastepaper basket without any adverse results for the purchaser. Nonetheless, there is a natural reluctance on the part of many solicitors to destroy original title deeds for historical or archival reasons. Certainly, no title deeds should be destroyed except with the express authority of the client to whom they belong. Many clients like to keep the title deeds for historical interest but lenders are not keen to store bundles of old Sasine titles.

To some extent, the position is covered by the 1979 Act s. 3(5). Once a title has been registered, any existing obligation (whether express or implied by s. 16) to assign or produce titles, other than a land or charge certificate, ceases to have any effect unless the Keeper has excluded indemnity.

It must also be kept in mind that the land certificate will not disclose a non-supersession clause or a warrandice obligation; and, if the purchaser requires to found on either of these clauses in any subsequent claim, he will have to rely on and produce the principal disposition containing these clauses.

The invulnerability of the registered title as compared to a Sasines title has already been commented on in Chapter 13.33, with particular reference to *Short's Trustee*.

### Dealings

### 33.100 Dealings with whole or part
Once the title has been registered, it remains permanently on the Land Register and only in very exceptional and rare circumstances can it be taken off the Land Register and transferred back into the Sasines Register. Accordingly, for practical purposes, once registered, every subsequent transaction with that title, whether by way of a transfer of the whole (which is the commonest case) or a transfer of part, or the granting of security or lease thereon is in every case a dealing with that registered interest.

### 33.101 Feu, disposition or lease
A sale and disposition of the whole property implies a transfer of the whole. In contrast, a feu or a lease of the whole property is treated as a transfer of part, because of the grantor's continuing interest as superior or landlord respectively. Likewise, any conveyance or lease of the whole but under exception of a part retained by the grantor is a transfer of part. On the other hand, a standard security granted by the registered proprietor over part of the registered subjects is classed as a dealing with whole, because heritable title remains with the grantor.

### 33.102 Transfer of whole
The title having been registered, identification of the property and the subsisting burdens are determined conclusively by the terms of the title sheet. It is of course possible either to transfer the whole or only a part thereof. The procedure in either case is substantially the same but, for convenience, transfers of whole are dealt with first; and thereafter the differences, such as there are, are noted in 33.114 *et seq*.

### 33.103 Pre-sale procedures – Practice Book G.3.01.  In contrast to first registration, the position here is more straightforward.
The seller's solicitor proceeds as follows:

(i) He examines the seller's land certificate, in particular, the title plan, and the real conditions in the burdens section D therein, in order to prepare for completion of missives. Only the land certificate need be consulted. Regardless of what earlier titles may have provided, there cannot be any subsisting real conditions other than the conditions set out in the burdens section and any overriding interests not disclosed in the title sheet. The only exception to this rule is where land in an operational area is feued and the original vassal registers his title to the *dominium utile*. It is thought that the charter conditions remain personally binding on the original vassal, even though omitted from his title sheet and land certificate which in any event is very unlikely.

(ii) He instructs a pre-sale report, using application Form 12. The seller's land certificate will show the position of the title as at the date to which it was made up; and that date will be shown, as the last date to which the land certificate was made to coincide with the title sheet, in the boxes on page 2 of the land certificate. But of course there may be later entries on the title sheet which are not reflected on the land certificate prepared down to the last date shown therein.

In the ordinary way, this will not occur because, for normal transactions, the land certificate has to be submitted along with any dealing and would be amended and updated at that time. But there are exceptions to this rule. For example, where the registered proprietor grants a second security or where an adverse title to part of the registered interest is also registered in name of an adjoining proprietor, the Keeper does not call in the land certificate – see Rule 18. It is also possible to obtain a substitute land certificate if the original has been lost. If it is subsequently found it may not be up to date.

**33.104 Application Form 12 – Practice Book F.12.** This is equivalent to Form 10, and is submitted in duplicate. It differs from the application Form 10 in that:

(i) The property is already defined exactly on the title sheet; and all that is required is to identify it by reference to the title number. It is unlikely that there will be any doubt as to the boundaries because the boundaries are exactly defined in the existing title sheet. If, however, there is a doubt as to boundaries, which can occur in unusual situations, then an application Form P17 is available, equivalent to the application Form P16 and serving that same purpose, requesting the Keeper to confirm that the occupational boundaries coincide with the title boundaries.

(ii) In the Form 12 Report, the registered proprietors are searched against automatically in the personal register. Normally, no other party would have to be searched against at this stage.

As with the Form 10 Report, so with Form 12, it can be updated shortly prior to settlement by a supplementary Form 13 Report.

Form 12 and Form 13 Reports or their equivalent can be obtained either from the Keeper or certain private searchers. See 1992 JLS 500 and 1993 JLS 9.

**33.105 Missives – Practice Book G.3.05.** Again, as on first registration, the only clause in the missives which requires adaptation is the marketable title clause; but further adaptation of that clause is recommended in the case of a dealing, taking account of the fact that the seller's title has already been registered. The suggested clause in the Practice Book reads:

'There are no outstanding charges, no unduly onerous burdens and no overriding interests adversely affecting the subjects of sale. In exchange for the purchase price there will be delivered a duly executed disposition in favour of the purchaser and there will be delivered or exhibited to the purchaser (i) a land certificate (containing no exclusion of indemnity), under s. 12(2) of the Land Registration (Scotland) Act 1979; (ii) all necessary links in title evidencing the seller's exclusive ownership of the subjects of offer; and (iii) a Form 12 Report, brought down as near as practicable to the date of settlement, and showing no entries adverse to the seller's interest, the cost, if any, of the said report being the responsibility of the purchaser. In addition, the seller will furnish to the purchaser such documents and evidence as the Keeper may require to enable the interest of the purchaser to be registered in the Land Register containing no exclusion of indemnity under s. 12(2) of the said Act. The land certificate to be issued to the purchaser will disclose no entry, deed or diligence prejudicial to the purchaser's interest other than such as are created by, or against, the purchaser, or have been disclosed to and accepted by the purchaser prior to the date of settlement. Notwithstanding the delivery of the disposition above referred to, this clause shall remain in full force and effect and may be founded upon.'

The last sentence is now otiose – see para. 33.84 above.

For a transfer of the whole, it is unnecessary to ask the seller to produce a plan since the subjects are aready defined on the title sheet and title plan; and no further definition is necessary. It may, however, be appropriate in such cases to require a P17 Report where one or more of the boundaries in the existing title sheet and land certificate are represented by dotted lines. Some adaptation of the missives may be necessary in these circumstances.

**33.106 Examination of title – Practice Book G.3.08.** 'It is on a sale or other dealing with a registered interest that the full practical changes under Registration of Title come into play.' Assuming the land certificate contains no exclusion of indemnity (and exclusions of indemnity are relatively rare) the purchaser's solicitor will examine:

(1) The land certificate. He will have to pay particular attention to:

(i) The identification of the subjects, to make sure that the land certificate covers the whole subjects of purchase in terms of the missives. But, since the missives usually refer to the land certificate, or at least a copy of its plan, no problem normally arises.

(ii) The proprietorship section and the destination therein, if any. This may also involve the checking of subsequent unregistered links in title.

(iii) The charges section, to make sure that all existing heritable securities are to be duly discharged by the seller.

(iv) The burdens section and the details of the burdens therein contained. Remember that no other burdens or conditions can affect the title except:

(*a*) the burdens and conditions set out in the land certificate; and

(*b*) any overriding interest.

In particular, there is never any need to examine prior titles unless the title contains an exclusion of indemnity. In that case, examination of the prior writs will normally be necessary to assess the risk of accepting the exclusion. Otherwise, examination of prior titles is not necessary because everything which affects the registered interest must appear in the land certificate unless it is an overriding interest; and, if the overriding interest was disclosed in the prior titles, the Keeper will have noted it on the title sheet, except for short leases and occupancy rights under the Matrimonial Homes Act. The land certificate will normally contain a statement (which is guaranteed) that there are no subsisting occupancy rights for the spouse of any previous proprietor.

The common law rights of common interest and common property, however, are overriding interests. Accordingly, when dealing with a flat in a tenement, examination of the titles of other flats in the same tenement is normally necessary in order to establish the common rights and mutual repairing obligations. In an increasing number of cases, the titles to the other flats in the tenement will have been registered and examination of the whole of the tenement titles is to that extent made easier.

It is just possible that there may have been other dealings, relating to the interest, but not yet registered. If so, it would normally be necessary to examine these.

(2) The Form 12 Report and any Form P17 Report.

(3) The draft application Form 13 which he will revise. The application Form 13 is lodged with the Keeper in duplicate.

Note particularly that the purchaser's solicitor need not concern himself with the validity of the title, because that is guaranteed by the Keeper unless there is an exclusion of indemnity. Likewise, the Keeper guarantees that any heritable security not appearing in the charges section has been discharged; and that any burden not entered in the burdens section is no longer enforceable. The Keeper does not, however, guarantee that the title is marketable. The purchaser's solicitor must examine the burdens section, in particular, to ensure that no reservation or burden or condition is so onerous as to render the title unmarketable.

**33.107 Deeds – Practice Book G.3.22.** In contrast to the registration system in England, no special forms of deed are provided in the Scottish system. Accordingly, traditional forms of deed are used to deal with registered interests in exactly the same style as for Sasines titles, but with certain differences in detail, summarised below. In particular, it is still competent to grant a feu charter, a feu disposition, a charter of novodamus, a disposition, a lease, a standard security, or any other document which, in the Sasines system, is capable of being recorded in the GRS; and any such document, when so used in relation to a registered interest, has exactly the same result as its counterpart in the Sasines system.

Reference has already been made to the decision in *Short's Trustee* where the House of Lords upheld the Court's refusal to grant an order on an application by a trustee in sequestration to register a decree of reduction of a gratuitous alienation as a dealing with whole, without recourse to s. 9 of the 1979 Act which regulates the circumstances in which rectification can be achieved, so as to restore to the estate of the bankrupt property conveyed by him at under-value before sequestration, on the footing that a decree of reduction did not affect the registered interest as such; and to allow the decree to be registered would substantially defeat the purpose of registration of title and the invulnerability of the title intended to be conferred by the 1979 Act. See Chapter 13.33.

On the other hand, the registered interest is exactly defined in the title sheet and title plan, and an exhaustive statement of the rights pertaining to, and of the burdens affecting, that interest is contained therein. This, taken together with the statutory provisions for the vesting of the interest in the 1979 Act s. 3, allow for substantial simplification in the content of deeds. Further, under s. 15(1), Rule 25 and Schedule B, a shorthand style of description is provided which should be followed in all cases.

Under s. 3 of the Act, registration has the effect of vesting in the registered proprietor a real right in and to the registered interest itself, and in and to any right, pertinent or servitude, express or implied, forming part of that registered interest; but subject to any adverse interests, including burdens, set out in the title sheet and to overriding interests. It follows, therefore, that there is no need, in describing a registered interest, to incorporate in the description any narration of, or reference to, parts, privileges or pertinents, servitudes and the like; and there is no need to refer to burdens. All these are inherent in the registration of the title. Accordingly, any dealing necessarily carries with it the benefit thereof and is necessarily subject thereto – see s. 15(1) and (2).

In the result, the Practice Book G.3.22(a) illustrates a disposition representing the transfer of the whole of a registered interest in the following simple terms:

> 'I, AB (design) in consideration of (state price or other consideration) hereby dispone to CD (design) ALL and WHOLE the subjects (here insert postal address of subjects where appropriate) registered under Title Number(s) (   ); With entry on; And I grant warrandice; (here insert stamp clause if appropriate).'

Note that no warrant of registration is required.

**33.108 Deeds by uninfeft proprietors.** In the Sasines system, the uninfeft proprietor, being a person having right to land by a title not recorded in the GRS, may complete his title by the recording of a notice of title under the 1924 Act s. 4.

Alternatively, such a proprietor may:

(*a*) grant a disposition (but not a feu charter or lease), so long as he deduces his title in that disposition in terms of the 1924 Act s. 3; or

(*b*) grant a standard security, so long as he deduces his title therein under the 1970 Act s. 12.

That rule continues to apply up to the point where a title is registered. So, it applies in operational areas to a disposition which will induce first registration. However, once an interest has been registered, the rule as to infeftment is modified by the 1979 Act s. 15(3), the general effect of which may be summarised thus:

(*a*) once a title has been registered, any subsequent uninfeft proprietor no longer has to use a notice of title to procure infeftment. Instead, he merely produces his link(s) in title to the Keeper with the appropriate application Form 2, and the Keeper will register him as proprietor; and

(*b*) where the person in right of a registered interest is not himself registered as proprietor, he can still validly grant a disposition or standard security. A clause of deduction of title is no longer necessary. Instead, the grantee simply produces the relevant deed (disposition or standard security) granted by the uninfeft proprietor in his favour, along with the unregistered links (*e.g.* confirmation) connecting the grantor to the last registered proprietor and the application form for registration of the disposition or standard security. This supplies the want of the formal deduction of title clause, which is now redundant.

On the other hand, notwithstanding the 1979 Act s. 15(3), where the registered proprietor grants a feu charter, feu disposition or lease, he must himself first be registered as proprietor, which, in registration of title, is equivalent to infeftment. At least, that is the theoretical position; and the Keeper will enforce that rule by requiring that the grantor of a feu charter, who is uninfeft, must first apply for registration before the vassal applies for the registration of his charter. If this is not done, the Keeper will accept the charter and register the vassal as proprietor of the *dominium utile*; but he will exclude indemnity in respect that the superior is uninfeft.

This underlines one of the major points of difference in the registration system. If, on a Sasines title in a non-operational area, a superior, uninfeft, grants a feu charter which the vassal records in Sasines, the vassal's right to the *dominium utile* is not made real by such recording since the superior has no infeftment. Accordingly, that right is automatically defeated if the superior, while still uninfeft, is subsequently sequestrated; and may be defeated in other comparable situations. In contrast, however, if the superior subsequently takes infeftment without any adverse right intervening, the vassal's title is then validated and made real by accretion. In registration of title, the position is quite different. Suppose that the person entitled to a registered interest is not himself registered as proprietor thereof, *e.g.* following on the death of the registered proprietor. Suppose that, without becoming registered himself, he grants a feu disposition in favour of a vassal of part or the whole of his interest; and the vassal applies for registration. The Keeper would not normally accept the vassal's application; and, if he did so, he would certainly exclude indemnity. If, however, for whatever reason the Keeper were to register the vassal's title without any exclusion of indemnity, notwithstanding that the superior is not himself the registered proprietor, the vassal would obtain an unchallengeable title as vassal, notwithstanding the lack of the superior's infeftment, whether he is holding uninfeft on a Sasines title or on a registered title. The reason is that, once the vassal's title is registered without exclusion of indemnity, then his real interest as vassal in the *dominium utile* vests under the 1979 Act s. 3; and no rectification of the register would be possible to deprive him of his interest so long as he retains possession.

**33.109 Letters of obligation.** Exactly the same letter of obligation is used for a dealing as is used on first registration; and the style provided, taken from the Practice Book, at para. 33.89 is appropriate, with minor adaptations to take account of the different number of questions in application Form 2 and the fact that the relevant reports are Forms 12 and 13, not 10 and 11.

**33.110 Settlement.** The procedure on settlement is substantially the same on a dealing as on first registration, but with differences in detail. At settlement, the purchaser's solicitors will take delivery of:

(i) the executed disposition in favour of the purchaser;

(ii) the discharge or deed of restriction of any outstanding standard security, duly executed;

(iii) the land certificate and charge certificate;

(iv) the links in title, if any, between the seller and the registered proprietor;

(v) the letter of obligation;

(vi) the Form 12 Report, updated, if appropriate, by the Form 13 Report;

(vii) the Form P17 Report, if any;

(viii) the keys.

**33.111 Application for registration.** The procedure for registering the title of the purchaser is basically the same on a dealing as on first registration, but with differences in detail:

(*a*) For a dealing involving a transfer of the whole, the blue application Form 2 should be used.

(*b*) An inventory Form 4 is required, listing the documents submitted to the Keeper with the application. The inventory is completed and lodged in duplicate; and the Keeper will acknowledge receipt by returning one copy of the inventory. As with first registration, so on a dealing, documents can be listed but marked 'To follow' if not available at the date of application. In contrast to first registration, however, the applicant must lodge the land certificate; but will not normally be asked to produce any other title deeds. If there are outstanding charges, then the charge certificate should be lodged along with the discharge thereof. If the two are lodged together, a separate application form for the registration of the discharge is not required; but the discharge should be listed in the inventory Form 4.

(*c*) In terms of the notes for guidance for completing Form 4, to accompany an application Form 2, the relevant deeds and documents to be listed are:

(i) the land certificate;

(ii) any relevant charge certificate;

(iii) all writs which affect the registration, including all writs containing burdens not already specified in the land certificate or varying or discharging burdens since the certificate was last issued – it is not likely that there will be any;

(iv) where appropriate, consents to leases, sub-leases and to assignations of recorded or registered leases;

(v) Form P17, if obtained;

(vi) matrimonial homes evidence under the Matrimonial Homes (Family Protection) (Scotland) Act 1981 as amended;

(vii) all unregistered links in title.

The Keeper may raise requisitions during the registration process and these should be responded to by the purchaser's solicitor within the appropriate time-limit.

**33.112 Concurrent standard security.** If the purchaser is obtaining a loan and has granted a standard security, then, as on first registration, so on a dealing, a separate application Form 2 should be lodged with the standard security itself for registration, which reduces the fees. Again, however, a separate Form 4 for the standard security is not required if the standard security is listed in the Form 4 lodged with the application Form 2 relating to the transfer of the interest.

**33.113 Procedure after registration.** In due course, following a transfer of the whole, the Keeper will issue to the applicant a land certificate and, if appropriate, a charge certificate for any standard security. The purchaser's solicitor should check the amendments made to the previous land certificate to ensure that it is correct. The land certificate is not a historic document; and alterations are not made simply by scoring out spent information and inserting new data. For example, on the sale of a registered interest, the proprietorship section and the charges section are freshly prepared, so that no trace appears in the new land certificate of previous proprietors nor of discharged securities. The new land certificate must be checked carefully to ensure that all entries therein are correct.

**33.114 Transfers of part**
A transfer of part occurs where only a part of the registered interest (as distinct from the whole or a *pro indiviso* share of the whole) is conveyed to a new proprietor. The most common example is the purchase of a new plot from a builder where the whole development is registered. The procedure for transfer of part follows almost exactly the procedure applicable to the transfer of the whole of the registered interest dealt with under para. 33.102 – Transfer of whole. Accordingly, in the case of dealing with part only but not the whole, paras. 33.100 to 33.113 above apply with minimal variations. The principal point of difference is that, on a transfer of part of the registered interest, it is necessary for the relevant deed to contain a description in identifying terms of the part dealt with in the particular transaction. This makes no difference whatsoever to the applicability of and procedure on:

33.103 – Presale Procedures.

33.104 – Application Form 12.

33.105 – Missives.

Here, however, there is this difference that, on a transfer of part, there are almost certain to be special provisions as between the part dealt with and the part retained, *e.g.* division boundary walls, servitude rights both serving and imposed on the respective parts, and a number of other possible special features. The fact that the title is registered, however, does not in itself produce any further specialty as compared with a transfer of part of a property held on a Sasines title. Aside from the foregoing difference, para. 33.105 – Missives, applies without variation. Para. 33.106 – Examination of title, involves exactly the same procedures. In para. 33.107, however, which deals with deeds, while the same general principles apply, the specialty above referred to must here be dealt with by the incorporation of the appropriate description of the part transferred. So, in contrast to the style of disposition illustrating a transfer of whole and incorporated in para. 33.107, the style of disposition on a transfer of part is illustrated in the Practice Book G.3.22. A skeleton disposition, following that form, might read:

'I, AB (design) in consideration of (state price or other consideration) hereby dispone to CD (design) ALL and WHOLE (describe the part conveyed in sufficient detail, preferably by reference to a plan, to enable the Keeper to identify it on the Ordnance Map) being part of the subjects registered under Title Number(s); but always with and under the following reservations, burdens and conditions *viz.*: (insert additional burdens or conditions where appropriate and otherwise adapt as required); with entry on (date of entry); and I grant warrandice; (here insert stamp clause if appropriate).'

Note, no warrant of registration will be required.

Chapter G.3.22 of the Practice Book then continues to discuss in some detail some of the specialties which may be encountered in a transfer of part including, in particular, the need to consider and, if need be, define parts, privileges and pertinents; conditions already imposed by prior disposals of parts; and new burdens now required to give effect to the rights of the disponee of part, and the rights of the disponer as registered proprietor of the remainder. All of this is, of course, familiar and the same general principles apply as in Sasines titles. But great care must be taken to deal with these in detail and exhaustively, as in a Sasine title. Since the transfer of part is to be registered, the applicant for registration will have to satisfy the Keeper on all the points in the transfer itself including the points above referred to. Otherwise, there is a risk that the Keeper may feel it necessary, at least to some extent, to qualify or limit his indemnity.

**33.115 Subsequent procedure on transfer of part**. There are only very minor variations in the subsequent procedure as compared with the transfer of the whole of the registered interest. These can be summarised thus:

33.109 – Letters of obligation. The same considerations apply.

33.110 – Settlement - likewise.

33.111 – Application for registration. The same general principles apply here but there is a special form of application for the registration of a transfer of part – Form 3 (yellow).

Form 3 follows the same pattern as Forms 1 and 2 but there are 13 questions to be answered compared with 8 questions in Form 2 and 14 questions in Form 1.

For practical purposes, however, the substance of the questions in all three Forms is identical, save only that, in Form 3, question 11 relates to boundaries, taking account of the fact that part only is being dealt with, whereas Form 1 contains detailed question 1 relating to identification.

**33.116 Inventory Form 4.** As with Forms 1 and 2, so with Form 3 on a transfer of part, the application form must be accompanied by a duly completed inventory Form 4 in duplicate but the content is identical with Form 4 supporting an application Form 2 on transfer of the whole and there are no specialties.

**33.117 Concurrent standard security**. Exactly the same considerations apply here as apply on a dealing with whole.

**33.118 Effect of transfer of part**. Following on a transfer of part, there are significant variations on the post-registration effects as compared with first registration. The point is, of course, that the existing registered interest, previously held on a single title sheet for which a single land certificate will have been issued, has now been sub-divided, part disposed of and part retained, with two separate proprietors. It logically follows that not only must the title sheet for the existing registered interest be amended or endorsed to show the part-disposal; but, in addition, a new title sheet must be created and a new title number allotted to the part disposed.

As a subordinate point, it is frequently the case that the original single registered interest, now sub-divided, was previously subject to one or more securities; and, in the ordinary way, the part disposed of will fall to be released from the heritable security over the original whole. Taking account of the special factors, the following points of difference apply.

(i) The land certificate in respect of the whole registered interest now sub-divided, will, of course, fall to be surrendered to the Keeper along with the application Form 3. That land certificate will be amended to show the part disposal and returned, so amended, on completion of the registration procedure. It will, however, retain its original title number. Depending on the nature of the part-disposal and the associated provisions, the original title sheet may either fall to be amended or a new title sheet may be made up, still retaining the old title number, probably to give effect to the provisions in the part-disposal. In addition, a fresh land certificate with a new title number will be issued to the applicant in respect of the part disposed of. Both certificates, the amended original, and the new certificate for the part disposed of, will be returned to the solicitor who applied for the registration of the title to the disposed part; and he in turn must, of course, return the original amended land certificate to the seller's solicitor.

(ii) Where the registered interest was subject to a real security, it would also be necessary for the applicant, when presenting Forms 3 and 4 to lodge with the documents the charge certificate(s) in respect of the secured interests. Unexpectedly, although the charge certificate(s) must be so lodged, the Keeper will not amend them to show the part-disposal, even although the part disposed of is released from the security. The reason is that, since we are dealing here with registered titles, a heritable security will not continue to operate as a security on any part of the subjects originally embraced therein unless, following on a part-disposal, the new title sheet of the part disposed of shows that security as a continuing charge thereon; and this will not happen if, as is usual, the part disposed of has been released from the security. But of course the Keeper must be satisfied on this point if he is to register the title of the part disposed of without showing the security in the charges section.

(iii) For this purpose, the charge certificate is required by the Keeper together with appropriate evidence of restriction in whatever form showing the part disposed of as released therefrom. This produces the somewhat unexpected consequence that a charge certificate which originally covered, say, 100 acres in a registered title, where the registered proprietor has subsequently disposed of substantial parts thereof, will still apparently operate as a security on the original 100 acres. Anyone therefore examining that charge certificate may be misled into thinking that the charge certificate still covers the original whole area. There will be nothing on the charge certificate to indicate any amendment to the extent of the security. The reason for this has already been explained but it can cause confusion.

(iv) The unamended charge certificate will also be returned to the solicitor for the applicant lodging the application to register the part-disposal and he in turn will, of course, return it to the seller's agents for transmission to the creditor.

### 33.119 Builder's development – Practice Book D.3.09; E.44 to 52
This is a further facility provided for the benefit of builders and developers who are to give off a number of separate titles to individual purchasers of houses on a developing estate.

In such cases the builder may, if he wishes, proceed as follows:

Firstly, the builder himself must have a registered title. The facility cannot be used where the builder's title is recorded in Sasines. But of course he may apply for a voluntary registration of his title to comply with this requirement, and this is the type of voluntary registration which the Keeper is most disposed to accept.

The builder submits a layout plan of the proposed development for approval by the Keeper before any transfer of part is made. This allows any initial questions on the development boundaries to be ironed out before sales proceed.

In the subsequent sales of individual houses, the Form 12 Report with an office copy of the title plan can be issued simply by reference to the plot number. Each disposition will contain a description appropriate for a transfer of part; but the description in the disposition is very much simplified by using an excerpt from the approved plan as the deed plan in each individual case. The solicitors for each purchaser can accept the approved layout plan as conclusive that the individual plot forms part of the registered title.

The requirement in Rule 18, that an application for registration, whether on a transfer of the whole or on a transfer of part, must be accompanied by the appropriate land certificate is avoided; and, instead, the builder's land certificate is deposited with the Keeper who, in turn, issues the builder with a deposit number. Each subsequent application for registration on a transfer of part (*i.e.* on the sale of each house) simply quotes the deposit number in the application Form 3 for registration of a dealing; and the applicant is not then required to produce the land certificate with that application. In association with this facility, the use of office copies conveniently surmounts the problem of several purchasers each seeking to examine the same title at the same time.

In the letter of obligation granted by the builder's solicitors, it would be appropriate to include a specific undertaking that the builder has not, and will not, deviate from the approved plan; but the seller's solicitor may not be prepared to grant such an obligation.

**33.120** Otherwise, subsequent procedure following on application for registration of a transfer of part creates no other specialties.

# Chapter 34

# A TYPICAL SASINES CONVEYANCING TRANSACTION

## 34.1 Sale and purchase of a dwellinghouse

This description of a typical conveyancing transaction involves a property which is not located in an operational area and illustrates the various stages through which it proceeds, and tries to set in context the various deeds and documents which are drafted and completed. It does not deal with any technical conveyancing points either in regard to the examination of title or to the drafting of deeds: for this reference will have to be made to the Diploma Styles Book, Appendix A and to the preceding chapters in this Manual. The sale of properties in operational areas involves registration of title, whether as a first registration or as a dealing with a registered interest. For a detailed consideration of the whole subject of registration of title and a checklist of points to follow in such transactions, reference is made to McDonald, *Registration of Title Manual*. See also Chapter 33.80–33.120. The transaction is divided into a number of phases, each of which is described in a separate section.

In describing a 'typical' Sasines conveyancing transaction, a number of assumptions have to be made since there is really nothing of the sort! The majority of transactions involve, so far as each solicitor acting for one client is concerned, the sale of one house and the discharge of a loan secured over it, coupled with the purchase of another house and the securing of a fresh loan over the new house. In this transaction, however, in the interest of clarity, the seller and the purchaser are treated as being involved only with the one property. In other words, the seller is selling his house and discharging the loan over it, but is not involved in buying a new house; while the purchaser is buying the seller's house and is securing his loan over that house, but is not involved in selling his own present house. Separate solicitors act for the seller and the purchaser respectively. If the seller were to buy a new house and if the purchaser were to sell his present house, the steps required would *mutatis mutandis* be the same as described here.

The outline of the transaction is therefore as follows. The seller is selling his house over which a building society hold a standard security in respect of the loan advanced when the house was bought. The purchaser is buying the house with the assistance of a loan from a building society and additional security is afforded by the purchaser/borrower assigning a life assurance policy to the society.

When moving house, the main difficulty is faced by the individuals and not the solicitors involved. There is no guarantee that, if you buy a house before selling your present one, you will in fact sell your present house either at a satisfactory price or at all; or that, if you sell your present house before buying a new one, you will find a suitable new house at a price you can afford. When houses are selling well, there is usually no problem, although there may be a difference between settlement dates. When the housing market is not flourishing, however, the problem becomes acute, *e.g.* the recent problems experienced by the housing market in South East England. It is up to the solicitor involved to try and ensure that houses are sold and bought with the minimum of worry and trouble to clients. Therein lies the way to a satisfied client. This is not always possible to achieve, however, and it should always be clearly explained to clients what the potential problems and liabilities are; for example, overdraft interest, hotel bills, etc. The key element is communication – in terms which the client can understand. With transactions running concurrently, you should ensure that the respective settlement dates are as closely matched as possible. Many clients prefer not to have to move out of their existing house and into the new one on the same day.

How long a particular sale/purchase transaction takes to complete will depend on the property and other factors such as price. The normal period considered as realistic between the conclusion of missives and settlement (when the price is paid, and entry to the house is given to the purchaser) is approximately six weeks.

It is normal practice for the solicitor who acts for a purchaser or seller also to act for the building society or other lending institution involved if the solicitor is on the building society's or institution's local panel of solicitors. This is not, however, an invariable practice and, since the interests of the purchaser and the society lending him the money to make the purchase will be different, it is always open for the society to instruct separate solicitors. If this does happen, it may cause delay in the transaction as well as increase the fees the purchaser has to pay. On the other hand, it does point out clearly that the interests of the purchaser (who is borrowing the money) and the society (which is lending the money) are distinct; and a solicitor instructed to act on behalf of both purchaser and society must remember that he is representing these separate interests and that he is not simply acting on behalf of the purchaser. Of particular interest to solicitors is the introduction in Rule 10 of the Solicitors (Scotland) Accounts Rules of the provision prohibiting a solicitor from acting for his or her lender in a house purchase. The prohibition extends to acting for his or her spouse, partner or other connected person. This prohibition was deemed necessary in an attempt to reduce the risk of fraudulent schemes being perpetrated. In the following sections, references to 'building society' should be taken to include also other lending institutions.

Conflict of interest is obviously of paramount importance. One must always take cognisance of this potential problem – especially in light of the Solicitors (Scotland) Practice Rules 1986. For convenience, the Rules are printed in para. 34.81 below.

### 34.2 Preparation for the sale

There is nothing to stop an owner advertising his own property for sale himself, either by press advertisement or by erecting a noticeboard in the front garden. He may go to an estate agent and the first you may hear of the sale is when offers have been received by the estate agent and they are passed to you for attention.

So far as is possible, however, you should ensure that every client consults you before selling a house. You should try and have a meeting with him. You should make clear that the assistance you can give does not relate simply to the actual transfer of the property. You should be aware of the state of the housing market both in general and in particular. If the market is buoyant and the house is in reasonable condition, is reasonably sited and is reasonably priced, then the sale should (hopefully) be accomplished relatively quickly, say in four weeks or so. Qualify any statement as to when a sale may be expected; there may be a house advertised one day and sold the following day but a similar house in an apparently similar location may hang fire for several months.

Fixing the correct level of price at which to advertise the house is of the utmost importance and, unless you are sure on the area, you should consult a valuer – always advising your client of this and getting his confirmation that he approves and will meet the fee. Your office may employ their own valuer/estate agent, whose services you may use. A price is generally better fixed at slightly under rather than slightly over the figure hoped for. Your client may have ideas about the enhanced value of his house based on what he has spent on it. This need not always be the case. Improvements such as central heating generally increase the value however but initially not by the same amount as that expended. Do not encourage the client to expect a top-of-the-market price but be realistic in your approach. Your indication of price should be as accurate as possible since this is a matter on which you will be holding yourself out as a professional adviser. Remember however that a successful sale involves there being a willing seller and a willing purchaser.

You will need to elicit information on various matters from your client, in addition to the date on which he hopes to move, to allow you to carry out your part in the sale. You will also have to obtain the following documents and information.

**34.3 (1) The title deeds of the house**. You should not advertise property for sale without having examined the title deeds or land certificate as the case may be (hereinafter referred to as the 'title deeds'). You should check not only the validity of the title itself, but the description given in the title against the property itself and any conditions which regulate the use of the property. This normally implies inspection of the property either by yourself or someone in your office; or by a surveyor.

Ask your client where the title deeds are held and if there is a loan secured over the property. If the client is an established one or if you bought the house for him, you should of course know this.

If there is a loan secured over the property, the title deeds will be held by the lender, in most cases a building society. If there is more than one loan secured over the property (for example, a building society loan with a second top-up loan from another lender), the title deeds will be held by the building society as first lender and the second lender will normally hold only the standard security granted in its favour, this, of course, should have been intimated to the first lender. You should obtain from your client the name of the building society, the branch at which the account is held and the roll number of the account. If there is a second loan you should obtain the same information about this loan. You should then write to the building society and request the title deeds. A few clients conveniently or inadvertently 'forget' the second loan, the most common example being postponed securities granted to secure double glazing and other types of home improvement. This is becoming an increasing problem. An interim report in the Property Register is therefore always advisable, at the outset. Given that the Presentment Book is now computerised, it is possible to obtain a search that is virtually up to date. For the implications of computerisation of the Presentment Book, see Chapter 33. Provided your firm is on their panel of solicitors, you will be sent the title deeds on loan subject to the condition that they are held by you to the order of the society and that they will not be allowed out of your control except in connection (temporarily) with the proposed sale and (permanently) on repayment of the balance of the loan outstanding. If the sale takes longer than anticipated, you will receive requests for information from the building society and you should keep them in the picture as to how the sale is progressing and as to why you still require the titles.

If there is no loan over the property, there will have been no requirement for the title deeds to have been lodged in any particular place. They may be in your own strong room if the client is an established one. If they are held for safe keeping on his behalf by a bank it is normally sufficient for you to write and request them, either enclosing a letter from your client or having previously asked him to contact the bank manager to arrange for their release. If they are held by another solicitor (whose client you have now gained), then you should obtain a mandate from your client and send this to the other solicitor requesting that the title deeds be sent to you. It is possible that a fee may be charged for forwarding the documents in such circumstances.

In a few cases the title deeds may have vanished and you will have to obtain extracts from the Scottish Record Office. The difficulty here is that if the title deeds have been lost, you will have to establish what they consist of either by inspecting the search sheets yourself or, more likely, by instructing a search. In the case of a property in an operational area, a replacement land certificate or charge certificate as the case may be can be ordered.

When you do receive the title deeds, always acknowledge receipt, after checking them to ensure that all the titles and other documents (for example, feuduty redemption receipt) listed as delivered are in fact present. Check whether there is a prescriptive progress of titles with a foundation writ, and that all the deeds referred to for description or burdens are there. If not, try and obtain them or get extracts or quick copies from the Scottish Record Office or direct from the searchers, as doing so at this stage will save time later. You should see all the titles, especially burden writs, before concluding a bargain; and it is more efficient if you can, after conclusion of missives, send the purchaser's solicitor all the deeds which he will require to examine. If there are titles which appear to be required and are not there, they may relate to larger property (of which your client's house forms only a part) and will be held by the solicitors who act for the owners of the remainder of that larger property or the superiors. Write to them and ask them for the prior writs. If they cannot be traced, or if the missing deed has obviously been mislaid, write to the Scottish Record Office in Edinburgh and request either a quick copy, which is simply a xerox copy of the deed and is not certified as a true copy, or an extract which is certified by the Keeper, takes longer to obtain, and is more expensive but has the same quality as the principal deed; Conveyancing and Feudal Reform (Scotland) Act 1970 s. 45.

You will be under obligation to exhibit or deliver a marketable title and the purchaser's solicitor is entitled to demand from you all that he (reasonably) needs to satisfy himself as to this. Solicitors holding titles on behalf of an estate, builder or superior will charge a lending fee to you if you wish to borrow these titles, and your client will have to meet this. Many solicitors however try and pass on the whole or at least half of the cost of Scottish Record Office copies or extracts to the purchaser's solicitor. If the deed is required to confirm the seller's title, the purchaser's solicitor should not be asked to pay. It may be, however, that it is not absolutely necessary to support the title, in which case there may be something (though not a lot) to be said for sharing the cost. There is no justification for the seller's solicitor requiring the return of a quick copy or extract which relates purely to the property being sold simply because he has had to pay for it. In the context of the average fee, the cost of the average quick copy (up to £15 plus VAT) is hardly of major importance.

**34.4 (2) Local authority certificates**. Property is or may be affected by numerous statutory controls; see Chapter 19. You should therefore request from the appropriate local authority and, if necessary, from the appropriate water authority, certificates confirming the position with regard to these various matters. To provide maximum protection, certificates should be obtained within the shortest practicable period prior to settlement. It is normal for a comprehensive enquiry letter (of which an example is given in the directory) to be sent, normally, to the Director of Planning and Transportation or Director of Law and Administration of the appropriate authority. In some cases specific additional information may be required and appropriate alterations should be made to the standard letter. The appropriate fee must accompany the request. Charges vary. Obtaining the replies may take anything up to four or five weeks and it may not always be possible to obtain a verbal report. For this reason, there are now several private firms of searchers who will provide the appropriate information more quickly and sometimes at a lower price than the local authorities. Their certificate is backed by indemnity insurance, unlike the local authorities' own certificates. Difficulties can be caused if the written reply is at variance with the verbal report. The difficulty with property enquiries comes when the enquiry produces information which may be unexpected, such as when the roads department proposes to route a major new road through the foot of your client's garden. In cases such as this, obviously, further enquiry has to be made and the client advised. Furthermore, it is often not enough simply to search against your client's property, since a proposal relating to a neighbouring property may adversely affect the subjects. The purchaser's agent may make provision for this in the contract of sale by introducing a warranty in respect of such matters. It is unusual for additional certificates to be requested. If possible, a plan of the subjects together with a note of adjoining roadways etc. might be annexed to the local authority enquiry letter.

**34.5 (3) Consents, etc., required under the Matrimonial Homes (Family Protection) (Scotland) Act 1981, as amended.** Unless the title to the property is in joint names of husband and wife, you should consider at this stage the necessary affidavit, consent or renunciation which will be required and arrange, in due course, for the appropriate party to sign or swear it. Offers for the house will contain a condition relating to the position under the Act.

Even where property is in joint names, it is prudent to establish, by discreet enquiry, that you are dealing with the same husband and wife as those named in the title, unless this fact is personally known to you. See Chapter 33.

**34.6 (4) Receipts for outgoings.** These may be required to confirm the amount or the position relative to feuduty and common charges, and will be needed in due course to vouch the state for settlement. Your client should be asked to produce them at an early stage. The outgoings include:

(*a*) *Feuduty*. If the feuduty has been redeemed, the certificate should be with the title deeds. If not redeemed, obtain the last receipt, or the current notice, or at least information about the superiors, from your client.

(*b*) *Common charges*. These will normally arise in tenement property or in housing estates where there are common areas maintained by the various house owners or community of feuars. Obtain the last receipt for charges or the current notice together with details of the factoring or other arrangements.

**34.7 (5) Superior's certificates and consents.** Having obtained the title deeds and examined them, you should deal with any matters in the title which may later give rise to problems. So, if there is a subsisting right of pre-emption, write formally to the person having right thereto. It is also common to find a provision requiring the seller to obtain certificates from the superior (if these are not with the titles) that the feuing conditions (except those of a continuing nature) have been complied with – for example that the house, fences, etc., have been completed to the superior's satisfaction. This is something which the solicitor acting for the first purchaser of a new property should deal with. If alterations have been made to the property however and appear to require prior approval in terms of the title, the appropriate certificate should be obtained. See Chapter 33.

**34.8 (6) Planning permission and building warrant.** Every house erected in recent years required planning permission and building warrant. Alterations to the structure of the house (*e.g.* dormer windows, kitchen extension, a garage) may require planning permission, and will normally need a building warrant followed by a completion certificate when the works are completed. Particular attention must be paid regarding the installation of double glazed units as practices differ among local authorities as to whether or not a building warrant is required. In all cases however, such windows must comply with the relevant regulations. Alteration to the use of the house or part of the house may require planning permission but will not, unless structural alterations are also required, need a building warrant.

So far as planning permission is required, you should check the position with your client and the planning authority if necessary as to whether any changes have taken place. In the case of a new house or a house where alterations have obviously taken place, the question of planning permission will almost certainly be raised by the purchaser's solicitor, and a copy of the permission or a letter confirming that the development in question was permitted without formal planning permission being necessary will be required. In the case of building warrant approval, the warrant and the certificate of completion (or certificate of habitation) will be required. In each case the relevant documents should be placed with the titles. See Chapter 33.

**34.9 (7) Other guarantees, certificates, etc.** Depending on the type and age of property, you should, for example, confirm that if the house was built within the last ten years there is a NHBC certificate or NHBC Buildmark ten-year notice and guarantee with the titles, or, if the house has had remedial treatment for rot or woodworm, that your client has the appropriate guarantee and the original survey reports and quotations for the work involved. If not immediately available, these should be obtained. It is also essential to ascertain whether the company which granted the guarantee is still trading. If it is not, the guarantee could be worthless.

**34.10 Advertisement**
You cannot sell property efficiently without having seen it for yourself. Once you have checked the title and the public land use position, you or your firm's property valuer or estate agent should visit the house. Check the boundaries against the titles and, if necessary, the planning permission. Discrepancies do occur where, for example, fences are replaced or extended or even erected on the wrong line. It is better to discover potential problems before you conclude missives rather than after, when rectification may be difficult and expensive. Confirm which fittings are to be left in the house and are included in the price (*e.g.* the stair carpet, kitchen fittings, etc.) and which may be available to a purchaser but at a separate – and additional – price. Explain to your client in what state he should leave the house – for example, if he wants to take the chandelier in the hall with him, he must replace it with a light socket and not just leave the wire hanging from the ceiling.

Discuss the advertising of the property, when and in what papers. Confirm the viewing arrangements. This will depend on the owner's wishes, but too restrictive arrangements do not make for an easy sale, except in the case of a very desirable property. 'Come at any time' will lead to a total disruption of your client's social life. It is better to stick to set hours (for example 2–4p.m. and 7–8p.m.) or viewing by individual arrangement with your client (arranged by telephone) on production of a card. Take care with unaccompanied viewing for security reasons. Similarly try to avoid placing your client's telephone number in the advertisement. Make sure you know how and when you can contact your client.

**34.11 Schedule of particulars.** You will now prepare a schedule of particulars of the house, with a photograph and plan, if possible, and a press advertisement. Confirm the details of these with your client remembering the terms of the Property Misdescription Act 1991 which prohibits the making of false or misleading statements about property matters in the course of estate agency and property development business. Instruct the advertisements in the press, remembering that you are advertising your client's house and not your firm. (The property days in local papers are listed in the *Memorandum Book* published by the Scottish Law Agents Society.) Lodge the schedule (with sufficient copies) in the local solicitors' property centre along with the appropriate fee. At the same time make the necessary arrangements in your office so that incoming calls in response to the advertisement will not be met by mystification on the part of your telephonist. Note down details of enquirers, have available a supply of schedules to send to them, and before the advertisements appear, advise your client of the dates on which they will appear.

The final matter which you should at this stage impress on your client is never to commit himself to any approach from a potential purchaser without consulting you first. You should explain in outline how the sale of property in Scotland is carried through so that he is aware of the binding nature of an offer once it has been accepted, especially in light of the terms of the Requirements of Writing (Scotland) Act 1995: see Chapter 3. You should discourage him from grasping at a tempting verbal offer when in fact it is possible that a higher offer may be negotiated or may be received later. The seller should be instructed simply to pass on any approaches to you and in the meantime to indicate that 'considerable interest has been expressed'. There can be an element of bluff at the selling stage; after all, the seller wants the highest price he can get.

Now begins the period of waiting – with fingers crossed!

**34.12 The problems for the purchaser**
The purchaser has in the meantime been looking for a house, and should have consulted his solicitor at an early stage, although all that his solicitor can do at this point is offer general advice, note that his client is actively looking for a new house, and discuss the price bracket in which the purchaser can operate. Unless the latter has won a large sum of money on the Lottery or has inherited a fortune, it is likely that the price he can pay will depend on (*a*) his income and the loan which that will support and (*b*) the price which his present house will fetch less the existing loan and outlays and expenses. This is particularly significant if the housing market is depressed and prices are falling with the result that the existing loan might exceed the price obtained after exposure on the open market. At settlement, the outstanding loan over a seller's house has to be repaid out of the proceeds of sale. Once the date of settlement is known, write to the building society for a note of the sum required to redeem the loan as at that date. It is sensible to ask the building society for information also at an earlier stage (if your client cannot produce the last annual statement of the mortgage account) so that the outstanding loan is known and the financial calculations as to purchasing the new house can be reasonably accurate.

A simple version of this costing might be as follows:

| Estimated sale price of present house | £32,000 |
| Repayment of outstanding building society loan | 17,000 |
| | £15,000 |
| New loan at 2½ times salary of £10,000 | £25,000 |
| | £40,000 |
| Estimated expenses of sale and purchase | 2,500 |
| | £37,500 |

The sum available 'to spend' is therefore of the order of £37,500. A potential purchaser should have some idea of his price range as well as the likely cost of outgoings and repayments on a house of this value and a loan of this size before he starts looking. While not wishing to over-extend a client financially, it is as well to point out that there are certain costs involved in making offers (for example, survey fees) which recur with each unsuccessful offer, and it may be more sensible (in the long run) for a purchaser to offer just a little more than he may comfortably be able to afford to secure a house.

**34.13 (1) Confirmation that funds are available**. The purchaser or his solicitor as an independent financial adviser should confirm at this stage that he will be able to obtain a loan of the likely amount he will need and on the date when he is aiming to buy his new house. In many instances a loan may be arranged by the purchaser direct with a building society, bank or insurance company. Care should be taken however so as to ensure that the type of loan selected is best for the client. An existing satisfactory borrower should have little difficulty in obtaining a new loan. It is for his solicitor, however, to advise him on the best type of loan for his particular needs and if necessary to arrange this loan for him. The client will have to complete the necessary documentation but, particularly in times when loans are in short supply, his solicitor may find it easier to arrange the funding. It should be possible for a loan to be arranged without the involvement of a mortgage broker. The purchaser's personal circumstances may make it practically impossible to arrange a loan any other way. He should beware the salesmanship of certain companies; if he does wish to take an endowment loan, he should wait until the loan has been confirmed before signing up for any new life policy.

What a purchaser needs at this stage is the promise of a loan to be available at the time when he is hoping to move into his new house.

**34.14 (2) Finding the property**. The purchaser, particularly if he is new to a district, should then be advised where to look for property; *i.e.* the local solicitors' property centre and the property pages of the local press. His solicitor can also circulate other solicitors in the area. Thereafter, the choice of a house is a matter for the client.

**34.15 Finance for house purchase**
For many years, a prospective house purchaser had few lending institutions to approach when requiring a mortgage. Building societies, who provided in excess of 90% of the demand, and other lenders, *e.g.* joint stock banks, were not consistent in their approach to this particular aspect of their business.

The economic climate in Britain has changed dramatically over the past ten years and no more so than in the area of mortgage finance. Building societies, the traditional lenders of house purchase finance, are now finding that their market share is being seriously attacked by other lending institutions and no longer can one assume that a mortgage is being granted by a building society. The UK joint stock banks, the Trustee Savings Bank, foreign banks, insurance companies and secondary banks are very active in this field.

This chapter is intended to give a broad outline of the lending terms from each of the main sources of mortgage finance. In addition, some detail is given regarding an individual's borrowing capacity, regulations regarding the valuation of a property, methods of repaying a mortgage, and tax relief. Lending terms tend to vary considerably, however, in response to market conditions prevalent at any one time.

## 34.16 Types of lender

**34.17 (1) Building societies.** Historically, the building society movement had over 90 per cent of the mortgage market in the UK and existed almost exclusively to attract investments from the general public and lend funds by way of a mortgage over the security of heritable property. The operations of the societies, until recently, were governed by the Building Societies Act 1962. However, in recognition of the new competitive markets that the building societies were facing, the Building Societies Act 1986 sought to relax the operating restraints on the societies; in particular, the raising of investment funds, not only from traditional but new sources, for example, UK and European money markets, and to relax the scope of the lending services that the societies could offer. In other words, the building society movement wished to provide for their clients not only an investment and mortgage service, but also a complete financial package consisting of insurance services of all types, secured and non-secured finance, estate agency services, conveyancing, money transmission services, etc. Notwithstanding all the new services which the societies now promote and operate, the main stream of their business will continue to be the provision of mortgage funds for house purchase.

On 1 January 1987, the greater part of the Building Societies Act 1986 came into operation. Included in that Act is an amendment to the Consumer Credit Act 1974 which means that all lending by building societies will fall into two categories: (1) house finance loans, and (2) personal loans. The first is related to house purchase lending, in other words the traditional method of lending funds, and the other to non-house purchase loans, that is regulated lending, as defined under the Building Societies Act. Regulated lending means loans granted which do not exceed £15,000, for the following purposes, e.g. re-mortgages, purchase of annuities for personal reasons (capital raising), and refinancing of unsecured borrowing for any purpose.

The building societies will continue to support, by allocation of a block of mortgage funds, housing association and local authority house purchase schemes, house builders, and will expand their entry into the commercial market, albeit somewhat limited compared to the banks. The most popular commercial properties might be good quality shops, offices, sub-post offices, nursing homes. Building societies are unlikely to consider farms, agricultural land, factories, schools, and petrol stations, however.

**34.18 (2) High Street banks**. Lending by way of mortgage is only one form of lending open to banks, who, in the past, have generally found it more profitable to lend to businesses and individuals on overdrafts and personal loans, etc. Their entry into the house mortgage market was previously spasmodic, but due to a variety of reasons, and in particular the economic situation whereby the demand for their normal lending facilities has not been as great as it had been in the past, their commitment to mortgage finance is now greater than ever before. They generally have not been in a position to offer such high percentage loans as the building societies, but they are now proving to be just as flexible, not only in their maximum lending amounts and the terms of their loans, but also their interest rates are comparable to the building societies. Banks, on the whole, are not restricting their applicants to their own customers but will consider applications from any member of the general public who can meet their requirements regarding credit-worthiness.

**34.19 (3) Secondary banks and finance houses**. Although in the past the secondary bank movement in the UK was not to the forefront in mortgage finance, they have recently begun to provide a far greater supply of mortgage funds than ever before. Again, as with the High Street banks, their lending terms, etc., are proving just as flexible as those offered by the building societies. In addition, they also provide top-up funds where a main lender may be restricted to a maximum of, say, 90 per cent; the bank then provides the further 10 per cent, generally secured by means of a second charge.

**34.20 (4) Insurance companies**. Generally the interest of insurance companies in the property market has been the provision of top-up finance, where they would also insist that the loan was repaid by means of an endowment policy taken out with their own company. With their main mortgage funding, however, the insurance companies are not as flexible as main lenders, particularly with regard to the method of repayment of the mortgage which is normally on an endowment basis, with a policy effected with the particular company in question.

### 34.21 Methods of repaying a mortgage

**34.22 (1) Capital and interest repayment**. For some time, this was the most popular method of repaying a mortgage. The applicant is charged interest on the capital sum being borrowed and repays instalments of the sum, plus interest, on a month-to-month basis. Obviously, the composition of that monthly payment will consist of capital and interest, with the interest being charged on the outstanding amount of the mortgage at the end of the financial year. This method is known as the annuity method of payment. With a mortgage of this type it is generally advisable that the borrower should make arrangements for some form of mortgage protection assurance. Such insurance is generally tailored to fit the capital outstanding at the outset of the mortgage and decreases over the period of the agreed term. Whilst at the outset future changes of interest rates cannot be forecast, the cover generally provided is enough in this relatively inexpensive type of insurance policy to discharge all or a very substantial proportion of the mortgage, on death occurring during the term of the mortgage. Alternatively, the borrower may take out a level-term assurance policy. This has the advantage, in later years, of providing more than enough cover on death to discharge the mortgage. In the earlier years, however, interest represents almost the whole of the month's payment; and so sufficient cover may not be available in the event of early death.

**34.23 (2) Endowment method.** With an endowment loan, the borrower pays only interest every month to the lender. The capital element of the mortgage is repaid at the end of the agreed term from the proceeds of an endowment policy taken out with an insurance company, or on earlier death. An endowment policy is an investment type of life assurance. The most popular type of policy being used as collateral security for a building society mortgage is known as a low-cost endowment plan. This type of policy comprises two parts: (1) a with-profits endowment policy which is designed in such a way that, if the company continues to achieve profits of only 80 per cent of its current level, there will be sufficient capital at the end of the term to repay the mortgage; and (2) decreasing term insurance such that the policy carries a minimum guaranteed death benefit which is never less than the original amount of the loan. In a recessionary climate however, even this type of loan can come under pressure in circumstances where the sum insured is insufficient to repay the loan.

Since 1 November 1986 member companies of the ABI provide quotations illustrating approximately the same maturity values for a given premium and not intended to form a basis of comparison between companies.

**34.24 (3) Personal pension plans.** This method of repayment of mortgage loans has risen in popularity in the last few years. The main points of relevance to the lender are that they are available mainly to people who are self-employed or in non-pensionable employment and the benefits normally can be taken by the policyholder only between the ages of 60 and 75 whether or not they have retired. There are however designated occupations where the retirement age is considerably less than 60 years. The policy cannot be assigned as collateral security for a loan.

An eligible person is entitled to invest a certain percentage of his relevant income in a personal pension plan policy. The policyholder is then entitled to tax relief at his highest rate on the premiums payable, which are then invested in a tax-free fund and consequently that fund grows at a much faster rate than a normal life fund. Unit linked pension plans will also be acceptable to the lender. At maturity, the policyholder is given the option of using all of the fund to purchase a pension or to take part as a tax-free lump sum with a reduced pension. It is the tax-free lump sum that the society looks to in order to repay the advance and which makes the scheme possible. As the pension plan policy cannot be assigned to the building society, the society requires a level-term assurance, which may be in the form of a separate policy or part of the pension plan, to be assigned to it.

It is also possible that another suitable life policy be used for this purpose. The borrower is then asked to sign an undertaking that he will, amongst other things, repay the outstanding debt from the proceeds of the personal pension policy. Generally, a building society's normal lending terms will not be altered because of this particular method of repayment. Note that certain aspects of executive/director's pension plan policies differ from personal pension plan policies.

### 34.25 Individual's borrowing capacity

This is normally calculated by taking the individual's gross annual salary and multiplying it by an appropriate factor. An average multiplier may be two and a half or three times, although this will obviously vary depending on the interest rate structure at any one time. In addition to the basic salary, a proportion of any commission or overtime worked on a regular basis can be taken into consideration, generally 50 per cent of this amount. Allowance will also be made for any secondary salary, *i.e.* that of a spouse. Such allowance is normally one year's secondary salary. Most lenders will, when considering a joint mortgage application, take the higher of the two salaries as the main salary irrespective of whether this is earned by the husband or the wife. Most lenders will also consider adding the joint gross salaries and multiplying them by an appropriate factor (lower than the factor used when multiplying an individual's gross annual salary). Prudent lenders will appreciate that the amount of the advance is not simply an automatic paper exercise. It is necessary to try to ascertain the applicant's existing or future financial commitments, and on receipt of all information, make the necessary decision. Most lenders now carry out a credit check against each borrower.

### 34.26 Survey and valuation of the property

A building society is required by law to obtain a valuation of a property on which an advance may be required and the regulations regarding that valuation are now contained in s. 13 of the Building Societies Act 1986. There will be generally three options available to a mortgage applicant and details of each are given below. This has already been referred to in Chapter 28.18.

### 34.27 Option 1 – See also para. 34.38.
A building society or indeed the purchaser's own solicitor will arrange a valuation/limited inspection of a property for mortgage purposes only and a copy of that report may be given to the applicant for his own information, and then probably only if an offer of advance is being made. This report is prepared solely to enable the society to decide how much to lend on the security of that property and on what terms. This is the most limited form of inspection and originates from an agreement between the building societies and the Royal Institution of Chartered Surveyors. A detailed structural survey will not be made by the valuer and therefore the applicant must under no circumstances assume that all parts of the structure are free from defect. Where the report does draw attention to certain defects, that does not mean that other defects do not exist. Any major defects which are visible and apparent at the time of inspection will be reported. Underfloor areas and mutual roof spaces, and any areas where special access is required will not be inspected. Floor coverings will not be lifted nor will furniture and effects be moved. According to RICS Guidelines however, private roof spaces will be inspected where the surveyor considers access to be reasonable and only to the extent of being visible from the access point. No attempt will be made

to gain access to communal roof spaces or other properties in a multi-occupancy building however. Such areas will be assumed to be non-detrimental. Roof coverings will be inspected from ground floor level only and serious visible defects will be reported. None of the services, water systems, heating or electrical circuits will be checked or tested. As mentioned above therefore, it must be recognised that this is the most limited form of inspection and a more comprehensive report is recommended.

**34.28 Option 2 – See also para. 34.39.**It should be possible for a building society to arrange a more detailed inspection of the property than that available under Option 1. This inspection is available for houses and bungalows up to 2,000 sq. ft. of floor area and not more than three storeys high. Period properties are however excluded. Although a full structural survey of the property will not be undertaken, the surveyor will provide a concise report on the condition and state of repair of the property together with an opinion as to its value. It is also possible to obtain a flat buyer's valuation report, where in addition to a detailed report on the flat in question, additional comment will also be made regarding the tenement block, the common parts and services, lifts, tenancies of the other flats, etc. The report can then be used by a building society for its own purpose and will also give guidance to a prospective purchaser. These reports will be prepared on the standard terms either from the RICS or the ISVA and are generally accompanied by a terms of engagement letter.

In addition to greater detail being available to the applicant, the most important distinction is that the report is provided for the sole use of the named client and is confidential to him and his professional advisers. In addition, the surveyor accepts responsibility to the client alone that the report will be prepared with the skill, care and diligence reasonably to be expected of a competent chartered surveyor, who will accept no responsibility whatsoever to any other person. There have, in the past, been many problems caused by verbal instructions followed by verbal reports. It is now common, where a building society accepts telephone instructions from an agent, that the society will acknowledge the telephone instructions and enclose an application form for completion by the client prior to the conclusion of missives. Some societies also ask intermediaries to make arrangements for their clients to sign an acknowledgement of the type of survey that has been instructed on their behalf.

**34.29 Option 3 – See also para. 34.40.** Finally, the applicant can arrange, via the building society, (or himself as the case may be) for a full structural survey to be carried out. It should be possible for the society to organise such a report and ask the valuer to complete a report for its purposes. It will also be necessary for the society and the applicant to negotiate with the valuer the question of fees, etc., and the exact terms of instruction.

**34.30 General percentage lending terms/insurance guarantees**
With more and more lenders in the market, it was, for a number of years, easy to obtain a maximum 100 per cent mortgage. However, in light of the recession and rising cases of default and subsequent repossession a greater realism is now being shown by most lenders, particularly the building societies, as to the wisdom of offering 100 per cent advances. 100 per cent mortgages are again the exception. Whilst the Building Societies Act 1986

came into effect on 1 January 1987, the regulations relating to insurance companies under the Building Societies Act 1962 are still current. Under the relevant sections, a building society normally cannot make an advance exceeding 75 per cent of the purchase price without additional security. This, however, does not mean that they are restricted to a maximum of 75 per cent; but may lend the balance by way of an excess which must not exceed 25 per cent of the purchase price. The excess advance under terms of s. 28 of the 1962 Act must be covered by some form of additional security which can take several forms. It can include a security over another heritable property, over funds deposited in the building society account, or assignation of a portfolio of shares, but typically the guarantee is given by an insurance company nominated by the building society. This indemnity guarantee policy provides that, in the event of a repossession by the building society and the sale of the property should a shortfall occur, this will be covered by the insurance company up to the amount of the excess advance. It should be remembered that in the event that the insurance company is required to indemnify the building society under the policy, the borrower remains personally liable for the capital sum. The insurance company receives a single premium for this facility which is normally deducted from the advance cheque when released from the society, although nowadays a variety of means are available for this premium to be paid by the applicants. Once again however, the recession in the property market has had an adverse effect on the level of such insurance with premiums increasing substantially over the last few years.

A form known as Form 1 is served on the borrower before the advance is entered into, advising him of the amount of the basic advance and the excess advance; and giving particulars of the security for the excess advance, which is to be taken from the third party. This notice is served in duplicate and one copy requires to be signed by the borrower and returned. At the same time, the society will serve a Form 3 notice on the applicant to the effect that, in the event of the society making an advance to assist in the purchase of a property, the making of such an advance will not imply any warranty by the society that the purchase price of the property is a fair and reasonable one.

### 34.31 Home loan scheme

This scheme was introduced to provide help to people buying lower-priced homes. It operated from 1979 to March 1990 when it was withdrawn. Any savers registered before March 1990 are entitled to claim benefits under the scheme.

The benefits under the scheme are (1) a cash bonus of up to £110 and (2) a loan of £600 which is normally added to the mortgage.

To qualify, the borrowers must have saved for at least two years after joining the scheme with a recognised savings institution, e.g. building societies, banks, trustee savings banks, etc., and have given notice to the lender that savings are being undertaken under the scheme. It is now quite unlikely that this scheme is of any continuing significance.

### 34.32 Tax relief

Tax relief is available on mortgages, provided the basic following criteria are met:

(1) the loan must be for the main or principal residence;

(2) the borrower is a UK resident for tax purposes; and

(3) the amount of the loan must not exceed £30,000.

Note that tax relief is not now eligile in respect of home improvements. The mortgate must be for the purchase or replacement of an existing qualifying loan.

From 5 April, 1983, provided the loan is for less than £30,000 and is taken out with a qualified institution, mortgage interest relief, given at source by the lender, is deducted at the basic rate of tax from the monthly payments. This is called MIRAS, for short.

From April 1987 all qualifying loans have had to be included in MIRAS. All loans in excess of £30,000 are eligible for tax relief on the first £30,000 and interest will be charged net on that first part.

### 34.33 Taking final instructions

It is recommended that the method of purchasing property in Scotland (the system of offers, surveys and so on) should be explained to the purchaser at this stage so that he is generally aware of the various steps which require to be taken. In particular, the purchaser should be advised not to write to the seller himself offering to purchase the property as, if accepted in writing, a binding contract may be created. See the Requirements of Writing (Scotland) Act 1995.

The purchaser having visited the seller's house, likes it and expresses interest to the seller; the seller, however, having been well briefed by his solicitor, indicates that offers should be made to his solicitor but may go on to add – without committing himself – that in principle the price, date of entry and so on indicated by the purchaser are acceptable. The purchaser should not push in these circumstances for a decision, however keen he may be on the house. The purchaser's solicitor will have advised him of the need for a survey to be made at least on behalf of the building society which will be providing the loan and the purchaser should find out when a surveyor will be able to obtain access. Throughout the sale period the seller and his solicitor should keep in touch and when there are any firm expressions of interest, the seller should notify his solicitor.

The purchaser now discusses the proposed purchase with his solicitor. The solicitor should obtain full details of the house. He should, if possible, obtain a copy of the schedule of particulars and any arrangements made as to other matters such as fittings and fixtures. At this stage, he is generally aware of his client's financial position and confirms that the price of the house is within his client's financial reach and that there appears to be no difficulty about a suitable loan. He will also discuss the date of entry with his client since this will have to take into account – so far as possible – completion of the sale of his client's present house to allow the financing of the sale and purchase to be simplified. If there is to be a period between the date of settlement of the new house and the date of settlement of the present house, some form of bridging loan for the purchase must be available on the date stipulated. It is as well to discuss this possibility with a client at this stage and to suggest he arranges the necessary bridging loan with his bank in the event of this being required. Banks will normally lend where a customer's house has already been sold and it is simply a question of waiting till a particular date for the sale proceeds (a 'closed bridge') but are most unlikely to agree to provide bridging finance on an open-ended basis where the present house has not been sold and there appears to be no other source from which funds to repay the bridging loan are likely to come.

### 34.34 Action by purchaser's solicitor

He contacts the seller's solicitor to confirm that the house is still on the market; if this is so, he 'notes his client's interest' in the property. Noting interest ensures (or should ensure) that the seller will not conclude the sale of the house without allowing all those who have noted interest to be given the opportunity of making an offer. He should also find out whether a 'closing date' has been fixed. This is the date by which offers have to be in the hands of the seller's solicitor. It is useful also at this stage to try and elicit information from the selling solicitor about the price level likely to be acceptable, the most suitable date of entry, the fittings to be included and so on. It is also becoming common for properties to be offered for sale at fixed prices whereby the first offer received at the advertised price will be accepted so long as there are no other unusual conditions.

**34.35 Offer price.** The price which the purchaser should offer is of the greatest importance since, if there are other interested potential purchasers, it will normally have to be higher than any other competing offer. In arriving at the final price to be offered various factors have to be borne in mind such as the amount of loan which may be obtained. This will depend both on the property and the purchaser's income, and the funds which the purchaser can himself raise, for example, from the sale of his present house. Two factors finally are present: the purchaser must be advised (if he has not already been) as to the likely cost of the move, both practical, *e.g.* removal costs, new carpets, curtains, etc., and legal, *e.g.* stamp duty, recording dues, legal fees, cost of survey, etc. He must weigh the total cost of the move against the fact that he may have to move again and that if he does not manage to buy this house he will incur further costs in trying to buy another house. The purchaser and his solicitor must therefore consider very carefully the price which the purchaser can and should offer, and whether, when the amount is settled on, this is likely to be successful. This is one area where the solicitor's experience and expertise is of great importance to the client who wants to buy the house but not to pay over the odds for it. The difficulties of fixing a price should not be under-estimated. One of the reasons for odd prices (for example, £2,507 or £40,253) being offered is not because it includes some fitment valued at £7 or £3 but so that, in theory, your client will have a slight edge (of £7 or £3) over another offerer.

### 34.36 Confirming loan arrangements

The purchaser has already asked about access arrangements and with this information he, or his solicitor, will now instruct a survey of the house. Alternatively, his building society will instruct a survey for loan purposes. The building society will normally instruct a valuation survey (carried out on their behalf, not the purchaser's) unless instructions are given for a more detailed form of survey. See para. 34.26. The purchaser's solicitor should advise the purchaser of the possible need for a more detailed survey. If a structural survey, for example, is necessary, it is possible for this to be done by the same surveyors and a reduced fee to be charged. A valuation survey can usually be carried out fairly quickly and if necessary the building society will advise the purchaser's solicitor by telephone of the result of the survey, the amount of the loan they are prepared to make and when the loan funds will be available. Ask the building society to confirm the actual amount of the loan which will be available on the date of settlement, and to indicate any deductions or retentions.

### 34.37 Surveys and valuation inspections
The importance of a survey has already been referred to in the context of finance for house purchase in para. 34.27 above. There are basically three types of inspections that can be instructed: mortgage valuation (normally for loan purposes); house buyer's report and valuation/private report; full structural survey. In addition there are various types of specialist survey.

**34.38 (1) Mortgage valuation.** This type of inspection is the most usual one and will be carried out by a chartered surveyor on instructions from a lending institution (*e.g.* a bank or building society) before the latter make an offer of loan on a property.

The valuation inspection is instructed by the institution although the prospective purchaser/borrower will pay for it and will also receive a copy of the report.

Its purpose is simply to assure the institution that the property provides adequate security for the loan. The intention of the inspection is to arrive at a value which reflects the value for mortgage purposes of the property. The surveyor will normally point out any immediate defects which are visible and apparent but will not inspect the underfloor area, roof spaces or any other area where special access is required. These will not be inspected and will, for the purposes of arriving at a valuation, be assumed to have no significant defects. Floor coverings (for example fitted carpets or vinyl) and furnishings will not be moved to gain access. The roof coverings will be inspected from ground level only and none of the services, *i.e.* water system, heating system or electrical circuits will be checked or tested. Comment may be made on systems which are obviously outdated or clearly defective. The surveyor will not normally note items which do not seriously affect the possible security value of the property such as rotten windowsills, frames, leaking gutters or broken windows. However, these items may be mentioned for the guidance of a prospective purchaser.

Particular problems arise with regard to tenement property. The surveyor will normally not attempt (or be able) to gain access to communal roof spaces or other common parts and for valuation purposes the condition of these areas will be assumed to be satisfactory, no regard being had to any mutual repair obligations.

If a retention is suggested, this may or may not reflect accurately the likely cost of repair; this is a matter for the purchaser/borrower to resolve himself. It is suggested that in this event an accurate estimate should be obtained from an appropriate contractor or other specialist and it would be advisable for a detailed inspection to be instructed.

**34.39 (2) House buyer's report and valuation/private report.** The purpose of this inspection is to establish the general condition and value of the house/flat. Whilst it is less detailed than a full structural survey it is more detailed than the inspection carried out for mortgage valuation. It will normally take the form of a pre-printed form which is completed by the surveyor and it should be noted that the surveyor is only obliged to answer accurately the questions asked on the form. Again, a surveyor will not be able to examine those parts of the property to which he cannot gain access, but he will inspect under the floors where access is available and roof coverings when visible from the attic windows or skylights or readily opened hatches.

He will also comment on drains, heating and electric, gas and water services. These services will not, however, be tested. The surveyor may also report on double glazing and any potential unauthorised alterations.

A private written report from the surveyor may be given as an alternative to the house buyer's report form.

The Royal Institution of Chartered Surveyors introduced this scheme and, of the major building societies/banks, Halifax, Alliance & Leicester and Nationwide and a number of others offer this type of survey scheme.

**34.40 (3) Full structural survey.** The purpose of this is to establish the full physical condition of the property and it is unlikely that a surveyor would carry this out in the absence of specific instructions.

A full structural survey is much more detailed and in the majority of cases requires to be specially instructed by the purchaser. Despite the term, however, the surveyor is unlikely to be able to look at parts of the property that he cannot get access to (for example if there are fitted carpets he is unlikely to lift these, and it may be impossible to obtain access to the foundations or the attic space). It is nonetheless the most comprehensive type of survey which is available and is normally essential when considering large or old property where an accurate idea of any defects and the necessary repairs to rectify these will be of importance. The surveyor will almost certainly comment on the services in addition to the state of the property, and he may be authorised to engage the services of such electricians or other specialist contractors as he may consider necessary in order to carry out his instructions properly. If damp or rot is suspected or obvious he may recommend further inspection by a specialist.

The cost of a full structural survey will depend on the property and the time spent by the surveyor (and any other specialists which he requires to instruct) but is unlikely to be less than £500 and will range upwards from that figure.

If the purchaser can arrange for the same surveyor to carry out the structural survey and any required valuation survey, the total cost to him is likely to be modified.

**34.41 (4) Specialist surveys.** Particularly when damp, woodworm or wet or dry rot is either obvious or suspected, the surveyor may well recommend obtaining a report from a specialist firm, and indeed it may be in the interest of the prospective purchaser to do this in any event. These surveys are normally free since they are carried out by firms who hope to carry out the work which they recommend, and it is sensible therefore to obtain a number of estimates since the quality and the thoroughness of the inspection do vary as in some cases do specialist opinions on the seriousness or complexity of the problem. A specialist surveyor should be instructed to examine all parts of a building, and not confine his inspection only to the areas where a surveyor has first noticed the likely defect.

A guarantee will be given on completion of the work, usually for 30 years, and again it is worth considering the length of time a firm has been in business when valuing the worth of a guarantee. Some guarantees are backed by an insurance company to reassure the customer. Such a guarantee is normally transmissible to successors in title without any formal assignation.

Other forms of specialist survey may relate to the wiring, drains, or if there is a potential problem with the structure, a structural engineer may be called in to investigate. These surveys are fee-based and can be expensive, depending on the extent of the work required.

**34.42 Surveyors**. Surveyors, other than specialists, are normally chartered surveyors, and members of the Royal Institution of Chartered Surveyors which operates a code of practice for members. Specialist surveyors may either be members of their own professional associations or, in certain cases, may not have a professional association, in which case reputation is what counts.

**34.43 The offers**
With confirmation from the building society about a loan and a satisfactory survey available, the purchaser is now in a position to go ahead. If a closing date is suddenly fixed and no time is available to obtain a survey or offer of loan, an offer can still be made provided it is made subject to suitable conditions.

The purchaser then instructs his solicitor to make an offer for the seller's house and should be asked to confirm in writing the property, the price, the date of entry, the fittings to be included in the price and those (if any) being bought separately. The name(s) of the purchaser(s) should also be confirmed. The purchaser's solicitor then prepares an offer for the house (which will no doubt follow his firm's standard form) which is subscribed by the purchaser or his solicitor and sends it to the seller's solicitor. The purchaser's solicitor should send a copy of the offer to the purchaser on the same day.

The offer will include (in addition to the price, a brief description of the subjects offered for, and the date of entry) such other – hopefully relevant – conditions as appear to the purchaser's solicitor and the purchaser as being necessary or appropriate. These will vary depending on the property and the circumstances. If a style offer is used, it should be altered to suit the property being offered for: for example an offer for a bungalow which includes conditions appropriate to a flat in a tenement is indicative of a careless conveyancer. It should be borne in mind also that the more stringent the conditions you attach, the more chance there is (unless there is only one offer) that a similar offer subject to fewer or less stringent conditions will be accepted. The aim of the solicitor making the offer is both to protect the purchaser's interests and buy the property for him; and the various factors involved should be balanced. The offer will usually conclude by stating the time limit within which an acceptance has to be received: this should be realistic. It is usual, unless a closing date has been fixed, for the formal offer to be sent with a simple covering letter. If a closing date has been fixed, the offer may well be enclosed in a further sealed envelope marked 'Offer for (property) to be opened at (noon) on (Friday, 26 June)'.

### 34.44 The bargain concluded

You, as the seller's solicitor, and the seller, in the meantime will have been gauging interest in the property. The noting of interest and a survey being carried out are indicative of serious interest in the property, and at this stage the seller's solicitor should consider with the seller whether to fix a closing date. If there are a number of interested parties, a closing date will probably be set, though it is difficult to be categoric about this; and every party who has noted interest or otherwise expressed interest should be notified. It is sensible to list those firms who have noted interest on behalf of clients on the inside of the file cover to avoid overlooking any of them. If a closing date has been fixed, you should adhere to it. Whether to set a closing date or to accept the first reasonable offer is a matter for agreement with the seller.

### 34.45 (1) No closing date.

If no closing date has been fixed, you will contact the seller when you receive any offer and will 'take instructions', though in most cases the seller will seek advice from the solicitor. The difficulties centre round the proverb 'a bird in the hand is worth two in the bush'. If a reasonable offer is received, even though it is possible that a higher one might come in, the seller may well consider accepting the present offer to avoid further disruption. The trauma which is often associated with buying and selling a house should not be lost sight of. In any event, a higher offer may not in fact materialise. The seller should, however, see the offer or have its terms summarised and he should be aware of all the relevant conditions, not just the price offered. It is then for the seller to instruct his solicitor whether to accept it or not.

### 34.46 (2) Closing date.

If a closing date has been fixed, the practice is for the offers to be opened at that time and not before. You may wish to consider having the seller present when the offers are opened at the 'appointed hour' on the closing date. The seller will, after all, be very interested in the proceedings. There is no need to have offerers present. The seller will then be advised of all the offers and terms. Price, date of entry, other conditions (particularly suspensive conditions) are all relevant in deciding which offer to accept. Even although a closing date has been fixed, the seller is not obliged in law to accept any offer; nor need he accept the highest. So, for example, an earlier date of entry may be preferable to a slightly higher price, while an offer subject to a survey condition is not as immediately acceptable as one without such a condition. The seller has to decide which offer he is to accept and he should formally advise his solicitor of this. You should therefore ensure that you can contact your client. On the other hand, there is no reason normally why the seller should be forced into taking an immediate decision, though it is unfair to keep offerers unnecessarily in suspense and most offers will have time limits. On the closing date, the seller should be advised that, although not bound to accept the highest or indeed any offer, if he or she instructs the solicitor to enter negotiations with a view to concluding a bargain with a party who has submitted an offer at the closing date, the solicitor will not be able to enter into any subsequent negotiations with or accept an offer from another party unless and until the negotiations with the original offerer have fallen through. In the event that the solicitor is instructed to negotiate with a third party in such circumstances, he should decline to act further in the sale.

**34.47 (3) Checking the successful offer.** Once the seller has confirmed which offer is to be accepted you will, if you have not done so already, check the conditions in the offer against the title deeds, the local authority and, if appropriate, water authority, certificate and any other relevant information. You will advise the solicitor who made the successful offer that it is to be accepted and will detail any qualifications which are to be made, probably by telephone initially. You will then accept the offer either (a) unconditionally, if there are no qualifications (which is unlikely) or (b) subject to any necessary qualifications. This letter of acceptance is a formal letter, and is usually sent subject to final acceptance being forthcoming within a brief time limit. If you as the seller's solicitor have received an assurance from the purchaser's solicitor that the qualifications are acceptable, you may also advise the other offerers that their offers were unacceptable: this should however be deferred if there is any doubt about the successful offer concluding the bargain.

The purchaser's solicitor confirms with the purchaser that the qualifications are acceptable, and then sends a further formal letter to the purchaser's solicitor to this effect 'holding the bargain as concluded'. It may be that a further exchange of formal letters will be required before this stage is reached; whether or not this is so, 'missives' – the comprehensive term for the various letters which comprise the bargain for the sale/purchase of heritage – must, before they can be considered to be concluded, deal with every point in the offer and the ensuing letters: both parties must be in agreement on all the points dealt with. At this stage the bargain for the sale/purchase of the property is complete.

It is unfortunately becoming increasingly common for the seller's solicitor to send the title deeds for the property to the purchaser's solicitor so that 'he can satisfy himself as to conditions A, B & C' of his offer. This practice, while sometimes necessary, ought to be avoided, where possible, as it leads to an inevitable delay in conclusion of missives and there is an increased possibility that either party may decide not to proceed. It is suggested that this is not in either party's best interests. The seller's solicitor ought to be able to stand by his client's title, having examined same pre-sale; and he should have obtained in advance all the documents and information referred to above.

**34.48 (4) Advising the clients.** As the seller's solicitor, you then advise the seller that the sale is concluded; cancel the advertising, withdraw the schedule of particulars from the local solicitors' property centre and remove any advertising signs from the house itself.

The purchaser's solicitor formally advises the purchaser that the purchase is concluded. He arranges temporary insurance cover for the property because the risk is deemed to have passed to the purchaser on conclusion of the bargain unless the seller accepts responsibility in terms of the missives. Temporary insurance cover is taken out normally in the name of the purchaser 'price unpaid' for the amount of the purchase price and covers the period from conclusion of missives until settlement, when permanent property insurance will be arranged. It is taken out either by arranging a separate policy with your firm's insurance company, at a likely cost of £20 or so, or by including details of the property on your firm's block insurance policy for property purchases. It is possible, if a building society loan is involved in the purchase, to arrange for the society to extend the insurance cover forward. If the missives provide for the seller to maintain the property and to insure it till settlement, the purchaser's name and the nature of his interest should be noted on the seller's insurance policy. While arranging such insurance, the possibility of 'double insurance' must not be overlooked; but there can be serious disadvantages to the purchaser if he has to rely solely on the seller's insurance policy.

Both the seller's solicitor and the purchaser's solicitor will mark the date of settlement and entry into their respective diaries or wall charts. This is now the date to which they will each work.

### 34.49 Titles and drafts

Once missives have been concluded, and indeed quite often before such conclusion, the next stage of a transaction proceeds. It includes the conveyancing and the examination of the title offered and commences with the seller's solicitor sending the purchaser's solicitor the following documents.

**34.50 (1) The title deeds.** The seller's solicitor checks the title deeds and removes any deeds or documents which are unnecessary or relate to the seller's financial affairs but which do not affect the title (for example an assignation of life policy, life policy and intimation thereof). He then lists the title deeds in the inventory of titles in chronological order separating (preferably) the estate title (the prior writs) and the security title (bonds, standard securities and discharges) from the property title. The search is noted as a final item on the inventory. It is normal to include in the inventory other relevant documents such as superior's certificates, the certificate of redemption of feuduty, etc. The inventory is prepared in duplicate so that the purchaser's solicitor can, after checking the titles against the inventory, acknowledge receipt on the duplicate copy and return that as a form of receipt to the seller's solicitor. If any titles have been sent already to the purchaser's solicitor (for example in explanation of any missive conditions) indicate this on the inventory or in the covering letter. Any relevant prior writs will also be exhibited.

**34.51 (2) The search and the draft memorandum for search.** The seller's solicitor is under obligation to deliver or exhibit a marketable title, which is why he forwards the title deeds to the purchaser's solicitor to allow the latter to examine them, and a clear search which will have to be continued to show the conveyance to be granted by the seller to the purchaser. This clearly cannot be done at this stage. What is required is an instruction to the searchers to complete the search when this becomes possible.

The seller's solicitor therefore drafts a memorandum for search (if there is no existing search or if there is a prior search relating to larger subjects and a new search is required for the property being sold) or a memorandum for continuation of search (if there is an existing search relating to the property). The memorandum is an instruction to the searchers to search or continue the search against a particular property and particular individuals from the date of the last entries (which will probably relate to the seller's purchase of the property) to the date on which the present sale is completed by the recording of the purchaser's title. It is unnecessary when preparing a draft memorandum to list every deed which has been recorded in the interim but only those which are crucial, such as the deed in favour of the purchaser. 'Search ... to disclose *inter alia* ...' is a useful phrase. Many firms use a pre-printed style to which information relating to the particular transaction is added. Certain firms of Searchers produce their own printed forms. Use of a style helps to prevent omissions and saves typing.

The draft which the seller's solicitor sends to the purchaser's solicitor will not be complete (he will not know the purchaser's full name and address, for instance). If the purchaser's solicitor also acts for the building society which will require a search to be made in the Personal Registers against the purchaser, he will extend the memorandum to provide for (*a*) disclosure of the standard security to be granted by the purchaser in favour of his building society and (*b*) a personal search against the purchaser/borrower. In these respects the revisals to the draft memorandum are made by the purchaser's solicitor who in the latter instance is acting on behalf of the building society. The seller is not bound to pay for the search being extended to disclose the purchaser's financial arrangements, but in practice no objection is normally taken. In the property search, only recorded writs will be disclosed; deeds which are not recorded such as the assignation of a life policy or a deed of assumption and conveyance will not be disclosed, but may be referred to in other entries.

**34.52 (3) The draft letter of obligation.** On the basis that the disposition, when granted, will supersede the missives, it has always been accepted that a letter of obligation to keep open the seller's obligation at the least to deliver a clear search is necessary at settlement. It is normal practice for a letter of obligation to be granted at settlement covering, principally, delivery of a clear search and, if the seller has a loan over the property, delivery of a recorded discharge of that loan. Other matters which have not been delivered or completed (e.g. a certificate of redemption of feuduty) will also be included.

The seller's solicitor drafts the letter of obligation, again perhaps using an office style or a pre-printed form, so long as it is in 'classic' terms. The importance (from the purchaser's point of view) of ensuring that the obligation is granted personally by the seller's solicitor and not 'on behalf of' the seller has already been stressed. See Chapter 33.45.

It will reflect the position as the seller's solicitor sees it and amendments may have to be made to it by the purchaser's solicitor now or at a later stage in the transaction. The scope of a letter of obligation should not be extended to extraneous matters or matters outwith the control of the seller's solicitor. A letter of obligation is still used even where, as is now commonplace, the non-supersession clause in the missives is also included in the disposition in favour of the purchaser. The purpose is to obtain the personal obligation of the selling solicitor to implement the undertakings in that letter. This personal obligation is, within limits, backed by the master policy, and is a valuable protection for the purchaser. It should be insisted on in every case. The remaining provisions kept alive by the non-supersession clause are the personal responsibility of the seller, not his solicitor. See Chapter 28 for further comment on the effect of a non-supersession clause.

**34.53 (4) A draft discharge of any security**.   The seller's solicitor will, if there is an outstanding loan secured over the property, draft a discharge of this security. In the case of a building society loan, a form of discharge will probably be printed on the principal standard security. If this form is to be adopted, one should photocopy the blank discharge, complete it with the necessary details and use this as the draft. If no printed or draft form of discharge is available, a style form is given in the 1970 Act. If there is more than one loan over the property, a separate draft discharge will be prepared for each loan.

**34.54 (5) The covering letter to the purchaser's solicitor**.   Having prepared the inventory of titles and the draft memorandum, letter of obligation and discharge, the seller's solicitor now sends to the purchaser's solicitor:

(*a*) the title deeds of the property (except those already sent) as listed in the inventory which is also enclosed in duplicate;

(*b*) the draft memorandum, letter of obligation and discharge;

(*c*) any other documents which are relevant and which have not already been sent to the purchaser's solicitor in support of any conditions in or qualifications to the missives (such as local authority certificates, affidavits, etc., under the Matrimonial Homes etc. Act 1981, as amended);

(*d*) any other draft deeds which may in the particular circumstances of the transaction be required – in straightforward transactions, there are unlikely to be any;

(*e*) a draft state for settlement and supporting vouchers, if any.

**34.55 (6) Draft retrocession of life policy**.   If the loan over the property is on an endowment or semi-endowment basis, the life policy or policies which is or are assigned as additional security to the building society will have to be re-assigned or retrocessed to the seller, as the life assured, on repayment of the loan and discharge of the principal security. In practice, however, some societies seem content simply to hold the policy without taking a formal assignation, in which case no retrocession is necessary. This practice is regarded by many as being fatally flawed however and is not recommended. While this part of the transaction has nothing to do with the purchaser or the purchaser's solicitor, it is sensible for the seller's solicitor at this stage to prepare the retrocession in draft. This will require to be intimated in due course to the building society so that the policy or policies may be released from the security, and the intimation form should also be prepared. One benefit of preparing the retrocession at this time is that the deed will be ready for execution by the building society at the same time as the discharge of the standard security. The life policy or policies will be with the deeds obtained from the building society. They should be retained by the seller's solicitor together with the relevant assignations and duplicate intimations and not sent to the purchaser's solicitor with the other titles.

When the life policy eventually matures, the insurance company will insist on seeing all assignations and retrocessions, all of which should therefore be carefully preserved with the policy itself.

Once the letter has been sent to the purchaser's solicitor, with the title deeds and usual drafts the seller's solicitor can sit back (if only briefly) since the ball is now firmly in the purchaser's court. The 'usual drafts' normally include the draft obligation, memorandum for search and discharge (if any).

### 34.56 Examination of title

This subject has already been dealt with in greater detail in Chapter 33 above. The purchaser's solicitor has to ensure that the title is, in accordance with the missives, 'a good and marketable title' and that the search is 'clear'. The purpose of examining the title is to ensure that this is so and that it will allow the purchaser freely to enjoy the use and ownership of the property and to be able in due course to sell it without difficulty. For the present, until a title has been registered in the Land Register, the practice is that in each transaction, whether on purchase or on obtaining a loan, the solicitor acting for the purchaser or the lender requires to make a full examination of title to ensure that his client's position is fully protected.

When the purchaser's solicitor receives a letter enclosing the title deeds and 'the usual drafts', he should check the enclosures and if all is in order he should acknowledge receipt by endorsing a receipt on to the duplicate of the inventory of titles and returning this to the seller's solicitor. If there are omissions from the enclosures, he should advise the seller's solicitor at once. Letters enclosing title deeds or other important documents should always be acknowledged without delay. If you can deal with the examination of title in the course of a day or so, you may feel that a separate acknowledgement is not necessary, but it is good practice to do so – there may be other causes of delay in an office.

Before examining a title, particularly if you did not yourself conclude the missives, check the file to see what has happened, and the missives to see that a proper contract has been completed and what special conditions it contains. Separate the title deeds into the property title (which will include the writs referred to for burdens) and the security title; in other words extract from the main body of titles all bonds, standard securities, discharges, etc.

### 34.57 (1) Procedure on examination of titles.

Check through the property title for the foundation writ. The foundation writ is the first recorded writ outwith the prescriptive period of 10 years. This may be a disposition, a feu disposition, a notice of title, etc. Assuming in the case of a particular transaction that the date of entry is to be 28 June 1997, you will require to find a deed recorded on or before 27 June 1987. In the case of a title where the property has not changed hands frequently, the foundation writ may be 20 or more years old; in other cases, it may be only a matter of days or weeks beyond the 10-year date. A review of the Sasines search may be helpful in ascertaining the foundation writ.

If the foundation writ is valid, there is no need to check any other prior writ. Where, however, the foundation writ, or indeed any other writ in the progress of titles, refers for description to a writ outwith the progress of titles and earlier than the foundation writ, then this writ should also be examined to confirm the accuracy of the description.

Having found the foundation writ, you will want to check that there is a continuous series of transfers of the property from that date down to the seller. The grantee in one writ should be the grantor of the next writ in the progress of titles; and if there is a gap or if the name of the grantee is not the same as the grantor of the next writ, further investigation should be made. For example, if the grantee was a company, it may have changed its name or alternatively a liquidator may have been appointed before the next deed was granted; or an individual grantee in one writ may have died and the grantor of the next writ may be his executor or trustee. In these cases the appropriate linking writs, such as a confirmation or special resolution, should form part of the progress of titles offered to allow the purchaser's solicitor to check the validity of the various links. All writs referred to for burdens should be examined, whether or not they are within the prescriptive progress of titles.

It is a matter of judgment as to whether the older titles, even if they are referred to for burdens, are required. Some resistance may sometimes be found on the part of sellers' solicitors to the production of these writs since it may be difficult to trace who holds them and the costs of obtaining the necessary extracts may be considerable. It is however for the seller's solicitor to produce such writs as are reasonably required by the purchaser's solicitor and there is no reason why the purchaser should meet the cost of obtaining extracts or quick copies of writs from the Scottish Record Office or the searchers. If a deed is referred to for burdens, it should be examined.

The purchaser's solicitor should compare the written description in the title and the plan (if any) against the missive description and against the actual property.

**34.58 (2) Inspection of property.** A solicitor acting for a purchaser should, ideally, always inspect the property which he is buying, preferably before missives are concluded, so that he has some idea of the property and so that he can foresee potential problems (for example a private roadway). What he should certainly do is to write to the purchaser (and possibly the surveyor if one was instructed) once he has the titles, sending him (or them) a copy of the description and the plan (if any) asking him (or them) to confirm that the description and the plan accurately define the property which is being purchased. The written description should also be checked against the survey report.

**34.59 (3) Burdens.** The purchaser's solicitor will also inform the purchaser of the burdens which affect the property and whether they are in conformity with the provisions of the missives. He will check the local authority and, if necessary, water authority, certificates (when he receives them) against the missives and he will check the superior's certificates (if any) against the title. If necessary he will require the seller's solicitor to obtain any other certificates.

If he requires to examine other writs, he will request these from the seller's solicitor. If he wishes further information about particular points he will raise these points also with the seller's solicitor. Before he reaches the point of raising these 'observations on title' he will have examined the title in detail.

**34.60 (4) Points to check.** The following list is not exclusive but indicates the main points which you should consider. It is helpful to have available some form of checklist which can be completed as the examination proceeds. This avoids any relevant points being omitted from consideration. See Chapter 33.

(*a*) Check that there is a prescriptive progress of titles, and that each writ is correctly framed, executed and recorded.

(*b*) Check the description of the property.

(*c*) Check the burdens in the title.

(*d*) If there are burdens in the title, were these referred to in the missives? If there is a right of pre-emption, does it affect the sale to your client? Have all the title conditions been complied with?

(*e*) What is the position with regard to feuduty? Has it been redeemed, and has a receipt been produced?

(*f*) If the property is modern (generally less than 10 years old), is there a superior's certificate as to implementation of feuing conditions? Have they been implemented? Is there an NHBC certificate? Is there a copy of the planning permission and building warrant?

(*g*) If the property is in a tenement, are there rights to *inter alia* the *solum* and are the obligations for maintenance apportioned on an equitable basis and conform to the missives?

(*h*) Check the local authority and, if necessary, water authority, certificates as to the planning position and as to whether the roads, pavements, water supply and main drains are publicly maintained. (In rural areas, this may well not be the case.)

(*j*) Check whether there have been any additions or alterations to the property and if so:

(i) check the planning position;

(ii) check the building warrant and completion certificate;

(iii) check that the superior/neighbouring proprietor(s) have consented, if such consent is required.

(*k*) Check any securities over the property. Have they been discharged?

(*l*) Check the search and, if necessary, the prior search for undischarged securities, etc.

(*m*) Check the position regarding Matrimonial Homes Act evidence.

**34.61 (5) Noting title.** It is normal and good practice to prepare notes on title (a summary of the salient points of each relevant deed in the titles). The property title should be dealt with first; thereafter, in order, the writs referred to for burdens, the security title, and the search. There is no need to repeat every word in every deed. It is always useful, particularly in the case of a deed of conditions in an estate title which is referred to for burdens, to photocopy the burdens section and, where there is a plan, it is helpful to attach a copy of this.

As well as providing confirmation of the sufficiency of the title, notes on title are a valuable record of the title which will be retained in the office once the transaction file is closed and once the title deeds are lodged elsewhere. Particularly if the titles have to be lodged with a building society, it is important that the notes on title are sufficiently full to answer any queries which may be subsequently raised on the title by the client. They provide an initial reference to the title, though if the query is important, you may need to obtain the actual titles. They may be useful also if you are buying or selling another house on the same estate. The notes on title may not be completed until other information is obtained from the seller's solicitor but they should be prepared as the purchaser's solicitor is going through the title.

**34.62 (6) Observations on title.** At the same time as the purchaser's solicitor is examining the title he will also note down any queries he may have and any points on which he wishes further clarification. These should be raised with the seller's solicitor at the same time as the purchaser's solicitor sends the draft disposition for revisal and returns the title deeds. If these observations relate to what may be serious defects in the title or if other information or other writs are necessarily required, then the observations will be raised before the purchaser's solicitor drafts (or can draft) the disposition. There is clearly no point in preparing a conveyance in favour of the purchaser if the validity of the title is in doubt, since, unless this can be rectified, the purchaser will resile from the bargain.

Examining and raising observations on the title require experience to carry out efficiently and selectively; having identified the points in the title on which further information is required, list them in order of importance, and, if certain are of minor if not minimal significance, you may consider that they can safely be ignored. Never, however, ignore points of any significance and do not feel embarrassed by raising them. In your letter to the seller's solicitor, however, rather than listing the points deed by deed, detail them in order of importance. In some cases, the seller's solicitor may consider some of the purchaser's solicitor's requests for information or confirmation less than reasonable; or some of the information sought may be unobtainable or not able to be confirmed (for example, a request to obtain an unrecorded feu charter of 1805 which is referred to for burdens, or a planning permission of 1962). Some degree of practical expediency is necessary when raising observations on title – but without ever compromising your duty as the solicitor acting for a purchaser as to the title being offered. If you overlook or accept something in the title which is incorrect, rest assured that when you are selling the property, a more meticulous conveyancer will raise the point and you will have to resolve it.

A letter raising observations on title should always be courteously phrased whatever you may think about the quality of the conveyanc-}ing offered. There are innumerable ways of requesting information and each letter will be different depending on the circumstances of the transaction.

The seller's solicitor is responsible for the title he is offering. It is up to him to satisfy the purchaser's reasonable doubts and to rectify any curable defects therein. On the other hand, you may wish to suggest a solution rather than leaving it to the seller's solicitor along the following lines: 'We note that' (the flaw) 'and await your comments. We would suggest that this might be rectified by . . .'.

The seller's solicitor should obtain the information, writs, etc., requested and deal with any queries raised: he must satisfy the purchaser's solicitor as to the validity and marketability of the title. If the latter is however satisfied, he then prepares the conveyance in the purchaser's favour.

**34.63 (7) Drafting the disposition.** In most sales, the conveyance to the purchaser is by way of disposition. The disposition is not a feu writ and is prepared by the solicitor acting for the purchaser. A feu writ, however, for example a feu disposition, is prepared by the solicitor acting for the seller/superior and is sent to the solicitor acting for the purchaser/feuar for approval.

Prior to concluding the missives, the purchaser's solicitor should have confirmed with his client the disponee(s) and the destination to be inserted in the disposition.

Over the years every solicitor will acquire his or her own personal set of styles (copies or drafts of deeds required to carry into effect out-of-the-ordinary transactions should always be retained). There are also published style books. In most ordinary cases, however, involving the straightforward conveyance of a whole property, the conveyancer will use the last disposition (in favour of the seller) in the title as a draft and by amending that disposition as necessary will produce the draft disposition in favour of the purchaser. While this is standard and convenient practice, it is also a frequent source of error. For example, if the last disposition describes the property by reference to an earlier deed, say 'by A B Limited in my favour . . .', 'my' is no longer appropriate in your draft.

**34.64 (8) Revisal/approval of seller's drafts.** The purchaser's solicitor will approve or revise the draft letter of obligation; will revise the draft memorandum by checking it against the search and amending it, if necessary, to take account of the purchaser's personal details and building society; and will approve (almost certainly) the draft discharge by comparing it with the standard security. So far as the search is concerned he will also ask for an interim report to be exhibited prior to settlement. If the seller is a limited company a search in the Register of Charges and the company's file will usually be required to be prepared or continued to a date 22 days after the date of recording of the disposition in favour of the purchaser. Certain other safeguards may also be insisted upon by the purchaser's solicitor such as a certificate of solvency by the directors or by a director and the company secretary, or a certificate of non-crystallisation of a floating charge (incorporating a deed of release) if appropriate. See Chapter 35.

The purchaser's solicitor then returns the title deeds to the seller's solicitor along with his draft disposition and the draft letter of obligation, memorandum and discharge all of which have been approved or revised. The purchaser's solicitor should not, if at all possible, accept an obligation which is dependent on his client's title being recorded within a short period after settlement. If, for some reason, the disposition is not recorded within that period, the seller's solicitor is released from his obligation.

### 34.65 The purchaser's loan

**34.66 (1) First stage**. The purchaser's solicitor has in this case (as is usual where building societies are involved) been instructed to act also – in a separate capacity – for the building society. Prior to the offer being made for the house, the purchaser's building society will have confirmed that a loan would be available if the particular property was suitable. The fact that a society is asked to survey a property does not necessarily mean that the purchaser proceeds with the purchase or, if he does so, that he is successful. When missives have been concluded, however, the purchaser or his solicitor will inform the building society that the offer for a particular property (which has been surveyed) has been successful and ask the society to start processing the loan.

The building society will then make an offer of loan (accompanied by the various statutory notices) to the purchaser/borrower, and, either at the same time, or once the offer has been accepted, will instruct the solicitor to act on its behalf in connection with the loan. Every society has slightly different procedures and it is sensible to read the instructions carefully. The client may well be at a loss and come to his solicitor for guidance. The type of loan (capital and interest repayment or endowment or pension-linked) will have been determined. What should be clearly explained are the various forms which accompany the offer of loan and the terms of the offer of loan itself. The purchaser himself will have to find any difference between the amount of the loan and the price of the house, and any deduction or retentions from the loan should be identified at the outset.

When a building society makes a loan, it will base the loan on the value placed on the property by its surveyor, not the price which the purchaser is prepared to pay for it. If, for example, the price offered is …20,000 but the property is valued at only £18,000 by the surveyor, and the loan offered is 90 per cent, then the sum which will be advanced is 90 per cent of £18,000; in other words the purchaser will receive by way of loan £16,200 and not the £18,000 which he might have expected had the value and the price been the same. This is the first point which should be explained to a potential borrower at the stage when you are discussing his general financial position with him.

**34.67 (2) Guarantees**. If a building society is lending more than their normal 75 per cent of valuation, any excess percentage will normally be covered by a single premium guarantee policy taken out by the society with an insurance company. The premium for this policy is paid by the borrower and will normally be deducted from the loan cheque, so that the loan advanced will be less (perhaps by anything up to £1,200) than expected. Some societies charge additional fees (such as acceptance fees) which may be deducted; or deduct the first interest payment from the advance cheque. Check the instructions and advise your client accordingly. There is also likely to be a survey fee payable by the borrower. See also para. 34.30.

**34.68 (3) Repairs**. If the property requires attention (such as the wiring) or if it is new (and, for example, the road has not been completed) the society may retain a proportion of the loan until such time as the condition giving rise to the retention has been satisfied. This can obviously cause financial problems. In the case of remedial work such as rewiring, not only will the purchaser not receive the sum retained until the work has been completed but he will also have to find the necessary cash to have the work done. In other words if (as in the previous example) the society is prepared to lend 90 per cent of the valuation of £18,000 and is then to make a retention of £2,000 to cover rewiring, the initial advance is £14,200 (being the advance of £16,200 less the retention). The purchaser will have to find the balance to complete the purchase on the date of settlement and also sufficient funds to carry out the rewiring before the retention can be released. The purchaser should, of course, be fully aware of those potential difficulties from the survey report and the loan conditions prescribed by the building society in the offer of loan. You should also point out to your client that a modest re-survey fee will be charged and deducted from the retention cheque to confirm that the rewiring has been properly completed. A building society may decide in more minor cases, or in cases where the loan is small in relation to the value of the property, for example a loan of £10,000 on a valuation of £50,000, not to retain any part of the advance (which is more favourable obviously to the borrower) but simply to obtain an undertaking from the borrower that the specified works will be carried out within a specified period having regard to the work required.

**34.69  (4) Acceptance of loan.**   Assuming that the purchaser/borrower is satisfied with the offer of loan, he should sign the acceptance and the duplicate copies of the attached statutory notices and relevant MIRAS forms if appropriate and return them as soon as possible to the society to allow the solicitor's instructions to be issued (if they have not already been issued) and the loan to be processed.

The loan instructions to the solicitor will include details of the society's procedures and blank copies (in duplicate to allow for a draft and a principal copy) of the various forms and other documents required. The loan instructions should be acknowledged and it should be confirmed that you are prepared to act on behalf of the society.

If there is a second loan, the procedures adopted by the lending institution, the borrower and the solicitor are *mutatis mutandis* similar; and details of what documents are required will also be given.

Before completing the security documents, the purchaser's solicitor should however wait until the seller's solicitor has approved and returned the draft disposition in case the latter has made any revisals which would affect the security documents.

**34.70  The disposition approved**
When you as the seller's solicitor receive the letter from the purchaser's solicitor returning the titles and the drafts, and enclosing the draft disposition, you will firstly deal with any queries and obtain any other information, documents or deeds required and send this/these on; and then will approve or revise the draft disposition and return this to the purchaser's solicitor. You will also send a copy of the memorandum for (continuation of) search (if there is one) to the searchers and instruct an interim report, usually brought down to a date shortly before settlement.

The revised memorandum will be retained on the file. The titles and approved/revised draft letter of obligation will be filed away pending settlement, and the approved draft discharge will be engrossed.

The purchaser's solicitor now engrosses the disposition. It will be compared to ensure its accuracy, and a schedule of signing attached. The engrossment, the schedule of signing and the draft 'for comparison and return' will then be sent to the seller's solicitor. The purchaser's solicitor should, however, ensure, before posting the draft and the engrossment, that he has either completed the standard security or has kept a copy of the draft to allow this to be done.

**34.71 (1) Loan – second stage**.  Complete the standard security in draft and have it engrossed; complete, if necessary, the assignation of life policy in draft – even if you do not have the details of the life policy as yet – and have this engrossed, at the same time completing in duplicate the notice of intimation of the assignation which will in due course be given to the assurance company (it is increasingly common for lenders only to require the deposit of the life policy offered in security – see para. 34.55 above); prepare, if this is required, in draft, the personal bond or other agreement regulating the terms of the loan and have this engrossed. These documents (with the exception of the notice intimating the assignation) all require to be signed by the purchaser and, while they can certainly be sent to him for this purpose, it may be sensible to ask him to call at the office. There is no shortage of witnesses there – the signatures will all require to be witnessed – and there may be points about the purchase on which he wishes further information. In any event, it is easier to explain verbally the purpose of the various deeds he is signing and where the signatures should appear than attempt to put this in writing in a letter. If you do have to send deeds out to a client to sign, explain clearly and concisely where the signature has to go and where the witness's signature (if required) has to go; and mark clearly in pencil exactly where each party has to sign. Always enclose a schedule of signing to be completed, even if details are to be given on the deed. Not infrequently, they are omitted there. Always send a stamped addressed envelope for the return of the signed deeds. At this point, if there is a shortfall between the price for the new house and the funds which will be received from the sale of the purchaser's present house and the new loan, it is wise to indicate what funds will be needed to settle and say when the cheque will be required. It is probably easier therefore to invite the client to the office both to sign the security deeds and to deal with settlement arrangements.

**34.72 (2) Signing the deeds**.  When the purchaser arrives for this meeting, the various deeds which he requires to sign should be ready; and his solicitor should be prepared for any explanation which is necessary. He should also have prepared (if this has not already been done) an estimated statement showing the various parts of the transaction from a financial point of view so that the client knows exactly what is required of him. The solicitor will require at settlement the full purchase price, plus or minus any outlays brought out in the state for settlement; and if these funds are not to be available (if the sale of his present house only settles after the purchase, for example) then bridging finance should be arranged, preferably by the client. If bridging finance is requested, an irrevocable mandate will be signed, in duplicate, by the purchaser; and the solicitor will require to confirm to the bank that he will implement the terms thereof when the loan cheque is encashed. If additional funds are to be found by the client, he should be made aware of this and he should be told that his cheque should be in your hands a few days before settlement to allow it to clear, though there is no personal reflection here on his credit rating. You should explain to him that stamp duty (if charged) and the recording/registration dues need to be paid immediately following settlement in order that the conveyance in his favour can be recorded and again you should be in funds to settle this. If a cheque in settlement of the amount of stamp duty and the recording/registration dues is not available, you should not delay stamping and then recording the disposition — especially if a standard security is being granted in favour of a lender. The solicitor also owes a duty of care to the lender if he/she is acting on behalf of the lender.

At the same time, once the security writs have been signed, the purchaser's solicitor will if he is satisfied with the title, confirm to the building society that the title is in order and will request the loan cheque to be made available shortly before the settlement date. Building society loan cheques, if not cashed within a brief period of issue (7 or 14 days), require to be returned for redating to the society. They should not therefore be requested for issue too soon before settlement.

### 34.73 Settlement

**34.74 (1) The seller's part.** When you, as the seller's solicitor, receive the engrossment of the disposition and the draft, you compare the one with the other and return the draft to the purchaser's solicitor. You will then arrange for the seller to sign the disposition and any forms under the Matrimonial Homes Act, if applicable. You may send the engrossment of the disposition to the seller for signature along with the schedule of signing; if so, you will explain clearly what signatures are required (including that of a witness), and enclose a stamped addressed envelope for the return of the signed disposition. Alternatively, you may suggest that the seller comes into your office to sign the deed. Remember to establish that the seller is going to be available to sign – there is nothing worse than a seller disappearing close to settlement, without having signed the necessary deeds. If the seller will be away at the relevant time, it is sensible to have him sign a power of attorney.

You will also engross the discharge (the draft of which was approved by the purchaser's solicitor since it is required to clear the title of the security writ encumbering it) and the retrocession (prepared by you and perhaps checked by another member of the firm) and send these documents to the seller's building society to execute, again accompanied by a schedule of signing. You will also request a note of the amount required to repay the outstanding balance of the loan on the settlement date and will undertake not to release the executed discharge and retrocession until payment of this balance has been made and the loan repaid.

You will prepare a state for settlement in draft, if you have not done so at an earlier stage in the transaction; and send this to the purchaser's solicitor for approval. The draft state will be accompanied by any relevant vouchers. A state for settlement is simply a cash statement of how much the purchaser requires to pay to the seller on the settlement date. The state for settlement will show the purchase price together with any other relevant item such as apportionment of unredeemed feuduty, interest on the price for a period of days, the cost of moveable items separately purchased, etc.

You will also forward the interim report on the search to the purchaser's solicitor when you receive it and at any rate prior to settlement.

When the seller has signed the disposition and the relative schedule of signing has been completed and the seller's building society returns the executed discharge and retrocession (again with a completed schedule of signing), you will complete as necessary the details of execution on the discharge and the retrocession (these are deeds affecting the seller) but will not put a testing clause on the disposition (this is a deed prepared on behalf of the purchaser). You will simply retain the signed disposition and schedule of signing with the titles. You will file the redemption figure for the loan. When the draft state for settlement is returned approved by the purchaser's solicitor, you will retype this if necessary and retain it on the file; you will also have typed the letter of obligation, dated for settlement, and will retain this and the draft on the file. You have arranged with the seller how the purchaser is to get access and where the keys will be. It is sensible for one key to be held by you; but, provided keys are not handed over until the price has been paid, any other suitable arrangements can be made. You may have to advise the seller on how to deal with services, such as gas and electricity. You are, however, at this stage now in a position to await the date of settlement.

**34.75 (2) The purchaser's part.** The purchaser has signed the security writs and these have been attested. The purchaser's solicitor has:

(*a*) requisitioned the building society loan cheque;

(*b*) instructed his client to let him have a cheque for any balance of price necessary (including outlays such as stamp duty) or has arranged for bridging finance to be available;

(*c*) approved the interim report sent to him by the seller's solicitor (he should examine the interim report carefully with particular reference to any entries in the Personal Register against the seller, and, if the purchaser is obtaining a loan, against the purchaser); and

(*d*) approved/revised and returned the draft state for settlement and supporting vouchers, if any.

He also is (or will be) in a position to settle. It is courteous, however, to confirm to the seller's solicitor that he is in funds and is in a position to settle.

Some days before settlement, he will confirm that the client's cheque has been received and banked. He will make the necessary arrangements with the seller's solicitor as to when settlement will take place. He will ensure that the loan cheque when it arrives is also banked on the day of settlement.

**34.76 (3) Procedure on settlement.** Settlements can be carried out by post or personally. The only difference is that, in the case of a postal settlement, arrangements have to be made to ensure that a signed cheque is on the desk of the seller's solicitor and the various documents, *etc.* (and keys) are on the desk of the purchaser's solicitor. So far as personal settlement is concerned, the arrangements will have been made by telephone, probably the same day, or some days before; the normal rule is that the purchaser's solicitor goes to the seller's solicitor. The purchaser often wishes settlement to take place early so that the removal can be got underway – especially if the purchaser is to be selling his existing house on the same day!

All the purchaser's solicitor requires is a signed cheque drawn on his client account and made out in favour of the seller's solicitor for the amount brought out in the state for settlement (the price plus or minus any outlays or apportionments). Remember to check the amount and to ensure that the cheque is signed. Before drawing this cheque, the purchaser's solicitor will have encashed (possibly some days before) any cheque from the purchaser to ensure that it is met; and, on the morning of settlement but not before, any bank cheque in respect of a bridging loan and the building society loan cheque. He will check (again), before he encashes the loan cheque, that the borrower/purchaser has signed the security writs. He should satisfy himself that he is in funds to settle before he draws the cheque in favour of the seller's solicitor. Particular care should be taken if a cheque in settlement of the purchase price is to be held as undelivered. It is not normally necessary for a solicitor to have specific consent to release a cheque since by the drawing and issuing of the general client cheque, a solicitor has given control of the transaction to the selling solicitor. If a cheque is to be held as undelivered, this should be clearly referred to either in the missives or in a subsequent exchange of correspondence.

In exchange for the cheque, the seller's solicitor will hand over:

(a) the disposition, signed by the seller, and the schedule of signing; the signatures and the schedule should be checked;

(b) the title deeds falling to be delivered;

(c) the executed discharge of the seller's loan; this will have been attested and completed by the seller's solicitor who will also have signed the warrant of registration. It will have attached to it a standard form of letter to the Keeper signed by the seller's solicitor and the selling solicitor's cheque for the appropriate recording dues payable to the Registers of Scotland. In some cases, the seller's solicitor retains the executed discharge, records it and delivers the recorded deed to the purchaser's solicitor in terms of the letter of obligation;

(d) the principal letter of obligation duly subscribed, together with the draft previously approved; check the one against the other there and then just in case the seller's solicitor has omitted any of your revisals;

(e) Matrimonial Homes Act affidavits (if applicable);

(f) feuduty redemption receipts (if available);

(g) non-supersession of missive back letters (if applicable);

(h) a receipted copy of the state for settlement; and

(i) the keys (unless other arrangements have been made), which is all that the purchaser is in fact really interested in!

### 34.77 After settlement

**34.78 (1) The purchaser**. Immediately following settlement, both the purchaser's solicitor and the seller's solicitor have a number of matters which should be attended to without delay.

The purchaser's solicitor will advise his client that settlement has now taken place; he will hand him the keys (if he received them at settlement) and will tell him that the removal vans can now roll, that he can start redecoration or digging up the garden if he wishes.

He will then prepare the testing clause for the disposition and type it on to the draft; after checking he will insert it on to the disposition; the deed will be stitched up or bound as the case may be, and he will sign the warrant of registration. He will (if he has not done so already) complete the testing clause on the standard security in favour of the purchaser's building society; and will sign the warrant of registration.

He will stamp or type (if this has not been done before) the name and address of his firm together with his firm's FAS Number for recording purposes on the bottom segment of the backing of both deeds so that they will be returned to the correct address. He will then complete and sign the standard form of letter to the Keeper, keeping a copy of this on the file, and the original will be attached to the disposition and the standard security along with a cheque for the appropriate recording dues payable to the Registers of Scotland. A computerised printed receipt is returned to the presenting agent as evidence of the provisional date of recording.

He will, if necessary, arrange for the disposition to be stamped, by sending it with the appropriate cheque and completed form Stamps 61 (Scotland) to the Controller of Stamps, 16 Picardy Place, Edinburgh. Thereafter, on its return he will send to the Keeper at Meadowbank House, Edinburgh, the disposition and standard security, accompanied by the relative Keeper's letter along with a cheque for the appropriate recording dues payable to the Registers of Scotland and the discharge of the seller's loan, accompanied by its Keeper's letter and the selling solicitor's cheque for the appropriate recording dues payable to the Registers of Scotland for the discharge. He will (if this has not already been done) complete the testing clause on the assignation of the life policy. He will prepare a notice of intimation of this assignation in duplicate and will, with a covering letter, send both copies to the head office of the life company which issued the policy. When the duplicate copy is returned endorsed with the life company's acknowledgement of the intimation, this should be placed with the assignation and the life policy being assigned and included with the title deeds of the property.

He will, if requested, advise the building society that the loan cheque has been encashed and the advance made, by returning the completion form duly completed.

He will cancel any temporary insurance cover taken out at the time missives were concluded. If a building society is involved, permanent property insurance will be arranged by the society. If the purchaser is buying from his own resources, a permanent property insurance should be arranged immediately.

He will pass the receipted state for settlement to the cash room.

He will file the letter of obligation, in accordance with office practice. It is not normally a good idea to file letters of obligation on a correspondence file since they may be overlooked there, but to file them on a separate 'Obligations' file where they can be reviewed at regular intervals.

He will then prepare a statement of the outlays incurred in connection with the purchase and loan, which will include his fee, and will either write to the purchaser for payment or, if he has requested payment in advance of settlement, will simply account to the purchaser. It is good practice to keep your client informed at all times, to advise him of the cost of whatever transaction he is involved in and to recover from him any outlays, such as stamp duty, before they are incurred. Otherwise the firm will effectively be lending the client the money. It is also good practice to render a statement of account before the date of entry or as soon as possible after the purchase has been settled. In any event, such a statement of account or a fee note must be rendered to the client either before or at the same time as the fees are debited.

He will, if the building society requires this, make an inventory and send to the society the title deeds which have been delivered to him. Most building societies, however, prefer that this be done only when the borrower's title – the disposition – and the standard security are returned duly recorded from the Scottish Record Office.

Finally, he will check through his file to confirm that everything which should have been done has been done; and he will note in his diary the appropriate dates on which the deeds at the Scottish Record Office should be returned and the search, etc., should be delivered. The golden rule, for both the purchaser's solicitor and the seller's solicitor, at this stage in any transaction, is to leave no loose ends in a file.

**34.79 (2) The seller.** Immediately following settlement, you as the seller's solicitor will cash the purchase cheque and will repay the outstanding balance of the seller's building society loan on the basis of the statement which was requested earlier. In due course the society will send the seller direct a statement of the mortgage account down to its close. The society will cancel the property insurance charged to the seller and will refund any balance of the premium due; further, if the seller only recently bought the house and a single premium guarantee policy was taken out by the building society, a proportion of this may also be repaid.

You should also intimate the change of ownership to the appropriate As-sessor giving details of the date of settlement, the purchaser and the purchaser's solicitor. For further information on the Council Tax, see Appendix C.

You will return any titles you have borrowed from other solicitors, and will, if you have not already done so, settle their lending fee.

You will ensure that you or the seller cancels any banker's orders or other debits in respect of monthly mortgage payments, etc.

You will prepare a notice of intimation of the retrocession (or reassignation or notice of release) of the life policy and will intimate this in duplicate to the life company which issued the policy, ensuring that the company are aware that the beneficial interest under the policy has reverted to the seller as the life assured. When the duplicate notice is returned, you will put it with the retrocession, the original assignation and the life policy. Note that the life policy and the associated documents (the assignation and the duplicate notice of intimation) are not part of the title so far as the purchaser is concerned but will have been retained by the seller's solicitor. They will also be required in the fullness of time when the policy matures and must be retained with the policy.

You will, if necessary, serve a notice of change of ownership on the superiors. You will also advise any factors of the change of ownership.

If the feuduty has not been and requires to be redeemed, you will arrange for this to be done and the receipt to be delivered to the purchaser's solicitor (no doubt in terms of the letter of obligation). If the feuduty was unallocated and apportioned in the state for settlement, you will serve a notice of change of ownership on the superior in the statutory form with the 25p fee. Some solicitors send a notice, whether the feuduty is redeemed or not.

You will then prepare a statement of outlays and your fee. If you have money in hand, it is necessary for you under the accounts rules to seek your client's approval before deducting the fee and outlays from the balance, leaving a net balance to be forwarded to the client, or as he may direct, or in response to a mandate, e.g. to a bank. If the client (for some reason) wants the full proceeds to be sent to him without first deducting the fee, you should retain sufficient to cover the outlays, and should ensure that the note of fee is submitted at the earliest possible moment.

You will pay any outlays which remain outstanding, for example, search dues or advertising accounts. Finally, you will check through your file once again to ensure that everything has been dealt with and that there are no loose ends.

### 34.80 Final stages

The final stages of a transaction take some time to complete. The process of recording deeds normally takes about three months. The production of an updated search takes approximately nine to twelve months. Some three to four months after the purchaser's solicitor sent the disposition, the standard security and the discharge to Register House, he will have returned to him duly recorded the disposition and the standard security (these being the two writs for which he was responsible and which were prepared by his firm). At that time, the seller's solicitor will have returned to him the duly recorded discharge, this deed having been prepared by his firm.

The letter of obligation granted by the seller's solicitor at settlement will in this case have provided for delivery of a 'duly recorded discharge'. The seller's solicitor now sends the purchaser's solicitor the duly recorded discharge 'in part implement of the letter of obligation ...'.

It is usual at this stage (if not earlier) if a loan is involved – but the building society instructions should have been checked – to forward the title deeds to the building society, when the disposition and standard security have been recorded. They should be listed in triplicate on the form provided and forwarded to the society.

Any other matters referred to in the letter of obligation will be dealt with as for the recorded discharge, but normally the only remaining matter concerns the search. When the memorandum for (continuation of) search was sent to the searchers before settlement, only an interim report could be supplied since the deeds to be included in the completed search had not at that stage been recorded. The process of recording may take three or four months and it is normal for a further period of three to six months to elapse before the search is completed by the searchers in accordance with the instructions in the memorandum. When this has been done, however, it is returned to the seller's solicitor who instructed it. He then passes it on to the purchaser's solicitor – and encloses for reference the draft memorandum (if he can still find it!) which was approved/revised by the purchaser's solicitor so many months before – 'in final implement of our letter of obligation ...'. If the search is in accordance with the memorandum, the purchaser's solicitor accepts it and returns the draft memorandum together with the letter of obligation marked as having been 'finally implemented'.

The reason for keeping a diary of dates when matters such as delivery of a discharge or search should take place, or placing letters of obligation (both incoming from other solicitors and those granted by your firm) on a separate file where they can be easily and regularly reviewed, is to avoid problems which may be caused by dilatoriness or forgetfulness in completing the final stages of a transaction. Indeed, with most missives now specifying varying periods during which they are to remain in full force and effect, it is essential that important dates are noted. If not, the purchaser can find himself without any recourse against the seller – although he probably may still have a justifiable complaint against his own solicitor.

So far as the seller's solicitor is concerned, when his letter of obligation is returned to him, the transaction is, finally, closed. The purchaser's solicitor will send the search on to his client's building society and when this is acknowledged he too can finally close his file ... always assuming of course that his fee has been paid!

### 34.81 Solicitors (Scotland) Practice Rules 1986
In the light of the comment in Chapter 34.1 on conflict of interest, these Rules are reproduced here for ease of reference.

**1.** (1) These rules may be cited as the Solicitors (Scotland) Practice Rules 1986.

(2) These Rules shall come into operation with respect to transactions commenced on or after 1 January 1987.

**2.** (1) In these Rules, unless the context otherwise requires:

'the Act' means the Solicitors (Scotland) Act 1980;

'client' includes the prospective client;

'Council' means the Council of the Society;

'established client' means a person for whom a solicitor or his firm has acted on at least one previous occasion;

'employed solicitor' means a solicitor employed by his employer for the purpose, wholly or partly, of offering legal services to the public whether or not for a fee;

'firm' includes any office at which that firm carries on practice and any firm in which that firm has a direct interest through one or more of its partners, or members;

'the Society' means the Law Society of Scotland established under the Act;

'solicitor' means a solicitor holding a practising certificate under the Act, or an incorporated practice;

'transaction' includes a contract and any negotiations leading thereto.

(2) The Interpretation Act 1978 applies to the interpretation of these Rules as it applies to the interpretation of an Act of Parliament.

**3.** A solicitor shall not act for two or more parties whose interests conflict.

**4.** Without prejudice to the generality of Rule 3 hereof an employed solicitor whose only or principal employer is one of the parties to a transaction shall not act for any other party to that transaction; provided always that such solicitor may, where no dispute arises or appears likely to arise between the parties to that transaction, act for more than one party thereto, if and only if:

(*a*) the parties are associated companies, public authorities, public bodies, or government departments or agencies;

(*b*) the parties are connected one with the other within the meaning of section 533 of the Income and Corporation Taxes Act 1970.

**5.** (1) Without prejudice to the generality of Rule 3 hereof, a solicitor, or two or more solicitors practising either as principal or employee in the same firm or in the employment of the same employer, shall not at any stage, act for both seller and purchaser in the sale or purchase or conveyance of heritable property, or for both landlord and tenant, or assignor and assignee in a lease of heritable property for value or for lender and borrower in a loan to be secured over heritable property; provided, however, that where no dispute arises or might reasonably be expected to arise between the parties and that, other than in the case of exception (a) hereto, the seller or landlord of residential property is not a builder or developer, this rule shall not apply if:

(*a*) the parties are associated companies, public authorities, public bodies, or Government Departments or Agencies;

(*b*) the parties are connected one with the other within the meaning of section 533 of the Income and Corporation Taxes Act 1970;

(*c*) the parties are related by blood, adoption or marriage, one to the other, or the purchaser, tenant, assignee or borrower is so related to an established client; or

(*d*) both parties are established clients or the prospective purchaser, tenant, assignee or borrower is an established client; or

(*e*) there is no other solicitor in the vicinity whom the client could reasonably be expected to consult; or

(*f*) in the case of a loan to be secured over heritable property, the terms of the loan have been agreed between the parties before the solicitor has been instructed to act for the lender, and the granting of the security is only to give effect to such agreement.

(2) In all cases falling within exceptions (*c*), (*d*) and (*e*) both parties shall be advised by the solicitor at the earliest practicable opportunity that the solicitor, or his firm, has been requested to act for both parties, and that if a dispute arises, they or one of them will require to consult an independent solicitor or solicitors, which advice shall be confirmed by the solicitor in writing as soon as may be practicable thereafter.

**6.** A solicitor shall unless the contrary be proved be presumed for the purposes of Rules 4 and 5 hereof to be acting for a party for whom he prepares an offer whether complete or not, in connection with a transaction of any kind specified in these Rules, for execution by that party.

**7.** A solicitor acting on behalf of a party or prospective party to a transaction of any kind specified in Rule 5 hereof shall not issue any deed, writ, missive or other document requiring the signature of another party or prospective party to him without informing that party in writing that:

(*a*) such signature may have certain legal consequences, and

(*b*) he should seek independent legal advice before signature.

**8.** Where a solicitor, or two or more solicitors practising as principal or employee in the same firm or in the employment of the same employer, knowingly intends or intend to act on behalf of two or more prospective purchasers or tenants (other than prospective joint purchasers or tenants) of heritable property (in this Rule referred to as 'the clients'), the clients shall be informed of such intention, and a single solicitor shall not, where he has given any advice to one of the clients with respect to the price or rent to be offered, or with respect to any other material condition of the prospective bargain, give advice to another of the clients in respect of such matters.

**9.** The Council shall have power to waive any of the provisions of these Rules in any particular circumstances or case.

**10.** Breach of any of these Rules may be treated as professional misconduct for the purposes of Part IV of the Act (Complaints and Disciplinary Proceedings).

# Chapter 35

# TRANSACTIONS WITH COMPANIES

## 35.1 General

Transactions with incorporated companies, including most commonly companies incorporated under the Companies Act 1985 and earlier Companies Acts, produce special problems. Some of these have been mentioned in earlier chapters; and, to some extent, the material in this chapter repeats what has gone before. The purpose of this chapter is to collect together and deal with, in one chapter, the main problems which the practitioner should be aware of when dealing with a company, on the sale or purchase of heritable property in particular and in certain other situations.

## 35.2 Foreign companies

The material in this chapter relates to companies incorporated under the Companies Acts and having their registered office either in Scotland or in England and Wales. Increasingly, in practice, practitioners find themselves dealing with companies registered abroad, particularly in tax havens. To a limited extent, some provision is made for such companies in UK statutes referred to later in this chapter; but, generally speaking, when dealing with a company registered outwith Scotland, England and Wales, advice should be sought from a lawyer in the country in which the company is registered, because the rules which apply to that company may well be different from the rules which would otherwise apply if the company were registered in Great Britain.

## 35.3 Company name

See Halliday's *Practice* 4–04.

As Halliday points out, it is peculiarly important that deeds granted by or in favour of an incorporated company should state the name of the company precisely as rendered in its certificate of incorporation or certificate of incorporation on change of name. The separate legal persona created on the incorporation of a company exists only in the company whose name is so registered. Accordingly, a deed granted by or in favour of a company whose name is not correctly and exactly reproduced is, in effect, a nullity. To this strict rule there are very limited exceptions. The abbreviation of the word 'Company' to 'Co.' has been held in England not to invalidate the document at common law – see *Banque de L'Indochine etc.* [1981] 3 All ER 198. But, in the case of a company called 'L & R Agencies Limited', an English court held that a document in which the '&' was omitted did not reproduce the company name correctly, which underlines the need for exactitude (*Jenice Ltd.* [1994] BCC 43).

If, in terms of the Companies Act 1985 s. 36B, a company chooses to have a common seal, the name of the company must be engraved on it. It is

594

thought that the name of the company must be rendered exactly correctly on the seal to comply with this direction; but the same special exceptions to the rule may apply also to the seal.

In the case of heritable titles, these rules may suffer some qualification in the case of foundation and earlier writs in the progress which may not be invalidated by the use of the wrong name because, in order to check whether or not the correct name has been used, extrinsic enquiry beyond the four corners of the deed is necessary, and that is excluded by the positive prescription.

## 35.4 Capacity

This has already been fairly fully dealt with in Chapter 3, to which reference is made. See also Halliday's *Practice* 2–100 (2nd edn. 2–116 *et seq.*).

In the ordinary case of sale and purchase under the Companies Act 1985, capacity did not normally present any problem because the company, in the objects clause in its memorandum of association, would almost invariably have the power to sell or purchase heritable property or borrow on the security thereof; under the Companies Act 1989 (introducing a new 1985 Act s. 35) the capacity of the company is not to be permitted to be called into question by reason of any limitation imposed in the memorandum. Non-observance of any limitations imposed in the memorandum can now only result in liability on the directors. As far as the power of the directors to bind the company was concerned, at least in a question with a person dealing with the company in good faith, prior to the 1989 Act, any transaction decided on by the directors was deemed to be one within the capacity of the company and there was no duty on the other party to make enquiry as to whether or not this was so. See the Companies Act 1985 s. 35 Under s. 35A and s. 35B (introduced in the 1989 Companies Act), the difficulties encountered with the *ultra vires* rule and the authority of a director to bind the company under the 1985 Act have been further ameliorated, at least as far as the duty of the third party to investigate the authority of directors is concerned. The third party is now presumed to be dealing in good faith (s. 35A(2)(c)). This presumption is not negated by a failure to investigate the powers of the directors, nor by actual knowledge of limitation on their powers (s. 35B).

For reasons later explained, the same applies in the case of an administrator.

Where a receiver has been appointed, he has statutory powers which cover sale, trading and borrowing on security. The liquidator, in a winding up, has statutory powers of sale and borrowing on security, but his power to continue trading is restricted.

Care must however be taken when dealing, not with companies, but with other bodies corporate not incorporated under the Companies Acts, to whom the *ultra vires* rule continues to apply. In *Piggins & Rix* 1995 SLT 418, the question arose as to whether the Montrose Port Authority had power to sell land which was surplus to requirements. In a special case presented to the Court, the answer was negative, although it was mentioned, *obiter*, that the Port Authority may have the power to grant long leases.

## 35.5 Execution of deeds

See Halliday's *Practice* 3–10 (2nd edn. 3–117).

The execution of deeds by companies has already been dealt with fairly fully in Chapter 2 and as was mentioned there, the Requirements of Writing (Scotland) Act 1995 refers to the execution of deeds by companies. The situation can be summarised thus.

(1) If executed on or before 30 July 1990 when the company is still a going concern, the execution of a deed intended to be probative should follow the provisions of the Companies Act 1985 s. 36(3). This required the affixing of the common seal of the company and the signatures of two directors or a director and the secretary on the last page of the deed and on the last page of each schedule or other addendum.

On 31 July 1989 the 1985 Act s. 36 was replaced by a new s. 36B in the Companies Act 1989. That section was not satisfactory and was in turn replaced on 1 December 1990, but with retrospective effect as from 31 July by the Law Reform (Miscellaneous Provisions) (Scotland) Act 1990 s. 72. The requirement under s. 36B is execution by two directors, or one director and the secretary, or by two persons authorised by the company to subscribe. In each case, witnesses are unnecessary and the deed need not be sealed. A deed so executed is probative. For more comment and for details of the probativity of deeds signed by a company under the Requirements of Writing (Scotland) Act 1995, see Chapter 2.21. For deeds executed on or after 1 August 1995, see Chapter 21.52).

For the execution of deeds by a foreign company on or after 16 May 1994, see the Foreign Companies (Execution of Documents) Regulations 1994 which provide that a foreign company may execute a deed by the subscription of two directors; by the subscription of a director and the secretary; or by the subscription of one person authorised to subscribe the document on behalf of the company.

(2) When a company is in liquidation, or a receiver or administrator has been appointed, the best view is that the deed runs in name of the company and of the liquidator, receiver or administrator, with a statement in the narrative, giving details of the liquidation or appointment of a receiver or administrator as the case may be following the style approved in *Liquidator of Style & Mantle Ltd.* 1934 SC 548. Given that the title remains vested in the company, it is not clear whether the liquidator, receiver or administrator need be, as co-grantor, conjoined in the deed, but this is standard practice. It rests on the argument that he is the person entitled to administer the estate.

The deed is signed by the liquidator, receiver or administrator as the case may be on the last page; and, in each case, the signature required attestation by two witnesses. The Requirements of Writing (Scotland) Act 1995 now requires that subscription need only be in front of one witness. For the same reason as stated above, some agents require the liquidator, receiver or administrator, as the case may be, to sign the deed twice, representing his dual capacity; although, again, it is doubtful if this is necessary. Any deed so executed before 31 July 1990 also required the common seal of the company; but, under s. 36B above referred to, a company no longer requires a common seal and accordingly sealing of the deed on or after 31 July 1990 is unnecessary in all cases.

## 35.6 Purchase of heritable property from a company as a going concern

This transaction is dealt with first because it is the transaction which causes most problems to practitioners.

It is well known that certain types of company, especially building and property development companies, are particularly vulnerable, and frequently go into liquidation or have an administrator or receiver appointed, in many cases with little or no warning.

The same fate may, of course, overtake an individual or a firm or partnership. Any of these may become insolvent; and may be sequestrated or have a judicial factor appointed.

## 35.7 (1) Floating charges.

The particular risk involved in dealing with a company arises out of the facility available to a company to grant a floating charge over the whole or certain specified assets, a facility which is not, of course, available to individuals or firms. The danger which the floating charge presents is that it can immediately become a fixed security on all the assets covered by the charge without prior notification and, in particular, without any entry appearing either in the Companies Register, the Register of Charges, or the Personal Register. This automatic conversion into a fixed security occurs immediately upon the liquidation of a company or on the appointment of a receiver in respect of the assets included in the charge. In practice, a floating charge normally extends to the whole assets of the company; but it may be restricted. The appointment of an administrator does not have the same effect. Admittedly, there are statutory provisions requiring notification of the liquidation or the appointment of a receiver or administrator in the Register of Charges and elsewhere; but the validity of the fixed security created immediately upon liquidation or on the appointment of a receiver is not dependent on such notification, and it is not affected by failure to register the appropriate information with the Registrar of Companies or to publish it in the Gazette or public press. A floating charge may also automatically crystallise on the happening of particular events as specified in the instrument of charge; and in that case notice of crystallisation must be lodged with the Registrar. For more details see Chapter 23. For an illustration of an automatic crystallisation, by special extra provision in the deed itself, subsequently followed by the appointment of a receiver, see *Norfolk House plc* 1992 SLT 235. It was held in the special circumstances of this case that the Insolvency Act 1986 s. 72, which deals with the cross-border operation of receiverships, was intended to bridge the transaction from the creation of the charge to the appointment of the receiver, to ensure that he could exercise his powers under the Act. It is also possible for a company to grant more than one security – for example, a floating charge and a fixed security. In these circumstances an agreement determining the order of ranking will be required. *AIB Finance Ltd.* 1995 SLT 2 involved a dispute as to ranking between a heritable creditor holding a fixed security and a creditor holding a floating charge. The ranking agreement failed in its purpose because of inept drafting.

A floating charge, when created, must be registered in the Register of Charges within 21 days after the date of its creation, with limited exceptions for charges created outwith the UK. Failure to register within the time-limit originally invalidated the charge. But, provided the floating charge is registered within that time limit, it takes effect from its date, not from the date of registration. Further, the Companies Act 1985 s. 462(5) expressly provides that the charge is fully effective, both as a floating charge and as a fixed security, notwithstanding that the deed creating it is not recorded in Sasines. In the result, at the date of settlement of a transaction with a company, there may be in existence an effective charge which has already become a fixed security on the heritable property in question without any official notification of these facts in any public register. Further, a charge which is still floating at settlement may, immediately thereafter, become a fixed security on the property, even after delivery of the disposition thereof to the purchaser against payment of the price. Prior to the decision of the House of Lords in *Sharp* v. *Woolwich Building Society* 1997 SLT (HL) 636 (previously referred to as *Sharp* v. *Thomson*) it was considered that this would apply even after delivery of the disposition to the purchaser against payment of the price. In *Sharp* a company signed and delivered a disposition to a purchaser. The disposition was recorded in the General Register of Sasines 12 days later. The day after the delivery of the disposition to the purchaser, a receiver was appointed to the company. The Court of Session held that the property remained vested in the company as the delivery of the disposition did not transfer property in land. Transfer of property occurred only when the disposition was recorded. However, the House of Lords reversed the decision and held that in receivership, on delivery of the disposition, the purchaser acquires a beneficial interest in the property which consequently no longer forms part of the property and undertaking of the company and thus will not be attached on crystallisation of the charge. For a discussion of the implications of the case, see Professor K. G. C. Reid, 'Jam Today: *Sharp* in the House of Lords' 1997 SLT 79. Under the Companies Act 1989 s. 95, the introduction of a new 1985 Act s. 400 was proposed where provision was made for the late registration of charges outwith the 21-day time-limit above referred to but subject to provisions which effectively protect anyone dealing with the company on the faith of the Register of Charges. Again, for more details see Chapter 23. This section is still not in force, and the indications are that it is unlikely that it will come into force without amendment.

**35.8 (2) Methods of protecting the purchaser**.  In the ordinary case, when purchasing heritage from a company as a going concern, the problems outlined above may be dealt with as suggested below.

**35.9** (*a*) *Power of sale*.  There are two possible limitations on the power of sale:

> (i) Improbably, but just conceivably, the company does not have power of sale in the objects clause of its memorandum of association. Some agents prefer to establish that the company has this power by examining the memorandum; but in practice, except in very unusual circumstances, a *bona fide* purchaser for value was fully protected by the Companies Act 1985 s. 35.
>
> From 16 November 1989 under the Companies Act 1985 s. 35 (introduced by the Companies Act 1989 s. 108), the validity of an act done by a company cannot be called into question on the ground of lack of capacity by reason of anything in the company's memorandum. This is discussed in more depth above.

(ii) If the company has granted a floating charge, it is perfectly competent and commonplace expressly to provide in the instrument of charge that the company will grant no other floating charge and no fixed security ranking prior to or *pari passu* with the floating charge itself. Occasionally, this provision goes further and prohibits the granting of any security, whether prior or postponed. Finally, some lending institutions include in their standard form of floating charge an absolute prohibition against disposal of any asset without the consent of the creditor.

**35.10** (*b*) *The 'floating' characteristics of a floating charge.* The whole essence of a floating charge is that property owned by a company 'floats out' of the charge on disposal and so, in the ordinary way, when purchasing from a company, the purchaser has no concern with the terms of a floating charge because, once disposed of, the charge no longer affects that property. So, Halliday's *Practice* at 21–87 states that, in strict theory, it is unnecessary to search the Register of Charges in the case of an outright sale, on the footing that a floating charge of its nature does not prevent the company from selling its heritable property. But he then points out that sale of a property may be an event which would precipitate the appointment of a receiver, and so convert the floating charge into a fixed security with possible adverse consequences.

Whether or not an absolute bar on disposal without the creditor's consent could in any circumstances affect a purchaser is doubtful; but conceivably an argument might be developed along the lines of the 'duty of enquiry' rule, as laid down in *Rodger (Builders) Ltd.* 1950 SC 482, on the footing that, since the charge is registered, a purchaser by implication is deemed to have notice of its terms and should therefore have enquired as to whether or not the creditor had consented to the sale. Against that, such an absolute prohibition in a floating charge can only be, in its nature, a personal contract between the creditor and the debtor therein, and on general principle should not be capable of affecting singular successors.

Clearly, however, to avoid future challenge, the best advice is to obtain the consent of the creditor.

**35.11** (*c*) *Title.* Apart from the situation outlined above where the floating charge totally excludes any disposal without consent, the existence of a floating charge does not of itself affect the title of the company to dispone. Accordingly, in the ordinary way, the selling company will grant a disposition in favour of the purchaser, without requiring any consent *in gremio*. On recording, the disposition will perfect the real right of the purchaser and give him a valid and marketable title free and disencumbered of the charge.

To ensure a marketable title as in other situations, all fixed securities, *e.g.* standard securities, etc., outstanding at the date of sale must either be discharged or restricted in order to release the part sold. This presents no particular difficulty and no specialties, as compared with taking a title from an individual.

**35.12** (*d*) *Risks inherent in floating charges.* In the case of floating charges, however, there are serious risks involved, against which precautions must be taken. The risks are that the company may go into liquidation before the transaction has settled, without the purchaser knowing anything about it; a receiver may be appointed; or similarly, one of the events as specified in the instrument of charge may have occurred. See *Norfolk House plc* above. In any event, when the disposition is delivered to the purchaser, the charge will already have become a fixed security and therefore the purchaser's title is burdened therewith. Further, until the disposition in favour of the purchaser is recorded, the company is arguably not finally divested. Therefore, liquidation or the appointment of a receiver even after settlement but before recording may create a fixed security on the property in the hands of the purchaser. When the disposition is delivered to the purchaser, the property will no longer form part of the property and undertaking of the company, and so on receivership a floating charge will not attach to the property. See *Sharp* above. However, in the case of liquidation or bankruptcy, there could still be a race to the register.

Under the Companies Act 1985 s. 403 (introduced by the Companies Act 1989 s. 98) a memorandum of satisfaction duly delivered to the Registrar of Companies renders the charge void as against a *bona fide* purchaser for value even if, in fact, the charge continues to be effective after the date of such registration. An informal release may also suffice to release the property from the floating charge. In *Scottish and Newcastle Breweries plc* 1994 SLT 1140 an informal letter from the creditor in a floating charge to the solicitors for the company amounted to a release of the properties specified in the letter. The letter did not require to be registered to be valid.

**35.13 (3) Necessary searches**. Searches will therefore be required:

(*a*) In the Property Register, to disclose the existence of any standard security or other fixed security affecting the property.

(*b*) In the Personal Register to disclose any diligence registered against the company, such as an inhibition.

(*c*) In the Companies Register, to disclose whether or not there are floating charges and, if so, whether or not a receiver has been appointed; whether the company has gone into liquidation; and whether the company has been struck off the Register and so ceased to exist.

**35.14** (*a*) *Search in the Companies Register*. In relation to searching in the Companies Register, see the article by Professor G. L. Gretton in 1989 JLS 50. As Professor Gretton points out, each individual company file is divided into three parts containing, separately, the annual return and accounts; general documents; and documents falling to be registered in the Register of Charges which does not exist as a separate self-contained register. Searching one part of the company file will not disclose information contained in another part. So, the general documents part of the company file will disclose liquidations and the like; and the charges section of the file will disclose the existence of floating charges and the appointment of a receiver. Both these sections must be searched to produce all the required information.

Where the title is registered, when a company is selling property, the Keeper relies on the answers given on the application forms; and does not take it on himself to search the Companies Register in order to ascertain the position as to floating charges; as to whether or not a receiver or administrator has been appointed; or whether or not the company has gone into liquidation; or whether or not the company has been struck off the Register. It is therefore entirely up to the agent to make these enquiries for himself by appropriate searches in the Companies Register.

**35.15** (b) *Period of search.* In order to ensure that all the necessary information is disclosed, the search in the Companies Register runs from 27 October 1961 (being the date from which floating charges first became competent in Scotland), or from the date of incorporation of the company if later, up to a date 22 days after the close of the search in the Sasines Register. The reason for the 22-day period is that:

(i) Until the disposition in favour of the purchaser has been duly recorded, the company is not divested. However, when purchasing from a company, the purchaser who has taken delivery of a disposition before the appointment of a receiver to that company under an existing floating charge but, who, for whatever reason, fails to record his disposition until after a receiver has been appointed, nonetheless obtains a personal right and a beneficial interest in the property so purchased which, in these special circumstances, will not be affected by the crystallisation of the floating charge. This creates a special exception to the standard rule above stated. It is thought that the same results will follow in other comparable insolvency situations See *Sharp* 1997 SLT (HL) 636 and the article by Professor Rennie in 1997 JLS 130.

(ii) The holder of a floating charge has 21 days within which to register the charge if it is to be fully valid. If a receiver is then appointed under that charge before the purchaser's disposition is delivered, the special situation referred to in (i) above is not applicable, and the floating charge becomes a fixed security on the property in the hands of the purchaser. The 21-day period might be extended by application to the court under the Companies Act 1985 s. 420, but it is very unlikely that the court would permit an extension of time to the prejudice of a third party purchaser. So, for practical purposes, a period of 22 days after the date of recording suffices.

The Companies Act 1985 s. 399 and s. 400 now allow for late registration of a charge but subject to safeguards which absolutely protect a person who acquires an interest in charged property, in *bona fide* and for value. If the relevant provisions of the 1989 Companies Act come into force, registration may be effected outwith the 21-day period, but again subject to the protection of rights acquired prior to registration (s. 399(2)(b) and 400(1)). See further Chapter 23.

**35.16** (c) *Searches in Property and Personal Registers.* When dealing with an individual and searching in the Property and Personal Registers, there is always a short gap between the closing date of the search and the settlement date during which, possibly, some adverse deed might be delivered or recorded. The purchaser or lender is protected by the seller's letter of obligation. When dealing with a company, a purchaser or lender will also be concerned to ensure that there have been no floating charges registered or receivers appointed prior to the delivery of the disposition. The registration of a floating charge may not show up until 21 days after the delivery of the disposition. Notice of appointment of a receiver should be delivered to the Registrar of Companies for registration within seven days of execution: Insolvency Act 1986 s. 53. Until computerisation of the Presentment Book for Sasines titles was introduced by the Keeper in 1992, there was a very real risk that the seller might record a standard security or other adverse deed during the gap of some months (as it then was) between the date of the close of the search on an interim report in the Property Register and the date of settlement. That risk in the Property Register is now virtually eliminated by computerisation. The Personal Register has always been up to date within 24 hours of close of search. See Chapter 33 for further comment on computerisation. Accordingly, the seller's solicitor can normally safely give an obligation to produce a clear search on behalf of an individual and in so doing does not incur any significant risk.

In the case of a selling company, however, the risks are thought to be greater, and, as a result, most solicitors, particularly when acting for the vulnerable building or development company, specifically provide in their missives that they themselves do not undertake to give a clear search in the Companies Register, and possibly in the other Registers as well.

**35.17 (4) Letter of obligation**. The letter of obligation traditionally granted at settlement undertaking to deliver clear searches in the Sasines and Personal Registers is personally binding on the solicitor who grants it, thereby effectively putting him in the position of a guarantor for the seller. Given computerisation of the Presentment Book and the comment above, the risk to the solicitor acting for a selling company in relation to the Property and Personal Registers is now generally thought to be acceptable; but, because of the special provisions for companies, already dealt with in Chapter 33, the agent acting for the selling company should not commit himself to produce a clear search in the Companies Register or Register of Charges. To ensure that he does not come under such an obligation and that settlement is not delayed on that account, a provision to this effect should be inserted in the missives. But of course the purchaser may not agree to such a provision.

**35.18 (5) Alternative methods of protecting the purchaser**. To protect the purchaser against unforeseen emerging fixed securities resulting from liquidation or the appointment of a receiver following on the granting of a floating charge, two devices are commonly adopted.

(i) The creditor in the floating charge(s) may agree to grant either:

(*a*) a certificate of non-crystallisation, in terms of which, again subject to certain conditions and usually within a fairly short time limit, the creditor undertakes that he will not take any steps to appoint a receiver or to put the company into liquidation. That is binding on the creditor; but it does not protect the purchaser against the possibility of liquidation at the instance of some other party, on which event the floating charge would automatically become a fixed security, notwithstanding the granting of the letter of non-crystallisation. The letter of non-crystallisation remains necessary even after the decision in *Sharp* to protect the purchaser for the period prior to the delivery of the disposition; or

(*b*) a deed of release in terms of which, possibly subject to certain conditions, he formally releases the property from the charge. This is similar to a deed of restriction of a standard security and is the most satisfactory solution because it avoids the risk referred to in (a) above.

Alternatively, an informal letter of release may suffice. See *Scottish & Newcastle Breweries plc*, above.

However, at least when dealing with a receiver, the lending institution who appointed that receiver very often has standard forms and a rigid policy of not departing therefrom. It may not, therefore, be possible to negotiate the protection for the purchaser which the agent would like to obtain.

> (ii) A certificate of solvency. This takes the form of a certificate, granted personally by one or more directors, or by a principal shareholder of the company concerned, warranting that, so far as they are aware, the company is solvent, that no steps have been or are about to be taken to put it into liquidation or to appoint a receiver, and that no floating charge has been granted which does not appear in the search of the Companies Register. The qualification 'so far as aware', though usual, seriously weakens the protection.

At first sight, it might be thought that this is a satisfactory solution to the problem; but such a certificate may well be worthless. In any event, it cannot amount to a release from the security and is at best a personal guarantee by the grantors thereof which, in turn, for its efficacy, depends on the honesty and financial standing of the grantors.

### 35.19 Purchase of heritage from an administrator

On the appointment of an administrator, the company remains a going concern and retains its corporate powers and title to its assets but the powers of directors are taken over by the administrator. The office of administrator has recently been introduced under the new insolvency provisions. The appointment is now dealt with in Part 2 of the Insolvency Act 1986. It involves an application to the court for an administration order. The general effect is that, on the making of an order, the administrator takes over the management of the company in place of its directors. The directors are not, however, removed from office although their powers are suspended during the period of administration. The main purpose of the administration order is to provide machinery to rescue an ailing company; but the order will not be granted unless there is a genuine prospect of success.

The administrator is required to intimate his appointment to the Registrar of Companies within 14 days of the making of the order under the Insolvency Act 1986 s. 21, and to the Keeper for insertion in the Personal Register.

### 35.20 (1) Disclaimer of contracts.

An administrator has no power to disclaim contracts entered into by the company before his appointment and so, even if the administrator is appointed after the property has been sold by the company, the contract is valid and binding. The following comments are therefore equally applicable whether the property was sold by the company before the administrator was appointed or was sold by the administrator himself under his administrative powers.

### 35.21 (2) Powers.

Under the Insolvency Act 1986 Schedule 1, an

administrator has power to sell by private bargain and, thereafter, to grant the necessary deeds. Under the Insolvency Act 1986 s. 14(6), there is a general provision to the effect that a person dealing with an administrator in good faith and for value is not concerned to enquire as to whether the administrator is acting within his powers. Accordingly, a purchaser can safely purchase property from an administrator, relying on these statutory provisions.

**35.22 (3) Title**. The appointment of an administrator has no effect on title; and all the company's assets remain vested in the company.

The question of searches and outstanding securities is less significant than when purchasing from a company as a going concern because, under the 1986 Act s. 15, the administrator has a further power to dispose of property of the company which is subject to a security as if the property were disencumbered. In the case of fixed securities, the consent of the court is required. Secured creditors are protected as against the administrator; but, under s. 14(6), that cannot affect a *bona fide* purchaser. In particular, under s. 16(1), a disposition by an administrator, when recorded, has the effect of disencumbering the property conveyed of all outstanding fixed securities, which of course would include standard securities and floating charges which have become fixed.

**35.23 (4) Moratorium on adverse actions**. Under the 1986 Act s. 11, during the period of administration, no effective resolution can be passed to put the company into liquidation; no steps can be taken to enforce any existing security; and no other proceedings and no diligence may be commenced or continued without consent of the court. The position of a pre-existing inhibition against the company, registered prior to the appointment of the administrator, is not entirely free from doubt but it is thought that, notwithstanding such an inhibition, the administrator has power to sell and to grant an unchallengeable title by virtue of the provisions of the 1986 Act s. 11(3)(*d*) which provides that no diligence may be 'continued' against the company or its property without leave of the court. The language does not fit easily into the concept of the Scottish inhibition but could arguably be interpreted as implying that, in a question with the administrator, the inhibition cannot prevent disposal, although the inhibiting creditor maintains his preference on the proceeds of sale. For the contrary view, see G. L. Gretton, 'Aspects of Insolvency Conveyancing' 1992 JLS 346 at p. 348.

### 35.24 Purchase of heritage from a receiver
If the company has granted a floating charge and if, thereafter, the creditor has appointed a receiver, the resulting position is dealt with in the Insolvency Act 1986 ss. 50–71.

In outline, the position is as follows.

**35.25 (1) Appointment**. Firstly, under s. 51, the holder of the floating charge over all or any property of the company has power to appoint a receiver; or he may apply to the court for such an appointment.

The circumstances justifying that appointment are prescribed in s. 52; and the mode of appointment in s. 53. In particular, under s. 53(7), on the appointment of a receiver, the floating charge attaches to the property included therein and has effect as if the charge was a fixed security over that property. In line with *Sharp*, the charge will not attach to property after delivery of the disposition. The receiver, when subsequently dealing with the property attached by the charge, does not rely on his security as such as conferring any powers, but on express statutory provisions as undernoted.

If the receiver is appointed by the creditor himself as is competent by instrument of appointment, a certified copy of that instrument must be notified to the Registrar of Companies within seven days after its execution under the 1986 Act s. 53(1).

Alternatively, if the receiver is appointed by the court under s. 54, the petitioner applying for the appointment is required to make intimation to the Registrar within the same period under s. 54(3).

**35.26 (2) Disclaimer of contracts**. As in the case of the administrator, the receiver has no power to disclaim contracts entered into by the company prior to his appointment. See the 1986 Act s. 57(4). So, if the company has sold the property prior to the appointment of a receiver he is bound to implement it according to its terms.

**35.27 (3) Powers.** The statutory powers relied on by the receiver are:

(*a*) the powers given to him by the instrument creating the charge; and

(*b*) the powers specified in Schedule 2 to the 1986 Act.

Under s. 55(4) a person dealing with a receiver in good faith and for value is not concerned to enquire whether the receiver is acting within his powers; but the powers do in fact include, under Schedule 2, power to sell or lease the property, power to use the company's seal which is no longer relevant as noted above, and power to grant deeds in name and on behalf of the company to implement the power of sale, etc.

**35.28 (4) Title**. The position as to title is somewhat anomalous. On the appointment of the receiver, the whole assets of the company, whether included in the charge or not, remain vested in the company which retains the title thereto.

The effect of the appointment is to convert the floating charge into a fixed security in terms of s. 53(7); but that section is not apparently intended to confer any titular powers; its purpose is simply to establish a preference. The receiver therefore relies on the powers referred to above which allow him, amongst other things, to deal with and dispose of property belonging to the company and attached by the charge.

The exercise of these powers is subject to the rights of any creditor holding a fixed security or floating charge having priority over the charge in question; and to the rights of any person who has effectually executed diligence on any of the property concerned.

**35.29 (5) Precedence among receivers**. Under the 1986 Act s. 56, if there are two or more floating charges subsisting, a receiver appointed under the prior charge takes priority over a receiver appointed under a postponed charge. In practice, if a receiver is appointed by the holder of a postponed charge, this simply triggers off the appointment of a receiver by the prior creditor so that, for practical purposes, in almost every case, one is dealing with the receiver under the first-ranking floating charge.

In the result, on examining a title, the agent is concerned with any fixed security ranking in priority to the first ranking floating charge and effectually executed diligence. In this context, however, an inhibition registered after the creation of the charge and before the appointment of a receiver but not followed by a decree of adjudication, is not effectually executed diligence and so for practical purposes falls to be ignored. So far as clearing the record is concerned, these statutory provisions produce a similar result to sale by a heritable creditor under a standard security in terms of the 1970 Act, for which see Chapter 22.

**35.30 (6) Consent of creditor or application to the court.** Under s. 61, if property under the control of the receiver is already subject to an effective fixed security or effectually executed diligence, and if the relevant creditor will not give consent, the receiver may apply to the court for authority to sell, and to disburden the property of the security or diligence in question. Where the court has approved of a sale under s. 61(2), the receiver grants to the purchaser or disponee a disposition of the property which, on being recorded, has the effect of disencumbering the property of the security and freeing it from any pre-existing effectual diligence under s. 61(8).

**35.31 (7) Searches.** As a result of these provisions, the position as to searches against the company is, again, of less significance than when a company is a going concern because of the disencumbering effect of the disposition in favour of the purchaser; but searches are, of course, still required, looking to the terms of the 1986 Act s. 61.

## 35.32 Liquidation

The winding-up of a company incorporated under the Companies Acts is now dealt with in ss. 73–219 of the Insolvency Act 1986, with some supplementary provisions in ss. 230–251. No attempt is made here to deal with the detail of the liquidator's appointment but, broadly speaking, there are two general liquidation situations.

(1) Where the company is solvent and the members decide nonetheless to terminate its activities. This is known as a members' voluntary liquidation.

(2) Where the company is insolvent, the company itself or any of its creditors may put the company into liquidation on the footing that it can no longer meet its obligations. In this situation, there are two alternatives: a creditors' voluntary winding-up where the company takes the initiative, passes a special resolution to wind up the company, and appoints a liquidator subject to confirmation by the creditors; or a winding-up by the court. This involves a petition to the Court of Session or the sheriff court in Scotland (High Court or County Court in England) applying for the winding-up of the company. There are technical differences in detail between these various methods of winding-up but, in all cases, a liquidator is appointed; the directors are no longer entitled to exercise any of their powers; the assets of the company remain vested in the company; but the liquidator alone can competently deal with them on behalf of the company. To this rule there is one exception in the case of a winding-up by the court where, under the Insolvency Act 1986 s. 145, in special circumstances, the court, may, on the application of the liquidator, direct that all or any part

of the assets of the company shall vest in the liquidator by his official name. This facility is rarely used.

**35.33 (1) Appointment and powers**. When the property in question belonged to the company at the date of liquidation and is to be sold by the liquidator, the position is relatively straightforward. Statutory powers are conferred on the liquidator by Schedule 4 to the 1986 Act. Certain of these powers require prior sanction. Others, including power to sell and power to execute in name of the company all deeds necessary for that purpose, require no prior sanction. In addition, in Scotland, under the 1986 Act s. 169(2), the liquidator has the same powers as a trustee in sequestration, subject to the rules prescribed in the 1986 Act. This relates principally to the relationship between the liquidator and secured creditors.

In contrast to what is thought to be the position of the administrator and is, by statute, the position of the receiver, a liquidator has at common law and by statute the right either to adopt and implement any contract entered into by the company prior to liquidation or to refuse to implement it, in which case, of course, the other contracting party has a claim for damages against the company but ranks only as an ordinary creditor. This means that, where the company has contracted to sell property prior to the liquidation but the sale has not yet been implemented by delivery of a disposition, the purchaser may or may not lose the benefit of his contract, depending on the decision of the liquidator.

**35.34 (2) Title**. In a sequestration, the appointment of the trustee operates as a general disposition in his favour of all estate, heritable and moveable, so that he takes over all the assets of the bankrupt in his own name. In a liquidation, in contrast, the assets remain vested in the company but the powers of the directors are suspended. Under the 1986 Act s. 145 referred to above, the liquidator may apply for a vesting order; and that would operate as a general disposition in his favour as an individual.

**35.35 (3) Fixed securities**. Liquidation has no direct effect on pre-existing fixed securities such as a standard security validly granted by the company and duly recorded and registered unless the same is cut down as an unfair preference. Further, on liquidation, any floating charge validly granted by the company and duly registered automatically becomes a fixed security, thereby securing a preference for the benefit of the holder of the charge.

Under the 1986 Act s. 185, which applies generally to all forms of winding up in Scotland, the Bankruptcy (Scotland) Act 1985 s. 37(1) to (6) and s. 39(3), (4), (7) and (8) are applied, *mutatis mutandis*, as they apply to a sequestration. The position generally speaking is as follows.

(*a*) If the liquidator is able to sell the property at a price more than sufficient to cover all securities on the property, then he is empowered to proceed with a sale without the consent of the secured creditors although they, of course, have a preference on the proceeds.

(*b*) If the liquidator intimates to a secured creditor that he intends to sell, that prevents the creditor from taking steps to enforce his security.

(*c*) Conversely, if a secured creditor has intimated to the liquidator that the creditor intends to embark on sale procedure under his power of sale, the liquidator is precluded from selling that asset.

Accordingly, in such cases, if the liquidator sells, existing securities will be discharged in the ordinary way; or, if a secured creditor sells, the sale will proceed under his statutory powers.

There is no equivalent provision in the Insolvency Act 1986 which would disencumber property of pre-existing securities if sold by a liquidator and this can cause problems.

In so far as diligence is concerned, there still seems to be some doubt as to whether or not an inhibition registered against the company prior to liquidation is effective to prevent disposal of heritable property in Scotland or not. See G. L. Gretton on *Inhibition* (2nd edn.) p. 174.

### 35.36  Second securities by companies

In the case of an individual, the granting of a second security is relatively straightforward. All that is required is a search in the Property Register and in the Personal Register to see what securities have already been recorded in Sasines and whether or not the debtor is under effective diligence, such as an inhibition. Because an individual cannot have granted a floating charge, there are no complicating factors. The position therefore is very similar to the position on purchase of heritage from a selling proprietor.

In the case of companies, however, again because of the floating charge facility, the position is more complex, whether a company is granting a first fixed security or a second or subsequent fixed security. The reason is that, if a company has granted a floating charge, a subsequent fixed security such as a standard security will normally take precedence over the floating charge under the Companies Act 1985 s. 464 which deals with ranking. But, in terms of that section:

(1)  under s. 464(1)(*a*), it is expressly provided that the instrument creating the charge may contain provisions prohibiting or restricting the creation of any fixed security having priority over or ranking *pari passu* with the floating charge in question. Accordingly, any such provision is undoubtedly effective in a question with a second creditor; and

(2)  a fixed security, if not so excluded under s. 464(1)(*a*), takes priority over a floating charge provided the right of the creditor thereunder is made real before the floating charge itself becomes fixed. For a discussion on ranking of charges see *Alloa Brewery Co. Ltd.* 1992 SLT 121.

For practical purposes, where a creditor is lending to a company as a going concern and securing the loan either by floating charge or by standard security, this presents exactly the same type of problem as confronts a purchaser from a company as a going concern, which is dealt with above in paras. 35.6 onwards.

# APPENDICES

# Appendix A

# STYLES

*Notes:*

(1) The styles which follow, as listed in this Inventory, are skeleton styles only, intended merely to illustrate the form and content of each writ. They are not meant to be used as styles in practice and indeed, in many cases, important clauses are either truncated or omitted altogether, rendering them quite unsuitable for use as practical styles.

(2) For full styles of the relevant writs, with variants to meet a number of special cases, see Halliday's *Practice*, and the *Coursework and Materials Style* volume for the Diploma in Legal Practice in the Scottish Universities ('the Diploma Styles').

(3) Registers of Scotland Forms 1, 4, 10 and 10A are Crown copyright. They are reproduced here with the kind permission of the Controller of Her Majesty's Stationery Office. New Forms were introduced in 1993, and have been used in these styles in substitution for the old forms.

(4) There is a deliberate error in the progress of titles. Would this have invalidated the title?

*Inventory of Style Writs*

1. Feu Charter by Andrew Brown in favour of County Developments Limited, recorded GRS Lanark 13 November 1980.

2. Floating Charge by County Developments Limited in favour of the Lanarkshire Bank Limited dated 15th and registered in the Register of Charges 23 March 1981.

3. Deed of Conditions by County Developments Limited recorded said GRS 20 June 1981.

4. Feu Disposition by County Developments Limited in favour of Mr. and Mrs. Edward Fox and the survivor recorded said GRS 28 December 1983.

5. Standard Security by the said Mr. and Mrs. Edward Fox in favour of The Larklanark Building Society recorded said GRS 20 January 1984.

6. Searches: Property, personal and company registers.

7. Death Certificate of Edward Fox (not reproduced).

8. Certificate of Confirmation in favour of the Executors of the late Mrs. Grace Fox issued from the Commissariot of South Strathclyde Dumfries and Galloway on 20 April 1992.

9. Discharge by The Larklanark Building Society in favour of the Executors

of the late Mrs. Grace Fox of Standard Security number 5 hereof, recorded said GRS 3 June 1992.

10. Missives of Sale and Purchase of dwellinghouse number 3 Larklanark Road, Lanark dated 12, 17 and 18 September 1992.

11. Disposition by the Executors of the late Mrs. Grace Fox in favour of Peter Quinn registered in the Land Register on 5 November 1992.

12. Application Form 10 and Form 10A Report thereon.

13. Application Form 1 for registration of the Disposition number 11 hereof and Inventory of Writs Form 4 accompanying same.

14. Land Certificate for 3 Larklanark Road, Lanark.

**1. Feu Charter by Andrew Brown in favour of County Developments Limited**
Stamp Duty: £2,000.

I, ANDREW BROWN, Accountant, residing at Larklanark House, Glasgow Road, Lanark (who and my successors as superiors of the subjects and others hereinafter disponed are hereinafter referred to as 'the Superiors') in consideration of the sum of One Hundred Thousand Pounds (£100,000) Sterling paid to me by COUNTY DEVELOPMENTS LIMITED incorporated under the Companies Acts and having their Registered Office at One Glasgow Square, Lanark of which sum I hereby acknowledge the receipt and of the feudal prestations hereinafter contained, HAVE SOLD and do hereby IN FEU FARM DISPONE to and in favour of the said County Developments Limited and their successors and assignees whomsoever but excluding assignees before infeftment on these presents and under declaration that these presents shall not be a valid warrant for infeftment after the expiry of six months from the date hereof (the said County Developments Limited and their foresaids as proprietors for the time being of the dominium utile of the Feu being hereinafter referred to as 'the Feuars') heritably and irredeemably ALL and WHOLE that plot or area of ground (hereinafter referred to as 'the Feu') situated on the south side of Glasgow Road, Lanark in the Parish of Larklanark and County of Lanark extending to Ten hectares or thereby and bounded as follows videlicet: on or towards the north by the north face of a stone wall separating the Feu from Glasgow Road aforesaid along which it extends two hundred metres or thereby; on or towards the east and south by the centre line of a post and wire fence separating the Feu from other subjects belonging to me along which it extends five hundred metres and two hundred metres respectively; and on or towards the west by the east face of a stone wall separating the Feu from other subjects belonging to me along which it extends five hundred metres or thereby, the Feu being delineated and outlined in red on the plan thereof annexed and signed by me as relative hereto (which plan is demonstrative only and not taxative) and forming part and portion of ALL and WHOLE the lands and estate of Larklanark in the said Parish and County more particularly described in and disponed by Disposition by the Testamentary Trustees of the late Bernard Brown in my favour dated Tenth and recorded in the Division of the General Register of Sasines for the County of Lanark on Fifteenth, both days of May, Nineteen Hundred and Sixty Six; and the Feu is hereby disponed TOGETHER WITH the whole fittings and fixtures therein and thereon, the whole parts, and privileges and pertinents of and effeiring thereto and my whole right, title and interest present and future in and to the dominium utile thereof; with free ish and entry to and from the Feu by Glasgow Road aforesaid; RESERVING to the National Coal Board constituted by the Coal Industry Nationalisation Act 1946 the whole coal and other minerals vested in them under that Act so far as situated in or under the Feu; but the Feu is disponed with and under the real burdens and conditions following videlicet: (First) the Feuars shall be bound in all time coming to maintain in good order and repair, and whenever necessary to re-erect or reconstruct with the like materials, the whole of the stone wall extending along the north boundary of the Feu except for that part thereof to be demolished in order to give access to the Feu from Glasgow Road aforesaid as hereinafter provided; (Second) . . .

*(Note: A number of further burdens would be included in this Feu Charter in practice in order to ensure a good standard of development and of future maintenance in order to preserve the amenity of the Superior's adjoining property.)*

All which real burdens and conditions hereinbefore specified are hereby declared to be real burdens and conditions on and affecting the Feu and shall be inserted in any infeftment hereon and inserted or validly referred to in any future conveyance or transmission of the Feu or any part thereof; Declaring further that, if the Feuars contravene or fail to implement any of the foregoing feuing conditions, then this Feu Charter and all that may have followed thereon shall, in the option of the Superiors, become null and void and the Feuars shall forfeit their whole right, title and interest in and to the Feu which, with all buildings thereon, shall revert to and belong to the Superiors free and disencumbered of all burdens thereon as if these presents had never been granted; With entry and vacant possession on Eleventh November, Nineteen Hundred and Eighty: TO BE HOLDEN the Feu of and under the Superiors as immediate lawful superiors thereof in feu farm, fee and heritage forever; and I grant warrandice: IN WITNESS WHEREOF I have subscribed these presents, consisting of this and the preceding page together with the plan annexed hereto, at Lanark on the Tenth day of November, Nineteen Hundred and Eighty before these witnesses John Smith and Allan Robertson, both Solicitors of Three Glasgow Square, Lanark.

John Smith, Witness

Andrew Brown

Allan Robertson, Witness

REGISTER on behalf of the within named COUNTY DEVELOPMENTS LIMITED in the REGISTER of the COUNTY of LANARK

Holdsworth & Hepburn, Solicitors, Lanark, Agents

Registers of Scotland
General Register of Sasines
County of Lanark Book 14132 Folio 5
Presented and recorded on 13th November, 1980.

This is the plan referred to in the foregoing Feu Charter by Andrew Brown in favour of County Developments Limited.

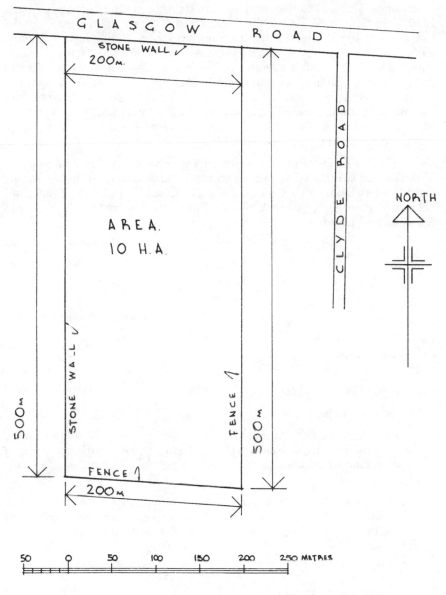

Andrew Brown

## 2. Floating Charge by County Developments Limited in favour of the Lanarkshire Bank Limited

Stamp Duty: Nil.

We, COUNTY DEVELOPMENTS LIMITED incorporated under the Companies Acts and having our Registered Office at One Glasgow Square, Lanark hereby bind and oblige ourselves to pay on demand to the Lanarkshire Bank Limited incorporated under the Companies Acts and having their Registered Office at Fifteen Glasgow Square, Lanark (hereinafter called 'the Bank') all sums due or which may become due by us to the Bank in any manner or way; And in security of our whole obligations hereunder we hereby grant in favour of the Bank a Floating Charge over the whole of the property (including uncalled capital) which is, or may be from time to time while this Instrument is in force, comprised in our property and undertaking . . . (*See Note 1 below*)

IN WITNESS WHEREOF these presents are sealed with the common seal of us the said County Developments Limited and subscribed for us and on our behalf by John Green, one of our Directors and George Black, our Secretary, together at Lanark on the Fifteenth day of March, Nineteen Hundred and Eighty One.

John Green, Director

Seal of
County Developments
Limited

George Black, Secretary

Registered 23rd March 1981
Companies House
Edinburgh

Company Number 654321

*Notes:*

*1. The foregoing writ contains the basic essentials of a Floating Charge, but in practice this document would contain a substantial number of supplementary obligations and conditions for the better protection of the creditor.*

*2. The Floating Charge would not have been recorded in the GRS but, to be valid, would have to have been registered with the Registar of Companies in the Register of Charges within 21 days of its date of execution.*

## 3. Deed of Conditions by County Developments Limited
Stamp Duty: 50p

We, COUNTY DEVELOPMENTS LIMITED incorporated under the
Companies Acts and having our Registered Office at One Glasgow Square,
Lanark, heritable proprietors of ALL and WHOLE that plot or area of
ground situated on the south side of Glasgow Road, Lanark in the County
of Lanark, extending to Ten hectares or thereby, more particularly described in and disponed by and delineated and outlined in red on the plan
annexed and signed as relative to the Feu Charter by Andrew Brown in our
favour dated Tenth and recorded in the Division of the General Register of
Sasines for the County of Lanark on Thirteenth, both days of November,
Nineteen Hundred and Eighty; CONSIDERING that we intend to develop
the said subjects by the erection of villa dwellinghouses thereon and to
dispone the same to individual purchasers and that it is desirable to execute
these presents in order to define the rights, interests, obligations and liabilities of the proprietor of each individual dwellinghouse to be erected on the
said subjects; THEREFORE we do hereby delare and provide as follows:

First    Definitions

In this deed, unless the context otherwise requires, the following expressions shall have the following meanings respectively, viz:

'the Development' means the said area of ground extending to ten hectares
or thereby.

'the Superiors' means us and our successors as proprietors for the time
being of the plenum dominium of the development or so much thereof as
has not been feued and of the dominium directum of those parts of the
whole of the development which, at the relevant date, have been feued.

*Notes:*

*1. Depending on the type of development proposed, a number of further
definitions will follow.*

*2. If the 1979 Act s. 17 has not been disapplied in this Deed of Conditions,
all the burdens and conditions therein will become real burdens affecting
the whole development and every part thereof immediately on recording
the Deed. Accordingly, a reference to this Deed in subsequent conveyances of parts of the development would be strictly unnecessary, although in practice the Deed of Conditions is always so referred to.*

*3. If Section 17 is disapplied, which is competent, the burdens and con-
ditions will become real, as regards each portion of the development subsequently feued or disponed if, but only if, the Feu Disposition (or
Disposition) of such portion expressly refers to the Deed of Conditions
for burdens.*

*4. The Deed of Conditions may contain a clause permitting the Superiors
to vary the terms thereof which can cause problems and must be carefully
drafted. Since such a clause is often desirable, s. 17 is commonly disapplied; but that does not solve all drafting problems.*

*5. For convenience, the definition clause in the Deed of Conditions may*

617

*contain provisions as to ownership in common of those parts of the development which are to remain common to the whole proprietors thereof, including internal roads and footpaths; lighting; parking and amenity areas; and possibly other special features. This is usually a necessary provision for the purpose of defining common repairing obligations. Whether or not the 1979 Act s. 17 is disapplied, a Deed of Conditions may conveniently be used to define and identify common parts, but it cannot of itself create any right of common ownership in those common parts. Such rights of common ownership must therefore be separately and explicitly conferred on each individual disponee in each subsequent Feu Disposition (or Disposition) of each Feu, normally by reference to the definition in the Deed of Conditions.*

SECOND The dwellinghouse erected on the Feu shall be used in all time coming as a private residence for use by one family only and for no other purpose whatsoever.

*Note: The foregoing clause is purely illustrative. A much fuller clause would normally be used and a substantial number of further clauses would normally then follow to provide for the maintenance and amenity of the development as a whole; the maintenance of common parts; insurance and reinstatement; the constitution, formation and powers of a feuars' association; the conferring of an express* jus quaesitum tertio *on each individual proprietor to enforce the conditions as against his neighbours; and a declaration of real burdens and irritancy clauses on the lines of these clauses as they appear in the Feu Charter No. 1 above.*

IN WITNESS WHEREOF these presents consisting of this and the (    ) preceding pages are sealed with the common seal of us the said County Developments Limited and subscribed for us and on our behalf by John Green, one of our Directors and George Black, our Secretary, together at Lanark on the Fifteenth day of June, Nineteen Hundred and Eighty One.

Seal of          John Green, Director

County Developments

Limited         George Black, Secretary

REGISTER on behalf of the within named COUNTY DEVELOPMENTS LIMITED in the REGISTER of the COUNTY of LANARK

Holdsworth & Hepburn, Solicitors, Lanark, Agents

Registers of Scotland
General Register of Sasines
County of Lanark Book 14134 Folio 20
Presented and recorded 20th June, 1981

**4. Feu Disposition by County Developments Limited in favour of Mr. and Mrs. Edward Fox and the survivor**
Stamp Duty: £1,200

We, COUNTY DEVELOPMENTS LIMITED incorporated under the Companies Acts and having our Registered Office at One Glasgow Square, Lanark, heritable proprietors of the subjects and others hereinafter disponed In Consideration of the sum of Sixty Thousand Pounds (£60,000) Sterling paid to us in equal shares by Edward Fox and Mrs. Grace Hunter or Fox, Spouses, presently residing at Sixteen Glasgow Road, Lanark, HAVE SOLD and do hereby IN FEU FARM DISPONE to the said Edward Fox and Mrs. Grace Hunter or Fox equally between them and to the survivor of them and to the executors and assignees whomsoever of the survivor (the said Edward Fox and Mrs. Grace Hunter or Fox and their foresaids as proprietors for the time being of the dominium utile of the Feu being hereinafter referred to as 'the Feuars') heritably and irredeemably ALL and WHOLE that plot of ground extending to twenty decimal or one hundredth parts of a hectare or thereby forming Plot 20 of the Development hereinafter referred to with the dwellinghouse and ancillary buildings erected thereon known as Three Larklanark Road, Lanark, in the County of Lanark all as the said Plot is delineated and outlined in red on the plan thereof annexed and signed as relative hereto, which said plot of ground hereinbefore in feu farm disponed is hereinafter referred to as 'the Feu' and forms part and portion of our Glasgow Road Development comprising ALL and WHOLE that plot or area of ground situated on the south side of Glasgow Road, Lanark in the said County extending to ten hectares or thereby, more particularly described in, in feu farm disponed by and delineated and outlined in red on the plan annexed and signed as relative to the Feu Charter by Andrew Brown in our favour dated Tenth and recorded in the Division of the General Register of Sasines for the County of Lanark on Thirteenth, both days of November, Nineteen Hundred and Eighty; and the Feu is so disponed together with (One) a right in common with all other proprietors of every part of the said Glasgow Road Development, including ourselves so long as we still remain heritable proprietors of any part of the dominium utile thereof, to the common parts of the said Glasgow Road Development all as the said common parts are more particularly described in a Deed of Conditions relative to the said Development, which said Deed of Conditions was granted by us dated Fifteenth and recorded in the said Division of the General Register of Sasines on Twentieth, both days of June, Nineteen Hundred and Eighty One; (Two) the whole parts, privileges and pertinents of the Feu; (Three) our whole right, title and interest, present and future in and to the dominium utile of the Feu; With free ish and entry to the Feu from Larklanark Road aforesaid fronting the Feu on the west side thereof: But always with and under the reservations, real burdens and conditions specified and contained in *(here refer to (i) the Feu Charter Number 1 hereof; and (ii) the Deed of Conditions Number 3 hereof. Note that, since the Deed of Conditions contains the whole conditions relative to the Development, including a declaration of real burdens and an irritant and resolutive clause, these clauses do not need to be repeated in this Feu Disposition)*; With entry and actual occupation to the Feu on Twenty First December, Nineteen

Hundred and Eighty Three; To be holden of and under the Superiors, as defined in the said Deed of Conditions, as immediate lawful superiors thereof in feu farm, fee and heritage forever; And we grant warrandice: IN WITNESS WHEREOF these presents consisting of this and the ( ) preceding page(s) together with the plan annexed hereto are sealed with the common seal of us the said County Developments Limited and subscribed for us and on our behalf by John Green, one of our Directors and George Black, our Secretary, together at Lanark on the Fifteenth day of December, Nineteen Hundred and Eighty Three.

Seal of            John Green, Director

County Developments

Limited        George Black, Secretary

REGISTER on behalf of the within named EDWARD FOX and MRS. GRACE HUNTER or FOX in the REGISTER of the COUNTY of LANARK

White & White, Solicitors, Lanark, Agents

Registers of Scotland
General Register of Sasines
County of Lanark Book 14139 Folio 215
Presented and recorded 28th December, 1983

This is the plan referred to in the foregoing Feu Disposition by County Developments Limited in favour of Edward Fox and Mrs. Grace Hunter or Fox.

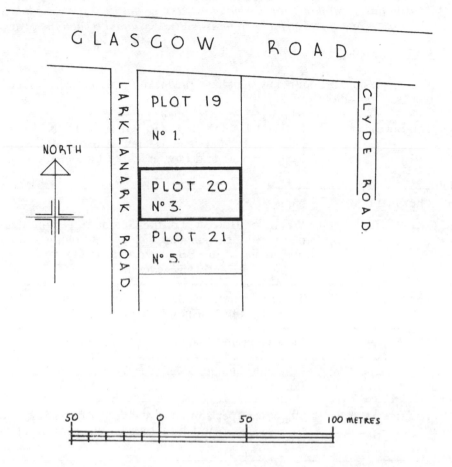

Seal of
County Developments
Limited

John Green, Director
George Black, Secretary

## 5. Standard Security by Edward Fox and Mrs. Grace Hunter or Fox in favour of the Larklanark Building Society

*Note: Building Societies normally use a boxed style of Standard Security as in this illustration. For alternative styles, see the 1970 Act Schedule 2 Forms A and B and styles in Halliday's* Practice *and the Diploma Styles.*

Stamp Duty: Nil.

The expressions set out below shall have the meanings and effects respectively set opposite them:

| | |
|---|---|
| The Borrower | EDWARD FOX and MRS GRACE HUNTER or FOX, both sometime residing at Sixteen Glasgow Road, Lanark and now at Three Larklanark Road there. |
| The Guarantor | None. |
| | Where the Borrower or the Guarantor is more than one person, the singular includes the plural and all obligations of the Borrower and the Guarantor are undertaken jointly and severally |
| The Society | The Larklanark Building Society having its Chief Office at Four Glasgow Square, Lanark |
| The Advance | Fifty Thousand Pounds (£50,000) Sterling |
| The Advance Date | Fifteenth January, Nineteen Hundred and Eighty Four |
| The Interest Rate | 10 per cent per annum or such other rate as may be fixed by the Society from time to time in terms of its Rules |
| The Property | Dwellinghouse No. 3 Larklanark Road, Lanark, being the subjects herinafter described. |

The Borrower hereby undertakes to pay to The Society The Advance made on The Advance Date and all other sums due and which may become due by The Borrower to The Society in respect of any further advances to be made by The Society to The Borrower with interest computed in accordance with the practice of The Society at The Interest Rate . . .

*Note: Special provisions will normally follow the foregoing undertaking to provide for,* inter alia, *repayment of capital by instalments, payment of interest and establishing the balance of capital outstanding and due to The Society under the security, together with arrears of interest, at any future date.*

For which The Borrower grants a Standard Security in favour of The Society over The Property, being ALL and WHOLE the plot or area of ground with the dwellinghouse and others erected thereon known as Three Larklanark Road, Lanark, in the County of Lanark, being the subjects more particularly described in, in feu farm disponed by, and delineated and outlined in red on the plan annexed and executed as relative to, the Feu Disposition by County Developments Limited in favour of The Borrower dated Fifteenth and recorded in the Division of the General Register of Sasines for the County of Lanark on Twenty eighth both days of December, Nineteen hundred and Eighty three.

The Standard Conditions specified in Schedule 3 of the Conveyancing and Feudal Reform (Scotland) Act 1970 as varied by the Rules of The Society and a Deed of Variation made by The Society dated Sixth and Registered in the Books of Council and Session on Sixteenth June Nineteen Hundred and Seventy One (a copy of which The Borrower hereby acknowledges to have received) and any lawful variation thereof operative for the time being shall apply;

And The Borrower grants warrandice; And The Borrower consents to the registration hereof and of any certificate granted in terms hereof as aforesaid for execution: IN WITNESS WHEREOF these presents, consisting of this and the preceding page, are subscribed by the said Edward Fox and Mrs. Grace Hunter or Fox both together at Lanark and on the Fifteenth day of January, Nineteen Hundred and Eighty Four before these witnesses Alan Brown and James Jones, both Solicitors, of Nine Glasgow Square, Lanark.

| | |
|---|---|
| Alan Brown    Witness | Edward Fox |
| James Jones    Witness | Grace Fox |

REGISTER on behalf of the within named THE LARKLANARK BUILDING SOCIETY in the REGISTER of the COUNTY of LANARK.

Brown & Jones, Solicitors, Lanark, Agents.

Registers of Scotland
General Register of Sasines
County of Lanark Book 14140 Folio 162
Presented and recorded 20th January, 1984

*Note: The County of Lanark became an operational area for registration of title on 3rd January 1984. The foregoing writ, although granted after the date on which Lanarkshire became operational, is not a writ which would induce first registration and therefore falls to be recorded in the Register of Sasines.*

**6. Searches: property, personal and company registers**

*MILLAR & BRYCE LIMITED*

# 𝔖𝔈𝔄ℜℭ𝔥 in ℜegister
# of ℭharges
# against

COUNTY DEVELOPMENTS LIMITED No. 654321 a

Company incorporated under the Companies Act

and having their Registered Office situated

in Scotland.

From 30 Sept. 1980 Date of Incorporation of Company

To 19 Jany. 1984

---

Date of Registration

23 March 1981

BOND AND FLOATING CHARGE dated 15 March 1981 by County

Developments Limited,- To Lanarkshire Bank,- of the

whole of the property and undertaking - for securing

all sums due or to become due. Under declaration as to

ranking.

SEARCHED THE REGISTER OF

CHARGES AND FOUND AS ABOVE

N.B. There were no adverse notices on the Company's

File relating to Liquidation, Receivership,

Administration Order, Winding Up or Striking off as at

19 January 1984

Authorised Signatory

# 𝔖𝔢𝔞𝔯𝔠𝔥 for 𝔍𝔫𝔠𝔲𝔪𝔟𝔯𝔞𝔫𝔠𝔢𝔰 𝔄𝔣𝔣𝔢𝔠𝔱𝔦𝔫𝔤

## 𝔄𝔩𝔩 𝔞𝔫𝔡 𝔚𝔥𝔬𝔩𝔢 that plot of ground extending
to 0.20 hectare, Plot 20 on Plan, together with the
dwellinghouse etc. erected thereon known as 3
Larklanark Road, Lanark, being the subjects more
particularly described in Feu Disposition by County
Developments Limited in favour of Edward Fox and his
wife Grace Hunter or Fox dated Fifteenth and recorded
in the Division of the General Register of Sasines
applicable to the County of Lanark on Twenty eighth
both days of December Nineteen hundred and eighty
three, which subjects are part of All and Whole
10 hectares of ground, bounded on the north by
Glasgow Road, Lanark, described in Feu Charter by
Andrew Brown in favour of County Developments Limited
dated Tenth and recorded in the said Division of
the General Register of sasines on Thirteenth both
days of November Nineteen hundred and eighty.

------

GEN: REG: OF SAS:

From 13 Novr. 1980

To 20 Jany. 1984

------

FEU CHARTER by Andrew Brown,- To County Developments
Limited,- of 10 hectares of ground, bounded on the
north by Glasgow Road, Lanark, in Parish of
Larklanark, part of the lands and Estate of
Larklanark /

2. **Millar & Bryce Limited**

Larklanark, reserving Minerals. Dated 10 November
1980.

NOTE:- Superiors interest and burdens, if any, by him
      or his Authors not traced.

| | |
|---|---|
| 20 June 1981<br>14134 - 20 | DEED OF CONDITIONS by County Developments Limited -<br>Declaring real burdens etc. affecting said 10 hectares<br>of ground. Dated 15 June 1981. |
| 28 Decr. 1983<br>14139 - 215 | FEU DISPOSITION by County Developments Limited,- To<br>Edward Fox and Grace Hunter or Fox, equally and<br>survivor,- of the Subjects of Search. Dated 15 December<br>1983.<br>NOTE:- Superiors interest not further traced. |
| 20 Jany. 1984<br>14140 - 162 | STANDARD SECURITY for £50,000 and further sums by<br>Edward Fox and Grace Hunter or Fox,- To Larklanark<br>Building Society,- over the Subjects of Search. Dated<br>15 January 1984. |

SEARCHED the General Register of Sasines for the County
of Lanark from the Thirteenth day of November Nineteen
hundred and eighty to the Twentieth day of January
Nineteen hundred and eighty four, both dates inclusive,

Inhibs: over
Page 1

and found as on this and the preceding page.

Authorised Signatory.

SEARCH 239283746          MILLAR & BRYCE LTD          Page 1

SEARCH

IN THE REGISTER OF

INHIBITIONS AND ADJUDICATIONS

AGAINST

COUNTY DEVELOPMENTS LIMITED

EDWARD FOX

GRACE HUNTER OR FOX

From 21 Jany. 1979

   To 20 Jany. 1984    2400 HOURS

8302345          5 April 1983
Notice of Letters of Inhibition, Michelangelo
and Partners, Chartered Architects, St. Peter's
Buildings, Rome Square, Glasgow,- against
COUNTY DEVELOPMENTS LIMITED, 1 Glasgow Square,
Lanark. Signetted 5 April 1983. Per L. Sharpe,
Writer, Edinburgh.

8303456          11 April 1983
Letters of Inhibition, Michelangelo and Partners,
Chartered Architects, St. Peter's Buildings,
Rome Square, Glasgow:- against COUNTY
DEVELOPMENTS LIMITED, 1 Glasgow Square,
Lanark. Per L. Sharpe, Writer, Edinburgh.

8306578          25 Octr. 1983
Discharge by Michelangelo and Partners,
Chartered Architects, St. Peter's Buildings,
Rome Square, Glasgow - of Inhibition (recorded
11 April 1983) against COUNTY DEVELOPMENTS
LIMITED, 1 Glasgow Square, Lanark. Per J. Bloggs,
Registers of Scotland.

SEARCHED THE REGISTER OF INHIBITIONS
AND ADJUDICATIONS AND FOUND AS ABOVE

AUTHORISED SIGNATORY.

**7. Death Certificate of Edward Fox – not reproduced here**

**8. Certificate of Confirmation in the estate of the late Mrs. Grace Hunter or Fox**

Certificate of Confirmation (Act of Sederunt 16th July 1971 Schedule D)

<u>Confirmation was issued</u> from the Commissariot of South Strathclyde Dumfries and Galloway on Twentieth April, Nineteen Hundred and Ninety Two in favour of Alan Brown and James Jones, both Solicitors of Nine Glasgow Square, Lanark as executors nominate of Mrs. Grace Hunter or Fox sometime of Sixteen Glasgow Road, Lanark and late of Three Larklanark Road, there who died on Tenth March, Nineteen Hundred and Ninety Two.

<u>DOMICILED IN SCOTLAND</u>

It is hereby certified that the said Confirmation contained *inter alia* the following item of estate situated in Scotland.

<u>HERITABLE ESTATE IN SCOTLAND</u>

1. ALL and WHOLE the dwellinghouse and pertinents
   known as Three Larklanark Drive, Lanark.                    £90,000

   Given under the seal of office of the Commissariot of South Strathclyde Dumfries and Galloway and signed by the Clerk of Court at Lanark the Twentieth day of April, Nineteen Hundred and Ninety Two.

John Gibson
Sheriff Clerk Depute                                          Seal

**9. Discharge by The Larklanark Building Society in favour of the Executors of the late Mrs Grace Hunter or Fox** (endorsed on the Standard Security No. 5 hereof)

We, The Larklanark Building Society having our Chief Office at Four Glasgow Square, Lanark IN CONSIDERATION of the sum of FIFTY THOUSAND POUNDS STERLING, being the whole amount secured by the Standard Security aftermentioned, paid to us by Alan Brown and James Jones both Solicitors of Nine Glasgow Square, Lanark, Executors Nominate of the late Mrs. Grace Hunter or Fox sometime of Sixteen Glasgow Road, Lanark and late of Three Larklanark Road, Lanark conform to Confirmation in their favour granted by the Sheriff of South Strathclyde Dumfries and Galloway at Lanark on Twentieth April, Nineteen Hundred and Ninety Two Do Hereby Discharge the foregoing Standard Security granted by Edward Fox sometime of Sixteen Glasgow Road aforesaid and late of Three Larklanark Road, aforesaid, and the said Mrs. Grace Hunter or Fox in our favour recorded in the Register for the County of Lanark on Twentieth January, Nineteen Hundred and Eighty Four: IN WITNESS WHEREOF these presents partly printed and partly typewritten on this page are sealed with our common seal and subscribed for us and on our behalf by David McDonald our Principal Deeds Officer at Lanark on the Thirtieth day of May Nineteen hundred and Ninety two before these witnesses, Evelyn Anderson and Linda Fisher both clerks and both at our Chief Office at Lanark.

Evelyn Anderson witness                            David McDonald
Linda Fisher witness                           Principal Deeds Officer
                    Seal of The Larklanark
                    Building Society

REGISTER on behalf of the within named Alan Brown and James Jones as Executors within mentioned in the REGISTER of the COUNTY of LANARK

                Brown & Jones, Solicitors, Lanark, Agents

Registers of Scotland
General Register of Sasines
County of Lanark Book 14203 Folio 21
Presented and recorded 3rd June, 1992

*Notes:*

*1. See Note on Writ No. 5.*

*2. Although this Discharge is endorsed on the Standard Security, the fore-going information relating to the Standard Security must be inserted in the endorsed Discharge to give the Keeper the required information for pur-poses of recording the Discharge in Sasines.*

*3. See Note on Writ 5 as to recording/registration.*

## 10. Missives of Sale and Purchase for number 3 Larklanark Road, Lanark

Messrs. Brown & Jones, Our Ref: JK/SR/JDM
Solicitors,                Your Ref:
9 Glasgow Square,
Lanark.

Messrs. King & Co.,
Solicitors,
10 Glasgow Square,
Lanark.

12th September, 1992

Dear Sirs,

Peter Quinn
3 Larklanark Road, Lanark

On behalf of our client Peter Quinn of 20 Clyde Street, Lanark, we hereby offer to purchase from your clients the dwellinghouse known as Three Larklanark Road, Lanark and garden ground pertaining thereto, together with the garage and garden shed at present erected thereon, and that on the following terms and conditions:-

1.     Price

The price will be Ninety Five Thousand Pounds (£95,000) Sterling payable on the date of entry hereinafter specified.

2.     Fittings and Fixtures

The purchase price includes all fittings and fixtures in and upon the subjects of sale and any items, the removal of which would cause damage to the fabric of the property, including all growing trees, flowers, plants and shrubs in the garden ground pertaining to the subjects of sale.

3.     Mineral reservations

The minerals are included in the purchase price in so far as the sellers have right thereto. In the event of the minerals being reserved to the sellers, the superior or some other third party, the titles of the subjects of sale contain a provision affording full rights of compensation to the proprietor in respect of any surface damage, damage to buildings or other damage occasioned by working of the minerals. In the case of coal and associated minerals, the statutory protection afforded by the Coal Mining Subsidence Act 1991 shall be deemed sufficient protection to the purchaser for the purposes of this clause.

4.     Maintenance, condition and existence of subjects of sale

(i)    The sellers will maintain the subjects of sale in their present condition (fair wear and tear excepted) until the purchase price is paid or the purchaser takes possession, whichever date is the earlier. In the event of the subjects being destroyed or materially damaged prior to that date, either party shall be entitled, but not obliged, to resile from the contract to follow hereon without penalty and without prejudice to any entitlement to claim damages from the other party.

(ii)   The risk of damage to or destruction of the subjects of sale will remain with the sellers until the purchase price is paid or the purchaser takes possession, whichever date is the earlier.

(iii) The sellers will be responsible for the cost of any repairs to the subjects of sale instructed prior to the date of entry. In addition, and without prejudice to the foregoing, the sellers will be responsible for the cost of any repairs required under Notices issued by the Local Authority or any other competent body prior to the date of entry.

5.    Entry

Entry with vacant possession to the whole subjects will be given on Thirty First October, 1992 or on such other date as may be mutually agreed.

6.    Interest on Price

It is a material condition of the bargain to follow hereon that (a) the purchase price will be paid on the date of entry and (b) the sellers will give entry with vacant possession to the whole subjects of sale on the date prescribed in Clause 2. Without prejudice to the foregoing, if (but only if) at the date of entry the sellers have (a) implemented all obligations incumbent on them in terms of the bargain to follow hereon and (b) are in a position to give possession of the whole subjects of sale to the purchaser, the purchaser will pay to the sellers interest on any part of the purchase price outstanding at said date at a rate of 4% per annum above the lowest base rate for lending charged by any of the Scottish clearing banks during the period of non-payment (together with any arrangement fee or other charges incurred by the sellers on any borrowing by them necessitated by the purchaser's failure to pay the purchase price timeously); and that notwithstanding consignation and whether or not the purchaser shall have taken occupation of the subjects of sale; and in the event of any part of the purchase price remaining unpaid on the expiry of a period of four weeks from the date of entry, the sellers will be entitled but not obliged, forthwith to resile from said bargain to follow hereon and to resell the subjects of sale, under reservation of all claims which may be competent to the sellers to recover from the purchaser all loss and damage sustained by the sellers on any such resale and interest as aforesaid.

7.    Retention for Repairs

In the event that the subjects of sale are affected by a District or Regional Council Notice ordering repairs to the subjects of sale, there shall be retained at settlement a sum which represents the proportion of the estimated cost to be borne by the sellers in respect thereof, augmented by 25%, and this sum shall be lodged on Deposit Receipt in the joint names of the sellers' and purchaser's solicitors against exhibition of the receipted final accounts for the works involved, whereupon the purchaser's solicitors will be bound forthwith to endorse said Deposit Receipt and deliver it to the sellers' solicitors. Failure to deliver the same so endorsed within 7 days will incur a liability to interest on the same terms as in Clause 6 hereof.

8.    Roads, sewerage and water supply, etc.

The sellers will provide at their expense a certificate prior to the date of entry from the appropriate local authority confirming (i) that the roadways, footways, waterchannels and sewers ex adverso and serving the subjects of sale have been taken over and are maintained by the local authority (ii) that there are no road proposals which will affect the subjects of sale and (iii) that the subjects of sale are connected to the public water supply and sewer. Furthermore, the sellers warrant that they are not aware of any proposals by or rights in favour of a public or local authority, statutory undertaker or other party which would affect the subjects of sale.

9.    Planning, etc.

The sellers will provide at their expense prior to the date of entry a certificate (dated not earlier than twenty eight days prior to the conclusion of the bargain to follow hereon) from the appropriate local authority confirming that the subjects of sale are (i) in an area designated in the Development Plan primarily for residential purposes (ii) not within a housing treatment or housing action area (iii) not adversely affected by any planning schemes, orders or proposals under the Town & Country Planning (Scotland) Acts or other Statutes, (iv) not included in any proposals or orders under the Housing (Scotland) Acts or other Statutes, (v) not subject to any such matters which are outstanding in the knowledge of the said local authority and (vi) not designated for compulsory acquisition for any planning purposes of the said local authority. The subjects of sale are not included in a list of buildings of special architectural or historic interest nor located within a conservation area.

10.    Amenity and Neighbourhood

The Sellers warrant:

(i)    that they are unaware of any proposals by any public or local authority, statutory undertaker or other party which would, in any way, materially and adversely affect the subjects of sale.

(ii)    that there are no pecuniary burdens affecting the subjects of sale.

(iii)   that the titles do not contain any provisions of an unusual or unduly onerous nature, which materially and adversely affect the said subjects, as to which the purchaser, acting reasonably, shall be the sole judge.

11.    Structural alterations, etc.

If the subjects of sale have been converted or altered in the 20 year period prior to the date of conclusion of the bargain to follow hereon, the sellers will provide at their expense such evidence as may reasonably be required by the purchaser that (i) the relevant works were carried out and completed in conformity with all necessary local authority permissions and warrants, and (ii) all other necessary consents and permissions, including that of the superior, were obtained and any conditions attaching thereto were fully implemented.

12.    N.H.B.C.

If the subjects of sale were constructed within ten years prior to the date of conclusion of the bargain to follow hereon (i) they were constructed by a contractor who was at the time a member of the National House Builders' Council ("N.H.B.C."), (ii) the subjects of sale were registered with the N.H.B.C. and are currently covered by all N.H.B.C. warranties available at the date of registration, and (iii) the sellers will deliver at their expense all relevant documentation pertaining to the said warranties together with the appropriate local authority certificate of completion.

## 13. Central Heating and Telephone

(i) The central heating system (if any is included in the price) shall be in full working order as at the date of entry. Any material defect in the system as at the date of entry, which is notified to the sellers or their agent within 7 days of the date of entry, will be remedied at the sellers' expense.

(ii) Any telephone apparatus in the subjects of sale which is not the property of British Telecom will be included in the price. The sellers will not cause the telephone to be disconnected.

## 14. Guarantees

The sellers are not aware of the existence in the subjects of sale of woodworm, dry rot, wet rot or rising damp and, in the event that a Guarantee has been issued in respect of any of these, said Guarantee is valid in all respects and the benefit thereof shall be transferred to the purchaser. Further, the said Guarantee, with the specification and estimate to which it refers, shall be delivered at settlement.

## 15. Title

In exchange for the price, the sellers will execute and deliver a valid Disposition of the subjects of sale in favour of the purchaser or the purchaser's nominee and will exhibit or deliver a valid marketable prescriptive progress of titles together with (i) a Form 10 or Form 11 report brought down to a date as near as practicable to the date of settlement and showing no entries adverse to the sellers' interest and (ii) at the sellers' expense will produce such documents and evidence, including a plan or plans, as the Keeper may reasonably require to enable him to issue a Land Certificate in name of the purchaser or the purchaser's nominee of the whole subjects of sale without exclusion or qualification of indemnity. Such Land Certificate will disclose no entry, deed or diligence prejudicial to the interests of the purchaser other than adverse interests created by the purchaser or disclosed to him and accepted by him in writing prior to settlement. Notwithstanding the provisions of Clause 18 hereof, the foregoing provision as to the Land Certificate will remain in force and may be founded on at any time after settlement within three months following the date of receipt by the purchaser of such Land Certificate.

## 16. Occupancy and other rights

At the date of entry there will be no subsisting occupancy rights of a non-entitled spouse in terms of the Matrimonial Homes (Family Protection) (Scotland) Act 1981, as amended, and the sellers will deliver appropriate evidence to that effect on or before the date of entry. In addition the sellers warrant that as at the date of entry (or the date of settlement, whichever is the later) the subjects of sale will not be affected by any court order in terms of the Family Law (Scotland) Act 1985 or any amendments thereto.

## 17. Time Limits

The sellers will provide all relevant documentary evidence of the matters specified in Clauses 8, 9, 11, 12, 14, 15 and 16 of the foregoing offer within 4 weeks of the date of conclusion of missives. If the said documentary evidence does not implement the obligations of the sellers hereunder or discloses matters materially prejudicial to the purchaser's position, the purchaser shall be entitled to withdraw from the missives to follow hereon without penalty by delivering written notice of his intention so to do to the sellers' solicitors within five working days from the date of receipt of the last of said items of documentary evidence. In the event of the purchaser failing to give notice as aforesaid within said period of five working days, he will be deemed to be fully satisfied in respect of all such matters and will have no further redress under Clause 18 hereof or otherwise.

18. **Non-Supersession Clause**

This offer and the missives following hereon will form a continuing and enforceable contract notwithstanding the delivery of the disposition in favour of the purchaser except insofar as fully implemented thereby. Without prejudice to the special provisions in Clause 15 hereof relating to the Land Certificate and in Clause 17 hereof, the missives will cease to be enforceable after a period of two years from the date of delivery of said disposition, except insofar as they are founded upon in any court proceedings which have been commenced within the said period. A clause to this effect will, at the option of the purchaser, be included in the disposition in his favour.

19. **The actio quanti minoris**

Notwithstanding any rule of law to the contrary the actio quanti minoris will be available to the purchaser.

20. **Letter of Obligation**

In exchange for the price there will be delivered a Letter of Obligation granted by the solicitors for the sellers in the form recommended by The Registration of Title Practice Book.

21. **Time Limit for Acceptance**

This offer is open for acceptance by letter reaching us not later than 5.00 pm on 19th September 1992.

Yours faithfully,

(King & Co.)

Our Ref : AB/TM     Brown & Jones,
Your Ref: JK/SR/JDM    Solicitors,
                          9 Glasgow Square,
                          Lanark.

17th September, 1992

**Messrs. King & Co,**
Solicitors,
10 Glasgow Square,
Lanark.


Dear Sirs,

### Mrs. Grace Fox's Executry

### Peter Quinn

### 3 Larklanark Road, Lanark

On behalf of and as instructed by our clients, the executors of **Mrs.** Grace Fox, late of 3 Larklanark Road, Lanark we hereby accept your offer of 12th September 1992 to purchase the above Subjects at the price and on the terms and conditions therein contained but that subject to the following qualification viz:

In Clause 11 of your said offer the period of 10 years shall be substituted for the period of 20 years therein specified.

This qualification is open for immediate acceptance only.

Yours faithfully,


(Brown & Jones)

```
Our Ref : JK/SR/JDM      King & Co.,
Your Ref: AB/TM          Solicitors,
                         10 Glasgow Square,
                         Lanark.
```

18th September, 1992

Brown & Jones,
Solicitors,
9 Glasgow Square,
Lanark.


Dear Sirs,

Peter Quinn

3 Larklanark Road, Lanark

<u>Mrs. Grace Fox's  Executry</u>


On behalf of  and  as  instructed by our client,  Peter Quinn,  we
hereby accept the  qualification  in your letter of 17th September
to our offer  of  12th September and hold the bargain as concluded
in terms of those two letters and this letter.

Yours faithfully,



(King & Co.)

## 11. Disposition by the Executors of Mrs Grace Hunter or Fox in favour of Peter Quinn
Stamp Duty: £950

We, Alan Brown and James Jones both Solicitors and both of Nine Glasgow Square, Lanark Executors Nominate of the deceased Mrs. Grace Hunter or Fox sometime of Sixteen Glasgow Road, Lanark and late of Three Larklanark Road, Lanark conform to Confirmation in our favour as Executors aforesaid issued from the Commissariot of South Strathclyde Dumfries and Galloway at Lanark on Twentieth April, Nineteen Hundred and Ninety Two and as such Executors, uninfeft proprietors of the subjects and others hereinafter disponed; IN CONSIDERATION of the sum of Ninety five thousand pounds (£95,000) Sterling now paid to us as Executors aforesaid by Peter Quinn of Twenty Clyde Street, Lanark of which sum we hereby acknowledge receipt, HAVE SOLD and do hereby DISPONE to and in favour of the said Peter Quinn and his Executors and Assignees whomsoever heritably and irredeemably ALL and WHOLE the dwelling-house and pertinents known as and forming Three Larklanark Road, Lanark in the County of Lanark being the subjects more particularly described in, in feu farm disponed by, and delineated and outlined in red on the plan annexed and executed as relative to, the Feu Disposition by County Developments Limited in favour of Edward Fox and another dated Fifteenth and recorded in the Division of the General Register of Sasines for the County of Lanark on Twenty eighth both days of December Nineteen Hundred and Eighty three TOGETHER WITH (One) the whole fittings and fixtures therein and thereon (Two) the whole parts, privileges and pertinents of the said subjects hereinbefore disponed and (Three) our whole right title and interest present and future as Executors aforesaid in and to the said subjects; BUT ALWAYS WITH and UNDER *(here refer to prior writs for burdens as in the Feu Disposition No. 4 hereof. Since there are no additional burdens in that Feu Disposition, it need not be referred to)*; WITH ENTRY and vacant possession on the Thirty First October Nineteen Hundred and Ninety Two; which said subjects hereinbefore disponed were last vested in the said Edward Fox sometime of Sixteen Glasgow Road, Lanark and late of Three Larklanark Road, Lanark and the said Mrs. Grace Hunter or Fox and the survivor of them and on the death of the said Edward Fox which occurred on Third November Nineteen hundred and Ninety, in the said Mrs. Grace Hunter or Fox alone; and from whom we acquired right as Executors aforesaid by the said Confirmation in our favour; and we, as Executors aforesaid, grant warrandice from our own facts and deeds only and, in so far as we can competently do so, we bind the beneficiaries entitled to the estate of said Mrs. Grace Hunter or Fox in absolute warrandice: IN WITNESS WHEREOF these presents on this and the preceeding page are subscribed by us the said Alan Brown and James Jones as Executors aforesaid both together at Lanark on the Twenty

Seventh day of October, Nineteen Hundred and Ninety Two before the witnesses hereto subscribing whose designations are appended below their respective signatures.

| | | |
|---|---|---|
| Witness | A. Smith | |
| Address | 9 Glasgow Square, Lanark | |
| Designation | Secretary | Alan Brown |
| Witness | J. Hughes | James Jones |
| Address | 9 Glasgow Square, Lanark | |
| Designation | Secretary | |

*Note: No Warrant of Registration is required on this Writ because it induces first registration. The relevant application forms 1 and 4 follow.*

## 12. Application Form 10 and Form 10A Report thereon

REGISTERS OF SCOTLAND EXECUTIVE AGENCY
(Land Registration (Scotland) Rules 1980 Rule 24(1))

**FORM 10**

FOR OFFICIAL USE

REPORT NUMBER

### APPLICATION FOR A REPORT PRIOR TO REGISTRATION OF THE SUBJECTS DESCRIBED BELOW

Note: No covering letter is required and an existing Search should not be submitted.

DATE OF RECEIPT

*Please complete in DUPLICATE and in BLACK TYPE*

SEARCH SHEET NOS.

VAT Reg No. GD 410

GB 888 8410 64

Typewriter Alignment Box
Type XXX in centre

FEE

FROM

Messrs King & Co.
Solicitors
10 Glasgow Square
LANARK

DX 829
LANARK

TO

Keeper of the Registers of Scotland

Meadowbank House
153 London Road
EDINBURGH EH8 7AU

Telephone: 0131 659 6111

| County | LANARK |
|---|---|

| Applicant's Reference | JK/SR/JDM | FAS No. | 1234 |
|---|---|---|---|
| Telephone No. | 01555 875436 | FAX No. | 01555 875346 |

FAX response required ☐ X here

**Postal Address of Subjects**

| Street No. | 3 | House Name | | Street Name | Larklanark Road |
|---|---|---|---|---|---|
| Town | Lanark | | | Post code | ML11 0TX |

Other: Description of Subjects

The above subjects being ~~XXXXXXXXXXXXXXXXXXXXXXXXXXXX~~ [2]
being (part of) the subjects described in [3]

Feu Disposition by County Developments Limited in favour of Mr and Mrs Edward Fox and the survivor recorded GRS Lanark 28th December 1983.

**I/We apply for a report**

(1) on the subjects described above, for which an application for registration in the Land Register is to be made, from

(a) the REGISTER OF SASINES and

(b) the **LAND REGISTER** stating whether or not registration of the said subjects has been effected [4]

1. Delete if inapplicable
2. A plan need not be attached if a verbal description will sufficiently identify the subjects
3. Describe by reference to a writ recorded in the Register of Sasines
4. If the subjects have been registered, the Keeper will supply an Office Copy of the Title Sheet only on specific request.
Faxed applications should not be followed up by a written request and may not be accepted if a plan is included.

and (2) from the Registers of Inhibitions and Adjudications for 5 years prior to the date of Certificate against

Typewriter Alignment Box
Type XXX in centre

**1. Surname(s)**

Fox

**Forename(s)**

Grace

**Address(es)**

Latterly of 3 Larklanark Road, Lanark

**2. Surname(s)**

Fox

**Forename(s)**

Grace, Exors of

**Address(es)**

**3. Surname(s)**

**Forename(s)**

**Address(es)**

**4. Surname(s)**

**Forename(s)**

**Address(es)**

**5. Company/ Firm/ Corporate body**

**Address(es)**

**6. Company/ Firm/ Corporate body**

**Address(es)**

**Note: Insert full names and addresses of the persons on whom a Report is required.**

Signature:...............................................................

Date:...............................................................

Printed in Scotland for HMSO by (13161)
Dd 8409700 C200 3/95

*Note: The style of the form shown above was not in place in 1992. It is used here for illustrative purposes.*

Form 10A

| REGISTERS OF SCOTLAND<br>(Land Registration (Scotland) Rules 1980 Rule 24(1))<br>**REPORT PRIOR TO REGISTRATION** | Report No.<br><br>4415/LAN/92 |
|---|---|

## REGISTER OF SASINES

1.  Prescriptive progress of titles

Deed                                                    Recording date

*Feu Charter* — *County Developments Ltd.* — *13 Nov. 1980*

*Feu Disposition* — *Edward Fox and another* — *28 Dec. 1983*

2.  Statement of Securities recorded within 40 years prior to the date of certificate and for which no final Discharge has been recorded.

*No deed.*

3.  Statement of Discharges (of Securities) recorded within the 5 years prior to the date of the certificate

*Discharge* — *Fox/Larklanark Building Society* — *3 Jun. 1992*

4.  Deeds, other than transfers or deeds creating or affecting securities, recorded within the 40 years prior to the date of the certificate.

*Deed of Conditions* — *County Developments Ltd.* — *20 Jun. 1981*

Certified correct to *10 September 1992*        Initials *XY*

## LAND REGISTER

The subjects have not been registered

~~The subjects have been registered under Title Number~~ ........................

~~An Office Copy is enclosed as requested~~

~~The subjects are in course of being registered under Title Number~~ ........................

~~An Office Copy will be sent in due course~~

Certified correct to *10 September 1992*        Initials *XY*

## REGISTER OF INHIBITIONS AND ADJUDICATIONS

See Report annexed

*No deed to 10 Sep. 1992*

**FOR OFFICIAL USE**

Nat. Grid ref.

## 13. Application Form 1 for registration of the Disposition and Inventory of Writs Form 4

| REGISTERS OF SCOTLAND EXECUTIVE AGENCY | **FORM 1** | *Please complete in BLACK TYPE* | Typewriter Alignment Box |
|---|---|---|---|
| (Land Registration (Scotland) Rules 1980 Rule 9(1)(a)) | | No covering letter is required | Type XXX in centre |

**APPLICATION FOR FIRST REGISTRATION**

**1 Presenting Agent. Name and Address** (see Note 1)

Messrs King & Co.
Solicitors
10 Glasgow Square
LANARK      DX 829, Lanark

**Part A**

Keeper of the Registers of Scotland
Meadowbank House
153 London Road
EDINBURGH EH8 7AU
Telephone: 0131 659 6111

| **2 FAS No.** (see Note 2) | **3 Agent's Tel No.** (include STD Code) | **4 Agent's Reference** |
|---|---|---|
| 1234 | 01555 875436 | JK/SR/JDM |

| **5 Name of Deed** in respect of which registration is required | **6 County** (see Note 3) | Mark X in box if more than one county |
|---|---|---|
| DISPOSITION | LANARK | |

**7 Subjects** (see Note 4)

| Street No. | 3 | Street Name | Larklanark Road |
|---|---|---|---|
| Town | Lanark | | |
| Other | | Post code | ML11 0TX |

**8 Name and Address of Applicant** (see Note 5)

1. Surname    Quinn         Forename(s)    Peter

Address    20 Clyde Street, Lanark

2. Surname         Forename(s)

Address

and/ or company/ firm or council, etc.         Mark X in box if more than 2 applicants

Address

**9 Granter/Party Last Infeft** (see Note 6)

1. Surname    Fox         Forename(s)    Grace (Party Last Infeft)

2. Surname         Forename(s)

and/ or company/ firm or council, etc.         Mark X in box if more than 2 granters

| **10 Consideration** (see Note 7) | **Value** (see Note 8) | **Fee** (see Note 9) | **Date of Entry** |
|---|---|---|---|
| £95,000.00 | | A £209.00 | |

**11 If a Form 10 Report has been issued in connection with this Application, please quote Report No.**    4415/LAN/92

**12 I/ We apply for registration in respect of Deed(s) No    8    in the Inventory of Writs (Form 4). I/ We certify that the information supplied in this application is correct to the best of my/our knowledge and belief.**

FOR OFFICIAL USE

Signature         Date

Notes 1-9 referred to are contained in Notes and Directions for completion of Applications for First Registration

**PART B**

Delete **YES** or **NO** as appropriate
N.B. If more space is required for any section of this form, a separate sheet, or separate sheets, may be added.

1. Do the deeds submitted in support of this application include a plan illustrating the extent of the subjects to be registered?     **YES/NO**
   If **YES**, please specify the deed and its Form 4 Inventory number:
   Feu Disposition by County Developments Limited in favour of Mr & Mrs Edward Ross. Item No. on Form 4.
   If **NO**, have you submitted a deed containing a full bounding description with measurements?     **YES/NO**

   If **YES**, please specify the deed and its Form 4 Inventory number:

   **N.B.** If the answer to both the above questions is **NO** then, unless the property is part of a tenement or flatted building you must submit a plan of the subjects properly drawn to a stated scale and showing sufficient surrounding features to enable it to be located on the Ordnance Map. The plan should bear a docquet, signed by the person signing the Application Form, to the effect that it is a plan of the subjects sought to be registered under the attached application.

2. Is a Form P16 Report issued by the Keeper confirming that the boundaries of the subjects coincide with the Ordnance Map being submitted in support of this Application?     **YES/NO**

   If **NO**, does the legal extent depicted in the plans or descriptions in the deeds submitted in support of the Application cohere with the occupational extent?     **YES/NO**

   If **NO**, please advise:-

   (a) the approximate age and nature of the occupational boundaries, or

   (b) whether, if the extent of the subjects as defined in the deeds is larger than the occupational extent, the applicant is prepared to accept the occupational extent as viewed, or     **YES/NO**

   (c) whether, if the extent of the subjects as defined in the deeds is smaller than the occupational extent, any remedial action has been taken.     **YES/NO**

3. Is there any person in possession or occupation of the subjects or any part of them adversely to the interest of the applicant?     **YES/NO**
   If **YES**, please give details:

4. If the subjects were acquired by the applicant under any statutory provision, does the statutory provision restrict the applicant's power of disposal of the subjects?     **YES/NO**
       N/A
   If **YES**, please indicate the statute:

5. (a) Are there any charges affecting the subjects or any part of them, except as stated in the Schedule of Heritable Securities etc. on page 4 of this application?     **YES/NO**
   If **YES**, please give details:

   (b) Apart from overriding interests are there any burdens affecting the subjects or any part of them, except as stated in the Schedule of Burdens on page 4 of this application?     **YES/NO**
   If **YES**, please give details:

(c)  Are there any overriding interests affecting the subjects or any part of them which     **YES/NO**
you wish noted on the Title Sheet?
If **YES**, please give details:

(d)  Are there any recurrent monetary payments (e.g. feuduty, leasehold casualties)     **YES/NO**
exigible from the subjects or any part of them?
If **YES**, please give details:
Variable annual service charge to Superiors/Feuars Association under Deed of
Conditions Item Number 2 on Form 4

6.  Where any party to the deed inducing registration is a Company registered under the
Companies Acts

                                              N/A
Has a receiver or liquidator been appointed?     **YES/NO**
If **YES**, please give details:

If **NO**, has any resolution been passed or court order made for the winding up of     **YES/NO**
the Company or petition presented for its liquidation?
If **YES**, please give details:

7.  Where any party to the deed inducing registration is a Company registered under the
Companies Acts can you confirm     N/A

(a)  that it is not a charity as defined in section 112 of the Companies Act 1989 and     **YES/NO**

(b)  that the transaction to which the deed gives effect is not one to which section     **YES/NO**
322A of the Companies Act 1985 (as inserted by section-109 of the Companies
Act 1989) applies?

Where the answer to either branch of the question is **NO**, please give details:

8.  Where any party to the deed inducing registration is a corporate body other than a
Company registered under the Companies Acts     N/A

(a)  Is it acting *intra vires*?     **YES/NO**
If **NO**, please give details:

(b)  Has any arrangement been put in hand for the dissolution of any such corporate     **YES/NO**
body?
If **YES**, please give details:

9.  Are *all* the necessary consents, renunciations or affidavits in terms of section 6 of the     **YES/NO**
Matrimonial Homes (Family Protection)(Scotland) Act 1981 being submitted in
connection with this application?

**N.B.** If sufficient evidence to satisfy the Keeper that there are no subsisting occupancy
rights in the subjects of this application is not submitted with the application then the
statement by the Keeper in terms of rule 5(j) of the Land Registration (Scotland) Rules
1980 will not be inserted in the Title Sheet or will be qualified as appropriate without
further enquiry by the Keeper.

10. Where the deed inducing registration is in implement of the exercise of a power of sale under a heritable security

**N/A**

Have the statutory procedures necessary for the proper exercise of such power been complied with?

**YES/NO**

11. Where the deed inducing registration is a General Vesting Declaration or a Notice of Title pursuant on a Compulsory Purchase Order

**N/A**

Have the necessary statutory procedures been complied with?

**YES/NO**

12. Is any party to the deed inducing registration subject to any legal incapacity or disability?

**YES/NO**

If **YES**, please give details:

13. Are the deeds and documents detailed in the Inventory (Form 4) all the deeds and documents relevant to the title?

**YES/NO**

If **NO**, please give details:

14. Are there any facts and circumstances material to the right or title of the applicant which have not already been disclosed in this application or its accompanying documents?

**YES/NO**

If **YES**, please give details:

### SCHEDULE OF HERITABLE SECURITIES ETC.
**N.B.** New Charges granted by the applicant should not be included

As per Item Number 4 on Form 4.

### SCHEDULE OF BURDENS

As per Item Numbers 1, 2 and 3 on Form 4.

Printed in Scotland for HMSO by (13161)
Dd8457055 C500 8/98

*Note: The style of form shown above was not in place in 1992. It is used here for illustrative purposes. There were 13 questions to answer in 1992 compared to 14 now.*

REGISTERS OF SCOTLAND EXECUTIVE AGENCY
(Land Registration (Scotland) Rules 1980 Rule 9(2))

FORM 4

Typewriter Alignment Box
Type XXX in centre

**INVENTORY OF WRITS RELEVANT TO APPLICATION FOR REGISTRATION** *(see Note 1)*
(to be completed in duplicate)

Messrs King & Co.
Solicitors
10 Glasgow Square
LANARK

DX 829, Lanark

FAS 1234

*(see Note 2)*

**Title Number(s)**
(to be completed for a dealing with registered interests in land.)

Subjects *(see Note 3)* 3 Larklanark Road, Lanark

Registration County LANARK

Applicant's Reference JK/SR/JDM

Please complete Inventory overleaf as in this specimen

| Item No. | Please mark "S" against writs submitted | Particulars of Writs *(see Note 4)* Writ | Grantee | Date of Recording |
|---|---|---|---|---|
| | | Land Certificate* | | |
| | | Charge Certificate* | | |
| 1 | – | Feu Charter | Upright Builders Ltd | 2 May 1938 |
| 2 | S | Feu Disposition | Smith | 4 Feb 1939 |

* Delete if inapplicable

Notes 1-4 referred to are contained in Notes and Directions for Completion of Inventory of Writs Relevant to Application for Registration.

FOR OFFICIAL USE ONLY

| APPLICATION NUMBER | DATE OF RECEIPT | TITLE NUMBER |
|---|---|---|
| | | |

The writs marked "S" on this inventory were received on the Date of Receipt stamped on this page.

**INVENTORY**

Particulars of Writs *(see Note 4)*

Typewriter Alignment Box
Type XXX in centre

| Item No. | Please mark "S" against writs submitted | Writ | Grantee | Date of Recording |
|---|---|---|---|---|
| | | ~~XXXXXXXXXX~~ | | |
| | | ~~XXXXXXXXXX~~ | | |
| 1. | S | Feu Charter | County Developments Limited | 13 NOV 1980 |
| 2. | S | Deed of Conditions | | 20 JUN 1981 |
| 3. | S | Feu Disposition | Mr and Mrs Edward Fox | 28 DEC 1983 |
| 4. | S | Standard Security | Larklanark Building Society | 20 JAN 1984 |
| 5. | S | Death Certificate of Edward Fox | | |
| 6. | S | Certificate of Confirmation | Fox's Executry | |
| 7. | S | Discharge of No. 4 hereof | Executors of the late Mrs Grace Fox | 03 JUN 1992 |
| 8. | G | Disposition | Peter Quinn | |

**Note:** Of the foregoing 10 Writs in this progress of Titles No:2 – The Floating Charge and No:9 – the Missives are not included in the foregoing Inventory Form 4 not being registrable or relevant to the Keeper's examination of the title.

\* delete if inapplicable

Printed in Scotland for HMSO by (13161)

*Note: The style of form shown above was not in place in 1992. It is used here for illustrative purposes.*

## 14. Land Certificate for 3 Larklanark Road, Lanark

(Land Registration (Scotland) Rules 1980 Rule 14)

**LAND REGISTER OF SCOTLAND**

# LAND
# CERTIFICATE

TITLE NUMBER: LAN91463

SUBJECTS: 3 LARKLANARK ROAD,
LANARK

This Land Certificate, issued pursuant to section 5(2) of the Land Registration (Scotland) Act 1979, is a copy of the Title Sheet relating to the above subjects.

**Statement of Indemnity**

Subject to any specific qualifications entered in the Title Sheet of which this Land Certificate is a copy, a person who suffers loss as a result of any of the events specified in section 12(1) of the above Act shall be entitled to be indemnified in respect of that loss by the Keeper of the Registers of Scotland in terms of that Act.

ATTENTION IS DRAWN TO THE NOTICE OVERLEAF AND GENERAL INFORMATION ON THE INSIDE BACK COVER OF THIS CERTIFICATE.

Dd 8387852 80M 4/92 28384

| 0 5 NOV 1992 | | | | |
|---|---|---|---|---|
| | | | | |
| | | | | |
| | | | | |

This Land Certificate may be made to agree with the Title Sheet at any time on payment of the appropriate fee. Application should be made on Form 8.

Please see inside back cover for General Information.

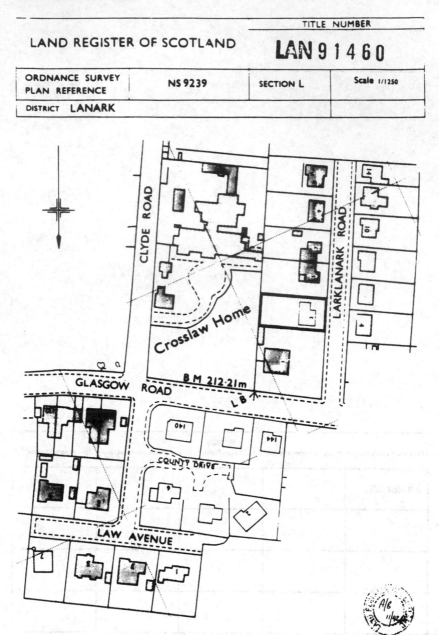

LAND REGISTER OF SCOTLAND

TITLE NUMBER LAN91460                        A 1

A. PROPERTY SECTION

Date of First
Registration
05 NOV. 1992

INTEREST                          MAP REFERENCE
Proprietor                        NS9239L

DESCRIPTION

Subjects 3 LARKLANARK ROAD, LANARK, edged red on the Title Plan;
Together with a right in common with all other proprietors of
every part of the Glasgow Road Development, to the common parts of
the said Development as described in the Deed of Conditions in
Entry 2 of the Burdens Section.

651

B. PROPRIETORSHIP SECTION

Entry no        Proprietor              Date of Registration


    1       PETER QUINN, 20 Clyde       05 NOV. 1992    Consideration
            Street, Lanark                              £95,000
                                                        Entry
                                                        31 OCT. 1992

    Note:   There are in respect of the subjects in this title no
            subsisting occupancy rights, in terms of the Matrimonial
            Homes (Family Protection) (Scotland) Act 1931, of spouses
            of persons who were formerly entitled to the said
            subjects.

TITLE NUMBER LAN91460          C 1

C. CHARGES SECTION.

Entry no               Specification               Date of Registra

**NO ENTRY**

TITLE NUMBER LAN91460                    D 1

D. BURDENS SECTION

Entry no                      Specification

1.        Feu Charter by Andrew Brown (who and whose successors are
          hereinafter referred to as "the Superiors") to County
          Developments Limited and their successors and assignees
          (hereinafter referred to as "the Feuars"), recorded G.R.S.
          (Lanark) 13 Nov. 1930, of 10 hectares of ground ("the
          Feu") of which the subjects in this Title form part,
          contains the following burdens:

          (First) the Feuars shall be bound in all time coming to
          maintain in good order and repair, and whenever necessary
          to re-erect or reconstruct with the like materials, the
          whole of the stone wall extending along the north boundary
          of the Feu except for that part thereof to be demolished
          in order to give access to the Feu from Glasgow Road,
          Lanark as hereinafter provided: (Second) ....
          Note: The burdens which are set out in the
                said Feu Charter No.1 above will be
                repeated here.

          Declaring further that, if the Feuars contravene or fail
          to implement any of the foregoing feuing conditions, then
          this Feu Charter and all that may have followed thereon
          shall, in the option of the Superiors, become null and
          void and the Feuars shall forfeit their whole right, title
          and interest in and to the Feu which, with all buildings
          thereon, shall revert to and belong to the Superiors free
          and disencumbered of all burdens thereon as if these
          presents had never been granted.

2.        Deed of Conditions, recorded G.R.S. (Lanark) 20 Jun. 1981,
          by County Developments Limited, proprietors of 10 hectares
          of ground, of which the subjects in this Title form part,
          contains burdens &c. in the following terms:

          CONSIDERING that we intend to develop the said subjects by
          the erection of villa dwellinghouses thereon and to
          dispone the same to individual purchasers and that it is
          desirable to execute these presents in order to define the
          rights, interests, obligations and liabilities of the
          proprietor of each individual dwellinghouse to be erected
          on the said subjects; THEREFORE we do hereby declare and
          provide as follows; FIRST: Definitions: In this deed,
          unless the context otherwise requires, the following
          expressions shall have the following meanings

## D. BURDENS SECTION

Entry no                    Specification

respectively, viz: "the Development" means the said area
of ground extending to ten hectares or thereby; "the
Superiors" means us and our successors as proprietors for
the time being of the plenum dominium of the development
or so much thereof as has not been feued and of the
dominium directum of those parts or the whole of the
development which, at the relevant date, have been feued;
SECOND: Each of the dwellinghouses erected on the
Development shall be used in all time coming as a private
residence for use by one family only and for no other
purpose whatsoever.

Note: The burdens which are referred to in the
said Deed of Conditions No. 2 above will
be set out in full here.

3.      Feu Disposition by County Developments Limited to Edward
Fox and Grace Hunter or Fox, recorded G.R.S. (Lanark) 23
Dec. 1983, of the subjects in this Title, contains no
further burdens.

## GENERAL INFORMATION

1.  OVERRIDING INTERESTS. A registered interest in land is in terms of section 3(1) of the Land Registration (Scotland) Act 1979 subject to overriding interests defined in section 28 of that Act (hereinafter referred to as "the 1979 Act") as amended by the Matrimonial Homes (Family Protection) (Scotland) Act 1981 as:

    in relation to any interest in land, the right or interest over it of

    (a)  the lessee under a lease which is not a long lease;

    (b)  the lessee under a long lease who, prior to the commencement of the 1979 Act, has acquired a real right to the subjects of the lease by virtue of possession of them;

    (c)  a crofter or cottar within the meaning of section 3 or 28(4) respectively of the Crofters (Scotland) Act 1955, or a landholder or statutory small tenant within the meaning of section 2(2) or 32(1) respectively of the Small Landholders (Scotland) Act 1911;

    (d)  the proprietor of the dominant tenement in a servitude;

    (e)  the Crown or any Government or other public department, or any public or local authority, under any enactment or rule of law, other than an enactment or rule of law authorising or requiring the recording of a deed in the Register of Sasines or registration in order to complete the right or interest;

    (ee)  the operator having a right conferred in accordance with paragraph 2, 3 or 5 of schedule 2 to the Telecommunications Act 1984 (agreements for execution of works, obstruction of access, etc.);

    (f)  the holder of a floating charge whether or not the charge has attached to the interest;

    (g)  a member of the public in respect of any public right of way or in respect of any right held inalienably by the Crown in trust for the public;

    (gg)  the non-entitled spouse within the meaning of section 6 of the Matrimonial Homes (Family Protection) (Scotland) Act 1981;

    (h)  any person, being a right which has been made real, otherwise than by the recording of a deed in the Register of Sasines or by registration; or

    (i)  any other person under any rule of law relating to common interest or joint or common property, not being a right or interest constituting a real right, burden or condition entered in the title sheet of the interest in land under section 6(1)(e) of the 1979 Act or having effect by virtue of a deed recorded in the Register of Sasines,

    but does not include any subsisting burden or condition enforceable against the interest in land and entered in its title sheet under section 6(1) of the 1979 Act.

2.  THE USE OF ARROWS ON TITLE PLANS

    (a)  Where a deed states the line of a boundary in relation to a physical object, e.g. the centre line, that line is indicated on the Title Plan, either by means of a black arrow or verbally.

    (b)  An arrow across the object indicates that the boundary is stated to be the centre line.

    (c)  An arrow pointing to the object indicates that the boundary is stated to be the face of the object to which the arrow points.

    (d)  The physical object presently shown on the Plan may not be the one referred to in the deed. Indemnity is therefore excluded in respect of information as to the line of the boundary.

3.  Lineal measurements shown in figures on title plans are subject to the qualification "or thereby". Indemnity is excluded in respect of such measurements.

4.  SUBMISSION OF LAND CERTIFICATE WITH SUBSEQUENT APPLICATIONS FOR REGISTRATION.

    In terms of Rule 9(3), this Land Certificate should be submitted to the Keeper of the Registers of Scotland with any application for registration.

5.  CAUTION. No unauthorised alteration to this Land Certificate should be made.

Dd F027 50M 2/92 25364

## Appendix B

# STYLES COMMITTEE –
# AGRICULTURAL LEASE

(Reproduced with kind permission of the Law Society of Scotland from
'Workshop' July 1980)

### LEASE
between

(who and whose successors as Landlord under this Lease are hereinafter
referred to as 'the Landlord')

### and

(hereinafter referred to as 'the Tenant')

IT IS AGREED between the parties hereto as follows:

The Landlord in consideration of the rent and other benefits and with and
under the reservations, conditions and others hereinafter specified, hereby
LETS to the Tenant, excluding successors, assignees and sub-tenants
whether legal or conventional without the written consent of the Landlord
ALL and WHOLE the Farm of

extending to                                                          all as
delineated on the plan thereof annexed and signed as relative hereto
together with the farmhouse and all other buildings thereon (which subjects are hereinafter referred to as 'the Farm').

The Farm is let from                                           for a period
of

The yearly rent payable by the Tenant will initially be          payable in
equal instalments at Fifteenth May and Eleventh* November in each year,
beginning the first payment at
for the term preceding
and the next payment at
and so forth half-yearly thereafter with interest on any sum outstanding
(whether in respect of rent or otherwise) at a rate three percentage points
above the Base Rate of the                                          Bank of

* Note: Now twenty-eighth – see Term and Quarter Days (Scotland) Act 1990.

in force from time to time. The Landlord will not at any time be barred from claiming damages from the Tenant for failure to implement any obligation under this Lease by reason of the fact that the rent may have been accepted by the Landlord.

The rent will be subject to review every three years, the first review date being                          and the subsequent review dates occurring at intervals of three* years thereafter. The new rent (which will take effect from the relevant review date) will be fixed by agreement between the Landlord and the Tenant, failing which by arbitration.

## RESERVATIONS

There are reserved to the Landlord:

(A) the whole ores, minerals and mineral substances, whether metalliferous or not, including precious and other metals, and sand, gravel and building stone on or under the Farm with full power to do everything necessary to prospect for, work, win and carry away, let or dispose of the same, including power to erect buildings and plant in connection therewith, but subject to payment for surface damage (which in the case of crops shall include temporary grass) or for damage to fixed equipment or other property of the Tenant and to an adjustment of rent which, failing agreement, will be fixed by arbitration;

(B) power to alter marches and excamb land with any neighbouring proprietor, an adjustment of rent being made on the basis of annual value of any additions to or deductions from the Farm, which adjustment will, failing agreement, be fixed by arbitration;

(C) power at any time to resume any part or parts of the Farm for any purpose other than agricultural purposes on giving at least     months' written notice;

(D) all water in rivers, streams, burns, springs, lochs, ponds, wells, reservoirs, dams, drains, conduits, canals, or underground channels with all necessary rights of access thereto subject to the use thereof by the Tenant for the proper purposes of the Farm only;

(E) the whole shootings and fishings on the Farm with the exclusive right of sporting, shooting, fishing, trapping and snaring, subject to the Tenant's common law and statutory rights; declaring that the Tenant is hereby granted permission to kill deer if found on arable land or enclosed pasture; and the period of twelve months ending Thirty-First October in each year will be substituted for the calendar year for the purposes of Section 52(1) of the Agricultural Holdings (Scotland) Act 1991; and the Tenant, so far as in his power and subject as aforesaid, will protect the game on the Farm and will prevent all poachers and others from trespassing thereon and will immediately give notice to the Landlord of poaching, suspected poaching or trespassing;

(F) all woods, trees, brushwood and plantations (with grass therein) and the ground occupied thereby on the Farm, with power on payment for surface

* Note: See now Agricultural Holdings (Scotland) Act 1991 s. 13.

damage (i) to cut, prune and remove the same and to plant others in their place; (ii) to fence the same and also the stools of trees and shrubs when cut; (iii) to enclose any unenclosed woods and plantations, all without compensation to the Tenant, it being understood that all such plantations or woodlands occupied by the Tenant will be so occupied by mere tolerance and such permission may be withdrawn by the Landlord at any time; and (iv) to cart wood through the Farm from the woods and plantations thereon or from neighbouring woods or plantations; declaring that if any trees, woods or plantations and the fences round the same are destroyed or injured by the Tenant or his employees or by the Tenant's machinery or by the Tenant's livestock, the Tenant will be liable to the Landlord for the damage so done;

**(G)** all existing rights of way, wayleaves and servitudes, with power to grant further wayleaves and servitudes, subject to payment for surface damage (which in the case of crops shall include temporary grass);

**(H)** a right to use all roads and means of access over the Farm to other lands and subjects;

**(I)** the right to enter and to authorise others to enter all parts of the Farm for the purpose of satisfying the Landlord that the conditions of this Lease are being properly carried out, or fulfilling the Landlord's obligations or exercising his rights hereunder;
declaring that if any ground damaged or resumed under any of the foregoing powers is restored to an arable state and if possession thereof is given to the Tenant at any time during the currency of this Lease, the abatement of rent in respect of such ground will cease and the Tenant will thereafter be bound to cultivate such land along with the rest of the Farm in accordance with the terms of this Lease.

## FURTHER CONDITIONS

**1** The Tenant will pay all rates, taxes and other charges, including water rates, usually payable by tenants or occupiers.

**2** The Landlord will reinstate or replace any building on the Farm which is damaged or destroyed by fire if its reinstatement or replacement is required to enable him to fulfil his obligation to manage the Farm in accordance with the rules of good estate management; and the Landlord will also effect in his own name a policy or policies of insurance against damage by fire for all buildings on the Farm to their full reinstatement value.

**3** The Tenant will in the event of the destruction by fire of harvested crops grown on the Farm for consumption thereon return to the Farm for full equivalent manurial value of the crops so destroyed insofar as the return thereof is required for the fulfilment of his obligation to farm in accordance with the rules of good husbandry; and the Tenant will insure to their full value against damage by fire, all live and dead stock on the Farm and all such harvested crops as aforesaid with an insurance office to be reasonably approved of by the Landlord and will exhibit the receipts for the premiums paid therefor to the Landlord and, if required, will assign the policy or policies of assurance to the Landlord who will be entitled to recover any sum due under the same and to apply such sum in payment of all or part of the rent due or current at the time and any other sums due by the Tenant to the Landlord, and if the Tenant fails to pay the premiums on the said policy or policies as they become due, the Landlord will be entitled to do so and recover payment thereof from the Tenant; [the Tenant will also insure the stock against anthrax and foot and mouth disease and brucellosis].

**4** The Landlord undertakes to put the fixed equipment on the Farm into a thorough state of repair, and to provide such buildings and other fixed equipment as will enable the Tenant, provided he is reasonably skilled in husbandry, to maintain efficient production as respects both the kind of produce specified in the Lease and the quality and quantity thereof; and will, during the tenancy, effect such replacement or renewal of the fixed equipment as may be rendered necessary by natural decay or by fair wear and tear.

**5** The Tenant agrees that the undertaking of the Landlord to put the fixed equipment on the Farm in a thorough state of repair has been duly implemented; and the Tenant binds himself during this Lease to maintain the fixed equipment on the Farm in as good a state of repair (natural decay and fair wear and tear excepted) as it was in immediately after it was put in repair as aforesaid, or, in the case of equipment provided, improved, replaced or renewed during the tenancy, as it was immediately after it was so provided, improved, replaced or renewed, the dykes and fences having the cope and wire on (as the case may be); and all being left 'slap free', natural decay and ordinary fair wear and tear alone being excepted.

Notwithstanding the foregoing, the cost of maintaining or replacing those fences which form the boundaries of the Farm will, where the Farm adjoins other subjects belonging to the Landlord, be shared equally between the Tenant and the Landlord.

**6** Without prejudice to the generality of the foregoing obligation to uphold the fixed equipment, the Tenant undertakes:
(*a*) to employ skilled tradesmen as necessary to replace loose or broken slates and glass, overhaul roofs, chimneys, rhones, gutters, pipes, roads and bridges, walls, dykes and fences, gates and gate pillars and to scour the ditches, drains and water courses;
(*b*) to keep all tile and surface drains and sewage disposal systems clear and efficient, and to repair all burst and choked drains;
(*c*) to dig and clean the roots of and switch all the hedges, and not to remove or destroy any hedges on the Farm;
(*d*) to cut down and spray all thistles, dockens and weeds on the Farm once before they come into flower and again in August in each year, and to take all practicable steps to prevent the growth of wild oats;
(*e*) to keep down all rabbits, moles, rats and other vermin and pests on the Farm;
(*f*) to paint, once in every                    years, the whole outside woodwork and ironwork of the buildings on the Farm in such manner as shall be approved by the Landlord;
(*g*) to paint, once in every                    years, the internal walls and woodwork of the farmhouse which have previously been painted in such manner as shall be approved by the Landlord;
(*h*) to whitewash or limewash, once in every                    years, all

those parts of the farmhouse and other buildings which have previously been whitewashed or limewashed.

If any of the foresaid operations is neglected or not duly performed, the Landlord shall have power to employ workmen to execute the necessary operation and the Tenant will be bound to meet the expenditure thereby incurred; and the Tenant will perform free of charge all cartage of materials required for any improvements or repairs, which may be executed or made on the Farm during the currency of this Lease. No capital improvements will be carried out by the Tenant except with the prior written consent of the Landlord.

**7**  The Landlord and the Tenant agree that a record of the condition of the fixed equipment on, and the cultivation of, the Farm will be made at the commencement of this Lease. At the termination of this Lease the Tenant will have a right to compensation for improvements and the Landlord to compensation for dilapidations.

**8**  The Tenant will not alter or add to any or erect new fixed equipment unless with the prior written consent of the Landlord.

**9**  The Tenant's fixtures are specified in Schedule I annexed hereto. At the termination of this Lease the Landlord or the incoming tenant will take over at valuation all the Tenant's fixtures. These fixtures will be kept in proper repair by the Tenant at all times.

**10**  The Tenant will always keep the Farm fully stocked and equipped with his own stock and crop and the Tenant accepts the Farm at entry in the then state of cultivation without claim or objection; and the Tenant will manage, manure, labour and crop the Farm as an arable and/or livestock rearing farm only, according to the rules of good husbandry in all respects and shall not use the Farm or any part or parts of it for any other business whatsoever; declaring that no permanent pasture land (or any part of the hill) will be broken up without the prior written permission of the Landlord, and in the last year of this Lease the Tenant will be bound to have the Farm under a rotation according to the rules of good husbandry as recognised and practised in the district; and the Tenant binds himself not to sell or remove from the Farm, but to consume thereon, the whole straw, turnips, and fodder (except potatoes and grain) growing yearly thereon and to apply to the Farm yearly the whole dung thereon and to manure the same and to leave the whole dung made thereon and not used at the expiry of this Lease to the Landlord or incoming tenant who will take over the dung at a valuation to be fixed, failing agreement, by arbitration.

**11**  The Tenant may burn one-tenth of the heather, muir, whins or bracken on the Farm in each year, but only on written intimation to the Landlord before the Twentieth day of March in each year. The Tenant will, when appropriate, give notice to neighbouring occupiers of his intention to burn and will take every precaution to avoid injuring any wood or trees and generally to control the burning.

**12**  The Tenant will ensure that no part of the Farm is used for camping or caravanning.

**13**  If the Tenant uses any part of the Farm as a market garden or for commercial flower or vegetable cultivation, or as a dairy farm, or for pig or poultry production, he will have no claim against the Landlord for alterations or improvements or for compensation at the termination of this Lease.

**14** The Tenant will at the proper season in the last year of this Lease, sow, if required so to do by the Landlord or incoming tenant, with such kinds and quantities of clover and grass seed as either of them may specify, such part of the Farm in grain crop in that year as may be fixed by the Landlord or incoming tenant; the Tenant will be bound to harrow and roll in said seed and protect the grass therefrom against injury by cattle or sheep or otherwise, all free of charge, the Landlord or incoming tenant paying for the grass seed; and further, in the last year of this Lease, the Tenant will allow the Landlord or incoming tenant to enter into such part of the Farm as may be intended to fallow at the separation of the penultimate crop from the ground and to labour, manure and dress the same accordingly; and generally in the last year the Tenant will allow the Landlord or incoming tenant access to the whole land under crop as soon as the crops are carried off the ground; and the Landlord or incoming tenant will take the whole of the waygoing fodder and grain crop and outgoing turnip crop of the last year of this Lease at a valuation to be fixed, failing agreement, by arbitration; and the Tenant further binds himself at the termination of this Lease to leave the Landlord or incoming tenant the one year old grass and all straw on the Farm, and to plough and harrow the fallow ground.

**15** The Tenant will reside in the farmhouse, and the habitable buildings will be occupied only by employees of the Tenant unless the Landlord agrees otherwise in writing.

**16** The Tenant will be bound at his own expense to reclaim any areas of waste ground on the Farm which are capable of being reclaimed as soon as it is practical to do so.

**17** If, during this Lease, the Tenant becomes notour bankrupt or grants a Trust Deed for behoof of his creditors or, without the prior written consent of the Landlord, assigns this Lease or sub-lets the Farm or any part or parts of it, or allows one half-year's rent to remain unpaid for one month after it has become due or for fourteen days after receipt of a written demand from the Landlord, whichever is the later, or fails to cultivate the Farm according to the rules of good husbandry, or if the farmhouse or buildings is or are not occupied in accordance with Condition 15 hereof, or if the Tenant fails within a reasonable time to remedy any breach, capable of being remedied, of any condition of this Lease, not inconsistent with his responsibilities as Tenant, or commits a breach of a condition of this Lease which materially prejudices the Landlord and is not capable of being remedied, then and in any of these events, it will be in the power of the Landlord by written intimation addressed to the Tenant at the Farm and sent by Recorded Delivery post or Registered Letter forthwith to put an end to this Lease and to resume possession of the Farm in whatever state it may then be without any declarator or process of law and without prejudice to the Landlord's claim for past, due and current rents and all other claims competent to him, and neither the Tenant nor any of his creditors will in such an event have any right or claim for improvements or otherwise against the Landlord.

*Note:* See new Law Reform (Miscellaneous Provisions) (Scotland) Act 1985.

**18** The Tenant binds and obliges himself to flit and leave the Farm vacant for the Landlord or incoming tenant at the termination of this Lease without the necessity of any warning or process of removing.

**19** And the parties consent to registration for preservation and execution:

IN WITNESS WHEREOF

### SCHEDULE I
### (Tenant's fixtures)

*An agricultural lease is frequently followed up by the conclusion of an Agreement between the parties to vary certain provisions of the lease, to an extent not inconsistent with statute, in the following terms.*

### AGREEMENT

between

(hereinafter called 'the Landlord')

and

(hereinafter called 'the Tenant')

The parties have agreed that their obligations under the lease of the Farm of

dated                                        be varied in manner underwritten:

**1** Notwithstanding the terms of the said Lease the Tenant hereby accepts the fixed equipment on the Farm as being in a thorough state of repair and sufficient in all respects to enable him to maintain efficient production, and further the Tenant undertakes that he will during the tenancy effect at his own expense on behalf of the Landlord such replacement or renewal of the buildings or other fixed equipment on the Farm as may be rendered necessary by natural decay or by fair wear and tear.

**2** Except in so far as varied hereby, the parties confirm the terms of the said Lease: IN WITNESS WHEREOF

# Appendix C

# THE COUNCIL TAX IN SCOTLAND

(Reproduced with the kind permission of the Law Society of Scotland
and Lothian Regional Council.)

**Information for Solicitors and their Clients**

*Introduction*
On 1 April 1993, the council tax will replace the community charge ('poll tax') as the way people contribute to the cost of local authority services. It will be levied by Regional and Islands Councils in respect of each dwelling in their area. In most cases either the owner-occupier or the tenant of the dwelling will be liable for the council tax, whether solely or jointly with others in the same position, or their spouses or partners. It follows that most changes in ownership or tenancy will therefore have implications as regards tax liability.

This leaflet highlights responsibilities placed on solicitors, with respect to the council tax, in connection with house sales and also procedural matters affecting sellers, buyers, and tenants – both outgoing and incoming – which solicitors might either draw to their clients' attention or look after on their behalf.

*Responsibilities of solicitors as estate agents*
Many solicitors undertake estate agency work in connection with house sales. They will therefore wish to be aware of the provisions of the Property Misdescriptions Act 1991 and the Property Misdescriptions (Specified Matters) Order 1992. Briefly, these impose on anyone carrying on an estate agency business a need to ensure that any statements made in advertising property concerning the level of council tax that the individual property would attract or the basis on which that sum is calculated are accurately stated. (The provisions of the Act do not apply to solicitors when they are engaged in conveyancing work.) Most obviously, solicitors and estate agents may therefore need to check, immediately before placing a house on the market, such information as its valuation banding and whether alterations have been carried out to the house since 1 April 1993 or under its present ownership which might give rise to a review of the valuation banding on sale. During the early years of the new regime, it may also be relevant to check whether the house attracts a transitional reduction on its council tax liability and, if so, how much.

The council tax valuation list, giving the valuation banding of a dwelling is on public display. Authorities may, however, make a charge for the provision of extracts from the list. The information concerning entitlement to transitional reduction may be available from the client, by examining their latest demand notice, though it may also be that further checks will have to be carried out with the levying authority to determine the authoritative position. In doing this, it must be remembered that the onus is on the estate agent to ensure that any statements which he or she makes are not false or misleading.

As regards the effect of alterations to a dwelling which might lead to a review of the valuation banding, on sale, it will be more difficult to ascertain the accurate position prior to sale and so care will need to be taken to ensure that no unsupportable undertakings are given as to the valuation band which will apply after the sale is completed. It is suggested that estate agents make their own enquiries of their clients to ascertain what works have been carried out since the dwelling was last banded. Assessors are unlikely, however, to be able to indicate hypothetical rebandings prior to a sale.

## The seller or outgoing tenant

Council tax is calculated on an accruing daily liability and therefore there is no apportionment of tax to be undertaken on a change in ownership or tenancy. It is, however, important for the seller or the outgoing tenant that the levying authority finance department knows promptly when their liability ceases so that amended bills can be issued to clarify the final amount of the liability that is being terminated.

If the levying authority is not informed that liability has changed then they will obviously expect the former liable person to continue paying the council tax in respect of the dwelling concerned. If it is not paid, then arrears enforcement procedures may be set in train. Although it will be possible to correct the liability records retrospectively this would obviously cause more trouble and could, in the meantime, cause worry for individuals who are being pursued for debts for which they are no longer liable. It is therefore highly desirable that levying authorities are notified of liability as soon as possible.

## The purchaser or incoming tenant

A purchaser or incoming tenant may become liable for the council tax in respect of their house. They should inform the levying authority finance department as soon as possible when they have taken entry of a property so that liability can be determined and demand notices issued on the correct basis. It is in their interest to do this promptly for the reasons explained below.

If the house is not someone's sole or main residence then there will be entitlement to a 50% discount and if only one person (or only one person who is not 'disregarded') resides there then a 25% discount will be due. The levying authority will only issue bills reflecting these discounts if it is aware of the relevant circumstances, so it is important that the owner or tenant provides the necessary details as soon as possible. There is a similar need to provide information promptly if a banding reduction is being claimed on account of someone's disabilities.

If a change of ownership or tenancy occurs in the first 9 months of the financial year (i.e. April to December) then the bill resulting from a new liability will normally be payable in instalments during the remaining months of the financial year, up to February. If, however, there is a delay in issuing the bill perhaps because the levying authority is not informed promptly of the new liable person's identity, then the liable person will receive a bill for the total accumulated arrears of council tax liability, from the date when they were first liable, and this will be payable promptly in a single lump sum. Action for the pursuit of arrears could be triggered promptly if it is not paid timeously. Most purchasers or incoming tenants are therefore likely to find it preferable to have their liability correctly established at an early date.

The purchaser of a property may also have an interest in ascertaining at an early date whether the property is going to be placed in a higher valuation band following completion of the sale (so as to avoid the possibility of a large bill for accrued arrears of tax being unexpectedly served on him at a later date). The position can be ascertained by the purchaser notifying the Assessor once the sale has been completed.

## Exemptions
In many cases solicitors may be aware that a dwelling is unoccupied and unfurnished for a few weeks at either side of the date of completion of a sale or that it is no longer anyone's sole or main residence following the death of the previous liable person. In these cases, and several others, the dwelling may be exempt from the council tax. A further description of the circumstances in which dwellings are exempt is proved in the leaflet on 'Liability (including Discounts and Exemptions)', prepared by The Scottish Office, which is available from levying authorities or The Scottish Office. Solicitors may wish to advise clients when they may benefit from exemption.

## Action for solicitors
It will be for consideration between solicitor and client (whether sellers or purchaser, outgoing or incoming tenant) as to whether solicitors will undertake notifications to the Regional or Islands Council, on behalf of their clients. But it is clearly in the interest of clients that notifications should be made promptly following any relevant transaction and it is therefore suggested that solicitors should either undertake this on their clients' behalf or draw their clients' attention to the need for them to make notifications and the advantages for them in doing so promptly.

# INDEX